# 2400
## Outlines, Notes, Quotes,
## and Anecdotes
## for Sermons

# *2400*
# Outlines, Notes, Quotes, and Anecdotes for Sermons

2 volumes in 1

Archibald Naismith

**BAKER BOOK HOUSE**
Grand Rapids, Michigan 49516

# Volume 1
# Scripture Outlines

# PREFACE

THESE outlines have been compiled by request. This book may form a fitting companion to my recent volume of *1200 Notes, Quotes and Anecdotes* which has had a good reception by Christian readers. As a young preacher, I was familiar with several books of skeleton outlines of sermons and found some of them useful for the orderly arrangement of my early discourses. For the preacher they provide useful mnemonics and give the audience points by means of which they can recall portions of messages that have been helpful or challenging. About 300 of the outlines in this compilation have been culled from others: the remainder are original.

In arranging these I have had recourse to my Loose-leaf study Bible which contains messages I have given over forty years in English and also in Telugu, one of the main languages of Southern India. I have felt that a systematic arrangement of these in Biblical order—from Genesis through Revelation—would be more suitable than a haphazard collection of sermon notes.

One of the criticisms of my book *1200 Notes, Quotes and Anecdotes* was that it might encourage preachers to be lazy. May I hope that this collection of Scripture outlines, as well as the previous volume, will, far from producing lazy preachers, stimulate users to further study and encourage the orderly presentation of Scripture texts. Skeletons are for students to examine, and become familiar with basic structures, but are powerless unless clothed with bodies and infused with some measure of vital energy.

This volume is not to be treated as a book of sermons: it does not claim to be that: and it is different, too, from an outlined Bible. But it is hoped that it will provide students, even if they are not preachers, with material for further Bible study and give some insight into the art of homiletics. Many may find an outline to be a good starting-point for the development of fresh lines of study or for the preparation of other original discourses.

As a further aid to the reader, preacher or student, I have prepared a general index of subjects treated and a full index of texts. It will be worth all the labour expended on the preparation of these outlines and indexes if some find real help from them.

A. NAISMITH

## GENESIS

### 1 Bible Study Acrostic

Study—
the *Scriptures*
    Jesus said, they testify
    of me          John 5. 39
    *Theology*
    —the knowledge of God
    —Jesus said, this is life
    eternal that they might
    know Thee, the only
    true God        John 17. 3
the *Universe*
    for — the heavens de-
    clare the glory of God;
    and the earth sheweth
    His handywork    Ps. 19. 1
    *Doctrine*
    Give attendance to
    reading—to doctrine    1 Tim. 4. 13
    *Yourself*
    Take heed unto thyself;  1 Tim. 4. 16
    study to shew thyself
    approved unto God    2 Tim. 2. 15

### 2 In the Beginning

  1 In the beginning of *all Creation*
    —*God* was there    Gen. 1. 1
  2 In the beginning of *God's Way*
    —*Wisdom* was there    Prov. 8. 22
  3 In the beginning of *Divine Revelation*
    —*the Word* was there  John 1. 1, 2, 18
  4 In the beginning of the *New Creation*
    —*the Son* was there    1 John 1. 1

### 3 A Creation Study

THE FIRST CREATION A TYPE OF THE NEW, as mentioned in 2 Cor. 5. 17; Gal. 6. 15; Eph. 2, 10; Eph. 4. 24.

1st DAY
'Let there be light'—ILLUMINATION
Compare Heb. 10. 32; 2 Cor. 4. 6; Eph. 5. 8

2nd DAY
'Let there be a firmament'—SEPARATION
Compare Gal. 1. 4; John 17. 16; 2 Cor. 6. 14

3rd DAY
'Let the dry land appear'—RESURRECTION
Compare Eph. 2. 5; Col. 3. 1; Phil. 3. 10, 11

4th DAY
'Let there be light'—IMPARTATION
(Light never shines for its own sake but for the benefit of others).
Compare the Sun and Mal. 4. 2; John 9. 5
Compare the Moon and Song of Sol. 6. 10; Matt. 5. 14
Compare the Stars and Phil. 2. 15; 1 Cor. 15. 41; Dan. 12. 3

5th DAY
'Let the waters bring forth'—MANIFESTATION
Compare the believer's progress through the world—1 Pet. 2. 11; Phil. 3. 12-14; Ps. 84. 7

Compare the believer's ability to rise above the world—Exod. 19. 4; Isa. 40. 31; Col. 3. 1

6th DAY
'Let us make man'—CONFORMATION
Compare Rom. 8. 29; Phil. 3. 21; 1 John 3. 2

7th DAY
'And God rested'—SATISFACTION
Compare Ps. 103. 5; Ps. 36. 8; Ps. 17. 15

                         G.H.

### 4 Divine Election

'The generations of'—a phrase occurring 11 times in Genesis—indicates the divisions of the book. It occurs altogether 13 times in the Old Testament, the other two being in Num. 3. 1 and Ruth 4. 18, and once only in the New Testament.

The occurrences in Genesis are—2. 4; 5. 1; 6. 9; 10. 1; 11. 10; 11. 27; 25. 13; 25. 19; 36. 1; 36. 9; 37. 2

GOD CHOSE—every family in Adam (Eph. 3. 15)
  SETH out of Adam's family    Gen. 5. 3
  SHEM out of Noah's family    Gen. 11. 10
  ABRAM out of Terah's family  Gen. 12. 1
  ISAAC out of Abraham's family Gen. 17. 19
  JACOB out of Isaac's family    Gen. 25. 23
  JUDAH out of Jacob's family  Gen. 49. 8-10

### 5 Sin and Death

In the day that thou eatest thereof, thou shalt surely die  Gen. 2. 17

  1 Sin is a FATAL DISEASE. This is
    the Operation of Physical
    Law              James 1. 15
  2 Sin is a TERRIBLE MASTER.
    This is the operation of
    Economic Law      Rom. 6. 23
  3 Sin is a PUNISHABLE OFFENCE.
    This is the operation of
    Criminal Law       Ezek. 18. 20

### 6 Eve—A Type of the Church

Compare Gen. 2. 18-25 with Eph. 5. 30-32

  1 Earth's ruler in Solitude—
    none to share his glory    Gen. 2. 18
  2 The Divine purpose for the
    man—'an help meet for
    him'              Gen. 2. 18
  3 The Means to accomplish it
    —'a deep sleep' (emblem
    of death)         Gen. 2. 21
  4 The Wounded Side of the
    man—'He took one of the
    ribs and closed up the
    flesh instead thereof'    Gen. 2. 21
  5 The Bride formed out of the
    man—'and the rib . . .
    made He a woman'    Gen. 2. 22

*Note.* The Hebrew word translated 'made' literally means 'built'

In Rev. 21. 9, 10 the glorified Church is seen both as a Bride and as a City

**7 Three Questions from the World's Oldest Books**

1 Where art thou?
THE SINNER — Gen. 3. 9
2 Where is the lamb for a burnt-offering?
THE SACRIFICE — Gen. 22. 7
3 Man dieth . . . and where is he?
THE SOUL — Job 14. 10

**8 Man's First Disobedience**
Gen. 3. 1-21

1 The serpent's 3-fold SUBTLETY—
Cast doubt on God's word, denied God's truth and defamed God's character — Gen. 3. 1, 4, 5
2 The woman's 3-fold REPLY—
Misquoted God's word, minimized the danger, and mistook God's purpose — Gen. 3. 3
3 Satan's 3-fold TEMPTATION—
Lust of the flesh, lust of the eyes and pride of life — 1 John 2. 16
4 The sinner's 3-fold ACT of disobedience—
With her eye she looked, with her hand she took, with her mouth she ate — Gen. 3. 6
5 Sin's 3-fold CURSE—
on the serpent, the woman and the ground — Gen. 3, 14-17
6 Transgression's 3-fold FRUIT—
Shame, Suffering, Separation — Gen. 3.8, 17, 24
7 God's 3-fold PROMISE—
'I will put enmity', 'it shall bruise thy head', 'thou shalt bruise his heel' — Gen. 3. 15

**11 Cain and Abel**
Gen. 4. 1-13

The way of Cain  Jude 11; Prov. 16. 25
The blood of Abel  Gen. 4. 10; Heb. 12. 24
MAN'S WAY—seen in Cain
(a) A WRONG APPROACH to God — Gen. 4. 3
(b) A WRONG ANSWER to God — Gen. 4. 5
(c) A WRONG ATTITUDE to his brother — Gen. 4. 8
GOD'S WAY—seen in Abel
*His Name*—that which ascends: Desire after God
*His Faith*—Heb. 11. 4
*His Offering*—'Shedding of blood' — Gen. 4. 4; Heb. 9. 22
*His Witness* — Gen. 4. 10; Heb. 11. 4
'he being dead yet speaketh'

**12 Enoch**
Gen. 5. 21-24

1 Enoch's *Conversion*—
at the age of 65, when Methuselah was born — Gen. 5. 22
2 Enoch's *Communion*—
From that time he 'walked with God' — Amos. 3. 3; Heb. 11. 6
3 Enoch's *Service*—
He prophesied—the first to tell of the Lord's coming — Jude 14, 15
4 Enoch's *Translation*—
'God took him'. Enoch was the only one for whom the funeral bell does not toll in Gen. 5 — Gen. 5. 24
But search parties went out to look for him — Heb. 11. 5
5 Enoch's *Commendation*—
'He pleased God' — Heb.11.5-6

**9 The Sentence of Death**

Gen. 3. 14-19; Rom. 5. 12
Seven Words—fulfilled in Christ on the Cross 'He bore on the tree the sentence for me.'

| SENTENCE— | on *The Sinner* | on *The Saviour* | |
|---|---|---|---|
| Sweat | Gen. 3. 19 | Luke 22. 44 | 'His sweat was as it were great drops.' |
| Thorns | Gen. 3. 18 | John 19. 2 | 'a crown of thorns . . . on His head.' |
| Curse | Gen. 3. 17 | Gal. 3. 13 | 'Christ . . . made a curse for us.' |
| Sorrow | Gen. 3. 17 | Lam. 1. 12 | 'See if there be any sorrow like unto my sorrow.' |
| Bruise | Gen. 3. 15 | Is. 53. 10 | 'Yet it pleased the Lord to bruise him.' |
| Sword | Gen. 3. 24 | Zech. 13. 7 | 'Awake, O sword, against my shepherd.' |
| Dust | Gen. 3. 19. | Ps. 22. 15 | 'Thou hast brought me into the dust of death.' |

**10 Man's Wardrobe**

1 The *Sinner's* Dress—Fig-leaves—MAN-MADE and CHEAP — Gen. 3. 7
(or filthy rags Is. 64. 6)
2 The *Believer's* Clothing—Coats of skin—GOD-GIVEN and COSTLY — Gen. 3. 21
(the best robe Luke 15. 21, 22)
3 The *Priestly* Dress—White Robes—BLOOD-WASHED and CLEAN — Rev. 7. 13-15
4 The *Pilgrim's* Attire—White Garments—SPIRIT-WROUGHT and CHOICE — Eccles. 9. 8
But the world (James 1. 27) and the flesh (Jude 23) may defile them.
5 The *Bridal* Gown—Fine linen clean and white—HAND-WOVEN and COMPLETE — Rev. 19. 7, 8

## 13 Walking with God

Gen. 5. 22. To walk with God involves—

1 Separation and Self-denial
1 Kings 8. 53

2 Holiness and moral purity
Heb. 12. 14; Matt. 5. 8
3 Grace and gentleness
Acts 4. 33; 1 Thess. 2. 7
4 Humility and tenderness
Acts 20. 19; Eph. 4. 32
5 Zeal and Energy
Ps. 119. 139; Phil. 2. 30
6 Patience and Longsuffering
Col. 1. 11
7 Faithfulness and uncompromising decision
Heb. 3. 2; Dan. 3. 18
FRANKLIN FERGUSON

## 14 Grace and its Concomitants

Gen. 6. 8 'Noah found grace in the eyes of the Lord'

This is the first mention of Grace in the Bible. The term occurs frequently and is used to denote—the Unmerited *Favour* of God (Rom. 3. 24; Eph. 1. 7; Eph. 2. 8; 1 Cor. 15. 10; Tit. 2. 11); the *Condescension* and *Sacrifice* of Christ (2 Cor. 8. 9); the *position* into which Divine favour brings the believer (Rom. 5. 2); *Divine help* in weakness (2 Cor. 12. 9); and Christian *liberality* (2 Cor. 8. 6).

CONCOMITANTS OF GRACE:

1 Grace and *Truth*—
came by Jesus Christ        John 1. 17
2 Grace and *Peace*—
Paul's salutation 13 times
in his letters
3 Grace and *Knowledge*—
Part of the process of
growth        2 Pet. 3. 18
4 Grace and *Mercy*
Grace for seasonable help Heb. 4. 16
5 Grace and *Apostleship*—
for God's servants        Rom. 1. 5
6 Grace and *Supplication*—
for Israel in the Millennium        Zech. 12. 10
7 Grace and *Glory*        Ps. 84. 11
'The God of all grace' has called us to eternal glory by Jesus Christ' (1 Pet. 5. 10).

## 16 The Raven and the Dove—Believer's Two Natures

Gen. 8. 6-12; Gal. 5. 16, 17

THE RAVEN an unclean bird that feeds on carrion:
was only sent out once. (There was another in the ark but it was not sent)
Found satisfaction in the old order, so did not return.

THE DOVE a clean bird: in Luke 3. 22 the form assumed by the Holy Spirit. It made three flights.

1 Found no satisfaction in that which had come under God's judgement

2 brought back an olive leaf, Emblem of peacefulness and Earnest of fruitfulness

3 did not return because God had provided for it in the new creation.

## 17 Abraham, the Man of Faith

Gen. 12. 1-8

'Simple faith honours God and God honours simple faith.'

1 Faith that *Justifies*
Gen. 15. 6; Rom. 4. 3
2 Faith of *Enterprise*
Gen. 12. 4; Heb. 11. 8
3 Faith that *Testifies*
Gen. 12. 7
4 Faith that *Sanctifies*
Gen. 12. 8; Heb. 11. 10, 13
5 Faith that *Multiplies*
Gen. 12. 2; Heb. 11. 11-12

## 15 Parallel Chapters

Genesis chapters 6, 7, 8 and Romans chapters 1 to 8

| | | |
|---|---|---|
| Rom. 1 | Gen. 6. 1-7, 11-13 | Man's Depravity |
| Rom. 2 | Gen. 6. 8-10 | A God-fearing few |
| Rom. 3 | Gen. 6. 14-22 | Salvation's Plan |
| Rom. 4 | Gen. 7. 1-15 | Believing God's Word |
| Rom. 5 | Gen. 7. 16-24 | Faith's Security |
| Rom. 6 | Gen. 8. 1-5 | Through the Waters (Death and Resurrection) |
| Rom. 7 | Gen. 8. 6-12 | The two natures, clean and unclean |
| Rom. 8 | Gen. 8. 13-22 | The New Creation |

## 18 Four Steps

1 *Separation*
   Abraham went forth     Gen. 12. 5
2 *Failure*
   Abraham went down     Gen. 12. 10
3 *Restoration*
   Abraham went up     Gen. 13. 1
4 *Progress*
   Abraham went on     Gen. 13. 3

W. W. FEREDAY

## 19 Calling on the Name of the Lord

It is recorded three times that Abraham called upon the name of Jehovah.

1 When he came into Canaan out of Ur (the world of the Natural man)     Gen. 12. 8

2 When he returned to Canaan from Egypt (the world of the Carnal man)     Gen. 13. 4

3 When he sojourned at Beer-sheba in the land of the Philistines     Gen. 21. 33

In each place he pitched his tent, the emblem of his pilgrim character. On the first and second occasions he built an altar in Canaan. On the third he went from Beer-sheba to Mount Moriah and built an altar there in obedience to God's call.

## 20 The Tragedy of a Delusive Choice

LOT—*looked* toward Sodom     Gen. 13. 10
*leaned* toward Sodom     Gen. 13. 12
*lived* in Sodom     Gen. 14. 12
*legislated* for Sodom     Gen. 19. 1, 9
   (Cp. Ruth 4. 1; 2 Sam. 15. 2)
*lost* his testimony in Sodom     Gen. 19. 14
*learnt* the ways of Sodom     Gen. 19. 30
   (His drunkenness)
*left behind* him the fruit of his backsliding     Gen. 19. 37
   (Moab and Ammon, progenitors of the enemies of God's people)

## 21 Experiences of the Man of Faith

1 GREAT CONFLICT
   A *Physical* encounter to deliver Lot     Gen. 14. 14-16
   A *Spiritual* conflict to overcome temptation     Gen. 14. 21

2 GRACIOUS CONSOLATION
   Body refreshed with bread and wine     Gen. 14. 18
   *Spirit* revived with divine blessing     Gen. 14. 19

3 GLORIOUS COMPENSATION
   'Thy *shield*'—Divine *Protection*     Gen. 15. 1
   'Thy exceeding great reward—Divine *Provision*     Gen. 15. 1

## 22 Sodom or Salem

*Two Kings* came to meet Abram, the victor—
   Of Sodom, city of Pleasure     Gen. 14. 17
   Of Salem, city of Peace     Gen. 14. 18

*Two Things* each brought to the victor
   Sodom—a purse and a curse     Gen. 14. 21
   Salem—bread and a blessing     Gen. 14. 18, 19

*Two Strengthenings* offered to the victor—
   Enrichment from the world     Gen. 14. 21
   Encouragement from heaven     Gen. 15. 1

## 23 Melchizedek

In *History*
   The King-Priest *Blessing*     Gen. 14. 18-20
   As king of Salem, he refreshed Abram
   As priest of the Most High God, he blessed Abram
   As king of righteousness, he received tithes

In *Prophecy*
   The King-Priest *Warring*     Ps. 110. 1

In *Doctrine*
   The King-Priest *Interceding*     Heb. 7. 1-21
   (Greater than Aaron and Abraham)

## 24 Bread and Wine

*1st* Mention—

   Abram *received* bread and wine     Gen. 14. 18
   (Together associated with blessing)
   Bread alone—associated with a curse     Gen. 3. 19
   Wine alone—associated with a curse     Gen. 9. 21-24

*2nd* Mention—

   Nehemiah *refused* bread and wine, because of the fear of God     Neh. 5. 14-15

*New Testament* Mention—

   John the Baptist *refrained from* them, because of his Nazariteship     Luke 7. 33

*Today*—

   Believers *rejoice in* the bread and wine, because of love to Christ     1 Cor. 11. 26

## 25 High-Priestly Blessing

There are three orders of Priesthood in the Bible: and the first act recorded of the high-priest in each is blessing

| | | |
|---|---|---|
| 1 *Patriarchal* Order | *Melchizedek*—Actual benediction recorded | Gen. 14. 19 |
| 2 *Levitical* Order | *Aaron*—Actual words are prescribed in Num. 6. 23-26 | Lev. 9. 22 |
| 3 *Spiritual* Order | *Jesus* the *Son of God*—Benediction is not recorded | Luke 24. 50-51 |

## 26 The All-Sufficient God

El-Shaddai—God all-sufficient, translated 'Almighty God'.
El—Strong One: Shaddai—Nourisher. The title occurs 31 times in Job.

To Abram it meant—

1 A New *Revelation* of God    Gen. 17. 1
2 A New *Walk* before God    Gen. 17. 1
3 A New *Covenant* with God    Gen. 17. 2
4 A New *Name* from God    Gen. 17. 5

(Abram became Abraham. The aspirate or 'breathing' was introduced into his name as the breath of God came into his life.)

## 27 The First Recorded Intercession
Gen. 18. 22-33

1 Abraham's ACCEPTANCE with God 'I know him'    Gen. 18.17-18
2 Abraham's ATTITUDE before God (stood before the Lord)    Gen. 18. 22
3 Abraham's APPROACH to God (drew near)    Gen. 18. 23
4 Abraham's APPEAL to God (he opened his heart to God)    Gen. 18. 24
5 Abraham's ASSURANCE from God (I will spare; I will not destroy)    Gen. 18. 26, 28, 30, 31, 32

## 28 Dust and Ashes yet Friend of God
Abraham is described

1 By himself as '*Dust* and *Ashes*'    Gen. 18. 27
2 By God as 'Abraham my *friend*'    Isa. 41. 8; James 2. 23
3 By Sarah, his wife, as her '*lord*'    1 Pet. 3. 6
4 By his unconverted neighbours—'*God is with thee*'    Gen. 21. 22
5 By those with whom he did business as 'a *prince* of God among us'    Gen. 23. 6 (Margin)
6 By his descendants as '*never in bondage*'    John 8. 33

## 29 The Promised Son
'Thine only son Isaac whom thou lovest' Gen. 22. 2
'His only begotten son' Heb. 11. 17; John 3. 16.

Gen. 21 *Birth* of the Promised Son    Isa. 9. 6

Gen. 22 *Offering up* of the Promised Son    Rom. 8. 32
Gen. 24 *Marriage* of the Promised Son    Rev. 19. 7

## 30 The Testing of the Man of Faith
'The Lord did tempt Abraham' Gen. 22. 1

1 His *Obedience* tested    Gen. 12. 1-4
2 His *Motives* tested    Gen. 13. 8
3 His *Faith* tested    Gen. 15. 2-4
4 His *Love* tested    Gen. 22. 1-3

## 31 The Divine Provision
*Jehovah-Jireh*—the Lord will provide Gen. 22. 8, 14.

1 The *Victim* appointed the only son    Gen. 22. 2; 1 Pet. 1. 20
2 The *Wood* cloven by the father    Gen. 22. 3; Acts 2. 23
3 The *Load* carried by the son    Gen. 22. 6; John 19. 17
4 The *Lamb* provided by God    Gen. 22. 8; John 1. 29
5 The *Substitute* available in the stead of his son    Gen. 22. 13; 2 Cor. 5. 21

## 32 Jehovah-Titles of God
Gen. 22. 14

Jehovah-jireh—The Lord will provide    Gen. 22. 14
Jehovah-nissi—The Lord my banner    Exod. 17. 15
Jehovah-shalom—The Lord send peace    Judges 6. 24
Jehovah-tsidkenu—The Lord our righteousness    Jer. 23. 6
Jehovah-shammah—The Lord is there    Ezek. 48. 35
F.K.

## 33 The Blessings of Obedience
Gen. 22. 15-18

1 Blessing of the *Productive* Life 'I will multiply thy seed' Gen. 22. 17
2 Blessing of the *Possessive* Life 'Thy seed shall possess the gate of his enemies' Gen. 22. 17
3 Blessing of the *Progressive* Life 'In thy seed shall all nations be blessed' Gen. 22. 18

## 34 A Bride for Isaac
Gen. 24

1 The *Purpose* of the *Father* (Abraham—Type of God the Father)   Gen. 24. 4
2 The *Mission* of the *Servant* (Eliezer—Type of the Holy Spirit)   Gen. 24. 10
3 The *Glory* of the *Son* (Isaac—Type of the Son of God)   Gen. 24. 36
4 The *Call* of the *Bride* (Rebekah—Type of the Church of God)   Gen. 24. 58

## 35 Steps of the Pilgrim Bride
Gen. 24. 56-67)
Her *Decision*
'I will go'   Gen. 24. 58
Her *Discipleship*
'She followed the man'   Gen. 24. 61
Her *Delight*
'She saw Isaac'   Gen. 24. 64;
(1 John 3. 2)
They met, not at Isaac's home nor at Rebekah's, but in between (Cp. 1 Thess. 4. 17).
Rebekah received the 'earnest of the inheritance' (Cp. Eph. 1. 14); the jewels that came from the father's house were brought and bestowed by the sent servant, and betokened the son's claim on her undivided affections.

## 37 Signs of Progress
'Isaac sowed in that land . . .; and the Lord blessed him   Gen. 26. 12

GOING
he went forward   Gen. 26. 13; Heb. 6. 1

GROWING
he grew   Gen. 26. 13; 2 Pet. 3. 18

GATHERING
he had possessions
Gen. 26. 14; 2 Pet. 1. 5-8

## 38 Wells
The Pilgrim's *Possession*
'Isaac digged again the wells of water'   Gen. 26. 17-18
The Pilgrim's *Preservation*
'Spring up, O well; the princes digged a well'   Num. 21. 17,18
The Pilgrim's *Consolation*
'Passing through . . . make it a well'   Ps. 84. 6
The Pilgrim's *Jubilation*
'With joy shall we draw water out of the wells of salvation'   Isa. 12. 3, 4

---

## 39 Four Beholds

| Gen. 28 | | | | |
|---|---|---|---|---|
| v. 12 | Behold a *Ladder* | From earth up to Heaven | Divine *Provision* | John 14. 6 |
| v. 12 | Behold the *angels* | From Heaven to earth | Divine *Protection* | Heb. 1. 14 |
| v. 13 | Behold the *Lord* | The Son of God in Heaven | Divine *Person* | John 1. 18 |
| v. 15 | Behold *I* am with thee | Heaven upon earth | Divine *Presence* | Heb. 13. 5 |

---

## 40 Jacob, Pilgrim and Priest

| | | |
|---|---|---|
| 1 Jacob *lift up* his *feet* | Pilgrimage began at Bethel | Gen. 29. 1 (margin) |
| 2 Jacob *lifted up* his *eyes* | Priesthood began at Peniel | Gen. 33. 1 |
| 3 Jacob *gathered up* his *feet* | Pilgrimage ended on earth | Gen. 49. 33 |
| 4 Jacob worshipped with *uplifted eyes* | Priesthood here and hereafter | Heb. 11. 21 |

---

## 36 A Young Man's Choice
'Esau despised his birthright'   Gen. 25. 27-34

1 A Choice of *Tremendous Importance* — between *present Pleasure* and *future Profit*   Gen. 25. 34
Every person has a 'Birthright' because 'born in sin' and 'Christ Jesus came into the world to save sinners'   1 Tim. 1. 15

2 A Choice of *Terrible Consequence*   Heb. 12. 16

3 A Choice of *Tragic Permanence*
('Found no way to change his mind')   Heb. 12. 17

## 41 What Peniel was to Jacob and is to us
Power with God and man   Gen. 32. 24
1 The Place of *Solitude*   Gen. 32. 24
2 The Place of *Subjection*   Gen. 32. 25
3 The Place of *Supplication*   Gen. 32. 26;
Hosea 12. 4
H.K.D.

## 42 Face to Face
Three men—Face to face with God
1 Jacob the *Suppliant*
Result—His *Character Transformed*   Gen. 32. 30
2 Moses the *Servant*
Result—*His Countenance Transfigured*   Exod. 33. 11
3 Gideon the *Soldier*
Result—His *Confidence Transferred* from idols to Jehovah   Judges 6. 22

## 43 The God of Bethel

'Arise, go up to Bethel'   Gen. 35. 1
What Jacob had in Bethel:

1 A *House*
  Bethel, *House of God*   Gen. 35. 1

2 An *Altar*
  Homage to God   Gen. 35. 3

3 A *Grave* for his idols
  *Holiness unto God*   Gen. 35. 4

## 44 Bethlehem and God in History

Bethlehem—House of Bread, the Divine Provision for man   John 6. 35

1 A *Death* at Bethlehem—
  Israel in *mourning*   Gen. 35. 19
  Out of death—a son (Isa. 9. 6)—
  Benoni—Son of my Sorrow, says Israel:
  Benjamin—Son of my Right Hand, says God   Gen. 35. 18

2 A *Birth* at Bethlehem—
  *Peace* on earth to men of goodwill   Matt. 2. 4-6

3 A *Marriage* at Bethlehem
  —*Joy* in heaven   Ruth 2. 4; 4. 13; (Rev. 19.7)

## 45 Joseph—A Type of Christ

1 The Beloved *Son*
  Gen. 37. 2-3; Matt. 3. 17

2 The good *Shepherd*
  Gen. 37. 2;   John 10. 11

3 The sent *Servant*
  Gen. 37. 13; 1 John 4. 14

4 The brother *Sold*
  Gen. 37. 28; Matt. 26. 15

5 The lonely *Sufferer*
  Gen. 39. 20; Isa. 53. 8

6 The honoured *Statesman*
  Gen. 41. 40; John 3. 35

7 The world's *Saviour*
  Gen. 41. 55; 1 John 4. 14

## 46 Two Dreamers and Two Destinies
Gen. 40

1 TWO OFFENDERS   Gen. 40. 1
  both were condemned—v. 3
  both were concerned—v. 6

2 TWO DREAMS   Gen. 40. 5, 8
  suited to their calling—vs. 9-11, 16, 17

3 TWO OFFERINGS   Gen. 40. 11, 17
  the butler's—What God had provided
  the baker's—What he himself had prepared

4 TWO DESTINIES   Gen. 40. 21, 22
  the butler was restored to favour and lived: the baker was rejected and died.

## 47 The Romance of the Twelve Brothers

How eleven bad were reconciled to one good brother. In this picture of righteous reconciliation we have

1 ROUGHNESS
  Spake *roughly* to them   Gen. 42. 7

2 REMEMBRANCE
  Put them all together in ward three days, time to talk and think   Gen. 42. 17

3 REPENTANCE
  'We are verily guilty,' also his blood is required   Gen. 42. 21, 22

4 RECOGNITION of Guilt
  'God hath found out the iniquity of thy servants'   Gen. 44. 16

5 RECONCILIATION
  'I am Joseph; . . . come near unto me; . . . they came near; . . . he kissed all his brethren   Gen. 45. 4, 15

6 SATISFACTION
  'It is enough'   Gen. 45. 28
        HENRY PICKERING

## 48 The Divine Purpose Through Joseph

'God sent me before you'   Gen. 45. 5, 7
'God meant it unto good'   Gen. 50. 20

1 To save life
  Gen. 45. 5; 50. 20; John 10. 10

2 To preserve a posterity
  Gen. 45. 7; Ps. 22. 30

3 To make him lord
  Gen. 45. 8; Ps. 105. 21; Acts 2. 36

4 To bring his brethren near
  Gen. 45. 10; Eph. 2. 13

5 To nourish his brethren
  Gen. 45. 11; Eph. 5. 29

## 49 All My Glory
  Gen. 45. 13

From a Pit and a Prison to be the Dispenser of immense wealth.

1 The Glory of REVELATION
  Gen. 41. 39, 45; John 1. 18

2 The Glory of RESURRECTION
  Gen. 45. 28;   1 Pet. 1. 21

3 The Glory of RULERSHIP
  Gen. 41. 40, 41; John 3. 35

4 The Glory of RANK
  Gen. 41. 42;   Heb. 2. 9

5 The Glory of RECOGNITION
  Gen. 41. 43;   Phil. 2. 9-11

6 The Glory of RELATIONSHIP
  Gen. 41. 45;   Eph. 5. 25

7 The Glory of RICHES
  Gen. 41. 55;   Eph. 3. 8

## 50 The Hope of the World
### TITLES OF CHRIST IN THE PENTATEUCH

1 SEED of the woman
Gen. 3. 15; Matt. 1. 23
2 SHILOH, Centre of gathering
Gen. 49. 10; Ps. 22. 27
3 SHEPHERD
Gen. 49. 24;  1 Pet. 2. 25
4 STONE of Israel
Gen. 49. 24;  1 Pet. 2. 4
5 STAR out of Jacob
Num. 24. 17;  Rev. 22. 16
6 SCEPTRE out of Israel
Num. 24. 17;  1 Cor. 15. 25

## 51 The Mighty God of Jacob
Gen. 49. 24

Contrast 'the Mighty One', the Almighty, with the 'worm Jacob' Isa. 41. 14.

1 The God of *Promise* to the
*Suppliant* man, *Jacob*  Gen. 49. 24
2 The God of *Power* to the
*Separated* man, *Joseph*
Gen. 49, 25, 26
3 The God of *Purpose* to the
*Sincere* man, *David*  Ps. 132. 2
4 The God of *Preservation*
to a *Saved* people,
*Israel*  Isa. 49. 26

---

## EXODUS

## 52 The Book of Redemption

Exodus—Going out. A Redeemed People leaving Egypt.

THE CHILDREN OF ISRAEL  Exod. 1. 1.

1 A Nation of Slaves
—in Egypt  Exod. 1. 1-12. 36
2 A Nation of Pilgrims
—on the way to Sinai Exod. 12. 37-18.27
3 A Nation of Learners
—at Sinai  Exod. 19. 1-24. 18
4 A Nation of Worship-
pers—Moses on the
Mount  Exod. 25. 1-31. 18
5 A Nation of Back-
sliders—at the foot of
Sinai  Exod. 32. 1-34. 35
(The Transgression of Israel, the Dis-pleasure of God, and the Renewal of the Covenant.)
6 A Nation of Builders
—preparing and
erecting the Tab-
ernacle  Exod. 35. 1-40. 38

## 53 Moses—A Hidden Man
Exod. 2. 3

1 Hidden in the house  Heb. 11. 23

2 Hidden in the ark on the
Nile  Exod. 2. 3

3 Hidden in the desert  Exod. 3. 1

4 Hidden in the mount  Exod. 32. 1

5 Hidden in the wilderness  Exod. 15. 22

6 Hidden in the rock  Exod. 33. 22

7 Hidden in the grave  Deut. 34. 6
T.B. and T.R.

---

## 54 Contrasts in Moses' Life

Exod. 2. 10

| | | |
|---|---|---|
| Moses was | the child of a slave, born in a hut, | yet the son of a princess yet brought up in a palace |
| Moses inherited | extreme poverty, | yet enjoyed immense wealth |
| Moses was | educated for a court, the mightiest of warriors | yet spent most of his life in a desert yet the meekest of men |
| Moses possessed | the wisdom of this world, | yet the faith of a child |
| Moses' funeral | was not attended by a single human creature, created no stir on earth, | yet the Creator Himself was present yet caused a great commotion in Heaven |

## 55 Lessons in the School of God
Exod. 3. 1-6; 4. 24-26

'My servant Moses' (Num. 12. 7); 'Moses the servant of the Lord' (Joshua 1. 1); 'Moses his chosen' (Ps. 106. 23).

Moses spent 40 years in Egypt learning to be Somebody; 40 years in the back-side of the desert, learning to be Nobody; and 40 years in the wilderness, learning how God can make a Somebody out of a Nobody. He had to be taught and trained for service.

1 Lesson of the *Shepherd duties*    Exod. 3. 1
(Gen. 46. 33: Shepherds were an abomination to the Egyptians; so Moses, like Paul, was made as the filth of the world   1 Cor. 4. 13)

2 Lesson of the *desolate place*    Exod. 3. 1
Horeb—'waste place' to man, but to Moses 'the mount of God'

3 Lesson of the *burning bush* Exod. 3. 2, 3
Only a thorn bush but aflame when God was in it; just what Moses and God's people Israel were to be

4 Lesson of the *unshod feet*    Exod. 3. 4-6
The Holiness of God

5 Lesson of the *sharp knife* Exod. 4. 24-26
To 'mortify the deeds of the body'

## 56 The Call of God
God's Call

to Moses—A COMMAND to be obeyed
Come now, therefore, and I will send thee    Exod. 3. 10

to Gideon—A COMMISSION to be fulfilled
Have not I sent thee?    Judges 6. 14

to Isaiah—A CALL to be heeded
Whom shall I send? Here am I, send me    Isa. 6. 8

## 57 The Divine Commission
Exod. 3. 10-12

1 Bring forth my people out of Egypt
IMMENSITY OF THE MANDATE

2 Who am I, that I should go?
INFIRMITY OF THE MESSENGER

3 When thou hast brought forth the people, ye shall serve God
INTENSITY OF THE MISSION

## 58 'I will' Exod. 3. 10-21

1 The Lord's Proposal
I will send thee    v. 10
2 The Lord's Presence
I will be with thee    v. 12
3 The Lord's Purpose
I will bring you out    v. 17
4 The Lord's Power
I will stretch forth my hand    v. 20
5 The Lord's Provision
I will give this people favour    v. 21

## 59 The Unwilling Servant's Excuses

It is a good thing to be humble, but it is a bad thing to be unwilling when God calls. Moses pleaded—

1 *Lack of Fitness* Who am I? Exod. 3. 11
God's answer, 'I will be with thee' *Divine Promise*

2 *Lack of Knowledge* What shall I say?    Exod. 3. 13
God's answer, 'I AM' hath sent you *Divine Plentitude*

3 *Lack of Authority* They will not believe me    Exod. 4. 1
God's answer, Signs and wonders *Divine Power*

4 *Lack of Utterance* I am not eloquent    Exod. 4. 10
God's answer, 'Who hath made man's mouth? Have not I, the Lord' *Divine Provision*

## 60 What is That in Thine Hand?
Exod. 4. 2

1 What is that in *thine hand*?
—A rod
Take it and use it for me, said God    Exod. 4. 2
(With it God made a way through the sea and brought water out of the rock)

2 What hast thou in *the house*?
—A pot of oil
Borrow empty vessels and pour it into them, said Elisha    2 Kings 4. 2
(With it she discharged her debt and her household responsibilities)

3 What have you in *your purse*?
—Two mites, a farthing
Put it into My treasury, says the Lord    Mark 12. 42
(The poor widow gave more than all the other donors)

4 What have you in *your treasure-chest*?—ointment of spikenard
With it anoint my beloved Son against His burial, said God    John 12. 3

5 What have you in *your memory*—The Scriptures 2 Tim. 3. 15
(Out of them Eunice instructed her young son, Timothy)

### 61 The Message of Moses
Exod. 5. 1-4

'Let My people go.' God purposed, and Moses preached, DELIVERANCE

| | |
|---|---|
| 1 To a land flowing with milk and honey | Exod. 3. 8 |
| 2 To a service for God on the mountain top | Exod. 3. 12 |
| 3 To a pilgrimage into the wilderness | Exod. 3. 18 |
| 4 To freedom from Egypt's bondage | Exod. 6. 6 |
| 5 To a sacrifice to God in the wilderness | Exod. 8. 27 |
| 6 To a festival 'unto the Lord' | Exod. 10. 9 |
| 7 To an annual memorial ordinance | Exod. 13. 10 |

### 62 Seven Great Promises of Jehovah
Exod. 6

| | | |
|---|---|---|
| I will bring you out | *Separation* | v. 6 |
| I will rid you . . . of their bondage | *Emancipation* | v. 6 |
| I will redeem you | *Redemption* | v. 6 |
| I will take you . . . for a people | *Selection* | v. 7 |
| I will be to you a God | *Adoration* | v. 7 |
| I will bring you in | *Admission* | v. 8 |
| I will give it you for a heritage | *Possession* | v. 8 |

### 63 The Uncompromising Servant of God

Satan, like Pharaoh, endeavours to induce the Lord's people to compromise.

*Four Subtle Suggestions* to which Moses said 'NO!'

1 *Sacrifice in the land*—in Egypt      Exod. 8. 25

Impossible, because—
  i. Such worship would be that of a servile people
  ii. Such worship would be that of an unseparated people
  iii. Such worship would be without Jehovah's presence
  iv. Such worship would be objectionable to the Egyptians

2 *Ye shall not go far away*—from Egypt      Exod. 8. 28
Satan tries to keep God's saints near the world in their interests and desires.

3 *Go, ye that are men*—and leave your families in Egypt      Exod. 10. 11
God's purpose was that their sons and daughters should accompany them.

4 Go, only *let your flocks and herds remain*      Exod. 10. 24
God's purpose was that not a hoof should be left behind. The flocks and herds were needed for sacrifices and food.

### 64 The Passover Lamb
'Take to them every man a lamb' Exod. 12. 3

'Christ our Passover is sacrificed for us' 1 Cor. 5. 7
A lamb for a man Gen. 4. 4; a lamb for a house Exod. 12. 3, 4; a Lamb for a nation Isa. 53. 6; a Lamb for the world John 1. 29.
In Exod. 12, the lamb is seen in three phases:—

1 A LIVING LAMB vs. 3-6, 'Jesus as He walked: without blemish, a male, and of the first year.

2 A SLAIN LAMB vs. 6, 7, 'a Lamb as it had been slain' (Rev. 5. 6). The people shed the blood and struck it on the doorposts: God saw the blood and sheltered His people (v. 13).

3 A LAMB ROAST WITH FIRE v. 8.

The Living Lamb—for *Examination*, the Slain Lamb—for *Emancipation*, the Lamb roast with fire—for *Enjoyment*.

### 65 Seven Requirements in Keeping the Passover
Exod. 12

| | |
|---|---|
| 1 Roasted Lamb (v. 8)— corresponding to Christ slain | 1 Cor. 5. 7 |
| 2 Bitter Herbs (v. 8)— corresponding to repentance | Luke 15. 10 |
| 3 Unleavened Bread (v. 8)— corresponding to holiness | 1 Cor. 5. 8 |
| 4 Girded Loins (v. 11)— corresponding to habits controlled | 1 Pet. 1. 13 |
| 5 Feet Shod (v. 11)— corresponding to Gospel testimony | Eph. 6. 15 |
| 6 Staff in Hand (v. 11)— corresponding to pilgrim character | 1 Pet. 2. 11 |
| 7 Eaten in Haste (v. 11)— corresponding to the Coming One | Rev. 22. 20 |

JS. FS.

## 66 Israel's Memorials

1 The Passover—
   The Redeemed life — Exod. 12. 14
2 Unleavened Bread—
   The Holy life — Exod. 13. 6-10
3 Defeat of Amalek—
   The Victorious life — Exod. 17. 14
4 Names of the tribes—
   The Sustained life — Exod. 28. 12, 29
5 Sound of the silver trumpets—
   The Guided life — Num. 10. 10
6 Broad plates on the altar—
   The Separated life — Num. 16. 40
7 Stones out of Jordan—
   The Resurrection life — Joshua 4. 4.7

## 67 Midnight Cries in Three Continents

IN AFRICA
   A Cry of Mourning over those who had perished — Exod. 12. 30

IN EUROPE
   A Cry of Assurance to an anxious soul — Acts 16. 28

IN ASIA
   A Cry of Expectation by those waiting for the bridegroom — Matt. 25. 6

IN ANY PART OF THE WORLD
   A Cry of Need from a needy friend — Luke 11. 5

## 68 God is Seen as

Redeemer through the Lamb — Exod. 12. 42

Leader in the Cloud — Exod. 13. 21

Saviour at the Sea — Exod. 14. 13

Healer at Marah — Exod. 15. 26

Provider in the Manna — Exod. 16. 15

Defender against Amalek — Exod. 17. 13

Ruler in the Tabernacle — Exod. 40. 16
JS. FS.

## 69 The Guiding Pillar
Exod. 13. 20-22

God's Provision for His pilgrims for their journeys.
Illustrates the Work of the Holy Spirit for the Believer in

1 Dwelling in him — Exod. 40. 38; 1 Cor. 6. 19
2 Comforting him — Ps. 105. 39; John 14. 16, etc.
3 Leading him — Neh. 9. 12, 19; Rom. 8. 14
4 Teaching him — Exod. 34. 5; John 14. 26, etc.
5 Witnessing to the world — Num. 14. 14; Acts 2. 4

## 70 Go Forward
Exod. 14. 15

Dr. Livingstone said, 'I shall go anywhere provided it is forward'.
1 *To Conflict*
   'Let us go up,' said Caleb — Num. 13. 30
2 *To Maturity*
   'Let us go on' — Heb. 6. 2
   Illustrations—
   Growth in a baby
   Progress by a student
   Superstructure of a building
3 *To Communion*
   'Let us go in' — Ps. 122. 1
4 *To Separation*
   'Let us go forth' — Heb. 13. 13

## 71 Habitations of God
'I will prepare Him an habitation'
Exod. 15. 2
'Let them make me a sanctuary, that I may dwell among them' Exod. 25. 8
1 The Tabernacle in the wilderness — Exod. 40. 34
2 The Temple in Jerusalem — 2 Chron. 5. 14
3 Jesus, the Incarnate Word — John 1. 14
4 The Church of God on earth — 1 Cor. 3. 16
5 The body of the believer — 1 Cor. 6. 19
6 The earthly Jerusalem in the Millennium — Ezek. 48. 35
7 The holy city, new Jerusalem, the Bride — Rev. 21. 3

## 72 Heaven's Fare for Earth's Wayfarers
'This is the bread which the Lord hath given you to eat' Exod. 16. 15
'I am the living bread which came down from heaven' John 6. 51
Manna was—

1 *Miraculous in its source—*
   The Bread of God — John 6. 33
   The Corn of Heaven — Ps. 78. 24
   Angel's food — Ps. 78. 25

2 *Mysterious in its nature—*
   Manna—what is it? — Exod. 16. 15; Deut. 8. 3

3 *Microscopic in its appearance—*
   a small, round thing (as small as the hoar frost on the ground) — Exod. 16. 14

4 *Marvellous in its sustenance—*
   Moses lived on it for 40 years — Deut. 34. 7
   Caleb lived on it for 40 years — Josh. 14. 10, 11
   Joshua lived on it for 40 years — Josh. 24. 29

## 73 The Manna and Its Meaning

1 Its taste—Sweet ............ Exod. 16. 31
  If ye have tasted ........... 1 Pet. 2. 3
2 Its price—Free ............. Exod. 16. 4
  Freely ye have received ..... Matt. 10. 8
3 Its colour—White ........... Exod. 16. 31
  Christ without sin .......... Heb. 4. 15
4 Its size—Small ............. Exod. 16. 14
  Christ in the manger ........ Luke 2. 16
5 Its form—Round ........... Exod. 16. 14
  Christ for Jew and Greek .... Rom. 1. 16
6 Its name—What is it? ....... Exod. 16. 15
  Christ unknown ............ John 1. 10
7 Its quantity—Sufficient ...... Exod. 16. 18
  Christ able to save ......... Heb. 7. 25
8 Where from—Heaven ........ Exod. 16. 4
  Christ from heaven ......... John 6. 38
9 Where it came to—The
  ground .................. Exod. 16. 14
  Christ in the world ......... John 17. 18
10 Who for—The people ....... Exod. 16. 4
  Christ for the world ........ John 6. 51
11 Who gathered it—Every man .. Exod. 16. 16
  As many as received Him .... John 1. 12
12 When overstored—Corrupted
                        Exod. 16. 20
  Christ came for judgment .... John 9. 39
                          JS. FS.

## 74 Wonders of the Spiritual Life
Exod. 16. 15

'They *wist not* what it was'

1 The Wonder of the
  *Divine Provision for us* ..... Exod. 16. 14, 15
  Bread from Heaven

2 The Wonder of the
  *Divine Process in us* ....... Exod. 34. 29
  Transformed life ........... 2 Cor. 3. 18

3 The Wonder of the
  *Divine Presence with us*
                 Judges 14. 6; 16. 20
  'I am with you alway' ....... Matt. 28. 20

## 75 Israel's First Battle
Exod. 17. 8-16

The Amalekites were bad masters (1 Sam. 30.13)
and terrible enemies: type of the flesh.

1 A Race of great antiquity
            Num. 24. 20
2 Had no fear of God
            Deut. 25. 18; Rom. 7. 18
3 Were the first enemy of God's people
            Exod. 17. 8; Rom. 8. 7
4 Attacked at the weakest point
  (The women and children were in the
  rear) Deut. 25. 18; 1 Pet. 2. 11
5 Were often in alliance with other foes
            Num. 14. 43, 45; Judges 6. 33;
            1 John 2. 16
6 God purposed their complete destruction
            Deut. 25. 19; Col. 3. 5
7 When permitted, bring disaster
            1 Sam. 15, 8, 9, 28; 1 Cor. 10. 6-8

## 76 Sinai
Mount Sinai, 'a granite mass, deeply cleft with
fissures', resembling in appearance a large altar.

1 THE MOUNT OF TRANSITION—
  a new epoch in God's ..... Exod. 19. 23;
  dealings with men ........ 20. 18

2 THE MOUNT OF TRANSCRIPTION—
  the writing of the Law by .. Exod. 24. 12;
  Jehovah .................. 31. 18

3 THE MOUNT OF TRANSMISSION—
  of the Old Covenant ...... Exod. 20. 19
  through Moses ........... John 1. 17

4 THE MOUNT OF TRANSGRESSION—
  worship of the golden calf .. Exod. 32. 4

5 THE MOUNT OF TRANSFIGURATION—
  the skin of Moses' face
  shone .................... Exod. 34. 29

## 77 The Decalogue

For Israel the righteousness of the Law was a
duty; for the Christian it is a joy.

Commandments 1 to 4—Duty to God Exod.
20. 3-11; Matt. 22. 37, 38

Commandments 5 to 10—Duty to our fellow-
men Exod. 20. 12-17; Matt. 22. 39

Our love to God must be whole-hearted: our
love to our neighbour must be unselfish.

First Commandment—Unique place of God
                   in our thoughts
Second Commandment—Unique honour due
                   to His Person
Third Commandment—Unique reverence
                   due to His Name
Fourth Commandment—Unique regard due
                   to His Day
Fifth Commandment—Filial respect due to
                   Parents
Sixth Commandment—Sanctity of our
                   neighbour's Life
Seventh Commandment—Sanctity of our
                   neighbour's wife or
                   husband
Eighth Commandment—Protection of our
                   neighbour's prop-
                   erty
Ninth Commandment—Preservation of our
                   neighbour's reputa-
                   tion
Tenth Commandment—Preservation of our
                   neighbour's honour

All transgression of the Law springs from
Selfishness, and is Sin 1 John 3. 4

Apostolic Teaching concerning the Law—

1 To the *Sinner*
  Impossibility of being justified by it
            Rom. 3. 27, 28; Gal. 3. 21
2 To the *Saint*—
  Love is the fulfilling of the Law
            Rom. 13. 10; James 2. 8

## 78 The Devoted Hebrew Slave
Exod. 21. 1-6

'Mine ear hast thou digged'
a type of Christ          Ps. 40. 6; Heb. 10. 5;
example to those who
are Christ's          John 12. 26

1 THE FACT—
I love my master—          Exod. 21. 5;
*The Cause*          2 Cor. 5. 14

2 THE ACT—
Bring him to the door—          Exod. 21. 6
*The Consecration*
Bore his ear through—          Exod. 21. 6
The sprinkled blood on the
doorpost declared,
'I *believe*'          Exod. 12. 23
The bored ear at the door-
post declared,
'I *love*'          Deut. 15. 17
The commandments written
on the doorpost declared,
'I *obey*'          Deut. 6. 9

3 THE PACT
He shall serve him for ever
*The Consequence*          Exod. 21. 6

## 79 The Tabernacle
Exod. 25. 8

1 GOD'S PATTERN FOR IT
'Things in the heavens'          Exod. 25. 40;
Heb. 8. 5
Four times Moses was instructed that it
must be 'according to the pattern' (Exod.
25. 9, 40; 26. 30; 27. 8)
Account of creation occupies 2 chapters,
of the tabernacle 14 chapters in Exodus.

2 GOD'S PURPOSE THROUGH IT
'That I may dwell among
them'          Exod. 25. 8
He 'walked' in Eden, and with Enoch and
Noah;
He visited Abraham, Isaac and Jacob;
but He wanted to dwell with His chosen
and redeemed people.

3 GOD'S PLACE IN IT
'in the midst'          Exod. 25. 8
God's Order in the design of the tabernacle
—From the Holiest out to the gate:
Israel's Order in their approach—From
the gate inward          Heb. 10. 19

Three Parts in the Tabernacle and their sizes—

THE COURT
100 cubits long, 50 cubits broad, 5 cubits high

THE HOLY PLACE
30 cubits long, 10 cubits broad, 10 cubits high

THE HOLIEST OF ALL
10 cubits long, 10 cubits broad, 10 cubits high

## 80 The Ark of the Covenant
Exod. 25. 10-22

1 *Its Composition*
Acacia wood overlaid
with gold          Exod. 25. 10, 11

Christ's incorruptible
humanity and His deity
and preciousness

2 *Its Crown*
Of gold          Exod. 25. 11
'Crowned with glory and
honour'          Heb. 2. 9

3 *Its Carriage*
with staves of acacia
wood          Exod. 25. 13-15

4 *Its Contents*
Pot of manna          Exod. 16. 33, 34
Tables of testimony, the
Law          Exod. 25. 16
Aaron's rod that budded          Num. 17. 10

5 *Its Covering*
the Mercy-seat          Exod. 25. 21

6 *Its Comprehensiveness*
the fullest type of Christ
of all the tabernacle
furniture: the gold—
His pre-existence, the
wood—His Incarna-
tion, the Tables of Law
—His sinlessness and
perfection, the manna
—His sustaining power
the rod that budded—
His resurrection and
life-giving power, the
Mercy-seat—His sacri-
fice, and the crown—
His coming glory.

## 81 Positions of the Ark

1 On the *Desert Sand*
beauty in contact with barrenness
Exod. 25. 10; Num. 5. 17

2 In the *Holiest of all*
within the veil   Heb. 9. 3, 4, 24

3 *Under* the *wings of the Cherubim*
1 Kings 6. 27, 28

4 In the *midst of the camp*
Num. 5. 3

5 On the *shoulders of the priests*
Deut. 10. 8

6 *Before the people* on a three days' journey
Num. 10. 33

7 First to go into Jordan and last to come out
of Jordan          Joshua 3. 11; 4. 11

## 82 Names of the Ark of the Covenant
Exod. 25. 10

1 Ark of the Testimony
chiefly in Exodus and Numbers

2 Ark of the Covenant
chiefly in Joshua and 1 Samuel

3 Ark of God, Ark of Jehovah
chiefly in Samuel, Kings and Chronicles

4 Ark of Jehovah—God
1 Kings 2. 26

5 Ark of Thy strength
2 Chron. 6. 41; Ps. 132. 8

6 The Holy ark
2 Chron. 35. 3

## 83 The Tabernacle Furniture
Exod. 25; 27. 1-8; 30. 1-10; 30. 17-21

In the Court—
THE BRAZEN ALTAR
Christ's full atonement for sin
Exod. 27. 1; John 1. 29
THE BRAZEN LAVER
Christ's cleansing truth for our walk
Exod. 30. 18; John 13. 5

In the Holy Place—
THE GOLDEN LAMPSTAND
Christ's Illuminating grace
Exod. 25. 31; John 8. 12

THE TABLE OF SHEWBREAD
Christ's sustaining power
Exod. 25. 23; John 6. 35
THE GOLDEN ALTAR
Christ's Priestly intercession
Exod. 30. 1; John 17

In the Holiest of all—
THE ARK OF THE COVENANT
Christ's all-comprehensive glory
Exod. 25. 10
THE MERCY-SEAT
Christ's work of propitiation and reconcilia-
tion          Exod. 25. 17; Rom. 3. 25

## 84 The Mercy-Seat
Exod. 25. 17
In the New Testament the word for 'mercy-
seat' occurs twice, in Heb. 9. 5 and Rom. 3.25
(translated there 'propitiation')

1 Where God dwelt and His glory was seen
Lev. 16. 2; Ps. 80. 1

2 Where the blood was sprinkled on Day of
Atonement          Lev. 16. 3, 14, 15

3 Where God can meet man and commune
with him          Exod. 25. 22; Num. 17. 4
Ps. 85. 10

## 85 Aaron and Christ Contrasted
Exod. 28. 1-2
AARON
Israel's first high priest
Called a high priest   Heb. 5. 1, 4
Taken from among men   Heb. 5. 1
Ministered on earth
Minister under the old covenant
Could not continue by reason of death
Heb. 7. 23
Offered sacrifices to God continually
Heb. 7. 27
Wore garments for glory and beauty
Exod. 28. 2

CHRIST
The Believer's only High Priest
Called a great High Priest   Heb. 4. 14
'Jesus, the Son of God'   Heb. 4. 14; 5. 5
Ministers in Heaven   Heb. 8. 1; 9. 24
Minister of the new covenant   Heb. 8. 6, 7
Continues ever
Heb. 7. 24
Offered up Himself—One sacrifice for sins
Heb. 7. 28
Is 'crowned with glory and honour'
Heb. 2. 9

## 86 Burdens the High Priest Bore

1 His people's names on his
shoulders          Exod. 28. 12
Jesus is
ABLE TO SUCCOUR   Heb. 2. 18

2 His people's names on his
breast (heart)          Exod. 28. 29
Jesus is
ABLE TO SYMPATHIZE   Heb. 4. 15

3 His people's 'judgment'
(guidance) on his heart Exod. 28. 30
Jesus is
ABLE TO SAVE TO THE UTTERMOST
Heb. 7. 25

4 The iniquity of his people's
holy offerings          Exod. 28. 38
Jesus is
ABLE TO SANCTIFY   Heb. 13. 12, 15

Ps. 68. 18—Thou hast ascended on high.
Ps. 68. 19—(R.V.) Who daily beareth our
burdens.

## 87 The Breastplate of Judgment
Exod. 28. 15-29

1 Its *Place*
on his heart, place of
affection          Exod. 28. 29
He loved them unto the
end          John 13. 1

2 Its *Space*

a span long and a span broad — Exod. 28. 16

No believer is outside the span of their High Priest's hand — Isa. 40. 12; John 10. 28

3 Its *Face*

precious stones differing in colour and brilliance, with his people's names — Exod. 28. 17-21

4 Its *Lace*

lace of blue through rings of gold, so that it could not be loosed, — Exod. 28. 28

Nothing can separate us from Christ's love — Rom. 8. 38, 39

## 88  The Urim and Thummim
Exod. 28. 30

The Breastplate was in the form of a bag or pouch and became the repository for the two articles, probably gems whose brilliance could shine through, called the Urim and Thummim —Lights and Perfections. By means of these God revealed to the high priest His will and gave guidance to His people when they asked for it.

Three Important Uses of the Urim and Thummim in Israel's history

1 To instruct God's chosen leaders — Num. 27. 18-23

2 To identify God's true priests — Ezra 2. 62, 63

3 To indicate God's sore displeasure with those who disobeyed Him — I Sam. 28. 6

## 89  The Mitre, Its Plate and Its Inscription
Exod. 28. 36-38

The mitre, which is the rendering of the Hebrew word meaning 'something wound round' the head, was like a turban. Aaron, Israel's high priest, of the tribe of Levi, could wear a mitre but not a royal crown. Israel's king of a later period, belonging to the tribe of Judah, could wear a crown but not a mitre (Heb. 7. 14; 8. 4).

One wicked prince of Israel in the past had the presumption to wear both and was punished. The Antichrist, who will be 'the man of sin' in the future, will also do this, but will be overthrown and have both his mitre and crown removed by 'Him whose right it is' (Ezek. 21. 27). When He, the true Messiah, comes, He will be 'a priest upon His throne' (Zech. 6. 13).

THE MITRE

1 Its *Parts*

Fine white linen— Christ's perfect righteousness — Exod. 39. 28

A lace of blue— Christ's heavenly ministry — Exod. 28. 37

A plate of gold— Christ's essential deity — Exod. 28. 36

2 Its *Plate*

bore the inscription— HOLINESS TO THE LORD — Exod. 28. 36

This may be rendered also 'Set apart to the Lord' — John 17. 19

3 Its *Purpose*

'that Aaron may bear the iniquity of the holy things which the children of Israel shall hallow in all their holy gifts'. — Exod. 28. 38; Heb. 13. 15

## 90  Acceptance Before God
Exod. 28. 38

1 No acceptance with God unless we come in His appointed way — Gen. 4. 7

2 Acceptance with God for those who 'lean their hand' on the sacrifice of Christ, the burnt offering — Lev. 1. 4 (The word translated 'lay' is the same word as in Ps. 88. 7, and means 'lean'. So we lean our soul on the same person on whom Jehovah leant His wrath)

3 Acceptance with God for those who repent, as did Job — Job. 42. 9

4 Acceptance of the believer in the Beloved, Jesus Christ — Eph. 1. 6

5 Acceptance of the believer's offerings through Christ — Exod. 28. 38; Heb. 13. 15

6 Acceptance of the first-fruits offered through the High Priest — Lev. 23. 11

7 Acceptance of the evangelist's priestly oblation of those converted through his preaching — Rom. 15. 16

## 91  Consecration of God's Priests
Exod. 29. 9

In the Old Testament four different Hebrew words are translated 'consecrate'. and together they provide a complete explanation of the act of consecration.

1 THE PURPOSE OF CONSECRATION
*Qadesh*, set apart — Exod. 28. 3; 30. 30

2 THE ACT OF CONSECRATION
*Male yad*, fill the hand — Exod. 29. 9, 29, 33, 35 (Also 1 Chron. 29. 5; 2 Chron. 29. 31)

3 THE STATE OF CONSECRATION
*Nazar*, separate — Num. 6. 12

4 THE SPIRIT OF CONSECRATION
*Charam*, devote, implying an attitude of devotion — Micah 4. 13

## 92 The High Priest's Service
Exod. 30. 1-10

1 The *Work of Atonement* at the brazen altar
Lev. 9. 7; Heb. 7. 28

2 The *Daily Ministry* within the Holy place
Lev. 24. 1-4;
Lighting of the lamps
Num. 8. 1-5; Eph. 5. 14
Offering of the incense
Exod. 30. 7; Rev. 5. 8

3 The *Exacting duties* within the camp, e.g.
Examination of lepers
Lev. 13. 1-3; 14. 8; Eph. 5. 26
Taking of the census
Num. 1. 44; 26. 1-4; John 18. 9

4 The *Pleasant ministrations* at the gate of
the tabernacle—
Blessing the people
Lev. 9. 22; Luke 24. 50
Consecrating the Levites
Num. 8. 11-12; Gal. 1. 15, 16

## 93 The Rites of the Sanctuary
Exod. 30. 11-38

1 *Redemption* by the
SILVER OF THE SANCTUARY
Exod. 30. 12, 13;
(Cp. 1 Pet. 1. 18)
Half a shekel for each person at each
census; after the Shekel of the Sanctuary:
i It was within the reach of all, the poor
as well as the rich
ii It was the same for all, the rich as well
as the poor
iii It was to make atonement for the souls
of all

2 *Cleansing* for the
SERVICE OF THE SANCTUARY
Exod. 30. 18, 19
The hands and feet of the priests must be
cleansed from defilement before they
entered the holy place    John 13. 8-10

3 *Anointing* for the
SANCTIFICATION OF THE SANCTUARY
Exod. 30. 29, 30
The Tabernacle, its furniture and the
priests must be sanctified with the holy
anointing oil.
i It was only for the priests of God
ii It must not be counterfeited

## 94 The Brazen Laver
Exod. 30. 17-21

1 Of what was it *made*?
Of Brass from the women's
mirrors. The Word of God is    Exod. 38. 8
a Mirror and contains water    James 1. 23;
for cleansing    Eph. 5. 26

2 What was its *size*?
No dimensions are given.
The Word of God is unlimited in its power and application

3 Where was it *placed*?
Between the Brazen altar and    Exod. 30. 18
the tabernacle    Heb. 10. 22

4 What was its *purpose*?
For Aaron and his sons to
wash their hands and feet    Exod. 30. 19

## 95 The Finger of God
Exod. 31. 18

1 The *Power* of God in
*Creation*    Ps. 8. 3

2 The *Holiness* of God in
*Legislation*    Exod. 31. 18

3 The *Righteousness* of God in
*Incarnation*    John 8. 6

4 The *Kingdom* of God in
*Emancipation*    Luke 11. 20

5 The *Wrath* of God in
*Condemnation*    Dan. 5. 5

## 96 God's Chosen Workmen
Exod. 31. 1-11; 35. 30-35
Bezaleel means 'Shadow of God' (Isa. 49. 2):
was of the tribe of Judah, praise. Aholiab
means 'Tent of my father' (Exod. 31. 7): was
of the tribe of Dan, judging. They were—

1 *Appointed* by the *Call of God* Exod. 31. 2
Those called by name to service—
Bezaleel    Exod. 35. 30
Israel the nation    Isa. 43. 1
Cyrus the Persian    Isa. 45. 1, 4

2 *Filled* with the *Spirit of God* Exod. 31. 3
Bezaleel was the first man said to be
filled with the Spirit

3 *Wise* in the *Work of God*    Exod. 31. 6

## 97 A Sinful People
Exod. 32

1 THE TEST
'Moses delayed to come    v. 1;
down'    Matt. 24. 48

2 THE FAILURE
'These be thy gods, O Israel' vs. 4, 6;
1 Cor. 10. 7

3 THE PLEADER
Moses 'besought the Lord' vs. 11, 31
He was a *Strenuous* pleader
a *Skilful* pleader, and
a *Successful* pleader

4 THE REMEDY
the sin must be put away    vs. 20, 26
the people must be penitent
the loyal must be set apart for Jehovah

5 THE CONSEQUENCES
God's wrath fell on the impenitent    v. 11
The tables of the law were
broken    v. 19
The hardened sinners were
punished    v. 28

98 **'My Presence Shall Go With Thee**
Exod. 33. 14

SALVATION
Silent in His presence    Zeph. 1. 7
Trembling in His presence Ps. 114. 7
Saved in His presence     Isa. 63. 9
POSITION
Standing in His presence  2 Chron. 20. 9
Hiding in His presence    Ps. 32. 7
Dwelling in His presence  Ps. 140. 13
CONDITION
Thankful in His presence  Ps. 95. 2
Singing in His presence   1 Chron. 16. 33
Joyful in His presence    Ps. 16. 11
  Yet sure, if in Thy Presence,
  My soul still constant were,
  Mine eyes would, more familiar,
  Its brighter glories bear.
                                    J.M.H.

99 **Communion With God**
Exod. 33. 17-23

1 The *Privilege* of Communion
  for those who have
  found grace in God's
  sight                   Exod. 33. 17
  through the Revelation
  of the Life of God      1 John 1. 3
  through the cleansing of
  the blood of Christ     1 John 1. 7
  through walking in the
  light by the Spirit     1 John 1. 7
2 The *Place* of Communion
  the Mount of God        Exod. 34. 1, 2
  on the Rock of ages     Exod. 33. 21, 22
  in the sanctuary        Exod. 33. 8
3 The *Purpose* of Communion
  to learn to know God    Exod. 33. 19;
                          John 17. 3
  to see the glory of God Exod. 33. 18, 22;
                          2 Cor. 4. 6
  to worship God          Exod. 34. 8
  to be transformed       Exod. 34. 29;
                          2 Cor. 3. 18
4 The *Preciousness* of Communion
  the Friendship of God   Exod. 33. 11;
                          James 2. 23

100 **The Radiance of Heaven**
Exod. 34. 27-35

Moses—
'The skin of his face
shone'                    Exod. 34. 29. 30

This Radiance was—
1 THE REWARD OF DESIRE
                          Exod. 33. 18; Ps. 90. 17

2 THE RESULT OF DILIGENCE
                          Exod. 34. 28; 2 Pet. 1. 5

Natural fears were Forgotten

Natural pleasures were Foregone

Natural appetites were Forsaken

3 THE REFLECTION OF DIVINE GLORY
                          2 Cor. 3. 9, 13

Moses 'wist not' that the skin of his face
shone. The radiance was apparent to all but
Moses.

101 **Jehovah's Appeal and His People's
Response**
Exod. 35. 4, 5, 20-29

The Lord said, 'In the hearts of all that are
wise-hearted have I put wisdom, that they may
make all that I have commanded' (Exod. 31. 6)
The Lord said, 'Whosoever is of a willing
heart, let him bring it' (Exod. 35. 5)

So *Whole-hearted Offerers*
  sought from their jewels
  and wealth an offering
  for the Lord            Exod. 35. 20-24

*Wise-hearted Workers*
  wrought with their hands
  in the work             Exod. 35. 25, 26

*Willing-hearted Givers*
  brought their contribu-
  tions for the tabernacle
  of the Lord             Exod. 35. 27-29

# LEVITICUS

## 102 Christ in Leviticus

Exodus tells of the Way Out of Egypt, and Moses, the Prophet, is prominent: Leviticus tells of the Way Into the Sanctuary, and Aaron, the Priest, is prominent.

'Christ is made unto us Wisdom, even righteousness, sanctification and redemption'
1 Cor. 1. 30

Chapters 1 to 10
The Guilty forgiven—made unto us Righteousness
The Character of God is revealed,

Chapters 11 to 22
The Defiled cleansed and sanctified—made unto us Sanctification
The Sacrifice of Christ is foreshadowed,

Chapters 23 to 27
The Disinherited and the Slaves are redeemed—made unto us Redemption
The Way of salvation is indicated and the Principles of legislation are enunciated.

2 The Meal Offering—
Man fallen and depraved needs as a substitute One Who is holy, harmless and undefiled and separate from sinners — Lev. 2
(Christ, God manifest in the flesh, sinless) — 1 Tim. 3. 16

3 The Peace Offering—
Man in heart alienated from God, needs reconciliation — Lev. 3
(Christ as our peace, having slain the enmity) — Eph. 2. 14-16 / Rom. 5. 1

4 The Sin Offering—
Man a sinner by nature and practice, needs an atoning sacrifice — Lev. 4
(Christ manifested to take away our sins) — Rom. 5. 6 / 2 Cor. 5. 21

## 103 Leading Characteristics of the Offerings

| | | | |
|---|---|---|---|
| 1 The Burnt Offering | FIRE | Christ's devotion to God's will | Lev. 1. 7, 8, 12, 17 |
| 2 The Meal Offering | OIL | Christ anointed with the Holy Spirit and with power | Lev. 2. 2, 4, 5, 6, 7, 15, 16 |
| 3 The Peace Offering | FAT | Christ making peace by the blood of His Cross | Lev. 3. 3, 4, 9, 10, 14, 15, 16 |
| 4 The Sin Offering | BLOOD | Christ's propitiation for sin by His death | Lev. 4. 5, 6, 7, 16, 17 18, etc. |
| 5 The Trespass Offering | AMENDS | Christ atoning for the injury sin inflicts | Lev. 5. 16; 6. 5 |

J. WEBB.

## 104 Holiness Unto the Lord, in Leviticus

1 Chapters 1 to 10
The *Platform* of holiness, Sacrifices and priesthood

2 Chapters 11 to 16
The *Principles* of holiness, Food, issues, leprosy

3 Chapters 17 to 25
The *Practice* of holiness, People, priests and periods

4 Chapters 26, 27
The *Promises* of holiness, God's to His people and the people's to God.

## 105 The Meaning of the Offerings

1 The Burnt Offering—
Man utterly unworthy in himself, without anything of his own to recommend him to God, needs to be identified with One Who is altogether worthy, and an object of divine favour, that he may be accepted — Lev. 1
(Christ obedient unto death) — Phil. 2. 8

## 106 The Burnt Offering
Lev. 1

All was for God — Eph. 5. 2
Christ in the Gospel of John

1 SELECTION OF THE OFFERING
Kind—Herbivorous and clean — Lev. 1. 2, 3, 14
Sex—Male, indicating strength
Description—without blemish

2 SACRIFICE OF THE VICTIM — Lev. 1. 4
The offerer presented it, laid his hands upon it, and killed it
The priest sprinkled the blood

3 SPECIFICATION OF THE OFFERING — Lev. 1. 3-19
It might be a bullock—Christ's patient endurance — Lev. 1. 3-9
It might be a sheep or goat —His perfect surrender — Lev. 1. 10-13
It might be turtle doves or young pigeons—Christ's poverty and meekness — Lev. 1. 14-19

## 107 The Sides of the Brazen Altar

| The *North* Side | the Sacrifice was slain | Condemnation | Lev. 1. 11 |
| The *East* Side | the Ashes of the victim were deposited | Justification | Lev. 1. 16 |
| The *South* Side | the Rivers of cleansing flowed out | Sanctification | Ezek. 47. 1 |
| The *West* Side | faced into the Holiest | Access by the Blood | Heb. 10. 19 |

## 108 The Meal Offering (A.V.—Meat-Offering)
Lev. 2

Christ in the Gospel of Luke

The Hebrew word for 'meal-offering'—minchah—occurs in many places, including Gen. 4. 3, 4, 5; 32. 13, 18, 20, 21, and means a present brought to a superior in recognition of his authority or to solicit a favour from a friend.

1 Its *Materials* —Fine flour—Christ's perfect Humanity ⎫ all burnt on — Lev. 2. 1, 2, 13
Oil—Christ's anointing by the Spirit ⎬ the altar; all
Frankincense—Christ's fragrant life ⎪ for God
Salt—Christ's incorruptible nature ⎭ — John 8. 29

But
NO HONEY —No mere natural sweetness that ferments in heat — Lev. 2. 11
NO LEAVEN —No malice or wickedness but sincerity and truth — 1 Cor. 5. 8

2 Its *Grades* —Different aspects of Christ's sufferings in life — Lev. 2. 1-3
Unbaked flour, burnt on the altar—Sufferings Godward,
Unleavened cakes, baked in the oven or roasted on a flat plate—Christ's sufferings among men, for righteousness, and in sympathy — Lev. 2. 4, 5
Unmilled firstfruits—beaten out and dried—Christ's prolonged sufferings at man's hands — Lev. 2. 14-16

3 Its *Uses* —For an Offering to God —Divine satisfaction — Lev. 6. 14-15
In the consecration of the priests—Divine service — Lev. 8. 2
For the food of the priests —Divine strength — Lev. 6. 18; 8. 31

## 109 The Peace Offering
Lev. 3; 7, 11-34

'He is our Peace' (or peace offering) Eph. 2. 14

1 A *Threefold Purpose*—
For thanksgiving Lev. 7. 12
For a Vow of Consecration Lev. 7. 16
As a Voluntary offering Lev. 7. 16

2 A *Threefold Selection*—
either male or female Lev. 3. 1, 7, 12
From the cattle—
Christ in service and sacrifice
From the sheep—
Christ in self-denying surrender
From the goats—
Christ as the sin-bearer

3 A *Threefold Application*—
The Blood— Lev. 3. 8, 13
sprinkled for atonement
the Fat—
all for God (Christ's excellencies) Lev. 3. 16
the Flesh—
eaten by the offerers Lev. 7. 15-21, 31, 34

4 A *Threefold Blessing*
to the offerer
Forgiveness, bringing peace with God Eph. 2. 16
Feasting, eating the flesh of the victim Lev. 7. 15
Fellowship with God and His priests Lev. 7. 33, 34

## 110 The Sin Offering
### Lev. 4

'This is the law of the sin-offering—it is most holy.' Lev. 6. 25

| | | |
|---|---|---|
| 1 *Sin* | —is Earth's deathblow (Gen. 3. 17), a Nation's shame (Prov. 14. 34), man's ruin (Rom. 5. 12), God's enemy (Col. 1. 21) and Satan's deadly weapon. | |
| 2 *The Sinner* | —might be a priest, a religious leader | Lev. 4. 3 |
| | might be the nation or congregation | Lev. 4. 13 |
| | might be a ruler of the people | Lev. 4. 22 |
| | might be one of the common people | Lev. 4. 27 |
| 3 *The Offering* | —must be a young animal | Lev. 4. 3, 14, 23, 28 |
| | (The Lamb of God was only 33 years when He offered Himself) | |
| | must be unblemished | Lev. 4. 3, 23, 28; 1 Pet. 1. 19 |
| | must be killed | Lev. 4. 4, 15, 24, 29; Acts 3. 15 |
| | Its blood must be sprinkled before the Lord | Lev. 4. 6, 17, 25, 30; 1 Pet. 1. 2 |
| 4 *The Offerer* | —brought his offering | Lev. 4. 4, 14, 23, 28 |
| | laid his hands on its head (token of transfer of guilt) | Lev. 4. 4, 15, 24, 29 |
| | was forgiven | Lev. 4. 26, 31 |
| | stood perfect and accepted before God | Heb. 10. 14 |

## 111 Christ Ever Available
### Lev. 6. 13

1 The Tabernacle gate into the Court was always open    Exod. 27. 16

2 The Fire on the brazen altar was always burning    Lev. 6. 13

3 The Water in the brazen laver was always sufficient    Exod. 30. 18-19

4 The Incense on the golden altar was always burning    Exod. 30. 8

5 The Shewbread on the table was always fresh    Exod. 25. 30

6 The Oil in the lampstand was always replenished    Lev. 24. 2, 4

7 The Shechinah glory was always with the camp    Neh. 9. 19

## 112 Consecration of the Priests
### Lev. 8

1 They were taken *
   SELECTION    Lev. 8. 2; 1 Pet. 1. 2; 2. 9

2 They were brought
   APPROACH    Lev. 8. 6; Eph. 2. 13, 18

3 They were washed
   REGENERATION
   Lev. 8. 6; Titus 3. 5

4 They were clothed
   RIGHTEOUSNESS
   Lev. 8. 7; 2 Cor. 5. 21

5 They were anointed
   UNCTION OF THE SPIRIT
   Lev. 8. 12; 1 John 2. 27

6 They laid their hands on the sin-offering
   SUBSTITUTION
   Lev. 8. 14; 1 Pet. 2. 24

7 The blood of the lamb of consecration, and the oil, were applied to their members
   CONSECRATION
   Lev. 8. 23, 30; 1 Cor. 6. 19

8 Their hands were filled
   SERVICE    Lev. 8. 27; Rom. 12. 1

9 They were set apart for God
   SEPARATION
   Lev. 8. 30; 1 Pet. 1. 2

10 They ate from the basket of consecrations
   PARTICIPATION
   Lev. 8. 31; 1 Cor. 11. 28

## 113 Three Kinds of Fire

1 The *Fire of Acceptance* that consumed the offerings    Lev. 9. 23, 24; 1 Kings 18. 38, 39

2 The *Fire of Transgression* 'strange fire' offered by Nadad and Abihu    Lev. 10. 1

Note that there was no flaw in their title, there was no neglect of prescribed rites    Lev. 8. 6-32

They were positionally right but conditionally wrong, because they were drunk with wine and could not distinguish between the holy and unholy, the clean and the unclean    Eph. 5. 18; Lev. 10. 9, 10

3 The *Fire of Retribution*    Lev. 10. 2; Heb. 12. 28, 29

**114 Personal Holiness**
Lev. 11. 44, 45

In Leviticus the exhortation to be holy is repeated six times.

HOLINESS is

1 The *Furtherance of God's Purpose for* His people Eph. 1. 4; 1 Thess. 4. 3

2 The *Evidence of God's Character in* His people Heb. 12. 11, 14, Holy Father (John 17. 11), Holy Son (Acts 4. 27), Holy Spirit (Rom. 1. 4)

3 The *Product of God's Grace through* His people Isa. 62. 11, 12; 1 Pet. 1. 15. As Redeemed (1 Pet. 1. 18), as sought (I Pet. 2. 25), as not forsaken (Heb. 13, 5, 6)

4 The *Display of God's Attributes by* His people Rom. 6. 22; Gal. 5. 22

These are—
Purity, modesty, chastity in ourselves,
Integrity, honesty, charity toward others,
Sincerity, sobriety, activity before God.

**115 Unclean! Unclean!**
Lev. 13. 1-3, 10, 45, 46

Leprosy in Scripture is presented as Defilement that needs cleansing rather than Disease that needs healing.

It begins inside and shows up outside, like sin, of which it is a type in—

1 ITS EXTREME LOATHSOMENESS
He shall be defiled            Lev. 13. 46

2 ITS INSIGNIFICANT BEGINNINGS
a swelling, a scab, a bright
spot in the skin             Lev. 13. 2

3 ITS INEVITABLE PROGRESS
spread much about           Lev. 13. 7, 8

4 ITS INSENSIBILITY
only detected by its appear-
ance when examined          Lev. 13. 5, 10,
                            17, 21. etc.

5 ITS INVOLVED SEGREGATION
outside the camp            Lev. 13. 46

**116 Cleansing of the Leper**
Lev. 14

In the Leper
A Life Tainted              Lev. 13. 20

For the slain bird
A Life Taken                Lev. 14, 4, 5

Two birds alive and clean were to be brought:
One was killed in an earthen vessel over running water, for a sacrifice was necessary for cleansing            Heb. 9. 14
In the living bird let loose
A Life Triumphant           Lev. 14. 7
(Type of Christ in resurrection)
It was dipped in the blood of the slain bird, and thus identified with its death.

**117 What Follows Cleansing?**
Compare Luke 5. 12-15

The Cleansed leper—
1 washed his clothes
Cleansed Habits             Lev. 14. 8
2 shaved his hair
Self-judgment               Lev. 14. 8
3 was brought into the camp
Nearness                    Eph. 2. 13
4 had the blood applied to his ear, thumb, and foot
Cleansed members            Lev. 14. 14
5 had the oil applied
Consecrated members         Lev. 14. 17
6 had his head anointed
The Spirit's anointing      Lev. 14. 18
7 offered sacrifices to the Lord
Worship                     Lev. 14. 19

**118 The Day of Atonement**
Lev. 16

Types of Christ, our propitiation 1 John 2. 2
1 The high priest who entered the holiest with the blood
                Lev. 16. 3, 14; Heb. 9. 7;
                Heb. 9. 11, 12
2 The bullock slain for the sin-offering
                Lev. 16. 6; Heb. 9. 14
3 The goat slain for the sins of the people
                Lev. 16. 15; Heb. 9. 14
4 The veil through which the Holiest was entered      Lev. 16. 2; Heb. 10. 20
5 The mercy-seat on which the blood was sprinkled     Lev. 16. 14; Rom. 3. 25
6 The scapegoat that bore away the confessed sins to the wilderness
                Lev. 16. 21, 22; John 1. 29
7 The bodies of the victims burned outside the camp      Lev. 16. 27; Heb. 13. 11, 12

### 119 The Atoning Blood of Christ
Lev. 17. 11

What the blood of bulls and goats could not do—atone for sin—Heb. 10. 4

What the blood of Christ does—

1 Makes atonement for sin
Lev. 17. 11

2 Ratifies the new covenant with God
1 Cor. 11. 24

3 Effects the justification of the sinner who believes in Jesus
Rom. 5. 9

4 Procures redemption for the believer
Eph. 1. 7

5 Brings the believer near to God
Eph. 2. 13

6 Reconciles the believer to God
Col. 1. 20

7 Looses the believer from his sins
Rev. 1. 7

8 Purges the believer's conscience from dead works
Heb. 9. 14

9 Gives the believer boldness of access into the Holiest
Heb. 10. 19

10 Cleanses the believer from all sins
1 John 1. 7

### 121 Golden Jubilee Year
Lev. 25. 8-17

Israel's Sacred Sevens—

the Sabbath, the Seventh day each week
Lev. 23. 3

the Year of rest, the Seventh year
Lev. 25. 4

There were two festivals each lasting seven days, and three Feasts in the Seventh month. The Feast of Pentecost was celebrated seven weeks after the previous set feast.

JUBILEE YEAR was the fiftieth year, after seven Sabbatic years had run their course. It brought—

1 *Reinstatement* to the *Dispossessed*—
Inheritance restored
Lev. 25. 28

2 *Redemption* to the *Downtrodden*—
Slaves emancipated
Lev. 25. 54

3 *Relief* for the *Distressed*—
Toilers rested
Lev. 25. 11, 12

The *Law of Liberty* was applied—

to the *Land*
vs. 13 to 18:

to *dwellings*
vs. 27 to 34:

to *bondslaves*
vs. 35 to 55.

### 120 The Feasts of Jehovah
Lev. 23

The Revised Version calls them 'set feasts' i.e., appointed, trysting times. In addition to the Sabbath day, the seventh day of the week, there were *Seven Feasts*.

1 *Passover*—
on 14th Abib (First month) | Death of Christ | Lev. 23. 5; 1 Cor. 5. 7

2 *Unleavened bread*—
15th to 21st Abib | Holiness of redeemed life | Lev. 23. 6-8; 1 Cor. 5. 8

3 *Firstfruits*—
also in Abib the 'Omer' (sheaf) | Resurrection of Christ | Lev. 23. 9-14; 1 Cor. 15. 23

4 *Pentecost*—
on the 6th Sivan (Third month) | The Church formed | Lev. 23. 15-21; Acts 2. 1
A new meal offering that had leaven was offered at Pentecost.

5 *Trumpets*
on 1st and 2nd Tisri (Seventh month) | Christ's Return to reign | Lev. 23. 23-25

6 *Atonement*—
on 10th Tisri | Israel's souls afflicted and Israel's sin put away | Lev. 23. 27-28; Zech. 12. 10-14; 13. 1

7 *Tabernacles* (booths) | 15th to 22nd Tisri | Lev. 23. 39-43;
The nations at peace with Messiah enthroned | Zech. 14. 16

# NUMBERS

**122   Israel's Camp with God in the Midst**
Num. 2

Four Directions with three on each cardinal point.

1 The *Way in for Worship*—
Clockwise—12 Tribes
(Judah—Praise—coming first)
Num. 2. 1-31

2 The *Way out for Service*—
Anti-clockwise—12 Oxen
(Facing out from the altar) 2 Chron. 4. 1-4

3 The *Way home for Reward*—
E, N, S, W—12 Gates
(Open for entry)          Rev. 21. 12, 13

**123   The Service of the Sanctuary**
Num. 3. 5-13

1 The *Selection of the Workers*
'I have taken the Levites' Num. 3. 12

2 The *Separation of the Servants*
'Thou shalt separate the Levites'          Num. 8. 14

3 The *Service of the Levites*
'Unto God'          Num. 8. 13;
Deut. 10. 8

unto Aaron, the high priest          Num. 18. 1, 2
unto the congregation   Num. 16. 9
unto the sanctuary       Num. 1. 50

4 The *Sustenance of the Ministers*
by the people's tithes      Num. 18. 21, 24
(They had no territorial inheritance)
Exhortation to the people
concerning the Levites      Deut. 12. 19

**124   The Levites and their Charge**
Num. 4

'The Kohathites upon their shoulders bear
The holy vessels covered all with care.
The Gershonites receive an easier charge,
Two waggons full of cords and curtains large.
Merari's sons four ponderous waggons load
With boards and pillars of the House of God.'
R. Murray McCheyne

1 Gershon—a Stranger here
*Gershonites' Charge*—
Curtains and Hangings
for gate and door
Coverings for the tabernacle—
THE EVANGELIST          Num. 4. 21-28

2 Kohath—assembly

*Kohathites' Charge*—
Vessels of the sanctuary
(Emblematic of Christ's
Person and Work)
THE TEACHER          Num. 4. 15

3 Merari—My bitterness
*Merarites' Charge*—
Framework of boards,
bars, pillars and sockets,
pins, etc—
THE PASTOR          Num. 4. 29-33

**125   The Princes in Israel**
Num 7

'A prince, a great man in Israel' 2 Sam. 3. 38
PRINCELINESS was seen in—

1 The Dignity of their Deportment          Num. 7. 2

2 The Wealth of their Possessions          Num. 7. 84

3 Their Appreciation of the Altar          Num. 7. 10

4 The Liberality of their Offerings          Num. 7. 3, etc.

5 The Conveyance of their Gifts          Num. 7. 3

**126   Seven Trumpets**

1 THE TRUMPET OF GATHERING
(Silver—Emblem of Redemption)
Num. 10. 2, 4

2 THE TRUMPET OF ALARM
Num. 10. 5, 6

3 THE TRUMPET OF BATTLE
Num. 10. 9; 1 Cor. 14. 8

4 THE TRUMPET OF GLADNESS
Num. 10. 10; Psa. 98. 6

5 THE TRUMPET OF VICTORY
Joshua 6. 4, 5; Judg. 7. 18

6 THE TRUMPET OF WARNING
Ezek. 33. 3

7 THE TRUMPET OF RESURRECTION AND
TRANSFORMATION
1 Cor. 15. 52

### 127 Three Prophets Who Wanted to Die

All were *called* by God, *sent* by God and *used* by God.

| | | | | |
|---|---|---|---|---|
| 1 MOSES | — | *Loss of Confidence* | — | after Testing in the Wilderness | Num. 11. 10-17 |
| 2 ELIJAH | — | *Loss of Courage* | — | after Triumph on the Mountain | 1 Kings. 19. 1-8 |
| 3 JONAH | — | *Loss of Concern* | — | after Testimony in the City | Jonah 4. 1-4 |

### 128 Faithful Servants of God

1 Moses the Prophet—
faithful in all his house  Num. 12. 7;
Heb. 3. 5

2 Abraham the Patriarch—
faithful before God  Neh. 9. 7-8

3 Daniel the President—
faithful in his duties  Dan. 6. 4

4 Paul the Preacher—
faithful in God's reckoning  1 Tim. 1. 12

5 Tychicus the Pastor—
faithful in service  Eph. 6. 21

6 Timothy the Pupil—
faithful in the Lord  1 Cor. 4. 17

7 Epaphras the Pleader—
faithful in prayer  Col. 1. 7; 4. 12

8 Onesimus the Partner—
faithful and beloved  Col. 4. 9;
Philem. 17

9 Silvanus (Silas) the Postman—
faithful to the saints  1 Pet. 5. 12

10 Antipas the Persecuted—
faithful unto death  Rev. 2. 13

S.T.

### 129 Good and Evil Reports

Joshua and Caleb, two of twelve spies sent to search the land of Canaan, brought back a good report.

1 THE COMMISSION
'Spy out the land of Canaan  Num. 13. 16

2 THE COMPARISONS
10 spies—like Grasshoppers
before Giants  Num. 13. 33
2 spies—God greater than
Giants  Num. 14. 8

3 THE CONCLUSIONS
10 spies—'We be not able'  Num. 13. 31
Caleb and Joshua—'We are
well able'  Num. 13. 30

### 130 Caleb, the Man who Followed Fully

It is *six times* said of Caleb that he followed the Lord fully:

Jehovah's testimony  Num. 14. 24; 32. 12;
Deut. 1. 36;
Joshua 14. 14
Moses' testimony  Joshua 14. 9
Caleb's own testimony  Joshua 14. 8

The Reason—he had
another spirit in him'  Num. 14. 24

Not the spirit of bondage
again to fear  Rom. 8. 15

Not the spirit of cowardice  2 Tim. 1. 7

Caleb's spirit displayed—

1 *Undaunted Faith*
in the Lord  Num. 14. 9

2 *Unswerving Loyalty*
to the Lord  Num. 14. 9

3 *Unbounded Zeal*
for the Lord's cause  Num. 13. 30

### 131 The Drink Offering, or Libation
Num. 15. 1-10

The Apostle Paul speaks of himself as a Libation to God. Phil. 2. 17; 2 Tim. 4. 6
The Drink Offering was—

1 The *Most Insignificant* of the offerings—
Paul's *Humility* Phil. 2. 17; Eph. 3. 8;
1 Tim. 1. 15; 1 Cor. 15. 9

2 *Always poured out on one of the great offerings*, especially the Burnt Offering
—Paul's *Devotion to Christ* Num. 15. 5;
2 Tim. 4. 6

3 An *Offering made by fire*—Paul's *Afflictions*
Num. 15. 10; 2 Cor. 11. 23-28

4 *Fragrant to the Lord*—Paul's *Ambition in life* or death Num. 15. 10; 2 Cor. 5. 9

5 *Measured to correspond* to the Value of the Burnt Offering—Paul's *Appreciation of Christ* Num. 15. 5; Gal. 2. 20

6 The *same measure as the measure of oil* offered with it—Paul's *Service by the Spirit* Num. 15. 4, 5, 6, 7, 9, 10; Phil. 1. 19

7 *Always a libation of Wine*—Paul's true estimate of the world's joys Num. 15. 5, 7; Gal. 6. 14

### 132 The Red Heifer
Num. 19

Purification from Defilement by the way, referred to in Heb. 9. 13-14. Truth taught—The Death of Christ brought to bear on a believer's conscience when defiled.

1 THE ANIMAL FOR SACRIFICE

a red heifer  Num. 19. 2

must be—without blemish—
Christ's Sinless nature

without spot—
Christ's stainless character

free from the yoke—
Christ's Freedom from sin

**2** THE SLAYING OF THE SACRIFICE
Num. 19. 3
Slain before the face of the priest—
Christ's sacrifice before His priesthood
Slain outside the camp, Christ suffered
without the gate Heb. 13. 12, 13
Blood sprinkled before the tabernacle—
Efficacy of Christ's sacrifice
Heb. 9. 14

**3** THE APPLICATION OF THE ASHES
Num. 19. 17-19
(a) along with running water—in the
Spirit's power:
(b) by a person who is clean
Num. 19. 9; Gal. 6. 1
(c) by one who has washed his clothes—
cleansed habits
(d) to one defiled by contact with death
Num. 19. 11-14
(e) to vessels defiled by a dead body
Num. 19. 15;
2 Tim. 2. 20, 21

**133   Mistakes Made by God's Famous Men**
1 Moses smote the rock
twice                    Num. 20. 10-12
2 Joshua believed the Gib-
eonites                  Josh. 9. 15
3 David trusted Ziba      2 Sam. 16. 4
4 Hezekiah received am-
bassadors               2 Chron. 32. 31
5 Peter separated from the
Gentiles                 Gal. 2. 12
6 Barnabas dissembled     Gal. 2. 13
7 John wanted fire from
heaven                   Luke 9. 54
JS. FS.

**134   Failure of Moses**
In Exod. 17 God said to Moses, 'Smite the
rock', and Moses obeyed.
'That Rock was Christ' (1 Cor. 10. 4, 5).
In Num. 20 God said, 'Speak to the rock',
and Moses disobeyed.

1 He *spoke inadvisedly*
with his lips       Ps. 106. 33
2 He *failed in* his
strongest point,
*meekness*          Num. 20. 10; 12. 3
3 He *struck* the *rock*
*twice*             Num. 20. 11
4 He *disbelieved God* Num. 20. 12
5 He *failed to honour
God* before the
people             Num. 20. 12

**135   The Brazen Serpent**
Num. 21 4-10; John 3. 14, 15
1 The *People*—
a *Sinful Race*, dying because of sin
Num. 21. 6
2 The *Provision*—
a *Suffering Redeemer*
Num. 21. 8

a Serpent 'lifted up'
John 3. 14;

i a Cursed creature: Christ was made a
curse          Gal. 3. 14

ii Uplifted on a pole, the Son of man
lifted up      John 3. 14

iii Made of brass, that could stand the fire
Heb. 12. 2

iv a fiery serpent, a burning one (same
word as 'seraph' in Isa. 6)
Isa. 6. 6

3 The *Purpose*—
a *Sure Recovery*
Num. 21. 8; John 3. 15
'Look and live', 'believe and live'

# DEUTERONOMY

**136   The Presence of the Unchanging God**

'The Lord thy God HATH BEEN
with thee
   *Past* of Yesterday,     Deut. 2. 7
'The Lord thy God IS with thee'
   *Present* of Today,     Joshua 1. 9
'The Lord God, even thy God,
WILL BE with thee
   *Future* and forever    1 Chron. 28. 20
'Jesus Christ, the same yester-
day and today and for ever.'
                Heb. 13. 8
                S.B.K.W.

**137   God's Calls on Our Attention**
     'Hear, O Israel!'

1 Concerning their enemies
          Deut. 1. 14 Chs 1-3
2 Concerning themselves
          Deut. 4. 1 Ch. 4
3 Concerning His moral law
          Deut. 5. 1 Ch. 5
4 Concerning the Implications of the Law
          Deut. 6. 3 Chs. 6-8
5 Concerning Special commands
          Deut. 9. 1 Chs. 9-20

**138   A Good Land for an Inheritance**
     Deut. 8. 7
          FOR ISRAEL
    Earthly and Material

1 Brooks, fountains, springs

2 Wheat and barley

3 Vines, figtrees and pomegranates

4 Oil olive

5 Honey

6 Iron and brass

7 Eating till satisfied
          FOR THE SAINTS
Heavenly and Spiritual
Purity and Delight of divine resources
Bread of life from Heaven
Fruitfulness in the life
The Spirit's power for witness
Sweetness from service
Treasures for diligent students of God's Word
Appetite to enjoy God's good provisions

**139   Inthe Land—In the Heavenlies**
     Deut. 12. 1; Eph. 1. 3
Deut. 12. 10-12
  1 The *Portion that God Conferred*

26

2 The *Place that God Chose*
3 The *Precepts that God Commanded*
4 The *Presents that God Claimed*

**140   Take Heed to Thyself**
  1 Care for *God's Place*     Deut. 12. 13
  2 Care for *God's Servants*   Deut. 12. 19
  3 Care for *God's Glory*     Deut. 12. 30

**141   Liberal Provision for the Liberated Pauper**
     Deut. 15. 14

'Thou shalt furnish him liberally'
OUT OF THY FLOCK—
the Lamb of God, in Redemption
        John 1. 29; 1 Pet. 1. 18, 19
OUT OF THY FLOOR—
the finest of the wheat, in God's Word
        Ps. 81. 16; Jer. 15. 16
OUT OF THY WINEPRESS—
the good wine, in Heavenly joy
        John 2. 10

**142   The Firstfruits**
     Deut. 26. 2

1 *What the Offerers brought* vs. 1-4
   i Firstfruits—
     *Quality* of the Gift, the
     best          Deut. 26. 2
   ii In a Basket—
     *Quantity* .of the Gift,
     limited       Deut. 26. 2
   iii Unto the Place—
     *Place* of giving, the Lord's
     choice       Deut. 26. 2
   iv Unto the Priest—
     *Presentation* of the Gift   Deut. 26. 3

2 *What the Offerers said* vs. 5-10
There was—
    *Remembrance*
    of their former condition    v. 5

    *Recognition*
    of God's goodness     v. 7

    *Review*
    of God's deliverance    v. 8

    *Rejoicing*
    in God's provision     v. 9

3 *What the Offerers did* vs. 10, 11
   Set their offering before the Lord
   Worshipped before the Lord
   Rejoiced before the Lord

**143    Ready—A Study For All**

1 Condition of the sinner—
*Ready* to perish Deut. 26. 5; Job 29. 13;
Prov. 31. 6; Isa. 27. 13
2 Compassion of the Lord—
*Ready* to pardon Neh. 9. 17; Ps. 86. 5;
Isa. 38. 20
3 Conduct of the saint
*Ready* to do 2 Sam. 15. 15
4 Commission of the servant
*Ready* to preach Rom. 1. 15
5 Coming glory and salvation—
*Ready* to be revealed 1 Pet. 1. 5
6 Complaint of the sorrowful—
*Ready* to halt Ps. 38. 17
7 Consequence of backsliding—
Grace *ready* to die Rev. 3. 2

F.E.M.

**144    The Perfections of God**

| | | |
|---|---|---|
| 1 | His *Work* is Perfect | Deut. 32. 4 |
| 2 | His *Way* is Perfect | 2 Sam. 22. 31 |
| 3 | His *Knowledge* is Perfect | Job. 36. 4 |
| 4 | His *Law* is Perfect | Ps. 19. 7 |
| 5 | His *Will* is Perfect | Rom. 12. 2 |
| 6 | His *Love* is Perfect | 1 John 4. 18 |
| 7 | He *Himself* is Perfect | Matt. 5. 48 |

T.B.

**145    Our God is the—**

| | |
|---|---|
| God of Truth | Deut. 32. 4; Jer. 10. 10 |
| God of all Grace | 1 Pet. 5. 10 |
| God of Peace | Phil. 4. 9 |
| God of Love | 2 Cor. 13. 11 |
| God of all Comfort | 2 Cor. 1. 3 |
| God of Patience | Rom. 15. 5 |
| God of Hope | Rom. 15. 13 |
| God of Glory | Acts 7. 2 |
| God of Judgment | Isa. 30. 18 |
| God of Mercies | 2 Cor. 1. 3 |

J.H.B.

**146    God is Sovereign Ruler**

'The Most High divided to the nations their
inheritance' Deut. 32. 8
God is sovereign in

1 the *Allotment of their territory*—
'according to the number of
children of Israel'              Deut. 32. 8

2 the *Appointment of their rulers*—
'whomsoever He will'              Dan. 4. 25

3 the *Attitude of the hearts* of
their kings—
'whithersoever He will'              Prov. 21. 1

4 the *Activities of their leaders*—
'Whatsoever Thy counsel
determined              Acts 4. 28
He is 'the blessed and only Potentate, the King
of kings and Lord of lords'              1 Tim. 6. 15

**147    The Last Days and Deeds of Moses**
Deut. 32. 44, 45
Five Great Chapters—
1 Deut. 31
The *Commands* of Moses,
the Messenger of God

| | |
|---|---|
| To Israel the nation | vs. 1-6 |
| To Joshua the leader | vs. 7, 8 |
| To the priests of Jehovah | vs. 9-13 |
| To the Levites | vs. 25-27 |

2 Deut. 32
The *Song* of Moses, the
Prophet of God              Deut. 31. 30;
                                      32. 44
3 Deut. 33
The *Blessing* of Moses, the
Man of God              Deut. 33. 1
4 Ps. 90
The *Prayer* of Moses, the
Man of God              Ps. 90, Title
5 Deut. 34
The *Death* of Moses, the
Servant of God              Deut. 34. 5

**148    Men of God**
First Occurrence of the title in the Bible
Deut. 33. 1. It is applied to—

1 *Moses* the servant
              Deut. 33. 1; Joshua 14. 6
2 *Samuel* the seer              1 Sam. 9. 6, 7, 8, 10
3 *David* the king              2 Chron. 8. 14
4 *Shemaiah* the messenger
              1 Kings 12. 22; 2 Chr. 11. 2
5 A *prophet* out of *Judah*
              1 Kings 13. 1, 4, 5, 7, 8, etc.
6 *Elijah* the Tishbite
              1 Kings 17. 18, 24, etc.
7 *Elisha* the son of Shaphat
              2 Kings 4. 7, 9, etc.
8 *Igdaliah*, a man of God              Jer. 35. 4
9 *Timothy*, the dearly beloved   1 Tim. 6. 11

**149    Places of Enjoyment**
1 A Place on *God's heart—Affection*
              Deut. 33. 3; Exod. 28. 29, 30
2 A Place in *His hand—Protection*
Graven on His palms
              Isa. 49. 16
Held in His hand
              John 10. 28, 29
Upheld by His hand
              Isa. 41. 10; 1 Pet. 1. 5
3 A Place at *His feet—Instruction*
              Deut. 33. 3; Luke 10. 39
4 A Place by *His side—Attraction*
              Deut. 33. 12; Song of S. 8. 5
5 A Place between *His shoulders*—
*Satisfaction* Deut. 33. 12; Luke 15. 5

G.G.

## 150 Seven Blessings for God's Nazarite
Deut. 33. 13-16

1 Precious things of heaven
Spiritual blessings in the
heavenlies     Eph. 1. 3

2 Precious fruits brought
forth by the sun
Fruit of the Spirit in our
lives     Gal. 5. 22

3 Precious things put forth by
the moon
Fruit of the light     Eph. 5. 9

4 Chief things of the ancient
mountains
Supremacy of God's com-
mands     Rom. 8. 4

5 Precious things of the lasting
hills
Triumphs of the Cross on
Calvary     Col. 2. 14. 15

6 Precious things of the earth
all things richly to enjoy     1 Tim. 6. 17

7 Goodwill of Him Who
dwelt in the bush
Preservation through trial     1 Pet. 5. 10

## 151 A Hind Let Loose
Deut. 33. 23

The Hind is a beautiful animal, exposed to danger and hunted. 'Hind of the morning'—Aijeleth-Shinar—title of Ps. 22.

1 'Let loose'—
FREEDOM Same word in Lev. 14. 7; Deut. 15. 18; Isa. 6. 8; Zech. 9. 11 (Let loose, send away)

2 'Hind's feet'—
FLEETNESS Ps. 18. 33; Hab. 3. 19

3 'Giveth goodly words'—
FRESHNESS (or 'spreadeth goodly antlers')
Gen. 49. 21

4 'Satisfied with favour'—
FAVOUR Isa. 9. 1, 2

5 'Full of Jehovah's blessing'—
FULLNESS Matt. 4, 15, 16

## 152 Satisfied
Deut. 33. 23

1 Satisfied in the days of famine
Ps. 37. 19

2 Satisfied in drought Isa. 58. 11; Jer. 31. 12

3 Satisfied with His goodness
Jer. 31. 14; Ps. 103. 5

4 Satisfied with the fatness of His house
Ps. 36. 8; 63. 5

5 Satisfied when we awake with His likeness
Ps. 17. 15

       E.A.H.

## 153 Asher's Blessing
Deut. 33. 24, 25

Asher—Happy; there was joy at his birth
Gen. 30. 13
HAPPY in

1 *Prosperity*—
'Fat bread'—prolific crops Gen. 49. 20

'Foot dipped in oil'—Olives and oil wells
'Iron and brass under foot'—Mineral
wealth

2 *Posterity*
'blessed with children'—no barrenness

3 *Partnership*—
'acceptable to his brethren'

4 *Provision*—
'as thy days, so shall thy strength (or rest)
be'

5 *Privilege*—
Anna, of the tribe of Asher, 'gave thanks',
and 'spoke of Christ' Luke 2. 36-38

## 154 The Eternal God
Deut. 33. 27

The *Eternal God* is the refuge of His saints,
who are

1 Called to
*Eternal Glory*     1 Pet. 5. 10

2 Blessed with
*Eternal Salvation*     Heb. 5. 9

3 According to an
*Eternal Purpose*     Eph. 3. 11

4 Based upon an
*Eternal Redemption*     Heb. 9. 12

5 and Sealed with an
*Eternal Spirit*     Heb. 9. 14

6 in Possession of
*Eternal Life*     John 10. 28

7 Pressing toward an
*Eternal Inheritance*     Heb. 9. 15

8 where they will have an
*Eternal House*     2 Cor. 5. 1

9 and Receive an
*Eternal Weight of glory*     2 Cor. 4. 17

10 under the rule of an
*Eternal King*     1 Tim. 1. 17
       T.B.

## 155 God's People
Deut. 33. 29

God's People are
1 A Saved People
2 A Unique people
3 A Happy People
4 A Sheltered People
5 A Defended People
6 A Persecuted People
and will be
7 A Triumphant People

       G.H.

**156 Moses, Representative of the Law**
Deut. 34

1 The Law was Given by
Moses John 1. 17
'Grace and truth came by
Jesus Christ'

2 The Glory of the Law
shone in Moses' face 2 Cor. 3. 7
The glory of the Gospel
in the face of Jesus
Christ

3 Moses' Vigour was un-
diminished (no lower-
ing of the standard) Deut. 34. 7
The Law made way for a
'better hope' Heb. 7. 19

4 Moses and the Law were
superseded Deut. 34. 10
The law was our peda-
gogue to bring us to
Christ Gal. 3. 24

5 Moses could not lead the
people into the Land, Joshua. 1, 2;
but Joshua did Rom. 8. 3

JOSHUA

**157 The Qualities of a Leader**
Joshua 1

1 *Dependence on God*
His name, originally
'Oshea', Saviour, be-
came Jehoshua, or
Joshua. Jehovah is
Saviour, and the Greek
form of this is 'Jesus'.
Addition of part of
Jehovah's name to his.
He no longer claimed
to be saviour but recog-
nized that 'Salvation is
of the Lord'. Num. 13. 16

2 *Confidence in God*
His tribe, Ephraim son
of Joseph—so he drew Gen. 49. 24;
his strength from God Joshua 1. 7

3 *Humility in Service*
His description— Joshua 1. 1;
Moses' minister
He had served with Exod. 24. 13;
humility 33. 11

4 *Prowess in Conflict*
His record of Victory as
leader in battle Exod. 17. 13

5 *Enduement with the Spirit*
God's Spirit was in him Num. 27. 18

6 *Appointment by God*
Not self-appointed Num. 27, 16, 17;
Deut. 1. 38

7 *Apprehension of God's Purposes*
His report of the land Num. 14. 30

**158 The Promised Land**
Sections of Joshua

The book covers a period of 25 years.

Chapters 1-5 Entering the Land
Chapters 6-12 Conquering the Land
Chapters 13-21 Dividing the Land
Chapters 22-24.8 Administering the Land
Chapters 24.2-33 Cemetery in the Land

**159 A Divine Command**
as given in Joshua 1. 8

This Book—shall not depart out of thy mouth

SPEAK OF IT
But thou shalt meditate therein

STUDY IT
Observe to do according to all that is written

SUBMIT TO IT
W.J.M.

**160 God's Message to His People**
as given in Joshua 1. 11

1 PREPARE—
yourselves for the journey v. 16
your food for the journey v. 11

2 PASS OVER—
Jordan together v. 2
armed v. 14

3 POSSESS—
the land promised by God v. 6
given by God vs. 3, 11
to be covered by them v. 3
occupied by enemies v. 4

## 161 Gentile Fellow-Heirs

Chapter 1
God's purpose of blessing for Israel, a people Elect, Redeemed, Sustained and Guided Rom. 9. 4

Chapter 2
God's purpose of blessing for Gentiles, Rahab and her household, chosen to be fellow-heirs. (They were strangers from the covenant of promise, having no hope and without God in the world) Eph. 2. 11. 12;

## 162 Rahab's Faith

| | | |
|---|---|---|
| 1 *Ground of Faith—*<br> *Revelation* | 'I know' | Joshua 2. 9 |
| 2 *Plea of Faith—*<br> *Mercy* | 'deliver our lives' | Joshua 2. 13; Heb. 11. 31 |
| 3 *Evidence of Faith*<br> *Witness* | 'line of scarlet thread' | Joshua 2. 18 |
| 4 *Works of Faith—*<br> *Reception of spies* | 'I shewed you kindness' | Joshua 2. 15, 16; James 2. 22 |
| 5 *End of Faith—*<br> *Salvation* | Joshua saved Rahab | Joshua 6. 25; 1 Peter 1. 9 |

## 163 An Untrodden Path

'Ye have not passed this way heretofore' Joshua 3. 4
The Hebrew word translated 'way' here means 'a trodden path', but for Joshua and his people it was untrodden.
It should be—

| | |
|---|---|
| GOD'S WAY | Deut. 13. 5 |
| a GUIDED WAY | Neh. 9. 19; Prov. 3. 6 |
| a GLOWING WAY | Prov. 4. 18 |
| a GOOD WAY | Judges 2. 22; Ps. 18. 32 |
| a GUARDED WAY | Ps. 17. 4, 5 |

## 164 Three Miracles in Joshua

| | |
|---|---|
| 1 Jordan's Waters—<br> Faith's Venture | Joshua 3. 15-17;<br>4. 10-24 |
| 2 Jericho's Walls—<br> Faith's Victory | Joshua 6. 1-24 |
| 3 Joshua's Words—<br> Faith's Vehemence | Joshua 10. 12-14 |

## 165 Two Cairns of Stones

1 Twelve Stones placed in a heap on Jordan's banks by representatives of the people (Joshua 4. 3) as—
 i A *Memorial* of God's *Power* Joshua 4. 7, 23-24
 ii A *Witness* to God's *Purpose*, an inheritance in Canaan Joshua 4. 5
 iii A *Declaration* of God's *Pattern*, unity of Israel Joshua 4. 7, 8
2 Twelve Stones set up by Joshua, the leader, in the bed of Jordan, as an Evidence that Jordan's fierce floods had once been held in check. (Emblem of Christ's Death and Resurrection)

## 166 Doing the First Works

| | |
|---|---|
| 1 Egypt's Reproach removed | Joshua 5. 9 |
| 2 Passover Feast observed | Joshua 5. 10 |
| 3 Wilderness Diet discontinued | Joshua 5, 12 |
| 4 Canaan's Fruit enjoyed | Joshua 5, 12 |

In Egypt the redeemed people ate the roasted lamb—Christ in Death

In the Wilderness they fed on the Manna—Christ the Bread of God

In Canaan they ate the corn of the land—Christ in Heaven

## 167 God's Conquering Hosts

Joshua 6

Faith is the victory that overcomes the world 1 John 5. 4

Three things happened at Jericho

| | |
|---|---|
| 1 Its walls fell down flat | Joshua 6. 20 |
| 2 All in the city destroyed | Joshua 6. 21 |
| 3 The city burnt with fire | Joshua 6. 24 |

Those who participated in the Victory:

1 The Invisible Captain
  Joshua 5. 13, 14

The word in the LXX is the same as that translated 'Prince' in Acts 3. 15; 4. 31, 'Captain' in Heb. 2. 10, and 'Author' in Heb. 12. 2

2 Battalions of angels
  Ps. 34. 7; 2 Kings 6. 16
3 Joshua, the human leader
  Joshua 6. 3, 6, 12, 16, 25
4 The Armed Soldiers
  Joshua 6. 3, 7, 9
5 The Trumpeters
  Joshua 6. 4, 5, 8, 9, 13, 16
6 The Priests carrying the ark
  Joshua 6. 8, 13
7 The Rescue Squad
  Joshua 6. 22, 23

**168  Three Divine Principles**
Jehovah—
1 asserted the Corporate Responsibility of His people                      Joshua 7. 11
2 demonstrated the Serious Nature of sin in a leader, Joshua 7. 18 for Achan was a prince belonging to the tribe of Judah                          1 Chron. 2. 7
3 demanded the exposure and punishment of the Joshua 7. 12; sinner                          1 Cor. 5. 13

**169  The Sin of Covetousness**
1 God's *Indictment*— 'Israel hath sinned'        Joshua 7. 11 They have taken the garment which should have been destroyed They have stolen the silver and gold which was for the Lord They have dissembled, and hidden the stuff to conceal their sin (Prov. 28. 13)
2 God's *Requirements*— 'Take away the accursed thing'                     Joshua 7. 13 Full confession was necessary                 Joshua 7. 19 Full restitution must be made              Joshua 7. 22, 23 Full retribution must be meted out            Joshua 7. 25
3 The *Sinner's Confession*— 'I have sinned against the Lord'                      Joshua 7. 20 'I saw' (Lust of the eye), 'I coveted' (Lust of the flesh), and 'I took!'

**170  The Valley of Achor**
1 A Valley of Trouble (Achor = trouble: Achan = troubler) Joshua 7. 26; 2 Cor. 7. 11
2 A Boundary of Separation Joshua 15. 7; 2 Cor. 6. 14-18
3 A Place of Rest Isa. 65. 10; Ps. 23. 2, 3
4 A Door of Hope Hos. 2. 15

**171  A Wily Foe**
'They did work wilily'        Joshua 9. 3, 4
'The wiles of the devil'       Eph. 6. 11
Gibeon was an important city in Southern Canaan, built on a hill and strongly fortified. The leaders of Israel succumbed to four Temptations—
1 To *Achieve* a desired end without paying the price Joshua 9. 15

2 To *Accept* a semblance of antiquity without questioning its authority       Joshua 9. 13
3 To *Agree* to an alliance without due investigation Joshua 9. 6-15
4 To *Act* on their own without seeking divine guidance                        Joshua 9. 14

**172  The Portion of the Overcomer**
'Give me this mountain,' said Caleb. Joshua 14. 12
Caleb had
1 A *Faith* that was Triumphant               Joshua 14. 7
2 A *Fortitude* that was Tireless                 Joshua 14. 11
Caleb got
3 A *Fellowship* that was Treasured              Joshua 14. 13 (Hebron means 'Fellowship')
4 A *Fullness* that was Transmitted To his own family        Joshua 15. 19 For the benefit of the priests of God         Joshua 21, 10, 11 For the shelter of the fugitive manslayer     Joshua 21. 13

**173  The Levites**
Chapters in their History—
Num. 3   *Census* of the Levites: their Pedigree.
Num. 4   *Charge* of the Levites: their Ministry
Num. 8   *Consecration* of the Levites: their Separation.
Num. 18  *Care* of the Levites: their Maintenance.
Joshua 21 *Cities* of the Levites: their Residence.

The Cities for the Levites were fixed—
1 By Divine Appointment Joshua 21. 2
2 By Definite Agreement  Joshua 21. 3
By Divisional Arrangement                  Joshua 21. 4, etc.

**174  The Downfall of Pride**
The children of Joseph said, 'I am a great people'. Joshua 17. 14; Isa. 28. 1

Those Ephraimites were characterized by—
Ambition without Discipline Joshua 17. 15
Jealousy without Reason   Judges 8. 1
Bravado without Courage   Ps. 78. 9-10

## 175 The Cities of Refuge
### Joshua 20

One who had killed somebody by accident—

1 Must flee to one of the appointed cities
Joshua 20. 3; Heb. 6. 18
2 Must plead his cause at the gate of the city
Joshua 20. 4; Job 33. 27, 28
3 Must make his home in that city
Joshua 20. 4; Phil. 3. 20
4 Was safe until the day of judgment
Joshua 20. 6; Rom. 8. 1
5 Was safe until the high priest's death
Joshua 20. 6; Heb. 7. 16, 17

THE ETERNAL GOD IS THY REFUGE Deut. 33. 27
The Cities of Refuge were—
In Elevated Positions. Our Refuge is at God's right hand in Heaven Heb. 6. 18.
Accessible from all Parts. Our Refuge is for 'every creature' in 'all the world' Mark 16. 15
Available for all in need, with ever open gates Matt. 11. 28.

## 176 Six Cities of Refuge
### Joshua 20. 7, 8

| | |
|---|---|
| 1 Kedesh—Holy | 2 Cor. 5. 21 |
| 2 Shechem—Shoulder | Luke 15. 5 |
| 3 Hebron—Friendship | Prov. 18. 24 |
| 4 Bezer—Stronghold | Ps. 31. 3 |
| 5 Ramoth—High place | Hab. 3. 19 |
| 6 Golan—Happy | Prov. 16. 20 |

J.E.B.

## 177 'As For Me'

| | |
|---|---|
| 1 Personal Resolution | Joshua 24. 15 |
| 2 Childlike Dependence | Ps. 55. 16 |
| 3 Individual Temptation | Ps. 73. 2 |
| 4 Earnest Intercession | I Sam. 12. 23 |
| 5 Self-Forgetfulness | Dan. 2. 30 |
| 6 Rendering Good for Evil | Ps. 35. 13 |
| 7 Eternal Satisfaction | Ps. 17. 15 |

G.H.

## 178 Three Graves in Canaan
### Joshua 24. 29-33

They buried—

Joshua, Captain of Israel's forces, Strong in the Lord

Joseph, Dispenser of Egypt's food, Strong in Faith

Eleazar, Leader of Israel's Worship, Strong in Grace

All died and were buried, and all await the day of resurrection. The Captain of our Salvation, the Supplier of our needs, and our great High Priest, died, was buried and rose again (1 Cor. 15. 3, 4) and is alive for evermore (Rev. 1. 18).

---

# JUDGES

## 179 Declension Among God's People
'Judges' contrasted with 'Joshua'.

| JOSHUA | JUDGES |
|---|---|
| Period of 25 years—One Leader | Period of 330 years—Thirteen Leaders |
| Israel possessing their inheritance | Israel neglecting their inheritance |
| Series of Victories | Series of Defeats |
| The spiritual life prominent | The carnal life prominent |
| Progress recorded | Retrogression recorded |

## 180 Power of God Through Weakness
God used—

1 Ehud with his left hand        Judges 3. 15
2 Shamgar with an ox-goad        Judges 3. 31
3 Deborah, as one of the weaker vessels        Judges 4. 4
4 Jael with a tent-pin        Judges 4. 21
5 Gideon's army of 300 with trumpets, pitchers and lamps        Judges 7. 7
6 A woman with a piece of millstone        Judges 9. 53
7 Samson, with the jawbone of an ass        Judges 15. 15

R.L.B.

## 181 Deborah
### Judges 5

Deborah was—

a *Prophetess*, knowing the will of God        Judges 4. 4

a *Bee* (meaning of her name), diligent in work        Judges 4. 4

a *Fighter*, victorious in battle Judges 4. 9

a *Singer*, praising the Lord        Judges 5. 1

a *Mother in Israel*        Judges 5. 7

Feeding, leading and pleading with her people: Loving God, braving the enemy, and saving her people.

**182   Call of Gideon**

When called by God, Gideon was—

EMPLOYED—

threshing wheat                Judges 6. 11

ENCOURAGED—

'mighty man of valour'        Judges 6. 12

EMBARRASSED—

'the least in my father's
house'                        Judges 6. 15

EMPOWERED—

'Surely, I will be with thee' Judges 6. 16

ENERGIZED—

threw down the altar of Baal  Judges 6. 25, 27

**183   Steps to Victory**

1 The *Tribes* that *Rallied*
their Forces                  Judges 6. 35

2 The *Tests* that *Revealed*
the Fit—Courage and
Zeal tested                   Judges 7. 3, 6, 7

3 The *Tools* that *Routed*
their Foes—Trumpets,
lamps and pitchers            Judges 7. 16

**184 Overcoming the Enemy**

Judges 7. 20

Gideon's Men

1 Blew their trumpets

2 Broke their pitchers

3 Held aloft their lamps

4 Shouted, 'the sword of
the Lord'

| Duties of God's Servants | PROCLAMATION | 1 Cor. 14. 8 |
| | CONSECRATION | 2 Cor. 4. 7 |
| | ILLUMINATION | 2 Cor. 4. 6 |
| | PENETRATION | Heb. 4. 12 |

**185   Parable of the Trees**

Judges 9. 7-15

Jotham's Parable. Jotham means 'Jehovah
is perfect'. Three Trees recognized a Divine
Purpose for them.

1 The *Recognition* Preserved
from unworthy ambitions

2 The *Response* Promoted usefulness to God and man

Olive Tree gave oil for the light—
Fatness and Witness        Judges 9. 9

Fig tree gave fruit to nourish—
Sweetness and Sustenance  Judges 9. 11

Vine gave wine to cheer—
Gladness and Lowliness    Judges 9. 13

(Wine was the element used
in the Drink offering)

3 The *Realization* produced glory to God.

Only the thorn bush (the bramble) consented
to 'wave idly' over the trees.    Judges 9. 15

**186   Training the Child**

Judges 13. 12

An Outline for Workers among the Young.
Four Questions, two in the Revised Version
and two in the Authorized Version, and how to
answer them.

1 What shall be the manner of the child?
(R.V)
Study the child's nature

2 What shall be his work? (R.V)
Study the child's bent

3 How shall we order the child? (A.V.)
Mould the child's character

4 What shall we do unto him? (A.V.)
Train the child by instruction (Prov.
22. 6)

**187   Samson, The Strong Man**

Judges 13

He had

1 Wonderful Parents      Judges 13. 3, 4, 19

2 A Wonderful Name,
meaning 'Serving as
the sun'                 Judges 13. 24

3 A Wonderful Calling,
a Nazarite unto God Judges 13. 7

4 A Wonderful Work to
do—begin to deliver—
Israel                   Judges 13. 5

5 A Wonderful Power to
use, the Spirit of the
Lord                     Judges 13. 25

**188   Tragedy of a Defective Consecration**

Samson's life was

1 A Life of Remarkable
Promise                  Judges 13. 5

2 A Life of Resplendent  Judges 13. 25;
Possibilities            14. 6; 15. 14

3 A Life of Relinquished
Purposes                 Judges 16. 4, 19

4 A Last Lap of Restored
Power                    Judges 16. 30

## 189 How Are the Mighty Fallen?

'Samson Agonistes' when 'the Lord had departed from him'                    Judges 16. 20

1 Lost *Strength*—'weak— like other men'         Judges 16. 17

2 Lost *Sight*—'the Philistines put out his eyes'       Judges 16. 21

3 Lost *Liberty*—'in the prison house'         Judges 16. 21

4 Lost *Dignity*—'he did grind         Judges 16. 21

---

# RUTH

## 190 The Book of Ruth

Two Bible books are named after women—

RUTH, a Gentile maiden who became the wife of a Jewish prince, and ESTHER, a Jewish maiden who became the wife of a Gentile king.

THE BOOK OF RUTH is read by the Jews at the Feast of *Pentecost*.

THE BOOK OF ESTHER is read by the Jews at the Feast of *Purim*.

1 The *Story* of Ruth has an appeal to young and old, rich and poor, master and servant, employer and employee, saint and sinner, sad people and glad people, lovers of history, nature and romance, and to all lovers of God.

2 The *Scenes* in Ruth move from the Riverside on the borders of Moab in Chapter 1, to the Fields of Bethlehem-judah in Chapter 2, the threshing-floor of Boaz in Chapter 3, and the City of Bethlehem in Chapter 4.

3 The *Sections* in Ruth are:

| | | | |
|---|---|---|---|
| Chapter 1 | Emigration | Faith's Choice | Ruth enters the Redeemer's Fold |
| Chapter 2 | Education | Faith's Comfort | Ruth enters the Redeemer's Field |
| Chapter 3 | Expectation | Faith's Courage | Ruth comes to the Redeemer's Feet |
| Chapter 4 | Emancipation | Faith's Conquest | Ruth enters the Redeemer's Family |

---

## 191 Evil Days
Ruth 1. 1

The days when the judges ruled (Judges 17. 6; 21. 25; Ruth 1. 1) were

1 Days of *Sinfulness* Judges 2. 11

2 Days of *Servitude* Judges 2. 14

3 Days of *Sorrow* Judges 2. 15

4 Days of *Scarcity* Judges 6. 6; Ruth 1. 1

## 192 Four Pairs in Ruth 1

1 Elimelech and Naomi— Two people Departing from Canaan's land         Ruth 1. 1

2 Mahlon and Chilion— Two men Disobedient to God's command         Ruth 1. 4

3 Ruth and Orpah— Two women Deciding for blessing or wrath         Ruth 1. 14

4 Naomi and Ruth— Two pilgrims Delighting in God's own path         Ruth 1. 19

## 193 A Famine in the Land
Ruth 1. 1

Famines may be sent as

1 A *Check-up* on our *Faith*         Gen. 12. 10; 1 Pet. 1. 6, 7

2 A *Chastisement* for our *Failure*         Heb. 12. 6

3 or *Child-training* for the *Future*         Heb. 12. 11

## 194 Results of Backsliding

1 Harmful Example to family and friends Ruth 1. 1; Rom. 14. 7

2 Formation of forbidden alliances (unequal yoke) Ruth 1. 4; Deut. 7. 3; 2 Cor. 6. 14

3 Shortening of life on earth Ruth 1. 3, 5; 1 Cor. 11. 32

4 Declension and spiritual poverty Ruth 1. 21

## 195 Ruth's Vow of Consecration
Ruth 1. 16-17

1 'Whither thou goest, I will go'— A new *Path* for her feet

2 'Where thou lodgest, I will lodge'— A new *Place* for her home

3 'Thy people shall be my people'—
A new *People* for her friends

4 'and thy God my God'  —
A new *Power* for her life

5 'Where thou diest, I will die'—
A new *Prospect* for the future

## 196   From Distance to Nearness

Ruth's choice brought her from Moab to Bethlehem (the house of bread), from poverty to wealth, and from widowhood to marriage.
Chapter 1
Ruth became a Fellow-citizen with Boaz
Ruth 1. 9; 2 4; Eph. 2. 19
Chapter 2
Ruth became a Fellow-labourer with Boaz
Ruth 2. 12; Phil. 4. 3
Chapter 3
Ruth became a Fellow-kinswoman to Boaz
Ruth 3. 12; 2 Cor. 6. 18
Chapter 4
Ruth became a Fellow-heir
Ruth 4. 10; Eph. 3. 6

## 197   A Mighty Man of Wealth

Boaz means 'In him is ability'; he is a type of Christ, mighty in seven ways (Prov. 23. 11).

1 In *Wealth*
Ruth 2. 1; 2 Cor. 8. 9; Eph. 3. 8
2 In *Grace*
Ruth 2. 4; John 1. 14, 16
3 In *Authority*
Ruth 2. 5; Matt. 9. 38
4 In *Supply*
Ruth 2. 14; John 6. 51; 7. 37
5 In *Kinship*
Ruth 2. 20; Heb. 2. 14
6 In *Redemption*
Ruth 4. 9-10; Gal. 3. 13
7 In *Fulfilment*
Ruth 4. 10; Rev. 19. 7

## 198   Under His Wings
Ruth 2. 12

His people find

| | |
|---|---|
| *Shelter* | Ps. 57. 1 |
| *Satisfaction* | Ruth 2. 12; Ps. 36. 7 |
| *Strength* | Ps. 63. 7 |
| *Security* | Ps. 91. 4 |

Contrast Matt. 23. 37-38—'Ye would not'.

## 199   In the Harvest Field

Ruth as a widow and a stranger was permitted by the Law to glean Lev. 19. 9-10.
Ruth *'found grace'*
1 to glean in the same field all the time
Ruth 2. 8
2 to glean among the sheaves
Ruth 2. 15
3 to gather handfuls dropped on purpose for her   Ruth 2. 16

She
4 was refreshed when thirsty
Ruth 2. 9; John 7. 37
5 was supplied with food when hungry
Ruth 2. 14; John 6. 35
6 was comforted in her loneliness
Ruth 2. 13; Heb. 13. 5
7 was rested when weary
Ruth 2. 14; Matt. 11. 28, 30

## 200   The Place of Fellowship

In the threshing-floor Ruth 3. 2

1 *Preparation* for communion
(Cleansing, anointing, clothing, waiting)   Ruth 3. 3
2 *Duration* of communion, 'until the morning'   Ruth 3. 13
3 *Occupation* during communion, 'hearing his word'   Ruth 3. 18; Luke 10. 39

## 201   The Kinsman-Redeemer

The Hebrew word *'Goel'* is translated *'kinsman'* in Ruth 2. 20; 3. 9, 12, 13 (four times); 4. 1, 3, 6, 8, 14; and *'redeemer'* in Job 19. 25; Ps. 19. 14; 78. 35; Prov. 23. 11; Isa. 41. 14; 43. 14; 44. 6; 44. 24; etc.

He must have—
the *Right* to redeem—as a Kinsman
the *Will* to redeem—as an interested party
and the *Power* to redeem—as a wealthy person

In 'Ruth' there was a nearer kinsman (Ruth 3. 12; 4. 1) who had the right and will, but not the power. Ruth 4. 6
Boaz had the *Right*, the *Will* and the *Power* to redeem Ruth 4. 9

## 202   Redemption Accomplished
Ruth 4. 1-11

1 by a *Public* Transaction at the city gate, the prescribed *Place*
2 by a *Witnessed* Transaction by ten elders, the authorized *People*
3 by a *Completed* Transaction according to the prescribed *Procedure*. The Claims and Conditions laid down by the Law were entirely fulfilled.

## 203   A Wonderful Union

The marriage of Boaz and Ruth was

1 A *New Union* of Redeemer and Redeemed (Ruth had been married before to Mahlon)   Ruth 4. 10; Rom. 7. 4
2 A *Joyous Union*—from Want to Wealth
Ruth 4. 14; 1 Cor. 3. 21
3 A *Fruitful Union*—when Obed (meaning service) was born
Ruth 4. 13-14
4 A *Purposive Union*—to give the Saviour to the world   Ruth 4. 22; Matt. 1. 1-5

# 1 SAMUEL

## 204 A New Era
1 Sam. 1; 2; 3

The Period between Samson the Judge and David the King

1 *A Period of Revelation*—
God as Lord of hosts, 1 Sam. 1. 3. 11
the first two occurrences
in the Bible, the only two { Rom. 9. 29;
occurrences in the N.T. { James 5. 4

2 *A Period of Revolution*—
Overthrow of existing
system of Government
by Israel  1 Sam. 8. 5-7
Israel's wicked priests
rejected by God  1 Sam. 2. 31, 35

3 *A Period of Retrogression*—
Like priests, like people 1 Sam. 2. 17; 7. 3

## 205 Wicked Men in the Priesthood
Eli's Sons—

*Their Wickedness*—
the sin of the young men
was very great  1 Sam. 2. 12-17

*God's Warning*—
'in one day they shall die 1 Sam. 2. 22-36

*Their Woe*—
'Israel is fled': thy two
sons are dead  1 Sam. 4. 18

## 206 The Godly in Evil Days
The *Piety* of a man, Elkanah 1 Sam. 1. 3

The *Prayerfulness* of a woman,
Hannah  1 Sam. 1. 12, 27

The *Power* of a lad, Samuel  1 Sam. 3. 19

## 207 Hannah's Paean of Praise
1 Sam. 2. 1-10

1 *Rejoicing* in God's Salvation, Holiness,
Omniscience  vs. 1-3

2 *Reversal* of man's order—the poor and
weak saved, the proud and mighty
humbled  vs. 4, 5

3 *Resurrection* and its benefits  vs. 6-8

4 *Regeneration* and its blessings  vs. 9, 10

## 208 What Jehovah Does
He—

1 Weighs men's actions  1 Sam. 2. 3
2 Humbles the sinner  1 Sam. 2. 6
3 Gives life to the dead  1 Sam. 2. 6
4 Enriches the poor  1 Sam. 2. 7
5 Exalts the humble  1 Sam. 2. 8
6 Keeps His saints  1 Sam. 2. 9
7 Judges the wicked  1 Sam. 2. 10

W.J.M.

## 209 The Word of God—In Those Days
1 Sam. 3. 1

It was precious to the godly, because it was 'rare'

1 in the days of *Samuel*,
when, with most,
it was a *Despised*
Book  Judges 21. 25
2 in the days of *Josiah*,
when it was a *For-
gotten* Book  2 Chron. 34. 18, 19
3 in the days of *Jere-
miah*, when it was a
*Neglected* Book  Jer. 15. 16
4 in the days of *Malachi*,
when it was a
*Rejected* Book  Mal. 2. 8
5 in the days of *Nero's
Persecutions*, when
it was a *Condemned*
Book  2 Tim. 4. 2-4
6 In the days of the
*Inquisition*, when it
was a *Forbidden*
Book
7 In modern times,
when it is a *Muti-
lated* Book

## 210 The Precious Word of God
1 Sam. 3. 1

It is precious because of—

1 Its *Intrinsic* Value
Ps. 19. 10; 119. 162
2 Its *Ethical* Value
Ps. 19. 11; 119. 11
3 Its *Spiritual* Value
2 Tim. 3. 16, 17
4 Its *Relative* Value
Ps. 138. 2
5 Its *Nutritive* Value
Jer. 15. 16
6 Its *Illuminative* Value
Ps. 119. 130
7 Its *Potential* Value
Heb. 4. 12; Ps. 126. 6; Luke 8. 11

## 211 Signs of the Times
Like these last days, the days of Samuel were characterized by—

1 A *Loosening* of Salutary
Controls—
in NATIONAL LIFE  Judges 17. 6
2 A *Lowering* of Moral
Standards—
in SOCIAL LIFE  1 Sam. 2. 17, 22
3 A *Lack* of Parental Restraint—
in DOMESTIC LIFE  1 Sam. 3. 13
4 A *Loss* of Divine Power—
in SPIRITUAL LIFE  1 Sam. 3. 3; 4. 2

## 212 The Tragedy of the Departed Glory

ICHABOD—'the glory is departed from Israel; for the ark of God is taken'. 1 Sam. 4. 21. Gone were

1 the *Judical* Glory—

ON the blood-stained mercy-seat by which atonement for sins was made once a year  Lev. 16. 34

2 the *Moral* Glory—

IN the ark. God's moral standard in the tables of the covenant  Exod. 25. 16

3 the *Shechinah* Glory—

OVER the ark. The guiding Pillar of cloud and fire  Exod. 40. 34

## 213 Restoration and Victory

as seen in the days of Samuel

1 Lamentation— the people lamented  1 Sam. 7. 2

2 Abrogation— They put away strange gods  1 Sam. 7. 3

3 Congregation— They gathered together  1 Sam. 7. 6

4 Expiation— They offered a sucking lamb  1 Sam. 7. 9

5 Subjugation— They gained the victory  1 Sam. 7. 10

6 Proclamation— They set up a testimony  1 Sam. 7. 12

7 Administration— Samuel continued in circuit to Bethel, Gilgal and Mizpeh, returned *home* to Ramah  1 Sam. 7. 16

SIR ROBERT MATHIESON

## 214 The Prayers of a Prophet

'I will pray for you unto the Lord' 1 Sam. 7. 5 Samuel prayed—

1 at *Mizpeh*, the *Watchtower*
1 Sam. 7. 5; Hab. 2. 1; 3. 1
when his people lamented after the Lord

2 at *Ebenezer*, the *Stone of help*
1 Sam. 7. 9, 12 (Contrast 4. 1)
when the people turned to the Lord

3 at *Ramah*, the *High Place*
1 Sam. 8. 4-6; Heb. 4. 16
when the people turned away from the Lord

4 at *Gilgal*, *Rolling*
1 Sam. 12. 18, 19
when the people wanted to serve the Lord

## 215 Hitherto

1 Sam. 7. 12

*Ebenezer*—'Hitherto hath the Lord helped us'.

1 Divine *Forbearance*  Exod. 7. 16
2 Divine *Forgiveness*  Num. 14. 19
3 Divine *Blessing*  Joshua 17. 14
4 Persevering *Prayer*  1 Sam. 1. 16
5 Divine *Assistance*  1 Sam. 7. 12
6 Divine *Guidance*  2 Sam. 7. 18
7 Divine *Sustenance*  Ps. 71. 17

G.H.

## 216 How Samuel Prayed

1 Sam. 12. 23

Samuel prayed 1 *Habitually* 2 *Ungrudgingly* 3 *Importunately*

His Prayers were—

*Individual*—'As for me'
*Intercessory*—'for you'
*Incessant*—'in ceasing'—'that I should sin against the Lord'
*Invocative*—'to pray'

## 217 A Man After My Own Heart

1 Sam. 13. 14

In choosing David, God—

1 sought a man  1 Sam. 13. 14
2 found a servant  Ps. 89. 20
3 took a shepherd  Ps. 78. 70
4 commanded a captain  1 Sam. 13. 14
5 provided a king  1 Sam. 16. 1

## 218 Regal but a Rebel

1 God's *Stern Command*—
'Go, utterly destroy Amalek'  1 Sam. 15. 3

2 Saul's *Sinful Compromise*—
'spared Agag and the best of the flock  1 Sam. 15. 9

3 Saul's *Self-Complacency*—
'I have performed the command'  1 Sam. 15. 13

4 Saul's *Sad Confession*—
'I have sinned'  1 Sam. 15. 24

5 Saul's *Sacrificed Crown*—
'the Lord hath rejected thee from being king'  1 Sam. 15. 26, 28

A. G. PHAIR

## 219 The Punishment of Disobedience

By disobedience Saul lost—

his *Kingship*—'the kingdom— given to a neighbour'  1 Sam. 15. 28

his *Fellowship*—'Samuel came no more to see Saul'  1 Sam. 15. 35

his *leadership*—'all Israel and Judah loved David'  1 Sam. 18. 16

his *Life*—'Saul—fallen in Mount Gilboa'  1 Sam. 31. 8

**220   'Send Me David'**
1 Sam. 16. 19

Who was David?

1 Son of Jesse the Bethlehemite
1 Sam. 16. 19; Ruth 4. 17;
Matt. 2. 5

2 Of the tribe of Judah
Matt. 1. 1; 3-6

3 a much loved man, (David means 'Beloved')     1 Sam. 18. 16

4 a Shepherd     1 Sam. 16. 11; 2 Sam. 7. 8

5 a Musician, a skilful player on the harp
1 Sam. 16. 18

6 A sweet Psalmist
2 Sam. 23. 1

7 A Hero in battle
1 Sam. 16. 18; 17. 50

8 A King of all Israel
2 Sam. 5. 3, 4

9 Founder of the city of Zion
2 Sam. 5. 7

10 Founder of a royal Dynasty
2 Sam. 7. 11

**221   Qualities of an Overcomer**

David, the overcomer, displayed—

1 *Fidelity* in *Doing* his *duty*  1 Sam. 17. 34-37

2 *Fervour* in *Defending*
God's honour     1 Sam. 17. 36-37

3 *Faith* in *Declaring* God's
power     1 Sam. 17. 44-47
(A faith born in secret
communion with God,
exercised in lonely
conflicts in the wilder-
ness, and triumphant
in the hour of danger.)

4 *Frankness* in *Discarding*
man's weapons     1 Sam. 17. 39
(too big for David,
too small for Goliath)

5 *Fearlessness* in *Delivering*
God's people     1 Sam. 17. 51-53

**222   David's Weapons**

1 A Shepherd's Crook
that became a royal     1 Sam. 17. 34;
Sceptre     2 Sam. 7. 8

2 A common Sling that     1 Sam. 17. 40;
grew into an army of     2 Sam. 23. 8;
mighty men

3 A tuneful Harp that     1 Sam. 18. 10
produced a Volume
of praise-songs     Book of Psalms

4 Five smooth stones
that were meant for
5 lords of the Phili-     1 Sam. 17. 40, 49;
stines     2 Sam. 8. 1

**223   Result of the Battle of the Champions**

1 *Triumph* of David     1 Sam. 17. 50

2 *Trophies* of David     1 Sam. 17. 51

3 *Tributes* to David     1 Sam.18. 7; 19. 5

4 *Throne* of David     1 Sam. 23. 17

**224   Wonderful Love**

'Jonathan loved him (David)
as his own soul'     1 Sam. 18. 1

'Thy love to me was wonderful' 2 Sam. 1. 26

1 Love's *Covenant*—     1 Sam. 18. 3;
made a covenant     20. 16; 23. 18

2 Love's *Consecration*—
Jonathan stripped himself 1 Sam. 18. 4

3 Love's *Confession*—
spake good of David     1 Sam. 19· 4

4 Love's *Communion*—
in the house, place of rest 1 Sam. 18. 1-3
in the field, place of toil 1 Sam. 20. 11
in the wood, place of re-
proach     1 Sam. 23. 16
but not in the cave, place of
hardship     1 Sam. 23. 18
(Jonathan went unto his
own house.)

**225   Attracted to David**

1 *Jonathan* in the hour of
his *Victory*     1 Sam. 18. 1

2 *David's men* in the hour
of his *Rejection*     1 Sam. 22. 1, 2

3 *Abiathar* the priest in
the hour of *Danger* 1 Sam. 22. 20, 21

4 *Abigail* in the hour of
his *Pleading*     1 Sam. 25. 8, 23

5 *Young man of Egypt* in
the hour of *Pursuit* 1 Sam. 30. 11

6 *Abner* the leader in the
hour of his *Vengeance* 2 Sam. 3. 8-10

7 Israel and Judah, the
*nation*, in the hour of
his *Power*     2 Sam. 5. 1, 5

**226   Wise Behaviour**
1 Sam. 18

1 David behaved himself *wisely*
when *honoured* by Saul     v. 5

2 David behaved himself *very
wisely* when *feared* by Saul     vs. 14, 15

3 David behaved himself still
*more wisely* when hated by
Saul     v. 30

The hatred of Saul grew out of *Envy* (v. 9),
led to cruelty (v. 11), and subtlety (v. 21)
God's *Grace* arising out of it
2 Sam. 15. 18, 19

**227 Changed Behaviour**
1 Sam. 21. 13

1 The *Cause of David's Declension—Fear*
1 Sam. 21. 10, 12; 27. 1
David was fearful when faithless, fearless when faithful.

2 The *Calamity of David's Deception—*
he acted a lie          1 Sam. 21. 13
affirmed a lie          1 Sam. 27. 10
assented to a lie       1 Sam. 28. 1, 2
'O what a tangled web we weave
When first we practise to deceive.'

3 The *Consequences of David's Defection—*
God's *Guidance* in spite of it
1 Sam. 29. 10
God's *Government* because of it
1 Sam. 30. 1, 2

**228 David's Men**
1 WHO THEY WERE
Those who joined him in the Cave of Adullam were
i *Debtors—*
Bitten by creditors     1 Sam. 22. 2
(Hebrew word means 'bitten')
ii *Distressed—*
Bereft of peace of mind
(Hebrew word means 'straitness')
iii *Discontented—*
(Hebrew word means 'bitter in spirit')
2 WHAT THEY DID
i Separated themselves unto David     1 Chron. 12. 8
ii Soldiered for David   1 Sam. 23. 5
iii Submitted their will to David     1 Sam. 26. 4
iv Served David faithfully     2 Sam. 23. 16
v Sided steadfastly with David     1 Chron. 11. 10
(Marg.)

**229 A Wise Woman and a Kind King**
1 Sam. 25

Abigail
*Made haste,* when she saw danger near     vs. 18, 34
*Came direct* to David himself     v. 20
*Prostrated herself* before David, in humility     vs. 23, 24
*Asked forgiveness* from David for her trespass     v. 28
*Expressed confidence* in David as chosen of God     vs. 28, 29
*Believed God's promise* to David concerning the kingdom     v. 30
*Became the wife* of David     v. 41

**230 Two Confessions Contrasted**
Confession of SAUL THE KING,
of the Tribe of Benjamin, who disobeyed the voice of the Lord     1 Sam. 15. 19

I have sinned
I have played the fool
I have erred exceedingly     1 Sam. 26. 21
Confession of SAUL THE APOSTLE
(Paul) of the tribe of Benjamin, who was not disobedient to the heavenly vision     Acts 26. 19
I have fought a good fight
I have finished my course
I have kept the faith     2 Tim. 4. 7
Saul the king lost an earthly crown, Saul of Tarsus, the Apostle, gained a heavenly crown.

**231 Greatly Distressed but Divinely Encouraged**
1 Sam. 30. 4

Greatly distressed by—
*Exile* from his home
*Ingratitude* of his people
*Deferment* of his hopes
*Loss* of his possessions
*Mutiny* of his men
Greatly encouraged in the Lord by—
1 *Strengthening himself* in weakness     2 Cor. 12. 9
(Same Hebrew word is used of *Jacob* in Gen. 48. 2)
2 *Taking courage* in time of trouble     Acts 28. 15
(Same Hebrew word is used of *Asa* in 2 Chron. 15. 8)
3 *Behaving himself valiantly* in face of mutiny     Acts 20. 24
(Same Hebrew word is used of *Abishai* in 1 Chron. 19. 13)
4 *Becoming mighty* in overcoming the enemy
(Same Hebrew word is used of *Benaiah* in 1 Chron. 27. 6)

**232 The Forsaken Slave**
1 Sam. 30. 13-15
The young man of Egypt was
1 *Foreign*—an Egyptian     1 Sam. 30. 11
2 *Friendless*     1 Sam. 30. 11
3 *Forsaken*
my master left me     1 Sam. 30. 13
4 *Famishing*     1 Sam. 30. 12
5 *Found*     1 Sam. 30. 11
6 *Fed*     1 Sam. 30. 11, 12
7 *Freed*     1 Sam. 30. 15
H.K.D.

**233 'To Whom Belongest Thou'**
1 Sam. 30. 13

1 Certainly not to yourself, for 'ye are not your own'     1 Cor. 6. 19
2 Possibly to the Devil, if still in your sins     John 8. 44; 1 John 3. 8
3 Happily to the Lord Jesus Christ, if you have received Him
John 1. 12; Mark 9. 41

# 2 SAMUEL

## 234 The Throne of David
Divisions of 2 Samuel:
1 David Came to the Throne 1. 1-5. 16
2 David Conquered from the
Throne 5. 17-11. 1
3 David Fled from the Throne 11. 2-20. 3
4 David Established on the
Throne 20. 4-24. 25

## 235 David's Prayer
2 Sam. 2. 1-3
Note concerning it—
1 How becoming it was—After this
David enquired v. 1
2 How direct it was—'of the Lord' v. 1
3 How brief it was—'Shall I go up?'
'Whither shall I go up?' v. 1
4 How simple was its subject—his
movements v. 1
5 How prevailing it was—the Lord
heard it v. 1
6 How speedily came the answer—'unto
Hebron' v. 1
7 How prompt was David's obedience—
David went up v. 2
A.C.B.

## 236 Died Abner as a Fool Dieth?
2 Sam. 3. 33
Abner's Folly consisted in—
1 *Unclaimed Privilege*—
at the gate of a city of refuge 2 Sam. 3.27
but failed to enter
2 *Unused powers*—
hands not bound and feet not
fettered 2 Sam. 3. 34
3 *Unwise parley*—
Joab took him aside to speak
quietly 2 Sam. 3. 27

## 237 David's Threefold Attitude
1 Lying before the Lord as a
Penitent 2 Sam. 12. 16
2 Sitting before the Lord as
a Worshipper 2 Sam. 7. 18
3 Standing before the Lord
as a Servant 1 Chron. 28. 2
N.B.

## 238 A King's Questions
1 'Who am I, O Lord God?
Man's Insignificance 2 Sam. 7. 18
2 'What is my house'
Man's Insufficiency 2 Sam. 7. 18
3 'Is this the manner of man?'
God's Sovereignty 2 Sam. 7. 19

4 'What can David say any
more unto Thee?'
God's Omniscience 2 Sam. 7. 20
5 'What one nation in the
earth is like Thy people?'
God's Redeeming Grace 2 Sam. 7. 23

## 239 Kindness Shown
1 It was *Kindness* the king showed (to
Mephibosheth and to Hanun)
2 Sam. 9. 1, 7; 10. 2; Jer. 31. 3
2 It was the *Kindness of God*
2 Sam. 9. 3; Tit. 3. 4
3 It was *Kindness for Jonathan's sake*
2 Sam. 9. 1, 7; Eph. 2. 7
4 It was *Kindness based on a covenant*
1 Sam. 20. 14, 15, 16
5 It was *Kindness that gave* its object a *new
status*—as one of the King's sons
2 Sam. 9. 11; 1 John 3. 1
6 It was *Kindness that gave* him a *new place*,
at the King's table
2 Sam. 9. 7; 1 Cor. 10. 31
7 It was *Kindness that restored* a *forfeited
inheritance*
2 Sam. 9. 7; 1 Pet. 1, 3, 4

## 240 The Kindness of God
Seven steps 2 Sam. 9
1 *Fallen*—in infancy 2 Sam. 4. 4
2 *Fatherless*—when Jonathan
was killed 1 Sam. 31. 2
3 *Friendless*—of the house of
Saul 2 Sam. 9. 1
4 *Famished*—in Lo-debar,
place of no pasture 2 Sam. 9. 4
5 *Favoured*—'that I may show
him kindness' 2 Sam. 9. 3
6 *Fetched*—King David sent
and fetched him 2 Sam. 9. 5
7 *Feasted*—ate continually at
the king's table 2 Sam. 9. 7-13

## 241 The King and the Cripple
2 Sam. 9
THE SOURCE—
1 He went in and sat before
the Lord
'According to Thine own
heart' 2 Sam. 7. 18
'For Jonathan's sake' 2 Sam. 9. 1
THE SUBJECT—
2 He was Lost. David had to
hunt for him
Lame on both his feet
Left—wellnigh left alto-
gether

THE STYLE

3 Powerfully—He sent and
fetched him
Peacefully—He said, 'Fear
not'
Perpetually—'Thou shalt
eat bread at my table
alway'

THE SEQUEL

4 Two Mephibosheths, One
Spared: the other Hanged
2 Sam. 21. 7, 8, 9
Which will you be in Eternity?

HYP.

## 242  At the King's Table

Associated in each mention with eating
2 Sam. 9. 7, 10, 11, 13
The Place where the hungry find abundant
satisfaction          Ps. 36. 7, 8

HOW LONG?—At his table continually, always
2 Sam. 9. 7, 10

IN WHAT CAPACITY?—As one of the king's sons
2 Sam. 9. 11

WITH WHAT THOUGHTS?—Lame on both his feet
2 Sam. 9. 13

(But his lameness was not seen while he was
seated at the king's table.)

## 243  David's Eyes

King David had—

first, *Wandering Eyes*      2 Sam. 11. 2
that, became *Wanton Eyes*   2 Sam. 11. 4
then *Weeping Eyes*          2 Sam. 15. 30
and finally, *Wishful Eyes*  2 Sam. 18. 24

## 244  From the Depths to the Heights

David's great *Sin*         2 Sam. 11
David's great *Sorrow*      2 Sam. 12
David's great *Suffering*   2 Sam. 13-18
David's great *Strength*    2 Sam. 19-23

## 245  'I Have Sinned'
2 Sam. 12. 13

This confession was made by—

1 Pharaoh—from a de-
sire to escape sin's
Penalty          Exod. 9. 27; 10. 16
2 Achan—with the
knowledge that his sin
had been exposed    Joshua 7. 19-21
3 Saul—from the desire
to save his face   1 Sam. 15. 24, 30
4 Judas Iscariot—from the remorse arising
from disappointment     Matt. 27. 3-5
5 David—from the fear
of God              2 Sam. 12. 13
6 the Prodigal son—from the longing to
return home          Luke 15. 21
7 Any truly Penitent—realizing the futility
of sin's course        Job. 33. 27

## 246  Sin Put Away
2 Sam. 12. 13

'The Lord also hath put away thy sin'
God never passes over sin but He can put it
away—

1 By covering it with the   Ps. 32. 1. 2;
blood                       Heb. 9. 22
2 By having it carried away
to a land uninhabited   Lev. 16. 21, 22
3 By removing it to a
distance                Ps. 103. 12
4 By casting it behind His
back                    Isa. 38. 17
5 By blotting it out as a
thick cloud             Isa. 44. 22
6 By consigning it to the
depths of the sea       Mic. 7. 19
7 By remembering it no
more                    Jer. 31. 34

## 247  The Young Man Absalom
2 Sam. 14. 21

*David's Way*—'Bring the young man Absalom
again' (with no mention of his crimes)
*God's Way*—'Yet doth He devise means that
His banished be not expelled from Him'
2 Sam. 14. 14

There is a difference between God's way and
man's way of bringing the banished criminal
back.

Absalom was brought back—

UNRIGHTEOUSLY—
as far as David was con-
cerned                      2 Sam. 14. 32
(Absalom had never been
brought to justice)

UNREPENTANT—
as far as he himself was concerned                    2 Sam. 15. 6, 13
(He very soon rebelled openly)

UNRECONCILED—
as far as both were concerned 2 Sam. 14. 24
('He saw not the king's face')

God's way is a *Righteous Way*  Rom. 3. 25, 26
commanding *Repentance*         Acts 17. 30
effecting *Reconciliation*      Rom. 5. 10

## 248  Three Loyal Followers of the Rejected King

*Ittai* the Gittite—

1 Yielded *himself* to
David: The *Loyalty*
of Love             2 Sam. 15. 19, 21
2 *Hushai* the Archite—
Yielded *his service* to
David: The *Labour*
of Love             2 Sam. 15. 32-37
3 *Barzillai* the Gileadite—
Yielded *his substance* to
David: The *Liberality*
of Love             2 Sam. 17. 27-29

**249 The Mount of Olives**

1 Under a *Cloud*—
The *Abjection* of a *Sinful*
king      2 Sam. 15. 30

2 In the *Sunlight*—
The *Acclamation* of a *Sinless* King      Luke 19. 37

3 In the *Moonlight*—
The *Anguish* of a *Sin-bearing* King      Luke 22. 39-42

4 In the *Spotlight*—
The *Ascension* of a *Saviour* King      Acts 1. 9-12

5 In the *Floodlight* of Glory—
The *Appearing* of a *Smiting* King      Zech. 14. 3, 4

**250 How Long? Three Questions**

1 'How long have I to live?'
makes us consider the
*Close of our Life*      2 Sam. 19. 34

2 'How long will ye love
vanity?' makes us consider the *Course of our Life*      Ps. 4. 2

3 'How long halt ye between
two opinions?' makes us
consider the *Challenge of our Life*      1 Kings 18. 21

**251 A Trinity of Truth**
2 Sam. 22. 31

1 A *Perfect Path*
'His way is perfect'. Amid the confusion
and contradiction in the world there is
one sure way. 'I am the way,' etc.
John 14. 6.

2 A *Tested Truth*
'The Word of the Lord is tried.' His
promises are not untried bridges on
which no foot has trod, but arches that
have borne thousands on their way to
heaven.

3 A *Present Protection*
'He is a shield,' e.g. Abraham, Job. etc.
                 W.R.

**252 David's Mighty Men**
2 Sam. 23. 8-39

The lion-faced—'faces—like the
faces of lions'      1 Chron. 12. 8

1 *Adino*—Lion-faced before overwhelming
forces of the enemy   2 Sam. 23. 8

2 *Eleazar*—hosts of Philistines      2 Sam. 23. 9, 10

3 *Shammah*—in defence
of a field of lentiles   2 Sam. 23. 11, 12

4 *Three mighty men*—lion-faced in breaking
through to the well
at Bethlehem      2 Sam. 23. 13-17

5 *Abishai*—Lion-faced in
using his spear against
the enemy      2 Sam. 23. 18, 19

6 *Benaiah*—before lion-like men of Moab      2 Sam. 23. 20

REWARDED because they were

*Separated* to David
*Steadfast* in purpose
*Strong* to Overcome
*Swift* to Pursue      1 Chron. 12. 8

**253 In Jeopardy of Their Lives**

Men who risked their lives

1 *David's three Mighty Men*—
to bring joy to their
Commander      2 Sam. 23. 14-17

2 *Barnabas and Saul*—
'hazarded their lives' to
bring glory to the
Name of Jesus      Acts 15. 25, 26

3 *Priscilla and Aquila*—
'laid down their necks'
to save the lives of
God's servants      Rom. 16. 3, 4

4 *Epaphroditus*—
'risked his life' (R.S.V.)
for the work of Christ   Phil. 2. 30

# 1 KINGS

**254 King Solomon**
1 Kings 2. 12

1 *Personally*—as a man he was
*Fittingly Humble*  1 Kings 3. 7-9
*Profoundly Wise*  1 Kings 4. 30
*Extremely Foolish, weak* and *wicked*
1 Kings 11. 1, 6, 9

2 *Officially*—as a king he
*Ruled* his people *righteously*
1 Kings 3. 28
*Chose* his ministers *wisely*
1 Kings 4. 1-20
*Extended* his dominions *peacefully*
1 Kings 4. 21-25

3 *Figuratively*—as a type. Compare
Ps. 72
i his *name*, Solomon—peaceable
Isa. 9. 6
ii his *coronation* twice
1 Chron. 23. 1; 29. 22
iii his *throne*, Jehovah's
1 Chron. 29. 23;
Rev. 3. 21
iv his *prosperity*  1 Kings 10. 21. 27;
Ps. 72. 15, 16
v his *authority*  1 Kings 4. 21;
Rev. 11. 15

**255 Reign of Solomon**
1 Kings Chs. 1-11

1 His *Appointment and Anointing*
Chs. 1 and 2

2 His *Wisdom and Wealth*
Chs. 3 and 4

3 *God's Temple and his house*
Chs. 5; 6; 7; and 8

4 His *Fare and his Fame* Chs. 3 and 10

5 His *Declension and Death*
Ch. 11

**256 Lampstands in the Temple**
1 Kings 7. 49

There was only *one* Lampstand in the Tabernacle Exod. 25. 31

There were *ten* Lampstands
in Solomon's *Temple*  1 Kings 7. 49

(The Unity of the nation
was about to end)

*No Lampstand* is required
in the *Millennial Temple,*
described in  Ezek. Chs. 40-42

10 Lampstands, 10 bases
for 10 lavers of brass,
and 10 tables for shew-
bread were in the Temple.

10 Commandments were
on the Tables of stone in
the Ark of the covenant.

10 Lampstands:
5 on the *Right*—to re-
present *Judah's* testi-
mony  1 Kings 11. 12-13;
15. 4

5 *Kings* of Judah kept the
Lamp of witness burn-
ing, namely, Asa, Jeho-
shaphat, Joash, Heze-
kiah and Josiah

5 on the *Left*—to re-
present *Israel's* testi-
mony  2 Kings 17. 18

5 *Prophets* in Israel who
witnessed for God,
namely, Nathan, Ahi-
jah, Elijah, Elisha, and
Jonah.

**257 A Royal Visitor to Solomon**
1 Kings 10. 1-13

The Queen of Sheba, the Queen of the South
Matt. 12. 42

1 *What she Heard*—
Solomon's Fame and Jehovah's Name
v. 1; Matt. 4. 24; 9. 31

2 *What she Did*—
she came  1; Matt. 11. 28

3 *What she Saw*—
8 things—*first* his wisdom, *last* his
ascending offering
v. 4; 1 Cor. 2. 6-8

4 *What she Said*—
'the half was not told me'
vs. 6-8; 1 Cor. 2. 9

5 *What she Got*—
his royal bounty  v. 13; Eph. 3. 8

**258 Causes of Solomon's Declension**
1 Kings 11. 9

'His heart was turned from the Lord God of
Israel by—

1 *Wealth*
1 Kings 10. 16-18, 23; Deut. 17. 17

2 *Vanity*
ivory, apes and peacocks
1 Kings 10. 22

3 *Horses*
1 Kings 10. 28; Deut. 17. 16

4 *Women*
1 Kings 11. 1-4; Deut. 7. 3

**259 Some Counterfeits**
1 Kings 12. 26-33

1 Counterfeit *God*  v. 28
2 Counterfeit *Priesthood*  v. 31
3 Counterfeit *Sacrifice*  v. 32
4 Counterfeit *Worship*  v. 32
5 Counterfeit *Feast*  v. 33

F. MCL.

## 260 A Man of God Sidetracked
1 Kings 13

In the Chapter the title '*man of God*' occurs
15 times
the '*word of the Lord*' 10 times

The man of God had the Word of the Lord
for his

| | |
|---|---|
| Guidance | 1 Kings 13. 1 |
| Message | 1 Kings 13. 2 |
| Power | 1 Kings 13. 5 |
| Authority | 1 Kings 13. 9 |

When he was off guard, he was 'disobedient
unto the Word of the Lord' v. 26.

1 *Satan's Time*—
after a great achievement for God
v. 5; 1 Kings 18. 40; 19. 4

2 *Satan's Disguise*—
the guise of a prophet
v. 18; 2 Cor. 11. 13, 14

3 *Satan's Aim*—
to get the man of God out of the will of God
v. 21; Eph. 5. 17

4 *Satan's Strategy*—
using something seemingly trivial (Eating
and drinking: coming and going)
v. 22; Eph. 6. 11

5 *Satan's Triumph*—
a carcase cast in the way (a live wire
become lifeless, a useful servant become
useless, a grand example become a
solemn warning)
v. 25; 1 Cor. 9. 27

## 261 Perilous Times

The times in which Elijah lived were marked by

1 *Departure* from the living God and spread
of Idolatry   1 Kings 12. 28; 15. 30, 34

2 *Division* among the people of God—2
kingdoms, Israel and Judah
1 Kings 12. 16

3 *Demoralization* of the leaders of Israel
1 Kings 16. 30-33

4 *Disobedience* to God's marriage laws—
the unequal yoke
1 Kings 16. 31; Deut. 7. 3, 4

5 *Defiance* of the word of God concerning
rebuilding Jericho (city of the curse)
1 Kings 16. 34; Joshua 6. 26

## 262 God's Word to Elijah
1 Kings 17. 3, 4

1 *A Definite Command*—
'Get thee hence'

2 *An Explicit Direction*—
'Turn thee eastward'

3 *A Timely Instruction*—
'Hide thyself'

4 *A Promised Supply*—
'I have commanded the ravens to feed
thee'

## 263 Character of Elijah

Elijah—My God is Jehovah: the Tishbite =
the converter. Man's Extremity is God's
Opportunity. Elijah was the man God chose
for those critical times.

He was—

1 *A Man of Passions*
1 Kings 19. 4; James 5. 17

2 *A Man of Prayer*
1 Kings 17. 20; James 5. 17

3 *A Man of Power*
1 Kings 17. 1; 2 Kings 2. 14, 15;
Luke 1. 17

4 *A Man of Patience*
1 Kings 17. 5-7

5 *A Man Protected* by God
1 Kings 18. 10

## 264 Marks of Divine Power in Elijah

1 In his *Boldness in Testimony* (Contrast Oba-
diah in 1 Kings 18. 3) 1 Kings 17. 1

2 In his *Obedience to divine
Commands* 'Hide thy-
self' (1 Kings 17. 3),
'shew thyself' (1 Kings
18. 1)        1 Kings 17. 2-5

3 In his *Dependence on
God's Supplies* Those
were—*natural*—a brook
*miraculous*—ravens;
and *divine*—a widow 1 Kings 17. 4-9

4 In his *Impartation of Life*
to the dead        1 Kings 17. 22

## 265 The Triumph of Faith

Elijah on Mount Carmel. *Carmel*—the
fruitful place: certainly fruitful for God.

1 *Faith's Challenge*—
he presented a fair
challenge        1 Kings 18. 24

2 *Faith's Confidence*—
he was certain his God
would act        1 Kings 18. 30

3 *Faith's Communion*—
he 'drew near' to God 1 Kings 18. 36, 37

4 *Faith's Conquest*—
Elijah's God answered
by fire        1 Kings 18. 38
*Vindication* of the true
God        1 Kings 18. 39
*Destruction* of the false
prophets        1 Kings 18. 40

## 266 How To Pray
1 Kings 18. 41-46

Pray as Elijah did—

| | |
|---|---|
| Intelligently | v. 41; Deut. 28. 12, 24 |
| Believingly | v. 41 |
| Humbly | v. 42 |
| Earnestly | James 5. 17 |
| Definitely | James 5. 17 |
| Persistently | v. 43; James 5. 18 |
| Successfully | vs. 44, 45 |

**267 God's Depressed Servant**
'Elijah arose and went for his life' 1 Kings 19.1-3
God's Grace is abundant in Elijah's weakness. Compare 2 Cor. 12. 9

1 *God Supplying*
His servant's need     1 Kings 19. 6-8
2 *God Seeking*
His servant's good     1 Kings 19. 9
3 *God Speaking to*
His servant's conscience     1 Kings 19. 9, 13
Elijah was absent from Jezreel just when his presence was most needed, so God had to say to him, twice, 'What doest thou here, Elijah?'
4 *God Sending*
His servant to act for Him     1 Kings 19. 15, 16
to anoint a successor to Benhadad in Syria
to anoint a successor to Ahab in Israel
to anoint a successor to himself in the prophetic office

**268 The Call of Elisha**
1 Kings 19. 19-21

1 *The Person* who was called—
Elisha = God is my Saviour     v. 19
2 *The Place* where he was found
Abel-meholah = Vale of the dance v. 16
3 *The Work* that he was doing—
Ploughing his field     v. 19
(called now to plough Jehovah's field)
4 *The Sign* that he was needed—
Elijah's mantle fell on him     v. 19
5 *The Response* that he gave—
'I will follow thee'     v. 20

**269 Anointed People**
1 Kings 19. 16-20

1 *The Priests* of the tribe of Levi
Exod. 28. 41; 40. 15; Lev. 8. 12
2 *The Kings* of Israel—Saul, David, Solomon, Jehu, Josiah
1 Sam. 15. 1; 16. 12, 13; 2 Sam. 2. 4;
5. 3; 1 Kings 1. 43, 45; 2 Kings 9. 6.
3 *The Prophet Elisha*
1 Kings 19. 16
4 *The Lord Jesus Christ* (Christ anointed)
Ps. 45. 7; Isa. 61. 1; John 12. 3;
Acts 10. 38; Heb. 1. 9
5 *The saints in the Church*
2 Cor. 1. 21; 1 John 2. 27

**270 Busy Here and There**
1 Kings 20. 35-43

A Story with three characters—

1 A wounded warrior with a responsibility

2 A king to whom he was accountable

3 A prisoner he was commanded to guard and hold

Observe—
1 *The Charge* committed to him—'keep this man'     v. 39

The Christian is commanded to keep, or hold, Heb. 6. 18
the hope set before us Heb. 6. 18
the Life that is life indeed 1 Tim. 6. 19
the Good Deposit of truth 2 Tim. 1. 14
Opportunities for service     Eph. 5. 15, 16

2 *The Excuse* for his negligence—'Busy here and there'     v. 40

Are we busy here and there—
in the struggle for a living?
in the affairs of the home?
in the business of life?
in the accumulation of wealth?
in the pursuit of pleasure?

3 *The tragedy* that resulted from his neglect—'he was gone'     v. 40

It was an irrecoverable loss.

**271 Micaiah, A Faithful Servant**

1 *Hated for his warnings*
that did not suit the king     1 Kings 22. 8

2 *Despised for his truthfulness*     1 Kings 22. 18

3 *Persecuted for his courage*     1 Kings 22. 24

4 *Imprisoned for his faithfulness*     1 Kings 22. 26, 27

5 *Afflicted for displeasing a wicked king*     1 Kings 22. 27
N.L.K.

## 2 KINGS

### 272 The Lesson of Elijah and Elisha

Elijah and Elisha are taking the last walk together. Elijah is about to be taken. Elisha will carry on the work. But what leads to him getting the power? 2 Kings 2.

1 PREPARATION—
Gilgal, 1; Bethel, 2; Jericho, 4; Jordan, 6
These places gave a fitness, a moral preparation for power.

2 PRAYER—
'Ask what I shall do for thee before I be taken from thee' (v. 9)

3 PROMISE (v. 10)—
'If ye see me when I am taken from thee.'

4 POSSESSION (vs. 14, 15)—
Spirit rests on Elisha

S.E.D.

### 273 The Way to Blessing

1 It was the
PATH OF PERSISTENCE
'I will not leave thee'     2 Kings 2. 2, 4, 6

2 It was the
PATH OF PROGRESS
'they two went on'     2 Kings 2. 6-8

3 It was the
PATH OF POWER
'the spirit of Elijah doth 2 Kings 2. 15;
rest on Elisha'     Luke 1. 17

The four places visited have significant meanings and had historic associations. He returned to the same places he had passed on his way, and in the same order.

He went to *get:*     he returned to *give*
He went to *see:*     he returned to *show*
He went to *hear:*     he returned to *heal*
He went to *learn:*     he returned to *lead*

### 274 The Double Portion
2 Kings 2. 9

was—

1 The Portion of
the *Firstborn son* Deut. 21. 17
Elisha wanted to
be considered
Elijah's firstborn
son, and to receive the portion
necessary to maintain Jehovah's
honour.

2 The Portion of
the *Well-beloved*
(Elkanah gave this 1 Sam. 1. 5 (Marg.);
to Hannah)     Song of Songs 7. 10

3 The Portion of
*one who endures
Trial*     Job. 42. 10; James 1. 12

### 275 The Spirit of Power

The Era of Elisha's miracles—double the number performed by Elijah.

1 Power in his *Works*—
the 'spirit of Elijah'     2 Kings 2. 14, 15

2 Power in his *Words*—
'the Word of Jehovah
is with him'     2 Kings 3. 12

3 Power in his *Walk*—
'an holy man of God' 2 Kings 4. 8, 9

### 276 The Unequal Yoke

'I am as thou art, my people as thy people'
2 Kings 3. 7
The Unequal Yoke in

1 Jehoshaphat's *Matrimonial* arrangements
2 Chron. 18. 1
The Result—Family disaster

2 Jehoshaphat's *Political* Alliances
2 Chron. 18. 2
The Result—National Discomfiture

3 Jehoshaphat's *Commercial* Partnership
2 Chron. 20. 35, 36
The Result—Financial Losses

### 277 Departure and Deliverance
2 Kings 3

1 The *Project Envisaged*—
a battle against Moab     v. 7

2 The *Plight Experienced*—
no water     v. 9

3 The *Provision Enjoyed*—
there came water     v. 20
by the *Word* of the Lord     v. 12
the *Joy* of the Lord     v. 15
the *Power* of the Lord     v. 18

### 278 A Debt and How it was Settled
2 Kings 4. 1-7

'The creditor is come v. 1
'Go, sell the oil, and pay the debt' v. 7

1 A *Transformation* that
took place by means
of—

2 A *Treasure* that was possessed—a pot of oil     v. 2; 2 Cor. 4. 7

3 A *Transfer* that was
negotiated—borrow
vessels, pour out     vs. 3, 4

4 A *Transaction* that was
completed—behind a
closed door, and led
to—     v. 5; Matt. 6. 6

5 A *Triumph* that was enjoyed.     v. 7
She paid the debt and
lived, with her family,
off the rest.

## 279  A Great Woman
2 Kings 4. 8

The woman of Shunem was—

1 Great in *Rank*
the Hebrew word for 'great'
indicates this)                                    v. 8
2 Great in *Discernment*—
'I perceive'                                          v. 8
3 Great in *Hospitality*—
'let us make a little chamber'            v. 9
4 Great in *Humility*—
'I dwell among my own people'      v. 13
5 Great in *Maternal Affection*—
'carry him to his mother'            v. 19, 20
6 Great in *Faith*—
'It is well' (with the child)              v. 26
7 Great in *Courage*—
'Drive and go forward: slack not'  v. 24


## 280  A Powerless Servant

Elisha's servant, Gehazi, lacked four great essentials—

1 Lack of *Pity*—
he came near to thrust her
away (though her soul was
vexed)                                    2 Kings 4. 27
2 Lack of *Prayer*—
(contrast Elisha in verse 33) 2 Kings 4. 31
3 Lack of *Preparation*—
used Elisha's staff only        2 Kings 4. 31
4 Lack of *Personal Touch*—
(contrast Elisha in verse 34) 2 Kings 4. 31


## 281  How to Raise the Dead

In the picture of the Shunammite's son we have the qualifications of the worker: 2 Kings 4

1 *Weakness*—
A young man and an ass              v. 22
2 *Zeal*—
'Drive and go forward, slack not'  v. 24
3 *Faith*—
The brokenhearted husband indifferent; child dead—'It is well'       v. 26
4 *Prayer*—
'He went in, shut the door, prayed
unto the Lord'                              v. 33
5 *Adaptation*—
Man and child made to fit, mouth
upon mouth, eyes upon eyes,
hands upon hands                        v. 34
6 *Patience*—
Walked to and fro, waited            v. 35
7 *Victory*—
Opened his eyes, 'take up thy son'
v. 35, 36
HYP.


## 282  The Problem of the Dead Child
(For Workers among the young)

1 THE MAN GOD USED—
Elisha—Jehovah is my Saviour
2 Kings 4. 27


2 THE MANNER HE FOLLOWED—
his Compassion for the sorrowing
his Concern for others
his Confidence in God
2 Kings 4. 26, 27; 4. 33

3 THE METHOD HE EMPLOYED—
Stretched himself upon the child
Personal touch and Adaptability
2 Kings 4. 34, 35
No teacher can hope for success who is not
able to put himself (herself) in the place
of the pupil.

4 THE MIRACLE GOD WROUGHT—
the child sneezed seven times
(Sign to those waiting outside the door)
the child opened his eyes
(Sign to the Lord's servant inside)
2 Kings 4. 35


## 283  The Model Maid

| | |
|---|---|
| She was *little* | 2 Kings 5. 2 |
| She was a *captive* | 2 Kings 5. 2 |
| She was an *Israelite* | 2 Kings 5. 2 |
| She *confessed God* | 2 Kings 5. 3 |
| She had *sympathy* | 2 Kings 5. 3 |
| She *told* of the *prophet* | 2 Kings 5. 3 |
| She was the *means of Salvation* | 2 Kings 5. 15 |

JS. FS.


## 284  Naaman's Mistakes

There are two Naamans in the Bible—
First in Gen. 46. 21—an Israelite, son of Benjamin: only one verse given to him. The other in 2 Kings 5; Luke 4. 27—a Gentile, a Syrian and a leper. A chapter in the Old Testament and a verse in the New Testament are given to him.

Naaman the leper—

1 *Engaged the Wrong
Person* for the job he
wanted done                2 Kings 5. 6
REASON—he did not
pay attention to the
message                      2 Kings 5. 3
2 *Expected the Wrong
Procedure* to be car-
ried out                       2 Kings 5. 10
REASON—he came
with his own precon-
ceived ideas—'I
thought'                      2 Kings 5. 11
3 *Entertained a Wrong
Prejudice* about the
plan of cleansing         2 Kings 5. 12
REASON—Natural and
national prejudices
influenced him
4 *Estimated the Wrong
Price* for his cleansing 2 Kings 5. 5, 15, 16
REASON—he did not
know the 'gift of God'
(10 Talents of silver, 6000 pieces of gold—
about equal to £16,000, but not enough to pay
for his cleansing)

**285  Elisha's Prescription**
2 Kings 5. 10

| | |
|---|---|
| 1 'Go' | *Responsibility* |
| 2 'Wash' | *Applicability* |
| 3 'In Jordan' | *Locality* |
| 4 'Seven times' | *Extremity* |
| 5 'And thou' | *Individuality* |
| 6 'Shalt be' | *Certainty* |
| 7 'Clean' | *Recovery* |

JS. FS.

**286  Five Steps Down**

Naaman—

1 Listened to a foreign, captive slave-girl          2 Kings 5. 4
2 Asked a favour of a defeated foe          2 Kings 5. 6
3 Waited outside a prophet's humble house          2 King's 5. 9
4 Divested himself of all his insignia of office          2 Kings 5. 13
5 Went down into Jordan and dipped seven times          2 Kings 5. 14

**287  Two Remarkable Men**

NAAMAN THE SYRIAN

| | |
|---|---|
| 'I thought' | 2 Kings 5. 11 |
| 'I know' | 2 Kings 5. 15 |

THE APOSTLE PAUL

| | |
|---|---|
| 'I thought' | Acts 26. 9 |
| 'I know' | 2 Tim. 1. 12 |

D. W-E-.

**288  A Story of Five Chapters**
2 Kings 6. 1-7

Picture of the community life of the people of God

1 *Enlargement*—
'the place—is too strait for us'          vs. 1, 2
2 *Encouragement*—
'Go ye' and 'I will go'          v. 3
3 *Employment*—
Felling down and building up          v. 4
4 *Embarrassment*—
'Alas, master, for it was borrowed'  v. 5
5 *Empowerment*—
'he put out his hand and took it'  v. 7

**289  Enlargement**
2 Kings 6. 2

The believer needs—

1 AN ENLARGED HEART—
for Increased Capacity to  Ps. 119. 32;
*Respond to Christ's Claims*  2 Cor. 6. 13
2 AN ENLARGED MOUTH—
for Increased Capacity to
*Receive God's Blessings*  Ps. 81. 10
3 AN ENLARGED DWELLING—
for Increased Capacity to
*Rejoice in the Lord*  Isa. 54. 2, 3
4 AN ENLARGED COAST—
for Increased Capacity to
*Refresh God's saints*  1 Chron. 4. 10

**290  Prayers for the Blind**

1 Elisha's for *his servant*—
'Lord I pray Thee, open his eyes'          2 Kings 6. 17
Paul's Prayer for *the saints* Eph. 1. 18

2 Elisha's for *his enemies*—
'Lord, open the eyes of these men'          2 Kings 6. 20
Paul's Preaching *to sinners* Acts 26. 18

**291  The Four Leprous Men**

| | |
|---|---|
| *Consultation* | 2 Kings 7. 3 |
| *Consideration* | 2 Kings 7. 4 |
| *Decision* | 2 Kings 7. 5 |
| *Salvation* | 2 Kings 7. 8 |
| *Proclamation* | 2 Kings 7. 9 |

H.K.D.

**292  'We Do Not Well'**
2 Kings 7. 3-9

1 A Remarkable Intervention
The Lord had made the hosts of the Syrians to hear a noise          vs. 5, 6

2 A Reprehensible Inactivity
We do not well: we hold our peace v. 9

3 A Regrettable Indifference
If we tarry—some mischief will come to us          v. 9

4 A Resolute Intention
Come—that we may go and tell v. 9

**293  A Day of Good Tidings**
2 Kings 7

Good Tidings, that was Noteworthy, Trustworthy, and Worthy of all acceptation
1 Tim. 1. 15

1 *Source*
of the Good Tidings—
God's Throne in Heaven
the Word of the Lord 2 Kings 7. 1

2 *Course*
of the Good Tidings—
Its Centre—the enemy's camp, outside the city wall, where the enemy was scattered by God without human aid, and where there was abundant provision for all 2 Kings 7. 8-15

3 *Force*
of the Good Tidings—
in the *Transformation* it brought about
in the *Transmission* it stimulated

The tidings was CENTRIPETAL—pointing to the centre outside the camp

It was CENTRIFUGAL—proceeding from the centre outside the camp

**294 Reception of the Good Tidings**

As with the Gospel, the Good news, of Christ—

1 Some received it *courteously*
    2 Kings 7. 11; Luke 2. 15
2 Some received it *coldly*—e.g. the king
    2 Kings 7. 12; John 5. 40
3 Some received it *cautiously*
    2 Kings 7. 13; Acts 17. 32
4 Some received it *contemptuously*—e.g. the
    lord on whose hand the King leaned
    2 Kings 7. 19; Acts 17. 32

**295 Fate of the Scoffer**

    2 Kings 7. 17-20

1 He rejected the Word of the
   Lord               v. 19
2 He perished in the midst of
   plenty             v. 19
3 He saw others enjoying the
   blessing he missed    vs. 19, 20

**297 A Picture of Grace**

2 Kings 25

1 *Emancipation*—
   Out of prison         v. 27

2 *Consolation*—
   Spake kindly to him    v. 28

3 *Exaltation*—
   Set his throne, etc.    v. 28

4 *Transformation*—
   Changed his prison garments    v. 28

5 *Acceptation*—
   Did eat bread continually before him v. 29

6 *Preservation*—
   A continual allowance every day, all
     the days of his life    v. 30
                            D.W.

**296 A Great Revival**

2 Kings 18. 3-7

| PERSONAL CONDITIONS | | NATIONAL CONDITIONS | |
|---|---|---|---|
| 1 Hezekiah did *right* in the sight of the Lord | 2 Kings 18. 3 | Temple doors were *opened* and *repaired* | 2 Chron. 29. 3 |
| 2 He *removed* the images | 2 Kings 18. 4 | A covenant was *made* with the Lord | 2 Chron. 29. 10 |
| 3 He *trusted* in the Lord | 2 Kings 18. 5 | The priests and Levites were *sanctified* | 2 Chron. 29. 15 |
| 4 He *clave* to the Lord | 2 Kings 18. 6 | The Temple was *sanctified* | 2 Chron. 29. 15 |
| 5 He *followed* the Lord | 2 Kings 18. 6 | The Temple was *cleansed* | 2 Chron. 29. 16 |
| 6 He *kept* His commandments | 2 Kings 18.6 | The sacrifice was *offered* | 2 Chron. 29. 22 |
| RESULT | | RESULT | |
| 1 The Lord *was with* him | 2 Kings 18. 7 | Hezekiah *rejoiced* | 2 Chron. 29. 36 |
| 2 The Lord *prospered* him | 2 Kings 18. 7 | There was *great joy* in Jerusalem | 2 Chron. 30. 26 |
| | | | J.G. |

# 1 CHRONICLES

**298  With the King**                1 Chron. 4. 23
1 *Conversion*—with the king
2 *Communion*—they dwelt
3 *Consecration*—for his work
4 *Continuation*—there

**299  Judah Prevailed**
        1 Chron. 5. 2
See Gen. 49. 8-12; Deut. 33. 7; Rev. 5. 5-8
Judah's Standard was a Lion: Judah's greatest
Son is 'the Lion of the tribe of Judah' (Rev. 5. 5)
Judah prevailed in—

WISDOM
in  construction—Bezaleel Exod. 31. 2, 3
WORSHIP
Judah's prince offered first
    day—Nahshon                Num. 7. 12
WARFARE
Judah first to go up to war  Judges 1. 2
WAITING
upon God—Prayer of
    Jabez answered            1 Chron. 4. 9, 10
WIELDING
the Sceptre                  Gen. 49. 8-10

**300  Very Able Men for the Work**
        1 Chron. 9. 13

God's Workmen must be—
1 *Competent*        1 Chron. 9. 13; 12. 33

2 *Whole-hearted*    Neh. 4. 6; 6. 3

3 *Valorous*         2 Chron. 32. 7, 8

4 *Diligent*         Ezra 7. 23; Neh. 4. 21

5 *Vigilant*         Neh. 4. 11, 18

6 *Undaunted*        Neh. 4. 11-14

7 *Dependent on God*
  for results        Neh. 4. 20

8 *God-honouring*    Neh. 5. 9; 6. 15

**301  Men With Whom the Holy Spirit Clothed
        Himself**
        1 Chron. 12. 18
1 With *Gideon*—
  for *Warfare*—Gideon's
    *Hands*              Judges 6. 34
  Resulting in three out-
    standing achievements
  Threshing wheat, show-
    ing his Zeal         Judges 6. 11
  Building an Altar, show-
    ing his faith        Judges 6. 24
  Hewing down a grove,
    showing his courage  Judges 6. 28

2 With *Amasai*—
  for *Wisdom*—Amasai's
    *Mind*               1 Chron. 12. 18
  'Thine are we, David,
    and on thy side'
  The Spirit gives 'the
    word of wisdom'      1 Cor. 12. 8
3 With *Zechariah*—
  for *Witness*—Zechariah's
    *Lips*               2 Chron. 24. 20
  For this he was made a
    martyr (Greek word
    for a 'witness')

**302  Issachar, the tribe that Improved**
        1 Chron. 12. 32
First, The *Weary Drudge*—
    *Slaves*             Gen. 49. 14, 15
  Compared to the Ass in
    love of ease and sub-
    mission to bondage.
Three Centuries later, the
    *Treasure Finder*—*Seekers*  Deut. 33. 18, 19
  Looking for treasures in
    the sea and on the shore
After one and a half Centuries,
    the *Warrior Tribe*—*Soldiers*  Judges 5. 15
  Out of Issachar came Tola,
    a Judge of Israel    Judges 10. 1
After two more Centuries, *Men
    of Understanding*—*States-
    men*                 1 Chron. 12. 32
  They knew what the nation
    ought to do.

**303  David's Mighty Men**
        1 Chron. 12. 8-33
They had Seven characteristics: they were—
1 *Attracted by* David—
  for his *Comeliness*   1 Sam. 16. 12, 13
2 *Separated unto* David—
  in the *Cave*          1 Chron. 12. 8
3 *Loyal servants* of David—
  in the *Camp*          1 Chron. 12. 23
  'to turn the kingdom of
    Saul to him'
4 *Wholly devoted* to David
  —in the *Court*        1 Chron. 12. 33
  Not men of double heart
These were moral traits. There were also three
characteristics in their Service—
5 *United in service*—
  they could keep rank   1 Chron. 12. 33
6 *Expert in service*—
  they could use both hands 1 Chron. 12. 2
7 *Intelligent in service*—
  they had understanding 1 Chron. 12. 32

## 304 A Challenge to Full Consecration

'Who then is willing to consecrate his service this day unto the Lord?'        1 Chron. 29. 5

1 THE EXAMPLE OF THE CHALLENGER
David said,        1 Chron. 29. 1-5
  'I have prepared with all my might'
  'I have provided according to my means'
  'I have planned with a willing mind'

2 THE EFFECT OF THE CHALLENGE
        1 Chron. 29. 6-9
The people offered with full hands, with willing minds, and rejoiced with perfect hearts.

3 THE EXTENT OF THE CLAIM
        1 Chron. 29. 5
'Who'—        The consecration must be *Personal*

'Is willing'—        it must also be *Voluntary*

'To fill his hands'—it must also be *Complete*

'This day'—        it must be *Immediate*

'Unto the Lord'—  it must also be *Devoted*

---

# 2 CHRONICLES

## 305 Reformation, but by Compulsion—King Asa

1 A *Sick Nation*—
Godless, ignorant and lawless
        2 Chron. 15. 3

2 A *Skilled Physician*—
Asa, whose name means 'Physician'

Personal righteousness: he was healthy himself        2 Chron. 14. 2

Unremitting zeal in attacking disease
        2 Chron. 14. 3

Wise foresight: Prevention better than cure
        2 Chron. 14. 6

Complete reliance on God to effect a cure
        2 Chron. 14. 11

3 A *Sensible Treatment*—
it was *Purgative* 2 Chron. 15. 8

it was *Resuscitative*
        2 Chron. 15. 8

it was *Cumulative*
        2 Chron. 15. 9-10

it was *Operative* 2 Chron. 15. 11

and it was *Subjugative*
        2 Chron. 15. 12-14

4 A *Sad Relapse*—
through the Unequal yoke
        2 Chron. 16. 3

through Reliance on man
        2 Chron. 16. 9

through Oppression and coercion
        2 Chron. 16. 12

Before long the Disease was again epidemic.

## 306 Reformation Without Separation—King Jehoshaphat

Revival began in the Heart and Life of the king.
Three Stages of National Revival—

1 *Appointment of Teachers*
Faithful ministers,
  Princes, Priests, Levites 2 Chron. 17. 7-9

2 *Appointment of Judges*
Impartial men to deal
  with problems        2 Chron. 19. 5

3 *Appointment of Singers*
to praise the Lord for
  His goodness        2 Chron. 20. 21

## 307 Reformation that Lacked Devotion—King Joash

1 *Coronation of the Lord's Anointed*
'God save the king' 2 Chron. 23. 11
The usurper was dislodged.

2 *Covenant of the Lord's people*
with their God        2 Chron. 23. 16

3 *Consecration of the Lord's priests*
to offer burnt-offerings
        2 Chron. 23. 18, 19

4 *Collection for the Lord's House*
in a chest at the gate
        2 Chron. 24. 8-14

The revival lasted until the death of the faithful priest, Jehoiada. Soon after, the king and the people displayed 'an evil heart of unbelief in departing from the living God'
Heb. 3. 12

### 308  A Great King who Transgressed
2 Chron. 26; Isa. 6. 1

King Uzziah was—

| | |
|---|---|
| a Great *Builder* | vs. 2, 10 |
| a Great *Warrior* | vs 6, 7, 11-13 |
| a Great *Farmer* | v. 10 |
| a Great *Engineer* | vs. 14, 15 |
| a Great *Ruler* | |
| for over half a century | vs. 3, 4 |

But he trespassed by usurping the priestly office and died a leper, *Unclean* 2 Chron. 26. 17-21

His sins were Sins of *Presumption, Pride*, and *Persistence in wrong-doing.*

In the year of his death God appointed a great prophet who confessed himself 'Unclean!' but was cleansed by Jehovah for His service Isa. 6.

### 309  The Proud and the Lowly
2 Chron. 26

1 The Lord hath respect unto

| the lowly | Ps. 138. 6 |
|---|---|
| Uzziah did what was right in the sight of the Lord | v. 4 |
| He sought God | v. 5 |
| God helped him | v. 7 |
| As long as he sought the Lord, God made him to prosper | v. 5 |
| He was marvellously helped until he was strong | v. 15 |

'BLESSED IS THE MAN THAT TRUSTETH IN THE LORD' — Jer. 17. 7, 8

2 The proud He knoweth afar

| off | Ps. 138. 6 |
|---|---|
| But when he was strong, his heart was lifted up | v. 16 |
| He transgressed against the Lord | v. 16 |
| He became presumptuous | vs. 16-18 |
| The Lord smote him | vs. 19, 20 |
| And he was cast out from His presence | v. 20 |

'CURSED IS THE MAN—WHOSE HEART DEPARTETH FROM THE LORD' — Jer. 17. 5, 6

E.A.H.

### 310  Three Commands to Three Companies— King Hezekiah

Hezekiah was the son of a very wicked father and the father of a very wicked son, but he did right in the sight of the Lord and was used in the reviving of God's people.

COMMANDS—

1 To the *Worshippers*—
'*Be not negligent*', a
*Right Relationship*
with God — 2 Chron. 29. 5, 11

Preparation in the
*Sanctification*
of Priests and Levites 2 Chron. 29. 15-19

*Sacrifice*
of the Sin-offering — 2 Chron. 29. 20, 21
*Song of the Lord*
at the Burnt-offering — 2 Chron. 29. 27-30
*Service*
of the consecrated
priests — 2 Chron. 29. 31, 32

2 To the *Workers*—
'*Be ye not stiffnecked*',
a *Real Return* to
God — 2 Chron. 30. 8
in the *Observance* of
the *Lord's Passover* — Chapter 30
and the *Offering* of
the *Lord's Portion* — Chapter 31

3 To the *Warriors*—
'*Be strong and courageous*', a *Resolute
Reliance* on God — 2 Chron. 32. 7

### 311  Good King Josiah

1 *Began to Reign*
at the age of 8—
*Tender years* and
*Early Responsibilities* — 2 Chron. 34. 1

2 *Began to Seek*
after the God of
David at the age of
16—*Tender Conscience* and *Early
Righteousness* — 2 Chron. 34. 3, 19

3 *Began to Purge*
Judah and Jerusalem
at the age of 20—
*Tender Heart* and
*Early Reformation* — 2 Chron. 34. 3, 27

For these reasons he

*Fulfilled the Divine Purpose* in prophecy — 1 Kings 13. 2

*Frustrated the Devil's
Plan* by cleansing his
heart, the temple, the
city and the land — 2 Chron. 34, 4, 7, 9

*Followed Divine Principles* contained in the
Scriptures.

### 312  The Book of the Law of the Lord

1 The *Book Preserved*—

| written first at Jehovah's command | Exod. 24. 4, 8 |
|---|---|
| kept before the priests and Levites | Deut. 17. 18 |
| entrusted to Joshua as they entered the land | Joshua 1. 8 |
| used by David in his charge to Solomon | 1 Kings 2. 3, 4 |
| the basis of teaching in Jehoshaphat's reign | 2 Chron. 17. 9 |
| found by Hilkiah the priest and given to Josiah | 2 Chron. 34. 14 |

**2** The *Book Found*—
but covered with rubbish
in the House of God     2 Chron. 34. 15

**3** The *Book Read*—
by Shaphan to the king 2 Chron. 34. 18

**4** The *Book Expounded*—
by the king to the people 2 Chron. 34. 30

**5** The *Book Obeyed*—
in three spheres—regulating

their *Condition of heart*     2 Chron. 34. 27

the *Cleansing of their lives* 2 Chron. 34. 33

their *Ceremonial observances*
     2 Chron. 35. 6

---

# EZRA

## 313   Divisions of the Book of Ezra

Chapters 1, 2   Registration of the Returned Exiles

Chapters 3, 4   Reconstruction of the Altar and Temple

Chapter 5   Interruption of the work

Chapter 6   Dedication of the rebuilt temple

Chapter 7   Proclamation of King Artaxerxes

Chapter 8   Liberation of the Jews

Chapter 9   Intercession of Ezra the priest

Chapter 10   Reformation of the people

## 314   Ezra the Prepared Priest
Ezra 7. 1-5

Ezra was—
a Servant and a Master
a Student and an Administrator of the Law
a Supreme authority, and yet a Subordinate

He became—

**1** An *Interceding Priest*
who had a Pedigree
Ezra 7. 1-5; 9

**2** An *Instructed Scribe*
who knew the Law
Ezra 7. 10, 11; Matt. 13. 52

**3** An *Inspiring Preacher*
who taught the people
Neh. 8. 2-5

For 'Ezra prepared his heart' Ezra 7. 10
*to seek the law* of the Lord: he searched the Scriptures
*to do it:* he regulated his life by the Scriptures,
and *to teach its statutes and judgments:* He taught the Scriptures to the people

## 315   Three Great Prayer Chapters
Ezra 9

In 457 B.C. Ezra thanked God for 'a little reviving' and confessed his own and his people's failure.

Neh. 9

In 445 B.C. Nehemiah thanked God for His care for Israel in the past and pleaded for help in their present distress.

Dan. 9

In 538 B.C. Daniel had confessed his own and his people's sins and pleaded with God to shine upon His sanctuary v. 17.

## 316   Revival and the House of God
Ezra 9. 8, 9

'Judgment must begin at the house of God', wrote Peter (1 Pet. 4. 17): so must Revival.

Setting up the House of God had to do with—

**1** The *Building of the House of God*
Ezra 5. 1, 2

*Commenced*—Ezra 5. 2

*Continued*—Ezra 6. 14

*Completed*—Ezra 6. 15

**2** The *Beautifying of the House of God*
Ezra 7. 27, 28

**3** The *Business of the House of God*
Neh. 11. 15, 16, 22; 12. 44, 45

carried on by
Overseers—     Willing Helpers
Singers—     Consecrated Helpers
Treasurers—     Faithful Helpers
Doorkeepers—Tactful Helpers

# NEHEMIAH

### 317  The Qualities of a Leader, Nehemiah

1 The *Earnestness of his Devotion*
Neh. 1. 4, 5

He prayed to his God and petitioned his king

2 His *Enthusiasm for the Work of God*
Neh. 1. 4; 2. 10, 19, 20

Commissioned by the king 2. 6

Chided by the enemy 2. 19

Constrained by his God 2. 20

3 His *Enterprise in every direction*
Neh. 1. 5-11; 2. 4, 5, 12; 4. 13-18
Examining the city's environs while others slept

Enrolling all willing Jews in the work

Equipping his workers for defence against their enemies

Examining grievances and investigating claims

4 His *Energy in the right direction*
Neh. 2. 20; 4, 6

5 His *Endurance in spite of opposition* and difficulties
Neh. 4. 21-23; 6. 6

### 318  The Work Comprised—Gates
Nehemiah Chs. 1-13

The Word comprised—

the Construction of Walls
and Gates                    Chapters 1 to 7

the Consecration of the
people, and                  Chapters 8 to 10

the Consolidation of
achievements                 Chapters 11 to 13

*Building Walls*—for Separation unto the Lord
*Repairing Gates*—for Communion with the Lord

The Work was—

1 *A Good Work*—
Good in Origin, Objective and Operation    Neh. 2. 18

2 *A Great Work*—
Extensive in character and compass         Neh. 4. 19

3 *A Grand Work*—
having Priority over everything else        Neh. 6. 3

4 *God's Work*—
for God was its Director and Dynamic       Neh. 3. 5; 6. 16

### 319  The Gates of Jerusalem
Neh. 3

*Gates*—the place of Coming and going—for Travellers

of Buying and selling—for Merchants

of Pleading and judging—for Judges and elders

of Reading the law—for Preachers

1 The *Sheep Gate*—on the North wall—
*Sacrifice*    Neh. 3. 1; John 1. 29
(Sheep led in to be offered on the altar)

2 The *Fish Gate*—on the North side—
*Evangelistic service*
Neh. 3. 3; Mark 1. 17
(Fishermen went in and out with their catch)

3 The *Old Gate*—Probably the Damascus
Gate—*Age-long Truths*
Neh. 3. 6; Jer. 6. 16

4 The *Valley Gate*—on the West—*Humility*
Neh. 3. 13; Phil. 2. 5

5 The *Dung Gate*—on the Western wall—
*Persecution* Neh. 3. 14; 1 Cor. 4. 13
(Filth was carried through this to the Valley of Hinnom)

6 The *Gate of the Fountain*—on the South-East—The *Spirit's Fulness*
Neh. 3. 15; John 7. 37-39
(Near the Pool of Siloah from which water was drawn for the temple)

7 The *Water Gate*—on the Eastern wall—
*Cleansing by the Word*
Neh. 3. 26; 8. 1; Eph. 5. 26,
(Where the people heard God's Word)  27

8 The *Horse Gate*—overlooking the Kedron
Valley—*Warfare*
Neh. 3. 28; 1 Tim. 6. 12;
Job 39. 19, 25
(Through which horses passed on the way to battle)

9 The *East Gate*—East of the Temple—
*Hope of Christ's Coming*
Neh. 3. 29; Rev. 22. 16

10 The *Gate Miphkad*—Appointment or Review—*Judgment Seat of Christ*
Neh. 3. 31; 2 Cor. 5. 10

## 320 God's Workmen
### Neh. 3

The Workers were not professional men, nor were they employed in a 'closed shop'. Who were they?

**A THE WORKERS**

1 The *Priests*—
very appropriately at the Sheep Gate, place of sacrifice    3. 1

2 The *Goldsmiths*—
successors of the artificers in gold for the temple    3. 8, 32

3 The *Apothecaries*—
medicine-makers, entrusted with the preparation of incense for the temple offering 3. 8

4 The *Rulers and their Daughters*—
elders who ruled well and their 3. 9, 12, 14, households    15, 16

5 The *Levites*—
specially appointed for sanctuary service    3. 17

6 The *Nethinims*—
the meanest Labourers in God's house, but there was skilled work for them to do 3. 26

7 The *Merchants*—
business men who had the Lord's work at heart    3. 32

**B THE SHIRKERS**

Their nobles put not their necks to the work of the Lord    3. 5

**C THE JERKERS**

Worked for a time but became discouraged because of the enemy    4. 10

## 321 Principles of Service
### Neh. 2. 18-20; 4. 17-18

1 *Principle of Selection*—
Excludes all who have no portion, right or memorial in God's city    Neh. 2. 20

2 *Principle of Specialization*—
every man to his work    Neh. 4. 15

3 *Principle of Priority*—
Home claims come first    Neh. 3. 10, 23, 28, 30

4 *Principle of Thoroughness*—
Earnestly and thoroughly repairing damage    Neh. 3. 20

5 *Principle of Dependence*—
on God's power    Neh. 4. 9; 6. 9

## 322 An Old Time Revival
### Neh. 4. 2

1 HINDRANCES TO REVIVAL—

i *Opposition* from the world    vs. 1-8

ii Much *rubbish* to be removed v. 10

2 ESSENTIALS TO REVIVAL—

i We made our *Prayer* unto God v. 9

ii The people had a mind to *Work* v. 6

iii We set a *Watch*    v. 9
   S.H.

## 323 Enemies of God's Work and Their Tactics
Cp. Enemies of the cross of Christ
   Phil. 3. 18, 19

THE ENEMIES—

1 *Sanballat the Antagonist*—
Public Enemy No. 1    Neh. 2. 10
He belonged to Horonaim and was therefore a Moabite    Neh. 13. 28

2 *Tobiah the Sarcastic*—
a freed slave, an upstart Neh. 2. 10; 4. 3
He was an Ammonite    Neh. 13. 1

3 *Geshem the Gossip*—
an Arabian    Neh. 2. 19; 6. 6

4 *Noadiah the Alarmist*—
Prophetess with Hebrew name—prostituted her gift to the enemy's cause    Neh. 6. 14

5 *Shemaiah the Catspaw*—
took bribes    Neh. 6. 10, 12

THEIR TACTICS—

1 *Chagrin*—
it grieved them    Neh. 2. 10

2 *Scorn*—
they poured ridicule on the workers    Neh. 2. 19; 4. 3

3 *Anger*—
they were wroth and took great indignation    Neh. 4. 1

4 *Conspiracy*—
conspired all of them together    Neh. 4. 8

5 *Cunning*—
'Come, let us meet together'    Neh. 6. 2-5

### 324   A Mind to Work

Nehemiah's heroic band recognized—

1 THE DIGNITY OF THE WORK  Neh. 3. 5; 6. 16

2 THE VARIETY OF THE WORK  Neh. 4. 17, 18

There were *Builders,
Burden-bearers, Buglers*
and others.

3 THE IMMENSITY OF THE
   WORK                     Neh. 4. 19, 20

Separated on the wall,
one far from the other.

Therefore they had to have a trysting place to
which they could resort.

We have such a place—
'Though sundered far, by faith we meet
Around one common Mercy-seat'
Heb. 4. 16

The work was completed quickly because there
was—

*Inspiration*, with 'Remember the Lord' as their
Watchword                Neh. 4. 14

*Aspiration*, the earnest desire to finish and do it
well                     Neh. 4. 15

*Perspiration*, for 'they
laboured in the work
from the rising of the
morning till the stars
appeared'                Neh. 4. 21-23

### 325   Go Your Way

1 *Sharing your Blessings*—
Eat the fat, drink the sweet,
and send portions unto
those for whom nothing is
prepared                 Neh. 8. 10

CONTEXT—From the worship
of God (Neh. 8. 6) and the
ministry of God's word
(Neh. 8. 8, 9)

2 *Showing your Purity of life*—
Let your garments be always
white and let your head
lack no ointment          Eccl. 9. 7, 8

CONTEXT—Into a world where
all is vanity and vexation
of spirit

3 *Serving your Lord*—
in view of the end time, and
the Judgment Seat of Christ Dan. 12. 13

### 326   Ready
Neh. 9.17

WHAT GOD IS READY TO DO

| | |
|---|---|
| Ready to Pardon | Neh. 9. 17 |
| Ready to Forgive | Psa. 86. 5 |
| Ready to Save | Isa. 38. 20 |
| Ready to Judge | 1 Peter 4. 5 |

WHAT PAUL WAS READY TO DO

| | |
|---|---|
| Ready to die | Acts 21. 13 |
| Ready to be offered | 2 Tim. 4. 6 |
| Ready to be bound | Acts 21. 13 |
| Ready to preach the gospel | Rom. 1. 15 |

J.A.

### 327   A Contrast oft repeated today
Neh. 9. 25-26

RECEIVING GOD'S GIFTS   Neh. 9. 25

1 They took
2 They possessed
3 They did eat
4 They were filled
5 They became fat
6 They delighted themselves

REJECTING GOD THE GIVER   Neh. 9. 26

1 They were disobedient
2 They rebelled
3 They cast Thy law behind their backs
4 They slew Thy prophets
5 They wrought provocations

H.P.J.

# ESTHER

### 328   Divine Providence in Esther

Observe that—In the book
God's Name is not mentioned
God Himself is veiled
but God's Actions are manifest

THREE LARGE SECTIONS—

1 *Great Danger—Infernal Plot
   developing*            Chs. 1-4

Two Women—Vashti and
Esther—prominent in     Chs. 1, 2
Two Men—Haman and
Mordecai—prominent in   Chs. 3, 4

2 *Great Deliverance—Infernal
   Plot thwarted*          Chs. 5-10

by Esther's Intercession in   Ch. 5
Mordecai's Exaltation in      Ch. 6
Haman's Downfall in           Ch. 7

3 *Great Delight*—

at the Deliverance of the
Jews and the Greatness of
Mordecai                Chs. 8-10

**329 Four Banquets in Esther**

1 The *Banquet of Deposition*
when Vashti was deposed     Esther 1. 3

2 The *Banquet of Coronation*
when Esther was crowned   Esther 2. 18

3 The *Banquet of Petition*
when Esther was a suppliant   Esther 5. 4-8

4 The *Banquet of Commemora-tion* when Deliverance was
celebrated     Esther 9. 17
                         T.B.

**330 Such a Time as This**
Esther 4. 14

1 For such a time as this—A TIME OF EXTREME URGENCY, because a decree had gone forth bringing to Esther's people *Danger, Death, Destruction.*

2 To the Kingdom—A PLACE OF EXCEPTIONAL OPPORTUNITY because of
Esther's Preparation to enter the king's presence
Esther's Preferment by the king
Esther's Position as Queen of the realm

3 Thou art come—A SENSE OF EXCLUSIVE RESPONSIBILITY because she was one of the condemned people and she alone could plead for them.

'Who knoweth?' asks a question. But Esther realized there was no question about it.

**331 How to Approach the Throne**
Esther 5. 1-4

1 Esther—*Arrayed in Royal Robes*     Esther 5. 1

The Believer—Covered with the robe of righteousness     Isa. 61. 10

2 Esther—*Standing in full view of the One on the throne*     Esther 5. 2

The Believer—'All things —opened to the eyes of Him'     Heb. 4. 13

3 Esther—*Expecting the king's favour*     Esther 5. 2

The Believer—'Access into this grace wherein we stand'     Rom. 5. 2

4 Esther—*Waiting for the royal sceptre to be extended*     Esther 5. 2

The Believer—All the authority of Heaven at his disposal     Matt. 28. 18, 20

5 Esther—*Ready to touch the golden sceptre*     Esther 5. 2

The Believer—Claiming the exercise of power on his behalf     Eph. 3. 14-16

6 Esther—*Listening for the king's voice*     Esther 5. 3

The Believer—'If any hear my voice'—communion     Rev. 3. 20

7 Esther—*Relying on the king's promise*     Esther 5. 3, 4

The Believer—obtaining mercy and grace for seasonable help     Heb. 4. 16

**332 The Two Posts**

'The posts went out' Esther 3. 15; 8. 14

FIRST POST with—

A MESSAGE OF DEATH—
to destroy, to kill, to cause to perish     Esther 3. 13

It brought mourning, fasting, weeping and wailing     Esther 4. 3

*Three Reasons* for that Message—

1 The people were scattered because of sin   Deut. 4. 26, 27

2 They were transgressing the king's laws   James 2. 10

3 They were unprofitable to the kingdom   Rom. 3. 12
(on a level with Spivs and Parasites)

SECOND POST with—
A MESSAGE OF LIFE—
bringing light, gladness, joy and honour     Esther 8. 16

because—

1 A competent Mediator had been found—   Esther 5. 1-4;
Esther     Heb. 8. 6

2 A powerful enemy had been defeated—   Esther 5. 14; 7. 10;
Haman     Heb. 2. 14-15

3 A despised Man had been exalted—Mor-   Esther 6. 6-11;
decai     Acts 2. 36

The Two Messages in one verse—Rom. 6. 23
'The wages of sin is death; but the gift of God is eternal life through Jesus Christ our Lord'.

# JOB

**333 The Book of Job** ──────────────────────────────

*Alfred, Lord Tennyson* called it 'the greatest poem of ancient and modern times'.
*Thomas Carlyle* called it 'a noble book, all men's book'.
*Martin Luther* described it as 'magnificent as no other book in Scripture'.

| 4 SECTIONS— | | |
|---|---|---|
| Chs. 1, 2 | *Historical* | —Job's *Calamities* |
| Chs. 3-31 | *Philosophical* | —Job's *Comforters* |
| Chs. 32-37 | *Evangelical* | —Job's *Condition* |
| Chs. 38-42 | *Experiential* | —Job's *Conversion* |

---

**334 Four Great Mistakes in Job**

1 *Satan's*—
   in thinking that Job served
   God for what he could get Job 1. 9, 10

2 *Job's Wife's*—
   in thinking that, with the loss
   of the visible and human,
   all was lost Job 2. 9, 10

3 *Job's Friends'*—
   in thinking that Job's suffering was the outcome of sin Job 22. 5

4 *Job's*—
   in thinking that God was
   unkind Job 27. 2
                     Dr. W. Graham Scroggie

**335 God's Servant Job**

God speaks of Job as '*My servant Job*' before

   his affliction began       Job 1. 8

   and after his affliction ended  Job 42. 8

Job's Experiences—

1 *Hedged about* by God    Job 1. 10

2 *Handed over* to Satan    Job 1. 12

3 *Harassed* by adversity    Job 1. 13-20

4 *Harnessed* to grief    Job 2. 7, 8

5 *Humiliated* before his
   friends    Job 2. 8, 12-13

**337 The Hypocrite**

1 The Hypocrite's *Hope*—
   shall perish    Job 8. 13

2 The Hypocrite's *Habitation*—
   shall be desolate    Job 15. 34

3 The Hypocrite's *Happiness*—
   is but for a moment    Job 20. 5

4 The Hypocrite's *Hell*—
   is for ever    Job 27. 8;
                   Isa. 33. 14
                   J.M.H.

**338 Man Dies and Where is He?**
      Job 14. 10

The *Agnostic's* answer—I don't know, neither
do I care
The *Evolutionist's* answer—He goes to dust
and ashes
The *Spiritist's* answer—His spirit exists in a
world of spirits
The *Transmigrationist's* answer—His soul goes
to be incarnate in another form
The *Christian* says—'Absent from the body,
present with the Lord' 2 Cor. 5. 8

The Christian's assurance is based on—

1 The Revelation of God in the Bible

2 The Distinctiveness of man

3 The Teaching of Christ, 'a Teacher come
   from God' John 3. 1

4 The Fear of death that is natural to man
   Heb. 2. 14, 15

**336 Job's Three Friends** ──────────────────────────

   Job 2. 11 ; 16. 24
He calls them 'miserable comforters'. THREE CYCLES OF SPEECHES—

| Cycle 1 | Chs. 4-14 | Job's friends are Harsh— |
| | Eliphaz is *Dogmatic* | Bildad is *Discourteous* | Zophar is *Didactic* |

Cycle 1    Chs. 4-14    Job's friends are Harsh—
   Eliphaz is *Dogmatic*  Bildad is *Discourteous*  Zophar is *Didactic*
Cycle 2    Chs. 15-21   Job's friends are Suspicious—
   Eliphaz is *Critical*  Bildad is *Cruel*  Zophar is *Caustic*
Cycle 3    Chs. 22-26   Job's friends are Abusive—
Observe the *Sophistry* of Eliphaz    The *Sagacity* of Bildad    The *Silence* of Zophar

Job's closing discourse occupies five chapters—Job 27-31.
Chapter 28 is a famous chapter, its theme being—'Where shall wisdom be found?' (v. 12).
Verse 28 is a famous verse—'The fear of the Lord, that is wisdom'.
Chapter 29 is the middle chapter in the Old Testament.

**339  My Redeemer**
Job 19. 25-27

With assurance Job speaks of his 'Kinsman-Redeemer' and expresses five great truths.

I KNOW—

a *Redeemer*
REDEMPTION            Eph. 1. 7

*My* Redeemer
RELATIONSHIP          Ps. 23. 1; Luke 1. 47

*Liveth*
RESURRECTION          Heb. 2. 14, 15; Rom. 1. 4

He *shall stand*
RETURN                Zech. 14. 4

I *shall see God*
REVELATION            Rev. 1. 7

**340  Acquaintance with God**
Job 22. 21, 22

1 *What to do—*
'Acquaint—with Him'
*Possible Acquaintance*    James 4. 8

2 *When to do it*—now
*Present Acquaintance*     2 Cor. 6. 2

3 *Who should do it*—thyself
*Personal Acquaintance*    John 3. 18

4 *How to do it*—be at peace
*Peaceful Acquaintance*    2 Cor. 5. 20

5 *Why to do it*—
good shall come unto thee
*Profitable Acquaintance*  Rom. 5. 10, 11
                          H.K.D. and A.N.

**341  The Fear of the Lord**
Job 28. 28

1 Is Wisdom                    Job 28. 28
2 Is to hate evil              Prov. 8. 13
3 Is strong confidence         Prov. 14. 26
4 Is a fountain of life        Prov. 14. 27
5 Is true riches, honour and life  Prov. 22. 4
6 Is quick understanding       Isa. 11. 3

**342  A Man with a Message from God**
Job 32. 20

Elihu—He is my God—

1 was *Younger* than Job's three
friends                        Job 32. 6
2 was *Born again* by the Spirit of
God                            Job 33. 4
3 was *Attentive* to the words of
the elders                     Job 32. 11
4 was *Impartial* in his attitude to
Job                            Job 32. 21
5 was *Commissioned* by God to
speak                          Job 33. 6
6 was *Constrained* by the Spirit
to speak                       Job 32. 18
7 was *Forthright* in all that he
said                           Job 33. 8

His Argument was—
God is greater than man: why
resist Him?                    Job 33. 12
God deals with man for his good:
why criticize Him?             Job 33. 14
God wants to deliver man: why
not come to Him?               Job 33. 24

**343  God and Man**
Job. 33. 14-30

1 *God's Dealings* with man—
are sometimes *Phenomenal*     v. 15
but always *Purposive*         v. 17
and always *Providential*      v. 18

2 *God's Feelings* toward man—
'He is gracious unto him' in
sending a messenger, and
providing a ransom             vs. 23, 24

3 *God's Healings* of men—
in enlightening them with the
light of the living            v. 30

**344  A Great Ransom**
Job 33. 24

1 *No Ransom* can be
found among men,
for 'all have sinned'  Ps. 49. 6-9

2 *A Ransom* has been
found by God for
men                    Job. 33. 24
That ransom is a
Messenger              Mal. 3. 1
an Interpreter of God
to men                 John 1. 18
One among a thou-
sand                   Song of Songs 5. 10

3 The *Son of Man* gave
Himself *a Ransom
for many*, as Sub-
stitute                Mark 10. 45

4 The *Man Christ Jesus*
gave Himself *a ran-
som, available for all*  1 Tim. 2. 5, 6

5 *No ransom*, however
great, is available
*after death*           Job 36. 18

**345  Blessings for the Penitent**
Job 33. 23-25

1 *Redemption*—
for a ransom has been found    v. 24

2 *Regeneration*—
for his flesh shall be fresher than a
child's                        v. 25

3 *Rejuvenation*—
for he shall return to the days of his
youth                          v. 25

4 *Relationship*—
for he shall pray to God       v. 26

5 *Reconciliation*—
for he shall see His face with joy  v. 26

## 346 Gates

1 *The Gates of Death*— Job 38. 17
  *Fools* because of their
  transgression draw
  near Ps. 107. 18
  God lifted *David* up
  out of them Ps. 9. 13
  The Son of God, the
  *Creator*, entered
  them John 10. 18, 19, 30
  The Son of Man, the
  *Conqueror*, came
  out of them Heb. 2. 14, 15
2 *The Gates of Heaven*—
  *Christ* passed through
  them into Heaven Heb. 9. 24
  *The Christian* goes
  through into his
  Father's house John 14. 3

3 *The Gates of Hell*—
  Opened to admit
  those who die un-
  repentant Luke 16. 22, 23

  Cannot prevail against
  Christ and His
  Church Matt. 16. 18

4 The *Gates of Right-
  eousness*—
  may be entered by
  faith, as Abraham
  and David entered
  them Ps. 118. 19, 20

---

# PSALMS

## 347 The Psalms and their Authorship
There are five Books of Psalms, corresponding
in theme to the five Books of Moses

  Book 1 Psalms 1-41 to Genesis
  Book 2 Psalms 42-72 to Exodus
  Book 3 Psalms 73-89 to Leviticus
  Book 4 Psalms 90-106 to Numbers
  Book 5 Psalms 107-150 to Deuteronomy

Many Psalms are

MESSIANIC
  e.g. Pss. 8, 16, 22, 24, 40, 45, 68, 69, 110,
  118

PENITENTIAL
  e.g. Pss. 6, 32, 38, 51, 102, 130, 143

PAEANS OF PRAISE
  e.g. Pss. 106, 111, 112, 113, 117, 135,
  146-150

DIDACTIC
  e.g. Pss. 1, 5, 7, 15, 50, 73, 94, 101

PILGRIMS' SONGS
  Pss. 120 to 134, called Songs of Degrees or
  Ascents

SUPPLICATORY
  e.g. Pss. 17, 86, 90, 102, 142

DEVOTIONAL
  e.g. Pss. 3, 16, 54, 61, 86, 122, 144

ALPHABETICAL
  e.g. Pss. 9, 10, 25, 34, 37, 111, 112, 119, 145,

73 Psalms are ascribed to David, 12 to Asaph
10 to the sons of Korah, 2 to Solomon, 1 to
Moses, 1 to Ethan, and 1 to Heman.

## 348 The Godly Man
Psalm 1

1 His *Purity*—
  he 'walketh not in the counsel of
  the ungodly' v. 1

2 His *Progress*—
  Three Negatives and Two Positives v. 1, 2

3 His *Piety*—
  Delights in, and meditates on,
  God's Law v. 2

4 His *Position*—
  'Planted by the rivers of water' v. 3

5 His *Prosperity*—
  Whatever he does prospers v. 3

Contrast the Ungodly—Like the chaff:
  Three Negatives—not so, not able to stand in
  the judgment, not in the congregation of the righteous.

## 349 Seats
Psalm 1. 1

1 The Seat of *God* Job 23. 3; Ezek. 28. 2

2 The Seat of *the Scornful*
  Ps. 1. 1

3 The Seat of *the Image of Jealousy*
  Ezek. 8. 3

4 The Seat of *Violence*
  Amos 6. 3

5 The Seat of *Moses* Matt. 23. 2

6 The Seat of *Satan* Rev. 2. 13

7 The Seat of *the Beast*
  Rev. 16. 10

1 The Seat of God is His throne in the heavens, on which He sits governing the nations Isa. 40. 22

2 The Seat of the Scornful is occupied by the 'despisers, who wonder, and perish' Acts 13. 41

3 The Seat of the Image of Jealousy answers to the 'Man of sin sitting in the Temple of God' 2 Thess. 2. 3, 4

4 The Seat of Violence is at present occupied by heartless men, in the oppression of the poor James 5. 4

5 The Seat of Moses, for the administration of law

6 The chief place of wickedness in any town can safely be called Satan's Seat.

7 The Seat of the Beast is his temporary headquarters during his brief reign on earth.

T.B.

## 350　A Cosmic Crisis
Psalm 2

| | |
|---|---|
| God the *Father* speaks | vs. 1-6 |
| The *Son* of God speaks | vs. 7-9 |
| The *Spirit* of God speaks | vs. 10-12 |

1 The *Division* of Mankind—
Heathen, people, kings, rulers, judges　vs. 1, 2, 10

2 The *Derision* of God—
'He that sitteth in the heavens shall laugh'　v. 4

3 The *Decision* of the Penitent—
to 'put their trust in Him'　v. 12

## 351　True Discipleship

1 Lead me in Thy righteousness Ps. 5. 8
2 Lead me in Thy truth and teach me　Ps. 25. 5
3 Lead me in a plain path　Ps. 27. 11
4 Lead me for Thy Name's sake Ps. 31. 3
5 Lead me to the Rock that is higher than I　Ps. 61. 2
6 Lead me in the way everlasting Ps. 139. 24
7 Lead me into the land of uprightness　Ps. 143. 10

F.S.B.

## 352　Christ in the Psalms

Christ's *Manhood*
　　Ps. 8. 4, 5
Christ's *Sonship* Ps. 2. 7; 110. 1
Christ's *Deity*　Ps. 45. 6, 11
Christ's *Holiness*
　　Ps. 89. 18, 19
Christ's *Priesthood*
　　Ps. 110. 4
Christ's *Kingship*
　　Ps. 2. 6; 89. 18, 19, 29; 110. 2
Christ's *Conquests*
　　Ps. 110. 5, 6
Christ's *Sovereignty*
　　Ps. 72. 8; 103. 19
Christ's *Return in Glory*
　　Ps. 98

## 353　What is Man?
The Question is asked five times in the Bible and answered in five ways.

1 In *Creation*—
the Object of *Divine Appointment*　Ps. 8. 4-8

2 In *Transgression*—
of *Divine Abhorrence*　Job 15. 14-16

3 In *Salvation*—
of *Divine Affection*　Job 7. 17

4 In *Christ*—
of *Divine Acceptance*　Heb. 2. 5-9

5 In *Judgment*—
of *Divine Attention*　Ps. 144. 3, 4

## 354　'I Shall Not Be Moved'

1 The *Sinner's False* Confidence　Ps. 10. 6
2 The *Saint's False* Confidence　Ps. 30. 6
3 The *Saint's True* Confidence　Ps. 16. 8

W.W.F.

## 355　A Condescending God
The Lord looked down from heaven—

to *see Ruin*　Ps. 14. 2
to *hear Repentance*　Ps. 102. 19
to *save—Redemption*　Ps. 33. 13-19
O Lord, look down from heaven,
and *visit us* with *Revival*　Ps. 80. 14

J.M.H.

## 356　Pleasant Things in Psalm 16

1 *Pleasant People*—
the saints, the excellent　v. 3

2 *Pleasant Portion*—
the Lord is the portion of mine inheritance　v. 5

3 *Pleasant Places*—
the lines are fallen unto me in pleasant places　v. 6

4 *Pleasant Position*—
at God's right hand　vs. 8, 11

5 *Pleasant Path*—
the path of life　v. 11

6 *Pleasant Prospect*—
pleasures for evermore　v. 11

## 357　Divine Secrets in Psalm 16

1 Secret of a *Life of Trust*—
I trust in Him　v. 1

2 Secret of a *Surrendered Life*—
I belong to Him　v. 2 (R.V.)

3 Secret of a *Separated Life*—
I side with Him　vs. 3, 4 (R.V.)

4 Secret of a *Happy Life*—
I am satisfied with Him vs. 5, 6

5 Secret of an *Instructed Life*—
I listen to Him　v. 7

6 Secret of a *Steadfast Life*—
I am engaged with Him　v. 8

F.F.

**358   Meditation on Psalm 17**

| | | |
|---|---|---|
| 1 'Hear the right' | v. 1 | *Supplication* |
| 2 'I am purposed' | v. 3 | *Resolution* |
| 3 'The word of Thy lips' | v. 4 | *Inspiration* |
| 4 'Keep me' | v. 8 | *Protection* |
| 5 'I will behold' | v. 15 | *Expectation* |
| 6 'I shall be satisfied' | v. 15 | *Satisfaction* |
| 7 'When I awake' | v. 15 | *Resurrection* |

JS. FS.

**359   Jehovah**

| | |
|---|---|
| 1 Thy presence to *search us* | Ps. 17. 2 |
| 2 Thy lips to *speak* to us | Ps. 17. 4 |
| 3 Thy paths to *separate* us | Ps. 17. 5 |
| 4 Thy right hand to *save* us | Ps. 17. 7 |
| 5 Thy wings to *shelter* us | Ps. 17. 8 |
| 6 Thy face to *shine* upon us | Ps. 17. 15 |
| 7 Thy likeness to *satisfy* us | Ps. 17. 15 |

W.J.M.

**360   As For**

1 *Divine Perfection*—
   'As for God, His way is
   perfect     Ps. 18. 30
2 *Human Frailty*—
   '*As for man*, his days are short' Ps. 103. 15
3 *Redemption's Hope*—
   '*As for me*, I shall be satisfied
   when I awake with Thy
   likeness'     Ps. 17. 15

**361  A Twofold Revelation of God**

   Psalm 19. 1-6

God in His Creation
God's Glory in Nature
Inarticulate expression
God known in His perfect arrangement
Our sun the Centre
What Creation says and sees

   Psalm 19. 7-14

God in His Law
God's Glory in His Word
Articulate expression
God revealed in His clear utterances
His Son the Centre
What God's Word is and does

**362   The Law of the Lord**
   Psalm 19. 7-10

1 It is His *Law*, converting the soul—
   It *Enlivens*     v. 7
2 It is His *Testimony*, making wise the
   simple—It *Edifies*     v. 7
3 It comprises His *Statutes*, rejoicing
   the heart—It *Enraptures*     v. 8
4 It is His *Commandment*, enlightening
   the eyes—It *Enlightens*     v. 8

5 It is His *Fear*, enduring for ever—
   It *Endures*     v. 9
6 It contains His *Judgments*, true and
   righteous—It *Establishes*     v. 9
7 It is more desirable than much fine
   gold—It *Enriches*     v. 10
8 It promises great reward to those
   who keep it—It *Encourages*     v. 11

**363   Visions of Christ**
   in Psalm 22

| | |
|---|---|
| 1 The *Reproached* One | v. 6 |
| 2 The *Rejected* One | v. 7 |
| 3 The *Risen* One | v. 22 |
| 4 The *Rejoicing* One | v. 22 |
| 5 The *Ruling* One | v. 28 |
| 6 The *Righteous* One | v. 31 |

W.J.M.

**364   Christ in the Midst**

THE CRUCIFIED—

1 In the midst of *Bulls* of
   Bashan—the *Jews*     Ps. 22. 12, 13
   (The bull—a clean animal)
2 In the midst of *Dogs*, the
   assembly of the wicked Ps. 22. 16
   (The dog—an unclean
   animal)—the *Gentiles*

   The Roman Governor,
   Pilate, delivered Him to
   be crucified: 'They
   pierced my hands and my
   feet'—the Cross.

THE GLORIFIED—

3 In the midst of the *Congregation*—the *Church*     Ps. 22. 22
   Declaring the Father's
   name to His brethren     Heb. 2. 11, 12
4 In the midst of *all people*
   and nations—the *World* Ps. 22. 27
   'All the kindreds of the
   nations shall worship
   before Thee'     Phil. 2. 10, 11

**365   The Lord's Hands**
   Ps. 22. 16

1 *Pierced* for His people's sins
        Ps. 22. 16
2 *Graven* with His people's
   names     Isa. 49. 16
3 *Healing* their infirmities  Mark 1. 41
4 *Opened* for their supply  Ps. 145. 16
5 *Uplifted* for their blessing Luke 24. 50
6 *Strong* for their defence  Ps. 138. 7
7 *Sustaining* them in their
   weariness     Song of S. 2. 6
8 *Reassuring* for their fears John 10. 28
9 *Hiding* them for their preparation
        Isa. 49. 2

**366   The Shepherd in Resurrection Power**
Psalm 23 and Luke 24

v. 2 Led beside Waters of Quietness—First to
*Mary Magdalene*        Luke 24. 10

v. 3 Soul restored and led in paths of righteousness—Next *Peter*        Luke 24. 12

v. 4 Walking through the valley of shadow—
*Two on way to Emmaus*   Luke 24. 13, 17

v. 5 Table prepared in presence of enemies—
*The eleven in the upper room*
                         Luke 24. 33, 41

v. 6 Attended by goodness and mercy, and
Dwelling in the house of the Lord—
*The Disciples at Bethany* Luke 24. 50-53


**367   Wilderness Provision**
Psalm 23

THE LORD IS MY SHEPHERD, I SHALL NOT WANT

REST                     v. 2
'He maketh me to lie down in green pastures'

REFRESHMENT              v. 2
'He leadeth me beside the still waters'

RESTORATION              v. 3
'He restoreth my soul'

COUNSEL                  v. 3
'He leadeth me in the paths of righteousness'

COMPANIONSHIP            v. 4
'For Thou art with me'

COMFORT                  v. 4
'Thy rod and Thy staff, they comfort me'

PROVENDER                v. 5
'Thou preparest a table before me'

POWER                    v. 5
'Thou anointest my head with oil'

ANYTHING HERE            v. 6
'Goodness and mercy shall follow me all the
days of my life'

ANYTHING HEREAFTER v. 6
'I will dwell in the House of the Lord for ever'
                              J.M.H.


**368   The Triumphs of Christ**
Psalm 24

1 *Triumph of the Prophesied—*
*Ascent* to the *Hill* of the Lord on earth
Ps. 24. 3-6

His triumphal entry into Jerusalem and
to the Temple on Mount Zion
Zech. 9. 9; Matt. 21. 5-12

2 *Triumph of the Crucified—*
*Ascension* into Heaven as Conqueror
Ps. 24. 7, 8
'Mighty in battle'
Mark 16. 19; Col. 2. 15

3 *Triumph of the Glorified—*
*Entry* with His people as Lord of hosts
Ps. 24. 9, 10; John 14. 3


**369   The Meek**
'The meek will he guide in judgment: and
the meek will he teach his way' Ps. 25. 9

'Blessed are the meek: for they shall inherit
the earth' Matt. 5. 5

'I am meek and lowly in heart' Matt. 11. 29

1 Shall be *satisfied*        Ps. 22. 26
2 Shall be *guided*           Ps. 25. 9
3 Shall be *taught*           Ps. 25. 9
4 Shall *have inheritance*    Ps. 37. 11
5 Shall be *saved*            Ps. 76. 9
6 Shall be *lifted up*        Ps. 147. 6
7 Shall be *beautified*       Ps. 149. 4
                              J.M.H.


**370   Lovingkindness**

Thy lovingkindness is before me     Ps. 26. 3
How excellent is Thy lovingkindness Ps. 36. 7
Thy lovingkindness and Thy truth    Ps. 40. 11
Thy lovingkindness is better than life Ps. 63. 3
Crowneth thee with lovingkindness   Ps. 103. 4
Praise Thy name for Thy lovingkind-
ness                                Ps. 138. 2
With lovingkindness have I drawn
thee                                Jer. 31. 3
                              J.A.


**371   Blessedness**

1 The *Saviour's* Blessedness—
'Blessed be the Lord for his marvellous
lovingkindness' Ps. 31. 21; 1 Pet. 1. 3

2 The *Believer's* Blessedness—
'Blessed is the man whose transgression is
forgiven'        Ps. 32. 1, 2; Rom. 4. 6-8

3 The *Church's* Blessedness—
'Blessed is the people whom the Lord hath
chosen'        Ps. 33. 12; Eph. 1. 3, 4


**372   The Forgiveness of Sins**
Psalm 32. 1

1 How *Procured for* us?—By the blood of
Christ           Rom. 3. 24-26

2 How *Secured by* us?—By faith in Christ
Acts 10. 43

3 How *Assured to* us?—By the Word of
Christ        Matt. 9. 2; Heb. 10. 17


**373   The Blessed Man**
SEVEN STEPS AS RECORDED IN THE PSALMS

1 Blessedly *Saved*          Ps. 32. 1, 2
2 Blessedly *Separated*      Ps. 1. 1, 2
3 Blessedly *Satisfied*      Ps. 34. 8, 9
(See also Ps. 84. 12 and 40. 4)
4 Blessedly *Sanctified*     Ps. 65. 4
5 Blessedly *Strengthened*   Ps. 84, 5, 6, 7
6 Blessedly *Subdued*        Ps. 94. 12, 13
7 Blessedly *Softened*       Ps. 112. 1-9
                              G.S.

**374  A Threefold Deliverance**
Psalm 34

Psalm 34 is an Alphabetical Psalm in which all the letters of the Hebrew Alphabet are used. Deliverance—

| | |
|---|---|
| 1 From all our *Fears*— if we seek the Lord | v. 4 |
| 2 From all our *Troubles*— if we cry to the Lord | vs. 6, 17 |
| 3 From all our *Afflictions*— if we are righteous before the Lord | v. 19 |

Thus we can 'look unto Him' and be radiant, and not be ashamed in spite of troubles v. 5

**375  Give God the Glory**

| | |
|---|---|
| 1 His Praise is sounded *Continually* | Ps. 34. 1 |
| 2 His Name is exalted *Collectively* | Ps. 34. 3 |
| 3 His Saints are exhorted *Compassionately* | Ps. 34. 9 |
| 4 His Ears are opened *Considerately* | Ps. 34. 15 |
| 5 His Servants are redeemed *Completely* | Ps. 34. 22 |

**376  Abundantly Satisfied**

Some of the provisions of His house Psalm 36. 8

| | |
|---|---|
| 1 His abundant mercy available for every sinner | Ps. 36. 5 |
| 2 His far-reaching faithfulness for every saint | Ps. 36. 5 |
| 3 His righteousness like a mountain high | Ps. 36. 6 |
| 4 His judgment as an ocean deep | Ps. 36. 6 |
| 5 His watchful care as a theme of praise | Ps. 36. 7 |
| 6 His lovingkindness ever true | Ps. 36. 7 |
| 7 His sheltering wing a refuge near | Ps. 36. 7 |
| | H.R.F. |

**377  The Upright Blessed by the Lord**

The Upright has complete security because—

| | |
|---|---|
| 1 his *Steps* are ordered by the Lord, so he is kept from *Straying* | Ps. 37. 23 |
| 2 his *Hand* is held by the Lord, so he is kept from *Stumbling* | Ps. 37. 24 |
| 3 his *Food* is provided by the Lord, so he is kept from *Starving* | Ps. 37. 25 |
| 4 his *Home* is assured by the Lord, so he is kept from *Suspense* | Ps. 37. 29 |
| 5 his *Seed* is blessed by the Lord, so he is kept from *Shame* | Ps. 37. 26 |

**378  The Story of the Redeemed**

| | |
|---|---|
| 1 *Sinking* in the miry clay | Ps. 40. 2 |
| 2 *Standing* on the Rock of ages | Ps. 40. 2 |
| 3 *Singing* to the God of his salvation | Ps. 40. 3 |
| 4 *Shining* in the midst of a perverse nation | Ps. 40. 3; Phil. 2. 15 |

**379  A Good Life**
Psalm 40

| | |
|---|---|
| A *Saved life*— 'He heard my cry' | v. 1 |
| A *Secure life*— 'He set me on a rock' | v. 2 |
| A *Satisfied life*— 'He put a new song in my mouth' | v. 3 |
| A *Surrendered life*— 'respecteth not the proud' | v. 4 |
| | F.J.S. |

**380  A Great Preacher's Subjects**
Psalm 40. 7-10

In the quotation of verses 6-8 in Heb. 10. 5-9, two words are omitted—'I delight'. Why?

In Psalm 40. 8 the Lord Jesus is viewed prophetically as the Servant of God in His life on earth.

In Heb. 10. 7, 9, He is viewed as the Sacrifice for sins in His death on the Cross.

HE PROCLAIMED—

| | |
|---|---|
| the Righteousness of God | v. 9 |
| the Faithfulness of God | v. 10 |
| the Salvation of God | v. 10 |
| the Lovingkindness of God | v. 10 |
| the Truth of God | v. 10 |

**381  Four Things David Did**
Psalm 42

| | |
|---|---|
| 1 David *Panting* | v. 1 |
| 2 David *Pouring* | v. 4 |
| 3 David *Pouting* | v. 5 |
| 4 David *Praising* | v. 11 |
| | T.B. |

**382  Things Touching the King**
Psalm 45

These were the outcome of Meditation, preparation and utterance v. 1

| | |
|---|---|
| 1 The GRACE OF THE KING— His Gracious *Person* His Gracious *Precepts* His Gracious *Positon* | v. 2 |
| 2 The GLORY OF THE KING— seen in His *Meekness* | v. 4 |
| seen in His *Majesty* | vs. 4, 6 |
| seen in His *Might* | v. 5 |
| 3 The GLADNESS OF THE KING— Gladness of *Anointing* | v. 5 |
| Gladness of *Achievement* | v. 8 |
| Gladness of *Association* | vs. 14, 15 |

**383   The Divine Helper**
Psalm 46. 1

1 A *Past* Helper—
'Thou hast been my help'
Ps. 63. 7

2 A *Present* Helper—
'a very present help in trouble'
Ps. 46. 1; Heb. 13. 6

3 A *Powerful* Helper—
'I have laid help upon One that is mighty'
Ps. 89. 19

4 A *Protecting* Helper—
'The Lord God will help thee'
Isa. 50. 7, 9

5 A *Precious* Helper—
'I will help thee'
Isa. 41. 10, 13, 14

6 A *Providing* Helper—
'the Helper of the fatherless'
Ps. 10. 14

7 A *Perpetual* Helper—
'The God of Jeshurun—is thy help'
Deut. 33. 26

**384   The Joy of Salvation**

Consists in

1 The knowledge of forgive-
ness                                     Ps. 51. 2
2 The enjoyment of God's
presence                              Ps. 51. 13
3 The realization of the
Spirit's power                       Ps. 51. 15
4 The pleasure of winning
souls                                    Ps. 51. 11
5 The offering up of praise Ps. 51. 11
6 The surrender of all to God Ps. 51. 16, 17
H.K.D.

**385   The Spiritual Losses of the Backslider**
Psalm 51

1 The Loss of *Heart Purity*—
'Blot out'                           v. 1
'Wash me'                          vs. 2, 7
'Cleanse me'                       v. 2
'Purge me'                         v. 7
'Create in me a clean heart' v. 10

2 The Loss of *Divine Fellowship*     v. 11

3 The Loss of the *Joy of Salvation* v. 12

4 The Loss of the *Power to Witness* v. 13

5 The Loss of the *Desire to
Worship*                           vs. 14-16

6 The Loss of *Concern for God's
Interests*                         v. 18
J. WEBB

**386   The Sacrifices of God**

1 A Broken spirit and a contrite heart
Ps. 51. 17

2 Consecration of our bodies for holy service
Rom. 12. 1

3 Offering of Praise and thanksgiving
Heb. 13. 15

4 Doing good and Giving to the Lord
Heb. 13. 16; Phil. 4. 18

5 Sinners won for Christ by priestly ministry
Rom. 15. 16

——————— 387 **The Imprecatory Psalms** ———————

Imprecation—derived from the Latin 'Impreco', I pray upon.
Psalm 55. 15 is an Imprecation, and there are several in the Books of Psalms.

In Book I,    out of a total of 616 verses, 11 verses are imprecatory
In Book II,   out of a total of 458 verses, 19 verses are imprecatory
In Book III,  out of a total of 358 verses, there are NONE imprecatory
In Book IV,   out of a total of 321 verses, there are NONE imprecatory
In Book V,    out of a total of 601 verses, 30 are imprecatory

Several imprecatory passages in the Psalms are quoted in the New Testament, and applied to Judas Iscariot who betrayed the Lord Jesus—Psalms 55. 12-15; 69. 22-28; 109. 5-20, 29-30.
But—
Not one Psalm is entirely imprecatory
Only one Psalm is half or more than half imprecation
Only 15 Psalms contain imprecations, i.e. 10%
Of these 15 Psalms the authorship of 11 is attributed to David, and the other 4 are anonymous
Some of the passages considered imprecatory are really predictive

The Imprecations reflect—

1 *David's Character*, and express his righteous indignation

2 *David's Circumstances*, for—
'David's Psalms had ne'er been sung
If David's heart had ne'er been wrung'

3 *David's Convictions*, that Jehovah, a righteous God, would take vengeance on his enemies

4 *David's Creed*—under Law—'an eye for an eye and a tooth for a tooth'

**388 Fear and Trust: Trust and Fear Not**
Psalm 56. 3-11

'What time I am afraid, I will trust in Thee,
—FEAR FOLLOWED BY FAITH v. 3

'In God I have put my trust, I will not be afraid—TRUST DISPELLING FEAR v. 11.

The Reasons—

1 God gives His
   BALM FOR OUR TERRORS            v. 4

2 God has His
   BOTTLE FOR OUR TEARS            v. 8

3 God keeps His
   BOOK FOR OUR TRAVELS           v. 8

**389 Changeful States of Soul**
Psalm 57

1 A *Trusting* Soul,
   taking refuge in God            v. 1

2 A *Tortured* Soul,
   among lion-like enemies         v. 4

3 A *Troubled* Soul,
   bowed down with grief           v. 6

4 A *Tuneful* Soul,
   singing and praising God        v. 7

5 A *Triumphant* Soul,
   rejoicing in God's mercy and
   truth                        vs. 9, 10

**390 Power Belongeth Unto God**
Psalm 62. 11

1 The *Searching* Power of
   *His Word*                   Heb. 4. 12

2 The *Saving* Power of *His
   Gospel*                     Rom. 1. 16

3 The *Keeping* Power of *God's
   Arm*                        1 Pet. 1. 5

4 The *Energizing* Power of
   *His Spirit*                  Acts 1. 8

5 The *Resurrection* Power of
   *His Son*                  1 Cor. 15. 43
                                    W.J.M.

**391 Captivity Led Captive**
Psalm 68. 18

This results in—

1 A *Great Emancipation* for
   the *Captives*             Judges 5. 12

2 A *Glorious Exaltation* for
   the *Conqueror*              Ps. 68. 18

3 A *Perfect Provision* for the
   *Church*                   Eph. 4. 8-12

4 A *World-wide Witness* to
   the *Gospel*             2 Cor. 2. 14-16

   ('Who—leadeth us in triumph in Christ'
   R.V.)

**392 The Burden-Bearer**
Psalm 68. 19

'Blessed be the Lord, Who daily beareth our burdens' (R.V.)

'Blessed be the Lord, Who daily beareth us up' (R.S.V.)

The Hebrew word used here for 'Lord' is 'Adonai', as in Psalm 110. 1—'my Lord'

God's Names in Psalm 68—

*Elohim*, the Triune God           v. 1

*Jah* (Jehovah), the Self-existing
   One                            v. 4

*El Israel*, the God of Israel        v. 8

*Adonai*, my Lord, (Plural)      vs. 11, 19

*Shaddai*, the Almighty—all-sufficient                         v. 14

*Jehovah-Elohim*, the Eternal,
   Triune God                    v. 18

*Jehovah-Adonai*, my Lord God     v. 20

THE SON OF GOD—Adonai—

1 The *Sin-Bearer* in the *Past*—the *Lamb of
   God*          John 1. 29; 1 Pet. 2. 24

2 The *Burden-Bearer* in the *Present*—my
   *Lord*                     Ps. 68. 19

3 The *Glory-Bearer* in the *Future*—the
   *King-Priest*        Zech. 6. 12, 13

**393 Christ's Millennial Reign**
Psalm 72

1 Solomon—Peaceable, type of Christ, the
   Prince of Peace   Title; Isa. 9. 6

2 The King, and the King's Son, King of
   kings, Son of God
                         v. 1; Rev. 19. 16

3 The Wisdom of His Administration
                           v. 2; Col. 2. 3

4 The Peace and Justice of His reign
                          v. 3; Isa. 32. 1

5 The Beneficence of His Authority
                      vs. 3-7; Isa. 32. 1, 2

6 The Extent of His dominions
                          v. 8; Zech. 9. 10

7 The Homage of this world's kings
                     vs. 10, 11; Phil. 2. 9-11

8 The Prosperity of His subjects
                       v. 16; Isa. 65. 21-23

9 The Universality of blessing through Him
                          v. 17; Gal. 3. 8

10 The Permanence and Excellence of His
   Name           v. 17; Heb. 13. 8

**394 The Prospect of God's Saints**
Psalm 73. 23-25

1 A *Lifetime of Grace*—
   enjoying God's presence and power v. 23

2 A *Future of Guidance*—
   guided by His counsel           v. 24

3 An *Eternity of Glory*—
   Afterward received to glory      v. 24

**395 The Years of the Right Hand of the Most High**
Psalm 77. 10

PSALM 77 has two parts, namely—
Verses 1-10     and     Verses 10-20

| | |
|---|---|
| My Infirmity | My Intercessor—at the right hand of the Most High |
| In the Shadow | In the Sunlight |
| The Sigh | The Song |
| Self is predominant | The Saviour is predominant |
| 22 Occurrences of the Pronoun in the First Person | Only three personal references |
| 11 References to God | 24 References to God |
| Trouble | Triumph |

The Psalmist's Remembrance—
| | | | | |
|---|---|---|---|---|
| 1 In the *Past* | — | 'was troubled' | — *Concern* | v. 3 |
| 2 In the *Present* | — | 'my song in the night' | — *Comfort* | v. 6 |
| 3 In the *Future* | — | 'Thy wonders' | — *Confidence* | v. 11 |

---

**396 God's Wrath Averted**
Psalm 78. 38

'Many a time turned He His anger away'

1 Because of the *Impassioned Intercession* of Moses, the *prophet*
Exod. 32. 11-14, 31, 32; Ps. 106. 21, 23

2 Because of the *Immediate Interposition* of Phinehas, the *priest*
Num. 25. 11

3 Because of the *Impartial Intervention* of Joshua, the *princely leader*
Joshua 7. 26

**397 The Man of God's Right Hand**

| | |
|---|---|
| 1 *Typified* in Benjamin (son of my right hand) | Gen. 35. 18 |
| 2 *Fortified* for God (made strong for thyself) | Ps. 80. 17 |
| 3 *Prophesied* by David—'Jehovah said unto my Lord' | Ps. 110. 1 |
| 4 *Identified* as the Son of man —before Caiaphas | Matt. 26. 64 |
| 5 *Glorified* as a Prince and a Saviour | Acts 5. 31 |
| 6 *Magnified* as Head of the Church, 'far above all' | Eph. 1. 20 |
| 7 *Satisfied* as the Princely Leader of faith | Heb. 12. 2 |

**398 The Valley of Baca**
Psalm 84. 6

Baca—Weeping
In Psalm 84 there are 3 Sections, punctuated by 'Selah'

1 The *Sanctuary* for a *Praising* People    vs. 1-4

2 The *Valley* for a *Pilgrim* People vs. 5-8
A place of *Pilgrimage*—'Passing through'
A place of *Prosperity*—'make it a place of springs' (R.S.V.)
'they go from strength to strength'

A place of *Prospect*—'every one of them appeareth before God in Zion' (R.V.)

3 The *Sanctuary* for a *Prosperous* People    vs. 9-12
There are Three 'Blesseds'—

i Blessedness of *Dwelling* in God's House    v. 4
ii Blessedness of *Drawing* upon God's Strength    v. 5
iii Blessedness of *Depending* on God's Provision    v. 12

**399 Mercy and Truth**

*Mercy and Truth* are met together at the Cross
Ps. 85. 10
By *Mercy and Truth* iniquity is purged
Prov. 16. 6; Heb. 1. 3
*Mercy and Truth* preserve the king
Prov. 20. 28
*Mercy and Truth* preserve God's righteous character    Rom. 3. 26
*Mercy and Truth* go before God's face for the saving of the sinner    Ps. 89. 14
*Mercy and Truth* shall be to them that devise good (i.e. the Enjoyment of them)
Prov. 14. 22

**400 The Faithfulness of God**

'Thy Faithfulness' occurs six times in Psalm 89. It is—

| | |
|---|---|
| *Established* in the heavens—a *Heavenly Place* | v. 2 |
| *Extended* in the congregation of the saints—a *Heavenly People* | v. 5 |
| *Encircling* the Lord of hosts—a *Heavenly Power* | v. 8 |
| *Exalting* the horn of the Lord's anointed —a *Heavenly Person* (Christ) | v. 24 |
| *Encompassing* the head of His people— a *Heavenly Provision* | v. 33 |
| *Expounded* by the godly in their hymns —*Heavenly Praises* | v. 1 |

**401  The Prayer of Moses the Man of God** ————————————

Psalm 90

**1 GOD'S WAYS—**

God as the Eternal Rest of the
redeemed                           v. 1

God as the Ruler of the Universe  v. 2

God as the Refuge of the Human
soul                               v. 3

**2 MAN'S DAYS—Few and Feeble—**
'as a sleep'                       v. 5
'like grass'                       v. 5
'as a tale that is told'           v. 9

**3 THE MAN OF GOD PRAYS—**
for a *Proper Approach* to Life's
Purpose                            vs. 12, 13
for a *Prayerful Appreciation* of
God's mercy                        vs. 14, 15
for a *Personal Appropriation* of
God's power                        vs. 16, 17

**402  Seven Precious Possessions of the Lord** ————————————

Psalm 100. 3, 4, 5

| | | |
|---|---|---|
| 1 His People | of His creation | He made us |
| 2 His Pasture | for His sheep | He leads us (Ps. 23. 2) |
| 3 His gates | for our entrance | Enter with thanksgiving |
| 4 His courts | for our dwelling | Enter with praise |
| 5 His Name | for our authority | Bless His name |
| 6 His mercy | for eternal ages | It is everlasting |
| 7 His truth | to all generations | It is enduring. |

D.F.

**403  Jehovah in His Relationship with Men** ————————————

(as seen in Psalm 103)

As Pardoner—
He forgiveth all my iniquities  vs. 3, 10, 12

As Redeemer—
He redeemeth my life from
destruction                     v. 4

As Physician—
He healeth all my diseases      v. 3

As Benefactor—
He satisfieth my mouth with
good                            v. 5

As Judge—
He executeth righteousness for
the oppressed                   v. 6

As Chastiser—
He will not keep His anger for
ever                            v. 9

As Father—
He pitieth them that fear Him   v. 13

As Creator—
He knoweth our frame            v. 14

As King—
His kingdom ruleth over all     v. 19

As Covenant-keeping God—
His mercy is from everlasting to
everlasting                     vs. 17, 18

E.A.H.

**404  The Music of the Praising Soul** ————————————

Psalm 103. 1-5

Psalm 103 begins and ends with the same words—Bless the Lord, O my soul.
The Music of the soul is the soul of music.
All that is within me          All I am for God
All His benefits               All I have from God

David sees himself in five Places—
1 A criminal in the Law courts who has been acquitted          Who forgiveth all
2 A Patient in the Hospital who has been cured                 Who healeth all
3 A Slave in the Slave-market who has been redeemed            Who redeemeth thy life
4 A Shepherd in the Throne Room who has been made king         Who crowneth thee
5 A Guest in the Banquet Hall who has had enough               Who satisfieth thy mouth

David knows the Lord in five Ways—
1 As Jehovah-Tsidkenu  (Jer. 23. 6)    Who forgives his iniquities righteously
2 As Jehovah-Ropheca   (Exod. 15. 26)  Who heals him completely
3 As Jehovah-Tsabaoth  (Isa. 47. 4)    Who redeemed him from death
4 As Jehovah-jireh     (Gen. 22. 14)   Who provides for him graciously
5 As Jehovah-Rohi      (Psa. 23. 1)    Who satisfies him and meets all his needs

David recounts his own experiences in five realms: Sins forgiven (Ps. 32. 1); Diseases healed
(Ps. 41. 8); Life spared (Ps. 9. 13); Compassed about with lovingkindness (Ps. 25. 3; 26. 3);
Satisfied with good things (Ps. 107. 9).

## 405  Three Immeasurable Blessings

Height—As high as the Heaven is
above the earth—Mercy that
cannot be comprehended     Ps. 103. 11

Breadth—As far as the east is from
the west—Forgiveness that cannot be rescinded     Ps. 103. 12

Depth—As a father pitieth his
children—Compassion that cannot be estimated     Ps. 103. 13

## 406  The Lord's Enduring Mercy
### Psalm 107. 1-31

They cried unto the Lord (vs. 6, 13, 19, 28)

FOUR CIRCUMSTANCES IN HUMAN EXPERIENCE—

1 The Struggles of the traveller    vs. 4, 5
2 The Sorrows of the sufferer    vs. 10, 12
3 The Sicknesses of the afflicted    vs. 17, 18
4 The Storms of the sailor    vs. 23-27

FOUR PERIODS IN ISRAEL'S HISTORY—

1 In the Wilderness they were
hungry and thirsty    v. 5
2 In the Promised Land they
rebelled    v. 11
3 In the times of the Kings they
transgressed    v. 17
4 In their scattering they do business in great waters    v. 23

FOUR EXPERIENCES OF THE REDEEMED OF THE
LORD—

1 A city of habitation for His
pilgrim people    v. 7
2 Bands of sin broken for His
enslaved people    v. 14
3 Healing by His Word for His
soul-sick people    v. 20
4 The storms calmed for His
worried people    v. 29

## 407  Right was the Pathway

'So He bringeth them unto their desired
haven' Psalm 107. 30

| | |
|---|---|
| Through the *waters* | Isa. 43. 2 |
| Through the *rivers* | Isa. 43. 2 |
| Through *fire* | Isa. 43. 2 |
| Through the *flood* | Ps. 66. 6 |
| Through the *depths* | Ps. 106. 9 |
| Through the *deserts* | Isa. 48. 21 |
| Through the *darkness* | Job 29. 3 |
| Through the great *wilderness* | Deut. 2. 7 |
| Through the *valley* of the shadow of death | Ps. 23. 4 |

N-B

## 408  Three Days of the Messiah
### in Psalm 110

1 The Day of His *Poverty and Passion*—
in the *Past*—    v. 7; Phil. 2. 5-8
2 The Day of His *Patience and Priesthood*—
in the *Present*    vs. 1, 4; Heb. 10, 12, 13
3 The Day of His *Power and Pre-eminence*—
in the *Future*    vs. 2, 3, 6; Rev. 19. 16

## 409  Four Figures of Christ's People

'Your people will offer themselves freely in
the day you lead your host in holy array.
From the womb of the morning, like dew your
youth will come to you' Ps. 110. 3 (R.S.V.)

1 Freewill Offerings—willing    Rom. 12. 1
2 Soldiers in Christ's army—
thy power (forces)    2 Tim. 2. 3
3 Priests in holy array—the
beauties of holiness    1 Pet. 2. 5
4 Drops of dew—the dew of
thy young men
(Youth is a collective noun here)

ORIGIN OF THE DEW—'from the womb of the
morning'

ONENESS OF THE DEW—composed of many
dewdrops

ORNAMENT OF THE DEW—sparkling in the
morning sun

## 410  God's Peculiar Treasure

Ps. 115. 9-13; 118. 1-4; 135. 19, 20—three
Concentric Circles with the Lord as Centre.

1 The House of *Israel*—
'an holy nation'    1 Pet. 2. 9
2 The House of *Aaron*—
'a royal priesthood'    1 Pet. 2. 9
3 Those that *fear the Lord*— 1 Pet. 2. 9;
'a peculiar people'    Mal. 3. 16, 17

What they do—
*Trust* in the Lord    Ps. 115. 9
*Testify* to the Lord's mercy Ps. 118. 1-5
*Praise* the Lord    Ps. 135. 19-21

'That ye should shew forth the praises of Him
Who hath called you'    1 Pet. 2. 9

## 411  The Death of His Saints
### Psalm 116. 15

'*Precious*', because 'costly' (1 Kings 5. 17);
'honourable' (Ps. 45. 9); 'excellent' (Ps. 36. 7).
All these words are translations of the same
Hebrew word.

Figures of the Death of His saints—

1 A SLEEP    John 11. 11; 1 Thess. 4. 13
2 A DEPARTURE—a vessel leaving its moorings
Phil. 1. 23; 2 Tim. 4. 6
3 AN EXODUS (decease)—a going out
Luke 9. 31; 2 Pet. 1. 15
4 A PUTTING OFF a garment, taking down a
tent    2 Pet. 1. 14; 2 Cor. 5. 1

## 412 According to Thy Word
Psalm 119

| | |
|---|---|
| 1 Cleansing | v. 9 |
| 2 Quickening (or Revival) | vs. 25. 107 |
| 3 Strengthening | v. 28 |
| 4 Saving | v. 41 |
| 5 Mercy | v. 58 |
| 6 Blessing | v. 65 |
| 7 Comforting | v. 76 |
| 8 Understanding | v. 169 |
| 9 Delivering | v. 170 |

D.F.

## 413 Love and Hate in Psalm 119

| | |
|---|---|
| 1 I love Thy law | vs. 97, 113, 163 |
| 2 I love Thy testimonies | vs. 119, 167 |
| 3 I love Thy commandments | v. 127 |
| 4 I love Thy precepts | v. 159 |
| 5 I hate the double-minded | v. 113 (R.V.) |
| 6 I hate every false way | v. 128 |
| 7 I hate falsehood | v. 163 (R.V.) |

W.W.F.

## 414 The Word of God
Psalm 119

| | |
|---|---|
| When *Received*—it gives light | v. 130 |
| When *Resorted to*—it cleanses | v. 9 |
| When *Retained*—it preserves | v. 11 |
| When *Relied on*—it strengthens | v. 28 |
| When *Read*—it instructs | v. 148 |
| When *Reverenced*—it sanctifies | v. 161 |
| When *Rejoiced in*—it enriches | v. 162 |

W.J.M.

## 415 The Word of God in the Heart
Psalm 119. 11

1 A *Good Provision* 'Thy Word'
2 A *Good Practice* 'have I hid'
3 A *Good Place* 'in my heart'
4 A *Good Purpose* 'that I might not sin against Thee'

## 416 Companions
'I am a companion of them that fear **Thee**'
Psalm 119. 63

Make your Companions

1 *Praying* Companions like Daniel
Dan. 2. 17
2 *Godly* Companions like David
Ps. 119. 63
3 *Loving* Companions like Paul Acts 19. 29
4 *Busy* Companions like Epaphroditus
Phil. 2. 25
5 *Holy* Companions like John Rev. 1. 9

L.W.

## 417 The Lord is Thy Keeper
Psalm 121. 5

1 THE PRAYER—
'Holy Father, *keep* through Thine own Name those whom Thou hast given me' John 17. 11

2 THE PROMISE—
'I will be with thee and *keep* thee' Gen. 28.15
'I will hold thine hand and will *keep* thee' Isa. 42. 6

3 THE PERSUASION—
'I know whom I have believed, and am persuaded that He is able to *keep* that which I have committed unto Him' 2 Tim. 1. 12

4 THE POWER—
'*Kept* by the power of God through faith unto salvation 1 Pet. 1. 5

5 THE PRAISE—
'Now unto Him that is able to *keep* you from falling, and to present you faultless before the presence of His glory with exceeding joy, to the only wise God our Saviour, be glory and majesty, dominion and power, both now and ever!' Jude 24, 25
T. Shuldman Henry

## 418 The Saint's Song of Degrees
as given in Psalm 126

| | |
|---|---|
| 1 Dreaming | v. 1 |
| 2 Laughing | v. 2 |
| 3 Singing | v. 2 |
| 4 Magnifying | v. 3 |
| 5 Weeping | v. 5 |
| 6 Reaping | v. 5 |
| 7 Rejoicing | v. 6 |
| 'We are glad' | HYP. |

## 419 Great Things and Greater

1 A *Grand Fact*—
'The Lord hath done great things for us' Ps. 126. 3

2 A *Good Meditation*—
'Consider how great things —for you' 1 Sam. 12. 24

3 A *Gracious Promise*—
'Rejoice, for the Lord will do great things' Joel 2. 21

4 A *Great Responsibility*—
'Go and shew how great things the Lord—' Mark 5. 19

5 A *Glorious Prospect*—
'Thou shalt see greater things than these' John 1. 50
J.M.H.

**420   From Toil to Reward**
      Psalm 126. 6
1 'He that goeth forth'—*Toil*
2 'Bearing precious seed'—*Treasure*
3 'And weepeth'—*Tears*
4 'Shall doubtless—with rejoicing—*Triumph*
5 'Bringing his sheaves with him'—*Trophies*

**421   The Service of the Lord**
1 The *Going* of the Servant—
   'He that goeth forth'          Ps. 126. 6
2 The *Flowing* of the Tears—
   'and weepeth'                  Ps. 126. 6
3 The *Sowing* of the seed—
   'bearing precious seed'        Ps. 126. 6
4 The *Mowing* of the Harvest—
   'bringing his sheaves with him' Ps. 126. 6

**422   Blessing in the House of God**
As seen in the Last Triad of the Songs of Ascents
1 *Priests* in the House of
   God—in *Purity*—*Bless-
   ing Expected*                  Ps. 132. 16, 17
2 *Brethren* in the House of
   God—in *Unity*—*Bless-
   ing Experienced*               Ps. 133;
3 *Servants* in the House of
   God—in *Activity*—*Bless-
   ing Emanating*                 Ps. 134

**423   Unity Among Brethren**
      Psalm 133
1 'Behold!' EXCLAMATION          v. 1
2 'How good and how pleasant it is'
   AFFIRMATION                    v. 1
3 Precious ointment, dew of Hermon
   ILLUSTRATION                   v. 2
4 'The blessing, even life for evermore'
   REALIZATION                    v. 3

**424   The Climax of the Songs of Degrees**
In Psalm 134 we have—
1 A *Compendium*—
   As last of the fifteen songs of degrees
2 A *Command*—
   To the watchers in the temple
3 A *Competency*—
   The servants, the priests, made so by God, could praise
4 A *Condition*—
   In holiness (marginal reading)
5 A *Compliance*—
   They responded and were blessed
6 A *Comprehension*—
   of God as Jehovah and Creator (His great Name and Work)
7 A *Channel*—
   Zion
                                  C.J.R.

**425   The Overwhelmed Soul**
'When my spirit is overwhelmed within me, then Thou knowest my path' Ps. 142. 3

Things that overwhelm—and overwhelmed David in light of the title of Ps. 142—

| | |
|---|---|
| SIN AND DECEIT | 1 Sam. 21. 12, 13 |
| SUFFERING AND EXILE | 1 Sam. 22. 1, 2 |
| SORROW AND LOSS | 1 Sam. 30. 3, 4 |

David found comfort in the realization that God knew his path, so prayed for deliverance from his PERSECUTORS, for 'they are STRONGER THAN I' (Ps. 142. 6)

'When my heart is overwhelmed, lead me to the ROCK THAT IS HIGHER THAN I' Ps. 61. 2
'That Rock is Christ', the Rock of ages.

**426   God's Servant David**
In the Psalter David is four times designated God's servant—

Ps. 78. 70  —David's Call to *Shepherd* God's people

Ps. 89. 20, 21—God's anointing to *Strengthen* His servant

Ps. 132. 9, 10—God's saints called to *Shout* for joy

Ps. 144. 9, 10—David begins to *Sing praise* to God for salvation

In Ps. 144 David is described as—
1 A *Warrior*—
   *Trained* by the Lord          v. 1
2 A *Ruler*—
   *Trusting* in the Lord         v. 2
3 A *Singer*—
   *Tuneful* for the Lord         v. 9
4 A *Father*—
   *Turning his people* to the Lord vs. 11, 12
5 A *Shepherd*—
   *Tending his flock* for the Lord v. 13

**427   Figures of the Christian Assembly**
      Ps. 144. 12-15
1 A *Family* with fruitful sons and
   graceful daughters             v. 12
2 A *Farm* having barns filled with
   every variety of grain         v. 13
3 A *Flock and Herd* that multiply
   abundantly and labour diligently                         vs. 13, 14
4 A *Fatherland*
   never *Despoiled* by invaders
   never *Deserted* by its citizens
   never *Defeated* by enemies

'Happy is that people—; yea, happy is that people whose God is the Lord.'

**428 David's Psalm of Praise**
Psalm 145

| WHAT GOD IS | | WHAT GOD DOES | |
| --- | --- | --- | --- |
| 1 Great | v. 3 | 1 Upholds | v. 14 |
| 2 Glorious | v. 5 | 2 Gives | v. 15 |
| 3 Gracious | v. 8 | 3 Satisfies | v. 16 |
| 4 Good | v. 9 | 4 Fulfils | v. 19 |
| 5 Righteous | v. 17 | 5 Hears | v. 19 |
| 6 Holy | v. 17 | 6 Saves | v. 19 |
| 7 Nigh unto all that call upon Him | v. 18 | 7 Preserves | v. 20 |

W.B.C.

# PROVERBS

## 429 The Tree of Life

The sin of the first man, Adam, excluded man from the Tree of life in 'Paradise Lost'. Salvation by the second man, Christ, admits man to the Tree of life in 'Paradise Regained'.

1 WISDOM is a tree of life to them that lay hold upon her — Prov. 3. 17, 18

2 THE WISDOM OF SOUL WIN-NING is a tree of life, 'for the fruit of the righteous is a tree of life, and he that winneth souls is wise' — Prov. 11. 30

3 THE WISDOM OF PATIENT WAITING is a tree of life, for 'when the desire cometh, it is a tree of life' — Prov. 13. 12

4 THE WISDOM OF RIGHT WORDS is a tree of life, for 'a wholesome tongue is a tree of life' — Prov. 15. 4

## 430 The Marks of a Lazy Person

1 *Love of Ease—*
a little more sleep — Prov. 6. 9. 10; 26. 14

2 *Lame Excuses—*
there is a lion in the way — Prov. 22. 13; 26. 13

3 *Loss of Energy—*
he hideth his hand in his bosom, and will not so much as bring it to his mouth — Prov. 19. 24; 26. 15

4 *Lack of Enterprise—*
the desire of the slothful killeth him, for his hands refuse to labour — Prov. 13. 4; 21. 25

## 431 The Commandment of the Lord

God's Word is—

a Chart and a Compass — Prov. 6. 22

a Lamp and a Light — Prov. 6. 23

a Provider and a Preserver — Prov. 6. 23, 24

It is—

*A Willing Guide,* for 'it shall lead thee' — Prov. 6. 22

*A Watchful Guardian,* for 'it shall keep thee' — Prov. 6. 22

*A Welcome Guest,* for 'it shall talk with thee' — Prov. 6. 22

## 432 Wisdom in the Book of Proverbs
Prov. 8. 12

In Proverbs 'Wisdom' is personified ,and corresponds to the Word (Logos) in John. Wisdom is seen as—

1 *A Preacher* — Prov. 1. 20
2 *A Treasure* — Prov. 2. 4
3 *A Tree of Life* — Prov. 3. 18
4 *A Promoter* — Prov. 4. 8
5 *A Sister* and Kinswoman — Prov. 7. 4
6 *A Counsellor* — Prov. 8. 14
7 *A Builder* — Prov. 9. 1

## 433 The Call of Wisdom
Prov. 9. 1

Two Persons in Prov. 9—Wisdom and the Foolish Woman. Both have—

*Attractions* to offer
An *Aim* in view
An *Appeal* to make

Three Sections in Prov. 9—

1 *Wisdom's Provision—* — vs. 1-6
A Perfect *Shelter—*
'Hath builded an house'

72

Perfect *Stability*—
'hewn her seven pillars'

A Perfect *Sacrifice*—
'killed her killing'

A Perfect *Supply*—
'furnished her table'

2 *Wisdom's Precepts*—
'Turn', 'come', 'eat and drink',
'forsake', 'live', 'go'    vs. 7-12

3 *The Foolish Woman's Pleasures*—
'stolen', 'sweet', 'secret'    vs. 13-18

## 434   Surety for a Stranger
Prov. 11. 15

Jesus—made surety of a better covenant
Heb. 7. 22

1 The *Stranger*—

Because of birth, a foreigner    Eph. 2. 12
Because of position, afar off    Eph. 2. 13
So has no claim and can give no guarantee.

2 The *Surety*—

Must be a *party* to all that's *involved*,
a *possessor* of all that's *promised*, and
*prepared* for all that's *required*.

3 The *Smart*—

'shall be sore broken' (Marginal reading):
'shall become evil for evil' (Literal
rendering).
Christ, the Surety, was 'made sin for us',
'made a curse for us', 'suffered, the just
for the unjust'.

## 435   Winning, Watching, Warning

'He that winneth souls is wise'—
Work of the *Evangelist*    Prov. 11. 30

'They watch for your souls'—
Work of the *Pastor*    Heb. 13. 17

'Warn every one night and day
with tears'—
Work of the *Teacher*    Acts 20. 31
T.B.

## 436   Women in Proverbs

1 The *Wise Woman*—

Builds her house    Prov. 14. 1

Establishes her home    Prov. 24. 3

Fills her house with wealth
Prov. 24. 4

2 The *Virtuous Woman*—

Has the full confidence of her husband
Prov. 31. 10, 11

Labours lovingly with her hands
Prov. 31. 13, 16, 19

Provides for her household
Prov. 31. 15, 21

3 The *Strange Woman*—
Flatters with her words
Prov. 2. 16; 5. 3, 4
Forsakes the guide of her youth
Prov. 2. 17; 5. 5
Forgets the covenant of her God
Prov. 2. 17; 5. 6

4 The *Foolish Woman*—
is Ignorant    Prov. 9. 13
is Insistent    Prov. 9. 14, 15
is Injurious    Prov. 9. 18

## 437   The Wrong Way—The Right Way
A WAY   Prov. 14. 12

1 Turned into    Isa. 53. 6
2 Trusted in    Hos. 10. 13
3 Taught to others    Jer. 2. 33
4 Turned upside down    Ps. 146. 9

THE WAY   John 14. 6

1 Turned to the Lord    Acts 11. 21
2 Trusted in    Eph. 1. 13
3 Taught to others    Acts 4. 2
4 Turned the world upside
down    Acts 17. 6
A.M.P.

## 438   A Wholesome Tongue—An Unwholesome Tongue
'Death and life are in the power of the tongue'
Prov. 18. 21

A WHOLESOME TONGUE

Is a tree of life    Prov. 15. 4
Is truthful    Eph. 4. 25; Col. 3. 9
Is pure    Eph. 4. 29; Col. 3. 8
Is peaceable    Prov. 15. 1; James 3.
13-18

AN UNWHOLESOME TONGUE

Is a tree of poison fruits    Prov. 25. 23
Is untruthful (an abomination) Prov. 6. 16, 17
Is impure    Eph. 4. 29; 5. 3
Is injurious, for it is—
'a sharp sword' that wounds    Ps. 57. 4
as 'an arrow shot out',    Jer. 9. 8
'a fire' that is kindled    James 3. 6

## 439   Pride Before Destruction
Prov. 16. 18

Some Examples—

1 *Lucifer*, son of the morning (Satan)    Isa. 14. 12-15
2 *Nebuchadnezzar*    Dan. 5. 20
3 *Belshazzar*    Dan. 5. 23, 24
4 *Amaziah*    2 Kings 14. 10
5 *Uzziah*    2 Chron. 26. 16
6 *Hezekiah*    2 Chron. 32. 25
7 *Prince of Tyrus*    Ezek. 28. 2, 17
8 *Herod*    Acts 12. 22, 23
R.C.B.

## 440 Jesus the Sinner's Friend

'A friend loveth at all times' (Prov. 17. 17):
'A friend that sticketh closer than a brother'
(Prov. 18. 24)

The Lord Jesus Christ is

a Friend Who gave His *all*    John 15. 13
a Friend Who loves *all* classes    Luke 7. 34
a Friend Who loves at *all* times  Prov. 17.17
a Friend Who loves in *all* states of soul
                  Prov. 27. 6; Heb. 12. 6
a Friend Who is needed by *all*
                Prov. 27. 10; John 6. 67, 68

## 441 Counsel

1 *Precept*—'hear' it—
'Hear counsel and receive
instruction'        Prov. 19. 20
2 *Possession*—of it—
'The Lord hath given me
counsel'          Ps. 16. 7
3 *Prayer*—for it—
'The Lord fulfil all Thy
counsel'          Ps. 20. 4
4 *Partnership*—in it—
'We took sweet counsel together'          Ps. 55. 14
5 *Prospect*—of it—
'Thou shalt guide me with
Thy counsel and afterward
receive me to glory    Ps. 73. 24
                      W.T.R.

## 442 'The Glory of Young Men is Their Strength'
(Prov. 20. 29)

'The Lord—my Strength' Exod. 15. 2
He is the Strength of
*Tempted young men*, like
Joseph          Gen. 49. 23, 24
He is the strength of
*Trustful young men* who
wait on the Lord    Isa. 40. 30, 31
He is the strength of
*Triumphant young men*
who overcome the
Wicked One      1 John 2. 13, 14

## 443 Qualified to Stand Before Kings
Prov. 22. 29

1 *Wisdom in the Head*—
'a wise servant'    Prov. 14. 35
2 *Right words on the
Lips*—
'a servant that speak-
eth right'    Prov. 16. 13; 22. 11
3 *Purity of Heart*—
a servant that 'loves
pureness of heart' Prov. 22. 11
4 *Diligence in business*—
'one diligent in busi-
ness'         Prov. 22. 29

## 444 In His Heart

'As he thinketh in his heart, so is he' Prov.
23. 7

1 *Abraham*—
Weakness of faith    Gen. 17. 17
2 *Esau*—
Revenge          Gen. 27. 41
3 *David*—
Unbelief         1 Sam. 27. 1
4 *Jeroboam*—
Subtlety        1 Kings 12. 26
5 *The evil servant*—
Worldliness       Luke 12. 45
                    W.W.F.

## 445 A Threefold Confession

1 The *Sinner of his sins*    Prov. 28. 13
2 The *Saint of his Saviour and
Lord*          Rom. 10. 9
3 The *Servant of his Sovereign* Matt. 10. 32
                    G.H.

## 446 Little Things and Their Lessons

1 The *Ants*—The *Wisdom of
Preparation*    Prov. 30. 25
They are *wise* and reason,
'Winter is coming'
They are *willing* and set about
preparing their food
They are *workers* and diligently lay in their store
2 The *Conies*—The *Necessity
for Precaution*    Prov. 30. 26
They are *feeble* so need a
strong place of shelter
They are *hunted* so need a
place of refuge
3 The *Locusts*—The *Secret of
Power*        Prov. 30. 27
They *lack leadership collectively*, yet march in rank
They *lack strength individually*, yet work in unity
4 The *Lizards*—The *Triumph
of Preservation*    Prov. 30. 28
'The lizard you can take in
your hands' (R.S.V.)
Not even the king's servants
will kill a lizard because
lizards destroy harmful
insects.

## 447 The Book of Ecclesiastes

*Key-verse*—'All is vanity and vexation of spirit'

*Key-phrase*—'Under the sun'

*Words used*—The Name of *God* throughout is
'*Elohim*'

Words for '*man*'—
Adam, red earth—40 times

*Ish*, strong, masculine man—6 times

*Enosh*, mortal man—twice

Words for '*fool*'—
*Kesil*, impious fool—16 times
*Saka*, stupid person—4 times

MAIN THEME OF THE BOOK—
What is good 'under the sun' for men at all
times and in all places.

ECCLESIASTES—was written by Solomon probably when he was near the end of his days
and had made proof of everything the world
can provide for man's benefit and pleasure.

THERE ARE THREE SECTIONS IN THE BOOK—
1 The Problem *Stated*        ch. 1. 1-11
2 The Problem *Studied*       ch. 1. 12-9. 6
3 The Problem *Solved*        ch. 9. 7-12. 14

## 448 Nature of Things Under the Sun
Eccles. 1. 2

1 *Vain*—'all is vanity'
Eccles. 1. 2; 2. 11; 2. 23; 2. 26

2 *Transient*—'One generation passeth away
and another generation cometh'
Eccles. 1. 4

3 *Restless*—'the wind—whirleth about continually' Eccles. 1. 6

4 *Unsatisfying*—'the eye is not satisfied—
nor the ear'
Eccles. 1. 8

5 *Recurring*—'it hath already been of old
time'    Eccles. 1. 9, 10

## 449 Men in the World

1 The *Unsatisfied* man—
looking for entertain-
ment for his eyes and
ears                         Eccles. 1. 7, 8

2 The *Affluent* man—
possessing houses and
lands, yet unsatisfied  Eccles. 2. 1-11

3 The *Bookworm*—
intent on acquiring know-
ledge                       Eccles. 2. 12-22

4 The *Selfish Bachelor*—
hoarding wealth for him-
self                         Eccles. 4. 7, 8

5 The *Sleepless Rich*—
afraid of robbers       Eccles 5. 12, 13

6 The *Wealthy Invalid*—
lacking the health to en-
joy his riches           Eccles. 6. 1, 2

7 The *Upstart*—
reversal of the social
order                        Eccles. 10. 5-7

8 The *Aged and Infirm*—
tottering to his grave   Eccles. 12. 1-7

## 450 The Work of God

'I know'—the Knowledge of
*man's ways*              Eccles. 3. 12

'I know'—the knowledge of
*God's work*              Eccles. 3. 14

GOD'S WORK—

1 There is *Permanence* in
it—'it shall be for
ever'                        Eccles. 3. 14

In *Revelation*—the
Word of God              1 Pet. 1. 23

In *Redemption*—the
Work of Christ           Heb. 10. 12

In *Regeneration*—the
Work of the Spirit      John 3. 5; 10. 28

2 There is *Perfection* in it
—'nothing can be put
to it'                       Eccles. 3. 14

'nothing can be taken
from it'                    Eccles. 3. 14

3 There is *Purpose* in it—
'that men should fear
before Him'              Eccles. 3. 14

Why should men fear before
Him—Because 'God re-
quireth that which is past'  Eccles. 3. 15

## 451 The Better Things

1 A Good Name—better than
precious ointment        Eccles. 7. 1
better than riches       Prov. 22. 1

2 The day of death—for the
righteous better than day
of birth                     Eccles. 7. 1;
                             Phil. 1. 23

3 The house of mourning—
better than the house of
feasting                    Eccles. 7. 2
(because the heart of the
wise is there)           Eccles. 7. 4

4 Sorrow—better than laughter
because it makes the heart
better                       Eccles. 7. 3

5 The Rebuke of the wise—
better than the song of
fools                        Eccles. 7. 5

6 The Completion of a business—better than the
beginning of it          Eccles 7. 8

7 The Patient in spirit—better
than the proud in heart  Eccles 7. 8
(Because pride goeth before
destruction and patience
worketh experience)     Rom. 5. 4

## 452 Four Exhortations
Eccles. 9. 7, 8

1 Go thy way—

A WAY FOR THE FEET
a Way of *Happiness* for oneself — Acts 8. 39
a Way of *Holiness* before
God — John 8. 11
a Way of *Helpfulness* to
others — Heb. 13. 16

2 Eat thy bread with joy and
drink thy wine with a
merry heart—

WORK FOR THE LORD—God—
accepteth thy works — Matt. 21. 28

3 Let thy garments be always
white—PURITY FOR THE
LIFE — 1 Tim. 5. 22

4 Let thy head lack no ointment—UNCTION FOR THE
HEAD — 1 John 2. 20

## 453 Man's Soul and its Redeemer
Eccles. 9. 14-16

1 Frail man's *Inherent Weakness*—'a little city', 'few
in it' — Eccles. 9. 14

2 The Arch-enemy's *Incessant* — Eccles. 9. 14;
*Warfare*—'a great king— — Eph. 2. 2;
besieged it' — 1 Pet. 5. 8

3 The Deliverer's *Incarnate
Wisdom*—in it 'a poor
wise man' — Eccles. 9 .15

Contrast—

'He saw that there was *no man*' — Isa. 59. 16
'There was found in it *a man*' — Eccles. 9. 15

He was—

A UNIQUE MAN—
'*Ish*', the Hebrew word used
in Exod. 15. 3—'Jehovah is
man of war'.

A POOR MAN—
'Rich yet became poor' — 2 Cor. 8. 9

A WISE MAN—
'all the treasures of wisdom' — Col. 2. 3

A KINSMAN—
the Kinsman-Redeemer—
'delivered the city' — Heb. 2. 14

A FORGOTTEN MAN—
'no man remembered' — Eccles. 9. 15

A DESPISED MAN—
'the poor man's wisdom is
despised' — Eccles. 9. 16;
Isa. 53. 3
AN UNHEEDED MAN—
'his words are not heard' — Eccles. 9. 16

## 454 Some Considerations in our Service
THREE ACTIVITIES within the PROVINCE of the
Lord's servants—

1 *Scattering*—
'Cast thy bread upon the
waters' — Eccles. 11. 1

2 *Sacrifice*—
'Give a portion to seven,
and—to eight — Eccles. 11. 2

3 *Sowing*—
'In the morning sow thy
seed' — Eccles. 11. 6

THREE PHENOMENA beyond the PREDICTION of
the Lord's servants—

1 '*Thou knowest not*' what
evil shall be upon the
earth—THE UNCERTAINTY
OF THE FUTURE — Eccles. 11. 2

2 '*Thou knowest not*' 'the way
of the spirit', 'the works
of God Who maketh all'
THE WONDERS OF GOD'S
WAYS — Eccles. 11. 5

3 '*Thou knowest not* whether
shall prosper—this or
that' THE RESULTS OF OUR
EFFORTS — Eccles. 11. 6

## 455 Youth's Opportunity
'In the days of thy youth'—

REJOICE, and walk in the ways of
thine heart, but know — Eccles 11. 9

REMEMBER *thy Creator* — Eccles. 12. 1
WHY?

1 The *Spiritual Senses* are
keen and undimmed — Eccles. 12. 1

2 The *Mental Faculties* are
clear and unimpaired — Eccles. 12. 2

3 The *Physical Powers* are
strong and undiminished — Eccles 12. 3-5

Then follow figures of failing powers which
may be explained as follows:

The *keepers of the house*—
The *Arms* for protection — Eccles. 2. 3

The *strong men*—
The *Shoulders* broad and
straight — Eccles. 12. 3

The *grinders*—
The *Teeth* (no dentures then) — Eccles. 12. 3

*Those that look out* of the
windows—
The *Eyes* in their sockets — Eccles. 12. 3

The *doors in the street*—
The *Lips and Ears*      Eccles. 12. 4

The *daughters of music*—
The *Vocal chords*      Eccles. 12. 4

The *Almond tree*—
The *Hair* turned white or the
*Head* become bald      Eccles. 12. 4

The *Silver cord*—
the *Breath of life*      Eccles. 12. 6

The *golden bowl*—
the *Brain*      Eccles. 12. 6

The *pitcher at the fountain*—
the *Heart and its Valves*      Eccles. 12. 6

The *wheel at the cistern*—
the *Circulation of the blood*      Eccles. 12. 6

## 456    The Wise Preacher

'Because the preacher was wise', we note these marks in Eccles. 12—

1 His *Perseverance*—
'he still taught'      v. 9
2 His *Preparation*—
'he gave good heed and sought out
proverbs'      v. 9
3 His *Planning*—
'he set in order many proverbs'      v. 9
4 His *Pleasure*—
'words of delight—acceptable'      v. 10
5 His *Production*—
'as goads and nails fastened by the
master of assemblies'      v. 11

HYP.

# THE SONG OF SOLOMON

## 457    'The Song of Songs, which is Solomon's'
Song of Sol. 1. 1

The *Subject*—Love      Song of Sol. 1. 2, 3, 4;
8. 6, 7

The *Sections*—five, the first four ending with a Chorus or Caesura—'I charge you, O ye daughters of Jerusalem.'

Section 1—The *Tenderness* of Love   1. 1-2. 7
Section 2—The *Touchstone* of Love   2. 8-3. 5
Section 3—The *Testing* of Love      3. 6-5. 8
Section 4—The *Testimony* of Love   5. 9-8. 4
Section 5—The *Triumph* of Love     8. 5-8. 14

## 458    The Love of the Beloved (Christ)

1 The *Expression* of Love—
'Kiss me'—*Affection*    Song of Sol. 1. 2
'Draw me'—*Attraction*    Song of Sol. 1. 4
'Tell me'—*Instruction*    Song of Sol. 1. 7

The Instruction is obtained—
'by the footsteps of the
flock'      Song of Sol. 1. 8
'beside the tents of the
shepherds'      Song of Sol. 1. 8

2 The *Excellence* of Christ's love—
'Better than wine'    Song of Sol. 1. 2
(Wine is of short dura-
tion and man-made;
Love is of God and
eternal in duration)

3 The *Experience* of Christ's Love—
His *Name*—an unction   Song of Sol. 1. 3
His *inner chambers*—
Communion      Song of Sol. 1. 4
His *remembrance*—joy   Song of Sol. 1. 4

## 459    Where Christ Brings His People

'The king has brought me' (Song of Sol. 1. 4): 'He brought me' (Song of Sol. 2. 4)

His saints are—

BROUGHT UP out of an
horrible pit      Ps. 40. 2
BROUGHT OUT of the place
of bondage      Deut. 26. 8
BROUGHT INTO a wealthy
place      Ps. 66. 12
BROUGHT TO the King's
*Apartments*—His *Rest-
ing Place*      Song of Sol. 1. 4

(Some of His apartments are—
His audience chamber,
where we listen,
His treasure house, where
we are enriched,
His conservatory, where
we gaze in wonder, and
His observatory, where
we look beyond.)

BROUGHT TO the King's
*Table*—His *Regal Pre-
sence*      Song of Sol. 1. 12
(Where we worship and
offer our spikenard)

BROUGHT TO the King's
*Orchard*—His *Royal
Provision*      Song of Sol. 2. 3
(Under His shadow
where we enjoy His
fruit)

BROUGHT TO the King's
*House of wine*—His
*Rallying Post*      Song of Sol. 2. 4
(Under His Banner
where we are refreshed
and cheered)

## 460 How the Lord Draws His People
Song of Sol. 1. 4

1 By the cords of love
Jer. 2. 2; Hos. 11. 4; 1 John 4. 19

2 By the Election of grace
John 6. 44

3 By the Cross of Christ
John 12. 32

## 461 Comeliness

1 The *Comeliness of Acceptance*—'I am black but comely'
Song of Sol. 1. 5

State by *Nature*—Black like the tents of Kedar, of black goat's hair

State by *Grace*—Comely as the curtains of Solomon Ezek. 16. 14

2 The *Comeliness of Character*—'thy cheeks', 'thy neck'
Song of Sol. 1. 10
(Graces that appear outwardly and are displayed)

3 The *Comeliness of Communion*—'thy countenance is comely'
Song of Sol. 2. 14
(Let me see thy countenance, let me hear thy voice')

4 The *Comeliness of Testimony*—'thy speech is comely'
Song of Sol. 4. 3
('thy lips are like a thread of scarlet'—the blood of the cross)

5 The *Comeliness of the Church glorious*—'Comely as Jerusalem'
Song of Sol. 6. 4; Rev. 21. 10

## 462 His Fruit Sweet to my Taste
Song of Sol. 2. 3

The 'apple tree' (or the citron tree), noted for its Foliage, Flowers, Fruit and Fragrance, is taken as a picture of Christ, the Beloved.

The Betrothed is 'under His shadow' and enjoying the fruit of that tree.

In John, Chapters 14, 15, 16, 17 Christ's 'own who are in the world' are 'Under His shadow', and His fruit is sweet to their taste.

WHAT FRUIT?

'My Peace—
to claim as a legacy          John 14. 27
'My Love'—
to continue to experience   John 15. 9
'My Commandments'—
to keep and obey              John 15. 10
'My Joy'—
to fill the heart and life      John 15. 11
'My Glory'—
to behold and share          John 17. 24

## 463 The Beloved

1 *Listening to* the Beloved    Song of Sol. 2. 8

2 *Leaning on* the Beloved    Song of Sol. 8. 5

3 *Longing for* the Beloved    Song of Sol. 8. 14
H.K.D.

## 464 The Beloved and His Betrothed

1 The *Visit of the Beloved*—
'Behold he cometh'
'Behold he standeth'
'he looketh forth'
'shewing himself'    Song of Sol. 2. 8, 9

2 The *Voice of the Beloved*—
but no response from
the betrothed    Song of Sol. 2 .10-13

3 The *Vigil for the Beloved*—
'I sought Him,' 'I will seek Him,' 'Saw ye Him whom my soul loveth?'    Song of Sol. 3. 1-3

4 The *Vision of the Beloved*—
'I found Him,' 'I held Him', 'I would not let Him go'    Song of Sol. 3. 4

## 465 The Call of the Beloved and the Unresponsive Heart

It was a call to—

1 *Unexplored Delights* with Him
*Flowers Magnificent* to the eye
*Songs* of birds *Melodious* to the ear
*Figs and grapes Mellifluous* to the taste
Song of Sol. 2. 10-13

2 *Unclaimed Privileges* from Him
Song of Sol. 2. 14
To commune with Him in His presence.

3 *The Unkept Vineyard*—to remove the 'little foxes' that were spoiling it
Song of Sol. 1. 6; 2. 15

## 466 My Beloved

'My Beloved is mine, and I am His'    Song of Sol. 2. 16

My Beloved—*Precious Possession*
1 Pet. 2. 7; Ps. 73. 25

Is          —*Present Possession*
Ps. 16. 5; Heb. 13. 6

Mine      —*Personal Possession*
Luke 1. 47; John 20. 28

I          —*Prized Possession*
Isa. 43. 4; Eph. 5. 25

Am        —*Permanent Possession*
John 6. 39; 10. 28

His        —*Purchased Possession*
1 Cor. 6. 20; Titus 2. 14
D.W.

**467 Gardens of the Lord**
Song of Sol. 4. 12

1 Garden of *Communion*—
Eden                    Gen. 3

2 Garden of *Conflict*—
Gethsemane              John 18. 1

3 Garden of *Conquest*—
Of Joseph of Arim-
athaea,                 John 19. 41

4 Garden of *Consummation*—
*Paradise of God*       Rev. 2. 7

5 Garden of the *Church*    Song of Sol. 4. 12

'Is there no other King's Garden? Yes, my
heart, thou art, or shouldest be, such. How do
the flowers flourish? Do the choicest fruits
appear? Does the King walk within and rest in
the bowers of my spirit?—Nor must I forget
the King's Garden of the Church. Rebuild her
walls, nourish her plants, ripen her fruits.'
                        C. H. Spurgeon

**468 A Barred Garden**
Song of Sol. 4. 12-16
A Garden barred but not barren, blown
upon but with nothing overblown, a Garden
beautified and its Owner satisfied.

1 The *Garden Barred*—
against the world's influences
against every kind of impurity
against every wind of heresy
                        Song of Sol. 4. 12
It has—
*Perennial Freshness* in itself
                        Song of Sol. 4. 12, 15
*Pleasant Fruits* for the Owner
                        Song of Sol. 4. 13
*Perpetual Fragrance* for all
                        Song of Sol. 4. 14

2 The *Garden under the Spirit's Breath*
The prayer is '*Blow*': the result is '*Flow*'
                        Song of Sol. 4. 16

3 The *Garden bringing Satisfaction to the
Owner*
'I *come*', 'I *gather*', 'I *eat*', I *drink*'
                        Song of Sol. 5. 1

**469 A Barred Door—Spiritual Desertion**

1 *Indifference* to her Beloved—'I sleep'
                        Song of Sol. 5. 2

He is not now the King sitting at His table
                        Song of Sol. 1. 12

nor the Lover showing Himself through
the lattice              Song of Sol. 2. 9

nor the Welcome Guest in her house
                        Song of Sol. 3. 4

nor the Owner finding satisfaction in His
garden                   Song of Sol. 4. 12

*but* the Patient Caller waiting for
admission                Rev. 3. 20

2 *Indolence* of the Betrothed—'I have put
off my coat; How shall I put it on?'
                        Song of Sol. 5. 3

3 *Indulgence* of the Betrothed—'I have
washed my feet; how shall I defile them?'
                        Song of Sol. 5. 3

**470 Fellowship in Service**
'Come, my Beloved, let us go—let us lodge—
let us get up—let us see.' 'HIS DESIRE IS TOWARD
ME'—He longs for such fellowship.

1 Going into the Field with Him—
*Preaching the Gospel*   Song of Sol. 7. 11

2 Lodging in the villages with Him—
*Pilgrimage of the Christian*
                        Song of Sol. 7. 11

3 Getting up early to the Vineyards—
*Pastoral care of the saints*
                        Song of Sol. 7. 12

4 Laying up pleasant fruits for Him—
*Produce of the Toiler*  Song of Sol. 7. 13

**471 The Triumph of Love**

| Song of Sol. 1. 1-4 | Song of Sol. 8. 5-7 |
| Love's Tenderness | Love's Triumph |
| Love's Sweetness | Love's Strength |
| Love's Attractiveness | Love's Achievements |
| Love's Gentleness | Love's Greatness |

THE LOVE OF CHRIST IS
*Unconquerable*    —    'strong as death' Song of Sol. 8. 6; John 15. 13
(Amor omnia vincit)

*Unquenchable*    —    'many waters cannot quench' Song of Sol. 8. 7; Ps. 69. 2

*Unfathomable*    —    it surpasses knowledge    Song of Sol. 8. 7; Eph. 3. 19

*Unpurchasable*    —    'all the wealth of a man's house would be utterly scorned'
                        Song of Sol. 8. 7

# ISAIAH

## 472 Two Sections in Isaiah

There is but one Author, the prophet Isaiah: but there are two distinct sections.

SECTION 1—Chapters *1 to 39*, corresponding to the 39 Books of the Old Testament, begins with Sin and Transgression in Ch. 1 and ends with Punishment and Captivity in Ch. 39.

SECTION 2—Chapters *40 to 66* (27 Chapters), corresponding to the 27 Books of the New Testament. Begins with comfort in Ch. 40 and ends with a New Heaven and a New Earth in Ch. 66.

CENTRAL CHAPTER OF SECTION 2—*Ch. 53*

CENTRAL THEME OF THE NEW TESTAMENT—*The Cross*

Section 2 has 3 Divisions each of 9 Chapters, each one punctuated by a warning—Chs. 40. 1-48. 22 'There is no peace, saith the Lord, unto the wicked'. Chs. 49. 1-57. 21 'There is no peace, saith my God, to the wicked'. Chs. 58. 1-66. 24 'Their worm shall not die, neither shall their fire be quenched'.

## 473 A Complete Sermon
### Isa. 1. 2-20

1 The Lord is the Speaker   Isa. 1. 2
2 The address is to the sinner   Isa. 1. 4
3 He reveals their disease   Isa. 1. 5, 6
4 He rejects their offerings   Isa. 1. 11, 15
5 He commands repentance   Isa. 1. 16, 17; Matt. 3. 2, 8
6 He announces pardon   Isa. 1. 18
7 He warns of judgment to come   Isa. 1. 20
H.P. JR.

## 474 A Study in Summaries
1 A Solemn Declaration   Isa. 1. 4
2 A Touching Lamentation   Isa. 1. 5
3 A Gracious Invitation   Isa. 1. 18
4 A Divine Conclusion   Isa. 1. 19, 20
G.H.

## 475 God's Call to Men
### Isa. 1. 18

'Come now'—*Invitation*

'Let us reason together'—*Conversation*

'Though your sins'—*Proclamation*

'they shall be as white as snow'—*Expiation*

## 476 Israel Represented by Four Trees
1 The *Vine*— 'the choicest vine'—Emblem of *Fruitfulness*   Isa. 5. 2
2 The *Olive*— 'fatness of the olive tree'— Emblem of *Testimony*   Rom. 11. 17
3 The *Fig*— 'firstripe in the fig tree'— Emblem of *Sweetness*   Hos. 9. 10
4 The *Fir*— 'I am like a green fir tree'— Emblem of *Freshness*   Hos. 14. 8
1 The *Vine*—Israel's *Spiritual Privileges*
2 The *Olive*—Israel's *Religious Privileges*
3 The *Fig*—Israel's *National Privileges*
4 The *Fir*—Israel's *Millennial Privileges*

## 477 Jehovah's Vineyard
### Isa. 5. 1-7

Spiritual History of Israel—
'A Vine out of Egypt'   Ps. 80. 8
'the choicest vine'   Isa. 5. 2
'a noble vine'   Jer. 2. 21
'an empty vine'   Hos. 10. 1

DEGENERATION IN 4 RESPECTS—
1 The sap went to wood, not to fruit   Ezek. 15. 1-4
2 The vine produced wild grapes   Isa. 5. 4
3 The vine had nothing for God, only for self   Hos. 10. 1
4 The vine was spoiled by wild beasts and locusts   Ps. 80. 13; Joel 1. 4-8

## 478 Six Woes in Isaiah 5
1 On the *Business of Self-advancement*   vs. 8-10
2 On the *Baseness of Self-indulgence*   vs. 11-17
3 On the *Bravado of Self-will*   vs. 18, 19
4 On the *Babbling of Self-opiniation*   v. 20
5 On the *Boasting of Self-satisfaction*   v. 21
6 On the *Blight of Self-Seeking*   vs. 22-25

## 479 Great Thrones of Scripture
1 Throne of *Pride*— Satan's   Isa. 14. 13
2 Throne of *Holiness*— Jehovah's   Isa. 6. 1
3 Throne of *Grace*— the *Father's*   Heb. 4. 16
4 Throne of *Worship*— the *Creator's*   Rev. 4. 2
5 Throne of *Righteousness*— the *King's*   Matt. 25. 31
6 Throne of *Judgment*— the *Judge's*   Rev. 20. 11
7 Throne of *Life*— God's and the Lamb's   Rev. 22. 3

**480 Holy, Holy, Holy, is the Lord of Hosts**
Isa. 6. 3

The Holiness of Jehovah is attested by—

1 The *Action of the Seraphim*—
faces and feet covered      Isa. 6. 2

2 The *Proclamation of the angels*—
'Holy, holy, holy'      Isa. 6. 3

3 The *Confession of the prophet*—
'Woe is me, for I am undone' Isa. 6. 5

4 The *Presence of the Altar*—
'a live coal from off the altar' Isa. 6. 6

**481 An Impressive Manifestation**

1 Impressive *Time*—
the year the leper king passed
away      Isa. 6. 1

2 Impressive *Way*—
he saw the Lord, heard the
seraphim, felt the posts of the
door move      Isa. 6. 1-4

3 Impressive *Effect*—
he said 'Woe is me!'—7th
'Woe' for himself      Isa. 6. 5

4 Impressive *Application*—
then flew one of the seraphim
—touched by a live coal from
the altar      Isa. 6. 6

5 Impressive *Commission*—
'Who will go?' 'Send me!'
'Go and tell'      Isa. 6. 8
     W.J.G.

**482 Four Monosyllables of the Gospel**

1 Isaiah's *'Woe!'*—
*Confession of the Sinner*    Isa. 6. 5

2 The seraph's *'Lo!'*—
*Cleansing from his sins*    Isa. 6. 7

3 Jehovah's *'Go!'*—
*Commission from the*
*Sovereign*      Isa. 6. 9

4 The servant's *'Ho!'*—
*Call of the Saviour*      Isa. 55. 1

**483 Immanuel, God with Us**
Isa. 7. 14; Matt. 1. 23

GOD—*His Person*—5 Unique Facts—

1 Numerous wonderful prophecies were
accurately fulfilled in Him

2 His virgin birth

3 His sinless life

4 His triumphant resurrection

5 His powerful influence on the world

WITH—*His Presence*—
Not only God *'over us'* as Sovereign Lord
Not only God *'for us'* as Gracious Lord
Not only God *'in us'* who believe as Living
Lord but
God 'WITH US' to the end of the age Matt.
28. 20

US—*His Purpose*—us sinners—He came into
the world to save sinners 1 Tim. 1. 15

**484 Wonderful Names of a Wonderful Person**
Isa. 9. 6

1 A *Wonderful Person*—
'a child born'—Son of Man
'a son given'—Son of God
'the government'—Son of David

2 A *Wonderful Birth*
Matt. 1. 23; Luke 1. 34, 35

3 A *Wonderful Teacher*
John 7. 45, 46

4 A *Wonderful Counsellor*
Isa. 9. 6

5 His *Wonderful Works*
Acts 2. 22; 10. 38

6 His *Wonderful Love*
John 15. 13

7 His *Wonderful Resurrection*
Luke 24. 22-24

**485 Lucifer, Son of the Morning**
Isa. 14. 12

Satan's Pride and Ambition—5 'I wills'.

'I will ascend into Heaven'    Isa. 14. 13

'I will exalt my throne'    Isa. 14. 13

'I will sit upon the mount of the
congregation'    Isa. 14. 13

'I will ascend above—the clouds' Isa. 14. 14

'I will be like the Most High'   Isa. 14. 14

**486 What of the Night?**
Isa. 21. 11-12

'What time of the night is it?' Question of the
scoffer, as in 2 Pet. 3. 4. 'The morning cometh
and also the night.' Answer given by the watchman.

THREE STAGES IN HISTORY AND IN INDIVIDUAL
EXPERIENCE

1 A *Cheerless Sunset*—Christ crucified
Luke 23. 33; 2 Cor. 4. 4

2 A *Cloudless Morning*—Christ coming
2 Sam. 23. 4

3 A *Ceaseless Night*—for the Christ-rejector
John 13. 30; 2 Pet. 2. 17

**487 Sure Things in Isaiah**

1 A sure *Place*—
*Christ our Support*      Isa. 22. 23

2 A sure *Foundation*
*Christ our Rock*      Isa. 28. 16

3 A sure *Covering*
*Christ our Defence*      Isa. 22. 17

4 A sure *Supply*—
*Christ our Life*      Isa. 33. 16

5 A sure *Resource*—
*Christ our Confidence*    Isa. 55. 4

## 488 Wonderful Things
'O Lord,—Thou hast done wonderful things'
Isa. 25. 1

WONDERFUL THINGS IN THE PAST: Jehovah has
been—

A strength to the poor and needy Isa. 25. 4

A Refuge from the storm     Isa. 25. 4

A Shadow from the heat     Isa. 25. 4

Has made—A Feast of fat things     Isa. 25. 6

WONDERFUL THINGS PROMISED: Jehovah will
remove—

Tears from all faces     Isa. 25. 8

Rebuke from His people     Isa. 25. 8

Jehovah will bring Salvation to His
waiting people     Isa. 25. 9

Rejoicing to His saved people     Isa. 25. 9

## 489 Other Lords—One Lord
Isa. 26. 13

1 *Dominion* of '*other lords*'
Isa. 26. 13
For *Israel*—Emperors of Babylon, Persia,
Greece, Rome, and Rulers of the nations
among whom they are scattered:
For the Christian—Sin, Lust, Covetous-
ness, Pride, Envy, etc. But sin 'shall not
have dominion over you'
Rom. 6. 14

2 *Acknowledgment* of '*one lord*', 'Thee only'
Isa. 26. 13; Zech. 14. 11
'Jesus as Lord' confessed with the mouth
Rom. 10. 9
'Christ as Lord' sanctified in the heart
1 Pet. 3. 15 (R.V.)

3 *Coming* of the *Universal Lord*, 'Thy Name'
—'Lord of all' Acts 10. 36
'King of kings and Lord of lords'
Rev. 19. 16

## 490 A Secure Hiding Place
Isa. 32. 2

1 *Secured* from the *wind*
(symbolical of Satan's
power), for 'your life is
hid with Christ in God' Col. 3. 3

2 *Sheltered* from the *tempest*
(the coming storm of
wrath), for 'we shall be
saved from wrath 1 Thess. 1. 10;
through Him'     Rom. 5. 9

3 *Satisfied* with *rivers of
water* (in a world which
is 'a dry and thirsty land'
'here no true satisfac-
tion is found)     John 7. 38

4 *Succoured* under the
*shadow of a great rock*
from the heat (the try-
ing influences all around
us)     Heb. 2. 18

## 491 Three Voices of Isaiah 40

1 The Voice of the *Herald*,
proclaiming *Preparation*
for the *Son of God*     Isa. 40. 3-5
(John the Baptist)     Luke 3. 4-6

2 The Voice of the *Spirit*, saying 'all flesh is as grass',
and proclaiming *Perman-* Isa. 40. 6-8;
*ence* of the *Word of God* 1 Pet. 1. 25

3 The Voice of the *Evangelist*,
lifted up—*Power* of the
*Gospel of God*     Isa. 40. 9-11

'O thou that tellest good
tidings to Zion' (Marginal
reading of verse 9)

## 492 'Behold Your God!'
Isa. 40. 9

'Behold *your King*!'
said Pilate to the Jews—
Gospel of *Matthew*     John 19. 14

'Behold *My servant*!'
said God to the world—
Gospel of *Mark*     Isa. 42. 1

'Behold *the Man*!'
said Pilate to the people—
Gospel of *Luke*     John 19. 5

'Behold *your God*!'
said (says) the Evangelist to all
men
Gospel of *John*     Isa. 40. 9

He has—

THE TENDERNESS OF THE GOOD
SHEPHERD     Isa. 40. 11

THE OMNIPOTENCE OF THE GREAT
CREATOR     Isa. 40. 12

THE WISDOM OF THE WONDERFUL
COUNSELLOR     Isa. 40. 13, 14

THE MAJESTY OF THE MIGHTY
POTENTATE     Isa. 40. 15

## 493 Waiting Upon the Lord
Isa. 40. 31

How to wait upon the Lord—

*Silently* to *Enjoy Communion*
Ps. 62. 1 (Margin)

*Patiently* to *Make Petition*
Ps. 40. 1

*Observantly* to *Hear Instruction*
Prov. 8. 33, 34

*Expectantly* to *Find Protection*
Isa. 33. 2

*Obediently* to *Receive Direction*
Ps. 25. 5

**494 Renewed Strength**

'They that wait upon the Lord shall change their strength' Isa. 40. 31

1 The *Source* from which we
  *Derive* this strength, 'the
  Everlasting God, Jehovah,
  the Creator'                    Isa. 40. 28

2 The *Secret* for those who
  *Desire* this strength, 'Wait
  upon the Lord'                  Isa. 40. 31

3 The *Spheres* in which to
  *Display* this strength—

  In the *Atmosphere of Heaven*
  —'mount up'                     Eph. 2. 6

  In the *Arena of Faith*—'run'   Heb. 12. 1, 2

  In the *Avenues of Daily* life
  —'walk'                         Eph. 4. 1

Thus we—

  OBTAIN FRESH STRENGTH FOR EACH NEW
  LENGTH,
  ATTAIN NEW HEIGHTS IN LOFTY FLIGHTS,
  MAINTAIN THE PACE THROUGHOUT THE RACE,
  SUSTAIN THE LOAD ALONG THE ROAD

**495 Helping Others**
  Isa. 41. 6-8

1 *Employment*—
  'they helped every one his
    neighbour'                    Isa. 41. 6
  'in Christ Jesus'              Rom. 16. 3
  'by prayer'                    2 Cor. 1. 11
  'to the truth'                 3 John 8

2 *Encouragement*—
  'the carpenter encouraged
    the goldsmith'               2 Chron. 35. 2

3 *Efficiency*—
  'he fastened it—that it
    should not be moved'         Isa. 41. 7

**497 Prophets and Prophecy**
  Isa. 41. 21-29

'God—spake in time past to our fathers by the prophets' Heb. 1. 1

'The Lord said unto Moses, Aaron thy brother shall be thy prophet' Exod. 7. 1

A PROPHET—from the Greek 'pro' and 'phemi' —is one who speaks instead of another, a Spokesman for God

PROPHET'S QUALIFICATIONS—the *Authority* to say what God reveals, and the *Ability* to give utterance to the revelation

TWO KINDS OF PROPHETS—Those who had the gift of prophecy, and those who, possessing the gift, were in the prophetic Office

PROPHECY—

1 Its *Purpose*—Proof of Divine Inspiration
    Isa. 41. 21-23

  The first recorded prediction was spoken
  by God direct

2 Its *Scope*—In the Old Testament—Messiah,
    the Jews and the Gentile nations

3 Its *Uses*—To reveal God's Plan
    to instruct men's minds
    to warn and comfort the hearts of God's
    people

**498 Jehovah's Servant**

In the Second Section of Isaiah Messiah is portrayed 3 times as *Jehovah's Servant* and 3 times as the '*Arm of the Lord*'

1 The Servant *Prophet*          Isa. 42. 1-4

2 The Servant *Priest*, making
    *Atonement* for our sins,
    *Amends* for our trespasses  Isa. 53. 10-12

3 The Servant *King, Exalted,
    Extolled* and *Eminent*      Isa. 52. 13-15

**496 Seven Perfect Assurances—Seven Perfect Replies**

| From my Lord to me   Isa. 41. 10 | From me to my Lord   Ps. 23. 4-6 |
|---|---|
| 1 Fear thou not | 1 Yea, though I walk, etc. |
| 2 For I am with thee | 2 For Thou art with me |
| 3 Be not dismayed | 3 Thy rod, etc.—comfort me |
| 4 For I am thy God | 4 Thou preparest a table, etc. |
| 5 I will strengthen thee | 5 Thou anointest my HEAD (Christ), my cup runneth over (Spirit's Fulness) |
| 6 Yea, I will help thee | 6 Surely goodness and mercy, etc. |
| 7 Yea, I will uphold thee | 7 And I will dwell . . . for ever |

H.J.B.

## 499   The Perfect Servant

1 The Father's Delight
   Isa. 42. 1; Matt. 3. 17

2 The Spirit-filled Man
   Isa. 42. 1; Matt. 3. 16

3 The Unobtrusive Teacher
   Isa. 42. 2; Matt. 12. 19

4 The Considerate Master
   Isa. 42. 3; Matt. 12. 20

5 The Infallible Conqueror
   Isa. 42. 4; Gen. 49. 10

## 500   Water Upon Him that is Thirsty
Isa. 44. 3

The *Container*—the water is
in 'the wells of salvation' Isa. 12. 3

The *Cost*—offered by God
to man freely      Isa. 55. 1; Rev.
                   22. 17

The *Course*—it flows as
'living water', emblem of
the Spirit            John 4. 14; 7. 39

1 The *Inflow—Appropria-
   tion*—God pours it,
   the Recipient drinks
   it. 'Jesus gave her
   water that was not in  Isa. 44. 3;
   the well'              John 7. 37

2 The *Overflow—Worship*
   —'She went away
   singing'               John 4. 14

3 The *Outflow—Service*—
   'She came back bring-
   ing Others for the
   water that was not in
   the well.'             John 7. 38, 39

## 501   A Polished Shaft

'He hath made me a polished shaft' Isa. 49. 2

HIDDEN—
   in the *Shadow of His Hand*—*Secret of Power*
   in His *Quiver*—*Security of Position*

POLISHED—Hebrew 'Bara' is translated—

| | |
|---|---|
| *Chosen* | 1 Chron. 16. 41 |
| *Purified* | Dan. 11. 35; 12. 10 |
| *Made bright* | Jer. 51. 11 |
| *Choice* | 1 Chron. 7. 40 |
| *Clear of speech* | Job. 33. 3 |

## 502   Four Members

Christ is said to have—in Isa. 50—

1 The *Tongue* of the learned     v. 4
   New Testament ref. 'Never
   man spake like this man' John 7. 46

2 The Opened *Ear*               v. 5
   New Testament ref. 'As I
   hear, I judge'               John 5. 30

3 The Smitten *Back*             v. 6
   New Testament ref. 'By whose
   stripes ye were healed'      1 Pet. 2. 24

4 The Flinty *Face*              v. 7
   New Testament ref. 'He
   steadfastly set His face to
   go to Jerusalem              Luke 9. 51
                                T.B.

## 503   Our Lord's Ear in Prophecy     Isa. 50. 4

1 *Digged* or *Pierced*—
   for *Incarnation* as Jehovah's Servant
                        Ps. 40. 6; Heb. 10. 5

2 *Wakened*—
   for *Instruction* as Learner and Teacher
                        Isa. 50. 4

3 *Opened*—
   for *Submission* as the Sacrifice for sins
                        Isa. 50. 5-7

## 504   The Pit Whence Digged, the Rock Whence Hewn
Isa. 51. 1

| Once, Sometime, In time past | Now | |
|---|---|---|
| 1 Disobedient | 1 Have obtained mercy | Rom. 11. 30 |
| 2 Not a people | 2 The people of God | 1 Pet. 2. 9, 10 |
| 3 Enemies | 3 Reconciled | Col. 1. 21, 22 |
| 4 Far off | 4 Made nigh | Eph. 2. 13 |
| 5 Darkness | 5 Light in the Lord | Eph. 5. 8 |
| 6 Unprofitable | 6 Profitable | Philem. 11 |
| 7 Persecuting | 7 Preaching | Gal. 1. 23 |

## 505 A Bad Bargain and a Great Gift
### Isa. 52. 3

'Ye have sold yourselves for nought'—A BAD BARGAIN

'Ye shall be redeemed without money'—A GREAT GIFT

*Bad Bargains—*
Esau's—sold his birthright
for a meal — Gen. 25. 33, 34
Ahab's—sold himself to work
evil — 1 Kings 21. 20
Judas's—sold his Master for
30 pieces of silver — Matt. 26. 15

*The Great Gift—*
*Redemption* purchased by the
precious blood of Christ — 1 Pet. 1. 18, 19
*Eternal Life* offered by God
in Christ — Rom. 6. 23
*Salvation* received through
faith in Christ — Eph. 2. 8


## 506 Five Views of the Saviour in Isaiah 53

1 The *Sinless Saviour*—
'the arm of the Lord' — v. 1
2 The *Silent Sufferer*—
'he opened not His mouth' — v. 7
3 The *Stupendous Sacrifice*—
'an óffering for sin' — v. 10
4 The *Satisfactory Settlement* He effected
'justify many' — v. 11
5 The *Strong Son of God*—
'a portion with the great' and 'the
spoil with the strong' — v. 12


## 507 The Subject of Isaiah 53

'He began at the same Scripture, and preached unto him Jesus' Acts 8. 35

1 The *Sensitive* One—
a tender plant — v. 2
2 The *Sorrowing* One—
a Man of sorrows — v. 3
3 The *Smitten* One—
smitten of God — v. 4
4 The *Suffering* One—
He was wounded — v. 5

5 The *Sin-bearing* One—
the Lord hath laid on Him — v. 6
6 The *Silent* One—
He opened not His mouth — v. 7
7 The *Stricken* One—
the stroke was upon Him — v. 8
8 The *Sincere* One—
No deceit in His mouth — v. 9
9 The *Submissive* One—
It pleased the Lord to bruise Him — v. 10
10 The *Satisfied* One—
He shall be satisfied — v. 11
11 The *Successful* One—
He shall divide the spoil — v. 12

H.K.D.


## 508 Christ's Sufferings

1 Christ's Sufferings from men—
Hatred — Isa. 53. 3
2 Christ's Sufferings with men—
Sympathy — Isa. 53. 4
3 Christ's Sufferings for men—
Atonement — Isa. 53. 5

W.W.F.


## 509 The Vicarious Sufferings of Christ
### Isa. 53. 5

For Our *Transgressions*, Sins of Commission—
He was Wounded — Isa. 53. 5

For Our *Iniquities*, Sins of Crookedness—
He was bruised — Isa. 53. 10

For Our *Peace*, the Reconciliation of enemies—
He was chastised — Zech. 13. 7

For Our *Healing*, the Salvation of our souls—
He was beaten with stripes — Matt. 27. 26

# JEREMIAH

## 510  Jeremiah's Times and Ours

Four Pairs—illustrating conditions in Jeremiah's day

**1** *Two Marred Things—*

A Linen Girdle—the *Priesthood* — Jer. 13. 1, 7

A Potter's Vessel—the *People* — Jer. 18. 4

**2** *Two Preachers—*

Jeremiah who spoke the words of the Lord — Jer. 2. 1

Pashur who 'prophesied lies' — Jer. 20. 6

**3** *Two Kings*—father and son

—Josiah repented at God's Word — 2 Kings 22. 19

Jehoiakim destroyed the scroll—God's Word — Jer. 36. 22, 23

**4** *Two Brothers—*

Baruch who served humbly as Jeremiah's secretary — Jer. 36. 1-6

Seraiah in high places, serving the king of Judah — Jer. 51. 59

## 511  The Prophet's Call to Preach
Jer. 1

Two Great and Godly Men—

*Jeremiah*—Whom Jehovah appoints—Words of a young Priest — Jer. 1. 2

*Josiah*—Whom Jehovah supports—Deeds of a young king — Jer. 1. 2

JEREMIAH'S CALL—

**1** Jeremiah heard the *Voice* of the Lord — Jer. 1. 3, 4

**2** Jeremiah felt the *Touch* of the Lord — Jer. 1. 9

**3** Jeremiah had a *Vision* from the Lord — Jer. 1. 11

Vision of the Almond Tree —Speeding of God's Purposes — Jer. 1. 11, 12

Vision of the Seething Cauldron—Evil out of the North — Jer. 1. 13, 14

## 512  Jeremiah's Questions

**1** *Ruin—*
How canst thou say, I am not polluted? — Jer. 2. 23

**2** *Redemption—*
How shall I pardon thee? — Jer. 5. 7

**3** *Regeneration—*
How shall I put thee among the children? — Jer. 3. 19

**4** *Retribution—*
How wilt thou do in the swelling of Jordan? — Jer. 12. 5

W.J.M.

## 513  Guidance

'My father, Thou art the Guide of my youth'
Jer. 3. 4

*Provisions* for Guidance—

| | |
|---|---|
| by His counsel | Ps. 73. 24 |
| with His eye | Ps. 32. 8 |
| by His hand | Ps. 78. 72 |

*Place* of Guidance—

| | |
|---|---|
| into the way of peace | Luke 1. 79 |
| into all truth | John 16. 13 |
| to Thy Holy Habitation | Exod. 15. 13 |

*Path* of Guidance—

| | |
|---|---|
| like a flock | Ps. 78. 52 |
| on every side | 2 Chron. 32. 22 |
| beside springs of water | Isa. 49. 10 |

*Period* of Guidance—

| | |
|---|---|
| in Judgment | Ps. 25. 9 |
| continually | Isa. 58. 11 |
| even unto death | Ps. 48. 14 |

J.M.H. and A.N.

## 514  A Message to Backsliders

| | |
|---|---|
| 1 A loving invitation | Jer. 3. 12 |
| 2 A gracious promise | Jer. 3. 12 |
| 3 A necessary confession | Jer. 3. 13 |
| 4 Additional promises | Jer. 3. 14 |

H.K.D.

## 515 Thus Saith the Lord
Jer. 6. 16

| To the Wanderer | | To the Weary | |
|---|---|---|---|
| 1 *Stand* in the ways | Jer. 6. 16 | 1 *Come* unto Me | Matt. 11. 28 |
| 2 *See* and consider | Jer. 6. 16 | 2 *Accept* the rest I offer | Matt. 11. 28 |
| 3 *Ask* for the old paths | Jer. 6. 16 | 3 *Take* my yoke upon you | Matt. 11. 29 |
| 4 *Walk* in them | Jer. 6. 16 | 4 *Learn* of Me | Matt. 11. 29 |

To BOTH—the Promise—'Ye shall find rest for your souls.'

**516 Message to Religious Sinners**
Jer. 7. 2

'The Daughter of My People' (but not 'My People') Jer. 8. 11, 19, 21, 22; 9. 1

1 Their *Sin*—
'the *hurt* of the daughter of
My people'                          Jer. 8. 11, 21
because of a Perpetual Back-
sliding                            Jer. 8. 5
a Refusal to Repent                Jer. 8. 6
a Rejection of God's Word Jer. 8. 9
a False Sense of Security          Jer. 8. 11

2 Their *Sorrow*—
'the *cry* of the daughter of
my people'                         Jer. 8. 19
'The harvest is past, the
summer is ended, and we
are not saved'                     Jer. 8. 20

3 Their *Sickness*—
'the health of the daughter
of my people'—not re-
covered                            Jer. 8. 22

4 Their *Slaughter*—
'the slain of the daughter of
my people'                         Jer. 9. 1

**517 Not Saved**
Jer. 8. 20

1 The *Progress of Time*—'
the harvest is past                Jer. 8. 20

2 The *Passing of Opportunities*—
the summer is ended                Jer. 8. 20
YET—the *Door* of Salvation
is still open                      John 10. 9
the *Day* of Salvation is still
present                            2 Cor. 6. 2
the *Desire* for Salvation is
still granted                      Isa. 45. 22

3 The *Peril of Delay*—
'we are not saved'                 Jer. 8. 20
Two Companies of the Lost—
Those who are lost and need
to be saved                        Luke 19. 10
Those who are lost and cannot
be saved                           Luke 16. 26

**518 Girdles that may be Marred**
1 The *Passover Girdle*—
Israel's, the pilgrim's            Exod. 12. 11
2 The *Priest's Girdle*—
Aaron's                            Exod. 28. 4
3 The *Prince's Girdle*—
Jonathan's                         1 Sam. 18. 4
4 The *Prizeman's Girdle*—
Joab's                             2 Sam. 20. 8

The Marred Girdle of Jer. 13 is
a Symbol of
*Marred Priesthood*                Jer. 13. 7
*Marred Pride*                     Jer. 13. 9
*Marred Purpose*                   Jer. 13. 11
*Marred Praise*                    Jer. 13. 11

**519 National Afflictions of a Sinful People**
*Five Pictures of Affliction*—
1 The People of Jerusalem
mourning                           Jer. 14. 2
2 The Children of the nobles
sent for water, and returning
with empty pots                    Jer. 14. 3
3 The Ploughman gazing in
despair on the hard, barren
ground                             Jer. 14. 4
4 The Hind deserting her new-
born calf to save her own life Jer. 14. 5
5 The Wild Asses with distended
nostrils vainly awaiting rain Jer. 14. 6
*Two Prayers of the Prophet*—Jer. 14. 7-9;
14. 19-22
The Answers to the Prayers—
'Pray not for this people for
good'                              Jer. 14. 11
'Though Moses and Samuel stood
before me, my mind could not
be toward this people'             Jer. 15. 1

**520 Jesus the Messiah, the Hope of Israel**
1 His *Glory*—
the Hope of Israel, its Saviour
in time of trouble                 Jer. 14. 8
2 His *Grace*—
a Stranger in the land, a Wayfarer pitching his tent at
night                              Jer. 14. 8
3 His *Grief*—
a Man ashamed, a hero that
cannot save—rejected               Jer. 14. 9

**521 Jeremiah's Prayers**
1 The *Person he addressed*—
Jehovah, the Hope of Israel        Jer. 14. 8
2 The *Prayer he expressed*—
*Consciousness* of what might
have been                          Jer. 14. 19
*Confession* of what was—sin
and backsliding                    Jer. 14. 20
*Confidence* in what could be,
God's power                        Jer. 14. 22
3 The *Plea of the distressed*—
on three grounds—                  Heb. 4. 12
the *Name* of the Lord
the *Throne* of the Lord
the *Covenant* of the Lord with
His people                         Jer. 14. 21

**522  Jeremiah—A Study**

1 A *Supplicant—*
   for *Preservation*            Jer. 15. 15

2 *Suffering—*
   from *Persecution*           Jer. 15. 15

3 *Strengthened—*
   by the *Words of the Lord*   Jer. 15. 16

4 *Satisfied—*
   with the *Word*              Jer. 15. 16

5 *Separated—*
   from *Scoffers*              Jer. 15. 17

6 *Supported*
   against *Sinners*            Jer. 15. 20

7 *Sustained—*
   by *Promise*                 Jer. 15. 20, 21
                                            W.J.M.

**523  The Marred Vessel**
     Jer. 18. 1-4

1 *Made* by the Creator         Jer. 18. 4

2 *Marred* by his sin           Jer. 18. 4

3 *Made again* in regeneration  Jer. 18. 4

**524  False Prophets**

The prophets who are against Jehovah and
against whom Jehovah speaks (Jer. 23. 25-32)
because—

1 they prophesy *Lies* and claim
   their message is from the
   Lord                         Jer. 23. 26

2 they encourage *Licence* among
   the people                   Jer. 23. 32

3 they are characterized by
   *Lightness*                  Jer. 23. 32

**525  Figures of the Word of God**

1 Compared to a *Hammer—*
   to break                     Jer. 23. 29

2 Compared to a *Fire—*
   to melt                      Jer. 23. 29

3 Compared to a *Lamp—*
   to shine                     Ps. 119. 105

4 Compared to a *Sword—*
   to smite                     Heb. 4. 12

5 Compared to a *Mirror—*
   to reveal                    James 1. 23

6 Compared to *Food—*
   to sustain                   1 Pet. 2. 2

7 Compared to *Water—*
   to cleanse                   Ps. 119. 9
                                            JS. FS.

**526  A Nation's Restoration**
     Jer. 30

'Radiant hopefulness falls like sunlight
across days of darkest gloom.'

1 *Return* of Messiah
2 *Regathering* of Israel
3 *Restoration* to the Land
   after scattering             Jer. 30. 1-3
   of a King after the day of
   Jacob's trouble              Jer. 30. 4-9
   of spiritual health after
   wounds                       Jer. 30. 10-17
   of Jerusalem and its
   palaces after being trod-
   den down                     Jer. 30. 18, 19
   of Israel, the nation, to
   God                          Jer. 30. 20-24

**527  The God of all the Families of Israel**
     Jer. 31

1 The Eternal Lover            vs. 1-8
2 The Good Shepherd            vs. 9-14
3 The Unfailing Comforter      vs. 15-17
4 The Compassionate Father     vs. 18-25
5 The Faithful Sower           vs. 27-30
6 The Righteous Redeemer       vs. 31-37
7 The Great Renewer            vs. 38-40

**528  The Hand of God in History**
     Jer. 32

1 The Purchase of Hope         vs. 1-25
2 The Rule of the Gentiles     vs. 26-35
3 The Return of Israel         vs. 36-40
4 The Promise of Homes         vs. 41-44

God's New Covenant will be an Everlasting
Covenant Jer. 32. 40

**529  Jehovah-Tsidkenu**
     Jer. 33. 16

'The Lord our Righteousness'—

1 In *Pardon* and Cleansing    Jer. 33. 4-8
2 In *Peace* and Justice       Jer. 33. 4-7
3 In *Prosperity* and Prestige Jer. 33. 9-10
4 In *Praise* and Gladness     Jer. 33. 11
5 In *Performance* and Fulfil-
   ment                        Jer. 33. 14
6 In *Princehood* and Righteousness                    Jer. 33. 15, 16
7 In *Priesthood* and Sacrifice Jer. 33. 17, 18

**530  Abundance of Peace**

1 The *Revelation* of it—
   'Reveal unto them the
   abundance of peace'         Jer. 33. 6
2 The *Jubilation* of it—
   'Delight themselves in
   the abundance of
   peace'                      Ps. 37. 11
3 The *Duration* of it—
   'Abundance of peace
   till there be no
   moon'                       Ps. 72. 7 (Margin)
                                            T.B.

**531 Jeremiah's Secretary, Baruch**

*Baruch*—means '*Blessed*' and displayed all the characteristics of the man described in the 'Beatitudes'.
1 *Employment* of a *Dedicated* man of God       Jer. 36. 4, 5
2 *Encouragement* of a *Despondent* minister of God   Jer. 45. 2-5
3 *Enrolment* of a *Dependable* messenger of God      Jer. 32. 12, 13

**532 The Book of the Words of the Lord**

The 'Book' was a Scroll in Jeremiah's day, not a bound volume.
1 The *Making of the Book*—
  the Agents—
  a Speaker, Jeremiah      Jer. 36. 2
  a Writer, Baruch        Jer. 36. 4
  Materials, ink and paper   Jer. 36. 18
  Readers            Jer. 36. 15

2 The *Message of the Book*    Jer. 36. 16
3 The *Marring of the Book*    Jer. 36. 23
4 The *Miracle of the Book*    Jer. 36. 32

Franklin D. Roosevelt said, 'Books cannot be killed by fire; people die but books never die'.

**533 Man's Quests**

1 The *Natural Quest*—
  Great things for oneself    Jer. 45. 5
2 The *Supreme Quest*—
  the kingdom of God and His righteousness      Matt. 6. 33
3 The *Spiritual Quest*—
  the things that are above    Col. 3. 1

---

## LAMENTATIONS OF JEREMIAH

**534 His Compassions Fail Not**    Lam. 3. 22

Jesus had compassion—and touched their eyes
     Matt. 20. 34

Jesus, moved with compassion—touched the leper—and he was cleansed
     Mark 1. 41, 42

Jesus said, I have compassion on the multitude, because they have nothing to eat
     Matt. 15. 32

He was moved with compassion toward them, and He healed their sick
     Matt. 14. 14

When He came out He was moved with compassion towards them, because they were as sheep having no shepherd
     Mark 6. 34

He, being full of compassion, forgave their iniquity    Ps. 78. 38; Luke 23. 34
          E.A.H.

---

## EZEKIEL

**535 Ezekiel—Prophet and Book**

The Prophet Ezekiel is about 100 times designated by the same name as that used by our Lord of Himself, 'Son of man'.

Observe words of frequent occurrence— 'know that I am Jehovah! KEYVERSE—'That they may know that I am Jehovah' Ezek. 20. 12

DIVISIONS OF THE PROPHECY OF EZEKIEL—
1 Chs. 1-5
  The *Prophet's Call*, introduced by a Time note 11.

2 Chs. 6-24
  *Predicted Calamities* on Judah and Jerusalem
3 Chs. 25-32
  *Proclaimed Condemnation* of Gentile nations
4 Chs. 33-39
  *Promised Cleansing* and restoration for Israel
5 Chs. 40-48
  *Precise Calculations*—Temple and its measurements

## 536 Preparation for Service

1 The *Vision Seen*—
Visions of God and
the Appearance of a
Man      Ezek. 1. 1. 26

2 The *Voice Heard*—
telling the prophet      Ezek. 1. 28; 2. 1-6
the *People* to whom he
must go      Ezek. 2. 3
the *Purpose* for which
he is sent      Ezek. 2. 7
the *Power* behind him
as he goes      Ezek. 2. 8

3 The *Volume Eaten*—
Hearing and Heeding
the Word of God      Ezek. 3. 1, 2

4 The *Victim Yielded*—
the Astonished Victim    Ezek. 3. 15
the Enchained Victim    Ezek. 3. 23-25
the Prostrate Victim    Ezek. 4. 4
the Nauseated Victim    Ezek. 4. 15

## 537 Four Figures in the Vision of Ezek. 1. 10

Four Living Creatures with Four Faces—

1 *A Man* (*front*)—
Sympathy, intelligence—corresponding to
the Gospel of Luke

2 *A Lion* (*right*)—
Majesty, power—corresponding to the
Gospel of Matthew

3 *An Ox* (*left*)—
Perseverance in service—corresponding to
the Gospel of Mark

4 *An Eagle* (*back*)—
Keenness of Vision—corresponding to the
Gospel of John.

                HYP.

## 538 Ezekiel's Roll
Ezek. 3. 1-17

was to him what the Bible should be to us.

1 *Intellectually* he had to 'eat it'
—get it into his head      Ezek. 3. 2

2 *Experientally* he had to 'digest it'—get it into his heart Ezek. 3. 10

3 *Practically* he was a watchman
to give warning—he had to
proclaim it with his lips      Ezek. 3. 17
                The Witness

## 539 These Three Men
Ezek. 14. 14

NOAH—'walked with God'—preserved through
the Flood      Gen. 6. 9; 1 Pet. 3. 20

DANIEL—'believed in his God'—delivered from
the lions' mouths      Dan. 6. 22, 23

JOB—'feared God'—blessed after many afflictions      Job. 1. 1; 42. 12

## 540 The Work of the Spirit of God

1 In *Regeneration*—
a new heart and a new
spirit      Ezek. 36. 26, 27;
(Life and Cleansing)    John 3. 5

2 In *Revival* of
Dead Bones in a Valley Ezek. 37. 1
Dry Bones in a Vision Ezek. 37. 2
A Voice—On first utter-
ance—a noise, shak-
ing and coming to-
gether—Conviction    Ezek. 37. 7
On next utterance—the
dead bones lived—
Regeneration      Ezek. 37. 10

3 In *Renewal*—
Stood on their feet—
Stability      Ezek. 37. 10
An Exceeding great
army—Activity and
Orderliness

## 541 The Laws of God's House
Ezek. 43. 12

1 The Law of *Supreme
Authority*—
'the place of His throne' Ezek. 43. 7

2 The Law of *Divine
Holiness*—
'the place of His holy
Name'      Ezek. 43. 7, 8, 12

3 The Law of *Heaven's
Pattern*—
'Measure the pattern'   Ezek. 43. 10
(Exod. 25, 9, 40; 1 Chron. 28. 11, 12, 19;
Heb. 9. 23)

4 The Law of *Priestly Service*—
must be *Priestly* (linen garments)
              Ezek. 44. 17, 18
must be *Pure* (linen breeches)
must be *Patient* (unhurried—no sweat)

## 542 The Waters from the Sanctuary
Ezek. 47

'The River of God—is full of water' Ps. 65. 9
Rivers of God—
in Eden      Gen. 2. 10
in the Wilderness      Ps. 78. 15, 16
in the Millennial capital   Ezek. 47. 1
in the Paradise of God above Rev. 22. 1, 2

1 Waters to the *Ankles*—'walk in the Spirit'
           Gal. 5. 16; Ezek. 47. 3

2 Waters to the *Knees*—'praying in the Spirit'
           Eph. 6. 18; Ezek. 47. 4

3 Waters to the *Loins*—serving in the Spirit
           Acts 20. 19; Ezek. 47. 4

4 Waters to *Swim in*—*Spirit-filled* life
           Eph. 5. 18; Ezek. 47. 5

when little of self is seen, there is a
loosening of the hold on the earth—life
in a new element.

# DANIEL

## 543 Daniel the Man Greatly Beloved

Daniel—means 'God is my Judge'.

1 His *Three Names*—
  *Hebrew* name—Daniel;
  *Chaldean* name—Belteshaz-
  zar                                    Dan. 1. 6, 7
  *Heavenly* name—
  Man greatly beloved            Dan. 9. 23;
                                         10. 11, 19

2 His *Three Spheres*—
  In *Private* Life—
    *Firm in Purpose*              Dan. 1. 8
  In *Public* Life—
    *Faultless in Practice*        Dan. 6. 4
  In *Prayer* Life—
    *Fervent in Prayer*            Dan. 9. 3

3 His *Three Outstanding Qualities*—
  his *Faithfulness* as a *Saint*  Dan. 1
  his *Fearlessness* as a *Sage*   Dan. 2; 4; 5
  his *Faultlessness* as a *States-
  man*                             Dan. 6

## 544 Dare to be a Daniel
  Dan. 1. 8

1 *Three Qualifications* required
  by the king—
  *Birth*—'of the king's seed'     Dan. 1. 3
  *Beauty*—'well-favoured'         Dan. 1. 4
  *Brains*—'skilful in all wis-
  dom and understanding'           Dan. 1. 4

2 *Three Purposes* at work—
  The *Divine* Purpose—'that
  they might stand'                Dan. 1. 5
  The *Devil's* Purpose—to
  make them defile them-
  selves                           Dan. 1
  through their *minds*            Dan. 1. 4
  through their *mouths*           Dan. 1. 5
  through their *manners*          Dan. 1. 10
  *Daniel's* Purpose—to keep
  himself pure                     Dan. 1. 8

3 *Three Traits* in Daniel's character—
  his *Conviction*—not to defile
  himself                          Dan. 1. 8
  his *Courage*—'he requested
  the prince'                      Dan. 1. 8
  his *Courtesy*—'Prove thy
  servants', 'as thou seest,
  deal with thy servants,'         Dan. 1. 12, 13

## 545 Daniel's God
  Dan, 2. 28

'There is a God in heaven'
Daniel's God is—
  a God Who *Reveals His will*  Dan. 2. 28
  a God Who *Rules His world*   Dan. 2. 28
  a God Who *Repays*—*His
  wages*                        Dan. 5. 23-26
  a God Who *Rescues*—*His
  work*                         Dan. 6. 22
No wonder Daniel 'believed in
His God'                        Dan. 6. 23

## 546 The Colossal Image of Nebuchadnezzar's Dream

1 The *Description of the Image*
                                 Dan. 2. 31-35
  ITS PHYSICAL SHAPE—
    a gigantic, awe-inspiring human form
    *Head* representing *Babylonian Empire*
    *Shoulders and arms*—*Medo-Persian*
    *Legs, feet and toes*—*Roman Empire*
    *Belly and thighs*—*Grecian Empire*

  ITS PROPHETIC SEQUENCE—
    Succession of kingdoms with universal
    dominion—from Head to feet

  ITS PARAMOUNT SPLENDOUR—
    Glittering metals, gold, silver, brass and
    iron that dazzled Nebuchadnezzar's
    senses so that he did not retain even a
    confused recollection of it.

  ITS PROPORTIONATE SIZES—
    Head—Babylon—shortest-lived
    Legs—Rome—longest-lived.

2 The *Deterioration of the Image* Dan. 2. 39
  *Commercially*, in the value of its metals
  *Chemically*, in their specific gravity
  *Constitutionally*, in the Quality of its rule

3 The *Destruction of the Image* Dan. 2. 34,
                                       35, 44
  The Stone—Christ and His coming
  kingdom—Smote the Image on its feet
  and brought all merely human Government to an end.

## 547 The Kingdom Set up by the God of Heaven
  Dan. 2. 44

It will be *Indestructible*—'shall never be de-
                                stroyed'
*Final*               —'shall not be left to
                        other people'
*Universal*           —'shall consume all
                        these kingdoms'
*Eternal*             —'shall stand for ever'

## 548 Without Hands
  Dan. 2. 45

1 Our circumcision is effected
  for us 'without hands'—
  not so with Israel             Col. 2. 11
2 Our holy places are made
  'without hands'—not so
  with Israel                    Heb. 9. 24
3 We have a house 'not made
  with hands' eternal in the
  heavens                        2 Cor. 5. 1
4 Christ is compared to a stone
  cut out of a mountain
  'without hands'                Dan. 2. 45
5 The Antichrist will be broken
  'without hands'                Dan. 8. 25
  (The Lord will destroy him
  with the Spirit of His
  mouth)                         2 Thess. 2. 8
                                 T.B.

G

### 549 The Fiery Furnace of Affliction
Dan. 3. 24, 25

| WHAT THE FIRE DOES | WHAT THE FIRE CANNOT DO |
|---|---|
| 1 Burns the bands that bind | 1 Cannot harm God's people—'no hurt' |
| 2 Affords opportunity to display an upright walk | 2 Cannot singe a hair of their heads (v. 27) |
| 3 Gives a precious experience of the Lord's companionship | 3 Cannot burn the clothes His people wear |
| 4 Convinces opposers of God's power and Providence (v. 28) | 4 Cannot leave its smell on them |

### 550 Principalities and Powers

These are the *four great Laws* governing the Universe—

1 The *Sovereignty of God*—
'King of kings'    Dan. 2. 37; 4. 25

2 The *Opposition of Satan*—
'Prince of the power of the air'    Eph. 2. 2; 6. 11

'prince of this world'    John 14. 30

Comes before the Judge of all the earth as accuser of those who fear God    Job. 1. 6; 2. 1; Zech. 3. 1

3 The *Activity of Angels* who—
minister to the heirs of salvation    Heb. 1. 14

discern the moral state of men    Dan. 4. 13

form a heavenly legislative court    Dan. 4. 17

4 The *Antagonism of Wicked Spirits in* heavenly places who    Eph. 6. 12

obstruct angelic messengers    Dan. 10. 12, 13

unite to oppose the angels of God    Dan. 10. 20

have a part in international affairs on earth    Dan. 4. 8

### 551 The Feast of Belshazzar
Dan. 5

1 A *Glamorous Feast*
Dan. 5. 1; Jer. 51. 39
(Millions are at Sin's feast, monarchs to menials, potentates to paupers)

2 A *Ghastly Fear*—
when the king saw the writing on the wall
Dan. 5. 6; Jer. 50. 43

3 A *Grievous Failure*—
to humble himself and repent
Dan. 5. 22, 23; Jer. 50. 31

4 A *Great Fall*—
'that night was Belshazzar—slain'
Dan. 5. 30; Jer. 50. 32

THE WRITING—

Mene—*Numbered*—the days of life

Tekel—*Weighed*—the ways of life

Peres—*Broken*—the thread of life

### 552 Daniel, the Man of Prayer
Daniel prayed—
1 as a *Humble Subject* of Nebuchadnezzar—by the *Compulsion* of a *Crisis*    Dan. 2. 18

2 as an *Honoured Statesman*—the *Custom* of a *Consecrated* life    Dan. 6. 10

3 as *Heaven's Suppliant*—the *Constraint* of a life of *Communion*    Dan. 9. 3

### 553 Daniel in Prayer
In the record of Daniel praying, four Hebrew words are used for 'pray', meaning—

1 'Bend, bow down'—
He prayed and gave thanks
Dan. 6. 10; Eph. 3. 14

2 'make petition'—
praying and making supplication
Dan. 6. 11

3 'judge self'—
praying and confessing
Dan. 9. 20

4 'offer praise'—
speaking in prayer
Dan. 9. 21; Phil. 4. 6

The Character of Daniel's Prayer Dan. 9

| His *Assurance* | Dan. 9. 2 |
|---|---|
| His *Approach* | Dan. 9. 3 |
| His *Appeal* | Dan. 9. 16 |
| the *Answer he received* | Dan. 9. 22 |

**554 The Touch**

1 The Touch of *Restoration*     Dan. 8. 18

2 The Touch of *Instruction*     Dan. 9. 21

3 The Touch of *Comfort*     Dan. 10. 10

4 The Touch of *renewed Assurance*     Dan. 10. 16

5 The Touch of *imparted Strength*     Dan. 10. 18

W. E. VINE

**555 The Seventy Weeks**
Dan. 9. 23-27

'Seventy weeks are determined (or decreed) upon thy people and upon thy holy city' Dan. 9. 24

1 The *Object of the Period Decreed*—

To finish, or restrain, transgression (Sins of *Commission*)

to make an end of sins (sins of *Omission*)

to make expiation for iniquity (Zech. 13. 1) —way of *Remission*

to bring in everlasting righteousness (door of *Admission*)

to seal up the Vision and Prophecy, because no longer needed (new mode of *Transmission*)

2 The *Order of the Period Decreed*—

Whole Period—70 Sevens of years—490 years, divided into periods

Period of Seven sevens—49 years—from Neh. 2. 1-8

Period of 62 sevens—434 years—till Messiah the Prince

Period of 1 seven—7 years—still future
The present Church period is an interval, when the 'holy city' is trodden down by the Gentiles.

3 The *Outcome of the Period Decreed*—

During the last period of seven years, still future, Dan. 9. 26, 27 will be fulfilled.

The Outcome—
i A *Commonwealth* of Israel established —already fulfilled

ii A *Covenant* with Israel confirmed— Isa. 28. 14-16—still future

iii A *Command* given to worship the Beast—Rev. 13. 3, 4

iv A *Cessation* of Jewish rites enforced— Dan. 9. 27

v The *Consummation* for Israel and the nations—at Christ's appearing, when 'that determined shall be poured upon the desolator'

**556 The Vision Glorious**
Dan. 10. 5, 6

Doubtless a Christophany. There is a close similarity between this and John's vision in Patmos, when he was 'in the Spirit on the Lord's Day' Rev. 1. 13-15
Seven Particulars are noted—externals first

1 His *Clothing*—Linen—Priesthood of Christ v. 5

2 His *Girdle*—Golden—Service of Christ John 13. 4

3 His *Body*—Beryl—Perfection of Form Song of S. 5. 14-16

4 His *Face*—Lightning—His Radiant Glory Matt. 17. 2

5 His *Eyes*—Lamps of Fire—Penetration and insight     Rev. 1. 14; 2. 2

6 His *Arms and Feet*—Polished Brass— Infallible judgment John 5. 27

7 His *Voice*—voice of a multitude—Authority of utterance

Matt. 7. 29; Rev. 1. 15

# HOSEA

## 557 A Heart to Heart Talk from God
Hosea 2. 14-18

'I will speak to her heart' Hos. 2. 14 Margin.

In Hos. 2 God is

| | |
|---|---|
| *Pleading with His people* | vs. 2-5 |
| *Punishing His people* for their sins | vs. 6-13 |
| *Promising blessing* to His people | vs. 14-22 |

In His words of promise are seen—

1 *His Grace*—
'I will allure her and bring her' Hos. 2. 14

2 *His Gifts*—
'I will give her *Vineyards*, a *Valley*, and the *Voice* of song Hos. 2. 15

3 *His Government*—
'thou shalt call me Ishi, Husband' Hos. 2. 16

## 558 The Unknown God
'No knowledge of God in the land' Hos. 4. 1
Lack of knowledge of God. Hos. 4. 6; 6. 6
False profession of the knowledge of God. Hos. 8. 2, 14
The God of whom men are ignorant is—

1 The Living God
Hos. 1. 10; 1 Thess. 1. 9

2 A Righteous God
Hos. 4. 6; Ezra. 9. 15

3 The Creator God
Hos. 8. 14; Isa. 40. 28

4 A Holy God
Hos. 9. 1; 1 Pet. 1. 16

5 A Gracious God
Hos. 14. 1; Exod. 34. 6

## 559 The Indictments in Hosea
'Israel' and 'Ephraim', the people addressed, are the same people, the nation of Israel, the Northern Kingdom, as distinct from the Southern Kingdom of Judah.

1 A Backsliding Heifer—
Declension                    Hos. 4. 16

2 Joined to idols—
Idolatry                        Hos. 4. 17

3 A Cake not turned—
Hypocrisy                     Hos. 7. 8

4 Ignorant of grey hairs here and there upon him—
Senile Decay                 Hos. 7. 9

5 A Silly Dove without understanding—
Foolish Ignorance         Hos. 7. 11

6 An Empty Vine—
Fruitlessness                 Hos. 10. 1

7 A Feeder on wind—
Vain Pursuits                Hos. 12. 1

8 Professing—'I am become rich'—
Smug Complacency        Hos. 12. 8;
                                      Rev. 3. 17

## 560 Words of Confession to God and Words of Promise from God
Take with you—

Words of *Repentance*—
'Take away all iniquity'      Hos. 14. 2

Words of *Faith*—
'In Thee the fatherless find mercy'      Hos. 14. 3

Words of *Entreaty*—
'Receive us graciously'        Hos. 14. 2

Words of *Praise*—
'the calves (offerings) of our lips'      Hos. 14. 2

The Promises of God—'I WILL'—three times—

I will heal their backsliding—
The *Goodness of God's Activity* Hos. 14. 4

I will love them freely—
The *Graciousness of God's Attitude*      Hos. 14. 4

I will be as the dew unto Israel—
The *Gentleness of God's Approach*      Hos. 14. 5

## 561 The Blessings of Revival
Seven Similes in Hosea 14

1 *Fair as the Lily*—in the Valley
Hos. 14. 5; Song of S. 2. 2

2 *Firm as the Cedar*—on the Hilltop
Hos. 14. 5; Eph. 3. 17

3 *Fat as the Olive*—on the Slopes
Hos. 14. 6; Judges 9. 9

4 *Fragrant as Lebanon's unnamed trees*—
on the Slopes Hos. 14. 6

5 *Flourishing as the Corn*—in the meadows
Hos. 14. 7; John 12. 24

6 *Fruitful as the Vine*—in the Vineyard
Hos. 14. 7; John 15. 1

7 *Fresh as the Cypress*—in the Woodlands
Hos. 14. 8

In the closing Dialogue

Ephraim says, 'What have I to do any more with idols?'

God says, 'I have heard him'

Ephraim says, 'I am like a green fir tree'

God says, 'From me is thy fruit found'

## JOEL

**562  Three Great Themes in Joel 1**

1  An *Historical Fact*—
the *Depredations* of Locusts  Joel 1. 4
(Swarms of locusts followed
by drought, famine and
other catastrophes)

2  A *Metaphorical Figure*—
the *Devastations* of a Hos-
tile nation  Joel 1. 6
As a result there were—
No Offerings for the Lord  Joel 1. 9, 13
No Tithes for the Levites  Joel 1. 9
No Harvest for the
Labourers  Joel 1. 10, 11
No Food for the people  Joel 1. 17
No fodder for Flocks and
Herds  Joel 1. 18

3  A *Prophetical Future*—
the Day of the Lord  Joel 1. 17
(frequently mentioned in
Joel's prophecy)

**563  The Years that the Locusts have Eaten**

'I will restore—the years that the locusts
have eaten' Joel 2. 25

1  The *Desolation Wrought*—
*Darkened Skies*—
Vision of Heaven ob-
scured  Joel 2. 2
*Deafening Sounds*—
Voice of God unheard  Joel 2. 5
*Desolate Scenes*—
Barren, fruitless land  Joel 2. 3

Figure of
i  The Sinners wasted years  Luke 15. 13, 14
ii  The Backslider's wasted
years  Ruth 1. 21
iii  The Family's wasted
years  1 Sam. 3. 12, 13
iv  The Local Assembly's
backsliding condition  1 Cor. 5. 7

2  The *Dedication Sought*—
Sound an alarm  Joel 2. 1
Summon a solemn as-
sembly  Joel 2. 15
Sanctify the congrega-  Joel 2. 16;
tion  Rom. 12. 1

3  The *Deliverance Wrought*—
The Lord's Promises—
I will send—food  Joel 2. 19
I will remove—the foe  Joel 2. 20
I will restore—the years  Joel 2. 25

**564  The Blessings of Restoration**

1  *Lost Years made good*—'I will restore the
years'  Joel 2. 23, 25; Ezek. 34. 26

2  *Sad Hearts made glad*—'Ye shall be
satisfied and praise'
Joel 2. 26

3  *God's Name made great*—'Know that I am
the Lord your God and none else'
Joel 2. 27

# AMOS

**565　Great Deliverance from Great Danger**
　　　　Amos 3. 12

1 *Brought up* out of an horrible
　　pit　　　　　　　　　Ps. 40. 2

2 *Taken out* of the mouth of the
　　lion　　　　　　　　Amos 3. 12

　(Two legs to flee from wrath,
　a piece of an ear to hear
　God's Word)

3 *Plucked out* of the fire　　Zech. 3. 2

4 *Delivered from* the power of
　　darkness　　　　　　Col. 1. 13

5 *Awakened out* of the snare of
　　the Devil　　　　　　2 Tim. 2. 26

In each there are—

A *Position of Danger*

the *Possibility of Destruction*

and a *Plan for Deliverance*

**566　God's Five Calls to Repentance**
1 Lack of necessities—
　Yet have ye not returned
　　unto Me　　　　　　Amos 4. 6
2 Envious surroundings—
　Yet have ye not returned
　　unto Me　　　　　　Amos 4. 7, 8
3 Reversal of prosperity—
　Yet have ye not returned
　　unto Me　　　　　　Amos 4. 9
4 Bereaving Visitation—
　Yet have ye not returned
　　unto Me　　　　　　Amos 4. 10
5 Marvellous providences—
　Yet have ye not returned
　　unto Me　　　　　　Amos 4. 11
Finally, 'PREPARE TO MEET THY GOD' —　4.12
　　　　　　　　　　　　　　　　F.S.B.

**567　Be Prepared**
　　　　Amos 4. 12
The Scout's Motto is God's Command.
1 A *Mandate from the Sove-*
　　*reign*　　　　　　Matt. 24. 44
2 A *Message to the Sinner*　Amos 4. 12
3 A *Maxim for the Servant of*
　　*God*　　　　　　　2 Tim. 2. 21
4 A *Motto for the Soldier of*
　　*Christ*　　　　　　Acts 21. 13

# OBADIAH

**568　Obadiah**

Several Obadiahs are mentioned in the Old
Testament. The first in order is the Pious
Steward of King Ahab, who feared the Lord
in the days of Elijah the prophet. The last
mentioned is the Prophet Obadiah who wrote
concerning Edom, the race descended from
Esau. Obadiah—means Servant of Jehovah.
CONCERNING EDOM

1 Their *Wantonness* Exposed　　vs. 5, 6

2 Their *Wise Men* Destroyed　　v. 8

3 Their *Warfare* Unsuccessful　　v. 9

4 Their *Wariness* Condemned　　v. 11

The Key phrase is—'*In the day*': the Key note
is—'*thou stoodest on the other side*'.
1 Taking the side of Israel's Invaders v. 11
2 Doing nothing to prevent their being
　carried captive　　　　　　　v. 12
3 Rejoicing at their destruction　　v. 12
4 Gloating over their distress　　　v. 12
5 Invading their cities and land　　v. 13
6 Withholding help from them in their
　affliction　　　　　　　　　　v. 13
7 Looting their property in their
　absence　　　　　　　　　　v. 13
8 Betraying those left behind to their
　enemies　　　　　　　　　　v. 14

# JONAH

## 569  Jonah the Man

1  A *Type of Christ* in Death and Resurrection
Our Lord boarded the Ship of Humanity
and paid the Fare
Cp. Jonah 1. 3

Our Lord—One Man—Became a victim
for all in the Ship
Cp. Jonah 1. 15

Our Lord entered a Prepared Grave
Cp. Jonah 1. 17

Our Lord came forth in Resurrection
after 3 days and 3 nights
Matt. 12. 40, 41

Our Lord preached judgment and produced repentance
Jonah 3. 4, 10

2  A *Sign to men*
Matt. 12. 39; Acts 17. 30, 31

3  A *Disobedient Servant*
in Ch. 1 *Fleeing* from God
in Ch. 2 *Fleeing* to God
in Ch. 3 *Flying* for God
in Ch. 4 *Flying* at God

## 570  Jonah in Four States

Jonah means '*Dove*':

In Ch. 1 A *Silly Dove* without
understanding          Hos. 7. 11

In Ch. 2 A *Trembling Dove*     Hos. 11. 11

In Ch. 3 A *Dove sent forth*     Gen. 8. 8-10

In Ch. 4 A *Mourning Dove*     Isa. 38. 14

Ch. 1 Jonah in the *Storm* at sea—A Rebel

Ch. 2 Jonah in the *School* of God—A Penitent

Ch. 3 Jonah in the *Service* of God—A Preacher

Ch. 4 Jonah in the *Shadows* with God—A
Learner

## 571  Six Personal Questions Jonah was Asked

1  'What meanest thou, O sleeper?'—
Asleep while men were perishing
Jonah 1. 6

2  'What is thine occupation?'—
A Disobedient servant of Jehovah
Jonah 1. 8

3  'What is thy country?'—
A citizen of the Promised Land
Jonah 1. 8

4  'Of what people art thou?'—
A Hebrew, a man from the other side
Jonah 1. 8

5  'Why hast thou done this?'—
I am afraid of losing my reputation as a
prophet          Jonah 1. 10; 4. 2

6  'What shall we do unto thee?'—
Take me up, and cast me out
Jonah 1. 11

## 572  Jonah's Four Attitudes

1  On his *Back—Sleeping*     Jonah 1. 5
2  On his *Knees—Praying*     Jonah 2. 1-9
(even though in the whale's belly)
3  On his *Feet—Preaching*  Jonah 3. 4
4  On his *Face—Mourning*   Jonah 4. 2, 3, 8

## 573  'Prepared'

The Keyword of 'Jonah' and the Solution of
all difficulties.
God—
1  Prepared (sent out) a great
*wind*—to turn the back-
slider          Jonah 1. 4
2  Prepared a great *fish*—to
swallow Jonah          Jonah 1. 17
(God made it for the purpose)
3  Prepared a *gourd* to cover
the despondent prophet     Jonah 4. 6
4  Prepared a *worm*—to wither
all man's hopes of earth     Jonah 4. 8
5  Prepared a silent east *wind*—
to cast him only upon
Jehovah          Jonah 4. 8
GREAT GRACE AT LAST (Verse 11).

HYP.

# MICAH

Micah—means 'Who is like Jehovah'.

**574 What is Good**
Micah 6. 8

1 To be like Jehovah (Micah), display His character to men—*Spiritual Character*    Micah 1. 1
2 To do what Jehovah requires of us—*Scriptural Principles* Micah 6. 8

3 To do justly—*Sincere Up-rightness*    Micah 6. 8

4 To love mercy—*Sympathetic Deportment*    Micah 6. 8

5 To walk humbly with our God—*Saintly Communion*    Micah 6. 8

# NAHUM

**575 God's People**

'He knoweth them that trust in Him' Nahum 1. 7

God's People are

1 *Harboured* in His *grace* for safety Nahum 1. 7; Joel 3. 16 (Margin); Amos 9. 11 (Margin)

2 *Holy* in His *holiness* for sanctification Deut. 7. 6; 14. 2, 21; 1 Pet. 1. 15, 16

3 *Helped* in His *strength* for suffering 2 Cor. 12. 9; Acts 26. 22; Heb. 4. 16

4 *Honoured* in His *fellowship* for service John 12. 26; 2 Tim. 2. 21

5 *Hidden* in His *presence* for communion Ps. 27. 5; 132. 7; Isa. 49. 2
6 *Happy* in His *love* for rejoicing Deut. 33. 29; Ps. 144. 15; 146. 5; Prov. 16. 20
F.E.M.

**576 Trust in the Lord**

1 The Lord knoweth them that trust in Him    Nahum 1. 7
2 Trust in Him—at all times    Ps. 62. 8
3 Trust in Him—for strength    Isa. 26. 4
4 Trust in Him—for guidance    Ps. 37. 5
5 Trust in Him—in the dark    Isa. 50. 10
6 Trust in Him—with the whole heart    Prov. 3. 5
7 Trust in Him—even if He slay thee    Job 13. 15
E.A.H.

# HABAKKUK

**577 Habakkuk's Four Experiences**

In Ch. 1 the prophet is a *Man with a Burden*—on the Ground looking round    Hab. 1. 1
In Ch. 2 he is a *Man with a Vision*—on the Watchtower looking out    Hab. 2. 1, 2
In Ch. 3 he is a *Man with a Prayer*—in the Sanctuary looking up    Hab. 3. 1, 2
In Ch. 3. 17-19, he is a *Man with a Song*—on the heights looking down    Hab. 3. 17-19

**578 The Just shall Live by his Faith**
Hab. 2. 4

1 The *Place of Trust*— the Watchtower    Hab. 2. 1
2 The *Pledge of Trust*— 'it will surely come'    Hab. 2. 3

3 The *Power of Trust*— 'live by his faith'    Hab. 2. 4
Verse 4 is quoted three times in the New Testament, with the emphasis as follows:

1 Who shall live by his faith?— the Justified    Rom. 1. 17
2 By what shall the just live?— by his Faith    Gal. 3. 11
(not by the works of the law but by faith)
3 What shall the just do by faith? —live for God    Heb. 10. 38
(as did those whose faith God honoured in Heb. 11)

**579 Habakkuk's Prayer**
Hab. 3. 2

1 *Revive Thy work* in the midst of the years
2 *Reveal Thy power* in the midst of the years (Make known)
3 *Remember mercy* in the day of Thy wrath

# ZEPHANIAH

## 580  Four Themes of Zeph. Ch. 3

1 *Failure* and God's *Punishments* vs. 1-7

2 *Faith* and God's *Promises*          vs. 8-13

3 *Fulness* and God's *Presence*       vs. 14-16
   He is 'IN THE MIDST'
       as the Righteous Lord      v. 5
       as the King of Israel        v. 15
       as the Mighty Saviour       v. 17

4 *Fellowship* and God's *People*      vs. 17-20

## 581  He Faileth Not—Zeph. 3. 5

1 When the *money* faileth—
   Times of *Financial
       Stringency*          Gen. 47. 14, 15

2 When my *strength* faileth—
   Times of *Poor Health*      Ps. 71. 9

3 When my *spirit* faileth—
   Times of *Nervous Strain*  Ps. 143. 7

4 When my *kinsfolk* have
   failed—
   Times of *Social Estrange-
       ment*              Job 19. 14

5 When *men's hearts* are
   failing them for fear—
   Times of *International
       Crisis*          Luke 21. 26

# HAGGAI

## 582  Consider Your Ways

Literal Translation—'Direct your hearts to your ways' Hag. 1. 5 (Consider how you are living)

1 *Unprofitable Lives*—
   Is it time for you to dwell in
       your ceiled houses?      Hag. 1. 4

2 *Unproductive Labour*—
   Ye have sown much and bring
       in little            Hag. 1. 6

3 *Unprovided Livelihood*—
   Ye are not filled: there is none
       warm              Hag. 1. 6

4 *Unpredictable Losses*—
   Wages—in a bag with holes   Hag. 1. 6

Consider what you should do (Hag. 1. 7)—

1 *Go up* to the mountain     Hag. 1. 8
2 *Bring down* materials      Hag. 1. 8
3 *Build* God's House         Hag. 1. 8
4 *Glorify* the Lord          Hag. 1. 8

## 583  The Lord's Message Through Haggai

'The Lord's Messenger in the Lord's Message' Hag. 1. 13

1 An *Expostulation*          1. 2-11

2 An *Exhortation*            2. 3-9

3 An *Encouragement*         2. 15-19

   CONSIDER (Lay to heart)
   What God has done          2. 15-17
   What God can do            2. 18
   What God will do           2. 18, 19

# ZECHARIAH

**584 Messages from the Lord of Hosts** —————————————————————————

Zechariah—mean's 'Whom Jehovah remembers'.

This book, of fourteen chapters, contains three sections after the Introductory verses (1-17).

| | |
|---|---|
| 1. 7-6.15 | Pictures and their Messages |
| 7. 1-8.23 | Problems and their Answers |
| 9. 1-14. 21 | Prophecies and their Meaning |

The Messages in the first six chapters are connected with their Visions or Symbols.

| CHARACTER OF THE MESSAGE | FAILURES IN ISRAEL | KEYWORD | Reference |
|---|---|---|---|
| 1 Call to Repent | Failure of the fathers | TURN | Zech. 1. 2-6 |
| 2 Message of hope | Failure of the nation | COMFORT | Zech. 1. 14-17 |
| 3 Word of assurance | Failure of the exiles | SURE | Zech. 2. 4-13 |
| 4 Promise of Cleansing | Failure of the priests | KEEP | Zech. 3. 7-10 |
| 5 Prediction of Blessing to come | Failure of the builders | GRACE | Zech. 4. 6-10 |
| 6 Note of warning | Failure of those who had returned | ENTER | Zech. 5. 3, 4 |
| 7 Preview of Coming Glory | No Failure | BUILD | Zech. 6. 9-15 |

**585  A Brand Plucked from the Fire**

In Zech. 3 three persons are introduced—

1 *Joshua* the high priest—
the *Accused*  Zech. 3. 1

2 *Satan* standing by—
the *Adversary*  Zech. 3. 1

3 *The Lord*—Jehovah—
the *Advocate*  Zech. 3. 1, 2

Joshua is—

*Rescued* from the fire—as a *Brand*

*Restored* to his office—as a *Priest*

*Recognized* by the people—as a *Sign*

For this he was—

1 *Chosen*—
a brand plucked out of the
fire  Zech. 3. 2

2 *Cleansed*—
I have caused thine iniquity
to pass  Zech. 3. 4

3 *Clothed*—
they—clothed him with garments  Zech. 3. 5

4 *Crowned*—
they set a fair mitre (turban)
upon his head  Zech. 3. 5

5 *Conditioned*—
if thou wilt walk in my ways Zech. 3. 7

6 *Commissioned*—
thou shalt judge—and keep Zech. 3. 7

7 *Compassed about*—
I will give thee places to walk Zech. 3. 7

**586  The Branch**

1 *My Servant* the Branch—
Christ in *Mark's* Gospel  Zech. 3. 8

2 The *Man* whose name is the
Branch—
Christ in *Luke's* Gospel  Zech. 6. 12

3 The *Branch of Jehovah*—
Christ in *John's* Gospel  Isa. 4. 2

4 The Branch out of *Jesse's
roots*—
Christ in *Matthew's* Gospel Isa. 11. 1

**587  The Golden Bowl**
Zech. 4. 2

In Zech. 4—

A *Question*—'Who hath despised the
day of small things?'  v. 10

An *Answer*—'Not by might nor by
power, but by My Spirit'  v. 6

A *Vision*—A Lampstand all of gold v. 2

In every era God has had His Lampstands of
testimony, shining for Him—

| | |
|---|---|
| In the *Wilderness* | Exod. 25. 31 |
| In the *City of Jerusalem* | 2 Chron. 4. 7 |
| In the *Land of Judea* (during the *captivity*) | Zech. 4. 2 |
| In the *World by His Church* | Rev. 1. 12, 13 |

The Fulness of oil to keep the Lamps burning
is supplied by the Golden Bowl, Christ.

The Golden Bowl—

1 Represented the Lord (Adonai) of the whole earth   Zech. 4. 14; Acts 10. 36

2 Was entirely of Gold—Christ's Preciousness   Col. 1. 12-16; 1 Pet. 2. 7

3 Was on the top—Christ's Pre-eminence   Col. 1. 17, 18

4 Was always full—Christ's Fulness   Col. 1. 19; 2. 3, 8, 9

5 Supplied every lamp from its fulness   Col. 2. 10; John 1. 16

6 Supplied the oil through golden pipes   2 Pet. 1. 4
(Partakers of the divine nature)

7 Maintained supplies from the two olive trees   Zech. 4. 3, 6, 12, 14
(sons of oil—'by My Spirit')

## 588 The Great Builder
Zech. 6. 9-15

'He shall build the temple of the Lord'

1 The Builder's *Name*—the Branch   Zech. 6. 12; Luke 1. 78
(Dayspring = Branch)

2 The Builder's *Activities*—in Creation   Prov. 8. 30
in the Church   Matt. 16. 18

3 The Builder's *Glory*—a priest on His throne   Zech. 6. 13; Eph. 3. 8

4 The Builder's *Counsel*—Peace   Zech. 6. 13; Eph. 2. 14
(breaking down the middle wall of partition and making both one)

## 589 Fasts Changed to Feasts

1 *Character* of the Fasts—not fasts to the Lord   Zech. 7. 3, 5

2 *Cause* of the Fasts—the Lord's punishment for sin   Zech. 7. 11-14

3 *Cessation* of the Fasts   Zech. 8. 9-13, 14-17
Conditions—A right relationship to God and to one another)

4 *Change of Fasts to Feasts*   Zech. 8. 19

The letter E breaks up Fasts and makes them Feasts: and E stands for Enlightenment, Emancipation and Enjoyment.

## 590 False Shepherds
Zech. 10. 3; 11. 5

The Flock of Israel was—

*Unfed*   Zech. 10. 3; Mark 6. 34
*Unprotected*   Zech. 11. 7; John 10. 12
(Flock of slaughter)
*Unprovided for*   Zech. 11. 7; Matt. 14. 15, 16

The Reasons—

1 Their *Possessors*, the Roman power—slew them   Zech. 11. 5

2 Their *Vendors*, Judah's civil rulers—sold them   Zech. 11. 5

3 Their *Shepherds*, The Jewish religious leaders, did not pity them   Zech. 11. 5

## 591 The True Shepherd
Zech. 11. 12-14; 13. 7

The Lord Jesus Christ is—

1 The *Shepherd of Israel*   Ps. 80. 1; Matt. 15. 24
2 The *Good* Shepherd   John 10. 11
3 The Shepherd *Servant*   Zech. 11. 12-14
4 The Shepherd *Sacrifice*   Zech. 13. 7
5 The *Great* Shepherd of the sheep   Heb. 13. 20
6 The *Chief* Shepherd   1 Pet. 5. 4
7 The Shepherd *King*   Zech. 9. 9; Matt. 2. 6

The Shepherd's Two Staves—
'His rod and His staff'   Ps. 23. 4
BEAUTY—the Beauty of Holiness   Zech. 11. 10
BANDS—the Bands of *Harmony*   Zech. 11. 14

## 592 Holiness Unto the Lord
Zech. 14. 9, 20, 21

One Holy Lord—'I sanctify myself'   John 17. 19

One Holy people—'Sanctify them'   John 17. 17; 1 Pet. 2. 9

HOLINESS UNTO THE LORD—on

1 The *Bells* (or *Bridles*) of the *horses*—Public life holy—Horse—animal of travel and war—Holy Walk and Warfare

2 The *Pots of the Lord's house*—Worship and service holy

3 The *Bowls before the altar*—Ministry of those specially called—holy

4 *Every pot in Jerusalem*—Family circle and Domestic life holy

# MALACHI

## 593   God's Messengers

Malachi—means 'My Messenger'.

1 The *Prophetic* Messenger—
  *Malachi*

  bringing the Word of the Lord
  to the people                    Mal. 1. 1

2 The *Priestly* Messenger—the
  *Levites*

  failing to teach the Law of the
  Lord to the people              Mal. 2. 7

3 The *Royal* Messenger—*John
  the Baptist*

  preparing the way of the Lord
  among the people                Mal. 3. 1

4 The *Messenger of the Covenant*
  —*Jesus* the Son of God
  coming to His house and His
  people                          Mal. 3. 1

## 594   God's Love for His People

'I have loved you', saith the Lord Mal. 1. 2
God's Love

*Declared*—I have loved you      Mal. 1. 2

*Denied*—Wherein hast thou loved
us?                               Mal. 1. 2

*Defined*—I loved Jacob          Mal. 1. 2

*Demonstrated*—Your eyes shall
see                               Mal. 1. 5

## 595   Wherein?—Questions in Malachi

A rebellious people ask the Lord—

1 Wherein hast Thou loved us?—
  *God's Love Denied*            Mal 1. 2

2 Wherein have we despised Thy
  name?—
  *God's Name Despised*          Mal. 1. 6

3 Wherein have we polluted Thee?
  *God's Table Defiled*          Mal. 1. 7

4 Wherein have we wearied
  Him?—
  *God's Providence Decried*     Mal. 2. 17

5 Wherein shall we return?—
  *God's Invitation Declined*    Mal 3. 7

6 Wherein have we robbed Thee?—
  *God's Treasury Defrauded*     Mal. 3. 8

7 What have we spoken—against
  Thee?—
  *God's Justice Defamed*        Mal. 3. 13

## 596   God's Covenant with His People

God's *Commandment* given to the
priests                           Mal. 2. 1

God's *Covenant* established with
Levi                              Mal. 2. 4

God's *Curse* overshadowing their
blessings                         Mal. 2. 2

Because—

1 His *Covenant* was corrupted   Mal. 2. 8

2 His *Holiness* was profaned    Mal. 2. 11

3 His *Ordinances* were forsaken Mal. 3. 7

4 His *Commandments* were transgressed                         Mal. 3. 14

## 597   The Prerequisites for Priestly Service

The Priest's—

1 *Heart* should fear the Lord    Mal. 2. 5

2 *Lips* should teach the Law of
  truth                           Mal. 2. 7

3 *Feet* should walk in the light of
  holiness                        Mal. 2. 8

4 *Aim* should be to turn many away
  from iniquity                   Mal. 2. 6

## 598   Failure in Four Spheres

Failure of Priests and People.

1 In the *Religious* Sphere—
  Failure of Priests and Levites Mal. 2. 7, 8

2 In the *Social* Sphere—
  Failure of the Husbands        Mal. 2. 14

3 In the *Spiritual* Sphere—
  Failure of the People as a
  whole                           Mal. 3. 5

4 In the *Material* Sphere—
  Failure of the Donors          Mal. 3. 8

## 599 The Record of the God-Fearing Remnant

'A book of remembrance was written before Him for them that feared the Lord' Mal. 3. 16
Right Condition and Right Position.

1 In their *Heart*—
'they feared the Lord'     Mal. 3. 16

2 In their *Mind*—
'they thought on His Name'     Mal. 3. 16

3 With their *Mouth*—
'they spoke often one to another'     Mal. 3. 16

4 In *God's Review*—
'the Lord hearkened and heard' Mal. 3. 16

5 In *God's Register*—
'a book of remembrance was written down'     Mal. 3. 16

6 In *God's Reckoning*—     Mal. 3. 17
His 'special treasure'     (Margin)

7 In *God's Record*—
'I will spare them as a man spareth His own son'     Mal. 3. 17

## 600 Elijah and John the Baptist

'Behold I will send you Elijah the prophet' Mal. 4. 5
'If ye will receive it, this is Elias which was for to come' Matt. 11. 14

1 Each was empowered by the Spirit of God for ministry
Luke 1. 17

2 Each had to do with a wicked king and a more wicked queen
1 Kings 19. 1, 2; Mark 6. 18, 19

3 Each received from God his daily provision—food and raiment
1 Kings 17. 4, 9; Mark 1. 6

4 Each was courageous in rebuking sin in high places
1 Kings 21. 20; Mark 6. 18

5 Each had a lapse into despondency when his life was in danger
1 Kings 19. 4; Matt. 11. 2, 3

CONTRAST—Elijah was taken to Heaven without dying: John was the last of the martyr prophets.

# MATTHEW

## 601 The King's Credentials of Royalty

'Matthew—Messiah, Israel's King, sets forth,
by Israel slain;

But God decreed that Israel's loss should be
the Gentiles' gain.'

(A) SEVEN GREAT EVIDENCES—

1 *Genealogical*—
Heir to the Throne, the
Promises and the
Land      Matt. 1. 1-17

2 *Angelic*—
Appearances to Joseph,
in the line of David   Matt. 1. 20; 2. 13

3 *Astronomical*—
'We have seen His star
in the east'      Matt. 2. 2

4 *Prophetic*—
John the Herald quoting
Isaiah's prophecy    Matt. 3. 1-3

5 *Divine*—
the voice of the Father
from Heaven      Matt. 3. 17

6 *Spiritual*—
Temptation and
Triumph over the
tempter      Matt. 4. 1-11

7 *Miraculous*—
Healing without medi-
cines      Matt. 4. 23-25

(B) SEVEN GREAT PROPHECIES FULFILLED—

1 *Emmanuel*—
by Isaiah (7. 14)    Matt. 1. 22, 23

2 *Bethlehem*—
by Micah (5. 2)     Matt. 2. 6

3 *Egypt*—
by Hosea (11. 1)    Matt. 2. 15

4 *Rama*—
by Jeremiah (31. 15)   Matt. 2. 18

5 *Nazareth*—
by an unknown prophet,
unrecorded prophecy   Matt. 2. 23

6 *Wilderness*—
by Isaiah (40. 3, 4)   Matt. 3. 3

7 *Galilee*—
by Isaiah (9. 1, 2)   Matt. 4. 14-16

## 602 Witnesses to the King's Greatness

Testimony of—

1 the Church by Matthew in
his Gospel

2 Angels      Matt. 1. 23

3 the Gentiles
(the Magi)      Matt. 2. 2

4 the Prophets
(John the Baptist)   Matt. 3. 11

5 God the Father    Matt. 3. 17

6 the devil
(the tempter)      Matt. 4. 11

7 His Jewish audience   Matt. 7. 28, 29

## 603 Five Women in Christ's Genealogy

Only God can bring a clean thing out of an
unclean    Job. 14. 4

1 *Tamar*—played the harlot
Matt. 1. 3; Gen. 38. 15

2 *Rahab*—a converted harlot
Matt. 1. 5; Joshua 2. 1

3 *Ruth*—a Moabitess, a foreigner
Matt. 1. 5; Ruth 4. 10, 17

4 *Bathsheba*—an adulteress
Matt. 1. 6; 2 Sam. 11. 3, 4

5 *Mary*— a virgin, the mother of Jesus, a
good and blessed woman, but not
immaculate
Matt. 1. 16; Luke 1. 28, 38, 48

## 604 King of the Jews
Matt. 2. 2

Jesus Christ was born King, not merely Heir
to the throne.

1 The *Appointed* King—   Micah 5. 2

2 The *Anointed* King—   Heb. 1. 8, 9

3 The *Assaulted* King—   John 19. 1-3

4 The *Ascended* King—   Acts 5. 30-32

5 The *Acclaimed* King—   Rev. 19. 11-16;
Phil. 2. 9-11

## 605 The Young Child

The descriptive phrase occurs nine times in
Matt. 2. Cf. Isa. 9. 6

1 Fulfiller of the Prophetic Scriptures      v. 8

2 Subject of Astronomical Study   v. 9

3 Object of Men's Worship   v. 11
Note—'the young child' (first)
with Mary His mother'

4 Centre of Angelic Ministry   v. 13

5 Target of Satanic Hostility   v. 13

6 Reason for a Nocturnal
Journey      v. 14

7 Centre of the Divine Plan   vs. 20, 21

**606  Words for 'Worship' in the New Testament** —————————————————

| | |
|---|---|
| 1 Proskuneo—I kiss the hand toward—60 times | Matt. 2. 2; Acts 24. 11; Rev. 22. 8 |
| 2 Eusebeo  —I am reverential, pious—twice | Acts 17. 23; 1 Tim. 5. 4 |
| 3 Therapeuo—I cure or serve—frequent, but not often 'worship' | Acts 17. 25 |
| 4 Latreuo  —I worship publicly—20 times | Acts 24. 14; Phil. 3. 3 |
| 5 Sebomai  —I venerate, revere—10 times | Acts 16. 14; 18. 7 |

---

**607  'If Thou be the Son of God'**
Matt. 4. 3, 6; 27. 40

1 A TITLE—

Son of God, implying Deity, equality with
God            Matt. 26. 63, 64; John 5.
17, 18; John 19. 7

2 A TEMPTATION—

If . . . ., command . . . .

If . . . ., cast Thyself down
Matt. 4. 3, 6

(It was within the Lord's power but
opposed to His principles)

3 A TAUNT—

If Thou be the Son of God, come down
Matt. 27. 40

4 A TRUTH—

He does COMMAND His people's Love, Lips,
Loyalty.

He has COME DOWN—in the Past to Redeem
us            1 Tim. 1. 15

He does COME DOWN—in the Present to
Refresh us    John 14. 21-23

He will COME DOWN—in the Future to
Receive us    1 Thess. 4. 16

**609  Verbal Accuracy of the Scriptures**
Matt. 5. 18

Inspiration of the Scriptures and their
Accuracy is seen to depend on—

| | |
|---|---|
| 1 A Phrase— 'yet once more' | Heb. 12. 27 |
| 2 The Voice of a verb— passive for active | Gal. 4. 9 |
| 3 The Tense of a verb— 'I AM'—present for past | John 8. 58 |
| 4 The Number of a noun— 'seed', not 'seeds' | Gal. 3. 16 |
| 5 A Single letter— an iota or a small stroke | Matt. 5. 18 |

**610  'O Ye of Little Faith'**

Four occasions in Matthew's Gospel when
the Lord rebuked His disciples for their
'LITTLE FAITH'.

| | |
|---|---|
| 1 Because they were worrying— CARE | Matt. 6. 30 |
| about their life | v. 25 |
| about their clothing | v. 28 |
| about their food | v. 31 |
| about their future | v. 34 |
| 2 Because they were terrified— FEAR | Matt. 8. 26 |
| 3 Because they, represented by Peter, were wavering— DOUBT | Matt. 14. 31 |
| 4 Because they lacked percep- tion— DULLNESS | Matt. 16. 8 |

---

**608  The Sermon on the Mount** —————————————————————
Matt. 5; 6; 7

The King issues the Laws of the Kingdom: THREE GREAT THEMES—

1 *Precepts*  —should be accompanied by *Rectitude of life*    —Heavenly Character Matt. 5
2 *Practices*  —should be accompanied by *Reverence of heart*  —Heavenly Computa-
tion    Matt. 6
3 *Profession*—should be accompanied by *Reality of behaviour*—Heavenly Conduct  Matt. 7

1 Matt. 5. 3-13 —Inner Qualities of the Heart: Metaphor—Salt    v. 13
  Matt. 5. 14-48—Outward conduct in the life: Metaphor—Light    vs. 14-16
2 Matt. 6. 1-4  —Heaven's Reckoning of our Almsgiving
  Matt. 6. 5-15 —Heaven's Reckoning of our Praying
  Matt. 6. 16-18—Heaven's Reckoning of our Fasting and Self-denial
  Matt. 6. 19-34—Heavenly Outlook on our Material possessions
3 Matt. 7. 1-5  —Judging others
  Matt. 7. 6-12 —Asking and Receiving
  Matt. 7. 13-20—Seven contrasted pairs—Gates, ways, destinies; Prophets; animals,
              fruit trees
  Matt. 7. 21-27—Empty profession and Active reality

**611 False Professors who say 'Lord! Lord!'**

1 Their *Foundation* all wrong—not on the Rock but on the Sand
Matt. 7. 21; Luke 6. 46

2 Their *Fruit* of the wrong kind—not the fruit of good trees
Matt. 7. 21; Luke 13. 25

3 Their *Foresight* entirely lacking—not prepared for Christ's return
Matt. 25. 11

**612 The Centurion's Faith**
Matt. 8

It was—

1 Personally presented     Matt. 8. 5

2 Pleadingly exercised     Matt. 8. 5

3 Practically illustrated     Matt. 8. 8, 9

4 Publicly honoured     Matt. 8. 10

5 Plentifully rewarded     Matt. 8. 13
H.K.D.

**613 Fourfold Assurance**
'Be of good cheer'

1 Assurance of Forgiveness     Matt. 9. 2

2 Assurance of Companionship     Mark 6. 50

3 Assurance of Victory     John 16. 33

4 Assurance of Eternal Safety     Acts 23. 11
I.W.P.

**614 'Even So'**

1 Of Submission     Matt. 11. 26

2 Of Resurrection     1 Thess. 4. 14

3 Of Expectation     Rev. 22. 20

4 Of Lamentation     Rev. 1. 7

5 Of Retribution     Rev. 16. 7

6 Of Communion     John 20. 21

7 Of Sustentation     1 Cor. 9. 14
T.B.

**615 The Great Invitation—Come!**

1 Come unto Me—the
*Person*     Matt. 11. 28
for Rest

for Communion—
'come and see'     John 1. 39

for the living water—
'come and drink'     John 7. 37

for the Bread of life—
'come and dine'     John 6. 35; 21. 12

2 All ye that labour and are heavy laden—
the *People*     Matt. 11. 28

3 I will give you—the
*Promise*     Matt. 11. 28

4 Rest: ye shall find rest
—the *Provision*     Matt. 11. 28, 29

5 Take my yoke upon you—the *Precept*     Matt. 11. 29

6 and learn of Me—the
*Privilege*     Matt. 11. 29

7 I am meek and lowly
in heart—the *Pattern*     Matt. 11. 29

**616 The Pre-Eminence of Christ**
Matt. 12. 41, 42

'Behold a greater'
Israel boasted in—

1 their *Race*, of which *Abraham* was the head and founder

2 their *Religion*, of which the *Temple* was the centre and expression

3 their *Royal Line*, in which *Solomon* was the greatest king

4 their *Revelation* through the prophets, *Jonah* having been sent with a message to the Gentiles

5 their *Resources* of wells and springs, *Jacob's* well being the most ancient

The Christian's boast, based on the words of Jesus, is CHRIST, GREATER THAN ALL—

1 Greater than Abraham in the *Pre-eminence* of His rank     John 8. 53, 58

2 Greater than the Temple in the *Magnificence* of His Glory     Matt. 12. 6

3 Greater than Solomon in the *Excellence* of His Wisdom     Matt. 12. 42

4 Greater than Jonah in the *Beneficence* of His Message     Matt. 12. 41

5 Greater than Jacob in the *Munificence* of His Gift     John 4. 12

**617 The Queen of the South**
Matt. 12. 42

1 A Lesson from the *Past*—

'she came from the uttermost parts of the earth to hear the wisdom of Solomon'
1 Kings 10. 1-3

2 A Challenge in the *Present*—

'behold, a greater than Solomon is here'

3 A Warning for the *Future*—

'shall rise up in the judgment with this generation and shall condemn it'

### 618 'Seven' in Scripture
See Matt. 13

It has been said that the constant occurrence in Scripture of the number 7 is the result of nothing short of Divine intention. This number has been traced in one form or another in nearly every book in the Old Testament and the New. It is wonderfully associated with the history of the life and teaching of our Lord.
Note—

1 The Seven stages of His history in Phil. 2. 6-9

2 The Seven characteristics of His wisdom in Prov. 3. 15-18

3 The Seven parables in Matthew 13

4 The Seven prayers in Luke Chs. 3, 5, 6, 9, 11, 22

5 The Seven miracles in John Chs. 2, 4, 5, 6, 9, 11

6 The Seven petitions in the Lord's prayer Luke 11. 2-4

7 The Seven sayings on the cross Luke 23. 34; John 19. 26-28; Luke 23. 43; Matt. 27. 46; John 19. 30; Luke 23. 46

8 The Seven blessings from the throne Rev. Chs. 1, 14, 16, 19, 20, 22

HENRY THORNE

### 619 Parables of the Sower and the Seed, the Wheat and the Tares

The first four parables of Matt. 13 were spoken by the *Seaside*  Matt. 13. 1-35

The first three parables deal with work in the *Countryside*  Matt. 13. 3-32

The first two parables tell of seed falling by the *Wayside*  Matt. 13. 19

The Fourth parable describes work in the *Inside*  Matt. 13. 33

The Fifth, Sixth and Seventh parables were spoken by the *Fireside*  Matt. 13. 36

Subjects of the first four parables of Matt. 13—
1 Conflict between good and evil
2 the work of the Lord Jesus
3 the work of the enemy, the devil
4 the seeming triumph of evil, and
5 the final triumph of Christ at the 'Consummation of the age'

In the PARABLE OF THE SOWER—there are—
One Sower  Matt. 13. 3
One Field
One kind of Seed
One Fertile soil out of 4 kinds mentioned

In the PARABLE OF THE TARES—there are—
One Owner  Matt. 13. 24
One Field
One Object
but—
Two Sowers  Matt. 13. 25-30
Two kinds of Seed
Two Destinies at time of Harvest

### 620 Parable of the Pearl of Great Price
Matt. 13. 45, 46

Five active Voice verbs describe the Merchantman's (gem-dealer's) activity—
SEEKING, FOUND, WENT, SOLD, BROUGHT.
The Merchantman is Christ.

The Pearl of great price—a pearl is the product of a living organism, the pearl-oyster, and is begotten of injury inflicted by the entry of a foreign substance.
Christ—

*Suffered* that He might *form* His pearl—The Oyster  Eph. 5. 25-27

*Sought* that He might *find* His pearl—The Diver  Luke 19. 10

*Sold all* that He might *free* His pearl—The Merchant  Matt. 13. 46

### 621 All That He (She) Had

1 The Merchantman, Christ, *sold* all that He had to obtain the pearl, and succeeded  Matt. 13. 46

2 The younger son, the sinner, *squandered* all that he had to obtain pleasure, but failed  Luke 15. 13, 14

3 The diseased woman *spent* all that she had to obtain health, but failed  Mark 5. 26

4 The destitute widow *surrendered* all that she had to the Lord, and obtained His commendation  Mark 12. 43, 44

### 622 A Parabolic Miracle
Jesus walking on the sea Matt. 14. 23-31

1 Jesus alone on the mountain, praying to His Father—His Present Priesthood

2 His disciples in the ship, sailing to the other side—His People's Pilgrimage

3 His disciples, tossed with the waves, facing danger—His People's Plight

4 Peter going to Him on the water and beginning to sink—Peter's Peril

5 The Lord an ever-present Helper, stretching out His hand—Christ's Pity and Power

## 623 'Whom Say Ye that I Am?'
### Matt. 16. 15

| | | |
|---|---|---|
| 1 'Thou art My Beloved Son,' | said the Father | Mark 1. 11 |
| 2 'I am the Son of God,' | said the Lord Himself | John 10. 36 |
| 3 'This is the Son of God,' | said John the Baptist | John 1. 34 |
| 4 'Thou art the Son of God,' | said Nathanael | John 1. 49 |
| 5 'Thou art the Son of God,' | said Peter | John 6. 69 |
| 6 'Thou art the Son of God,' | said Martha | John 11. 27 |
| 7 'This was the Son of God,' | said the Centurion | Matt. 27. 25 |
| 8 'Thou Son of God,' | said the Demons | Matt. 8. 94 |

JS. FS.

## 624 The Negatives of the Self Life

'This shall not be unto Thee' Matt. 16. 22·
'Not' in Greek is 'ou me', the emphatic
negative, rendered by Rotherham 'in no wise'.
Peter's use of the expression—

1 The NEVER of Self-pity          Matt. 16. 22
2 The NEVER of Self-will          John 13. 8
3 The NEVER of Self-confidence
              Matt. 26. 33-35: Mark 14. 31
4 The NEVER of Self-righteousness
                      Acts 10. 14; 11. 8
   (an even stronger expression incorporating
   both particles)
5 The NEVER of Self-depreciation 2 Pet. 1. 10

## 625 The Transfiguration of Our Lord
### Matt. 17. 1-9, 24-27

There are four accounts of the Transfiguration—

1 Matthew's—
   emphasis on the King's face: Moses the
   Lawgiver has priority
2 Mark's—
   emphasis on the Servant's livery: Elias the
   Prophet has priority
3 Luke's—
   emphasis on the Prayer of the Dependent
   Man: 'two men'
4 Peter's—
   emphasis on the Voice—'Jesus only':
   Peter had learnt his lesson  2 Pet. 1. 17,
   18:
In Matthew's account—PETER'S MISTAKES—
   i 'Jesus only'—
   Glorious Isolation: Peter ranked the Lord
   with Moses and Elias (Matt. 17. 8):
   ii 'For me and Thee'—
   Gracious Identification: Peter ranked the
   Lord with strangers (Matt. 17. 26, 27).

## 626 The Charter of Gathering
### Matt. 18. 20

| | | |
|---|---|---|
| 1 Divine Place | 'Where' |
| 2 Divine Testimony | 'two or three' |
| 3 Divine Assembly | 'are gathered' |
| 4 Divine Fellowship | 'together' |
| 5 Divine Authority | 'in My name' |
| 6 Divine Presence | 'there am I' |
| 7 Divine Centre | 'in the midst of them' |

AUTHOR UNKNOWN

## 627 Things to Come

1 The Regeneration of all
   things                    Matt. 19. 28
2 The Redemption of all
   things                    Eph. 1. 14
3 The Restitution of all things Acts 3. 21
4 The Reconciliation of all
   things                    Col. 1. 20
5 The Restoration of all things Eph. 1. 10

H.K.D.

## 628 Bethany
### Matt. 21. 17

On the Fig tree, emblem of Israel
nationally—NO FRUIT for God's
Anointed                     Matt. 21. 19

In the Temple, centre of Israel's
worship—NO FELLOWSHIP with
God's Anointed               Matt. 21. 23

In Bethany the Lord Jesus found
both FRUIT and FELLOWSHIP     Matt. 21. 17

He found—a Lodging there
                             Matt. 21. 17

He got—a Hearing there
                             Luke 10. 38-42

He had—a Response there
                             John 11. 18-26, 31, 32

He received—a Welcome there
                             John 12. 1-7

He led—His followers there
                             Luke 24. 50

## 629 The King's Son

1 The Murder of the King's Son—
   at Golgotha
                  Matt. 21. 37-39; John 19. 14
2 The Marriage of the King's Son—
   in Heaven
                  Matt. 22. 2; Rev. 19. 7
3 The Manifestation of the King's Son—
   on Earth  Matt. 25. 31; 2 Chron. 23. 11

**630   The Parable of the Marriage Feast**
      Matt. 22. 1-14

Five Classes who received the invitation and
their attitude—

1 Those who *refused* the invitation      v. 3

2 Those who *excused* themselves
   (begged off)                            v. 5

3 Those who *abused* the messengers       v. 6

4 Those who *used well* the opportunity   v. 10

5 Those who *refused* the King's provision                                 v. 11

**631   What Think Ye of Christ?**
      Matt. 22. 42

This is a vital question and demands a
definite answer.

'What think ye of Christ?' is the test to try
both your state and your scheme: You cannot
be right in the rest unless you think rightly of
Him.'

What does the true Christian answer?

1 As to His Person,
   He is the Revealer of
   God the Father          John 1. 1, 2, 18

2 As to His Work,
   He is the Redeemer of
   sinners                 John 1. 29

3 As to His Influence,
   He is the Renewer of
   men                     1 Tim. 1. 12, 13

**632   The Great Tribulation**
      Matt. 24. 21

Our Lord describes it as—

1 UNIQUE IN HISTORY—
  'such as was not—nor ever shall be' v. 21

2 UNEQUALLED IN SEVERITY—
  'except these days should be shortened, there should no flesh be
  saved'                              v. 22

3 UNEXCELLED IN PROVIDENCE—
  'for the elect's sake, these days shall
  be shortened'                       v. 22

It is called—
  The Day of the Lord          Joel 2. 1, 2
  The Tribulation the great one Rev. 7. 14
  The Time of Jacob's trouble  Jer. 30. 7

The Period will have four characteristics—

1 The Cumulation of De-
  ception and Depravity Matt. 24. 5, 12

2 The Culmination of Dis-
  tress                 Matt. 24. 21

3 The Curtailment of its
  Duration              Matt. 24. 22

4 The Consummation of
  the Dispensation      Matt. 24. 29, 30

**633   Behold the Bridegroom!**
      Matt. 25. 1-13

Christ's Second Advent—
  to the True Church, His
  Bride—'Behold the Bridegroom cometh'            Matt. 25. 6
  to the nation of Israel—
  'Behold thy King cometh' Zech. 9. 9, 10
  to the Gentiles and the
  world—'Behold He cometh
  with clouds'             Rev. 1. 7

──────── **634   Parable of the Talents** ────────
Matt. 25. 14-30

A Comparison with the Parable of the pounds in Luke 19. 11-27

| PARABLE IN LUKE 19 | PARABLE IN MATTHEW 25 |
| --- | --- |
| Time—After Jericho, before entry into Jerusalem | After entry into Jerusalem |
| Context—Preceded by a verse on Christ's First Advent | Preceded by a verse on Christ's Second Advent |
| A Nobleman going to receive a kingdom | A man taking a journey into a far country |
| Number of servants given—10 | Three Samples of servants given |
| Currency—Pounds | Currency—Talents |
| (A pound is about £3-10-0 in value) | (A Talent is about £240 in value) |
| Enemies who opposed are punished | No mention of enemies |

The Servants in relation to their Lord—three matters of intimate concern—

1 The Return of their Lord      Matt. 25. 19; Luke 19. 15

2 The Review of their Lives     Matt. 25. 19-28; Luke 19. 15-26

3 The Reward of their Labours   Matt. 25. 20-23; Luke 19. 16-19

The Reward of the Faithful Servants was Threefold—
   Commendation of the Master
   Confidence of their Master
   Commission from the Master   Matt. 25. 21, 23; Luke 19. 17, 19

## 635 The Throne of His Glory
Matt. 25. 31

The King—

'Born King of the Jews'—All the credentials of royalty     Matt. 2. 2

'Behold your King'—Thorns for His crown, a cross for His throne
    John 19. 14

'The King of glory'—Heaven's gates open to receive Him     Ps. 24. 6, 8

'My King'—on the Throne of His glory
    Ps. 2. 6; Matt. 25. 31

During His Millennial reign—

Satan bound for 1000 years     Rev. 20. 2

Wicked dead still in their graves     Rev. 20. 3

Saints and martyrs reign with Him     Rev. 20. 4-6

Characteristics of His Reign—

1 The Resurrection of Life
    Rev. 20. 4, 5

2 The Restraint of sin and death
    Isa. 65. 20; 1 Cor. 15. 26

3 The Rejoicing of the New Creation
    Rom. 8. 19-23; Isa. 51. 11; 65. 19

4 Righteousness established
    Isa. 32. 1; 11. 3-5

5 Reign of peace
    Isa. 32. 17, 18; Ps. 46. 9

6 The Regathering of Israel
    Isa. 43. 5; 54. 6-8; Jer. 29. 14

7 The Restoration of prosperity
    Isa. 60. 16-20; Amos 9. 13

## 636 The Sword of Jehovah
Matt. 26. 31

A sword Preventing access to the Tree of Life Gen. 3. 24

A Sword Preparing a way of access to the Tree of Life Matt. 26. 31

1 The Smiting Sword—'I will smite'     Matt. 26. 31

2 The Slain Shepherd—'the Shepherd'

3 The Scattered Sheep—'the sheep of the flock shall be scattered'

4 The Saviour's Strength—
'After I am risen again, I will go before you'     Matt. 26. 32

## 637 He Went a Little Farther
Matt. 26. 39

1 To Gethsemane's Torment—the Cup of Suffering
(Only 3 of the 12 were near, Peter, James and John)

2 To Gabbatha's Trial—the Crown of Thorns
(Only 2 of the 12 were near, Peter and John, and Peter not so near)

3 To Golgotha's Torture—the Cross of Shame
(One only of the 12 was near, John, and the Lord Jesus went farther than anyone else could go—the Sin-offering)

## 638 A Question that Demands an Answer
'What shall I do then with Jesus—called Christ?' Matt. 27. 22

How was it answered?

*Caiaphas* the high priest—
influenced by Religious considerations     Matt. 26. 65

*Judas Iscariot* the traitor—
influenced by Love of material gain     Matt. 26. 14-16

*Pilate* the Governor—
influenced by Desire for popularity     Matt. 27. 24

The *Penitent Thief*—
influenced by the Sense of his need     Luke 23. 40-43

## 639 Three Classes at the Cross

1 Apathy—'sitting down'     Matt. 27. 36
2 Antipathy—'passing by'     Mark 15. 29
3 Sympathy—'standing by'     John 19. 25
               H.K.D.

## 640 Christ's Five Resurrection 'Alls'

1 ALL HAIL!—
Christ's *Greeting* to His own     Matt. 28. 9

2 ALL POWER is given unto Me—
Christ's *Gift* from His Father     Matt. 28. 18

3 ALL NATIONS—
'make disciples of', 'baptizing them', Christ's *Guidance* for His servants     Matt. 28. 19

4 ALL THINGS—
'whatsoever I have commanded you', Christ's *Gospel* for His messengers     Matt. 28. 19; Mark 16. 15

5 ALL THE DAYS—
'Lo I am with you—even to the consummation of the age'—Christ's
*Guarantee* of His presence     Matt. 28. 20
               T.B. and A.N.

**641 Our Responsibility**
Matt. 28. 19, 20

Command and Promise—

To Abraham—Command—'Get thee out',
and Promise—'I will bless thee'
Gen. 12. 1, 2

To Andrew and Peter—Command—'Follow
Me', and Promise—'I will make you—'
Matt. 4. 19

To the Apostles—Command—'Go', and
Promise 'I am with you all the days'
Matt. 28. 19, 20

The Responsibility to believe and obey is
ours: Our Response to God's Ability.
Five possible attitudes to Responsibility—

1 We may Shirk it, because afraid to undertake it

2 We may Shelve it, because anxious to
defer it

3 We may Shoulder it, because ready to
fulfil it

4 We may Shed it, because tired of bearing it
OR
5 We may Share it, and be wise in distributing it

# MARK

**642 John the Baptist**

A DIVINE TESTIMONY CONCERNING HIM—

1 God the Father's—
'My messenger'   Mal. 3. 1; Mark 1. 2

2 The Spirit's—
'A Voice crying in
the wilderness'   Isa. 40. 3; Matt. 3. 3

3 The Son's—
'A burning and a
shining light'   John 5. 35

B HUMAN TESTIMONY CONCERNING HIM—

1 John's father's—
'Prophet of the Highest'   Luke 1. 76
(A spokesman for God)

2 The Apostle John's—
'a Witness' of the Light'   John 1. 7

3 John's own words—
'a friend of the Bridegroom'   John 3. 29

**645 Three Great Magnets**
Mark. 4. 19

The cares of this world—Distraction
The deceitfulness of riches—Abstraction
The lusts of other things—Attraction
HYP.

**646 Degrees of Faith**

NO FAITH—
in time of *Danger*, yet they were
the Lord's disciples   Mark 4. 40

LITTLE FAITH—
in time of *Doubt*, yet anxious to
venture to Him   Matt. 14. 31

GREAT FAITH—
in spite of *Discouragement*, and
willing to take the outcast's
place   Matt. 15. 28

SO GREAT FAITH—
in spite of *Distance*, and owning
personal unworthiness   Matt. 8. 10

**643 The Saviour and the Sinner**

1 The Pattern Preacher —giving—Pardon for the Sinner   Mark 2. 2, 5
2 The Powerful Physician—giving—Power for the Saint   Mark 2. 10, 11
3 The Pilgrim's Guide — and —Praise for the Saviour   Mark 2. 12, 14
W.J.M.

**644 Christ in the Home**
'It was noised that He was in the house'
Mark 2. 1
His presence in the home means—

1 The Exhibition of Fellowship
Mark 1. 30; 2. 2; Luke 10. 38; 19. 7-9

2 The Exercise of Faith
Mark 2. 5; 2 Tim. 1. 5

3 The Experience of Forgiveness
Mark 2. 5; Acts 10. 43, 44

4 The Exposure of Fault-Finding
Mark 2. 8; 9. 33, 34; Luke 10. 41

5 The Enjoyment of Fulness from Him
Mark 2. 12; John 12. 3

**647 The Satan-bound Woman**

1 Her Condition—
had a haemorrhage for twelve
years   Mark 5. 25

2 Her Concern—
had spent all that she had on
physicians   Mark 5. 26

3 Her Conviction—
'If I may touch but His
clothes, I shall be whole'   Mark. 5. 28

4 Her Cure—
'she was healed of that plague'   Mark 5. 29

5 Her Confession—
the woman came—and told
Him all the truth            Mark 5. 33
6 Her Comfort—
'Go in peace and be whole of
thy plague'                 Mark 5. 34
D. WARD

**648   From Somebody to Nobody to Everybody**
The woman with the issue of blood
Was—A NOBODY in the crowd—
'a certain woman'            Mark 5. 25
1 A NOBODY who *Tried*—many
physicians                  Mark 5. 26
Some of the physicians' sick sinners are trying—
Dr. Reformation, who prescribes Treatment
and Transfusions
Dr. Relaxation, who prescribes Tranquillizers
Dr. Recreation, who prescribes Television,
sports and entertainment
Dr. Religion, who prescribes Tabloids and
Tonics
Result—'Nothing bettered but
rather grew worse.'         Mark 5. 26
2 A NOBODY who *Trusted*—She
said, If I may touch—, I
shall be whole              Mark 5. 28
3 A NOBODY who *Touched*—'she
—touched His garment        Mark 5. 27
She became SOMEBODY who *Testified*—'Somebody hath touched
me'                         Luke 8. 46
'she came—and told Him all' Mark 5. 33
She *told* EVERYBODY in the crowd—
'before all the people'     Luke 8. 47
Why she came, what she did and
how she was healed.

**649   Three Flocks and Their Shepherds**
First Flock mentioned—
Disciples of John Baptist—
had lost their shepherd     Mark 6. 29
Second Flock mentioned—
Apostles of Jesus Christ—
came to their Shepherd      Mark 6. 30
Third Flock mentioned—
The people in the crowd—
were 'as sheep not having a
shepherd'                   Mark 6. 34

**650   'Come Ye Apart'**
Mark 6. 31, 32
1 For Intercession on behalf of others—
the Lord Himself    Matt. 14. 13, 22, 23
2 For Rest from journeys and toil—
His apostles        Mark 6. 31, 32
3 For Visions of His glory—
His intimate disciples
Mark 9. 2
4 For Instruction after failure—
His powerless disciples
Mark 9. 28, 29

**651   The Feeding of the Five Thousand**
Five simple sentences of five short words each,
spoken by the Lord Jesus to His servants—
1 'Give ye them to eat'—
revealing the Sympathy of
their Master                Mark 6. 37
2 'How many loaves have ye?'
the Slenderness of their
Means                       Mark 6. 38
(5 barley loaves, 2 small fishes)
3 'Bring them hither to me',
revealing the Surrender of
their Materials             Matt. 14. 18
4 'Make the men sit down'—
the Supervision of their
Ministry                    John 6. 10
(N.E.B.)
5 'Collect the pieces left over'—
signifying the Satisfaction of
the Multitude               John 6. 12

**652   Remarkable Units**
1 One thing lacking—
to take up the Cross and
follow Christ               Mark 10. 21
2 One thing certain—
Once I was blind, but now
I see                       John 9. 25
3 One thing needful—
to sit at Jesus' feet and hear
His word                    Luke 10. 42
4 One thing predominant—
This one thing I do—I press
toward the mark of the
high calling                Phil. 3. 13, 14
5 One thing remembered—
The Lord is not slack concerning His promise. One
day is with the Lord as
a thousand years.           2 Pet. 3. 8, 9
6 One thing desired—
That I may dwell in the
house of the Lord for
ever                        Ps. 27. 4
7 One thing not discovered—
Not one thing hath failed
of all the good things
which the Lord your God
spake                       Joshua 23. 14
W.R.

**653   Blind Bartimaeus**
1 His Condition—
Blind and Begging           Mark 10. 46
2 His Conviction—
Heard of Jesus, and cried for
mercy                       Mark 10. 47
3 His Call—
Jesus called him            Mark 10. 49
4 His Conversion—
He came to Jesus            Mark 10. 50
5 His Consecration—
He followed Jesus           Mark 10. 52
W.J.M.

113

## 654 The Lord at His Treasury

1 Where Jesus sat—

over against the treasury Mark 12. 41

2 What Jesus saw—

people casting in money,
the rich casting in
much, a poor widow
casting in two mites       Mark 12. 41, 42

Note—The Greek word
—Ballo, I cast—occurs
seven times in this
story. It is translated
'cast' in connection
with 'seed' in Mark
4. 26, 'poured' on
Jesus' body in Matt.
26. 12, 'put to' the ex-
changers in Matt. 25.
27

3 What Jesus said—

This poor widow has
cast in more than they
all—all that she had—
all her living           Mark 12. 43, 44

## 655 The Central Cry on the Cross
Mark 15. 34

Of the Seven Sayings of our Lord on the Cross,
ONLY ONE—the Fourth—is addressed to God
by the name 'God'
ONLY ONE—the Fourth—is a quotation from the
Old Testament prophecies Ps. 22. 1
ONLY ONE—the Fourth—was misunderstood
by the bystanders Matt. 27. 46, 47
This was the Central cry of the seven—
'My God, my God! Why hast Thou for-
saken Me?'

Me —signifies the *Aloneness* of the
Saviour, as Sacrifice and Sin-
Bearer

Thou —addressing His God—signifies the
*Alienation* that was His as 'made
sin'. The answer to the question—
Ps. 22. 3—'Thou art holy'.

Forsaken—signifies His *Abandonment* in the
hour of His agony and anguish:
Rejected by His own people, left
by His own disciples, and forsaken by His God.

Why? —signifies the *Agony* He was enduring
while His friends and His God
were silent

---

# LUKE

## 656 Individual 'Fear Nots' in Luke

1 The 'Fear not' of Assurance to
Zacharias              Luke 1. 13

2 The 'Fear not' of Approval to
Mary                   Luke 1. 30

3 The 'Fear not' of Announcement to the shepherds  Luke 2. 10

4 The 'Fear not' of Affirmation
to Peter               Luke 5. 10

5 The 'Fear not' of Alleviation
to Jairus              Luke 8. 50

## 657 'Salvation' Hymns in Luke

1 Mary's 'Magnificat'—
a Personal Salvation—'my
Saviour'               Luke 1. 46-58

2 Hymn of Zacharias—
a National Salvation—'an
horn of salvation'     Luke 1. 67-79

3 Angelic Chant—
Salvation for the world—a
Saviour—Christ the Lord Luke 2. 10-12

4 Simeon's Paean of praise—
Salvation for Jew and
Gentile—'Thy salvation' Luke 2. 29-32

## 658 Waiting for His Coming

The 'pious ones', the God-fearing of Mal.
3. 16, 17, called the 'Chasidim', were eagerly
waiting to welcome the Messiah. The Greek
word—Prosdechomai—which means 'I wait in
order to welcome', is used of—

1 Simeon (meaning 'Hearing'—
an Attitude)
Waiting for a Prophet, 'the
consolation of Israel'  Luke 2. 25

2 Anna (meaning 'Gracious'—
an Attribute)
Waiting for a Priest, 'redemption in Jerusalem'      Luke 2. 38

3 Joseph of Arimathaea (meaning 'Adding'—an Activity)
Waiting for a King, 'the kingdom of God'             Luke 23. 51

SIMEON was 'just and devout',
living righteously and godly   Titus 2. 12

ANNA was 'serving God with fast-
ings and prayers, night and day',
living soberly and godly       Titus 2. 12

JOSEPH was 'a good man and a
just', living soberly and righteously'                        Titus 2. 12

All were looking for (same Greek word as in
Titus 2. 13) the Hope of Israel.

## 659  The Widows of Luke's Gospel

1 A Widow who served and worshipped    Luke 2. 37

2 A Widow who was honoured and provided for    Luke 4. 26

3 A Widow who sorrowed but was comforted    Luke 7. 12

4 A Widow who prayed and was answered    Luke 18. 3

5 A Widow who was commended and extolled    Luke 21. 3

W.J.M.

## 660  Two Couples who Lost Jesus

1 Mary His mother and Joseph
Luke 2. 40-52
(a) were unconcerned at first and concerned later    Luke 2. 43, 44
(b) were glad when they ought to have been sad    Luke 2. 44
(c) thought Jesus was in their company when He was not  Luke 2. 44
(d) went back to Jerusalem with sad hearts till they found Him
Luke 2. 45

2 The two disciples going to Emmaus
Luke 24. 13-24
(probably Cleophas and his wife)—one home, one heart    Luke 24. 30, 32
(a) were unbelieving until they recognized Him    Luke 24. 25, 31, 32
(b) were sad when they ought to have been glad    Luke 24. 17
(c) thought Jesus was not in their company when He was    Luke 24. 18
(d) went back to Jerusalem with glad hearts to tell others    Luke 24. 33

## 661  Baseless Suppositions

1 'Supposing Him to be in the company'—the Unconcerned Mind    Luke 2. 44

2 'Supposing Him to be the gardener'—the Unenlightened Eye    John 20. 15

3 'They—supposed that they had seen a spirit'—the Unbelieving Heart    Luke 24. 37; Mark 16. 14

## 662  God's Business Men in the World

Busy in God's affairs, and minding their own business (1 Thess. 4. 11) but not busybodies in other people's affairs (2 Thess. 3. 11).

1 JESUS—'About my *Father's* business' Luke 2. 49

2 DANIEL—*Faultless* and *Faithful* in business (Had always time for God's business) Dan. 6. 4

3 CHRISTIANS—Not slothful but *fervent* in business    Rom. 12. 11; Eccl. 9. 10; Col. 3. 17, 23

## 663  Jesus the Man of Prayer

1 At Baptism while praying, the Holy Ghost came upon Him    Luke 3. 21, 22

2 After He had healed many sick    Mark 1. 35

3 When His fame spread and multitudes came to hear    Luke 5. 16

4 Before appointing His disciples    Luke 6. 12

5 When He had fed 5000    Mark 6. 46

6 Before telling His disciples He must suffer and be slain    Luke 9. 18

7 When He was transfigured Luke 9. 28

8 Before raising Lazarus from the dead    John 11. 41

9 Before teaching His disciples to pray    Luke 11. 1

10 When His soul was troubled    John 12. 27

11 When about to leave His disciples    John 17

12 In the Garden of Gethsemane    Matt. 26. 36

13 On the Cross, for His persecutors    Luke 23. 34

14 On the Cross, when resigning His breath    Luke 23. 46

## 664  Followers and Fishers

1 A NIGHT OF FAILURE— toiled all the night, taken nothing    Luke 5. 5

2 A MORNING OF FAITH— 'at Thy Word I will let down the net'    Luke 5. 5

3 A DAY OF FULNESS— a great multitude of fishes    Luke 5. 6

4 A LIFETIME OF FELLOWSHIP— their partners—come and help them    Luke 5. 7

5 A MAXIM FOR FISHERS OF MEN— 'Launch out' and 'Let down'    Luke 5. 4

## 665  Peter and His Lord

1 The Sinner's Confession— 'I am a sinful man, O Lord' Luke 5. 8

2 The Saviour's Consolation— 'Fear not'    Luke 5. 10

3 The Servant's Commission— 'thou shalt catch men'    Luke 5. 10

**666 Forgiveness**

'He said unto her, Thy sins are forgiven'
Luke 7. 48

Divine Forgiveness is—

1 Full—Who forgiveth *all* thine
  iniquities                     Ps. 103. 3

2 Free—when they had *nothing
  to pay*                        Luke 7. 42

3 Frank—he *frankly* forgave
  them                          Luke 7. 42

4 Final—their sins and iniquities
  will I remember no more    Heb. 10. 17

**667 Salvation**

'Thy faith hath saved thee'    Luke 7. 50
'Thy faith hath made thee whole' Luke 8. 48
In both statements the words in Greek are
exactly the same.

Four Occurrences of the same Verb, meaning
'SAVE'—

1 A Sinsick woman received
  Spiritual Health             Luke 7. 50

2 A Demoniac man received
  Mental Health              Luke 8. 35, 36

3 A Diseased woman received
  Physical Health             Luke 8. 48

4 A Dead girl received Life
  from the dead               Luke 8. 50

**668 'The Seed is the Word of God'**
  Luke 8. 11

What the Bible does for spiritual life—

1 We are born of the Word    1 Pet. 1. 23

2 We grow by the Word       1 Pet. 2. 2

3 We are cleansed by the Word John 15. 3

4 We are sanctified by the
  Word                        John 17. 17

5 We are protected by the
  Word                        Eph. 6. 17

6 We are edified by the Word Acts 20. 32

7 We are illuminated by the
  Word                        Ps. 119. 105

8 We are converted by the
  Word                        Ps. 19. 11

9 We are satisfied by the Word Ps. 119. 103
                    DR. GRIFFITH THOMAS

**669 The Perfection and Power of the Lord
Jesus**
  Luke 8

1 His Power in Discourse—
  nine references to hearing in   vs. 4-21

2 His Power over the Devil—
  He stilled the storm           vs. 22-25

3 His Power over Demons—
  a legion of demons cast out    vs. 26-40

4 His Power over Disease—
  a sick woman healed            vs. 41-48

5 His Power over Death—
  the daughter of Jairus
  restored to life               vs. 49-56

**670 Life from the Son of God**

Three dead people to whom he restored life

1 Daughter of Jairus, a
  girl of twelve—an only
  daughter, newly dead,
  in her home                   Luke 8. 53-55

2 Son of a widow of Nain,
  a young man—an only
  son, on way to burial,
  in the street                 Luke 7. 11-15

3 Lazarus—age not known
  —an only brother, four
  days in the grave, in the
  cemetery                      John 11. 38-44

THREE FACTS COMMON TO ALL THREE INCIDENTS—

1 Only One Person was able
  to give life—Jesus, the
  Son of God                    John 5. 25, 26

2 Only one way for the dead
  to receive life—hearing
  His voice                     John 5. 25

3 All three gave evidence of
  life received—

Food for the girl of twelve
  —'give her meat'             Luke 8. 55

Fellowship for the young
  man—delivered to his
  mother                        Luke 7. 15

Freedom for Lazarus—
  'loose him and let him
  go'                           John 11. 44

**671 Failures of Christ's Disciples**
  Luke 9

| | | | |
|---|---|---|---|
| 1 The Inconsiderate 12 | —'send the multitude away' | —Lack of Sympathy | v. 12 |
| 2 The Impotent 9 | —they could not | —Lack of Power | v. 40 |
| 3 The Intimate 3 | —heavy with sleep | —Lack of Vigilance | v. 32 |
| 4 The Impatient 2 (James and John) | —'command fire'—'consume them' | —Lack of Love | v. 54 |
| 5 Impetuous Peter | —not knowing what he said | —Lack of Discretion | v. 33 |
| 6 Intolerant John | —He followeth not with us | —Lack of Tolerance | v. 49 |
| 7 The Important 12 | —which should be the greatest | —Lack of Humility | v. 46 |

**672 The Transfiguration of Jesus**

Four speakers on the Mount—

1 The Lord Jesus—
to His Father—
He prayed      Luke 9. 29

2 Moses and Elias—
to the Lord Jesus—
'spoke of His decease'    Luke 9. 31

3 Peter—
to Jesus—
'let us make three taber-
nacles'      Luke 9. 33

4 God the Father—
to the disciples—
'This is my Beloved Son:
hear Him'      Luke 9. 35

The voice came out of the cloud, the Shechinah glory

from the excellent glory    2 Pet. 1. 17
from heaven      2 Pet. 1. 18

The words were a rebuke to Peter who recalled and recorded them (2 Pet. 1. 16-18) They seemed to say—'Why three tabernacles? The kingdom on earth and the Feast of booths have not yet come.' The TRUE TABERNACLE (John 1. 14 where the Greek word 'dwelt' is the verb 'tabernacled') and the KING are in your midst.'

**673 Candidates for Discipleship**

1 The Whole-hearted Scribe (Matt. 8. 19)
Jesus reminded him of the Cost of Discipleship    Luke 9. 57, 58

2 The Cold-hearted Adherent (Matt. 8. 21)
Jesus reminded him of the Claims of Discipleship    Luke 9. 59, 60

3 The Half-hearted Follower
Jesus reminded him of the Conditions of Discipleship    Luke 9. 61, 62

Looking back—looking to the things behind (Greek)      John 6. 66
Contrast Paul—forgetting the things behind      Phil. 3. 14

THE CONDITIONS ARE—

Full Consecration to Christ
     Matt. 16. 24, 25
Continuance in His word
     John 8. 31
Courage to count the cost
     Luke 14. 26, 27, 33

**674 Attitudes of Men to Fellow-Men**

1 The Robber Attitude—
'What's mine's mine and what's thine's mine if I can get it'    Luke 10. 30

2 The Legal Attitude—
'What's mine's mine and what's thine's thine if you can keep it'    Luke 10. 31, 32

3 The Christ-like Attitude—
'What's thine's thine and what's mine's thine if you need it'    Luke 10. 33, 37

**675 The Good Samaritan—Example of Christian Service**

'Go thou and do likewise' Luke 10. 37

1 He went to him—BENDING over him
Luke 10. 34

2 He bound up his wounds—MENDING him (Pouring in oil and wine)
Luke 10. 34; Gal. 6. 1

3 He took care of him—TENDING him
Luke 10. 34; 1 Tim. 3. 5

4 He took two pence and gave them to the host—SPENDING for him
Luke 10. 35; 2 Cor. 12. 15

5 He said, 'I will repay thee'—LENDING to the Lord    Luke 10. 35

**676 The Gospel in the Story of the Good Samaritan**

The man that fell among thieves is a picture of the sinner

1 His Ruin—'went down'
—his Direction; 'to Jericho'—his Destination (Place of a curse);
stripped, wounded,
half-dead—his Distress Luke 10. 30

2 His Religion—The priest
and Levite—repre-
sentatives of the Law,
passed by but did
nothing    Luke 10. 31, 32

3 The Redeemer—'a cer-
tain Samaritan', des-
pised, one whom the
Jewish lawyer refused
to name    Luke 10. 33

4 The Remedy—oil and
wine: wine to cleanse
—conviction; oil to
cure—conversion    Luke 10. 34

5 His Recovery—Taken care
of and nursed back to
health    Luke 10. 34

**677 At the Feet of Jesus**

Mary of Bethany, sister of Martha and Lazarus—

1 Waiting at the feet of the
Prophet—to hear His
word    Luke 10. 39

2 Weeping at the feet of the
Priest—to receive His sympathy    John 11. 32

3 Worshipping at the feet of
Jesus the King—to anoint
Him against the day of His
burial    John 12. 3

## 678 The Rich Farmer's Four Big Mistakes

1 In planning for himself, he forgot his neighbour — Luke 12. 17

2 In reckoning his goods, he forgot the Giver — Luke 12. 18

3 In providing for his body, he forgot his soul — Luke 12. 19
(He planned to enjoy his treasure, leisure and pleasure)

4 In counting on time (many years) he forgot eternity — Luke 12. 20

## 679 'Salvation' Questions in Luke's Writings

1 'Are there few that be saved?—asked out of *Idle Curiosity* — Luke 13. 23
Our Lord's two answers—
See that you enter in yourself — Luke 13. 24
Many from every part will be saved — Luke 13. 28, 29

2 'Who then can be saved?' asked out of *Incredulous Concern* — Luke 18. 26
Our Lord's two answers—
Impossible with men but not with God — Luke 18. 27
Even the rich are being saved — Luke 19. 9, 10

3 'What must I do to be saved?' asked out of *Intense Conviction* — Acts 16. 30
Only one answer—
'Believe on the Lord Jesus Christ and thou shalt be saved.' Acts 16. 31

## 680 Parable of the Great Supper

'A certain man made a great supper and bade many'—Why Great?

1 Because of the *Great Preparation* and what it Involved — Luke 14. 16
the Costliness it entailed
the Carefulness it displayed
the Completeness it revealed — Luke 14. 17

2 Because of the *Gracious Invitation* and whom it Includes Luke 14. 17, 21, 23
those originally invited
the poor, maimed, halt and blind in the streets of the city
the homeless in the highways and hedges

3 Because of the *Glad Proclamation* and what it Intimates — Luke 14. 22
'Yet there is room'

4 Because of the *Grave Declaration* and what it Implies — Luke 14. 24
Those who reject the invitation will not enjoy the provision.

## 681 Excuses a Man Makes for not Accepting God's Invitation

1 I have bought a piece of land— his Land and its Claims Luke 14. 18

2 I have bought five yoke of oxen— his Labour and its Commitments — Luke 14. 19

3 I have married a wife— his Lady and her Company Luke 14. 20

## 682 Seven Proofs of Discipleship

Leaving kindred — Luke 14. 26
Hating his own life — Luke 14. 26
Bearing the cross — Luke 14. 27
Forsaking possessions — Luke 14. 33
Continuing in Christ's Word — John 8. 31
Loving one another — John 13. 35
Bearing fruit for God — John 15. 8

Note—Wives and husbands are not included among the kindred to be left, for 'God hath joined together' husband and wife.

## 683 The Lost Sheep
Luke 15. 1-7

Love's Loss — —If he lose one
Love's activity — —goeth after it
Love's persistency — —till he find it
Love's provision — —layeth it on his shoulders
Love's joy — —rejoicing
Love's consummation— —when he bringeth it home
Love's fellowship — —He calleth together friends and neighbours

T.B.

## 684 A Threefold Parable
Luke 15

Christ's Attitude to sinners—
'receiveth sinners and eateth with them'

Sinner's Attitude to Christ—
'drew near—to hear Him'

The Lord's Parable—

1 A LOST SHEEP— out of the Flock—1% Loss—Lost in a place of Danger

2 A LOST SILVER COIN— out of the Funds—10% Loss—Lost in a place of Darkness

3 A LOST SON— out of the Family—50% Loss—Lost in a place of Distance

Common Features—
In each there were 2 Classes, one needing reclaiming and the other appearing not to need it.

In each there was—
1 a Loser
2 something lost
3 sorrow over the loss
4 suffering till found
5 satisfaction over the recovery

## 685 The Prodigal Son
Luke 15. 11-32

Five Chapters in the History of the younger son—

1 He was Rebellious—
kicking over the traces    vs. 12-16

2 He was Repentant—
'I will arise and go to my father'    vs. 17, 18

3 He was Returning—
He arose and came to his father    v. 20

4 He was Reconciled—
His father ran—and kissed him    v. 20

5 He was Rejoicing—
They began to be merry    v. 24

## 686 Simple Setting of the Prodigal Son
Luke 15. 11-32

1 The Prodigal's Consideration of his position and prospects

2 The Prodigal's Conviction of his sin

3 The Prodigal's Contrition for his wickedness

4 The Prodigal's Confession of his wrongdoing and ruin

5 The Prodigal's Conversion through his Father's forgiving mercy
       C.R.H.

## 689 A Message Never Delivered, Yet Recorded
Luke 16. 28

1 The Person who sent it—
a rich man    Luke 16. 22

2 The Place from which it was sent—hell    Luke 16. 23

3 The Punishment that prompted it—I am tormented    Luke 16. 24

4 The Prospect that necessitated it—a great gulf fixed    Luke 16. 26

5 The Petition contained in it—'send to my father's house'    Luke 16. 27

6 The People for whom it was intended—five brothers    Luke 16. 28

7 The Purpose in recording it—that men may repent    Acts 17. 30, 31

The Message was —

one of Concern—'Testify unto them'

one of Caution—'lest they also come into this place'

one of Confession—'If one went from the dead, they would repent.'

## 687 The Elder Brother
Luke 15. 25-32

| HIS ARGUMENT | HIS FATHER'S ANSWER | HIS LOSS |
|---|---|---|
| These many years do I serve thee | Son | Privilege of sonship despised |
| Neither transgressed I at any time | Thou art ever with me | Blessing of Fellowship unclaimed |
| Thou never gavest me a kid | All that I have is thine | Riches of Heirship ignored |

## 688 Three Pairs of Men in Luke

Two men in Life—

one justified and the other condemned    Luke 18. 10-14

Two men in Death—

one repentant, and the other railing    Luke 23. 39-43

Two men in Eternity—

one comforted, the other tormented    Luke 16. 19-26

## 690 Some Things to Remember

1 Jesus said, 'Remember Lot's wife'—Solemn Reflection    Luke 17. 32

2 The preacher said, 'Remember thy Creator'—Timely Reminder    Eccles. 12. 1

3 The Lord Jesus said, 'Remember Me'—Loving Request    Luke 22. 19, 20

4 Abraham said, 'Son, remember'—Eternal Regret    Luke 16. 25

5 The penitent thief said, 'Lord, remember me'—Genuine Repentance    Luke 23. 42

**Luke**

**691 Prayer**

Need for prayer—Men ought
(owe it) — Luke 18. 1

Time for prayer—always — Luke 18. 1

Place for prayer—everywhere — 1 Tim. 2. 8

Subjects for prayer—all men — 1 Tim. 2. 1

D.T.B.

**692 Desires Granted**

1 Sight for the blind—
a Final Opportunity — Luke 18. 41

2 Springs for the barren
land—a Favourable
Occasion — Judges 1. 12-15

3 Spirit of power for the
faithful servant—a
Farewell Offer — 2 Kings 2. 9

4 Spirit of wisdom for
the young ruler—
Future Obligations — 2 Chron. 1. 7-10

**693 Four Rich Men**

One was Saved—
Zacchaeus the tax-gatherer — Luke 19. 2, 6, 9

One in life—

a religious leader—went
away sorrowful, rejected
the Word — Luke 18. 23

One in death—

a prosperous farmer—cut
off, forgetting God — Luke 12. 16, 23

One in eternity—

Dives—lifted up his eyes in
hell — Luke 16. 19

**694 A Gospel Study of Zacchaeus**

1 A rich man—
unsatisfied — Luke 19. 2

2 An anxious man—
hindered — Luke 19. 3

3 An earnest man—
in a hurry — Luke 19. 4

4 An obedient man—
brought down — Luke 19. 6

5 A genuine convert—
received Jesus — Luke 19. 6

6 A happy man—
joyful in the Lord — Luke 19. 6

7 A real man—
owning Jesus as Lord — Luke 19. 8

W.J.M.

**695 Until He Come**

1 We are occupied in service
for the Lord — Luke 19. 13

2 We show forth the Lord's
death — 1 Cor. 11. 26

3 We suffer with long patience — James 5. 7, 8

4 We are to hold fast what
we have — Rev. 2. 25

5 We should live honestly
before unbelievers — 1 Thess. 4. 12

**696 Tears Shed by Different Persons**

1 The Saviour's Tears
Luke 19. 41; John 11. 35

2 The penitent sinner's Tears
Luke 7. 38-44

3 The saint's Tears
John 20. 11; Acts 20. 37

4 The servant's Tears
Acts 20. 19-31; Phil. 3. 18

5 The backslider's Tears — Luke 22. 62

6 The lost sinner's Tears — Matt. 8. 12; 22. 13

W.J.M.

**697 The Gentile Nations**

1 Times of the Gentiles—
Political—Dominion beginning with the
Babylonian Empire — Luke 21. 24

2 Riches of the Gentiles—
Spiritual—Gospel blessing beginning
with household of Cornelius — Rom. 11. 12

3 Fulness of the Gentiles—
Universal—Return of Christ as the
Deliverer—Israel saved — Rom. 11. 25

**698 The Guest-Chamber**
Luke 22. 11

'Where is the guest-chamber?' The same
Greek word is translated 'inn' in Luke 2. 7.
There was no room in that guestroom for Jesus
at His birth: there was room for Him and His
apostles in another guestroom just before the
Cross.

Where was it?
In the city of Jerusalem — Luke 22. 10

How was it reached?
By the path of humility and
purification — Luke 22. 10

How is it described?
A large upper room furnished — Luke 22. 12

For what purpose?
For the Lord to eat the Passover
with His disciples — Luke 22. 11

THE LORD JESUS WAS—
the Perfect Host — Luke 22. 11
the Passover Lamb — Luke 22. 11
the Humble Servant — John 13. 5

He washed their feet, trained their memories,
comforted their hearts and instructed their
minds in that Upper room

## 699 The Lord in Gethsemane
Luke 22. 39-44

1 The Retreat of the Master—
Judas knew the place    John 18. 2

2 The Regularity of His visits—
went as He was wont    Luke 22. 39

3 The Reason for this visit—
He offered up prayers    Heb. 5. 7

4 The Reverence of His attitude—
He kneeled down and
prayed    Luke 22. 41

5 The Resignation of His spirit—
'not My will but Thine'    Luke 22. 42

6 The Reward of His prayer—
'there appeared an angel—
strengthening Him    Luke 22. 43

7 The Rigour of His sufferings—
His sweat was as it were
great drops of blood    Luke 22. 44

## 700 Divine Openings in Luke 24

1 The Opened Sepulchre—
to let the women look in    v. 3

2 The Opened Eyes—
to recognize the Lord Jesus    vs. 16, 31

3 The Opened Scriptures—
to expound the things concerning Himself    vs. 27, 32

4 The Opened Understanding—
to enable them to understand
the truth concerning Jesus    v. 45

5 The Opened Heaven—
to receive the Lord Jesus    v. 51

## 701 He is Risen
Luke 24. 6

The Resurrection of the Lord Jesus Christ from the dead is confirmed

1 By the Simplicity of the Narratives

2 By the Sincerity of the Witnesses (John 20. 9)

3 By the Stability of the Scriptures

4 By the Supersedence of the Sabbath, for He rose on the first day of the week

## 702 Four Heart Experiences in Luke 24

1 The Sad heart—
failing to understand the
Lord's purpose    v. 17

2 The Slow heart—
failing to believe the witnesses
to the Lord's resurrection    v. 25

3 The Burning heart—
seeing Christ revealed in the
Scriptures    v. 32

4 The Glad heart—
exulting in the Lord's exaltation and priestly ministry for
His saints    vs. 52, 53

## 703 The Burning Heart
Luke 24. 29-32

The two disciples on the way to Emmaus were probably Mr. and Mrs. Cleopas. They lived together and together invited the Lord to stay in their home. HEART (verse 32) is a singular noun with a plural possessive pronoun. The meal was probably an Act of Hospitality (entertaining strangers), also an Expression of Mourning for the Crucified Christ (Jer. 16. 7 Margin), and became a Supper of Remembrance as they recognized Jesus. Their heart then burned with the flame of devotion. We need the Burning Heart, set aflame by

1 The Fire of Meditation Ps. 39. 3

2 The Fire of Adoration Ps. 45. 1, (Margin) 2

3 The Fire of Proclamation    Jer. 20. 9

## 704 Led Out and Brought In

1 Separation to God's Anointed Leader—He
led them out    Luke 24. 50

2 Association with God's Appointed Heirs—as
far as Bethany    Luke 24. 50

3 Contemplation of God's Ascending Son—they
looked steadfastly toward Heaven    Acts 1. 10

4 Adoration by God's Assembled priests—they
were continually in the
temple, praising    Luke 24. 52, 53

# JOHN

## 705 Christ in John 1

| | | |
|---|---|---|
| 1 | Christ the Word | John 1. 1 |
| 2 | Christ the Light | John 1. 8 |
| 3 | Christ the Lamb of God | John 1. 29, 36 |
| 4 | Christ the Son of God | John 1. 34, 49 |
| 5 | Christ the Anointed (Messias) | John 1. 41 |
| 6 | Christ the King of Israel | John 1. 49 |
| 7 | Christ the Son of man | John 1. 51 |

## 706 The Word

| | | |
|---|---|---|
| 1 | His Eternity—in the beginning | John 1. 1 |
| 2 | His Equality—was with God | John 1. 1 |
| 3 | His Deity—was God | John 1. 1 |
| 4 | His Humanity—was made flesh | John 1. 14 |
| 5 | His Testimony—' told the Father out' (Margin) | John 1. 18 |

H.K.D.

## 707 In Him was Life

| | | |
|---|---|---|
| 1 | Life manifested in Him | John 1. 1 |
| 2 | Life obtained from Him | John 3. 16 |
| 3 | Life possessed by trusting Him | John 4. 14 |
| 4 | Life sustained by Him | John 6. 35 |
| 5 | Life ministered through the Spirit | John 7. 38 |
| 6 | Life abounding from Him | John 10. 10 |
| 7 | Life and Resurrection through Him | John 11. 24, 25 |

## 708 Christ, The True One

| | | |
|---|---|---|
| 1 | The True Light | John 1. 9 |
| 2 | The True Bread | John 6. 32 |
| 3 | The True Vine | John 15. 1 |
| 4 | The True God | 1 John 5. 20 |
| 5 | The True Witness | Rev. 3. 14 |
| 6 | Faithful and True | Rev. 15. 3 |

'WE KNOW THAT THOU ART TRUE'

J.A.

## 709 John's Four Sights

And we beheld His glory John 1. 14

| | | |
|---|---|---|
| 1 | Revealed Glory at His Transfiguration | Mark 9. 2 |
| 2 | Redemption Glory at His Crucifixion | John 19. 26 |
| 3 | Risen Glory at His Resurrection | John 20. 20 |
| 4 | Returning Glory at His Revelation | Rev. 19. 11, 12 |

A.C.B.

## 710 The Tabernacle in John's Gospel

The Word became flesh and tabernacled among us. John 1. 14; Heb. 8. 2

The Court Chs. 1-13—Jesus as He walked
John 1. 36

The Wall of Fine Linen—Full of grace and truth John 1. 14

The Victim at the Altar of brass—Behold the Lamb of God John 1. 29

The Laver of brass—He began to wash the disciples' feet John 13. 5

The Holy Place Chs. 14-16—By me—enter
John 10. 9

The Table of Shewbread—'I am the Bread of life' John 6. 35

The Lampstand—lighted—'I am the Light of the world' John 9. 5

The Golden Altar of incense—Prayer to the Father in John 12. 27, 28

The Rent Veil—'It is finished'
John 19. 30

The Great High Priest in the Holiest of all—
John 17

The Shechinah Glory—Christ in Resurrection
John 20. 20; 21. 7

The Mercy-Seat—'He shewed them His hands and His side' John 20. 20; Rom. 3. 26

## 711 'Behold the Lamb of God'
John 1. 29

| | | |
|---|---|---|
| 1 | The Lamb of God *prophesied* | Gen. 22. 8 |
| 2 | The Lamb of God *typified* | Exod. 12. 5, 6 |
| 3 | The Lamb of God *identified* | John 1. 29 |
| 4 | The Lamb of God *crucified* | Isa. 53. 7 |
| 5 | The Lamb of God *glorified* | Rev. 5. 6 |
| 6 | The Lamb of God *magnified* | Rev. 5. 12 |
| 7 | The Lamb of God *satisfied* | Rev. 19. 7; 21. 9 |

## 712 Christ is the Answer

'We have found the Messias' John 1. 41; 'we have found Him' John 1. 45

He is the answer to the *Sin* Question—the Lamb of God John 1. 29

He is the answer to the *Self* Question—the Messias (God's anointed Ruler)
John 1. 41

He is the answer to the *Social* Question—Jesus of Nazareth (the sinner's friend)
John 1. 45; 9. 35-38

## 713 Nathaniel's Conversion

| | |
|---|---|
| 1 His Arrest | John 1. 45 |
| 2 His Doubt | John 1. 46 |
| 3 His Character | John 1. 47 |
| 4 His Question | John 1. 48 |
| 5 His Confession | John 1. 49 |
| 6 His Faith | John 1. 50 |
| 7 His Prospect | John 1. 51 |

JS. FS.

## 714 Four Meals in John's Gospel

| | |
|---|---|
| 1 The *Marriage Feast* in Ch. 2—the Lord Jesus a Guest | John 2. 2 |
| 2 The *Thanksgiving Supper* in Ch. 12—the Lord Jesus the Guest of honour | John 12. 2 |
| 3 The *Passover Feast* in Ch. 13—the Lord Jesus the Fulfilment | John 13. 1 |
| 4 The *Morning Breakfast* in Ch. 21—the Lord Jesus the Host | John 21. 12, 13 |

## 715 Not Yet (Greek—Oupo)

| | |
|---|---|
| 1 Mine hour is NOT YET come | John 2. 4 |
| 2 Jesus was NOT YET come to them | John 11. 30 |
| 3 The Holy Ghost was NOT YET given | John 7. 39 |
| 4 We see NOT YET all things put under Him | Heb. 2. 8 |
| 5 It doth NOT YET appear what we shall be | 1 John 3. 2 |

## 716 Water Made Wine

| | |
|---|---|
| 1 The Vessels *employed*— Clean waterpots | John 2. 6; 2 Tim. 2. 21 |
| Filled waterpots | John 2. 7 |
| Used waterpots | John 2. 8 |
| 2 The Change *effected*— by the word of the Lord | John 2. 5 |
| by the power of the Lord | John 2. 9 |
| for the glory of the Lord | John 2. 11 |
| 3 The Provision *enjoyed*— *Proved* good by tasting | John 2. 9 |
| *Pronounced* good by the host | John 2. 10 |
| *Productive* of faith in the Lord Jesus | John 2. 11 |

## 717 Personal Soul-Winning

John 3. 1, 2; 4. 7

The Lord Jesus the Great Example, winning souls one by one

| JOHN 3 | JOHN 4 |
|---|---|
| A man | A woman |
| Respected and Religious | Sinful and Shunned |
| A Jew | A Samaritaness |
| Came at midnight to Jesus | Met Jesus at midday |
| Introduced the conversation | Jesus introduced the conversation |
| Became for a time a secret disciple | Became immediately a public witness |

## 718 The New Birth

AS TAUGHT BY A 'TEACHER SENT FROM GOD'

Jesus was *acknowledged* to be such by a Jewish leader

The fact was *attested* by His great miracles

The truth was *affirmed* by Jesus Himself, the Greatest of all teachers

| | |
|---|---|
| 1 The Necessity of the New Birth— 'ye must be born again' | John 3. 7 |
| 2 The Nature of the New Birth— a New experience—'again' a New creation—anew a New origin—from above | |
| 3 The Nobility of the New Birth— born of God | John 1. 12, 13 |
| born of the Spirit | John 3. 8 |
| born by the Word of God | 1 Pet. 1. 23 |

Those born again ('bairns' of God)

| | |
|---|---|
| Are the Objects of the *Father's* love | 1 John 3. 1 |
| Display the *Son's* likeness | 1 John 3. 2 |
| Are subject to the *Spirit's* leading | Rom. 8. 14 |

## 719 A Message from Heaven

John 3. 16

1 Heaven's Brightest Beam— 'For God so loved the world'

2 Earth's Greatest Theme— 'that He gave His only-begotten Son'

3 God's Simplest Scheme— 'that whosoever believeth in Him should not perish'

4 Life's Purest Stream— 'but have everlasting life.'

**John**

**720 Ten Points of Salvation in One Precious Verse**
John 3. 16

1 The SOURCE of Salvation—
For *God*

2 The SUPERLATIVENESS of Salvation—
*So* loved

3 The SUBJECTS of Salvation—
the *world*

4 The SPONTANEITY of Salvation—
that He *gave*

5 The SECURER of Salvation—
His only-begotten *Son*

6 The SCOPE of Salvation—
that *whosoever*

7 The SIMPLICITY of Salvation—
*believeth* in Him

8 The SOLACE of Salvation—
should *not perish*

9 The SURENESS of Salvation—
but *have*

10 The STABILITY of Salvation—
*everlasting* life

AUTHOR UNKNOWN

**721 The Stream of Eternal Bliss**
John 3. 16

1 The Fountain Head—
God so loved the world

2 The Channel Stream—
He gave His only-begotten Son

3 The Receptacle filled—
whosoever believeth in Him

4 The Life-giving Draught—
should have everlasting life.

**722 God Loves the Whole World**
John 3. 16

1 God's Attitude towards the World—
Loves the world

2 God's Attitude towards us—
Hates sin

3 God's Attitude towards His Son—
Gave His only-begotten Son, the object of God's delight, given for the world, for you and me

4 God's Attitude towards Believers—
Have everlasting life

5 God's Attitude towards Unbelievers—
Perish

DR. TORREY

**723 The Woman of Samaria**

1 Conversation commenced—
'give me to drink' John 4. 7

2 Confidence gained—
'Sir, give me this water' John 4. 15

3 Conscience reached—
'he whom thou now hast is not thy husband' John 4. 18, 19

4 Conversion experienced—
'I know that Messias cometh 'I that speak unto thee am He' John 4 .25, 26

5 Change manifested—
'Come, see a man—Is not this the Christ?' John 4. 29
W.J.M.

**724 Communicated by the Spirit of God**

1 The Fountain of life springing up John 4. 14

2 The Bread of life coming down John 6. 35

3 The Rivers of life flowing out John 7. 38

4 The Light of life shining in John 8. 12
H. BELL

**725 Worship**

Worship is the Bowing of the soul before God in wondering and adoring contemplation.

1 The Act of Worship—
9 times the verb, once the noun—from 'Proskuneo', I kiss the hand toward John 4. 20-24

2 The Object of Worship—
the Father John 4. 21, 23

3 The Place of Worship—
'neither in Jerusalem' nor in this mountain (Gerizim) John 4. 21

4 The Offerers of Worship—
'the true worshippers' whom the Father seeks John 4. 23

5 The Manner of Worship—
in spirit and in truth John 4. 23

**726 Prerequisites to Worship**

Before we can worship there must be—

1 RELATIONSHIP—
The Father seeketh such John 4. 23

2 REVELATION—
We know what we worship John 4. 22

3 RECOGNITION—
God is a Spirit John 4. 24

4 REDEMPTION—
Salvation is of the Jews John 4. 22
H. BELL

124

**727 Power for the Impotent**

'Wilt thou be made whole?' John 5. 6

Consider

1 WHERE THE IMPOTENT MAN WAS—

In Jerusalem, the holy city
and religious centre    John 5. 2

By the Sheep Gate, the place
of sacrifices    John 5. 2

By the Bathing Pool of Beth-
esda, place of washing    John 5. 2
and there

At Festival time, a specially
appointed time of worship    John 5. 1

2 IN WHAT STATE THE IMPOTENT MAN WAS—

*Helpless*, because impotent    John 5. 3

*Harmless*, because he lay
there unable to harm any-
one    John 5. 3, 6

*Hapless*, because he had nobody who could help him    John 5. 7

*Hopeless*, because each time
someone else got in before
him    John 5. 7

3 WHAT THE IMPOTENT MAN DID—

*Waited*—for the moving of
the water    John 5. 3

*Willed*—Are you willing to be
made whole?    John 5. 6

*Walked*—he took up his bed
and walked. He believed
Jesus could heal him,
obeyed the command of
Jesus, acted at once, and
did what seemed impos-
sible.    John 5. 9

*Witnessed*—he told the Jews
Jesus had made him whole    John 5. 15

**728 Five Solemn Negatives**

in John 5. 40-47

1 Ye will not—come    v. 40

2 Ye have not—the love of God in you    v. 42

3 Ye receive not—me    v. 43

4 Ye seek not—the honour that cometh
from God    v. 44

5 Ye believe not—his writings    v. 47

G.H.

**729 Essentials For All**

1 Life—'Come unto Me'
John 5. 40; Eph. 2. 1; John 10. 10

2 Light—'he that followeth Me'
John 8. 12; 1. 9

3 Rest—'come unto Me'
Matt. 11. 28

4 Food—'he that cometh unto Me'
John 6. 35

5 Drink—'come unto Me'
John 7. 37

**730 Jesus Walking on the Sea**

John 6. 19

The Sea is the domain of the Lord Jesus Christ

1 He calmed the stormy sea    Matt. 8. 24, 26

2 He walked on the stormy
sea    John 6. 19

3 He directed fishermen to
the fish    John 21. 6

4 He knew where the fish
that had the silver coin
was    Matt. 17. 27

5 He called men from the
sea to follow Him    Mark 1. 16-18

The Fish was the symbol of the early Christians.
The letters of the Greek word for 'Fish' gave
the initials of the words—'Jesus, Christ, of
God the Son, Saviour'.

**731 The New and Living Bread in John 6**

1 It is True—My Father giveth you
the true Bread    v. 32

2 It is Living—Jesus said, I am the
Living Bread    v. 51

3 It is Life-giving—Jesus said, It gives
life to the world    v. 33

4 It is Life-sustaining—He said, I am
that Bread of life    v. 48

5 It is Satisfying—The eater shall never
hunger    v. 35

6 It is Enduring—That which endures
unto life eternal    v. 27

7 It is Divine—The Bread of God
which gives life    v. 33

8 It is Heavenly—The Bread from, or
out of, Heaven    v. 41

H. J. VINE

**732 Seven 'I Ams' of Christ**

(Meeting man's need)

1 I am the Bread (for the unsatisfied one)    John 6. 35

2 I am the Light (for the blind
one)    John 9. 5

3 I am the Door (for the unsafe
one)    John 10. 9

4 I am the Shepherd (for the
lost one)    John 10. 11

5 I am the Way (for the ignorant
one)    John 14. 6

6 I am the Life (for the dead
one)    John 11. 25

7 I am the Vine (for the fruitless
one)    John 15. 1

A.G.A.

### 733 The Great Divide

'A division because of Him'—a Division among men because of—
1 WHO HE IS—His Person
    John 7. 12, 13, 37-43
2 WHAT HE SAID—His Teaching
    John 6. 50, 52, 60-68; 10. 19, 20
3 WHAT HE DID—His Work
    John 9. 14-16; 12, 9, 10
4 HOW HE DIED—His Cross
    Luke 23. 39-43

### 734 The Handwriting of God

Jesus stooped down and wrote on the ground
    John 8. 6

1 On a Mountain—
    Law of *Righteousness* Exod. 31. 18
2 On a Palace Wall—
    Law of *Retribution* Dan. 5. 5
3 On the Ground of the Temple court—
    Law of *Redemption* John 8. 6, 8
4 On the Hearts of men—
    Law of *Regeneration* Heb. 10. 16, 17

### 735 Conscience in Seven Stages

'Convicted by their own conscience' John 8. 9

1 An Evil Conscience — Heb. 10. 22
2 A Convicting Conscience — John 8. 9
3 A Purged Conscience — Heb. 9. 14
4 A Good Conscience — Acts 23. 1
5 A Pure Conscience — 1 Tim. 3. 9
6 A Weak Conscience — 1 Cor. 8. 12
7 A Seared Conscience — 1 Tim. 4. 2

An *evil* conscience once *convicted* may become *good* through being *purged* by the blood of Jesus, and afterwards may become *pure*, or *weak*, or *seared*, according to the measure of obedience the believer gives to the Scriptures.
    T.B.

### 736 The Man Born Blind

Three Questions about Jesus—
WHERE IS HE?—
His answer—
    I know not — John 9. 12
WHAT DID HE TO THEE?—
His answer—
    He hath opened mine eyes — John 9. 26, 30
WHO IS HE?—
His answers—
1 A man that is called Jesus — John 9. 11
2 He is a prophet — John 9. 17
3 He is 'of God' — John 9. 33
4 'the Son of God' — John 9. 35
5 'Lord!' — John 9. 38; Rom. 10. 9

### 737 Every Whit—Altogether

1 Altogether (every whit) born in sins—
    the Blind man — John 9. 34
2 Every whit whole—
    the Lame man — John 7. 23
3 Every whit clean—
    the Regenerate man — John 13. 10
4 Every whit of gold—
    the Shining light — Zech. 4. 2
    (same word in the LXX as in the other Scriptures above)

### 738 Two Doors of John 10

THE DOOR FOR THE SHEPHERD—
the Prophetic Scriptures — John 10. 2

1 The Shepherd, the Stone of Israel — Gen. 49. 24
2 The Shepherd of Israel — Ps. 80. 1
3 'Feed His flock like a shepherd' — Isa. 40. 11
4 'Awake, O sword, against My Shepherd' — Zech. 13. 7

THE DOOR FOR THE SHEEP—
Jesus said, I am the Door — John 10. 9

1 The sheep He purchases by giving His life for them — John 10. 11
2 My sheep He knows and is known by them — John 10. 14
3 *His own* sheep He puts forth and goes before them — John 10. 4
4 *Other* sheep He must bring into the one fold — John 10. 16

### 739 Marks of Christ's Sheep

1 They enter by the door — John 10. 9
2 They go in and out, find pasture and feed — John 10. 9
3 They hear the Shepherd's voice — John 10. 3, 27
4 They follow the Shepherd — John 10. 4, 27
5 They will not follow a stranger — John 10. 5
6 They receive eternal life from their Shepherd — John 10. 28
7 They are eternally secure— 'never perish' — John 10. 28

**740 One Flock and One Shepherd**
John 10. 16

All believers are—

1 Disciples—
in the same school—
One Master      Acts 20. 7

2 Children—
in the same family—
One Father      John 11. 52

3 Sheep—
in the same flock—
One Shepherd      John 10. 16

4 Saints—
in the same covenant—
One Rank      Rom. 1. 7

5 Stones—
in the same building—
One Foundation      1 Pet. 2. 5

6 Members—
of the same Body—
One Head      Rom. 12. 5

7 The Bride (future)—
in the same glory—
One Bridegroom      Rev. 21. 2, 9
                   M.I.R.

**741 Four Outlooks in Face of Death**

1 The Pessimistic Outlook—
'that we may die with
Him'—Thomas      John 11. 16

2 The Optimisitic Outlook—
'I know that he shall
rise again'—Martha      John 11. 24

3 The Realistic Outlook—
'Lazarus is dead'—the
Lord Jesus      John 11. 14, 15

4 The Idealistic Outlook—
'If thou wouldest believe,
thou shouldest see the
glory of God'—the
Lord Jesus      John 11. 40

**742 Story of Lazarus of Bethany**

1 Lazarus is dead—
DEAD      John 11. 14; Eph. 2. 1

2 He that was dead came forth—
ALIVE      John 11. 44; Eph. 2. 1

3 Bound hand and foot—
BOUND      John 11. 44

4 Loose him and let him go—
FREED      John 11. 44

5 Lazarus—sat at the table with Him—
SEATED      John 12. 2; Eph. 2. 6

6 They came—that they might see Lazarus—
WITNESSING      John 12. 9

7 Consulted that they might put Lazarus to
death—SUFFERING      John 12. 10

**743 Four Worship Scenes**
John 12. 1-26

*One* Theme—Worship: *Two* days (John 12. 12)
—the Church age and the Millennium:
*Three* Companies—a family gathering, a
national ovation and a company of Greeks:
*Four* Symbolic Pictures—a supper, a box of
ointment, palm branches and a field of corn.

FOUR WORSHIPPING COMPANIES

1 Collective Worship—
They made Him a
supper      John 12. 2

2 Individual Worship—
Mary—anointed the
feet of Jesus      John 12. 3
Martha was a Silent
Worker—Service
Mary was a Silent
Worshipper—Worship
Lazarus was a Silent
Wonder—Communion

3 National Worship—
in the city of the
great king—'Blessed
is the King of
Israel that cometh
in the name of the
Lord'      John 12. 13

4 Universal Worship—
We would see
Jesus: the world is
gone after Him      John 12. 19, 20, 21

**744 Sevenfold Presentation of the Cross**

1 The Cross and Glory—the
Son of man should be
glorified      John 12. 23

2 The Cross and Blessing—a
corn of wheat—much fruit   John 12. 24

3 The Cross and Discipleship—
he that loveth his life shall
lose it      John 12. 25

4 The Cross and Suffering—
now is my soul troubled   John 12. 27

5 The Cross and Attraction—I,
if I be lifted up, will draw   John 12. 32

6 The Cross and Condemna-
tion—'Now is the judg-
ment of this world      John 12. 31

7 The Cross and Expulsion—
Now shall the prince of the
world be cast out      John 12. 31
                 H. BELL

**745 The Christian Life**

1 Confession of Christ      John 12. 42
2 Cleansing by Christ      John 13. 10
3 Communion with Christ      John 13. 23
4 Chastening unto Christ      John 15. 2
5 Consecration to Christ      John 15. 14
6 Conflict for Christ      John 15. 19
7 Comfort in Christ      John 16. 33

**746 His Own in the World**
John 13. 1

'Ye are Christ's' 1 Cor. 3. 23

How we become Christ's—

| | |
|---|---|
| 1 By Deed of Gift | John 17. 6 |
| 2 By Right of Purchase | 1 Cor. 6. 19 |
| 3 By Act of Choice | John 1. 12 |

In John's Gospel this Relationship is unfolded in increasing intimacy in the names the Lord Jesus gives to 'His own'.

| | |
|---|---|
| 1 My sheep—<br>follow the Shepherd | John 10. 26, 27 |
| 2 My Servants—<br>follow the Master | John 12. 26 |
| 3 My Disciples—<br>love one another | John 13. 35 |
| 4 My Friends—<br>do what the Lord commands | John 15. 14 |
| 5 My Brethren—<br>to them He is not ashamed to give that name | John 20. 17;<br>Heb. 2. 11 |

**747 Christ's Ministry for His Own**

| | |
|---|---|
| 1 He washes their feet—<br>His Example | John 13 |
| 2 He comforts their hearts—<br>His Promises | John 14 |
| 3 He opens their lips to witness—<br>His Pruning | John 15 |
| 4 He opens their ears to hear—<br>His Instruction | John 16 |
| 5 He protects their lives—<br>His Intercession | John 17 |

**748 Washing the Disciples' Feet**
John 13

| | |
|---|---|
| 1 THE BATH—<br>'Ye are clean'—the eleven disciples 'but not all'—Judas was not clean | John 13. 10 |
| 2 THE BASON—<br>He poureth water into a bason | John 13. 5;<br>Eph. 5. 26, 27 |
| (Three infinitive verbs—<br>*Began to wash* His disciples' feet | John 13. 5 |
| *Needeth to wash* his own feet | John 13. 10 |
| *Ought to wash* one another's feet | John 13. 14 |
| 3 THE BOSOM—<br>Leaning on Jesus' bosom—Communion | John 13. 23 |
| 4 THE BADGE—<br>By this shall all men know—if ye have love one to another—Discipleship | John 13. 35 |

**749 Christ's Legacies to His Disciples**

| | |
|---|---|
| 1 His Example of lowly love | John 13. 15 |
| 2 His Promise of a Home above | John 14. 2, 3 |
| 3 His Spirit as their Comforter | John 14. 16-18 |
| 4 His Peace to keep them from fear | John 14. 27 |
| 5 His Joy to remain with them | John 15. 11 |

**750 Christ Our Example**

| | |
|---|---|
| 1 In Loving—<br>Love one another AS I have loved you | John 13. 34 |
| 2 In Receiving—<br>Receive one another AS Christ also received us | Rom. 15. 7 |
| 3 In Forgiving—<br>Forgive one another AS Christ forgave you | Col. 3. 13 |

H.K.D.

**751 The Questions of Three Apostles**
John 14

| | |
|---|---|
| 1 Thomas's Question—<br>he did not know the Way | vs. 1-7 |
| 2 Philip's Question—<br>he did not know the Truth | vs. 8-21 |
| 3 Judas's Question—<br>he did not know the Life | vs. 22-31 |

The key verse (verse 6) answers all three questions

1 The Way—of man to God—
    Christ's Work

2 The Truth—of God to man—
    Christ's Word

3 The Life of God in man—
    Christ's Will

H. BELL

**752 The Coming One**
John 14. 3

| | |
|---|---|
| I | —The Person |
| I will | —The Power |
| I will come | —The Promise |
| I will come again | —The Prospect |
| And receive you unto Myself | —The People |
| That where I am | —The Place |
| There ye may be also | —The Purpose |

D. WARD

**753 The Comforter—The Holy Spirit**

1 His *Coming* was made dependent
    on Christ's Absence
        John 16. 7
    on Christ's Ascension
        John 14. 28
    on Christ's Advocacy
        John 14. 16

2 His *Comfort*—making Christ dearer, the Word clearer and Heaven nearer
        John 16. 13, 14, 15

3 His *Companionship*. The Holy Spirit in the
   believer is

| A SEAL | Eph. 1. 13; 4. 30 |
| AN EARNEST | Eph. 1. 14; 2 Cor. 1. 22 |
| A RESIDENT | Rom. 8. 11; 1 Cor. 6. 19, 20 |
| AN UNCTION | 2 Cor. 1. 21; 1 John 2. 20 |
| A WITNESS | Rom. 8. 16; 1 John 5. 10; Heb. 10. 15 |

**754   The Holy Spirit of God**
   John 14. 16, 17

He is called the Spirit of life, of truth, of
grace, of adoption, of power, of comfort and
of holiness.

| He strives with sinners | Gen. 6. 3 |
| He reproves (convicts) of sin | John 16. 8 |
| He helps our infirmities | Rom. 8. 26 |
| He comforts | Acts 9. 31 |
| He teaches | John 14. 26 |
| He guides | John 16. 13 |
| He sanctifies | Rom. 15. 16 |
| He testifies of Christ | John 15. 26 |
| He glorifies Christ | John 16. 14 |
| He searches all things | 1 Cor. 2. 10 |
| He works according to His own will | 1 Cor. 12. 11 |
| He dwells in saints | John 14. 17 |
| He may be grieved | Eph. 4. 30 |
| He may be vexed | Isa. 63. 10 |
| He can be resisted | Acts 7. 51 |
| He can be tempted | Acts 5. 9 |
| He can be quenched | 1 Thess. 5. 19 |

D. WARD

**755   Life, Light and Love**
   John 14. 19-21

The three great Themes of the Fourth Gospel

1 Life in the Son of God      v. 19
2 Light through the Spirit of God      v. 20
3 Love from the Father and the Son      v. 21

**756   Three Statements about the 'Prince of this World'**

The prince of this world *cometh*
   and hath nothing in Me      John 14. 30
   Coming to the last Adam in
   temptation
The prince of this world is *judged* John 16. 11
   Satan defeated by the Cross
The prince of this world—cast out John 12. 31
   The final dislodgement of Satan

T.B.

**757   The Vine and the Branches**

1 Chosen by Christ for Fruitbearing
      John 15. 16
2 Chosen in Christ for Holiness
      Eph. 1. 4
3 Consecrated to Christ for 'fruit unto
   holiness'      Rom. 6. 22
4 Abiding in Christ for Fruitbearing
      John 15. 4
   Without the Vine the Branch can do
   nothing
   Without the Branches the Vine will do
   nothing

5 Desire of Christ is FRUIT, ADDED FRUIT,
   ABUNDANT FRUIT, ABIDING FRUIT
      John 15. 2, 4, 5, 8, 16
   All the Branch has belongs to the Vine
   All the Vine has is communicated to the
   Branches

THREE KINDS OF BRANCHES—
      John 15. 2
1 The Fruitful branch, with the promise of
   greater fruitfulness
2 The Fruitless branch, removed as useless
3 The Pruned branch, purged with the object
   of producing more fruit

**758   The Lord's Prayer for His Own**
   John 17

There are three parts in the Prayer—

Christ and His Father—
   His Work      vs. 1-5
Christ and His disciples—
   God's Word      vs. 6-19
Christ and all believers—
   Man's World      vs. 20-26

CHRIST AND HIS FATHER

Christ's Glory—

1 Glory of His Personal
   Greatness—with the
   Father      v. 5
2 Glory of His Official Position—as Interceding High
   Priest      v. 1
3 Glory of His Completed
   Work—'I have finished' v. 4
4 Glory Reflected in His
   people—'glorified in
   them'      v. 10

Christ's Work—

'I have finished the work that
   Thou gavest me to do'      v. 4
1 Revealing the Father—'I
   have manifested Thy
   name'      v. 6
2 Redeeming His people—
   'I have set myself apart'   v. 19
3 Restoring what He took not
   away—'I have given
   them'      vs. 2, 14

CHRIST AND HIS DISCIPLES—

'Those that Thou hast given
   Me'      vs. 2. 6, 9, etc.
He prays—
for their Preservation from
   Disunity      v. 11
for their Separation from evil v. 15
for their Sanctification
   through the Truth      v. 17

CHRIST AND ALL BELIEVERS—

| They are in the world | v. 13 |
| They are not of the world | vs. 14, 16 |
| They are sent into the world | v. 18 |
| They are to display oneness to the world | v. 21 |

129

### 759 Four Hours in John's Gospel

1 The Hour of the Saviour's
Suffering     John 17. 1

2 The Hour of the Sinner's
Salvation     John 5. 25

3 The Hour of the Saint's
Service     John 4. 23

4 The Hour of the Son's
Supremacy     John 5. 28, 29
             G.W.B.

### 760 The Father's Seven Gifts to the Son

1 John 17. 2 —Authority or
power over all—
His position     Matt. 11. 27

2 John 17. 4 —The work to
do
His mission     John 1. 8

3 John 17. 6 —The men out
of the world—
His people     John 6. 37-40

4 John 17. 7 —All things
whatsoever—
His endowments     John 3. 35

5 John 17. 8 —Sayings or
words to give to them—
His message     John 7. 16

6 John 17. 22—The glory of
redemption—
His reward     2 Thess. 1. 10

7 John 17. 24—The glory of
Eternal Creatorship—
His pre-eminence     Col. 1. 18

As the Obedient Son He acquired a glory which
He shares with His own.

As the Co-eternal Son He has an essential
glory which is incommunicable.
             F.S.B.

### 761 The Master and the Servants

1 Where He found them—
out of the world     John 17. 6

2 What He gave them—
life, the words and the
glory     John 17. 2, 8, 22

3 Where He sends them—
into the world     John 17. 18

4 What He does for them—
I pray for them     John 17. 9

5 Where He brings them—
to behold His glory     John 17. 24
             A.H.

### 762 The Christian and the World

1 The Christian is given to
Christ out of the world John 17. 6

2 The Christian is left in the
world     John 17. 11, 15

3 The Christian is not of the
world     John 17. 14

4 The Christian is hated by
the world     John 17. 14

5 The Christian is kept from
the world     John 17. 15

6 The Christian is sent into
the world     John 17. 18

7 The Christian is to preach
the Word to the world John 17. 20
             N.B.

### 763 'Before' and 'From' the Foundation of the World

THREE THINGS that took place *before* the
Foundation of the world—

1 Christ was loved of God     John 17. 24

2 Christ was foreordained
to die     1 Pet. 1. 20

3 Believers were chosen in
Christ     Eph. 1. 4

FIVE THINGS that have taken place *from* the
Foundation of the world—

1 The Lamb was slain     Rev. 13. 8

2 The works of God were
finished     Heb. 4. 3

3 The Kingdom was prepared Matt. 25. 34

4 Names were written in the
book of life     Rev. 17. 8

5 Secrets (to be revealed later)
were kept     Matt. 13. 35

### 764 Christ's Crowns

1 A Crown of *Mockery*—a crown of thorns
             John 19. 5

2 The Crown of *Majesty*—crowned with
glory and honour     Heb. 2. 9

3 Crowns of *Monarchy*—many crowns (diadems)     Rev. 19. 12, 16

4 The Crown of *Mastery*—Christ as Lord in
your heart     1 Pet. 3. 15 (R.V.)

### 765 The Risen Lord
John 20

At His crucifixion the Lord Jesus Christ is seen as the last Adam 1 Cor. 15. 48

In His resurrection He is seen as the Second Man 1 Cor. 15. 49

OUR RISEN LORD—

1 We share in His *Peace*
John 20. 19; Col. 3. 1

2 We draw on His *Power*
Matt. 28. 18-20

3 We join in His *Praises*
Heb. 2. 11

4 We become conformed to His *Pattern*
Rom. 8. 29

### 766 A Resurrection Retrospect

John 21 comes between Peter's Denial of the Lord in John 18 and Peter's Discourse at Pentecost in Acts 2. It is the Period of Peter's Transformation. In it Peter had FIVE RE-MINDERS OF THE PAST—

1 The multitude of fishes—a Reminder of his *Confession* John 21. 6; Luke 5. 8

2 The words—'it is the Lord'—a Reminder of his *Cry* 'Lord, save me'
John 21. 7; Matt. 14. 30

3 The fire of coals—a Reminder of his *Compromise* John 21. 9; 18. 18

4 The third time the Lord asked him the same question—a Reminder of his *Cowardice* John 21. 17; Matt. 26. 75

5 The bread and fish—a Reminder of the Lord's *Compassion*
John 21. 13; 6. 9-11

### 767 Resurrection Numbers
John 21

'And Peter'

In the Gospel of John
'Simon Peter' occurs 17 times
'Peter' occurs 17 times

In Chapter 21 (the last)
'Simon' occurs 8 times
'Peter' occurs 9 times: together 17 times

In Chapter 21
7 Apostles are mentioned in v. 2
The Lord Jesus is the eighth Person, v. 4

In Chapter 21
153 fishes were caught and counted—v. 11
153 is a multiple of 9 and 17

The sum of all the numbers from 1 to 17 adds up to 153

17 is the 9th odd number and the 7th prime number

9 is the middle number between 1 and 17

8 numbers come before 9 and 8 after 9 between 0 and 18

8 is the number of Resurrection

In Chapter 21

Jesus showed Himself to His disciples for the third time—i.e. after His resurrection v. 14

Jesus said to Peter the third time, 'Simon, son of Jonas, lovest thou me?' v. 17

3 is the number of the Trinity

It was the Lord's seventh appearance in Resurrection

7 is the number of spiritual perfection

# ACTS

## 768　The Book of Acts

of the Holy Spirit through the Apostles. The finest record of missionary enterprise ever penned—full of incidents that are Heart-warming and Hair-raising.

| THE NARRATIVE BEGINS | THE NARRATIVE ENDS |
|---|---|
| In Jerusalem, the Jewish Capital | In Rome, the Gentile Capital |
| With the apostle to the Jews, Peter, prominent | With the apostle to the Gentiles, Paul, prominent |
| With God's salvation offered to the Jews | With God's salvation sent to the Gentiles |

Three great Themes run through the Book of Acts—

1 The *Purpose* of GRACE—repentance and remission of sins preached in Christ's name among all nations　　　　　　　　　　　Luke 21. 47

2 The *Punctuation* of GOD—Five Punctuation marks, then the full-stop　Acts 28. 31

3 The *Progress* of the GOSPEL—Each punctuation mark is one of progress—
The Word of God increased—in Jerusalem　　　　　　　　　Acts 6. 7
Then had the churches rest and were edified (throughout Palestine)　Acts 9. 31
The Word of God grew and multiplied (Antioch in Syria)　　　　Acts 12. 25
The churches (in Asia Minor) were established in the faith and increased in number daily　　　　　　　　　　　　　　　　　　　Acts 16. 5
So mightily grew the Word of God and prevailed (in the great cities)　Acts 19. 20

## 769　The Holy Spirit in Acts

Endued the disciples with power Acts 1. 8
Inspired the sacred Scriptures Acts 1. 16
Gave utterance to the preachers Acts 2. 4
Witnessed concerning Jesus Christ　　　　　　　Acts 5. 32
Comforted the churches　　Acts 9. 31
Gave guidance when needed　Acts 10. 19
Directed in missionary enterprise　　　　　　　Acts 13. 2
Sent forth the missionaries　Acts 13. 4
Guided them in their movements　　　　　　　Acts 16. 6, 7
Appointed overseers in the churches　　　　　　Acts 20. 28

THE HOLY SPIRIT—

1 Was received as an *Endowment*
Acts 2. 38; 8. 15-19; 19. 2

2 Came on believers as an *Enduement*
Acts 1. 8; 10. 44; 11. 15; 19. 6

3 They were baptized in, as an *Element*
Acts 1. 5; 1 Cor. 12. 13

4 Was poured out, as an *Effusion*
Acts 2. 17, 18; 10. 45

5 Filled believers as an *Empowerment*
Acts 2. 4; 4. 8; 4. 31; 6. 5; 7. 55; 9. 17; 13. 9

## 770　Witnesses Unto Christ

Witnessing is mentioned in Acts 1. 8, 22; 2. 32; 3. 15; 4. 33; 5. 32 'YE SHALL BE WITNESSES UNTO ME' Acts 1. 8 'In the early Church it became the most sacred duty of the new convert to diffuse among his friends the inestimable blessing which he himself had received.'

GIBBON

1 The Duration of our Witness—From Christ's Ascension till His Return　　　　Acts 1. 7, 9-11

2 The Direction of our Witness—Jerusalem, Judaea Samaria, and to the uttermost parts of the earth.　　　　Acts 1. 8

3 The Dynamic of our Witness—Power (dunamis) after that the Holy Ghost is come upon you Acts 1. 8

## 771　How to Secure Abiding Results

As at the beginning—in Acts 2—so today in the Twentieth Century—

1 UNITED DISCIPLES—
Peter, standing up with the eleven　　　　v. 14

2 UPLIFTED CHRIST—
Jesus of Nazareth—crucified—raised up —to sit on the throne vs. 22, 23, 24, 30
A Rejected—Risen—Reigning Christ

3 UNPARALLELED BLESSING—
the same day there were added unto them 3000 souls　　　　　v. 41
The *same* mind (v. 1), the *same* Jesus (v. 36), the *same* day　　(v. 41)

4 UNWAVERING STEADFASTNESS—
They continued stedfastly　　　　　v. 42

5 UNEQUALLED GLADNESS—
the result—praising God and having favour with ALL the people v. 47

HYP.

**772 Peter's Sermon at Pentecost**

He commenced with an Explanation of the rare manifestation  Acts 2. 14-21
He continued with an Exposition of the Scriptures  Acts 2. 22-36
He concluded with an Exhortation to repentance and faith  Acts 2. 38-40
His message was—
STRUCTURAL, SCRIPTURAL and SPIRITUAL

**773 The Cross of Christ**
Acts 2. 22-24

Four factors behind the Cross—

1 God's Eternal Purpose—the determinate counsel—of God  v. 23
2 Man's Sinful Hatred—ye have taken and—crucified and slain  v. 23
3 Christ's Submissive Will—a man approved of God  v. 22
4 Satan's Infernal Opposition  John 12. 31, 32; 14. 30

The Cross was—
The Glorious Climax of the Eternal Plan
The Greatest Crime of sin-benighted man
The Gravest Crisis of a sinless Life
The Grandest Crown of Christ's Triumphant strife

**774 At Pentecost the Spirit of God Produced**

1 Conviction of Sin  Acts 2. 38
2 Conversion to God  Acts 2. 38
3 Confession of faith in Christ  Acts 2. 41
4 Continuance in the ways of God  Acts 2. 42
5 Consecration to God  Acts 2. 45
6 Community of joyful Christians  Acts 2. 46, 47

G.H.

**775 Products of Preaching**

in Apostolic Days
3000 believed  Acts 2. 41
5000 men believed  Acts 4. 4
Multitudes believed  Acts 5. 14

A great company of the priests believed  Acts 6. 7
The people of the city of Samaria gave heed  Acts 8. 6
All who heard received the Holy Ghost  Acts 10. 44
A great number believed and turned to the Lord  Acts 11. 21
Much people was added to the Lord  Acts 11. 24
A household believed  Acts 16. 34
Many—not a few—believed  Acts 17. 12
Many myriads (R.V.) of Jews believed  Acts 21. 20
Why not now?  HYP.

**776 The Lame Made to Walk**

Note—
1 His *Disease*—
lame from his mother's womb  Acts 3. 2
2 His *Distance*—
at the gate of the temple—could not enter  Acts 3. 2
3 His *Decrepitude*—
they laid him there daily  Acts 3. 2
4 His *Destitution*—
asking alms of them that entered  Acts 3. 2

'MADE WHOLE'—
same word translated 'SAVED'  Acts 4. 9, 12
1 He sprang up—with an effort—
Obedience of Faith  Acts 3. 8
2 He stood up—straight—
Stability of Faith  Acts 3. 8
3 He walked about—
Walk of Faith  Acts 3. 8
4 He leaped (Isa. 35. 6) as a hart—
Exuberance of Joy  Acts 3. 8
5 He praised God—
Praise for Healing  Acts 3. 8
6 He entered into the temple—
Privilege of Nearness  Acts 3. 8
7 He held Peter and John—
Fellowship of saints  Acts 3. 11

**777 The Name of Jesus**

1 Unique in its Provision—
He shall save His people from their sins  Matt. 1. 21
2 Unique in its Power—
Healing in His name (Acts 3)  Acts 4. 10
Forgiveness in His name  Acts 10. 43
3 Unique in its Proclamation—
among all nations  Luke 24. 47

**778 Moses, A Type of Christ**

as revealed in Acts 3. 22—'a prophet like unto me'.

1 Preserved at birth in spite of Satan's attempts to destroy him
Exod. 1. 22; 2. 9; Matt. 2. 13-15
2 Humbled himself to visit his brethren
Acts 7. 22, 23; Phil. 2. 6-8
3 Was rejected by his brethren
Exod. 2. 11-14; John 1. 11
4 Was God's appointed Deliverer
Exod. 3. 10; 1 John 4. 14
5 Suffered in obscurity in preparation for his life's work
Exod. 3. 2; Heb. 5. 8, 9
6 Was the meekest man of his time
Num. 12. 3; Matt. 11. 29
7 Was God's prophet, becoming his people's mediator
Heb. 8. 9, 10; 1 Tim. 2. 5, 6

## 779 Salvation for the Worst

as revealed in Acts 3. 26

THE WORST FIRST—

Unto you first

Rebels red with the blood of Christ three months after the crucifixion

THE WORST BLESSED—

Sent Him to bless you

They cursed but could receive blessing instead of 'blasting' Deut. 28. 22

THE WORST TURNED—

by turning every one of you from his iniquities

Not blessed *in* sin, but by being turned *from* sin

HYP.

## 780 Things to Know

1 Be it known—
The Knowledge of Resurrection     Acts 4. 10
2 Be it known—
The Knowledge of Justification     Acts 13. 38
3 Be it known—
The Knowledge of Salvation     Acts 28. 28
JS. FS.

## 781 The Resurrection of the Lord Jesus Christ

1 Witness of His Resurrection—
an Essential Fact in Christian Evidence     Acts 4. 33
2 Likeness of His Resurrection—
an Essential Feature of the Christian Ordinance     Rom. 6. 5
3 Power of His Resurrection—
an Essential Factor in Christian Experience     Phil. 3. 10

## 782 Barnabas, Son of Exhortation (or Consolation)

1 A *Separated Levite*, tribally and spiritually     Acts 4. 36, 37
Sold an Earthly Heritage and left an Earthly Home for the service of Christ.
2 A *Selected Labourer*—'I have called'     Acts 11. 22; 13. 2
as a MINISTER OF CHRIST     Acts 11. 23; 13. 43; 14. 22
a MESSENGER OF THE CHURCH     Acts 11. 30
a MISSIONARY OF THE CROSS     Acts 13. 2
a MOUTHPIECE OF THE CHRISTIANS     Acts 15. 12, 30
3 A *Spiritual Leader*—a good man, full of faith and the Holy Ghost     Acts 11. 24
GRACIOUS—
in introducing the converted persecutor Saul     Acts 9. 27
in bringing Saul to help at Antioch     Acts 11. 25, 26
in taking second place in service     Acts 13. 43

## 783 Ananias and Sapphira

1 Hidden Deceit—
'kept back part' and 'lied to the Holy Ghost'     Acts 5. 2, 3, 9
2 Sudden Death—
fell down and gave up the ghost     Acts 5. 5, 10
3 Great Dread—
great fear fell upon the church     Acts 5. 5, 11

## 784 Names of Christ's Followers in 'Acts'

1 Believers—
who were 'added to the Lord'     Acts 5. 14
2 Disciples—
whose number was multiplied     Acts 6. 1
3 Saints—
who were persecuted by Saul     Acts 9. 13
4 Brethren—
who accompanied Saul to Caesarea and helped him to escape     Acts 9. 30
5 Christians—
who received the name first at Antioch     Acts 11. 26

## 785 The Witness of Stephen

Stephen was—

Filled with the Spirit     Acts 6. 5
Fearless in witness     Acts 6. 10
Faithful in service     Acts 6. 14
Forbearing in love     Acts 7. 60

THE WITNESS OF HIS LIFE—

full of faith and power     Acts 6. 8

THE WITNESS OF HIS LABOURS—

did great wonders     Acts 6. 8

THE WITNESS OF HIS LEARNING—

his wisdom and the spirit by which he spake     Acts 6. 10

THE WITNESS OF HIS LOOKS—

his face—as the face of an angel     Acts 6. 15

THE WITNESS OF HIS LOVE—

Lord, lay not this sin to their charge Acts 7. 60
He cast the crown of his life at his Master's feet and went in to receive the crowns promised to the faithful—

the Victor's Crown, incorruptible     1 Cor. 9. 25
the Martyr's Crown of life     Rev. 2. 10
the Soul-winner's Crown of rejoicing     1 Thess. 2. 1
('Stephen' means 'crown')

**786 Stephen's Sermon**
Acts 7

Stephen was accused of—

Disloyalty to his Religion     Acts 6. 14

Blasphemy against God's Law  Acts 6. 11, 13

Disparagement of the Temple  Acts 6. 13

In his answer he quoted from the Scriptures and gave an Epitome of Israel's history, proving that God had revealed Himself to Abraham, and His Moral standard to Moses.

THE CHAPTER BEGINS WITH THE 'GOD OF GLORY' AND ENDS WITH THE 'GLORY OF GOD'.

His Defence—

1 *Affirmation* from Israel's Scriptures                   vs. 2-36

2 *Application* of Israel's history    vs. 37-50

3 *Arraignment* of Israel's children  vs. 51-53

**787 Philip the Evangelist**
Acts 6. 5; 21. 8

Not to be confounded with Philip the Apostle who is not mentioned after Acts 1. 13

1 The *Man*—

his personal character —full of the Holy Ghost and wisdom— his public reputation —of honest report     Acts 6. 5

2 His *Movements*—

all under the Holy Spirit's control
Directed by circumstances          Acts 8. 4-6
Dictated by Heavenly messengers      Acts 8. 26, 27
Diverted by the Holy Ghost            Acts 8. 29, 30

3 His *Ministry*—

He heralded aloud the message of God  Acts 8. 5
He spoke in ordinary tones the Gospel  Acts 8. 6
He evangelized— preached the Gospel  Acts 8. 12, 35, 40

4 His *Methods*—

'went down' to Samaria,           Acts 8. 5
'ran' to join the eunuch in the chariot, Acts 8. 30
toured the cities on his way to Caesarea, Acts 8. 40
His evangelism was *Public, Personal* and *Peripatetic*

5 His *Message*—

Christ, the Kingdom of God, the name of Jesus Christ, and Jesus   Acts 8. 5, 12, 35

**788 Essentials for an Evangelist**

1 He must know the Scriptures          Acts 8. 32-34
2 He must reach the Sinner Acts 8. 29, 30
3 He must preach the Saviour Acts 8. 35
4 He must be ready to baptize the Saved    Acts 8. 38

**789 The Conversion of the Ethiopian Eunuch**

Three Notable Conversions in three Consecutive Chapters of Acts—

In Chapter 8—a Descendant of Ham— Chancellor of the Exchequer of Ethiopia

In Chapter 9—a Descendant of Shem— Member of the Jewish Sanhedrin

In Chapter 10—a Descendant of Japheth— Officer in the Roman army

THE ETHIOPIAN EUNUCH'S CONVERSION—

1 A Seeking Sinner—
a man of Ethiopia      Acts 8. 27
the WORD HE READ (Isa. 53) Acts 8. 28
the WORK HE RELIED ON  Acts 8. 32
the WISH HE RECORDED   Acts 8. 36

2 A Sent Servant— Philip the Evangelist   Acts 8. 29

3 A Suffering Saviour— 'Jesus'         Acts 8. 32-38

4 A Singing Saint— the converted Eunuch  Acts 8. 39

**790 Conversion of Saul of Tarsus**

'Of the tribe of Benjamin' Phil. 3. 5—

First a Wolf devouring the prey        Gen. 49. 27
Later—the beloved of the Lord          Deut. 33. 12

HOW CONVERTED—

A Time when—at midday Acts 26. 13
A Place where—near Damascus           Acts 9. 3
A Vision seen—light from Heaven        Acts 9. 3
A Voice heard—'Saul, Saul, why?'       Acts 9. 4
His eyes opened, scales removed        Acts 9. 17, 18
Baptized by Ananias    Acts 9. 18
Straightway became a preacher of Christ Acts 9. 20

WHAT HE GOT—

I obtained mercy       1 Tim. 1. 12-16
Having obtained help of God            Acts 26. 12
To the obtaining of the glory          2 Thess. 2. 14

135

**791 A Pattern Young Christian**

The Apostle Paul in Acts 9. 6; 22. 10—
'What shall I do, Lord?' What he did, any
young believer may be safe in following—

1 He PRAYED—
Behold he prayeth     Acts 9. 11

2 He WAS BAPTIZED—
Brother Saul—was baptized   Acts 9. 17, 18

3 He PREACHED CHRIST—
that He is the Son of God   Acts 9. 20

4 He JOINED THE DISCIPLES—
on the testimony of Barnabas to one thing—'that
he was a disciple'     Acts 9. 26, 27

5 He CONTINUED STEADFAST—
with them, speaking boldly
in the Name     Acts 9. 28, 29
           HYP.

**792 Peter's Vision and its Purpose**

'In a trance I saw a vision'    Acts 11. 5

1 It was Given on a *Special
Occasion*—to prepare Peter
to receive the Gentiles approaching his house    Acts 10. 9

2 It was Given with a *Special
Significance*—to proclaim
God's far-reaching grace in
blessing Gentiles     Acts 10. 17

3 It was Given for a *Special
Purpose*—to produce a
change in Peter's attitude to
the Gentiles     Acts 10. 28

**793 The Great Sheet Let Down From Heaven**

1 It was GREAT—
from a Great God, sending
a Great Salvation,
through the preaching of
a Great Gospel     Acts 10. 11

2 It had FOUR CORNERS—
literally four beginnings—
yet was knit in one—
Christ in the Four
Gospels     Acts 10. 11

3 It came FROM HEAVEN—
from which comes every-
thing worthwhile and
lasting, through 'the
Lord from Heaven'    Acts 10. 11

4 It COMMANDED ATTENTION—
I fastened mine eyes (looked
attentively)     Acts 11. 6

5 It CAME EVEN TO ME—
said Peter—the Gospel to
every creature Acts 11. 5; Mark 16. 15

THE OCCUPANTS OF THE SHEET—
1 *Classified*, as the world sees
them     Acts 10. 12
Fourfooted beasts, wild
beasts, creeping things,
and fowls of the air    Acts 10. 14

2 *Common*—or defiled—as
Peter saw them     Acts 10. 14

3 *Cleansed*—as God saw
them     Acts 10. 15; 1 Cor. 6. 9-11

**794 Jesus Christ, He is Lord of All**
Acts 10. 36

1 Lord from Heaven—
His Incarnation 1 Cor. 15. 47

2 Lord of the Sabbath—
His Ministry on Earth
Matt. 12. 8

3 Lord of Glory—
His Crucifixion 1 Cor. 2. 8

4 Lord both of the dead and living—
His Resurrection
Rom. 14. 9

5 Lord of the Harvest—
His Exaltation Luke 10. 2

6 Lord of Sabaoth (Hosts)—
His Priestly Ministry of Intercession
Rom. 9. 29; James 5. 4

7 Lord of lords—
His Return in Glory
Rev. 19. 16

**795 An Ideal Address**

1 A Consecrated Life    Acts 10. 38
2 A Criminal's death    Acts 10. 39
3 A Confirmed resurrection Acts 10. 40, 41
4 A Coming judgment    Acts 10. 42
5 A Complete salvation    Acts 10. 43
6 A Converted company   Acts 10. 44
7 A Command obeyed    Acts 10. 48
         H.K.D.

**796 The Church at Antioch**
The First Missionary Home-base
It was—

1 GROUNDED
in the Gospel of Christ   Acts 11. 19-21

2 GROWING
in the Grace of God    Acts 11. 23

3 GENEROUS
in its Giving to the Lord   Acts 11. 29
(Gifts were *Spontaneous*,
*Systematic* and *Symptomatic*)

4 GARNISHED
with the Gifts of the
Ascended Lord     Acts 13. 1

**797 Christians**
To God—Christ's ones, servants of the
Anointed Saviour.
In the World—
A Separate People     Acts 11. 26
A Reproached People    Acts 26. 28
A Suffering People     1 Pet. 4. 16

## 798 Three Characters in Acts 12

HEROD—

stretched out his hand ⎫
slew James ⎬ —the Devil's tool
sentenced his soldiers ⎭

Acts 12. 1, 2, 19

THE ANGEL—

shone a light in the prison ⎫
smote Peter on the side ⎬ —God's
spoke to Peter ⎭ messenger

Acts 12. 7, 8

PETER—

was Prisoner ⎫
was Prayed for ⎬ —the servant of the Lord
was Preserved ⎭

Acts 12. 4, 5, 19
JS. FS.

## 799 Types of Missionaries in Acts

1 Barnabas the Exhorter
Acts 11. 23; 13. 43; 14. 22
2 Saul the Teacher (Apostle to the Gentiles)
Acts 11. 26; 13. 1; 20. 27
3 John Mark the Attendant
Acts 13. 5
4 Silas the Evangelist
Acts 15. 40
5 Timothy the Pastor
Acts 16. 1-3; Phil. 2. 19, 20
6 Luke the Doctor (the beloved Physician)
Acts 16. 11 (we); Col. 4. 14
7 Apollos the Orator
Acts 18. 24
8 Aquila the Tentmaker
Acts 18. 18; Rom. 16. 3, 4
9 Priscilla the Deaconess
Acts 18. 18; Rom. 16. 3, 4

## 800 Prerequisites of a Missionary

1 Conversion—Example—Saul of Tarsus
Acts 9. 1-11
2 Consecration—Example—Barnabas
Acts 4. 36, 37
3 Call—Examples—Barnabas and Saul
Acts 13. 2
4 Commission—Paul the Apostle
Acts 26. 16-19; 2 Tim. 1. 11
5 Commendation to the grace of God
Acts 14. 26; 15. 40

## 801 The Great Missionary Venture
Acts 13, 1-4

1 The Activity of the Spirit—
Suggesting the plan            Acts 13. 2
Selecting the Persons         Acts 13. 2
Sending out the Preachers Acts 13. 4
2 The Responsibility of the
Saints—Separate me          Acts 13. 2
They fasted, prayed, laid hands
on them, let them go.
3 The Liberty of the Servants—
they departed                     Acts 13. 4
No salary was promised, no
period prescribed and no
control proposed.

## 802 Fivefold Denunciation of Elymas the Sorcerer
Acts 13. 5-11

1 A Downright Deceiver—full of all
subtilty                               v. 10
2 A Mischievous Villain—full of all
mischief                             v. 10
3 A Child of the Devil              v. 10
4 An Enemy of righteousness      v. 10
5 A Perverter of the ways of God   v. 10

## 803 Forgiveness of Sins
Acts 13. 38

Forgiveness of sins and the knowledge of it
are features common to the whole family of
God 1 John 2. 12

1 It is a Divine forgiveness—
God Himself has lifted the
mighty load from off the
conscience, saying, 'I, even
I, am He that blotteth out
thy transgressions'          Isa. 43. 25
2 It is a Personal forgiveness—
The Saviour Who spoke
to the weeping penitent at
His feet, said to me,
'Thy sins are forgiven'      Luke 7. 48
3 It is a Frank forgiveness—
no reserve in His heart—
'He frankly forgave'         Luke 7. 42
4 It is an Eternal forgiveness
and forgetfulness — The
Holy Ghost has come
from Heaven as God's
witness to us, saying,
'Their sins and their iniquities will I remember no
more'                            Heb. 10. 17
5 It is Forgiveness for Christ's
sake—It must therefore be
complete and perfect and
God-like in character.
'Your sins are forgiven
you for His name's sake.' 1 John 2. 12
The believer's sins are all forgiven, forgotten,
purged, borne and cast behind Jehovah's back.
w.s.

## 804 The Forgiveness of Sins

1 The Message—
is preached unto you        Acts 13. 38
2 The Source—Jesus, a
Prince and Saviour           Acts 5. 31
3 The Ground—
for His name's sake          1 John 2. 12
4 The Means—
through His blood             Eph. 1. 7
5 The Condition—
if we confess our sins        1 John 1. 9
6 The Extent—
all trespasses                   Col. 2. 13
7 The Measure—
the riches of His grace      Eph. 1. 7
8 The Result—
forgiving one another        Eph. 4. 32
I.W.P.

## 805 The Common Salvation
Acts 13. 38, 39

Here is—

A Royal Proclamation—
preached

A Purchased Salvation—
through this Man

A Personal Salvation—
unto you

A Plenteous Salvation—
all that believe

A Present Salvation—
is preached

A Perfect Salvation—
justified from all things

A Peerless Salvation—
could not be justified by the law of Moses
J. MCA.

## 806 Paul's Sermon in Pisidian Antioch
Acts 13. 16-51

1 HIS APPROACH—
'Men of Israel! Divine Government vs. 16-25
(The God of Israel chose,
exalted, suffered, gave, raised
up)

2 HIS APPLICATION—
To you is the word of this
salvation sent vs. 26-37

3 HIS APPEAL—
Believe (v. 39), Beware (v. 40),
Behold (v. 41)

Results—

Propagation of the Word of the
Lord v. 49

Persecution of the preachers of the
Word v. 50

Perseverance of the missionaries
of Christ v. 51

## 807 The Things Spoken by Paul
Acts 13. 45

HOW WERE THEY SPOKEN?

| | |
|---|---|
| In a *Wooing* tone | Acts 20. 20 |
| With *Weeping* eyes | Acts 20. 19, 31 |
| With a *Warning* note | Acts 20. 28-31 |

WHAT THINGS WERE SPOKEN?

1 Repentance toward God and
Faith toward our Lord
Jesus Christ (Epistles to
Romans and Galatians) Acts 20. 21

2 The Gospel of the grace of
God (1 and 2 Corinthians) Acts 20. 24

3 The Kingdom of God (1 and 2
Thessalonians) Acts 20. 25

4 The whole counsel of God
(the Prison Epistles) Acts 20. 27

5 The words of the Lord Jesus
(the Pastoral Epistles) Acts 20. 35

HOW THEY WERE RECEIVED?

With opposition and blasphemy
by the Jews—Hostile Critics Acts 13. 45

With reverence and receptivity
by Lydia—True believer Acts 16. 14

With indifference and inattention by Eutychus—Careless
Backslider Acts 20. 9

With courtesy and rejection by
the Centurion — Friendly
worldling Acts 27. 11

## 808 The Work the Missionaries Accomplished

1 Proclamation of the Gospel Acts 14. 21
2 Impartation of the truth Acts 14. 21
3 Confirmation of the disciples Acts 14. 22
4 Exhortation of the believers Acts 14. 22
5 Ordination of elders Acts 14. 23
6 Supplication for the saints Acts 14. 23
7 Commendation of the saints
to the Lord Acts 14. 23

## 809 The Council at Jerusalem
Acts 15

1 *What it was*—
a meeting of the local church, the
first assembly Conference on
record vs. 4, 6

2 *Where it was held*—
in Jerusalem v. 4

3 *Why was it convened?*
To consider a matter of the utmost
importance in missionary work vs. 4-6

4 *Who met in conference?*
Apostles, elders, missionaries and
delegates from the assembly at
Antioch vs. 4-6

5 *How did it proceed?*
With reports from missionary
workers, Peter, Paul and Barnabas.

Peter's Address—vs. 7-11

An *Intimation*—
Gentiles, hearing the Word he preached,
believed, were cleansed and received the
Holy Ghost

An *Inference*—
Salvation comes to them, as to the Jews, by
the grace of our Lord Jesus Christ, through
faith, and not by the law of Moses

An *Inconsistency*—
Why then put upon them a yoke they had
not borne—circumcision and the Mosaic
law—which neither the Jews in the past nor
then were able to bear?

Barnabas and Paul reported the conversion of
Gentiles and the marvellous change in their
lives, without circumcision v. 12

James, an elder in Jerusalem, summing up, gave
his judgment on the matter vs. 13-21

The decision of the Conference was recorded
and reported by letter to the local churches
vs. 22-29

**810 Paul's Visions**

1 Near Damascus—a man in sin
Acts 9. 12; 26. 19

2 Outside Lystra—a man in Christ
Acts 14. 19; 2 Cor. 12. 1-4

3 At Troas—a man in the Spirit
Acts 16. 9

4 In Corinth—a man in communion
Acts 18. 9, 10

5 In the castle, Jerusalem—a prisoner in chains          Acts 23. 11

**811 Prayer Meetings and Conversions in Acts 16**

1 Before a Prayer Meeting—
Conversion of a slave girl
under Satanic control          vs. 16-18

2 During a Prayer meeting—
Conversion of Lydia, a seller
of purple          vs. 13, 14

3 After a Prayer meeting—
Conversion of the jailor and
his household          vs. 25-33

**812 Lydia, an Asiatic, the First Convert in Philippi**

1 Her Ears were opened to hear
the Word spoken by Paul   Acts 16. 14

2 Her Heart was opened to
accept the Lord Jesus
Christ          Acts 16. 14

3 Her Mouth was opened to
confess the Lord          Acts 16. 15

4 Her Home was opened to receive the Lord's servants   Acts 16. 15

**813 The Conversion of the Philippian Jailor**

1 Sudden Shaking—
the foundations of the
prison were shaken          Acts 16. 26

2 Alarmed Awaking—
the keeper — awaking —
would have killed himself  Acts 16. 27

3 Unwonted Quaking—
he—sprang in and came
trembling          Acts 16. 29

4 Earnest Seeking—
Sirs, what must I do to be
saved?          Acts 16. 30

5 Faithful Speaking—
Believe on the Lord Jesus
Christ, and thou shalt be
saved, and thy house      Acts 16. 31

6 Decision making—
Believing in God with all
his house          Acts 16. 34

7 Joyous Partaking—
Set meat before them, and
rejoiced          Acts 16. 34

**814 Paul in Athens**

WHAT GOD SAYS OF THEM
The people of Athens were—

*Steeped in Idolatry*          Acts 17. 16
*Soaked in Philosophy*          Acts 17. 18, 21
*Sunk in Superstition*          Acts 17. 22

WHAT THEY SAID OF PAUL—

1 An Ignorant Plagiarist, picking up scraps of knowledge Acts 17. 18
('Babbler'—Greek 'Spermo-
logos'—a seed-picker)

2 An Announcer of foreign
Deities          Acts 17. 18

3 A Teacher of new Doctrines Acts 17. 19

4 A Propagator of Strange
Teaching          Acts 17. 20

WHAT PAUL TOLD THEM—
The God Whom they did not know is

1 the Ruler of the Universe   Acts 17. 24
2 the Source of all life          Acts 17. 25
3 the Creator of all mankind Acts 17. 26
4 Regulator of world events   Acts 17. 26

The God Whom they did not know
Commands all men to repent   Acts 17. 30
Has appointed a day of judg-
ment          Acts 17. 31
Raised Jesus from the dead to be
the judge of all          Acts 17. 31

**815 God's Horizon**

Occurrences of the Greek verb 'Horizo', from which 'Horizon' is derived, and which is translated—determine, determinate, declare, limit, etc.

On the Horizon of God are—

1 the Epochs of History          Acts 17. 26
2 the Frontiers of Geography Acts 17. 26
3 the Road to Calvary          Luke 22. 22
4 the Death of Christ on the
Cross          Acts 2. 23
5 the Resurrection of Jesus   Rom. 1. 4
6 the Opportunities to hear
God's voice          Heb. 4. 7
7 the Coming Judgment and
the Judge          Acts 10. 42

**816 Repentance**

1 The Authority of God commands it          Acts 17. 30
2 The Goodness of God leads
to it          Rom. 2. 4
3 The Longsuffering of God
waits for it          2 Pet. 3. 8
4 The Grace of God grants it Acts 11. 19
5 The Love of God rejoices
over it          Luke 15. 7

W.W.F.

139

### 817 By Royal Command
Acts 17. 30, 31

1 Who commands? God
2 When? now
3 Whom? all men
4 Where? everywhere
5 What? to repent
6 Why? day appointed and Judge appointed

### 818 Sinners Paul Addressed

1 The *Careless* Sinner—Gallio Acts 18. 17
Indifference is a deadly enemy of the Gospel, and is a marked characteristic of men in these last days (Jonah 1. 6; Amos 6. 1)

2 The *Convicted* Sinner—Felix Acts 24. 25
Conviction is not conversion (Prov. 27. 1)

3 The *Calculating* Sinner—Agrippa Acts 26. 28
'With a little persuasion you would like to make me a Christian.'
'Even from the Gates of Heaven there was a way to Hell'—Bunyan

All three perished, as far as the Scriptures enlighten us.

**W.A.T.**

### 819 Prisca the Faithful

Prisca—means 'old woman', though she does not appear to have been old when Paul met her.

Paul always uses the proper form of her name Prisca (Cf. the R.V.)

Luke always uses the diminutive or endearing form, Priscilla.

She was the wife of Aquila, a Jewish tent-maker, and they are always mentioned together.

She was—

1 Of high rank: it has been suggested that her social status was higher than her husband's

2 Of a Hospitable nature—
'Paul abode with them' Acts 18. 3

3 Of Holy deportment—a helper of Paul in Christ Rom. 16. 4

4 Well instructed in the Scriptures—expounded to Apollos the Word of God more perfectly Acts 18. 26

5 Full of courage:—she and Aquila 'risked their necks' Rom. 16. 4

6 Ready for self-sacrifice for Paul's sake Rom. 16. 4

7 Greatly loved by the saints in all the churches Rom. 16. 4

### 820 Apollos the Eloquent Preacher

Apollos was—
1 Skilful in the Scriptures Acts 18. 24
2 Forceful in his Fervour Acts 18. 25
3 Useful in his Utterances Acts 18. 25
4 Powerful in his Preaching Acts 18. 26
5 Helpful in his Humility
Acts 18. 26; 1 Cor. 3. 6
6 Faithful in his Friendship
1 Cor. 3. 4; 16. 12
7 Tactful in his Teamwork
1 Cor. 3, 4; 16. 12

### 821 Apollos the Missionary from Africa

1 His *Antecedents*—a Jew by birth, an African by nationality Acts 18. 24
2 His *Ability* in the Scriptures
His *Discourses* were Scriptural—'mighty in the Scriptures'
His *Delivery* was Splendid —'eloquent in speech' Acts 18. 24
3 His *Ardour* of spirit—'fervent in spirit', full of enthusiasm Acts 18. 25
4 His *Activity* in service—
He taught Acts 18. 25
he spoke boldly Acts 18. 26
5 His *Achievements* among the saints—
He helped the believers much Acts 18. 27
he watered the young churches 1 Cor. 3. 6

### 822 Paul's Ministry at Ephesus

Paul's Address to the elders of the church at Ephesus comprised—

1 His Personal Activities during his three years there Acts 20. 18-27
2 His Pastoral Advice for the church's future welfare Acts 20. 28-31
3 His Practical Application of his example and teaching Acts 20. 32-35

His ministry among them was—

1 Unostentatious—with all humility Acts 20. 19, 20
2 Gracious—with many tears Acts 20. 19
3 Profitable — kept back nothing that was profitable Acts 20. 20
4 Faithful—testifying repentance Acts 20. 21, 26
5 Fearless—I have not shunned to declare Acts 20. 27
6 Full—the whole counsel of God Acts 20. 27
7 Far-seeing—I ceased not to warn every onenight and day Acts 20. 29-31

## 823  Elders and their Work
### Acts 20. 17, 28

Elders of the church should be—
1 Shepherds—to feed the flock
Acts 20. 28; 1 Pet. 5. 2
2 Guides—to lead the saints
Heb. 13. 7 (Margin)
3 Guardians—to watch for the souls of believers  Heb. 13. 17
4 Overseers—to take the oversight of the church  1 Pet. 5. 2, 3
5 Teachers—to instruct the disciples
1 Tim. 3. 2
6 Fathers—to give counsel and comfort
1 Thess. 2. 11
7 Examples—to show the character of the Head of the Church
1 Pet. 5. 3, 4

## 824  The Flock of God
### Acts 20. 28; 1 Pet. 5. 2

1 Sought by the loving Shepherd when going astray  Luke 15. 4
2 Bought by the Good Shepherd with His precious blood  Acts 20. 28
3 Brought by the Great Shepherd into the one flock  John 10. 16
4 Taught by the Under-shepherds to feed on the Word 1 Pet. 5. 2, 4
The Under-shepherds
are the gift of the Chief Shepherd  Eph. 4. 11
are to be examples to the flock  1 Pet. 5. 3
will be rewarded by the Chief Shepherd  1 Pet. 5. 4

## 825  The Word of His Grace

The message of God's free bounty has a wonderful effect on the hearts of believers. Paul, in concluding his address to the Ephesian elders, shows its practical application—
1 The Word of His grace
and what it does—
sets apart for God
builds up
gives an inheritance  Acts 20. 32
2 The Example of Paul and
what it shows—
not to covet
not to be idle
to help others  Acts 20. 33, 34
3 The Saying of our Lord
and what it means—  Acts 20. 35
Happiness is greater in giving to others than receiving from others.

## 826  A Remarkable Contrast in Acts 21
1 Four women filled with the Spirit  Acts 21. 9
2 Four men filled with religion Acts 21. 23

W.W.F.

## 827  Things to Come
### Acts 24. 25

1 A Life to come  1 Tim. 4. 8
2 An Age to come  Matt. 12. 32
3 A World to come  Heb. 2. 5
4 Judgment to come  Acts 24. 25
5 Wrath to come  Matt. 3. 7

## 828  Paul's Obedience to God's Call
### Acts 26. 19

The Call came through—
the Voice of the Lord and  Acts 26. 14
the Vision of the lost  Acts 26. 18
(The lost—blind, in darkness, under Satan's control, guilty sinners and disinherited.)
to—the Vocation of a Lifetime
—a minister and a witness  Acts 26. 16

His Obedience was—

*Immediate* — Whereupon, O King Agrippa  Acts 26. 19

*Implicit*—I was not disobedient Acts 26. 19

*Impelling*—but showed first unto them that they should repent Acts 26. 20

## 829  Paul's Voyage and Shipwreck
### Acts 27

1 DIVINE PROTECTION—
Julius, although a Roman Centurion, is kindly disposed toward Paul and brings him safely to Rome. God was at the back of the arrangement v. 1

2 PERILOUS REJECTION—
Paul's wise advice to the mariners was rejected, like the Gospel today  vs. 10, 11

3 PREVAILING INTERCESSION—
During the great storm Paul had been praying for the safety of the 275 lives on board  vs. 21. 22

4 COMPLETE SALVATION—
All lives saved  v. 22

5 PERSONAL DEVOTION—
'Whose I am'—Possession
'Whom I serve'—Consecration  v. 23

PERFECT RESIGNATION—
The storm was unabated. Paul did not trust the ship, for it was doomed, nor the sailors, a bad lot, but against all appearances he trusted God v. 25

J.G.

## 830 Life's Voyage

The Voyage of life is like the voyage described in Acts 27.

1 WHAT KIND OF VOYAGE—
  *Difficult*—the wind not suffering
    us                                         v. 7
  *Dangerous*—sailing was now
    dangerous                                  v. 9
  *Detrimental*—with hurt and
    much damage                                v. 10

2 WHAT MEN TRUST ON LIFE'S
  VOYAGE—
  the Voice of Experience—the
    master and owner                           v. 11
  the Way of Expediency—the
    haven was not commodious                   v. 12
  the Drift of Circumstances—
    the south wind blew softly                 v. 13

3 WHAT MANY DO IN LIFE'S STORMS—
  Are Deaf to Revelation—do not
    heed the things spoken by
    Paul                                      vs. 10. 11
  Desire Reformation—lighten
    the ship                                   v. 18
  Are Driven to Desperation—all
    hope—taken away                            v. 28

4 THE TRUE HOPE OF THE SOUL—
    the four anchors                           v. 29

1 Christ our Redeemer—Whose
    I am                                       v. 23
2 Christ our Lord—Whom I
    serve                                      v. 23
3 Christ our Comforter—Fear
    not                                        v. 24
4 Christ our Counsellor—it was
    told me                                    v. 25

## 831 Three Great Storms in the Bible Story
Acts 27

1 Jonah asleep in a storm—
    the Disobedient servant,
    unconcerned                       Jonah 1. 4, 5

2 Jesus asleep in a storm—
    the Perfect Servant, un-
    perturbed                          Matt. 8. 24

3 Paul awake in a storm—
    the Zealous servant, un-
    flinching                        Acts 27. 18, 21

# ROMANS

## 832 The New Testament Epistles

PAUL wrote *to*, and *of*, the Church
  of God—                              13 Letters
PETER wrote *to*, and *of*, the Flock
  of God—                               2 Letters
JOHN wrote *to*, and *of*, the
  Family of God—                        3 Letters
JAMES wrote *to*, and *of*, the People
  of God—                               1 Letter
JUDE wrote *to*, and *of*, the Saints
  of God—                               1 Letter

The Epistle to the Hebrews—the author uncertain—was written to Hebrew Christians and contains, more than any other letter, citations from, and allusions to, the Old Testament Scriptures.

## 833 Divisions of the Epistle to the Romans

1 God's Grace—
    Doctrinally stated                  chs. 1-4

2 God's Grace—
    Practically applied                 chs. 5-8

3 God's Sovereignty—
    seen in His purposes—for
    Israel and the nations              chs. 9-11

4 God's Sovereignty—
    in the life of the individual
    Christian, in the church and
    in the State                        chs. 12-15

5 Paul's SALUTATIONS                     ch. 16

## 834 The Facts of the Gospel Unfolded

1 *Condemnation* of sinful men, opposed to
    God—Reprobate minds and Dis-
    honoured bodies          Rom. 1. 1-32

2 *Explanation* of God's Dealings with men,
    and God's verdict of Guilt
                             Rom. 2. 1-3, 18

3 *Propitiation* for sin by the death of Christ,
    a sinless sacrifice      Rom. 3. 19-26

4 *Justification* through faith in Christ
                             Rom. 3. 27-31

5 *Illustration* of how God justifies the
    believer in Christ       Rom. 4. 1-25

## 835 Christ's Resurrection and Ours in 'Romans'

1 The Proof of Christ's Deity  Rom. 1. 4
2 The Pledge of our justifica-
    tion                     Rom. 4. 24, 25
3 The Pattern of new life in
    Christ                   Rom. 6. 4, 5, 9
4 The Power for the expres-
    sion of that life        Rom. 7. 4
5 The Promise of our resur-
    rection                  Rom. 8. 11
6 The Provision for our
    peace of mind            Rom. 8. 34
7 The Profession of our
    faith for salvation      Rom. 10. 9

**836 Don't be Ignorant, Brethren**

Seven things about which brethren are not expected to be ignorant.

| | | |
|---|---|---|
| 1 | Fruitbearing | Rom. 1. 13 |
| 2 | God pleasing | 1 Cor. 10. 1 |
| 3 | Spiritual Gifts | 1 Cor. 12. 1 |
| 4 | Confidence in God | 2 Cor. 1. 8, 9 |
| 5 | Reunion of saints | 1 Thess. 4. 13 |
| 6 | Cutting off of Israel | Rom. 11. 25 |
| 7 | Faithful Promises | 2 Pet. 3. 8 |

HYP.

**837 The Christian's Debts**

1 To all men, Jew and Gentile, to preach the Gospel — Rom. 1. 14

2 To God, to live after the Spirit, mortifying the deeds of the flesh — Rom. 8. 12

3 To all the saints, to love one another — Rom. 13. 8

4 To the poor saints and to those who minister spiritually, to give — Rom. 15. 26, 27

**838 Why Preach the Gospel?**

1 Because of what man is, a sinner irrespective of colour, culture, class or creed
Rom. 1. 15; 1. 17; 3. 23

2 Because of what God is, a Saviour holy, just and unchanging. 'TIME WRITES NO WRINKLE ON THE BROW OF THE ETERNAL'.
Rom. 1. 17; 3. 26

3 Because of what the Gospel is, good news and God's power unto salvation
Rom. 1. 16

4 Because of what Christ is, the theme of the Gospel and the Judge of all men
Rom. 1. 3; 2. 16

5 Because of what we Christians are, Trustees of the Gospel, Debtors to our fellow-men, and Ambassadors for Christ
Rom. 1. 5; 1. 14; 2 Cor. 5. 20

**839 Not Ashamed**

1 The Christian is not ashamed of the Gospel of his salvation — Rom. 1. 16

2 The Servant of Christ is not ashamed of suffering for Christ — 2 Tim. 1. 12

3 God is not ashamed to be called the believer's God — Heb. 11. 16

4 Christ is not ashamed to call His saints 'Brethren' — Heb. 2. 11

**840 Things Which may be Despised**

1 The riches of God's goodness — Rom. 2. 4

2 The chastening of the Lord — Heb. 12. 5

3 One of Christ's little ones — Matt. 18. 10

4 The Church of God — 1 Cor. 11. 22

5 Prophecy — 1 Thess. 5. 20

6 Other people by those who are self-righteous — Luke 18. 9

7 Masters by their servants (Employers by their employees) — 1 Tim. 6. 2

T.B.

**841 Justification**

1 We are justified by God—The SOURCE of it — Rom. 3. 26

2 We are justified by grace—The SPRING of it — Rom. 3. 24

3 We are justified by blood—The GROUND of it — Rom. 5. 9

4 We are justified by resurrection—The ACKNOWLEDGEMENT of it — Rom. 4. 25

5 We are justified by faith—The PRINCIPLE of it — Rom. 5. 1

W.S.

**842 Seven Things about Justification**

1 The Source—It is God that justifieth — Rom. 8. 33

2 The Spring—Being justified freely by His grace — Rom. 3. 24

3 The Ground—Being now justified by His blood — Rom. 5. 9

4 The Proof—He was raised again because of our justification — Rom. 4. 25

5 The Means—Being justified by faith — Rom. 5. 1

6 The Evidence—By thy words thou shalt be justified — Matt. 12. 37

7 The Fruit—By works a man is justified — James 2. 24

G. GOODMAN

**843 What Shall We Say?**

1 God is the righteous Judge of the world — Rom. 3. 5

2 Abraham was justified by faith, not works — Rom. 4. 1

3 We who are dead to sin (confessed at Baptism) must not continue in sin — Rom. 6. 1

4 The Law is right and good, but the trouble is the sinful nature within us — Rom. 7. 7

5 God is for us and greater than anything that may seem to be against us — Rom. 8. 31

6 God is sovereign but never acts unrighteously — Rom. 9. 14

7 Gentiles who do not have the law of righteousness are counted righteous through faith in Christ — Rom. 9. 30

## 844 The Righteous

NONE RIGHTEOUS—'No, not one' of the human race                    Rom. 3. 10

ONE RIGHTEOUS—the centurion's confession
Luke 23. 47

SOME RIGHTEOUS—made righteous by the obedience of One          Rom. 5. 19; 1 Cor. 1. 30

ALL RIGHTEOUS—Of a future day it is written, 'My people also shall be all righteous' Isa. 60. 21; Rev. 21. 27

W. LUFF

## 845 Man's Destitution

| | |
|---|---|
| 1 No righteousness | Rom. 3. 10 |
| 2 No understanding | Rom. 3. 11 |
| 3 No desire for God | Rom. 3. 11 |
| 4 No goodness | Rom. 3. 12 |
| 5 No peace | Rom. 3. 17 |
| 6 No fear of God | Rom. 3. 18 |
| 7 No defence | Rom. 3. 19 |

H.K.D.

## 846 Abraham's Faith

Two illustrations of justification by faith in Rom. 4, Abraham and David. Neither could be justified by the works of the Law, for Abraham lived before the Law was given, and David broke the Law.

1 Circumcision—
the SEAL of faith: Abraham's faith was Prospective          Rom. 4. 11

2 Experience—
the STEPS of faith: Abraham's faith was Progressive        Rom. 4. 12

3 Progeny—
the SEED of faith: Abraham's faith was Productive (natural and spiritual)    Rom. 4. 16

4 Confidence—
the STRENGTH of faith: Abraham's faith was Persuasive Rom. 4. 20

## 847 The Steps of Abraham's Faith
Rom. 4. 12

Observe that it does not say—'who walk in the steps of our father Abraham', for sometimes he took false and wrong steps, but 'who walk in the steps of that FAITH of our father Abraham' See Heb. 13. 7

Step number One—Leaving all for God
Gen. 12. 5; Heb. 11. 8

Step number two—Leaving all with God
Gen. 13. 9, 14

Step number three—Finding all in God
Gen. 15. 1

Step number four—Yielding all to God
Gen. 22. 16

## 848 The Believer's Confidence

1 His past—
Justified by faith                  Rom. 5.1

2 His present—
This grace wherein we stand Rom. 5.2

3 His prospect—
The glory of God                  Rom. 5.2

4 His experience—
Tribulations also                  Rom. 5. 3

5 The Outcome—
Hope, and the love of God shed abroad in our hearts by the Holy Ghost          Rom. 5. 5

J.H.

## 849 The Four Freedoms in Romans

1 Freedom from sin's guilt in Christ our new Head   Rom. 5. 12-21

2 Freedom from sin's dominion as servants of a new Master                 Rom. 6. 12-33

3 Freedom from the Law's bondage, married to a new Husband           Rom. 7. 1-6

4 Freedom from the law of sin and death by the Spirit, a new Guide      Rom. 8. 1-14

## 850 Triplets in Romans
Romans 5. 1-20

1 v. 1 Peace with God—as to the past
v. 2 Access into this grace—our present standing
v. 3 Hope of the glory—our future prospect

2 Faith in v. 1, Hope in v. 2, Love in v. 3

3 Patience, experience, hope in v. 4

4 Peace with God in v. 1, Loving God in v. 5, Joy in God in v. 11

5 We rejoice in hope v. 2, in tribulation v. 3, in God v. 11

6 In vs. 6 and 7—Ungodly man, righteous man, and good man

7 Christ died for the ungodly v. 6, for sinners v. 8, for His enemies v. 10

8 The Trinity—God the Father in v. 1, God the Holy Ghost in v. 5, and the Lord Jesus Christ in v. 11.

9 Grace in v. 15, Abundant grace in v. 17, superabundant grace in v. 20.

J.M.H.

## 851 What Sin has Done

| | |
|---|---|
| 1 Made man a transgressor | Rom. 5. 14 |
| 2 Made Satan a tyrant | Heb. 2. 14 |
| 3 Made God a worker | Isa. 65. 17 |
| 4 Made Christ a sufferer | I Pet. 3. 18 |
| 5 Made earth a wilderness | Rom. 8. 22 |
| 6 Made punishment a necessity | Matt. 25. 46 |
| 7 Made hell a reality | Luke 16. 23 |

T.B.

## 852  The Free Gift
Rom. 5. 15, 16, 18

There are five things about this gift in Romans 5.

1 THE GIVER—GOD v. 15

He is the God of peace—Peace with
God                                    v. 1
He is the God of glory—Glory of
God                                    v. 2
He is the God of love—Love of God vs. 5-8
He is the God of reconciliation—
'reconciled to God'                   v. 10
He is the God of joy—Joy of God      v. 11
He is the God of grace—Grace of God v. 15

2 THE GIFT—JESUS CHRIST vs. 15-17

He was the Promised Gift Gen. 12. 5-7
with Gal. 3. 16
He is a Precious Gift 1 Pet. 2. 7
He was a Providing Gift for He has
provided

Peace with God v. 1, an access to God v. 2, the joy of hope v. 2, the Holy Ghost v. 5, Salvation vs. 6, 8, 9, 16, Eternal life v. 21, Justification vs. 1-9.

3 THE GROUND OF THE GIFT—THE GRACE OF GOD v. 15

The Source of Grace—God v. 15

The Subjects of Grace—the strengthless v. 6, sinners v. 8, enemies v. 10, the disobedient v. 19, the dead in sin v. 12, the condemned v. 18, the separated v. 11.

The Standing of Grace—sure standing place v. 21

The Surmounting of Grace—Much more v. 20

Submitting to Grace—so might grace reign v. 21

4 THE GLORY OF THE GIFT—Hath abounded unto many v. 15

5 THE GRACIOUSNESS OF THE GIFT—The free gift v. 15

W.J.D.

## 853  Early Stages of the Christian Life

1 The sinner in his poverty accepts the *Gift* of righteousness        Rom. 5. 17

2 The believer, dead with Christ, enters a *Grave*— 'buried with Him in baptism'           Rom. 6. 4

3 The believer, risen with Christ, is planted in a *Garden* 'Planted together in the likeness of His resurrection'    Rom. 6. 5

4 The believer, yielded to God, moves toward a *Goal* — Holiness and everlasting life       Rom. 6. 13, 22

## 854  Baptism unto the Name of the Lord Jesus
Rom. 6. 1-4

This is not dedication but a Figure of Death, Burial and Resurrection with Christ. It is—

1 A sign of repentance and faith in the Lord Jesus Christ    Mark 16. 16; Acts 2. 38

2 The Appeal (interrogation—R.V.) of a good conscience
1 Pet. 3. 20-22

3 A figure of burial with Christ and death unto sin    Rom. 6. 3, 4; Col. 2. 12

4 The beginning of a new life of holiness
Rom. 6. 4, 22

5 The putting on of a new and beautiful robe, Christ    Gal. 3. 27

6 An initial step in discipleship
Matt. 28. 19 (R.V.)

7 An act of public testimony before men
Acts 9. 18

The word 'unto' (Greek—eis) used in Acts 2. 38; 8. 16; 10. 48; 19. 5, signifies that the baptized person becomes the sole property of the person indicated after 'eis'—'Ye are not your own' 1 Cor. 6. 19 'Ye are Christ's' 1 Cor. 3. 23

## 855  The Cross of Christ in Paul's Epistles

ROMANS—The Believer on the Cross—crucified with Him—The *Identity it Produces*
Rom. 6. 6

I CORINTHIANS—the Preaching of the Cross—The *Mystery it Unfolds* 1 Cor. 1. 18

GALATIANS—The Offence of the Cross—Why do I yet suffer persecution? The *Ignominy it Implies*        Gal. 5. 11

EPHESIANS—The Power of the Cross—reconcile both unto God—The *Unity it Effects*
Eph. 2. 16

PHILIPPIANS—The Death of the Cross—became obedient unto death—The *Humility it Displays*        Phil. 2. 8

COLOSSIANS—The Blood of the Cross—'Having made peace'—The *Victory it Achieves*
Col. 1. 20; 2. 14, 15

## 856  Life's Greatest
Rom. 6. 23

1 Life's greatest reality—
Sin

2 Life's greatest certainty—
The wages of sin is death

3 Life's greatest offer—
The gift of God

4 Life's greatest issues—
'Death' and 'Life'

5 Life's greatest choices—
'Wages' or 'Gift'

6 Life's greatest medium—
Through Jesus Christ

## 857 The Impeccability of Our Lord Jesus Christ

Jesus Christ was Immaculate—'He did no sin' 1 Pet. 2. 22

He was also Impeccable—for 'In Him was no sin' 1 John 3. 5

Yet He came 'in the likeness of sinful flesh' Rom. 8. 3 His Humanity was different from ours which is sinful: His was sinless: His Humanity was different from Adam's which was at first innocent: yet 'He knew no sin' 2 Cor. 5. 21

Adam and Eve were capable of not sinning, but not incapable of sinning.

1 Jesus was born without sin—'that holy thing that shall be born of thee' (No other person was called holy at birth) Luke 1. 35

2 His Temptations were real, yet 'sin apart' Heb. 4. 15

3 His response to temptation was different from ours, for He had no 'lust' within Him to respond James 1. 14

4 His temptations were under the severest circumstances—in a wilderness at the beginning of His ministry, in a Garden (Gethsemane) before the Cross, and related to His perfect fulfilment of the Father's will Matt. 4. 4; 26, 38

5 His suffering in temptation was a real experience, so He is able to succour them that are tempted Heb. 2. 18

## 859 The Spirit

| | | |
|---|---|---|
| 1 | The Possession of the Spirit | Rom. 8. 11 |
| 2 | The Leading of the Spirit | Rom. 8. 14 |
| 3 | The Witness of the Spirit | Rom. 8. 16 |
| 4 | The Firstfruits of the Spirit | Rom. 8. 23 |
| 5 | The Help of the Spirit | Rom. 8. 26 |
| 6 | The Intercession of the Spirit | Rom. 8. 26 |
| 7 | The Mind of the Spirit | Rom. 8. 27 |

H.K.D.

## 860 The Effect of Receiving the Spirit

| | | |
|---|---|---|
| 1 | Godward—Prayer | Rom. 8. 15 |
| 2 | Soulward—Conflict | Gal. 5. 17 |
| 3 | Churchward—Love | Acts 4. 31 |
| 4 | Worldward—Separation | Acts 5. 13 |

JS. FS.

## 861 The Glory of the Lord
### as revealed in—

| | | |
|---|---|---|
| 1 | The Liberty of His glory | Rom. 8. 21 |
| 2 | The Gospel of His glory | 2 Cor. 4. 4 |
| 3 | The Body of His glory | Phil. 3. 21 |
| 4 | The Power of His glory | Col. 1. 11 |
| 5 | The Appearing of His glory | Tit. 2. 13 |

H.K.D.

## 858 The Holy Spirit in Five Realms in Rom. 8

| | | | |
|---|---|---|---|
| 1 | In the Realm of Control | Keyword 'law' | —A Principle that Emancipates vs. 2-4 |
| 2 | In the Realm of Thought | Keyword 'mind' | —A Power that Elevates vs. 5-7 |
| 3 | In the Realm of Action | Keyword 'deed' | —A Process that Eradicates v. 13 |
| 4 | In the Realm of Environment | Keyword 'hope' | —A Prospect that Exhilarates vs. 22-25 |
| 5 | In the Realm of Prayer | Keyword 'intercession' | —A Paraclete Who Educates vs. 26, 27 |

## 862 God for Us

Rom. 8. 31

### AGAINST US

1 The Guilty Past (things behind) Col. 2. 13

2 Fleshly lusts (things within) 1 Pet. 2. 11

3 Adverse circumstances (things without) Gen. 42. 36

### GOD FOR US IN

1 The Gift of righteousness Rom. 5. 16, 17

2 The Power of the Spirit Rom. 8. 4, 13

3 The Gift of His Son Rom. 8. 32

**863 He Spared not His Son**
Rom. 8. 32

Here is—

1 God's answer to our Opponents—'Christ that died'—His crucifixion
Rom. 8. 34

2 God's answer to our Accusers—Christ risen again—His resurrection
Rom. 8. 33, 34

3 God's answer to our Sentence of Condemnation—Christ's Exaltation—Christ at God's right hand    Rom. 8. 1, 34

4 God's answer to our present sufferings—Christ our Intercessor—His Priesthood
Isa. 53. 12

**864 No Separation from God's Love in Christ**
Rom. 8. 38, 39

1 By death or life          2 absolute states

2 By angels, principalities or powers, whether evil or good    3 spiritual forces

3 By things present or things to come
2 time states

4 By height or depth       2 relative worlds

5 By anything else in creation not in the list of 9 (Number of finality) already named.

THE REASON—

God's Purpose for us        Rom. 8. 29, 30
God's Provision for us      Gal. 5. 22, 23

**865 God's Earthly People and God's Effectual Purpose for Them**

1 Their Peculiar Privileges  Rom. 9. 3-5
(Nationality, sonship, glory, covenants, the Law, priestly service, the promises, the fathers, the Messiah)

2 Their Preference by God  Rom. 9. 13
(Isaac, not Ishmael: Jacob, not Esau—chosen)

3 Their Present Hardness —Eyes blinded, ears deaf to God      Rom. 11. 7, 8

4 Their Provocation to Jealousy at the blessing of the Gentiles     Rom. 11. 14

5 Their Predestined Preservation — all Israel shall be saved (Nationally, not individually) Rom. 11. 15, 26

**866 The Goodness and Severity of God**
Rom. 11. 22

God's Goodness is seen in—

The Kindness of a LOVING GOD Titus 3. 4

The Grace of a LIBERAL GOD     Eph. 2. 7

The Forbearance of a LONG-SUFFERING GOD            Rom. 2. 4

God's Severity (Greek—the Sheerness of a rock or precipice: the word is only found here in the New Testament) is seen in—
The sudden descent of judgment—
at the Flood       Gen. 7. 10; Matt. 24. 39
on Sodom and Gomorrah
Gen. 19. 24
on the Egyptians' firstborn
Exod. 12. 29
on backsliding Israel
Rom. 11. 11

**867 The Greatness of God**

1 The Greatness of His wisdom Rom. 11. 33
2 The Grandeur of His judgments          Rom. 11. 33
3 The Graciousness of His ways           Rom. 11. 33
4 The Glory of His power     Rom. 11. 36

**868 Through Him are all Things**
Rom. 11. 36

We have *peace with God* through our Lord Jesus Christ       Rom. 5. 1
We have received *the atonement* through our Lord Jesus Christ Rom. 5. 11
We have *joy in God* through our Lord Jesus Christ       Rom. 5. 11
We have *eternal life* through our Lord Jesus Christ       Rom. 6. 23
We have the *victory over death* through our Lord Jesus Christ 1 Cor. 15. 57
To God be the glory through our Lord Jesus Christ       Rom. 16. 27
E.A.H.

**869 Divine Sovereignty in Seven Spheres**
Rom. chs. 12-15

1 In the individual Christian's life      Rom. 12. 1, 2
2 In the Church of God      Rom. 12. 3-16
3 In the world of men       Rom. 12. 17-21
4 In the government of the State        Rom. 13. 1-7
5 In the Kingdom of God  Rom. 13. 8-14
6 In view of the Judgment seat         Rom. 14. 1-23
7 In the service of His people        Rom. 15. 1-33
(to the Saviour, to the saints and to sinners)

**870 Full Consecration**
Rom. 12. 1, 2

1 The Salvation of God—by the mercies of God

2 The Presentation of our bodies—present your bodies

3 The Dedication of our lives—a living sacrifice

4 The Renovation of our minds—by the renewing of your mind

5 The Transformation of our whole being—be ye transformed

## 871 One Body
### Rom. 12. 5

The expression occurs eight times in the New Testament.

1 The individual member of the Body and his ministry      Rom. 12. 3-9
2 The inter-relationship of the members and their importance      1 Cor. 12. 13-27
3 The inter-dependence of the members and the Head in heaven      Col. 2. 18, 19
4 The interpretation of the character of the Head by the members Eph. 4. 11-17

## 872 The Spiritual Barometer

1 Fervent in spirit      Rom. 12. 11
2 Active in service      Rom. 12. 11
3 Rejoicing in hope      Rom. 12. 12
4 Patient in tribulation      Rom. 12. 12
5 Importunate in prayer      Rom. 12. 12
6 Liberal in hospitality      Rom. 12. 13
7 Impartial in love      Rom. 12. 14

## 873 Christ as Lord

Spheres in which the Lordship of Christ in the believer is emphasized—

1 In the Recognition of the liberty of each believer      Rom. 14. 6-11
(Lord—8 times in 6 verses)
2 In the Remembrance of the Lord at the Lord's Supper      I Cor. 11. 20-32
(Lord—7 times in 13 verses)
3 In the Relationships of daily life      Col. 3. 16 to 4. 1
(Lord—8 times in 11 verses)
4 In the Return of the Lord Himself to the air for His own      1 Thess. 4. 13-18
(Lord—5 times in 4 verses)

## 874 Be Like-Minded
### Rom. 15. 5

1 A Right Mind      Luke 8. 35
2 A Sound Mind      2 Tim. 1. 7
3 A Pure Mind      2 Pet. 3. 1
4 A Spiritual Mind      Rom. 8. 6
5 A Guided Mind      1 Pet. 1.13
6 A Garrisoned Mind      Phil. 4. 7
7 A Renewed Mind      Rom. 12. 2

JS. FS.

## 875 The Evangelist's Priestly Service
### Rom. 15. 16

'Offering up'—'sacrificing' (Margin)—is the same word used of the sacrifices under the Law, of Christ's sacrifice and of the 'spiritual sacrifices' of the 'holy priesthood' in 1 Pet. 2. 5

They are offered to—
the GOD OF PATIENCE      Rom. 15. 5
the GOD OF HOPE      Rom. 15. 13
the GOD OF PEACE      Rom. 15. 33

—God in the threefold Benediction—
and are obtained by the threefold Benefaction of—
the Divine Deacon, Jesus Christ      Rom. 15. 8
the Evangelistic Deacon, Paul Rom. 15. 16
the Ecclesiastical Deacon, the treasurer of the churches      Rom. 15. 26
in carrying out a threefold Benevolence—
the strong helping the weak      Rom. 15. 1
the taught teaching the uninstructed      Rom. 15. 14
the rich contributing for the poor      Rom. 15. 26

## 876 The Names in Romans Chapter 16 and their Spiritual Teaching

1 PHOEBE: Shining and pure—
We are 'light in the Lord' Eph. 5. 8 and 'Let your light shine before men, that they may see your good works, and glorify your Father which is in Heaven' Matt. 5. 16
2 ANDRONICUS: 'a man excelling others'—
We are to 'covet earnestly the best gifts' 1 Cor. 12. 31
3 URBANE: 'civil and courteous—
'Let your speech be always with grace, seasoned with salt.' Col. 4. 6
4 ARISTOBULUS: the best counsellor—
In our ministry for Christ—'preach the Word' 2 Tim. 4. 2
5 PHLEGON: zealous—
'Zealous of good works' Tit. 2. 14
6 OLYMPAS: heavenly—
'Partakers of the heavenly calling' Heb. 3 .1
'Not of the world' John 17. 14
7 TIMOTHEUS: honoured of God—
'Ye are a chosen generation, a royal priesthood, an holy nation, a purchased people'—'ye are now the people of God' 1 Pet. 2. 9 10

F.F.

## 877 Approved
### Rom. 16. 10

1 Approved in Christ—
Apelles was      Rom. 16. 10
a man in Christ 2 Cor. 12. 2, blessed in Christ Eph. 1. 3
2 Approved by God—
Paul was      1 Thess. 2. 4
'to be put in trust with the Gospel'
3 Approved unto God—
Timothy was to aim to be 1 Tim. 2. 15 'Handling aright the Word of truth'
4 Approved of men—
Those who serve Christ acceptably are      Rom. 14. 18
But we must be careful not to be Disapproved (meaning of 'a castaway' in 1 Cor. 9. 27)

**878   The Discipline of Avoidance**

| | |
|---|---|
| 1 Of Divisive teachers | Rom. 16. 17 |
| 2 Of Doctrinal heretics | Rom. 16. 17 |
| 3 Of Disorderly brethren | 2 Thess. 3. 6 |
| 4 Of Disobedient believers | 2 Thess. 3. 14 |
| 5 Of Dishonest trustees | 2 Cor. 8. 20 |

**879   The Mystery of the Gospel**
Rom. 16. 25-27

This mystery is—
'God's magnificent, world-embracing plan in the Gospel when preached at His command to all nations'          Eph. 6. 19, 20

The Good news itself is not a mystery, for it was 'preached before unto Abraham'
Gal. 3. 8.

THE GOSPEL—

| | |
|---|---|
| 1 Its Uniqueness | Col. 2. 2 |
| 2 Its Utterance | Col. 4. 3 |
| 3 Its Unity | Gal. 1. 6-9 |
| 4 Its Universality | Rom. 16.26 |

# 1 CORINTHIANS

**880   How 10 Church Problems were Solved**

| THE PROBLEM | THE SOLUTION |
|---|---|
| 1 Divisions among the saints<br>1 Cor. 1. 11; 3. 3 | Paul's example in the ways of Christ<br>1 Cor. 4. 17 |
| 2 Discipline necessary because of immorality          1 Cor. 5. 1-7 | Putting away from among them the wicked person          1 Cor. 5. 13 |
| 3 Defilement and Defrauding one another<br>1 Cor. 6. 8, 13-16 | Treating their bodies as the temples of the Spirit of God          1 Cor. 6. 19 |
| 4 Marriage and Divorce in the Christian community          1 Cor. 7. 1-5 | Marry 'only in the Lord' 1 Cor. 7. 39 |
| 5 Eating and Drinking and meats offered to idols          Chs. 8-10 | Do all to the glory of God  1 Cor. 10. 31 |
| 6 Divinely-appointed Headships<br>1 Cor. 11. 1-16 | Submission to God's order in the assembly gatherings          1 Cor. 11. 14, 16 |
| 7 Disorders at the Lord's Supper<br>1 Cor. 11. 20-22 | Self-examination before partaking<br>1 Cor. 11.28 |
| 8 Distribution and exercise of spiritual gifts<br>Chs. 12-14 | Do everything to edification, and decently and in order          1 Cor. 14. 26, 40 |
| 9 Denial of the resurrection by false teachers<br>1 Cor. 15 | Testimony of the Scriptures and of eye-witnesses          1 Cor. 15. 4-8 |
| 10 Donations to the Lord by the saints<br>1 Cor. 16. 1-8 | Lay aside on the first day of the week as God prospers          1 Cor. 16. 2 |

**881   Seven Things of God**

| | |
|---|---|
| 1 The Will of God | 1 Cor. 1. 1 |
| 2 The Church of God | 1 Cor. 1. 2 |
| 3 The Faithfulness of God | 1 Cor. 1. 9 |
| 4 The Power of God | 1 Cor. 1. 18 |
| 5 The Wisdom of God | 1 Cor. 1. 21 |
| 6 The Testimony of God | 1 Cor. 2. 1 |
| 7 The Deep things of God | 1 Cor. 2. 10 |

H.K.D.

**882   Your Calling**

1 Saints by calling—
Partakers of Christ's Holiness          1 Cor. 1. 2

2 Calling on the name of the Lord Jesus—
Acknowledgement      of Christ's Lordship          1 Cor. 1. 2

3 Called unto the fellowship of His Son—
Enjoyment   of   Christ's Fellowship          1 Cor. 1. 9

4 Unto them that are called, Christ the power of God—
Experience   of   Christ's Power          1 Cor. 1. 24

**883   The Saints at Corinth**

1 The Message by which they were called— 'Jesus Christ and Him crucified'
1 Cor. 2. 2

2 The Method by which they were constrained to believe   1 Cor. 2. 3
NOT by the Oratory of a Declaimer
NOR by the Persuasion of a Political candidate
NOR by the Worldly Wisdom of a Philosopher   1 Cor. 2. 1-6

3 The Men who were Chosen—
Socially weak, despised, unlearned
1 Cor. 1. 26-29
Morally-living in gross sin
1 Cor. 6. 9-11
Spiritually idolators   1 Cor. 12. 2

4 The Manner in which they were changed—
1 Cor. 6. 11
Washed, sanctified, justified

**884   What God has Prepared for His Own**
1 Cor. 2. 9, 10

Revealed by the Spirit of God in the Word of God to the child of God.

1 A Marriage Feast   Matt. 22. 2
2 Good works   Eph. 2. 10
3 A Place in the Father's house John 14. 2, 3
4 A City which has foundations   Heb. 11. 16
5 An Inheritance in His kingdom   Matt. 25. 34

**885   Three Classes of Men**

1 THE NATURAL MAN—
in his sins and unregenerate   1 Cor. 2. 14
Is a child of wrath   Eph. 2. 3
Does not receive the things of the Spirit
1 Cor. 2. 14
Does not know them   1 Cor. 2. 14
Counts them foolish   1 Cor. 2. 14
Does not understand them   1 Cor. 2. 14

2 THE CARNAL MAN—
regenerate but living after the flesh
1 Cor. 3. 1; Rom. 7. 14
Rom. 8. 7, 8
Cannot take strong meat but only milk
Has not grown in grace
Is sold under sin
Is not submissive to God's will
Cannot please God

3 THE SPIRITUAL MAN—
regenerate and spiritually healthy
1 Cor. 2. 13, 15
Knows the things God has freely given him   1 Cor. 2. 13, 15
Compares spiritual things with spiritual
1 Cor. 2. 13, 15
Has good discernment
1 Cor. 2. 13, 15
Is able to receive and comprehend the deep things of God
1 Cor. 2. 13, 15
Can restore a brother who has been overtaken in a fault
Gal. 6. 1

**886   God's Building**
1 Cor. 3. 9

1 The Habitation of God—Its Purpose
Eph. 2. 22
2 The Temple of God—Its Character
1 Cor. 3. 16, 17
3 The House of God—Its Responsibility
1 Tim. 3. 15; 1 Pet. 2. 4, 5
(Pillar and Prop of God's truth on earth)
4 The Tabernacle of God—Its Destiny
Rev. 21. 3, 10
5 The City of God—Its Glory
Rev. 21. 10, 11
(God is its Architect and Builder)

**887   Believers Are**

Labourers with God   1 Cor. 3. 9
the Husbandry of God   1 Cor. 3. 9
the Building of God   1 Cor. 3. 9
the Temple of God   1 Cor. 3. 16
the Property of God   1 Cor. 3. 23
H.K.D.

**888   Seven Forms of Judgment in 1 Corinthians**

1 Motive Judgment   4. 5
2 Self-judgment   11. 31
3 Divine judgment   11. 32
4 Assembly judgment   6. 5
5 World judgment   6. 2
6 Angelic judgment   6. 3
7 Civil judgment   6. 6
'JUDGE YE'
T.B.

**889   The Corinthians Were—**

1 Begotten through the Gospel   1 Cor. 4. 15
2 Brethren, in Christ   1 Cor. 2. 1
3 Built by God and for God 1 Cor. 3. 9.
4 Bought with a price   1 Cor. 6. 20
5 Baptized into one Body   1 Cor. 12. 13
6 Body of Christ, members in particular   1 Cor. 12. 27
7 Beloved by the apostle   1 Cor. 15. 58
JS. FS.

**890   Forms of Discipline in the Assembly**

1 Excommunication for grievous Moral Delinquency   1 Cor. 5. 11-13
2 Rejection for serious Doctrinal error
2 John 9, 11
3 Public Rebuke for less serious Sin
1 Tim. 5. 20
4 Avoidance and Disassociation for Disorderly conduct   1 Thess. 5. 14
5 Solemn Warning to Formers of factions
Tit. 3. 10
6 Silencing of vain and unprofitable Talkers
Tit. 1. 10, 11
7 Withdrawal of recognition for Defiance of the church   Matt. 18. 15-17

**891   Let us Keep Festival**
   1 Cor. 5. 7, 8

'Keep the feast' (A.V.) is the translation of one Greek word. The context shows it to be a reference to the Feast of Unleavened bread which immediately followed the Passover and lasted for seven days.

HOW TO KEEP IT—

1 With the Happiness of a
   Redeemed people          Exod. 5. 1
2 With the Holiness of
   an Unleavened people   Exod. 12. 14, 15
3 With the Homage of a
   Grateful people          Deut. 16. 15-17
4 With the Hopefulness of
   an Expectant people      Deut. 16. 15-17

**892   What God says of Believers**

'YE ARE'—

1 The 'Ye are' of Purification   1 Cor. 6. 11
2 The 'Ye are' of Sanctification  1 Cor. 6. 11
3 The 'Ye are' of Justification   1 Cor. 6. 11
4 The 'Ye are' of Association    1 Cor. 6. 15
5 The 'Ye are' of Possession
   by Christ                 1 Cor. 6. 19
   (Union with Christ)
6 The 'Ye are' of Redemption
   by Christ                 1 Cor. 6. 20
7 The 'Ye are' of Transforma-
   tion                       1 Cor. 6. 20
   (A Life like Christ)

                                   G.H.

**893   The Laws of the Christian Life**

1 The Law of Liberty—
   'all things are lawful unto me'
                          1 Cor. 6. 12; 10. 23
2 The Law of Authority—
   'I will not be brought under the power of
   any'                    1 Cor. 6. 12
3 The Law of Expediency—
   'All things are not expedient'
                              1 Cor. 6. 12
4 The Law of Edification—
   'all things edify not'
                              1 Cor. 10. 23, 24

**894   The Believer's Body Is—**

1 The Tabernacle of his spirit, his 'ego'
                              2 Cor. 5. 1, 6
2 A Member of the Body of Christ
                          1 Cor. 6. 13, 15; 12. 27
3 The Temple of the Holy Ghost
                              1 Cor. 6. 19, 20
4 A Vessel containing a Divine treasure
                              2 Cor. 4. 7
5 A Living Sacrifice to present to God
                              Rom. 12. 1

**895   The Lord's Free Man**
   1 Cor. 7. 22

Yet—'the slave of Jesus Christ' Gal. 1. 10
The two classes in the Roman world were the free men and the slaves.

MADE FREE—

1 By the Son             John 8. 36
2 By Christ              Gal. 5. 1
3 By the Truth           John 8. 32
4 By the Law of the
   Spirit of life         Rom. 8. 2
5 By the Spirit of God   2 Cor. 3. 17, 18

**896   Married in the Lord**
   1 Cor. 7. 39

When Christ is present and pre-eminent—

1 ON THE WEDDING DAY—
   He supplies any lack—    John 2. 2
   Marriage under the
   Happiest possible con-
   ditions

2 IN THE HOME—
   He provides for every
   emergency—              Mark 2. 1
   Home Life amid the
   Healthiest possible cir-
   cumstances

3 ON LIFE'S JOURNEY—
   He changes sadness to
   gladness—               Luke 24. 18-32
   Married Life with the
   Highest possible com-
   fort

**897   Service and Reward**
   1 Cor. 9. 16-18

1 Reasons for Service—
   necessity is laid upon
   me                      1 Cor. 9. 16
   that I might gain them  1 Cor. 9. 20, 21
   for the Gospel's sake   1 Cor. 9. 23
2 Requirements for Service—
   Willingness             1 Cor. 9. 17
   Faithfulness            1 Cor. 4. 2
   Lowliness               1 Cor. 9. 19
   Thoroughness            1 Cor. 3. 14
3 Rewards for Service—
   In measure as we shine here, we shall
   shine in the day of His glory
                              Dan. 12. 3
   In measure as we suffer here, we shall
   reign with Him in glory
                              2 Tim. 2. 12
   In measure as we serve here, we shall
   have authority when He returns
                              Luke 19. 17-19
   In measure as we are soul-winners here,
   we shall have joy and rejoicing in His
   presence              1 Thess. 2. 19, 20
   In measure as we shepherd the flock, we
   shall be commended when the Chief
   Shepherd appears    1 Pet. 5. 4

## 898  Spiritual Athletics

1 The short sprint—a race
  to win the prize (Greek
  —Stadion, a furlong
  —220 yards)                1 Cor. 9. 24

2 The boxing ring—not
  beating the air, practis-
  ing without an oppo-
  nent, but giving the
  opponent — self — the
  knock-out blow            1 Cor. 9. 26, 27

3 The Relay race—passing
  on the truth to the
  next in line               2 Tim. 2. 2

4 The obstacle race—over-
  coming the obstacles
  in the way                 Gal. 5. 7

5 The wrestling match—
  observing and con-
  forming to the rules       2 Tim. 2. 5

6 The Marathon—a long
  race—running without
  weights or sin that
  would trip up, running
  with endurance             Heb. 12. 1, 2

7 The last lap—concentrating on reaching the
  goal                       Phil. 3. 12-14

  Therefore 'Exercise
  (Greek — Gymnastise)
  thyself unto godliness'   1 Tim. 4. 7, 8

## 899  The Lord's Supper
### 1 Cor. 11. 20

'THIS DO'—

WHY DO IT?

1 Because of its Divine Institution
  Luke 22. 19, 20
  (In the Father's counsels, by the Son's
  command, with the Spirit's confirmation)

2 Because of its Historic Inauguration
  1 Cor. 11. 23

3 Because of its Apostolic Interpretation
  1 Cor. 10. 16, 17; 11. 26

WHAT WE DO?

1 We remember a Unique Person
  1 Cor. 11. 24

2 We proclaim a wonderful Death
  1 Cor. 11. 26

3 We celebrate a notable Victory
  1 Cor. 15. 4
  (the Lord's Resurrection)

4 We express a world-wide Fellowship
  1 Cor. 10. 16, 17

5 We anticipate a glorious Event
  (till He come)   1 Cor. 11. 26

HOW SHOULD WE DO IT?

There should be by all partakers—

1 Mental comprehension—discerning the
  Lord's body   1 Cor. 11. 29
2 Moral conformity—worthily
  1 Cor. 11. 28
3 Mutual consideration—one for another
  1 Cor. 11. 33

---

## 900  The Spirit of God

as revealed in 1 Corinthians 12

| | | | |
|---|---|---|---|
| 1 Confession of the Spirit | v. 3 | 2 Baptism in the Spirit | v. 13 |
| 3 Drinking in the Spirit | v. 13 | 4 Gifts of the Spirit | v. 8 |
| 5 Dividing by the Spirit | v. 11 | 6 Working of the Spirit | v. 11 |
| 7 Manifestation of the Spirit | vs. 7-10 | THE AIM—'to profit withal' | v. 7 |

T.B.

---

## 901  Spiritual Gifts

Greek—Charismata—gifts of grace—occurs 17 times in the New Testament. They are different
from the 'gifts' in Eph. 4. 8 where the Greek word is 'Domata', gifts.

| 1 COR. 12 | EPH. 4 |
|---|---|
| Gifts of the Spirit of God | Gifts of the ascended Lord |
| Abilities for ministry | Persons and classes of ministry |
| Exercised chiefly in the local church | Exercised usually in the whole Church |

1 Cor. 12—the Possession and Purpose of the gifts
1 Cor. 13—the necessary accompaniment of the gifts
1 Cor. 14—the exercise of the gifts for edification

SPIRITUAL GIFTS—

| | |
|---|---|
| The Holy Spirit is the Bestower ('by the Spirit'—five times) | 1 Cor. 12. 1-11 |
| The Holy Spirit through the gifts brings the recognition of Christ as Lord | 1 Cor. 12. 3, 8 |
| The Holy Spirit is the Distributor of the gifts | 1 Cor. 12. 7-12 |
| The Holy Spirit is the Controller of the recipients of gifts | 1 Cor. 14. 32 |

**902   The Laws of the Body of Christ**

1 The Law of Unity—
One body        1 Cor. 12. 12, 13, 20

2 The Law of Diversity—
many members   1 Cor. 12. 20, 23

3 The Law of Sympathy—
the same care for
one another    1 Cor. 12. 25, 26

4 The Law of Activity—
the effectual work-
ing of every part Eph. 4. 16

5 The Law of Authority—
holding the Head  Col. 2. 18, 19

**903   Love**

1 Cor. 13

'Charity' is a wrong translation. The Greek
word 'Agape' is used here, the same word as in
'God is love' 1 John 4. 8

1 Love is *Indispensable*—
Without it I say nothing, even
with the gift of tongues
Without it I am nothing, even
with knowledge and faith
Without it I gain nothing, even
though I make the utmost
sacrifice              vs. 1-3
A brilliant life—but love absent

2 Love is *Invaluable*—
Has 2 Positive qualities, patience
and kindness
Has 7 Negative qualities—'not'
Has 2 Relative qualities, 'rejoices
not in—but in—'
Has 4 Superlative qualities, 'all
things'                vs. 4-7
A beautiful life—with love evident

3 Love is *Infallible*—
Gifts of prophecy, tongues and
knowledge are impermanent   vs. 8-10
A blessed life—and love permanent

**904   Edification**

1 The Process of Edification—
building up  1 Cor. 14. 3, 5; Eph. 4. 12

2 The Profit from Edification—
individually  Acts 20. 32
collectively   1 Cor. 14. 4, 12, 19
corporately   Eph. 4. 16

3 The Provisions for Edification—
Gifts for men
            Eph. 4. 11
spiritual gifts 1 Cor. 14. 1

**905   Spirit-Guided Ministry**

1 No Presiding minister is
appointed      1 Cor. 14. 26

2 The edification of the
church and of each
member is the objec-
tive            1 Cor. 14. 26

3 There is no confusion,
only one speaking at
a time          1 Cor. 14. 31

4 There is a limit to the
number who speak
publicly        1 Cor. 14. 27, 29

5 The women present
keep silent and listen 1 Cor. 14. 34, 35

**906   Four Last Things in 1 Cor. 15**

The Last Witness—
Last of all He was seen of me        v. 8
The Last Adam—
The last Adam a quickening spirit    v. 45
The Last Enemy—
The last enemy—is death              v. 26
The Last Trumpet—
At the last trump                    v. 52
                                     T.B.

**907   'If Christ did not Rise Again'**

1 The Scriptures are false and unreliable, for
'He rose again the third day ACCORDING
TO THE SCRIPTURES'
1 Cor. 15. 4

2 Jesus is not declared to be the Son of God
with power
Rom. 1. 4

3 No atonement for sin has been made by
His death 'Ye are still in your sins'
1 Cor. 15. 17

4 We have not a Living Saviour
Acts 5. 30, 31

5 The Christian Church has no solid foundation and no Head
Matt. 16. 18; Eph. 1. 22; 2. 20

6 The believer has no hope beyond the grave
and is therefore 'of all men most
miserable'
1 Cor. 15. 18, 19

7 There is no divine power for the Christian
life    Gal. 2. 20; Phil. 3. 10; Col. 3. 1

**908   If the Dead Rise Not—Seven Terrible
Calamities in 1 Cor. 15**

Christ is not raised                 v. 13
We are yet in our sins               v. 17
Our faith is vain                    v. 14
Our preaching is vain                v. 14
We are false witnesses               v. 15
Those who have fallen asleep have
perished                             v. 18
We are of all men most miserable     v. 19
                                     T.B.

**909   Stand Fast**

1 Equality—Stand fast in the
faith as saints            1 Cor. 16. 13

2 Fraternity—Stand fast in one
spirit as brethren         Phil. 1. 27

3 Authority—Stand fast in the
Lord as disciples          Phil. 4. 1

4 Liberty—Stand fast in the
liberty as free men        Gal. 5. 1

# 2 CORINTHIANS

## 910  Paul, the Minister of Christ

1 His Salutation    2 Cor. 1. 1, 2

2 His Sufferings and Solace    2 Cor. 1. 3-11

3 His Sincerity    2 Cor. 1. 12-22

4 His Solicitude    2 Cor. 1. 22-2. 13

5 His Sufficiency    2 Cor. 2. 14-3. 18

He is—

a Minister of God    2 Cor. 6. 4

a Minister of Christ    2 Cor. 11. 23

a Minister of the New Covenant    2 Cor. 3. 6

a Minister of the Gospel Eph. 3. 7

## 911  The Apostle's Change of Purpose
2 Cor. 1. 15

His purpose had been to visit Corinth and minister to the saints there. Paul explains that the change in his plans was—

1 Not due to levity or lack of serious consideration    2 Cor. 1. 17

2 Not due to carnal desires    2 Cor. 1. 17

3 Not due to inconsistency in not being a man of his word 2 Cor. 1. 18

4 Not due to vacillation because of an unstable mind    2 Cor. 1. 21

5 BUT due to his desire to spare them further reproof and sorrow    2 Cor. 1. 23; 12. 21

## 912  Aspects of Christian Ministry

1 A Ministry of glory to all 2 Cor. 3. 9, 10

2 A Ministry of Reconciliation to the unsaved    2 Cor. 5. 18, 19

3 A Ministry of Suffering for the minister of Christ    2 Cor. 6. 4-10

4 A Ministry of Fellowship with the saints    2 Cor. 8. 4

5 A Ministry of Liberality to the needy    2 Cor. 9. 10, 11

## 913  Fourfold Fragrance

1 The Fragrance of the Knowledge of God    2 Cor. 2. 14

2 The Servant of God a Fragrance of Christ    2 Cor. 2. 15

3 The Fragrance of Death unto death    2 Cor. 2. 16

4 The Fragrance of Life unto life    2 Cor. 2. 16
     T.B.

## 914  Divine Sufficiency

Who is sufficient for these things? 2 Cor. 2. 16

Paul's answer—

1 Our sufficiency is of God    2 Cor. 3. 5

2 The sufficiency of the Gospel 2 Cor. 3. 6

3 The sufficiency of God's Grace    2 Cor. 12. 9

4 The sufficiency of His Glory 2 Cor. 3. 18; Col. 1. 12

## 915  Superiority of the New Covenant over the Old
2 Cor. 3. 6-9

It is a 'BETTER COVENANT' Heb. 7. 22

| THE OLD | THE NEW |
| --- | --- |
| Given by Moses, a prophet | Came by Jesus Christ, Prophet, Priest and King |
| The letter was important | The letter and the spirit are important |
| A ministry of death | A ministry of the Spirit of life |
| A ministry of condemnation | A ministry of justification |
| Made glorious | Excelling in glory |
| Its glory was transient | Its glory is permanent |
| Israel was blind to its true message—a veil not removed | The Christian can behold the glory of the Lord with unveiled face |

**916 The Minister of the New Covenant**
2 Cor. 3. 6

| | |
|---|---|
| Is one ANOINTED by the Spirit of God | 2 Cor. 1. 21 |
| Is an AROMA of Christ | 2 Cor. 2. 15 |
| Is an AMBASSADOR for Christ | 2 Cor. 5. 20 |

**917 The Veil that Covers the Face or Head**

Two Greek words are translated 'veil' in the New Testament, one used of the veil of the temple meaning 'a curtain'; the other used of the 'veil' on Moses' face (Greek-kalumma) meaning 'a covering'.

The 'Vail' in 2 Cor. 3. 13-18 is—

1 The Veil that *imposed Restrictions*    2 Cor. 3. 13, 15
'Moses put a vail over his face'
Israel—'the vail is upon their heart'
To the lost the Gospel is veiled    2 Cor. 4. 3

2 The Veil that *implores Removal*    2 Cor. 3. 16
When the nation of Israel turn to the Lord, the veil will be removed.
Already the veil is removed from the believer, who 'with unveiled face' can behold the Lord's glory    2 Cor. 3. 18

3 The Veil that *implies Recognition*    1 Cor. 11. 5, 13
Recognition, in the church and before the angels, of God's appointed Headships and of the authority of Christ.

**918 The Image of God**
2 Cor. 4. 4

1 In Creation man was made in the image of God    Gen. 1. 26, 27

2 By sin and disobedience the image of God in man was defaced
Gen. 5. 3

3 All mankind bears the image of the earthy
1 Cor. 15. 49

4 In Incarnation Jesus Christ came as 'the image of the invisible God'
2 Cor. 4. 4; Col. 1. 15

5 God's purpose is that the believer should be 'conformed to the image of His Son'
Rom. 8. 29

6 By beholding the glory of the Lord the believer is being changed daily into that image    2 Cor. 3. 18

7 At Christ's return saints will 'bear the image of the heavenly'
1 Cor. 15. 49; Phil. 3. 21

**919 The Judgment Seat of Christ**
2 Cor. 5. 10

The Greek word 'Bema'—translated 'judgment seat'—means primarily a step from which orations were made. Then it came to be applied to a Roman magistrate's Tribunal. In Rom. 14. 10 and 2 Cor. 5. 10 it is used for the tribunal before which all believers will stand and be made manifested.

1 THE TIME—'the day', 'the day of Christ' (Phil. 1. 10), 'the day of the Lord Jesus' (1 Cor. 5. 5), 'the day of Jesus Christ' (Phil. 1. 6)

2 THE JUDGE—'the Lord the righteous Judge'
2 Tim. 4. 8; John 5. 22

3 THE PERSONS JUDGED—'we all', i.e. all believers    2 Cor. 5. 10

4 THE STANDARD USED—Faithfulness, not success    1 Cor. 4. 1-5

5 THE SEVERITY OF THE TEST—tried by fire
1 Cor. 3. 13

6 THE RESULTS OF THE TEST—reward or loss
1 Cor. 3. 14, 15

7 THE GOAL OF ALL—eternal glory
1 Pet. 5. 4, 10

**920 Five Great Urges in Christian Service**

1 The urge of a Tremendous Responsibility    2 Cor. 5. 11
('Knowing—the terror of the Lord, we persuade men')

2 The urge of a Mighty Love —the love of Christ constraineth us    2 Cor. 5. 14

3 The urge of a Profound Gratitude—hath reconciled us to Himself    2 Cor. 5. 18

4 The urge of a Lofty Privilege—we are ambassadors for Christ    2 Cor. 5. 20

5 The urge of a Present Opportunity—now is the day of salvation    2 Cor. 6. 1, 2

**921 Seven Things—Old and New**

1 The old and the new creation
2 Cor. 5. 17; Col. 3. 10

2 The old and new Head
Rom. 5. 17

3 The old and new covenants
Heb. 8. 13

4 The old and new man
Col. 3. 10

5 The old and new commandment
1 John 2. 7

6 The old and new treasures
Matt. 13. 52

7 The old and new heavens
2 Pet. 3. 5-13

JS. FS.

**922  The Cross to the Glory**

1 Redeemed—
  He hath made Him to
  be sin for us                    2 Cor. 5. 21

2 Reconciled—
  Hath reconciled us      2 Cor. 5. 18;
  Made peace by the
  blood of His cross        Col. 1. 20

3 Righteous—
  made the righteousness
  of God in Him               2 Cor. 5. 21

4 Regenerated—
  in Christ — a new
  creature: 'created in
  Christ Jesus'               2 Cor. 5. 17;
                              Eph. 2. 10

5 Reviewed—
  made manifest unto
  God                        2 Cor. 5, 10, 11
                                    W.J.M.

**923  The Constraining Love of Christ**
       2 Cor. 5. 14, 15

1 A Crucified Lord—
  One died for all

2 A Consecrated Life—
  Live—unto Him Who died for them and
  rose again

3 A Constraining Love—
  the love of Christ constraineth us

CONSTRAIN—

  Luke uses the same Greek word, 'sunecho', in

  Luke 4. 38—of the Grip of a fever

  Luke 8. 45—of the Pressure of a crowd

  Luke 12. 50—of the constraint of a task to be
  accomplished

  Luke 19. 43—of the siege of a city, with no
  way out

  Luke 22. 63—of the Grip of officers arresting
  a prisoner

**924  Ambassadors for Christ**
       2 Cor. 5. 20

An ambassador is—

  A deputy appointed by his ruler

  a foreigner in the land in which he resides
  temporarily

  a stranger who must not participate in the
  politics of the land

  a mediator who endeavours to maintain a
  state of peace

  a Plenipotentiary who is honoured for the
  sake of his ruler.

CHRIST'S AMBASSADORS—

1 Their Appointment—
  'for Christ' and by Christ

2 Their Approach—
  'we pray', 'we beseech'

3 Their Appeal—
  'be reconciled to God'

**925  'Be Ye Reconciled to God'**

1 The Way of Peace—
  God in Christ recon-
  ciling                     2 Cor. 5. 19
  Christ made peace by
  the blood of His cross Col. 1. 20

2 The Work of Christ—
  a Sinless Saviour Who
  'knew no sin'              2 Cor. 5. 21
  a Stupendous Sacrifice
  —'made sin for us'        2 Cor. 5. 21
  a Satisfactory Settle-
  ment 'made the right-
  eousness of God in
  Him'                      2 Cor. 5. 21

3 The Word of Reconcilia-
  tion—
  'be ye reconciled to
  God'                     2 Cor. 5. 17, 20

'Get right with God' and do it now,
Get right with God—He tells you how.
Oh, come to Christ Who shed His blood,
And at the cross get right with God.'

**926  Credentials of the Minister of Christ**
       'IN ALL THINGS APPROVING OURSELVES'
       2 Cor. 6. 4

The Greek word translated 'commend' occurs
16 times in the New Testament, 9 times in
2 Corinthians.

1 The Fruit of his ministry—
  ye are our epistles
       2 Cor. 3. 1-3; 1 Thess. 2. 19, 20
2 The Character of his ministry—
  not crafty or dishonest
       2 Cor. 4. 1, 2
3 The Motive of his ministry—
  the love of Christ
       2 Cor. 5. 12-14
4 The Conduct of his ministry—
  giving no offence
       2 Cor. 6. 3-10
5 The Spirit of his ministry—
  when I am weak, then am I strong
       2 Cor. 12. 10, 11

**927  Giving to God**
GIVING is called
1 A Grace                    2 Cor. 8. 6
The Examples—
  God's unspeakable gift     2 Cor. 9. 15
  The Lord Jesus giving His
  all                        2 Cor. 8. 9
  The indigent saints in
  Macedonia                  2 Cor. 8. 1, 4, 5
The Exhortation—
  'see that ye abound in this
  grace'                     2 Cor. 8. 7
The Encouragement—
  'God is able to make all
  grace abound toward
  you'                       2 Cor. 9. 8

2 A Bounty (or liberality) 2 Cor. 9. 5
seven Principles to
follow—

Give spiritually     2 Cor. 8. 5
Give willingly     2 Cor. 8. 3
Give gratefully     2 Cor. 8. 7
Give proportionately     2 Cor. 8. 12
Give liberally     2 Cor. 9. 5, 6
Give purposefully     2 Cor. 9. 7
Give cheerfully
(hilariously)     2 Cor. 9. 7

3 A Sowing—
with a harvest to come 2 Cor. 9. 6, 9, 10

## 928   Motives for Giving to the Lord

1 The Example of Christ
Who 'became poor' and
'sold all that He had' 2 Cor. 8. 9

2 The Expediency of the
occasion — ministering
to the saints     2 Cor. 8. 4, 10

3 The Easing of the burdens
of poorer saints and the
Lord's servants     2 Cor. 8. 13

4 The Equalizing of means
by the supply of others'
needs from our abund-
ance     2 Cor. 8. 14

## 929   The Grace of our Lord Jesus Christ
    2 Cor. 8. 9

1 His Unlimited Possessions—
He was rich

2 His Unparalleled Poverty—
He became poor

3 His Unswerving Purpose—
that ye through His poverty might be
rich

## 930   He is Able
    2 Cor. 9. 8

What the Lord Jesus is able to do for us—

To save to the uttermost     Heb. 7. 25
To keep us from stumbling     Jude 24
To build us up and give us an
inheritance     Acts 20. 32
To make us stand—to hold us up   Rom. 14. 4
To succour them that are
tempted     Heb. 2. 18
To subdue all things to Himself   Phil. 3. 21
To make all grace abound to-
ward us     2 Cor. 9. 8
To do exceeding abundantly
above all we ask     Eph. 3. 20
To perform what He has
promised     Rom. 4. 21
    J.E.W.

## 931   'Thanks be unto God'

1 For what He has given in
the Past—His unspeak-
able gift     2 Cor. 9. 15

2 For what He is giving in the
Present — a place in
Christ's triumphal pro-
cession     2 Cor. 2. 14

3 For what He will surely
give in the Future—
Victory over death     1 Cor. 15. 57

## 932   The Three Unspeakables
'Unspeakable' is only used three times in the
New Testament—

1 His unspeakable gift     2 Cor. 9. 15
2 Heard unspeakable words     2 Cor. 12. 4
3 Rejoice with joy unspeakable 1 Pet. 1. 8

Each word translated 'unspeakable' is a totally
different word in Greek. Reconstructing the
passages by Liddell and Scott's Lexicon, we
get—

1 Thanks be unto God for His 'indescribable'
gift

2 Caught up into paradise and heard 'un-
published' words

3 We rejoice with joy 'unutterable' and full
of glory

    LIEUT. G. MARCULL

## 933   God's Unspeakable Gift
    2 Cor. 9. 15
The Gift of God—

His Son, Jesus Christ     John 3. 16
Living water     John 4. 10
Eternal life     Rom. 6. 23
Salvation of the soul     Eph. 2. 8
the Holy Spirit     Acts 2. 38

1 ITS ADVANTAGES—
its Inestimable cost     1 Pet. 1. 18
its Imperishable character—'eternal'
its Immediate conferment—'now'

2 ITS ACCEPTANCE—
by faith, and without payment Eph. 2. 8

3 ITS AVAILABILITY—
'Now is the day of salvation'   2 Cor. 6. 2

## 934   The Subtlety of Satan

1 Satan's works—
the Son of God came to
destroy them     1 John 3. 5

2 Satan's devices—
thoughts, plans, schemes,
mind     2 Cor. 2. 11

3 Satan's craftiness—
cunning     2 Cor. 11. 3

4 Satan's snare—
trap     1 Tim. 3. 7;
    2 Tim. 2. 26

## 935 Ministers of Satan

In 2 Corinthians 11, Paul writes of, and warns against—

| | |
|---|---|
| Satan's Methods | v. 13 |
| Satan's Machinery | vs. 12, 14 |
| Satan's Ministers | v. 15 |

SATAN'S MINISTERS—

1 Corrupt God's Word — 2 Cor. 2. 17
2 Trade on letters of commendation — 2 Cor. 3. 1
3 Measure themselves by themselves — 2 Cor. 10. 12
(Proverb—'The one-eyed is king among the blind')

4 Preach a counterfeit gospel — 2 Cor. 11. 4
5 Will reap the consequences of their evil deeds — 2 Cor. 11. 15

## 936 Spending and Being Spent

Paul's service was the service of—

1 A Surrendered life — 2 Cor. 4. 7
2 A Suffering love — 2 Cor. 6. 4-10
3 A Spendthrift loyalty — 2 Cor. 12. 14, 15 (spending and being spent out)
4 A Sorrowful longing — 2 Cor. 12. 21

---

# GALATIANS

## 937 The Centrality of the Cross in Galatians

The Cross is—

1 The Centre of God's Purpose for us
Deliverance from this present evil age — Gal. 1. 4

2 The Centre of God's Power in us
Deliverance from the bondage of the Law — Gal. 2, 19, 20

3 The Centre of God's Promise to us
Deliverance from the curse of a broken law — Gal. 3. 13, 14

4 The Centre of God's Patrimony for us
Deliverance from servitude to the world — Gal. 4. 4-7

5 The Centre of God's Provision for us
Deliverance from the works of the flesh — Gal. 5. 22-24

6 The Centre of our Jubilation and Boast
Deliverance from glorying in the flesh — Gal. 6. 13, 14

## 938 Why Christ gave Himself
Gal. 1. 4

1 To bring glory to God in doing the Father's will — Eph. 5. 2; Heb. 10. 7
2 To pay the ransom price for our redemption — 1 Tim. 2. 5, 6
3 To deliver us from this present evil age — Gal. 1. 4
4 To redeem us from all iniquity and purify us to Himself — Titus 2. 14
5 To present us to Himself, holy and blameless — Eph. 5. 25-27

## 939 Not I But—

THE PERSON—
'I live, yet not I, but Christ liveth in me' — Gal. 2. 20

THE POWER—
'Yet not I, but the grace of God —with me' — 1 Cor. 15. 10

THE PROCLAMATION—
'We preach not ourselves, but Christ Jesus' — 2 Cor. 4. 5

## 940 'Who gave Himself for Me'
Gal. 2. 20

He—

Gave His head to wear the thorns for me — John 19. 2
Gave His eyes to weep tears for me — Luke 19. 41
Gave His cheek to be smitten for me — Lam. 3. 30
Gave His tongue to pray for me — Luke 23. 34
Gave His shoulders to bear me to His home — Luke 15. 5
Gave His back to be ploughed for me — Ps. 129. 3
Gave His side to the spear-thrust for me — John 19. 34
Gave His hands to the nails for me — Ps. 22. 16
Gave His feet to the iron spikes for me — Ps. 22. 16
Gave His precious, precious blood for me — Acts 20. 28
Gave His soul a sin-offering for me — Isa. 53. 12
Gave His life for me — John 10. 11
Gave all His riches and became poor for me — 2 Cor. 8. 9
Will never rest till He comes again for me — John 14. 3

J.A.

**941  A Sevenfold Unity, the Basis of all Others**

1 I have been crucified with Christ, and still am — Gal. 2. 20

2 I was buried with Him in baptism — Rom. 6. 4

3 I have been quickened with Him — Eph. 2. 1

4 I have been raised again with Him — Eph. 2. 6; Col. 3. 1

5 I am seated in Heaven in Him — Eph. 2. 6

6 I am suffering with Him — Rom. 8. 17

7 I shall be glorified, and reign with Him — Rev. 20. 4

'CHRIST IS ALL AND IN ALL'

DR. W. P. MACKAY

**942  The Development of the Spirit in Galatians**

1 The Spirit promised — Ch. 3. 14

2 The Spirit sent forth — Ch. 4. 6

3 The Spirit ministered — Ch. 3. 5

4 The Spirit received — Ch. 3. 2

5 The Spirit — A beginning made in—the Spirit — Ch. 3. 3

6 Living in the Spirit — Ch. 5. 25

7 Led by the Spirit — Ch. 5. 18

8 The conflict of the Spirit against the flesh — Ch. 5. 17

9 Sowing to the Spirit — Ch. 6. 8

10 Fruit of the Spirit — Ch. 5. 22, 23

11 Waiting for the hope of righteousness through the Spirit — Ch. 5. 5

T.B.

**943  Concerning Abraham**

1 Abraham's Faith — Gal. 3. 6

2 Abraham's Children — Gal. 3. 7

3 Abraham's Blessing — Gal. 3. 14

4 Abraham's Seed — Gal. 3. 16-29

5 Abraham's Inheritance — Gal. 3. 18

H.K.D.

**944  The Gospel Preached to Abraham**

Gal. 3. 8

1 One Gospel through one seed, Christ
Gal. 3. 16

2 For all nations of the earth
Gen. 12. 3; Gal. 3. 14

3 A message and a source of blessing
Gen. 12. 3; Gal. 3. 14

4 The Basis of Abraham's greatness
Gen. 12. 4; 17. 5; Rom. 4. 1

5 Given before the Law and cannot be annulled by it
Rom. 4. 13-15; Gal. 3. 17, 18

**945  Four Views of the Cross by the Believer**

1 First he sees his Saviour crucified—'made a curse for us' — Gal. 3. 13

2 Next he sees himself crucified—'I have been crucified with Christ' — Gal. 2. 20

3 Then he sees the flesh and its passions and lusts crucified — Gal. 5. 24

4 Finally he sees the world system crucified to him, and himself to it — Gal. 6. 14

**946  Five Points of Time**

1 The fulness of the time—the Birth of Christ — Gal. 4. 4

2 The consummation of the ages—the Cross of Christ — Heb. 9. 26

3 The end of the age—the Close of Christianity — Matt. 13. 39

4 The fulness of the times—the Millennium — Eph. 1. 10

5 The end of time—Beginning of the day of God — 1 Cor. 15. 24

W.W.F.

**947  In the Spirit**

1 As Warriors—
Walk in the Spirit and ye shall not fulfil the lusts of the flesh — Gal. 5. 16

2 As Redeemed ones—
Having begun in the Spirit—continue — Gal. 3. 3

3 As Suppliants—
Praying always with all prayer and supplication in the Spirit — Eph. 6. 18

4 As Worshippers—
who worship God in the Spirit — Phil. 3. 3

5 As Brethren—
your love in the Spirit — Col. 1. 8

6 As United ones—
have our access in one Spirit — Eph. 2. 18 (R.V.)

7 As Obedient ones—
If we live in the Spirit, let us also walk in the Spirit — Gal. 5. 25

**948  Conflict and Crucifixion**

1 A Conflict—
The flesh lusteth against the Spirit and the Spirit against the flesh — Gal. 5. 17

2 A Contrast—
The works of the flesh and the Fruit of the Spirit — Gal. 5. 19-23

3 A Crucifixion—
They that are Christ's have crucified the flesh — Gal. 5. 24

4 A Conformity—
Live in the Spirit and walk in the Spirit — Gal. 5. 25

## 949 The Fruit of the Spirit
Galatians 5. 22, 23

1 LOVE is the Source of Obedience
2 JOY is the Flower of Holiness
3 PEACE is the Outcome of Trustfulness
4 LONGSUFFERING is the Partner of Patience
5 GENTLENESS is the Daughter of Love
6 GOODNESS is the Activity of Grace
7 FAITH is the Faithfulness of Courage
8 MEEKNESS is the Trait of Christ
9 TEMPERANCE is the Mastery of Faith.

C.C.

## 950 The Spirit of Meekness
The spiritual Christian has—

1 The Spirit of the Master
    Gal. 6. 2; Matt. 11. 29
2 The spirit of Meekness
    Gal. 6. 1; 1 Pet. 3. 14, 15
3 The spirit of Mercy
    Gal. 6. 1, 2; Rom. 12. 8
4 The spirit of Mending
    Gal. 6. 1; Luke 10. 34
(Note—'Restore' is translated 'mend' in
Mark 1. 19)

## 951 Bearers in Galatians 6

1 The Helpful Partner—
    'Bear ye one another's
    burdens' (Burden — weight) Gal. 6. 2
2 The Responsible Steward—
    'every man shall bear his own
    burden' (Burden — ballast,
    loading or cargo of a ship) Gal. 6. 5
3 The Devoted Slave—
    'I bear in my body the marks
    of the Lord Jesus' (Marks—
    stigmata, brands) Gal. 6. 17

## 952 Why Glory in the Cross?
Gal. 6. 14

It is—

| | |
|---|---|
| the Measure of man's guilt | Acts 3. 13-15 |
| the Manifestation of God's love | Rom. 5. 6-8 |
| the Means of salvation | John 3. 14, 15 |
| the Mark of separation | Gal. 6. 14 |
| the Motive for service | 2 Cor. 5. 14, 15 |
| the Melody of Heaven | Rev. 5. 8-10 |

F.F.

## 953 The Israel of God
Gal. 6. 16

1 They are not all Israel which
   are of Israel         Rom. 9. 6
2 He is a Jew which is one inwardly, and circumcision is
   that of the heart     Rom. 2. 29
3 Neither because they are the
   seed of Abraham are they
   children         Rom. 9. 7
4 They which are of faith, the
   same are the children of
   Abraham        Gal. 3. 7
5 Abraham believed God, and it
   was accounted unto him for
   righteousness     Rom. 4. 3
6 There is neither Jew nor Greek
   —ye are all one in Christ  Gal. 3. 28
7 If ye be Christ's, then are ye
   Abraham's seed according to
   promise        Gal. 3. 29

E.A.H.

## EPHESIANS

### 954 Spiritual Blessings

1 An Election that can never be annulled—chosen in Him    Eph. 1. 4

2 A Relationship that can never be severed—unto the adoption of Children    Eph. 1. 5

3 An Acceptance that can never be gainsaid—accepted in the Beloved    Eph. 1. 6

4 A Redemption that can never be challenged—through His blood    Eph. 1. 7

5 A Forgiveness that will never be rescinded—forgiveness of sins    Eph. 1. 7

6 An Abundance that can never be exhausted—He hath abounded toward us in all wisdom and prudence    Eph. 1. 8

7 A Revelation that will never be superseded—the mystery of His will    Eph. 1. 9

8 An Inheritance that can never fade away — we have obtained    Eph. 1. 11, 14

9 A Seal that can never be dissolved — sealed with that Holy Spirit    Eph. 1. 13

10 A Pledge that will never be dishonoured—the earnest    Eph. 1. 14

### 955 The Heavenlies in Ephesians

1 Our Blessings are there    Eph. 1. 3

2 Our Saviour is there    Eph. 1. 20

3 We are there    Eph. 2. 6

4 Observant Principalities and powers are there    Eph. 3. 10

5 Our Warfare against wicked spirits is there    Eph. 6. 12

### 956 Themes of the Ephesian Epistle

Chapter 1—Blessings that can never be Depleted    Eph. 1. 3

Chapter 2—A Building that can never be Demolished    Eph. 2. 21

Chapter 3—A Bequest that can never be Disputed    Eph. 3. 8

Chapter 4—A Body that can never be Decomposed    Eph. 4. 12, 16

Chapter 5—A Bride that can never be Divorced    Eph. 5. 27

Chapter 6—A Battalion that can never be Defeated    Eph. 6. 13

### 957 Past, Present, Perfect

1 A PREVIOUS PURPOSE—
Chosen—before the foundation of the world    Eph. 1. 4

2 A PRESENT INTENTION—
To the intent that *now* unto principalities and powers    Eph. 3. 10

3 A FUTURE DISPLAY—
That in the ages *to come* He might show    Eph. 2. 7

AUTHOR UNKNOWN

### 958 In Love

About 32 years after Paul wrote this letter to the church at Ephesus, our Lord sent to the same church by John another letter in which He said, 'Ye have eft your first LOVE'.

LOVE IS—

1 The Spring from which the saints are enriched in the Household of God    Eph. 2. 4; 6. 23

2 The Sphere in which the saints move in the Presence of God    Eph. 1. 4

3 The Soil in which the saints are planted in the Garden of God    Eph. 3. 17

4 The Subject in which the saints are instructed in the School of God    Eph. 3. 19

5 The Spirit by which the saints are characterized in the Family of God    Eph. 4. 2

6 The Sustenance by which the saints grow in the Church of God    Eph. 4. 15

7 The Street along which the saints travel to the City of God    Eph. 5. 2, 25

'WALK IN LOVE'

### 959 The Riches of His Grace
Eph. 1. 7

1 The greatest wonder in the world
Redemption

2 The blessing Redemption brings
Forgiveness of sins

3 The Person through whom it comes
Our Lord Jesus Christ

4 The means by which it is accomplished
through His blood

5 The way we become possessed of it
United to Him 'in whom ye also trusted'

6 The great fountain-head of all
the riches of His GRACE

PROF. JAMES ORR

**Ephesians**

## 960 Things Worth Knowing

1 The Mystery of His will      Eph. 1. 9
2 The Hope of His calling      Eph. 1. 18
3 The Riches of His glory      Eph. 1. 18
4 The Greatness of His power      Eph. 1. 19
5 The Wisdom of God      Eph. 3. 10
6 The Love of God in Christ      Eph. 3. 19
7 The Son of God      Eph. 4. 13

           H.K.D.

## 961 Christ's Headships

To head up all things in the Christ Eph. 1. 10—
New Translation

1 In the Universe      Eph. 1. 10; Col. 2. 10
2 In the Church of the redeemed
           Eph. 5. 23; Col. 1. 18
3 In the Human Race
           1 Cor. 11. 3

## 962 The Exceeding Greatness of His Power
     Eph. 1. 19

This is one of the 'HYPERBOLE' BLESSINGS.
Compare Eph. 2. 7; 3. 19

1 How Apprehended—
     the eyes of your hearts
     being enlightened      Eph. 1. 18

2 How Exemplified—
     in three ways—
     in Christ's Resurrection   Eph. 1. 20
     In His Triumph      Eph. 1. 21
     in our Relationship to
     Him      Eph. 1. 22, 23

3 How Appropriated—
     by faith—to us-ward who
     believe      Eph. 1. 19

4 How Operative—
     in producing likeness to
     Christ—
     morally      Col. 2. 12;
           Phil. 2. 13
     corporately      Eph. 3. 7; 4. 16
     physically      Phil. 3. 21

## 963 Past Condition—Present Position—Future Prospect

A study in Ephesians 2

**(A) A PAST CONDITION**

1 In times past—
     walking according to the course of
     this world, according to the
     prince of the power of the air    v. 2

2 In times past—
     fulfilling the desires of the flesh
     and of the mind; by nature children
     of wrath      v. 3

3 In times past—
     Gentiles in the flesh called Un-
     circumcision; without Christ;
     aliens from the commonwealth of
     Israel; strangers from the coven-
     ants of promise; without hope
     and without God      v. 11

4 In times past—
     far off      v. 13

**(B) PRESENT POSITION**

1 *Now* 'in Christ Jesus made nigh by
     blood'      v. 13
2 Now 'by grace are ye saved'      v. 8
3 Now 'we are His workmanship'    v. 10
4 Now 'we have access—unto the
     Father'      v. 18
5 Now 'ye are fellow-citizens with the
     saints'      v. 19
6 Now 'ye are built upon the founda-
     tion'      v. 20

**(C) FUTURE PURPOSE AND PROSPECT**

1 *In the ages to come*
     He might show the exceeding riches
     of His grace in His kindness to-
     ward us through Christ Jesus    v. 7
2 *In the ages to come*
     'all the building—a holy temple in
     the Lord'      v. 21

           W.H.

## 964 'Togethers' in Ephesians

1 Quickened together with Christ Eph. 2. 5
2 Raised up together (in Christ) Eph. 2. 6
3 Seated together in the heaven-
     lies      Eph. 2. 6
4 Framed together — an holy
     temple in the Lord      Eph. 2. 21
5 Builded together for an habita-
     tion of God      Eph. 2. 22
6 Joined together—the whole
     Body      Eph. 4. 16
7 Gathered together—all things
     in Christ      Eph. 1. 10

           JS. FS.

## 965 Exceeding Riches
     Eph. 2. 7

The Hyperbolical Blessings (the same Greek word in each)

1 The Excelling Glory of the
     Gospel      2 Cor. 3. 10
2 The Exhilarating Grandeur
     of our Prospect      2 Cor. 4. 17
3 The Exhaustless Gift of
     Christ's Love      Eph. 3. 19
4 The Exceeding Greatness of
     God's Power      Eph. 1. 19
5 The Extreme Goodness of
     His Grace      Eph. 2. 7

**966   Peace with God**
Eph. 2. 14

1 PEACE PROCURED—
Having made peace through
the blood of His cross        Col. 1. 20
So making peace              Eph. 2. 15

2 PEACE PROCLAIMED—
Christ came and preached
peace to you                 Eph. 2. 17

3 PEACE POSSESSED—
Being justified by faith, we
have peace with God          Rom. 5. 1

4 PEACE PERSONIFIED—
He is our Peace              Eph. 2. 14
A.J.P.

**967   He Is Our Peace**

1 Christ IS our Peace (or Peace-
offering)                    Eph. 2. 14
The letter to the Ephesian
saints is the Epistle of the
Peace-offering.   Believers,
God's priests, feast on the
Heave-shoulder of the Offer-
ing, Christ's power (Eph. 1.
19) and the Wave-breast,
His affection (Eph. 3. 19)

2 Christ MADE Peace by His
blood                        Eph. 2. 15

3 Christ PREACHED peace to
Gentiles that were afar off
and to Jews that were nigh   Eph. 2. 17

**968   The Mystery of Christ and the Church**
Eph. 3. 4; 5. 32

1 The Foundation of the
Church—the work of
Christ                       1 Cor. 3. 11

2 The Composition of the
Church—Saved Jews and
Gentiles                     Eph. 3. 6

3 The Relationships in the
Church—Fellow-heirs, of
the same body, and part-
ners of His promise          Eph. 3. 6

4 The Hope of the Church—
Glory, for Christ dwells in
it                           Col. 1. 27

**969   Links of Fellowship**

1 Fellow-heirs—
of one inheritance           Eph. 3. 6

2 Fellow-members—
of one body                  Eph. 3. 6 (R.V.)

3 Fellow-partakers—
of one calling               Eph. 3. 6 (R.V.)

4 Fellow-citizens—
of one home                  Eph. 2. 19

5 Fellow-labourers—
of one Master                Phil. 4. 3

6 Fellow-soldiers—
in one warfare               Phil. 2. 25

7 Fellow-prisoners—
with one hope                Rom. 16. 7
F.F.

**970   The Fulness of the Godhead**

1 The Fulness of God         Eph. 3. 16-19
2 The Fulness of Christ      Eph. 4. 7-13
3 The Fulness of the Spirit  Eph. 5. 18-21

THE PARTAKERS OF THAT FULNESS—the Church
which is His Body, the Fulness of Him that
filleth all in all           Eph. 1. 23
'For in Him dwelleth all the fulness of the
Godhead bodily, and ye are filled full in Him'
Col. 2. 9, 10; John 1. 16
E.A.H.

**971   Fulness for the Believer**

1 Fulness for his Heart, when
Christ's Worth is appreciated Eph. 3. 19

2 Fulness for his Mind, when
Christ's Will is apprehended Col. 1. 9

3 Fulness for his Life, when
Christ's Ways are assimi-
lated                        Phil. 1. 11

**972   Walking Worthy**
Eph. 4. 1

1 'Walk *worthy of God*, who
hath called you unto His
kingdom and glory'           1 Thess. 2. 12
Walk in keeping with the
truth that the living God
has implanted, supplant-
ing your former dead
idols, and set you to wait
for His Son from heaven.

2 'Walk *worthy of the Lord*
unto all pleasing'           Col. 1. 10
Christ is exalted as the
'Head' in Colossians,
and we are to own Him
practically as such. We
need not go to the wis-
dom of man for help, for
all resources are stored
up in that exalted Lord
in glory.

3 'Walk *worthy of the vocation* wherewith ye are
called'                      Eph. 4. 1
It is in keeping with the
truth of the Church un-
folded in this Epistle in
Chapter 2—Association
with Christ and one
another in resurrection
as a new creation, access
as worshippers to the
Father, and builded to-
gether for an habitation
of God through the Spirit
Thus the individual
walk and the collective
walk are to be in keeping
with the grace in which
we stand.
M.I.R.

## 973 Gifts to the Church from the Ascended Lord

1 A PERFECT PROVISION—
Apostles, and prophets for the foundation work    Eph. 4. 10, 11
Evangelists, pastors and teachers for the super-structure

2 A PREDOMINANT PURPOSE—
the Edifying of the Body of Christ    Eph. 4. 12

3 A PRESENT PROGRAMME—
Speaking the truth in love, may grow up unto Him in all things—
By the effectual working in the measure of every part    Eph. 4. 15, 16

4 A PARAMOUNT PROSPECT—
Till we all come—unto a perfect man, unto the measure of the stature of the fulness of Christ    Eph. 4. 13

## 974 The Unity of the Faith

As the Faith accepted is one, so believers who accept it are one.

1 THE BASIS OF UNITY—
The Unity of the Faith    Eph. 4. 13
One Building in Eph. 2
One Body in Eph. 4
One Bride in Eph. 5

2 THE BOND OF UNITY—
The Unity of the Spirit    Eph. 4. 3
With one mind    Phil. 1. 27
Of one accord, of one mind    Phil. 2. 2
Of the same mind in the Lord    Phil. 4. 2

3 THE BLESSINGS OF UNITY—
Life for evermore    Ps. 133. 3
(First mention of everlasting life in Scripture)

## 977 Christlike Conduct in Four Spheres

WALK

1 In love—forgiving one another—in the Family of God    Eph. 4. 32; 5. 2

2 In light—shining for Christ in the World    Eph. 5. 8

3 In wisdom — circumspectly, using our time properly    Eph. 5. 15

4 In the Spirit—singing and making melody to the Lord    Eph. 5. 18
   Gal. 5. 16

## 978 Redeeming the Time

Eph. 5. 16

The words might be translated 'buying up the opportunities'. How people use their time—

1 Some KILL TIME—
until Time kills them

2 Some WASTE TIME—
Heedless as to how the days are passing

3 Some PASS TIME—
in trivial and unprofitable pastimes

4 Some SPEND TIME—
as they would money, some carelessly, others carefully

5 Some TAKE TIME BY THE FORELOCK—
seizing the opportunities as they come

## 975 Positive and Negative Commands

| Ephesians | | | | | Ephesians |
|---|---|---|---|---|---|
| 4. 14 | Be no more deceived | BUT | Grow up into Christ | | 4. 10 |
| 4. 29 | No corrupt words | BUT | that which is good | | 4. 29 |
| 4. 28 | Steal no more | BUT | Give | | 4. 28 |
| 5. 4 | Nor foolish talking | BUT | Giving of thanks | | 5. 4 |
| 5. 15 | Walk not as fools | BUT | as wise | | 5. 15 |
| 5. 17 | Be not unwise | BUT | Understanding | | 5. 17 |
| 6. 6 | Not men pleasers | BUT | Servants of Christ | | 6. 6 |

JS. FS.

## 976 The Christian's Walk and Talk

HIS WALK—

The Negatives—

| | |
|---|---|
| Not in Vanity | Eph. 4. 17 |
| Not in Darkness | Eph. 4. 18 |
| Not in Alienation from God | Eph. 4. 18 |
| Not in Uncleanness | Eph. 4. 19 |
| Not in Greediness | Eph. 4. 19 |

HIS TALK should be characterized by

| | |
|---|---|
| Truthfulness | Eph. 4. 25 |
| Temperance | Eph. 4. 26, 27 |

The Positives—

| | |
|---|---|
| After the example of Christ | Eph. 4. 20 |
| According to the teaching of Christ | Eph. 4. 21 |
| in the way of truth | Eph. 4. 21 |
| in righteousness | Eph. 4. 24 |
| in holiness | Eph. 4. 24 |
| Timeliness | Eph. 4. 29 |
| Tenderness | Eph. 4. 31, 32 |

## 979  The Spirit-Filled Life

BE FILLED WITH THE SPIRIT
Eph. 5. 18

1 A Joyful life—
singing and making melody Eph. 5. 19

2 A Thankful life—
giving thanks                    Eph. 5. 20

3 A Graceful life—
Wives, submit yourselves    Eph. 5. 22
Husbands, love your wives  Eph. 5. 25

4 A Peaceful life—
Fathers, provoke not your
children                        Eph. 6. 4

5 A Hopeful life—
the same shall he receive of
the Lord                        Eph. 6. 8

6 A Powerful life—
strong in the Lord and in the
power of His might            Eph. 6. 10

7 A Prayerful life—
praying always with all
prayer                          Eph. 6. 18

## 980  Christ and His Church

1 The Purchase Price—
Christ—gave Himself for it Eph. 5. 25

2 The Purifying Process—
that He might sanctify and
cleanse it                      Eph. 5. 26

3 The Perfect Preparation—
by washing of water, by the
Word                            Eph. 5. 26

4 The Personal Presentation—
present it to Himself a
glorious church                Eph. 5. 27

## 981  The Christian Soldier

Has—

1 An Impregnable Position    Eph. 6. 10

2 An Impenetrable Armour   Eph. 6. 14-17

3 An Invincible Sword         Eph. 6. 17

## 982  The Panoply of God

Called—

THE ARMOUR OF LIGHT        Rom. 13. 12

THE ARMOUR OF RIGHT       2 Cor. 6. 7

Is—

THE ARMOUR OF MIGHT       Eph. 6. 10

We are exhorted to—

BE    1 Belt of Truth—for the
loins                   Eph. 6. 14

2 Breastplate of Right-
eousness—for the
heart                   Eph. 6. 14

STRONG  3 Shoes of the Gospel of
peace—for the feet Eph. 6. 15

in      4 Shield of Faith—for
the left hand           Eph. 6. 16

HIM,   5 Helmet of Salvation—
for the head            Eph. 6. 17

STRONG in 6 Sword of the Spirit—
for the right hand Eph. 6. 17

HIM     7 Heliograph of Prayer
—for the eyes, ears
and mouth               Eph. 6. 18

---

# PHILIPPIANS

## 983  The Christian's Mind in Philippians

Chapter 1—The Happy Mind
vs. 3, 4, 18, 25, 26

Chapter 2—The Humble Mind
vs. 5-8, 20, 25

Chapter 3—The Heavenly Mind
vs. 12-14, 20, 21

Chapter 4—The Holy Mind
vs. 7, 8

## 984  Christ and His People in the Epistle

Chapter 1—Christ our Passion—
Living for Christ—           vs. 1, 21
The Christian Testimony     vs. 18, 27

Chapter 2—Christ our Pattern—
Labouring for Christ—The
Christian's Temperament     vs. 5, 16

Chapter 3—Christ our Prize—
Looking for Christ—The Chris-
tian's Treasure              vs. 8, 14, 21

Chapter 4—Christ our Power—
Learning of Christ—The Chris-
tian's Triumph               vs. 4, 12, 13

## 985  The Saviour and the Saint

1 Our Position—
in Christ                   Phil. 1. 1

2 Our Purpose—
to live Christ              Phil. 1. 21

3 Our Privilege—
to preach Christ            Phil. 1. 15

4 Our Prize—
to win Christ               Phil. 3. 8

5 Our Prospect—
to be with Christ           Phil. 1. 23

6 Our Perfection—
like Christ                 Phil. 3. 21

W.J.M.

## 986 Fellowship
Phil. 1. 5

In secular Greek the word 'koinonia' had three implications—

1 Commercial—signifying a business Partnership
2 Marital—signifying matrimony, fellowship in marriage
3 Social—signifying a share in actions done or activities carried on

In Paul's letters there are four Aspects of Fellowship—

1 Spiritual Fellowship—Sharing the same life    Phil. 2. 1; 3. 10; 1 Cor. 1. 9
2 Social Fellowship—Sharing mutual love
Phil. 1. 5; Acts 16. 34; 2. 46
3 Operational Fellowship—Sharing labour in service   Phil. 1. 27-29
4 Practical Fellowship—Sharing material things   Phil. 4. 14, 15
(Communicate—Greek 'Koinoneo', have fellowship with)

## 987 The Perfect Work of a Perfect Saviour
1 Commencement—
He has begun a good work
in you    Phil. 1. 6
2 Continuation—
It is God who works in you   Phil. 2. 13
3 Completion—
Who shall change our vile
(humiliated) body    Phil. 3. 21
       G.H.

## 988 To me to live is Christ
Phil. 1. 21

Christ is Supreme in the Scriptures (John 5. 39) and in the Divine purpose (Eph. 1. 10). He should be Supreme in the believer's life. The Christian's life should be, as Paul's was—

1 A Display of the Mind of Christ   Phil. 2. 5
2 A Demonstration of the Magnificence of Christ    Phil. 1. 20
3 A Declaration of the Message of Christ    Phil. 1. 27

## 989 A Roman Citizen from Tarsus to Roman Citizens in Philippi

'Conversation' in Phil. 1. 27 means 'Conduct as citizens': in Phil. 3. 20—'citizenship'.

Wherever they were, Roman citizens spoke the Latin language, owned loyalty to the Roman Emperor and moulded their lives after the fashion of the Romans. The people of Philippi were a colony of Rome in Philippi: the Christians there a colony of Heaven on earth.

1 Their Language was to be the language of Heaven
2 Their Loyalty was to the Lord Jesus in Heaven
3 Their Lives were to be directed by the Laws of Heaven

## 990 The Responsibility of Heaven's Citizens on Earth
Phil. 1. 27-30

1 As Saints—
to shine brightly for the
display of the Gospel   Phil. 2. 15, 16
2 As Soldiers—
to stand firmly for the
faith of the Gospel   Phil. 1. 27
3 As Servants—
to strive unitedly for the
spread of the Gospel   Phil. 1. 27
4 As Subjects—
to suffer willingly for the
Christ of the Gospel   Phil. 1. 29

## 991 The Mind of Christ
Phil. 2. 5-8

A Before He 'emptied Himself' He was—

1 In the form of God   Phil. 2. 6
2 The image of God   Heb. 1. 3
3 Equal with God    Phil. 2. 6; John 1. 1, 2

B After He 'emptied Himself' He became—
1 in the form of a
bondservant   Phil. 2. 7
2 in the likeness of
men    Phil. 2. 7; Heb. 2. 14
3 lower than the
angels in order to
die    Heb. 2. 9

THE SON OF GOD—
Remained what He always was, God
Became what He had not been before, man
Retains what He had voluntarily assumed, humanity
and
Regained what He had not lost, Paradise

## 992 Pour Contempt on all my Pride
'Let this mind be in you, which was also in Christ Jesus' Phil. 2. 5

HIS LIFE HAD NO PRIDE OF—

BIRTH AND RANK—Is not this the Carpenter?
Mark 6. 3

WEALTH—The Son of Man hath not where to lay His head
Matt. 8. 20; Luke 9. 58

RESPECTABILITY—Can there any good thing come out of Nazareth?
John 1. 46; Matt. 2. 23

PERSONAL APPEARANCE—No form nor comeliness: Marred more than any man
Isa. 53. 2; 52. 14

REPUTATION—Gluttonous and a wine bibber; a friend of publicans and sinners
Matt. 11. 19; Luke 7. 34

INDEPENDENCE—Many—ministered unto Him of their substance
Luke 8. 3

LEARNING—How knoweth this man letters, having never learned
John 7. 15

SUPERIORITY—I am among you as He that serveth
Luke 22. 27; Phil. 2. 8; Gal. 3. 13

SUCCESS—He came unto His own and His own received Him not
John 1. 11

Neither did His brethren believe in Him
John 7. 5

ABILITY—I can of my own self do nothing
John 5. 19, 30

SELF-WILL—I seek not Mine own will, but the will of the Father who hath sent Me
John 5. 30

I do nothing of myself
John 8. 28

And was subject to them
Luke 2. 51

INTELLECT—As My Father hath taught me, I speak these things
John 8. 28

BIGOTRY—Forbid him not—for he that is not against us is on our part
Mark 9. 39, 40

RESENTMENT—Father, forgive them.
Luke 23. 34

Friend, wherefore art thou come?
Matt. 26. 50

SANCTITY—This man receiveth sinners and eateth with them
Luke 15. 2

AUTHOR UNKNOWN

## 993   Four Examples of Lowliness

In Philippians 2 we have four examples of 'Lowliness'—

1 THE LORD HIMSELF—
Unselfishness brought Him from above
Phil. 2. 5-8

I can learn a great deal from my Brethren, but I can see perfection only in the Man, Christ Jesus.

2 PAUL (Verse 17)—
Offered upon the sacrifice
Margin reads 'poured out'. He likens the faith of the Philippians to the 'bullock', and his martyrdom to the 'cup of wine' poured on the offering. Forty years buffeted.

3 TIMOTHEUS (Verse 19)—
'Like-minded'. All seek their own, but Timotheus 'cared for you'.

4 EPAPHRODITUS (Verse 25)—
The man who could carry a parcel for Paul from Philippi to Rome at the risk of his life (verse 30). When sick he thought not of his sickness, but of their anxiety about his sickness (verse 26).

W.W.F.

## 994   Paul in the Stripping Room and in the Arena

1 Paul enters, immaculately dressed in seven spotless garments
Phil. 3. 5, 6

The Divinely-appointed Badge of Circumcision

The National Garb derived from the privilege of birth—'of the stock of Israel'

The Tribal Robe of Benjamin's lineage

The Rabbinical Gown of a Hebrew

The Denominational Dress of a Pharisee

The Uniform of a Zealot —'persecuting the church'

The gaudy Robe of self-righteousness, as a candidate for Heaven's approval.

2 The disciple of Christ divests himself of all seven —'What things were gain to me, those I counted loss for Christ'
Phil. 3. 7

3 Paul the servant of Jesus Christ renounces all claim to any honour—'I have suffered the loss of all things—that I may win Christ'
Phil. 3. 8

4 The Apostle of Jesus Christ, running in the arena, says —'This one thing I do,— I press toward the mark for the prize
Phil. 3. 13, 14

5 The prisoner of Jesus Christ exhorts all Christ's disciples to 'Mind the same thing'.
Phil. 3. 16

## 995   The Power of His Resurrection
Phil. 3. 10

It is—

1 A Militant Power       Eph. 1. 19-23

2 A Motivating Power     Rom. 6. 4, 5

3 A Magnetic Power       Col. 3. 1, 2

4 A Magnifying Power     Phil. 1. 20

'That Christ may be magnified in my body'

**996  Paul and His Lord**

1 Paul Committed himself as a Personal Trust to 'Christ Jesus my Lord'  Phil. 3. 8

2 Paul Coveted for himself a Precious Treasure—'the surpassing knowledge of Christ Jesus my Lord'  Phil. 3. 8

3 Paul Contemplated his experience of a Present Transition—'be found in Him'  Phil. 3. 9

For this he Consecrated all his Energies  Phil. 3. 8, 12

On this he Concentrated all his Efforts  Phil. 3. 13

and his Lord would Compensate him with 'the prize of His high calling'  Phil. 3. 14; 2 Tim. 4. 8

**1000  Sweet Aromas**
Phil. 4. 18

1 The Sacrifice of Christ is 'a sweet savour to God'  Eph. 5. 1, 2

2 The Believer led in the triumphal procession of Christ—is 'a sweet savour of Christ'  2 Cor. 2. 15, 16

3 The Worship offered to the Lord—is a sweet savour 'filling the house'  John 12. 1-3

4 Gifts to the servants of Christ are 'well-pleasing to God'  Phil. 4. 18

5 The Unity of brethren in Christ—is like the holy anointing oil  Ps. 133. 1, 2

---

**997  'Stand Fast'—'Hold Fast'**

| FOUR POSITIONS IN WHICH TO 'STAND FAST' | | FOUR THINGS TO 'HOLD FAST' | |
|---|---|---|---|
| 1 Stand fast in the LORD | Phil. 4. 1 | 1 Hold fast the confidence of the hope | Heb. 3. 6 |
| 2 Stand fast in the FAITH | 1 Cor. 16. 13 | 2 Hold fast our profession | Heb. 4. 14 |
| 3 Stand fast in the LIBERTY | Gal. 5. 1 | 3 Hold fast the form of sound words | 2 Tim. 1. 13 |
| 4 Stand fast in one SPIRIT | Phil. 1. 27 | 4 Hold fast that which is good | 1 Thess. 5. 21 |

We are called upon first to 'Stand fast' and afterwards to 'Hold fast'. The man who has a poor foothold cannot possibly have a firm 'hand-hold'. In our 'Tug of war' with sin we want both.

T.B.

---

**998  Four Positions in Philippians 4**

Registered—
'names are in the book of life'  v. 3

Rejoicing—
'in the Lord'  v. 4

Restful—
'the peace of God—shall keep'  v. 7

Rewarded—
'the God of peace shall be with you'  v. 9
G.H.

**999  The Value of a Gift Sent to The Lord's Servant**

1 It is—
fragrant to God  Phil. 4. 18

2 It brings—
fruit to the account of the donor  Phil. 4. 17

3 It expresses—
fellowship with the recipient  Phil. 4. 15

**1001  A Blank Cheque**
Phil. 4. 19

The Firm—My God
The Promise—Shall supply
The Amount—all your need
The Capital—His riches
The Address—in glory
The Signature—Christ Jesus

D. L. MOODY

**1002  All Your Need**
Phil. 4. 19

Our various and varied needs traced through the New Testament—

1 Our Material or Temporal needs  Matt. 6. 32
2 Our Physical need—Health  Luke 9. 11
3 Our Personal need—Spiritual food  Luke 10. 42
4 Our Moral need—Cleansing  John 13. 10
5 Our Social need—Fellowship  1 Cor. 12. 21
6 Our Spiritual need—Patient endurance  Heb. 10. 36
7 Our Intellectual need—Wisdom  James 1. 5

## COLOSSIANS

**1003  Christ in Colossians**

Chapter 1—The Pre-eminence of Christ
Col. 1. 15-23

Chapter 2—The Plenitude of Christ
Col. 2. 2, 3, 9, 10

Chapter 3—The Preciousness of Christ
Col. 3. 1-17

Chapter 4—The Preaching of the Mystery of Christ
Col. 4. 2-6

**1004  Knowing and Doing the Will of God**
Col. 1. 9

The Knowledge of God's will produces—

1 Worthy conduct, pleasing to God                    Col. 1. 10

2 Good works in a fruitful life Col. 1. 10

3 Increase in the knowledge of God                    Col. 1. 10

4 Accession of spiritual power    Col. 1. 11

5 Thanksgiving to the Father      Col. 1. 12

**1005  The Course of Every Believer**

ONCE—

Ruined—in darkness               Col. 1. 13

NOW—

Rescued—delivered from the power                     Col. 1. 13

Redeemed—by His blood            Col. 1. 14

Reconciled—through His death                     Col. 1. 21, 22

Rich—with 'all riches'           Col. 2. 2

Rooted—and built up in Him  Col. 2. 7

Risen—with Christ                Col. 3. 1

FINALLY—

Rewarded—ye shall receive the reward             Col. 3. 24
S.E.D.

**1006  Our Lord**

Precedes all things—
His Priority                     Col. 1. 17

Created all things—
His Power                        Col. 1. 16

Upholds all things—
His Preservation                 Heb. 1. 3

Fills all things—
His Position                     Eph. 4. 10

Subdues all things—
His Pre-eminence                 Phil. 3. 21

Reconciles all things—
His Propitiation                 Col. 1. 20

Owns all things—
His Patrimony                    Heb. 1. 2
H.K.D.

**1007  The Glory of Christ**

1 All things were created by Him Col. 1. 17

2 All things were created for Him Col. 1. 16

3 All things are reconciled by Him Col. 1. 20

4 All things consist by Him       Col. 1. 17

5 All things came into being after Him                        Col. 1. 17

6 All things are under Him        Col. 1. 18

7 All fulness dwells in Him       Col. 1. 19

'This is my Friend' (Song of Sol. 5. 16)
JS. FS.

**1008  Failure Through the Inroads of Heresy**
in the churches at Colosse and Laodicea

1 Foot Disease—
not walking in Christ Jesus
Jesus the Lord                   Col. 2. 6

2 Heart Trouble—
not being filled with Christ's
Fulness                          Col. 2. 10;
Eph. 3. 19

3 General Debility—
not holding the Head for
nourishment                      Col. 2. 19

4 Mental Aberration—
not setting their minds on
things above                     Col. 3. 2

5 Fleshly Indulgence—
not mortifying the members
on earth                         Col. 3. 5

**1009  The Mystery of God and of the Father
and of Christ**
Col. 1. 21

1 Its Commencement—
Christ's Fulness        Col. 1. 19; 2. 3, 9

2 Its Course—
Christ's Incarnation    Col. 2. 9

3 Its Crisis—
Christ's Crucifixion    1 Cor. 2. 7, 8

4 Its Conclusion—
Christ's Millennial
Reign                   Eph. 1. 9, 10

5 Its Consummation—
Christ's Supremacy      Eph. 3. 9, 10

**1010  Let No Man**

1 Let no man *spoil you* through
philosophy and vain deceit Col. 2. 8

2 Let no man *judge you* in respect
of meat, drink or days    Col. 2. 16

3 Let no man *beguile you* of your
reward                    Col. 2. 18
(Beguile—bribe the umpire to
decide against)

## 1011 Triumphs of the Cross of Christ
God by the Cross of Christ—

1 Forgave us our trespasses when
we believed   Col. 2. 13
2 Blotted out the handwriting of
ordinances that declared us
guilty   Col. 2. 14
3 Nailed the accusing document
to the Cross   Col. 2. 14
4 Removed it out of the way
entirely   Col. 2. 14
5 Disarmed the infernal forces
that opposed and threatened
us   Col. 2. 15
6 Led them captive in His
triumphal procession   Col. 2. 15
7 Made an exhibition of them to
their shame   Col. 2. 15

## 1012 Things Above
Col. 3. 1-4
Things above—at God's right hand
With Christ (Col. 1. 5)—in Heaven
That is the Place where

1 Our Home is   John 14. 1-3
2 Our Head is   Eph. 1. 21-23
3 Our Hope is   Col. 1. 5
4 Our Hidden Life is   Col. 3. 3
5 Our Hearts should be   Col. 3. 2

## 1013 With Christ
Risen with Christ—
a Past Experience   Col. 3. 1
Hid with Christ in God—
a Present Enjoyment   Col. 3. 3
Appearing with Christ in glory—
a Future Ecstasy   Col. 3. 4

## 1014 Christ Our Life
Col. 3. 4
He is—
The Source of our Life Eph. 2. 1; Gal. 2. 20
The Sustenance of our Life
John 6. 51
The Solace of our Life Heb. 13. 5
The Object of our Life Phil. 1. 21
The Pattern of our Life
Phil. 2. 5
The Crown of our Life 1 John 3. 2

S.E.R.

## 1015 Paul's Companions
TYCHICUS, a Gentile and an Asiatic, a Faithful
minister and *Paul's Fellow-servant*
Col. 4. 7; Acts 20. 4;
Titus 3. 12; 2 Tim. 4. 12
ONESIMUS, a runaway slave—a beloved brother
and *Paul's own heart*
Col. 4. 9; Philem. 10
ARISTARCHUS, a Thessalonian and a Hebrew
Christian—*Paul's Fellow-prisoner*
Col. 4. 10; Acts 20. 4; 27. 2
JOHN MARK, a citizen of Jerusalem—*Paul's
restored Fellow-servant*
Col. 4. 10; 2 Tim. 4. 11
JESUS CALLED JUSTUS—a Hebrew believer—
*Paul's Fellow-worker*
Col. 4. 11
EPAPHRAS—a brother from Colosse—*Paul's
Fellow-helper in prayer*
Col. 1. 7, 8; 4. 12
LUKE, a Gentile believer, the beloved physician,
*Paul's Fellow-traveller*
Col. 4. 14; 2 Tim. 4. 11
DEMAS, a Gentile believer—for a time *Paul's
Fellow-labourer*   Col. 4. 14; 2 Tim. 4. 10

## 1016 Luke the Beloved Physician
Col. 4. 14
'Luke is with me' 2 Tim. 4. 11
With Paul—
In his Travels—joined him at
Troas—'we'   Acts 16. 10
In his Troubles—came after
his sickness in Galatia   Gal. 4. 13
In his Triumph—was with
him at the end   2 Tim. 4. 6, 11
LUKE THE AUTHOR—a Greek, a Gentile convert

1 His Conversion—there is no record of it
2 His Courtesy—toward all: he keeps himself in the background
3 His Culture—Luke's Gospel has been
called 'the most literary of the Gospels'
and 'the most beautiful book in the
world'
4 His Companionship—He probably re-
received from Paul material for his
Gospel narrative
5 His Constancy—When Demas left, Luke
remained: he was Beloved by Paul and
Beloved by all

# 1 THESSALONIANS

## 1017  The Faith of the Thessalonians

1 Your work of faith                                      1 Thess. 1. 3
2 In every place your faith—
  is spread abroad                                        1 Thess. 1. 8
3 Sent Timotheus—to com-
  fort you concerning your
  faith                                                   1 Thess. 3. 2
4 I sent to know your faith                               1 Thess. 3. 5
5 Timotheus — brought us
  good tidings of your faith                              1 Thess. 3. 6
6 We are comforted — by
  your faith                                              1 Thess. 3. 7
7 We might perfect that
  which is lacking in your
  faith                                                   1 Thess. 3. 10
8 Putting on the breastplate
  of faith                                                1 Thess. 5. 8
9 We—thank God that your
  faith groweth exceedingly                              2 Thess. 1. 3
10 We glory—for your faith in
  all your persecutions and
  tribulations that ye en-
  dure                                                    2 Thess. 1. 4
BUT THE LORD IS FAITHFUL  2 Thess. 3. 3
                                                          J. SN.

## 1018  A Model Church—In Triplets

1 Model pastors of God's flock—Paul,
  Silvanus, Timotheus
                                                          1 Thess. 1. 1
2 A Model ministry—Praying, preaching,
  persecuted            1 Thess. 1. 2, 5; 2. 2
3 A Model Message—In power, in the Holy
  Ghost, in much assurance
                                                          1 Thess. 1. 5
4 A Model Response—turned—to serve—
  and to wait           1 Thess. 1. 9, 10
5 A Model activity—work of faith, labour
  of love, patience of hope
                                                          1 Thess. 1. 3
6 A Model prayer for them—with thanks-
  giving, remembrance and knowledge
                                                          1 Thess. 1. 2-4
7 A Model programme followed—they be-
  came recipients of the Word, imitators
  of the apostles, and examples to the
  believers             1 Thess. 1. 6, 7

## 1019  What Each Local Church Should Be

1 A Centre of Gospel testimony
                                                          1 Thess. 1. 8
2 A Nursery for spiritual babes
                                                          1 Thess. 2. 7, 8
3 A Target for the Devil
                                                          1 Thess. 2. 14, 15; 3. 5
4 A Family Circle with love prevailing
                                                          1 Thess. 3. 12
5 A Sphere of Divine discipline
                                                          1 Thess. 4. 6
6 A School for character development and
  for instruction     1 Thess. 4. 9-13
7 A Hospital for the spiritually weak
                                                          1 Thess. 5. 14

## 1020  Past—Present—Future

1 Conversion—

  turned to God from idols
  —the Sphere of Faith                                    1 Thess. 1. 9

2 Consecration—

  serve the living and true
  God—the Domain of
  Love                                                    1 Thess. 1. 9

3 Contemplation—

  wait for His Son from
  heaven—the Realm of
  Hope                                                    1 Thess. 1. 10
                                                          W.R.

## 1021  The Lord's Coming

The word is 'Parousia' which signifies presence,
that is, not only motion to a place but stay in a
place.

1 Connected with the Salvation of the
  Believer                   1 Thess. 1. 10

2 Connected with the Service of the Soul-
  winner                     1 Thess. 2. 19

3 Connected with the Steadfastness of the
  Saint                      1 Thess. 3. 13

4 Connected with the Sorrow of the Bereaved                     1 Thess. 4. 15-18

5 Connected with the Sanctification of the
  Sons of light              1 Thess. 5. 23, 24

## 1022  The Life of Faith

1 The Commencement o their faith—God's
  servants are grateful  1 Thess. 2. 13

2 The Consummation of their faith—God's
  servants are hopeful   1 Thess. 2. 19

3 The Confirmation of their faith—God's
  servants are careful   1 Thess. 3. 2, 6

4 The Concomitants of their faith—God's
  servants are prayerful 1 Thess. 3. 10-13

## 1023  Satanic Opposition

1 By External trials, persecutions and bodily
  afflictions
              1 Thess. 2. 14, 15; 3. 3; 2 Cor. 12. 7

2 By Internal temptations, subverting the
  faith of some
              1 Thess. 3. 5; 2 Cor. 11. 3

3 By Infernal hindrances and false doctrines
              1 Thess. 2. 18; 2 Cor. 11. 13-15

## 1024    Ambition

STUDY TO BE QUIET 1 Thess. 4. 11

The word translated 'study' (Philotimeomai) means literally, 'I love the honour', or 'I am ambitious', and occurs three times in the New Testament—

1 Study to be quiet—the Ambition of every Christian                                        1 Thess. 4. 11

2 So have I strived to preach the Gospel, not where Christ is named — the Ambition of every Pioneer Missionary                       Rom. 15. 20

3 We labour that—we may be accepted of Him—the Ambition of every Servant of Christ                     2 Cor. 5. 9

## 1025    The Rapture of the Saints
1 Thess. 4. 13-18

1 THE EVENT—

The Fulfilment of Christ's Promise                              John 14. 2, 3

The Display of Christ's Power                                 1 Thess. 4. 16

The Realization of Christ's Presence                            1 Thess. 4. 17

2 THE ACCOMPANIMENT—

the Shout of a King            1 Thess. 4. 16

the Voice of the Chief messenger                           1 Thess. 4. 16

the Trump of God              1 Thess. 4. 16

(The Lord Himself as Prophet, Priest and King)

3 THE FULFILMENT—

Resurrection of sleeping saints                                1 Thess. 4. 16

Rapture of living saints        1 Thess. 4. 17

Reunion of all saints          1 Thess. 4. 17

## 1026    Sons of Light
1 Thess. 5. 5

1 In relation to times and seasons
1 Thess. 5. 1, 2
(Our Lord's return will find some unconcerned and some unprepared)

2 In contrast to children of darkness
1 Thess. 5. 8
(Watchful and sober while children of darkness are asleep and drunken)

3 In association with one another
1 Thess. 5. 11
(ministering mutual comfort and edification)

4 In their attitude to spiritual exercises
1 Thess. 5. 16-22

5 In anticipation of the Lord's return
1 Thess. 5. 23, 24

## 1027    Some Neglected Exhortations

1 'Know them' that are over you                                1 Thess. 5. 12
HOW? By the services they render to the saints

2 'Remember them' that are over you                         Heb. 13. 7
WHY? As an example worthy to follow

3 'Obey them' that are over you                                Heb. 13. 17
HOW? By submitting yourselves, because they feel the responsibility for your soul's welfare and growth in grace.

4 'Salute them' that are over you                                Heb. 13. 24
J.W.W.

## 1028    Believers in Relation to One Another

1 Our Attitude to *Equals* in the assembly        1 Thess. 5. 11, 13
Comfort and edify one another, and be at peace with all

2 Our Attitude to *Elders* in the assembly        1 Thess. 5. 12, 13
Know who they are and esteem them highly

3 Our Attitude to *Erring* *saints* in the assembly 1 Thess. 5. 14
Support the weak and be patient toward all

## 2 THESSALONIANS

### 1029 Four Pairs of Events at Christ's Second Advent

The Greek word 'Parousia', translated 'coming', means 'presence' and, when used of our Lord's return, refers to a period with a commencement (the rapture of the saints), a continuation (when believers appear before the Judgment seat of Christ), and a consummation (the appearing of Christ in glory).

2 Thess. 2. 1 refers to the commencement, 2. 8. to the consummation.

There will be—

1 A Descent (shall descend) and an Ascent (caught up)    1 Thess. 4. 16, 17

2 A Recall (of him who restrains) and a Downfall (of Satan)
2 Thess. 2. 7; Rev. 12. 9

3 A Cessation (of the proclamation of the Gospel of the grace of God) and a Continuation (of the preaching of the Gospel of the kingdom)
Acts 20. 24; Matt. 24. 14

4 A Strong Consolation (for those who have the 'blessed hope')
Heb. 6. 18
and a Strong Delusion (for those who have rejected the Gospel)
2 Thess. 2. 11

### 1030 Portion and Prospect

Of believers in Christ
1 Chosen to Salvation    2 Thess. 2. 13
2 Called to Glory    2 Thess. 2. 14
3 Consoled through grace    2 Thess. 2. 16
4 Comforted in service    2 Thess. 2. 17

H.K.D.

## 1 TIMOTHY

### 1031 Paul's Picture of a Local Church

Over the entrance—'How—to behave in the house of God'    1 Tim. 3. 15

Over the rostrum or platform— 'Be a good soldier of Jesus Christ'    1 Tim. 4. 6

The Text—'Great is the mystery of godliness'    1 Tim. 3. 16

The Theme of the sermon— GODLINESS

Chapter 1—
The Apostle instructs his child in the faith, giving him the charge received from the Lord    1 Tim. 1. 5

Chapter 2—
The Prayer-room, the men in prayer, the women in Heaven's adornment

Chapter 3—
The Oversight, elders and deacons

Chapter 4—
The Preacher, his life and doctrine

Chapter 5—
The poor widows and wise elders and deacons

Chapter 6—
The congregation, composed of rich and poor, and the collection

### 1032 The Christian is Exhorted in 1 Timothy

1 To unfeigned faith    Ch. 1. 5

2 To hold faith and a good conscience    Ch. 1. 19

3 To hold the mystery of the faith in a pure conscience    Ch. 3. 9

4 To be nourished up in words of faith    Ch. 4. 6

5 To be an example in faith    Ch. 4. 12

6 To follow after faith    Ch. 6. 11

7 To fight the good fight of faith    Ch. 6. 12
Faith is the victory that overcomes the world    1 John 5. 4

J.M.A.

### 1033 Sound Doctrine

concerning—

1 The Salvation of Sinners
1 Tim. 1. 15

2 The Inspiration of the Scriptures
2 Tim. 3. 16

3 The Incarnation of Christ
1 Tim. 3. 16

4 The Condition of the last days
1 Tim. 4. 1; 2 Tim. 3. 1

5 Intercession for all men
1 Tim. 2. 1

6 The Position of women
1 Tim. 2. 9-12

7 The Qualifications of overseers
1 Tim. 3. 1-7
And 'any other thing that is contrary to sound doctrine'
1 Tim. 1. 10

H.K.D.

**1034 'Faithful Sayings' in Paul's Pastoral Epistles**

THIS IS A FAITHFUL SAYING concerning—

1 The Gospel of Jesus Christ      1 Tim. 1. 15

2 The Oversight in the assembly      1 Tim. 3. 1

3 The Profit derived from godly living      1 Tim. 4. 8, 9

4 The Reward of endurance      2 Tim. 2. 11, 12

5 The maintenance of good works      Titus 3. 8


**1035 The Gospel Paul Preached**
1 Tim. 1. 15

This is a faithful saying   —the Proclamation

worthy of all acceptation—the Plea

Christ Jesus         —the Person

Came into the world    —the Place

to save             —the Purpose

sinners            —the People


**1036 Paul the Pattern**
1 Tim. 1. 16

1 As a Man—in the Miracle of his Conversion—'I obtained mercy'

2 As a Minister of Christ—in the Moulding of his Character—in three stages—

his Energy in travels and preaching—Primary Epistles

his contentment in trials and prison—Prison Epistles

his foresight in teaching and providing—Pastoral Epistles

3 As a Missionary in the Mapping of his Course as evangelist, teacher and pastor.


**1037 Good Works in Evil Days**

Adorned with good works      1 Tim. 2. 10

Well reported for good works      1 Tim. 5. 10

Diligently following good works   1 Tim. 5. 10

Manifesting good works      1 Tim. 5. 25

Rich in good works      1 Tim. 6. 18

Prepared unto every good work    2 Tim. 2. 21

Perfected unto all good works    2 Tim. 3. 17

God's salvation is not obtained by good works      Eph. 2. 9

God's Christianity is full of good works      Acts 9. 36

Faith without works is dead      James 2. 20

J.M.H.


**1038 Words Describing Various Kinds of Prayer**
1 Tim. 2. 1

1 Supplications—earnest entreaty
Heb. 5. 7
(Originally the suppliant held an olive branch in his hand)

2 Prayers—the general term for all prayer

3 Intercessions—an approach to a ruler with a petition, prayer on behalf of others
1 Tim. 4. 5; Rom. 8. 26

4 Thanksgiving—Greek—'eucharistia', expressions of gratitude
Eph. 5. 4

5 Requests—expression of a desire: prayer for something desired
Phil. 4. 6


**1039 Godliness in 1 Timothy**

Godliness—Piety—

| | | |
|---|---|---|
| 1 The Profession of Godliness | — its Responsibility | 1 Tim. 2. 10 |
| 2 A Life of Godliness | — its Desirability | 1 Tim. 2. 2 |
| 3 The Mystery of Godliness | — its Visibility | 1 Tim. 3. 16 |
| 4 The Exercise of Godliness | — its Availability | 1 Tim. 4. 7 |
| 5 The Doctrine of Godliness | — its Reliability | 1 Tim. 6. 3 |
| 6 The great Gain of Godliness | — its Utility | 1 Tim. 6. 6 |
| 7 The Pursuit of Godliness | — its Advisability | 1 Tim. 6. 11 |

## 1040 Overseers—Bishops or Elders

1 Their Ordination—in the assembly by the Spirit
  Acts 20. 28

2 Their Confirmation—before the assembly by recognition
  Acts 14. 23; Titus 1. 5; 1 Thess. 5. 12

3 Their Qualifications—for oversight—
Personal Devotion to Christ
  John 21. 15-17; 1 Pet. 5. 1
Blameless Character
  1 Tim. 3. 2-5
Desire emanating from Devotion
  1 Tim. 3. 1
Ability to rule well in their own families
  1 Tim. 3. 4, 5; Titus 1. 6
Doctrinal Soundness
  Titus 1. 9
Maturity and Experience
  1 Tim. 3. 6
A good reputation among men
  1 Tim. 3. 7

4 Their Occupation—
to feed the flock of God
  1 Pet. 5. 2
to take the oversight of the assembly
  1 Pet. 5. 2
to watch for the souls of the saints
  Heb. 13. 7

5 Their Compensation—a fadeless crown of glory at Christ's return
  1 Pet. 5. 4

## 1041 The Mystery of Godliness
  1 Tim. 3. 16

Six Great Facts are stated—
  ⎰God was manifest in the flesh
  ⎱justified in the spirit

  ⎰seen of angels
  ⎱preached unto the nations

  ⎰believed on in the world
  ⎱received up into glory

INDICATING—

1 The Manifestation of the Incarnate Son of God

2 The Mediation of the Crucified Christ

3 The Mystery of the Exalted Saviour

## 1042 In the Latter Times

1 Some shall depart from the faith
  1 Tim. 4. 1

2 Some shall deny the faith
  1 Tim. 5. 8

3 Some shall cast off their first faith
  1 Tim. 5. 12

4 Some shall be seduced from the faith
  1 Tim. 6. 10 (Margin)

5 Some shall err concerning the faith
  1 Tim. 6. 21

6 Some shall overthrow the faith of others
  2 Tim. 2. 18

7 Some shall be reprobate concerning the faith
  2 Tim. 3. 8

In Jude 3, Christians are exhorted to 'contend earnestly for the faith'.

  J.M.H.

## 1043 Christian Contentment

'Godliness with contentment is great gain'
  1 Tim. 6. 6

Contentment is—

1 An Evidence of Conversion—Be content with your wages
  Luke 3. 14

2 The Exclusion of Covetousness—Be content and take two
  2 Kings 5. 20-27

3 An Expression of Confidence in God—Having food and raiment therewith to be content
  Heb. 13. 5, 6

4 An Exhibition of Comradeship—Be content and go with thy servants
  2 Kings 6. 2, 3

5 The Essence of Consecration—I have learned, in whatsoever state I am, therewith to be content
  Phil. 4. 11

## 1044 Money and its Uses

1 From the World's Viewpoint Money is a Measure of Human Greatness
  1 Tim. 6. 17

2 From the Pastor's Viewpoint it is a Menace to true Godliness
  1 Tim. 6. 9

3 From the Christian's Viewpoint it is a Manifestation of God's Grace
  1 Tim. 6. 17

4 From the Recipient's Viewpoint it is a Means of doing Good
  1 Tim. 6. 18

5 From the Divine Viewpoint it is Material for eternal Gain
  1 Tim. 6. 19; Luke 16. 9

## 1045 The Man of God—Four Portraits

1 A Man Fleeing (Illustration—Joseph)
  1 Tim. 6. 11; 2 Tim. 2. 22; Gen. 39. 12

2 A Man Following (Illustration—Elisha)
  1 Tim. 6. 11; 2 Kings 2. 6

3 A Man Fighting (Illustration—Paul)
  1 Tim. 6. 12; 2 Tim. 4. 7

4 A Man Furnished (Illustration—Timothy)
  2 Tim. 3. 16, 17

# 2 TIMOTHY

## 1046　Paul's Picture of a War Memorial

Chapter 1—
The Sentry guarding the
Treasure　　　　　　2 Tim. 1. 14

Chapter 2—
The Soldier on the field enduring hardships　　　2 Tim. 2. 3

Chapter 3—
The Cadet in the Military
School training and in the
Armoury being equipped 2 Tim. 3. 14-17

Chapter 4—
The Veteran Warrior review-
ing his campaigns　　2 Tim. 4. 6, 7

## 1047　Divisions of 2 Timothy

1 The Steward of God and
his Trust—Fidelity in
Defending the truth　2 Tim. 1

2 The Servant of God and
his Tests—Fidelity to
Christ's Claims　　2 Tim. 2. 1-13
Fidelity to Christ's
Word　　　　　2 Tim. 2. 14-17
Fidelity to Christ's
Name　　　　　2 Tim. 2. 18-26

3 The Man of God and his
Treasure—Fidelity in
days of Declension　2 Tim. 3

4 The Martyr of God and
his Triumph—Fidelity
in view of Departure
to be with Christ　2 Tim. 4

## 1048　Perils of the Last Days and God's Un-failing Resources

1 The Peril of the Faint Heart—Hold fast
the form of sound words
2 Tim. 1. 8, 13, 14

2 The Peril of the Wandering Feet—Handle
aright the Word of truth
2 Tim. 2. 15, 18

3 The Peril of the Double Life—Heed carefully the Scriptures　2 Tim. 3. 5, 14, 15

4 The Peril of the Itching ears—Hold forth
the Word of God　　2 Tim. 4. 2, 3

## 1049　The Believer's Confidence
2 Tim. 1. 12

I am not ashamed, for I know—and am persuaded
—A Demonstration of Confidence

I know whom I have believed
—A Declaration of Trust

He is able to keep that which I have committed
unto Him
—A Deposit of Value

Against that day
—A Day of Reckoning

## 1050　Names of Believers

| | | |
|---|---|---|
| 1 Sons | 2 Tim. 2. 1 |
| 2 Soldiers | 2 Tim. 2. 3 |
| 3 Athletes | 2 Tim. 2. 5 |
| 4 Husbandmen | 2 Tim. 2. 6 |
| 5 Workmen | 2 Tim. 2. 15 |
| 6 Vessels | 2 Tim. 2. 21 |
| 7 Servants | 2 Tim. 2. 24 |

H.K.D.

## 1051　Meet for the Master's Use

'Meet'—Greek—euchrestos, meaning 'useful', 'profitable'—occurs three times in the New
Testament—

1 Any believer who has
purged himself from
unclean things　　2 Tim. 2. 20, 21

2 John Mark, who went
back and was restored 2 Tim. 4. 11

3 Onesimus, a runaway
slave who was con-
verted through Paul　Philem. 11

## 1052　Seven Signs of the Times

1 Departure from the faith 1 Tim. 4. 1
2 Disobedience to parents 2 Tim. 3. 2
3 Despisers of good 2 Tim. 3. 2
4 Devotion to pleasure 2 Tim. 3. 4
5 Denial of the power of
godliness 2 Tim. 3. 5
6 Distress among nations Luke 21. 25
7 Downtrodden Jews aris-
ing Luke 21. 24, 30

H.K.D.

## 1053　The Last Days in Second Epistles

In 2 Timothy—
Departure and Declension 2 Tim. 3. 1-9

In 2 Corinthians—
the Devil and his Decep-
tions 2 Cor. 11. 3-15

In 2 Thessalonians—
Antichrist and Apostasy 2 Thess. 2. 3-10

In 2 Peter—
Deniers of the Lord and
their Doom 2 Pet. 2. 1-16

In 2 John—
Deceivers and their Doc-
trines 2 John 7-10

## 1054 Objects of Love in the Last Days

A WHAT WORLDINGS LOVE—
1 their own selves
    2 Tim. 3. 2
2 money ('covetous' = lovers of money)
    2 Tim. 3. 2; 1 Tim. 6. 10
3 pleasures    2 Tim. 3. 4
4 the world    2 Tim. 4. 10; 1 John 2. 15-17

B WHAT GOD'S SAINTS LOVE—
1 the form of sound words
    2 Tim. 1. 13
2 all that is good (Greek)
    2 Tim. 3. 3
3 God    2 Tim. 3. 4
4 Christ's appearing
    2 Tim. 4. 8

## 1055 Characteristics of the Last Days

1 Morally—Lowering of ethical standards—vice and violence (Perilous times—fierce seasons)    2 Tim. 3. 1. 3. 6
2 Spiritually—No fear of God and no time for God—so many will follow Antichrist    2 Thess. 2. 3, 4, 9
3 Intellectually—Men of conceited demeanour, communistic ideals, and corrupt minds    2 Tim. 3. 2-8

## 1056 The Scriptures

1 Contain the Word of Salvation—given by God    2 Tim. 3. 16
2 Confirm the Way of Salvation—through faith in Christ Jesus    2 Tim. 3. 15
3 Convey the Wisdom for Salvation—make thee wise    2 Tim. 3. 15

They are for the child to learn, for the adolescent to prove and be assured of, for the mature Christian to profit by, and for the man of God to obey    2 Tim. 3. 14-17

## 1057 The Word in 2 Timothy
2 Tim. 4. 2

1 A Treasure to guard    1. 14
2 Teaching to commit to others    2. 2
3 Truth to handle aright    2. 15
4 A Textbook to study    3. 15
5 A Trumpet to sound    4. 2

## 1058 The Life Worth Living
2 Tim. 4. 6-8

1 An Aspect—Paul's Reckoning of his life—
Surrendered, as a drink offering poured out    Phil. 2. 17
Selfless because Christ-centred and controlled    Phil. 1. 21
Spent out, as a ship about to be loosed    2 Tim. 4. 6
2 A Retrospect—Paul's Review of his life—
as a soldier, a runner and a steward    2 Tim. 4. 7
3 A Prospect—Paul's Reward for his consecrated life—
a crown of righteousness    2 Tim. 4. 8

Paul had been treated unrighteously by men on earth. The righteous Judge would reward his sufferings with the crown of righteousness in Heaven.

## 1059 Four Men in 2 Timothy 4

1 LUKE—began well and ended well
    2 Tim. 4. 11; Col. 4. 14
2 DEMAS—began well and ended badly
    2 Tim. 4. 10; Col. 4. 14
3 MARK—began badly and ended well
    2 Tim. 4. 11; Acts 13. 13
4 ALEXANDER—began badly and ended badly
    2 Tim. 4. 14

# TITUS

## 1060 The Church and the Citizens of Heaven—in Titus

Chapter 1—An Orderly Church—
with its Councillors, the elders

Chapter 2—A Sound Church—
with the Common Citizens (aged men, aged women, young women and their husbands, young men, employers and employees)

Chapter 3—A Practical Church—
the Charter of the citizens, their privileges and responsibilities

## 1061 Three Appearings in Titus 2

1 Past (verse 11)—Appearing in Grace at His coming to suffer

2 Present (verse 12)—Appearing in Godliness in His people's lives now

3 Future (verse 13)—Appearing in Glory at His Coming to reign

J.M.H.

## 1062 That Blessed Hope
### Titus 2. 13

'Looking for'—Greek—Prosdechomai, I wait to welcome, I am looking out for—occurs 14 times in the New Testament.

'Blessed'—is the word of Christ's Beatitudes and occurs 50 times in the New Testament. It is translated 'happy' six times.

The HOPE is BLESSED because—

| | | |
|---|---|---|
| 1 | It Believes in the Coming of Christ which will be Personal, Physical and Pre-millennial | John 14. 1-3 |
| 2 | It Breathes the Comfort of Christ | 1 Thess. 4. 18 |
| 3 | It Begets more Confidence in Christ | 1 Thess. 1. 10 |
| 4 | It Brings full Conformity to Christ | 1 John 3. 2 |
| 5 | It Bestows the Companionship of Christ | 1 Thess. 5. 9, 10 |

# PHILEMON

## 1063 A Model Letter

Of the thirteen letters containing Paul's signature—

nine were written to local churches and are Doctrinal

three were written to fellow-workers and are Practical and Pastoral

one was written to a friend, and is Fraternal

This letter to Philemon is the shortest, and the only private letter Paul wrote. It deals with an incident in domestic life. It was been called 'a true little chef d'oeuvre in the art of letter-writing'.

It is—

1 A Model of Christian Commendation, commending a converted thief to the master he had robbed (verse 18), commending an absconder to the household from which he had escaped (verse 15), commending a sheep that had gone astray to an Under-shepherd, Archippus (Col. 4. 17), commending a young believer to a local church

2 A Model of Christian Concern—for the spiritual progress, social fellowship and future Christian career of Onesimus

3 A Model of Christian Courtesy, for Paul does not command Philemon but requests him (Verses 8, 9) and is confident of his willing response (verse 21). He also suggests that he will come to Colosse as the guest of Philemon (Verse 22)

4 A Model of Christian Courage, pleading for an absconder, a thief, a good-for-nothing

## 1064 Three People with very Different Backgrounds

'I'—the Writer—First Person—Paul the apostle, a Jew by birth and training, who has become a prisoner of Jesus Christ (v. 1), an ambassador of Jesus Christ (v. 9 R.V. margin), and the guarantor for Onesimus (vs. 18, 19)

'Thee'—the person addressed—Second Person—Philemon, the slave-owner, a Gentile convert (v. 16), Philemon means 'loving'. (His love is mentioned in vs. 5, 7, 9)

'He'—the subject of the letter—Third Person—Onesimus, a slave socially, a thief morally, an outlaw legally, yet saved by the grace of God.

Yet what love and fellowship existed because they were 'all one in Christ Jesus'.

## 1065 The Transforming Power of the Gospel

The Gospel of Christ which Onesimus had received and believed had made him—

| | | |
|---|---|---|
| 1 | Paul's child in the faith | v. 10 |
| 2 | A brother beloved | v. 16 |
| 3 | A Partner in the greatest Firm in Heaven and on earth | v. 17 |
| 4 | Paul's own heart, greatly loved | v. 12 |
| 5 | A profitable servant of Christ | v. 11 |

## HEBREWS

### 1066 Prophet, Priest and King

1 The Son of God as Prophet—
'God—hath—spoken unto
us by His Son' — Heb. 1. 1, 2

He is the Perfect Revealer of
God

the Creator of all things in the
past

the Upholder of all things in
the present

the Heir of all things in the
future

2 The Son as Priest—'When He
had by Himself purged our
sins, sat down' — Heb. 1. 3

His efficacious sacrifice—
purged our sins

His completed work — sat
down

His exalted position—on the
right hand of the Majesty
on high

3 The Son as King — 'Thy
throne, O God, is for ever
and ever' — Heb. 1. 8
He is the perfect Ruler of an
eternal kingdom

### 1067 Seven Things about 'His Son'

1 The nearness of His relationship—Son — Heb. 1. 2, 5, 8

2 The word of His power — Heb. 1. 3

3 The excellence of His
Name — Heb. 1. 4

4 The duration of His
throne — Heb. 1. 8

5 The sceptre of His kingdom — Heb. 1. 8

6 The unchangeableness of
His person — Heb. 1. 11

7 The triumph of His cause Heb. 1. 13

H.K.D.

### 1068 The Exalted One

'On the right hand of the majesty on high'

Four Times in Hebrews—

1 As Son of God—
His Sonship — Heb. 1. 3

2 As High Priest—
His Sanctuary — Heb. 8. 1

3 As the Man in the glory—
His Sacrifice — Heb. 10. 12

4 As the Sustainer—
His Supremacy — Heb. 12. 2

### 1069 Christ as the 'Son' in Hebrews 1 and 2

1 His Rank—Son of God, His
Deity — Heb. 1. 1
His Pre-eminence is proved
by 6 quotations from the
Psalms and one from 2
Samuel 7.

2 His Revelation—Son of man,
His Humanity — Heb. 2. 6
'made a little lower than the
angels'

3 His Rule—Son of David, His
Sovereignty — Heb. 2. 8, 9
'all things in subjection under
His feet'

4 His Role—Son of Abraham,
His Nationality — Heb. 2. 16
'He took hold of—the seed of
Abraham'

### 1070 What Believers Inherit

1 Heirs of Salvation—served by
God's angelic messengers Heb. 1. 14

2 Heirs of promise—with the
sure and steadfast hope of
an entry into Heaven — Heb. 6. 17

3 Heirs of Righteousness—by
faith in the unchanging
Word of God — Heb. 11. 7

4 Heirs of the world—through
the righteousness of faith Rom. 4. 13

5 Heirs of the kingdom—by the
election of God, as poor yet
rich in faith — James 2. 5

6 Heirs according to the hope
of eternal life—by the grace
of God that justifies us — Titus 3. 7

7 Heirs of God and joint-heirs
with Jesus Christ, because
'children of God' — Rom. 8. 17
JS. FS.

### 1071 Angels—the Ministering Spirits sent by God
Heb. 1. 14

Angels—

1 Point out the way for God's Pilgrims
Exod. 23. 20; 32. 34

2 Prepare the hearts of God's People
Judges 6. 11, 12

3 Provide the sustenance for God's Prophets
1 Kings 19. 5

4 Protect the lives of God's Prisoners
Dan. 6. 22; Ps. 34. 7;
Acts 12. 7

5 Prescribe the sphere of God's Preachers
Acts 8. 26

## 1072　Seven Safeguards for Saints

1 Hearing—Give heed to the things which we have heard LEST at any time we should let them slip　Heb. 2. 1

2 Heeding—Take heed, brethren, LEST there be in any of you an evil heart of unbelief　Heb. 3. 12

3 Exhorting—Exhort one another daily LEST any of you be hardened through the deceitfulness of sin　Heb. 3. 13

4 Labouring—Labour, therefore, to enter into that rest LEST any man fall after the same example of disobedience (Marg.)　Heb. 4. 11

5 Considering—Consider Him LEST ye be wearied and faint in your minds　Heb. 12. 3

6 Making—Make straight paths for your feet LEST that which is lame be turned out of the way　Heb. 12. 13

7 Looking—Looking diligently LEST any man fail of the grace of God, LEST any root of bitterness, springing up, trouble you　Heb. 12. 15
F.E.M.

## 1073　So Great Salvation
Heb. 2. 3

1 Salvation so great—because
Announced by an Incomparable Preacher　Heb. 2. 3
Attested by many Infallible Proofs　Heb. 2. 4
Accomplished at an Infinite Price　Heb. 2. 9
Administered by an Invincible Prince　Heb. 2. 10
Accompanied by many Inestimable Privileges　Heb. 2. 11-15

2 Neglect so easy — Same word is translated 'made light of' in Matt. 22. 5

3 Escape so impossible—'How shall we?'—an unanswerable question.

## 1074　We See Jesus
Jesus—without the accompaniment of any of His other names or titles—occurs eight times in Hebrews.

1 Jesus—crowned with glory and honour　Heb. 2. 9

2 Jesus—the Apostle and High Priest of our confession　Heb. 3. 1

3 Jesus—made an High Priest for ever after the order of Melchisedec　Heb. 6. 20

4 Jesus—made Surety of a better testament　Heb. 7. 22

5 Jesus—the new and living way into the Holiest　Heb. 10. 19

6 Jesus—the Author and Finisher of faith　Heb. 12. 2

7 Jesus—the Mediator of the new covenant　Heb. 12. 24

8 Jesus—the One Who sanctifies the people because He suffered without the gate　Heb. 13. 12
R.A.H.

## 1075　Three Precious Things
Heb. 3. 1

1 Our Character—holy brethren　Heb. 3. 1

2 Our Calling—Heavenly　Heb. 3. 1

3 Our Contemplation—Consider Jesus, the Apostle and High Priest　Heb. 3. 1
H.K.D.

## 1076　Danger Signals—the Red Light, then the Green

1 Do not drift away, but pay earnest heed to directions　Heb. 2. 1

2 Do not waver, but hold fast your confidence　Heb. 3. 6, 14

3 Do not lag behind, but endeavour diligently to enter　Heb. 4. 11, 12

4 Do not turn back to the rudiments, but go on to maturity　Heb. 6. 1-3

5 Do not be carried away by false doctrines, but be anchored to God's grace　Heb. 13. 8, 9

## 1077　Hear or Harden

'Today, if you will hear His voice, harden not your hearts' Heb. 3. 7, 15; 4. 7

THREE TIMES IN TWENTY VERSES
'TODAY' Five times in twenty verses.

Two Alternatives Proposed—
'Hear His voice' or 'Harden your hearts'

Three hardening forces indicated by the word 'LEST'

1 An evil heart of unbelief　Heb. 3. 12

2 The deceitfulness of sin　Heb. 3. 13

3 Falling short of God's promises　Heb. 4. 1

Two Answers Possible—
'Today' or 'Some time'　Prov. 27. 1

## 1078 The Heart in Hebrews
Seven marks—

| | | |
|---|---|---|
| 1 | The Erring Heart | Heb. 3. 10 |
| 2 | The Hardened Heart | Heb. 3. 8-15 |
| 3 | The Evil Heart of unbelief | Heb. 3. 12 |
| 4 | The Discerned Heart | Heb. 4. 12 |
| 5 | The Sprinkled Heart | Heb. 10. 22 |
| 6 | The True Heart | Heb. 10. 22 |
| 7 | The Established Heart | Heb. 13. 9 |

T.B.

## 1079 God's Chosen Priest
1 His Person—Jesus the Son of God
Heb. 4. 14, 15; 5. 5

2 His Preparation—through suffering
Heb. 5. 8

3 His Purpose as Priest—to offer sacrifices
Heb. 5. 1

4 His People—the redeemed
Heb. 6. 20

5 His Place—Heaven itself
Heb. 9. 24

6 His Pattern and order—Of Melchisedec
Heb. 5. 10

7 His Power—Almighty—able to save
Heb. 7. 25

JS. FS.

## 1080 The Throne of Grace
Heb. 4. 14-16

The Mercy-seat on earth Ps. 85. 10; Exod. 25. 21, 22; Rom. 3. 25

The Throne of Grace—Where?—In Heaven Ps. 11. 4; 103. 19

For how long?—For ever Heb. 1. 8

Five reasons for boldness of approach to the Throne of Grace—

1 We have a great High Priest—able to save, succour, sympathize
Heb. 7. 25, 26; 2. 17, 18; 4. 15

2 He has passed through the heavens into Heaven itself
Heb. 4. 14; 9. 24

3 He is Jesus the Son of God, truly man and truly God
Heb. 4. 14

4 He is able to be touched with the feeling of our infirmities
Heb. 4. 15

5 He has been tempted as we are, sin apart
Heb. 4. 15
(NO SIN 1 John 3. 5; 2 Cor. 5. 21; 1 Pet. 2. 22)

## 1081 Our Great High Priest

| | | |
|---|---|---|
| 1 | His Ordination—<br>by God | Heb. 5. 5, 6 |
| 2 | His Obedience—<br>as Man | Heb. 5. 8, 9 |
| 3 | His Omnipotence—<br>as High Priest | Heb. 4. 14-16 |

## 1082 Seven Eternal Verities
In the Epistle to the Hebrews

| | | |
|---|---|---|
| 1 | Eternal Salvation—<br>Christ the Author | Heb. 5. 9 |
| 2 | Eternal Judgment—<br>a Fundamental doctrine | Heb. 6. 2 |
| 3 | Eternal Redemption—<br>obtained by the blood of<br>Christ | Heb. 9. 12 |
| 4 | Eternal Spirit—<br>through Whom Christ<br>offered Himself | Heb. 9. 14 |
| 5 | Eternal Inheritance—<br>promised to them who are<br>called | Heb. 9. 15 |
| 6 | Eternal Covenant—<br>ratified by the blood of<br>Christ | Heb. 13. 20 |
| 7 | Eternal Perfection—<br>in the Son of God, our High<br>Priest | Heb. 7. 28 |

J.H.E.

## 1083 Three Figures of Stinted Growth in Believers
1 The Infant—still on milk when he should be full-grown Heb. 5. 13; 1 Pet. 2. 1, 2

2 The Student—still at the alphabet when he should be a teacher
Heb. 5. 12

3 The Building—still at the foundation stage when the super-structure ought to be going up
Heb. 6. 1, 2

## 1084 The Hope Set Before Us
Heb. 6. 18

| | |
|---|---|
| It is a 'better hope' | Heb. 7. 19 |
| It is a 'blessed hope' | Titus 2. 13 |
| It is a hope laid up in Heaven | Col. 1. 5 |
| It is a 'sure and steadfast' hope | Heb. 6. 19 |
| ABRAHAM—against hope believed in hope | Rom. 4. 18 |
| SOLOMON said—Hope deferred maketh the heart sick | Prov. 13. 12 |
| DAVID said—Hope thou in God | Ps. 42. 5, 11 |

Note—

| | | |
|---|---|---|
| 1 | The Purpose of the Hope—a<br>Refuge | Heb. 6. 18 |
| 2 | The Power of the Hope—an<br>Anchor | Heb. 6. 19 |
| 3 | The Place of the Hope—a<br>Sanctuary | Heb. 6. 19 |
| 4 | The Person Who is our<br>Hope—Jesus our High<br>Priest | Heb. 6. 20 |

OUR HOPE—

| | | |
|---|---|---|
| 1 | Is Based on a Solemn Con-<br>firmation | Heb. 6. 16 |
| 2 | Brings a Strong Consolation | Heb. 6. 18 |
| 3 | Establishes a Sure Commun-<br>ication | Heb. 6. 20 |

## 1085   The Order of Melchisedec

Like Melchisedec, Jesus—

1 Is Ordained by God
   Heb. 6. 20

2 Is a Priest of the Most High God
   Gen. 14. 18-20

3 Is King of Righteousness and of Peace
   Heb. 7. 2; 1. 8; Isa. 9. 6

4 Is a Priest without primogeniture or pedigree   Heb. 7. 3

5 Inaugurated His Priesthood by an act of blessing   Luke 24. 50; Heb. 7. 6

6 Receives homage and tithes from God's chosen   Luke 24. 51; Heb. 7. 8

7 Holds His office to perpetuity
   Heb. 7. 15, 16

## 1086   Consider how Great this Man is

Greater than Aaron—

1 Because Abraham gave him tithes   Heb. 7. 4

2 Because he blessed Abraham Heb. 7. 6, 7

3 Because Abraham is dead, and He has an endless life   Heb. 7. 16

4 Because of God's oath conferring priesthood   Heb. 7. 21

5 Because of His one complete sacrifice   Heb. 7. 27

But note—

While in these respects our Lord is identified with Melchisedec, the appearance of Melchisedec to Abraham in Gen. 14 was not a Christophany, nor was Melchisedec an angel from Heaven but a man, and as a man a Type of Christ, 'made like unto the Son of God' (Heb. 7. 3) Who is 'another priest after the similitude of Melchisedec' (Heb. 7. 15)

## 1087   God has Sworn

about these Things

1 The Priesthood of Christ
   Heb. 7. 21

2 The Security of the Christian
   Heb. 6. 16-20

3 The Subjection of the Impenitent
   Isa. 45. 23; Rom. 14. 11
                                T.B.

## 1088   Perfect Salvation
   Heb. 7. 25

1 ABILITY—'He is able to save' (7. 25), to sympathize (4. 15), to succour (2. 18), to make stand (Rom. 14. 4), to stablish (Rom. 16. 25), to keep from falling (Jude 24), to build up (Acts 20. 32), to subdue (Phil. 3. 21), to do exceeding abundantly (Eph. 3. 20).

2 ACTIVITY—'able to keep on saving' (literal translation)—past, present, future

3 ASSURANCE—'He ever liveth to make intercession' For the unsaved—His work on earth; for the saved—His work in Heaven

4 APPROACH—'Them that come unto God by Him' (Literally 'them that draw near', or 'them that come right up'.
                          DR. GRIFFITH THOMAS

## 1089   The Better Ministry of Christ

1 A Better Priest—
   High Priest of good things   Heb. 9. 11

2 A Better Sanctuary—
   A greater and more perfect
   tabernacle   Heb. 9. 11

3 A Better Sacrifice—
   not blood of bulls and
   calves—His own blood   Heb. 9. 12

4 A Better Method—
   offering once for all   Heb. 9. 12

5 A Better Blessing—
   Having obtained eternal
   redemption for us   Heb. 9. 12

6 A Better Guarantee—
   the eternal Spirit   Heb. 9. 14

7 A Better Result—
   a purged conscience and
   service to the living God   Heb. 9. 14
                          DR. GRIFFITH THOMAS

## 1090   Sanctification

Its Meaning—setting apart for a holy use; becoming like a holy God.

1 In connection with the Divine Purpose for us   Jude 1; 1 Cor. 1. 2; 1 Pet. 1. 2

   Three Different writers—
   Jude—by God the Father ⎫ THE
   Paul—in Christ Jesus      ⎬ TRINITY
   Peter—of the Spirit       ⎭

2 In connection with the Believer's Position
   Heb. 9. 13, 14; 10. 10, 14; 13. 12

3 In connection with the Believer's Practice
   1 Thess. 3. 13; 4. 3, 4

4 In connection with the Believer's Progress
   Heb. 12. 14; 2 Cor. 7. 1

## 1091   Divers Washings—Various Baptisms

Baptisms (plural) in Heb. 6. 2—translated 'washings' in Heb. 9. 10.

1 Ceremonial Washings
   Heb. 9. 10; Mark 7. 4

2 One of the initial rites for proselytes to Judaism

3 John's baptism unto repentance
   Matt. 3. 11; 21. 25; Acts 19. 3, 4

4 Christ's sufferings and death
   Luke 12. 50

5 The Spirit's baptism
   1 Cor. 12. 12, 13

6 Baptism of believers in Christ
   Acts 8. 36-38; 9. 18; 10. 47, 48

7 Baptism of judgment (with fire)
   Luke 3. 16, 17

## 1092  Three Appearings

1 Past—Christ's Appearing on earth to put away sins by the sacrifice of Himself     Heb. 9. 26
2 Present—His Appearing in Heaven to intercede for His own as Priest     Heb. 9. 24
3 Future—His Appearing on earth to them that look for Him, as King     Heb. 9. 28

## 1093  Christ and the Heavenly Sanctuary

1 He has opened it     Heb. 9. 11, 12
2 He has cleansed it     Heb. 9. 20-23
3 He intercedes for us in it     Heb. 9. 24
4 He has secured for us access to it     Heb. 10. 19-22
5 He offers our sacrifices of praise in it     Heb. 13. 15; 1 Pet. 2. 5

## 1094  The 'No Mores' of Hebrews 10

1 No more conscience of sins as far as the believer is concerned     v. 2
2 No more remembrance of sins as far as God is concerned     v. 17
3 No more offering for sin as far as Christ is concerned     v. 18
4 No more sacrifice for sins as far as the apostate is concerned     v. 26

## 1095  The Lord's Body

1 Prepared in Incarnation    Heb. 10. 5
2 Offered in Sacrifice    Heb. 10. 10
3 Broken in Judgment    1 Cor. 11. 24
4 Buried in Death    John 19. 40
5 Handled in Resurrection    Luke 24. 39
6 Glorified in Ascension    Phil. 3. 21
7 Discerned in Communion    1 Cor. 11. 29

The Lord Jesus has TWO bodies—His own human body, and the Church, which is His Body. The one 'marred more than any man's', the other 'without spot or wrinkle or any such thing'. These two bodies will be side by side through all eternity. The first body is the explanation of the second, and the second is the outcome of the first.

T.B.

## 1096  The First Superseded by the Second
Heb. 10. 9

Heb. 1—In the past God spoke by prophets: now He speaks in His Son

Heb. 2—In the past the Word was spoken by angels: afterwards Salvation was preached by our Lord

Heb. 3—Moses was a servant in God's house: Christ is a Son in God's house

Heb. 4—Rest was not enjoyed in the week: rest is abiding for the people of God

Heb. 5—Israel's high priests were taken from among men: our High Priest is the Son of God from Heaven

Heb. 6—God's promise was to Abraham: God's promise now is to Abraham's spiritual seed

Heb. 7—Priests could not continue by reason of death: Jesus has an unchangeable priesthood 'in the power of an endless life'.

Heb. 8—Israel worshipped in an earthly sanctuary: we worship in a Heavenly sanctuary

Heb. 9—Animal sacrifices could not take away sin: Christ offered Himself one sacrifice for sins, once for all

Heb. 10—The way into the Holiest was not open: we have boldness of access into the Holiest

Heb. 11—Those of old died in faith, not having received the fulfilment of the promises: God has provided some better thing for us

Heb. 12—Those of old came to Mount Sinai: we have come to Mount Sion

Heb. 13—Israel's priests had an altar and could eat of the bodies of victims offered: we have an altar whereof they have no right to eat

## 1097  The Perfection of Christ's Sacrifice

The Proofs—

1 'One sacrifice'—offered once for all—no need for repetition     Heb. 10. 12

2 He 'sat down': Israel's priests always stood     Heb. 10. 11, 12

3 He is 'on the right hand of God' so God has been perfectly satisfied     Heb. 10. 12

4 He is 'expecting till his enemies be made His footstool'—not expecting to have to make atonement for sins again    Heb. 10. 13

5 He 'has perfected for all time them that are sanctified'     Heb. 10. 14

6 The Holy Spirit is a witness to the efficacy of Christ's work     Heb. 10. 15

7 We have now boldness of access to a Holy God    Heb. 10. 19

**1098  Inside the Veil**

The word for 'veil' in the Gospels and in Hebrews means 'curtain'.

1 The Veil of the Tabernacle, and of the Temple, on earth (The way into the Holiest of all was not yet made manifest) Exod. 26. 31; 2 Chron. 3. 14; Heb. 9. 8

2 The Veil of the Temple rent from top to bottom at Christ's death
Matt. 27. 51
Five events took place then—
the Veil was rent
the Earth was shaken
the Rocks were rent
the Graves were opened
the Onlookers were convinced

3 The Veil, that is to say, His flesh—the body taken in Incarnation
Heb. 10. 19, 20

4 The Veil of the Heavenly temple
Heb. 6. 19
'SOON THY SAINTS SHALL ALL BE GATHERED
—INSIDE THE VEIL'

**1099  Three Important Exhortations**

1 Let us draw near—*Our Worship*　Heb. 10. 22
'with a true heart'—Composed
'in full assurance of faith'—Confident
'having our hearts sprinkled'—Cleansed

2 Let us hold fast the confession of our faith—*Our Witness* Heb. 10. 23

3 Let us consider one another to provoke unto love and to good works—*Our Work*　Heb. 10. 24

**1100  Full Assurance**
Heb. 10. 22

One word in Greek—Plerophoria—occurring four times in the New Testament

1 Full assurance of the Gospel message　1 Thess. 1. 5
2 Full assurance of faith　Heb. 10. 22
3 Full assurance of understanding　Col. 2. 2
4 Full assurance of hope　Heb. 6. 11

**1101  God's Picture Gallery and its Sections**
Heb. 11

Section 1
The Antedeluvian section—
Abel, Enoch, Noah　Heb. 11. 3-7
Section 2
The Patriarchal section—
Abraham, Sarah, Isaac, Jacob, Joseph　Heb. 11. 8-22
Section 3
The Mosaic section—
Moses' parents, Moses, Moses' people　Heb. 11. 23-29
Section 4
The Promised Land section Heb. 11. 30-39

Section 5
The Present day section—
'for us'　Heb. 11. 40
In Section 1 the few were doing what none of the rest of the world was doing

In Section 2 the few were looking for something in which others were not interested

In Section 3 the few were choosing what no one else was choosing

In Section 4 the few were enduring what none of the rest of the world would endure

In Section 5 the few are running in a race in which the rest of the world is not competing.

**1102  The Way of Faith**
Hebrews 11

1 The Definition of Faith—'title deeds' and 'evidences'　Heb. 11. 1
Faith's Confidence v. 1
Faith's Commendation v. 2
Faith's Comprehension v. 3
2 The Demand of Faith—Gateway to the Presence of God and Guarantee of an audience with God Heb. 11. 6
3 The Declaration of Faith—We 'seek a city' (God's Promises accepted, embraced and confessed)　Heb. 11. 14
4 The Demonstration of Faith—Through faith　Heb. 11. 28, 33, 34
5 The Devotion of Faith—not accepting deliverance　Heb. 11. 35-38

**1103  The Manifestation of Faith**
Hebrews 11

1 Faith's Worship—
a more excellent sacrifice　v. 4
2 Faith's Witness—
Enoch pleased God　v. 5
3 Faith's Work—
Noah prepared an ark v. 7; 2 Pet. 2. 5
4 Faith's Walk—
Abraham went out　v. 8
5 Faith's Waiting—
He looked for a city　v. 10
6 Faith's Willingness—
Sarah received strength vs. 11, 12
7 Faith's Welcome—
These all were persuaded—confessed—a better country　vs. 13-16
DR. GRIFFITH THOMAS

**1104  Heroes of Faith**
as seen in Heb. 11

1 Abel—the Sacrifice of Faith
2 Noah—the Simplicity of Faith
3 Abraham—the Sojourn of Faith
4 Isaac—the Sanguinity of Faith
5 Moses—the Suffering of Faith
6 Rahab—the Salvation of Faith
7 The Rest—the Supremacy of Faith (vs. 32, etc.)
H.K.D.

## 1105 Living Pictures of Faith
### Heb. 11

Abel—
| | |
|---|---|
| Faith that Justifies | v. 4 |

Enoch—
| | |
|---|---|
| Faith that Sanctifies | v. 5 |

Noah—
| | |
|---|---|
| Faith that Testifies | v. 7 |

Abraham—
| | |
|---|---|
| Faith of Enterprise | v. 8 |

Sarah—
| | |
|---|---|
| Faith that Multiples | v. 11 |

Isaac—
| | |
|---|---|
| Faith that looks onward | v. 20 |

Jacob—
| | |
|---|---|
| Faith that looks upward | v. 21 |

Joseph—
| | |
|---|---|
| Faith that looks homeward | v. 22 |

Moses' Parents—
| | |
|---|---|
| Faith of a Mother | v. 23 |

Moses—
| | |
|---|---|
| Faith of a Man | v. 34 |

Moses' People—
| | |
|---|---|
| Faith of a Multitude | v. 29 |

Rahab—
| | |
|---|---|
| Faith that Receives | v. 31 |

Others—
| | |
|---|---|
| Faith that Achieves | vs. 33, 34 |

Martyrs—
| | |
|---|---|
| Faith that Endures | v. 35 |

Martyrs—
| | |
|---|---|
| Faith that Assures | v. 35 |

## 1106 Moses' Choice

Moses said 'NO!' to—

1 The Pleasures of sin—
   as Transient — Heb. 11. 25
2 The Treasures of Egypt—
   as Tawdry — Heb. 11. 26
3 The Vainglory of earth—
   as Temporal — Heb. 11. 24

These comprise all that is in the world, the lust of the flesh, the lust of the eye and the pride of life 1 John 2. 16

Moses said 'YES!' to—

1 The Reproach of Christ — Heb. 11. 26
2 The Riches of Christ — Heb. 11. 26
3 The Recompense of the
   reward — Heb. 11. 26

## 1107 Characteristics of Moses' Choice

1 'By faith'—It was a *Faith*
   Choice — Heb. 11. 24, 27
2 'he had respect to—the
   reward'—It was a *Fore-
   seeing* Choice — Heb. 11. 26
3 'he forsook Egypt'—It
   was a *Farewell* Choice — Heb. 11. 27
4 'Not fearing the wrath'—
   It was a *Fearless* Choice — Heb. 11. 27
5 'he endured' to the end—
   It was a *Final* Choice — Heb. 11. 27

## 1108 Moses, the Man of Purpose and Power

| 1 Refusing Honour | Heb. 11. 24 |
|---|---|
| 2 Choosing Suffering | Heb. 11. 25 |
| 3 Esteeming Reproach | Heb. 11. 26 |
| 4 Respecting Recompense | Heb. 11. 26 |
| 5 Forsaking Egypt | Heg. 11. 27 |
| 6 Enduring Wrath | Heb. 11. 27 |
| 7 Keeping the Passover | Heb. 11. 28 |
| 8 Overcoming all obstacles | Heb. 11. 29, 30 |

The secret of his success—'By faith'. 'By faith' the Christian is saved (Eph. 2. 8; 1 Pet. 1. 9), lives (Heb. 10. 38), walks (2 Cor. 5. 7), and overcomes (1 John 5. 4)

J.M.K.

## 1109 The Race Set Before Us

'Run with patience', i.e. with endurance Heb. 12. 1

The same word in 10. 32 and in 10. 35: also in 12. 2 and 3 (of Jesus our Example). CONSIDER—

1 The Witnesses that Encompass
   us (those in Heb. 11 who
   testify to Faith's victory) — Heb. 12. 1
2 The Weights that Encumber us — Heb. 12. 1
3 The Wickedness that Entangles
   us — Heb. 12. 1
4 The Weariness that Encounters
   us — Heb. 12. 3
5 The Winner Who Encourages
   us — Heb. 12. 2

He is Jesus, the Dependent Man: He is File Leader, the Pace-setter: He is the Perfecter, having completed the course: He is the Survivor, having endured the cross and shame: and He is the Exalted Man at God's right hand.

## 1110 The Path of the Christian
### Heb. 12

The Example of the Saviour—
Looking off unto Jesus — Heb. 12. 1-3
The Experience of sons—
Chastisement, child-training Heb. 12. 4-6
The Endurance of saints—
Partakers of His holiness — Heb. 12. 7-11
The Entreaty of the servant—
Lift up the hands that hang
down and the feeble knees Heb. 12. 12-17
The Encouragement of the
shepherd—
ye are come to Mount Sion Heb. 12. 18-24

## 1111 God's Ways of Testing and Training

Five very short words of one syllable each—
ROD, YOKE, FIRE, CROSS, THORN: but what a depth of meaning!

1 The Training of the Rod
   (Chastisement means 'child-training')
   — Heb. 12. 6
2 The Teaming of the Yoke — Matt. 11. 29
3 The Testing of the Fire
   — Job 23. 10; 1 Pet. 1. 7
4 The Travail of the Cross — Mark 8. 34
5 The Throbbing of the Thorn — 2 Cor. 12. 7

## 1112 The Glory of God the Father

He is 'the God and Father of our Lord Jesus Christ' Who revealed Him as—

1 THE FATHER OF LIGHTS—
in the Gospel of Matthew    James 1. 17
2 THE FATHER OF SPIRITS—
in the Gospel of Mark    Heb. 12. 9
3 THE FATHER OF MERCIES—
in the Gospel of Luke    2 Cor. 1. 3
4 THE FATHER OF GLORY—
in the Gospel of John    Eph. 1. 17

## 1113 Terrors of the Old Covenant and Triumphs of the New

The Seven Terrors of the Old Covenant to which the Christian HAS NOT COME—

1 The Mountain that was
material and tangible    Heb. 12. 18
2 The fire that enveloped it    Heb. 12. 18
3 The blackness that covered it    Heb. 12. 18
4 The darkness that surrounded
it    Heb. 12. 18
5 The tempest that swept over it    Heb. 12. 18
6 The sound of a trumpet of
warning    Heb. 12. 19
7 The voice of words, the letter
of the law    Heb. 12. 19

The Eight Triumphs to which the Christian HAS COME—

1 Mount Sion of which glorious
things are spoken    Heb. 12. 22
2 The Heavenly Jerusalem, the
city of the living God    Heb. 12. 22
3 An innumerable company of
angels ministering    Heb. 12. 22
4 The Church of the firstborn
ones    Heb. 12. 23
5 God the Judge of all    Heb. 12. 23
6 The spirits of just men made
perfect    Heb. 12. 23
7 Jesus the Mediator of the New
Covenant    Heb. 12. 24
8 The blood of sprinkling that
calls for forgiveness and not
for vengeance    Heb. 12. 24

## 1114 Lest We Forget

We are exhorted to REMEMBER—

God's Strangers and Pilgrims—
Hospitably    Heb. 13. 2
God's Sufferers and Prisoners—
Sympathetically    Heb. 13. 3
God's Spokesmen and Preachers—
Gratefully    Heb. 13. 7
God's Servants and Pastors—
Benevolently    Heb. 13. 16, 17

There are two keywords in Heb. 13—'Remember' and 'Obey' vs. 7. 17

## 1115 The Guides

'They that have the rule over you'—mentioned three times in Heb. 13—are the Guides.

ATTITUDE OF THE CHURCH TO THE GUIDES—

1 Recognition of them    1 Thess. 5. 12
2 Respect for them    1 Tim. 5. 17
3 Submission to them
   Heb. 13. 17; 1 Pet. 5. 5
4 Remembrance of them    Heb. 13. 7
5 Emulation of them    Heb. 13. 7
6 Entreaty of them    1 Tim. 5. 1
7 Confidence in them    1 Tim. 5. 19

## 1116 An Unchanging Christ in a Changing World
Heb. 13. 8

He is the unchanging Lord of creation in Heb. 1. 10, 11 in contrast to the heavens and earth that will pass away and be changed.

He is the unchanging Christ in glory in Heb. 13. 8 in contrast to the passing of other guides and helpers.

God's Word is unchanging (Matt. 24. 35): God's Kingdom cannot be moved (Heb. 12. 26) and God's Christ is immutable (Heb. 13. 8) In the Epistle to the Hebrews the following are described—

1 The Woeful Change that sin had wrought
2 The Blessed Change the blood has brought
3 Changes with which man's world is fraught
4 The Christ of God Who changes not

## 1117 The Sin-Offering
Heb. 13. 12

1 The Person—Jesus
2 The Purpose—to sanctify the people
3 The Price—His own blood
4 The Place—outside the gate

H.K.D.

## 1118 God's Good Pleasure
Heb. 13. 20, 21

1 The Title of God's pleasure—God of peace
   Rom. 15. 33; 1 Thess. 5. 23
2 The Man of God's pleasure—Our Lord
Jesus    Prov. 8. 30
3 The Act of God's pleasure—brought
again from the dead
   Acts 2. 22, 24
4 The Sacrifice of God's pleasure—the blood
of the everlasting covenant
   Isa. 53. 10
5 The People of God's pleasure—make YOU
perfect    Eph. 1. 5, 9
6 The Purpose of God's pleasure—to do His
will    Heb. 10. 36
7 The Process of God's pleasure—working
in you that which is well-pleasing in His
sight through Jesus Christ
   Heb. 13. 21

This is all 'ACCORDING TO THE GOOD PLEASURE OF HIS WILL'    Eph. 1. 5

# JAMES

## 1119 Perfection in James's Epistle

1 The Perfect Gift of God    James 1. 17

2 The Perfect Law of Liberty    James 1. 25

3 The Perfect Work of Patience James 1. 4

4 The Perfected Faith by Works James 2. 22

5 The Perfected Man by Restraint    James 3. 2
                                        T.B.

## 1120 Let Every Man Be

SWIFT to Hear—the Ear in Subjection

SLOW to Speak—the Tongue in Subjection

SLOW to Wrath—the Temper in Subjection

SEPARATED FROM all filthiness and superfluity of
naughtiness    James 1. 19 21
                        T.D.W.M.

## 1121 How Conviction is Wrought

1 By the Law of God, when God's requirements are known
                        James 2. 9

2 By our own Conscience, when God's voice is heard    John 8. 9; Rom. 2. 14, 15

3 By the Light that came into the world, Jesus Christ
                        John 3. 20

4 By the Holy Spirit, the Comforter, directly
                        John 16. 8

5 By the Holy Spirit through the lives of God's saints
                        Eph. 5. 11

6 By the Lord in His Church, through His chastening    Heb. 12. 5; Rev. 3. 19

7 By the faithful Word spoken by elders in the assembly
                        Titus 1. 9

8 By the Lord Jesus at His return
                        Jude 15; Rev. 1. 7

---

# 1 PETER

## 1122 Strangers Scattered Abroad
### 1 Pet. 1. 1

The saints addressed by the Apostle Peter were

1 Displaced Persons—
    strangers    v. 1

2 Dispersed People—
    scattered    v. 1

3 Disinherited People—
    homes destroyed    v. 1

4 Dependent People—
    on the Triune God    v. 2

5 Distressed People—
    through manifold trials    v. 6

## 1123 The Doctrine Enunciated by Peter

1 Foreordination, according to God's foreknowledge    1 Pet. 1. 2

2 Sanctification, set apart by the Spirit of God    1 Pet. 1. 2

3 Regeneration 'unto a living hope'    1 Pet. 1. 3

4 Expectation of an inheritance in Heaven    1 Pet. 1. 4
    (though disinherited on earth)

5 Preservation by the power of God    1 Pet. 1. 4

6 Jubilation because of what is to be revealed    1 Pet. 1. 5

7 Temptation—in heaviness because of various trials    1 Pet. 1. 6

8 Valuation—faith—more precious than gold    1 Pet. 1. 7

9 Salvation—the end of their faith    1 Pet. 1. 9

10 Revelation—Prophecies of the grace to come    1 Pet. 1. 10

## 1124 Reserved

1 An Inheritance for the saints, who are preserved for it    1 Pet. 1. 4

2 Judgment for the angels that sinned, who are in chains    2 Pet. 2. 4

3 Punishment for men who are ungodly    2 Pet. 2. 9

4 Conflagration for the heavens and earth    2 Pet. 3. 7

5 The Blackness of darkness for Christless professors    Jude 13
                        T.B.

## 1125 Faith and its Actings

1 The Operation of Faith—through faith unto salvation   1 Pet. 1. 5
2 The Probation of Faith—that the trial of your faith   1 Pet. 1. 7
3 The Exultation of Faith—believing, ye rejoice with joy unspeakable   1 Pet. 1. 8
4 The Consummation of Faith—receiving the end of your faith   1 Pet. 1. 9
W.E.V.

## 1126 Exhortations based on Doctrine

The 'WHEREFORE' of 1 Pet. 1. 13 links what follows with the doctrine that precedes it.
1 The Mind of the Christian—Sobriety enjoined because of the Revelation   1 Pet. 1. 13, 14
2 The Morality of the Christian—Holiness enjoined because of our Relationship   1 Pet. 1. 15-17
3 The Motive of the Christian—Reverential Fear enjoined because of our Redemption   1 Pet. 1. 18-21
4 The Mainstay of the Christian—Fervent love enjoined because of our Regeneration   1 Pet. 1. 22-25

## 1127 The True Church and Divine Revelation

1 ITS CREED—
an Authoritative Ground for our faith—'Who believe in God'. Doctrines of Redemption, Regeneration, and Revelation   1 Pet. 1. 17-25
2 ITS CODE—
an Infallible Guide for our life—the pure milk of the Word   1 Pet. 2. 1-3
3 ITS CONSTITUTION—
an Established Government for our society—built up a spiritual house   1 Pet. 2. 4-10

## 1128 Redemption—Man's Price and God's Purchase

1 Pet. 1. 19, 20

| THE MOST MAN CAN OFFER | THE PRICE GOD REQUIRES |
|---|---|
| 1 Silver and gold | Precious blood |
| 2 Comes from the earth | the Lamb of God from Heaven |
| 3 Inanimate | the living Lord |
| 4 Human currency | Divine currency |
| 5 Only temporary in value | Eternal in efficacy |
| 6 Corruptible | Incorruptible |
| 7 Defiled | 'Without blemish and without spot' |

## 1129 Christ the Divinely-Appointed Saviour

1 The Appointed Lamb for our Redemption   1 Pet. 1. 19
2 The Appointed Lord for our Salvation   Acts 2. 36
3 The Appointed High Priest for our Representation   Heb. 7. 16
4 The Appointed Head of the Church   Eph. 1. 20-22
5 The Appointed Heir of all things   Heb. 1. 2
6 The Appointed Judge of the world   Acts 17. 31

## 1130 'The Word of the Lord Endureth for Ever'

1 Pet. 1. 25

Because of—
1 The Uniqueness of its Production and Preservation (Preserved from Corruption and Extirpation)
2 The Unity of its Structure and Spirit—Contents of the O.T. and N.T. are Historic, Didactic and Prophetic—in that order
3 The Uniformity of its Teaching and Testimony concerning God and man, with Jesus Christ the central Figure
4 The Universality of its Application and Appeal

## 1131 A Precious Threefold Link

1 Peter's Precept—
that ye may grow   1 Pet. 2. 2
2 God's Purpose—
that ye should show   1 Pet. 2. 9
3 Paul's Prayer—
that ye may know   Eph. 1. 18
W.T.R.

## 1132 'As' in 1 Peter 2

As Newborn Babes—in God's family   v. 2
As Living Stones—in God's house   v. 5
As Stranger Pilgrims—in God's world   v. 11
As God's Servants—with God's freedom   v. 16
As Wandering Sheep—returned to God's fold   v. 25

188

## 1133 A Spiritual House and a Spiritual Priesthood
1 Pet. 2. 9

1 A SPIRITUAL HOUSE AND ITS CONSTRUCTION
Its Basis—the living Word of God     1 Pet. 1. 23
Its Bond—all united to a living Head in Heaven     1 Pet. 2. 4
Its Building—living stones built up     1 Pet. 2. 5
2 A SPIRITUAL HIERARCHY AND ITS COMPOSITION—
Holy Priests     1 Pet. 2. 5
Royal Priests     1 Pet. 2. 9
3 A SPIRITUAL SANCTUARY AND ITS CONSECRATION—
'to God by Jesus Christ'
4 SPIRITUAL SACRIFICES AND THEIR COSTLINESS

## 1134 The Priesthood of All Believers
AN HOLY PRIESTHOOD—
Founded on Christ, the chief corner stone     1 Pet. 2. 6
Feeding on the Word of God     1 Pet. 2. 2
Freed from all malice and guile     1 Pet. 2. 1
Furnished with acceptable offerings for God     1 Pet. 2. 5

A ROYAL PRIESTHOOD—
Chosen by God
Called into God's marvellous light
Sanctified—set apart for God
Showing the graces of Christ     1 Pet. 2. 9

## 1135 A Precious Person and Precious Things
HIMSELF—'He is precious' (or the Preciousness)     1 Pet. 2. 7
A Precious Corner Stone—elect, precious     1 Pet. 2. 4-6
Precious Blood—the precious blood of Christ     1 Pet. 1. 19
Precious Faith—of the believer     2 Pet. 1. 1
The Trial of Faith—more precious than gold     1 Pet. 1. 7
Precious Promises—given to us     2 Pet. 1. 4
E.A.H.

## 1136 Christ Our Example
Christ—leaving us an example—Greek 'Hupogrammos', the headline of a copy book, a different word from that used in John 13. 15, where the word is 'Hupodeigma', a Demonstration lesson.

TO THE INDIVIDUAL BELIEVER He has left an Example, a Headline to copy:

TO THE CHURCH He has given an Example, a Demonstration lesson of love. John 13. 15
He has left us an Example—
1 in His Actions—
Who did no sin     1 Pet. 2. 22
2 in His Affirmations—
No guile found in His mouth     1 Pet. 2. 22
3 in His Attitude—
reviled not again—Non-retaliation     1 Pet. 2. 23
4 in His Appeal—
to Him that judgeth righteously     1 Pet. 2. 23

## 1137 Christ and His People
1 The Man on earth—
His Example—
Follow His steps     1 Pet. 2. 21
2 The Man on the cross—
His Expiation—
Healed by His stripes     1 Pet. 2. 23
3 The Man on the Throne—
His Exaltation—
upheld by His strength     1 Pet. 2. 25

## 1138 Four Blessed Statements
Concerning Jesus
In His Nature—
Sinless     1 Pet. 2. 22
In His Life—
Blameless     1 Pet. 2. 23
In His Death—
Vicarious     1 Pet. 2. 24
In His Resurrection—
Victorious     1 Pet. 2. 25
T.B.

## 1139 As Sheep Going Astray
1 Pet. 2. 25

Compare also Isa. 53. 6, 7; Jer. 50. 6
1 Sought by the Kind Shepherd
Luke 15. 4; 19. 10; Ps. 119. 176
2 Bought by the Good Shepherd
John 10. 11; Acts 20. 28
3 Thought of by the Overseeing Shepherd
1 Pet. 2. 25
4 Brought home by the Glad Shepherd
Luke 15. 5
5 Taught by the under-shepherds
1 Pet. 5. 2

## 1140 Wives and Husbands
CHRISTIAN WIVES—
1 Their Conduct—manner of life     1 Pet. 3. 1
2 Their Chastity—chaste manner of life     1 Pet. 3. 2
3 Their Cosmetics—a meek quiet spirit     1 Pet. 3. 3, 4
(Adorning—Greek—Kosmeo, from which 'cosmetics is derived)
4 Their Character—holy women     1 Pet. 3. 5

CHRISTIAN HUSBANDS—
1 Their Courtesy—giving honour unto the wife
2 Their Considerateness—as unto the weaker vessel
3 Their Concord—heirs together of the grace of life
4 Their Communion—that your prayers be not hindered     1 Pet. 3. 7

**1141 Heirs Together of the Grace of Life**
1 Pet. 3. 7

'HEIRS TOGETHER'—if both are believers—
Fellow-pilgrims to glory     Heb. 11. 9
Fellow-heirs of Christ's
Riches     Rom. 8. 17
Fellow-members of the
Church of God     Eph. 3. 6
This Marital Partnership is—
a Physical Partnership—one
flesh     Matt. 19. 4, 5
an Economic Partnership—
an help meet for him     Gen. 2. 18
a Spiritual Partnership—the
grace of life     1 Pet. 3. 7
The Grace of life—
1 Grace—Greek—Charis = thanks, favour. A Life filled with gratitude for Divine favour:
2 Charis = Pleasingness, A Life well-pleasing to the Lord and pleasant to one another
3 Charis = Grace of character, A Life expressing the beauty of Christ's character

**1142 Five Negatives Concerning Evil**
1 Not rendering evil for evil     1 Pet. 3. 9
2 Not speaking evil or guile     1 Pet. 3. 10
3 Not following evil but peace     1 Pet. 3. 11
4 Not doing evil but good     1 Pet. 3. 12
5 Not suffering for evil doing
but for well doing     1 Pet. 3. 17

**1143 Three Precious Truths in One Verse**
1 Propitiation—
Christ hath once suffered
for sins     1 Pet. 3. 18
2 Substitution—
the Just for the unjust     1 Pet. 3. 18
3 Reconciliation—
that He might bring us to
God     1 Pet. 3. 18
    H.D.

**1144 Faith, Hope and Love**
1 Pet. 4
The Order here is Faith, love and hope.
1 A Living Faith—
condemns the Past life
of sin in light of
Christ's Sufferings     1 Pet. 4. 1-3
considers the Future life
in light of coming
judgment     1 Pet. 4. 5, 6
conditions the Present
life in terms of vigilance and prayer     1 Pet. 4. 7
2 A Fervent Love—
in a Forgiving attitude
to Erring ones     1 Pet. 4. 8
in a Hospitable attitude
to Every one     1 Pet. 4. 9
in a Helpful attitude to
Each one     1 Pet. 4. 10, 11
3 A Joyful Hope—
based on a Privileged
Partnership in Christ's
sufferings     1 Pet. 4. 12, 13
based on a Present
Participation in
Christ's reproach     1 Pet. 4. 14-16
based on a Placid Presentation of ourselves
to Christ     1 Pet. 4. 17-19

**1145 Crowns as Rewards**
1 The Athlete's Crown—Incorruptible, unlike the fading laurel wreath
1 Cor. 9. 25
2 The Martyr's Crown—of life, for all who
endure trial     James 1. 12; Rev. 2. 10
3 The Watcher's Crown—of righteousness,
for all who love His appearing
2 Tim. 4. 8
4 The Soul-winner's Crown—of rejoicing,
for those who win souls
1 Thess. 2. 19
5 The Shepherd's Crown—of glory, for
those who feed the flock
1 Pet. 5. 4

**1146 He Careth for You**
1 Pet. 5. 7
As a Mother comforting you     Isa. 66. 13
As a Shepherd seeking you     Ezek. 34. 12
As an Eagle bearing you up     Deut. 32. 11
As a Father pitying you     Ps. 103. 13
As a Hen gathering you together     Matt. 23. 37
As a Bridegroom rejoicing over
you, His bride     Isa. 62. 5

**1147 God's Care for His Own**
1 Pet. 5. 7
1 He knows our names
John 10. 3
2 He numbers the hairs of our head
Matt. 10. 30
3 He counts the steps of our feet
Job 14. 16
4 He writes down the thoughts of our hearts
Mal. 3. 16
5 He bottles the tears from our eyes
Ps. 56. 8
6 He holds our right hand in His hand
Isa. 41. 13; Ps. 73. 23
7 He supplies all our needs
Phil. 4. 19

## 1148  2 Peter Compared and Contrasted with 1 Peter

This Epistle was written by Peter shortly before his martyrdom (2 Pet. 1. 14), as 2 Timothy was written by Paul shortly before his (2 Tim. 4. 6).

1 Peter and 2 Peter both begin with 'GRACE AND PEACE'.

| 1 PETER | 2 PETER |
|---|---|
| Ends with 'Love and peace' | Ends with 'Grace and knowledge' |
| The Sufferings of Christ and Christians | The knowledge of our Lord Jesus Christ |
| Triumph in Trial | Triumph over corruption |
| Christ's Precious blood shed for our Redemption | Our Precious Faith obtained through God's Righteousness |

2 Peter—

Chapter 1—Give Diligence
Chapter 2—Get Deliverance
Chapter 3—Grow and Develop

# 2 PETER

## 1149  The Knowledge of God in 2 Peter

It is—

1 Enriching Knowledge—
Grace and peace multiplied
through it                               2 Pet. 1. 2

2 Energizing Knowledge—
Keeping us from being idle
or unfruitful                           2 Pet. 1. 8

3 Emancipating Knowledge—
freeing us from the corrup-
tions of the world                    2 Pet. 2. 20

4 Edifying Knowledge—
providing growth in grace    2 Pet. 3. 18

## 1150  The Superlative Christian Life

Is—

1 The Reward of the utmost
possible diligence—all
diligence                                2 Pet. 1. 5

2 Acquired by the best possible process—adding in
(not 'to')                               2 Pet. 1. 5

3 The Expression of the
highest possible char-
acter (made up of faith,
valour, knowledge, con-
tinence, patience, piety,
brotherly kindness and
love)                                    2 Pet. 1. 5-7

4 Productive of the happiest
possible results—a fruit-
ful life, a clear vision, an
unswerving course, and
an abundant entrance.      2 Pet. 1. 8-12

## 1151  Diligence in 2 Peter

To add in our faith the various
graces of Christian character    2 Pet. 1. 5

To make our calling and election
sure                                    2 Pet. 1. 10

To bring to others' remembrance
things that pertain to life and
godliness                            2 Pet. 1. 15

To aim at being found blameless
when the Lord returns            2 Pet. 3. 14

## 1152  The Longsuffering of God

1 The Patience of a Long-
suffering God — 'waited'
when men were interested
only in their own affairs
and indifferent to God          1 Pet. 3. 20

2 The Provision of a Longsuffering God—'salvation'    2 Pet. 3. 15

3 The Purpose of a Long-
suffering God—'willing—
that all should come to
repentance'                         2 Pet. 3. 9

191

# 1 JOHN

**1153 Triumphs in 1 John**

1 Triumph of Light over Darkness
Ch. 1. 1-2. 11
2 Triumph of Life over Death
Ch. 2. 12-29
3 Triumph of Love over Hatred
Ch. 3. 1-24; 4. 7-21
4 Triumph of Truth over Error
Ch. 4. 1-7
5 Triumph of Faith over the World
Ch. 5. 1-21

**1154 The Family of God**

Chapter 1 The Family Relationships—Father, Son, and little children

Chapter 2 The Family Representatives— fathers, young men and babes

Chapter 3 The Family Responsibilities—Purity before God, righteousness before men and love to all believers

Chapter 4 The Family Resistance—to the spirit of Antichrist, to false teachers and to every form of error

Chapter 5 The Family Resources—by faith

**1155 Great Manifestations**

That which was from

| | |
|---|---|
| the beginning was manifested | 1 John 1. 1 |
| the Love was manifested | 1 John 4. 9 |
| the Light was manifested | John 1. 9 |
| the Life was manifested | 1 John 1. 2 |
| the Father was manifested | John 14. 9 |
| the Son of God was manifested | 1 John 3. 8 |
| His glory was manifested | John 1. 14 |

E.A.H.

**1156 Names of Our Lord in 1 John**

| | |
|---|---|
| The Word of Life | 1 John 1. 1 |
| The Eternal Life | 1 John 1. 2 |
| The Advocate | 1 John 2. 1 |
| The Righteous One | 1 John 2. 1 |
| The Propitiation | 1 John 2. 2 |
| The Saviour of the World | 1 John 4. 14 |
| The Son of God | 1 John 5. 5 |

H.K.D.

**1157 Our Fellowship**

1 The Meaning of Fellowship—
partnership, sharing    1 John 1. 3
2 The Medium of Fellowship—
light    1 John 1. 5-7
3 The Maintenance of Fellowship—
by walking in the light  1 John 1. 7
by confessing our sins  1 John 1. 9
by cleansing from all unrighteousness  1 John 1. 9

4 The Manifestation of Fellowship—
in relation to God    1 John 2. 3, 4
in relation to ourselves 1 John 2. 6, 7
in relation to others  1 John 2. 9, 10

**1158 As He Is**

1 1 John 1. 7 'We walk in the light *as He is* in the light' His communion with the Father is ours as sharing eternal life.

2 1 John 4. 17 '*As He is* so are we in the world'. We are in a world under sentence, but His relationship to judgment is ours; as associated with Him, we have boldness in the day of judgment.

3 1 John 3. 2 'We shall be like Him for we shall see Him *as He is*'. The world will never see Him thus: they will see Him in a judicial character and as the King, but we know Him as the second Man in glory, the firstfruits in resurrection, and the firstborn from the dead, the pattern of the kind of people God will have in the glory by and by.

4 1 John 3. 3 'He that hath this hope in Him purifieth himself *even as He is* pure'. The practical effect on our ways now of all these glorious expectations to be realized at His second Coming for all His saints.

M.I.R.

**1159 The Sin Question in 1 John**

| | |
|---|---|
| 1 A bold profession— No sin | 1 John 1. 8 |
| 2 A self-deceiver— deceive ourselves | 1 John 1. 8 |
| 3 A false position— truth is not in us | 1 John 1. 8 |
| 4 A necessary confession— confess our sins | 1 John 1. 9 |
| 5 A complete absolution— forgiven and cleansed | 1 John 1. 9 |
| 6 An important admonition— sin not | 1 John 2. 1 |
| 7 A gracious provision— if we sin, we have | 1 John 2. 1 |

H.K.D.

**1160 Marks of a True Child of God**

| | |
|---|---|
| 1 Believes that Jesus is the Christ | 1 John 5. 1 |
| 2 Does righteousness | 1 John 2. 29 |
| 3 Keeps His commandments | 1 John 2. 3 |
| 4 Does not practise sin | 1 John 3. 9 |
| 5 Is hated by the world | 1 John 3. 13 |
| 6 Loves the brethren | 1 John 3. 14 |
| 7 Overcomes the world | 1 John 5. 4 |

W.T.M.

## 1161　Tests of Profession

'He that saith'—three times in 1 John 2, indicating profession and what should accompany it—

1　A Life of obedience to Christ's
　　commandments　　　　vs. 2. 3
　　Profession tested by God's character

2　A Life of communion in walking
　　as Christ walked　　　　v. 6
　　Profession tested by Christ's walk

3　A Life of love to our brethren　v. 10
　　Profession tested by the Spirit's
　　teaching

## 1162　Grades in God's Family

Little children—Greek TEKNIA—John's term of endearment for all in God's family: occurs in 2. 12, 28; 3. 1, 7, 10—God's bairns

Little children—Greek PAIDIA—babes, infants

1 John 2. 12 Sins are forgiven for Christ's sake—True of all born of God

1 John 2. 28 Looking for Christ's coming—true of all born of God

Two Orders in the New Testament—

1　Order of Grace—from the least to the
　　greatest: e.g. Luke 15.

2　Order of Responsibility—from the greatest
　　to the least: e.g. John 8. 9; 1 John 2.

Three Grades—

1　*Fathers*—Paul would call
　　them the elders in the
　　assembly
　　Peter calls them shep-
　　herds of the flock
　　John calls them fathers in
　　the family
　　They 'have known Him
　　that is from the begin-
　　ning'　　　　1 John 2. 13, 14
　　Life in Maturity—the
　　Fruit of Experience

2　*Young men*—
　　'ye have overcome'　1 John 2. 13-17
　　Life in Activity—the
　　Prize of Strength
　　The Danger—the world
　　and the things of the
　　world

3　*Babes*—
　　'Ye have known the
　　Father'　　　　1 John 2. 18-27
　　Life in Enjoyment—the
　　Sense of Relationship
　　The Danger—Antichrist
　　and false doctrine
　　But they have God's pro-
　　vision—the Anointing,
　　the Holy Ghost

## 1163　The Love of God

1　The Father's Love—
　　that we should be called the
　　children of God　　　　1 John 3. 1

2　The Son's Love—
　　because He laid down His
　　life for us　　　　1 John 3. 16

3　The children's Love—
　　Let us love one another　1 John 4. 7

## 1164　What Manner of Love

1　Our Privilege—
　　What we are—
　　　　children of God　　　1 John 3. 1

2　Our Prospect—
　　What we shall be—
　　　　'like Him'　　　　1 John 3. 2

3　Our Practice—
　　What we should be—
　　　　'pure'　　　　1 John 3. 3
　　Pure in thought　　　Phil. 4. 8
　　Pure in Word　　　　Eph. 4. 29
　　Pure in deed　　　　1 Tim. 5. 22

## 1165　Truth and Error

CHARACTERISTICS OF TEACHERS OF ERROR—

Alien in origin　　　　1 John 2. 19
Separatist in attitude　　1 John 2. 19
Erroneous in doctrine　　1 John 2. 22
Infernal in objective　　1 John 2. 26
Doomed to defeat　　　1 John 4. 4

ANOINTING OF THE SPIRIT OF TRUTH—

1　as a permanent Gift　　John 16. 13
2　as an Indwelling Person　1 John 2. 27
3　as a Perfect Teacher　　1 John 2. 27
4　as a Present Benefactor　1 John 4. 4

## 1166　The Love that Casts out Fear

1　The Source of that Love—
　　it 'is of God'　　　　1 John 4. 7

2　The Standard of that Love—
　　God *so* loved us　　　1 John 4. 11

3　The Sphere of that Love—
　　in God　　　　　　1 John 4. 16

4　The Security of that Love—
　　boldness in the day of
　　judgment　　　　1 John 4. 17

5　The Scope of that Love—
　　God and his brother also　1 John 4. 21

**1 John**

**1167   Try the Spirits** ————————————————————
1 John 4. 1

| 1 Lying spirit | 1 Kings 22. 22 | Spirit of truth | John 16. 13 |
|---|---|---|---|
| 2 Evil spirit | Luke 7. 21 | Good spirit | Neh. 9. 20 |
| 3 Unclean spirit | Matt. 12. 43 | Holy Spirit | Eph. 1. 13 |
| 4 Dumb spirit | Mark 9. 17 | Spirit speaketh expressly | 1 Tim. 4. 1 |
| 5 Spirit of a man | 1 Cor. 2. 11 | Spirit of God | 1 Cor. 3. 16 |
| 6 Spirit of python | Acts 16. 16 | Spirit of power | 2 Tim. 1. 7 |
| 7 Spirits many | Mark 5. 9 | One Spirit | Eph. 4. 4 |

T.B.

**1168   The Resources of God's Children**
1 John 5

| 1 Faith in the Son that Achieves | vs. 1-5 |
|---|---|
| 2 Witness of God that Affirms | vs. 6-9 |
| 3 Witness within that Agrees | v. 10 |
| 4 Record of God that Assures | v. 11 |
| 5 Life of the Son that Aspires | v. 12 |
| 6 Prayer of faith that Appropriates | vs. 14-17 |
| 7 Knowledge of Truth that Apprehends | vs. 18-20 |

**1169   The Triumph of Faith**
1 John 5. 4, 5

| 1 The Enemy—<br>the Devil that Overturns | 1 John 5. 19 |
|---|---|
| 2 The Enemy—<br>the World that Overpowers | 1 John 5. 4, 5 |
| 3 The Equipment—<br>the Faith that Overcomes | 1 John 5. 4, 5 |
| The Ground of Faith—<br>the witness of God | 1 John 5. 9 |
| The Sphere of Faith—<br>God has given us eternal life<br>in His Son | 1 John 5. 11 |
| The Activity of Faith—<br>whatsoever we ask | 1 John 5. 15 |
| The Assurance of Faith—<br>we know | 1 John 5. 18 |

**1170   What Christ Is—The True God**
1 John 5. 20

1 He is 'the Truth' John 14. 6—
Let us *believe* Him

2 He is 'the true God' 1 John 5. 20—
Let us *adore* Him

3 He is 'the true Bread' John 6. 32—
Let us *feast* upon Him

4 He is 'the true Vine' John 15. 1
Let us *abide* in Him

5 He is 'the Holy and the True' Rev. 3. 7—
Let us be *holy and true* to Him

6 He is the 'true Light' John 1. 9—
Let us *be illuminated* by Him

7 He is 'the true Witness' Rev. 3. 14—
Let us *listen* to Him

As the Truth He delivers us from error

As the True God He is the Object of our worship

As the True Bread He makes us independent of earth's joy

As the True Vine He enables us to be fruitful to the Father

As the Holy and the True He is the Pattern of what the Church should be

As the True Light He is the pillar to guide us in the world's darkness

As the True Witness He would restore our souls when lukewarm

M.I.R.

## 2 JOHN

### 1171 Antichrist in John's Epistles
2 John 7

He is called—
'Antichrist' as opposed to God and His Christ
'Deceiver' in relation to men
'Not in the doctrine of Christ' as opposed to God's Word v. 9

John writes of—
1 A Personal Antichrist to come—'the man of sin' 1 John 2. 18; 2 Thess. 2. 3-10
2 The Forerunners of Antichrist—all who oppose Christ now
1 John 2. 22
3 The spirit of Antichrist—opposed to the Spirit of God
1 John 4. 3

### 1172 Words of Counsel to the Elect Lady
2 John

Three interpretations are given of the addressee, 'the elect lady'

1 Either an unknown sister addressed as 'lady' (Greek 'kuria', feminine of 'lord')
2 Or a believer whose name was 'Kuria'
3 Or a community, a local assembly

The writer, the aged Apostle John, gives her a three-fold counsel—

1 LOVE one another—the Command v. 5
2 LOOK to yourselves—the Warning v. 8
3 LEARN the doctrine—the Advice v. 9

## 3 JOHN

### 1173 Three Men in 3 John

This short letter contains—

1 A THREEFOLD COMMENDATION of Gaius, to whom the letter is addressed.

He was spiritually prosperous v. 2

loyal to the truth of God vs. 3, 4

hospitably disposed to all vs. 5, 6

2 A THREEFOLD INDICTMENT of Diotrephes vs. 9, 10

3 A THREEFOLD TESTIMONY concerning Demetrius from all men, by the truth and from the apostle vs. 11, 12

### 1174 Diotrephes
3 John 9-11

What he loved—to have the preeminence —his Personal Pride v. 9
What he spoke—malicious words—his Slanderous Tongue v. 10
What he did—
rejected true brethren in Christ, forbade others to receive them, cast out those who would—his Overbearing Manner v. 10
What motivated him—had not seen God—his Godless spirit v. 11
(i.e. was out of fellowship with God)
What he deserved—the rebuke of the apostle—his Everlasting Shame v. 10
What we may learn—to 'follow not that which is evil' v. 11

W.H.S.

# JUDE

## 1175 Three Stages of Apostasy
Jude 11

1 The Way of Cain, the Self-righteous—Natural apostasy—opposed to Christ, the Way

2 The Error of Balaam, the Self-interested—Sacrificial apostasy—opposed to Christ the Truth

3 The Gainsaying of Core, the Self-willed—Ecclesiastical apostasy—opposed to Christ the Life

The end of those who

Go in the way of Cain—is to be banished, like Cain     Gen. 4. 14, 16

Run greedily after the error of Balaam—is to be admonished, like Balaam     2 Pet. 2. 16

Follow in the gainsaying of Core—is to be punished, like Korah     Num. 16. 32

## 1176 Six Metaphors Describing the Wicked
Jude uses

| | |
|---|---|
| six illustrations from Old Testament history | vs. 4-11 |
| six metaphors from classical writings | vs. 12, 13 |
| six epithets of his own | vs. 15, 16 |

The six Metaphors are—

1 Brute beasts wallowing in their corruption     v. 10

2 Spots in the Christians' 'love-feasts'     v. 12

3 Clouds without water, driven before the wind     v. 12

4 Trees without fruit, plucked up by the roots     v. 12

5 Waves of the sea, foaming out their own shame     v. 13

6 Wandering stars, to whom is reserved the blackness of darkness     v. 13

# REVELATION

## 1177 The Time Scheme and the Great Themes of Revelation

The Book of Revelation covers three periods, past, present and future, as indicated in Rev. 1. 19

PAST—the things John saw in his vision in Patmos     Ch. 1

PRESENT—the things which are, the seven churches     Chs. 2, 3

FUTURE—the things which will take place hereafter     Chs. 4-22

The Central Figure is the Lamb. John saw—

1 a Lamb as it had been slain     Rev. 5. 6

2 a great multitude whose robes were made white in 'the blood of the Lamb'     Rev. 7. 14

3 144,000 undefiled men who 'follow the Lamb'     Rev. 14. 4

The Themes of the Book are—

1 The FRIENDS of the Lamb     Chs. 1-11

2 The FOES of the Lamb     Chs. 12-18

3 The FAME of the Lamb     Chs. 19-22

## 1178 Revelation 1. 1-3
Tells us—

WHAT THIS BOOK IS—'The Revelation (or unveiling) of Jesus Christ.' How precious!

WHOM IT IS FOR—The servants of God. Am I one?

WHY IT WAS WRITTEN—To show them 'things that must shortly come to pass'

WHO THE WRITER WAS—'His servant John': what a Privilege to write for God!

WHAT HE RECORDS—
1 The Word of God
2 The Testimony of Jesus Christ
3 The Things that he saw
(a threefold testimony to the truth of what is written)

WHO MAY BE BLESSED—the reader of the book the hearer of its words, and those that 'keep the things written therein'.
(Make sure of the blessing by doing all these three)

WHY SUCH INDUCEMENTS ARE OFFERED—'The time is at hand.'
(There is no time to lose if you would read this book. 'The coming of the Lord draweth nigh.')

W.H.S.

## 1179 The 'Amens' of John's Writings

'Amen!' means 'so be it!' or 'So it is'.

1 The AMEN of Gracious Affirmation—25 times, and always double in John's Gospel, translated 'Verily! Verily!' in the A.V.

2 The AMEN of Grateful Adoration      Rev. 1. 6, 7

3 The AMEN of Glorious Annunciation      Rev. 3. 14

4 The AMEN of Glad Anticipation      Rev. 22. 20

## 1180 In the Spirit

Four times in Revelation John says he was 'in the Spirit', and each time a vision of outstanding imagery and importance was granted to him.

1 The Vision of the Glorified Christ      Rev. 1. 10

2 The Vision of God on the Throne and the Lamb      Rev. 4. 2

3 The Vision of Babylon the Great, the scarlet woman, and her overthrow (Apostate Christendom)      Rev. 17. 3

4 The Vision of the Glory of the true Church, the holy City, the Bride, the Lamb's Wife      Rev. 21. 10

## 1181 The Message to Smyrna, the Persecuted Church

1 The Comfort of the Saviour   Rev. 2. 8, 9

2 The Constancy of the Saints   Rev. 2. 10

3 The Courage of the Sufferers   Rev. 2. 10

4 The Crown of the Slain      Rev. 2. 10

## 1182 The Church with a Worldly Orthodoxy, Pergamos

1 The Infernal Satanic Atmosphere—Where Satan's throne and residence were   Rev. 2. 13

2 The Church's Steadfast Attitude—thou holdest fast my name and hast not denied my faith      Rev. 2. 13

3 The Devil's Staggering Attack—with the doctrine of Balaam and the doctrine of the Nicolaitanes   Rev. 2. 14, 15

4 The Lord's Satisfied Appreciation—the hidden manna and a white stone for the overcomer      Rev. 2. 17

## 1183 Four Women in Revelation

1 Jezebel—her false position, false claim and false teaching—Popery      Rev. 2. 20

2 The Sun-clothed woman, Israel      Rev. 12. 1

3 Babylon—Reunited Christendom      Rev. 17. 5

4 The Bride of the Lamb—the true Church      Rev. 19. 7

     W.W.F.

## 1184 The Church of Brotherly Love, Philadelphia

Loved by the Lord Rev. 3. 9

On account of its Feebleness—a little strength      Rev. 3. 8

Because of its Faithfulness—thou hast kept my word      Rev. 3. 8

and because of its Fearlessness—hast not denied my name      Rev. 3. 8

The Overcomer in Philadelphia was promised three names      Rev. 3. 12

as Born of God, the name of the God and Father of the Lord Jesus Christ

as Citizen of Heaven, the name of the city of God, the new Jerusalem

as a Christian witness, the new name of Christ the Lord

## 1185 Open Doors

'Behold, I have set before thee an open door' Rev. 3. 20

1 A Door that remains open—'no man can shut it', God has opened 'a door of faith to the Gentiles'      Acts 14. 27

2 A Door of Opportunity in Ephesus, but 'many adversaries'—Opposition of infernal powers      1 Cor. 16. 9

3 A Door for Evangelism in Troas, but 'I could not rest'—Distraction of internal problems      2 Cor. 2. 12

4 A Door for Teaching 'the mystery of Christ' out of prison but—Delay because of indefinite prayers      Col. 4. 2, 3

## 1186 The Lukewarm, Complacent Church, Laodicea
     Rev. 3. 14-22

1 Its Threefold Boast—Rich, increased in goods, lacking nothing      v. 17

2 Its Threefold Folly—Self-sufficient, self-important and self-satisfied      v. 17

3 Its True Condition—wretched, miserable, poor, blind, naked      v. 17

4 Its Threefold Need—Gold tried in the fire, white raiment and eyesalve      v. 18

5 The Lord's Threefold Counsel—Be zealous, repent, hear my voice      vs. 19, 20

## 1187 The Cross in Heaven

The title of Christ—the Lamb—used 28 times in Revelation, presents our Lord in His sacrificial aspect, and thus constitutes wherever it is used a direct reference to the Cross.

1 The Cross is our only title to Heaven and Glory    Rev. 7. 9-15
2 The Cross is the Centre of Heaven's Government    Rev. 4. 2; 5. 6
3 The Cross is the source of Heaven's life    Rev. 22. 1
4 The Cross is the brilliance of Heaven's Light    Rev. 21. 23
5 The Cross is the scene of Heaven's Worship    Rev. 21. 22
6 The Cross is the theme of Heaven's Song    Rev. 5. 9
7 The Cross is the incentive of Heaven's Service    Rev. 22. 3
8 The Cross is the basis of Heaven's Triumph    Rev. 12. 11
9 The Cross is the subject of Heaven's Rejoicing    Rev. 19. 7
10 The Cross will be the terror of Heaven's enemies    Rev. 6. 12-17

R. J. G. VOISIN

## 1188 Heavenly Worshippers

In Revelation, Chapters 4 and 5, there are five companies of Worshippers—

1 The Four Living Creatures worship the Eternal God   Rev. 4. 8
2 The Four and twenty Elders worship the Creator, God   Rev. 4. 10, 11
3 The Living Creatures and the Elders worship the Redeemer    Rev. 5. 8-10
4 The Living Creatures, Elders and Angels worship the Lamb, the Conqueror of Death    Rev. 5. 11, 12
5 Every Creature, in heaven, on earth and under the earth, worships the Ruler of the universe    Rev. 5. 13, 14

## 1189 The Lamb in Revelation

'Worthy is the Lamb'

1 The Wrath of the Lamb    6. 16
2 The Blood of the Lamb    7. 14
3 The Book of life of the Lamb    13. 8
4 The Song of the Lamb    15. 3
5 The Marriage of the Lamb    19. 7
6 The Supper of the Lamb    19. 9
7 The Throne of the Lamb    22. 1

I.J.B.

The Blood of the Lamb—shed for our Redemption
The Book of life of the Lamb—kept for our Registration
The Bride of the Lamb—title of our Relationship

## 1190 The Lamb in the Midst of the Throne

1 Offering the Sacrifice for sin—

'as it had been slain'    Rev. 5. 6
The Sinless Lamb    1 Pet. 1. 18, 19
The Sin-bearing Lamb    John 1. 29

2 Occupying the Seat of power—'in the midst of the throne' The Lamb will rule and He will rule as the Lamb.    Rev. 5. 6

3 Opening the Seals of the Book—'hath prevailed to open the book'    Rev. 5. 5; 6. 1

4 Overcoming the Satellites of Satan—'the Lamb shall overcome them'    Rev. 17. 13, 14

## 1191 Christ in the Midst

Rev. 5. 6

1 Listening, and asking questions—
the Teacher    Luke 2. 46

2 Dying on the Cross in agony—
the Sacrifice    John 19. 18

3 Risen from the dead in power—
the Risen Lord    John 20. 19

4 Walking among the lampstands—
the Head of the Church   Rev. 2. 1

5 Dwelling among His people now—
the Lord of glory    Matt. 18. 20

6 Praising and leading the praises—
the Princely Leader    Heb. 2. 12

7 Standing in the midst of the throne—
the Lamb of God    Rev. 5. 6

## 1192 The New Song

As given in the Book of Revelation 5. 8

1 The highest note—'Thou art worthy'
2 The greatest sacrifice—'Thou wast slain'
3 The sweetest theme—'Redeemed by blood'
4 The widest result—'Every kindred, tongue and people and nation'
5 The newest relationship — 'kings and priests'
6 The brightest hope—'We shall reign'

H.K.D.

**1193  The Worthy One**
Rev. 5. 9-12

1 The Person who is worthy—
He Who has the Majesty of a lion
and the Meekness of a lamb          v. 9

2 The Proclamation of His worth—
He has paid for us the Price of
Redemption          v. 9
He has conferred on us the Privil-
ege of Priesthood          v. 10
He has given to us the Prospect of
Reigning          v. 10

3 The Proof of His worth—
He receives the worship of the
angels in Heaven and the redeemed from the earth          v. 11

**1194  The Sevenfold Ascription of Praise to the
Lamb**
Rev. 5. 12

1 Power (authority Matt. 28. 18)—Nebuchadnezzar received power but proved
unworthy Dan. 2. 37; 4. 27

2 Riches Eph. 3. 8—Jehoshaphat had riches
in abundance but proved unworthy
2 Chron. 18. 1

3 Wisdom Col. 2. 3—Solomon received
wisdom but proved unworthy 1 Kings
4. 29

4 Strength Isa. 63. 1—Samson was given
strength but proved unworthy
Judges 16. 19, 20

5 Honour Heb. 2. 9—Adam had honour
conferred by God but proved unworthy
Gen. 1. 27; 3. 24

6 Glory Heb. 2. 9—Aaron wore garments of
glory but proved unworthy Exod. 28. 2;
32. 4

7 Blessing (praise)—Many men have been
blessed and praised, but all have proved
unworthy e.g. Acts 12. 22, 23

**1195  White Raiment**
Those arrayed in white robes in Revelation—

1 The Redeemed out of great tribulation—
'washed in the blood'  Rev. 7. 13, 14

2 The Remnant—undefiled—worthy to walk
with Christ          Rev. 3. 4

3 The Radiant—overcomers—walking in
the light          Rev. 3. 5

4 The Reverent—elders—worshipping before the throne          Rev. 4. 4, 10

5 The Raptured—saints who waited for the
Bridegroom          Rev. 19. 8

**1196  The Great White Throne**
Rev. 20. 11-15

1 The Imperial Throne—
Great because of its Immensity
Great because of the Importance of the
assize
Great because of the One Who occupies
it

2 The Impartial Judge—A White Throne
because of the Purity of the Judge
because of the Impartiality of His
judgment as Son of man John 5. 22, 27

3 The Incriminating Records—the books
opened—
Book of works Rev. 20. 12
Book of Christ's words John 12. 48
Book of life Rev. 20. 12

4 The Irrevocable Sentence—
'cast into the lake of fire' Rev. 14. 11;
20. 15; 21. 8

**1197  'No Mores' in Revelation**

1 No more sea          Rev. 21. 1
2 No more sorrow          Rev. 21. 4
3 No more crying          Rev. 21. 4
4 No more pain          Rev. 21. 4
5 No more curse          Rev. 22. 3
6 No more night          Rev. 22. 5
7 No more death          Rev. 21. 4

R.G.

**1198  The Great City, the Holy Jerusalem**
Rev. 21. 10

Contrast to man's cities on earth—

ENOCH, the first city, built by the first
murderer, Cain had—
Supplies of food by Jabal-Cain
Metal Industries by Tubal-Cain
Musical Entertainment by Jubal-Cain
It was destroyed by the
Flood.          Gen. 4. 17, 21

BABEL, the city built after the
flood had Skyscrapers,
but the citizens were
scattered and it too was
destroyed          Gen. 11. 1-9

UR of the Chaldees, that
Abram left—'wholly given
to idolatry          Josh 24. 2, 3

THE CITY FOURSQUARE is in Heaven, and its
citizens, the Bride, the Lamb's Wife, are
identified with their city.

1 The Eternal City—the city for which
Abraham and the patriarchs looked, and
for which all believers look
Heb. 11. 10, 16; 13. 14

2 An Impregnable City—has foundations
with the apostles' names in them
Heb. 11. 10; Rev. 21. 19

3 A Planned City—has a Perfect Architect,
God          Heb. 11. 10

4 A Constructed City—has an infallible
Builder, God          Heb. 11. 10

5 A Resplendent City—has the Glory of God
Rev. 21. 11

6 An Accessible City—has twelve open gates
of pearl          Rev. 21. 21

7 An Undefiled City—'Nothing that defileth' shall enter it          Rev. 21. 27

8 A Perfect City—perfect in every dimension,
the height, breadth and length being
equal          Rev. 21. 16

1199  **The Throne of Life—Perfection at Last**

1 The Proclamation from the
Throne—'All things new'  Rev. 21. 5

2 The Perfection of the Transformation—'a new heaven  Rev. 21. 1;
and a new earth'  2 Pet. 3. 13

Perfect Provision—the tree
of life  Rev. 22. 2

Perfect Blessing—'no more
curse'  Rev. 22. 3

Perfect Government—'the
throne of God and the
Lamb'  Rev. 22. 3

Perfect Service—'His ser-
vants shall serve Him'  Rev. 22. 3

Perfect Vision—'they shall
see His face'  Rev. 22. 4

Perfect Reflection — 'His
name—in their fore-
heads'  Rev. 22. 4

Perfect Illumination—'no
night there'  Rev. 22. 5

1200  **God's Last Messages to Men**

God's Revelation is complete and perfect
Rev. 22. 18, 19

1 The Last Proclamation—'I am Alpha and
Omega'  Rev. 22. 13

2 The Last Promise—'I come quickly '(three
times)  Rev. 22. 7, 12, 20

3 The Last Prayer—'Even so come, Lord
Jesus'  Rev. 22. 20

4 The Last Prediction—'I Jesus—the bright
and morning Star'  Rev. 22. 16

5 The Last Provision—'the water of life
freely'  Rev. 22. 17

# INDEX OF TEXTS

202

208

## Index of Texts

# GENERAL INDEX

# General Index

Volume 2

# Notes, Quotes, and Anecdotes

# PREFACE

IT is just over a decade since the volume of 1200 *Notes Quotes and Anecdotes* was published. Since then it has undergone several reprints, an indication that it has had a good reception. This further collection of 1200 illustrations and quotations will be found to comprise many that are more up-to-date, besides a few that formed part of the stock of some of the older preachers. The purpose of this, another volume of 1200, is the same as of that previously published—to provide the preacher with quotations and historical and biographical illustrations, to convey to the reader the teaching of Scripture on a variety of themes, and to recount the experiences of some who have proved for themselves the infallibility of divine revelation and the veracity of God's great and precious promises. While it is hoped that this collection will prove interesting to the casual reader, those who study the Scriptures diligently and preach for the spiritual welfare of their fellow-men will doubtless regard this volume as a book of reference also.

To facilitate the relation of the several items in prose and poetry to the teaching of the Bible, I have endeavoured to indicate what I consider relevant Scripture texts, and this forms one of the indexes appended. With the object of adding further to the interest, an index of the names of persons, peoples and places has been added. While the Scripture and general indexes have been made as complete as possible, this added reference list will not be found to contain all the names, some of which are little known and of a very limited interest today. When the author's name is known with certainty, this is indicated in or after the item concerned; and while some of the authors may not be so well known, their names will be found in alphabetical order in the index.

Here I wish to express my indebtedness and gratitude to all who have helped. I am indebted to the writings of the prince of preachers, C. H. Spurgeon, for a number of his illustrations. To Patricia St. John I acknowledge my indebtedness for the record of some of the unique experiences of her father, Mr. Harold St. John. The gifted evangelist, Mr. Charles McEwen of Exeter, very willingly co-operated with me by sending his wide collection of illustrations and permitting me to make a selection from it. I acknowledge also my indebtedness to my friend, Mr. Alex Allan, a tireless spiritual and social worker in prisons and detention centres, who has supplied several interesting instances of lives transformed by the Gospel. I am truly grateful also to Mrs. William Gorrie, whose beautiful little lyrical verses on various subjects appear under the author's name, May Gorrie. My own initials are attached to the few that have had their origin in my own experience or thoughts.

A. NAISMITH

**1 Abandoned Obelisk—The.** Lying in its bed in the quarry of Aswam in South Egypt is an unfinished obelisk. There it has remained, in its present state, for several thousand years. It is believed to be the work of Pharaoh Thothmes III, and was to have been the tallest obelisk ever made. It measures 14 ft. by 14 ft. at its base, and the estimated weight is 1170 tons. How is it that it never graced an Egyptian temple, or adorned a modern city? Because, after the workmen worked on it for some time and shaped three of its four sides, a fault was found in it. Therefore it was abandoned as unfit for the position it was intended to have occupied. It is a beautiful piece of granite, but faulty.

The Egyptians refused to place a faulty obelisk before one of their temples. The living God has likewise decreed that nothing that defiles, nothing faulty, nothing sinful, will ever enter heaven: so all men in their natural state are excluded. The preacher said, ' There is not a just man upon earth that doeth good and sinneth not.' But by the death and resurrection of One who is faultless and perfect in every way, sinful men can be cleansed from every sin and be accorded a place in Heaven.
(Eccl. 7. 20)

**2 Adoption.** I heard of some youngsters who were teasing an adopted boy at school. They said to him, ' You aren't the real son of your father.'

He stood it as long as he could, but at last flashed back at them, ' All I can say is that my father chose me, and your folks couldn't help accepting you.'
                           Harold Wildish
(Eph. 1. 5; Rom. 8. 15)

**3 Advent—Awaiting Christ's.** Scripture sets down seven steps of His advent:
1 THE ARRIVAL of the Lord from heaven— ' The Lord Himself shall descend from heaven '.
2 THE ANNOUNCEMENT FROM THE AIR—' with a shout '.
3 THE ARCHANGEL'S VOICE—' with the voice of the archangel '.
4 THE ALARM OF THE TRUMPET—' with the trump of God '.
5 THE AWAKING OF THE BELIEVING DEAD—' the dead in Christ shall rise first '.
6 THE ASCENT of the believers in the clouds —' we which are alive and remain shall be caught up—in the clouds '.
7 THE ASSEMBLY with the Lord for ever— ' to meet the Lord in the air, and so shall we ever be with the Lord '.
(1 Thess. 4. 16,17)

**4 Advent—Prepared for the.** When Shackleton was driven back from his quest of the South Pole, he left his men on Elephant Island and promised to come back for them. Working his way as best he could to South Georgia, he tried to get back to his men to fulfil his promise and failed; tried again and failed. The ice was between him and the island, so he could not get near it. He had promised his men to come and, being unable to come, he could not rest. Though the season was adverse, though they told him it was impossible to get there in his little boat *Yaliho* because of the thick ice barrier between, he tried it again. It was the wrong time of year, but, strange to say, as he got nearer to the island, there was an open avenue between the sea and the place where he had left his men. He ran his boat in at great risk, got his men, all of them, on board and came out again before the ice crashed in. It was all done in half an hour. When the excitement was partly over he turned to one of his men and said, ' Well, you were all packed and ready.' In reply, the man said, ' You see, Boss, Wild (the second in command) never gave up hope and whenever the sea was all clear of ice he rolled up his sleeping bag and said, "Roll up your sleeping bags, boys: the boss may come today ".' Christians, roll up your sleeping bags: the Lord may come today.

**5 Advent—Ready for Christ's.** During his presidency of the U.S.A., Dwight Eisenhower was once vacationing in Denver. His attention was called to an open letter which told how six-year-old Paul Haley, dying of incurable cancer, had expressed a wish to see his President. Spontaneously, President Eisenhower decided to grant the boy's request. One Sunday morning in August, a big limousine pulled up outside the Haley home, and out stepped the President. He walked to the door and knocked. Mr. Donald Haley, unshaven and wearing blue jeans and an old shirt, opened the door. Behind him stood his little son, Paul. Eisenhower said to the sick lad, ' Paul, I understand you want to see me. I'm glad to see you!' Shaking hands with the boy, he led him to see the presidential limousine, then took his leave. But Mr. Haley can never forget how he was dressed when he opened the door. ' What a way to meet the President of the U.S.A.!' he said. Will you be ready when Jesus comes?
(Matt. 24. 44; 1 John 2. 28)

**6 Advent—Second.**

*If He should come today and find my hands*
   *so full*
*Of future plans, however fair,*
*In which my Saviour has no share,*
   *What would He say?*

*If He should come today and find my love*
   *so cold,*
*My faith so weak and dim*
*I had not even looked for Him,*
   *What would He say?*

*If He should come today and find I had*
   *not told*
*One soul about my heavenly Friend,*
*Whose blessings all my way attend,*
   *What would He say?*

*If He should come today, would I be glad—*
   *quite glad?*
*Remembering He had died for all*
*And none through me had heard His call,*
   *What would He say?*

**7  Advocate—Christ Our.** Christ's work as Advocate comes into operation as soon as we sin. He is an Advocate with the Father, indicating a family relationship. We have a lovely word in Africa used to express this idea. An advocate or comforter is sometimes called a *kasendo mukwashi*. The first word *kasendo* means ' a blood brother ', one with whom a solemn covenant sealed in blood has been made. The second word *mukwashi* means ' one who helps by laying hold '. The Lord is both to us.
T. Ernest Wilson

The twofold function of a kinsman who has sealed His new covenant with His blood and takes hold, not of angels but of Abraham's seed, is expressed in Heb. 2. 14-16.
(1 John 2. 1.)

**8  Affliction—Profit by.** C. H. Spurgeon said that affliction was the best bit of furniture in his house, for all the grace he got out of comfortable, easy times might almost lie on a penny, but the good received from his pains and griefs was incalculable. Great was his debt to the fire and the file, the crucible and the bellows, and the Hand that thrust him into the heat.

A young girl of twenty years was afflicted with spinal meningitis. She knew that her case was incurable, and that her life would be one of chronic invalidism. A friend, calling on her, seemed to see the dark side only, and remarked in a commiserating tone, ' Yes, affliction colours everything in one's life '. ' Yes ' the young girl replied brightly, ' but I choose the colours '.

**9  Affliction—Profit through.** There are all kinds of hidden blessings in the trials that beset us. An American evangelist was stricken with polio, but he began at once a ministry of writing which God has blessed to thousands. Dr Joseph Parker was nearly beside himself with grief when his beloved wife was suddenly taken from him, but those who used to listen to him at the City Temple, London, said that he was quite different after the tragedy. He was more powerful, more sensitive to other people's needs and more effective as a preacher and a pastor. Miss Corrie ten Boom could not speak as well as she does all over the world if she had not been in the fires of affliction where she suffered at the hands of men.
Francis W. Dixon

**10  Affliction that Incites to Courage.** In the Greek annals there is an old story of a soldier under Antigonus who had a disease about him, an extremely painful one, likely to bring him soon to the grave. Always first in the charge was this soldier, rushing into the hottest part of the fray as the bravest of the brave. His pain prompted him to fight that he might forget it; and he feared not death, because he knew that in any case he had not long to live. Antigonus, who greatly admired the valour of his soldier, discovering his malady, had him cured by one of the most eminent physicians of the day; but alas! from that moment the warrior was absent from the front of the battle. He now sought his ease; for, as he remarked to his companions, he had something worth living for—health, home, family and other comforts, and he would not risk his life now as aforetime. So, when our troubles are many, we are often by grace made courageous in serving our God; we feel that we have nothing to live for in this world, and we are driven, by hope of the world to come, to exhibit zeal, self-denial and industry. But how often is it otherwise in better times!
C. H. Spurgeon

**11  Affliction—Virtue from.** In cases of deep affliction nothing, nothing, nothing will do but to be assured in our inmost souls of the infinite wisdom of God, of the power of God. Nothing else will do but to hold fast what we read in Scripture (Ps. 119. 50), to believe that it is in our inmost soul to be meant literally as God our Father has told us in His Word. Then we have peace, then we look calmly and quietly at everything and are assured in our inmost soul that good, nothing but good, will come out of it all, whatever the trial, whatever the difficulty, whatever the bereavement, however great and heavy it may be. Our business is to look at the heart of our heavenly Father which is ever for us, and to look at the mighty arm of God. He brought us low and He can lift us up.
George Muller

(Ps. 34. 19; 2 Cor. 4. 16-18)

**12  Affliction—Virtue from.**

*The Christian suffers but to gain*
*And every virtue springs from pain,*
*As aromatic plants bestow*
*No spicy fragrance while they grow,*
*But, crushed or trodden to the ground,*
*Diffuse their balmy sweets around.*

(2 Cor. 6. 4; 1 Pet. 1. 7)

**13  Age—This Present.**

*Age of the atom! Power, immense, unknown*
*Man's puny hand would harness, make his own;*
*Grim plaything of an adolescent race*
*Who seek a playing field in outer space!*

*Age of invention! Vision, motion, sound,*
*Bombard the heavens and to the earth rebound,*
*While the inventor, man, in comfort curled,*
*Views in his home the horizons of the world.*

*Age of the cults! Like mushrooms, cancers,*
   *flies,*
*At home—abroad, they spread Satanic lies,*
*When truth, on falsehood's trail, lags far*
   *behind*
*While error's poison taints the human mind.*

*Age of amusement! In abandoned glee*
*Man to the goddess Pleasure bows the knee,*
*While empty churches cry the truth abroad—*
*Man loves his pleasure better than his God.*

*Age of expectancy! He comes at last,*
*King of the coming ages and the past:*
*The Bridegroom cometh! Church of Christ,*
   *arise!*
*He comes to claim thee, His eternal prize!*
William Montgomery

**14 Agnosticism Answered.** On a voyage across the Atlantic, Dr Meyer was asked by the Captain to preach in the saloon at the Sunday morning service. His subject was 'Answered Prayer', and he gave several illustrations. An agnostic who was present was asked what he thought of the sermon and replied, 'I don't believe a word of it.'

That afternoon Dr Meyer was speaking to the tourist class passengers. Picking up a couple of oranges, the agnostic put them in his pocket and made his way to the meeting. On the way, as he passed an old woman with silvery hair sitting asleep in a deck chair, with her hands open on her lap, he took the two oranges from his pocket, placed them in her open hands and went on to the meeting.

When he came back the old lady was eating one of the oranges and he said to her,

'You seem to be enjoying your orange!'

'Yes!' she said, 'my Father is very good.'

'Your father! Your father can't be living!'

'Oh!' said she, 'He is very much alive.'

'What do you mean?' he asked.

'Well!' she replied, 'I have been seasick for five days. This morning I longed for an orange. I knew there were some in the saloon but I wondered how I could get them in the tourist class, so I asked the Lord to send me an orange. I must have fallen asleep and—would you believe it, sir?—when I opened my eyes, He had not only sent me one but two!'

'Why,' said the agnostic, 'is that true?'

'Absolutely true,' she said. The bottom fell out of his agnosticism there and then. God answers prayer and sometimes uses infidels to carry the answer.

(Matt. 6. 8)

**15 Alive Unto God.** Frances Willard, when a student in Northwestern College for Women, wrote in her journal: 'Dr Foster closed the Bible after his discourse at the University Chapel yesterday with these words: "With most men life is a failure." These words impressed me deeply; there is sorrow in the thought, and tears and agony are wrapped up in it. Oh, Thou who rulest above, help me that my life may be valuable—that some human being shall thank Thee that I have lived and toiled.' If I had a dozen lives to live, I might afford to waste one of them, but I have only one life to invest or lose.

E. J. Fry

*Only one life for service, one talent to lay*
*at His feet;*
*And effort and prayers are needed, and*
*workers in every street.*

(Rom. 6. 11; 2 Cor. 5. 15)

**16 Almost Home, but Lost.** In the days when the world was still on the gold standard there was a ship with a cargo of gold en route from Australia to Liverpool. The civic authorities of Liverpool had arranged a reception for the captain, officers and crew of the expected vessel.

The hosts, assembled in the banqueting hall to await the arrival of their guests, wondered why they were so late. Then the news came through that the ship had been driven off its course and wrecked at Maulsperry Point, and all aboard had been drowned.

A very close friend of one of the officers who perished was in the banqueting hall when the shipwreck was announced and hastened to his friend's home to break the sad news to the wife, now a widow. When he rang the bell, the door was hurriedly opened by a little girl who came running out with outstretched arms, crying 'Daddy!' When she saw the visitor, and not her Daddy, she drew back as if half ashamed of her impetuosity. The mother came to the door and apologised, saying that her little girl had been expecting her Daddy all day. Then the friend gently broke the sad news to the bereaved widow who threw up her hands, and exclaimed, 'My God! so near home, yet lost after all.' (Mark 12. 34; Luke 13. 28)

**17 Alone—Dare to Stand.** It is human to stand with the crowd: it is divine to stand alone. It is man-like to follow the people, to drift with the tide: it is God-like to follow a principle, to stem the tide. It is natural to compromise conscience and follow the social and religious fashion for the sake of gain or pleasure: it is divine to sacrifice both on the altar of truth and duty.

'No man stood with me, but all men forsook me,' wrote the battle-scarred apostle in describing his last appearance before Nero to answer for his life for believing and teaching contrary to the Roman world. Truth has been out of fashion since man changed his robe of light for a garment of fading leaves. Noah built and voyaged alone. His neighbours laughed at his strangeness and perished in style.

Abraham wandered and worshipped alone. Elijah sacrificed and worshipped alone. Jeremiah prophesied and wept alone. Daniel dined and prayed alone. Jesus loved and died alone.

Wanted today men and women, young and old, who will obey their convictions of truth and duty at the cost of fortune and friends, livelihood and life itself!

Selected

*Dare to be a Daniel, dare to stand alone:*
*Dare to have a purpose firm and dare to*
*make it known.*

(Dan. 1. 8; 2 Tim. 4. 10,16)

**18 Alone Yet Not Alone.** About the year 1754, when war was raging between the French and the British in Canada, and when the Indians took the part of the French, one day a party of Indians surrounded the house of a poor family from Germany at a time when the mother and one of the sons were absent. The father, the eldest son, and two little girls named Barbara and Regina, were at home. The savages burst into the house, killed the men and carried off the little girls along with other children of the same age, leading them by forced marches in order to escape pursuit. At that time Barbara was ten years old, Regina nine. What became of Barbara was never known, but Regina was given to an old widow who was very cruel to the little girl. Here she remained till she was about nineteen years of age, but she did not forget her early home training. She said her prayers night and morning, often repeated verses from the Bible, and sang little hymns which she had learnt at home. One she often sang was:

*Alone, yet not alone am I,*
*Though in this solitude so drear.*

She constantly hoped and prayed that the Lord would in His own time restore her to her friends. In 1764 the long deferred hope was realised. A British colonel discovered the Indian encampment, attacked it, and took it by storm. A condition of peace was the surrender of the prisoners, and no less than 400 captives were handed over by the Indians to the British. Many of them had quite forgotten their native language, and were so altered in appearance that their own mothers could not recognize them. They were fed and clothed, and then taken to a town named Carlisle. It was announced in the daily newspapers that all parents who had had children carried off by the Indians might come and reclaim them. Amongst those who came to Carlisle was Regina's sorrowing mother. She searched up and down the lines of captives but nowhere could she discover her daughters. So great was her disappointment that she burst into tears. The bystanders endeavoured to console her, and the colonel, in order to help her, asked the weeping mother if she could recall anything by which her children might be discovered. She replied that there was a hymn she used to sing to them, and at the colonel's request she sang:

*Alone, yet not alone, am I*
*Though in this solitude so drear;*
*I feel my Saviour always nigh.*
*He comes the weary hours to cheer.*
*I am with Him and He with me—*
*Even here alone I cannot be.*

She had only sung a few words when Regina rushed from the crowd and began to sing it too; then she threw herself into her mother's arms. The early training in that Christian home thus brought about that happy reunion.
(2 Tim. 3. 15)

**19  Always Abounding.** A woman 24 years of age was told that her husband, two years older, would soon die of an incurable disease. This was a terrible blow and it caused a night of gloom to settle about this pair. After prayerful meditation they decided they would pack every day with helpful service and joyous companionship. They were not careless of a single hour and lived every day to its full in view of his

early death. But years were added to the young man's life and the doctor attributed this to their wholesome, unselfish living—'always abounding in the work of the Lord '.
(1 Cor. 15. 58)

**20  Always Trusting.** The hymn 'Simply trusting every day' first appeared as a poem in a newspaper, and someone handed it to D. L. Moody who went through it and found it sound doctrinally and helpful spiritually. At his request Ira D. Sankey set it to music.

But 'every day' seemed too long, so the verses of 'I need Thee every hour' took shape. The chorus of this beautiful hymn has often been sung as a prayer, and the writer has heard it time and again sung thus by the lads in a Borstal Institution at their Bible Class before the opening prayer by the leader.

During one World Fair in Chicago, where meetings were being held, this hymn, 'I need Thee every hour', was frequently sung. Henry Varley, an evangelist who was present, remarked to a friend that he felt he needed Christ not only every hour, but every moment of the day and night. Varley's friend Major Whittle, was led by this remark to write the hymn with the chorus,

*Moment by moment I'm kept in His love:*
*Moment by moment I've life from above,*
*Looking to Jesus till glory doth shine;*
*Moment by moment, O Lord, I am Thine.*

(Job 7. 18; Lam. 3. 22,23)

**21  Ambition—A Vampire.** Ambition is like the sea which swallows all the rivers and is none the fuller; or like the grave whose insatiable maw for ever craves for the bodies of men. It is not like an amphora, which being full receives no more, but its fullness swells it till a still greater vacuum is formed. In all probability, Napoleon never longed for the sceptre till he had gained the baton, nor dreamed of being Emperor of Europe till he had gained the Crown of France. Caligula, with the world at his feet, was mad with a longing for the moon, and could he have gained it the imperial lunatic would have coveted the sun. It is in vain to feed a fire which grows the more voracious the more it is supplied with fuel; he who lives to satisfy his ambition has before him the labour of Sisyphus, who rolled uphill an ever-rebounding stone, and the task of the daughters of Danaus, who are condemned for ever to attempt to fill a bottomless vessel with buckets full of holes. Could we know the secret heart-breaks and wearinesses of ambitious men, we should need no Wolsley's voice crying, 'I charge thee, fling away ambition', but we should flee from it as from the most accursed blood-sucking vampire which ever uprose from the caverns of hell.
                                                    C. H. Spurgeon

**22  Ambition—Worldly.** Dr Joseph Parker in his great lecture on 'Clocks and Watches' told the following story:

A little watch, delicately made but dissatisfied with its little sphere in a lady's pocket, envied Big Ben as one day he passed with her ladyship over Westminster Bridge. 'I wish I could be up there,' said the delicate little watch, 'then I could serve the multitude.' 'You shall have your opportunity,' said the lecturer. Then he graphically described the little chronometer being drawn up the tower by a slender thread. When it reached the top the lecturer said 'Where are you, little watch? I cannot see you.' Then, after a pause, he said, 'Its elevation has become its annihilation.'

C. S. Lewis said, 'Aim at heaven and you will get earth thrown in. Aim at earth and you will get neither.'
(Jer. 45. 5; Luke 22. 24-26)

**23  Amusements—Doubtful.**  A young Christian, defending her constant attendance at some rather suprising places of amusement, said, 'I think a Christian can go anywhere.'

'Certainly she can,' rejoined her friend, 'but your words remind me of an incident last summer when, with a party of friends, I went to explore a coal-mine. One of the young women came dressed in a dainty white dress. When her friends remonstrated with her, she appealed to the old miner acting as guide to the party. 'Can't I wear a white dress down into the mine?' she asked. 'Yes ma'am,' returned the old man, 'there's nothing to keep you from wearing a white dress down there, but there will be plenty to keep you from wearing one back.'
(James 1. 27; Jude 23)

**24  Angelic Ministry.**  A wonderful story is told by a Moravian missionary in connection with angelic protection. An American missionary and his wife bravely went to their mission station where, twenty years before, two missionaries had been killed and eaten by the natives. As they took up their work, it seemed as if they were surrounded not only by hostile natives but by the very powers of darkness, which were so real that night after night they were forced to get up and strengthen their hearts by reading the Word of God and praying.

One day a man came and said, 'I would like to see your watchmen close at hand.' The missionary replied, 'I have no watchmen, only a cook and a little boy. What watchmen do you mean?'

The man asked permission to look through the missionaries' home. After searching thoroughly every corner of the house, the man came out disappointed. When the missionary asked the man to tell him about the watchmen to whom he referred, he answered, 'When you and your wife came here we determined to kill you as we did the missionaries twenty years ago. Night after night we came to carry out our intention but there always stood around your house a double row of watchmen with glittering weapons, and we dared not come near. At last we hired a professional assassin who said he feared neither God nor devil. Last night he came close to your house, brandishing his spear. We followed at a distance. There stood the shining watchmen, and the killer fled in terror. So we have given up our purpose to kill you; but tell me, who are the watchmen?'

The missionary opened the Word of God and read: 'The angel of the Lord encampeth round about them that fear Him and delivereth them.'
(Ps. 34. 7)

Of these angelic ministers the poet, Edmund Spencer wrote:

*How oft do they with golden pinions cleave*
*The flitting skies, like flying pursuivant*
*Against foul fiends to aid us militant?*

**25  Angelic Ministry.**  C. H. Spurgeon believed in the ministry of angels, and wrote: 'Angels are the unseen attendants of the saints of God; they bear us up in their hands lest we dash our foot against a stone. Loyalty to their Lord leads them to take a deep interest in the children of His love: they rejoice over the return of the prodigal to his father's house below and they welcome the advent of the believer to the King's palace above.

'To what dignity are the chosen elevated when the brilliant couriers of heaven become their willing servitors! Into what communion are we raised when we have intercourse with spotless celestials! To whom do we owe this? Let the Lord Jesus be for ever endeared to us, for through Him we are made to sit down in heavenly places far above principalities and powers. He it is whose camp is round about them that fear Him.'
(Heb. 1. 14)

**26  Anonymous Servants of God.**

*They lived and they were useful : this we know*
*And naught beside;*
*No record of their names is left to show*
*How soon they died;*
*They did their work and then they passed away,*
*An unknown band,*
*And took their places with the Heavenly host*
*In Glory land.*

*And were they young or were they growing old,*
*Or ill or well,*
*Or lived in poverty, or had much gold—*
*No one can tell.*
*One only thing is known of them—they were*
*Faithful and true,*
*Disciples of the Lord and strong through*
    *prayer*
*To live and do.*

*But what avails the gift of empty fame?*
*They lived for God;*
*They loved the sweetness of another Name,*
*And gladly trod*
*The rugged ways of earth that they might be*
*Helper or friend,*
*And in the joy of this, their Ministry,*
*Be spent and spend.*

*No story clusters round their names on earth;*
*But in God's heaven*
*Is kept a book of names of greatest worth,*
*And there is given*
*A place for all who did the master please,*
*Although unknown,*
*And their lost names shine out in brightest rays*
*Before the Throne.*

*O take who will the boon of fading fame,*
*But give to me*
*A place among the workers, though my name*
*Forgotten be;*
*And if within the Book of life is found*
*My lowly place,*
*Honour and Glory unto God redound*
*For all His grace.*

(Phil. 4. 3)

**27 Answer—A Soft.** When C. H. Spurgeon was still a boy preacher, he was warned that a certain lady intended to give him a tongue-lashing. ' All right,' he replied, ' but that's a game two can play.'

Not long after she met him and assailed him with a flood of abuse. He smiled and said, ' Yes thank you, I am quite well: I hope you are the same.' Then came another burst of vituperation pitched in a yet higher key, to which, still smiling, he replied, ' Yes, it does look rather as if it might rain; I think I had better be going on.'

' Bless the man!' she exclaimed, ' he's as deaf as a post. What's the use of storming at him?' So her railings ceased and she never tried it on again with C. H. Spurgeon.

A Quaker had a troublesome neighbour whose cow often broke into the Quaker's well-cultivated garden. One morning, having driven the cow from his premises to the owner's, the Quaker said to him, ' Friend I have driven thy cow home once more, and if I find her in my garden again . . .' ' Suppose you do,' the neighbour angrily interrupted, ' What will you do?' ' Why!' replied the Quaker, ' I will drive her home again.'

The cow never troubled him again.

*The Indian Christian*
(Prov. 15. 1)

**28 Answer—Before Prayer.** When the telegraph wires were being erected in Shetland, a fellow who was considered simple, stood looking at the wires on the poles. A shrewd man of business said to the boy, ' What a wonderful thing! When these wires are finished, you will be able to send a message two hundred miles or more, and get an answer within an hour.' ' Nothing very wonderful about that,' said the lad. ' Why?' asked the keen man of the world. ' Did you ever hear of getting an answer before they send?'

God's answer comes sometimes before He is addressed in prayer, and His help and provision is on the way long before the need occurs. On one occasion in India we had just drawn all the money to our credit in the Bank, which was just sufficient for our personal needs and the end-of-the-month payments. The Sunday had been spent preaching in a neighbouring town, and it was a fiercely hot day. That evening the wallet with all the money it contained was stolen: everything had gone. Our only resource was prayer—in homes and in the local assembly. Within a few days, and just as payments became due, the postman brought us a Money Order sent several weeks before by a Christian brother in Scotland whom we did not know and had never met. The amount sent and received by us was exactly the equivalent of the money that had been stolen, and was sufficient to meet our needs for that week. God says, ' Before they call I will answer; and while they are yet speaking I will hear.'

A.N.

(Isa. 65. 24)

**29 Answer—Christ is the.** In a college in California, U.S.A., a debate on the Bible was arranged. After preliminaries an agnostic Professor called on a Christian young man to read his paper in defence of the Bible. Then he called on a young man of outstanding ability, chosen by himself, to read his paper in refutation of the authority of the Bible. The student said, ' I have spent many hours reading the Bible, looking for evidences of untruthfulness and contradictions. I read through the New Testament three times, and the more I read and studied the Book, the more I became convinced that it is not of human origin. Not only do I believe that the Bible is the Word of God, but I have found Jesus Christ in it and accepted Him as my Saviour.'
(John 5. 39; 2 Tim. 3. 16)

**30 Answering Fools.** In one of Clarence Darrow's first recorded court battles the veteran who opposed him sought repeatedly to belittle him in the eyes of the jury by referring to him as ' my beardless adversary '. Darrow concluded his summation by remarking, ' My honourable opponent seems to condemn me for not having a beard. Let me reply with an anecdote. The King of Spain once entrusted a youthful liege with an important message to the court of a neighbouring monarch. The latter flew into a rage and cried, ' Does the King of Spain lack men that he sends me a beardless boy?' The young ambassador answered, ' Sire, had my king known you imputed wisdom to a beard, he would have sent you a goat!' Young Darrow won the case and was launched on one of the most brilliant careers in the history of the bar.

His answer to his venerable opponent was in accordance with one of wise King Solomon's three thousand proverbs.
(Prov. 26. 5)

**31 Anxiety—Its Cause and Cure.** Basic to all personal problems is anxiety. It dwells in the primal abyss of human life, the very stuff of which humanity consists.

Anxiety is a many-headed hydra. The Greek

legend of Perseus narrates his encounter with one of the Gorgons, three sisters. To look upon them a man was turned to stone. Only one of them, Medusa, was mortal. Perseus attacked and slew her by seeing her reflection on his shield. This legend illustrates our experiences. We cannot face anxiety, and when we are obsessed by it, our hearts turn to stone, petrified and reduced to some neurotic state. Yet we cannot destroy all our anxieties, else we would be deprived of life itself. Only the mortal elements we see reflected in our personal defences can we endeavour to destroy.

Medusa wears many serpents coiled around her mind. There is economic insecurity, with the concern we have for our jobs, the prospects of our careers, or even the more vital needs of food and clothing. There are bodily causes of worry in ill-health or the sickness of dear ones. Insomnia, undiagnosed symptoms we fear may be cancer, or clinical changes of the body with puberty, maturity or old age, are all causes of anxiety. Then there are social causes in our inner lives—the lack of self-confidence that displays a sense of inferiority, or fears to accept responsibility. By seeing these reflected in our personal defences we can assail and destroy them—as in the legend Perseus slew Medusa.

The cure for Anxiety:

*Though doubt and dismay should enfold you*
*And hope of relief become dim,*
*Remember that Someone has told you*
*To cast all your care upon Him.*
*The world is unkind and friends may not mind,*
*But it matters to Him.*

*If sorrow and trouble o'ertake you*
*And grief fill your cup to the brim,*
*There is One who will never forsake you,*
*So ' cast all your care upon Him.'*
*He will not pass on or bid you begone,*
*For it matters to Him.*

*When mourning the loss of the dearest*
*And tears make your couch seem to swim,*
*' Tis then that the promise is clearest*
*To cast all your care upon Him.*
*The world may not grieve, but you must believe*
*That it matters to Him.*

*If worried and worn, you've neglected*
*The lamp that He gave you to trim,*
*Even then by His Word you're directed*
*To cast all your care upon Him.*
*His coming is near, though some may not care,*
*But it matters to Him.*

F. W. Pitt

(1 Pet. 5. 7)

The Berkeley Version renders this: Throw all your anxiety upon Him for His concern is about you.

**32  Apocrypha—The.** The Apocryphal books are: I & II Esdras, Tobit, Judith, the rest of the Chapters of Esther, the Wisdom of Solomon, Ecclesiasticus, Baruch, a letter of Jeremiah, the Song of the Three, Daniel and Susanna, Daniel Bel and the Snake, the Prayer of Manasseh, I & II Maccabees.

Apocrypha means ' hidden things '. It has been published in English as a separate volume by the Joint Committee that published *The New English Bible* and also along with the Scriptures of the Old and the New Testament in *The New English Bible with Apocrypha*.

'When I was at Chestnut College, my colleague at that time teaching Hebrew was a great scholar, Owen Whitehouse. I had great joy in his fellowship. We were talking once about the Apocrypha. He was a man with knowledge of all the Semitic languages. I asked him what his feeling was about the Apocrypha. He replied, "I know the Apocrypha well and this I know, that a close and intimate study of the Hebrew Scriptures and those of the Apocrypha leaves me without a doubt that there is no comparison between them. There is something about all the Hebrew Scriptures that has the very breath of God in them." That is the Bible we have, God-breathed writings. Those are what we are called upon to teach.'

Dr G. Campbell Morgan

(2 Pet. 1. 21)

**33  Apology—A Duke's.** The Duke of Wellington had rung his bell three times. At length, after immense delay, the footman, quite at his leisure, happened to appear. Wellington fired at him a perfect volley of indignant words. ' Your grace,' stuttered the poor fellow, ' the bell is broken.' ' Broken is it? Oh, I was not aware of that. I am really very sorry, William. I beg your pardon.' A little girl was present. ' My dear,' said the Duke beautifully, ' learn something; whenever you are in the wrong, own it.'

*The kindest and the happiest pair*
*Will find occasion to forbear,*
*And something every day they live*
*To pity and perhaps forgive.*

*Choice Gleanings*

(Acts 23. 5; James 5. 16)

**34  Apostles—Deaths of the.** The deaths of Judas Iscariot and of James, the brother of John, are recorded in the New Testament, but for the others we are dependent entirely on tradition for what it is worth. Tradition says that:

Matthew was slain with the sword in Ethiopia.
John was put into a burning cauldron in Rome but escaped death. He died a natural death in Ephesus.
James the Great, John's brother, was beheaded in Jerusalem.
Bartholomew (Nathanael) was flayed alive at the command of a barbarous king.
Andrew was crucified; bound to his cross, he preached to the people till he died.
Thomas was run through the body with a lance in Madras, India.
Peter was crucified upside down.
Jude was shot to death with arrows.

13

Simon Zelotes (called the Canaanean) was crucified in Persia.

Matthias was first stoned, then beheaded.

James the Less (of Alphaeus) was beaten to death with a club.

Philip was hanged against a pillar at Hierapolis in Phrygia.

**35  Appeal for Missionaries.**  Dr Alexander Duff of Calcutta, on furlough in Scotland, was giving a report before the Assembly of the Church of Scotland and had begun to appeal for workers for India when he was taken suddenly ill, collapsed and was carried off the platform unconscious. A doctor who was called bent to examine his heart. Presently Dr Duff opened his eyes. 'Where am I?' he asked, ' Where am I?' ' Lie still!' said the doctor, 'your heart is very weak.' ' But,' exclaimed the old warrior, ' I must finish my appeal. Take me back. I haven't finished my appeal yet.' ' Lie still!' said the doctor again, ' you are too weak to go back.' But the aged missionary struggled to his feet, his determination overcoming his weakness; and with a doctor on one side and the moderator on the other, the old white-haired warrior was led again to the platform. As he mounted the pulpit steps, the entire Assembly rose to do him honour. Then he continued his appeal:

'When Queen Victoria calls for volunteers for India ', he exclaimed, ' hundreds of young men respond; but when the Lord Jesus, heaven's King, calls, no one goes.' Then he paused. ' Is it true ', he asked, ' that Scotland has no more sons to give for India?' Again he paused 'Very well,' he concluded, ' if Scotland has no more young men to send to India, then, old and decrepit though I am, I will go back, and even though I cannot preach, I can lie down on the banks of the Ganges and die in order to let the peoples of India know that at least one man in Scotland cares enough for their souls to give his life for them.'

In a moment young men sprang to their feet, crying out, ' I'll go! I'll go!' After the good missionary went home to glory, many of those young men found their way to India.
(2 Cor. 4. 15,16)

**36  Ark of the Covenant.**  The Ark of the Covenant symbolised God dwelling in the midst of His people and foreshadowed Christ in the midst of His saints.

Israel, defeated by the Philistines, treated it as a CHARM, a mascot to bring them victory in their war against the national enemy; so they carried it from Shiloh into the field of battle. ' Fetch the Ark: it may save us,' they cried. The nation was out of touch with God, and vile men —the priests of Israel, Hophni and Phinehas were in charge of the sacred Ark.

It was captured by the Philistines and for Israel ICHABOD was the result. The blood-stained mercy-seat was in the hands of the enemy. Gone were the glories it symbolised, the Judicial glory of divine pardon through the blood sprinkled on and before it, the moral glory of God's holy law, His perfect standard for His people, contained in it, and the spiritual glory of God's visible presence in the Shekinah.

The disasters the Ark brought upon its captors compelled the Philistines to restore it to Israel, and it found for a time a new centre in the house of a godly Edomite, Obed-Edom. Of this Harold St. John has written:

' Now it is a very serious thing to bring the Ark of the Covenant into the centre. A man was smitten to death, and the Ark was swept aside into the house of an Edomite. It stayed there for three months, and you can imagine the woman's fears—the mother with about seven or eight children—for there was that terrible blood-stained box, and the man who touched it fell dead; and here she is shut up in her cottage with her children, and she says, "How can I ever prevent their touching the Ark?" But, as usually happens, all their fears turn out to be mistakes, and the blessings descended on that house, so everyone was talking about it. There is a place where Christ is absolutely central, and such a change has come over those Edomite children, they are so easy to manage, and the house runs as if on oiled wheels. What has happened? Christ has got His place.'
(1 Sam. 4. 5,11; 2 Sam. 6. 12)

**37  Armour of God.**  Here is a footnote from the Emphatic Diaglot: The Grecian armour consisted of two sorts—Defensive and Offensive armour. The apostle selects from these the following which he calls the panoply, or complete armour of God.

1  The Girdle, or military belt, used to brace the armour tight to the body and cover the two parts of the breastplate where they joined; and to support daggers, short swords, etc.

2  The Breastplate consisted of two parts, one reaching from the neck to the navel and the other hanging from thence to the knees.

3  The Greaves, made of gold, silver, brass or iron designed to defend the front of the legs and feet.

4  The Helmet, made of various metals and used to protect the head.

5  The Shield, sometimes round and sometimes square, was made of strong, thick leather or hides: sometimes of wood covered with brass or iron.

6  The sword was an offensive weapon.

He who had all these was completely armed for combat.

The panoply of God is thus a complete equipment for the Christian in every part of his being and life. Not one of the parts of armour can be dispensed with. The Christian must put on the whole armour of God. It is called the panoply of God because it is the ' armour of light ' (Rom. 13. 12), the ' armour of right ' (2 Cor. 6. 7) and ' the power of his might ' (Eph. 6. 10).

Paul in his prison, surrounded by the Praetorian guard and perhaps manacled to one

of them, was in an excellent position to observe their armour. There was no armour for the back so no soldier was envisaged as fleeing from the enemy. The expression—the Achilles' heel—signifying the vulnerable part of Achilles, the Greek who was supposed to be invulnerable, is applied to one who has come through battles unscathed but in the long run has been overcome through one weak spot, a defect in his defensive armour. Achilles was supposed to have been dipped in the River Styx by his mother to render him invulnerable, but in dipping him she had to hold him by the heel. That heel proved to be his vulnerable part.
(Eph. 6. 11-18)

**38  Arms—The Everlasting.**  There are many believers like Sancho Panza in *Don Quixote*, who in fear hung all night from the ledge of a window and found by the light of day that his toes were about an inch from the ground. Many trembling souls fall short of the rest of faith because they are afraid to ' let go ' and simply trust Him. To the trusting soul who is standing on the definite promise of the Word, the worst that can happen is to fall into the ' everlasting arms '. ' Let go and let God.'

*Oh, the everlasting arms, how they hold me,*
*Ever hold me and enfold me!*
*Underneath and all around,*
*And whatever may surround,*
*Are the mighty everlasting arms.*

*Choice Gleanings*
(Deut. 33. 27)

**39  Aseptic—Making Oneself.**  Dr Maltbie D. Babcock was on one occasion invited to attend a banquet on a Saturday evening but declined the invitation. Being pressed for a reason, he replied, ' When a surgeon is about to perform an operation, he is at particular pains to make himself aseptic, that he may carry no foreign substance, no poisonous matter of any kind to his patient. On Sunday I am to preach the Word: I am to be a physician and surgeon of souls. I must do all that I can to keep myself absolutely aseptic. I must not allow even the possibility of carrying to those to whom I minister anything that might vitiate my ministry or lessen its beneficial effect.' For this reason he was accustomed to set apart Saturday evening as a preliminary preparation for his Sunday services.

*The Indian Christian*
(James 1. 27)

**40  Ashamed of Jesus.**  A Hindu of high rank was disturbed in mind on the subject of a future state. He had heard of Christians and desired to converse with them about their religion and to gain information about the Lord Jesus Christ. He visited Great Britain provided with introductions to leading people. At a great banquet he said to the gentleman sitting next to him, ' Can you tell me something about Christ?' ' We do not speak about such subjects at dinner parties,' was the reply. Later he was invited to a fashionable ball and took the opportunity of asking his partner for information about Jesus Christ. Again he was told that a ball was no place for such a subject. ' How strange these Christians in England are!' said the Hindu, ' They seem ashamed to speak about their religion and of Christ, its Founder.'
(Rom. 1. 16; 2 Tim. 1. 8,12,16)

**41  Ashamed of You, Mother?**  In the State of Georgia there was a widowed mother who had an only son. She was very poor, and had to work hard to support herself and her son, so took in washing. But the boy was bright; he graduated at the top of his class. He took the ' Valedictory ', which was given only to the highest man in the class, and a gold medal for special excellence in a particular study. The graduation day came—Commencement Day as it is called in America—and he said to his mother: ' Mother, it is Commencement Day, and I graduate today. Why are you not getting ready for the Commencement exercises?' ' Oh,' she said, ' I am not going: I have nothing fit to wear. The grandest people in the town will be there, and you will be ashamed of your old mother in her faded dress.' His eyes just beamed with admiration as he answered, ' What! Mother, ashamed of you! Never! I owe everything I have in the world to you and I won't go unless you do.'

He insisted and his mother consented. He helped her to make herself as tidy looking as possible and started down the street with his mother's hand on his arm. They entered the hall where the exercises were to take place and took her to one of the best seats among the grandest people in town; and there she sat in her faded dress among the silks and elegance. Her son took his place on the platform and when his turn came delivered his Valedictory address. He received much applause, was given his diploma and his special gold medal; and no sooner had he received it than he walked right down from the platform straight to where his mother was sitting, pinned the gold medal on her dress and said: ' There, Mother, that belongs to you! You earned it.'

As Dr Torrey told the story, tears were streaming down the cheeks of many, and, amidst their applause, he said, ' You do well to applaud, but I want to tell you a better way to applaud. By imitating him. You owe everything to Jesus Christ. Stand up and confess HIM.'
(Matt. 10. 32)

**42  Assurance of Salvation.**  Many years ago in Glasgow, Major Whittle held some meetings at one of which a poor woman was saved after listening to an address on John 5. 24: ' Verily, verily, I say unto you, he that heareth my word and believeth on Him that sent me hath everlasting life, and shall not come into condemnation but is passed from death unto life.' The evangelist wrote the verse on a little card and gave it to her. Accompanied by her little son who had been with her in the service, she took the card home, rejoicing in the knowledge of salvation.

In the morning she came down to breakfast feeling very gloomy, her face overclouded, and inwardly utterly discouraged after a night of conflicts, doubts and fears. Her little boy asked what was the matter. She burst into tears saying ' Oh, it is all gone. I thought I was saved but I feel just as bad as ever.' Looking puzzled, the lad said, ' Why, Mother, has your verse changed? I'll go and see.' He ran and fetched her Bible with the little card in it and read again the message of John 5. 24. ' Why, Mother,' he said, ' it hasn't changed a bit. It's just the same as it was last night.' His mother looked up with a smile now overspreading her face. Her son's simple trust had dispelled her depression.

### 43　Assurance—Words of.

*If all the SHALLS in Scripture meant*
　　*PERHAPS,*
*And all the HATHS meant simply HOPES*
　　*TO HAVE,*
*And all the ARES depended on an IF,*
*I well might doubt;*
*But since our Saviour-God means what He says*
*And cannot lie,*
*I trust His faithful Word and know that I*
*Shall surely dwell to all eternity*
*With Him Whose love led Him for me to die,*
*E'en Christ Himself.*

Isaac Watts wrote the hymn in which occurs the verse:

> *My faith looks back to see*
> *The burden Thou didst bear*
> *When hanging on the accursed tree,*
> *And HOPES her guilt was there.*

Charles Wesley changed one word in the last line to read—and KNOWS her guilt was there.

### 44　Atheism Avowed.

In the month of November, 1793, with the fall of the monarchy in France, the revolutionists decreed that God did not exist and that Reason was to be worshipped in His stead.

A veiled woman was brought into the Convention and one of the leaders said, ' Mortals, cease to tremble before the powerless thunders of a God whom your fears have created. Henceforth acknowledge no divinity but Reason. I offer you its noblest and purest image: if you must have idols, sacrifice only to such as this.' The veil was then removed. With open blasphemy the woman was taken in a beautiful carriage to Notre Dame and elevated upon the altar there. She then received adoration from the crowds that gathered. In this manner the France of the Revolution decreed that God did not exist.
(Ps. 14. 1; 53. 1; Rom. 1. 22-25)

### 45　Atheism—Evil Power of.

Some years ago a man by the name of Martin Thorn was electrocuted at Sing Sing prison, thus paying the extreme penalty for murdering a man. Shortly before his death he said to the Christian worker who had been visiting him in prison: ' I was not always bad. I was a good boy and a good man at first. I believed in the Bible, in God and in a future life. I liked the company of Christians and good-living folks. The fatal mistake of my life was the reading of a book written by the atheist, Ingersoll. I am sorry that atheist ever lived. I am sorry I ever read a line of his. The reading of that book was the first step away from God and heaven. My course has been downward ever since till I have come to a black crime and am now to face a shameful death.'
(Ps. 53. 1)

### 46　Atheist and a Peasant Woman.

Some years ago an atheist lecturer was travelling up and down the country pouring out his barrage against the very thought of God, and heaping ridicule on all those he deemed foolish enough to believe in God and in the Bible as the Word of God.

On one occasion he addressed a group gathered in a large hall in which his eloquence stirred them to a high pitch. Proudly considering himself master of the situation, he hurled a challenge to Almighty God to reveal Himself by smiting him to death. When nothing happened, he exclaimed, ' See, there is no God!'

Thereupon a little peasant woman rose to her feet and addressed the lecturer: ' Sir, I cannot answer your arguments: your learning is beyond me. You are an educated man while I am only a peasant woman. With your superior intelligence will you answer me one question?

' I have been a believer in Christ for many years, rejoicing in His salvation and enjoying reading my Bible. His comfort has brought me immense happiness. If when I come to die I learn that there is no God, that Jesus is not the Son of God, that the Bible is not true, and that there is no salvation or heaven, what have I lost through believing in the Lord Jesus Christ during this life?'

The room was very still as the audience now quickly grasped the logic of the woman's question. The atheist to whom the audience now turned, answered quietly, ' Madam, you will not stand to lose a thing.'

The peasant woman spoke again, ' Sir, you have been kind enough to answer my question. Permit me to ask another. If, when it comes your turn to die, you discover the Bible is true, that there is a God and Jesus is His Son, and that there is a heaven and a hell, what, sir, will you stand to lose?'

The logic was so overwhelming that the crowd leaped to its feet and shouted; but the atheist was silent. He had no answer.
(Prov. 27. 12)

**47 Audience of One.** One stormy night a servant of Christ went to preach in a remote place in one of the States of the U.S.A. The meeting had been arranged and announced beforehand, and many had promised to attend, but owing to the inclemency of the weather only one turned up. The preacher began to question in his mind if it was worth while preaching to only one man. However, remembering that God had sent him there, he spoke with all the earnestness of one with a great burden on his heart and a great work to do. As soon as the preaching was ended he endeavoured to contact the man who had composed his entire audience but found he had gone. Years later he was accosted by a man who asked, ' Do you remember me?'

' No!' was the preacher's reply.

' Do you remember preaching one wet night to only one man?'

' Yes, I do, and I tried to have a talk with him afterwards, but he went off before I could reach him.'

' Well!' he said, ' I am that man. That sermon led to my conversion, and now this neighbourhood is full of the fruits of that one sermon to one man.'

(John 4. 28, 29, 39)

**48 Authenticity of the Bible.** It is said that on January 1, 1863, President Lincoln set his name and seal to the proclamation which set four million slaves free. The proclamation was written on four pages of ordinary foolscap in the President's own handwriting. A few months later this document was given to the manager of a Fair held in Chicago in the interests of the Sanitary Commission, and they sold it to a resident for a large sum. It perished in the great Chicago fire of 1871.

Suppose some slave-owner should then have seized one of his former slaves, challenged him to produce Lincoln's proclamation as his charter of liberty, and threatened that, if he did not produce it, he would hold him still in slavery. What would the ex-slave do? He could not produce the original since it was long ago destroyed by fire; but though he could not produce that document, he could recover and produce the text of the original message. How? By copies of it in public documents, newspapers of the period, books, private letters and so forth; and also by translations of it in French, German and other languages, and quotations from it in speeches, periodicals, books, etc. By comparing and combining all these he could establish to the satisfaction of a Court of Law the original message granting him liberty.

In the case of the Bible there is a wealth of manuscripts, copies and versions such as no other ancient book can command. For every ten manuscript copies of a classic like Virgil there are a thousand manuscript copies of the Bible. We may well be satisfied, therefore, with the proof which we have of the genuineness and authenticity of the Bible.

Kemp

**49 Backsliding.** Remember, brethren, that decay in grace and backsliding are usually very much like the fall of autumn leaves. You are watching the trees, for even now they are beginning to indicate the coming fall. They evidently know that their verdant robes are to be stripped from them, for they are casting off their first loose vestments. How slowly the time of the brown leaf comes on! You notice here and there a tinge of the copper hue, and anon the gold leaf or the bronze is apparent. Week after week you observe that the general fall of the leaves is drawing nearer, but it is a matter that creeps slowly on. And so with backsliders.

God save us from falling by little and little! The devil's little strokes have felled great oaks. Where Satan captures one man by force of strong temptation, he captures ten by the gradual process of sapping and undermining the principles which should rule within.

C. H. Spurgeon

**50 Backsliding—Gradual.** In Colorado, U.S.A., there is the ruin of an enormous tree, a seedling when Columbus discovered America and only half grown when the Pilgrim Fathers landed at Plymouth. Fourteen times it had been struck by lightning and had survived the storms of centuries. Age did not wither it, lightning did not blast it, nor did avalanche move it, but it fell—gradually—before an army of tiny beetles. Read the story of Samson in the Book of Judges. He stood up to storms with undiminished strength but fell before the daily pressure of a woman.

(Prov. 14. 14; Jer. 8. 5)

**51 Banner—Heaven's.** Many years ago a Swedish newspaper carried this story. On his morning ride through Copenhagen the King of Denmark, Christian X, noticed a swastika waving over a public building in violation of the agreement Hitler made with their country. ' Take it down,' the king commanded. The German officer refused. ' It's up there by new orders from Berlin,' he said tersely. ' That flag must be removed before 12 o'clock, otherwise I shall send a soldier up to do it,' the monarch declared. ' Any soldier who tries that will be shot,' warned the Nazi officer. ' Ah, but I shall be that soldier!' replied the king. The swastika came down, for the Nazis at that point dare not shoot Denmark's king.

The Lord from heaven, the King of kings, came to earth to tear down the enemy's banner and defeat Satan, the prince of this world, and He has done this and hoisted Heaven's banner.

(Heb. 2. 14; 1 John 3. 8; Song of Solomon 2. 4)

**52 Barley Cakes.**

*The Midianite is in the land, and Israel's*
*hard bestead.*
*There's poverty on every hand, and scarcity*
*of bread:*
*But brawny Gideon beats at night the threshing*
*of his floor,*
*And by the winepress, out of sight, conceals*
*his precious store.*

*How well his honest heart esteems the food*
*  his God has given!*
*A plain unleavened cake he deems fit for a*
*  guest from Heaven.*
*Here is a man whom God can tell, ' Go thou*
*  in this thy might':*
*Yes, Midian's tents shall prove how well a*
*  ' barley cake ' can fight!*

*A lesson learn from Gideon's floor: nutritious*
*  food for you*
*Is in the Word; abundance more than ever*
*  Canaan grew.*
*And if you wish to serve the Lord (for still*
*  His foes assail),*
*If you would learn to use the sword, first*
*  learn to use the flail.*

James S. Tait

(Judg. 7. 13; 2 Tim. 3. 16, 17)

### 53 Bartimaeus.

*One day I saw a blind man by the way:*
*He heard but could not see, the passers-by:*
*His time was spent in begging for his bread,*
*But few were they who stopped to hear his cry.*

*He heard one day the multitude draw nigh,*
*And listened as they talked of Christ the King.*
*He cried, ' O Lord, be merciful to me;*
*My darkness take away and healing bring.'*

*The great Physician heard him as he cried,*
*While those around rebuked him in their zeal.*
*' What wilt thou?' was the question that*
*  He asked:*
*' My sight, O Lord, restore, my blindness heal.'*

*The Saviour heard his plea and cried, ' I will!'*
*He touched his eyes and forthwith gave him*
*  sight.*
*He saw the sun, the flowers, the face of man,*
*And praised the One who took away his night.*

*With joy untold he followed Christ that day;*
*For ever bound was he by love's decree.*
*O matchless grace! O wondrous love divine!*
*The Son of God has made the blind to see.*

(Mark 10. 46-52)

### 54 Beacon from the House of God.

Arbroath Abbey, in Angus, Scotland, high on the hill behind the town, still rears its towering seaward gable pierced by a vast circular aperture, the ' O ' of Arbroath. On a platform behind this, centuries ago, monks lit the huge bonfire which served as a beacon on stormy nights to ships passing the wild and perilous North Sea coast and the dreaded Inchcape Rock. The beacon offered at once, to native and foreigner alike, warning, guidance and cheer, and it shone from the house of God. Even so should the Church of God in every age shine in this dark world.
(Ps. 119. 105; Ezek. 3. 17; 33. 2,3)

### 55 Beauty from Ashes.

A handful of sand is deposited by the Lord in the heart of the earth. Great heat is applied from beneath and ponderous weight from above, until, when found by man, it has become a beautiful fiery opal. God does the same with clay and man finds a lovely amethyst. He does the same thing with black carbon, and man finds a glorious diamond. How? I don't know. I only know He can take a life that is drab, useless and fruitless and transform it into a beautiful garden full of the sweetest graces for His glory. Now the works of the flesh are . . .

But the fruit of the Spirit is love, joy, peace, . . . Galatians 5. 19-23. Is my life a factory or an orchard?
(Isa. 61. 3)

### 56 Beauty—Spiritual.

Spiritual beauty is loveliest when it is unconsciously possessed. Self-conscious virtue is lean and uncrowned. Moses had been closeted with God. The glory of the Lord had been poured upon him, bathing him in unearthly brightness, so that when he returned to the mountain base, his countenance shone like the light. The same transformation is effected every day and by the same means. Spiritual communion alters the fashion of a countenance. The power of a beautiful spirit makes many a plain face lovely. But Moses ' wist not ' that his face shone. That is the supreme height of spiritual loveliness; to be lovely and not to know it. Surely this is a lesson we need to learn; virtue is so apt to be self-conscious and thus lose its glow.

Humility is very beautiful when we see it unimpaired: it is exquisite with the loveliness of Christ. But there is a self-conscious humility which is only a very subtle species of praise. Humility takes the lowest place and does not know that her face shines. Self-consciousness always tends to sour humility and pervert it to pride.

J. H. Jowett, D.D.

### 57 Beauty—Spiritual.

*You may not have beauty*
*That most crave today:*
*But then, it is only skin deep, they say.*

*There are hidden beauties*
*That one can acquire—*
*More precious by far than the looks some*
*  desire.*

*There are priceless virtues*
*That you can display,*
*Opportunities coming with each passing day:*

*In being kind-hearted,*
*Loving and true,*
*Sincere and patient and humble too.*

*These are the beauties*
*That shine from within,*
*Lasting for ever, much deeper than skin.*

May Gorrie

(Exod. 34. 29; Ps. 90. 17; 2 Cor. 3. 18)

### 58 Beauty Unrealised.

An old brier was growing in a ditch. A gardener came along with a spade, dug around it and lifted it out. ' What is he doing this for? Doesn't he know that I am an old worthless brier?'

The gardener took it and put it in his garden. ' What a mistake he has made—planting an old brier like myself among such roses!' But the gardener came once more and with his keen-edged knife made a slit in the brier and ' budded ' it with a rose; and by and by when the summer came, lovely roses were blooming on the old brier. Then the gardener said: ' Your beauty is not due to what came out of you but to what I put into you.'

The human heart is no better than the old brier, but the Heavenly Gardener can graft in the divine life, and the impossible happens. Heavenly virtues bloom where once weeds abounded. Spiritual graces are found and abound because of what He put into us.

By accident a relative of John Ruskin spilt ink over a beautiful silk handkerchief. She wept until her heart literally ached. Then Ruskin came in and smilingly took it from her. Going to his studio he set to work on that blot, draw-ing figures upon it; then with delicate brush movements he painted a beautiful picture and returned the handkerchief. ' Oh,' she said, ' this is not my handkerchief!' ' Yes, it is yours. I simply took the ugly blot and transformed it into a picture.' So God does with us when we truly repent of our failures and mistakes and sins and yield ourselves to Him.
(Isa. 61. 3; Ezek. 16. 14; Col. 3. 9,10)


59   **Before and Beside.**

*Before me is a future all unknown,*
*A path untrod;*
*Beside me is a Friend, well-loved and known;*
*That Friend is God.*

*Before me lies a new and unseen way*
*'Mid shadows dim;*
*Beside me is my Guide, and day by day*
*I walk with Him.*

*Before me may be trials dark and strange,*
*And loss and pain;*
*Beside me is the One whose love will change*
*Earth's grief to gain.*

*Before me I discern but barren land*
*And desert waste;*
*Beside me is the Lord, and His dear hand*
*My path has traced.*

(Exod. 33. 14,15; Heb. 13. 5)


60  **Beginning—In the.** Frank Borman, an only child born in Gary, Indiana on March 14, 1925, was sickly in childhood, plagued with sinus, mastoid, tonsil and adenoid troubles. At 15 he began taking flying lessons and, after finishing High School, entered the U.S. Military Academy at West Point. There he graduated with honours and immediately transferred to the U.S. Air Force and earned his Wings in 1951. Colonel Borman was a child of God by

faith in our Lord Jesus Christ and proved himself to be a man of faith. Sustained by his faith in God, and living a disciplined life, he went on the Apollo 8 orbit round the moon. He was concerned before the take-off about sending out of space a unique message for a Christmas service for all people everywhere on earth, and there came the suggestion of the Creation story, which was typed into the flight plan. This was read, each of the three astro-nauts taking part, as they were making their last turn into the dark. Gen. 1. 1-10 was the portion they read, commencing with ' IN THE BEGINNING GOD . . .'. These first four words of the Bible may be taken as the Christian's life motto. In everything begin with God—in companionships, marriage, business partner-ships, every day and always. In other words, we must get our priorities right.
(Matt. 6. 33)


61  **Bells and Pomegranates.**

*With holy awe and reverent pace,*
*The Priest approached the Holy Place;*
*Attired in garments that became*
*The Place where God had set His Name.*
*His ephod shone with gold and gems,*
*While softly from the wreathen hems*
*The mellow music rose and fell*
*From a ' pomegranate and a bell,*
*A pomegranate and a bell.'*

*Today there's still a Holy Place,*
*An Altar, and a priestly race,*
*A godly order still obtains,*
*The ' pattern of the House ' remains.*
*Shall I invade that sacred shrine*
*And jingle through its calm divine*
*With clamorous notes that plainly tell*
*' No pomegranates but a bell,—*
*Another bell—and another bell?'*

*O for the grace that knows to suit*
*The outward sound to inward fruit;*
*That knows how well the music blends,*
*When lips confess and life commends;*
*That, though with boldness coming, brings*
*No reckless touch to holy things;*
*But hems the priestly garment well,*
*With ' a pomegranate and a bell,*
*A pomegranate and a bell.'*

James S. Tait

(Exod. 28.34; Heb.13. 15,16)


62  **Beloved—My.**

*What is thy Beloved more than another*
*Beloved?*
*O what is thy Beloved? They oft enquire of me,*
*And what in my Beloved so passing fair I see?*
*Is it the heavenly splendour in which He*
*shines above,*
*His riches and dominion, that won my heart's*
*best love?*

O no! 'tis not His glories. He's worthy of
  them all!
'Tis not the Throne and Sceptre, before
  which angels fall:
I view with heart exulting each crown His
  head adorns:
But O, He looks most lovely, wearing His
  crown of thorns.

I'm glad to see His raiment, than snow
  more spotless white,
Refulgent with its brightness, more dazzling
  than the light;
But more surpassing lovely His form appears
  to me
When stripp'd and scourged and bleeding,
  He hung upon the tree.

With warmest adoration I see Him on the
  throne
And join the loud hosannas that His high
  virtues own;
But O, most blessed Jesus, I must confess
  to Thee
More than the throne of glory I love that
  sacred tree.

I joy to see the diadems upon Thy royal brow,
The state and power and majesty in which
  Thou sittest now;
But 'tis Thyself, Lord Jesus, makes Heaven
  seem Heaven to me,
Thyself, as first I knew Thee, uplifted on the
  tree.

Though higher than the highest, most mighty
  King Thou art,
Thy grace, and not Thy greatness, first
  touched my rebel heart;
Thy sword it might have slain me, Thine
  arrows drunk my blood,
But 'twas the cross subdued me and won my
  heart to God.

Thy sceptre rules creation, Thy wounded
  hand rules me;
All bow before Thy footstool, I but the nail-
  prints see.
Aloud they sound Thy titles, Thou Lord of
  lords most high.
One thrilling thought absorbs me—this Lord
  for me did die.

O, this is my Beloved. There's none so fair
  as He:
The chief among ten thousand, He's all in all
  to me.
My heart just breaks with longing to dwell
  with Him above
Who wooed me first and won me by His
  sweet dying love.

J. G. Deck

**63  Beloved—My.**

Treasure beyond all telling,
Friend when the trusted fail,
Comfort in Jordan's swelling,
Strength when the foes assail,
Rock when the sands are shifting,
Anchor in storm-tossed sea,
Surety in aimless drifting—
All this is He to me.

Joy to the sorrowing spirit,
Rest after fruitless toil—
Forgiven alone through his merit,
Healed by anointing oil:
Light when the dark clouds hover,
In the unknown way a Guide:
All this, O Matchless Lover,
All this and Heaven beside.

E.M.G.

(Song of Solomon 5. 9-16)

**64  Benefits—All His.**  Reverse had befallen a
prosperous merchant and he failed in business.
With haggard countenance and breaking heart,
he said to his wife as the family gathered round
the table in his home, ' My dear, I am ruined.
I have lost my all.' 'All?' queried his wife, ' No!
I am left!' 'All!' said his eldest son, ' but you
have me too!' 'And I am still with you,' said his
affectionate daughter, putting her arms round
her father's neck. 'And you have your health
left, darling!' said his wife. 'And your hands
still strong to work!' added his daughter. 'And
your feet, Dad, to carry you about, and your
eyes to see with,' said his youngest son.
  Granny then chipped in: ' You have also
God's promises which are exceeding great and
precious.' And mother topped the list of mercies
with:— 'And a kind, good Father, and a
heavenly Home before you.'
  ' God forgive me!' said the merchant, ' I
haven't lost all. Indeed, I haven't lost much
compared with the inestimable wealth that is
left to me.'
(Ps. 103. 2)

**65  Bereavement and God's Will.**  J. D. Tippit
was the policeman shot dead by Lee Oswald,
the assassin of President John Kennedy.  The
Tippit story began in Red River County, Texas,
U.S.A., in 1946, just after J. D. Tippit came
home from service in the World War. He took
Marie to a revival meeting, and from that first
date there developed a friendship and love that
culminated in marriage on December 26, 1946.
  Marie Tippit and her husband had been
Christians for over a year, and they were
members of, and regular attenders at, a church
in Red River County until they moved to Dallas.
In 1952 J. D. Tippit joined the police force to
provide a livelihood for his wife and family.
Though they realised they could not be effective
workers for the Lord without belonging to a
local church, they allowed many things to keep
them out of active service. In 1962 they re-
dedicated their lives to the Lord and became
active Christian workers. About that time their

son Allen and daughter Brenda were saved and baptised.

After the death of her husband God spoke again to Marie Tippit, and her response was a full committal of her life to the Lord. ' The experiences that have come during this period of bereavement ', she said, ' have drawn me closer to God than I have ever been before. I could never have got through the experiences of the past months without God's presence and power. I can truly say I have been able to forgive Lee Oswald for the crime he committed in killing my husband. My desire is to live a simple normal life by raising my children and helping them to find the will of God for their lives. I have the assurance that I shall see my husband and be reunited to him in that eternal city that Jesus has gone to prepare for all who trust Him as Saviour and Lord.'

## 66  Best for God—The.

One of India's many widows had two young sons, one sturdy and robust, the other puny, sickly and not likely to live to be any stay or support to her. She took them on a long pilgrimage to the banks of the sacred River Ganges at Varanasi, and there, after hugging him lovingly to her bosom and covering his face with kisses, she flung the sturdy lad into the river, ' a living sacrifice '. Asked later why she did not give the younger, puny boy as a sacrifice to her god, instead of the strong, sturdy elder brother, she replied, ' My gods demand the best from me, don't they?'

Do we give God our best?

Crawford J. Tilsley
(Lev. 22. 20,21; Rom. 12. 1)

## 67  Bethlehem—The Babe of.

*Was Jesus God, the Babe of Bethlehem*
*Who took upon Himself the form of man?*
*Was He in very deed the great I AM,*
*Who came to carry out the Father's plan?*

*Yes, He was God, and He is God today.*
*No other could have paid the price of sin.*
*'Twas God Who trod earth's road so long ago,*
*And yet He deigns to dwell my heart within.*

Oswald J. Smith

*Even in Lowly Bethlehem where crowds all*
*   day had trod,*
*Some shepherds sought the Saviour and found*
*   the Lamb of God.*

*Even in peaceful Bethlehem with all the*
*   town asleep,*
*They saw in Him the shepherd who would*
*   die to save His sheep.*

*Even in blessed Bethlehem as sheep beneath*
*   His rod,*
*The shepherds returned praising and glorifying*
*   God.*

*Even in humble Bethlehem with all the*
*   world asleep,*
*They knew Him as their Shepherd and*
*   followed as His sheep.*

C. A. Lufburrow
(Luke 2. 12-15)

## 68  Beulah.

' Beulah ' is one of the names given to Israel's land, and it occurs only once in the Bible. It is celebrated in some of our hymns as the dwelling-place of God's heavenly people today; and it is also the name of individual homes and a personal Christian name, especially of women. Its use has given rise to an amusing story. A preacher was explaining the meaning of the names in Isaiah 62. 4, and had just pointed out that ' Hephzibah ' signifies ' My delight is in her '. Then he went on to state, 'and "Beulah" means "to be married" '. Just at that moment a young lady, ' Beulah ' by name, rather late in arriving at the service, took her seat, her face all suffused with blushes at what she thought was the announcement of her intentions which she had till then only confided to a few of her friends.

## 69  Bible—A Library.

George Brealey, founder and evangelist of the Blackdown Hills' Mission, was on one occasion staying in the home of a minister of the Gospel who offered him the use of his well-stocked library. ' Thank you,' he replied, ' but I carry my library with me—66 books.' ' It's a shame to have to carry all these with you,' said his host. ' No!' replied Mr. Brealey, ' they pack quite small.' Producing his Bible, he said, ' Here they are! All 66 books in one volume: 39 in the Old Testament and 27 in the New.'

This wonderful library has a catalogue of its books on one of its front pages, and contains history, ethnology, law, ethics, poetry, drama, medical science, prophecy, political economy, social studies, and biographies. Every book has a main theme and they all centre round one outstanding Person, the Lord Jesus Christ, who said, ' They testify of Me.'

When imprisoned during the years of the Second World War for his faithfulness to the Word of God, Pastor Martin Niemoller found this library a great source of consolation, and said, ' The Word of God was simply everything to me—comfort and strength, guidance and hope, master of my days and companion of my nights, the bread of life which kept me from starvation and the water of life that refreshed my soul.'

In the darkness of solitary confinement in Marxist China, Geoffrey Bull was for a long time without his library. But what a relief he experienced when he had his Bible restored to him and could read it!

*O Library of books! O Word of words!*
*The only Book whose title is ' the Lord's ':*
*Thy theme—the Truth, the Light, the Life,*
*   the Way,*
*That leads from darkness to eternal day.*

## 70  Bible and its Author.

The books of the Bible were written by over forty different men, but all have but one Author, God.

*This Book contains the Author's mind, His*
*   great eternal Plan,*
*The waywardness of human kind, the state*
*   of God-made man.*

Salvation's way is here made plain, the
   sinner's doom foretold;
The Christian's happiness and gain its pages
   here unfold.

How holy its doctrinal Truth, its precepts
   how secure,
Its histories of age and youth, decrees so firm
   and sure!

True wisdom it unfolds to all who read its
   sacred page
And, answering the loving call, a war with
   sin will wage.

Their safety in belief is found, their holiness
   in use.
It snaps the chains that sin had bound, sheds
   light on themes obtuse.

Its daily food support will give to comfort
   and to cheer,
For if we by its precepts live our hearts need
   know no fear.

It is the pilgrim traveller's guide, the staff that
   gives him aid,
The pilot's compass o'er life's tide, the soldier's
   trusty blade,
The Christian's charter in this world, his balm
   for every ill,
His banner glorious which, unfurled, reveals
   his Master's will.

Here Paradise restored is seen and Heaven's
   open gate,
And Hell disclosed in frightful mien, the
   sinner's awful fate.

Christ is its grand eternal Theme, God's glory
   its chief end
Designed to make their joy supreme who trust
   the sinner's Friend.

The memory should with it be filled, the heart
   obeys its rule;
The rod for all who are self-willed, for ' babes
   in Christ ' the school.

Peruse its sacred page with care: to it have oft
   recourse,
And by sincere and earnest prayer you'll reach
   that blessed Source
And find within a mine of wealth, a paradise
   of bliss.
For souls impoverished in health the healing
   Water this.

How great the onus it involves on teachers of
   its truth
Whose precepts are their firm resolve,
   instructing errant youth!

What great reward is theirs who seek its
   message to impart,
And for their blessed Master speak a word
   to cheer the heart.

To those who trifle with the Word or apathy
   assume
Will come the judgement of the Lord Who
   will pronounce their doom.

C. R. Caie

(Ps. 119. 9,105,130; Heb. 4. 12,13)

**71  Bible—Buying a.** Señor Antonio Parisi, Bible Society Colporteur in Northern Argentina, stopped at a humble hut. The woman who lived there wanted to buy a Bible but did not have sufficient money to pay for it. ' Wait until my son returns from the village: he will pay for it,' she said. Time passed but the son had not returned. ' Just a little longer,' pleaded the mother; but the colporteur had a long distance to travel to Quilimif and wanted to get there before nightfall. He and his wife got into their jeep but could not get it to start. Meantime the son returned from the market and a child ran out with the price of the Bible. When the colporteur next pressed the starter, the jeep roared into life.

A few days later, at a general store beside a petrol pump, the jeep again refused to start. The colporteur, knowing what God wanted him to do, grabbed his satchel of books, entered the store and sold a Bible to the man in charge. Again the engine started up immediately and they were able to proceed.

But there is a sequel. Recounting these experiences at a course for Scripture distributors held in San Pedro de Jejuy some time later, the colporteur was thrilled when one of the students stood up and said, ' I am the son who returned in time to buy my mother a Bible.' That was 900 miles from San Pedro de Jejuy.
(Prov. 23. 23)

## 72  Bible—Facts about the.

1  The Bible is one of the simplest books in the world, for where is the child who does not understand and enjoy its delightful stories?

2  The Bible is the most profound book in the world, for it contains also the deep things of God.

3  The Bible is the cheapest book in the world for its size; yet more money has been expended for a single copy than for any other book in the world. (£100,000 was paid for the Sinaitic Version.)

4  The Bible is the most available book in the world, printed in more languages and dialects than any other book.

5  The Bible has had the greatest moral influence in the world, enlivening man's conscience, elevating womanhood, and sanctifying family life. It condemns falsehood, covetousness, hatred, impurity and idolatry in all its forms.

6  The Bible is the most quoted book in the world—by all classes, creeds, and persuasions. Men cannot get away from its wisdom, knowledge and influence.

7  The Bible is the most hated book in the world, for men have sought to destroy it and to forbid its possession.

8  The Bible is the most loved book in the world among all classes and all nations in all lands. Some have sold their all to obtain a copy and walked long distances to obtain it and hear it read.

**73 Bible Features.** The Bible contains 66 books, 39 in the Old Testament and 27 in the New Testament. The Old Testament has 929 chapters and 23,214 verses; and the New Testament has 270 chapters, and 7,931 verses. The whole Bible has 1,199 chapters and 31,145 verses. Proverbs is the middle book of the Old Testament, Job. 20 the middle chapter and 2 Chronicles 26. 17 the middle verse. 2 Thessalonians is the middle book of the New Testament, Romans 13 and 14 the middle chapters, and Acts 11.17 the middle verse. The middle verse of the Bible is Psalm 117. 8: the longest verse is Esther 8. 9: the shortest is John 11. 35. There are four verses alike in Psalm 107, viz. verses 8, 15, 21, 31. The English Bible contains about four times as many words as are found in a book of average length. In the Authorised Version only about 6000 different words are used, which is very small compared with 20,000 in the writings of William Shakespeare. The average word in the Bible contains five letters, and many of these short words—grace, faith, glory, Jesus—are full of the most profound meaning.

Of the Bible Sir Walter Scott, the well-known novelist and poet, wrote:

*Within this wondrous volume lies*
*The mystery of mysteries;*
*Happiest they of human race*
*To whom their God has given grace*
*To read, to fear, to hope, to pray,*
*To lift the latch and find the way;*
*And better had they ne'er been born*
*That read to doubt, or read to scorn.*

**74 Bible—Heaven's Ledger.**

*O Book! infinite sweetness! let my heart*
*Suck every letter, and a honey gain,*
*Precious for any grief in any part,*
*To clear the breast, to mollify all pain.*

*Thou art all health, health-thriving till it make*
*A full eternity; thou art a mass*
*Of strange delights, where we may wish and take.*

*Ladies, look here; this is the thankful glass,*
*That mends the looker's eyes; this is the well*
*That washes what it shows. Who can endear*
*Thy praise too much? Thou art heaven's ledger here,*
*Working against the states of death and hell.*

*Thou art joy's handful: heaven lies flat in thee,*
*Subject to every mounter's bended knee.*

*O that I knew how all thy lights combine,*
*And the configurations of their glory!*
*Seeing not only how each verse doth shine,*
*But all the constellations of the story.*

*Stars are poor books, and oftentimes do miss;*
*This book of stars lights to eternal bliss.*

A. C. Rose

(Ps. 19. 10; 119. 89)

**75 Bible—Memorising the.** Some years ago a humble villager in Eastern Poland received a Bible from a colporteur who visited his hamlet, read it, was converted and passed it on to others. Through that one Bible two hundred more people became believers. When the colporteur, Michael Billester, revisited the town, the group gathered to worship and listen to his preaching. Billester suggested that, instead of giving the customary testimonies, they all recite verses of Scripture. Thereupon a man asked, ' Do you mean verses or chapters?' ' Can some of you recite chapters of the Bible?' the colporteur asked in astonishment. The villagers had memorised whole books of the Bible. Thirteen people knew Matthew, Luke, and half of Genesis, and one had committed the Psalms to memory. Together they knew practically the whole Bible. The old book had become so worn that its pages were hardly legible.
(Ps. 119. 11; Acts 12. 24)

**76 Bible—Reading the.** A young lady, lately married to a faithful and devoted missionary, was on her way to the port from which she was soon to sail with her husband for South Africa. On the journey their stage coach changed horses early in the morning in the town where her brother was at school. Running up into his bedroom to bid him Goodbye, she said to him very earnestly, ' Robert, read your Bible.'

About forty years later the head of a large Mission school in India who had done a great work for Christ among lads of high caste, lay dying. A fellow missionary standing by his bedside asked, ' Is it true that your sister's words led you to read the Scriptures?' ' Yes!' he replied, ' she told me to read my Bible and I have done it: I've done it!' Then Robert passed away.
George Everard

**77 Bible Remains for Ever.** Writing on the Bible, Sir Winston Churchill said:

' Let men of science and learning expand their knowledge and prise and probe with their researches every detail of the records which have been preserved to us from those dim ages. All they will do is to fortify the grand simplicity and essential accuracy of the recorded truths which have lighted so far the pilgrimage of men.

*Captains and conquerors leave a little dust,*
*And kings a dubious legend of their reigns;*
*The swords of Caesar now are left to rust;*
*God's Word, the Bible, evermore remains.'*
(Ps. 119. 89,99)

**78 Bible Solves Problems.** The Bible demands for itself our obedience, for to the degree in which we obey, to that degree the divine Author will reveal its secrets and answer the deepest problems of our enquiring minds. The Bible—
(a) gives the only reasonable explanation of the origin of the world:
(b) gives a clear simple explanation of the cause of human failure, sin and suffering:
(c) solves the problem of death and gives a sure and certain hope of eternal life:
(d) Provides a way of salvation in Christ whereby sinful men can find peace and acceptance with God:

(e) Solves the problem of the future of the race in giving promise of a new heaven and a new earth wherein dwells righteousness.

Which then will you have? Atheism and ignorance? Or God and the Bible?

**79  Bible—Source of Comfort.** The Royal Albert Hall was filled some years ago with people who came in their thousands to render testimony to the value of the Bible. Here is the testimony given by the Emperor Haile Selassie, exiled then from his land, Ethiopia: ' From early childhood I was taught to appreciate the Bible, and my love for it increases with the passage of time. All through life I have found it a cause of unfailing comfort . . . For myself I glory in the Bible.'

**80  Bible—Suited to all Circumstances.**

*If thou art merry, here are airs;*
*If melancholy, here are prayers:*
*If studious, here are those things writ*
*Which may deserve thy ablest wit.*
*If hungry, here is food divine;*
*If thirsty, nectar, Heavenly wine.*

*Read then, but first thyself prepare*
*To read with zeal and mark with care:*
*And when thou read'st what there is writ,*
*Let thy best practise second it.*
*So twice each precept writ should be,*
*First in the Book, and then in thee.*

(Job 23. 12)

**81  Bible—Transforming Power of.** Vicente, the witch-doctor, announced one day to his wife, ' This town is so terrible that we shall have to move. We can't raise our children here.'

The little town in the mountains of Cuba where Vicente lived had indeed degenerated through drunkenness, gambling, lust and crime, so that even Vicente, whose nefarious religious traffic was largely responsible for much of this condition, feared for his family.

Soon after his decision to move, while visiting a nearby city, Vicente discovered a Bible. He did not know what it was except that it appeared to be a religious book; and, being a religious man, he bought it and took it home. A spiritualistic seance was scheduled for his home that night, but instead of the usual programme Vicente decided to read his newly acquired Bible to the people who had gathered. As he read, they were all greatly impressed and wanted more. So night after night Vicente read the Bible to those mountain people.

When some of the listeners wanted Bibles for themselves, Vicente went back to the city, bought additional copies and brought them to his followers. Soon lives began to be transformed. Drunkards stopped their drinking: gamblers began to earn honest livings. People were praying and telling their acquaintances what a wonderful thing it was to have a friend like the Jesus of the Bible.

Vicente was much surprised at what was happening and especially at what had happened in his own life through reading the Book.

Hearing that there were Christian churches that used the Bible, he found the address of a missionary and invited him to come. The missionary came, found many people convicted of sin and some converted. As a result a church of born-again, committed Christians was formed and Vicente became their preacher and teacher. He began to visit nearby villages and witnessed to the people, with the result that spiritual miracles took place in many places.

The Bible always bears fruit—in Cuba or anywhere else in the world.

Christian Literature and World Crusade
(Ps. 119. 130; Heb. 4. 12,13)

**82  Bible Translation.** An editorial in the *Bible Translator* ran as follows:

Not infrequently the Editor's postbag contains a letter from some unknown correspondent giving details of an old copy of the Bible of which he is the proud and optimistic possessor. First comes the detailed description of the book, its age and peculiar features, etc., then the inevitable question, ' Can you tell me what this Bible is worth?'—in terms of hard cash, of course! The year 1964 marks the centenary of the translation of one of the most significant Bibles in Modern history, that of Van Dyck into classical Arabic. Scattered throughout the Arabic-speaking world, especially in Egypt, the Lebanon and the Near and Middle East, there must be many thousands of copies of this now venerable translation. One wonders if anyone could begin to offer an estimate as to their worth—in terms of spreading the Gospel of truth, transforming human lives, founding churches, challenging error, silently but eloquently witnessing in the very heart of the Islamic world to the perfect plan of God for the redemption of men by His Son, Jesus Christ.

The truth is that in terms like these no one can begin to estimate the value of any Bible, and least of all this particular translation.

W. J. Bradnock (October, 1964)
(1 Sam. 3.1; Ps. 119. 72)

**83  Bible—Uniqueness of the.** A colporteur was offering the Bible to some Moslems who were sitting in a coffee shop. One of them asked, 'Are you a preacher?' The colporteur replied, ' No, I am just a colporteur.' Then another man spoke up. ' Beware, this man is worse than the preacher who speaks to you and then goes away. This man leaves with you a Book which is able to convert you to Christianity.'

Professor Max Muller knew the sacred books of the East as few scholars have known them, and he said that it only enabled him to say with a new assurance: ' I am not ashamed of the gospel. The Bible is altogether unique in its unity, its purity, its authority and its power to uplift and bless. It means just what it says.'

*There are some who believe in the Bible,*
*There are some who believe a part,*
*Some who trust with a reservation*
*And some with all their heart;*

*But I know that every promise*
*Is firm and sure always;*
*It is tried as the precious silver*
*And it means just what it says.*

A. B. Simpson

(Ps. 19. 10; John 17. 17)

## 84  Bitter Fruit Made Sweet.

*Lokman the faithful had a lord he served*
*With constant zeal that never flagged nor*
*swerved.*
*So closely knit were they in one accord*
*You scarce could tell which slave was,*
*which was lord.*
*One day the master a bitter melon gave,*
*Unconscious of its taste, to his dear slave,*
*Who ate as though 'twere something to enjoy*
*And gave no sign of shrinking or annoy.*
*But when one slice was left of that harsh fruit*
*His master thought that he would follow suit*
*And swallow it. Then, for one moment he*
*Was dumb; and then, his wonderment set free,*
*With eyes that watered, throat all burning hot,*
*He questioned Lokman: ' Whence is it you got*
*Such patience as an eagle's reach exceeds?'*
*Lokman replied, ' My Lord, so many deeds*
*Of kindness hast thou shown to thy poor slave*
*With your dear hand, that if, for once it gave*
*A bitter fruit, should I then hesitate*
*Or, weakly querulous, bemoan my fate?'*
*Love makes the bitter sweet if love be real,*
*Trusting the purpose, though the clouds conceal.*

A Persian Legend

(Rev. 10. 9,10)

## 85  Blessings or Mercies.
The late H. P. Barker, a master of illustration, tells of a visit to a shut-in child of God. He sat by her bedside, reading the Word and talking of the things of God. Then he asked, ' What is your favourite hymn?'

' There are so many, Mr. Barker: I don't know which one I like best.'

' Try to think of your favourite,' said H. P. Barker.

' Well, I am very fond of " Count your many blessings ".'

They sang it together. Then he said, ' Now, we must do it, must we not? Let us have a few of your blessings.'

' Oh,' she replied, ' there are so many I couldn't begin to count them.'

' You are not going to wriggle out of it like that. Let me hear you begin to count a few of your blessings.'

' Well, it's springtime now and with the coming of the lovely sunshine, somehow the rheumatism in my knees gets a bit easier, and that's a blessing.'

' Let's have another,' said Mr. Barker.

' You know,' the lady went on, ' last year the potatoes grew wonderfully in my garden. A friend of mine dug them up and there was such a stock of them that they've lasted all through the winter. That's a great blessing these hard times.'

' Well, another?'

' You know, I've got a son who lives in Manchester and every now and then he writes to me and he pops a ten shilling note in the letter, and in these hard times it's a great blessing.'

' Listen, sister,' said H. P. Barker, ' you'll be surprised and shocked when I tell you that none of the things you have mentioned are blessings.'

' Indeed they are,' she exclaimed, ' they are great blessings to me.'

' No!' he said, ' these are not blessings. These are what God calls **Mercies**. God does not give His blessings to everyone, but in wondrous grace He gives His mercies to everyone. He only gives His blessings to those who are in Christ Jesus. You can share your mercies with others, but you cannot share your blessings!'

Harold Wildish

(Ps. 103. 1,2)

## 86  Blind from Birth.
A preacher in Hyde Park had just finished what he had to say when a man stepped from the crowd and addressed the company thus:

' Ladies, and gentlemen, you have been listening to this chap talking about God, heaven and Jesus Christ. He has had a lot to say about sin and death, the devil and hell. I hope you won't believe a word of it. I don't. I refuse to believe what I cannot see.' In this manner he went on for some time, ridiculing faith in the invisible.

As he finished, another man elbowed his way forward and he, too, addressed the company. ' Friends,' he said, ' I hear that not very far from here runs a river. I don't believe it. Many declare the grass hereabouts is a beautiful green. I don't believe it. And some also say that by these walks are pretty shrubs which yearly blossom to please the eye of man and make the surroundings pleasant. Again, let me declare, I don't believe it. Now I am sure that most of you standing here will decide that I am talking like a fool, but I am not a fool. I am really serious.

' I have never seen a river. I have never seen the grass and never looked upon a beautiful flower, for I was born blind. The more I talked to you as I have done, the more it would appear to you that I must be blind, and unless sight is given to me, I shall never see the flowers, the grass, the river that flows silently into the sea. But—does this justify my insisting that what I cannot see I will not believe? Certainly not!'

Then, turning in the direction of the other man, the blind man went on: ' You, sir, by your statements disprove nothing the preacher has said. What you do prove, however, is that you are blind—spiritually blind—and that is why you do not understand what many people here know to be true.'

*The Indian Christian*

(John 9. 40,41; 2 Cor. 4. 4)

## 87  Blind Once—Now I See.
A young man had suffered for many years from a direful disease which gradually rendered his limbs immovable. One who had witnessed many

cases of severe bodily suffering stated that he had never seen anything to compare with that with which this dear man was afflicted for so many years. Finally his sight also completely failed. When in this state he called someone to him to write down from his lips the good matter which his heart was inditing, and he spoke as follows:

> Once I could see, but ne'er again
> Shall I behold the verdant plain
> Jewelled with flowers of colour bright,
> Bathed in a flood of golden light.
> The birds, the brilliant butterflies,
> These all in thought before me rise;
> The shining rivulet whose song
> Comes sweetly murmuring along;
> The sky, the clouds, the grass, the trees,
> All waving, glancing in the breeze—
> I see them pictured in my mind,
> But there alone, for I am blind.
>
> Blind, did I say? How can it be
> Since I, by faith, my Saviour see
> Exalted on the throne above,
> Beaming with mercy, grace and love?
> A view like this is better far
> Than sun or moon or glittering star,
> Or glowing landscape, sunny skies,
> Or sight that's fair to mortal eyes.
> I THANK my God that He has put
> A veil before my eyes, and shut
> All earthly objects from my sight
> And Christ revealed in glory bright.
> Henceforth my word shall ever be—
> Once I was blind but now I see.

(John 9. 25)

88 **Blood of Christ.** An American evangelist, friend of Dr H. A. Ironside, was involved in a car accident and taken to a Roman Catholic Hospital where he lay for several months. On a nearby bed lay a young priest, evidently a sincere and earnest man, but greatly troubled in view of his possible death. An aged priest came from time to time to hear his confession and grant him absolution.

The evangelist longed to speak to him but found him very difficult to approach. One day, however, as the older priest was about to leave, he heard the young man say to him, ' Father, it is very strange. I have done everything I know to do. I have endeavoured to carry out all the church has asked, and yet I have no peace. How can I be sure that God has put away my sins?'

The older priest looked at him compassionately and then exclaimed: ' Surely the blood of Christ ought to count for something.' As though a flash of divine light had entered his soul, the young man's countenance changed. Then he looked up eagerly to exclaim, 'Ah, yes, it counts for everything. I can trust that.'

And it was evident afterwards that his soul had entered into peace.

(Rom. 3. 20,24; 1 John 1. 7)

89 **Blue Eyes or Brown.** Amy Carmichael of Dohnanur, India, a great missionary, a poetess and the author of many interesting missionary books, was the eldest of a family of seven. While still very young, she began to notice that her godly mother's prayers meant something, for God heard and answered them. She decided to try an experiment in prayer on her own. She greatly admired her mother's beautiful blue eyes and was very disappointed that her own were brown. So one night, full of hope, she knelt down and asked God to change her eyes and make them blue instead of brown. Early next morning, her heart pounding with excitement, she pushed a chair over to the dressing table and clambered up to examine her new blue eyes in the mirror. She nearly fell off the chair with disappointment when she found that her eyes were still brown. It was no good: God had not answered her prayer. Then she seemed to hear a quiet voice saying to her, ' God said "NO!"—isn't "No" an answer?' Someone has put this incident into verse:

> Just a tiny little child three years old
> And a mother with a heart all of gold:
> Often did that mother say
> Jesus hears us when we pray,
> For He's never far away,
> And He always answers.
>
> Now that tiny little child had brown eyes,
> And she wanted blue instead, like the skies;
> For her mother's eyes were blue
> Like forget-me-nots. She knew
> All her mother said was true;
> Jesus always answered.
>
> So she prayed for two blue eyes, said ' Goodnight!'
> Went to sleep in deep content and delight;
> Woke up early, climbed a chair
> By a mirror: where, oh where
> Could the blue eyes be? Not there!
> Jesus hadn't answered;
>
> Hadn't answered her at all. Nevermore
> Could she pray. Her eyes were brown as before.
> Did a little soft wind blow?
> Came a whisper sweet and low,
> ' Jesus answered: He said "NO!"
> Isn't "no" an answer?'

Many years later, when as a missionary she worked among the brown-eyed Indian women and girls, she thanked the Lord that He had said ' No ' to her prayer and had not given her blue eyes. Sometimes the Lord says ' Not yet!', sometimes ' Not your way!' Sometimes He says, ' Yes, of course!' and sometimes He says ' No!' He always gives us what is best for us, as Amy Carmichael proved when she went to serve Him in India.

90 **Boat—Peter's.**

> I owned a boat a while ago
> And sailed the morning sea without a fear;
> And whither any breeze might fairly blow
> I steered my little craft afar or near;
> Mine was the boat and mine the air,
> And mine the sea without a care.

*My boat became my place of nightly toil.*
*I sailed at sunset for the fishing ground.*
*At morn the boat was freighted with the spoil*
*That my all-conquering work and skill had*
*    found;*
*Mine was the boat and mine the net,*
*And mine the power and skill to get.*

*One day there passed along the silent shore,*
*As I my net was casting in the sea,*
*A man who spoke as never man before:*
*I followed Him: new life began in me;*
*Mine was the boat but His the voice,*
*And His the call, but mine the choice.*

*Oh! 'twas a fearful night out on the lake,*
*And all my skill availed not at the helm—*
*Till Him asleep I wakened, crying, ' Take,*
*Take Thou command lest waters overwhelm;'*
*Mine was the boat but His the sea,*
*And His the peace o'er all and me.*

*Once from this boat He taught the curious*
*    throng,*
*Then bade me let down nets into the sea;*
*I murmured but obeyed: nor was it long*
*Before the catch amazed and humbled me.*
*His was the boat and His the skill,*
*And His the catch, and His my will.*

(Matt. 4. 18-20; Mark 4. 37-41; Luke 5. 1-9)

## 91   Bondslave of Jesus Christ.

*I'm but a slave!*
*I have no freedom of my own:*
*I cannot choose the smallest thing,*
*Nor e'en my way.*
*I am a slave!*
*Kept to do the bidding of my Master:*
*He can call me, night and day.*
*Were I a servant, I could claim wages,*
*Freedom—sometimes anyway.*
*But I was bought!*
*Blood was the price my Master paid for me,*
*And I am now His slave,*
*And evermore will be.*
*He takes me here, He takes me there;*
*He tells me what to do.*
*I just obey—that's all;*
*I trust Him too.*

M. W. Booth
(Rom. 1. 1; 1 Cor. 6. 19,20; 1 Pet. 1. 18,19)

## 92   Book—The Agnostic's.

Lew Wallace, the author of *Ben Hur*, told this story to a friend. He said:

I had always been an agnostic and denied Christianity. Robert C. Ingersoll was one of my most intimate friends. It was generally known that I was an agnostic. I had been appointed Governor of Arizona, and after serving my term, was returning East together with Ingersoll. As we neared St. Louis, in conversation on ordinary things, we both noticed a forest of church spires. ' Isn't it a shame ', Ingersoll remarked, ' that so many apparently intelligent people continue to believe the foolish doctrines that are being taught under these church spires? When will the time arrive that the teachings of the so-called Bible will be thrown out as foolishness?'

Suddenly Ingersoll looked me in the face and said: ' See here, Wallace, you are a learned man and a thinker. Why don't you gather material and write a book to prove the falsity concerning Jesus Christ, that no such man has ever lived, much less the author of the teachings found in the New Testament. Such a book would make you famous. It would be a masterpiece, and a way of putting an end to the foolishness about the so-called Christ and the Saviour of the world.'

This thought made a deep impression on me and we discussed the possibility of such a book. I said I would try to gather material and have it published as the masterpiece of my life and the crowning glory of my work.

I went to Indianapolis, my home, and told my wife my purpose. She was a member of the Methodist Church and naturally did not like my plan. But I decided to do it and began to collect material in libraries here, and in the old world. I gathered everything over that period in which Jesus Christ, according to saying, should have lived. Several years were spent in this work. When I had accumulated all possible proof I began to write the book. I had written nearly four chapters when it became clear to me that Jesus Christ was just as real a personality as Socrates, Plato, Caesar and other ancient men. The conviction became certainty. I knew that Jesus Christ had lived on earth because of the facts connected with the period in which He had lived.

I was in an uncomfortable position. I had begun to write a book to prove that no such person as Jesus Christ had ever lived on earth. Now I was face to face with the fact that He was just as historic a personage as Julius Caesar, Mark Antony, Virgil, Dante, and a host of other men who had lived in the olden days. I asked myself candidly—If He was a real person (and there was no doubt) was He not then also the Son of God and the Saviour of the world? Gradually the consciousness grew that, since Jesus Christ was a real person, He probably was the One He claimed to be. The conviction became so strong that one night it grew into certainty.

I fell on my knees to pray for the first time in my life, and I asked God to reveal Himself to me, forgive my sins and help me to become a follower of Christ. Towards morning the light broke into my soul. I went into my bedroom, woke my wife and told her that I had received Jesus Christ as my Lord and Saviour. ' O Lew,' she said, ' I have prayed for this ever since you told me of your purpose to write this book—that you would find Him while you wrote it!'

Pilgrim Tract Society

## 93   Books—The Making of.

The present age is an era of books. The world is being flooded with all kinds of literature. Solomon said, ' Of the making of books there is no end.' This is not to despise books or the messages they seek to convey, but there is a need to keep books in their proper place.

That man of God, J. N. Darby, said near the end of his life that it was the Scriptures that gave him authority to keep his small library. There had been a period in his life when he had thought of dispensing with all his books and concentrating only on the Bible. At that particular time God spoke to him through the words of Paul in 2 Tim. 4. 13.

J. S. McNaught

**94  Bottle in the Smoke.** ' I am become like a bottle in the smoke.' This is an Oriental metaphor. The Asian peasantry keep many articles, dry or liquid, in leather bottles of kid or goatskin for security, and suspend them from the roof or hang them against the walls. Hanging there, they become black with smoke in rooms that have no chimneys. The smoke escapes through an aperture in the roof or by the door. The bottles feel the full influence of the smoke as minute particles of soot rest on them. When empty of solids or liquids, they appear shrunk and shrivelled.

This is the picture that the Psalmist gives of himself in Psalm 119. His soul is faint yet he hopes in the Lord; his eyes fail, yet he finds comfort from the Lord: his days on earth are few, yet each day his strength is renewed. When he encounters trials and endures troubles, he is enriched by testing and can say, ' I do not forget Thy commandments.'

*The path of sorrow, and that path alone,*
*Leads to the land where sorrow is unknown.*

(Ps. 119. 83)

**95  Bought with a Price.** A lady went into a hotel in Glasgow, Scotland, shut her bedroom door and turned on the gas to end her miserable life. Then she saw a book lying on the table, took it up, opened it at random and began to read. It was a Gideon New Testament. She read one sentence, then got up, went to the gas, turned it off, opening the door to let the fumes escape. The words she had read were, ' Ye are not your own: ye are bought with a price.'
(1 Cor. 6. 19,20)

**96  Boys—Essay on.** Boys are found everywhere—on top of, underneath, inside of, swinging from, running around or jumping to. Mothers love them, little girls hate them, older sisters and brothers tolerate them, adults ignore them, and heaven protects them.

A boy is Truth with dirt on its face, Beauty with a cut on its finger, Wisdom with bubble gum in its hair and the Hope of the future with a frog in its pocket.

A boy is composite. He has the appetite of a horse, the digestion of a sword swallower, the energy of a pocket-size atomic bomb, the curiosity of a cat, the lungs of a dictator, the imagination of a Bunyan, the shyness of a violet, the audacity of a steel trap, the enthusiasm of a fire-cracker; and when he makes something he has five thumbs on each hand.

A boy is a magical creature. You can lock him out of your workshop but you can't lock him out of your heart. You can get him out of your study but you can't get him out of your mind. Might as well give up—he is your captor, your jailer—a freckle-faced, pint-sized, cat-chasing bundle of noise. But when you come home at night with only the shattered pieces of your hopes and dreams, he can mend them like new with two magic words—' Hi dad!'

Alan Beck

(Gen. 48. 9)

**97  Brahmin's Testimony—A.** ' I am Babudas Masih, son of the late Pujari Brahmin of Hamirpur, U.P. After passing intermediate examination, I went to Benares to study Hindu religious books, and to be taught in the ordinances of that religion. After I returned from there, I used to be engaged in reciting Ramayana, etc., along with my father. Later we got settled in Saugor District, my father being Priest of a temple. I was not only an orthodox Hindu but was also anti-Christian.

' Once when I went to Bhopal in connection with my job some Christians were selling gospels and distributing tracts in the midst of a crowd. From them I bought a copy of John's gospel and received a tract, the title of which was "Repent or Perish", which I read through. While reading John's gospel I happened to notice Ch. 1. 12 as well as 3. 16. Then I said to myself that if I succeed in completing my work today, I will meet the addressee. By God's grace my work was completed and I went to Bhopal in search of Mr K. M. Mathai. There I was given a New Testament and also the addresses of M/s Gulam Masih and T. A. Kurien at Saugor. I did in due course meet with them for acquiring knowledge of the Bible. In those days I had made a comparative study of Christianity and Hinduism. I did seek salvation but could not find it till I was taught by Brother T. A. Kurien to accept Jesus as Lord according to the Bible.

'As soon as I became a Christian I was ousted from my post as a Pujari. People in my locality requested the police that an enquiry be made concerning me. I was thus summoned to the police station, where I got a good opportunity to witness for the Lord. After this, they sent a wire to my uncle, who came with the family to reconvert me to Hinduism. But when he didn't succeed, he pestered me for about a week. He even conspired to take my life. But the Lord delivered me from all dangers. My uncle then forced me to sign a typed paper which turned out to be my resignation from office. He also auctioned my personal properties, took away money, clothes and all personal belongings except a small bag in which I had hidden my Bible.

'At last he decided to take me to Hamirpur in a train which providentially halted at a place from where I escaped and took shelter with Brother T. A. Kurien at Saugor. But as there was cause to fear, by night he took me to Indore, from where I witnessed for the Lord in those regions along with other brethren. I was then baptised at Indore.'

(Ps. 119. 59)

**98  Brand out of the Fire.** A man with whom I spent my apprenticeship was the most blasphemous person I have ever met, though his wife and son were both active Christians. In many ways he made my life a misery during those apprenticeship years. He boasted openly that he had lived in defiance of God all his life and would never change his attitude so long as there was breath in his body. Even hardened sinners were shocked by his defiance of God and blasphemous language. Then he took ill and knew in his heart that his end was near. In fear and trembling I visited him and asked if I could read to him. To my surprise he agreed to this, and we read Psalm 103, the psalm through which God had spoken to me at my own conversion. 'As the heaven is high above the earth, so great is His mercy toward them that fear Him. As far as the east is removed from the west, so far hath He removed our transgressions from us.' That night the old blasphemer could not rest till he had a talk with his son and trusted the Saviour: and next day he had gone into eternity. The text at the graveside was most apt: 'Is not this a brand plucked out of the fire?' He had asked that all his old associates should be told about his repentance and faith and be urged to learn from his example that it is possible to wait too long before accepting the mercy of the Lord.

' *He rescued me, He rescued me—*
*A brand from the burning He rescued me.*'

(Zech. 3. 2)        Alex Allan

**99  Bread of Life.** Robert E. Speer tells the story of a boy at Yale who inherited a small fortune. Not wanting to waste it, he went to one of his old friends, a wise and successful man, and asked him for his advice. How should he invest his life and this money of his?

' My son!' said the old man, ' I will tell you what to do. Attach yourself to one of the great feeding interests. Don't manufacture things that can be dispensed with. There will come times when men will give up their luxuries, but there never will come a time when men will not have to eat. And if you want to be identified with one of the secure interests of mankind, attach yourself to one of those which feed the hunger of the world.'

That is more than good business advice: it is a Christian challenge. The world is hungry: feed it!

There is a greater hunger than the hunger for bread. It is the hunger of the soul for Christ, the living Bread; and two thirds of all the people who die, die in that hunger, and without Him. That is the greatest single need in the world today. Give your life to feeding the hunger of the world.     Samuel Hugh Moffat

(Mark 6. 37; John 6. 35, 48, 51, 57, 58)

**100  Breastplate—The High Priest's.** Scholars tell us the Hebrew word for ' breastplate ' means ' ornament '. It certainly had twelve brilliant jewels in it. Christ first beautifies us, then wears us on His breast ' for glory and beauty ', as He says, ' Behold I and the children which God hath given me.'

Dr Andrew Bonar says, ' It would almost seem as if the breastplate of the high priest pointed back to Eden, promising to Israel readmission into its glories.

*On His heart, amidst the glory,*
*Bearing all our grief and care,*
*Every burden, ere we feel it,*
*Weighed and measured in His prayer.*

*As of old the Man of sorrows*
*Pleads before the Father's face,*
*Knowing all the needed solace,*
*Pleading all the needed grace.*

*We, so faithless and so weary,*
*Serving with impatient will,*
*He, unwearied in our service,*
*Gladly ministering still.*

(Exod. 28. 15; Ezek. 28. 13; Heb. 2. 13, 17, 18)

**101  Brightness of His Glory.** ' I should like to see your God,' said the Emperor Trajan to a Jewish Rabbi. ' No mortal eye can look upon Him,' the rabbi replied. When the Emperor insisted, the rabbi said, ' Well, suppose we begin by looking on one of His ambassadors '; and bade the Emperor gaze at the midday sun in a cloudless sky. ' I cannot,' the emperor confessed, ' the light dazzles me.' ' If, then,' said the rabbi, ' you cannot endure the glory of one of His creatures, how could you behold the unclouded glory of the Creator?'

(Acts 26. 13; 2 Cor. 4. 6; Heb. 1. 3)

**102  Brother—A Beloved.** Under the title *Brother Beloved*, Frank Holmes has beautifully portrayed the holy life of the late Robert Cleaver Chapman of Barnstaple.

In the following brief verses, another beloved brother, now with the Lord—D. Bell of Winnipeg, Canada—has portrayed the character of an unnamed brother, greatly beloved.

*A beloved brother, what a precious title*
*For one who once had trod the downward road!*
*Rebellious, stubborn, self-willed and defiant,*
*Now justified and made a child of God.*

*A beloved brother, what a blest relation*
*For one who was a sinner far from God!*
*But now made nigh, redeemed, all sins forgiven,*
*Yea, reconciled and saved through Jesus' blood.*

*A beloved brother, what a gracious record*
*For one who laboured 'mongst the saints*
*of God!*
*Who sought to build them up in things most*
*holy,*
*Instructing always from the sacred Word.*

*A beloved brother, what a goal to aim at,*
*To be beloved of all who love the Lord!*
*Because of deep, sincere and real devotion*
*To Him who sits upon the throne, adored.*

*A beloved brother, what a commendation*
*From Him who sees and knows as none can*
*know!*
*Lord, give us grace to have this aspiration*
*That we may more into Thine image grow!*
(Eph. 6. 21; Rom. 16. 5,12; Col. 4. 9,14;
Philem. 16; 1 Tim. 6. 2)

**103 Brothers—Pair of.** There were two boys
in the Taylor family. The older said he must
make a name for the family, so he turned to
politics, and Parliament and fame. His younger
brother gave his life to the service of Christ, so
he became a missionary to China. Hudson
Taylor, founder of the China Inland Mission,
died, beloved and known in many countries.
The account of the other, his brother, was
summed up in the Encyclopaedia in these words,
'the brother of J. Hudson Taylor'.
(Heb. 11. 5)

**104 Brothers—Two.** On a motor drive near
Guelph, Ontario, my host pointed to a cemetery
and said, 'David Livingstone's brother is buried
there.' I said, 'I did not know David Livingstone
had a brother.' 'Yes,' he said, 'John Livingstone
died one of the richest men in Ontario. The two
boys grew up together in a simple Scottish home
under the same instruction. Both made decisions affecting their whole lives. John lived in
luxury and died in wealth. Dr David Livingstone lived for God, accomplished great things
for God at great personal sacrifice, and died in
a miserable hut in the heart of the dark continent. When John died, there was a brief note in
the newspapers telling that he was the brother of
David Livingstone, the well-known missionary
in Africa.'

A.N.

In the days of Jeremiah the prophet, Baruch,
his secretary, wrote down the revelations the
weeping prophet received from God and went
out with the scroll to publish abroad the Lord's
message to His people, sharing the prophet's
persecution and penury. His brother Seraiah,
the king's chief chamberlain, is mentioned
briefly in a few verses in Jeremiah, Chapter 51;
Baruch occupies a prominent place in the
narrative in Chapters 32, 36, 43 and 45.

**105 Brothers—Two Saved.** D. L. Moody,
the great evangelist, had been deeply attached
to his brother, and when he died the evangelist
went to pay his last tribute. With tears streaming from the eyes, D. L. Moody said:
'Friends and neighbours, I thank God that
He ever gave me a brother. I thank Him also
that He permitted me to lead him to Jesus. I
thank God that I can now look down into
his face and know that I shall see him again.'
Standing for a moment with hands uplifted,
he suddenly shouted in triumphant tones in the
hearing of the crowd gathered around him, 'O
death, where is thy sting? O grave, where is thy
victory?'
(1 Cor. 15. 55)

**106 Brothers—Unbelievers.** The brother of
Colonel Ingersoll, the great infidel orator, died;
and, being greatly attached to his brother,
Ingersoll went to pay his last tribute to his
memory. With one hand resting on his brother's
coffin, the tears coursing down his cheeks, he
said:
'Life is a dark and barren valley between the
cold ice-clad peaks of two eternities. We strive
sometimes to look beyond the darkness for the
light. Sometimes we cry for help, but there
comes back to us nothing but the echo of our
own cry.'
Then he bowed his head and sat down weeping.
(Isa. 48. 22)

**107 Brotherhood—The.** On his first visit to
Merrion Hall, Dublin, Henry Moorhouse began
his address in the following strain:
'Beloved friends, this is the first time I have
ever spoken to an audience of rich and learned
people. I don't know how to speak to you,
though I am sure we are all one in the sight of
our God and Father. When I was at home the
other day, a rich lord went with me to the
meeting, and we knelt together in prayer. I said,
"Our Father", and he said "Our Father"; and
he and I were brothers. Soon after I visited a
poor beggar, and he prayed and I prayed. He
said, "Our Father", and I said, "Our Father",
and the beggar and I were brothers. And thus
it is, rich or poor, learned or ignorant, all around
the globe, every believer in the Lord Jesus
Christ is united by an indissoluble bond, one to
the other, to form one brotherhood in Christ.'
(Matt. 23. 8; John 20. 17; 1 Pet. 2. 17)

**108 Builders.** A lady standing in front of a
noble cathedral heard someone behind her say,
'Didn't we do a fine piece of work here?'
Turning round, she saw a man in plain working
clothes and said to him, 'Pray, what did you do
to help?' 'I mixed the mortar across the street
for two years,' was the cheerful reply.
God's work needs cheerful, patient and
diligent mortar mixers. Mixing mortar is one of
the hardest and most disagreeable things to do
in the rearing of a building. But what sort of a
building could be made without mortar?
*Sunday School Times*
(Neh. 4. 17; 1 Cor. 3. 10)

**109 Burden-Bearing.** Henry Moorhouse
was once in very trying circumstances. His
little daughter, who was paralysed, was sitting
in her chair as he entered the house with a
package for his wife. Going up to her and
kissing her, he said, 'Where is Mother?'
'Mother is upstairs,' she replied. 'Well, I have
a package for her.' 'Let me carry the package
to mother,' said his daughter. 'Why, Minnie
dear, how can you carry the package? You
cannot carry yourself.' With a smile on her face
Minnie said, 'Oh no, papa, but you give me the

package and I will carry it, and you will carry me.'

Then the word of the Lord came to Henry Moorhouse that this was just his position in the work in which he was engaged. He was carrying the burden, but was not the Lord carrying him?
*Sunday School Times*

## 110   Burden-Bearing Recompensed.

*All through the desert's sultry day a weary
  load to carry:*
*Who envied them the toilsome way of Kohath
  and Merari?*

*Now priest and ark alike find rest where God
  His temple raises,*
*And they who served with burdens presssed
  now only serve with praises.*

*How perfect are the ways of God! How just
  His compensation!*
*How low the path they humbly trod, how high
  the exaltation!*

*No needless load on thee He'll lay, no
  unrequited sorrow:*
*The burden-bearer of today is the singer of
  tomorrow.*
James S. Tait
(Num. 4. 37; 11. 12; 1 Chron. 6. 31; 1 Pet. 5. 7)

## 111   Burial of a Saintly Leader.

William Pell, a well-known Christian leader, finished his course and went to be with Christ at his earthly home in Grand Rapids, Michigan, U.S.A., on March 30, 1972: ' absent from the body, with the Lord at Home '. Saved in early life, he was baptised soon after conversion, along with his brother Peter who is a very gifted evangelist. Owner and manager of the ' Folio Press ', he produced year after year the Calendar, *Choice Gleanings*, with its interesting and instructive comments on, and illustrations of, the daily texts. In his life he exemplified in a marked degree the meaning of being instant in season and out of season, and always abounding in the work of the Lord. At his burial service a Scottish evangelist living in St. Catharines, Ontario, read the following lines which were found in Will Pell's Bible:

*And, brethren, when you gather
To lay my senseless clay
To rest among the tombstones
Until the break of day,
And when you roll the green turf
Above my lonely bed,
And wake the slumbering echoes
In the city of the dead:*

*Then preach the grace of Jesus
To all who gather round,
And heave no sigh of sorrow
As you lay me in the ground:
But let the praise of Jesus
Upon the winds be borne—
An overture of blessing
On the resurrection morn.*

*So preach the glorious gospel
When you carry forth my bier,
And tell them of the rapture
That left no room for fear,
And point them to the Saviour
Who bore my sins away,
And press them all to meet me
At the breaking of the day.*

(1 Thess. 4. 13-18)

## 112   Called to Preach or?

*The sun blazed down upon the cotton field,
And Sam, poor silly creature,
Said, ' Mother, I won't pick cotton any more
For I'm called to be a preacher.*

*' Last night I watched the clouds go by
And " G.P.C." they were forming,
Which surely stands for " Go, preach Christ ",
So I mustn't neglect the warning.'*

*But his wise old mother shook her head,
Saying, ' Son, you have forgotten
That " G.P.C." can equally stand
For the three words, " Go pick cotton." '*
M. Colley
(1 Cor. 7. 20)

## 113   Calling—The High.

*Child of the eternal Father,
Bride of the eternal Son,
Dwelling-place of God the Spirit,
Thus with Christ made ever one;
Dowered with joy beyond the angels,
Nearest to His throne;
They are ministers attending
His beloved one.*

*Granted all my heart's desire,
All things made my own;
Feared by all the powers of evil,
Fearing God alone;
Walking with the Lord in Glory
Through the courts divine,
Queen within the royal palace,
Christ for ever mine.*

*Say, poor worldling, can it be
That my heart should envy thee?*
Gerhardt Ter Steegen
(Ps. 45. 9)

## 114   Calvary.

*Deepest of mystery,
Record of history,
Purposed and planned in counsels divine;
Human extremity,
Unfailing remedy,
Love evermore in fullness doth shine.*

*Holy and wonderful,
Excellent, beautiful,
' Grace upon grace ' in fullest display;
'Tis indispensable,
Incomprehensible,
Heavenly thoughts in grandest array.*

*Guilt inexcusable,*
*Wrath inescapable,*
*Judgement and death, decided, deserved!*
*Perfect the substitute,*
*Wonderful attribute,*
*Clearing for ever—forgiven, preserved.*

*Mercy so bountiful,*
*Sweetest, unchangeable,*
*Pardon and peace imparted, possessed;*
*Forgiving finally,*
*Receiving joyfully,*
*Blessed redemption—Accepted and blessed!*

*Perfect security,*
*Hope for eternity,*
*Present possession with future in view;*
*'Love to the uttermost',*
*Word of the heavenly host,*
*Ransomed, redeemed and all things made new.*

                                                      **J. H. Bathgate**

(Luke 23. 33)

### 115  Camel—The Kneeling.

*The camel kneels at the close of day,*
*Kneels down upon the sandy plain*
*To have its burden lifted off*
*And rest again.*

*My soul! thou too should'st to thy knees*
*When daylight draweth to a close,*
*And let thy Master lift thy load*
*And grant repose.*

*Else how canst thou tomorrow meet*
*With all tomorrow's work to do,*
*If thou thy burden all the night*
*Dost carry through?*

*The camel kneels at the break of day*
*To have its guide replace the load,*
*And rises up anew to take*
*The desert road.*

*O soul, thou too should'st kneel*
*At morning dawn,*
*That God may give thy daily care,*
*Assured that He no load too great*
*Will make thee bear.*

(Dan. 6. 10; Eph. 3. 14)

### 116  Canon of Scripture.

**The Old Testament.**  'Canon' is derived from the Greek 'Kanon', a rule or measuring line. It signifies the collection of divinely-inspired writings.

The Old Testament was divided by the Jews into three parts: TORAH, the Law: NEBIIM, the Prophets: and KETHUBIM (or Hagiographa), the Holy Writings. The Prophets were in two compartments, the former prophets—Joshua, Judges, Samuel and Kings—and the latter prophets—Isaiah, Jeremiah, Ezekiel and Hosea to Malachi (in one book). The TORAH —the Pentateuch—was the Jewish Bible until the captivity: The NEBIIM—the Prophets, were all convinced that they were Jehovah's spokesmen, the true witnesses for Jehovah to a divine Kingdom among men, the expositors and the exponents of its laws. The prophetic writings were completed about the beginning of the third century B.C. The influx of anti-Jewish Hellenic philosophy and literature after Alexander the Great stimulated Israel to put the Nebiim on the same footing as the Torah. Finally the Kethubim were also included among the divinely-inspired writings. ECCLESIASTICUS, an apocryphal book written about 200 to 180 B.C., refers to the Torah, the Nebiim and portions of the Hagiographa.

When the Christian era began there was already a fixed body of writings called 'SCRIPTURE' recognised to be of divine origin. Our Lord Jesus and His apostles frequently refer to those. Josephus recognised twenty-two sacred books of the Jews as divinely-inspired.

**The New Testament.**  Before A.D. 50 Christian writings began to appear (Luke 1. 1-4). Luke's Gospel was written about A.D. 57.

Recognition of the New Testament Scriptures was in four stages:

i The apostles to A.D. 120. The gospels were well known by the end of the first century. Polycarp, born A.D. 69, makes reference to 18 New Testament books, Hebrews included. The first reference to Mark and Matthew was made by Papias in A.D. 126. He quoted from 1 John and 1 Peter and acknowledged Revelation to be divinely-inspired.

ii A.D. 120-170—Christian writings attacked by heretical writers were defended by Church leaders. Justin Martyr mentioned the Gospels as used on Sundays interchangeably with the prophets. Tatian, a disciple of Justin, wrote a Harmony of the four Gospels, and seems to have known Acts and some of the Epistles.

iii A.D. 170-303—was the rapid expansion of Christianity and the rise of Christian writers in Asia, Egypt and North Africa. Irenaeus alludes to every New Testament book except Philemon, James, 2 Peter, 1 John and Jude. Clement of Alexandria uses all the New Testament books except James, 2 Peter and 3 John; and Origen accepted the divine authority of the same books as Clement did and placed them on equality with the Old Testament Scriptures.

iv A.D. 303-397—The Council of Carthage acknowledged the Gospels, Acts, Paul's Epistles, 1 Peter, 1 John and Revelation. James, 2 Peter and 2 and 3 John were disputed. Athanasius acknowledged all the New Testament books as we have them. The Council of Carthage confirmed them.

### 117  Captain—The Greatest.
When a sixteenth-century sailor who sailed all his life with Sir Francis Drake returned home, someone ridiculed him. 'You haven't much to show for all these years, have you?' Said the sailor, 'No, I haven't much. I've been cold, hungry, desperately frightened often enough in life—even shipwrecked. But I'm sure of one thing—I've been with the greatest captain that ever sailed the seas.'

                                                      *Sunday School Times*

(Heb. 2. 10; 12. 1,2)

                                                      **32**

## 118  Captive Maid—The.

*I'm only a captive Jewish maid*
*From the land of Israel,*
*But for all my humble origin*
*I've a wondrous tale to tell.*

*I lived in a land where God was known*
*Till the Syrians brought me here,*
*For they cruelly raided our Jewish homes*
*And filled our hearts with fear.*

*I felt lonely and strange in an unknown land*
*With a strange new way of life,*
*But I found my work was just to learn*
*To wait on my master's wife.*

*So although the tears would often fall*
*As I thought of my far-off land,*
*I knew the Lord was still my God*
*And would lead me by His hand.*

*Now it came to pass that this Syrian home*
*Was shadowed by tragedy,*
*For my master was suddenly stricken down*
*By the dreaded leprosy.*

*I was grieved when I saw my mistress weep,*
*But prayed for courage to tell*
*That I knew my God could work a cure*
*Through a prophet of Israel.*

*I hoped and prayed that my single words*
*Might be used by God that day,*
*And my heart was light as I watched with joy*
*The procession start on its way.*

*For my master went in his chariot grand*
*With horses and servants too,*
*And travelled to far Samaria*
*With his splendid retinue.*

*It would take too long for me to relate*
*The story they told to me,*
*But I'll simply tell how the cure was wrought*
*That dispelled his leprosy.*

*When the chariot stopped at the prophet's gate,*
*Elisha sent forth his decree:*
*' You must bathe in Jordan seven times*
*To be rid of your leprosy.'*

*My master had hoped for a show of power*
*Befitting his rank and age,*
*But when told to bathe in Jordan's stream*
*He turned away in rage.*

*His servants then, in respectful tones,*
*The prophet's words reviewed,*
*Till my master turned towards Jordan's stream,*
*His anger now subdued.*

*Then seven times Naaman dipped himself—*
*A leper so defiled—*
*When lo! his flesh became pure and clean*
*As that of a little child.*

*Once more to the prophet he repaired*
*The joyful news to tell;*
*' Behold I now know that there is no God*
*Save here in Israel.'*

*My master has now returned to us*
*Full of health and vigour too,*
*And his trust in the God of Israel*
*Is deep and strong and true.*

*Yes, I'm only a captive Jewish maid*
*From a land so far away,*
*But still I can serve my father's God*
*In a simple humble way.*

(2 Kings 5)

## 119  Careful and Troubled.

*Careful and troubled! Is that true of me?*
*Careful and troubled! Why should I be?*
*Faith in His wisdom my Saviour desires;*
*Trust in His guidance He always requires.*
*Careful and troubled! But that is not trust:*
*Trust means to leave all, happen what must:*
*Trust means to live free from worrying care,*
*Casting on Jesus my burden to bear.*
*' Careful and troubled' dishonours His love;*
*Do not His past dealings all faithful prove?*
*' Careful and troubled' dishonours His power:*
*Will not His strength hold hour after hour?*
*Alter your motto, then trouble no more;*
*Go to the book of heavenly lore.*
*' Careful for nothing,' there written I see;*
*Saviour, I thank Thee: Make that true of me.*

(Luke 10. 41; John 14. 1; Phil. 4. 6)

## 120  Cares—Your.

*It is God's will that I should cast*
*My care on Him each day.*
*He also asks me not to cast*
*My confidence away.*
*But oh! how stupidly I act*
*When taken unawares,*
*I cast away my confidence*
*And carry all my cares.*

Paul's and Peter's advice is—' You do all the casting: He will do all the caring.'

*All your anxieties, all your care*
*Bring to the mercy-seat: leave it there.*

(1 Pet. 5. 7)

## 121  Caring for Your Interests.

*' Prepare to leave thy trading and do my work*
*  instead:*
*Prepare to go my errand across the sea,'*
*  she said.*
*' Your Majesty, my fortunes will certainly*
*  decline.'*
*' If you will care for my things, I shall take*
*  care of thine.'*
*So spake in days far distant Elizabeth the*
*  Queen;*
*And often, when discouraged, I contemplate*
*  the scene,*
*For One who is all kingly has made the*
*  promise mine—*
*' If you will care for my things, I shall take*
*  care of thine.'*

(Matt. 6. 33,34)

## 122  Carrying Capacity.

John Rollo tells the story of a customer who one day went into a draper's shop and saw a small boy standing with outstretched arms, while the proprietor of the shop placed package after package from the

shelves into his waiting arms. As the pile grew higher and higher and the weight increased, the customer turned to the boy and said, ' My lad, you'll never be able to carry all that.' Turning round, the boy replied with a smile, ' My father knows how much I can carry.'
(1 Cor. 10. 13)

**123 Challenge.** At Felixstowe a sentry's challenge resulted in the conversion of a sergeant. The fort there was jealously guarded. One day Gipsy Hawkins had been out for a walk and entered the fort by a different route. He was halted by a strange sentry who did not know him. Not having a pass, he was placed in the guard room and the sentry was summoned. The gipsy's credentials were examined and found to be in order, so he was allowed to proceed. Before going, he said to the sergeant, ' Have you got a pass for heaven, Sergeant?' ' I'm afraid not!' was the reply. ' Then you'd better get one at once,' said the gipsy, ' for if they are half as particular there as you are here, you won't stand the ghost of a chance of getting in.' Four days later the sergeant accepted Christ as his Saviour. He gripped the gipsy's hand and said, ' Thank God, I've got my pass for heaven.'

**124 Chamber—A Prophet's.**

*The little chamber ' built upon the wall '*
*With stool and table, candlestick and bed,*
*Where he might kneel in prayer and lay*
*    his head*
*At night or sultry noontide; this was all*
*A prophet's need; but in that chamber small*
*What mighty prayers arose, what grace was*
*    shed!*
*What gifts were given, potent to wake the dead,*
*And from its viewless light a soul recall!*
*And still, what miracles of grace are wrought*
*In many a lonely chamber with closed door,*
*Where God our Father is in secret sought*
*And shows himself in mercy more and more.*

(2 Kings 4. 10; Matt. 6. 6)

**125 Changes and the Unchanging God.**

*Every tide has its ebb and flow,*
*Every sun has its spot*
*Every year has its winter drear,*
*Every copy its blot.*

*Every substance a shadow casts,*
*Every rose has its thorn;*
*Every bee has honey and sting,*
*Every eve has its morn.*

*So every life has its changing moods,*
*Its rise, its flow, its fall;*
*Its light, its shade, its gleam, its gloom,*
*But God is over all.*

                                        Tom Baird

(Mal. 3. 6)

**126 Character—Its Meaning.** The word ' character' comes from a root which means ' to

tear, cleave, cut in, engrave, cut into furrows.' Thus it has come to mean that which is engraved or cut on anything. In life, therefore, it is that which experiences engrave in the soul. We have missed one of the greatest facts in human history if we have not seen that out of the process of pain have sprung the greatest literature, poetry, paintings and philosophies. All have blossomed into the sunlight of beauty out of the darkness of suffering.
                                        F. Cundick

*The mark of rank in nature*
*Is capacity for pain,*
*And the sadness of the singer*
*Makes the sweetness of the strain.*

Patience is seen in Job (James 5. 11): faith in Abraham (Heb. 11. 17): meekness in Moses (Num. 12. 3): prayerfulness in Elijah (James 5. 17,18): wisdom in Solomon (Matt. 12. 42): courage in Daniel (Dan. 6. 10): devotion in John (John 13. 23): boldness in Peter (Acts 2. 14): goodness in Barnabas (Acts 11. 24): eloquence in Apollos (Acts 18. 24): zeal in Paul (Rom. 10. 1).

**127 Charity Begins at Home.** In Texas, U.S.A., they tell the story of the days when the redoubtable Ma Ferguson first entered the political arena. Returning to her home after a succession of stump speeches all over Texas State, she reported to her husband cheerfully, ' Looks as if I'm going to sweep Texas.'
Pa Ferguson, casting his eyes round the room, suggested, ' How about starting with this living room?' ' Beginning at Jerusalem ' (Luke 24. 47), the early Christians ' turned the world upside down ' (Acts 17. 6).

**128 Cheer—Everyday.**

*We have nothing to fear*
*Though the journey be long,*
*Though our weakness be great*
*And our enemies strong.*

*There is nothing to fear;*
*Perfect love claims the right*
*To direct us by day*
*And defend us by night.*

*He knoweth our frame,*
*Counts it nothing but dust,*
*But He calls us by name*
*And delights in our trust.*

*He sees all that's future,*
*Understands all that's past,*
*And knows how much longer*
*The journey will last.*

*For our comfort He'll care*
*Every step of the road,*
*Till His glory we share*
*In the house of our God.*

*Though some of His ways*
*May be past finding out,*
*The thought of His love*
*Must exclude every doubt.*

*These myst'ries, when solved*
*In His presence above,*
*Will but add further charms*
*To the story of love.*

George Cutting

(Matt. 14. 27)

**129  Cheque—God's Blank.**  Dr Wilbur Chapman in a time of great personal sorrow took a trip into the far West. One of his elders, a banker, came to see him, and as he was taking his leave slipped a bit of paper into Dr Chapman's hand. It was a cheque made out in his name and signed by the banker, but there was no amount in the figures' column. 'Do you mean you are giving me a signed blank cheque to be filled in as I please?' asked Dr Chapman. 'Yes!' replied the banker. 'I did not know how much you might need and I want you to draw any amount that will meet your needs.' Dr Chapman did not use the cheque but it gave him the happy comfortable feeling that he had millions at his disposal. God has given us a signed blank cheque in Philippians 4. 19.

**130  Child Training.**  Years ago Lord Shaftesbury said, 'Give me a generation of Christian mothers and I shall undertake to change the face of society in twelve months.' The parents of Samuel were both on speaking terms with God. A little fellow was once asked why he was such a model of behaviour in the Chapel service, and answered, 'That's easy. My father is on speaking terms with God and my mother is on spanking terms with me.' Sometimes the order is reversed.

A man who attained a high position in life attributed his success to two factors. He said, 'I was brought up at the knees of a devoted mother and across the knees of a determined father.' It has been said that a child's character can be improved by a pat on the back provided that pat is administered often enough, hard enough and low enough.

(1 Sam. 1. 20,21; Prov. 13. 24; Eph. 6. 4)

**131  Christ All-Sufficient.**  The Christ of the Father's throne, the Christ of the central cross, the Christ of the empty tomb, is sufficient for all our need and meets every circumstance. We have learned by experience His eternal power and Godhead. We acknowledge His strong government. We rely upon His intercession. We seek to follow in His steps. We learn to think His thoughts. His glory is our triumphant joy. His coming again is our hope. His everlasting kingdom is our reward.

A. C. Rose

(1 Cor. 1. 30)

*This hath He done, and shall we not adore*
  *Him?*
*This shall He do, and can we still despair?*
*Come, let us quickly fling ourselves before Him,*
*Cast at His feet the burden of our care;*
*Flash from our eyes the glow of our*
  *thanksgiving,*

*Glad and regretful, confident and calm.*
*Then through all life and what is after living,*
*Thrill to the tireless music of a Psalm.*
*Yea, through life, death, through sorrow and*
  *through sinning*
*He shall suffice us, for He hath sufficed;*
*Christ is the end, for Christ is the beginning,*
*Christ the beginning for the end is Christ.*

F. W. Myers

(Jude 24)

**132  Christ—Consider.**

*Consider Him; let Christ thy pattern be,*
*And know that He hath apprehended thee*
*To share His very life, His power divine,*
*And in the likeness of thy Lord to shine.*
*And thus transformed, illumined thou shalt be,*
*And Christ's own image shall be seen in thee.*

*Marvel not that Christ in glory*
*All my inmost heart hath won—*
*Not a star to cheer my darkness*
*But a light beyond the sun.*
*All below lies dark and shadowed,*
*Nothing there to claim my heart*
*Save the lonely path of sorrow*
*Where of old He walked apart.*

*I have seen the face of Jesus—*
*Tell me naught of aught beside:*
*I have heard the voice of Jesus!*
*All my soul is satisfied*
*In the radiance of the glory*
*First I saw His blessed face,*
*And for ever shall that glory*
*Be my home, my dwelling-place.*

(2 Cor. 3. 18; 4. 6; Phil. 2. 15; 3. 12)

**133  Christ—Greatness of.**  Christ's claims for Himself are of the profoundest importance. He claimed to transcend the Mosaic Law (Matt. 5. 21,22,27,28). He continuously preached Himself. He promised that prayer offered in His name would be answered (John 14. 13). He declared His pre-existence (John 8. 58). He claimed to be Lord of the realms of death. He invited men to trust in Him as they trusted in God (John 14. 1). He said that love of Him was proof that one was a child of God (John 8. 42). He affirmed that no one knew God but Himself and those to whom he revealed Him (Matt. 11. 27). He accepted the confessions of Nathanael and Peter that He was the Son of God. He said that whoever had seen Him had seen the Father (John 14. 9,10). He affirmed that He had the power to forgive sins and to give eternal life (John 10. 28). He claimed absolute authority for His teaching. He declared that He had universal power (Matt. 28. 18), and He asserted that God and He were one (John 10. 30).

No one in history, unless blasphemously, has ever made such claims; and if they be not true He Himself was the greatest of blasphemers.

W. Graham Scroggie

He wrote on Bethlehem the story of His birth, on Nazareth the story of His Manhood, on the mountain side the story of His prayers, on Capernaum the story of His mighty works, on Olivet the story of His tears, on Gethsemane the story of a broken heart, on Calvary the story of a finished work, on the throne of God the story of the world's redemption, and He writes on human hearts the story of divine love and peace.

### 134 Christ—Greatness of.

*Christ for sickness, Christ for health,*
*Christ for poverty, Christ for wealth,*
*Christ for joy and Christ for sorrow,*
*Christ today and Christ tomorrow;*
*Christ my life and Christ my light,*
*Christ for morning, noon and night,*
*Christ when all around gives way,*
*Christ my everlasting stay.*
*Christ my righteousness divine,*
*Christ for me, for Christ is mine:*
*Christ supreme from shore to shore,*
*Christ who all things will restore*
*Christ of God, oh glorious sight!*
*Christ the Head in glory bright,*
*Christ my song, my joy shall be,*
*Christ the great I AM. 'Tis He*
*Now and through eternity.*

         Thomas Holliday (abbreviated)

(Rom. 9. 5)

### 135 Christ Only, for Salvation.

In the dark ages a man called Antonio Palerio wrote a book entitled *The Benefits of the Death of Christ*. He was arrested and tried for heresy. The inquisitors said, ' We shall ask him three questions, that in his answers he may have every opportunity to say something that will exalt the Church.' So they asked him, ' What is the first means of salvation?' He replied, ' Christ!' ' And what is the second means of salvation?' To this he gave the same answer—' Christ.' Once more they enquired, ' What is the third means of salvation?' The brave confessor answered the third time—'Christ.' 'Take him away,' they said, ' and burn him: he is a heretic.' But was he?

                       T. H. Lyttle

(Acts 4. 12)

### 136 Christ—The Living.

For five or six nights in succession, a young Jew had attended Gospel meetings conducted by the Armenian preacher and hymn-writer, A. H. Ackley. One night he stayed behind for a conversation. ' Why should I worship a dead Jew?' he asked. Mr. Ackley replied, ' He lives! I tell you He is not dead, but lives here and now. Jesus Christ is more alive today than ever before. I can prove it by my own experience as well as by the testimony of thousands of others.' Later he wrote the hymn—' He lives! He lives! Christ Jesus lives today.'

(Rev. 1. 18)

### 137 Christ—The Living.

*' So the Nazarene is dead,'*
*Caiaphas the high priest said.*
*' His wonder-working days are o'er:*
*He will trouble us no more.*
*May blasphemers such as He*
*Perish on the shameful tree,*
*And our holy temple law*
*Be kept free from every flaw!*
*For the temple must hold sway*
*Till heaven and earth shall pass away.*
*So the Nazarene is dead,'*
*Caiaphas the high priest said.*

*' So the Nazarene is dead',*
*In his palace Pilate said.*
*' Good His words and just His life,*
*But the priests who stirred up strife*
*Said His followers will be*
*From Imperial Rome set free.*
*Vain their plotting and their care:*
*All—the yoke of Rome must bear,*
*Rome that will for ever stand*
*Mighty Lord of every land.*
*So the Nazarene is dead,'*
*Pilate in his palace said.*

*The temple now has passed away;*
*Ended Rome's Imperial sway;*
*But the Nazarene still lives—*
*Peace to myriad souls He gives,*
*Lives in gentle words and deeds,*
*In all that meets the spirit's needs.*
*And the Cross on which He died*
*By His death is sanctified.*
*Hosts in many lands proclaim—*
*Christ is risen: praise His name!*
*In such faithful hearts is seen*
*The ever-living Nazarene.*
*Priest and Pilate both have said*
*That the Nazarene is dead.*
*False their wisdom, false their lore—*
*Jesus lives for evermore.*

(Rev. 1. 18; Heb. 7. 25; Gal. 2. 20)

### 138 Christian—A Committed.

Jimmy was a fine Christian lad who got an after-school job in a grocery store. One day a customer entered and, after making a purchase of fruit, whispered, ' Throw in a few extra. The boy who was here before used to give me a large portion in return for a tip from me!' ' No!' said Jimmy, ' I can't do that: the boss wouldn't approve.' ' But,' said the man, ' the boss isn't in.' ' O yes, He is,' said Jimmy, ' my boss is always in. You see, I'm a Christian.'

(Acts 6. 3)

### 139 Christian—A Consistent.

*Could I be called a Christian if everybody*
   *knew*
*My secret thoughts and failings, and every-*
   *thing I do?*
*Oh! could they see the likeness of Christ*
   *in me each day*
*Or could they hear Him speaking in every*
   *word I say?*

*Could I be called a Christian if other folk
could know
That I am found in places where Jesus would
not go?
Oh, could they hear His echo in every song
I sing?
In eating, drinking, dressing—is Christ in
everything?
Could I be called a Christian if judged by
what I read,
By all my recreations, and every thought
and deed?
Could I be counted Christlike as I now
work and play—
Unselfish, kind, forgiving to others every day?*

(Col. 3. 22,23; Acts 11. 26; 1 Pet. 2. 9; 4. 16)

## 140   Christian—A True.

*He has a mind and knows it;
He has a will and shows it;
He sees the way and goes it;
He draws the line and toes it.*

*He has the chance and takes it,
A friendly hand and shakes it,
A rule and never breaks it.*

*He loves the truth, stands by it
Whoever may deny it
Or openly defy it.*

*He hears a lie and slays it;
He owes a debt and pays it;
And, as I've heard him phrase it,
He knows the game and plays it.*

*He walks the path his Saviour trod
And grasps the loving hand of God.*

(1 Cor. 3. 23)

## 141   Christian Living.

*Christ has no hands but our hands to do His
work today;
He has no feet but our feet to lead men in
the way;
He has no tongue but our tongues to tell men
how He died;
He has no help but our help to bring them
to His side.*

*We are the only Bible the careless world
will read;
We are the sinner's gospel, we are the
scoffer's creed;
We are the Lord's last message given in deed
and word.
What if the type is crooked? What if the
print is blurred?*

(2 Cor. 3. 2,3)

## 142   Christians in the Early Church.
In the second or third century the following was written in a letter to Diognetus: 'They (the Christians) live, each in his native land but as though they were not really at home there. They share in all the duties like citizens and suffer all hardships like strangers. Every foreign land is for them a fatherland and every fatherland a foreign country... They dwell on earth, but they are citizens of heaven. They obey the laws men make, but their lives are better than the laws ... In a word, what the soul is to the body, Christians are to the world. The soul is distributed to every member of the body, and Christians are scattered in every city of the world. The soul dwells in the body, and yet it is not the body.'
(John 17. 16)

## 143   Christianity—True or False?
In his autobiography, *Time Remembered*, the late Canon Anthony Deane recalls his undergraduate days at Cambridge. For a while it seemed to him that the only wise course was to keep an open mind about Christianity. He refused to come to a decision: he would not commit himself: but, when he gave the whole matter deeper consideration, the attitude of neutrality that he proposed to adopt seemed ridiculous. Christianity was either true or false. If true, it mattered more than anything else in the world. If false, the sooner a person abandoned it the better. As a mere matter of common sense, it was essential to come to a definite decision.

That was what the Spirit of God led him to do. He accepted Christianity by accepting Christ: he acknowledged it was true by owning Christ as Lord.
(1 John 5. 20)

## 144   Christmas
is celebrated the world over, but millions who celebrate the day are ignorant of its meaning.

A young woman went into a bookshop in Kenya and was looking through the Christmas cards. Suddenly she threw down the one she held in her hand and said to her friend as she stamped angrily out of the shop, 'Imagine bringing religion into Christmas!'

Two women were viewing the window of a departmental store in which there was a display of Christmas gifts and in the centre a painting of the 'young child', Jesus. One remarked to the other, 'I suppose those religious fanatics are going to try to cram Christianity into Christmas and spoil our fun.'
(Luke 2. 11)

## 145   Christmas and our Calendar.
Dr Charles S. Robinson once asked a prominent business man, 'What does Christ mean to you?' He replied, 'I never think of Jesus Christ.' 'When were you born?' The man gave the date. 'B.C. or A.D.?' The question brought him into confusion, for he had been dating his letters with dates that commemorated the first Christmas when Jesus Christ was born, yet gave no thought to the Person from whose advent into the world those dates were calculated.
(Matt. 1. 18-21; 1 Tim. 1. 15)

## 146 Citizens of Heaven.

*We are citizens of heaven!*
*And as one who has no ear*
*For the turmoil of the journey*
*When the home he loves is near,*
*One whose step is onward hasting*
*Where his heart went long before,*
*We are now in spirit dwelling*
*Where earth's discord all is o'er.*

*All our longing and endeavour*
*Is to reach Him whom we love;*
*'Tis Himself our hearts are set on*
*Who first drew our hearts above:*
*What alone we count as pleasure*
*Is to lean on Jesus' breast:*
*All things here may fade and perish;*
*We press onward to our rest.*

*'Tis the love of Christ attracts us*
*Like a magnet to His heart;*
*On the wings of faith borne upward,*
*Lord! we see Thee as Thou art.*
*All our joys and tribulation*
*Now are open in Thy sight;*
*All our life and conversation*
*Soon shall be declared in light.*

*What if men proclaim it madness*
*Not to seek a portion here?*
*We can bear it with all gladness*
*And endure the worldling's jeer:*
*For the One soon coming for us*
*Died from earth to set us free.*
*We are the citizens of heaven*
*Where with Christ we soon shall be.*

(Phil. 3. 20)

## 147 City Foursquare—The.

*They tell me of a country beyond the starry*
*skies*
*Where 'mid celestial glories a foursquare city*
*lies;*
*Its wall is built of jasper; its street is paved*
*with gold;*
*Its wonder and its beauties can never half*
*be told.*
*It is God's 'holy City' eternal, pure and fair,*
*Where shadows never darken and night is*
*never there;*
*And nothing that defileth can ever enter in,*
*No sickness, death or sorrow, no taint or*
*stain of sin.*
*No sad farewells are spoken; no heartaches,*
*cares or fears;*
*And God from all our faces will wipe away*
*all tears.*
*We'll meet again our loved ones who have*
*gone on before*
*And now are watching, waiting, upon that*
*further shore.*
*There wind no lonely pathways or mountains*
*steep to climb,*
*That foursquare city's builded beyond the*
*hills of Time.*
*Unheard the noise of battle and stilled the*
*cannon's roar,*

*Earth's foes for ever vanquished—there shall*
*be war no more.*
*But this would not be heaven if Jesus were*
*not there,*
*The chiefest of ten thousand, the Fairest*
*of the fair.*
*In His effulgent glory and seated on His*
*throne,*
*The Lamb of God, all worthy, is worshipped*
*by His own.*

(Heb. 11. 10; Rev. 21. 10-27)

148 **City—The Pilgrim's.** God has a path for heaven-bound pilgrims. Many have found it and by faith trodden it. In Hebrews 11, where Old Testament saints have a memorial before God, their immortal names are enshrined. They would tell us that the treasure they found in divine companionship cannot be valued—no, not with the gold of Ophir. They estimated that the reproach of Christ far outweighed the world at its best. What was all earthly status to them? Their far-seeing eye had espied the city which hath the foundations whose architect and builder is God. This is our path in the land wherein we are strangers, and it leads to the ' land that is fairer than day '.

Franklin Ferguson

The dwellers in that city enjoy restfulness from labour (Rev. 14. 13), clearness of vision (Rev. 22. 4), fullness of knowledge (1 Cor. 13. 12), holiness of environment (Rev. 21. 27), painlessness of condition (Rev. 21. 4), busyness in service (Rev. 22. 3) and brightness of glory (Rev. 22. 5).

*We've no abiding city as through the world*
*we roam;*
*We are but pilgrims travelling on to reach*
*our heavenly home.*
*We seek a city out of sight, for this is not*
*our rest:*
*We long to lay our weary heads upon our*
*Saviour's breast.*
*Our city is both bright and fair: there all is*
*joy and peace.*
*There no cold wintry blasts can blow: there*
*storms for ever cease.*
*There billows all are hushed to rest and no*
*more tears are shed:*
*There we shall never part again or weep*
*above our dead.*

149 **Claims of Christ—The.** A raging fire was sweeping through a humble dwelling and the clang of the fire-engine mingled with the shouts and cries of the gathering crowd. At an upper window a pale, small face appeared, but no one ventured into that seething inferno of crackling flames and blinding smoke. Then a man broke from the crowd, darted past the line of safety and past the firemen, to what seemed certain death. Taking off his coat and throwing it over his head and face he plunged into the room. Clutching the little mite and sheltering her with his arms and hands from the flames, he sped down the flaming hallway, raced down

the stairs and staggered out into the arms of the firemen.

Weeks elapsed. Friends and neighbours filled the courtroom of the town, and in it, near the kindly-faced judge, sat a little girl with golden curls. The judge spoke. ' You all know the circumstances of this child's parents' deaths in the fire that burnt their home to the ground. Her parents were poor, and there is no one of kin to claim her. Who will take this child, give her a home and bring her up as their own?'

The little girl, with her wistful, sad eyes and blonde curls, made an appealing picture, and there were many who wanted to adopt her. Offers were made of lovely homes and happy children for her companions. Childless parents, too, offered to give her a home and a good upbringing.

From the back of the courtroom a man with face and hands swathed in bandages cried out, ' I claim the child. I saved her from the raging fire and these burns are the evidence I submit in support of my claim.' Pointing to the scars on his face, he held up two arms of seared flesh, wrapped in bandages.

' Does anyone oppose this man's claim?' asked the judge. Not a dissenting voice was heard. The judge went on: ' We all know Jim Brown. He does not have a wife but he has a good home, a good position and can, I feel certain, be both father and mother to this lass whom he rescued at the risk of his own life. The court therefore gives this child to Jim's care, for him to rear, educate and love!'
(Isa. 52. 14; John 10. 11)

## 150   Clean Hands.

*Once in my boyhood days long dead,*
*I watched a supper table being spread*
*By busy hands, and eagerly I said,*
*Wishing to help, ' Please may I bring the*
*   bread.'*
*Gently, reprovingly, a kind voice said,*
*'Are your hands clean?'—Abashed, I hung*
*   my head.*

*Oft when I see the multitude unfed*
*And waiting, hungering for the living bread,*
*My heart and hands are eager to be sped*
*To bring the manna that they may be fed.*
*But a voice says, ev'n as a voice once said,*
*'Are your hands clean?'—I only bow my head.*

(Ps. 24. 4)

## 151   Cleansing from Sin.
In 1893, at the World's Fair in Chicago, a great Parliament of religions was held. The apostles of the East, representatives of Confucianism, Buddhism, Hinduism, Islam, etc., had presented their arguments and spoken eloquently of their several philosophies. Edward Everett Hale had expounded Unitarianism. The plea for the Gospel of Jesus Christ was made by a Christian named Joseph Cook. In the course of his convincing address he turned to the men who had already spoken and said:

' Gentlemen, I beg to introduce you to a woman who has a great sorrow. She has blood stains on her hands and do what she will, she cannot wash them out. She exclaims, "All the perfumes of Arabia will never sweeten this little hand." In her distress and desperation, and through the long hours of the night she has been crying, " Out, damned spot! Out damned spot!" but it will not "out", for it is the blood of one she has murdered. Is there anything in your philosophies that will tell this woman how to get rid of this great sin?' As though expecting an answer, the speaker turned to one and another. Then he added, ' You have said nothing that tells how the stain of sin can be washed from a human life.' Then lifting his eyes he said, 'I shall put my question to another. "John, will you tell this woman how she can get rid of this awful sin?" ' Tarrying for a moment as if waiting for an answer, he continued, ' Listen! John is speaking—" If we confess our sins, He is faithful and just to forgive us our sins and to cleanse us from all unrighteousness," for "the blood of Jesus Christ His Son cleanseth us from all sin." '
(1 John 1. 7,9)

## 152   Cleansing Power of God's Word.
The little stone by the roadside receives dust from every passing wind. The showers have often cleansed it but always again it has become soiled. Another stone of the same lustre lies near by, but within the brook. It is perpetually cleansed and kept clean by the flowing waters. Clouds of dust may pass over it but they do not reach it, and it always reflects the clear rays of the sun. All its cleaning, all its purity is the stream itself.

Now it is the blood of Christ which saves and it is the same blood which cleanses and sanctifies; and as we had to come to Jesus to be plunged into the fountain, so we have to abide in Jesus by fellowship to grow up into Christlikeness.

The Word of God, too, read and assimilated, and applied to the conscience and life by the Holy Spirit, cleanses from sin and unrighteousness.

A. E. Kittredge
(Ps. 119. 9; John 17.17; 1 John 1. 7)

## 153   Climbing Heavenward.
Miss Amy W. Carmichael of the Dohnavur Fellowship wrote a little poem on ' Climbing '.

*Like staircase in ancient homes,*
*Long winding and strangely dim,*
*It is faith that is needed for climbing—*
*Faith rather than length of limb.*

*But there's light at the different landings*
*And rest in the upper room,*
*And a larger range of vision*
*And glorious thoughts to come.*

*How much of our life resembles*
*Time lost in going upstairs!*
*What days and weeks seem wasted,*
*But we're climbing unawares.*

**154 Climbing Higher.** In December, 1941, there appeared a poem written by a nineteen-year-old flyer. This youth, John Gillespie Magee, was the son of a former missionary in China. Three months before he was shot down he wrote:

*Oh, I have slipped the surly bonds of earth*
*And danced the skies on laughter-silvered*
    *wings;*
*Sunward I've climbed and joined the tumbling*
    *mirth*
*Of sunsplit clouds and done a hundred things*
*You have not dreamed of—wheeled and*
    *soared and swung*
*High in the sunlit silence. Hov'ring there,*
*I've chased the shouting wind and flung,*
*My eager craft through footless falls of air.*
*Up, up the long delirious, burning blue*
*I've topped the wind-swept heights with*
    *eager grace,*
*Where never lark or even eagle flew;*
*And while with silent lifting mind I've trod*
*The high untrespassed sanctity of space,*
*Put out my hand and touched the hand of God.*

        Elizabeth Andrews Houghton
(Ps. 139. 7,8)

**155 Coals of Fire.** A hot-tempered officer in the army struck a common soldier, a young man noted for his courage. He felt the insult deeply, but military discipline forbade his returning the blow. He could only retaliate with words, and so he said, ' I'll make you repent.'

One day, in the heat of a furious battle, the young soldier saw an officer wounded and separated from his company, gallantly trying to force his way through the enemies surrounding him. Recognizing his former insulter, the courageous soldier rushed to his assistance, supporting the wounded man with his arm. Together they fought their way through to their own line. With emotion the officer grasped the hand of the young soldier and, stammering out his gratitude, said, ' What a return for an insult so carelessly given!' The young man pressed his hand in return and, with a smile, said gently, ' I told you that I would make you repent.' From that time they were friends.

        *The Indian Christian*
(Rom. 12. 20)

**156 Coincidence or Providence?** It was Christmas time 1958. In a town in Northern England was an evangelical church the Lord had greatly blessed, but many people had left the district and some had died. The building itself was dusty and unattractive and the elders and faithful saints there were distressed.

After preparing for a special service on Christmas Day, they were grieved when a great storm blew up during the night, completely undoing all the labour they had expended on the building. A great piece of plaster had been blown down from the cracked wall, leaving a large hole in the wall. The Christians again brought their brushes and dusters, swept up the debris, and polished the tables and seats once more.

On his way home for lunch, the pastor passed an auction room, slipped in to the auction sale, bid for a 15 feet tablecloth and got it for a few shillings. It would, he felt sure, exactly cover the hole in the wall and would look beautiful as it was white with gold embroidery.

Outside at the bus stop he saw a woman standing with tears on her cheek, in seeming distress. He invited her into the building and gave her a seat in a pew. While repairs were going on, she rose and, pointing to the cloth, said, ' That cloth is mine. My husband gave it to me, and if you look in that corner you will see three initials—mine.'

Then she narrated how she and her husband formerly lived in Vienna. During the war he was put into a concentration camp and his death there had been reported to her. Escaping to Great Britain, she answered an advertisement for a governess for children in that town. Finding the post already filled, she was about to return to the town where she lived. The pastor, touched by her story, said she could have the cloth but she declined. Then she left to go back to the town in which she resided.

The Hall was filled that evening for the service, and the congregation dispersed to return to their homes; but one man remained. He approached the pastor and said, ' I gave that tablecloth to my wife in Vienna. During the war we were separated and my wife was sent to a concentration camp where, I was told, she died. I crossed to England and have settled as a clockmaker in this town. The Pastor, astonished, wanted to get in touch with the man's wife as soon as possible but could only remember the name of the people to whom she had applied for the post. They were able to produce her letter with her address. That night they went by car to the town in which she was living and arrived in the early hours of morning. Husband and wife met again in a happy reunion, and she came to live with her husband. Both are devoted Christians and regularly attend ' the church of the tablecloth '.
(Ps. 86. 15; 145.9)

**157 Collapse and its Cause.** Nobody noticed when the first little parasite wormed its way beneath the bark of the handsome tree; nobody noticed the way the parasites multiplied, boring and drilling their way through its once-sound heart. Nobody noticed that the great tree swayed increasingly in the winter gales. Then one morning when everyone awoke it was on the ground; and they said, ' Look! it's down! It seemed so solid: fancy crashing like that.' Probably nobody notices if you forget to read your daily portion of the Bible; nobody notices if you let prayer slip for a week; but if you continue, there will one day come a crash, and others will say, ' Fancy So-and-so! Used to be so keen!' The strength of your character, the usefulness of your life, is in direct proportion to the measure in which you know God. (Dan. 11. 32)

**158  Colonies of Heaven.** Paul and Barnabas visited, and evangelized in Pisidian Antioch, a Roman colony in Asia, in A.D. 45 or 46. Paul, Silas and Timothy, with Luke, the beloved physician, evangelized and planted a Christian church in Philippi, a Roman colony in Europe, several years later. In each of these cities a colony of heaven on earth was established.

Antioch in Pisidia (Asia Minor), situated on a plateau 3,300 feet above sea level, was a Roman colony and a military base in the Roman Empire. A colony was a fragment of Rome transplanted in another province and at a distance from the imperial capital, a bastion of the Roman Government in an unsettled area. Latin was the official language, and a Roman tone permeated the government, recreations and festivals of the people. Paul and Barnabas, heaven's ambassadors, revisited this colony of heaven confirming the disciples of Christ, exhorting the colonial believers, ordaining elders in the Christian church, and praying for them all.

Philippi in Macedonia, named after its founder Philip, the father of Alexander the Great, was made a Roman colony in 42 B.C. and after a century had elapsed, some of those Roman citizens became a colony of heaven when they received heaven's messengers and submitted to heaven's King—'another king, one Jesus.' Accustomed to obedience to the laws of Rome and loyalty to the Emperor, their liege-lord, and familiar with the Latin language, they began to fulfil the law of Christ, to display a new loyalty to their Lord and Saviour, Jesus Christ, and to speak to one another in the language of heaven. Their names were entered in heaven's burgess roll, the Book of life.

In the letter to the Philippian saints, Paul, a Roman citizen, in a Roman prison, writes to the Roman citizens in Philippi from the Roman capital, and discourses on the principles that were to guide their conduct as citizens of heaven, and on their hope of entering their fatherland with the Lord from Heaven. (Acts 13. 14,48; 16. 12; Phil. 1. 27; 3. 20,21)

**159  Come.**

*Come first to Bethlehem where Christ was born:*
*See Him, the heavenly King, that Christmas*
*    morn*
*Low in a manger laid: No pomp or show—*
*'Twas His eternal love that bade Him go.*

*Come to Gethsemane—Watch Jesus there:*
*Witness His agony, kneeling in prayer.*
*Great drops of blood He sweat 'neath our*
*    sin's load:*
*Yet He endured it all, made peace with God.*

*Come to dark Calvary: look there and see*
*Christ Jesus crucified there, on the tree.*
*Cruel His sufferings, pierced hands and head,*
*Our sin's tremendous load crushing Him dead.*

*Come to the empty tomb: Jesus is risen,*
*Ascended from the grave back into heaven.*
*One day He will return to claim His own*
*And reign eternally, King on His throne.*

                                May Gorrie
(Luke 2. 15; 22. 41,42; 23. 33; 24. 1,6)

**160  Come—Just as you are.** Charlotte Elliott was the granddaughter of John Venn, an outstanding preacher, and was in early life light-hearted and gay. When a godly preacher from Switzerland, a friend of her parents—Dr Malan—was staying at their home, Charlotte very abruptly told him to mind his own business when he asked her if she was a Christian. He did not reply to the rude rebuff, but Charlotte was evidently troubled in conscience, and one day, when Dr Malan was strolling in the garden, she approached him, apologised for her rudeness to him and said, ' I should like to come to Christ but I don't know how.' ' Come just as you are,' was his immediate reply. It was not long before she came to the Saviour.

Years later, at the age of forty-five, in ill-health and great weakness of body, while all the other members were attending a service, she lay in bed overcome with the thought of her own uselessness. She then took pen and paper and wrote the hymn, ' Just as I am without one plea ', little realising that it would be used by God in days to come to the blessing and salvation of many souls. (Matt. 11. 28)

**161  Comfort from a Hymn.** Dr Oswald J. Smith's sister, Mrs. Clifford Becker, and her husband were missionaries in Peru. Clifford Becker was killed in a motor accident just before their furlough was due. His wife thus became a widow at 26. Dr Oswald Smith wrote the lovely poem, since set to music, ' God understands ', and sent it to her. Arriving, as it did, just before she sailed for furlough, it proved to be a great comfort to her.

*God understands your sorrow,*
*He sees the falling tear*
*And whispers, ' I am with thee,'*
*Then falter not, nor fear.*
*He understands your longing;*
*Your deepest grief He shares;*
*Then let Him bear your burden—*
*He understands and cares.*

**162  Comfort of the Scriptures.** One Sunday C. H. Spurgeon left the Bible closed when the time for the reading of the Scripture lesson came. ' Some have found fault with me ', he said, ' thinking I am too old-fashioned because I am always quoting from the Bible and do not say enough about science. Well, there's a poor widow here who has lost her only son, a fine regenerate Christian lad. She wants to know if she will ever see him again. Let's turn to science for the answer. "Will she see him? Where is he? Does death end all?"' There was a long pause. 'We are waiting for an answer,' said the preacher: 'this woman is anxious to know.' Another long pause. 'What? nothing to say? Then we'll turn to the Book!' And Spurgeon clinched the point by reading the wonderful promises concerning eternal life and heaven.

(Acts 9. 31)

**163  Coming Today.**  A traveller chanced on a beautiful villa situated on the shores of a beautiful lake in Switzerland, far from the beaten track of tourists. He knocked at the garden gate and an aged gardener unlocked it and bade him enter. The old man, seemingly glad to see him, showed him round the garden. 'How long have you been here?', asked the traveller. 'Twenty-four years,' replied the gardener. 'How often has your master been here meanwhile? When was he here last?' 'Twelve years ago.' 'He writes often?' 'Never once!' 'From whom do you receive your pay?' 'His agent in the mainland.' 'But he comes here often?' 'He has never been here.' 'Who does come then?' 'I am almost always alone. It is very, very seldom that a stranger ever calls.' 'Yet you have the garden in such perfect order as if you were expecting your master's coming tomorrow!' 'As if he were coming today, sir, today!' exclaimed the old man.

(Mark 13. 34,35)

**164  Commandments—The Ten.**

*In vain we call old notions fudge*
*And bend our conscience to our dealing:*
*The ten commandments will not budge*
*And stealing will continue stealing.*

James Russell Lowell
(Exod. 20. 1-17; James 2. 10)

**165  Commission—The Great.**  Daniel Crawford, late of Luanza, Garenganze, and author of *Thinking Black*, wrote:

Query—(on Matt. 28. 19,20)—How can we claim His 'LO!' if we ignore His 'GO!'?

*Came a vision of St. Paul:*
*Scene—within a Roman Hall:*
*Face lit up with holy gladness—*
*Festus twitted him with madness.*
*'Noble Festus, nay, not mad,*
*But a heart supremely glad!*
*All my soul is now aglow,*
*For I've heard the Master's "GO"*
*And His "LO!" I'm ever with you,*
*Prove I daily this is true!*
*Caesar could not order so;*
*Christ said "GO" and also "LO!"'*

*Came the echo down the ages,*
*Record true of saintly sages;*
*Came the witness all sublime*
*Of those conquerors of time,*
*Whether living they or dying*
*This their shout, all time defying;*
*'Men of God, the order's so—*
*Ours that "GO!" and His that "LO!"'*

*Came the vision of the years,*
*Of the lonely pioneers;*
*Came their sob of hope forlorn*
*For the breaking of the morn;*
*Came the rugged tug of doubt,*
*Then, anon, the victor's shout,*
*And the routing of the foe*
*To Christ's tune of 'GO!' and 'LO!'*

*Comes the warning of the Lord*
*To all readers of the Word;*
*His appeal of love and yearning*
*That we hasten His returning;*
*Warning us lest we forget*
*That the Christ must tarry yet*
*While His servants are so slow*
*Forth to 'GO' and prove His 'LO!'*

*Comes a message from the throne*
*Answering the heathen groan.*
*Comes a voice from God's right hand,*
*Word of hope for every land—*
*'Go ye into all the world,*
*Let My banner be unfurled;*
*Widen out your ranks and GO,*
*And I'll flood them with my LO!'*

**166  Committal—A Millionaire's.**  J. Pierpont Morgan's greatest business transaction was:

'I commit my soul into the hands of my Saviour in full confidence that, having redeemed it and washed it in His most precious blood, He will present it faultless before the throne of my heavenly Father; and I entreat my children to defend at all hazard and at any cost of personal sacrifice, the blessed doctrine of the complete atonement for sin through the blood of Jesus Christ once offered, and through that alone.'

(2 Tim. 1. 12)

**167  Commonplaces of Life.**

*'A commonplace life,' we say as we sigh;*
*But why do we sigh as we say?*
*The commonplace sun in the commonplace sky*
*Make up the commonplace day;*
*The moon and the stars are commonplace things,*
*The flower that blooms and the bird that sings;*
*But dark were our world and sad our lot*
*If flowers failed and the sun shone not.*
*But God who well knows each separate soul*
*Of commonplace things makes a beautiful whole.*
*Ere He placed the sun in the commonplace sky*
*He had wonderful thoughts to bring us nigh*
*In image, and like to His Son so dear,*
*To behold His glory, and that without fear,*
*To gaze upon His face so fair*
*With gladness, without either pain or care—*
*God all in all, in majesty blest,*
*Satisfied then, in His love will rest.*

## 168  Communion.

*My beloved spake to me, and so winning was*
 *His tone,*
*' O arise, my love, my fair one, come away!'*
*For the winter time is past: lo, the rains are*
 *overblown,*
*And the sward with new-bloomed flowerets*
 *all is gay.*
*Hark, the turtle's voice is cooing*
*Gentle love-notes, softly wooing;*
*All the air's athrill with gladsome song today.*
*Here the fig-tree yields its flavour,*
*There the vine gives forth its savour.*
*O arise, my love, my fair one, come away.*
*(NO RESPONSE)*
*' O my dove that dwellest safe, with the Clefted*
 *Rock thy seat,*
*Thou that shelterest in the secret of the stair;*
*Let me hear thy voice, my love, for thy voice*
 *indeed is sweet,*
*Turn thy countenance to me, divinely fair.*
*(NO RESPONSE)*
*Ah, but let us, quickly hasting,*
*Seize the little foxes, wasting*
*All the tenderest grapes that grace our*
 *vineyard rare.*
*For alas, what fruits are sweetest,*
*They would rob and spoil the fleetest,*
*Oh then, guard thy vintage well, thou only-fair.'*
*Then with heart all welling o'er, to my love*
 *I answered low:*
*' My beloved, I am His and He is mine.*
*Where He tends and feeds the flock 'mong*
 *the lilies I will go;*
*Where He makes them rest at noon will I*
 *recline*
*Till thy soft day-dawn awaking,*
*Through the fleeing shadows breaking,*
*Bring the One I love to me: for Him I'll pine.*
*O that, like the young hart bounding,*
*Thou would'st skip those hills surrounding,*
*That they nevermore might sever Thee and*
 *Thine.*

         James S. Tait

(Song of Solomon 2. 10-17)

## 169  Communion of Saints.

*How sweet communion is with saints*
*For soul can soul inspire;*
*The brand that soon goes out alone*
*With others makes a fire:*
*So 'tis our Father's will that we*
*Should heavenward walk in company.*

*But just as blessed 'tis to know:*
*Commune with one's own heart*
*The hidden manna there to eat*
*When Jesus draws apart,*
*For while they lose who keep at home,*
*They lose much more who always roam.*

*But oh, 'tis truly best of all*
*Communing with our Lord,*
*To breathe our secrets in His ear*
*And catch each whispered word;*
*One hour with God is better far*
*Than years of toil without Him are.*

*Then let me prize communion dear*
*With loved ones on the road,*
*But prize as well the hours alone,*
*And most the hour with God.*

         J. Dickie

(Mal. 3. 16)

## 170  Commuter's Contacts—A.

November, 1942. The Allies had commenced the invasion of North Africa—a move which was to lead to the eventual defeat of Hitler's forces. The dining car of the Newcastle to London train was packed to capacity. Little conversation was to be heard as each passenger eagerly scanned the morning newspaper with its unexpected and exciting news. Soon, however, the silence was broken as passengers who were strangers to one another discussed the news and its possible effects on the whole course of the war.

From the far end of the carriage one voice could be heard above all others. It came from a clergyman who had been asked by two airmen sitting opposite him, ' What do you think will happen now?' He had a strident voice and, although his remarks were addressed to the two airmen, all the carriage could hear the conversation that followed. ' Well, I don't know much about these things,' he said. ' I don't know what is likely to happen next—but I do know how it is all going to end! Would you like to know?' He then proceeded to tell his listeners that whatever course this war took it was bound to be followed by an amazing series of events which would culminate in universal rule being set up, the power being in the hands of one man who would bring in universal peace. There would be no more war, no more poverty or hatred or injustice, but the whole world would enjoy peace and happiness! The centre of His government would not be London nor Washington and certainly not Berlin or Rome. It would be Jerusalem!

A somewhat stunned silence followed as these unexpected views were heard by all in the carriage. Then one of the airmen asked: ' That sounds too good to be true, but how do you know that, sir?' ' On the very best authority of all,' he replied, ' on the authority of the Word of God.' At this point he produced a Bible, saying, ' Would you like to hear?' He began to read, in the same penetrating voice, the whole of Daniel's prophecy, chapter 2, verses 31-45—the description of the great image of a man having a head of gold but with feet and toes of a mixture of iron and clay. He then skilfully outlined the meaning of the passage, pointing out how the autocratic Kingdom of Babylon, of which Nebuchadnezzar was the head, would yield to another inferior kingdom (Medo-Persian). This in turn would be followed by the Grecian Empire after which there would emerge the iron rule of Rome—an empire which itself would later be divided, the iron finally giving place to the admixture of iron and clay. This would be particularly evident in the feet and ten toes of the image; and this, said he, is already becoming apparent in the Democracy of today.

'But', he continued, 'notice now what is said about this Stone "cut out without hands" which smote and destroyed the image, itself becoming a great mountain which filled all the earth.

'Now,' said the speaker to his fascinated hearers, 'the whole point is—What is that stone, or rather, who is He?' Whereupon he told them at once that the Stone is none other than the Rock of Ages, the Lord Jesus Christ, the Son of God to whom God has given all power in heaven and on earth. It is He who will be enthroned, and under His beneficent rule there will at last be universal peace. 'And now,' said he, 'Listen! You men can enjoy now what the whole earth will enjoy then. If you will let Christ reign in your hearts, if you will accept Him now as your Saviour and Lord, you can enjoy now the peace of God which passes all understanding.'

The effect was apparent on all. Some smiled condescendingly, some were obviously annoyed. Two sailors sitting opposite me smiled and tapped their foreheads! But I was probably not the only one who prayed earnestly for that faithful servant of His absent Lord, truly an 'ambassador for Christ'.

At this point the train slowed down and stopped at York. The man sitting next to the clergyman alighted. I went up the carriage and asked if I might speak to these two airmen. I told them I had heard all that had been said to them and, like them, was greatly impressed, especially at the claim that all who truly receive Christ as Lord and Saviour can experience now that inward peace and joy for which the whole world is longing today. 'But', I said, 'you are being asked to make the biggest decision of your lives. I want to warn you that you have no proof that what this gentleman has said is true. But now I have come to offer you what is lacking: I am the proof!'

The preacher, for the moment, disconcerted, soon recovered from his surprise and urged me to take the vacant seat. What a joy it was to tell those men of a decision made in boyhood, proved in manhood and never to be regretted!

A. E. Barnes

**171 Companionship—Divine.** In his essay on 'Sir Ernest Shackleton's Text' Dr F. W. Boreham writes: 'Flame or Fire: it makes no difference.'

1,2,3,4—counted King Nebuchadnezzar—at the fiery furnace in Babylon.

1,2,3,4—exclaimed the explorer amidst the snowdrifts and glaciers in the Antarctic. 'We all felt that there were not three but four of us!' said Sir Ernest Shackleton, speaking at the banquet in London given in his honour and describing the thrilling adventures of the Rescue Expedition as, after the sinking of the *Endurance*, they made their way in an open boat, crawled and clambered over dizzy peaks and slippery glaciers in South Georgia to obtain succour for their twenty comrades marooned on Elephant Island. 'I cannot doubt that our party was divinely guided. Worsley said to me, " Boss, I had a curious feeling on the march that there was another Person with us." Crean confessed to the same idea.'

'The form of the fourth was like unto the Son of God!'

(Dan. 3. 25; Matt. 28. 20)

**172 Companionship of Christ.** Can it be that any of you are grieving Him by waywardness and wilfulness in neglecting to cultivate this holy companionship? Philip Henry, the father of the famous commentator, had fallen in love with a Miss Matthews of Worthenbury; but her people rather objected to the engagement on the ground that they did not know much about him or where he came from. 'Yes,' was her reply, 'that is more or less true; but I do know where he is going and I want to go with him.' And surely it is to our eternal advantage to enter into close and intimate fellowship with our divine Lord as we journey along the highways and by-ways of life's pilgrimage.

Harvey Farmer

(Heb. 13. 6)

**173 Company—Bad.** A farmer, seeing a lot of crows picking up the seed he had sown in one of his fields, took his gun and fired at them. All the birds flew away except one that lay wounded on the ground. Going to the wounded bird, the farmer found to his astonishment that it was his own pet parrot. It had escaped from its cage and flown out to join the crows in the field. Its wing was broken with the shot. Picking it up, the farmer said, 'Ah, Polly, this is what comes of keeping bad company.' He put the wounded parrot under his coat and returned home.

As he neared the house, his little girl ran out to meet him. 'Have you shot any crows, Dad?' she asked. 'I have shot Polly,' replied the farmer. Before he could tell his daughter how it happened, the parrot put out its head and exclaimed, 'Bad company, bad company!'

(1 Cor. 15. 33)

**174 Compassion in Christian Service.** Dr A. J. Gordon used to say, 'I have long ceased to pray, "Lord, have compassion on a lost world." I remember the day and the hour when I seemed to hear the Lord rebuking such a prayer. He seemed to say to me, "I have compassion on a lost world, and now it is for you to have compassion."'

We can preach without compassion, sing without compassion, give without compassion. Preaching fails, singing fails, giving fails, but individual concern never fails.

*When I am dying, how glad shall I be*
*That the lamp of my life has been blazed*
*    out for Thee.*
*I shall be glad in whatever I gave,*
*Labour or money, one sinner to save.*

(Ps. 112. 4; Matt. 14. 14; 15. 32)

**175  Computers—The Greatest of all.** Mrs. McNamara, the wife of the U.S.A. Defence Secretary, when asked if computers will replace the human brain, answered:

'The human brain is the most magnificent bit of miniaturization in the universe. It weighs only three pounds and contains ten billion cells, with 25,000 possible inter-connections with other nerve cells. To build an electric computer large enough to have that range of choice would require an area equal to the entire earth's surface.'

(Ps. 139. 14)

**176  Confession—A Humble.**

*Father of spirits, God of light,*
*Great Source of all forgiving grace,*
*Before whose searching, awful sight*
*We stand and smitten, seek Thy face!*
*Have mercy on Thy saints, O Lord,*
*And grant to us Thy pard'ning Word!*

*For senseless pride and godless greed*
*That shame us on the busy mart,*
*For conduct that belies our creed,*
*For faithless and divided heart,*
*O spare Thy erring children, Lord,*
*And speak to us Thy pard'ning Word!*

*For coward lips that would not speak*
*When silence was a shameless wrong,*
*For thoughtless word that drove the weak*
*To think that right was with the strong,*
*Have mercy on Thy saints, O Lord,*
*And grant to us Thy pard'ning Word!*

*For cautious age, for hasty youth,*
*For well-set sails to catch the breeze,*
*For fear that dares not face the truth*
*But welcomes base and trait'rous ease,*
*For thousand sins have mercy, Lord,*
*And speak to us Thy pard'ning Word!*

*For all that oft Thy Spirit grieved,*
*The petty faults of every day,*
*For shunning light we have received*
*To show the path where duty lay,*
*For passions that denied Thy Word*
*Have mercy on Thy saints, O Lord!*

*And while we humbly kneel to pray,*
*Confessing sins and wrongs we've done,*
*Grant us the grace anew to say*
*For love of Thy enthroned Son,*
*We'll walk more closely to Thy Word*
*For all Thy mercies, Sovereign Lord.*

A. Borland

(Ezra. 9. 6; Dan. 9. 4,5)

**177  Confession of Faith.** H. J. Heinz who became world famous as the head of the great preserving and pickling firm established in Pittsburgh gave the following striking testimony in the opening paragraph of his final testament, dated January 11, 1919: 'Looking forward to the time when my earthly career shall end, I desire to set forth at the very beginning of this will, as the most important thing in it, a confession of my faith in Jesus Christ as my Lord and Saviour; I also desire to bear witness to the fact that throughout my life, in which were the usual joys and sorrows, I have been wonderfully sustained by my faith in God. To Him I attribute any success I may have attained during my lifetime.'

(Rom. 10. 9)

**178  Confidence in Father.** A party of scientists and botanists were exploring certain almost inaccessible regions of the Alps in search of new species of flowers. One day they spied through a field glass a flower of such rarity and beauty as would add great value to botanic science. It lay in a deep ravine with perpendicular cliffs on both sides. To obtain this rare plant someone would have to be lowered over the sheer precipice by means of a rope and this was a very dangerous undertaking. Approaching a lad nearby who was watching them with curiosity, they said, 'We'll give you five dollars if you'll let us lower you down into the valley below to obtain that lovely rare flower for us.' The youngster, taking a long look down into the dizzy depths, replied, 'Just a minute. I'll be back shortly.' When he returned he was accompanied by an older man. Approaching one of the botanists, he said, 'I'll go over the cliff and get that flower for you if this man holds the rope. He's my father.'

(Ps. 118. 8,9)

**179  Confidence in Man or God.** A certain Scotsman had been converted under the preaching of Dr Andrew Bonar and blessed through his subsequent ministry. Indeed, his whole spiritual life seemed to depend on the famous preacher. When Bonar died, this man was overcome with grief and seemed dazed and helpless, with no spiritual energy. In this state, some days later, he was walking despondently in a nearby park. Close by, a nannie was wheeling two children in a little carriage, and one of them happened to have been named after the distinguished minister. The other child was lolling against this little brother at the time they were passing the Scotsman, and the nannie said sharply, 'Sit up! You mustn't lean on Andrew Bonar.'

The grief-stricken Scot, hearing these words, felt that this was a message from God to him, as it made him realise that he had been leaning for spiritual succour on one of the Lord's servants instead of on the Lord Himself.

(Ps. 118. 8,9 the middle verses of the Bible)

**180  Conscience—A clear.** At the time when Samuel Budgett, afterwards called 'the Successful Merchant', went into business, pepper was laid under a heavy tax. In consequence it was very commonly adulterated and in almost every store might be seen a cask marked 'P.D.'— pepper dust, a dust resembling pepper with which the pepper was mixed before it was sold. This had become a recognized custom of the trade.

In Henry Budgett's store was a cask marked 'P.D.' As soon as Samuel entered the firm, his conscience began to trouble him. That 'everyone did so' carried no weight with him. Some called it 'only a trick of the trade', but the more Samuel thought about it, the more he hated the sight of that cask. He felt sure he could not ask God's blessing on the use of P.D. So one night he went into the store, rolled out the barrel of P.D. into an old quarry behind the building, broke it up and scattered the P.D. to the four winds.

Then his conscience was clear and at rest.
(1 Pet. 3. 16)

**181 Conscience Money.** A big surprise was in store for Mr F. Humphrey as he made his customary trek to collect his mail from the post-office in Waynesboro, Georgia. A strange-sized envelope caught his attention and when he opened it, to his great surprise, he found four one-hundred-dollar bills and two fifty-dollar bills, five hundred dollars in all. Then came an even greater surprise, an enclosed unsigned letter which read, 'This money I stole from you. I am now a Christian and I must give it back to you. The Lord forgave me: will you?'

From whom could the letter have come? He examined the postmark on the envelope but that afforded no clue as to the sender, for the postmark was illegible. Floyd Humphrey is still wondering who this former employee might be, though he does remember times when he missed some money, but not that exact amount.

Under the law of the Trespass Offering a Jew would have brought a ram without blemish as a trespass offering to obtain divine forgiveness on the ground of atonement made. The lamb would be slain by a priest, and the guilty man would have added to the amount stolen one fifth of its value.
(Lev. 5. 15,16; 6. 4)

**182 Conscience—Needle of.** An old pilot, trusted and wise, was one night many years ago taking his vessel up between the coasts of Wales and Ireland. He had been over the course innumerable times without disaster. This particular night nearing port and home, he was running full steam ahead. With his keen eye he watched compass and chart. Suddenly with a sickening crashing sound, the vessel was on the hidden rocks. Loss of life and loss of ship marked the wreck.

Later, upon entering the pilot-house which still survived, close examination revealed the fact that someone, in seeking to clean or tamper with the compass, had slipped a thin knife blade into the compass box near the needle, and the little blade had broken off. That little piece of foreign steel was sufficient to deflect, though only slightly, the needle by which the old clear-eyed pilot was steering the boat. Such a little thing—such a mighty wreck!

Ask yourself the question: what has slipped into my life that is deflecting the needle of conscience and leading me off the true course?
Selected

(Acts 24. 16; Tit. 1. 15)

**183 Consecration for Service.**

*No cross too hard to bear, no stoop too low,*
*No task too menial to undertake*
*For One who humbly bore for sinners' sake*
  *the cross of woe:*
*No sacrifice too great, no cost too high,*
*No offering of love could e'er compare*
*With His: Oh, boundless love— none else*
  *would dare for us to die.*

Mary C. Dunlop

(John 15. 13)

**184 Consecration for Success.** Someone asked General William Booth on one occasion what was the secret of his success. He replied, with tears in his eyes, 'God has had all there is of me to have.'

*Give God thy best! In service true and willing*
*Pour out thy life that He may live in thee.*
*Though frail the vessel He will do the filling,*
*Make thee a blessing in the years to be.*

*Give God thy best! In true heart consecration*
*Offer to Him thy fragrant morning hours.*
*Think not to find His reconciliation*
*When darkness falls and thou hast spent*
  *thy powers.*

*Give God thy best! In unreserved surrender*
*Yield Him thy life in all its youthful prime.*
*Wait not until thy sun hath set in splendour*
*And thou hast nothing but the evening time.*

(Rom. 12. 1; 6. 13; 2 Cor. 12. 15; Phil. 2. 17)

**185 Consecration—Full.** 'Lord, I give up my own purposes and plans, all my own desires and hopes and ambitions (whether they be fleshly or soulish), and accept Thy will for my life. I give myself, my life, my all utterly to Thee, to be Thine for ever. I hand over to Thy keeping all of my friendships; all the people whom I love are to take a second place in my heart. Fill me and seal me with Thy Holy Spirit. Work out Thy whole will in my life, at any cost, now and for ever. To me to live is Christ. Amen!'

Nine years later, on December 8, 1934, Betty Scott Stam and her husband calmly and bravely laid down their lives for Christ when they were martyred by Chinese Communists. As Mrs Scott spoke of lessons of trust and faithfulness from the lives of John and Betty, she said that Betty's victory over the power of the enemy in that dark hour in 1934 had been won at Keswick in 1925. Betty was victor in the crisis because, years before, she had utterly yielded herself to the Lord Jesus Christ and trusted Him to be her Victor.

*The Prairie Overcomer*

(Ps. 143. 10; Phil. 1. 20,21)

**186 Consecration—More.**

*Bye and bye, when I look on His face,*
*Beautiful face, thorn-shadowed face,*
*Bye and bye, when I look on his face,*
*I'll wish I had given Him more.*

*Bye and bye, when He holds out His hands,*
*Welcoming hands, nail-riven hands,*
*Bye and bye, when He holds out His hands,*
*I'll wish I had given Him more.*

*Bye and bye, when I kneel at His feet,*
*Wonderful feet, nail-pierced feet;*
*Bye and bye, when I kneel at His feet,*
*I'll wish I had given Him more.*

*In the awe of that heavenly place,*
*Light from His face, beautiful face,*
*In the awe of that heavenly place,*
*I'll wish I had given Him more:—*
*More, so much more,*
*Treasures unbounded for Him I adore.*

(Rom. 12. 1)

### 187   Consecration of the Home.

*Take our home and let it be*
*Consecrated, Lord, to Thee.*
*Take thy servants here who dwell:*
*May they do Thy bidding well!*

*Take our books: let them impart*
*Wisdom to each seeking heart!*
*Take the door and let it be*
*Ever open, Lord, for Thee.*

*Take the food and, every day,*
*Bless; accept our thanks, we pray.*
*Take the table: at each meal*
*Thy sweet Presence may we feel!*

*Take our pictures: may they be*
*Pure and pleasing, Lord, to Thee!*
*Take the ivories and raise*
*Music always to Thy praise!*

*Take the garden: always there*
*Nature's beauties may we share!*
*Take the telephone and use*
*Every call as Thou shalt choose.*

*Take control at dawn of day—*
*In our lives, Lord, have Thy sway:*
*Take, and nail to Calvary's tree*
*All that dims our sight of Thee.*

                                        E.H.
(2 Kings 20. 15; Prov. 31. 27; Luke 10. 38)

**188   Consistency.** After the death of Robert Murray McCheyne, a letter addressed to him was found in his locked desk, a letter he had showed to no one while he lived. It was from one who wrote to tell him that he had been the means of leading the writer to Christ, and contained these words: 'It was nothing you said that made me wish to be a Christian; it was the beauty of holiness which I saw in your very face.' His deportment was consistent with his doctrine, his conduct with his creed.
(1 Cor. 11. 1)

**189   Consistent Life.** An American teacher was employed in Japan with the understanding that during school hours he should not utter a word on the subject of Christianity. His word was kept, but so beautiful was his life, so blameless his character, and so Christ-like his example, that forty of those students,

unknown to him, met secretly in a grove and signed a covenant to abandon idolatry.

*Pray, who is my neighbour who reads me*
*    day by day*
*To learn if I am living right and walking as*
*    I pray?*
*Oh, he is with me always to criticise or blame,*
*So worldly-wise in his own eyes, and 'sinner'*
*    is his name.*

(1 Pet. 2. 9)

**190   Constrained by Christ's Love.** To Henry Martyn, after he had completed a brilliant course as a student, came the Lord's call to serve him abroad. Though several attractive, lucrative vocations were open to him, he said, 'Here I am, Lord: send me to the ends of the earth. Send me even to death itself if it but be in Thy service and in Thy kingdom!'

When he fell deeply in love with a girl named Lydia, he told her of his call from God to live and minister in India. Was this agreeable to her? he asked, and pleaded that it might be. But it was not. If he would stay in England, he could have her as his bride. If he went to India, he must do without her. The question came like a drum-beat in his brain—India or Lydia? Lydia or India?

Henry Martyn was a mastered man, mastered by love and love's Master, constrained by the love of Christ. The mastery was his in a crisis involving a crucial choice. 'My dear Lydia and my duty call me different ways, yet God has not forsaken me. I am born for God only, and Christ is nearer to me than father or mother or sister. So he went to India to "burn out for God".'
(2 Cor. 5. 14)

**191   Contentment.** William C. Burns wrote, 'The happiest state of a Christian on earth seems to be this—that he should have few wants. If a man have Christ in his heart and heaven before his eyes, and only as much of temporal blessings as is needful to carry him safely through life, then pain and sorrow have little to shoot at; such a man has little to lose. To be in union with Him who is the Shepherd of Israel, and to walk very near to Him who is a sun and a shield, that comprehends all that a poor sinner requires to make him happy between this and heaven.

*I am content. In trumpet tones my song let*
*    people know;*
*And many a mighty man with thrones and*
*    sceptres is not so.*
*And if he is, I joyful cry,*
*'Why, then he's just the same as I.'*

Not many today are like the coloured boy the late Charles M. Alexander tells about. He was helping him to pack his case and said to him, 'Mister Charlie, would you have any old clothes you aint makin' use of?'

'Well, Sam,' said Mr. Alexander, 'now what about shoes, and what size do you wear?'

'Well,' Sam replied, 'that mostly 'pends on

who gives 'em. Sometimes I wear sixes and sometimes elevens.'

He had learned what a lot of Christians haven't. He had learned 'In whatsoever shoes I am, therewith to be content.'

Tom. A. Taylor

(Phil. 4. 11)

### 192 Contentment.

*I'll take what Thou art pleased to send*
*And yield if Thou no longer lend;*
*I'll come if Thou the way wilt show*
*And flee where Thou forbid'st to go.*

*Come joy or grief, content I'll rest*
*And feel myself supremely blest,*
*Since nought in earth or heaven can part*
*The Saviour from the loving heart.*

Alfred Edersheim

(Phil. 4. 11; 1 Tim. 6. 8; Heb. 13. 5)

### 193 Contentment a Treasure.

*There is a jewel which no Indian mine can buy,*
*No chemist's art can counterfeit;*
*It makes men rich in greatest poverty,*
*Makes water wine, turns wooden cups to gold,*
*The homely whistle to sweet music's strain;*
*Seldom it comes—to few from heaven sent—*
*That 'much in little', 'all in nought,' CONTENT.*

### 194 Continuance.

*I must go on: my hand is put upon the plough.*
*The wind turns cold; the sluggard leaves the*
 *sod unturned*
*Nor cares that in the time of harvest he must*
 *beg!*
*But I have seen a ploughman, spite the wind*
 *and snow,*
*Plough an unbending furrow to the end*
*And, ceaseless in his toil, break up the*
 *fallow ground,*
*And through the mist and murk of*
 *unpropitious days*
*Lay up in store the summer's golden harvest*
 *joy.*
*That ploughman is the master of my soul;*
*Therefore, in spite of storm and stress, like*
 *Him I must go on.*

*I must fight on: I have in conscience drawn*
 *the sword.*
*The fight is hard: the armed Ephraimites*
 *may flee*
*And fill the streets of Gath and Askelon*
 *with mirth:*
*But I have seen a Warrior take the field*
 *alone,*
*Unsheath the sword against infernal foes*
*And, with undaunted soul, cut through the*
 *serried ranks;*
*And, though forsaken of the men He came to*
 *save,*
*Pour out His blood to win for them the*
 *Victor's crown.*
*That Warrior is the Captain of my soul,*
*And I, though I should stand alone—like Him*
 *I must fight on.*

*And I must Love: my heart is longer not my*
 *own.*
*The world allures and fickle hearts may turn*
 *aside,*
*Nor care that ashes mark the place of*
 *yester's flame.*
*But I have seen a Lover, spite the scorn and*
 *hate,*
*Love through an agony of blood and tears*
*And, ceaseless in His love for ev'n His enemies,*
*Lay down His life, forsaken of earth and skies,*
*And rising, win a bride and ring the marriage*
 *bells.*
*That Lover is the Lover of my soul*
*And I, unto the endless end, like Him—*
 *I too must love.*

Dr J. T. Shields

(John 21. 18,19; Phil. 3. 14)

### 195 Continuance with the Lord.

In a notice of a Bible Study Convention held in March, 1963, the following mild, but tasty, Printer's Pie appeared:

Our prayer is that the Lord's people may continue to continue to value this tremendous privilege of Bible study.

Very emphatic, isn't it? But we cannot sufficiently emphasize the need for persevering prayer and continuous Bible study.

*Some of us stay at the Cross,*
*Some of us wait at the tomb—*
*Quickened and raised together with Christ*
*Yet lingering still in the gloom.*
*Some of us bide at the Passover feast*
*With Pentecost all unknown;*
*The triumphs of grace in the heavenly place*
*That our Lord has made our own.*

*If the Christ who died had stopped at the Cross*
*His work had been incomplete;*
*If the Christ who was buried had stayed in*
 *the tomb,*
*He had only known defeat;*
*But the way of the Cross never stops at the*
 *Cross,*
*And the way of the tomb leads on*
*To victorious grace in the heavenly place*
*Where the risen Lord has gone.*

*So let us go on with our Lord*
*To the fullness of God He has brought,*
*Unsearchable riches of glory and good*
*Exceeding our utmost thought.*
*Let us grow up into Christ,*
*Claiming His Life and its powers,*
*The triumphs of grace in the heavenly place*
*That our conquering Lord has made ours.*

Annie Johnson Flint

(John 15. 9; Acts 2. 42; 26. 22; Heb. 6. 1)

### 196 Controlled Life—The.

The story is told of that great preacher and writer of the last century, Professor Henry Drummond. He used to spend his summer holidays with some friends in Scotland. On one such occasion, as he was just leaving, his hostess said to him, 'Oh, we've just remembered something we were going to ask you to do for us. We're very troubled about John, our coachman. He's drinking heavily. We've warned him again and again, and he's on his last chance now. Could you speak to him and try to help him?' When the coachman brought round the carriage to take him to the station, Henry Drummond got up beside him. He began to talk to the man about his horses, and as they came round a very dangerous bend in the road he said, 'John, what would happen if you lost control of these two horses and they ran away with us here?' 'It'd be a bad job for both of us!' said the man. 'But if, when you found that they were out of your control,' said Henry Drummond, 'you knew that I could control any horse, what would you do?' 'That's easy to answer,' said John, 'I'd give you the reins.' 'John,' said Henry Drummond, 'do you ever feel as though there was something in you like a pair of wild horses that threatens to run away with you again and again?' John hung his head with shame, for he knew only too well what a defeated man he was. Then the professor said, 'I know of One who can control all these wild passions if you will only let Him into your life to do it for you.' As he parted from him at the station he said, 'John, will you give Him the reins?' A year later the professor met the coachman again, and as Henry Drummond came along the platform of the station his face lit up as John touched his hat and said, 'I've given Him the reins, sir.'

**197 Controversies—An Allegory.** In the days when knights wore armour and challenged one another to mortal combat on the slightest pretext, a certain Baron Veritas was said to have suspended a gigantic shield over the path which ran past the drawbridge of his castle. One day a Black Knight, riding up from the South, stopped to gaze at the shield as it shone brightly in the sun. A White Knight, just then approaching from the other direction, saw the other man gazing up at the shield and reined in his horse so that he too could have a look at it. Thus halted on their way, the Black Knight hailed the White Knight and loudly praised the magnificence of Baron Veritas who had placed that splendid golden shield in their path.

'Truly Veritas is a great lord!' shouted back the White Knight, 'But you are mistaken in saying that the shield is golden: any churl could tell you it is silver.' 'Sir knight,' scoffed the one in black, 'look again. Those northern mists must have dulled your sight. If you had the advantage of living in our southern climes, you would have known at a glance that the shield is golden!' At this the White Knight retorted in a rage, that, whether a man came from the North or the South, he ought to know silver when he saw it. With rising anger the Black Knight thundered out, 'Not silver but gold! Gold! Gold!'

After hurling insults at one another the gauntlet was thrown down, and each drew back his horse and lowered his lance, ready for the charge. They galloped furiously at each other and met with a terrific crash right under the shield. Neither was badly hurt, though the White Knight was unseated and fell to the ground. At this the Black Knight wheeled his horse round so that he could return and demand submission from his routed adversary; but happening to raise his eyes to the shield, discovered, to his surprise, that it was not gold after all, but silver.

Being fair-minded as well as hot-headed, he apologised to his opponent. 'Forgive me!' he said, 'I was wrong. The shield is made of silver after all.' Meanwhile the White Knight had picked himself up and was leading back his horse. Raising his head he saw from his position in the South the shield gleaming golden in the sunlight. Again mad with rage, the White Knight bellowed, 'You have defeated me in fair combat, but don't insult me by trying to humour me as if I was a child. You pretend you were mistaken. It was I who was wrong. The shield is, after all, not silver but golden.' 'Not silver!' cried the Black Knight, greatly offended. 'Of course it is silver, man!' So once again they began to hurl insults at one another, the one crying 'Silver! Silver!' and the other 'Gold! Gold!' until it was clear that they both must have another tilt at each other.

Just at that moment Baron Veritas came walking over the drawbridge to enquire about the quarrel. Calling the Black Knight to the South side where the White Knight was standing, he bade them both look up. The shield was gleaming gold. Then Lord Veritas requested them to pass to the North and look again. This they did and saw then that the shield was made of silver.

'What a pity you had all that argument and fighting,' he said to them, 'for the shield is gold on the South side and silver on the North. You were wrong because you only knew in part. You needed me to give you all the truth.'

Having said this, Baron Veritas withdrew to his castle to wait for the next travellers who would quarrel over his famous shield.

In the history of the Church, different leaders have seen the same doctrine from different viewpoints and, like those knights, have quarrelled and denounced each other because they only knew in part. How much better to look to the Spirit of truth to lead us into all truth!
(John 16. 13; Tit. 3. 9)

**198 Conversion.** In his essay on 'Hugh Ogilvy's Soliloquy,' Dr F. W. Boreham tells the conversion story of Samuel Kane, for which a former poet-laureate, John Masefield, was awarded the Edmond De Poignac prize of £100 by the Academic Committee of the Royal Society of Literature. The title of the poem is 'The Everlasting Mercy', and it is narrated by Samuel Kane, a desperate and abandoned profligate, in the convert's own wild, eloquent speech.

Dr Boreham goes on to say that conversion is like the love of a maiden answering to the love of a man, like the petals of a rose unfolding to the kiss of the sun. He describes it as the natural response of an internal impulse to an external appeal, as the most sublime, the most mysterious, the most majestically miraculous operation that our world ever witnesses, and as 'the mighty ministry of God the Father, God the Son and God the Holy Spirit in the theatre of the human soul'.
(Luke 18. 10-14)

**199 Conversion—A Brahmin's.** In the early years of the twentieth century a party of Brahmins set out on a pilgrimage to Kasi (Benares). One of the families had a boy, an only child, born after the mother had performed many rites at various temples because of her barrenness. The parents had named him Sanjeevi, wishing long life for him. At the time of the pilgrimage Sanjeevi was about eleven.

Great was the rejoicing of the pilgrims on reaching the holy city, Kasi, one of India's 'punyakshetrams'. Someone met the Pondicherry party and told them there was in the city a certain Swami whom all the pilgrims visited before going down to the river to bathe. The Swami, attired in yellow robes, had long hair and a beard. What arrested the lad's attention was his long, claw-like finger nails. The older folks in the party had some conversation with him which was unintelligible to the youngster. The Swami then took a large bitter gourd and with his claws tore off chips from it, and gave one to each pilgrim, saying, 'Bind this on your hand and go through the ceremonies without taking it off. After your holy bath come back and see me.'

The party proceeded through the crowd of pilgrims to the waterside. Sanjeevi's group sought out one of the priests repeating 'mantras', received instructions, went down into the water repeating prayers and bathed without removing the gourds from their hands. Then they went back to the Swami who bade them taste the vegetable on their hands. 'How does it taste now?' he asked each, and all replied, 'It is still bitter.' Then the Swami asked, 'If the Ganges water cannot wash away that bitter taste, how can it wash away your sins?' He then began to preach to them about the blood of Jesus Christ, God's Son, that cleanses from all sin. The party went straight to find a 'Christian' priest and were baptized in a Roman Catholic church. They then returned to Pondicherry.

Sanjeevi was a thoroughly spoilt boy, disobedient to his parents, and a truant at school, and went about collecting and selling for a few annas all the empty bottles he could find. The priests in Pondicherry would buy liquor in the bazaar, drain the entire contents and throw away the empty bottles, which Sanjeevi would pick up and sell.

Sanjeevi knew nothing of the Bible. When in his middle teens he went to hear the preacher, Tamil David, the preacher took a fancy to Sanjeevi, adopted and educated him with the consent of Sanjeevi's mother and called him Sanjeevi David. Tamil David enrolled him as a boarder in a Mission School. There, night after night he would break the rules, jump over the wall into the next street and run around the town. To escape detection when the warden made his nightly visit, he would bribe a fellow from the sick-room to come and occupy his bed till he returned. During those nights he often attended dramas in the town.

One night on his way to the theatre, he saw a crowd assembled in an open space under a gas light and joined the crowd out of curiosity, keeping himself out of sight. A missionary was preaching and said, 'Here, you compound-wall jumper!' Sanjeevi felt his head beginning to swim and his knees giving way, for he thought he had been recognised and would be reported; but being afraid to run away, he stood transfixed.

The preacher, Walker of Tinnevelli, did not know Sanjeevi and was not aware of anyone present who had broken hostel rules, but was familiar with the escapades of boarding-school boys, and his sermon brought conviction to Sanjeevi who that night yielded to the claims of the Lord Jesus Christ and became a new creature in Christ Jesus. He soon began to preach the Gospel, though persecuted by fanatical Roman Catholics, and thus Tamil David left a successor to continue his work.

H. Kaveri Bai (abridged)

**200 Conversion—A British Journalist's.** Mr. Malcolm Muggeridge, a journalist and TV personality with a ready wit and an acid tongue, and an acknowledged master of English, resigned on moral grounds from the Rectorship of Edinburgh University. In his address delivered at St. Giles Cathedral after his resignation, he took as his text 'Another King, Jesus', and told of his conversion. Referring to the incident of the two disciples on their journey to Emmaus and their realization that the person who joined them was not a stranger but their Saviour, he added, 'As my friend and I walked along, like Cleopas and his friend, we recalled, as they did, the events of the Crucifixion and its aftermath in the light of our utterly different and yet similar world. Nor was it a fancy that we two were joined by a third presence.'

In the course of his sermon, he said, 'I should like my light to shine even if only very fitfully, like a match struck in a dark cavernous night. . . . I came back to where I began, to that other King, one Jesus; to the Christian notion that man's efforts to make himself personally and collectively happy in earthly terms are doomed to failure. He must indeed, as Christ said, be born again. As far as I am concerned, it is Christ or nothing.

'I am more convinced than I am of my own existence that the view of life Christ came into the world to preach and died to sanctify, remains as true and as valid as ever, and that all who care to, young and old, healthy and infirm, wise and foolish, with or without A or O levels, may live thereby finding in our troubled, confused world, as in all other circumstances, an enlightenment and a serenity not otherwise attainable.'
(Acts 17. 7)

**201 Conversion—A Hit Song-Writer's.** Scott Lawrence was a born musician. From childhood he composed melodies with beautiful chords and words to suit. In youth, drink took its toll and King Alcohol ruled his life. The enormous sums of money he earned by his musical compositions were soon spent on drink, dope and gambling.

One day he wrote a hit song, 'I'll never be good enough', in twenty minutes and gave the premier performance of it in the saloon in which he had just composed it. What most of his mates did not know was that there was a girl, Victoria Barnes, connected with the song. She liked Scotty and he almost worshipped her, but Victoria was a Christian. One day, when he asked her why she was so cold to him, and why she would not change her ways, she asked him if he really wanted her to live the ungodly, wild life he was living. He admitted he did not. Then he tried to convince her that she could marry him and change him. 'No!' she told him, 'I can't marry you, though I love you and see so many talents in you, for I cannot change you.' At this he became furious and shouted, 'God doesn't love me and I don't need Him or anyone else—not even you.'

The song—'I'll never be good enough'— grew to popular hit proportions and Victoria knew it had been written for her. She waited and prayed, and for ten years wrote to various rescue missions asking prayer for this wayward soul. During that time Scotty was arrested for stealing and jailed. After his release he took to sleeping on two broken boxes in an alley. One morning at 1 a.m. he stumbled into the Pacific Garden Mission where Mrs. Taylor, the composer of the hymn 'Calvary covers it all', took his name, sat down prayerfully beside him and read John 1. 12 'To as many as received Him to them gave He power to become the children of God even to them that believe on His name'. There and then Scott Lawrence received the Lord Jesus Christ as his Saviour.

After a few falls and failures he began to live for Christ and wrote hymns instead of pop songs. From one State to another he travelled, giving his testimony, and wrote the chorus, 'Whisper a prayer!' One day, when it was introduced in a large New York auditorium, the composer was asked to come forward. Victoria was in the audience and as he moved down the aisle she went to meet him and together they mounted the platform.

Soon afterwards they were married and had five wonderful years of married life and service among the under-privileged children of New York city.

Scott went to an early grave because of his previous dissipation. The scars of sin took their toll. Before he died he wrote the beautiful hymn, 'He loves even me!'

*When I think of the Saviour's great love*
*In coming from heaven above*
*To die on the tree for a sinner like me,*
*I am sure that He loves even me.*

Orella Sabre Shafer (abridged)

**202 Conversion—A Preacher's.** In the *Banner of Truth*, F. W. Krummacher told how a preacher was converted in an unusual way. His preaching was usually the plain 'word of the cross', so he had his share of enemies. One opponent, a learned man, did not attend his services, but one Sunday night thought he would go once more to hear the stern minister. The subject was 'The Narrow Way', which he made neither smaller nor wider than our Lord made it.

The opponent went to him and said, 'I was in your audience when you preached on the only way of salvation, and I want to know if you can prove your assertions. The minister replied with assurance that he had spoken God's Word which was the infallible truth. 'O my God!' the man exclaimed, 'is it so? If it is, what will become of us?' The word *US* startled the preacher, but overcoming his momentary disquietude, he began to expound the doctrine of redemption and to exhort him to repentance and faith. Interrupting, his questioner repeated anxiously, 'My dear sir, if it is the truth, what shall we do?' The preacher really staggered by the plural personal pronoun, thought, 'What does this *WE* mean?' Again he resorted to explanation and exhortation till his visitor, with tears in his eyes and in a voice that might have moved the very stones, desperately exclaimed, 'My dear man, if it is the truth, we're lost.' The preacher, pale and trembling, cried with a sob in his voice, 'My friend, let us get down in the dust and pray.' They prayed: the stranger took his departure: the preacher locked himself in his study. For two Sundays he was unable to preach. On the third Sunday he appeared before his congregation a new man, pale from the experience he had had alone with God, yet filled with heavenly joy and peace, and commenced his sermon by telling his audience that he himself had only recently entered through the narrow gate into life eternal. The Holy Spirit had used the *WE* and *US* to convict and convert the preacher.
(Matt. 7. 13,14)

**203 Conversion—A Robber's.** Only the clip-clop of the horse's shoes touched the deep silence of the forest as the lonely traveller wended his homeward way upon the night road. Suddenly it was broken by the leaping of a figure from a nearby covert and the hoarse cry of 'Halt! Halt!' A rough hand seized the bridle. 'Quick now! Your money, or your life!'

The traveller emptied his pockets of the few coins he carried. Then to the highwayman's surprise, he invited a search of the saddlebags. After a suspicious pause, there was the eager stripping.

'Bah! Nothing but books! What good are they?'

Then the traveller leaned over and whispered, 'But I do have something of value to give you: of great value. . . .' There was a pause. 'You may not think so now. But the time will come when you will bitterly regret this kind of living. When it comes, then remember this: "The blood of Jesus Christ, God's Son, cleanseth us from all sin." Remember it, for then it will serve as your only hope.'

With an ugly snarl the highwayman turned and fled. The other sat for a long moment as if in deep thought.

The years passed. The traveller went about his work of preaching the gospel from place to place. And then one day he came to a particular town. At the close of a meeting one of the leading townsmen begged a word. Tears filled his eyes as he spoke.

'God bless you, sir, God bless you indeed! And your text! "The blood of Jesus Christ, God's Son cleanseth us from all sin". Why, it was the very word you whispered in my wild, young ears those many years ago.' He paused as the other eyed him with quick interest. 'Yes, I was that highwayman who robbed you in the forest. And that word you gave me just kept after me like a hound, dogging me everywhere I went, until at last it led me to Christ in confession and faith! And all that I am now, I owe to the blessed Lord and to you, Sir. So I say, "God bless you indeed, sir!" '

The man on horseback was John Wesley, and the highwayman was one of thousands he led to Christ.

(1 John 1. 7)

**204 Convictions.** Opinions, wrote A. T. Pierson, are like spider webs, beautifully spun but easily broken. Convictions are the forces that move the world. The world will never be moved by flabby Christians who believe their doubts and doubt their beliefs.

Man is unsure of himself and feels the deep need of help and supernatural guidance to navigate the deceptive and ever-changing river of life. Sin has put the compass out of order! Man must get right with God first and then the Supreme Guide will take over the direction of the life put under His control.

When God comes into our lives He undertakes to guide and direct us, but not necessarily by supernatural means. Having created us intelligent beings and redeemed us, He is not going to by-pass either our intelligence or the convictions produced within us by the Holy Spirit.

Neville J. Taylor

**205 Corn of Wheat.** In the *Encyclopaedia Britannica* there is the account of a notable experiment at Wolverhampton, England. One grain of wheat was planted and produced several distinct stalks with ears of wheat. Each grain was transplanted. The grains produced by each were again separated and transplanted. In two years 32,500 grains of wheat were produced from one single 'corn of wheat'. —It bringeth forth much fruit.

(John 12. 24)

**206 Creator—The Great.**

*The spacious firmament on high*
*With all the blue ethereal sky*
*And spangled heavens, a shining frame,*
*Their great Original proclaim.*
*The unwearied sun, from day to day,*
*Does his Creator's power display,*
*And publishes to every land*
*The work of an Almighty hand.*

*Soon as the evening shades prevail*
*The moon takes up the wondrous tale,*
*And nightly to the listening earth*
*Repeats the story of her birth;*
*While all the stars that round her burn,*
*And all the planets in their turn*
*Confirm the tidings, as they roll*
*And spread the truth from pole to pole.*

*What though in solemn silence all*
*Move round this dark terrestrial ball?*
*What though no real voice nor sound*
*Amidst their radiant orbs be found?*
*In Reason's ears they all rejoice*
*And utter forth their glorious voice,*
*For ever singing as they shine,*
*'The hand that made us is Divine!'*

Joseph Addison

(Job 38. 7; Ps. 19. 1-3)

**207 Credulity and Incredibility.** The story is told of an aged lady taking her first journey in a railway train. She was very interested in everything she saw and very loquacious. Two young men in the same compartment were greatly amused by her exclamations and questions. She enquired the use of the wires strung along the posts beside the railway track. The young men kidded her by saying they were put there by the railway company so that passengers could hang their washing out to dry as they went along their journey. 'How thoughtful!' said the lady. A gentleman in the same compartment, overhearing the conversation, could stand it no longer, and explained that the telegraph wires were there to convey messages from one city or town to another. 'Now,' said the old lady, 'and do you think I'd be for believing that?'

**208 Creed—A Simple.** In the north of Ireland recently, before the terrible outbreaks

of violence and assassinations, a taxi-driver, waiting to be hired, was found reading a book by the person who engaged him. As they drove along, the passenger asked, 'What book was that I saw you reading?' 'The Bible, sir!' was the reply. 'Why do you read that book?' he was asked. 'I love it, sir, and the Saviour of whom it tells,' replied the taxi-driver. 'To what denomination do you belong?' 'To none, sir! I love all who love Christ!' 'But haven't you any creed?' the passenger persisted. 'Yes, a very simple one of three articles: Believe all that God has said: obey all that Christ has commanded: and expect all that He has promised!'
(Deut. 29. 29)

**209 'Crimond'—The Tune.** Our gracious Queen Elizabeth and Prince Philip celebrated their Silver Wedding anniversary in 1972. On the evening of November 19, 1947, a telephone rang at Westminster Abbey and a voice asked for Canon Elliott. He was called to the 'phone and heard the following: 'This is Buckingham Palace and I am ringing on behalf of Princess Elizabeth. She would like to speak to Canon Elliott.'

It turned out that the Princess, who was to be married on the following day, had, with her mother and sister, visited the Abbey to listen to the rehearsal of the music. Talking over things afterwards, the three royal ladies agreed that the setting of 'Crimond' to the twenty-third Psalm was very different from the setting to which they were accustomed. The bride-elect therefore determined to ring the Abbey.

'When we are in Scotland,' she explained to the Canon on the 'phone, 'Mother, Margaret and I often sing the twenty-third Psalm but the setting of "Crimond" as it was rendered in the Abbey this afternoon doesn't seem quite the same as that with which we are familiar. We wondered if it could possibly be altered.'

Consternation in the Abbey! Then, with the Canon, organist and precentor listening intently, the ladies at the Palace sang the Psalm over the 'phone. At length the gentlemen at the Abbey requested that they might be permitted to come to the Palace and practise with the ladies the amended setting of 'Crimond' and next day the Abbey resounded to the music that the bride, now our gracious queen, had so often enjoyed in Scotland.
(Ps. 98 4,5)

**210 Cross and Crown.** 'We want to begin a High School magazine, and we need first to have a school motto: can you suggest one?' asked the Mission High School Principal. 'Not at the moment,' replied the missionary, 'but we shall pray about it and think about it. Come again to me in a day or two and I may have thought of one by that time.' Within a week the missionary had found a motto: 'Bear the Cross: wear the crown.'    A.N.

(Luke 18. 28-30)

**211 Cross of Christ—The.** The sacrifice of the cross is the wonder of all wonders, the theme of all themes, the mystery of all mysteries, the song of all songs.

*O mystery of mysteries! of life and death the*
   *tree,*
*Centre of two eternities*
*Which look with rapt, adoring eyes, onward*
   *and back to Thee—*
*O Cross of Christ where all His pain*
*And death is our eternal gain!*

On the South coast of China, on a hill overlooking the harbour of Macao, Portuguese settlers built a massive cathedral. But a typhoon proved stronger than the work of man's hands, and some centuries ago the building fell in ruins, except for the front wall. High on the top of that jutting wall, challenging the elements down through the years is a great bronze cross. In 1825 Sir John Bowring was shipwrecked near that place. Clinging to the wreckage of his ship, he at last caught sight of that great cross which showed him where he could find safety. The dramatic rescue moved him to write the words that are familiar to millions:

*In the Cross of Christ I glory;*
*Towering o'er the wrecks of time;*
*All the light of sacred story*
*Gathers round its head sublime.*

(Gal. 6. 14)

**212 Cross—Sign of the.** A crowd of University students were coming home from an evening of pleasure. Their drunken leader noticed on the steeple of a church a cross illuminated by the moonlight, and shouted. 'Ye mathematicians, look at God's plus sign.'

One of the students could not sleep that night. Toward morning he stepped into the leader's room and told him that the vision of the Cross as God's plus sign had made him decide to uphold that cross as the symbol of God's abundant love for mankind. Seven other university men very soon took the same step.

*The Watchman Examiner*

Someone bought a house in Scotland. The previous owner had laid out the front garden in the form of a large cross. As the weeks passed, he noticed that the outline of the cross began to fade and soon was difficult to trace. Nothing had happened, but weeds and tufts of grass were springing up and obliterating the cross.

H. P. Barker

(Gal. 2. 20; 5. 24,25)

## 213 Cross—Splendour of the.

*The cross that Christ would have us bear is
    not a cross of wood:*
*It is the suffering of a heart that seeks
    another's good;*
*It is the tender heart that bleeds o'er pilgrims
    on the road;*
*It is the gracious heart that bends to lift
    another's load.*

*The tomb that He would have us seek is not
    a tomb of rock:*
*'Tis one where we can bury self with all its
    evil stock,*
*From which we rise in newest life to live for
    Him alone,*
*To count ourselves as dead to sin, for which
    He did atone.*

*The crown that He would have us seek does
    not belong to earth:*
*The potentates of time know not its vast and
    peerless worth.*
*It is no gain of skilful arms, no gift of
    scheming choice:*
*Its splendour has no place in speech: no word
    its worth can voice.*

*The glory He would have us prize is not the
    praise of man*
*Which fills the heart with subtle pride and
    evil passions fan:*
*Befriending those who have no friend—'tis
    here true glory lies*
*Unseen, unknown, yet serving all—this glory
    never dies.*

F. H. Oakley

(Matt. 16. 24)

## 214 Crosses—Cheap.

A Filipino Christian tells of an experience on Good Friday in Manila. As he passed a large Roman Catholic church, he noticed that the area around the church was crowded, not only with worshippers, but with many vendors selling incense, candles, veils and rosaries. Among the busy merchants were small boys running about selling crosses, and calling, 'Cheap crosses for sale! Buy a cheap cross!'

This struck me as having a meaning beyond what was intended. Some people like an easy religion, one that is all sweetness and light, one that makes no demand on their interests, no claim on their time and strength. As if the cross could be cheap!

The cross of Calvary was no cheap cross. Christ gave up His throne in glory to come and live in this world of sin, and give His life as a ransom on the cross in order to redeem us. There was nothing cheap about what He did for us. He calls us to take up our cross and follow Him. It is not a cheap, easy way, but it is a way filled with the light of His presence and blessed with opportunities to serve. One day the cross will be exchanged for a crown.

(Gal. 6. 14; Mark 8. 34)

## 215 Crowd is often Wrong.

Adam Thompson of Cincinnati, Ohio, filled the first bath tub in the U.S.A. in the year 1842. Doctors predicted rheumatism and inflammation of the lungs from such a newfangled idea. The city of Philadelphia put a ban on baths between November and March. Other towns imposed extra heavy water rates. All these facts are right, and off the records. But the crowd was wrong!

Dr Samuel Johnson said in the eighteenth century that no one could travel at more than ten miles an hour and live. In 1896 Britain still had a law prohibiting any power-driven vehicle from travelling at more than four miles an hour on the public highways. Furthermore it required that such a vehicle should be preceded by a man bearing a red flag. Yet the crowd was wrong again.

Samuel Morse had adverse criticism from Press and Government: but today the click of the telegraph, heard the world over, proved the crowd was wrong.

Alexander Bell was called a fool when he exhibited his telephone. Today we talk around the world as a result of his invention. Once more the crowd was wrong.

The first reaper and binder was derided as a cross between a chariot, a wheelbarrow and a flying machine. Yet the inventor was right and again the crowd was wrong.

When Westinghouse proposed to stop a railway train with wind (the Westinghouse air-brake) he also was called a fool, but very soon the crowd was proved wrong.

Goodyear was 'booed' by everyone but his wife working eleven years on vulcanizing rubber. Today every motor car uses his invention. The crowd was wrong.

Jenner was jeered when he discovered vaccination. Some serious-minded men went so far as to say that all the animal diseases would be transferred to the human race. Some said horns had actually grown out of the foreheads of innocent people. Yet Jenner eliminated the smallpox scare by using his vaccine. The majority was mistaken.

Robert Fulton had only words of discouragement from the crowd as they watched him work on his steamboat. They called it in derision 'Fulton's Folly'. Steamboats in large numbers cross the seas daily and displace the sailing ship. The crowd is daily proved to have been wrong.

Madame Curie sorted through tons of waste material in search of radium. The crowd laughingly asked, 'What is radium?' It is today a valuable asset in fighting disease, and many have owed their lives to its beneficent powers. Again the crowd was mistaken.

Have you ever thought that the majority may be wrong about their attitude to the Lord Jesus Christ? Are you part of that crowd that ignores His claims?

(Num. 13. 30,31)

**216 Crown of Righteousness.** At a Farewell meeting in New York, at the conclusion of Andrew Bonar's only visit to America, several speakers eulogised him, and in closing one man said, 'Think of the crown of righteousness which the Lord, the righteous judge, will give to Andrew Bonar in that day.' The dear man walked to the front of the platform, held up his hand toward heaven and completed Paul's words to Timothy: 'and not to me only, but unto all them that love His appearing.'

*Sunday School Times*

(2 Tim. 4. 8)

**217 Crucified.** Head down, hands in pockets, feet lagging, he was on his way to the waterfront when a startling word sounded out into the night. A man's voice exclaimed, 'Crucified! They crucified Him!'

The young man stopped in his tracks and glanced up. There, quite near, he saw light streaming from the open door of a little Mission Hall, and the speaker on the platform, beginning his evening's discourse. Churches and preachers had never meant much in John Scott's life; but tonight that brutal word had hit him where he lived, for he had seen man's inhumanity to man. He stepped inside and sat down.

A year before, the lad had gone to war, had suffered serious wounds and illness. Discharged from the British army, unfit for war or work, he had walked the streets of Bristol. 'Nobody cares,' he thought, 'nobody!' And he planned to end his life that night.

But now the preacher's words held his attention. 'A few months ago,' he was saying, 'the British were engaging the Germans on a certain sector in France. One British soldier, badly wounded, lay helpless in a shell hole between the lines; his friend shouted to the officer, "My buddy's out there! I'm going out to get him!"

'So Bill dropped to the ground and crawled out toward Jack—nearer and nearer until he was almost there. Then an enemy patrol spotted him, clubbed him over the head and dragged him back to their lines. They stretched him out against the wall of a wooden shed, and because of the hatred in their hearts they crucified him and left him there to die.'

At the repetition of that word 'crucified' a shadow crossed Scott's face.

'They thought Jack was dead, and so didn't touch him. He lay there in a shell hole and saw it all—the brutality, the suffering, the lingering death. As long as he lives the wounded man will never forget that sight. He will never forget how his buddy died for him.

'Friends,' the preacher continued, 'Have you forgotten that once a Man died in agony for you? Have you received Him? Have you done anything to show Him your love?'

As the service closed and young Scott moved toward the door, the preacher met him with outstretched hand, 'My lad,' he said, 'have you received the Lord?'

'No, sir,' he answered, 'but I want to. I never knew before what the Gospel was all about. But tonight I begin to understand. You see, I was the man in the shell hole. I saw my buddy die for me!'

The two knelt in prayer, while Jack Scott, led by the preacher, accepted the Lord Jesus as his Saviour and thanked Him for all He had done. Jack understood and believed the truth presented in Romans 5. 6, 'For when we were yet without strength, in due time Christ died for the ungodly.'

**218 Crucified Life—The.** I remember how, on one occasion, in South America, some engineering works had begun, but owing to malaria had to be abandoned. The ground was thickly wooded forest land, and before leaving, the engineers set light to a broad belt of land, hoping thus to cleanse the infected area, and for months the brushwood was smouldering. About two years after, the workmen returned to resume operations and were surprised to find the blackened ground covered with a new and unknown type of plant with an exquisite blue flower. Specimens were gathered and forwarded to the Botanical Gardens at Washington and elsewhere, but no one could identify this apparent produce of the action of fire. How many times have I seen in the realm of the soul, a crucified, cauterized life giving birth to new flowers and fruit of the Spirit!

H. St. John

(Gal. 2. 20; 5. 19-23)

**219 Crucified with Christ.** Here is a news clipping! Turning for a final glimpse of Gordon's Calvary, you recall the recent experience of a member of your party. While visiting that place, Dr R. G. Lee, a beloved Baptist pastor, had turned to his Arab guide with an unusual request: 'I'd like to go up there,' he said, pointing to the crest of the hill. 'You can't,' said the guide. But Dr Lee was not to be refused. 'I'm going,' he insisted. 'Then I'll go with you,' the guide answered, and together the two made their way to the top of the hill. Once on the crest, Dr Lee removed his hat to stand with bowed head, greatly moved. 'Sir,' the guide asked abruptly, 'have you been here before?' 'Yes!' replied Dr Lee without hesitation, 'two thousand years ago.' When Christ died, he died: 'crucified with Christ.'

Silas Fox

(Gal. 2. 20; 2 Cor. 5. 17; Rom. 13. 14)

**220 Custodianship.** Seen on a Wayside Pulpit: 'The Church is not the custodian of things that are ageing but of things that are ageless.'

(2 Tim. 1. 14; Jude 3)

**221 Dancing.** A fluffy young girl about sixteen years of age asked the late Harold St. John, 'Do you think a young Christian should dance?' He replied, 'first of all, I'm glad you say a young Christian. An old Christian doesn't want to; his bones are too stiff. Now you've asked me a very great question much too hard for me to answer. If you had asked me something simple, like the meaning of Ezekiel's wheels, or the wings of the seraphim, I could have told you at once; but to a question as deep as that I must say I cannot answer you.' And there were fifteen disappointed faces.

Then, by way of helping them to answer the question themselves, he got a piece of paper, drew a line down the centre, and put a cross on the centre, writing on one side of the cross B.C. and on the other A.D. 'Now!' he said, 'everything on the left will be what is suitable to the days before you knew Christ, and everything on the right hand suitable to the days after you knew Christ.' He then began to name quickly a number of activities, bringing dancing in about twelfth place, and like a flash it went down on the left-hand side.
(2 Cor. 5. 17)

**222 Dancing.** C. H. Spurgeon wrote: 'When I hear of a dancing party I feel an uneasy sensation about the throat, remembering that a far greater preacher had his head danced off in the days of our Lord. However pleasing the polkas of Herodias might be to Herod, they were death to John the Baptist. The caperings and wantonings of the ballroom are death to the solemn influences of our ministry, and many an ill-ended life first received its bent for evil amid the flippancies of gay assemblies met to trip away the hours.'
(Matt. 14. 6-8)

**223 Dancing—Is it wrong?** After a meeting three girls came to Montague Goodman. They wore the Crusader badge and he knew they were professing Christians. They said, 'Mr. Goodman, we want to ask you why you say it is wrong to dance.'

He answered, 'I never said such a thing.' 'Oh, well, you implied it,' said one. 'We'll leave that alone for the present,' he replied. 'But do you mind my asking you a question? Do you mind telling me, do you want to be holy?'

One after the other, the girls answered, 'Yes, I do!' 'Well!' he said, 'I have only one other question to put to you. In your experience, do you find dancing helps in that direction?'

They opened their eyes with a look of astonishment and said, 'No!' 'Well,' he said, 'I don't think we need to discuss the merits of dancing, for if you are determined to be holy and you find that dancing doesn't help you, you won't dance, will you?'
(Eph. 1. 4)

**224 Dangerous Amusements.** J. Wilbur Chapman, the evangelist, frequently told the story of a young lady who grasped an electric wire in front of her father's house and amused herself by pulling it along and watching the sparks fly. Suddenly, as her hand moved to a bare spot on the wire, a tremendous sweep of electricity surged through her body. She screamed in agony but was unable to let go because the current contracted the muscles of her hand. Her mother appeared on the scene and the girl cried out in anguish, 'Mother, save me! My hands are burning up.' The mother tried but was hurled to the ground as if she had been coshed. Finally a man with an axe severed the wire and the girl's life was saved: but she was fearfully burned and disfigured.

In the spiritual realm similar tragedies are daily taking place. Many tamper with sin and enjoy the sparks and kicks and thrills of sinful pleasures. The devil's enticing 'wires' lure them along the path of danger until they are unable to let go and so perish in their sin.
(1 Kings 13. 34)

**225 Daybreak.** A man whose youth and early manhood had been spent in evil ways was converted and one night was giving his testimony. During the week he had met an old former drinking pal who had chaffed him about turning pious. 'I'll tell you what I said to him. "Bill," I says, "you know what I am" (he was a lamp-lighter). "When I goes round turning out the lights, I looks back, and all the road over which I've been walking is all blackness, and that's what my past life is like. I looks on in front and there's a long row of twinkling lights to guide me, and that's what my future is like since I found Jesus." "Yes," says my friend, "but by and by you gets to the last light and turns it out, and where are you?"

'"Then," says I, "Why! when the last light goes out it's dawn, and there ain't no need for lamps when the morning comes"'
George Jackson
(Prov. 4. 18)

**226 Death—A Ship.**

*When men go down to the sea in ships,*
*'Tis not to the sea they go;*
*Some isle or pole the mariner's goal,*
*And thither they sail*
*Through calm and gale*
*When down to the ship they go.*

*When souls go down to the sea by ship,*
*And the dark ship's name is Death,*
*Why mourn and wail at the vanishing sail?*
*Though outward bound, God's world is round,*
*And only a ship is Death.*

Robert Freeman

**227 Death—A Sleep.** Sir Winston Churchill, in his radio tribute to King George VI, said: 'During these last months the king walked with death, as if death were a companion, an acquaintance whom he recognised and did not fear. In the end death came as a friend, and after a happy day of sunshine and sport, he fell asleep, as every man who strives to fear God and nothing else in the world may do.'

Prince Albert, Queen Victoria's husband, who died aged forty-two, left this testimony just before his death: 'I have had wealth, rank and power. But if this were all I had, how wretched I should be now!' He too fell asleep, with the words of his favourite hymn filling his mind: Rock of ages, cleft for me, Let me hide myself in Thee.
(John 11. 11,14)

**228  Death Abolished.** In 2 Timothy 4. 6, behold Paul standing there on the high deck of a great ocean liner (and the name of the good ship is 'Death') awaiting the moment of unmooring when the hawser will be slipped from the mooring post. The moment arrives and slowly, gradually feeling her freedom, the great ship drifts with the tides away from the dock; those on the shore wave it off with tears of affection; slowly those loved faces fade from the vision; the ship catches her stride and sails off beyond the horizon.

Jesse H. Baird

**229  Death Behind Us.** 'I do not expect to die,' said the old lady to Mr Needham, when he had asked her, 'You are not afraid to die?' 'You mean,' answered he, 'you are trusting the Lord and he has taken away the fear.' 'No, I'm not going to die.' Thinking that her mental balance was disturbed, and that he would humour her, he said, 'Why should you be exempt?' 'I have died already,' said she. Seeing the puzzled look on his face, she continued, 'You do not seem to understand. When Jesus died, I died: when He was crucified, I was crucified; when He rose, I rose. I am a child of the resurrection. Death is behind me: I shall only "sleep in Jesus".'
(2 Tim. 1. 10)

**230  Death Ends All.** I was talking to an atheist one day, and he said, 'I do not believe, Dr Wilson, what you are preaching.'

'You have not told me what you do not believe,' I said and then I asked: 'Perhaps you will tell me what you do believe.'

'I believe that death ends all,' was the reply.

'So do I,' I said. 'What! You believe that death ends all?'

'I certainly do,' I answered. 'Death ends all your chances for doing evil; death ends all your joy, all your projects, all your friendships, all your ambitions. Death ends it all for you, and you will go out into outer darkness.

'As for myself, death ends all my wanderings, all my tears, all my perplexities, all my disappointments, all my aches and pains. Death ends it all, and I go to be with my Lord in glory.'

'I never thought of it in that way,' he said. The outcome was that I led that man to Christ by agreeing that death ends all.

Walter Lewis Wilson
(Job 14. 10,14; Rev. 14. 13)

**231  Death in the Pot.** A story is told of an ancient who made a wonderful cup. When filled with wine, it appeared like other cups. When drained to the dregs there lay a serpent curled upon the bottom, with gleaming eyes and extended fangs.

When the prophet Elisha was dining with the prophets at Gilgal, they cried out after tasting the meal, 'O man of God, there is death in the pot.'

Beware of the fatal cup. There is a serpent coiled amid the flowers of worldly pleasure, lurking in the bowers of fleshly lust, hidden in the cup of sensual pleasure. The serpent lies low but poisons every drop. There is death in the 'pot' of drugs; at the bottom of the alcoholic cup lies the serpent ready to bite and sting. Here noble men bury their greatness and soil their honour and glory. Beware of the serpent in the cup: beware of the death in the pot.
(2 Kings 4. 40; Prov. 23. 31,32)

**232  Death of a Martyr.** In the days of the Scottish Covenanters—1660-1688—many men, women and even children, loyal to the Lord Jesus, were slaughtered for their faith in the Saviour. Those were the 'Killing Times.' One wee laddie, on his way to a Conventicle, was taken prisoner by the 'dragoons' of John Graham of Claverhouse. He refused to give the soldiers any information as to where the meeting was being held. His name was Jamie Douglas. The troops led him to the edge of a ravine, bade him to look down and see how deep it was, and threatened to drop him over into the ravine if he did not give them the information they demanded. He looked down, shuddered, and refused to tell them where the Lord's faithful followers were meeting that day, adding, 'Sae drap me doon there if ye will: it's nae sae deep as hell.' And they did.

**233  Deaths of Jesus and Alexander.** With three centuries intervening, these two outstanding men died at approximately the age of thirty-three, one in Babylon and the other outside Jerusalem. Jesus, the Son of God, was called great before His birth in Bethlehem: Alexander, the son of Philip of Macedonia, was given the title 'the Great' by historians after his death.

*Jesus and Alexander died at thirty-three:*
*One lived and died for self, One died for*
*  you and me.*
*The Greek died on a throne, Jesus died on*
*  a Cross:*
*One's life a triumph seemed, the other's but*
*  a loss.*

57

*One led vast armies forth, the other walked
    alone:*
*One shed a whole world's blood, the other
    gave His own.*
*One won the world in life and lost it all in
    death,*
*But Jesus gave His life to win our love and
    faith.*

*Jesus and Alexander died at thirty-three:*
*One died in Babylon and One at Calvary.*
*One gained all for himself; Jesus Himself
    He gave:*
*One conquered every throne, the other every
    grave.*
*One made himself a god: true God made
    Himself less:*
*The one lived but to blast: the other lived
    to bless.*
*When died the Greek, for ever fell his throne
    of swords,*
*But Jesus died and lives for ever, Lord of lords.*

*Jesus and Alexander died at thirty-three:*
*The Greek made all men slaves, but Jesus
    makes men free.*
*One built a throne on blood, the other built
    on love:*
*The one was born of earth, Jesus came from
    above.*
*One won the whole of earth to lose both
    earth and heaven:*
*The other gave up all, and all to Him is
    given.*
*The Greek for ever died: Jesus for ever lives.*
*He loses all who gets and wins all things
    who gives.*

(John 5. 25,26)

**234  Deathbeds.** The French nurse who was present at the deathbed of Voltaire the infidel, being asked to attend an Englishman whose case was critical, said, 'Is he a Christian?' 'Yes!' was the reply, 'he is a Christian in the highest and best sense of the word, a man who lives in the fear of God; but why do you ask?' 'Sir,' she answered, 'I was the nurse who attended Voltaire in his last illness, and for all the wealth of Europe I would never see another infidel die.'
*The Sunday School Times*

Two men died in the same year in America, Colonel Ingersoll, the acknowledged leader of American infidelity; and D. L. Moody, the leader of Christian activity. The death of Ingersoll was sudden and without a ray of cheer or brightness, and his funeral utterly pitiful. His wife and daughter despairingly clung to his decaying body: it was all they had. The scene at the crematorium, as described in the daily newspaper, was enough to make the heart of anyone ache.

On the other hand, the death and funeral of Mr. Moody were triumphant in every detail. On the morning of his departure his eldest son, sitting beside his bed, heard his father say in a low tone of voice, 'Earth is receding, heaven is opening, God is calling.' The family, summoned to his bedside, heard him say, 'Is this death? There is no valley. This is bliss: this is glorious!' He rallied, rose from his bed and walked to the window, then, feeling faint, again was helped back into bed. His daughter Emma began to pray for his recovery, but he said, 'No, no, Emma, God is calling. This is my coronation day. I have been looking forward to it.' The heroic warrior then entered the presence of the King.

All was triumphant at the funeral. There was nothing of sadness in the service.

**235  Debt Cancelled.** Lord Congleton devised a plan for teaching his tenants how by faith they could receive the forgiveness of sins, but be shut out from the promises of the Gospel through unbelief.

His tenants, some of them years behind in their payment of rent, had reason to be apprehensive that their landlord might take action against them through the 'Land Court'. To their astonishment, a notice was posted up all over the estate promising remission of rent to any tenant who would meet Lord Congleton in his office at certain stated hours on a certain day. The tenants, suspicious, spent the intervening days trying to find out what plan Lord Congleton had to trick them.

On the appointed day Lord Congleton sat in his office awaiting his tenants' response to his offer, while they, on their part discussed their landlord's offer. The hours fixed were the morning hours, ten to twelve o'clock, but it was not till nearly midday that one of the tenants, unavoidably delayed, rushed into the office and claimed the promised remission.

'Do you really expect your debt to be forgiven?' asked Lord Congleton.

'Indeed I do, my lord,' was the reply.

'And why do you?' asked his landlord.

'Because your lordship has promised.'

'And do you believe the promise?'

'Of course I do, my lord.'

'Why?'

'Because your lordship would not deceive a poor man.'

'But you are a good man, are you, industrious and hard-working?'

'Oh, my lord, your notice said nothing about that.'

'And so, believing the notice and finding no condition attached, you have come for your receipt?'

'Yes, my lord.'

Lord Congleton wrote the receipt and handed it to the tenant who waved the paper above his head and shouted, 'I knew you wouldn't deceive us. God bless your lordship.'

He was making for the door to show it to his fellow-tenants but Lord Congleton asked him to wait a few minutes till the hour struck, since the promise of remission was to faith, and only to faith, and the specified time ended at twelve noon.

At twelve o'clock he rushed out with the receipt, shouting, 'I've got it. My debt is cancelled.'

Other tenants then rushed to the office but found the door shut. Unbelief had kept them from obtaining cancellation of their debt.

(Acts 13. 38,39; Heb. 3. 19; 2 Cor. 6. 2)

**236 Debt—Christian's to Christ.** All who were present at the annual Missionary meetings held in the Central Hall, Westminster, on the occasion when the late J. B. Watson gave the closing message on the Lord's parable of the unjust steward will never forget the emphasis he laid on the question, 'How much owest thou unto my lord?' He said:

'The issue has been stated strikingly thus. The voice of truth enquires of you, "How much owest thou unto my lord?" The answer is plain, "An hundred measures of oil." And then the spirit of the unjust steward whispers within, "Sit down quickly and write fifty." "No, no, it will not do. Acknowledge your debt, and be ready as much as in you is to discharge it. Sit down quietly and deliberately and write 'One hundred!' And then, having given your note of hand, go forth and honour it by diligent and conscientious labour till the end of the day." '

(Luke 16. 6,7)

*O what a debt we owe to Him who shed His blood,*
*And cleansed our souls and gave us power*
*To stand before His God!*
*Saviour and Lord! we own the riches of Thy grace;*
*For we can call Thy God our God—*
*Can bow before His face.*
*Thy Father, too, above, we worship as our own,*
*Who gave with Thee the Spirit's cry,*
*To us His sons foreknown.*

G. V. Wigram

**237 Debt Paid.** It is a happy custom in some Jewish quarters of great cities for a wealthy Jew to seek out needy compatriots and try to help them. Up and down the streets of the ghetto he goes, scanning each door for a tell-tale white paper fluttering in the breeze. At last he sees one. It is a bill which the tenant of the cottage cannot pay, and by pinning it to his door declares the fact to any interested neighbour or inquisitive passer-by.

Going softly to the door, the would-be benefactor withdraws it, takes it to the creditor and pays the bill in full. Then, folding the receipted bill in half, with fine delicacy he again tiptoes to the door and pins it where he found it. With what happiness the poor bankrupt discovers next morning that his debt is fully paid, righteously discharged, and he holds in his hand the legal receipt.

Ransome W. Cooper

(Col. 2. 14)

**238 Debt Paid and Receipted.** It was the Monday of Easter week and a ring at the bell brought me to the door to find two young men who smilingly introduced themselves: 'We are two from a party of fourteen, sponsored by a Commonwealth organisation, whose assignment is to interview anyone kind enough to talk to us. That way we gain confidence in ourselves and learn what other people think.'

I soon learned that one was from Newcastle and had some three or four years' hotel training to his credit. The other was from Edinburgh where he had learned engineering: but being fond of figures he had decided to join his friend in running a hotel. Both felt confident that they could make money in the hotel business. Tactfully I reminded them that a great deal of hard work lay behind the successful hotelier, and that the most capable and courteous hotel proprietor I knew in England had spent some years learning the business in Switzerland, starting with scrubbing the kitchen floors.

'Which of you will look after the financial side of things?' I enquired. It was an unnecessary question, for the Scot at once asserted his intention of doing so.

We each asked and answered many more questions until I felt that I had a more important topic to discuss with them. Rather bluntly I said, 'Have you fellows ever realised that you owe a great debt to God which you can never pay?'

Sudden shocked silence.

'You and I are sinners, adding every day to our sin-debt, never able to reduce it. All we can ever do is tell God we are sorry; but that does not remove a single sin and the debt mounts higher daily.'

Turning to the would-be hotel proprietor, I said, 'Suppose a man comes along to your hotel—when you have one—and stays a few days with you. In the usual run of things you present your bill for, shall we say, fifteen pounds. He comes along to the office and says, rather shamefacedly, "I'm very sorry, but I don't possess a brass farthing." You look as astounded as you feel; but before you can express yourself forcefully he says: "But I'll tell you what—I promise I won't run into debt any more with you!"

'Now,' said I to them both, 'would that promise satisfy you? Would that clear your books of the fifteen pounds he owes you? No, I agree with you, it wouldn't wipe out the debt he owes. Nor will our repentance or promises to reform put away the sin-debt we owe to God.

'But now the man on the mat says, "Do you mind if I ring up a friend of mine?" You hand him the telephone and there in your office he talks to his friend. "I've got myself into trouble; I've run up a bill I cannot meet. Can you come round to the hotel and help me?"

'The friend comes round, takes out his wallet and produces three five-pound notes. Would that satisfy you? Yes, I'm sure it would. But it doesn't satisfy the friend who tenders the money. "Will you kindly give me a receipt?" he asks, and Mr Accountant, you are glad enough to do so. "Received cash with thanks, signature and date."

'Why does he need the receipt? Because the debtor wants legal proof that the debt was paid, though he himself did not pay it.

'This is Easter week, and next Friday is Good Friday. It was then that my Saviour went to the cross to pay a debt which I owed to God's righteousness and could never pay. When He had paid it, He cried, "It is finished!" That death cleared for ever my sin-debt and satisfied every claim which God had against me. But next Sunday is Easter Sunday, and that is the day when my Saviour rose again. That is my receipt. I see Him at God's right hand and I say, "There is the One Who paid my debt." He was delivered for our offences and raised again for our justification' (Romans 4. 25)

The two young men shook hands and departed; perhaps they carried with them some thoughts which may prove of eternal benefit to them.

Ransome W. Cooper

**239  Debt to Mother.** Tommy made out a bill for his widowed mother, which read something like this:

MOTHER OWES TOMMY

| | |
|---|---:|
| For chopping sticks ... ... ... ... | 20 cents |
| For fetching water ... ... ... ... | 20 cents |
| For odd jobs ... ... ... ... ... | 10 cents |
| Total ... ... ... | 50 cents |

Placing the bill on the table, he awaited developments and was thrilled when he found a bright half-dollar from mother's tattered old purse on his plate.

'Whoopee!,' he cried, 'now I've something to spend with the boys.'

Then he noticed his mother also had made out a bill and put it on his plate. It read like this:

TOMMY OWES MOTHER

| | |
|---|---:|
| For clothing ... ... ... ... ... | 0 |
| For food ... ... ... ... ... ... | 0 |
| For love and care ... ... ... ... | 0 |
| Total ... ... ... | 0 |

Tommy rushed into the kitchen and flung himself into his mother's arms and cried:

'O mum, I'll do anything for you.' Mother got her fifty cents back.

Harold Wildish

(James 1. 17)

**240  Debtors.** Katar Singh, a Tibetan, for professing his faith in Christ, was sentenced to be sewn up in a yak skin and exposed to the heat of the sun. The slow process of contraction of this death trap is the most awful means of torture ever devised by human cruelty. At the close of the day the dying man asked to be allowed to write a parting message. It was as follows:

> *I give to Him who gave to me*
> *My life, my all, His all to be.*
> *My debt to Him how can I pay,*
> *Though I may live to endless day?*
> *I ask not one, but a thousand lives,*
> *For Him and His own sacrifice.*
> *Oh, will I then not gladly die*
> *For Jesus' sake, and ask not why.*

(Heb. 11. 35,36)

**241  Deceit.** Abraham Lincoln said, 'We may deceive all the people sometimes: we may deceive some of the people all the time, but not all the people all the time, and not God at any time.'
(Jer. 9. 5)

**242  Deceivers.** The expression 'face the music' is said to have originated in Japan. In the Imperial Orchestra was a person of great wealth and influence who had demanded a place in the group that played before the emperor, though he didn't know music and could not play a note. The conductor agreed to let him sit in the second row of the orchestra. When the music began he would raise the flute to his mouth, pucker his lips and go through all the motions of playing but never made a sound. This deception continued for two years, and apparently he had fooled everyone.

Then a new leader of the orchestra took over who required a personal audition on the part of each player. One by one each rendered a solo before the conductor. Then came the flautist's turn. Frantic with worry, he acted sick when the time came. A doctor was called and declared him perfectly well, so he had to appear and prove his ability to play the flute. Shamefacedly he had to confess himself a fake, so he was unable to face the music.

**243  Decision for Christ.** In the year 1879 a young student at Yale University attended one of D. L. Moody's meetings and was counselled after the service by a man who accompanied him to the gate of his house, urging him to accept Christ as his Saviour. As they reached the house, the young man said, 'Now I must decide this question tonight. If I cross this line, my life shall be for Christ; if I go round it, it will be for the world.' For half an hour he stood with the line at his feet, uncertain and undecided. Then, praying, 'O God, help me to decide aright!' he stepped over the line and went straight to his father's room to tell him of his decision. The next night, the young man's father, who was a preacher, told the story at Moody's meeting.

The hymn 'Over the line, it is only a step!', commencing 'O tender and sweet was the

Master's voice!' was written by Ellen K. Bedford when she heard of the incident. (Josh. 24. 15)

**244 Decision—The Wrong.** George Gould and another evangelist were conducting a gospel campaign in a village in Northern Ireland. One day a farmer who lived in the vicinity met him and said, 'I want you to come to my house to meet my family, and to get my wife and daughter to attend your meetings.'

'And why not come to the meetings yourself?' asked Mr. Gould.

'It would not help me any,' said the farmer, decisively.

On being asked to explain why, the farmer said, 'There was an evangelist, named David Rea, preaching in the same schoolhouse about forty years ago. I went to hear him preach every night, and I was really anxious to be saved at that time. In the neighbourhood there was some opposition. My uncle knew that I was attending the meetings and he did not like it at all, so one day he said to me,

'"Look here, John, this one hundred acre farm of mine is one of the finest farms around here, and I am going to leave it to you if you quit going to those meetings in the schoolhouse. Now understand me, keep on going if you like, and we shall still be friends, but you will never get this farm unless you quit going."

'You can be sure I didn't sleep a wink that night. I was anxious to be saved but I wanted the farm too. The struggle that night and all the next day was terrific. Finally I decided to quit attending the meetings and take the farm, thinking there was plenty of time and there would be other meetings in the schoolhouse some day. I reckoned I could go then and be saved. So I left off attending the meetings and inherited my uncle's farm. I shall show you the very spot where I made this tragic decision.'

The farmer led Mr Gould across the yard and pointed out the very spot on which he had stood when he decided to take the farm and refuse the Saviour.

'Now,' said the farmer, 'it would be useless for me to come to the meetings because I am not anxious to be saved any more. I have come back to this spot with tears in my eyes and pleaded with God to let me reverse my decision, but in vain. It is too late for me now to change it, but ask my wife and daughter to come to the meetings. Perhaps they will decide for Christ and be saved, but for me it is too late.' (Gen. 6. 3; Mark 8. 36)

**245 Decisions—Making.** Trust in God to help you make the right decisions. The Psalmist said, 'Thou wilt guide me with Thy counsel and afterward receive me to glory.' The Psalmist believed that God's wisdom is available to people and that, if we will avail ourselves of His guidance, He will see to it that everything works out all right.

A friend of mine told me that when he has a decision to make, he prays, 'Lord, I want to do the right thing and if Thou wilt show me what the right thing is, I promise Thee I shall do it regardless of what the cost may be.' He says he usually has very little trouble in reaching a decision after that.

Charles Allen in *Reader's Digest*
(Ps. 27. 11; 86. 11)

**246 Dedication—A Covenant of.** A servant of Christ, who for many years served her Lord in the Congo, wrote what she called her COVENANT OF DEDICATION, and signed it with her blood. It was worded:

'Lord Jesus, I belong to Thee from head to foot, and will always be Thine, for Thou hast redeemed me. Thou art the King of my life and hast absolute and undivided rule over all my affections and will and desire. My chief aim in life shall be to please Thee, so do Thou change me and cleanse me and use me as Thou wilt. I ask Thee to help me loyally to keep this covenant which I seal with my own blood because I am willing to lay down my life for Thy sake, if Thou should'st ask me.' (Rom. 12. 1; Phil. 1. 21)

**247 Deity and Divinity.** The word 'Divinity' is sometimes confounded with 'Godhead' and 'Deity'. Godhead and Deity are faithful translations of the Greek word 'theotees' which occurs only in Colossians 2. 9. The word means 'Godhead in the absolute sense' (J.N.D.) and is distinct in meaning from 'theiotees', occurring in Romans 1. 20, which signifies the character of God rather than God Himself.

The word in Romans is applied by the apostle to what may be observed of God in the works of nature—His creative majesty, might and wisdom. These attributes are included in His Godhead, but are not His essential Being. On the other hand, all the fullness of the Godhead dwells in Christ bodily.

To make this important distinction between the two words, 'Godhead' in Romans 1. 20 is replaced by 'divinity' in the R.V., in the New Translation and in other translations. 'Godhead' is reserved for the rendering of 'theotees' in Colossians 2. 9, where Deity in the fullest, most absolute sense is required both by the word and its context.

It is always wise to note the inspired values of Scriptural words, particularly of those relating to the Person of our adorable Lord. In view of the prevailing denials of the ever-blessed Son, it is specially important to mark the distinction between the terms 'Deity' and 'Godhead' on the one hand, and 'divinity' on the other, and to remember that the latter should never be regarded as a synonym or as the equivalent of the former two.

W. J. Hocking

(Acts 17. 29)

**248  Deity of Christ.**

*The king? If King of Heaven, had He no*
*  power*
*To stay the surging evil of that hour?*
*He had—but out He went, and there He died*
*That sinners might be cleansed and justified,*
*Brought back to God. The wonder of this*
*  thing—*
*A pauper's pardon purchased by a King!*

*The King. Today mankind still turns Him*
*  down,*
*Still scourges, spits and plaits a thorny crown,*
*Still mocks His precious Name, still treads*
*  roughshod*
*Upon His claims—We have no time for God!*
*And so the royal Saviour is denied*
*The souls for whom He once was crucified.*

*The King. Creator of all living things;*
*The Lord of Hosts; the mighty King of kings;*
*The conqueror of Death; the perfect One;*
*The Judge of all the earth, God's only Son;*
*The Christ of God is King! No power is known*
*To match in majesty His heavenly throne.*

*The King. Today this question comes anew—*
*Will you have Jesus to reign over you?*
*His hands and feet are pierced, His brow is*
*  scarred,*
*But there is glory in that face once marred.*
*He reigns! His claim outrivals everything.*
*Will you have Jesus Christ to be your King?*

Maurice Cox
(Matt. 2. 2; John 19. 15; Rev. 19. 16)

**249  Deliverer—The Great.** In the middle of
the seventeenth century, when Dr Doddridge
lived at Northampton, there was a poor
Irishman sentenced to be executed for sheep-
stealing. The cruelty of this decree stirred the
sympathetic doctor to the depths of his heart.
He felt there was insufficient proof of the
man's guilt and so he travelled many miles,
and toiled and tried hard to get that man a
reprieve. But his efforts, his eloquence and his
earnestness were all unavailing. The man was
hanged. It also broke the good doctor's heart.

The road to the execution led the convict
past Dr Doddridge's house, but the doctor
who could not bear to see the sad procession
stayed in his room, pouring his grief into the
ear of God. On reaching the place, the prisoner
persuaded the sheriff to stop the cart at Dr
Doddridge's residence and, kneeling down,
exclaimed, 'God bless you, Dr Doddridge.
Every vein in my heart loves you, every drop
of my blood loves you, for you tried to save
every drop of it.'

J. T. Mawson tells of a native of East
Africa who summed up the story of the
impotent, helpless man in John 5 in two
sentences: The man said, 'I have no man.'
and Jesus said, 'I am your man!' He had
learnt the wonderful and soul-emancipating
truth that, where all others fail, power and
deliverance lie in Christ alone. For the
disappointed seeker, the soul condemned to
eternal death, Jesus is the Man mighty to
save, the great Deliverer.
(John 5. 7; Rom. 7. 24)

**250  Denominations of Christendom.** Harold
St. John loved to look back to the origin of
the great denominations and claim his own
share in the doctrines for which their founders
lived and died. He maintained that the great
blunder of the Corinthian church and the
cause of all their party spirit was that they
said, 'I belong to Paul or Apollos' instead of
'Paul, Apollos, belongs to us'. 'They were
putting the cart before the horse,' said Mr.
St. John. They didn't belong to Paul; Paul
belonged to them. If we understand that, all
the sectarianism in the church would disappear
tomorrow. You would not say, 'I belong to
Martin Luther' but 'He belongs to me'. Look
at Chapter 3 of 1 Corinthians—'All things
are yours; whether Paul, or Apollos, or
Cephas—all are yours!' What did he mean?
He means that all the great spiritual men and
ministers of the past belong to us, everyone.
I have a share in—Martin Luther, John
Bunyan, C. H. Spurgeon. Everyone belongs
to me but I belong to none of them.

Patricia St. John
(1 Cor. 3. 4, 21-23)

**251  Denunciation of Sin.** One of the
chaplains of King Charles II was wont to
denounce sin very sternly. Warned by the
king to alter his message and manner of
preaching, he replied courageously, 'I will,
your Majesty, when you alter your manner
of living.'
(Ezek. 33. 11)

**252  Depression and its Remedy.** Dr Martyn
Lloyd-Jones writes:

'I am always very distrustful of any Christian who tells me he or she knows nothing about
depression. There is a chorus which says,
"And now I am happy all the day". I do not
believe that. There will be times when you are
unhappy. There are these states and conditions
of the soul, and the sooner you learn to deal
with them and how to handle them, the
better it will be for you and for those with
whom you live and work.'

Experience confirms the words of Dr
Martyn Lloyd-Jones, for there are very few
people indeed who never feel out of sorts,
who are always 'on top of the world' and
never 'under the weather'; who never have
'a touch of the blues' because they are always
'in the pink'.

Dr Martyn Lloyd-Jones found an unfailing
remedy in a book by Dr Sibbes entitled—
*The Bruised Reed, The Soul's Conflict.* He
says, 'It was balm to my soul at a period in
my life when I was overworked and badly
overtired, and therefore subject to the on-
slaughts of the devil in an unusual manner.
That book quietened, soothed, comforted,
encouraged and healed.'
(Ps. 42. 5,11)

**253 Depths of the Sea.** When Nansen, the Norwegian explorer, tried to measure the depth of the ocean in the far North, he used a long measuring line, and when he discovered it had not reached the bottom he wrote in his record: 'Deeper than that'. The next day he tried a longer line only to have to write again, 'Deeper than that'. Several times he tried until finally he fastened all his lines together and let them down, but his last record was like the first, 'Deeper than that'. He left without being able to ascertain the depth of the ocean at that point.

Billy Bray, the Cornishman, was alone in a friend's house. He looked round for a Bible but could only find a Geography book. Opening it, he read that in certain parts of the great oceans the depth is measured in miles. Then he shouted, 'Praise the Lord!' and quoted Micah 5. 19:

*I will cast in the depths of the fathomless sea*
*All thy sins and transgressions, whatever they be*
*Though they mount up to heaven, though they*
*    sink down to hell,*
*They shall sink in the depths and above them*
*    shall swell*
*All the waves of My mercy, so mighty and free.*
*'I will cast all thy sins in the depths of the sea.'*

**254 Desires.** I asked a student what three things he most wished for. He said, 'Give me books, health and quiet and I care for nothing more.'

I asked a miser and he said, 'Money, money, money.'

I asked a pauper and he faintly said, 'Food, clothes and warmth.'

I asked a drunkard and he loudly called for strong drink.

I asked the crowd around me and they clamoured for wealth, pleasure and fame.

I asked a workman and he replied, 'More wages, more leisure and more amusement.'

I asked a poor man who had long borne the character of a consistent Christian. He replied that all his desires could be met in Christ. He continued: 'I greatly long for three things: that I may be found in Christ, that I may be like Christ, that I may be with Christ.' (Phil. 3. 8,9)

**255 Despair to Joy.** 'Hell could be no worse', I thought as I turned toward the bathroom. I hated my stubborn, good-looking husband. I didn't like being a mother. I couldn't stand washing dishes and house cleaning. Life was just one horrible day after another. Our marriage was on the rocks and I decided that suicide was the only way out.

Reaching into the medicine chest, I deliberately got a razor blade. As I lowered the sharp blade to my wrist, the telephone rang. I let it ring. No one had any answers for me. But the caller was insistent.

Now beyond the place of being hurt or

helped, I picked up the telephone and said, 'Hello.' That call, in May, 1958, saved my life.

I was born in a parsonage. My parents prayed that God would give them a girl—a girl who played the piano and sang. When I was born they rejoiced and named me Joyce.

I loved music and before reaching my eighth year I knew I wanted to be a concert pianist. I wasn't leaving God out—and yet I was! I sang and played in church, but I was living on my folk's salvation. My Christianity consisted of the too common list of 'do's' and 'don'ts'.

At the age of fifteen I told my mother, 'Let me love God in my own way; I don't want to be a Christian fanatic.' I could run my own life. If things really got beyond me I would, I thought, have enough sense to call for His help. In emergencies, God could bail me out, but I must not be hindered from reaching the bright lights.

I put my career at the top of the list. Then I found a man I could love. When he asked me to be his wife I was ready with the answer. We started our home, we thought, on the premise of loving God. We both became active in the church. Eighteen months later we welcomed blue-eyed Ricky. Two years after that, lovely Laurie joined our family.

A handsome husband, two lovely children, and a singing career should be enough to make any woman happy. But I was neurotic and miserable. Our marriage, only five years old, was on the rocks.

I couldn't get it through Dick's stubborn head that I was talented, creative, sensitive and musical, and that I was meant to be vivacious, charming and appreciated. He insisted that I should care for the children, wash dishes and clean the house. By this time neither of us was talking with God. As a matter of fact we talked very little with one another. We simply retreated into our own private worlds and never discussed the real issues of life. Soon there was no hope and I knew it. There was no love—only hate. I was filled with disgust for living. I was through.

And then that telephone rang! A Christian I had met when singing for Youth for Christ answered my 'Hello' with, 'I don't know what you are doing, Joyce, but whatever it is, stop and listen to me!'

Instantly I knew he was going to quote the Bible—and I was furious. I knew the Bible, and felt it had no answers for me. But I listened as he quoted Ephesians 5. 17, 'Firmly grasp what you know to be the will of God' (Phillips). Sensing I was in no mood to listen, he shouted, 'Joyce, the Bible says, "Having done all to stand".'

He was still talking as I slammed down the receiver. I walked back to the bathroom and picked up the razor. As I did so, the enormity of what had just happened startled me. I put down the blade and asked, 'God, do you care about me?' The Lord answered me with a verse I had learned as a child, 'The Son of man is come to seek and to save that which was lost' (Luke 19. 10).

In the living room I dropped to my knees by a chair. During the next hours the Lord showed me that I had rebelled against God, parents, husband, home and children. Tenderly He spoke to me, assuring me that if I confessed my rebellion, He would forgive me, and cleanse me as well.

A miracle took place as the rebellious Joyce Landorf became the rejoicing Joyce Landorf. I jumped to my feet a new girl with a new song. My joy was interrupted with the disturbing question, 'But what about Dick? Can love once dead live again?'

I was cooking supper when Dick came in. I turned off the oven and shared my story with him. He moved closer and put his arm round me. I knew he was trying to hide wet eyes.

'Joyce,' he said, 'I want to tell you my side of the miracle. Perhaps we should call it Chapter Two. Today I gave up. I locked my office door and wrote you a hateful letter filled with the words of a defeated man. On the envelope I wrote, "To Joyce. When you find this I will be dead."'

'But, Joyce, as I sealed that letter the Lord said, "Dick, suicide is not the answer: I am the answer. I am all you need. I will give you abundant life."' As Dick told his chapter I reached for the Kleenex box and we wept together, and in that unforgettable moment, we stepped into the sunlight of a brand new life.

Has that been your experience? Have you found the sunlight of that new life? In the midst of all the cares and pressures of life—in the face of those trying circumstances that inflict fear and discouragement and sometimes despair—God offers the victory of true joy. Turn your despair into joy.

Joyce Landorf in *Concerning Himself*

**256 Devil—Deliverance from the.** A Christian negro slave in America was overheard by his master, groaning, weeping and praying to God for deliverance from the devil. 'Pompey,' said his master, 'you seem to have a good deal of trouble with the devil, and he never bothers me at all. Yet you are a good praying man, and I am not a Christian. How comes that, Pompey?'

To this the slave replied, 'Ah, Massa, I will soon explain that. When you are out shooting ducks, which do you send the dog after first? The ones that fall dead or the ones that are wounded a little and are trying to get away?'

'Why, Pompey, the wounded ones, of course. The dead ones we are sure of, and can take our time to pick them up.'

'Just so, Massa. And so it is with Satan. He has got all those that are not born again, fast and sure. But those that know the Lord he always sets his dogs after. He knows he can pick up the others by and by.'

'We are not ignorant of his devices' (2 Cor. 2. 11).

**257 Devil—Works of the.** At a church conference in the early 1960s the delegates decided to give the devil seven more years, but not in jail—in a more respectable place, the Catechism. The conference had before it a suggestion that, in these modern times, the section requiring the church members to 'renounce the works of the devil' should be removed.

*Men don't believe in a devil now,*
*As their fathers used to do.*
*They have opened their door to the broadest creed*
*To let his majesty through.*

The conference decided that the devil must stay in the catechism for at least another seven years.

'The whole world lies in the wicked one', wrote the apostle John. He also wrote, 'The Son of God was manifested that He might destroy the works of the devil.'

John Selfridge writes, 'The syncopation of "Rock 'n' Roll" and "The Twist" and the bodily contortions which they produce are similar to what the missionary can hear and see day by day in heathen villages'—and he might have added, 'all through the night', where numbers of them are demon-possessed. (1 John 3. 8; 5. 19)

**258 Devil Worship.** The 'spirit of divination' from which Paul the apostle, in the name of Jesus Christ, delivered the girl possessed by it, as recorded in Acts 16. 16-18, was a spirit of Python, a snake god. They regarded the god they worshipped by the name Apollo as embodied in a snake. In the Old Testament version the same word is used of the witch of Endor who had 'a familiar spirit', (1 Sam. 28. 7) and it is also employed by Plutarch to indicate 'ventriloquists'. That spirit made the witch of Endor and the girl in Philippi do and say things beyond their own control, because it was under the control of the devil.

A Sunday School teacher in London recently discovered that some of the boys were going directly after morning Sunday School to some mysterious place of meeting. He learned where the meeting was held and went one morning to the place, a large room formed by enclosing a railway arch. Knocking at the door, he was admitted by one of his own Sunday School boys and found within several boys and girls from his own Sunday School. Asking what they were doing, he was told they were going to have Sunday School. Presently a woman, their leader and teacher, came in, formed them into a ring after telling them to put all their Bibles on a shelf, and led the children in singing hymns.

One of the songs was addressed to 'Mother Lotus'. The children next circled round a gilt serpent hanging from the roof, all holding up hands and pointing with their forefingers to this serpent, while they called out repeatedly,

'O glorious Apollo!' Some of the girls had rings on their fingers in the form of a serpent with its tail in its mouth.

Later, the teacher who found this out called a meeting of the other teachers and related what he had seen. On making further enquiries, they found that many of their scholars attended that place and were quite aware that they were being taught to worship the devil. One girl of thirteen or fourteen, warned by her Sunday School teacher said quite seriously, 'Oh, miss, the devil's very kind: he'll give me whatever I want.' It was further discovered that this was only one of a considerable number of similar 'Sunday Schools' in England.

(1 John 5. 19)

**259 Devilish Drugs.** LSD used to signify a value in sterling, pounds, shillings and pence. Now these three initials identify a tincture with terrifying effects. By this new weapon hell is invading the very minds of men.

LSD is described as a 'psychedelic drug', that is, a 'consciousness expanding' drug. Compared with this, the well-known narcotics are like a walk in the park on a Sunday afternoon. One ounce of this drug can make 300,000 doses, each one dropped on a sugar cube being potent enough to derange the mind of the taker for ten hours and dangerous enough to make permanent the mental deterioration it produces.

The disciples of this devilish drug say, 'No one has really lived until he has taken a trip via LSD.' It is estimated by some that this year one million doses will be swallowed by people who just as eagerly swallowed the lie.

The users of this drug have developed into a cult with strong religious overtones. They speak of using 'altars' and of 'officiating priests', and of administering a 'host' to the communicants.

If ever there was a 'table of devils' this surely is one. One user, describing his sensations while on a 'trip', said he felt as though there was a serpent writhing within him. Another saw within himself 'hideous shapes ...horrible,...a flood of bogeymen'.

The hellish origin of this latest craze is undeniable and its dangers terrifying. A few pounds of it dumped into the water supply of a city would be sufficient to disorientate mentally a multitude of its inhabitants, men, women and children.

It is not only the young set, but many who feel the limitations of the stiffened muscle, the grey hair and the not-so-elastic artery who are experimenting with the drug.

*Food for the Flock*

(1 Cor. 10. 21)

**260 Disaster.** November 28, 1942, was a gala Saturday night and about eight hundred merrymakers were packed in the Coconut Grove. Some were boys about to return to service in the Army camps and some were members of a wedding party. Many more were there to celebrate a Holy Cross football victory over Boston College that afternoon.

In the Melody Lounge downstairs a pianist was banging out jazz tunes. The war being on, young women in evening gowns were dancing in the main floor dining-room with men in uniform.

The bridegroom had planned to take his bride to their new apartment at 10 p.m. sharp but they lingered on a few fateful minutes. The floor show was scheduled to start at 10.15 p.m. so the dance floor upstairs had been cleared and the band leader stood poised to lead the crowd in the singing of the 'Star Spangled Banner'.

Suddenly a girl rushed across the room screaming 'Fire!' Panic followed. At the downstairs bar, a bus boy apparently had struck a match to see how to screw a light bulb into its socket. The flame touched one of the artificial palm trees that gave the Coconut Grove its atmosphere. The fire quickly devoured the palm tree and racing along silk draperies was sucked upward through the stairway, leaping along ceilings and walls.

The flimsy hangings turned to balloons of flame, falling on tables, people and floor. But it was the hysteria and panic of the screaming, clawing crowds, more than the flames and the stifling smoke, which added the tool of death in this terrible catastrophe. Men and women, maddened with fear, fought their way toward the revolving door. The push of bodies jammed the exit.

Nearby was another door but it was locked tight. Then the lights went out. Now there was nothing to be seen but flames, smoke and moving torches that were men and women with clothing and hair afire. The people pushed, fought, fell and were trampled upon.

Firemen breaking down the revolving door found it blocked by the bodies of the dead, six deep. The final count showed that 501 people lost their lives. It was the worst U.S. disaster of its kind since the 1903 Iroquois Theatre fire in Chicago when 572 persons perished.

Our hearts are heavy at the reminder of this horrible holocaust, but there is a soul-searching lesson for all in this story. We are living in a world that is doomed for destruction under the righteous judgement of God. The wise will seek the door that leads to salvation and eternal security before the way of escape is removed. The Lord Jesus says, 'I am the Door; by me if any man enter in he shall be saved.'

(John 10. 9)

**261 Discontent.** One day Abraham Lincoln was walking along a street in his home town, Springfield, Illinois, with his two small sons, both of whom were crying lustily. A neighbour stopped and enquired, 'What's the matter with the boys?' 'Just the same as what's the

matter with the whole world,' replied Lincoln. 'I've got three walnuts and each of the boys wants two.'
(Heb. 13. 5)

**262  Divided Interests.**  Michael Faraday, the great scientist, was in his youth a newsboy in England. A big iron gate to the paper offices was locked one morning when he waited for his papers. He sat on the rod that was part of the gate and put his hands and his head through the palings. The trunk of his body was on the outside, his hands and head on the inside. As a youthful philosopher he began to reason: 'With my hands and head on one side, and my heart on the other, on which side am I?' While he was debating, somebody opened the gate, and the wrench that he received taught him a lesson. For effective service in any sphere the head, hand and heart must be on the same side. A divided house, or kingdom, or person, is a misfit.
*Sunday School Times*
(Matt. 12. 25)

**263  Division because of Christ.**  In his splendid historical account of the 'Killing Times' in Scotland, Dr Alexander Smellie in *Men of the Covenant* tells of two men who died within a few hours of each other on July 26, 1681. They were the Earl of Rothes and Donald Cargill. Companions in youth and fellow-students at St Andrews University, they made in early manhood different decisions that divided them and influenced the course of their lives. Donald Cargill, after a life devoted to the cause of the Lord Jesus Christ, died as a martyr at Mercat Cross, Edinburgh. After a life of sinful pleasure and dissipation the Earl of Rothes died of disease in his own stately home. Nearing the end of his life, the Earl said, 'We all thought little of what Cargill did in excommunicating us, but I find that sentence binding and it will be binding to eternity.'
High up in the Alps are two lakes, Lago Nero (the Black Lake) and Lago Blanco (the White Lake), about a stone's throw apart, on two sides of a watershed. The overflow of Lago Nero runs in a river to the Black Sea, and the overflow of the other to the calm waters of the Adriatic, 'one to darkness and the frozen tide, one to the peaceful sea'. 'There was a division among the people because of Him.'
(John 7. 43; 9. 16; 10. 19)

**264  Doctor's Bible—The.**  W. P. Mackay left home to attend college and medical school at the age of seventeen. His mother was a very godly Christian, and upon his departure she gave him a Bible, writing her name and his, and a verse of Scripture upon the fly-leaf. He had no use for his mother's God, or the Bible she had given him. He did not consult its pages; and soon after, while drunk, he pawned it to purchase whisky.

His studies engrossed him and the Bible was forgotten. Eventually he graduated with high honours and became the head of a large hospital. He also took the lead in an infidel club where they practised everything that was licentious and vile.

The only thing that seemed to give him any thrill at all was when an ambulance would unload a dying victim of an accident; or a patient came under his care whose condition was so critical that the chances of survival were slim. This nerved him to pit his skill against what his colleagues would term the impossible.

One day an accident victim was brought to the hospital, the lower part of whose body was crushed and horribly mangled. In spite of this condition, on his face was a serene look of peaceful calm, so unusual that it amazed Dr Mackay, who was accustomed to seeing people suffer.

'What's the diagnosis?' asked the patient with a smile.

'Oh, I guess we'll pull you through,' replied Dr Mackay.

'No, doctor, I don't want any guess,' the man said, 'I want to know if it is life or death. Just lay me down anywhere, doctor. I am ready. I am not afraid to die, because my trust is in the precious shed blood of the Lord Jesus Christ. But I would like to know the truth: just what is my condition?'

The patient's face was radiant with Christ's love and joy.

'You have at the most three hours to live.' Hardened as he was, Dr Mackay could not but feel sympathy for the dying man. 'Is there anything special you would like us to do for you?' he asked.

'Thank you', said the man. 'In one of my pockets is a two weeks' pay cheque. I wish you would send it at once to my landlady and ask her to send me the book.'

'What book is that?' asked the doctor. 'Oh, just the book,' the man answered.

Dr Mackay arranged for the man's request to be carried out, and then started on his rounds through the hospital; but those words kept ringing in his ears—'I am ready, doctor. Just lay me down easy, anywhere. I am ready.'

Dr Mackay had never been known to inquire about a patient for any personal motive, but for the first time in his life, he wanted to know how this one was getting along.

He returned to the ward where the injured man had been placed, and seeing the nurse whom he had assigned to the case, he asked her how the man was.

'He died a few minutes ago,' the nurse informed him.

'Did he get the book?' asked the doctor. 'Yes, it arrived shortly before he died.' 'What was it, his bank book?'

'No, it wasn't his bank book,' said the nurse. 'It's still there, though, if you want to look at it. He died with it under his pillow.'

Dr Mackay went to the bedside, reached

under the pillow, and pulled out the man's book. It was a Bible. As he picked it up, the Bible opened, and the pages turned over to the fly-leaf. There in his mother's handwriting was his own name, his mother's name and a verse of Scripture. It was the Bible given him by his mother when he had left home to attend college—the one he remembered pawning, while drunk, to buy more whisky. He slipped the Bible under his coat, blushing with shame to think that he had despised it so, and rushed upstairs to his private office. There he fell upon his knees and asked God to have mercy on his soul. In repentance he accepted Christ as his Saviour and came into the realisation that God was his Father, the Lord Jesus Christ his Saviour, and Heaven his home.

### 265   Drug Addict Won for Christ.

A Christian preacher, Stephen Brown, spoke of the Lord Jesus Christ to a girl of fourteen who was already, at that early age, a drug addict, and suggested that she should find some Christian friends at once. He introduced her to a group that met regularly for Bible study and prayer. Among the members were some who had formerly been drug users. Her experience, as related by herself, was: 'I was at first afraid to attend because I thought they would be examining me to be sure I was good enough; but they accepted me right away and it was the best thing that ever happened to me. Now, when tempted to use dope, I know those Christians would be disappointed if I did.'

This girl's experience emphasizes the Christian's responsibility to love others who have fallen, to be compassionate and kind to such and to share our faith with them. (Jude 22. 23)

### 266   Drug Addict's Conversion.

Visiting one of the lads who had been converted in prison through my Bible Class lessons and who, on his return to his home, had persuaded fifteen of his neighbours to study Bible Lessons, I met this young woman who was a drug addict. The area in which this Christian young man of nineteen lived with his wife was one of indescribable squalor and filth, but his own home was showing signs of practical Christianity in the removal of some of the layers of filth that had accumulated over years, and he had been moving around among his neighbours telling them of the Saviour he had found in prison.

He had given the young woman (the drug addict) a course of lessons, which she had returned to me, requesting that I should call upon her. She told me a fascinating story. She was twenty-eight years of age: her husband was in prison: and she had been left to bring up three young children. She showed the puncture wounds on both arms and said she had been on drugs for twelve years. On one particular day, she had decided that when she had put the children to bed in the evening, she would take an overdose of tablets and be finished with her unbearable life. When evening came she still intended to go through with this, but the young man I had come to see, Robert by name, had knocked at her door, told her of the change in his life since he had accepted Jesus Christ as his Saviour, and persuaded her to accept the Bible Lessons he had brought. So she put off the suicide attempt for an hour or two while she looked through the book. As she did so, she became fascinated with its teaching which seemed to hold out for her a new and happy life. It was a great joy to point her to the Saviour, and it is an added joy to know that she goes on well after five years, with the drug habit completely broken.

The fruitfulness of Robert's work for his Lord can be gathered from this excerpt from the Church of the Nazarene magazine: 'Over the past year the church at ............... has increased its membership by fifteen, all of these directly due to the witness of a young man who returned from prison, having found the Saviour there.'

Alex Allan

### 267   Drug Addiction a Tragedy.

The following was found in a telephone box in Sunderland:

*King Heroin is my shepherd, I shall always want;*
*He maketh me to lie down in the gutters.*
*He leadeth me beside the troubled waters:*
*  he destroyeth my soul.*
*He leadeth me in the paths of wickedness for*
*  the effort's sake.*
*Yea, I shall walk through the valley of poverty*
*  and fear all evil, for thou, Heroin, art with*
*  me.*
*They stripped the table of groceries in the*
*  presence of my family; thou robbest*
*  my head of reason, my cup of sorrow*
*  runneth over.*
*Surely heroin addiction will stalk me all the*
*  days of my life, and I will dwell in the*
*  house of the damned for ever.*

On the back of the card on which this was typed, there was the following postscript:

'I am a young woman, twenty years of age and for the past year and a half I have been wandering down the nightmare alley of the junkie. I want to quit taking dope and I try, but I can't. Prison didn't help me, nor did the hospital for long. It would have been better and indeed kinder if the person who first got me hooked on dope would have taken a gun and blown my brains out, and I wish she had. How I wish she had!'

How sad! how tragic! There are thousands of our young people in a similar plight, beyond human or medical or psychiatric skill, but 'there is nothing too hard for the Lord'. The poor girl who wrote the above parody on the grand twenty-third Psalm was evidently familiar with the Scriptures, but alas! had no experience of the saving power of the Lord Jesus Christ. (2 Tim. 2. 26)

**268  Duty to God and to the State.** Professor Ferenc Kiss of Hungary was an outstanding example of 'Render unto Caesar the things which are Caesar's and unto God the things that are God's' in his life and ministry. Mr Ransome Cooper visited him in the company of Mr E. H. Broadbent, and stayed with the Professor and his wife in the spacious flat provided by the University. This flat had been wonderfully provided for them. When it had become vacant, he applied for its use to the Rector of the University, stating plainly that if it were put at his disposal he intended to use it for the preaching of the gospel. The Rector, a Roman Catholic, allocated it to him and it became the home of the young assembly in that city. He preached the gospel so effectively that soon there was a large local church of over one hundred consisting mainly of professional men—doctors and dentists— and of converted Jews. His lounge was so large that there was ample room for all who attended the meetings on Sundays.

When the hall in which the assembly met was closed, in the difficult days of Hitler's dictatorship, he told the Christians, 'We use all the liberty the law allows us. We shall all meet outside the hall at the usual time on Sunday morning and go for a walk in the field.' They walked round the fields in little groups, the saved ones explaining the gospel to the unsaved. Until the hall was again opened for their use they followed this pattern.

Professor Kiss was an acknowledged authority on his subject, anatomy, and his books commanded international respect. In the lectures he gave in Britain, U.S.A. and other countries he boldly testified to his faith in Christ before atheistic and materialistic colleagues, and he was respected for his transparent honesty. In the assembly he taught the Christians their duty to God and to the State, and led his flock into the green pastures. (Matt. 22. 21)

**269  Dying Daily.** In his book *The Sky is Red*, Geoffrey Bull tells of how he was impressed by the words written in an autograph book, 'When Christ calls a man, He says to him, "Come and die".' Paul could say, 'I die daily.'

In the city of Hamilton, Ontario, there used to be a sign over the entrance to a small Dyers' and Cleaners' establishment:

We live to dye, we dye to live;
the more we live, the more we dye:
the more we dye, the more we live.

The pun, appropriate to the tradesmen who displayed it, is as appropriate to the Christian who responds whole-heartedly to Christ's call. It needs but the change of one letter in the word 'dye'.
(2 Cor. 5. 14,15)

**270  Dying is Gain.** We are told that on one occasion Moody said to a friend of his: 'One day you'll see in the paper "Moody is dead." Don't you believe it! I'll be more alive than ever.'

C. H. Spurgeon tells of a child who once found some beautiful eggs in a bird's nest. A week later he went back again and then returned to his mother crying, 'Mother, I had some beautiful eggs in this nest, and now they're destroyed! There's nothing left but a few pieces of broken shell.' But his mother said, 'The eggs weren't destroyed. There were little birds inside those eggs, and they've flown away and are singing in the branches of the trees.'

'And,' said Spurgeon, 'so it is that when we look at our departed loved ones we are apt to say, "Is this all thou hast left us, ruthless spoiler?" But faith whispers, "No, the shell is broken, but among the birds of paradise, singing amid unwithering bowers, you shall find the spirits of your beloved ones; their true manhood is not here, but has ascended to its Father, God." You see, it is not a loss to die; it is gain, a lasting, a perpetual and an unlimited gain!'

When Richard Baxter lay dying, racked with pain and disease, a friend asked him, 'Dear Mr Baxter, how are you?' 'Almost well!' replied Baxter—and he was right. (Phil. 1. 21)

**271  Dying Words of the Impenitent.**
T. Hobbes—I am taking a fearful leap in the dark.
Mirabeau—Give me laudanum that I may not think of eternity.
Voltaire—I am abandoned by God and man! I shall go to hell! O Christ O Jesus Christ.
Charles IX of France—What blood, what murders, what evil counsels have I followed! I am lost!
Tom Paine—I would give worlds if I had them, if the *Age of Reason* had never been published. Stay with me! It is hell to be left alone.
Francis Newport—Millions and millions of years will bring me no nearer to the end of torments than one poor hour. O eternity, eternity!

**272  Dying Words of Saved Sinners.**
D. L. Moody—This is glorious! earth recedes: heaven is opening. God is calling me.
Margaret Prior—Eternity rolls before me like a sea of glory.
Dr Cullen—I wish I had the power of writing. I would describe how pleasant it is to die.
S. Bangs—The sun is setting: mine is rising. I go from this bed to a crown.
John Arthur Lyth—Can this be death? Why, it is better than living. Tell them I die happy in Jesus.
Samuel Rutherford—Amid the shades of evening, while sinks life's lingering sand, I hail the glory dawning in Immanuel's land.

Lord Shaftesbury—I am touching the hem of His garment.

John Newton—I am still in the land of the dying. I shall be in the land of the living soon.

(Num. 23. 10)

**273  Eagles' Wings.** The eagle's flight is majestic, effortless, without the flicker of a feather, swift and graceful. Professor Aggrey, the great educator of Africans, tells this story.

A young eagle, caught by a farmer, was so tame that it fed with the chickens in the poultry yard. One day, some time later, a stranger visited the farmer.

'Why, that's an eagle,' he said.

'Yes, but it behaves like a chicken,' replied the farmer.

It greedily swallowed scraps of food thrown to it by the farmer.

The stranger suggested an experiment. Early next morning before sunrise, he took the eagle and, with the farmer, climbed a mountain facing the east. The stranger took the eagle and said, 'You are no chicken: you are an eagle.' Then he tossed it into the air. It fell down to the ground and began to eat some scraps the farmer threw to it. 'It's a mere chicken,' said the farmer.

A second time the stranger threw it up, but again without success. Then he turned the eagle toward the east, and the glorious sun shone on it. The eagle began to raise its wings gave a piercing cry, spread out its wings and flew straight into the sunlight. It never returned to the poultry yard.

The eagle builds his eyrie on an inaccessible crag, high above the surrounding landscape. The mother bird uses twigs and tough long thorns which form an elastic, comfortable bed for the young as they grow into sturdy young birds. But her mother instinct teaches her unerringly that it is not good for them to have such comfortable quarters indefinitely; they will never learn to fly unless compelled. So she stirs up the nest until the sharp points of the thorns and sticks make further rest impossible. Then, one by one, she pushes each young eaglet out into space to make it use its wings. As it falls it screams with terror and flutters madly; then at the right moment the mother bird swoops underneath the struggling eaglet and bears it safely back into the security of the nest again.

There is probably not one child of God who does not pass through this experience at some time of his life.

Ransome W. Cooper

(Exod. 19. 4; Isa. 40. 31; Deut. 32. 11,12)

**274  Earnest of the Spirit.** In early times when land was sold, the owner cut a turf from the greensward and cast it into the cap of the purchaser as a token that it was his; or he tore off the branch of a tree and put it into the new owner's hand to show that he was entitled to all the products of the soil; and when the purchaser of a house received seizin or possession, the key of the door, or a bundle of thatch plucked from the roof, signified that the building was yielded to him.

The God of all grace has given to His people all the perfections of heaven to be their heritage for ever, and the earnest of His Spirit is to them the blessed token that all things are theirs. The Spirit's work of sanctification and comfort is a part of heaven's covenant blessings, a turf from the soil of Canaan, a twig from the tree of life, the key to mansions in the sky.

C. H. Spurgeon

(Eph. 1. 13,14)

**275  Earth and Heaven.**

*There is a land that to the eye seems fair;*
*Yet, strange to say, a poison haunts the air.*
*Within its borders sin and sorrow reign,*
*And death grasps all within its massive chain,*
*AND THAT IS EARTH.*

*But there's a land where sorrow is unknown,*
*Where seeds of pain and death have not been*
*   sown.*
*Its atmosphere is always bright and clear;*
*No soul is ever faint and weary there,*
*BUT THAT IS HEAVEN.*

*There is a land where hearts are often broken*
*And parting words—alas! too oft are spoken;*
*Where briny tears are very often shed*
*By mourners as they gaze upon their dead,*
*AND THAT IS EARTH.*

*But there's a land where tears will never fall,*
*Where peace and joy sit smiling upon all.*
*Within its gates no dead are ever found;*
*No warrior's grave is marked by grassy mound,*
*AND THAT IS HEAVEN.*

S. Britton

**276  Earth and Heaven—Knowledge in.** Dr Schulyer English's little leaflet, *The Pilgrim*, carries this story. A local minister delivered a most effective sermon on the subject: 'Shall we know each other in heaven?' He showed from the Scriptures definite clues proving that we shall know each other there. In the course of a day or two he received a letter which ran:

'Dear Sir, I wonder if you would preach next Sunday on the subject, "Do we know each other on earth?" I have attended your church for the past twelve months and to date no one has taken any notice of me whatsoever.'

It would be well if all of us were more friendly toward strangers and other Christians who attend our church services.

J.B.W.

(1 Cor. 13. 12; Heb. 13. 1,2)

**277  Easter Flowers.** A florist joined an evangelist in his garden a few days before Easter. The preacher said, 'Have you noticed that most of the flowers that bloom at Easter time have a cross somewhere in the blossom?'

The florist had not noticed this and questioned its veracity. They went to see. The florist examined one blossom after another and found that, due to the arrangement of the stamens, a cross did appear.

(Acts 2. 23,24)

### 278 Easter Meditation—An.

*And so hate nailed Him to the tree,*
*Nor would His grace and mercy see;*
*While love, which laid Him in the tomb,*
*Saw naught therein but hopeless gloom.*
*Shall we as thoughtless be today?*
*Shall we be blinded as were they?*

*Death and the grave—*
*The sealed grave*
*Wherein the Saviour lay;*
*Doubting and fear,*
*But needless fear—*
*'Who'll roll the stone away?'*

*And so they came their tears to shed,*
*To minister unto the dead;*
*Amazed, they found an empty tomb,*
*And grief to joy and hope gave room.*
*Shall we in doubt and fear remain*
*Or sing, with them, 'He lives again!'*

Fred Shepard

(1 Cor. 15. 3,4,20)

### 279 Election and Free Choice.
A brother of Arminian principles, about to pay a Cornish miner who was a Calvinist a sum of money, addressed him thus: 'Malachi, is it decreed that I should pay thee this money?' The miner promptly replied, 'Put it into my hand and I will tell you.'

(2 Thess. 2. 13)

### 280 Encouragement.
One Monday morning, after a barren Sunday, D. L. Moody sat weeping in his study, depressed with the thought that there was no pleasure in working for God if there was no fruit. A Sunday School teacher visited him and on enquiring about the previous day's meetings got the reply from Moody, 'It was as dark a Sunday as ever I had!' By way of contrast the Sunday School teacher said, 'But I had one of the best times I ever had in my life! I was preaching on Noah. If you think you are doing nothing, you read about Noah!' Moody turned to his Bible and began to study the life of the great patriarch. Here was a preacher who laboured and talked for over one hundred years without a convert but he did not get discouraged. He never led even one soul to the Lord except from his own family. Moody put down his Bible and went out to the meeting with his head held high and all thoughts of darkness and depression gone. As he sat in his chair in the meeting a man came forward trembling and said, 'My friend, I am lost. Would you please pray for my soul?' Moody thought to himself, 'What would Noah think of that?'

(Gen. 6. 8; Heb. 11. 7)

### 281 Enemies—Loving our.
During the Armenian atrocities a young woman and her brother were pursued down a street by a Turkish soldier. Finally they were cornered and the brother was brutally slaughtered. The young woman escaped down an alley. Later as a nurse, she was forced to labour in a hospital. One day the Turkish soldier who had murdered her brother was brought into the hospital ward where she was on duty. He was desperately ill and the slightest inattention would have ensured his death; and nobody would ever have known. But she did all in her power to restore him to health. The Turkish soldier, recognising her, asked her why she did not let him die. She replied, 'Because I am a follower of Him who said, "Love your enemies and do good to them that hate you".' The soldier was silent, pondering over her words, then said, 'I never knew there was such a religion. If that is your religion, I want to embrace it. Tell me more about it.'

*Sunday School Times*

(Matt. 5. 44)

### 282 Envy.
In the Arena Chapel, in Padua, the pioneer of fresco painting, Giotto, has given allegorical representations of the Deadly Vices and their opposing Virtues, facing each other in pairs on opposite walls. Envy is a female figure who has long wide ears to catch every breath of rumour that may hurt a neighbour's reputation; out of her mouth issues a serpent's tongue, swift to poison all things sweet and tender. This serpent coils back on itself and stings the eyes of the envious one to blindness; and the figure stands in flames, representing the fierce fire that consumes the heart that takes pleasure in others' injuries and is made bitter by their prosperity.

(1 Pet. 2. 1)

### 283 Estimate of Worth—Man's or God's.
For more than twenty years Olive Davies had served the people in a small Welsh mining community, and Dr A. J. Cronin resented the inadequate salary with which her selfless work was rewarded. After a particularly strenuous case he ventured to protest to her. 'Nurse,' he said, 'why don't you make them pay you more? It is ridiculous that you should work for so little. God knows you're worth it.' There was a pause. She smiled, but her gaze held a gravity, and intensity, that startled him. 'Doctor,' she said, 'if God knows I'm worth it, that's all that matters.'

(2 Tim. 2. 15)

### 284 Eternal Punishment.
A venerable preacher preached a sermon on eternal punishment. Next day some thoughtless young men who had been present agreed to draw him into an argument on the subject in order to make a fool of him and his doctrine.

One of them, whom they appointed to introduce the argument, commenced his talk by saying, 'I believe there is a dispute between you and me, sir, and I would like to settle it.'

'Oh!' said the preacher, 'What is it?'

'Why,' the young man replied, 'you say that the unregenerate and the wicked will go into eternal punishment and I do not think they will.'

'Oh!' said the minister, 'if that is all, there is no dispute between you and me. If you will read Matthew 25. 46 you will find the words, "And these shall go into eternal punishment but the righteous into life eternal." The dispute is between you and the Lord Jesus, and I advise you to go immediately and settle it with Him.'

**285  Eternity.** In *Uncle Tom's Cabin*, a book by Harriet Beecher Stowe, there is a chapter that gives a vivid picture of the cruelty of slave owners and the sufferings of their poor slaves.

Uncle Tom, having fallen into the hands of the brutal Legree, had been thrashed within an inch of his life and lay bleeding and writhing in anguish in the old slave shed. But his soul was not in the shed. Without shuddering or trembling he heard the voice of his persecutor saying, 'How would you like to be tied to a tree and have a slow fire lit around ye? Wouldn't that be pleasant, Tom?' 'Mas'r, I know ye can do dreadful things but after ye've killed the body, there ain't no more ye can do. And oh! there's all eternity to come after that!'

'Gentlemen,' exclaimed old Rabbi Duncan to his students, as he dismissed them at the end of the year, 'Many will be wishing you a Happy New Year. Your old tutor wishes you a Happy Eternity.'

**286  Eternity—Where?**

*Time has run long—moments! minutes! hours!*
*Days! weeks! months! nigh six thousand years*
*Await thy dawn—ETERNITY!*

*Moments! brief space draw time apace,*
*As link by link to thy dread brink*
*They come, they sink—ETERNITY!*

*Days quickly pass, too soon alas!*
*Stormy or bright, how swift their flight*
*From morn to night—ETERNITY!*

*Eternity! What will it be*
*For you and me, when o'er life's sea*
*Our barque shall be?*

*When wrath foretold all lands enfold,*
*When rocks shall rend, when time shall end:*
*Where will you spend ETERNITY?*

*With Christ to reign, His bliss to gain?*
*Or—endless pain from sin's deep stain,*
*With sad refrain—ETERNITY!*

**287  Ethiopian Eunuch—The.** It is a remarkable fact that in the public reading of the Scripture in the Synagogue on the Sabbath day, the selection for one Sabbath reading ends at Isaiah 52. 12, but on the following week the Book of the Roll is opened at Isaiah 54, thus omitting the whole of Isaiah 53.

A question may be raised as to what share Gentiles can have in Jehovah's suffering Servant, but a full answer to this is given in the picture Luke paints in Acts 8. We are shown a maimed and nameless negro, shut out from God's temple by a pitiless law, reading the story of Messiah's woes. To him comes a true evangelist who, 'beginning at the same Scripture, preached unto him Jesus'; and when the two have parted, may we not imagine the Ethiopian picking up the Roll again and reading, a few verses further on, these cheering words:

Neither let the son of the stranger that hath joined himself to the Lord speak, saying, The Lord hath utterly separated me from His people: neither let the eunuch say, Behold, I am a dry tree.

Harold St. John

(Isa, 56. 3-7)

**288  Evangelism.** The chief business of every Christian in the world today is to evangelize. No consideration of age or sex, poverty or rank, allows you to escape. May I say that your first thought is not your wife, nor your baby, nor yet your business; these are side issues only. The one controlling thing that lies before you is that your business in the world is to preach the gospel to every creature, if you bear the name of Christian at all. When you meet Jesus face to face, the first thing He will ask you will not be, 'How did you conduct your business in the world?' but 'How did you preach the Gospel? How did you care for my interests?'

It is the responsibility of the Church of God to wipe out the stain that rests upon her, that half the world has as yet heard nothing of Christ, and yet it is 1900 years since our Lord stood in Galilee and said, 'Go ye into all the world and preach the gospel to every creature.'

Harold St. John

(Mark 16. 15; 1 Cor. 9. 16)

**289  Evangelism among Savages. Dr H. C.** Mabie tells the story of Edward Payson Scott who served the Lord many years ago among the Nagas, a hill tribe in India. Before setting out on his trip to the Naga country he managed to master their language. The venture was considered very dangerous, and friends tried earnestly to dissuade Scott from his perilous undertaking, The British official offered him a military escort which he declined as incompatible with the Gospel of peace.

Being a musician and a gifted violinist, he carried his fiddle with him on the three or four days' journey up the mountains into the Naga country. Hearing of his approach, the natives came out and surrounded him, with their spears levelled at his heart. Any moment threatened to be his last.

Led by the Spirit of God, he took out his violin and began to play and sing in the Naga tongue, a hymn he had previously translated,

*Alas and did my Saviour bleed,*
*And did my Sovereign die?*
*Would He devote that sacred head*
*For such a worm as I?*

By the time he had completed that verse the spears were lowered and all the savages were listening to the words Scott was singing. It was the first word of the Gospel that they had ever heard. He went on, singing the hymn through to the end. When he had finished, some were shedding tears and all signs of hostility had disappeared. Scott was welcomed by them and spent the rest of his life ministering to them.
(John 19. 17,18)

**290 Evangelist's Aim and Influence—The.** Lord Beaverbrook once said, 'The evangelist is the man who has the greatest capacity for doing good and, therefore, if I was in the position to influence the life of a sincere young man today, I would say to him, "Rather choose to be an evangelist than a Cabinet Minister or a millionaire! When I was a young man I pitied my father for being a poor man and humble preacher of the Word. Now that I am older I envy him his life and his career".'
This will be the aim of the true evangelist:

*I do not ask that crowds may throng the*
  *temple,*
*That even standing room be highly priced:*
*I only ask that, as I voice the message,*
*They may see Christ.*

*I do not ask for churchy pomp or pageant,*
*Or music such as wealth alone can buy:*
*I only ask that, as I preach the Gospel,*
*He may be nigh.*

*I do not ask that men may sound my praises,*
*Or praiseful headlines spread my name abroad;*
*I only pray that, as I speak of Jesus,*
*Hearts may find God.*

*I do not ask for earthly place or laurel,*
*Or of the world's distinction any part;*
*I only ask, when I have voiced the message,*
*My Saviour's heart.*

(Gal. 1. 10,11)

**291 Ever-ready.** Admiral Porter, when he was at the head of the United States Navy, had a young staff officer whom he could never catch napping. No matter what day or what hour of the day or night he was wanted by the admiral, the young officer promptly turned up, dressed correctly, a smile on his lips and ready for duty. One day the admiral said to him, half jocosely, that he would recommend him for promotion if he would tell him the secret of his always being ready for service. To this the youngster replied, 'Waking or sleeping, I have trained myself to be ready, no matter what the emergency.

When awake, I plan what I must do if called when I am asleep. When I am asleep, I do not need to worry: I am drilled for the call. There's no secret about it, sir!'
                                    *The Sunday School Times*
(Matt. 24. 44; 25. 10)

**292 Evidence Brought to Light.** Suppose 30 Bible students with 500 copies of the original texts examine them one by one. In some a number of leaves are found to be missing. In others there are disagreements in the text itself. How can they secure a reliable text? Their method is simple. By careful comparison they find 400 out of the 500 in essential agreement. The missing leaves are supplied from complete documents. By consulting the many ancient documents they can detect, and correct by the accumulated evidence of correct readings, any mistake or omission found.
The three earliest and most important manuscripts of the Bible are:
1 *The Vatican MS.* The oldest, dating from the fourth century, kept in the Vatican in Rome for over 500 years. It is written in beautiful style but is not quite perfect.
2 *The Sinaitic MS.* Said to be the second oldest in existence, dating also from the fourth century. It was found in a monastery on Mount Sinai in Arabia by Dr Tischendorf. The New Testament is complete.
3 *The Alexandrian MS.* Dates from the fifth century and is kept in the British Museum in London. Ten leaves are missing from the Old Testament and several from the New Testament.
Translators have taken and carefully compared these three manuscripts. From them they have obtained the correct and entire set of the original writings.
Another exceedingly important source of evidence is found in the writings of the early fathers.
                                            R. F. Bayles

A Professor of Secular History recently said to a colleague who was a Professor of Theology, 'If we treated our historical sources as some theologians treat your Biblical sources, there would be no history at all, for there is far less evidence for our sources than for yours.'
(Luke 1. 1,4; Acts 1. 3)

**293 Evidence from Bible Morality.** The Scriptures possess a moral power that transforms and elevates human life. The morality of the gospel is not of man.

**The Bible's attitude to sin.—**In the Bible, sin is everywhere spoken of as an evil against God, but men view sin in respect to its effect on individuals and society. Sin is represented in the Bible as evil because it is dishonouring to God. The great object of all the writers in the Bible is to lead men to estimate all things according to the will and thoughts of a holy

God. In the Bible man is seen as sinful, and God alone is exalted.

No evidence for the Bible and Christianity could possibly be stronger than the moral and spiritual transformation of men once polluted by sin and the vilest practices.

R. F. Bayles

(Ps. 19. 11; Heb. 4. 12)

**294 Evil.** Edmund Burke, the great eighteenth-century British statesman, once said, 'All that is necessary for the triumph of evil is that good men do nothing.'

**295 Evil Overcome with Good.** Dr Stuart J. Holden asked a British sergeant who was a Christian how he was led to the Lord Jesus Christ. 'Before we were drafted here to Egypt,' he replied, 'we were in Malta. A private in my company there was converted and was not ashamed to witness to the Lord. We gave that chap an awful time, but it did not seem to matter to him.

'One night we all came to the barracks very wet and very tired. Before getting into his bed, this man got down on his knees and began to pray. I sure let him have it! My boots were heavy with damp mud, and I hit him on one side of his face with one boot and on the other side with the other; but he kept on praying.

'Next morning,' the sergeant continued, 'I found these very boots lying by the side of my bed beautifully polished. That was the private's reaction to my cruelty, and it broke my heart. That very day I was saved.'

**296 Evil overcome with Good.** A Salvation Army officer tells of an old Maori woman who had earned the name of 'Warrior Brown' by her fighting prowess when drunk or enraged. She was wonderfully converted and spiritually transformed by the grace of God. When giving her testimony one evening at an open-air meeting, someone hit her a nasty blow with a potato. Had this happened a week before, the cowardly insulter would have had to make himself scarce in double quick time, or take what he got from Warrior Brown; but 'Warrior' without a word picked up the potato and put it in her pocket. Nothing further was heard of the incident until harvest festival, when Warrior brought a small bag of potatoes and explained that she had cut up and planted the potato that had been thrown at her, and was presenting to the Lord the entire crop that had sprung from it.

(Rom. 12. 20,21)

**297 Evolution.** Henry Drummond lived when Darwin's theories were all the rage. In one of his books—*The Ascent of Man*—he propounded evolutionary theories which he thought were a part of divine revelation, but that book is the least enduring of his works. He mistook the theories of his day for eternal verities and so built much on the sand.

He had great influence over young men and his great gifts were not all misspent, for he pointed very many to the Saviour.

Let us take warning and refuse to be moved by fashionable theories which conflict with the Bible. Use historic sense and remember how the 'assured results' of yesterday are on the scrap heap today. Be sure that, as men like Newton and Faraday laid the foundations of modern science, so our Lord and his apostles laid the foundations of truth on which we may safely build.

(Rom. 3. 3,4)

**298 Example—A Bad.** One Saturday night a young couple were involved in a car crash. The young man was killed and his sweetheart, a popular High School girl of seventeen, seriously injured. They were taken to hospital and the parents of the girl were called. The mother had been unable to sleep that night, for she thought she had seen a bottle in the young man's pocket as the couple left home. At the hospital the parents learned that both had been intoxicated at the time of the accident, and a half-empty bottle had been found in the car. The girl's father flew into a rage and exclaimed, 'If I can find the person who sold these children that whisky, I'll kill him.' On returning home, the father felt he must have a drink to steady his shattered nerves, so he went to his secret cache of liquor. Instead he found a note in his daughter's handwriting, 'Dad, we hope you won't mind our taking your whisky with us tonight.' It had been the father's own liquor that had intoxicated the young couple, resulting in the critical injury of his daughter and the death of her boy-friend.

(Gal. 6. 7)

**299 Example—Christ our.** An example is a pattern by which persons model their behaviour. There is no pattern so perfect as the Lord Jesus. It would be well if His people modelled their behaviour in accord with His in all things. He is the perfect Pattern in suffering (1 Pet. 2. 21), in gracious forgiveness (Col. 1. 14), and the great Example of divine affection (John 13. 34).

Some years ago in our newspapers there was published a picture of Prince Charles now the Prince of Wales. During an inspection of the armed forces, he followed his father, the Duke of Edinburgh. He adopted the same gait, held his arms in the same manner, and cocked his hat at the same angle. In fact he looked like Prince Philip, Duke of Edinburgh, in miniature.

Peter and John, close followers of the Lord Jesus in His three and a half years of ministry, both speak of Him as our Example, but use different Greek words. Peter speaks of Him as leaving us the perfect Headline of a copy book to follow, and John tells us that the Lord, in washing His disciple's feet, told them He had given them a demonstration of what they should do for one another (John 13. 15). May we so follow the example of Christ that those who watch us may see Christ in our behaviour!

> *Ye who look for great examples*
> *Over the historic page—*
> *Teachers who with good ensamples*
> *Would the thoughts of youth engage!*
> *To the sacred record turning,*
> *There behold the perfect Man!*
>
> *There, the light for ever burning!*
> *Match its lustre if you can.*
> *Imitate the great Example*
> *Humbly as a Christian should,*
> *Ever, like that bright Ensample,*
> *Speaking well and doing good.*

(Col. 2. 6,7)

**300 Example—Good.** A chaplain on a battlefield came to a man who was lying in a shell hole, desperately wounded.

'Would you like me to read you something from this Book, the Bible?' he asked.

'I'm so thirsty, I'd rather have a drink of water,' the soldier said. Hurrying away, the chaplain soon brought the water. Then the wounded man said, 'Could you put something under my head?'

The chaplain took off his raincoat, rolled it up, and gently placed it under the man's head for a pillow. 'Now,' said the suffering man, 'if I just had something over me—I'm cold'.

There was just one way to meet that need, and the chaplain took off his coat and spread it over the man.

The wounded soldier looked up into his face then and said, 'If there is anything in that Book in your hand that makes a man do for another what you have just done for me, please read it to me.'

*The Gideon*

(Matt. 5. 42)

**301 Expansion.** Some years ago on a visit to Rome, I stood gazing at some superb paintings by Italy's famous sculptor and artist, Michelangelo; they were in the dome of St. Peter's and other churches. Someone present told the story of how Michelangelo one day entered his studio to appraise the productions of a group of his pupils. He stood for some time contemplating the painting of a favourite pupil. Then, to the amazement of all present, he seized a brush and marred the painting by writing something across it—*Amplius*, meaning 'larger'. The master was in one sense pleased with his pupil's work. It showed skill and was commendable as far as it went, but it did not go far enough: the picture was cramped, its design too limited.

I believe God is writing *Amplius* across all our missionary vision and effort.

Robert Hall Glover

(2 Cor. 10. 16; Col. 1. 28,29)

**302 Expectation.** Queen Victoria was much loved. She made unexpected calls on the farm folks who lived in cottages. Any day might be a royal day, and the Scots had a chair prepared for her visit. Their houses were kept spotless. They were a clean and wholesome people, but her unannounced visits added to the joy of keeping their homes lovely. The old people who remembered her visits in their youth charmed visitors by the expression used in the residences on Deeside. They would say, 'Perhaps today, she'll come my way.'

> *Perhaps today the clouds will part asunder,*
> *Reveal a glory brighter than the sun;*
> *And we shall view, with transport, joy and*
> *    wonder,*
> *The hope of earth and heaven's beloved one.*

(Tit. 2. 13; Phil. 3. 20)

**303 Experience.**

> *All experience is an arch where through*
> *Gleams that untravell'd world whose margin*
> *    fades*
> *For ever and forever when I move.*
> *How dull it is to pause, to make an end;*
> *To rust unburnished, not to shine in use!*
> *As if to breathe were life. Life piled on life*
> *Were all too little, and of one to me*
> *Little remains.*

Alfred, Lord Tennyson

**304 Experience—Varied.** A Christian's experience is like a rainbow, made up of drops of the grief of earth and beams of the bliss of heaven.

John Ruskin says: 'Break off an elm bough three feet long, in full leaf, and lay it on the table before you, and try to draw it, leaf for leaf. It is ten to one if in the whole bough (provided you do not twist it about as you work) you find one form of a leaf exactly like another; perhaps you will not even have one complete. Every leaf will be oblique, or foreshortened, or curled, or crossed by another, or shaded by another, or have something or other the matter with it; and though the whole bough will look graceful and symmetrical, you will scarcely be able to tell why or how it does so, since there is not one line of it like another.'

There is this infinite variety in creation, and we may expect to find it in the experience of the saints. Uniformity is not a rule of the spiritual life. All the saints, like ourselves, are led in the right way, but no two in exactly the same way. If we reject all believers who have infirmities or are marred with faults our fellowship will be extremely limited. Experiences of each individual differ in the course of his or her life: some are pleasant, some sorrowful; some are bright with the sunshine of the divine smile; others are dark under the chastening hand of our Father in heaven.

**305 Extravagance—Love's.** Love is not love if it merely calculates the cost. Love gives its all, and love's only regret is that it has not still more to give.

O. Henry, the master of the short story, has a moving story called *The Gift of the Magi.* This was a young American couple, Della and Jim, who were very poor but very much in love. Each had one unique possession. Della's hair was her glory. When she let it down it almost served her as a robe. Jim had a gold watch which had come to him from his father and which was his pride. It was the day before Christmas, and Della had exactly one dollar eighty-seven cents to buy Jim a present. She did the only thing she could do: she went out and sold her hair for twenty dollars. And with the proceeds she bought a platinum fob for Jim's precious watch. Jim came home at night. When he saw Della's shorn head he stopped as if stupefied. It was not that he did not like it or love her any less. She was lovelier than ever. Slowly he handed her his gift: his gift was a set of expensive tortoiseshell combs with jewelled edges for her lovely hair—and he had sold his watch to buy them for her. Each had given the other all he or she had to give. Real love cannot think of any other way to give.

Dr William Barclay

(John 12. 1-3; 2 Cor. 8. 2-5)

**306 Extravagance or Content.**

*Oh! Extravagance saileth in climes bright*
*   and warm!*
*She is built for the sunlight and not for the*
*   storm;*
*Her anchor is gold, and her mainmast is*
*   pride—*
*Every sheet in the wind doth she dashingly*
*   ride!*
*But Content is a vessel not built for display,*
*Though she's ready and steady, come storm*
*   when it may;*
*So give us Content as life's channel we steer—*
*If our pilot be Caution, we've little to fear.*

**307 Facts—Insist on.** One day a committee called on Abraham Lincoln to discuss a matter of public concern. Their case was built largely on suppositions. After listening for a while, Mr. Lincoln asked, 'How many legs would a sheep have if you called its tail a leg?' As he expected, they promptly answered 'Five!' 'No!' he said, 'it wouldn't; it would only have four. Calling a tail a leg does not make it one.'

Lincoln was right. Giving something a new name does not change its character. Yet we are often guilty of trying to do that very thing. We seem to think that by calling a falsehood 'a white lie', it ceases to be a prevarication. When we repeat a juicy bit of information about someone, we ensure that it is not really 'gossip' if we present the facts without any embellishment or exaggeration.

When a person falls into a bad habit, calling it a 'shortcoming' does not make it any different from the sin that it is.

(1 Pet. 3. 10)

**308 Faith.** Faith is the brightest star in the firmament of grace. It treads down seeming impossibilities, and it strides to victory over mountains of stupendous hindrances. It enthrones Jesus as King of the inner man. It kindles and fans the flame of love and it opens the lips of praise and prayer.

Henry Law

*Faith is the grasping of Almighty power,*
*The hand of man laid on the hand of God—*
*The grand and blessed hour*
*In which the things impossible to me*
*Become the possible, O Lord, through Thee.*

Based on this is the exhortation:

*Put thy trust in God; in duty's path go on;*
*Walk in His strength with faith and hope,*
*   so shall thy work be done.*
*Commit thy ways to Him, thy works into*
*   His hands,*
*And rest on His unchanging word who heaven*
*   and earth commands.*

(Heb. 11. 33; 1 John 5. 4)

**309 Faith, Hope and Love.**

*Faith will outlast the bitter hour:*
*Hope will outshine the darkest fear:*
*Love will outmatch the strongest power*
*That threatens all the soul holds dear.*
*For Faith will conquer, Hope abide,*
*And Love will reign, the throne beside,*
*Where sin and fear and death have died.*

*Give me the love that leads the way,*
*The faith that nothing can dismay,*
*The hope no disappointments tire,*
*The passions that will burn like fire.*
*Let me not sink to be a clod:*
*Make me thy fuel, Flame of God!*

Amy Wilson Carmichael

(1 Cor. 13. 13; 1 Tim. 1. 5)

**310 Faith in Christ.** The late Dr Harry Rimmer was once travelling in Egypt, and while negotiating with the Secretary of State at that time, a refined and cultured Egyptian, engaged him in conversation concerning religion and revelation.

'We believe that God has given to man three revelations of Himself,' said Dr Rimmer.

'We too believe that,' said the Secretary of State, a Moslem.

'We believe that God has revealed Himself in a book, the Bible.'

'We Moslems believe that God has revealed Himself in a book, the Koran.'

'We Christians believe that God has revealed Himself in a man, and that man is Jesus Christ'.

'We too believe that God has revealed

Himself in a man, and that man is the prophet Muhammad.'

'We believe that Jesus died to save His followers,' said Dr Rimmer.

'And we believe that Muhammad died for his people,' was the Moslem's reply.

'We believe,' said Dr Rimmer, 'that Jesus is able to substantiate His claims because He rose from the dead.'

The Egyptian hesitated, then his eyes fell, and finally he replied, 'We have no information concerning our prophet after his death.'

The Lord Jesus Christ is the only one who conquered death and triumphed over the grave. He is alive and able to save all who call upon His name in faith.
(1 Cor. 15. 17)

**311  Faith in God.**  A city Missioner records the conversation he had with Communists.

'I don't believe in God but I do believe in the teaching of Jesus Christ: you see, I'm a Communist!' These words were spoken to me by a young man in his mid-twenties. 'If you believe in Jesus Christ,' I replied, 'you must believe in God, because He taught us about God. Jesus said, "I am the Way, the Truth and the Life; no man comes to the Father but by Me." Jesus taught us the prayer which begins —"Our Father" Jesus told us to have faith in God.' I went on to testify to my faith in God through knowing Jesus Christ as my personal Saviour. The young man was interested and said he had never seen it like that before, but admitted it did make sense. I was invited into his home and met his wife who asked me if I had read the works of Voltaire and Thomas Paine, particularly the latter author's book, *The Age of Reason.* I replied that I had not, and asked her if she knew that each of those writers, when dying, cried to God to have mercy on his soul, and that Thomas Paine regretted having written *The Age of Reason.* I gave the lady a booklet entitled *The Impossibility of Atheism*, which recorded the facts I had told her, and she promised to read it.
Oscar Penhearow
(Mark 11.22; Heb. 11.6)

'Lord, I believe.' Many fail because they miss the most important part. This man did not say to Jesus, 'I believe': He said, 'Lord, I believe.' There is a tremendous difference.

This is where psychology or psychiatry alone fall down. You cannot do it by yourself. The Christian faith has in it all the principles and techniques of psychology and psychiatry, and it has so much more. At the very centre of the Christian faith is an eternal, all-powerful God. When one starts with God, putting belief first in Him, it makes the major difference. You cannot do it by yourself, but with His help you can eventually really know what Paul meant when he said, 'I can do all things through Christ which strengtheneth me.'
*Reader's Digest*
Mark 9. 24)

**312  Faith—Justified by.**  Dr A. J. Gordon, while travelling on a train, fell into debate with a fellow passenger on the subject of justification by faith. Said the man, 'I tell you, God deals with men, not with a little bit of theological scrip called faith: and when the Almighty admits one to heaven, He makes rigid inquiry about his character and not about his faith.' Dr Gordon said, 'Did you notice how the conductor always flashes his light on the ticket and takes no pains to inspect the passenger?'

Faith alone entitles a man to the saving grace that is able to produce a character. 'Without faith it is impossible to please God.'
L. A. Banks
(Rom. 4. 16; Heb. 11. 6)

**313  Faith—Little.**  'Ah!' said the convert to the missionary, 'I used to treat the Lord as if He were a poor man and had very little to give. I prayed, "Lord, give me a little more faith!" or "Oh, I beseech Thee, Lord, bestow on Pompey rather more grace." Then a man came to preach at Lagos and he described how great the Lord was and what His riches in glory must be. That night I said to myself, Pompey, you have been praying as if the Lord owned only a sago palm and as if his heart were as hard as the shell of a dry coconut, when all the time every beast in the forest is His! and I just acted on what I found out.'
*Choice Gleanings*
(Matt. 6. 30; Luke 17. 5)

**314  Faith of a Mother.**  In the far North of Argentina, attracted by the sound of singing, a soldier entered a little mission hall and heard the Gospel preached. He stayed behind and spoke to the preacher, who asked him if he were a Christian.

'Yes, I am' he replied.

'Where did you hear the Gospel?'

'From my mother.'

'Where does she live?'

'She lives a long way from here and she has never heard a preacher, and would be glad to see you.'

The missionary went, and away on a distant farm, where no missionary had ever been, he found this Christian woman. She told him that years before a colporteur who passed that way had left a copy of the Word. She had read it and had come to know Jesus Christ as her Saviour. That old woman was the mother of fourteen children, the youngest twelve years old, each of whom she had led to Christ through reading them the message from the Scriptures.
*Workers Together*
(Ps. 119. 130)

**315  Faith—Saving.**  A sceptical doctor said to a Christian patient, 'I could never understand this saving faith. I believe in God and I suppose I believe in Jesus Christ. I am not conscious of any doubts. I believe that Jesus Christ was the Son of God, and I believe the Bible, yet I am not saved. What is the matter with me?'

'Well!' said the patient, 'a week ago I believed in you as a very skilful doctor. I believe that if I come to you when I am sick you can help me. In other words I trusted you. For two days I have been taking some mysterious stuff out of a bottle. I don't know what it is. I don't understand it, but I trust you. Now, when you turn to the Lord Jesus and say, "Lord Jesus, Christianity seems to be full of mysteries—I do not understand them, but I believe Thee to be trustworthy and I trust Thee and commit myself to Thee," that is faith.'

Very simple, is it not? The faith of the patient did not heal him; it was the remedy that healed him. But faith took the remedy. (Mark 9. 23,24)

316 **Faith—Simple.** Huxley, the great agnostic, was a member of a house party at a country house. Sunday came round and most of the members of the party prepared to go to church; but very naturally Huxley did not prepare to go. He approached a man known to have a simple and radiant faith and said to him, 'Suppose you don't go to church. Suppose you stay at home and you tell me quite simply what your Christian faith means to you, and why you are a Christian.'

'But,' said the man, 'you could demolish all my arguments in an instant. I'm not clever enough to argue with you.'

Huxley said quietly, 'I don't want you to argue with me. I just want you to tell me simply what Christ means to you.'

The man stayed and told Huxley very simply of his faith. When he had finished there were tears in Huxley's eyes. 'I would give my right hand,' he said, 'if I could believe that.'
(1 Pet. 3. 15)

317 **Faith Tested.** Vast crowds watched the brilliant performance of Blondin, the tightrope artist at Niagara Falls. Balancing a rod in his mouth, he pushed a wheelbarrow across the rope over the Falls. Seeing among the cheering people a small lad, Blondin said to him, 'Sonny, do you think I could push the barrow back again?' 'Yes, sir!' was the lad's unhesitating reply. 'Do you think I could take you across?' 'Yes, sir!' 'Good! Jump in and I will take you.' 'No, sir!'
(Matt. 9. 28,29)

318 **Faith that Prevailed.** Many years ago when Hudson Taylor first went to China, he went on a sailing vessel. Of necessity the boat was routed very close to the shores of a cannibal island. Suddenly the wind died down. The becalmed vessel began to drift toward the nearby beach. The evil-looking savages quickly gathered, eagerly anticipating making a feast of the passengers. The captain, in much distress, came to Mr. Taylor and asked him to pray for the help of God. 'I will,' said Taylor, 'provided you set your sails to catch a breeze.' The captain declined to make himself a laughing stock by unfurling the canvas in a dead calm. Taylor said, 'I will not undertake to pray for the vessel unless you unfurl the sails.' So, reluctantly, the old sailor yielded to the missionary's wishes. Later, while engaged in prayer, there came a knock on the door of the stateroom of the man of God. 'Who is there?' he called. The captain's voice responded, 'Are you still praying for wind, Taylor?' 'Yes!' 'Well, you'd better stop, for we have more wind now than we can manage.' The magnet of Hudson Taylor's faith had brought down the power of God! The cannibals who at one time were less than one hundred yards from the ship, were thus cheated out of their human prey.

*Sunday School Times*

(Matt. 17. 20)

319 **Faith the Title-Deeds.** Moulton & Milligan, in their book, *The Vocabulary of the Greek New Testament*, maintain that in all cases of the use of the word translated in the A.V. (King James Version) 'substance', in the papyri there is the same central idea of something that underlies visible conditions and guarantees a future possession, and suggest that the meaning of Hebrews 11. 1 is 'Faith is the title-deeds of things hoped for'. The possession of the title-deeds of realities should prove an effective power in the believer's life.

In a certain region of South India it is common to find each house standing in its own compound where the owner grows tapioca, rice and fruit for his household's needs. In many cases the house has mud walls and a thatched roof, and is very sparsely furnished. A primitive cot, one or two chairs, a stool and a table, often form the entire furnishings. But there is one article of furniture that the owner values above all others. It is a strong box, perhaps two or three feet long and eighteen inches broad, constructed of durable wood. If he has treasures to preserve they are kept there. Even in the absence of any other things of value, one possession may be seen safely secured within the box, namely the title-deeds of his homestead. It is of supreme importance that the title-deeds should be secure, for this precious document proves that the property is his very own.

Faith is the title-deeds of the inheritance of the saints, and the Lord Jesus prays for us, as He did for Peter, that our faith may be preserved intact.

320 **Faith—Turning from the.** In the centre of Detroit, Michigan, U.S.A., a beginning has been made to establish a great Islamic centre.

It is planned to have educational facilities there, and it is hoped that many Americans will embrace Islam. We are living in days when we may see another upsurge of Islam. Churches that have lost the vital life that is in Christ Jesus may be swept away before the onroads of Muhammadanism, as those in North Africa were swept away by the Moslem armies in the seventh century A.D.

In Luke 18. 8 the Lord Jesus raises the question, 'When the Son of man comes will He find faith on the earth?' As modern heresies and false cults spread and increase, true faith will decrease.

(1 Tim. 1. 19; 2 Tim. 2. 18)

**321  Faith—Venture of.** The following item appeared in a Scottish daily newspaper:

John Berkeley is a young Scottish doctor with a love of climbing. This week he leaves to begin an assault on a very different kind of mountain. He is going to West Bengal as a medical missionary. There he will help in the fight against the mountain of fear, suspicion and doubt surrounding one of the world's oldest diseases—leprosy.

John Berkeley at thirty-nine is throwing up his house and his job to work in a leper hospital. In terms of family and finance it doesn't make sense. He will leave behind a wife and three teenage children. He hopes Mrs Berkeley will be able to join him sometime next year but this is not certain.

The basic pay of a missionary is £400 a year, though Dr Berkeley will earn a bit more because of family commitments, bringing him to about a quarter of what he would earn as a G.P. in this country.

He leaned back in the chair of his Edinburgh home, a tanned, athletic-looking man, and smiled: 'You could say that no one does it for the money.'

So why is he going?

'On a human level you might put it that I have come to know the work and the problems of the work among lepers. My wife has been on the North of Scotland Committee of the Leprosy Mission. I became very interested and wanted to help. But that is not the reason I am going.

'I am going to India because I believe it is God's will that I should. My whole family believes this, even the children. You could argue that Indian doctors should do this work for their own country—many of them do. You could say that there was plenty for me, as a Christian, to do here.

'Of course it will be an awful wrench leaving the children, but we believe that this is part of a plan for us all. Yes, it is a question of faith. There is so much to do for people with leprosy. Drugs and modern methods of surgery have helped tremendously, but there is a need to rehabilitate these people, to help them to regain a place in the community.'

What is this but a venture of faith?

(Heb. 11. 8)

**322  Faith versus Fear.** A party of friends was visiting the Niagara Falls. At a place called the 'Cave of the Winds', a marvellous view of the mighty waterfall can be obtained. Led by the guide, they passed down through the rocks out to the edge of the river. Then by winding paths, across narrow bridges and through the flying spray that drenched them, the tourists emerged upon a rather shaky footbridge in front of the American Fall. That plank bridge with its single wooden rail must be crossed in order to reach the 'Cave of the Winds'.

The party followed the guide across, but one lady lost her nerve midway and stood still, clinging to the handrail. The guide, sensing the situation, stepped back quickly and said calmly in a kind voice, 'Your hand in the guide's hand, please.' With an effort the lady transferred one hand to the guide's hand but clung more tightly to the rail with the other, and no progress was made.

Then the guide, with an understanding smile, said, 'Both hands in mine, please!' For a moment there was a struggle, fear defying faith. Then faith won; she ventured, trusting both hands and her safety to the guide, and in a moment stood safely on a ledge of rock in the 'Cave of the Winds'.

(Ps. 56. 3)

**323  Faith—Walking by.**

*When we the way can understand*
*It needs no faith to take His hand,*
*And walk along the way we see is best:*
*But when the path ahead is veiled*
*And we, by doubts and fears assailed,*
*Lean hard on Him and in His Word find rest;*
*When in His strength we are made strong*
*And in His joy we find a song,*
*That is the faith by which our souls are blest.*

*That faith can wait His blessed will*
*And at His bidding can stand still*
*When we in zeal would like to interfere.*
*He knows the time, He knows the way:*
*His to command, ours to obey—*
*He always speaks into the listening ear:*
*And He who, sovereign over all,*
*Still notes the lonely sparrow's fall,*
*Will guide His child through every passing*
*  year.*

*At last He'll call us to the air*
*And take us to His home so fair,*
*Where sorrow and where sin shall never be.*
*He then shall wipe all tears away,*
*And through an endless, cloudless day*
*We'll dwell with Him through all eternity.*
*But till He comes He in His love*
*Would guide us in our every move,*
*And lead us still by paths we cannot see.*

                              Mrs Alex C. Murray
(2 Cor. 5. 7)

**324  Faith—Warmth of.** The Golden Age of Nestorian Missions in Central Asia was from the end of the fourth till about the end of the ninth centuries, and thereafter till the thirteenth century they extended their activities to Mongolia, China and Southern Siberia.

They pitched their tents in the camps of the wandering Tartar: the Lama of Tibet trembled at their words: they stood in the rice fields of the Punjab: they taught the fishermen at the Sea of Aral. They struggled through the vast deserts of Mongolia, and the memorable inscription of Hsa an fu attests their victories in China.

They braved alike pagan and fire worshipper, the burning suns of Tiflis and the feverish swamps of Imeretia; and they planted a colony halfway up the great mountain of Ararat. Merchant and physician travelled and made it their task to win souls. Sailors with the same object in view manned vessels and sailed the seas. Jerome speaks of Huns as having learnt the Psalms from Syrian merchants 'who burn by the very warmth of their faith'.

Vanbery speaks of the feverish activity of the Nestorians in spreading abroad their faith. A passion gripped them. They said, 'He loved me and gave Himself for me', therefore 'we glory in tribulation' was the language of life and lip. It was this self-abnegation that gave them the secret of the multiplied life and, having drunk of the living water themselves, from them flowed rivers of living water.

Christ was very real to those early Christians, and they practised the teaching of the Word of God amongst the people and won them by their sheer reality. Every believer was a missionary. They served as secretaries and physicians to Turks, Mongols and others; in fact, they did everything in their power to help, even inventing alphabets for them. Such zeal in order to win men for the Lord had a wonderful harvest.

*The Treasury*

(Heb. 11. 38,39)

### 325 Faithfulness—God's.

*Praise the Lord and leave tomorrow in thy*
  *loving Father's hands;*
*Burden not thyself with sorrow, for secure the*
  *promise stands.*
*He is faithful! Leave thy troubles in His hands.*

*Trust today and leave tomorrow; each day*
  *has enough of care,*
*Therefore, whatsoe'er thy burden, God will*
  *give thee strength to bear.*
*He is faithful! Cast on Him thy every care.*

*Pray today and let tomorrow bring with it*
  *whate'er it may;*
*Hear thy loving Father promise strength*
  *according to thy day.*
*He is faithful! Trust Him, therefore, come*
  *what may.*

*Watch today and leave tomorrow, for tomorrow*
  *may not come,*
*For today the loving Saviour may appear to*
  *take thee home.*
*He is faithful! Look for Him, the coming One.*

*Thus, by trusting, watching, praying each day,*
  *as our time rolls on,*
*We shall find the promised blessing, strength*
  *restored when strength is gone.*
*He is faithful! He will come to take us home.*

(1 Cor. 1. 9; Heb. 10. 23)

326 **Fall of an Empire.** The historian Gibbon listed in 1787 five reasons for the fall of the Roman Empire, which certainly present a remarkable forecast of present-day conditions. These were:
1 The rapid increase of divorce; the undermining of the home, which is the basis of human society.
2 Ever increasing taxes and the spending of public monies for free bread and entertainments for the people.
3 The mad craze for pleasure, sports becoming every year more riotous and more brutal.
4 The building of gigantic armaments when the real enemy was the decadence of the people.
5 The decay of religion, faith fading into mere formalism, losing touch with life and impotent to guide the people.
(2 Tim. 3. 1-9,13)

327 **False Doctrine.** 'What is a false doctrine?' asked the teacher. 'False doctoring,' answered one little boy in the class, 'is when a doctor gives the wrong stuff to sick folks.' False doctrine *is* giving the wrong medicine to those who are sick with the disease of sin. There is but one remedy for that disease, and it is found in the Gospel of the Lord Jesus Christ. Nothing a sinner can do will save his soul. The only thing that can save is what the Lord Jesus has already done.

Vivian D. Gunderwon

(Heb. 13. 9)

328 **Family—Basis of Society.** 'Our Western civilization is sunk,' exclaimed one of the lawyers from our town. We had been comparing present moral conditions with those of Rome just before the collapse of that World Empire.

A great American leader has also said, so it is rumoured, 'Our own moral laxity will soon destroy us, even if the Communists don't.'

The family is that basic unit of society, the home the corner-stone of the community. If these basic units deteriorate, what hope is there for the Western Nations, or for the world at large? None whatever!

Quotations from the Press at various

79

sources confirm these statements, and indicate the extent of this deterioration in many, many homes. 'Home is the empty house to which junior returns from school, the place where the only sound he hears is the echo of his own voice when he cries in vain for his mommie.'

Marital breakdown is the break for which some persons wait, but what kind of a break is it? Broken vows, broken laws, broken hearts, broken homes, broken and fragmented minds, and broken and split personalities!

James Gunn

(Ps. 68. 6)

**329  Family Life.** In one of the early Christmas broadcasts by the monarch of Great Britain, King George VI said, 'The foundations of national glory are set in the homes of the people. They will only remain unshaken while the family life of our nation is strong and simple and pure.'

Had there been time, he might have added that the foundations of such homes and such families are set in what W. E. Gladstone called 'The Impregnable Rock of Holy Scripture'.

**330  Family Training—Lack of.** Mr Harold St. John would never speak a disrespectful word about anybody. On one occasion he was having supper with a Christian family in whose home he was visiting when one of the young daughters began to criticize and sneer at some godly old evangelist, and another member of the house made some withering remark about another body of believers. Mr St. John turned quietly to his host and, rising from the table, said, 'You won't mind if I go now, will you?' 'But', said his host in surprise, 'we're only just starting supper.' 'Well!' replied Mr St. John, 'I've made it a rule never to sit in the company of people who are speaking disparagingly of God's servants. I must ask you either to excuse me or change the subject.'

The subject was changed and the meal proceeded, but the next morning, when the family had gone off, the hostess came to Mr St. John in tears and said, 'I could not sleep last night for thinking of what happened. We've got into the habit of criticizing other Christians, and my boys have grown up to despise preachers. Neither of them was at the meeting last night; if only we could start again and have things different!'

(1 Pet. 3. 9,10)

**331  Far above all.**

*The kings of earth in festooned glory rise,*
*Bedecked in pompous robes, the sceptre,*
*  crown and rings;*
*Yet in a day soon hence, beyond the skies,*
*Their knees will bow before the King of kings.*

*The lords of land, of wealth, of might and*
*  slave,*
*Who sprawl in goods and mock the God who*
*  gives,*
*Will stand before the one who died to save*
*And worship at the throne of one who lives.*

*The crofter of the hidden hill and plain*
*Who loves the Lord of glory as his own,*
*Will sing the song of Him, the Lamb once*
*  slain,*
*And at the spike-pierced feet lay down his*
*  crown.*

*The sum of life held dear this side of Heav'n*
*Consisteth not in things, in money, land,*
*But in the blood of Christ, our sins forgiv'n,*
*And Him, in majesty at God's right hand.*

*What is the price set by the heedless throng*
*Upon the blood that ransoms from the fall?*
*He is rejected as they move along,*
*And, in their path, the trampled 'Life for all'.*

*But far above the wheeling galaxies,*
*Beyond the realm of cramping time and space,*
*There, far above all principalities,*
*My Saviour sits and holds the highest place.*

J.B.N. Jr.

(Eph. 1. 21)

**332  Fate Fixed.** In reply to the question by a reader of *The Harvester*, a monthly magazine, 'Is it true that everything we do, and everything that happens to us, is fixed unchangeably in advance long before our birth?' Professor F. F. Bruce wrote:

No! This idea is bound up with pagan notions of fate, and has nothing to do with the Biblical teaching about God's foreordaining grace and Fatherly providence. For example, when I start to deal with a question like this, I decide in my own mind how to answer it. I am well aware that many antecedent factors in my life, and very probably in my heritage, influence the way in which I answer it, but the final decision about the answer lies within my free choice. If everything were fixed unchangeably in advance, our personal responsibility for our actions would be dissolved; but nothing is taught more clearly in the Bible, than that each of us shall give account of himself to God. In fact, this needs to be specially stressed today, when so many schools of thought minimise personal accountability, so that people plead that their actions are the result of parentage or their environment, or just of 'something that came over them'.

(Rom. 14. 12)

**333  Favours Divinely Bestowed.**

*Grace, knowing my every sin,*
*Grace, dying to make me clean,*
*Grace that ran to bring me in*
*Suits a heart like mine.*

*Love proved on the cross of shame,*
*Love worthy of God's great name,*
*Love eternally the same*
*Wins a heart like mine.*

*Joy, fruit of the Father's kiss,*
*Joy, foretaste of heavenly bliss,*
*Joy that springs from love like this*
*Fills a heart like mine.*

*Peace, sea of glass still and vast,*
*Peace, knowing the judgement's past,*
*Peace that will for ever last*
*Calms a heart like mine.*

*Lord, while in this world below,*
*Still more of Thy love I'd know,*
*So shall sweeter praises flow*
*From a heart like mine.*

George Cutting

(2 Cor. 12. 9; Gal. 5. 22)

**334   Fear of God.**   The great British Statesman and Prime Minister between 1868 and 1894, W. E. Gladstone, on his last visit to Oxford, sat in the senior common room of Christ Church College and talked at some length about the happy changes he had witnessed in his lifetime in the lot of the British people. His outlook was so radiantly optimistic that it aroused a challenge. One of the students said, 'Sir, are we to understand that you have no anxieties for the future? Are there no adverse signs?' The grand old man answered slowly, 'Yes, there is one thing that frightens me—the fear of God seems to be dying out in the minds of man.'
(Prov. 9. 10; Rom. 3. 18)

**335   Fears Dispelled.**   The road was long and lonely, and the night so dark as they were homeward bound after the mid-week prayer meeting. Ominous shadows and weird songs came from the trees and bushes as the wind blew through the branches. It was enough to send shivers up the spine. The two little girls sitting in the back seat of the horse-drawn vehicle were asked, 'Are you not frightened?' 'Oh no!' they replied, 'You see, Father is with us, and we are never afraid when he holds the reins.'
(Isa. 43. 2; Acts 18. 9,10)

**336   Feast of Tabernacles** (sometimes called the Feast of Booths). Professor F. F. Bruce answers a question in *The Harvester* as to which was the 'great day', the last day of the feast:
Our principal source of information is the tractate 'Sukkah' in the Babylonian Talmud, from which we gather that the ceremony of the water-pouring was enacted on the first seven days of the feast, but not on the eighth day (although prayer for rain was offered on that day). If our Lord's proclamation was made on the day when there was no water-pouring, His point would be that while no material water was poured on that morning, yet spiritual and life-giving water was available to all who would come to Him. His announcement was essentially a repetition of that in Isaiah 55. 1-3, whereas there it is Jehovah through His prophet who says, 'come unto me' (verse 3); here it is the Son who says so in person. (It has indeed been held that 'the last day, the great day of the feast' was the seventh day, on which the feast proper came to an end, the eighth day being an additional festival; but on the whole it is probable that the eighth day is intended.)
(John 7. 37-39)

**337   Feet—Beautiful.**      'What ugly feet!' exclaimed a little girl, pointing to another girl who was walking along the street outside the window where she was seated. To her surprise her mother replied, 'I think Caroline (the girl in the street) has more beautiful feet than any girl in the village.'
'Why Mother, just look at them!' her daughter said, pointing with her finger. Then her mother answered,

*'Beautiful feet are they that go*
*Swiftly to lighten another's woe*
*Through summer's heat and winter's snow.'*

Caroline's feet are carrying her on errands of mercy, sometimes to read to blind Peggy, sometimes to amuse poor lame Eddy West, sometimes to hunt up new Sunday School scholars among neglected children.

**338   Feet—Dear.**   In 1868 in Stuttgart, Samuel Hebich, a fearless witness for God, was summoned into the presence of the One he had served with great singleness of purpose. A day or two before he died Dr Gundert visited him. One can well imagine how much he would be cheered by this visit of a much-loved colleague. After Dr Gundert left, the dying saint said, 'That is a dear man, a hard-working man! He is very diligent with his pen. Compared with him I am a lazy fellow!' A day or two before, when his friends were washing his feet, he smiled and said, 'These are dear feet. They have carried peace far and wide. They have made many long walks for the Lord.'
Elise Revington, missionary from Dublin to India, served the Lord faithfully in the jungle areas of the Reddiseema for many years. She took little thought for her personal comfort or health, so engrossed was she in winning souls and so constrained by the love of Christ. On her feet she wore the kind of leather sandals worn by the Indian people, that exposed the instep and ankle to the fierce rays of the tropical sun. As she lay dying from chronic malaria in the Mission Hospital, Narsapur, she pointed to her sun-browned feet and said, 'Aren't they beautiful?' Truly they had been shod with the preparation of the Gospel of peace.
(Song of Solomon 7. 1; Rom. 10. 15)

**339  Feet—Hind's.**  The gazelle's footprints
—those of the 'hind' of the Bible—are very
dainty. The hind has a clean, polished foot,
tiny yet strong, delicate yet powerful. The hind's
feet are:

*Smooth feet, and so they are very beautiful
    and even,*
*Strong feet, enabling it to travel great distances
    day after day; stronger than a man's, yet
    only 45 square inches to bear 100 lbs.
    weight,*
*Sure feet, soaring sometimes 20 to 30 feet,
    yet never slipping or sliding,*
*Swift feet, that travel faster than hunters
    when danger is near,*
*Steady on high ground when crops fail and
    everything around is breaking down.*

Well might we pray, 'Lord, plant my feet
on higher ground!'
(Ps. 18. 33; Habak. 3. 19)

**340  Fellowship.**  In classical and secular
Greek the New Testament word translated
'fellowship' is found in three main associations:
i. *In the Commercial sphere.* In a Papyrus a
man speaks of his 'brothers with whom I have
no fellowship'. He did not mean that they
were not on speaking terms or that there was
no coming and going with them in the social
realm, but that they had no business connection:
they were not business partners. In the Gospel
two pairs of brothers—Andrew and Peter,
and James and John—were partners in the
fishing business.
ii. *In the sphere of Matrimony.* Two people
just married were said to have entered upon a
'fellowship of life', in which everything was
supposed to be shared by husband and wife.
The New Testament sums up this marital
partnership for the Christian household in
the words—'Heirs together of the grace of
life'.
iii. *In Experience.* Sharing an action, an opinion
or a course, whether good or bad. In one
papyrus it is stated that the authorities were
unable to trace a criminal and therefore
concluded that those in fellowship with him,
that is, those who had a share in his misdeeds,
were sheltering him. 'Have no fellowship with
the unfruitful works of darkness but rather
reprove them'.
(Luke 5. 7; 1 Pet. 3. 7; Eph. 5. 11)

**341  Fellowship of Suffering.**

*The vessel must be shapen for the joys of
    Paradise;*
*The soul must have her training for the service
    of the skies;*
*And if the great Refiner in furnaces of pain,*
*Would do His work more truly, count all His
    dealings gain;*
*For He Himself hath told thee of tribulation
    here.*
*Be still! and let Him mould thee for the
    changeless glory there.*

*From vintages of sorrow are deepest joys
    distilled,*
*And the cup outstretched for healing is oft at
    Marah filled;*
*God leads to joy through weeping, to quietness
    through strife,*
*Through yielding unto conquest, through death
    to endless life!*
*Be still! He hath enrolled thee for the
    Kingdom and the Crown.*
*Be silent! let Him mould thee who calleth
    thee His own.*

*Such silence is communion, such stillness is a
    shrine;*
*The fellowship of suffering an ordinance
    divine.*
*And the secrets of abiding most fully are
    declared*
*To those who, with the Master, Gethsemane
    have shared.*
*Then trust Him to uphold thee 'mid the
    shadows and the gloom.*
*Be still! and He shall mould thee for His
    presence and for home.*

(Phil. 3. 10)

**342  Fellowship with God.**  'Truly our fellowship is with the Father and with His Son,
Jesus Christ'.

*To walk with God—is this some dreamer's
    dream*
*Reserved for ancient men of different caste
Than me? For men of slowly moving years?
And must I think such holy joy is past?*

*And can it be that as from distant Ur
There is a path that leads from idol shrine,
Marked out by tent, by altar and by fire,
Yet points me to the glory that is Thine?*

*And is it so, that I may walk with Thee?
May hear Thy voice above earth's din below?
And like old Sinai's sage and warrior saint
May find Thy ways and see Thine afterglow?*

*How can I see invisibility?
Or how with finite mind reach to confide
Transcendent thoughts: or how with halting
    thigh
Draw near, and keep apace Thy mighty stride?*

*A Mystery? There is a way for all
Who thirst for God, not trod by feet but heart;
An eye, not needing man's external aids,
A mind the schools of earth cannot impart.*

*'The Way' to reach the inaccessible,
'The Truth' the great Inscrutable to know,
'The Life', and thus it opens up the eye
To see, the mind to grasp, the way to go.*

*To walk with God—'tis not too late to join
That holy band who soared above the sod
Of transient things, of weights, besetting sins,
And feel the mighty pulse of Life with God.*

J.B.N.

(Gen. 5. 24; 6. 9: 1 John 1. 3)

**343   Fervour of Love.**

*O pardon us, Lord, that our love to Thy name*
*Is so faint, with so much our affections to*
   *move!*
*Our coldness might fill us with grief and with*
   *shame*
*So much to be loved, and so little to love.*

*O kindle within us a holy desire,*
*Like that which was found in Thy people of old*
*Who tasted Thy love, and whose hearts were*
   *on fire*
*While they waited, in patience, Thy face to*
   *behold.*

It was with tearful eyes and mingled shame
and sorrow that, some time ago, we sang
those verses in company with others. How we
longed for the fire of a holy enthusiasm, for
the burning zeal of a Paul, the fervour of a
Peter, and the all-absorbing love to Christ of
a John! Power was the distinguishing feature
of the apostolic age. Under Pagan and Papal
Rome, love to Christ was the prominent
characteristic of the beloved saints who, for
His sake, counted not their lives dear unto
them. In our day and generation an all-
consuming personal devotedness to Christ
and His interests is but lightly valued, and
intelligence in the things and Word of God is
rated at a high degree. This may be our last
appeal to our beloved fellow-members of one
body united to Christ in glory, and in the
deepening sense that we are about to pass
into His presence we would say to one and all,
give yourselves wholly, heartily and freely to
Christ. Let 'Christ for me! Christ for me!' be
the aim and object of life.

                                           Walter Scott
(Rom. 12. 11)

**344   Fight of Faith—The Good.**

   *Great is the facile conqueror,*
   *Yet haply he who, wounded sore,*
   *Breathless, unhorsed, all covered o'er*
   *With blood and sweat,*
   *Sinks foiled, but fighting evermore,*
   *Is greater yet.*

(1 Tim. 6. 12; 2 Tim. 2. 3; 4. 7)

**345   Filled with the Spirit.**   Paul tells us that
to live victoriously and to avoid excesses of
the flesh, we should be sure that we are filled
with the Spirit. Moody once illustrated the
truth as follows: 'Tell me,' he said to his
audience, 'how can I get the air out of this
glass?' One man said, 'Suck it out with a
pump.' Moody replied, 'That would create a
vacuum and shatter the glass.' After many
impossible suggestions, Moody smiled, picked
up a pitcher of water, and filled the glass.
'There,' he said, 'all the air is removed.' He
then went on to show that victory in the
Christian life is not by 'sucking out a sin here
and there', but rather by being filled with the
spirit.
                                    *Sunday School Times*
(Eph. 3. 19; 5. 18)

**346   Finding Men for Christ.**   Captain James
Haldane, a swearing young naval officer in
command of the battleship *Melville Castle*, was
converted through the words of a young
Christian sailor on his ship whose name has
been forgotten. Abandoning his career in the
Navy, Captain Haldane became an evangelist
and served the Lord in this capacity for over
half a century. He led his brother Robert to
Christ, and Robert in turn was used by the
Lord to the conversion of Felix Neff, a
philanthropic, Swiss Protestant leader; of
Merle D'Aubigne, the famous historian of
the Reformation; and of Fredrick Monod, an
eloquent preacher. These four or five men,
and hundreds of others, will be the joy and
crown of rejoicing of that anonymous Christian
seaman in the day of rewards at the Judgement
Seat of Christ.
(John 1. 41; Acts 2. 41; 1 Thess. 2. 19)

**347   Finest Christian in the Prison.**   George
came to us in prison, convicted of the double
murder of a teenage girl and her father who
came on the scene and tried to defend her.
At the age of seventeen he was a powerful
lad, with strong hands and muscular arms. He
had strangled both his victims.

Although he had protested his innocence
right through the Courts, he confessed to me
after Bible Class one Sunday that he was
guilty of the crime. He said that God was
dealing with him now, and he could not lie
or pretend to God; and he added, 'You tell
us that God is a God of love and forgiveness,
but He could never forgive the kind of thing
I have done: I am lost for ever.' We pointed
out to him that no one could ever minimise
the horror of what he had done, but that
God in His mercy offered forgiveness even to
the murderers of His own Son if only they
would repent and seek His mercy. I shall
never forget how George wrung his hands in
real anguish, then clasped them together in
prayer as he asked the Lord for forgiveness
and salvation. Within a week he was transferred
to another prison to which I had no access,
and I lost touch with him for four years.
Then, asked to speak in another prison
entirely, I was delighted to find George sitting
in the front seat, radiating the peace of
Christ.

He told me of his having been transferred
to the first prison just after his conversion and
of doubt having been sown in his mind about
the reality of his experience with God, which
had been described as 'hallucination and
emotion'. But he kept on reading his Gideon
Bible, presented to him before he left us,
and receiving assurance from the Word of
God. With the joy of salvation evident in his
life, he became a real power for good and
was described openly by the Governor as
'the finest Christian in the Bible Class this
evening'.

George is still in prison and will be there
for a long time to come, but his witness for

the Lord is bright and clear, and he is maturing steadily in his knowledge of the Lord Jesus Christ.

Alex Allan

**348   Finished.**

*The sculptor laid his tools aside;*
*Unfinished, though he was, he died.*

*The artist, with his work undone,*
*Laid down his brush at set of sun.*

*The writer, with his tale half told,*
*No longer to his life could hold.*

*The farmer put away his plough.*
*Sod still unturned, he's resting now.*

*God's Son alone, triumphant, died,*
*For 'It is finished!' Jesus cried.*

*The price is paid, the battle's won,*
*The great work of salvation done.*

*Because He finished all for me,*
*Complete in Him, I know I'll be.*

Edih Selindh Bergman

(John 19. 30; Col. 2. 10)

**349   Fire in the Church.** Samuel Chadwick used to say, 'Men ablaze are invincible: Hell trembles when men kindle: the strongholds of Satan are proof against everything but fire.'

An old country church building was burning and all hands in the village were busy helping to put out the flames. In the bucket line the minister came face to face with the village infidel, and he could not help saying, 'This is the first time I have ever seen you at my church'. There came the instant rejoinder, 'Yes, sir, but this is the first time I have seen your church on fire.'

(Jer. 20. 9)

**350   Fishers of Men.**   Much patience is needed in man-fishing. Though we have toiled all night and caught nothing, we are to continue steadfast and unmovable in His blessed service. Carey, Moffat, and Morrison worked seven years before they saw fruit. Dr Chalmers called on an infidel twenty-four times, and on each occasion was repelled. Then the door opened, for the dying man wanted to see the man who loved his soul so much as to stand twenty-four rebuffs.

A. Marshall

(1 Cor. 15. 58)

**351   Fitted for Service.**

*Balanced and shaped the arrow must be*
*Hid in His quiver, God's armoury.*
*Polished and oiled the sword must stand*
*Waiting the grip of the owner's hand.*
*Silent, inactive, ready to use,*
*Rustless, not restless, for Him to choose.*

*One smooth stone in a shepherd's sling*
*A giant to his end will bring.*
*Simple trumpets joyfully blown*
*And a mighty army is overthrown.*
*Trumpet or stone, Lord, let me be*
*In the battle for right, some use to Thee.*

*In Thy great house there are vessels indeed*
*For every purpose and every need;*
*Clean and empty, and ready today;*
*Lord, here I am, use me, I pray,*
*To bring life-draught to some thirsty soul,*
*Or word of comfort, to make men whole.*

*Thou canst take a Saul and make him be*
*A chosen vessel unto Thee;*
*The past forgiv'n, new theme, new power,*
*To bear Thy name till his latest hour.*
*In some small measure I would be*
*Chosen, fitted and used of Thee.*

Ransome W. Cooper

(Isa. 49. 2; Acts 9. 15)

**352   Five of Spades.**   A preacher returning from the West of England was travelling by train to Paddington. Into his compartment came five men who immediately began to play cards. After a while they invited the preacher to join them. This he steadfastly refused to do, but after a time he offered to tell their fortune from the pack. To this they all readily agreed.

The preacher then said, 'I shall need one special card, the five of spades.' The men handed him the card, and he then got out his Bible and read from Revelation 1. 7, 'Behold He cometh with clouds, and *every eye* shall see Him.' Then from Philippians 2. 8-11, stressing the words, '*Every knee* shall bow and *every tongue* shall confess that Jesus Christ is Lord to the glory of God the Father.' Holding up the card, the five of spades, he pointed to the two black spots at the top. 'These', he said, 'represent your two eyes; the two spots at the bottom are your two knees, and the one in the middle is your tongue. "Behold He cometh." Your two eyes will see Him, your two knees will be forced to bow to Him, and all your tongues will confess that Jesus Christ is Lord.'

By this time the card players had packed up their cards and had begun to look uncomfortable. The preacher then went on to say, 'This card tells me something else about you. These five spades represent five real spades existing at this very moment, waiting to dig your own five graves when the time comes.'

At this moment the train stopped at Didcot Junction, and the five men all bundled out of the door as fast as they could.

Some years later the preacher went out for an evening walk in a London suburb. As he walked someone came behind and touched him on the shoulder. 'Do you remember me, sir?' 'No, I don't think I have seen you before.' 'Do you remember telling five men their fortune in a railway carriage?' 'Yes, of course I remember! They all bundled out at Didcot and didn't even stop to pay the fortune teller his fee.'

Then the stranger said, 'I was one of the five men and this is my story. On that very day I had been to see my old mother. She was desperately ill and passed away soon after. While I was there she read to me the very same words that you read to us on the train. Some time later, when I was out for a walk, I came upon an open-air meeting and stopped to listen. A young man stepped on to the rostrum and read out the same words from his Bible. He then preached and urged people to respond.

'I was greatly moved and went back to my lodgings and there at my bedside I confessed my need of a Saviour and accepted Christ.'

The preacher then asked, 'What about the rest of the men?' The stranger's face grew sad. 'I am sorry to say, sir, that the grave-digger's spade has already dug the graves of the other four men; yet I by God's grace have bowed my knees and confessed Christ to be my Lord and Saviour, and am alive to bear witness to His salvation.'

353  **Flag—The Faded.**   It was very mysterious. The matter was discussed and debated but no satisfactory solution could be arrived at. The signalman's statement, corroborated as it was by others, was positively contradicted by the engine-driver's. Who was speaking the truth?

**Terrible Accident in U.S.A.**—Excursion train from Kingston, North Carolina had run on to the drawbridge which crosses the Elizabeth River.

*Driver's Account.* Signal directed him to proceed—hung from the signal box—but one of the sections of the bridge was open and before the brakes could be applied, the engine and two front coaches plunged into the river. Many lives lost. Farm labourer on bank helped to save thirty-five of the passengers.

Why had the train been allowed to proceed on to the bridge while a section was still open?

*Signalman's Account.* He said he had displayed the red flag in time for the train to be stopped. This was confirmed by other employees.

The driver, severely injured, maintained that it was a white flag that was shown, indicating that the way was clear.

The flag was then produced and the mystery solved. The flag, in use so long, was once red but the colour had faded from it, and it might easily have been mistaken for a white one.

The faded red flag is a picture of the doctrine of redemption by blood left out of the message. Well-meaning hands are still waving such flags, saying 'Peace, peace, when there is no peace.'

H. P. Barker

354  **Flame—The Unfed.**

*Are you on fire for God?*
*Or does the flame burn low?*
*Are the red embers burning out*
*Till there is no more glow?*

*Why has the fire burnt down?*
*Why is the flame all gone?*
*Simply because there's no more fuel*
*To keep it burning on.*

*If you would blaze for God,*
*Your soul must ever be*
*Fed daily from His holy Word,*
*Praying continually.*

*Then will the flame burn bright*
*As you live close to Him.*
*This is the fuel that feeds the fire.*
*The flame won't then grow dim.*

May Gorrie

(Ps. 39. 2,3)

355  **Food and Colour.**   Many different plants will furnish daily food an insect needs; but it always takes the colour from the leaf on which it feeds. Christians often from the Bread of heaven turn to earthly fare, but a little change of colour—to their shame—they always wear. If on Christ, the Lamb, we're feeding we'll present a heavenly blue, but the tastes of earthly follies change us to another hue.

(John 6. 56,57)

356  **Forget it.**

*If you see a tall fellow ahead of the crowd,*
*A leader of men, marching fearless and proud,*
*And you know of a tale whose mere telling*
    *aloud*
*Would cause his proud head in anguish to*
    *be bowed,*
*It's a pretty good plan to forget it.*

*If you know of a skeleton hidden away*
*In a closet and guarded, and kept from day*
*In the dark, whose showing and sudden display*
*Would cause grief and sorrow and lifelong*
    *dismay,*
*It's a pretty good plan to forget it.*

*If you know of a spot in the life of a friend*
*(We all have spots hidden, world without end)*
*Whose touching, his heartstrings would sadden*
    *or rend,*
*Till the shame of its showing no grieving*
    *could mend,*
*It's a pretty good plan to forget it.*

*If you know of a thing that will darken the joy*
*Of a man or a woman, a girl or a boy,*
*That will wipe out a smile or the least way*
    *annoy*
*A fellow, or cause any gladness to cloy,*
*It's a pretty good plan to forget it.*

Claude A. Ries

357  **Forgiven.**

*Not far from New York, in a cemet'ry lone,*
*Close guarding its grave stands a simple*
    *headstone,*
*And on it is graven this one word alone—*
*FORGIVEN!*

*No sculptor's fine art has embellished its form,*
*But constantly there, through the calm and the*
*storm,*
*It bears this one word from a poor fallen worm,*
*FORGIVEN!*

*It shows not the place of the silent one's birth,*
*Reveals not his frailties nor lies of his worth,*
*But tells out its tale from those few feet of*
*earth,*
*FORGIVEN!*

*The name is unmentioned, the date is untold;*
*Beneath lies the body, corrupted and cold;*
*Above rests the spirit, at home in the fold—*
*FORGIVEN!*

*And when from the skies the Lord shall*
*descend,*
*This stranger will rise and to glory ascend,*
*Well-known and befriended, to sing without*
*end—*
*FORGIVEN!*

(Luke 7. 48)

**358  Forgiven by the King.** During King George III's visits to the royal stables, one of the stable boys attracted his attention. Something about the boy won his master's favour, and the king treated him kindly in many ways.

But a time of temptation came, and the poor lad fell into disgrace. He had stolen some oats from the royal bins and, being detected, he was disgraced by the head groom. There seemed to be no idea of speaking to the poor lad about the sin of stealing the oats and abusing the confidence of his master, but only a determination to treat him as he deserved and dismiss him.

Not long afterward, when the king again visited his stables, he noticed that the boy was absent and asked one of the men what had become of him. The man, fearing to tell the truth, yet not liking to tell a falsehood, said he had left. His Majesty was not satisfied with the groom's reply and, suspecting something wrong, called the head groom to him and made the inquiry again.

'I have discharged the boy, sir,' answered he.

'Why?' asked the king.

'He was discovered stealing the oats from one of the bins,' was his reply, 'and I sent him away.'

The king felt very sorry for the poor boy who had thus disgraced himself, and gave the order for him to be sent for immediately. The order was obeyed, and without loss of time the boy was brought to the king. What a scene that was! Face to face with Britain's king stood the boy, a convicted thief!

'Well, my boy', said his Majesty when the lad, not knowing what awaited him, stood before him, trembling and looking very pale: 'is this true that I hear of you?' The lad could not look up into the king's face but, with head bent down, his only answer was a flood of tears. He knew he was guilty: he stood condemned and without excuse.

The king, seeing the stable boy was truly sorry for his sin, spoke to him of the evil, showing him that he had not only taken what was not his own but had abused the confidence reposed in him.

'Well, my lad,' said his Majesty, putting his hand kindly on the boy's head, 'I forgive you.' Then, turning to the head groom, he said, 'Let the boy have his former place and let him be cared for.'

What a thrill of joy filled the lad's heart when the king uttered those three words, 'I forgive you!' Instead of being punished and disgraced, he was restored to favour and reinstated in the place he had lost.

*Indian Christian*

(Ps. 103. 3,4,10)

**359  Forgiven Sincerely.** Prince Bismarck was once asked by Count Enzenberg to write something in his album. The page on which he was to write contained the autographs of Guizot and Thiers. The former had written, 'I have learned in my long life two rules of prudence. The first is, to forgive much; the second is, never to forget.' Under this Thiers had written: 'A little forgetting would not detract from the sincerity of the forgiveness.' Bismarck added, 'As for me, I have learned to forget much and ask to be forgiven much.'

*Sunday School Times*

(Matt. 18. 21,22)

**360  Forgiveness for the Worst Sinners.** Brownlow North, one of the great preachers of his time, was to speak in one of the largest churches in the city of Aberdeen and it was thronged with people who had come to hear him. In the vestry—before the service—he had a note handed to him from an old companion of his unregenerate days, challenging him to enter the pulpit, and saying, 'I know your past history. I followed you to Paris years ago and I know all your career of vice. I have a record of your life at Liverpool also, and I know how you carried on at Manchester. I challenge you to stand in a Christian pulpit and preach: I dare you to do it.'

Brownlow North went into the pulpit and commenced the service by reading the letter, omitting nothing, and, having read out the long list of vile sins, he said, 'My friends, it is all true, and a good deal more than my companion has written here. But I want to tell you there came a day in my life when I heard the Saviour's voice saying, "Brownlow North, go in peace: thy sins are forgiven thee"; and if there was mercy for me, there is mercy for all of you here.'

The service did not continue as arranged, for men and women were broken down there and then. Many hundreds, weeping, decided for Christ that night, and a mighty work began in the granite city where they still speak of it.

**361 Forward!** Dr David Livingstone, great missionary and explorer, said, 'I shall go anywhere provided it is forward.' He did go forward as a pioneer in a strange land, an explorer, a pathfinder, an evangelist, a healer of the sick, and a builder of bridges of faith and courage.

*Pioneers who go exploring into unknown lands*
*Have to span the foaming torrents, making*
*    bridges with their hands,*
*Bridges over roaring streams and rivers deep*
*    and wide*
*Or they would never reach the goal upon the*
*    other side.*

*When difficulties bar the way and obstacles*
*    appear,*
*Do not shrink from facing them through*
*    hopelessness and fear;*
*But dare to build a bridge across the*
*    cataracts of fate,*
*A bridge of faith, a bridge of courage*
*    that will take your weight.*

Patience Strong
(Exod. 14. 15)

**362 Foundations of Faith** Someone said to C. H. Spurgeon, 'I hear you are opposed to works.' 'No,' he replied, 'I am not, nor to chimney-pots; but I would not put them at the foundation.'
(Rom. 4. 4,5)

**363 Founders of Empires.** Founders of world-empires there have been; great as the world counts greatness. But where are Egypt, Babylon, Medo-Persia, Greece, Rome, and their founders? The names of Simon and Andrew, of James and John, however, are hewn in the rock foundations of that church against which the very gates of hades shall not prevail. Nay, when earth kingdoms shall *all* have perished, and Messiah reigns gloriously, then shall these righteous ones shine forth in the kingdom of their Father. When the holy city Jerusalem descends from heaven to be the seat of government of the kingdom of heaven, manifested in all the glories of fulfilled prophecies, earth shall read the Galilean names again. In the dazzling vision of the prophet of Patmos, where all is glory and perfection and brilliance, amid the blazonry of heaven itself, brought down for terrestrial view, we can see twelve names only (Rev. 21. 14), and they include these four, once scored as proof of ownership, on a couple of fishing cobles on the Galilean lake. This is a marvellous record, and where shall we match it?

W. J. Hocking

**364 Found Out.** The missionary, returning before midday to his bungalow after a morning of travel and preaching, found a visitor awaiting his coming. Observant by nature, he noticed that his little travelling alarum was missing from its usual place on the shelf. Suspecting that his visitor had stolen it, he said nothing but managed to keep his visitor until the hour set for the alarum to go off. Then, to the dismay of the thief, the clock made its presence known and revealed the visitor's guilt. 'Be sure your sin will find you out.'
(Num. 32. 23)

**365 Friend—The Sinner's.** When in Canada in 1970 we visited and photographed the tomb and Memorial of Joseph Scriven, the writer of the beautiful familiar hymn, 'What a friend we have in Jesus!' A young Irishman, Joseph Scriven, emigrated in 1845 to Canada where he died in 1886 at the age of 66. He consecrated his life to the Lord after the accidental death by drowning of his fiancée on the eve of their wedding day. His fiancée's death brought him indescribable grief. Shortly before his death a neighbour who came in to help him during his illness found some lines in manuscript in his room and asked him how he came to write them. He replied that he had written them to comfort his mother in her sorrow, and had intended them only for her. As to the composition of the poem, he declared, 'The Lord and I did it between us.' The poem, set to music and now sung to several different tunes, became the well-known hymn, 'What a friend we have in Jesus!' Two lines in the hymn as we know it are different from the poet's original words. These are:

*Are we cold and unbelieving,*
*    cumbered with a load of care?*
*Here the Lord is still our refuge:*
*    Take it to the Lord in prayer.*

His tomb, with the verses of the hymn engraved on the headstone, and his memorial can be seen not far from the city of Peterborough, Ontario.
(Prov. 17. 17; 18. 24)

**366 Fruit of the Spirit.** 'The fruit of the Spirit is love,' love in action. Joy is love rejoicing, peace is love resting, longsuffering is love's patience: gentleness is love's touch, goodness is love's character, faith is love's trust: meekness is love's humility, and temperance is love's strength. In newspaper English, the words of Galatians 5. 22, 23 have been rendered:

'The fruit of the Spirit is an affectionate lovable disposition, a radiant spirit and a cheerful temper, a tranquil mind and a quiet manner, a forebearing patience in provoking circumstances and with trying people, a sympathetic insight and tactful helpfulness, generous judgement and big-souled charity, loyalty and reliableness under all circumstances, humility that forgets self in the joy of others, in all things self-mastered and self-controlled, which is the final mark of perfection.

**367  Fruit out of Martyrdom.**  It has been said that the blood of the martyrs is the seed of the Church, and this has been constantly proved true.

Five young missionaries were martyred in the uncharted jungle of Eastern Ecuador. The father of one—Mr Elliot—on hearing of his son, Jim's, death, said, 'Oh, may God bring those very Aucas who threw the lances to slay our loved ones to stand by our boys in Glory and praise the Saviour for ever!' Not only have all the five Auca men who killed the missionaries become baptised believers, but one of them and three other Christian Aucas have announced their desire to visit the only other tribe of Aucas known to exist, and to tell them about the Lord Jesus Christ. This second tribe, several days' journey through the jungle from the first tribe, is as isolated and as savage as the first tribe of Aucas was years ago. Those Auca missionaries go forth, armed with copies of the Gospel of Mark in the Auca language. This edition, translated by Miss Rachel Saint, sister of one of the martyred missionaries, was printed in Mexico, and is the result of ten years of painstaking labour.

*Indian Christian*

**368  Funeral—A Royal.**  I was idly listening to the B.B.C. programme when I realised that a commentary was being broadcast on the funeral of ex-Queen Wilhelmina of the Netherlands in December, 1962. It will be recalled that it was an unusual funeral in one respect. It was a white funeral. The family mourners were dressed in white, and the horses which drew the hearse were white, at the special request of the ex-Queen herself.

But the greatest surprise came when a hymn was sung in the Cathedral: what was the hymn? The hymn selected was No. 872 in Sankey's Sacred Songs and Solos:

> *There is sunshine in my soul today*
> *More glorious and bright*
> *Than glows in any earthly sky,*
> *For Jesus is the Light.*
> *Oh there's sunshine, blessed sunshine*
> *When the peaceful, happy moments roll;*
> *When Jesus shows His smiling face*
> *There is sunshine in my soul.*

If I heard aright, the listeners were told by the commentator that the ex-Queen had first heard the hymn in Norway and had asked that it should be sung at her funeral. She had been strangely moved by it and attracted to it, and Queen Juliana had translated it into her mother's language and mother tongue. One envisaged the great congregation being introduced to it and singing it with the royal mourners.

**L. R. Plover** in *Life of Faith*

(2 Cor. 4. 6)

**369  Garden of Delight—A.**  In the garden of the poet Tennyson in Freshwater, Isle of Wight, now the grounds of a fashionable hotel, stands a sundial on the edge of the goldfish pond, bearing the Latin inscription—*HORAS NON NUMERO NISI SERENAS*—and the names Alfred, Emily and Hallam. A short verse of poetry, expressive of the poet's feelings when the three met, is also inscribed:

> *And unto greeting when we meet*
> *Delights a hundredfold accrue:*
> *For every grain of sand that runs*
> *And every space of shade that seals,*
> *And every kiss of toothed reels*
> *And all the courses of the suns.*

Before sin entered this earth, a garden—Eden—was the meeting place of God and man, the Creator and the creature, and that converse was a delight until 'man's first disobedience'. Jehovah of hosts found delight in His orchard until His vine, the house of Israel, brought forth wild grapes.
(Gen. 2. 8; Isa. 5. 7)

**370  Garden of Flowers—A.**

> *Only a cottage garden, but it fills my heart*
> *with pleasure*
> *As I muse on the Creator who made each*
> *floral treasure.*
> *These flowers are truly wondrous, dressed by*
> *the Master-hand.*
> *Look on each bloom so perfect, and you will*
> *understand*
> *That only God can form them, those lovely*
> *blossoms rare,*
> *With colours that delight the eye, fragrance*
> *that scents the air.*
> *And they are filled with sweetness: there's*
> *nectar in each bloom.*
> *Fair flowers full of goodness as well as sweet*
> *perfume.*
> *Oh God! I pray that my life may be full of*
> *sweetness for Thee,*
> *Shedding a fragrance on life's road*
> *To draw men heavenward to God.*

**May Gorrie**

(Song of Solomon 4. 12-15)

**371  Garment of Love.**  'Put on love, the bond of perfection.' The picture in the apostle's mind is that of one who is putting around his body the loose and flowing robe, the garment of antiquity. It occurs to him that these loose garments, no matter how fine or beautiful they may be, can never be worn with comfort or grace until they are clasped with a girdle. And Paul says this uniting band is love, which is the girdle of every grace, the final touch that beautifies the whole, that turns the task into delight and perfects every relationship.

**G. H. Morrison**

> *It is not the deed we do,*
> *Though that deed be never so fair—*
> *But love that is always the priceless thing,*
> *Hidden with holy care*
> *In the heart of the deed so fair.*

(Col. 3. 14)

**372 Gentleness.** An elderly Christian who in youth had had a violent temper became remarkable for his gentleness. When asked how he had managed to overcome his temper, he replied very briefly and very wisely, 'By praying to God and speaking low.' When people are angry and ill-tempered, they naturally raise their voices and speak loudly. That elderly gentleman had learnt the lesson of gentleness.

'He shall not cry, nor lift up, nor cause His voice to be heard in the streets,' was said prophetically of Jehovah's servant, our Lord Jesus who could declare, 'I am meek and lowly in heart.'

(Isa. 42. 2; James 2. 17)

**373 Gift of God—The.** A friend of mine whose face always seems to radiate the love of God defies convention, and by his genial and pleasant manner breaks down prejudice wherever he goes. He is a personal worker, and his methods of approach are varied. Here is one of them.

Entering a large shop whose windows are advertising a sale currently proceeding, he asks an assistant in the Men's Department, 'Have you a free-gift department in this shop?'

'No, sir,' replies the salesman, 'but there are splendid bargains while our sale is on.'

'Yes, I have no doubt there are,' says my friend, 'but I'm not looking for bargains: it's something for nothing I want. So there's no free-gift department?'

'I'm sorry there's none here, and I don't think you'll find one in any shop in this town.'

'Thank you! I believe you're right,' says the enquirer, 'but, you see, what man hasn't got, God has. Have you ever been to His free-gift department? This is it—The gift of God is eternal life through Jesus Christ our Lord.'

So the Word is left with the salesman, and a free booklet, too, if he will accept it.

One day, however, my friend met his match. When he asked for the free-gift department in a Canadian store, the salesman said, 'Oh yes, we have! Would you like to visit it?' 'Certainly I would,' was my friend's reply.

'O.K. I'll come with you.' The assistant took him to the very top floor where there was a wide balcony, and led him out to it.

'There you are, sir,' he said, 'You are now in the free-gift department and may enjoy God's free fresh air.'

Twenty-seven centuries ago, through the Prophet Isaiah, God extended a wonderful invitation to His free-gift department, and His words have re-echoed down through the centuries ever since: 'Ho, every one that thirsteth, come ye to the waters, and he that hath no money; come ye, buy and eat; yea, come, buy wine and milk without money and without price.' 'The gift of God is eternal life through Jesus Christ our Lord,' wrote Paul in the first century A.D.

A.N.

(Isa. 55. 1; Rom. 6. 23)

**374 Gifts—Spiritual.** Dr A. T. Pierson has stated seven great principles of spiritual gifts. These are:
1 Every believer has some gift, therefore all should be encouraged.
2 No one has all the gifts, therefore all should be humble.
3 All gifts are for the Body, therefore all should be harmonious.
4 All gifts are for the Lord, therefore all should be contented.
5 All gifts are needful and mutually helpful, therefore all should be faithful.
6 All gifts promote the whole Body's health therefore none can be dispensed with.
7 All gifts depend on the Holy Spirit's fullness and power, therefore none should be out of fellowship with Him.

The leading of the Spirit in the public exercise of gifts operates in close connection with the believer's spiritual judgement.

**375 Gifts—Variety of.** Mr Fearing, who often despaired that his labour was in vain, said to John Wesley, 'If I could preach like you, I should be happy.' 'Sir,' said Mr Wesley, 'we are building God's temple. Go now, read the third chapter of Nehemiah and learn that he who repaired the dung gate was counted of as much honour as he who touched the gate of the fountain. All did their bit; you and I can do no more.'

(Neh. 4. 17; Mark 14. 8)

**376 Giving all to Christ.**

*God does not ask for much.*
*He does not ask that I*
*Should yield great gifts and high,*
*Things I do not possess,*
*Character, nobleness,*
*Riches and strength and such;*
*God does not ask for much:*
*But—howsoever small—*
*He asks for all.*

M. E. Procter

In Rabindranath Tagore's 'Gitanjali' the following story is told:

I had gone a-begging from door to door in the village path, when thy golden chariot appeared in the distance like a gorgeous dream, and I wondered who was this King of all kings! My hopes rose high and methought my evil days were at an end, and I stood waiting for alms to be given unasked and for wealth scattered on all sides as the dust.

The chariot stopped where I stood. Thy glance fell on me and thou camest down with a smile. Then of a sudden thou did'st hold out thy right hand and say: 'What hast thou to give to me?'

Ah, what a kingly jest was it to open thy palm to a beggar to beg! I was confused and stood undecided, and then from my wallet I slowly took out the least little grain of corn and gave it to thee.

But how great my surprise when at the day's end I emptied my bag on the floor to find a least little grain of gold among the poor heap. I bitterly wept and wished that I had the heart to give thee MY ALL.

William Walker

Jesus says, '*My all I gave for thee!*
　　　　*What hast thou given to me?*'

## 377　Giving and Getting.

*Give, though your gifts be small,*
*Still be a giver!*
*Out of the little fount*
*Proceeds the river.*

*Out of the river's gifts*
*Gifts soon will be*
*Pouring their waters out,*
*Making a sea.*

*Out of the sea again*
*Heaven draws its showers,*
*And to the fount imparts*
*All its new powers.*

*Thus in a cycle borne*
*Gifts roll around,*
*And in the blessing given*
*Blessing is found.*

(Prov. 3. 9,10; 19. 6)

## 378　Giving—Blessedness of.

How little can I spare for God and satisfy His claims and my conscience? We should invert the terms and ask, How little can I expend upon myself and yet satisfy my actual needs, and how much can I thus spare for God? The missionary age affords new opportunity and incentive for the culture of this supreme grace. Giving will bring its true blessing, its greater blessing only when systematic and self-denying.

One of the foremost incentives to missions is found in the blessedness of giving. Christ spake a new beatitude, recorded and preserved by Paul who said to the Ephesian elders:

'Remember the words of the Lord Jesus how he said, It is more blessed to give than to receive!' The full meaning and truth of the last beatitude is yet to be known, and can be known only as this work of missions is done as He meant it to be done.

A. T. Pierson

## 379　Giving brings Blessing.

*It's a funny thing with giving that it spreads*
　　*out far and wide,*
*As a stone that drops into a pond sends*
　　*ripples to the side;*

*If one person meets another and gives a*
　　*cheerful smile,*
*That can spread 'mong other people till it's*
　　*travelled many a mile;*

*One kindly word that's spoken to a stranger*
　　*on the way*
*Can multiply and multiply before the end*
　　*of day.*

*And I think you'll know the story of five*
　　*thousand people fed*
*When a boy gave just two fishes and five*
　　*tiny loaves of bread:*

*So, when you give your money, just think*
　　*what it might do,*
*How many people might be blessed by the*
　　*gift that comes from you.*

(Esth. 9. 22; Acts 20. 35)

## 380　Giving for Others.

Dr Donald Barnhouse explains the lesson of our Lord's parable of the unjust steward in this way:

If by our giving to missions souls may be saved on the other side of the world, if by our giving in the church at home young people may be saved who shall carry on the torch of truth at home and abroad in the next generation, then when our control of money fails, when death relaxes our hold upon the possessions to which we have so tightly held, we shall find on the other side in the presence of God those whom we have blessed with our gifts, the souls who have been reached through the money we have expended for the Lord, those who have been blessed through the teaching of the Word because we have 'communicated unto him that teacheth in all good things'—these will be there to welcome us, in our reception, to our reward.

(Luke 16. 9,10; Gal. 6. 6)

## 381　Giving—Greatest Illustration of.

None of us like to be told what to do with our money and yet, if we turn a deaf ear to the great spiritual principle of stewardship, we shall miss the blessing of the Lord, and the eternal reward that the Lord Jesus called treasure in heaven.

Jesus stood by the treasury and noticed a widow cast in two mites (a farthing) and from this gave the greatest illustration on true giving. This, the greatest illustration on giving in the Bible, was about the smallest amount ever given. The crowd gave out of their abundance but she gave her all. The real test is not what we give out of our pockets but what we have left.

(Luke 21. 24)

## 382　Giving is more Blessed.

*More blessed it is to give than receive:*
*I wonder how many this great truth believe,*
*For, in this big selfish world today*
*People keep grabbing but don't give away.*
*You have heard of the man whom some*
　　*folks thought mad,*
*The more he gave, the more he had!*
*I, like that 'madman', have proved it true;*
*What is willingly giv'n comes back double*
　　*to you.*
*So don't be a grabber, but scatter abroad:*
*There's real joy in giving as unto the Lord.*

May Gorrie

(Acts 20. 35)

**383  Giving—Keep on.**

*Withhold not the gospel from souls needing
     bread,*
*For giving is living, the bright angel said.*
*'But must I be giving and giving again*
*And empty my storehouse for ungrateful men?'*
*'Oh no!' said the angel whose glance pierced
     me through,*
*'Just give till the Master stops giving to you.'*

(Prov. 3. 9,10)

**384  Giving Liberally.**  John Wesley had a
friend Samuel Bradburn who was in straitened
circumstances. Mr Wesley sent him the
following letter:

   'Dear Sammy,
              Trust in the Lord and do
good; so shalt thou dwell in the land and
verily thou shalt be fed.
                    Yours affectionately,
                          John Wesley'

With the letter he enclosed two £5 notes.
The reply was prompt:

   'Rev. and Dear Sir,
                I have often been struck
with the beauty of the passage of Scripture
quoted in your good letter, but I must confess
that I never saw such useful expository notes
on it before.
   I am, reverend and dear sir,
      your obedient and grateful servant,
                          S. Bradburn'

John Wesley was throughout his life a
liberal giver. He lived economically and
simply, and gave half and often more than
half of his income to the Lord.
(Heb. 13. 15,16)

**385  Giving Methodically.**  William Ewart
Gladstone kept a careful account of his
giving. Later this showed that his gifts aggre-
gated fully half a million. In a letter which he
wrote to one of his sons at Oxford he offered
the following suggestions as to the use of
money.
   'In regard to money, there is a great advantage in its methodical use. Especially is it
wise to dedicate a certain portion of our
means to purposes of charity and religion,
and this is more easily begun in youth than
in after life. The greatest advantage of making
a little fund of this kind is that when we are
asked to give, competition is not between
self on the one hand and any charity on the
other, but between the different purposes of
religion and charity between which we ought
to make the most careful choice. It is desirable
that the tenth of our means be dedicated to
God, and it tends to bring a blessing on the
rest. No one can tell the richness of blessing
that comes to those who thus honour the
Lord with their substance.'
(1 Tim. 6. 18)

**386  Giving One's Best.**

*Then to the branching of the way I came*
*And paused to see which way the path should
     lead,*
*And while I stood He called me by my name*
*And said, 'Seek not a life of fame—*
*For I have many lambs for you to feed.'*

*And though I lacked the perfect Shepherd
     heart*
*I gave out knowledge and I sought to live*
*As He, the Shepherd, lived, from sin apart,*
*And when I fell, He lifted me again to start,*
*And whispered, 'Walk with me, and give,
     and give, and give.'*

*And so I gave, and as I gave my best,*
*I found that I had more than all*
*Which I had previously possessed:*
*For I had God's own peace and rest,*
*And maybe some young lambs had heard His
     call.*

                          Mona Laird

The above was found among Miss M. R.
Laird's papers in a handwritten book of
poems.

**387  Giving or Only Singing?**  The late Dr
Peter Marshall once selected for use in a
service the familiar hymn of consecration,
'Take my life and let it be.' He requested the
congregation to give particular thought to the
words:

   *Take my silver and my gold—*
   *Not a mite would I withhold.*

Explaining the practical sense of the words,
'Not a mite would I withhold,' he asked all
who could not sing the line with literal sincerity to refrain from singing it at all.
   The effect was a dramatic commentary on
the glib, thoughtless manner in which we
all too often sing the hymn. Hundreds of
voices, with the organ accompaniment, sang
vigorously up to the designated point. Then
suddenly there was only the sound of the
organ music. Not a single voice ventured to
so challenging a height.
                    *Sunday School Times*

(Mark 12. 41-44)

**388  Giving Sacrificially.**  Sitting over
against the treasury of the temple, the Lord
detected that day the difference between the
ostentatious gifts of the rich and the humble
two mites of the widow. Wuest's translation
of Mark 12. 41 is, 'He was viewing with a
discerning eye how the crowd throws money
into the treasury.'

The world sees what a man gives: Christ sees
   how he gives.
The world looks at the amount: Christ looks
   at the motive.
The rich gave of their abundance: the widow
   gave all that she had.
There was no sacrifice in the one: there was
   no reserve in the other.

The fable is told of a pig and a hen walking together along the road when they saw a large notice directing them to an 'Egg and Bacon Barbecue'. 'How about going along?' asked the hen. 'Not I,' replied the pig, 'You can go if you wish, for you only give a contribution. For me it is a sacrifice.'

(Mark 12. 44)

### 389  Giving—Standard of.

I said to a rich orthodox Jew whom I knew, who lived in the East of London, 'What is your method of giving to God? Do you give a tenth of your income?' He replied, 'If I gave a tenth of my income, that would not be giving at all. The tenth is Jehovah's. What I give above a tenth, that, I reckon, is my giving.' If all Christians gave like that, there would be no lack of funds for the foreign mission field. But the Christian's standard of giving should be much higher if we read 1 Corinthians 16 aright.

Mark Kagan

(1 Cor. 16. 2)

### 390  Giving While You're Living.

*Do your giving while you're living,*
*Then you're knowing where it's going.*

A man once said to a servant of God, 'Why is it that everybody is always criticising me for being miserly when they know that I have made provision to give everything to charity when I die?' 'Well,' said the other, 'let me tell you about the pig and the cow. Said the pig to the cow, "Everybody likes you, yet you give only milk and cream, while I give much more. I give bacon and ham, I give bristles, and they even pickle my feet! Still nobody likes me. Why is this?" The cow thought for a minute and then said, "Well, maybe it's because I give while I'm still living."'

### 391  Giving While You're Living.

*Use your money while you're living,*
*Do not hoard it to be proud;*
*You can never take it with you,*
*There's no pocket in a shroud.*

*Gold can help you on no further*
*Than the graveyard where you lie;*
*Even though you're rich while living,*
*You're a pauper when you die.*

*Use it, then some lives to brighten,*
*Those who ever weary plod;*
*Place your bank account in heaven*
*And grow richer toward God.*

*Use it wisely, use it freely,*
*Do not hoard it to be proud*
*You can never take it with you—*
*There's no pocket in a shroud.*

John Alexander Joyce

(Luke 12. 33,34)

### 392  Glamour.

We live in an age of glamour: people love it, and desire it. Something within them seems satisfied if they can bring some glamour into their everyday lives. With some it is expressed by the glittering lights of a big city like Paris or New York, and they can walk about after dark revelling in the brilliant illuminations that help them to escape from reality. With others it is pin-up pictures on the wall (most of them probably quite harmless ones)—photographs of famous footballers or leading sportsmen or of some film star.

We went into a room once that had some pictures on the wall, all taken from magazines. There was nothing improper about any of them, but they seemed all to be summed up by the central one, which was a head and shoulders of some 'glamour girl'. The story beside the picture was of her success in her career and her ambition to remain at the top, whatever might come along. And it told of the steps she took with great care to remain among the stars of the film world.

Most people like some glamour brought into life. Fun and games—or films—or sports—or something else that breaks the monotony of life is what so many are seeking. Experience proves the transient nature of these things, but people mostly learn the hard way, and have to find out for themselves the shallowness of worldly glamour. There is undoubtedly an enchantment about many of the things that we encounter, a 'magic' whereby the mind can be taken up with a desire for something—an experience, a possession, a sense of ownership or or of realization...and it is only in the end that we awaken to the futility of these things to satisfy life's deepest longings.

Touchstone in *The Witness*

### 393  Glorifying God.

The chief end of man is to glorify God and to enjoy Him for ever, says the Shorter Catechism once taught in Scottish schools: and it speaks truly. God is a God of infinite variety, and it is given to His own to bring glory to Him in an infinite variety of ways: some through sickness and through death, some through life and health; some through joy and some through sorrow; some in bonds and imprisonment, some in labours more abundant; some in poverty, some in wealth; some in ill-repute, some in good repute. What matters the circumstances so long as in them we bring glory to God and in them bear testimony to God's faithfulness.

R. Sheldrake

(1 Cor. 10. 31)

### 394  Glory—Aftermath of.

*The Cross looked like the victory of evil*
*    over good,*
*The cruel crucifixion of a Man misunderstood.*
*It seemed that death had conquered love*
*    when in the grave He lay.*
*But after came the glory of the resurrection*
*    day.*

*While the night still wrapped the garden in a*
*   shroud of gloom,*
*Mary, weeping, stood aghast before the empty*
*   tomb;*
*But after came a voice she knew upon the*
*   morning air,*
*Saying, 'Mary!' Then she turned to see*
*   the Master there.*
*And with a heart that sang for joy, by*
*   certainty made bold,*
*She ran to tell the greatest tidings that was*
*   ever told.*

Patience Strong

(1 Peter 1. 11)

**395 Glory—Reflected.** God does not reveal
Himself hurriedly to the man on the jump. He
does not unveil His heart to the one who
wants only a curious casual glance. He does
not manifest His glory to the spiritual tourist,
but to the one who comes up to Him on the
Mount. The reflected glory on Moses' face as
he came forth from his forty days of communion
with God was not produced by a snapshot,
but by a time exposure.

*Choice Gleanings*

(Exod. 34. 28,29; 2 Cor. 3. 18)

**396 Goal—The Christian's.**

*God give you strength to view the heights*
*   sublime*
*And count the cost, nor hesitate to climb!*
*May you achieve that to which you aspire*
*And, gaining, set your standard ever higher;*
*Content, like Him we follow, to endure*
*Because the goal is set, the prize is sure,*
*Content because, although He leads the way,*
*He walks Himself with you from day to day—*
*Himself the goal, Himself the Prize again,*
*Himself the strength by which you will attain.*

(Phil. 3. 8)

**397 Goal—Travelling to a.**

*From the day we were born*
*Till the day that we die*
*We are travelling toward a goal;*
*And—whether we face the fact or no—*
*To the destiny of the soul.*

*These bodies will perish,*
*For mortals are we,*
*But everyone has a soul*
*Which will still live on in eternity,*
*And heaven or hell is the goal.*

*It is good to be ready,*
*For there is no lease*
*Of our life in this world here below;*
*And sometimes the call comes suddenly—*
*Without notice we must go.*

*There is only one way*
*To the heavenly land:*
*The blood of the Lamb is the sign.*
*If I come as a sinner and trust in that blood,*
*Then heavenly bliss will be mine.*

May Gorrie

**398 God.** What is God? The telescope by
which we hold converse with the stars, the
microscope which unveils the secrets of nature,
the crucible of the chemist, the knife of the
anatomist, the reflective faculties of the
philosopher, all the common instruments of
science, avail not here. On the threshold of
that impenetrable mystery, a voice arrests
our steps. From out of the clouds and darkness
that are round about God's throne, the
question comes, 'Canst thou by searching
find out God? Canst thou find the Almighty
to perfection?'

Thomas Guthrie

Running like a Gulf-stream through the
sea of time, comes the affirmation that God
has manifested Himself to man, and the best
men have affirmed it most persistently. Where-
ever this affirmation has made its way, the
icebergs of scepticism have disappeared, the
temperature of virtue has risen, and the sweet
fruits of charity have ripened. If the belief
be false, then a lie has blessed the world,
and the soul is so organised that it reaches
the highest state of development in an atmosphere of deception; for it is a fact that man
is purest and woman most virtuous where
belief in God's manifestation is most intense
and real.

O. P. Gifford

(Gen. 1. 1)

**399 God for us.** Philip Melancton, the most
lovable of all the Reformers, and a great
friend of Martin Luther, was outstanding for
his moderation, love of order and profound
scholarship. He often quoted the words, 'If
God be for us, who can be against us?' in
his correspondence, and found great comfort
from them when his life was threatened by
powerful foes.

On his deathbed Paul Eber was with him
and read those words, and Melancton said,
'Read these words again. That's it! That's it!'
He passed away peacefully on April 19, 1560.

When John Bunyan, the Bedford tinker,
was on the horns of a dilemma, he read the
words and said, 'Just the words I needed.'
William of Orange, too, was encouraged by
the words as, at the Battle of the Boyne, he
faced the armies arrayed against him.

(Rom. 8. 31)

**400 God—Heart-knowing.** The precise
meaning of the divine epithet 'Shaddai' has
been a matter of etymological speculation for
a long time. In a recent article Norman
Walker suggests a new etymology and meaning
for 'Sadday' (Shaddai) which seems worth
considering. He takes as his starting-point
the divine name SHA (G) -ZU, which appears
in the seventh Babylonian Creation Tablet.
In this context the title of the Deity means
'One who knows the heart (or inward parts)
of man'. Walker then shows how an etymological development to Hebrew Sadday

(Shaddai) could be possible. Thus the meaning 'Heart-knower' seems assured.

There are several considerations to support the idea. First, the self-revelation of God to Abraham who lived much of his life in the Akkadian sphere of influence is by His name El-Shaddai; and this is a title with which he was probably familiar. Second, it seems characteristic that the initial appearances of divine epithets occur in contexts in which the meaning of that epithet is a key factor. As a divine epithet, Shaddai occurs in connection with Abraham's great desire to have a son and heir. The meaning 'Heart-knower' for Shaddai seems particularly appropriate in other occurrences in Genesis; and the term 'kard-iognosta' used by the apostles as a vocative of Deity seems to echo this meaning of the divine title 'Shaddai'.

Henry R. Moeller

(Gen. 17. 1; Ps. 139. 2,4,6)

**401  God—Immeasurable.**  Colonel Glenn, the first American astronaut, said, 'Although you cannot measure God in scientific terms, or feel, smell or touch Him, yet you can know Him.' This may seen unreasonable, but when you come to think of it, many of the greatest forces of life are beyond reason.

The only true guide to life comes from God Himself by revelation in the Bible, for the Bible tells us first of all that life is a gift of God and owes its existence to the sustaining power of God. Little wonder that the great Jewish Rabbi who became the great Christian missionary, the apostle Paul, exclaimed in an ecstasy of wonder: 'O the depth of the riches, both of the wisdom and knowledge of God! how unsearchable are His judgements, and His ways past finding out!'

God's wealth is incomputable, His wisdom incomparable, His ways incomprehensible.

(Rom. 11. 33)

**402  God—Is He Dead.**  'Is God dead?' That would seem to be a question occupying many minds these days, and it would almost seem as if some of our modern theologians find it hard to give a satisfactory answer. Our Dominican Christians would have no difficulty answering the question, as they have abundant proof in these days that God is not dead and that even in these modern days in which we hear so much, it is still no vain thing to trust in the Lord.

At the end of July we commenced an extension to our chapel. No appeals have been made for money, and the Lord has supplied every need in a wonderful way. The Christians have been putting the needs before the Lord in prayer, and so have received ample evidence that God hears and answers prayer, so, how could God be dead? It has been an experience of great value for them and for us.

Duncan M. Reid

(Heb. 11. 6)

**403  God of the Stars.**  How good it is that we are able to put our lives into His hands in the knowledge that we have a relationship infinite and eternal! Above the things and the physical bodies which hold too many men prisoners we can find everlasting meaning in the One who made the stars. Amy Carmichael wrote:

*I am the God of the stars;*
*They do not lose their way;*
*Not one do I mislay.*
*Their times are in My hand:*
*They move at My command.*

*I am the God of the stars,*
*Today as yesterday,*
*The God of thee and thine,*
*Less thine they are than Mine:*
*And shall Mine go astray?*

*I am the God of the stars.*
*Lift up thine eyes and see*
*As far as mortals may*
*Into eternity,*
*And stay thy heart on Me.*

(Isa. 57. 15)

**404  God's Delight.**

*A well-kept heart is God's delight:*
*Then let thy heart be clean,*
*For out of it life's issues flow,*
*The mighty and the mean.*

*A well-stored mind is God's delight;*
*Then fill thy mind in youth,*
*Draw deeply from the hidden springs*
*Of God's eternal truth.*

*A well-trained eye is God's delight;*
*Then train thine eye to trace*
*The glories of thy Father's house*
*Where thou shalt see His face.*

*A well-drilled ear is God's delight;*
*Then strain thine ear to hear*
*The whisper of thy Father's voice,*
*Who walketh ever near.*

*A well-ruled tongue is God's delight;*
*Then guard thy tongue right well;*
*'Tis full of poison, full of strife,*
*'Tis set on fire by hell.*

*A well-placed foot is God's delight,*
*Then bring thy foot straight down;*
*Stand on the solid rock of right,*
*Ignore the proud world's frown.*

*A well-shaped course is God's delight;*
*Then have thy course defined:*
*Pursue it with blood earnestness,*
*Nor cast one glance behind.*

Thomas Baird

**405  God's Majesty.**

*Thou God all transcending,*
*Of life never ending*
*The source, in whose hand is the key:*
*The only Inscrutable,*
*Ever Immutable;*

*Broken hearts mending,*
*To feeblest cry bending,*
*In love Thy Son sending*
*To save a poor sinner like me.*

*O God all pervading,*
*Of glory unfading,*
*Who art Thine own vast Dwelling Place;*
*Thou God of antiquity,*
*Far-flung ubiquity;*
*Hell's host invading,*
*Their prisoners aiding,*
*In Secret Place shading*
*The weary who rest in Thy grace.*

*O God, praise is blending*
*And worship ascending;*
*Thy Majesty burns as a flame*
*Of Light unapproachable,*
*Rights unencroachable;*
*Yet condescending,*
*The wanderer tending,*
*The Comforter sending*
*To all who have called on Thy name.*

                                     J.B.N.

(1 Tim. 6. 13-16)

**406 God's Manuscripts.**

> *And Nature, the old nurse, took*
> *The child upon her knee,*
> *Saying, 'Here is a story-book*
> *Thy Father hath written for thee.'*
> *'Come, wander with me,' she said,*
> *'Into regions yet untrod,*
> *And read what is still unread*
> *In the manuscripts of God.'*

                Henry W. Longfellow
(Rom. 1. 20)

**407 God's Names.** 'God' is our most important word, and one of the most difficult. In many languages there is a common usage: e.g. 'Allah' in about 50 languages; 'God' in nearly 40 (Gott, etc.); 'Ishwar'—in India in about 40, 'Parameshwar' in 10, 'Deva' in about 20 (and the kindred words 'Dieu', 'Dios' in various European ones), 'Khuda' in some 25, 'Mulungu' in about 30 East African languages, 'Nyambe' in about 30 in Zaire.

Our difficulty as translators is always with what lies *behind* a word. Very rarely do we have to invent a word for 'God'; the word is there already, but along with it are all sorts of imperfect, sub-Christian ideas of God. There is a belief in a Supreme Being, or at any rate in minor deities, a belief in the supernatural, but it does not come up to the Christian belief.

In India 'Deva' and its forms really imply only minor deities. Carey prefers 'Ishwar', Lord, Ruler. Others have added 'Param', Supreme, to which objection is taken that it might imply 'supreme among many deities'.

It may well be considered whether the Sanskrit language might not aim at uniformity, and whether 'Ishwar' is not, taking everything into consideration, the most satisfactory term.

     H. K. Moulton in *The Bible Translator*

**408 Godliness.** 'There is,' said Dr F. B. Meyer, 'a street in London, near St Pauls', which I never traverse without very peculiar feelings. It is Godliman Street. Evidently the name is a corruption of *godly man*. Did some saint of God once live here, whose life was so holy as to give a sweet savour to the very street in which he dwelt? Were the neighbours, who knew him best, the most sure of his godliness?'

> *So let our lips and lives express the holy*
> *Gospel we profess;*
> *So let our works and virtues shine, to prove*
> *the doctrine all divine.*

                *Choice Gleanings*
(Ps. 4. 3; Tit. 2. 12)

**409 Gold.** Men adopt as their motto—'Win gold'. The vain man adds—'and wear it': the generous man adds—'and share it': the miserly man adds—'and spare it': the prodigal adds—'and spend it': the usurer adds—'and lend it': the gambler adds—'and lose it': the wise man adds—'and use it'.

The Pope's ambassador, sent to bribe Martin Luther to return to the corrupt church, exclaimed in disappointment and disgust, 'That German beast does not care for gold.' (Job 28. 12-17)

**410 Gold Standard.** Devaluation is an expression used in commerce when for one reason or another it becomes necessary to lower the standard. The classical example of this was seen when Britain found it necessary to go off the gold standard. Prior to that time the sterling currency had been supported by gold reserves. For each pound note there was in reserve its equivalent in gold. At the time of the great depression it was found that such a standard was no longer feasible and so it was lowered and put on a basis that was related to trade and productivity. Briefly, the standard was what the nation could produce. Later debts, and adverse trade balances caused a further devaluation. By following such a procedure there is an impression created of prosperity within the nation.

While devaluation may be politically expedient, it should never be spiritually expedient. But we are living in days when the standards are slowly but surely being removed. This has happened before. The prophet Isaiah had to cry to the people that the gold had become dim and the silver had turned to dross. The high spiritual aims of the law had gone and expediency coupled with material prosperity was the standard. This devaluation points to a serious spiritual decline, and generally precedes the judgement of God. It was so in the days before the flood: it was so at the time of the Exile: and it is so today.

This spiritual devaluation characterised the church at Laodicea. They were rich and prosperous, but the Lord had to tell them that it was necessary to buy gold that had been tried in the fire.

J. S. McNaught

(Rev. 3. 17,18)

## 411  Golgotha.

*Nailed upon Golgotha's tree—*
*Faint and bleeding. Who is He?*
*Hands and feet so rudely torn,*
*Wreathed with crown of twisted thorn:*
*Once He lived in heaven above,*
*Happy in His Father's love,*
*Son of God, 'tis He, 'tis He*
*On the Cross at Calvary.*

*Nailed upon Golgotha's tree—*
*Mocked and taunted. Who is He?*
*Scorners tell Him to come down,*
*Claim His kingdom and His crown.*
*He it was who came to bless,*
*Full of love and tenderness.*
*Son of Man, 'tis He, 'tis He*
*On the cross at Calvary.*

*Nailed upon Golgotha's tree—*
*As a Victim. Who is He?*
*Bearing sin, but not His own,*
*Suff'ring agony unknown.*
*He, the promised Sacrifice,*
*For our sins has paid the price.*
*Lamb of God, 'tis He,'tis He*
*On the cross at Calvary.*

*Throned in glorious majesty,*
*Lord triumphant. Who is He?*
*E'en the same who came to die,*
*Now in heav'n exalted high.*
*With adoring hearts we now*
*At His blessed feet would bow.*
*Lord of all, 'tis He, 'tis He,*
*Throned in glorious majesty,*

(John 19. 17,18)

## 412  Goodness of God.

In a town on the coast of Kent there lived a sailor who had spent over thirty years at sea. Like many others, he had no thought of God or eternity. He passed through the horrors of Dunkirk and was wounded in the battle for Crete, but he still remained careless and indifferent to his eternal welfare. Some months later the vessel on which he served was torpedoed, dive-bombed, and sunk in the Southern seas. All the lifeboats except two were destroyed before they could be launched. One of the two boats which did get away was bombed and sank with all its occupants. The sailor of whom I write was in the other boat. They were in a shark-infested sea and expected to be blasted at any moment by dive bombers. Yet nothing seemed to touch the sailor's heart or conscience.

Suddenly something strange happened. A sea mist completely enveloped the boat, coming, it seemed, from nowhere. Those in the boat realised that this wonderful deliverance could only come from the mercy of God. They went down on their knees and thanked God for His deliverance. Thus the sailor who had till then been an atheist came to believe that God was good and merciful. So touched was he by the goodness of God that when he returned to his home town he listened with avid interest to a preacher on the street proclaiming the story of God's love in giving His Son to die for sinners, believed the gospel message and accepted Christ as his Saviour.
(Rom. 2. 4)

## 413  Gospel of Christ—The.

Archibald G. Brown once said: 'The gospel is a fact, therefore tell it simply; it is a joyful fact, therefore tell it cheerily; it is an entrusted fact, therefore tell it faithfully; it is a fact of infinite moment, therefore tell it earnestly; it is a fact about a Person, therefore preach Christ.'

After 41 years of service for the Lord in one place, Dr Baldwin said: 'I testify that at 30, after examining as best I could the philosophies and religions of the world, I said, "Nothing is better than the gospel of Christ." At 40, when burdens began to press and years seemed to hasten, I said, "Nothing is as good as the gospel." At 50, when there were empty chairs in the home, and the mound builders had done me service, I said, "There is nothing to be compared with the gospel." At 60, when my second sight saw through the delusions and vanities of earthly things, I said, "There is nothing but the gospel." At 70, amid many limitations, I sing,

*Should all the forms that men devise*
*Attack my faith with treacherous art,*
*I'd call them vanities and lies*
*And bind the gospel to my heart.'*

(Rom. 1. 1,9,16)

## 414  Gospel—The Life Plant.

E. L. Langston in one of his books says: 'There is a strange plant in Jamaica called the life-plant. It is called this because it is almost impossible to kill or destroy any portion of it. When a leaf is cut off and hung by a string, instead of shrivelling up and dying like any other leaf, it sends out white, threadlike roots and thus gathers moisture from the air and begins to grow new leaves. The gospel is the Life Plant of the moral and spiritual world. Circulate the gospel anywhere, and it will soon take root in the affections and hearts of mankind.'
(Rom. 1. 16)

## 415  Gospel—The World's Only Hope.

The Right Hon. W. E. Gladstone, three times Prime Minister of Britain, declared:
'If I am asked what is the remedy for the deeper sorrows of the human heart, what a man should chiefly look to in progress through

life as the power that is to sustain him under trials and enable him manfully to confront his afflictions, I must point to something which in a well-known hymn is called "the Old, Old Story", told in an old, old book and taught with an old, old teaching, which is the greatest and best gift ever given to mankind ... Talk about questions of the day, there is but one question and that is the gospel. It will correct everything that needs correction. My only hope for the world is in bringing the human mind into contact with divine revelation.'
(1 Cor. 9. 16)

## 416   Gospels—The.

*Holy writings of the Person of the Blessed*
*    Son of God,*
*Precious records of the pathway which the feet*
*    of Jesus trod:*
*Treasured pages of His doings, rich reminders*
*    of His days,*
*Skilful touches, by the Spirit, of His ever*
*    perfect ways.*

*Scenes whose rich delineations are the work*
*    of heaven's art,*
*Words whose wonderful unfoldings meet the*
*    longings of the heart,*
*Here we trace the Man of Sorrows, here we*
*    see the Holy One*
*On the earth amongst His creatures in the*
*    person of the Son.*

*By the Galilean waters, in the busy city street,*
*On the highways, in the deserts, or where*
*    congregations meet;*
*In the house of Simon Peter; sitting wearied*
*    at the well;*
*'Mid disciples on the hillside with the truth of*
*    God to tell.*

*Sharing Levi's entertainment with the outcast*
*    and the lost,*
*Or asleep upon a pillow in a vessel tempest-*
*    tossed;*
*Healing multitudes at sunset, praying through*
*    the night alone,*
*As the Lord of Sabbath walking through the*
*    cornfields with His own.*

*Cleansing here the pleading leper, opening*
*    there the darkened eye*
*Of the beggar by the wayside—He a stranger*
*    passing by;*
*Standing radiant on the mountain, meeting*
*    unbelief below,*
*Bearing grief, sustaining sorrow, calming*
*    fear, dispelling woe;*

*Bowed in sorrow in the garden, standing*
*    silent in the hall,*
*Crowned with thorns upon the pavement and*
*    rejected there by all;*
*Cast away by men as worthless, He, Jehovah's*
*    Holy One,*
*Walking meekly to Golgotha, there for sinners*
*    to atone.*

*Wrapped in linen with the spices, lying fragrant*
*    in the grave,*
*Rising from the tomb triumphant and*
*    omnipotent to save;*
*Stretching out to loved disciples hands of*
*    blessing and of grace,*
*Carried upward into heaven, there to have the*
*    Victor's place;*

*Down the ages comes the impress of His*
*    Person and His ways;*
*Not a myth of man's devising, but the theme*
*    of heaven's praise;*
*Breathings of the Holy Spirit whom the*
*    Father hath sent forth.*
*Bringing blessed declarations of the Son's*
*    surpassing worth.*

H. J. Miles

417   Gospels—The.   Archibald Rutledge wrote: 'For more than 30 years it was my business to study and try to teach literature. To anyone earnestly engaged in this there naturally comes a certain ability to distinguish the genuine from the spurious, the authentic from the invented. Every time I read the Gospels I am impressed more deeply with the conviction that the narratives concerning Christ do not belong to the realm of fancy or tradition or folklore. There is about them the ingenuous reality of life itself. The incidents are such that they could never have been invented; and their effect on the world for nearly 2000 years has been such as no inventions could have produced. These stories possess the transparent validity that belongs to truth.'
Everywhere in the Gospel narratives Jesus is in the midst:

> *A mocking crowd who taunt and jeer,*
> *A few whom grace has taught to fear,*
> *The priests and rulers filled with pride,*
> *A dying thief on either side*
> *And Jesus in the midst.*
>
> *Now, owning Christ alone as Lord*
> *And cleaving firmly to His word,*
> *In faith the saints the promise claim*
> *That they who gather in His name*
> *Have Jesus in the midst.*

418   **Gossip.**   'Can you guess who I am?' was the query at the head of a magazine article. Then followed the description that provided the clue and answer:
I have no respect for justice and no mercy for defenceless humanity. I ruin without killing: I tear down homes: I break hearts and wreck lives. You will find me in the pews of the pious as well as in the haunts of the unholy. I gather strength with age. I have made my way where greed, distrust and dishonour are unknown; yet my victims are as numerous as the sands of the sea, and often as innocent. MY NAME IS GOSSIP.
(Ps. 101. 5; Prov. 20. 19)

**419 Grace—Amazing.** In a corner of the churchyard of Olney Parish Church, of fourteenth-century architecture, there is a large tombstone on which the inscription is as follows:

'John Newton, clerk, once an infidel and libertine, a servant of slaves in Africa, was by the rich mercy of our Lord and Saviour Jesus Christ preserved, restored and appointed to preach the faith he had long laboured to destroy.'

Newton was the son of a sea captain engaged in Mediterranean trade. His mother died when he was 6, and after two years at school he joined his father's ship at the age of 11. Immorality, debauchery and failure followed. Rejected by his father and finally jailed and degraded, he later served on slave ships where he so incurred the hatred of his employer's negro wife that he became a 'slave of slaves'.

He was brought to his senses by reading the *Imitation of Christ* by Thomas à Kempis. His conversion was the result of a violent storm in which he almost lost his life. At 39 he became a minister of the Gospel and was Pastor at Olney for 15 years. He wrote many hymns and, with William Cowper, his friend, he published a hymnal. His personal experience is recounted in the hymn.

> *Amazing grace! how sweet the sound*
> *That saved a wretch like me.*
> *I once was lost but now am found,*
> *Was blind but now I see.*

> Dr Billy Graham

By a strange providence that hymn has become the top of the pop songs of today. Young people sing it without, perhaps, realising its truth or experiencing the power of God's matchless grace.

Dr J. H. Jowett has said: 'Grace is more than mercy. It is more than tender mercy. It is more than a multitude of mercies. Grace is more than love. It is more than innocent love. Grace is holy love in spontaneous movement going out in eager quest toward the unholy and unlovely.'

**420 Grace and Glory.** The grace of God undertakes our salvation, supervises our education, guarantees our glorification, demands our santification, and deserves our attention.

D. L. Moody said, 'Grace is glory in the bud; glory is grace in the flower.'
Thomas Spurgeon wrote:

> *'Grace for grace,' and 'grace sufficient'—*
> *'Grace abounding,' grace that reigns:*
> *Grace the guarantee of glory:*
> *Grace, not law,—How sweet the strains!*

**421 Grace of God.** Two or three years before the death of John Newton, when his sight was so dim that he was no longer able to read, a friend and colleague in the ministry called to have breakfast with him. Their custom was to read the Word of God following mealtime, after which Newton would make a few remarks on the Biblical passage, and then prayer would be offered. That day there was silence after the words of Scripture—'By the grace of God I am what I am.' Several minutes passed, then John Newton said:

'I am not what I ought to be. How imperfect and deficient I am!

I am not what I wish to be, although I abhor that which is evil and would cleave to that which is good:

I am not what I hope to be. Soon I shall put off mortality, and with it all sin and imperfection.

Though I am not what I ought to be, nor what I wish to be, nor yet what I hope to be, I can truly say I am not what I once was, a slave to sin and Satan. I can heartily join with the apostle and say that by the grace of God I am what I am.'
(1 Cor. 15. 10)

**422 Grace Sufficient.** I like that dream of Josephine Butler's when her life passed into deep shadow: 'I thought I was lying flat, with a restful feeling, in a smooth, still sea, a boundless ocean with no limit or shore on any side. It was strong and held me up and there was light and sunshine all around me. And I heard a voice say, "Such is the grace of God."'

> J. H. Jowett

(Gen. 6. 8)

**423 Grace Sufficient Always.** Bishop Handley Moule has attested the authenticity of the account that has often been told of an esteemed servant of Christ who, in an hour of deep trial, was agonizing before the Lord, praying, 'Let Thy grace be sufficient for me.' Momentarily lifting his tear-filled eyes, a newly hung wall plaque met his gaze, which bore the words, 'My grace is sufficient for thee.' The 'IS' was brightly and conspicuously painted, and the text came home to his heart with such freshness and blessing that he rose to a new life of peace and power in Christ.

> *My Lord never said that He would give*
> *Another's grace without another's thorn.*
> *What matter, since for every day of mine*
> *Sufficient grace for me comes with the morn.*
> *And though the future brings some heavier*
> *      cross*
> *I need not crowd the present with my fears:*
> *I know the grace that is enough today*
> *Will be sufficient still through all the years.*

(2 Cor. 12. 9)

**424 Graduation Prayer.**

> *Beside life's ocean, vast, untried,*
> *We stand; the young, the strong, the brave;*
> *And know tomorrow's rolling tide*
> *Must bear us out across its wave:*
> *O Father God, we look to Thee!*
> *Guide Thou our course o'er life's wide sea.*

*We know not what may lie before,*
*Or shoal or shallow, reef or bar;*
*We know not how we'll come to shore—*
*Or harbour near or wreck afar:*
*O Pilot, trusted, true and tried,*
*Be Thou with us our course to guide!*

*Come deepest darkness, Thou art light;*
*Come tide and tempest, Thou art peace;*
*Come wrong and warring, Thou art right;*
*Come fear and failure, Thou—release!*
*Almighty God, be Thine to keep*
*Our souls from peril on the deep!*

*O Pilot of our souls, with Thee*
*We fear no fierce or stormy gale;*
*We fear no restless, rolling sea,*
*For Thine is skill that will not fail;*
*O Father God! we trust in Thee*
*To guide our course o'er life's wide sea!*

E. Margaret Clarkson

(Ps. 77. 19)

**425 Gratitude of Love.**   In January, 1858, Frances Ridley Havergal was staying in the home of a German Christian minister and, as Count Zinzendorf had done many years before, stood spellbound before Steinberg's picture of Christ crucified, which hung in her host's study. 'All this I did for thee!' The words came home with a strong appeal to her heart, so she took a piece of paper and wrote the poem, 'All this I did for thee: what hast thou done for me?' She was later visiting an elderly woman and quoted the words to her. The old lady was delighted and spoke in appreciation of the words. She then copied them out and showed them to her father who wrote the tune 'Baca' to them.
(Gal. 2. 20)

**426 Grave—Born in a.**   Take an oak of a hundred years' growth. How was that oak born? In a grave! The acorn was planted in the ground; a grave was made for it that the acorn might die. It died and disappeared, and it cast roots downward and it cast shoots upward, and now that tree has been standing for one hundred years. Where is it standing? In its grave—all the time in the very grave where the acorn died. Yet all the time, though it stood in the very grave where it had died, it has been growing higher and stronger and broader and more beautiful. And all the fruit it bore, and all the foliage that adorned it year by year, it owed to that grave in which its roots are cast and kept.
Dr A. Bonar

(Rom. 6. 4; Col. 2. 12)

**427 Grave—The Opened.**   In a cemetery at Hanover, Germany, there is a grave on which great slabs of granite and marble are piled, cemented together, and fastened with steel clasps. It is the grave of a woman who did not believe that Jesus rose from the dead, nor that she nor anyone else would live again after death. In her will she ordered her grave

to be made so secure that if there were a resurrection of the dead it could not reach her. On the stone these words were engraved:

'This burial place must never be opened.'

A little seed, however, chanced to be covered over by the stones and, beginning to grow, it tried to find its way to the light. You would not think a little growing plant could wrench those steel clasps from their sockets and burst the cemented stone slabs, but it did. That little seed has become a full grown tree and the great stones have fallen over to give it room.
Caiaphas and other enemies of Jesus thought when the tomb in which His body had been laid was made secure, it could not be opened; but the power of God that worked through a little seed in Hanover worked in a more marvellous way to open that tomb near Jerusalem.
Aquila Webb

(Matt. 28. 2)

**428 Great Men Need God.**   General Grant had just professed faith in Christ. The minister who spoke to him ventured to say, 'God's kingdom has gained a great acquisition in your conversion, General.' General Grant replied, 'God does not need great men, but great men need God.'
*Choice Gleanings*

(1 Cor. 1. 26)

**429 Greatness of Christ.**   The first Napoleon said to those around him, 'I am doing now what will fill thousands of volumes in this generation. In the next, one volume will contain all; in the third, a paragraph; and in the fourth a single line.'
How different with Christ! Beginning with 'the seed of the woman shall bruise the head of the serpent' the record increases, till we are told of the things that He did, that should they be written every one, even the world itself could not contain the books that should be written.
Andrew Miller

(Luke 24. 27; John 21. 25)

**430 Greatness of God.**   As we have sung it on many occasions, all of us have been impressed with the theme of Boberg's song, 'How great Thou art' the majesty and greatness of our God. Two and a half to three thousand years ago another writer, one of the great literary masters of all time, took up his pen. His name was Isaiah, and his subject that of Boberg's song, 'How great Thou art!' Isaiah declares in wonderful language the glory and the immensity, the greatness and the majesty of God. In Isaiah 40. 12 it is contrasted with the physical creation and in this wonderful verse the prophet uses the analogy of four of God's measurements.
The first of these is the measurement of

volume. 'He hath measured the waters in the hollow of His hand.' How much water can you measure in the hollow of your hand? I tried it one day recently. Do you know how many gallons I put in the palm of my hand? I put two teaspoonfuls in it, but when I put in the third teaspoonful I had great difficulty in keeping the first two teaspoonfuls from leaking out of the hollow of my hand. What about the hollow of God's hand? In it He has measured the waters of Lake Ontario, of Lake Erie, of the St Lawrence River, of the Mississippi, the Amazon and the Nile, and the waters of the Atlantic, Pacific, Indian and the other great oceans. Four hundred million cubic miles of waters God has measured in the hollow of His hand! What a great God is ours!

We note also that God has a measurement for distance. We read that He meted out the heavens with His span. What is your span? I measured mine that same night and found it to be about eight or nine inches. But God measures out the heavens with His span—all those starry heavens that we look out upon on a lovely night. In that heaven in the brightness of day there is a glorious sun which by human calculation is so large that one and a quarter million earths could go into it. I am told that if you took an express train tonight in the direction of the nearest star, it would take you sixty million years to reach it. Men go faster than express trains nowadays. They go at fast rocket speed: but if men were to start for a star in a rocket it would take 25,000 years to reach the nearest star. And suppose you could travel at the speed of light, 186,000 miles in a second (around the world seven times in one second) you would require four years or more to reach the nearest star and two million years to the nearest galaxy. Our minds stagger at the enormity of these figures: they are too great for us to comprehend: but that is the measure of God's span. 'How great Thou art!'

God has a measure, too, of dry capacity. He comprehends the dust of the earth in His measure—not a truck load of dust, or a few truck loads, but the dust of all the earth. It is reckoned that all of the earth's surface that men have worked on, to make buildings, ships, houses and cars, would occupy less than a hundred cubic miles, but the dust of the earth that God takes in His measure occupies 260,000 million cubic miles.

The fourth measure of God is weight. How does God measure weight? He weighs the hills in scales and the mountains in a balance, Everest, Kunchenjunga, all the mountains of the Himalayas, the Alps, the Rockies and the Andes. Put them all together and they all can go into God's scales. That is how God measures weight. How great, how infinite, how majestic, is our God!

Read down a few verses in Isaiah 40 to verse 15. Here we read of the creature, the great nations of men, evidencing God's greatness:

China with over 600 million people, India with 500 million, Russia and the U.S.A., each with over 200 million, Canada with nearly 20 million people. These great and populous nations, and all the lesser peoples—they are nothing to God, just like a drop in a bucket. Have you ever filled a bucket with water at the tap and carried it along the road full? Perhaps, as you filled it, there was a little spilled over the side, a little drop hanging from the bucket. As you walked along the road with your bucket full of water, that little drop fell off the bucket. Did you notice how much lighter the bucket was after that drop fell off? Of course you didn't: you didn't notice the drop falling to the ground and it did not make the slightest difference to the weight. There is another picture of these nations in the same verse: they are counted as the small dust of the balance. We may take the trouble to dust the balance we use in our home, but it is not because the dust adds anything to the weight of what we put in the balance. No! the fine dust on the balance does not make the slightest difference to the weight. The nations of the world, great and small, are together like the fine dust of the balance.

God takes up the Isles of the earth, large and small, and all the great continents of men, with their teeming millions—for the continents are but islands surrounded by water in God's eyes—and He counts them a very small thing, a speck of dust, a flake of powder. What an evidence of God's greatness in contrast to the nations of men. 'How great Thou art!' Nebuchadnezzar, after living among the beasts of the fields and there realising the power and glory of God, spoke these words, 'All the inhabitants of the earth are reputed as nothing before God.'

Dr J. T. Naismith

(Isa. 40. 12-16)

**431  Greatness of God's Creation.**  Astronomers say that our Milky Way has no less than 100 billion stars, and also that there are 50 million other galaxies, some larger, some smaller than our own. One star—called Beteleguese—is 215,000,000 miles in diameter. All this is almost beyond our imagination. Our great God created the stars, all of them.

*The Heavens declare Thy glory,*
*The firmament Thy power;*
*Day unto day the story*
*Repeats from hour to hour.*
*So let my whole behaviour,*
*Thoughts, words and actions be,*
*O Lord, my strength, my Saviour,*
*One ceaseless song to Thee.*

*Choice Gleanings*

(Neh. 9. 6)

**432  Grieving the Lord.**  In seeking revival it is essential that we avoid doing things that will dishonour God or grieve Him. How can we grieve God? There are two major ways in which we can do this. There is unrestrained passion, and there is a lack of concern for others, i.e. self-assertion and selfishness. These sins are most common in our day.

We tend to overlook the weakness of human nature and excuse the passionate outburst as due to provocation. We should never forget that for this very sin Moses was excluded from the promised land. Moses was not unconcerned with God's honour; in fact, he was grieved because the people were dishonouring God. He allowed his personal feelings to overrule his obedience to the Word of God, and God said that he had failed to honour Him before the people. If it was thus with Moses, how much more have we grieved God in our day!
(Num. 20. 12; Eph. 4. 30)

**433  Growth—Spiritual.**  'Growth is the evidence of spirituality', said the undersized preacher, 'but don't look at me.' Yet that preacher, though short in physical stature, was a spiritual giant.

It is good to note in Ephesians 4 that if we are well grown we shall not be tossed to and fro by every wind of doctrine. The higher we go, the safer we are; hence Satan tries to prevent us from going to the top.

Spiritual growth is a mystery. It is more evident in some than in others. It is common for us to think that when we enjoy most of God in the way of manifestation, then we grow most in the divine life: whereas it is when we are in our own view in the lowest case and frame of soul that we have the quickest perception and insight into the deadly nature of inherent sin and pollution, and this leads us to look wholly and immediately to Christ for life and salvation. That is a certain sign of spiritual growth, for it makes us see more and more our need of depending continually on the Person, work, intercession and words of the Lord Jesus. We then become more spiritual in worship, esteeming ordinances more by divine quickening, and by God-glorifying and Christ-exalting thoughts created in us by the eternal Spirit.
(Eph. 4. 15; 2 Pet. 3. 18)

A. N. Groves

**434  Grumbling.**  There is a proverb in Arabic that reads: 'I had no shoes and I grumbled till I saw a man with no feet.'

*Today upon the bus I saw a lovely girl with*
*  golden hair:*
*I envied her, she seemed so gay, and wished I*
*  were as fair.*
*When suddenly she rose to leave, I saw her*
*  hobble down the aisle;*
*She had one leg and wore a crutch, and as*
*  she passed—a smile.*
*O God, forgive me when I whine.*

*I have two legs. The world is mine.*

*And then I stopped to buy some sweets. The*
*  lad who sold them had such a charm:*
*I talked with him—he seemed so glad—if I*
*  were late 'twould do no harm:*
*And as I left he said to me, 'I thank you:*
*  you have been so kind.*
*It's nice to talk with folks like you. You see,'*
*  he said, 'I'm blind.'*
*O God, forgive me when I whine.*

*I have two eyes. The world is mine.*

*Later walking down the street I saw a child*
*  with eyes of blue.*
*He stood and watched the others play: it*
*  seemed he knew not what to do.*
*I stopped a moment, then I said, 'Why don't*
*  you join the others, dear ?'*
*He looked ahead without a word, and then I*
*  knew—he could not hear.*
*O God, forgive me when I whine.*

*I have two ears. The world is mine.*

*With legs to take me where I go,*
*With eyes to see the sunset's glow,*
*With ears to hear what I would know—*
*O God, forgive me when I whine.*

*I'm blessed indeed. The world is mine.*

Dot Aaron

(Ps. 107. 1,2)

**435  Guidance.**

*Lead Thou me on! I am content to follow:*
*Thou only, Lord, Thou only art my Guide.*
*Be it by lotus pools of tranquil beauty,*
*Earth's bliss is sweeter with Thee by my side.*

*Be it up cliffs that sheer in steep gradation,*
*At thy command they shall become a plain:*
*The loss that seems too great for compensation*
*With Thee, Lord, is immeasurable gain.*

*Lead Thou me on! I would not choose the*
*  pathway;*
*I know it leads but to the journey's end.*
*I cannot wander if Thou walk beside me:*
*I cannot falter if Thou be my Friend.*

F.C.D.

(Deut. 32. 10)

**436  Guidance by Curious Methods.**

1 *The Lucky Dip Method.* Rowland Hogben tells of a young prospective missionary who hoped for some oracular confirmation concerning his missionary career. He turned to the Scriptures in a haphazard fashion and was rewarded with the words, 'the eyes of a fool are in the ends of the earth.' Though his method of seeking guidance was rebuked, his call was not revoked.

2 *The Sudden Impulse Method.* A man read in Deuteronomy 2. 3, 'Ye have compassed this mountain long enough; turn you northward!' On the strength of it he sold his farm at the foot of the mountains and went to reside in the north, becoming a burden to the believers there.

101

3 *The Hunch Method.* For every hunch that is right nine are wrong. One can neither solve life's problems nor walk in the paths of righteousness by guess-work.

4 *The 'Feeling led' Method.* This hackneyed expression covers everything from an excuse for unspiritual ministry to justification for thoughtless actions. According to the Scripture we do not 'feel' led: we are led by the Spirit of God.

5 *Natural Preference* is a basically dishonest method and often consists in an unadmitted decision to go in a certain direction irrespective of the Word and will of God.

6 *The Majority Vote Method.* One does not find guidance by consulting many friends usually favourably disposed, and accepting the counsel of the majority.

Neville J. Taylor

(Ps. 25. 9,10)

**437 Guidance—Means of.** Guidance is for everyday life in Christian experience. God gives guidance to His people by His Word, by His Spirit using His Word, and by circumstances He makes to work together in the lives of His people.

In the wilderness, as Israel journeyed to Canaan, the cloud and the fire, and thereafter until the captivity, indicated to the nation the leading of Jehovah. Shadow in the day and light in the night, the 'Shekinah' was the visible manifestation of the presence of God among His people, leading and protecting them.

The Urim and Thummim in the breastplate of the High Priest indicated in some way the mind of the Lord for those who asked counsel of Him. To those who earnestly seek the mind of the Lord today, guidance will surely be vouchsafed, so that we can say, 'All the way my Saviour leads me.'

The silver trumpets also indicated when, and for what purpose, Israel's armies and families had to bestir themselves and be active in progress, warfare or service. The advice of godly elders co-operating with Moses in counselling the people when advice was needed, was a recognised way of guidance among Israel's tribes.

In the early Church the voice of the Spirit was frequently heard by God's servants, Philip the evangelist, Barnabas and Saul, and the responsible ministers in the church at Antioch are examples of this. To Paul visions also were granted, and by him voices were heard. Spiritual discernment was required to determine when the Lord was speaking, and to recognise the voice of the Lord and His leading.

(Ps. 32. 8)

**438 Hand of God.** In his Christmas broadcast in 1939 King George VI said: 'And I said to the man who stood at the gate of the year, "Give me a light that I may tread safely into the unknown", and he replied, "Go out into the darkness and put your hand into the hand of God. That will be to you better than light, and safer than a known way." '

That part of his speech was a quotation from M. Louise Haskins, who wrote:

*So I went forth and found the hand of God,*
*Trod gladly into the light.*
*He led me toward the hills*
*And the breaking of the day in the East.*
*So, heart, be still!*

*What need our little life to know*
*If God hath comprehension?*
*In all the dizzy strife of things both high and*
*   low*
*God hideth His intention.*

**439 Hands of Christ.**

*We're in His hand, that mighty Hand*
*That flung a universe in space,*
*That guides the sun and moon and stars*
*And holds the planets in their place.*

*We're in his hand, that skilful hand*
*That made the blinded eyes to see,*
*That touched the leper, cleansed and healed,*
*And set the palsied sufferer free.*

*We're in His hand, that loving Hand*
*That lifted children to His breast,*
*That fed the hungry multitudes*
*And beckoned weary hearts to rest.*

*We're in His hands, those pierced Hands*
*Once nailed to Calvary's cruel tree*
*When there, in agony and blood,*
*He paid the price to set us free.*

*And none shall pluck us from that hand.*
*Eternally we are secure.*
*Though heaven and earth shall pass away,*
*His word for ever shall endure.*

*Those hands are still outstretched to bless,*
*His people's wayworn feet to guide,*
*Till dawn shall break and shadows flee*
*When He will come to claim His bride.*

Mrs. M. E. Rae

(Deut. 33. 3; John 10. 28)

**440 Hands of God.** The Christian life is like the dial of a clock. The hands are God's hands, passing over and over again. The short hand is the hand of discipline, the long hand the hand of mercy. Slowly and surely the hand of discipline must pass, and God speaks at each stroke. But over and over passes the hand of mercy, showering down a twelvefold blessing for each stroke of discipline and trial. Both hands are fastened to one secure pivot, the great unchanging heart of our loving God: for

*Every joy or trial cometh from above,*
*Traced upon our dial by God's hand of love.*

(Ps. 101. 1)

**441  Hands Pierced.**  A Christian young man, shown over a lace works in an industrial town in Great Britain, turned to thank the manager who had guided him round, and gratefully to shake his hand. He was surprised to find his guide's hand soft, limp and flabby. Seeing his look of surprise, the manager said, 'You must excuse my hand. When I was an apprentice I had an accident: a nail was driven through it and I have never been able to close it since.' Immediately expressing, as well as showing sympathy, the young Christian said, 'May I shake hands with you again, sir? And may I tell you something? Nearly 2000 years ago one left the glory of heaven and came as a child to earth. His people crucified Him, and nails were driven through His hands. Like you, He has never closed them since but stretches them out to a needy world.'

> *Oh! the wounded hands of Jesus,*
> *Bearing nail scars for men's sins,*
> *Still extend salvation's blessings*
> *Where true penitence begins.*

(Ps. 22. 16)

**442  Hands Uplifted.**

> *No fiery chariot was sent:*
> *The Lord, in right divine alone,*
> *Up to the heav'n of heavens went,*
> *Ascending to the Father's throne—*
> *From Bethany, by Zion set;*
> *How blest thy memories, Olivet!*
>
> *The parting benediction said,*
> *O glorious attitude of love!*
> *His pierced hands o'er every head*
> *He raised, and slowly rose above.*
> *That blessing lingers with us yet;*
> *How bright thy memories, Olivet!*
>
> *With lifted hands, as from that hill,*
> *Light, mercy, from a loftier sphere,*
> *From the high throne, He showers still*
> *On every waiting pilgrim here;*
> *All fears allayed, all sorrows met*
> *As when He rose from Olivet.*
>
> *Lord! give us to receive of Thee*
> *(Should e'er our fainting spirits fail)*
> *Fresh power, fresh grace and energy,*
> *That Amalek may not prevail.*
> *O give us never to forget*
> *That blest return from Olivet.*

                                        E. L. Bevir

(Luke 24. 50,51)

**443  Harmony in our Lives.**  We once saw a man draw some black dots. We looked and could make nothing of them but an irregular assemblage of black dots. Then he drew a few lines, put in a few rests, then a Clef at the beginning, and we saw that these black dots were musical notes. On sounding them we were singing, PRAISE GOD FROM WHOM ALL BLESSINGS FLOW.

There are many black dots and black spots in our lives, and we cannot understand why they are there. But if we let God come into our lives, He will make a glorious harmony.

                                        *Prophetic News*

(Eph. 5. 19,20)

**444  Heart—Slow of.**

> *How burdened, sad and lonely*
> *Were two sad hearts that day;*
> *Bewildered in their sorrow,*
> *They journeyed on their way,*
> *Too hopeless to remember*
> *That step they knew so well,*
> *Too cumbered by their trouble*
> *His blessed voice to tell.*
>
> *O tireless love that found them*
> *All faithless as they went,*
> *And drew forth all the sadness*
> *That in their hearts was pent—*
> *The doubts, the fears, the reasonings*
> *That pressed upon the soul,*
> *The yearnings for their Master!—*
> *He made them tell the whole.*
>
> *Then showed the wondrous meaning*
> *Of what o'erwhelmed their faith,*
> *Sin and the devil vanquished,*
> *His victory over death.*
> *O wonderful expounding!*
> *Well might their hearts then burn.*
> *He spoke but one reproachful word—*
> *'Oh! slow of heart to learn.'*
>
> *Those lips had often taught them*
> *And told that tale before;*
> *They might have known Him better,*
> *They might have trusted more.*
> *We read the gracious history*
> *And worship and rejoice,*
> *But are we quick to know His step,*
> *To worship and rejoice.*
>
> *And do we tell our questionings,*
> *Unveiling every part—*
> *The loneliness, the faithlessness,*
> *The secret of our heart?*
> *'Fools,' 'slow of heart,' Oh, Master,*
> *Well may'st Thou say it still!*
> *Our hearts that miss Thy purposes,*
> *That stagger at Thy will.*
>
> *Too slow to understand Thee,*
> *Thy tireless love and true*
> *That waits upon our wilfulness*
> *To win our hearts anew,*
> *Those wayward hearts too faithless*
> *To comprehend the grace*
> *That chastens but to bring us*
> *Back to Thy blessed face;*
>
> *That face that knows no changing,*
> *No shading to its love,*
> *That shines down still to meet the eyes*
> *Upturned to Thee above.*
> *Yes, hearts are slow to know Thee*
> *In heaven, O Lord, today,*
> *As were those eyes by sorrow dimmed*
> *Beside Thee in the way.*

                                        Ora Rowan

(Luke 24. 25)

**445 Heart Touched by Contrition.** When King Henry II, in centuries gone by, was provoked to take up arms against his ungrateful and rebellious son, he besieged him in one of the French towns, and the son, being near to death, desired to see his father and to confess his wrongdoing; but the stern old sire refused to look the rebel in the face. The young man, being sorely troubled in his conscience, said to those around him, 'I am dying; take me from my bed and let me lie in sackcloth and ashes, in token of my sorrow and ingratitude to my father.' Thus he died, and when the news was reported to the old man outside the walls that his son had died repentant for his rebellion, he threw himself on the ground, and like another David said, 'Would God I had died for him!' The thought of the boy's broken heart touched the heart of the father. God our Father delights to see the broken heart and the contrite spirit.
(Ps. 51. 17)

**446 Heart Unfolded to Christ.**

*To Thee, Lord, my heart unfoldeth*
*As the rose to the golden sun;*
*To Thee, Lord, mine arms are clinging,*
*The eternal joy begun.*
*For ever through endless ages*
*Thy cross and Thy sorrow shall be*
*The glory, the song and the sweetness*
*That makes heaven heaven to me.*

*Let one in his innocence glory,*
*Another in works he has done;*
*Thy blood is my claim and my title—*
*Beside it, O Lord, I have none.*
*The scorned, the despised, the rejected,*
*Thou hast won Thee this heart of mine:*
*In Thy robes of eternal glory*
*Thou welcomest me to Thine.*

(1 Cor. 1. 31)

**447 Heathen—What about the.** The question is often asked, 'If a heathen lives up to the light he has, will he be saved?' The fact is—there are none living up to the light they have. Dan Crawford said of the Africans he knew through years of intimate touch with them: 'The pagans in the heart of Africa are sinning against a flood of light.'

When Charles E. Scott was asked if he believed the heathen would be saved by living up to the light they had, he replied that he had never met one in China who was living up to his light. More than that, they know they are not living up to the light they have: so they are 'without excuse'.
(Rom. 1. 19,20)

**448 Heaven—Admission to.** 'I cannot understand why a man who has tried to lead a good moral life should not stand a better chance of heaven than a wicked one,' said a lady. The answer? 'Simply for this reason! Suppose you and I wanted to go to a concert where the admission was a dollar. You had

half a dollar: I had nothing. Which of us would stand the better chance of admission?' 'Neither of us.'

'Just so! Therefore the moral man stands no better chance than the terrible sinner. But suppose a kind person presented a ticket of admission to each of us at his own expense, what then?' 'Well, then, we would both alike go in.'

'The Lord Jesus saw our perplexity: He came, died on the Cross and obtained eternal redemption for us, and now offers to each of us a free ticket to heaven. Only take care your "half-dollar" does not make you too proud to accept His free ticket, and so be refused admittance.'
(Rom. 3. 23; 10. 12)

**449 Heaven—A Place in.** Matthew Henry said:

'To Christians heaven is a house, a dwelling-place, a resting place, their everlasting home, their Father's house where there are many mansions. It is a house in the heavens that as far excels the palaces of this earth as the heavens are high above the earth. It is a city whose builder and maker is God, and it is eternal in the heavens. The most marvellous thing about it is that God has prepared it for those who love Him.'

At one time Frederick the Great had as his guest the infidel philosopher, Voltaire, who, when dinner was served to those attending the banquet in Cleve's Palace, began to cast aspersions on the many Christians present. Finally he said: 'Why, I would sell my seat in heaven for a Prussian dollar.' One of the guests at the banquet, a distinguished counsellor and a devout believer in the Lord Jesus Christ, shocked at Voltaire's words rose from his seat and rebuked the blasphemer with the words, 'Sir, you are in Prussia where we have a law which requires that one who wishes to sell anything must first prove ownership. Are you prepared to establish the fact that you have a seat in heaven?' Surprised and rather embarrassed, Voltaire had little more to say for the rest of the evening.
(1 Pet. 1. 4,5)

**450 Heaven—A Song of.**

*Let me sing you a song of heaven,*
*Of the golden land on high*
*Where the heart shall find no sorrow,*
*And the breast shall know no sigh;*
*Where no wasting grief or sickness*
*Can assail those forms we love,*
*Where the blood-washed dwell for ever*
*In their royal home above.*

*Oh! home of the loved and loving*
*Where the heavenly praises ring,*
*I would that my lips could utter,*
*I would that my voice could sing*
*Of the bliss, the rapturous glory,*
*The rest and the joyful song,*
*That rolls like the sound of the ocean*
*From the glorious 'white-robed' throng.*

*Home where the Bride in her glory,*
*The Bridegroom's joys shall share,*
*But deepest joy of her joying—*
*The Bridegroom Himself is there.*
*Glory! O glory of glories—*
*To gaze on His loving face,*
*And sing, till the wide hall echo*
*The marvels of matchless grace.*

S. Trevor Francis
(Rev. 4. 1)

**451 Hebrew Verb—Conjugation.** A lecturer was addressing a school, giving the young people sound advice, and he said to them, 'All of you know the verb which says, "I am, thou art, he is", and you all know that verbs in English, French, German, Italian and Latin run in the same way—"I love, thou lovest, he loves"; or "I walk, thou walkest, he walks". But how many of you know that this is a very bad way for a verb to run? How many of you know that the Old Hebrew people arranged their verbs the other way round—He is, thou art, I am?'

Then he told them, 'That is the way to look at life. Say to yourself, looking up to God, "He is", then look at your neighbour and say, "you are", and last of all think of yourself and say, "I am". First God, then your neighbour, then yourself. That is the best way to think and to live.'

A friend was so struck by this discovery that he could not get it out of his mind, so he made it his business to find a Hebrew scholar to ask him if it was really true that Hebrew verbs are conjugated in this manner. 'Yes', said the scholar, 'that is the way the Hebrew verb is conjugated; but why do you ask?' The friend then told of the lecturer's words to the school children.

'Well!' cried the scholar, 'I have been studying Hebrew all my life and never once has it occurred to me that Hebrew verbs can have that beautiful significance.' He sat for some moments, saying, 'He is; thou art; I am. How beautiful! Yes, to be sure—He is; you are; I am! It is wonderful, wonderful!'

**452 Hell.** A profane man, who was being taken down a coal mine by a Christian miner, said as they descended the shaft and the air grew hotter and hotter, 'It's terribly hot. I wonder how far it is to hell.'

The miner solemnly replied, 'I cannot tell you the distance in terms of metres or miles, but if one link of that chain were to give way, you might be there in a minute, and you and I would be separated for ever.'

**453 Hell—Doctrine of.** A. W. Rainsbury wrote: 'Time was when the doctrine of hell caused men to tremble, but it no longer does so, for the doctrine of hell has been relegated to the rubbish heap by the Modernists. They think they are wiser than the Lord Jesus. They do not believe in hell any more; indeed most are more concerned with the dangers

of nuclear war than the dangers of hell. I tell you in the name of God that the danger of hell is far more real, far more certain, infinitely more terrible, and for some far more imminent than the danger of nuclear war.

'Religious leaders say that when Jesus talked about hell He did not really mean what He said. He meant something else; or if He did mean what He said, He did not know what He was talking about.

'The king of Hades, the father of lies and the enemy of souls, does all in his power to keep our minds off the subject. He does not like people to discuss hell unless they mention it now and again, of course, as a joke. We are not likely to lose much sleep when we have a good laugh over it.'
(Luke 16. 22,23)

**454 Hell—Torments of.** In reply to a sceptic who, when asked to trust Christ for salvation, said, 'I'm not afraid of hell: all the hell we have is here on earth,' the preacher said, 'I'll give you three reasons why this cannot be hell. First, I am a Christian and there are no Christians in hell. Secondly, there is a place round the corner where you can slake your thirst, and there is no water in hell. Thirdly, I have been preaching Christ and His gospel to you, and there is no gospel in hell.'

John Wesley, powerful evangelist of the eighteenth century who turned many to righteousness, preached often on 'hell'. When he was a lad of six, he was rescued from his home when it was destroyed by fire, and all his life he spoke of himself as 'a brand plucked out of the fire'. Some of his messages on eternal punishment contained these words:

'Settle it in your heart, and let it be ever uppermost in your thoughts, that if you are on the broad way, you are in the way that leadeth to destruction. If many go with you, as sure as God is true, both they and you are going to hell!

'The moment a soul drops the body and stands naked before God, it cannot but know what its portion will be to all eternity. It will have full in its view, either everlasting joy or everlasting torment.

'All the torments of hell are without intermission. They have no respite from pain, but "the smoke of their torment ascendeth up day and night". No sleep accompanies that darkness. And be their suffering ever so intense, there is no possibility of fainting away, no, not for a moment.'
(Matt. 7. 13; Rev. 14. 11)

**455 Helpers.** When St Paul's Cathedral was being built, the architect, Sir Christopher Wren, used to go round talking to the workmen. 'What are you doing?' he asked one, who replied, 'I am earning my daily wage.' The next man to whom he put the question replied, 'I am breaking these stones.' The third man whom he approached with the same question,

105

answered, 'Why, I am helping to build this Cathedral.' The third man was evidently enjoying his work because he was conscious of its purpose.

The owner of a beautifully kept farm was asked by a friend who was admiring the magnificent sheep how he had been able to rear such fine flocks. The owner's answer was, 'I take care of my lambs.'
(Neh. 4. 17,18)

456   **Helpfulness.**   Sir Bartle Freer, a governor of Cape Colony prior to the Boer War, was a very devoted Christian and a great philanthropist, given to helping folk around him. While he was absent for some time from his home in London, in those days before motor cars, his coachman resigned and his wife engaged a new coachman; and on the day of her husband's expected return by rail called the new coachman and told him to take the carriage to meet her husband at the station in London at which he was due to arrive. 'But,' said the coachman, 'I have never met Sir Bartle: how shall I identify him?' Lady Freer thought for a moment, then said with a smile, 'When the train comes in, look for a great big man helping somebody: you cannot mistake him.'

The coachman went off; the train arrived on time; and the people in large numbers emerged from their compartments. Looking up and down the platform, he saw a woman trying to get out of a compartment with a lot of luggage, a big case, a small case, a hat box, a bandbox, and a bundle. No porter went anywhere near her to help, but presently a gentleman stopped beside the compartment and said politely, 'Madam, allow me to assist you.' Loading himself up with her baggage, he helped her out of the compartment and asked her where she wanted to go. Then he called a cab, saw her into it and piled her luggage on top, raised his hat, and faced the station entrance as the cabby drove off.

As Sir Bartle turned, he was met by a man in the uniform of a coachman, who asked, 'Are you Sir Bartle Freer, sir?' and received the reply, 'Yes, who are you?' 'I am your coachman, sir' 'Oh yes! I had forgotten. My wife did tell me the other man had left. I am glad to see you.' Then he asked, 'But how did you know me?'

The coachman replied, 'Lady Bartle said I was to look for a great big man helping somebody, and you were the only person in the crowd that answered that description.'
(Isa. 41. 6)

457   **Helps.**   A devoted, aged missionary, widow of a faithful servant of the Lord but with no great gift for instructing the Indian women, used to say. 'I'm glad that HELPS is mentioned among the Spirit's gifts. I'm just one of these.' One sister like that missionary, but who never heard the call to serve the Lord in other lands, wrote the following:

*God has not called me, so I cannot go.*
*I cannot preach—my lips are too slow:*
*I cannot teach—my knowledge is too small:*
*I cannot heal—I have no power at all:*
*BUT I CAN HELP.*

*Yes! I can help: full well I know the way.*
*I surely can, for I can always pray,*
*And I can give, and this to Him, I know,*
*Is service precious in this world below.*
*YES, I CAN HELP.*

*And with this help some other one may go*
*And preach the Word as I could never do;*
*And when, one day, we've left this world*
  *behind,*
*Up there in glory I shall some souls find*
*BECAUSE I HELPED.*

                     G. W. Marsh

(1 Cor. 12. 28)

458   **Hereafter.**
*I know not now why schemes were spoiled*
*And lofty aspirations foiled;*
*I know not now why briar and thorn*
*Should mar ambitions nobly born.*
*Hereafter, I shall know, shall see*
*These very things were best for me.*

*I know not now why—needing aid—*
*It did not come or was delayed;*
*I know not now why burning tears*
*Should fall so often through the years.*
*Hereafter, I shall know, shall see*
*These very things were best for me.*

*I know not now why friends should fail,*
*And enemies my faith assail;*
*I know not now why clouds should burst*
*And flood and tempest do their worst.*
*Hereafter, I shall know, shall see*
*These very things were best for me.*

*I know not now why sorrow's dart*
*Should penetrate and wound my heart;*
*I know not now why death drew near*
*And led away my loved ones dear.*
*Hereafter, I shall know, shall see*
*These very things were best for me.*

*O Master, I believe Thy Word—*
*Hereafter, I shall know, O Lord,*
*Shall fully see Thy plan, Thy care,*
*Thy skill, Thy love beyond compare.*
*Hereafter, I shall know, shall see*
*These very things were best for me.*

                     A.G.

(John 13. 7)

459   **Highbrow Talk.**   Every Christian speaker and writer should have a copy of *Thorndike's English Dictionary* which is exceptional among dictionaries in that it gives an indication of word frequency. In many an address and article, expressions are used which occur on an average but once in one or two million words of written or printed English.

One of the underlying causes of this highbrow rash is the almost universal obsession with academic learning in the world today and this tendency has invaded the Church.

It is essential to get a balanced view on this matter. Everyone instructed in the Scriptures knows that the Authorised Version is misleading in Acts, chapter 4, verse 13, when it used the terms 'unlearned and ignorant men' in relation to Peter and John. The plain sense, of course, is that they were not 'professionals' and as such were held in contempt. Actually they were fully literate. No one would for a moment suggest that the task of communication in the local church should be entrusted to men who are ignorant in the current sense of the word, though it is noteworthy that many a great work of God has been pioneered by men of no special educational qualification. The growth of this highbrow is certainly in part the cause of the middle-class character of much of our church activity, and the failure to reach out to what in an older notation were called 'the masses'.

Herbert Dennett

(Neh. 8. 8)

### 460 Himself.

*Once it was the blessing—*
*Now it is the Lord;*
*Once it was the feeling—*
*Now it is His Word;*
*Once His gifts I wanted—*
*Now the Giver own;*
*Once I sought for healing—*
*Now Himself alone;*
*Once 'twas painful trying—*
*Now 'tis perfect trust;*
*Once a half salvation—*
*Now the uttermost;*
*Once 'twas ceaseless holding—*
*Now He holds me fast;*
*Once 'twas constant drifting—*
*Now my anchor's cast;*
*Once 'twas busy planning—*
*Now 'tis trusting prayer;*
*Once 'twas anxious caring—*
*Now He has the care.*
*Once 'twas what I wanted—*
*Now what Jesus says;*
*Once 'twas constant asking—*
*Now 'tis ceaseless praise.*
*Once it was my working—*
*His it hence shall be.*
*Once I tried to use Him—*
*Nòw He uses me;*
*Once the power I wanted—*
*Now the Mighty One;*
*Once for self I laboured—*
*Now for Him alone.*
*Once I hoped in Jesus—*
*Now I know He's mine;*
*Once my lamps were dying—*
*Now they brightly shine.*
*Once for death I waited—*
*Now His coming hail;*
*And my hopes are anchored—*
*Safe within the veil.*

A. B. Simpson

(Luke 24. 15)

**461 Hitherto and Henceforth.** Away in a little mission within view of the mighty Himalayas, Mary Reid, the lady missionary, watched a visitor start on his homeward way down a steep, zig-zag path. At each turn he looked back and saw Miss Reid watching; he might be her last visitor for months. At last he reached the turn which would take her out of his sight, and with a shout he sent a message up to the lonely listener— 'HITHERTO!' A wave of her white handkerchief showed that the word had been received. In a moment, as he waited, there came down faintly yet clearly the brave response— 'HENCEFORTH!'

*Hitherto the Lord hath blessed us, guiding all*
*the way;*
*Henceforth let us trust Him fully, trust Him*
*all the day.*
*Hitherto the Lord hath loved us, caring for*
*His own;*
*Henceforth let us love Him better, live for*
*Him alone.*

*Choice Gleanings*

(1 Sam. 7. 12; 2 Cor. 5. 15)

**462 Holding Forth the Word.** The word used for 'holding forth' is suggestive of offering food and drink to others. During the very hot months in South India we have often witnessed Hindus at the railway stations with a bucket of water and a small metal container offering a drink of water to any thirsty passengers. They do it as a deed of merit. But the believer individually and the assembly collectively is to hold out the Water of life and minister the Bread of life to their fellow-travellers to eternity.

J. M. Davies

(Phil. 2. 12,13)

**463 Holding the Rope.** During the holiday season some years ago, at a fishing village in Cornwall, a crowd had gathered to watch the turbulent waves of a rough sea pounding against the harbour wall. Suddenly there was a cry; a boy had been seen in the water, and the waves tossed him up as though he were a cork and carried him away. Suddenly a man ran forward and forced his way through the crowd with a coil of rope. Tying one end of the rope round his waist, he shouted, 'Someone take hold of the rope.' Then, quickly diving into the sea, he battled with the waves and slowly reached the boy. Grasping him safely in his arms, he shouted to the crowd on the harbour wall, 'Pull on the rope.' But alas! in their excitement, no one had bothered to take hold of the rope, which had slipped into the sea and was drifting out of reach. Two lives were lost because no one bothered to hold the end of the rope.

**464 Holiest—Way into the.** The blood of our 'brothers', like that of Abel, keeps us out, for it calls for punishment and cries out for vengeance. We can enter only by the 'blood of Jesus' shed for rebels, shed for sinners.

Our own way, that is, the way we followed, took us in the wrong direction. Jesus said, 'I am the Way'; He is the 'newly-slain' yet living way to God.

The veil of blue, purple, scarlet and fine twined linen that signifies the perfections and glories of Christ's own Person and character barred the way and shut us out, until Christ rent the veil of the temple when His body was torn in His death on the cross, for our approach is now through another veil, 'that is to say, His flesh'.

The high priest of Israel, and He alone, could enter into the most holy place in the tabernacle where the Shekinah glory was, and only once a year, and not without blood, the blood of a victim slain. That meant that all others were forbidden to enter. Our great High Priest, Jesus the Son of God, has entered, and it is He who bids us now draw near.

*'The gate is open wide: the new and living Way
Is clear and free and bright with love and
    peace and day.
Into the holiest we may come,
Our present and our endless home.*

(Heb. 10. 19-22)

465  **Holiness.** Holiness is not human life brought up to the highest possible development, but it is divine life brought down to the lowest possible level of condescension. First, the recipient of God's life of holiness must be brought down to the lowest level of contriteness before the Lord.

Dr Stuart Holden

We must distinguish between cleansing and holiness. You cannot be holy without being cleansed, but you can be cleansed without being holy. The Book of Leviticus is divided into two parts: the first part is about cleansing and the second part is about holiness. Cleansing is by an act: holiness never is. There can be no holiness until there is cleansing. Cleansing is never progressive: holiness always is, and they are intimately related.

Dr W. Graham Scroggie

(1 Pet. 1. 15)

466  **Holy Communion Service—A.** Some of us will never forget a communion service a number of years ago in Sacramento, California, when an unconverted Japanese was present. We had barely replaced the bread and cup upon the table before this heathen man rose to his feet in great emotion and burst out in prayer, as follows:

'O God! I all broke to pieces. I a poor sinner. For long time, for one whole year, I fight you hard; but here I see your people eat the bread and drink the wine that show how Jesus He die for sinners. O God, I can fight no more—I all break down. I take Jesus; He be my Saviour now.'

And that very day, at his earnest request, he was baptized as owning his personal faith in Christ. For years he has been in fellowship as simply gathered to the name of the Lord. Alas, that such scenes are not more common!

Dr H. A. Ironside

(1 Cor. 11. 26)

467  **Home Above—The.** A year or two before Queen Victoria's death she visited a poor, aged woman who had reached the age of 104. The elderly Christian lady, pleased that her Sovereign had come to visit her, heartily expressed her deep gratitude. As she was a fearless witness for the Lord, she said to her royal visitor in a trembling voice, 'May I ask your Majesty one question?' 'You may ask me anything you like,' answered the queen. Slowly and earnestly the centenarian asked, 'Shall we meet again in the home above?'

Bending her head, the queen with tears replied, 'Yes, we shall greet each other again in heaven by the grace of God and through the blood of our Lord Jesus Christ who is my Saviour too.'

(John 14. 2,3)

468  **Home on Earth, Home in Heaven.**

*One less at home:
The charmed circle broken—a dear face
Missed day by day from its accustomed place,
But cleansed and saved and perfected by grace;
One more in heaven.*

*One less at home:
One voice of welcome hushed, and evermore
One farewell word unspoken. On the shore
Where parting comes not, one soul landed
    more—
One more in heaven.*

*One less at home, where, cramped in earthly
    mould,
The sight of Christ is dim, our love is cold;
But there, where face to face we shall behold,
Is home and heaven.*

*One less on earth—
Its pain, its sorrow and its toil to share,
One less the pilgrim's daily cross to bear;
One more the crown of ransomed saints to
    wear,
At home in heaven.*

*One more in heaven:
Another thought to brighten cloudy days,
Another theme of thankfulness and praise,
Another link on high our soul to raise
To home and heaven.*

*One more at home,
That home where separation cannot be,
That home where none are missed eternally!
Lord Jesus, grant us all a place with Thee
At home in heaven.*

Sarah Geraldine Stock

(2 Cor. 5. 6,8)

## 469   Home—The Christian.

*When Jesus came to our home,*
*Praise God, He came to stay.*
*We hadn't even washed the hearth*
*Nor cleared the cups away.*
*We didn't see Him enter*
*But knew that He was there;*
*The sunshine of His presence*
*Spread radiance everywhere.*
*'Twas in a time of trouble;*
*Our hearts were sore, opprest:*
*He didn't seem to notice*
*How poorly we were dressed.*
*He drew us sweetly to Him*
*And gazed so tenderly,*
*Our children gathered near us*
*And grouped around His knee.*
*He took us as He found us,*
*All stained with sin within,*
*And told us how He loved us*
*And made us all love Him.*

*He spoke of heaven's treasures*
*And joy that ours should be*
*When gathered in the glory*
*Beside the crystal sea.*
*He didn't seem to notice*
*The things He knew were wrong.*
*He knew that His dear presence*
*Would give us a new song.*
*He looked at our piano*
*And all the hymnbooks there;*
*It pleased Him that our Bibles*
*Spoke of His love and care.*
*We're glad now He lives with us*
*To guard and guide each act,*
*And know His grace is given*
*To furnish all we lack.*
*With His name on our doorpost*
*As Head, not merely Guest,*
*We find new strength to battle*
*Yet know a perfect rest.*

          Theresa Meachen, *Prophetic News*
(Mark 2. 1)

## 470   Home—The Eternal.

*The Home beyond the shadows has neither*
*    pain nor tears;*
*But, through its cloudless regions, the Light of*
*    life appears*
*Dispelling ev'ry sorrow, removing ev'ry care,*
*And giving rest eternal to all who enter there.*
*Far beyond the shadows through gates that*
*    never close*
*The King Himself will lead us where the*
*    living water flows.*
(Rev. 21. 4)

## 471   Home—The Welcome.

*What will it be when our eyes behold*
*The Lamb on His kingly throne,*
*When He welcomes us to the heavenly fold*
*And the joy of the Father's home?*
*As we bow at His blessed nail-pierced feet*
*To worship and adore,*
*Ah, that will be ecstasy full, complete,*
*Abiding for evermore.*

*Then let us with patience carry on*
*To the end of our pilgrim way,*
*For glory waits at the setting sun*
*And joy at the close of day;*
*And the Saviour stands at the gates ajar,*
*With His arms outstretched in love*
*To welcome His own who have journeyed far,*
*To the warmth of His home above.*

## 472   Homeward Bound.

*Enough, thus far His hand has led!*
*The promised blessings from His hand have*
*    flowed;*
*The water sure and daily bread*
*In constant faithfulness have been bestowed.*
*Enough, my soul! Approve His will!*
*He doeth all things well! Be still!*

*Nor fear, though dark the future be!*
*Though loud the storm and fearsome thunders*
*    roar,*
*He rules the raging of the sea,*
*And bids the surging waves to toss no more.*
*Nor fear, my soul! He fills thy cup!*
*No needless drop is there! Look up!*

*Be strong the conflict to endure!*
*Though Satan's host in dread array assail;*
*His power the vict'ry will assure,*
*Nor evil touch thee, nor shall foe prevail.*
*Be strong, my soul! It will not last!*
*The conflict soon shall cease: stand fast!*

*Rejoice, the glorious dawn appears!*
*The Morning Star already gilds the gloom;*
*His hand shall wipe away all tears,*
*And wrench the vict'ry from the vanquished*
*    tomb.*
*Rejoice, my soul! forget the past:*
*Haste homeward; Lo, He comes! At last!*

                                    L.W.G.A.

(Ps. 4. 4; Rev. 22. 20)

**473   Honoured by His Sovereign.**  In the
Crimean War the British sustained tremendous
loss of men. After the termination of that
disastrous war, a State function was held in
order to give away the rewards to all those who
had faithfully fought in it. Queen Victoria
herself was present and the great men of the
realm were also there. The queen confronted an
ocean of faces. Many received rewards from
the hands of the sovereign. A soldier who had
gallantly fought in the war was brought before
the queen on a litter. He had lost his legs and
arms, and was almost just a lump of flesh. The
heart of the gracious queen was melted at that
pathetic sight and tears began to trickle down
the royal cheeks. Many of those present also
wept. The weeping queen bent down and
pinned a badge on the breast of the mutilated
soldier, then placed an affectionate kiss on his
brow. Rising with all imperial gravity, she
exclaimed, 'Well done, good and faithful
servant!'
    What an approbation for that battle-scarred,
mutilated warrior!
(Matt. 25. 21,23)

**474 Hope Amid Fears.** John Calvin wrote: 'Fear and hope may seem opposite and incompatible affections; yet it is proved by observation that the latter never comes into full sway unless there exists some measure of the former. In a tranquil state of mind there is no scope for the exercise of hope. David feared, and yet trusted; was sensible of the greatness of his danger, and yet quieted his mind with the confident hope of the divine deliverance.'

C. H. Spurgeon commented on the same theme: 'As though he were two men the psalmist talks to himself—"Why art thou cast down, O my soul . . . hope thou in God." His faith reasons with his fears, his hope argues with his sorrows. These present troubles, are they to last for ever? The rejoicings of my foes, are they more than empty talk? Why this deep depression, this faithless fainting, this chicken-hearted melancholy? As Trapp says, "David chideth David out of the dumps." And herein he is an example for all desponding ones. To search out the cause of our sorrow is often the best surgery for grief. A clearer view will make monsters dwindle into trifles.'
(Ps. 42. 11)

**475 Hope—Door of.**

*I will fling open wide a door of hope,*
*And I will give you back*
*Years that the locusts have devoured;*
*No good thing shall you lack.*
*Lift up your head and trust me to fulfil*
*My utmost word,*
*Till I make plain the record of a love*
*That never erred.*

Nancy Hansen
(Hos. 2. 15; Joel 2. 25)

**476 Hope of Our Heart.** The following verses were written by Daniel Otsing, a Russian Christian:

*O Lord, with our ears and heart open,*
*Awaiting Thy shout would we be,*
*The summons that calls us to heaven*
*For ever to be, Lord, with Thee.*
*Thy Word and Thy Spirit, blest Lover,*
*The earnest, are giv'n to Thy bride;*
*Thou'rt near to faith's vision, O Saviour,*
*But soon she will be at Thy side.*

*O come then, Lord Jesus, we're watching,*
*And take now Thy spouse home to Thee!*
*Thine absence awakens deep yearning,*
*The bride her loved Bridegroom to see.*
*Thy heart, O Lord Jesus, is throbbing*
*With love deep, eternal, we know;*
*Our hearts in response, with love's burning,*
*Await Thee, with lamps all aglow.*

*The Spirit and bride are united*
*In saying, 'Come, Lord, yea, come soon!'*
*Throughout the long night she has waited*
*To see Thee, her faithful Bridegroom.*
*Gross darkness the earth doth now cover,*
*And night, like a pall, shrouds the land;*
*The flock is still here, Shepherd Lover,*
*The sheep Thou hast kept by Thy hand.*

*Midst darkness faith clearly sees beaming*
*The light of Thy coming afar;*
*We watch for the dawn of the morning*
*And hail Thee, the bright Morning Star.*
*The Word of Thy patience we're keeping;*
*Thy radiancy draws us apart,*
*A beacon us homeward attracting*
*To meet Thee, the Hope of our heart.*
(Rev. 22. 20)

**477 Hope—The Blessed.** The Christian has a hope that the man of the world has not. It is:

*A better hope than the Law could devise,*
*A bigger hope than man's biggest prize,*
*A brighter hope than the world can afford,*
*A blessed hope, the return of the Lord.*
(Col. 1. 5; Tit. 2. 13; Heb. 7. 19)

**478 Hope—The Christian's.** The following 'Quote' appeared in the *Reader's Digest*:

'No mariner ever enters upon a more un-charted sea than does the average human being in the twentieth century. Our ancestors knew their way from birth through to eternity; we are puzzled about the day after tomorrow.'

Walter Lippman

But the 'committed Christian' is NOT the average human being in the twentieth century, for he has a hope.

Hope, said H. W. Webb-Peploe, is a greater grace than faith. Faith deals with details; hope with the largeness of life. Faith has definite objects: 'All things, whatsoever ye shall ask in prayer, believing, ye shall receive.' But hope is content to leave large scope to the Lord. It does not wish to fix on any one boon, but prays with Abraham, 'Lord God, what wilt Thou give me?' Hope is ready to say, 'I will leave all choice to Him; I cannot ask for this or that; I only know He is greater than I can think, richer than I can conceive.'

**479 Horizon of Love.** Dr John MacBeath tells a beautiful story of two little girls who stood on the deck of a liner in mid-ocean, looking out on the sea. The elder of the two exclaimed, 'What a wonderful day! Look at the horizon!' 'What is the horizon? Where is it?' asked the younger girl. 'See,' answered the other, pointing with her finger, 'where the sea seems to meet the sky, and the sky seems to meet the sea, that is the horizon; and when you get there, there is another one, and then another, and then another. You never really reach it. It's always further on.'

That, he said, is like the love of God in Christ. There is no end to it: it is always further on.

R. B. Owen

Note: the Greek word 'horizo', of which 'horizon' is a derivative, occurs in Acts 2. 23; 17. 26; 17. 31; Romans 1. 4

**480 Hospitality—Given to.** The late A. C. Rose, who held an important and responsible post on the Madras and Southern Mahratti

Railway and Mrs. Rose, his wife, while in Madras had an open house for the Lord's people. Their gracious hospitality was well known in Southern India. On the desk of their guestroom was a card with the following lines: One of the joys of our life is to welcome to our house the friends of our love and choice. It is good to have you with us. May your visit be restful and happy! And when the time comes for you to leave us, we hope you will carry away with you fragrant thoughts and happy memories.

On the other side of the card were these beautiful lines in verse:

*Sleep sweetly in this quiet room, o thou*
  *whoe'er thou art!*
*And let no mournful yesterdays disturb thy*
  *questing heart,*
*Nor let tomorrow mar thy rest with dreams of*
  *coming ill!*
*Thy Master is Thy changeless friend: His*
  *love surrounds thee still.*
*Forget thyself and all the world: put out each*
  *glaring light.*
*The stars are waking overhead—Sleep sweetly*
  *then: Goodnight!*

**481  Hospitality Offered.** Brethren in an assembly in a bilingual city met to discuss arrangements to be made for the visit of a ministering brother who had been invited for two months' meetings. Where was the preacher to stay? Who was going to entertain him during the campaign? One French brother, whose knowledge of English was very good but not just perfect, said, 'Well! we have talked it over and shall be delighted to hospitalise him.'

We do not 'make a man an offender for a word'.
(Isa. 29. 21)

**482  Host—Choosing Your.** John Nelson Darby, an eminent servant of God, arrived on one of his preaching tours at the railway station and was met by a number of brethren. One of them, a wealthy brother with a carriage and pair, came forward to claim the distinguished minister as his guest. Mr Darby, grasping the situation in a moment, hastily enquired, 'Who generally receives the Lord's servants?' A humble brother, with no means of conveyance, was pointed out to him. 'Then,' said Mr. Darby, 'I shall stay with him.' The rich brother went home alone in his carriage. Perhaps, if he cared for some of God's humble servants, he would have had J. N. Darby as his guest on that occasion.
(Rom. 16. 23)

**483  House in Heaven.** 'In My Father's house are many mansions,' said Jesus. The true home life is in the Father's house in heaven, with the Father's heart the spring of all the affection there and the Saviour's presence the pledge of its permanence.

A young girl, taking a walk with her father, was very quiet for a long time. When her father asked what she was thinking about, she replied, 'I was just thinking if heaven with its stars is so beautiful wrong side out, how wonderful it must be on the right side.'

*Soon the journey will be over; His own voice*
  *will bid us come;*
*Rest and welcome will enfold us, once within*
  *the realms of home.*
*Home! where loved ones fast are gath'ring,*
  *Home! where all is joy and light:*
*Home! where doors are barred for ever 'gainst*
  *earth's sorrows and its night:*
*Home! where love that never ceases has for*
  *us a 'place prepared',*
*Where the angels wait to serve us, there*
  *shall joys with Him be shared.*

                              Eleanor M. Tucker

(John 14. 2,3)

**484  House—The Earthly.** A Christian lady of 94 wrote the following lines:

*I hail once more my natal day,*
*Still in my tenement of clay*
*With every favour blest;*
*And He who placed the structure here*
*Can prop it up another year*
*If He should think it best.*

*Long has it stood through snows and rains*
*And braved life's fearful hurricanes*
*While many a stronger fell;*
*The reason why I cannot see,*
*And what to us seems mystery*
*The Builder knows full well.*

*But now it's weather worn and old:*
*The summer's heat, the winter's cold*
*Pierce through the walls and roof;*
*'Tis like a garment so worn out—*
*To mend there seems no whereabout.*
*But now it's weather worn and old,*
*So gone is warp and woof.*

*Its tottering pillars now are weak;*
*The poor old rusty hinges creak;*
*Its windows too are dim:*
*But let defects, discomforts pass,*
*For, looking darkly through the glass,*
*I catch a hopeful gleam.*

*Nature and scripture tell us all*
*This withered frame at last must fall,*
*Though when or how's unknown;*
*I leave that to the architect,*
*And trust his wisdom to direct*
*The taking of it down.*

*But when you see it prostrate lie,*
*Let not sad tears bedim your eye;*
*The tenant is not here:*
*For just beyond time's little space*
*She finds with Christ a resting-place,*
*No more to date her year.*

*And when she walks with you no more*
*The world will move just as before.*
*Let each his house in order set*
*That he may leave without regret*
*Whenever called to go.*

(2 Cor. 5. 2)

**485   House—This Earthly.**

*You tell me I am getting old, but that's not*
*   really so;*
*The house I live in may be worn and that, of*
*   course, I know.*
*It's been in use a good long while and*
*   weathered many a gale;*
*I'm therefore not surprised to find it's*
*   getting somewhat frail.*

*You tell me I am getting old, you mix my*
*   house with me;*
*You're looking at the outside—that's all that*
*   most folks see.*
*The dweller in the little house is young and*
*   bright and gay,*
*Just starting on a life that lasts through long,*
*   eternal day.*

*The colour changing of the roof, the windows*
*   looking dim,*
*The walls a bit transparent and getting rather*
*   thin,*
*The foundations not so steady as once it used*
*   to be,*
*And that is all that you observe, but that's*
*   not really me.*

*I patch the old house up a bit to make it*
*   last the night,*
*But soon I shall be flitting to my home*
*   of endless light;*
*I'm going to live for ever there; my life goes*
*   on—it's grand;*
*How can you say I'm getting old? You do*
*   not understand.*

*These few short years can't make me old;*
*   I feel I'm in my youth.*
*Eternity lies just ahead, full life and joy and*
*   truth.*
*We shall not fret to see this house grow*
*   shabby day by day,*
*But look ahead to our new home which*
*   never will decay.*

*I know that I have been made fit for that*
*   blest land above,*
*Cleansed in the precious blood of Christ and*
*   growing still in love.*
*The beauty of that glorious home no words*
*   can ever say;*
*'Tis hidden from these mortal eyes but kept*
*   for me some day.*

*My house has been made ready in the land*
*   beyond the sky:*
*Its architect and builder is my Saviour now on*
*   high;*
*But I rather think he's leaving the*
*   furnishing to me,*
*So it's 'treasure up in heaven' I must store*
*   each day, you see.*

(2 Cor. 4. 16; 5. 1)

**486   Humanism.** This cult, represented by
the Peace Corps and other such organizations,
says: 'We don't worry about your soul, but we
do care about your body, and we do care about
your mind, we do care about your home, we do
care about your country.' And to these secon-
dary needs they are giving themselves. Jesus
said, 'What shall it profit a man if he gain the
whole world and lose his own soul? Or what
shall a man give in exchange for his soul?'
(Mark 8. 36,37; Isa. 38. 17)

**487   Humanity and Deity of Christ.**

*Our blessed Lord combined in one*
*Two natures, both complete—*
*In perfect manhood all sublime,*
*In Godhead all replete.*

*As man He entered Cana's feast,*
*A humble guest to dine;*
*As God He moved the water there*
*And changed it into wine.*

*As man He suffered weariness,*
*And rested on a well;*
*As God He pierced a sinner's heart*
*And saved her soul from hell.*

*As man He climbed the mountain's height*
*A suppliant to be;*
*As God He left the place of prayer*
*And walked upon the sea.*

*As man He wept in heartfelt grief*
*Beside a loved one's grave;*
*As God He burst the bands of death,*
*Almighty still to save.*

*As man He lay within a boat,*
*O'erpowered by needful sleep;*
*As God, He rose, rebuked the wind,*
*And stilled the angry deep.*

*As man he yielded to His foes,*
*Submitting to be bound;*
*As God, His presence overawed*
*And threw them to the ground.*

*Such was our Lord in life on earth,*
*In dual nature one;*
*The woman's seed in very truth*
*And God's eternal Son.*

*O Child! O Son! O Word made flesh!*
*May Thy high praise increase;*
*Thou wonderful, Thou mighty God,*
*Eternal Prince of peace!*

                                   Thomas Baird

(Rom. 9.5)

**488   Humble Prince—A.** An American travelling in Norway made much ado one day
because he was given an upper berth on a
train. 'I'll change with you,' offered a young
man. The offer accepted, the two men sat
together for a pleasant talk. The next morning
the young man had to change to another train.
'Goodbye,' he said, shaking hands with the
American. 'I hope sometime you will think of
Prince Bernadotte. I am on my way to preach
the gospel to the Laplanders.' Shame flushed
the face of the American, for he knew then
that the better place had been given him by
the son of Sweden's king, the son who had
given up his succession to the throne to become
a missionary. 'For ye know the grace of our
Lord Jesus Christ that, though He was rich,
yet for your sakes He became poor, that ye

through His poverty might be rich.' The servant is not greater than his lord. That missionary servant of God was like his Lord.

*Sunday School Times*

(2 Cor. 8. 9)

### 489 Humble Walk With God—A.

*Lord, help me thus to walk with Thee*
*Each day in true humility,*
*Nor ever from Thee stray.*
*Do Thou all needful strength impart,*
*And by Thy grace incline my heart*
*Thy precepts to obey!*
*Lord, help me thus to walk with Thee*
*And make me ever quick to see*
*The leading of Thy will;*
*For I would lose my will in Thine,*
*Nor ever murmur or repine,*
*But in Thy love be still.*

*Lord, help me thus to walk with Thee,*
*So that where'er my lot may be*
*I may be unafraid;*
*For Thou wilt hold my trembling hand*
*And in Thy strength I strong shall stand,*
*Nor ever be dismayed.*

*Lord, help me over life's rough road*
*To share my brother's heavy load,*
*Since Christ bore mine for me.*
*So shall my pathway all along*
*Become one glad, triumphant song:*
*And thus I walk with Thee.*

S. E. Burrow

(Micah 6. 8)

### 490 Humble Work Preferred.
An Irish king who came into the banquet hall and sat down in the lowest place was entreated by his courtiers and nobles to go and take his place at the head of the table. 'Where the king sits, there is the head of the table,' was his answer.

He who is in closest fellowship with his Master in service in the lowest place, and even in suffering and reproach, asks no other place. In man's estimate it may be very low, but it is still the head place.

> *Door-keeping is humble work,*
> *Yet through heavenly grace,*
> *He who takes the lowest task*
> *Finds the highest place.*

(Ps. 84. 10; Luke 14. 10)

### 491 Humbler Days Remembered.
There is a Persian story of one who had been raised from a lowly station in life to a high position in royal favour. In his palace one room was dedicated as a 'Chamber of Memory'. There he kept the memorials of his early days when he was a poor shepherd. In it was his crook, and his wallet, a water cruse and a coarse dress. Every day he spent an hour in this room. Here he lived again with the memories of his youth. These recollections not only kept him humble, but contributed to his gratitude and happiness and also gave him a warm and sympathetic heart for the common people.

(Deut. 24. 18)

### 492 Humility.
If you want to be high, stoop low; if you want to go up, go down; but go as low as e'er you will, the Highest has been lower still.

William Carey, missionary to India, was one of the humblest men that ever ministered to the welfare of the world, and one of the greatest too. He was never ashamed of the position he once occupied, for in it he had conscientiously ministered to his fellow-men. On one occasion, when at the table of the Governor-General of India, he overheard an officer asking another in a voice loud enough for all the guests to hear, whether Carey had not once been a shoemaker. 'No, sir!' said William Carey who had translated the Bible into several Indian languages, 'only a cobbler.'

J. Hudson Taylor, founder of the China Inland Mission, was to address a crowded meeting in Melbourne, Australia. The chairman, introducing him, referred to him as our 'illustrious guest'. Quietly Mr Taylor stood for a moment, the light of God on his face, and in a way that won all hearts said, 'Dear friends, I am only the little servant of an illustrious Master.'

On one occasion Hudson Taylor was travelling with a young missionary not so used to roughing it as Dr Taylor, his companion, now grey-headed in the service of the Lord Jesus. The first night the young man put his boots outside his bedroom door, forgetting that he was no longer at home where a servant would clean and polish them. Next morning, however, he found them cleaned and polished. Hudson Taylor had got up early before his young companion was awake, and brushed his boots. (Phil. 2. 5)

### 493 Humility—Clothed with.
Moses, Gideon and David were great men, each with no knowledge of the fact that he was great. Peter wrote in his first letter: 'Be clothed with humility: humble yourselves . . . that ye may be exalted in due season, casting all your care upon Him for He careth for you.' It is impossible with a proud spirit to cast our burden on the Lord.

During William Carey's last illness in 1834 he was visited by the Scottish missionary, Dr Alexander Duff, who, in prayer with him, referred to him as 'Dr Carey'. As Mr Duff was leaving, the aged missionary said, 'Mr Duff, you have been speaking of Dr Carey. When I am gone, say nothing of Dr Carey; speak about Dr Carey's Saviour.'

(1 Pet. 5. 5-7)

### 494 Humility of Christ.

*Lord, I must not, cannot rest*
*Till I Thy mind obtain,*
*Chase presumption from my breast*
*And all Thy meekness gain.*
*Give me, Lord, Thy gentle heart,*
*Thy lowly mind my portion be.*
*Meek Redeemer, now impart*
*Thine own humility!*

*Let Thy cross my will control;*
*Conform me to my Guide!*
*In the manger lay my soul*
*And crucify my pride.*
*Give me, Lord, a contrite heart,*
*A heart that always looks to Thee!*
*Meek Redeemer, now impart*
*Thine own humility!*

Augustus Toplady
(Phil. 2. 5)

**495  Hurricane Warning.** Some years ago a man who lived on Long Island, U.S.A., bought himself a very fine barometer. When it arrived at his home he was extremly disappointed to find that the indicating needle appeared to be stuck, pointing to the sector marked 'HURRI-CANE'. After shaking the barometer vigor-ously several times, its new owner sat down and wrote a scorching letter to the store from which he had bought the barometer, and posted it the following morning from his office in New York. That evening he returned to Long Island to find not only the barometer missing, but his house also. The barometer's needle had been right after all: there was a hurricane.

How many are there who disregard the warnings of the Bible, not realizing that those warnings mean what they say and are given to lead us to escape from the wrath to come and to find a refuge in Jesus Christ, the only Saviour.
(Heb. 3. 12)

**496  Hurry and Bustle.** 'Slow down and stay alive!' says the sign on the highway. The admonition is much needed in this day of frantic rushing about. Lives by the thousand are lost for lack of taking it seriously. Year by year the carnage increases while speeds are stepped up still further. But speed is not confined to the highways. In every department of our life the pace is being accelerated. So many things clamour for our attention! And we feel that we must somehow keep in touch with all that goes on, and participate actively in as much of it as is humanly possible. We busy ourselves doing four or five things at once, or at least desperately trying to. If nerves protest, as they surely will, we soothe (?) them with more noise and still more bustle. We badly need to escape from the mad scramble, but then we might 'miss something'! Or we might be looked upon as eccentric, and dare we risk that?

'There is too much hurry and bustle . . . to allow the calm working of the Spirit on the heart.' So wrote Robert Murray McCheyne, not yesterday but before 1840. If he felt it then, what would he say if he could witness the scene today? The mortality on our highways would surely shock him. But much more staggering to his sensitive soul would be the defeat being suff-ered by so many Christians for the simple reason that they will not learn to 'let the world go by'.

F. W. Schwartz

**497  Husband's Lament—A.**
*I never knew how much she was to me;*
*I never knew how patient she could be;*
*I never realized until she went away*
*How much a woman helps a man each day.*
*And Oh! I never knew how thoughtless I*
*Had been at times, until I saw her die.*
*I never knew the crosses that she bore*
*With smiling patience, or the griefs that tore*
*Upon her heart-strings as she toiled away:*
*I only saw her smiles and thought her gay.*
*I took for granted joys that were not so;*
*I might have helped her then but didn't know.*
*I thought she worried needlessly, and yet*
*I see her life was bounded by regret;*
*I might have done much more for her had I*
*But known her sorrows, or had thought to try;*
*But now that I'm alone, at last I see*
*How much of pain her smiling hid from me.*
*I never knew how much I leaned upon*
*That little woman till I found her gone,*
*How much her patience, gentleness and cheers*
*Had meant to me through all those early years,*
*How many little things she used to do*
*To smooth my path. Alas, I never knew!*

Edgar A. Guest

Some day many of us will wake up and wish we had 'spread a little honey' to our loved ones—'a little balm and a little honey.'
(Gen. 43. 11)

**498  Hymn-Writer Isaac Watts.** Isaac Watts who has been called the 'father of English hymnody', was a versifier from a very early age. One morning, while at family prayers, his laughter interrupted his father's prayer and brought down the godly minister's wrath on his frivolous son. When he was asked to explain why he had laughed, he replied:
*'There was a rat for want of stairs*
*Climbed up the rope to say its prayers.'*
When his father was about to chastise him, he cried,
*'Oh father, do some pity take*
*And I shall no more verses make.'*

In those days only the Psalms were sung in public worship, and at the age of fifteen young Isaac said to his father, 'The singing of God's praise is the part of worship nighest to heaven, and its performance among us is the worst on earth.' His father replied, 'Young man, give us something better.' He did so in over 600 hymns. One of the finest and best known has as its theme 'The Cross of Christ' and commences—'When I survey the wondrous cross on which the Prince of glory died.'
(Eph. 5. 19)

**499  Hypocrite's Hope—The.** Some time ago there came to Los Angeles a so-called human fly. He announced that on a given day he would climb up the face of one of the large department store buildings. Long before the time thousands of eager spectators gathered. Slowly and care-fully he mounted aloft. Up and up he went against great difficulties. At last he was nearing the top. He was seen to be looking for something to support his weight and to carry him further. Soon he seemed to spy what looked to the spectators like a piece of grey stone protruding from the smooth wall. He reached for it but it was beyond his reach. He ventured all on a cat-like spring, grasped the grey-like object, fell to the ground and was dashed to pieces. In his dead hand was clutched a spider's web.

Dr H. A. Ironside

The hypocrite's hope shall perish . . . whose trust shall be a spider's web.
(Job 8. 13,14)

**500   Hypocrite's Marks—The.** The late R. T. Archibald, for many years a S.U. evangelist in India, used to narrate the following fable which made a very great impression on our High School students in Narsapur. The allegory has since been recounted by an Indian Christian, R. R. Rajamani, in his book *Monsoon Daybreak* as follows:

This crow was lazy and instead of foraging for himself he planned to benefit from the food put out for some tame pigeons. So he rolled in a heap of ashes to disguise himself. This done, he joined them, decked in his pale grey plumage; but in his eagerness to reach the food he quickly forgot to walk like a pigeon, and hopped along. The housewife recognised him as a fraud and drove him away, So he went off and practised diligently, and by next day he had mastered the pigeon's gait and walked bravely around with them. But this time temptation was his undoing: he became diverted by a piece of rotting meat, and so revealed to them his appalling taste in food. Now it was the pigeons' turn to chase him off. At length by the third morning he had perfected his disguise and was quite at ease feeding among the pigeons: but not, alas, for long. By chance an old friend flying overhead, recognised and greeted him. 'Caw! Caw!' the 'pigeon' replied vigorously, and again the secret was out.

Three times, and by three things—his walk, his taste and his talk—his true nature was revealed: it could not be changed.

The word for 'hypocrite' in the New Testament means a play-actor, one who acts a part to deceive others.

A.N.

**501   Hypocritical Conduct and Confessions.** Great swarms of beggars make their way to all the big Hindu Festivals held in the sacred places in India. Here is a man with one leg tied up skilfully by interested friends or relatives, moaning that he has only one leg. Here are others with their faces and hands covered with ugly coloured stuff to simulate loathesome ulcers. Others again have their eyes treated in order to counterfeit blindness in a more impressive way so that the pious pilgrims passing to bathe in the sacred rivers or worship in the temples of their gods may commiserate them

and bestow upon them pity and alms. In one of his sermons John Berridge, using a similar illustration, says, 'Why, this is just your case, sir, when you go to the church a-praying, which is begging, you tie your righteous heart up, and then make woeful outcry for mercy on us miserable sinners!' Such hypocrites will be found out and due retribution meted out. Some of the severest woes pronounced by our Lord were against hypocrites.

A.N.

(Matt. 23. 13-33)

**502   Idle—The Violinist.** In January, 1962 a newspaper in Pembroke, Wales, reported:

One hundred and sixteen violins, four of them 'Strads' worth thousands of pounds, were today discovered in a deserted house owned by a hermit who was buried five months ago, without a single mourner. Neighbours said they often heard the oddly-dressed recluse, Mr. Herman Idle, playing a violin but never believed him when he told them he had a valuable collection. Although devoted to the violins, the recluse had deprived the world of their music. Many Christians, like Mr. Idle, treasure their salvation, the gift of God, but keep it to themselves.
(Rom. 12. 11)

**503   Idols Destroyed.** In the year A.D. 627 Edwin, the Saxon king of Northumbria, was in council with his nobles discussing a subject of great importance, fraught with immense consequences for our land.

At that time our Saxon forefathers were mostly idolators. A Christian missionary had come to Northern England and told the king and his men of the true God and of His Son who died for us that we might have a hope beyond the grave, the hope of life eternal. Even the heathen priest had been impressed and spoke in favour of the gospel. Then one of the nobles said that during supper he had seen a swallow enter the hall in which a fire was burning. The swallow enjoyed the warmth for a few moments, then flew out into the raging storm and the cold outside. 'Such,' said the noble, 'is the life of man. But if this new doctrine can really teach us anything more certain, it deserves to be followed.' Others agreed.

The pagan priest wanted to hear more, and at the king's bidding the evangelist was called in to preach to them. The priest and the king embraced the truth and were converted, and many of their followers followed suit.

'Who will be the first to profane the idol temple?' said the king. 'I will,' said the priest. 'I who worshipped those idols in folly shall give an example to others in destroying them, by the wisdom given me by the true God.' The idolatrous shrine was burned to the ground, and Bede, the Saxon historian, who records this story, says the place where this happened was still shown in his time, not far from the city of York.
(1 Thess. 1. 9,10)

504   **If.**   (with apologies to Rudyard Kipling)

*If you can keep the 'faith' when those about*
   *you*
*Are losing it and seeking something new;*
*If you can stand the firmer though they flout*
   *you*
*As being simple and old-fashioned too;*
*If you can put your hand in Christ's and,*
   *feeling*
*The marks of Calvary's scars upon your palm,*
*Can gladly say 'Amen' to all His dealing*
*Or change the sigh into a joyous psalm;*
*If you can laugh when human hopes are*
   *banished,*
*When castles fall and cherished prospects die,*
*And just keep on though earthly props have*
   *vanished,*
*Content to see the pattern by and by;*
*If you can meet abuse without complaining*
*And greet your unkind critic with a smile;*
*If, conscious that your human love is waning,*
*You claim a Calvary love that knows no guile;*
*If you can bear the unjust imputation*
*Without a murmur of revengeful thought,*
*And even forfeit rights and reputation*
*Because HIS glory is the one thing sought;*
*If you can give an honest commendation*
*To him whose work looms larger than your*
   *own,*
*Or scorn to speak the word of condemnation*
*To him who falls or reaps what he has sown;*
*If you can give consent to Calvary's dying*
*And live again in resurrection power;*
*If you can claim the victory, not by trying,*
*But resting in His triumph every hour;*
*If you can be content with his provision*
*Though others seem to prosper and succeed,*
*Nor let repining mar the heavenly vision*
*And simply trust in God for every need;*
*If you can let the mind of Christ possess you,*
*To think on 'things of good report', and true,*
*And ever let the love of Christ obsess you,*
*Constraining everything you say and do;*
*If you can find in Him your highest treasure,*
*Let Him hold sway o'er heart and soul and limb,*
*Then LIFE is yours, and blessing without*
   *measure,*
*And—what is more—YOU'LL LIVE AND*
   *REIGN WITH HIM.*

                              Reginald Wallis

(Phil. 4. 15)

505   **If for Thy Glory.**

*If for Thy glory, Lord, this life of mine*
*Could in some measure help Thy work divine,*
*If in some humble task my heart could ache,*
*My very self could suffer for Thy sake,*
*For Thee, dear Lord, they would be used,*
*They would be bruised.*

*If these two feet could walk some rugged hill*
*Of sacrifice for Thy most holy will,*
*If these two hands could minister for Thee*
*In loving toil where'er Thou'dst have me be,*
*Use them, O Lord, they are Thine own,*
*For Thee alone.*

*If any intellect or gift Thou hast bestowed*
*Could in Thy service help to bear the load,*
*If Thou dost need the treasures of my heart*
*In Thy great plan to play a little part,*
*Take them, dear Lord, they are for Thee*
*Wholeheartedly.*

                              P. Dunning

506   **Ifs.**   How much depends on that little word 'If'! Philip of Macedon sent a threatening message to the Lacedaemonians, 'If I enter Laconia, I will level Lacedaemon to the ground.' Their answer is well worth remembering. It was to send back the little word 'IF'. That tiny word told the proud ruler that their brave men would be able to resist his invasion. There are two grand 'IFS' in the letters of Paul the apostle, which are not conditional, but assuring: 'If God be for us, who is against us?' Romans 8. 31. The meaning is—'Since God is for us.' 'If ye then be risen with Christ, seek those things which are above.' Again this meaning is 'Since'—Because God is for us, no enemy that opposes us can prosper; and because we are risen with Christ, our mind is to be occupied with heavenly things.

507   **Image of His Son.**

*A block of hardest marble stood*
*Before the sculptor; where he would*
*He smote with hand well skilled,*
*And thus with blow fulfilled*
*The image of his mind.*
*At first with chisel coarse and stroke*
*Unspared, the corners off he broke,*
*And soon the form appeared;*
*But then with finer tools he wrought,*
*And finer yet, until he brought*
*The perfect image forth*
*So with unerring skilfulness,*
*With cunning hand and sure,*
*'Tis as the marble groweth less,*
*The likeness groweth more.*
*So God divinely works with those*
*He in eternal ages chose*
*To show His works of grace,*
*And thus with blow on blow to trace*
*The image of His Son.*

*Though sharp the blows, yet skilled the hand:*
*If we but feebly understand*
*The reason of each stroke,*
*How blest to know that He who holds*
*The tools—before His eye beholds*
*His own beloved One!*
*The cares and troubles day by day,*
*The sorrows that o'ershade the way,*
*Together work for good.*
*For nothing e'er by chance befalls*
*The one whom God in purpose calls,*
*In whom His love is found.*
*And when we have the glory gain'd,*
*And Christ's full image have attain'd,*
*We'll praise His wondrous skill,*
*And bless the hand that dealt each blow*
*Upon the marble here below*
*In working out His will.*

                              A. J. H. Brown

(Rom. 8. 29)

**508 Image Projected** The Brand image is a factor of great importance in the field of modern advertising. It is the composite of the many characteristics that goes to identify a product or service. The operation is largely by implication, and a whole aura of subjective meanings concerning persons or things is registered on the subconscious mind, ready to flash on the inner eye through the stimulation of any of the senses. The Brand image seeks to convey through imaginative symbols and forms an overall impression of which there is a constant build up. For instance, the symbol of a bird gliding in the sky intuitively reminds us of air travel. Every individual, society and nation has its own peculiar brand image. Each nation wants to project the best possible image of herself to the world outside, and this explains the existence of Information Wings attached to most Foreign Missions.

We as Christians have an image for projection to the world. That Image is the Christ of God. 1 Peter 2. 9 tells what we are through God's wondrous grace. Christ is as great and glorious on earth as His people make Him.

**509 Imitation or Real?** A professor, demonstrating to his friends among whom were many magnificently dressed ladies wearing rare and costly jewellery, the wonders of the Röntgen or X-ray, said, 'Ladies and gentlemen, the effect of these rays upon diamonds is really marvellous!' Lowering the lights in the room, he turned the X-rays on the sparkling gems worn by the ladies. Immediately the real diamonds sparkled in all their brilliancy, but the beautiful paste diamonds—only imitations—had lost all their lustre. The X-rays discovered which were real and which were imitation, much to the annoyance of some of the ladies.
(John 3. 20,21)

**510 Incarnation.**

*From His unmeasured, yearless state He came,*
*Of the eternal God the timeless Son,*
*Choosing a moment to be part of time,*
*To have beginning, who had ne'er begun.*

*An hour of birth was His; an infant hour*
*When to the beating pulse was added breath,*
*Sight, hearing, touch and every human sense,*
*The joy of living and the fear of death.*

*Now the Infinite binds Himself in days,*
*The hours of mortal life His heart beats out.*
*He knows the irretrievable past of man,*
*The fleeting present and the future doubt.*

*I AM can say, 'I was' and 'I will be',*
*Confined within the scope of day and night,*
*Setting aside an hour to pray, to teach,*
*Knowing a moment's sorrow or delight.*

*How great the purpose was that made Him man*
*And brought Him to restriction and restraint!*
*How unrestricted, unrestrained the love*
*That had no time for hesitant complaint!*

*Our Saviour came in wondrous willingness,*
*Binding Himself in time to set us free,*
*Slowly enduring hours that brought Him death*
*That We with Him might live eternally.*

*Time is the measure of our shadowy days,*
*But yet within that measure must we choose.*
*Within the little limits of our span,*
*A deathless life is ours to take or lose.*

J. A. Nye

(Matt. 1. 23)

**511 Incarnation and the Cross.**

*God gave His only Son to know*
*The darkness of a virgin's womb,*
*The sweetness of a virgin's love,*
*The sorrow of her tears which bathed*
*The Baby face, as she foreviewed*
*The sword-thrust that would pierce her heart,*
*When cruel men would wreak their hate*
*On Innocence—her Son—and God's.*
*Her agony our hearts can feel;*
*But what of His—the Father's heart?*
*Such agony the perfect gauge*
*Of God's great love for humankind,*
*The burning and eternal proof*
*Redemption was not cheaply bought,*
*Nor could be bought but at the price*
*Of Incarnation and the Cross;*
*The end to justify the means.*
*The bringing sons to glory can*
*Alone appease and justify*
*Unprecedented agony,*
*That found its first expression in*
*The manger, and its last—the Cross.*
*Oh glorious manger, halo crowned,*
*The cradle of incarnate God!*
*Oh Cross of Christ, my glorying*
*By which the world to me is dead,*
*And I in Christ am crucified:*
*God's justice in it satisfied,*
*God's love eternally expressed.*

F.C.D.

(Luke 2. 35)

**512 Incarnation—Assurance from the.** Like other truths, the Word made flesh can speak both to comfort and strengthen, and also to warn of the danger of disregarding what is true and just. Mary E. Coleridge has written:

> *I saw a stable, low and very bare,*
> *A little child in a manger.*
> *The oxen knew Him, had Him in their care.*
> *To men He was a stranger.*
> *The safety of the world was lying there,*
> *And the world's danger.*

Because the Word is truth, it throws into sharp relief the hypocrisies and prejudices with which men so often buttress their lives. At first sight it may seem that to stress the darker side of man's nature spoils the simple joy of Christmas; but what man is without God must be set alongside of what man can be with God. Man needs an assurance that life has a meaning and purpose, and that the things of the Spirit are true and lasting. That is the assurance given us in the Word made flesh.

## 513  Incarnation—Miracle of the.

O the miracle of redeeming Love,
God's blessed Son, wrapped in our mortal clay:
Down laid His sceptre in the courts above,
Forsook the realms of heaven's perpetual day,

Bend low: a lower stoop He needs must take;
Peer where the guttering flame sheds light so
   mild;
Witness in quiet wonder—for man's sake—
God and His creature framed within a child.

From earth's far distant climes, behold them
   come—
The seeking magi hastening to His birth,
Laden with costly presents, yet with some
Strangely symbolic meaning of His worth.

The shepherd's ceaseless watch upon bleak
   hills,
Clustered around the wood fire's leaping flame,
When light and voice celestial the sky fills,
Heav'n's sign and psalm, to magnify His name.

Far down the avenue of yester-year
To Bethlehem thy willing journey ply;
Now wing thy thoughts: faith's chariot draws
   near
To bear its precious burden up on high.

Edward Freestone in The Witness
(Matt. 2. 1; Luke 2. 13-15)

## 514  Incarnation of Christ.

How painfully and wearily 1000 years of the world's history rolled on, and no Christ: 2000 years and no Christ: 3000 years and no Christ: 4000 years and no Christ. 'Give us a Christ,' had cried Assyrian and Persian and Chaldean and Egyptian civilizations, but the lips of the earth and the lips of the sky made no answer. Then Christ came, Son of Mary, Son of God, Child of a day, Monarch of eternity. Omnipotence was sheathed in that Babe's arm; omniscience resided in the optic nerve of that Child's eye.

Dr Talmage

(Gal. 4. 4,5)

## 515  Incarnation of Heaven's King.

My Lord, how strange, Thou cam'st to earth
In infant form, through human birth.
And though Thou couldst have chosen other,
Yet didst Thou, in wisdom choose
A Hebrew maid, as mother.

My Lord, how strange that Thou shouldst
   scorn
All hint of splendour when wert born
Thou, Who with splendour decked this sphere,
Elected for Thyself no court
Whilst on Thy sojourn here.

My Lord, how strange Thou hadst no home,
Nor for Thy head soft, pillowed foam;
No resting place was ever found
For Thee whose hands had shaped this world:
No bed, but stony ground!

My Lord, how strange Thou wert so poor
To live behind a stable door:
Thou who placed gold in the hills
And precious stones, to make us rich:
No wealth Thy pocket fills.

And yet, my Lord, what other king
Can cause the heavenly choirs to sing?
Or cause a star, with blinding light
To broadcast news in distant lands
And sleeping shepherds fright?

What other king could heretofore
Fulfil the prophecies of yore?
What king can lay claim as Son of God
Or talk about His heavenly home
As earthly paths He trod?

What other king could wield such power
Within a stable's makeshift bower?
Behold three wise men on their knees:
Their gifts true recognition of
A greater King than these.

Nor did those shepherds think it odd
That here was born the Son of God
In poverty; and midst the oxen smell
They saw within that infant form
The holy Godhead dwell.

Do I then see an infant stranger
Lying in a humble manger?
Can I not see, as those of old
That with this wondrous birth took place
The greatest story told?

Those kings were rich, the shepherds poor
Yet both knelt down on stable floor;
This new-born King had power to reach
And draw all men and listen to
The lessons He would teach.

Those lessons teach to me, I pray,
And guide my steps, Lord, day by day.
With kings and shepherds now I stand
To give my heart—a gift to Thee—
And touch Thy blessed hand.

Those hands outstreched through all the years
To take my hands and dry my tears!
Oh! Saviour Christ, I yield Thee all
And seek Thy Christmas blessing now
Whilst kneeling at Thy stall!

Elizabeth M. Bell

## 516  India.

Verses of a lady missionary in India

We live in a land where such delights
As prickly heat and blistering nights
And smallpox, and mosquito bites
Are free to all;
Where drinking water must be boiled
That dread diseases may be foiled;
Where ox-cart wheels are never oiled
But squeak and squall;

Where white ants eat your books in holes
And red ants tackle sugar bowls,
And black ants harrow up your souls
And look for more;

*Where brown ants, biting like a vice,*
*And big ants, little, middle-size,*
*Have held the land since Adam's rise,*
*Maybe before;*

*Where mildew sits upon your shoes*
*And rust your precious cycle chews,*
*And from your pores the sweat drops ooze*
*Through half the year;*
*Where spots come in your China silk*
*And water mingles with the milk,*
*And centipedes and all their ilk*
*Drop in to cheer;*

*Where serpents add their charm to spring,*
*Where jackals make the welkin ring*
*And insects myriad-minded sting*
*And leave their mark;*
*While jackals rest, the dogs take on*
*And whoop it up from morn till dawn,*
*When crows their horrid cacophone*
*Keep up till dark;*

*Where spiders spread expansive legs*
*And hens lay microscopic eggs,*
*And rain, by bucketfuls and kegs,*
*Falls from the sky;*
*Creating on the earth morass*
*So thick and deep that none may pass*
*Until the shifty gummy mass*
*At last can dry.*

*Goats scale your compound wall's defence*
*And squirm beneath your barbed wire fence,*
*And munch your hedge, however dense,*
*And ruin all*
*The precious plants you strove to save*
*From cochineal and clownish knave,*
*And other pests that, wave on wave,*
*Would work their fall.*

*Where dust lies on your table tops*
*In drifts, howe'er one dusts and mops,*
*And fish moths are perennial crops*
*Always on hand.*
*Nor have I yet begun to tell*
*The sweet delights of those who dwell*
*Within the lotus-charmed spell*
*Of this fair land.*

### 517   Indifference to Others' Needs.

*What if your own were starving,*
*Fainting with famine pain,*
*And you should know*
*Where golden grow*
*Rich fruits and ripened grain;*
*Would you hear the wail*
*As a thrice told tale*
*And turn to your feast again?*

*What if your own were thirsting*
*And never a drop could gain,*
*And you could tell*
*Where a sparkling well*
*Poured forth melodious rain,*
*Would you turn aside*
*While they gasped and died,*
*And leave them to their pain?*

*What if your own were darkened*
*Without a cheering ray,*
*And you alone*
*Could show where shone*
*The pure, sweet light of day;*
*Would you leave them there*
*In their dark despair,*
*And sing on your sunlit way?*

*Indian Christian*

(1 Cor. 9. 22)

**518   Indolence.** There once lived in Ghent a beggar who was accustomed to collect alms upon the pretence that he had a secret disease lying in his bones and weakening his whole body, and that he dare not for shame mention the name of it. This appeal was exceedingly successful until a person in authority, more curious than the rest, insisted upon following him and examining him at home. At last the beggar confessed—'That which pains me you see not; but I have a shameful disease in my bones, so that I cannot work; some call it sloth, and others term it idleness.' Alas! that so many in our churches should be so far gone with this same sickness.

*C. H. Spurgeon*

(Prov. 6. 9-11)

**519   Infidel and Editor.** An infidel farmer in Illinois wrote to the editor of a newspaper as follows: 'I have a field of corn which I ploughed on Sunday; I planted it also on Sunday; I did all the cultivating it received on Sunday; I gathered the crop on Sunday; and on Sunday I hauled it into the barn: and I find I have more corn than has been gathered by my neighbours during this October.'

The editor of the newspaper was not a professor of religion, and the farmer evidently counted on obtaining his sympathy. He did not get it, however, for the editor simply added these words at the bottom:

'God does not always settle His accounts in October.'

**520   Infidel Notions Banished.** Some years ago the well-known infidel lecturer, Charles Bradlaugh, after an address to pitmen and others in a colliery district, invited discussion should any of his audience have anything to say about the arguments he had brought forward and the inferences he had drawn. He waited some time, probably congratulating himself that he had carried his hearers to his own conclusions, when one of the colliers, rising to his feet, quietly addressed the lecturer as follows:

'Mr Bradlaugh, a while ago there was a man working in the pit along wi' me, and he was a very bad man, as all of us knew. After a while he became converted and was a very good man. But he got along wi' a set of you infidel chaps, and they did him a lot of harm, they did, Mr Bradlaugh; and he went on very bad again something like what he had been before, when one day a great big coal fell on the top of his head, and what did it do but knock him right down on his knees in the pit, Mr Bradlaugh, and he began crying to the Lord with all the strength he'd got to have mercy on him. Well, we got him out very quickly and that great big coal did his head a power of good, for it just knocked out of him those infidel notions of yours for good and all. And I think how a great big coal like that might do you a lot of good, too, Mr Bradlaugh.'

           W. Rickard

**521 Infidelity Tested.** A professed infidel on board a ship was troubling all around him with his peculiar belief, broaching the subject whenever he could get anyone to listen to him. But a terrible storm arose, and it seemed as if all must be drowned. No one was as greatly frightened as the infidel. In his extremity he sought out a Christian on board. 'Oh, Dr Witherspoon,' he said, 'we're all going; we have only a short time to stay.' The doctor turned solemnly to him and replied: 'No doubt we are going, but you and I don't go the same way.' There is nothing like the brink of eternity for testing a man's infidelity.
(Job. 8. 13)

**522 Influence of Preachers.** Three centuries have not dimmed the bright light Samuel Rutherford held aloft for Christ in Scotland. The Person of Christ became everything to him. Multitudes of lives were influenced by this Christ-impassioned man. An English minister who visited Scotland and heard several outstanding preachers reported: 'I came to Irvine and heard a well-favoured proper old man with a long beard (David Dickson) who showed me all my heart. Then I went to St Andrews where I heard a sweet majestic-looking man (R. Blair) and he showed me the majesty of God. After him I heard a little fair man (Samuel Rutherford) and he showed me the Loveliness of Christ.'
(Song of Solomon 5. 15)

**523 Ingratitude.** Years ago there was a shipwreck in Lake Michigan. A powerful swimmer who was then a student at Northwestern University rescued twenty-three persons before he finally collapsed. Some years after in Los Angeles, Dr R. A. Torrey told the story about this young man's concern and his heroic deed. To his astonishment he found out that the young man, now an old man, was in the audience. In talking with the rescuer he asked him what was the most significant thing about the rescue, the thing that stood out most in his memory after all the intervening years. The rescuer dropped his eyes and in a low voice said, 'Not one said, Thanks!'
(Luke 17. 15-18)

**524 Ingratitude.** E. P. Hammond once visited a man in Detroit, Michigan, who had a large scar on his face. During his visit he noticed that this gentleman was constantly looking out of the window, and one day, when he visited him, he got him to explain why he did so. The man said, 'Nine years ago, standing at my window, I saw one day a carriage run past with a little girl in it. Seeing her great danger, I ran out, stopped the carriage and succeeded in saving her from what would have been certain death; but I was carried into the house seriously injured, and the doctors told me I should never recover my health, as the injury was extremely severe. When I first regained consciousness after the accident, I asked, "Is the little girl safe?" "Yes!" they said, "she is safe and unhurt." "And she has never come to thank me for saving her life?" "No!" they replied, "Nor her father, nor any of her relatives?" I asked. "No! neither the girl nor her parents, nor any of her people have ever looked near to thank you or to enquire how you are." For these nine years I have waited for some expression of thanks, but I have been disappointed. I did not want payment for what I did, only gratitude.' Then, with tears streaming from his eyes, he said, 'Oh, if she had just come to thank me!'

**525 Ingratitude for Salvation.** A fisherman told Mark Guy Pearce that once when he was lying aboard his boat in Plymouth Sound, he heard a splash in the water. He knew there was another fishing boat not far off, and the man on board was a drinking man. Finding the man in the water and praying to God for help, he managed to pull him out and worked over him for more than an hour. Then he made him as comfortable as possible and left. Next morning he pulled over to see how the man was, and found him leaning over the side of his craft. 'How are you this morning?' he asked; and the man replied gruffly, 'What's that to you?' 'Why!' said his rescuer, 'I can't help taking an interest in you. I saved your life last night.' With a curse the rescued man yelled, 'Get out of here, liar.' The fisherman at this point said to Pearce, 'My heart was like a thing broke. I looked up to heaven and said, "My blessed Lord Jesus, I am sorry for Thee. That is how the world is always treating Thee."'
(Isa. 53. 3)

**526 Inheritance in Christ.** A man took one of his friends to the top of his house to show him the extent of his possessions. Waving his hands about, he said, 'There, that is my estate.' Then, pointing to a great distance on one side, he continued, 'Do you see that house? That belongs to me.' Then his friend said to him, 'Do you see that village over yonder?' 'Yes!' 'Well, there lives a poor woman in that village who can claim that she has a bigger estate than this.' 'How's that? What can she claim?' 'Why, she can say, "Christ is mine."' The wealthy gentleman looked confounded but said not another word.
(1 Cor. 3. 22,23)

**527 Inquiry Room Surprise.** Dr G. Campbell Morgan told of a unique meeting in the inquiry room after a Gospel service. Into the inquiry room came a gaunt old man, hoary in the service of sin and Satan, but realizing his need of Christ. Dr Campbell Morgan knelt down at his side and spoke to him of the blood of Christ that cleanses from all sin. Just as he was speaking, someone touched him on the shoulder and said, 'Won't you speak to this man?' Turning toward the person indicated he saw the Mayor of the city kneeling by his side. The Mayor was about the same age as the other man, but had all the marks of culture and refinement; and he had sentenced the other man to hard labour. That sentence had just expired. They were side by side, and Dr Campbell Morgan had to turn from one to talk to the other. The light dawned in the hearts of both as each realised that his need was met by the blood of Christ.

The Mayor rose and went to the other man, and said, 'Well, we didn't meet here the last time.' Then the old fellow looked up and said, 'No! and we shall never meet again as we did the last time, praise God.'
(2 Cor. 5. 17)

**528 Instrument of Ten Strings.** At a prayer meeting one of those present addressed the Lord as follows: 'Lord, we praise Thee. We will praise Thee with an instrument of ten strings.' As he continued his prayer, the people present learnt what he meant by 'an instrument of ten strings'. 'We will praise Thee with our eyes as we look only to Thee, with our ears as we listen to Thy voice, with our hands as we employ them in Thy service, and with our feet by walking in the way of Thy statutes. We will praise Thee with our tongue, bearing testimony to Thy loving-kindness, and our heart will send up its note of praise in love for Thee, our loving God. We thank Thee, Lord, for this instrument. Lord, keep it in tune and ring out on it the melodies of Thy grace; keep it in perfect harmony, and may its music tell the world of Thy Glory.'
(Ps. 33. 2; 92. 1-3; 144. 9)

**529 Intercession.** The late C. E. Stokes, for many years a missionary in Africa, used to tell of a visit he made to a lady who for thirty years had been paralysed from the waist down and suffering intense pain. She was very poor and had no near relatives. Expecting to see a face that was drawn in sorrow and bitterness, he was surprised to see one radiant with joy. Soon he discovered the reason. On the little table beside her bed was an open book, and a note-book which had been ruled into four columns. The first column contained the names of the persons for whom she was praying, the second column their special needs, and the third column the date she began to pray for each. In the fourth column she entered the date when she believed God answered her prayers. In the eyes of the world she was a useless burden.

In the eyes of God she was a greatly used servant of her Lord Jesus Christ. Though unable to understand her affliction, she had accepted it as coming from the hands of a loving Father in heaven, and God was using her in a wonderful way in the service of intercession.
(Ps. 119. 50)

**530 Intercession of Judah.** Judah's intercessory utterance in Genesis, Chapter 44, is one of the great orations of Scripture. Sir Walter Scott said it was the most complete pattern of genuine, natural eloquence extant in any language. Sir Walter continues, 'When we read this generous speech, we forgive Judah all the past and cannot refrain saying, "Thou art he whom thy brethren shall praise." '

Judah the intercessor raised his voice with telling effect in Egypt. Simeon was released, Benjamin was delivered, and aged Jacob was preserved. The whole family was set on the way to promised greatness. Therefore Moses prays, 'Hear, O Lord, the voice of Judah.' Human ears had heard it with amazing results. Then let the Lord hear it, for the divine ear would surely hear and heed its call, and yield heaven's treasures to its pleadings.

A. Soutter
(Gen. 44. 33; Deut. 33. 7)

**531 Interest—Lost.** Mr Bingham used to tell of a young couple who left Toronto years ago to go out to Nigeria as missionaries. They had splendid success in learning the language. They had tremendous joy as they reported that a church had been established soon after they began to preach. But, after a few years, a child that had been born to them died. Then the woman became sick and another baby died. Finally the wife herself died. The man came home broken and unannounced. He came into Toronto late in the afternoon, had supper, and went to his home church. He came into the prayer meeting and sat there through the entire service. The pastor said, 'Is there anything else before we dismiss?' Just about the time he was about to pronounce the benediction the missionary began to sob convulsively: he could not control himself. Somebody reached over and said, 'Friend, what's the matter?' And as he caught a glimpse of the missionary's face, he said, 'Why, it's our missionary! Our missionary has come back! Don't you have something to say to us?'

When he could control himself, the missionary said, 'I wasn't going to say anything, but I am now. The last time I saw you, you stood at the railway station: and you ran down the platform as the train started, waving and shouting, "We'll pray for you until the Lord comes." ' The missionary continued, 'I wondered why we learned the language so well. It's because you prayed for us. I wondered why the Lord blessed in the church so much, but I know it's because you prayed. Then, after two and a half years, you lost interest in praying. I

searched my heart, thinking that it was sin in my life. I've nearly driven myself crazy trying to find out where I've sinned against God to bring this judgement on me. But now,' he said, 'I know. I've sat through this entire prayer service, and you've not once mentioned the name of your missionary.'
(1 Sam. 12. 23)

**532 Interest—With Compound.** The farmer sat humped over the book on the table, his face matching the weather outside where the heavy grey clouds were dropping rain faster every moment. In the book were his accounts, and when he had done arithmetic and checked it with more arithmetic, he knew he was not mistaken.

His farm was doing badly. But what could you expect, with weather like this? It was all very well having a harvest thanksgiving service last Sunday, but the Almighty governed the weather, and just *look* at it!

Then the farmer found himself thinking about the reading from the Bible at that service. 'All the tithe of the land, whether of the seed of the land, or of the fruit of the tree, is the Lord's: it is holy unto the Lord' (Lev. 27. 30) He'd never thought that. He couldn't really grumble about the Lord sending bad weather if he didn't do his share.

The farmer stood up and banging the table with his fist, said aloud: 'I'll do it, that I will. I'll give Thee a tenth, Lord, of every harvest of corn for ten years.'

It was a small patch of only a few square yards in his garden where the farmer sowed his small bag of corn. He cut the harvest by hand one morning; ground some by hand and made some bread. One loaf of bread went to the pastor of the local church. The remainder of the corn went into half a small field behind his house. In the fall he cut the second harvest by hand in a day, and gave a tenth to the harvest thanksgiving service. With the remainder he sowed a complete large field. He harvested it with a tractor and cutter; sold a tenth and gave the money to the Lord. With the remainder he was able to sow three large fields.

For the fourth harvest he employed a helper; the fifth year he needed two; the following summer he had six men with three machines—and no more land. His sowing had reached the boundaries of his farm. But after a tenth of his money had gone to the Lord's work, he had plenty with which to purchase more land.

Seventh year ... eighth year ... ninth year.

'What an odd advertisement!' said Farmer Brigg to his wife over breakfast. 'It says here, "Farmer wishes neighbouring farmers to join him in large-scale test of Bible promise—to give over portion of farmland for sowing of corn provided by advertiser, to harvest same for own use with exception of one-tenth to go into the work of the church." I'll do it! Where's my pen to write?'

'Sounds an interesting advertisement,' Farmer Capon was saying. 'I'm going in on this!'

'It's an original idea—but all of us could do with more trust in God,' said Farmer Driver as he slipped his reply into the letter box.

And in the tenth summer after the farmer's promise, he and ten others were reaping corn off many acres of land with many machines and hired men. His face was serene and smiling now, though ten years older. At harvest thanksgiving the pastor read: 'The earth is the Lord's and the fullness thereof ...' and the farmer nodded, murmuring to himself, 'Aye; and the Lord never lets us down. Praise the Lord!'
(2 Cor. 9. 6,7)

**533 Interpretation—Laws of.** David L. Cooper often repeated the time-tested rule of interpretation: 'When the plain sense of Scripture makes common sense, seek no other; therefore take every word at its ordinary, usual, literal meaning unless the facts of the context indicate clearly otherwise.'

This rule has never been controverted, and when applied, the Word of God unfolds as a consistent whole. By ignoring it we meet with confusion or resort to conjecture.
(Neh. 8. 8)

**534 Invisible—Seeing The.**

*With my eyes upon the Saviour*
*I can walk the sea of life*
*With its waves and billows round me,*
*With its tempests, storms and strife.*

*Should I look upon another,*
*Look at self or turn my gaze*
*On life's problems and temptations,*
*I would sink beneath the waves.*

*Saviour, let me walk beside Thee,*
*Let me feel my hand in Thine!*
*Let me know the joy of walking*
*In Thy strength and not in mine!*

                               John Sidebotham
(Heb. 11. 27)

**535 Inward Man—The.**

*It is not clothes that make the man*
*Though dandy he may be;*
*It's something more important than his dress*
*For all the world to see.*

*It is a radiant beauty from within*
*That fills a man with power,*
*And permeates and glows and floods the life*
*Each day, and every hour.*

*But this is something money cannot buy,*
*For priceless is its worth:*
*It only comes from God Himself on high*
*Who sends it down to earth.*

*Through Jesus Christ alone these beauties come*
*To captivate the heart:*
*No earthly dress or pomp or show of any kind*
*Can in this have a part.*

*Sincerity, simplicity and love divine,*
*A contrite humble soul,*
*Are gifts the Holy Spirit gives to those*
*Whom Christ makes whole.*

*He then transforms the life and makes it glow*
*With virtuous gifts, God-given,*
*To shine for Him while here on earth below*
*And take right up to heaven.*

May Gorrie

(1 Pet. 3. 3,4)

**536  Israel and the Bible.** Mr David Ben Gurion in his Independence Day broadcast to the nation of Israel said, 'The profound and growing attachment to the Bible that we are witnessing in Israel is unequalled by anything known during the Dispersion. The study of the Scriptures which, for the last two hundred years, was almost monopolized by the Gentiles, is becoming a characteristically Israeli subject, and it is no longer possible to study and understand the books of the Bible without the fruits of Bible research in Israel. And yet we are only at the beginning of our work in this field.

*Sunday School Times*

(John 5. 39)

**537  Israel's Lost Tribes.** Ezekiel prophesied during the exile period to Israel (Ch. 37). Jeremiah the prophet links Judah and Israel. So does Daniel the prophet. 1800 families during the exile, made up of Levites, Nethinims and the children of Israel, went up to Jerusalem. The Dispersion consisted of 'twelve tribes scattered abroad' (James 1. 1). Jew and Israelite became synonymous terms from about the time of the captivity. In the book of Ezra the remnant is only eight times called Jews, and forty times 'Israel'. In the book of Nehemiah, the remnant is only eleven times called Jews, and twenty-two times 'Israel'.

In the New Testament Anna was a Jewess living in Jerusalem, but of the tribe of Aser (Luke 2. 36). At the dedication of the temple in Ezra's day the offerings were 'according to the number of the tribes of Israel'.

At Pentecost in Jerusalem Peter addressed his audience—'Ye men of Israel' (Acts 2. 22). In Pisidian Antioch Paul addressed his audience—'Ye men of Israel' (Acts 13. 16,17). In his defence before Agrippa Paul recognizes the existence of the twelve tribes of Israel (Acts 26. 6,7).

David Baron

Therefore we conclude that there are no lost tribes.

**538  Jealousy Overcome.** In Henry Varley's life story mention is made of a neighbouring pastor whose ministry was attracting some of Varley's congregation who were frequently missing from his own audience. To his intense loathing the green-eyed monster set its claws on his soul, followed by a strong sense of guilt and sin. 'Was I really showing inability to rejoice in another worker's service?' he thought. The grace of God then gave him the victory over the foul image of jealousy.

Dr F. B. Meyer used to say he found it easier to pray for Dr Campbell Morgan when the latter was in America than when he returned to England and took Westminster Chapel, not far from Christ Church (Dr Meyer's place) and got larger audiences than he himself had. He found this jealousy eating away the joy of his life and set out to overcome it. He prayed about it; then, calling together the elders of his church, he suggested that they should officially invite Campbell Morgan and his family to their church and give them a reception. To this they all agreed. At the reception he told his congregation of his love for Campbell Morgan, of his daily remembrance of them in prayer, and of the conflict within his heart arising from jealousy. Then he told them how he prayed often for Campbell Morgan and his ministry and for C. H. Spurgeon, and found that the more he prayed for them and their ministry, the less he needed to wrestle in prayer for himself and his ministry. The result was that God filled the Chapel and the Tabernacle so full that they overflowed, and his own congregation was bigger than ever before.

(Ezek. 8. 5)

**539  Jehovah's Titles.** Our problem is not to know how the Lord will make His presence real to us, only to know who has made the promise; He is faithful to fulfil it. Thus we learn that Jehovah-jireh (Gen. 22. 14) is our hope, our Provider. Jehovah-rapha (Exod. 15. 26) is our Healer. Jehovah-nissi (Exod. 17. 15) is our Heart, our Praise. Jehovah-Shalom (Judg. 6. 23,24) is our Haven of Rest, our peace in the midst of perplexity and impossibility. Jehovah-ra-ah (Ps. 23. 1) is our unfailing Helper, our Protector. Jehovah-tsidkenu (Jer. 23. 5,6) is our Holiness, our Purity. Jehovah-shammah (Ezek. 48. 35) is our Home, our unfailing Presence made real to us by the ever-present, indwelling Holy Spirit.

G. R. Erdman

**540  Jerusalem Besieged.** It was nearing Christmas day in December, 1917. The ancient city of Jerusalem was besieged by a section of the British army under the command of General Allenby. The Turks, possessors and occupiers of the city, refused to surrender. Allenby could have bombed and captured it by force, but, being a Christian general with a desire to preserve the lives of the residents and to keep Jerusalem intact, if possible, he cabled to the British Premier for instructions.

The reply to his cable—from the King—was 'Consult your Master!'—which meant, 'Pray about it.' Just then the Turks ran up the white flag and surrendered. General Allenby, bare-headed and leading his horse, entered Jerusalem at the head of his troops, almost nineteen centuries after the Lord Jesus,

Jerusalem's King entered it in triumph, seated on an ass's colt.

(Zech. 9. 9)

## 541 Jesus Himself.

*A dusty road, a setting sun,*
*Two hearts weighed down with fear,*
*A present grief, a future blank,*
*Then—Jesus Himself drew near.*

*A little group and close-shut doors,*
*(No ray of hope is here)*
*A voice they heard, 'Peace unto you',*
*And Jesus Himself drew near.*

*Just two or three, together met,*
*In that blest name so dear,*
*Agreed on earth, a thing to ask,*
*And Jesus Himself is near.*

*The blackest day, the dullest hour,*
*When clouds ne'er seem to clear;*
*Our hearts can sing, for this we know*
*That Jesus Himself is near.*

Ray Guyatt

(Matt. 18. 20)

## 542 Jesus Himself.

*There is an eye that sees, an ear that hears,*
*And close at hand is One whose presence*
*cheers*
*When faded hopes have left us in despair*
*And disappointment meets us ev'rywhere.*

*Jesus Himself drew near in gracious form*
*And resurrection might—Hushed was the storm*
*That round Him raged and in its fury fell.*
*Had He not said that He dread death would*
*quell?*

*And of Himself he spoke—Oh, mighty theme!*
*Longed not their hearts for Him who would*
*redeem*
*Not Israel only but creation vast,*
*O'er which rebellious powers their spell had*
*cast?*

*Perchance they saw the nail-prints in His*
*hands!*
*The burning heart, enlightened, understands.*
*The Christ who suffered is the Christ who lives:*
*What solace to the aching heart He gives!*

*Jesus Himself amidst His own appears;*
*His charming word of peace dispels their*
*fears,*
*And overwhelming joy fills ev'ry heart;*
*Yes! blessedness immortal is their part.*

*To Olivet the Saviour leads His own,*
*From thence ascends to grace the eternal*
*throne;*
*His servants true, with never-failing zest,*
*Will make the souls of men their life-long*
*quest.*

*The Lord Himself from heaven will return;*
*Till then our hearts can only for Him yearn:*
*And He the travail of His soul shall see,*
*And 'satisfied' our loving Lord will be!*

A. H. Storrie

(Luke 24. 15)

## 543 Jesus Our Lord.

A big lump of something like stone lay for a long time in a shallow limpid brook in North Carolina. People passing that way saw only an ugly lump and passed on. A poor man passing one day saw the heavy lump—a good thing to hold his door ajar—and took it home. A geologist who stopped at the poor man's door saw a lump of gold, the biggest lump of gold ever found east of the Rockies.

Many people looked upon Jesus. Some saw only a Galilean peasant and turned away. Some saw a prophet and stopped to listen. Some saw the Messiah and worshipped. Some saw the Lamb of God and looked to Him to save them from their sins. There are people today who see in Jesus only a perfect man, and they get nothing more from Him than the example of His life. Others see the Lamb of God, the divinely chosen sacrifice and Saviour—and, realizing that their greatest need is to be saved, they go to Him for Salvation.

*Sunday School Times*

(Matt. 16. 13,15)

## 544 Jesus Slept: Jesus Wept.

*When the storm was fiercely blowing*
*While the sea was wildly flowing,*
*Angry wind and angry billow*
*Only rocked the Saviour's pillow—*
*JESUS SLEPT.*

*But when sudden grief was rending*
*Human hearts in sorrow bending,*
*When He saw the sisters weeping*
*Where the brother's form was sleeping,*
*JESUS WEPT.*

(Matt. 8. 24; John 11. 35)

## 545 Jesus—Sovereign Lord.

Jean Paul Richter described the Lord Jesus as the Holiest among the mighty, and the Mightiest among the holy, who has lifted with His pierced hands empires off their hinges, turned the stream of centuries out of its channel, and still governs the ages.

Canon Rock wrote of Him:

*He is the lonely Greatness of the world*
*(His eyes are dim):*
*His power it is holds up the Cross*
*That holds up Him.*

(Luke 1. 32)

## 546 Jewels All Dedicated.

Frances Ridley Havergal wrote her famous consecration hymn 'Take my life and let it be' in 1874, but it was not till 1878 that the lines appeared in print. When she read the second stanza in print— 'Take my silver and my gold; not a mite would I withhold'— she was suddenly convicted of her own failure to do just that, for she had an amazing collection of exquisite jewellery, most of which came by gift or inheritance; and among them an unusually fine jewel cabinet.

Miss Havergal immediately packed the jewel box full (except for half a dozen pieces

which were special memorials of her parents and relatives) and sent it to her church missionary society. Then, just to be sure, she included a cheque to cover the monetary value of the jewels she had chosen to keep. 'I don't think I need to tell you that I have never packed a box with such pleasure,' she exclaimed.
(1 Chron. 29. 9)

**547 Jewry on the Move.** There are great movements in Jewry today, and they are undoubtedly an indication that the Lord is about to come. The Jew in the synagogue still recites at the morning prayer his faith in the coming of the Messiah when he says,

'I believe with all my heart, with all faith, in the coming of the Messiah, and though He tarry yet will I wait for Him daily.'

The former Prime Minister of Israel, David Ben Gurion, made an appeal to the Jews of the world when he told them that the only country where they would be welcomed was the land of Israel. The last sovereign State existed in Judaea in the days of Zedekiah, approximately 500 B.C., Jeremiah's predictions being literally fulfilled.

The Jews are returning to Palestine from over one hundred different countries. It is true that they are going back in unbelief, but the regathering must come first and their conversion afterwards.

The Jews can bring a criminal to justice today because they have their own courts. It will be remembered that Eichmann was charged and condemned before a Jewish court; and the whole world admired the dignity with which the proceedings were conducted, because barristers and judges of the High Court were all trained in Oxford and Cambridge.
(Isa. 1. 26; Jer. 31. 8)

**548 Jews in Russia.** Emmanuel Litvinoff, author of *Crown for Cain* and *Lost European*, writing in *The Listener* for January, 1963, recounts the following incident:

'With a companion I got into a train in the Moscow subway. We were talking in English, and people stared at us with avid curiosity. A young man followed when we alighted, and his close scrutiny of my features made me a little uncomfortable. 'You are Jewish?' he asked in English with an uncertain accent. I nodded. He stood on the escalator at my side, with a curiously irresolute smile, then suddenly bent close and whispered 'SHEMA ISRAEL'; and hurried away as if afraid to be detained in conversation. These are the opening words of the familiar Jewish prayer, 'Hear, O Israel, the Lord thy God; the Lord is one'—a strange thing to have murmured in one's ear in the capital of the Marxist world. Many Jews visiting Russia have had such tentative encounters. It was 1956, the year Khrushchev first spoke out against Stalin, and I have often wondered if that young man would feel it necessary to be so cryptic now. Perhaps not, but he would still have to think before speaking,

and there are some things he would prefer to leave unsaid.'

Among Soviet intellectuals one of the hallmarks of quality is to be outspokenly opposed to anti-Semitism. Consider the poem 'Balu-Yar' by the young Russian poet Yentushenko, in which he declared:

'*Let the Internationale ring out
When the last anti-Semite on earth is buried.*'

This poem was a manifesto, a declaration of faith, endorsed by these Soviet humanists. Many poems on similar themes are written in other countries, but they would scarcely make news. It is some indication of conditions in Russia that the young people of Moscow went wild with enthusiasm over the poet who wrote 'Balu Yar', and that in Soviet synagogues the poem is read.
(Deut. 6. 4,5)

**549 John Chapter 5, Verse 24.** John 5. 24 is the middle verse of the fifth chapter of John's Gospel. In it there are five verbs, that connote—attention, reception, possession, exemption and transition (hear, believe, have, shall not come—into judgement, passed from—unto—). Here are five-finger exercises in the melody of heaven, five pillars in the House of Salvation, five links in the chain of life, five strands in the lifeline of grace, five spans in the bridge from sin to God; and it has been used by the Spirit of God to bring to many the knowledge of salvation by faith in the Lord Jesus Christ.

*Rejoice with me, and praise the Lord
Both now and evermore
For that blest portion of His word,
John five and twenty-four.*

*I trusted in Christ's finished work:
My soul could ask no more.
This banishes all doubts that lurk—
John five and twenty-four.*

*No condemnation now for me:
No judgement lies before:
Exemption in Christ's words I see—
John five and twenty-four.*

*I know eternal life is mine
Since Christ my judgement bore:
In Him I have the life divine—
John five and twenty-four.*

*Until I see Christ face to face
I'll preach the whole world o'er
To men of every clime and race
John five and twenty-four.*

A.N.

**550 Journey Through Life.** What a blessed word is this word 'through'! Are you in the valley of sorrow, disappointment, trial or darkness? Are the dark shadows falling depressingly across your path? Listen—you are travelling THROUGH! There is radiant brightness and perfect joy for you at the end of the journey, if the Lord is your Shepherd.

In Damascus there is a long, dark lane which ends in a tunnel. The traveller descends and passes through the tunnel, and on the other side he emerges into the courtyard of a beautiful oriental palace, flashing with colour and sunlight. We are now in the valley, the tunnel, but we are going through to the sunlight of our heavenly home. What a prospect!

Francis W. Dixon

(Ps. 23. 4; 84. 6)

**551 Journey Through Life.** Life's journey has been described under various similitudes. It has been likened to a voyage of which Dean Alford writes:

> My barque is wafted to the strand
> By breath divine;
> And on the helm there rests a hand
> Other than mine.
>
> One who is known in storms to sail
> I have on board,
> Above the raging of the gale
> I hear my Lord.
>
> Safe to the land, safe to the land,
> The end is this;
> And then with Him go hand in hand
> Far into bliss.

It is well known that the New Testament likens life to an athletic contest or to a conflict in the arena. The going may be hard, and the real enemy is the devil who, using well tested tools, goes about seeking whom he may devour. Such an enemy demands watchfulness on the part of those whom he singles out for attack.

Arthur Hugh Clough writes of life as a long struggle during which one is apt to succumb, but his advice is:

> Say not, the struggle naught availeth;
> The labour and the wounds are vain,
> The enemy faints not nor faileth,
> And as things have been they remain.

However, it is to John Bunyan, the 'tinker out of Bedford', that the world of literature in general and the Christian fraternity in particular, are indebted for the fascinating description of spiritual experience as a journey from the doomed City of Destruction to the Celestial City on Mount Zion. A thousand pities it is that *The Pilgrim's Progress* is not better known today. The rising generation has lost its taste for that remarkable allegory.

A. Borland

**552 Joy.**

> You can be blessed and have joy to the full
> If you will follow this simple, wise rule—
> Give Jesus first place in all that you do;
> Let others come next and finally you.
> This surely spells Joy, Joy, Joy, lasting and true.

May Gorrie

(Phil. 1. 25)

**553 Joy in doing God's Will.**

> 'Grant me the secret of Thy joy,' I prayed.
> He pointed me a path of thorns and snares
> Which I must tread alone; forsaken there
> By those I loved and trusted. Dark the way;

> Wet with the dew of heaven and drenched by spray
> Of mountain torrent; slippery the stones,
> And sharp the rock beneath my feet. 'And must
> I joy in this?' I asked Him. 'Yes!' He said,
> 'This is the way the Father's will appoints.'
>
> And in an instant His strong loving arm
> Was round me, and we journeyed side by side,
> He lifting me over the rough places,
> I thrilling in His love felt no more pain,
> Or weariness, or loneliness. With Him
> The cost was far too small to count,—engulfed
> In something wonderful, ineffable.
>
> And in a moment of revealing light
> I knew that He had granted my request—
> The secret of His joy—the Father's will.

F.C.D.

(Neh. 8. 10)

**554 Joy in the Morning.**

> The dream had ended; hope had fled.
> There in that tomb their Lord lay—dead.
> The night was filled with weeping,
> But in the morning—joy!
>
> Without the presence of their Lord
> The seven toiled at Peter's word
> All night—no harvest reaping;
> But in the morning—joy!
>
> Have high hopes tumbled to the ground?
> Is life beset with trials round?
> Christ lives! We're in His keeping.
> Watch for the morning joy.
>
> The Spirit's leading let us learn
> While we await our Lord's return;
> There's just this night of weeping
> And in the morning—JOY!

(Ps. 30. 5)

**555 Joy Restored.** In 1895, writes Dr G. Campbell Morgan, I went to Douglas, in the Isle of Man, and in one of my afternoon meetings there came to me a young lady who said that all the joy had gone out of her life four years ago.

'Praise God!' I said. 'What about?' she asked. 'That you know when it went, because if you know when it went, you know how it went.'

She said, 'I do not think I do.' 'Yes, you do. You are very definite about the time; now go back four years and tell me what happened.'

She hung her head for a while, and I knew that something had happened. 'What was it?' I asked. She replied, 'I disagreed with my oldest friend. We were both Christians, and I wanted to tell her that I was wrong but I did not; and she has left the country.'

'Well!' I said, 'it is at least evident that you know the reason of your failure.' 'What am I to do?' she asked. 'Write to her and tell her that you were wrong. That is what the Master wanted you to do then.' 'I cannot do that,' she said. 'Well, you will never get back your joy until you do.'

She came all through the series of meetings and fought against God. She had all the knowledge of the blessed life that had come to her from her past experience, and yet was in darkness and distress because she would not go back to the point of disobedience, and be obedient.

The next year I went back to Douglas, and my first meeting was a meeting for workers. One of the first persons I spoke to was that young woman. I said, 'You have sent that letter!' She said, 'Yes!' Every line on her face convinced me that the joy had returned. She said, 'I wrote it last night. I have been fighting God for twelve months about that letter, and all last week, as I looked forward to this mission, I have been in anguish, and at last I said, "Oh God, I cannot bear this any longer. I shall give in!" I wrote that letter, sealed it, carried it at midnight and dropped it in the letter box, and as that letter went into the box, heaven came back into my heart.'
(Ps. 51. 12)

**556 Judgement Day.**

*When all the great plants of our cities*
*Have turned out their last finished work;*
*When our merchants have sold their last*
 *yard of silk*
*And dismissed the last tired clerk;*
*When our banks have raked in their last*
 *dollar*
*And paid out the last dividend;*
*When the Judge of the earth says, 'Close for*
 *the night!'*
*And asks for a balance, what then?*

*When the choirs have all sung their last*
 *anthem*
*And the preacher has prayed his last prayer,*
*When the people have heard their last sermon*
*And the sound has died out in the air;*

*When the Bible has closed on the lectern*
*And the pews are all empty of men,*
*And each one stands facing his record*
*And the great books are opened, what then?*

*When the actors have played their last drama,*
*The comedian has made his last pun,*
*And the talkie has flashed its last picture*
*And the bill-board displayed the last run;*

*When the crowds seeking pleasure have*
 *vanished*
*And gone out in the darkness again;*
*When the trumpet of ages has sounded*
*And we stand up before Him, what then?*

(Rev. 20. 11-15)

**557 Justice and Mercy.**

*The perfect righteousness of God*
*Is witnessed by the Saviour's blood:*
*'Tis in the cross of Christ we trace*
*His righteousness and wondrous grace.*

*God could not pass the sinner by;*
*Justice demanded he should die;*
*But in the Cross of Christ we see*
*How God can save, yet righteous be.*

*The judgement fell on Jesus' head,*
*And by His death sin's debt was paid.*
*Stern justice could demand no more*
*And Mercy can dispense her store.*

(Rom. 3. 26)

**558 Justice Satisfied.** Schimel was the leader of a Caucasian people that had long resisted the Russian advance in lands between the Black and Caspian Seas. Among his people bribery and corruption were on the increase, so Schimel passed a severe law that after a certain date any person convicted of bribery should be brought to the whipping post and receive one hundred lashes on the bare back.

The first offender was Schimel's own mother. Would he spare her? Or would the one hundred lashes be inflicted on his mother's back? Love said, 'Release her!' Justice said, 'Punish her!' The people, appealing to him for a final decision, waited to see what he would do. Then came the sentence, 'Take her to the whipping post.' Schimel attended personally. After five strokes had descended on her bare back, Schimel said, 'Stop! Release her!'

Then, stripping off his uniform and shirt, he said, 'I shall take the rest.' As his mother looked on ninety-five strokes fell on his bare back. Justice was satisfied, and love bore the brunt of the penalty. But the love of God goes beyond that: 'Jesus paid it all'; and the sinner may go free, for justice has been completely satisfied.

**559 Justified Legally and Absolutely.** Some years ago Captain Dreyfus, a French military officer, was charged with betraying secrets to Germany. After an unfair trial and in spite of strong evidence in his favour, he was convicted of treason and sentenced to life imprisonment. His friends, knowing him to be innocent, appealed on his behalf and a fresh trial was granted, but again he was pronounced guilty. Public opinion in his favour was so strong that the French President pardoned him and he was freed.

Captain Dreyfus, however, was not satisfied. He was pardoned, it is true, but not absolved from the charge of treason. Very soon the whole world, realising that injustice had been done, brought pressure to bear on the French Government, and a third trial was granted at which Dreyfus was absolutely and unequivocally justified, and his innocence established.
(Acts 13. 38,39)

**560 Key—The Master's.** One day a mechanic, who questioned the wisdom of God's ways in governing the universe, was marvelling at an intricate piece of machinery. He was told that all the movements were controlled from the centre which was in a chest. When he expressed a desire to see it he was informed that the master had the key. The words—'the master has the key'—came to him as the answer to his perplexities about the control of the universe.

*Life is a mystery; here the tangled skein
Unravelled cannot be.
The threads are too knotted, and 'tis vain
To try and get them free.*

*Yes! life is strange and tangled here below;
There seems but scant design.
In heaven a living, loving God will show
'Twas wrought with skill divine.*

S.T.F.

(John 13. 7)

**561 Kindness for Christ's Sake.** The night was cold and the wind was blowing up a storm. Conrad Cotta, an esteemed citizen of a little town in Germany, was playing his flute while his wife Ursula was preparing supper. Suddenly they heard a sweet but weak voice singing outside, 'Foxes to their holes have gone, every bird into its nest; but I have wandered here alone, and for me there is no rest.'

Hearing a knock at the door, they opened it and saw a half-frozen, ragged lad who asked for charity in the name of Christ. 'Come in, young man,' said Mr Cotta, 'we'll give you some food and a place to stay tonight.' Ursula immediately began to prepare a meal, but before it was ready the lad fainted from weariness and hunger. They tenderly cared for him, gave him a nourishing broth, and put him to bed. He seemed such a worthy teenager that, after praying about it, they decided to treat him as their own son. They sent him to school and he later entered a monastery where he found a Bible and he eagerly read it. From it he learned the way of salvation.

Unable to keep the good news to himself, he spread abroad the message of Romans, Chapter 5—'Being justified by faith we can have peace with God through our Lord Jesus Christ.' Little did Conrad and Ursula know when they took that young singer into their home in the name of Christ that they were nourishing the one who was to become the great champion of the Reformation, for the lad was none other than Martin Luther.

(Matt. 25. 40)

**562 Kindness—Human.** When John Huss of Bohemia was going to his death for his faith in Christ, an old friend stood out from the crowd and gave the martyr a powerful grip of his hand. It was a brave act, as it was dangerous to show sympathy for Huss. 'Only God and he himself,' said Huss, 'knew what that handshake meant to him in that time of supreme test.'

J. E. Harris

*Did you give him a lift?
He's a brother of man,
And bearing about
All the burden he can.*

*Did you give him a smile?
He was downcast and blue,
And the smile would have helped him
To battle it through.*

*Did you give him a hand?
He was slipping downhill,
And the world, so I fancied,
Was using him ill.*

*Did you give him a word?
Did you show him the road
To the heart of the Lord,
To the heavenly abode?*

(Luke 10. 31,32)

**563 Kindness of God.** The measurement of God's kindness is beyond calculation. His kindness is heavens high and worlds wide; that is its measurement in terms of space. In terms of charity, He heals our sicknesses and crowns us with loving-kindness; in terms of life He renews our youth like the eagles; in terms of sympathy He is better than the best of fathers to His children. Language sinks exhausted in its attempt to express at all adequately the kindness of our God.

John MacBeath

(Ps. 103. 3-5,11)

**564 Kindness to all Creatures.** President Lincoln, walking one day with his secretary, stopped at a little shrub and looked into it; then he put his hand down through the twigs and leaves as if to take something out. His secretary said to him, 'What do you find there, Mr Lincoln?' 'Why,' said he, 'here is a little bird fallen from its nest, and I am trying to put it back again.'

*Choice Gleanings*

(Luke 6. 35)

**565 King—Born To Be.**

*Some humble shepherds awestruck stood
Before a manger-cradle rude;
They gazed upon Emmanuel,
But did not know—How could they tell?*

*That Child enwrapt in swaddling bands,
Enwrapt in tender mother hands,
Was heaven's answer to man's need,
The Saviour of the world indeed.*

*Behold that child to manhood grown
Crowned on a cross and not a throne,
Dying accursed upon a tree
That guilty man might ransomed be.*

*By God's immutable decree
King over all destined to be,
Why should I not my tribute bring
And gladly own Him Lord and King?*

Andrew Borland

**566 King—No Place for the.**

*He had no place to lay His head,
He who was born a King;
Yet foxes had their resting-place
And birds their sheltering.*

*He had no place to lay His head;
While others calmly slept,
He on the darksome mountainside
A lonely vigil kept.*

*He had no place to lay His head*
*Except upon a tree*
*Erected by unwitting hands*
*On shameful Calvary.*

*But I've a place to lay my head,*
*Thanks to the Cross He bore;*
*And to the platted painful crown*
*Of thorn He quietly bore.*

*I lay my head upon His breast,*
*And hear Him sweetly say—*
*'Thy many sins are all forgiven;*
*Peace shall be yours alway.'*

J. S. Borland

(Luke 2. 15,16; Matt. 8. 20)

## 567   King of Kings.

*A king? They call him King! Is homage due*
*To such a one? A King? Can it be true?*
*The lowly Jew, born in far Bethlehem?*
*Men from all nations say He died for them*
*And rose from death, to hold a heavenly sway*
*To which all men must bow the knee some day.*

*'The king? He's not our king!' the Jews once*
   *cried—*
*'Away with Him! Let Him be crucified!*
*His claim is false. He is no king of Jews.*
*Away with Him! Kill! Crucify! We choose*
*Barabbas.' So a robber goes out free,*
*While Jesus Christ is led to Calvary.*

## 568   Kings' Son—A.
When Cyrus the Great was a baby, his grandfather, out of jealousy and fear that Cyrus would one day take the Persian throne from him, called a servant and charged him to take the baby away and destroy him. Instead of killing the baby, the servant gave him to a childless shepherd living in a distant province. Cyrus grew up supposing he was only a shepherd's son. One day he learned that he was a prince of the royal blood and an heir to the throne of Persia. After that there was no minding the sheep for him, for he immediately began to fit himself to rule the kingdom, and eventually became King of Persia. The turning point in his life was when he realized whose child he was, and that was the first great step toward the fulfilment of God's purposes for him.

Have we who have been born by regeneration into God's kingdom and are heirs of God and joint-heirs with Jesus Christ realized that God has a purpose for us to fulfil in His kingdom?
(Isa. 45. 1-3; Rom. 8. 16,17)

## 569   Kingdom of Christ.
Napoleon Bonaparte said, 'I have inspired multitudes with such affection for me that they would die for me. God forbid that I should compare the soldiers' enthusiasm with Christian charity which are as unlike as their cause. But, after all, my presence was necessary—the lightning of my eye, my voice, a word from me; then the sacred fire was kindled in their hearts. I do indeed possess the secret of the magical power which lifts the soul, but I could never impart it to anyone. None of my generals ever learnt it from me, nor have I the secret of perpetuating my name and love for me in the hearts of men, and to affect these things without physical means.

'Now that I am at St Helena, now that I am alone, chained to this rock, who fights and wins empires for me? Where are any to share my misfortune, any to think of me? Who bestirs himself for me in Europe? Who remains faithful to me? Where are my friends? Yes, two or three of you who are immortalised by this fidelity, ye share, ye alleviate my exile. Such is the fate of great men. So it was with Caesar and Alexander, and I, too, am forgotten. The name of a conqueror and an emperor is a college theme; our exploits are forgotten, and are tasks given to pupils by their tutors, who sit in judgement upon us, according us censure or praise. Such is soon to be the great Napoleon.

'What a wide abyss between my deep misery and the eternal kingdom of Christ, which is proclaimed, loved, adored, and which is extended over all the earth!'
(Luke. 1.33)

## 570   Kingdom Song

*Break forth, O earth in praises!*
*Dwell on His wondrous story;*
*The Saviour's name and love proclaim—*
*The King who reigns in glory.*
*See on the throne beside Him,*
*O'er all her foes victorious,*
*His royal bride, for whom He died,*
*Like Him for ever glorious.*

*Ye of the seed of Jacob!*
*Behold the royal Lion*
*Of Judah's line in glory shine,*
*And fill his throne in Zion.*
*Blest with Messiah's favour,*
*A ransomed, holy nation,*
*Your offerings bring to Christ your King,*
*The God of your salvation.*

*Come, O ye kings! ye nations!*
*With songs of gladness hail Him!*
*Ye Gentiles all, before Him fall,*
*The royal Priest in Salem.*
*O'er death and hell triumphant*
*Your conquering Lord hath risen,*
*His praises sound, whose power hath bound*
*Your ruthless foe in prison.*

*Hail to the King of glory!*
*Head of the new creation—*
*Thy ways of grace we love to trace,*
*And praise Thy great salvation.*
*Thy heart was pressed with sorrow,*
*The bonds of death to sever,*
*To make us free that we might be*
*Thy crown of joy for ever.*

E. Denney

(Rev. 15. 3)

129

## 571 Kinsman-Redeemer.

*'Sold under sin!' What a pitiful fate!*
*Where can we find a Redeemer?*
*Earning full wages both early and late—*
*Oh, for a Kinsman-Redeemer!*
*'Wisest of men, can you help us?' we cry,*
*'Seraphim holy, archangels on high,*
*Unfallen angels?'—they mournfully sigh,*
*'We cannot be your Redeemer!'*

*Hark! from the bound of eternity swells—*
*'Lo, I will be your Redeemer!'*
*Type, shadow, off'ring successively tells*
*Promise of coming Redeemer.*
*Author of life, yet in Bethlehem's stall*
*Born of a virgin—but God over all.*
*Low at his feet we adoringly fall,*
*Jesus, long-promised Redeemer.*

*See Him ascending up Calvary's hill,*
*Jesus, our Kinsman-Redeemer.*
*Come is the Surety to settle the bill,*
*Come is our blessed Redeemer,*
*Payment is made to the very last mite;*
*Signed is the contract and finished the fight;*
*'Settled' is writ o'er the bill in God's sight—*
*'Finished!' O glorious Redeemer.*

*See on the third day triumphant He stands;*
*Death cannot hold our Redeemer.*
*Marks of His passion in feet, side and hands,*
*Risen ascended Redeemer!*
*Soon will He gather His blood-purchased Bride,*
*Freed, furnished, fitted to sit at His side,*
*Reign then as Monarch where He meekly He died;*
*Hail to Thee, Kinsman-Redeemer!*

Ransome W. Cooper
(Heb. 2. 14, 15; Job. 19. 25)

## 572 Knit Together.

The interesting expression 'knit together' occurs twice in the Epistle to the Colossians, and these occurrences picture two separate pictures of God's people; the first, the phalanx as formed by the ancient Macedonian army; the second, the human body.

It is not difficult to envisage these, and this we shall do, but in an inverted order, the body first and then the phalanx.

The body suggests an organic union; the phalanx an operative unity. The body suggests a union in Christ; the phalanx a unity for Christ. The body emphasizes the union of life in Christ; the phalanx the unity of love through Christ.

The Spirit of God uses the picture of the body correctly to rectify what was wrong at Colosse, and He uses the picture of the phalanx defensively to protect the saints from further danger. (Col. 2. 9, 19)

## 573 Knowledge—Excellency of the.

'We are living in a more highly educated world than ever before and hence the servant of the Lord needs more education.' That's what the ad. said. Nor would I for a moment put a premium on academic ignorance, However, there is apparently a difference between education and wisdom.

In those days in which there was less emphasis on academic attainment we produced more young people who were wise enough to count the service of Jesus Christ as the happiest, holiest, highest goal of life. Today with all our vaunted preparation and our hard-earned accreditation, we are producing fewer missionaries proportionately than before. And who is there to say that those we are producing are doing a better job than the faithful servant of yore whose only claim to fame was a working knowledge of the Bible and a passion to reach souls for Christ?

Perhaps we have taken 'the excellency of the knowledge' out of its context. Perhaps we should rethink it in the light of Paul's full statement: 'Yea doubtless, and I count all things but loss for the excellency of the knowledge of Christ Jesus my Lord: for whom I have suffered the loss of all things, and do count them but dung, that I may win Christ.'

Dr Don. W. Hillis
(Phil. 3. 8)

## 574 Knowledge of God.

Mrs Cobley of Leicester, England, was a devoted hospital visitor. One day in the wards a young doctor accosted her with the words: 'Well, Mrs Cobley, I suppose you have been telling these people that God answers prayer.' 'Yes!' 'I am very glad to hear it, for I am very hard up. Do you think if I asked God for a five-pound note that he would give it me?'

The group around awaited her answer with some curiosity. She replied: 'Suppose you were introduced to the Prince of Wales today, Doctor, do you think that you could at once ask him for a five-pound note?'

The doctor haltingly responded, 'No I suppose I should need to wait till I got to know him better.'

'Yes, and you will have to know my Father better before you can ask Him for a five-pound note.'

## 575 Knowledge of God's Ways.

*I know not how that Bethlehem's Babe*
*Could in the Godhead be;*
*I only know the Manger Child*
*Has brought God's life to me.*

*I know not how that Calvary's Cross*
*A world from sin could free;*
*I only know its matchless love*
*Has brought God's love to me.*

*I know not how that Joseph's Tomb*
*Could solve death's mystery;*
*I only know a living Christ,*
*Our Immortality.*

Major Henry Webb Farrington
(1 John 5. 13)

## 576 Knowledge of God's Ways.

*Now know we not the meaning of life's sorrow;*
*Now know we not the pattern God has planned;*
*But comes the dawning of his glorious morrow—*
*Then shall we know—then shall we understand.*

*Now know we but in part our life's long story;*
*Now see we through a darkened glass and dim;*
*Then shall we see our God in all His glory,*
*Then shall we know as we are known of Him.*

*Then shall we know the love that passeth*
*measure,*
*Then shall we read the mysteries of grace;*
*Then shall we know eternal truth and treasure,*
*Then shall we see our Saviour face to face!*

E. Margaret Clarkson

(1 Cor. 13. 12)

**577   Knowledge of Self.**

*'Go to your bosom,*
*Knock there and ask your heart*
*What it doth know?'*

are the words of William Shakespeare.

Wise is the counsel of the poet, George Herbert:

*'By all means use sometimes to be alone:*
*Salute thyself, see what thy soul doth wear!*
*Dare to look in thy chest, for 'tis thine own,*
*And tumble up and down what thou find'st there.*

The great Apostle Paul said, 'I know that in me, that is, in my flesh, dwelleth no good thing.' (Rom. 7. 18.)

**578   Lamb—Christ's.** 'John, is the Christian life a hard one? Some boys say they are so persecuted.' 'Well,' said John, 'it's far easier than I thought. There are a hundred fellows down at our place, and four I work for are infidels. One day in the dinner hour all four attacked me. I bore it some time, and then, taking my Bible, I said, "My answer is in the Psalms" and I began to read as quietly as I could, "The Lord is my Shepherd; I shall not want." I didn't get through the psalm, though—they all sneaked out and I had to finish the psalm to myself. They have given me up. All they said was that if I had a Shepherd, I must be a lamb, and I was dubbed "lamb" by the whole hundred but that doesn't hurt. I might be something worse than a lamb.'

*Jesus is my Shepherd, guess who I am!*
*Such a lovely secret, I'm His little lamb.*

*Choice Gleanings*

(Ps. 23. 1)

**579   Lamb Lost and Found.** In 1861, as General Garibaldi was going home one evening, he met a Scandinavian shepherd lamenting the loss of a lamb out of the flock. Garibaldi at once turned to his Staff and announced his intentions of scouring the mountain in search of the lamb. A grand expedition was organized. Lanterns were brought, and old officers of many a campaign started off on the search. But no lamb could they find and the soldiers returned to their beds. Next morning Garibaldi's attendant found him in bed, fast asleep. Surprised at this, for the General was always up before anybody else, the attendant went out softly. Returning in half-an-hour, he found Garibaldi still asleep. After further delay, the attendant awoke him. The general rubbed his eyes and so also did the attendant when he saw the old warrior take the lost lamb from under the covering and bid him convey it to the shepherd. The general had kept up the search through the night till he found it. (Luke 15. 4,5)

**580   Lamb of God.** 29 times in Revelation (once without the article) this title, 'the Lamb,' is found. Singularly it is a diminutive term, which describes a young, weak lambkin. Yet marvellously everywhere in the Apocalypse, 'the Lamb' is not feeble or helpless, but the strong, mighty Lamb. He is not the lamb to be 'fed' but 'feeding'; not the lamb to be 'led' but 'leading'; not the lamb 'following' but 'followed'; not the lamb 'meek' but 'wrathful'; not the lamb 'slain' and dead, but 'alive' and slaying His enemies.

A. C. Gaebelein

(John 1. 29; Rev. 17. 14)

*Lamb of God! Thou soon in glory*
*Wilt to this sad earth return;*
*All Thy foes shall quake before Thee,*
*All that now despise Thee mourn.*

**581   Lamb—Saved by a.** In the town of Woeden in Germany, on the tower of a fine church building is the carved figure of a lamb. It was placed there to commemorate the remarkable escape from death of a workman who fell from the high scaffolding when the tower was being built. The men working with him saw him fall and were transfixed with fear. When they rushed down the scaffolding to the ground with the utmost haste, they found their companion virtually unhurt. At the moment of his fall a flock of sheep was being driven by, and he had fallen on one of the lambs, which was crushed to death. The carved figure of the lamb was placed there to commemorate the incident, and also to remind all who came that way of the Lamb of God who died to save sinners. (Isa. 53. 5-7; John 1. 36)

**582   Lamb's Book of Life.** Dean Stanley used to tell a lovely story of two soldiers from the north of England who were undergoing some weeks of artillery practice in Woolwich. After their practice was over they had a day of sight-seeing in London, before their return to the North and arrived one evening at the door of Westminster Abbey just as the officer was locking up. Disappointed, they were about to walk away when a voice behind them enquired, 'Would you like to look over the Abbey now?' Turning round, they thanked the gentleman who addressed them and gratefully accepted his offer. The Dean, for it was he, led them round, showed them the wonderful architecture of the Abbey and its statuary, and paused before a monument erected in memory of one of Britain's foremost warriors. After reading the inscription to the attentive soldiers, he said, 'You may never obtain honour in this world such as that general received or have your deeds recorded on a monument like this, but if your names are written in the Lamb's Book of life, that will be your best possible memorial.'

As the men left, Dean Stanley warmly invited them to the early morning service on the following day and promised to meet them then.

Next morning the soldiers were again at the Abbey and were treated to the hospitality of the generous Dean. In parting he placed a small gift in the hand of each, adding fervently, 'Well, we may never meet again on earth, but be sure to have your names written in the Lamb's Book of life, and we shall meet above.'

The two soldiers travelled homeward and each received a warm loving welcome from the folk at home. One of them told his wife of their visit to the Abbey and added, 'A mighty kind gentleman was the Dean, but twice he used a sentence that neither of us could understand. He told us to be sure to have our names written in the Lamb's Book of life.' At this a tear fell from his wife's eye and he asked her what was the matter. 'It reminds me,' said she, 'of what my Sunday School teacher used to tell me. I know what the Dean meant by the Lamb's Book of life.' Then she explained the meaning as best she could to her husband. The result was that the two men went to a place where they could learn more: both were converted and became bright witnesses to the Lamb of God who took away their sin and in whose 'Book of life' their names were written.

(Phil. 4. 3)

### 583   Lamp of God—The.

*We need a light to shew the way when night*
    *grows dim,*
*A lamp to shine upon the road—all bright*
    *and trim—*
*That sheds a glow about our feet and lets us*
    *see*
*And guides us safely through the dark, from*
    *fear set free.*

*The Bible is the lamp God gave to light our*
    *way*
*And lead us on, through this dark world, to*
    *realms of day*
*So let us read this holy Book and we shall*
    *prove*
*Its Word to be a light indeed, and God is*
    *Love.*

                        May Gorrie

(Ps. 119. 105,130)

### 584   Lamp Unlit.

A gateman saw a motor car approaching a railway crossing one dark night. He quickly caught his lamp, and rushed out, swinging the lamp. The motorist came on and was killed by the oncoming train. The gateman was charged and taken to court. He was asked, 'Did you, or did you not, swing the lamp to that motorist?'

With trembling lips the gateman replied, 'Sir, before God, I declare I did swing the lamp.' He was discharged.

The gateman's best friend said to him afterwards, 'George, when you were giving evidence, why did you shake so?'

George answered, 'I did swing my lamp, but, may God forgive me, there was no light in the lamp.'

So today in many places of worship where the glad tidings and warning notes of the gospel should be sounded out, there is no light in the lamp, and therefore no guiding ray, and multitudes of travellers to eternity dash on to destruction.

(Matt. 5. 16)

### 585   Lampstand of Gold.

*Pure gold—pure precious gold—and yet*
*It doth not all the beauty show*
*That God hath willed, nor could it get*
*Such, save by many a hammer blow.*

*Like to the golden cherubim*
*That shadowed o'er the mercy-seat—*
*A holy thing—a type of Him*
*In whom all truth and mercy meet.*

*Nor could the lampstand, golden, pure,*
*Shining with sevenfold brightness so,*
*A glory of itself procure;*
*It needed many a hammer blow.*

*'One beaten work,' and formed by one*
*In whom the Holy Spirit dwelt,*
*Completing all the work begun;*
*The gold has skilful handling felt.*

*And there within the holy place*
*Their beauty met the eye of Him*
*Who planned the pattern in His grace,*
*Who dwelt between the cherubim.*

*O Father, let me ne'er despise*
*The chastening of Thy loving hand;*
*In all Thy working thou art wise;*
*Perfect I would before Thee stand.*

*It may mean many a hammer blow,*
*But if in all Thy hand I trace,*
*What is it, if thereby I shew*
*My Saviour's loveliness and grace.*

(1 Pet. 1. 7)

### 586   Land of The Living.

Someone said to a dying man, 'Well, you are in the land of the living yet.' 'No!' said he, 'I am in the land of the dying yet; but I am going to the land of the living where they live and never die.'

                      D. L. Moody

*It is not death to fling aside this lowly dust,*
*And rise on strong exulting wing to LIVE*
    *among the just.*

*Jesus, Thou Prince of life, Thy chosen cannot*
    *die!*

*Like Thee, they conquer in the strife to reign*
    *with Thee on high.*

(2 Cor. 5. 4)

**587 Last Letter of an Officer.** H. F. Hargood, a young officer of the Middlesex Regiment, aged 19, was killed in action, and the following letter to his parents was found in his kit:

'My dearest parents, I don't suppose you will ever get this, and I certainly hope you won't, as it is only to be sent to you if I am killed on the "Trench Stunt". I expect you have wondered (or will do so) how I regarded the prospect of death, for of course the possibility of it is always before me. As you know, I have always been expecting it, so it has not taken me by surprise. As for the rest, well, I have never been able to express it to myself, so I don't suppose I can do any better to you. Although I have not regarded the prospect with pleasure, yet I can say that it caused me no fear. I have, of course, such feelings to buck me up as the thought of being an Englishman, the descendant of soldiers and so on; but when it comes to the point such things are of little or no value.

'No, I have an assurance which is of far more use to me than any of these things, the knowledge of Jesus Christ as my Saviour; and He will be with me after death, the same as He has been with me the last three or four years. This has been of the greatest comfort to me, and—under God—I owe it all to you, my dearest parents, and I could never, if I lived a thousand years, tell you what I would want to, or thank you for all that you have done for me, and especially the best thing of all, in bringing me up in the knowledge of my Saviour. And if I am killed, remember that it is our Lord's will, and He who is our Friend knows far better than we what is good for us; and after all none of us would wish it otherwise, would we? I know you wouldn't, and though it means more for you than for me, yet I'm sure you wouldn't.

'And now, as I hope you will never get this, I will leave off. Goodbye, my dearest parents, don't sorrow.'

(Ps. 91. 1)

**588 Law of the Spirit of Life.** A father and his little son were walking in the springtime when the display of early beauty was at its best. 'What is gravitation, Dad' asked the boy. 'Gravitation, son, is the law or principle of nature by which everything is drawn to the earth. If you drop a stone or an apple, the earth draws it down, and so it falls, as they say, to the earth.'

'But, Dad,' objected the lad, 'look at these lovely tulips. They all go upwards. They are not drawn down.'

'True, my boy; but that is because another law is at work in them, the law of life, which is stronger than the law of gravitation and has freed them from it as long as they live. If I destroy the life of one by cutting it off, it falls to the ground.'

George Goodman

(Rom. 8. 2)

**589 Lawful or Unlawful Pleasure.** John Wesley's wise mother wrote this good advice to him in his college days. 'Would you judge of the lawfulness of pleasure? Take this rule: whatever weakens your reason, impairs the tenderness of your conscience, obscures your sense of God, or takes away the relish of spiritual things; whatever increases the authority of your body over your mind, that thing is sin.' (Heb. 3. 13)

**590 Lazarus Raised from the Dead.** Dr Harry Rimmer preached a sermon on the raising of Lazarus from his grave, and with a triumphant shout, proclaimed: 'Then Jesus came; that changed everything.' Homer Rodeheaver who was present was deeply impressed. Later, he narrated the sermon to Oswald J. Smith who took up the theme and wrote the poem, 'Then Jesus came'. That same day Mr Rodeheaver composed a musical setting for the poem.

*When Jesus comes the tempter's power is broken,*
*When Jesus comes the tears are wiped away.*
*He takes the gloom and fills the life with glory,*
*And all is changed when Jesus comes to stay.*

(John 11. 38)

**591 Leadership.** During the American Civil War, when the rival forces of the North and the South were engaged in fierce battle in the great conflict of the Shenandoah Valley, General Sheridan, in command of the Northern forces, hearing the roar of the artillery and the rattle of the musketry, rode down the valley to see how it fared with his forces, and was horrified to find the entire Northern Army being driven before the Southern troops. The moment was a critical one. Was it possible for his army to be saved from complete defeat? Rising in his stirrups and flashing his sword in the air, he shouted, 'We are going the wrong way, boys; we are going the wrong way!' The next moment that rabble, retreating host was transformed into a compact army. Facing about, with their trusted General leading them on, they rushed upon the enemy and converted flight and defeat into pursuit and victory. Following their leader, they won the day.

(2 Cor. 2. 14; 1 John 5. 4)

**592 Leadership in the Church.** That the church in India is faced with a serious lack of true leadership is patent to any thoughtful mind. While this fact in itself should cause concern, the problem assumes even greater proportions when we realise that there is still little indication that any such leadership is under emergence. Now why is it so? On the secular level, India has achieved solid gains since our political independence in 1947, and almost in every field of human endeavour, our nation has shown foresight, industry and acumen. Our leaders do count, and are held in respect in the highest councils of the world and, given further opportunity, there is no reason why we should stand behind any other country in national development within a few years. But when it comes to the Christian sphere, we are still largely dependent; without individuality, vision and vigour. We need a heart-searching, surely.

Most of the Christian groups in India are still but off-shoots of foreign organisations. Some of these groups might claim technical autonomy, but are largely ineffective as an instrument for the spread of the Gospel, because they have merely stepped into the shoes of foreign personnel and just maintain status quo without heavenly vision or passion for souls. It is still a fact that foreign missions will not freely and voluntarily support any true indigenous effort unless they have at least a remote control. This is foreign to the simple unencumbered plan of Christian missions taught by our Lord and His apostles. Yet God in His sovereignty is often pleased to bless the honest efforts of His people, however faulty and imperfect their vision.

We believe the Scriptures provide the answer. Spiritual leadership goes exclusively to men who are born of the Spirit, who accept without questioning the Word of God as verbally inspired and authoritative, and yield obedience in respect to every detail of life and service. In other words, the leader is one who himself is 'led,' one who has heard God's specific call to him, and endowed with confirmatory spiritual gifts, calls to other spiritual men.

　　　　　　　　　　　Justus Samuel, Bombay

(Heb. 13. 7,17 RSV)

**593　Leading Lambs to Slaughter.** The following is from a newspaper column: Charlie the ram is a born leader. Other sheep follow him—like lambs to the slaughter. Which is exactly why Charlie has been employed at the Tiverton Junction abattoir of Messrs. Lloyd Maunder. There he works a five-day week, pulling the wool over the eyes of the other sheep, and leading them straight into the arms of waiting slaughtermen.

Before his arrival, workmen had the greatest difficulty in persuading sheep to participate in the abattoir's production routine until someone hit on the idea of employing a 'wolf in sheep's clothing'. Charlie, previously a pet lamb on a local farm, received a few days intensive training from a stockman and soon got the hang of leading other sheep into the receiving pens at the abattoir. As often as fifty times a day Charlie leads unsuspecting groups of sheep into the stunning pens and then waits patiently to be let out at a side door. Nor does he look even a little sheepish as he bids his friends farewell. Although Charlie is the black sheep of the family, no one would think of sending him to the butcher's, for he is too valuable alive.

(Matt. 7. 15; Acts 20. 29,30)

**594　Liberator Lincoln.** In Springfield, Illinois, the birthplace of Abraham Lincoln, the President of the U.S.A. who emancipated the slaves, there is a museum which displays some relics closely connected with the life and history of the great liberator. One of these museum pieces is an eighteen inch square of silk stained with blood in a glass case.

The story behind the blood-stained silk is this. The President was shot while seated in a large opera house. As he fell over, a young lady wearing a white silk dress, seated in the next box, let him rest his head on her dress to make him as comfortable as possible. When she returned to her home, her first impulse was to have her dress laundered, but on reflection she decided to cut out the blood-stained piece and send it to the city fathers at Springfield. This she did, and they put it in the museum, with the inscription, 'To the man who liberated the slaves.'

That is what the Springfield citizens thought of the blood of the man who freed the slaves. Do we, the freed slaves redeemed by the blood of Christ, the greatest Emancipator of all, attach infinite value to the precious blood of our redemption?

(1 Pet. 1. 19,20)

**595　Life Apostrophised.** Mrs Barbauld in extreme old age wrote:

*Life! we have been long together*
*Through pleasant and through cloudy weather;*
*'Tis hard to part when friends are dear:*
*Perhaps 'twill cost a sigh, a tear;*
*Then steal away, give little warning—*
*Choose thine own time;*
*Say not 'Good-night!' but in some brighter*
*　clime*
*Bid me 'Good-morning!'*

(James 4. 14)

**596　Life Dedicated.** When H. M. Stanley found David Livingstone in Central Africa, he asked Livingstone to come back to England with him. Livingstone refused to go and two days later wrote in his diary, 'March 19th. My birthday. My Jesus, my King, my Life, my All, I again dedicate my whole self to Thee. Accept me and grant, O gracious Father, that ere the year is gone I may finish my work. In Jesus' name I ask it, Amen!' A year later his servants found him dead upon his knees.

His heart was buried in Africa, his body in Westminster Abbey, London; and on the day of his funeral to Westminster Abbey, the following verse appeared in a secular magazine:

*Open the Abbey gates and let him in*
*To sleep with king and statesman, chief and*
*　sage,*
*The missionary come of weaver kin*
*Yet great by work that brooks no lower wage.*
*He needs no epitaph to guard a name*
*That man shall prize where worthy work is done*
*He lived and died for God: be this his fame!*
*Let marble crumble—this is Livingstone.*

(Rom. 12. 1)

**597　Life Eternal.** 'Discovery of eternal life' is one of the items in the long-term research plan of the Soviet Academy of Sciences. Announcing it, Alexander Topchiev, Vice-President of the Academy, said the main biological target in the plan was the solution of the problem of ageing, and of what LIFE is.

But life for many is full of trouble, perplexity and pain. To discover a way to make it endless in this world is surely a doubtful blessing. Many in their misery seek death.

Eternal life is offered to all here and now by the Lord Jesus Christ. It is the life that is life indeed: it is abundant life here on earth and an eternal life of bliss in heaven. (John 5. 40; 6. 68)

**598  Life of Usefulness.**  A young lawyer sat at his desk and carried on this conversation with himself:

What are you going to do when you finish your apprenticeship? Answer: Hang out my shingle and practise law, of course!
What then?—Answer: Why, make a lot of money!
What then?—Answer: When I get rich I shall retire!
What then?—Answer: Well, I'll die!
What then?

His whole body trembling, Charles G. Finney rushed out of the office and ran to a park some few yards distant. He remained there in prayer, vowing he would not return to his office or to his room until he had settled his life-work. He saw himself as he was, selfish, ambitious, sinful. He gave himself for the Lord to use. Leaving the park, Finney stepped forth strong in faith in God, to a life of usefulness rarely paralleled in the last two centuries.

Moses had to make a choice between a trivial life and a life that counted. He turned his back on earthly fame, riches and comfort. He spurned the pleasures of sin. He saw all that the world had to offer as bubbles. To him the important thing was to serve God and to serve his neighbour. Because he chose as he did, we know him as we do.
(Heb. 11. 24,25)

**599  Life-Saving Squad.**  The late Dr R. A. Torrey related the following story: 'A number of years ago, in a university in a Mid-west State, a group of students organized themselves into a life-saving squad. Their purpose was to go to the rescue of drowning people in Lake Michigan. Early one bleak November morning, urgent word came to this group that the *Lady Elgin* with its human cargo had been caught in the jaws of a violent storm and was rapidly going to pieces. The college youths hurried to the scene of the wreck. In the life-saving group was an athletic young man named Ed. Spencer. Hurriedly he tied a rope about his waist and threw himself into the choppy, chilly waters of the lake. Swimming back and forth to the wrecked vessel he rescued fifteen persons. Finally, utterly exhausted, shivering with cold and hardly able to stand, he paused to warm himself at the fire. As he stood there, he suddenly saw a spar rising and falling on the waves, and above it he faintly discerned the head of another man. "Boys," he said, "I'm

going after that fellow." His friends tried to dissuade him from going, as his strength was gone; but he said, "I'll try anyway," and plunged back into the chilly waters and accomplished the rescue. Completely exhausted he was carried to his room in a delirious condition. As his mind cleared, he would intermittently ask, "Did I do my best?" "Yes, Ed," came the answer, "you saved sixteen!" But Ed replied wearily, "Yes, but did I do my best, my level best?" and all that night he kept mumbling, "Oh, if I could only have saved one more!"
(1 Cor. 9. 22)

**600  Life's Jig-saw Puzzle.**  I have heard many versions of the story of the jig-saw puzzle: this is the one I like best. A father, reading his Sunday paper and wishing not to be disturbed by his little girl, cut up a map of the world, gave it to her, and told her to put it together. He thought this would keep her quiet for some time. After a short while she returned with it and every piece was in its place. Very much surprised, the father said: 'Why, how did you do it? You don't know anything about geography.' The little one replied, 'There was a picture of Jesus on the other side, and I knew when I had Jesus in the right place, the whole world would be all right.'

The Lord Jesus in the right place! 'To be in all things alone supreme.' Thus Paul describes the right place. Christ must be pre-eminent in our lives if we want our lives to come out right. Christ must be first in our affections, even before family or friends. First and supreme in our thoughts, motives, purposes and above all before self: then everything else will be in place.
                                                    A. Hughes in *New Life*
(Col. 1. 18)

**601  Life's Lessons.**
*Sometime when all life's lessons have been*
    *learned*
*And suns and stars for evermore have set,*
*The things which our weak judgements here*
    *have spurned,*
*The things o'er which we grieved with lashes*
    *wet,*
*Will flash before us out of life's dark night,*
*As stars shine most in deeper tints of blue;*
*And we shall see how all God's plans are*
    *right*
*And what had seemed reproof was love most*
    *true.*

*But not today! Then be content, poor heart;*
*God's plans like lilies pure and white unfold.*
*We must not tear the close-shut leaves apart;*
*Time will reveal the calyxes of gold.*
*And if, through patient toil, we reach the land*
*Where weary feet, with sandals loosed, may*
    *rest,*
*Where we shall clearly see and understand,*
*I'm sure we then shall say, 'God knew the*
    *best!'*

(John 13. 7)

**602 Lifeboat Refused.** Some time ago in one of those tremendous gales which occasionally sweep the coast of Cornwall, England, a shipwreck occurred in the middle of the night. The signals of distress were heard and speedily answered by the gallant lifeboat crew at Penzance.

On reaching the wreck they witnessed a scene of unusual sadness. The captain of the ill-fated vessel, under the influence of liquor, was standing on board and would not enter the lifeboat, madly refusing to avail himself of the messenger of mercy sent to him in that moment of imminent danger. Not only did he refuse to enter the lifeboat himself, but, drawing his revolver, threatened to shoot the first man who would dare to jump from the sinking wreck into the lifeboat. All the entreaties of the coastguard men were in vain. The drunken captain, bent on his own and his crew's destruction, obstinately refused to leave the wreck.

Six of the crew, perhaps under the influence of drink also, joined the captain in his foolish refusal to enter the boat.

At length, the commander of the lifeboat sadly and reluctantly ordered his men to row to shore with those of the ship's crew who had braved the captain's wrath. Far on in that dark night there came a lull in the storm, and over the waters came the wailing cry, 'Lifeboat! Lifeboat!' Once more the gallant men pushed off toward the wreck, but alas! it was too late. The wretched captain and his six men had sunk beneath the boiling surf. They had vainly called for the rejected lifeboat when it was too late.

C. H. Mackintosh

(Heb. 2. 3; 12. 25)

**603 Light of the World.** Alexander the Great was regent of Macedonia at the age of 16, a victorious general at 18, a king at 20. He died before he was 33, having conquered the then known world. His father was Philip of Macedon, also a military genius who invented the famous 'Greek Phalanx'. While Alexander was still in his early teens, Philonicus the Thessalonian offered to sell Alexander's father his horse, Bucephalus, a trained but vicious animal. Philip took his son along to see the horse go through his paces, but the stallion proved so unmanageable that none of the men could even mount him. Alexander noted that he seemed to be afraid of his own shadow, so he quieted the horse by turning its head toward the sun. Then Alexander mounted the horse and by keeping him headed toward the sun, got him under control.

Millions today are afraid of their own shadows, but let some faithful Christian point them to Christ, and their shadows immediately fall behind them for Christ is 'the Light of the world'. All who follow Him 'shall not walk in darkness but shall have the light of life'. The closer one walks to Him the more light one has; and the further one walks from Christ, the deeper are the shadows.

(John 8. 12)

**604 Light Rays.** Science tells us that pure light is made up of three primary colours, and that when intercepted by rain or a glass prism, it is broken up into its seven hues, forming the spectrum. It further tells us that, apart from the rays of pure light, all plant life is colourless, and that a rose is red only because it is capable of imbibing the red rays of pure light and that a leaf is green because it is capable of imbibing the green and blue rays of pure light and excluding the red.

It is a solemn thought that that which we reflect is only that which we are capable of imbibing, whether it be good or bad. We may not only look upon the glory of the Lord but we may catch from it and reflect a radiance that will be apparent to others.

R. G. Thompson

(2 Cor. 3. 18)

**605 Lights along the Shore.** Walking after dusk with a friend along the harbour at Teignmouth, we had our attention drawn to two prominent red lights. Our friend explained that when a ship was entering the harbour, the skipper guided it toward those danger lights so long as they appeared in line. But he must not proceed too far, so at a certain point two green lights were seen to his left in line with the ship at that point, and he then turned the boat in the direction of the green lights which led into the wharf.

On one occasion, we were told, the skipper entrusted the wheel to his brother who was also a skilful navigator. As he was steering the ship in toward the red lights, he suddenly became aware of the beauty of the smaller lights that sparkled all along the harbour, and exclaimed, 'What a magnificent display of lights!' 'Never mind those lights,' sang out his brother 'keep your eye on the main lights.'

In our lives the two main lights are the Word of God and the Spirit of God: sometimes they are red and warn us of danger: sometimes they are green and bid us go forward.

A.N.

(Ps. 119. 105)

**606 Light's Characteristics** are:
1 the nearer we are to the source, the brighter the light appears:
2 light reveals; the brighter the light, the more revealing it is:
3 light reflects more clearly from a clean surface:
4 light reveals uncleanness but cannot itself be adulterated:
5 light is nothing to the blind: they cannot see it or appreciate it:
6 a person walking with his face away from the light walks in his own shadow, hence in darkness:
7 a person walking toward the light walks in the light:
8 light cannot dwell with darkness nor darkness with light.

C. F. Bundy

(John 1. 4,9; 3. 19; 9. 5)

**607   Lights Shining in the Dark.** D. L. Moody related in one of his meetings the story of a shipwreck on a dark and tempestuous night when not a star was visible. A ship was approaching Cleveland Harbour with the pilot on board. Noticing only one light—that streaming from the lighthouse—the Captain asked the pilot if he was quite sure it was Cleveland Harbour toward which they were sailing, as other lights should have been seen at the harbour mouth. The pilot replied that he was quite sure. The Captain then asked, 'Where are the lower lights?' To this the pilot replied, 'Gone out, sir!' 'Well, then, can you make the harbour?' was the captain's next question, to which the pilot replied, 'We must, sir, or perish.' Alas! in the darkness he missed the channel, and the ship struck a rock. Many lives were lost.

In his appeal, after telling the story, D. L. Moody said, 'Brothers, the Master will take care of the great lighthouse. Let us keep the lower lights burning!' This inspired P. P. Bliss to write the hymn, with the chorus, Let the lower lights be burning:

> *Let the lower lights be burning:*
> *Send a gleam across the wave.*
> *Some poor fainting, struggling seaman*
> *You may rescue, you may save.*

(Matt. 5. 16; Phil. 2. 15)

**608   Lion and Law.** India, formerly part of the British Empire, became a Commonwealth Republic in 1950, having been granted Independence in August, 1947. It has an area of over 1¾ million square miles and a population of over 600 millions.

The lion on the Asoka pillar at Sarnath, where Buddha preached his first sermon after his supposed enlightenment, was adopted as the emblem of the Republic of India. Its flag of saffron, white and green, has in its centre the Dharma Chakra, the wheel of the Dharmashastra or Law. So its people revere a dead lion and are under the Law. (Dharmashastra is the word consistently used to translate the word 'Law' in the Bible into several of the Indian languages.)

The Christian who acknowledges the Lordship of Christ is exhorted to stand fast in the liberty wherewith Christ has made us free. The symbol of our triumph and liberty is that of a living Lion, the Lion of the tribe of Judah, who breaks every chain and gives the victory. The believer is 'free from the law' and is exhorted not to become again entangled in the yoke of bondage.

'We are not under law but under grace', for it is by amazing grace that we are free.

A.N.

(Rom. 6. 15)

**609   Lions in the Way.** The kind of lions that trouble us need to be met with a firm hand and a courageous heart. Our adversary the devil goes about like a roaring lion seeking whom he may devour, but we are to resist the devil.

Mary Slessor, the intrepid missionary, who,

single-handed, turned back two tribes of warriors and stopped an inter-tribal war in the heart of savage Africa, once met a lion coming toward her on the path. She was alone and didn't even know how to shoot, if she had had a gun. She had only an umbrella which she aimed at the lion and prayed to God to help her, looking the beast straight in the eyes. She stood still and said firmly, 'Get out of here in the name of the Lord Jesus.' The lion stopped in his tracks and sniffed at the point of her umbrella. Nothing daunted, Mary Slessor repeated, 'Get out of here in the name of the Lord Jesus.' The lion turned and ambled away through the bush, leaving Mary alone. She did not go home and brag about her faith. We would not know the story except through men who came on the scene.

(Prov. 26. 13)

**610   Lions Roaring but Chained.** In John Bunyan's Immortal Dream, 'The Pilgrim's Progress,' Christian is seen approaching the Palace Beautiful where warmth, welcome and refreshment awaited him. Just as he drew near to the palace, he met two lions who roared at him, and he stood trembling in the path. One of the men in the palace, Watchful by name, saw Christian and called out in a loud voice, 'Stay in the middle of the path. The lions are chained and cannot hurt you if you stay in the middle of the path.' Christian did that and safely passed the lions. It took a lion on either side of the path to convince Christian that safety lay in the middle of the path. Lion's serve God's purpose, and sometimes God has to use the terrific roar of the lion to force the believer into the place where he would have him; and he can use the roar of the lion to awake the sleepy Christian.

When lions are known to be about, it is not necessary to call the flock together, for the sheep instinctively cling to each other. The soul among lions is driven closer to God. The very proximity of danger makes the believer's tower of safety more evident; and prayer is spontaneous when danger is imminent. The name of the Lord is a strong tower: the righteous runneth into it and is safe.

(Ps. 57. 4; Prov. 18. 10)

**611   Literature—Christian.** D. M. Panton wrote: 'Christian literature never tires, never grows disheartened, never flinches and never shows cowardice: it is never tempted to compromise, it travels cheaply and requires no hired hall: it works long after we are dead. Christian literature is a visitor which gets inside the home and stays there: it always catches a man in the right mood, for it speaks to him only when he is reading it; it always sticks to what it says and never answers back, and it is bait left permanently in the pool. The printed messenger is deathless: you can destroy one but the press can produce millions more; as often as it is martyred it is raised again—the ripple started can widen down the centuries until it reaches the shores of eternity.'

Dr Oswald J. Smith wrote: 'What was it that gave us the Reformation? You say it was Martin Luther's preaching. I do not believe that it was. Martin Luther wrote nearly 100 books and circulated them throughout Western Europe, and as a result of the WRITINGS of Martin Luther, there came the Reformation. Where would you have been today if it had not been for the Reformation?

'I believe that the greatest miracle of our day and generation is the increasing literacy around the world. Three million people learn to read every seven days. What does that mean?

'It means that last week three million people who could not read a single word are able to read this week. It means that next week another three million people who cannot read a single word this week will be able to read next week. Three million people every week—150 million people a year.

'That has never happened before in the 6,000 years of man's history on earth. Up until our generation only a handful of people have been able to read in comparison to the vast number unable. But today the peoples of the world are learning to read.

'But what are they going to read? The Communists have the answer. They know something of the power of the printed page. Do you know what you would see if you were to visit the Asiatic world and look at the bookstalls? You would see beautifully coloured magazines. They are the magazines of the Communists. The Communist presses are going day and night turning out ton upon ton of literature. Very little of it is being sent to the Western world. Most of its goes to Africa and the different Asiatic countries.

'Why, they even claim they won China by the printed page. Now they want to win the whole world. Do you know how many pieces of literature the Communists printed in one year? Within just one year they printed two pieces of literature for every man, woman, every boy, and every girl on the face of the earth. The Communists are on the job.

'What else would you see on the bookstands? You will see another series of beautifully printed magazines. They are put out by Jehovah's Witnesses. Do you realise that Jehovah's Witnesses have one press, which is the largest religious press in the world, and that it runs day and night? It prints no less than 500 magazines a minute. That means 84,000,000 magazines a year. They are sent to the Asiatic world, to Africa and to many other countries. They are going to win them to their cult if at all possible. They put their money where it will count most. They put it into the printed page, into the messsage.

'Do you know how much money the Seventh Day Adventists put aside in one year for the printed page? They set aside over £5,000,000. They know something of the power of the printed page and are determined to get their message out.

'I know of no other way by which we can carry out the Lord's command to reach every creature, apart from the printed page. I know of no method to compare with the printed page. It is needed on every field. Let us put out simple salvation messages, filled with Scripture, and let us circulate them far and wide.

**612  Longevity of the Kings of Judah.** Only one, the first, lived to be threescore and ten.

David died at 70: Solomon at 60: Rehoboam at 58: they each reigned 40 years. Jehoshaphat died at 60: Jehoram at 40: Ahaziah at 43: Joash at 47: Amaziah died at 54: Uzziah at 68: Jotham at 41: Ahaz at 36: Hezekiah at 54: Manasseh died at 67: Amon at 24: Josiah at 39: Jehoiakim at 36: Zedekiah (or Jehoiachin) lost his eyes at 32 and was taken captive to Babylon: yet Jehoiada, God's high priest, lived to be 130.

**613  Looking Back.** Roger Bannister was the first man to run a mile in four minutes. Three months later John Landy topped his record by 1.4 seconds. Three months later the two met together for a historic race. As they moved into the last lap, the other contestants were trailing far behind. Landy was ahead. It looked as if he would win, but as Landy neared the finish he was haunted by the question: Where is Bannister? As Landy reviewed the race for The Time reporter, he said, 'If I hadn't looked back, I would have won the race.'

'Back' in Luke 9. 62 means 'the things behind'. (Luke 17. 32; Phil. 3. 13)

**614  Looking Off.** Prince Charlie was waiting at the head of a glen to see if the Highlanders would come to his call and rally round his standard. Lochiel had heard of the landing of the Prince and brought the Camerons to meet him. On his way he visited his brother, and the advice which his brother gave him was this: 'Better go back. If you set eyes upon him, you will do all he asks.' So great was the attraction of that romantic figure.

It is true of a nobler and more stirring cause, that those who set eyes upon the Leader are willing to follow and obey Him.

A gay, worldly officer was wounded during a siege and became a cripple for life. As he lay through long weary months on his couch he read the Gospels and the lives of Christian heroes and martyrs, and he set his eyes upon Jesus Christ. He became His soldier and tried to serve Him, being irresistibly attracted to the Leader.

A certain Gallic nobleman was being led forth to die for his faith, together with some Christians of humble birth. He noticed that because of his rank he had not been bound with chains as they were. Then he said to the officer in whose charge he was, 'Let me not be deprived of any of my honours. I, too, for love of Jesus, would wear a chain.' He had set his eyes upon Jesus.
(Prov. 23. 5; Heb. 12. 1,2)

**615  Looking Up.** Over a century ago the French tight-rope walker astonished the world by crossing on a tight-rope the gorge just below Niagara Falls. Disdainfully discarding his balancing pole, he walked across the 1,100 foot cable without mishap.

At his farewell appearance Blondin carried a man across the gorge on his back. The volunteer was Harry Colcord. Halfway across, Colcord felt the cable swaying, took one agonizing look at the swirling river far below, and in a panic dug his finger nails into Blondin's back.

Before starting, Blondin had warned him, 'Don't look down.' Now he warned him, 'If you don't stop shaking I'll put you down.' That did it. The passenger stopped looking down at the angry, swirling waters and the rocks below.

The Christian should learn the lesson Blondin impressed on Colcord, 'DON'T LOOK DOWN!' If you don't look down, you will be looking up.

**616  Lord—Finding a Word for.** Bruce Moore writes of an interesting experience in looking for a word for 'LORD' in the Colorado language of Ecuador. 'How do you find a word to translate "LORD" to a tribe which has lost its chieftain system with the coming of the national government?'

Nothing in contemporary Colorado society seemed to fit the concept of 'LORD' and the Spanish—señor—meant only 'mister' to them. The one word we did find was MIYA: it alone seemed to have a meaning similar to Lord. But we were puzzled to find a variety of reactions when we wanted to call Jesus our MIYA. One informant said definitely 'yes' but others were undecided, and most rejected the term as applied to Jesus Christ.

We began to dig. What did a 'miya' do? Who could be a 'miya'? Was the local witch-doctor considered a 'miya'? The sheriff in town? The president of the country? Eventually a picture began to take shape, and then it became clear why they didn't want to call Jesus a 'miya.' A miya is one to whom obedience and allegiance is given—a very good parallel for 'LORD': but for most of the Colorados Jesus was nothing more than the statue of a helpless man on a cross, and certainly not a 'miya'. In short, they were rejecting the term as applied to Jesus not because 'miya' doesn't mean Lord, but because for them Jesus was simply not Lord! We had found our word.

*Translation*, magazine of
Wycliffe Bible Translators

(Acts 10. 36)

**617  Lord Jesus Christ.** We believe that this is 'the name that is above every name', and not the name of Jesus alone; for while many have borne the name of Jesus, our Saviour alone bears the name—Lord Jesus Christ.

In the early nineteenth century, Simon Greenleaf, Professor of Law at Harvard University, wrote:

'The great character portrayed in the Gospels is perfect. It is the character of a sinless Being, of one supremely good. It exhibits no error, no sinister intention, no imprudence, no evil passion, no impatience; in a word no fault; but all is perfect uprightness, innocence, wisdom, goodness and truth. The mind of man has never conceived the idea of such a character, even for his gods; nor has history or poetry shadowed it forth. The doctrines and precepts of Jesus are in strict accordance with the attributes of God, agreeably to the most exalted idea of which we can form of them, either from reason or from revelation. They are strikingly adapted to the capacity of mankind, and yet are delivered with a simplicity and majesty wholly divine. He spake as never man spake. He spake with authority, yet addressed Himself to the reason and understanding of men; and He spake with wisdom which none could either gainsay or resist. In His private life He exhibits a character not merely of strict justice, but of overflowing benignity. He is temperate, without austerity; His meekness and humility are signal; His patience is invincible; truth and sincerity illustrate His whole conduct; every one of His virtues is regulated by consummate prudence; and He both wins the love of His friends and extorts the wonder and admiration of His enemies. He is represented in every variety of situation in life, from the height of worldly grandeur, amid the acclamations of an admiring multitude, to the deepest abyss of human degradation and woe, apparently deserted of God and man. Yet everywhere He is the same; displaying a character of unearthly perfection, symmetrical in all its proportions, and encircled with splendour more than human.'

(1 Tim. 3. 16)

**618  Lord of My Heart.**

*Wonderful in Majesty, glorious and bright,*
*Fullness of Deity, Love, Life and Light;*
*Powerful in movement, mighty in word,*
*Sovereign eternity, creation's Lord.*
*Judgement and righteousness before Thy throne,*
*None to compare with Thee, Thou God alone.*

*Yet in Thy Majesty, boundless in love,*
*Grace in abundance caused Thee to move;*
*Wondrous compassion, bringing God's grace,*
*Showing His glory in Thy dear face;*
*Patient and tender was Thy sweet word,*
*None to compare with Thee, my Sovereign*
  *Lord.*

*Going to Calvary, bearing Thy cross,*
*There to atone for me, pleading my cause,*
*Giving Thy life and blood, ransomed my soul,*
*Loving me fondly, spending Thy all.*
*Calling God's pardon from heaven's throne,*
*Lord of my heart art Thou; reign there alone.*

William Wilson

**619 Lord's Supper—The.** Hymn for the remembrance meeting:

*O God most holy, turn we now to Thee,*
*Set Thou our minds from care and conflict free;*
*Humble our hearts as here we lowly wait,*
*Be this blest place as heaven's gate.*

*No rite nor bounden duty calls us here,*
*But the glad knowledge that our Lord is near;*
*Close all our thoughts to everything but Christ,*
*As in Thy courts we keep the tryst.*

*Thine was the grace that brought us from afar,*
*Thy changeless mercy made us what we are;*
*All that our ransomed beings can command*
*Humbly we bring with open hand.*

*Touch us anew with gratitude divine,*
*Draw from each soul love's true response to*
                                          *Thine;*
*Here as before Thy throne we bow the knee,*
*No man save Jesus, may we see.*

*So as around Thy table thus we meet,*
*Our hearts aglow in union pure and sweet;*
*With single purpose, and with voice as one*
*Sing we the praise of Thy dear Son.*

(Luke 22. 19,20)

**620 Love.** May not the failure that we some-times experience be due to lack of love? I find the following paraphrase of 1 Corinthians 13, suggested by an Indian translation, very chal-lenging.

If I have the language ever so perfectly and speak like a native and have not love for them, I am nothing. If I have diplomas and degrees and know all the up-to-date methods, and have not His touch of understanding love, I am nothing. If I have been able to argue success-fully against their beliefs and make fools of them and have not the wooing note, I am nothing. If I give my clothes and money and have not His love for them, I am nothing. If I surrender all prospects, leave home and friends and make the sacrifices of a missionary career and turn sour and selfish amid the daily annoyances of a mis-sionary life, and though I give my body to be con-sumed with the heats and fevers of the tropics, and have not the love that yields its rights, its leisures and its pet plans, I am nothing. Virtue has ceased to go out of me. If I can heal all manner of sicknesses and diseases, but wound hearts and hurt feelings for want of His love that is kind, I am nothing. If I can write articles and publish books that win applause, but fail to transcribe the word of the cross in the language of love, I am nothing.

R. Hurrell in *Workers Together*

**621 Love.**
*Though I, the tongue of men and angels have,*
*And, in the gift of speech, all men surpass,*
*I am become, if I possess not LOVE,*
*As tinkling cymbal or as sounding brass.*

*Though I, my knowledge of all mysteries prove,*
*And have prophetic gifts, all men above;*
*Though I have faith that mountains could*
  *remove,*
*I am as nothing, if I have not LOVE.*

*Though all the poor to me for food have turned,*
*And I to them have all my goods made free;*
*Though I may give my body to be burned*
*And have not LOVE, it doth not profit me.*

*For LOVE doth suffer long, and it is kind,*
*And envieth not, and vaunteth not itself;*
*Is not puffed up, nor hath unseemly mind,*
*And seeketh not her own in ease or pelf.*

*LOVE is not easily provoked to wrath,*
*Nor evil thinks, nor in iniquity*
*Doth it rejoice, but in the truthful path*
*And beareth all things in adversity.*

*LOVE hopeth and believeth in all things,*
*And LOVE endureth and shall never fail;*
*For should there be prophetic utterings,*
*Or tongues, or knowledge, they shall not*
  *prevail.*

*We now but know and prophesy in part,*
*But when that which is perfect comes to stay,*
*And understanding gives to every heart,*
*Then that which is in part, is put away.*

*When I was but a child, I spake as one,*
*And understood and thought with childish mind;*
*But when I had in manhood's state begun,*
*Then did I leave these childish things behind.*

*For now we see but darkly through a glass,*
*And only part before our eyes is shown,*
*But then, as face to face, shall vision pass,*
*And we shall even know as we are known.*

*And now of all the virtues that abound,*
*There doth these three abide the rest above;*
*Of FAITH and HOPE and LOVE; that which*
  *is found*
*To be the greatest of them all is LOVE.*

                                Charles R. Caie

(1 Cor. 13)

**622 Love Everlasting.**
*Master! Thou hast never failed me;*
*And when Satan's spite assailed me,*
*Broke my heart and stilled my song;*
*As I fell in fear before Thee,*
*Sweet Thy whisper floated o'er me,*
*'Loved so well and loved so long!'*

*Sharp the thorns that rise around me,*
*But the love that sought and found me*
*Stills the sigh and wakes the song.*
*Can He fail me? Never, never!*
*I am His and His for ever,*
*Loved so well and loved so long!*

(Jer. 31. 3)

**623 Love for God's Son.** A wealthy man lost his wife when his only child was very young. Then there came into his home a housekeeper to take care of that boy. He lived till he was of age and then died. The man had no other relatives, and after his boy's death he died heart-broken. He had no heir to his enormous wealth and there was a question as to what would become of his possessions. No will was found so it looked as if it would all pass over to the State. At last the State took it over, and they held an auction sale to dispose of his personal effects at the mansion where he had lived.

The old housekeeper who had brought up the boy from infancy, not having any money of her own, went to the sale. She could not buy the furniture; she could not buy the expensive rugs; but there was on the wall of the house a picture of the boy.

She loved the boy: he had been like a son to her. When the picture came up for sale no one else wanted it, so she bought it for a small sum and took it home. As it had been on the wall some considerable time, she began to take the back off and remove the glass in order to clean and polish it. But when she took it apart, some papers that looked important fell out. She took them to a lawyer who said to her, 'I guess you have landed on your feet this time. This gentleman has left all his wealth to the one who loved his son enough to buy the picture!'

God gives everything to those who love His Son, the Lord Jesus Christ: they are 'heirs of God and joint heirs with Christ'.

Edward Drew

(Rom. 8. 17; 1 Cor. 2. 9)

**624 Love for Lost Souls.** Nothing wins like love. It is the Saviour lifted up on the cross, thus revealing His infinite love, who draws men unto Him, and we, by our love to men, can win them for the Saviour.

At the close of a meeting in one of the suburbs of Chicago, the first person that rose was a very large man. I was attracted by his appearance, and afterwards spoke to him. He told me he had attended church and prayer meetings for years but had only gone to criticize; when men got up to speak in the prayer meeting he would take out his notebook and 'keep the tab on them', writing down what they said and then comparing it during the week with the way they lived.

At last he was taken very sick and was supposed to be dying. A minister of the town called upon him.

'You can pray if you want to,' the sick man had said.

'But as the minister knelt to pray,' he told me, 'I kept tab on him too. I thought I was dying, but I lay there with my eyes open, watching the preacher to see if he was real; thinking nothing about my soul, but about him. As I watched, I saw a tear stealing down his face, and I said, "This man is real. He loves me, though I am nothing to him," and that broke my heart.'

The man recovered and became an untiring worker for Christ, but he was not won by my sermon or by my dealing with him, but by the other minister's love. That minister never knew what he had accomplished by his prayer.

Selected

(2 Cor. 12. 15)

**625 Love for Sinners.** D. L. Moody said of his early preaching, 'I preached that God hated sinners, that He was standing behind sinners with a double-edged sword, ready to cut off their heads.'

In Dublin, at the close of a service, he heard a voice, 'Ah'm Harry Moorhouse. Ah'll coom an' preach for you in Chicago.' Looking round, he saw a beardless youth, very short, just up to his shoulder.

Moody was away when Moorhouse came to Chicago. On his return his wife said, 'He preaches a little different from you: he preaches that God loves sinners.'

'He is wrong!' said Moody. 'But,' said Mrs Moody, 'he backs up everything he says with the Bible.' Thereafter Moorhouse preached night after night on John 3. 16.

(1. John 4. 10)

**626 Love of Christ.**

*Love which gave Himself for me,*
*Love that suffered on the tree,*
*Love told out at Calvary,*
*My Saviour's love!*

*See Him in Gethsemane,*
*Prostrate there for such as me—*
*Sinless, spotless, holy He*
*In His great love!*

*Yes, He measured all the deep,*
*Distance, too, without relief,*
*Bowed in agony and grief—*
*Surpassing love!*

*For the guilty and the lost*
*Dying there upon the cross,*
*Oh! how infinite the cost—*
*What peerless love!*

*'It is finished!' loudly cried,*
*Every claim is satisfied,*
*God the Father glorified—*
*Triumphant love!*

*Out of death's dark tomb arisen,*
*Now He lives for me in heaven;*
*All He is to me is given,*
*For He is love!*

*Soon He's coming thence for me;*
*I shall all His glory see,*
*With Him then for ever be—*
*Eternal love!*

*Oh! what love to Thee I owe,*
*To the One who loves me so:*
*Ever deepen, Lord, that flow—*
*Responsive love!*

John Light

(1 John 4. 19)

**627 Love of Christ—Wonderful.** Thy love to me, Lord Jesus, was wonderful. When I was a stranger wandering far from Thee, fulfilling the desires of the flesh and of the mind, Thy love restrained me from committing the sin which is unto death, and withheld me from self-destruction. Thy love held back the axe when Justice said, 'Cut it down! Why cumbereth it the ground?' Thy love drew me into the wilderness, stripped me there, and made me feel the guilt of my sin and the burden of my iniquity. Thy love spake thus comfortably to me when I was sore dismayed—'Come unto Me, and I will give thee rest.' Oh how matchless Thy love when, in a moment, Thou didst wash my sins away! How Thou didst commend Thy love when Thou didst whisper in my ears, 'I am thine and thou art Mine!' Never shall my soul forget those chambers of fellowship where Thou hast unveiled Thyself to me!'

C. H. Spurgeon

*Himself He could not save;*
*Love's stream too deeply flowed:*
*In love Himself He gave*
*To pay the debt we owed,*
*Obedient to the Father's will:*
*And love to Him did all fulfil.*

### 628   Love of God.

*The manger where He lay*
*Newborn upon the hay,*
*The bench at which He toiled,*
*The hands His labour soiled,*
*The simple words He said,*
*The multitudes He fed,*
*The grave by which He sighed,*
*The cross on which He died,*
*His resurrection face*
*Bright with celestial grace—*
*All the long way He trod*
*Still speaks the love of God.*

Reginald Glanville

(John 3. 16)

### 629   Love of God—Sacrificial.

The emergency the world is in through sin calls for sacrifices that bring great pain of spirit. A young man in a small college in the Middle West in U.S.A. was stirred by the needs of a foreign mission field. He determined to offer his life and service to help to meet that need. But before committing himself actively he wrote to his mother, telling her of the burning desire in his heart, and asking her consent. By and by the answering letter came, blotted with tears. Its pages brought up a vivid picture of that mother's face and heart. She replied, in effect giving her consent, and then writing down these words, 'I never knew until now how much it cost God to give His Son.'

S. D. Gordon

(John 3. 16)

### 630   Love of God—Unending.

*All things that are on earth shall wholly pass*
  *away*
*Except the love of God, which shall live and*
  *last for aye.*
*The forms of men shall be as they had never*
  *been;*
*The blasted groves shall lose their fresh and*
  *tender green;*
*The birds of the thicket shall end their pleasant*
  *song*
*And the nightingale shall cease to chant the*
  *evening long;*
*The kine of the pasture shall feel the dart that*
  *kills,*
*And all the fair white flocks shall perish from*
  *the hills;*

*The goat and antlered stag, the wolf and the*
  *fox,*
*The wild boar of the wood and the chamois of*
  *the rocks,*
*And the strong and fearless bear, in the*
  *trodden dust shall lie;*
*And the dolphin of the sea and the mighty*
  *whale shall die,*
*And realms shall be dissolved and empires be*
  *no more;*
*And they shall bow in death who ruled from*
  *shore to shore;*
*And the great globe itself (so the holy*
  *writings tell)*
*With the rolling firmament where the starry*
  *armies dwell,*
*Shall melt with fervent heat—they all shall*
  *pass away*
*Except the love of God which shall live and last*
  *for aye.*

(Jer. 31. 3)

### 631   Love Others.

*Can it be hard to love and thus to follow Thee?*
*A life of love your footsteps trod, and you say,*
  *'Follow Me.'*

*Can it be hard to love when help comes from*
  *on high?*
*When power comes to keep Thy words—'Love*
  *others, love as I!'*

*A word so small, yet great: so simple, yet*
  *sublime;*
*A word so vast, so infinite—to pour on all*
  *mankind.*

*Can it be hard to love? Your Spirit walks*
  *with me:*
*He'll lead me in that life of love and thus I'll*
  *follow Thee.*

*Oh, Lord, please love through me; your spirit*
  *is the key,*
*The key that will unlock my heart that love*
  *might pour from me.*

*From me, my precious Lord, from me to all*
  *mankind:*
*Shed forth Thy love within my heart from me*
  *to all mankind!*

Carole Swaim

(Eph. 5. 2)

### 632   Love Proclaimed.

Early in the seventh century the good King Oswald of Northumbria requested the Scots to send a missionary to his people. The brethren of Iona sent them an austere, though well-meaning man named Cormac. He soon returned dispirited, saying the people were too obstinate to be converted.

'Ah!' said Aidan, standing by, 'had thy love been offered to them, O my Saviour, many hearts would have been touched. I will go and make Thee known, Thee who breakest not the bruised reed.'

He went and told the Anglo-Saxons of the Saviour's love. Wondering multitudes welcomed him, listened to his words, wept and were won by love.

(Rom. 5. 8)

**633  Love Sacrificial.**  One Christmas Day a young African woman came to give her sacrificial offering of thanksgiving. African Christians are extremely poor and can only give a handful of vegetables or a bunch of flowers.

The newcomer handed the missionary a silver coin worth a dollar. The missionary was amazed and at first refused to accept it, but finally did. At the close of the service the lady missionary asked the girl, 'Where did you get such a fortune?' Smilingly, the girl said, 'I went to a neighbouring planter and sold myself as a slave for the rest of my life to obtain that coin. I wanted to give to Jesus an offering which satisfies my heart.' She had brought the financial equivalent of her life and laid it down, in a single gift, at the feet of her Lord.
(Rom. 12. 1)

**634  Love Surpassing Knowledge.**

*I bore with thee long weary days and nights,*
*Through many pangs of heart, through many*
*tears;*
*I bore with thee, thy hardness, coldness,*
*slights,*
*For three and thirty years.*

*Who else had dared for thee what I have*
*dared?*
*I plunged the depth most deep from bliss above;*
*I not My flesh, I not My spirit spared:*
*Give thou Me love for love.*

*For thee I thirsted in the daily drought,*
*For thee I trembled in the nightly frost:*
*Much sweeter thou than honey to my mouth;*
*Why wilt thou still be lost?*

*I bore thee on My shoulders and rejoiced.*
*Man only marked upon My shoulders borne*
*The branding cross; and shouted hungry-*
*voiced,*
*Or wagged their heads in scorn.*

*Thee did nails grave upon My hands; thy name*
*Did thorns for frontlets stamp between Mine*
*eyes;*
*I, Holy One, put on thy guilt and shame,*
*I—God, Priest, Sacrifice.*

*A thief upon My right hand and My left,*
*Six hours alone, athirst in misery;*
*At length in death one smote My heart, and*
*cleft*
*A dwelling place for thee.*

*Nailed to the racking cross, than bed of down*
*More dear, whereon to stretch Myself and*
*sleep:*
*So did I win a kingdom—share My crown;*
*A harvest come and reap.*

Christina G. Rossetti

(Eph. 3. 19)

**635  Love to Christ.**  A little girl was playing with her doll while her mother was busy writing. When she had finished writing, she said, 'You can come now, Alice; I have done all I want to do this morning.' The child ran to her mother, exclaiming, 'I am so glad, for I wanted to love you so much.' 'But I thought you were happy

with your dolly,' said her mother. 'Yes, Mother, I was, but I soon get tired of loving her, for she cannot love me back.' 'And is that why you love me—because I can love you back?' 'That is one why but not the first or the best why,' said the little girl. 'What is the first and best why?' asked her mother. 'Because you loved me when I was too little to love you back.' The mother's eyes filled with tears, as she whispered 'We love Him because He *first* loved us.'

Indian Christian

(1 John 4. 19)

**636  Love! What is Love?**

*What is this thing called love?*
*Can tongue or pen describe*
*Its meaning or its heights or depths,*
*Its majesty ascribe?*

*Love bore our sins away;*
*Love gave us life anew;*
*Love opened wide the gates of heaven;*
*Love gave us work to do.*

*Love is of God, we read.*
*How can we take it in,*
*That He should love enough to give*
*His only Son for sin?*

*God has so loved the world,*
*But how can they know this*
*Apart from love I offer them,*
*An overflow of His?*

*Love nailed Him to the tree*
*For those who sin and hate;*
*Loving is giving, e'en to death,*
*A sacrifice so great.*

*God give me grace to love*
*As thou hast loved me,*
*That others too might share the wealth*
*Of riches found in Thee.*

*Have they no right to know*
*God loves without reserve?*
*Yes, truly they must see his love*
*As my life they observe.*

Ruth A. Atwell

(1 John 4. 7,11)

**637  Love's Conquests.**  Meditation on John 19

*What mighty love is here displayed*
*By Thee, the Father's only Son,*
*When Thou didst bow in death Thy head*
*To purchase thus a world undone!*
*The ransom price—Thy own heart's blood*
*There shed for me, O Lamb of God.*

*.O Love that moved Thee thus to die*
*To fit me for the land of bliss!*
*The Law's demands to satisfy*
*No price was found but blood like this.*
*What sorrows rent that form divine*
*To bear away such sin as mine?*

*The scourge, the spitting and the thorn—*
*What word can well explain the half*
*Of all Thy grief—the bitter scorn,*
*The nails, the spear, the mocking laugh;*
*Thy pains and cries upon the tree?*
*'Why has my God forsaken me?'*

*By Thee are all my needs supplied:*
*Thou hast for me the victory won.*
*Thy cross my refuge, let me hide,*
*For I am helpless and undone.*
*I in Thy wounds my healing see*
*And know that Thou hast ransomed me.*

E.C.

## 638   Love's Constraint.

*The Shepherd found me in his boundless grace*
*Before I even knew that I was lost.*
*My tiny footsteps scarcely had begun*
*To tread the path of danger ere I saw*
*The shepherd close beside me. 'Twas enough!*
*No sense of danger made me seek His arms:*
*I did but catch a sight of His dear face,*
*Then gladly let Him lift me to His breast,*
*And only after that, when I was safe*
*And felt His arms encircling me with love*
*Did He Himself point out the road beneath*
*And make me see the precipice below.*
*I saw His love before I saw my need:*
*I knew my safety long before I knew*
*The awful death from which He rescued me.*
*And though I cannot tell when this took place*
*Or when I first was clasped in His embrace,*
*I only knew He found me—I was His!*

Ada R. Habershon

(Jer. 31. 3; Hos. 11. 4)

## 639   Lowest Place.

W. Hake and R. C. Chapman, the Barnstaple patriarchs, lived together for sixty years. Mr Chapman once told a visitor, 'Brother Hake and I have been contending for sixty years,' and then naively added, 'but it has been for the lowest place.'
(Luke 14. 7-11)

## 640   Loyalty to Christ.

A young Jewess in Chicago was wonderfully converted and commenced immediately to witness to her fellow-employees. As some objected, the president of the firm told her she must stop talking religion to the other workers. 'All right,' she replied, 'then I shall have to leave, for I cannot work where I cannot take my Saviour and witness for Him.'

'O.K.' said the president, 'if that's how you feel about it, then you will have to give up your position.' Having an aged mother to support, she did not know where she could find other employment, but she answered, 'As you say, I shall give up my position, but I cannot be disloyal to Jesus Christ.'

On Saturday of that week a note from the president was laid on her desk. Opening it, expecting it was a notice of discharge, she read, 'We have a place of greater responsibility than the one you now occupy, with a larger salary. We consider you are the right person for that job, so we are offering it to you.'

One who is loyal to her Lord is one who will be loyal to her boss, if he does not ask her to do anything of which her Saviour would not approve.
(Col. 3. 23,24)

## 641   Loyalty to the King.

When Robert Bruce was fleeing from the English he came to a poor old Highland woman's house and asked for a night's lodging. 'Who are you?' she asked 'I am a stranger and a traveller,' said the king. 'All strangers and travellers are welcome here,' said she, 'for the sake of one,' 'And who is that one?' asked the king. 'Our good King Robert the Bruce,' said she, 'whom, though he is hunted by hounds and horns, I acknowledge to be the rightful King of Scotland.' She could not enthrone him except in her heart, but she would if she could; and in his rejection she acknowledged him as her rightful king.
(Jer. 14. 8)

## 642   Lydia's Opened Heart.

The Providence of God brought together in the first century A.D., in the Roman colony of Philippi in the continent of Europe, evangelists from Asia and a merchant lady from a Macedonian colony in Asia Minor. Lydia, the lady merchant, came from Thyatira, a city in Lydia, which was specially famous for its dyers of cloth. Possibly she took the name Lydia from her native province. Lydia was a 'seller of purple,' a cloth that received its name from a purple dye made from shellfish. The fluid from them was first placed on wool which turned it blue, then exposed to the sunlight which turned it first green, and finally purple. Then after washing in water it became a brilliant crimson. The material was then very popular and worn by the wealthy, for it fetched a high price. By this merchandise Lydia had doubtless become a very wealthy lady, carrying on a lucrative business in Philippi. She was also a religious woman, for Acts 16 introduces us to her at a prayer meeting composed, no doubt, of devout Jewish women. Guided by the Holy Spirit to the riverside where those praying women were in the habit of meeting, Paul, Silas and Timothy joined them, and Paul preached the Gospel to them. At that meeting Lydia was converted and became the first convert in Greece—or Macedonia, rather. How did her conversion take place? First, she opened her ears and 'attended to the things spoken by Paul'. 'Faith cometh by hearing and hearing by the Word of God.' Then the Lord by His Spirit opened her heart, and she received the Word with joy and faith. Then she opened her mouth to ask for baptism, and finally her home was opened to receive hospitably the Lord's servants.
(Acts 16. 14,15,40)

## 643   Madness—For Men's Salvation.

Rowland Hill, the noted evangelist, was often told that he was mad. To this he would reply, 'While I passed along yon road, I saw a gravel pit cave in and bury three men alive. I hastened to the rescue and shouted for help until they heard me in the town, almost a mile away. Nobody called me a madman then. But when I see destruction about to fall on sinners and entomb them in an eternal mass of woe, and cry aloud,

if perchance they may realize their danger and escape, they say I am beside myself. Perhaps I am, but oh that all God's children might be filled with a desire to save their fellows. More of this madness is needed.
(Jer. 20. 9; Ezek. 33. 6)

**644  Magnificence of Christ.**  'Christ shall be magnified in my body.'

*I dare not say I must succeed in life's divine*
*   pursuit;*
*'Tis mine to sow the precious seed but God*
*   must give the fruit*
*Thus will I serve, that Christ may be in all*
*   things magnified in me.*
*The way is often cold and drear, the burden*
*   hard to bear,*
*With many a sigh and many a tear, and many*
*   an anxious prayer:*
*Still I press on that Christ may be in all things*
*   magnified in me.*
*When enemies God's Word deny and unbelief*
*   assails,*
*When adversaries terrify and courage almost*
*   fails,*
*Lord make me bold, that Christ may be in all*
*   things magnified in me.*
*I hope the Lord will come again ere death my*
*   light shall dim;*
*If not, my hope is not in vain, for I shall go to*
*   Him;*
*And Christ, by life or death, shall be in all*
*   things magnified in me.*

*Choice Gleanings*
(Phil. 1. 20)

**645  Man for Me—The.**  A Christian gentleman was travelling in an out-bound train from London and, when it stopped at one of the stations, a mill-girl entered singing a pop song describing a man who must be kind, handsome, rich, loving and clever, each verse ending with the words—'And that's the man for me!'

Listening till she had finished, the Christian man asked, 'Well, have you found that man yet?' 'No!' she replied, 'I'm afraid they're few and far between.' Then the Christian man said, 'I know a Man who answers in every respect to what you have been singing. I was speaking to Him this morning, and I know He has an interest in you. In fact, He loves you.' Her curiosity aroused, she asked, 'Well what's His name?' 'His name is Jesus,' he replied. Nothing more was said till the end of her journey, one stop before the Christian man's. As she alighted and was closing the door, she said gently, 'And that's the Man for me.'

**646  Man who Died for Me—The.**

*My pilgrim days are waning; the voice of Him*
*   I love*
*Has called me to His presence in My Father's*
*   house above.*

*Long, long by faith I've known Him, but now*
*   I'm going to see*
*The Man who sits in heaven, the Man who*
*   died for me.*

*But ere I left the desert I longed that I might*
*   know*
*What joy His blessed presence could give me*
*   here below;*
*These few short fleeting moments, oh! I would*
*   nearer be*
*To Thee, my precious Saviour, the Man who*
*   died for me.*

*He gave me all I asked for, yea, more than I*
*   can tell;*
*He filled my soul with rapture, with joy*
*   unspeakable;*
*The hand of Jesus on my soul seemed laid so*
*   tenderly,*
*I had for my Companion the Man who died*
*   for me.*

*To fall asleep in Jesus, 'tis that I think of now,*
*To be forever with the Lord, before Himself to*
*   bow,*
*Ah, yes with Him who stayed to call Zacchaeus*
*   from the tree,*
*With Him who hung upon the Cross, the Man*
*   who died for me.*

*To be alone with Jesus, Himself to gaze upon,*
*To see the Man I've read about oft in the*
*   eighth of John,*
*To leave this scene of sadness, oh! wondrous*
*   Lord to see*
*The glory of Thy presence—the Man who died*
*   for me.*

*It is the Man Christ Jesus with whom I'm going*
*   to dwell,*
*The weary Man of Sychar who sat upon the*
*   well,*
*Whose matchless love filled that poor heart,*
*   and gave her eyes to see*
*That He was God's anointed one, the Man who*
*   died for me.*

(Gal. 2. 20; 1 Tim. 2. 5,6)

**647  Management or Submission?**  A good lesson was once taught to the whole family of critics by the wise George Muller. When one of his boys was brought before him charged with finding fault with the way things were done, Mr Muller received the boy with a deep bow of respect and immediately proposed that the lad should take his seat while he stepped down among the boys. 'Now,' said he, 'I understand that you do not like the way I manage things, and I propose, therefore, that you shall manage things, and I now wait for your orders for the rest of the day.'

The boy, greatly embarrassed, began to cry and to beg Mr Muller to take his own place and let him be a boy again, promising to obey orders and to support the government of the house in every way.
(Heb. 13. 17)

**648   Management—Under New.**   In a Midland town where they make pottery—a grimy, smoky place—was a man, unable to read or write, who had been living a very bad life. One day he received Christ as his Saviour at a Salvation Army meeting, and gave clear evidence that he was truly converted.  One Sunday morning he came home from the morning service very miserable.

'What's the matter with you?' asked his wife. 'I thought you said you'd been converted.'

'I am,' he said, 'but I'm so miserable today because everyone had red jerseys on but me.'

'Oh,' replied his wife, 'I'll knit you one.'

So she knitted him a red jersey and the next Sunday he went to the meeting proudly wearing it.

He came back home miserable. 'What's the matter with you now?' asked his puzzled wife.

'Well, you see,' he said, 'everybody else had some lovely white letters on their red jersey, but I had none.'

'What are we going to do about that?' wondered his wife, for she could not read either. She noticed that across the street a shop had put up a new banner, so she decided to copy the letters and sew them on to her husband's jersey. The next Sunday he came home radiant.

'Do you know, my dear,' he said, 'everybody said that I had the best jersey of anyone there!'

What was written on it? 'UNDER NEW MANAGEMENT'!

That was nothing less than the truth, for when Christ takes control of a man's heart and life all things become new.

(Tit. 3. 5)

### 649   Manger's Message—The.

*Was it not strange that Jesus should be treated*
*As if He were an outcast, and undone,*
*When high on heaven's throne He had been*
  *seated*
*Long, long before man's history had begun?*

*Was it not strange that when the manger held*
  *Him,*
*The men of David's city failed to see*
*That in this fashion prophets had beheld Him,*
*Rejected—from the Manger to the Tree?*

*Yes, it was strange. But is it not still stranger*
*That multitudes from Him still turn away?*
*Shall we not heed the Message of the Manger*
*And open wide the door for Him today?*

A. Soutter

(Luke 2. 12)

### 650   Manner of Some—The.

*The manner of some is to stay away*
*From the table spread on the Lord's own day.*
*A dinner hot or an hour in bed—*
*Such are the things they prefer instead.*
*'I met a friend and he hindered me,'*
*Can any friend such as Jesus be?*
*He said, 'This do!' and can they forego*
*Thus to give Him joy who loves them so.*

*By the manner of some, when the Gospel's told*
*You would think their hearts would be very cold:*
*It has no music to charm their ear,*
*Or sure they would come its message to hear.*
*And yet by that their souls were saved*
*Unless, as I fear, they were self-deceived.*
*To have no care for the tidings glad,*
*While still they believe them, is terribly sad.*

*The manner of some is never to see*
*The place where prayer 'is wont to be';*
*Where saints together approach the Throne*
*Is where, alas, they are never known.*
*Yet where in petition the saints agree,*
*'I am there in the midst of two or three,'*
*Are the Saviour's words, and the promise is*
  *plain*
*But those that don't ask, how can they obtain?*

*The manner of some, when they can spend*
*A holiday—month, week or week-end—*
*Is to choose a spot where none are found*
*To gather together on scriptural ground.*
*Yet many a 'two or three' would be*
*Delighted a brother's face to see.*
*But some—alas prefer to choose*
*Some other place and fellowship lose.*
(Heb. 10. 25)

**651   Marital Affection.**   A Christian husband used to display his love for his wife in thoughtful gifts. One day he went to a florist's shop and selected some flowers, remarking, 'They are my wife's favourites.'

'Oh, I wish to express my sympathy, sir,' the clerk at once exclaimed: 'I trust your wife's illness is not serious.' 'Illness!' laughed the man, 'my wife is as well as you are, thank you.' The clerk apologised and added, 'I beg your pardon, sir, but to tell the truth, husbands don't usually buy flowers for their wives unless they are ill or dead.

*Act kindly! 'tis a little thing dropped in the*
  *heart's deep well;*
*The good, the joy that it may bring eternity*
  *will tell.*

(Rom. 12. 10; Eph. 5. 25)

**652   Marks of the Lord Jesus.**   Garibaldi promised his followers 'wounds, scars, bruises and perhaps death':

Churchill promised his people blood and tears, toil and sweat:

The Lord Jesus promises His disciples sacrifice, suffering, the daily cross and the crown of life.

*Have you no scar?—*
  *No hidden scar on foot, or side, or hand?*
  *I hear you sung as mighty in the land:*
  *I hear men hail your bright ascendant star:*
  *Have you no scar?*

*Have you no wound?—*
  *Yet I was wounded by the archers—spent,*
  *Transfixed upon the tree to die, and rent*
  *By ravening wolves that compassed me*
    *around:*
  *Have you no wound?*

*No wound, no scar!—*
*Yet, as the Master, shall the servant be,*
*And pierced are the feet that follow Me,*
*But yours are whole. Can he have followed far*
*Who has no wound or scar?*

(Gal. 6. 17)

### 653   Marriage Day and After.

*As at the marriage altar now you stand,*
*Dear ones, united in love's holy bond,*
*The Saviour reaches forth His nail-pierced hand*
*And bids you walk with Him the path beyond.*
*He offers your unfailing Guide to be*
*Along life's devious and uncertain way:*
*To every worthwhile joy He holds the key—*
*Joys He would have you know from day to day.*
*Within your doors He ever would abide*
*The blessing of His presence to impart,*
*To be your Counsellor, whate'er betide,*
*For you are precious to His loving heart.*

*Grant at your table He shall have a place:*
*Yea, yield to Him the Headship of your home.*
*Let all your plans be guided by His grace,*
*And your desire never from Him to roam.*
*Let His blest word be your unfailing light,*
*His promises your bulwark day by day,*
*His power your ceaseless source of strength and*
*    might,*
*His love your sunshine all along the way.*
*So shall the future, dear ones, for you hold*
*Joy which no storm or stress can ever sway:*
*Peace from above He never will withhold*
*And glory that will never pass away.*

Avis B. Christiansen

### 654   Marriage Hymn.

*O perfect day, with joy anticipated,*
*When Christ shall take unto Himself His*
*    Bride!*
*With patient grace for this He long has waited*
*To share the glory with her by His side.*

*The nuptial day—a transcript of the heavenly—*
*Has once more dawned; and now their vows*
*    they take*
*To love and cherish one another wholly*
*And live their lives for Christ, the Saviour's*
*sake.*

*May blessings rich and rare abound toward*
*    them*
*As through the busy world their way they wend!*
*The sunshine of His smile beam ever on them*
*These favours from their never-failing Friend!*

*May peace be theirs surpassing understanding,*
*And grace sustain them all along the way,*
*With love enjoyed that ne'er shall know an*
*    ending*
*Till Home is reached in God's unclouded Day!*

W. Fraser Naismith

(Rev. 19. 7)

### 655   Martha and Mary.

*Martha was cumbered and weary*
*As the cares of life took their toll,*
*But Mary talked much with Jesus*
*And Mary had peace in her soul.*

*Are you a Martha or a Mary?*
*Do you sit at His feet every day?*
*Have you looked on the face of Jesus?*
*Do you read God's good Word and pray?*

*Or, like Martha who did much serving,*
*Am I always too busy to be*
*Seated down at the feet of Jesus*
*And seeking His will for me?*

*Jesus loved Martha and Mary*
*Both were most dear to His heart;*
*But remember, He said this of Mary,*
*'She hath chosen the better part.'*

May Gorrie

(Luke 10. 41,42)

### 656   Martyr Polycarp.
At the command of the
governor of Smyrna, Polycarp, the best and most
influential Christian in Smyrna, was dragged
before him and asked, 'Are you a Christian?'
'Yes, I am a follower of Jesus,' he replied. 'You
must renounce Jesus and sacrifice to the idols or
I will throw you to the lions to be torn limb
from limb.' Polycarp refused. The governor,
furious, said, 'Unless you renounce Jesus, I will
have them burn you at the stake.' The aged
servant of God, ninety-five years old, replied,
'These eighty-six years have I served my Lord.
He never did me any harm, and I cannot deny
my Lord and Master now.'
They took him out, tied him to the stake,
piled the faggots around him and kindled the
fire with a torch. Hotter and hotter grew the
flames, and Polycarp's flesh began to burn, but
the aged saint endured the excruciating pain
and the death pangs, rejoicing that he was
counted worthy to suffer for the name of Jesus.
(Heb. 11. 35;  Rev. 2. 10)

### 657   Martyr Triumphant.
One of the most
noble Scottish martyrs during the persecutions
under Charles II was Archibald Campbell,
First Marquis of Argyll. Accused of treason
because of his adherence to the National
Covenant of 1638, he was condemned to be
beheaded at Edinburgh Cross.
He spent the two days' respite granted him
discharging numerous duties, consoling his
wife, and bravely facing, without signs of fear,
the ordeal of execution. Both nights he slept
soundly, and on the morning of the execution
rose early, seemingly possessed of an unearthly
gladness about which he declared, 'I thought to
have concealed the Lord's goodness, but it will
not do.' As he descended the stairs from his
prison room he was heard to say, 'I could die a
Roman but I choose rather to die like a Christian.' He embraced James Guthrie who was soon
to follow to a martyr's death, and Guthrie
encouraged him with these words, 'God has
been with you, He is with you, and He will be

with you.' When he was standing on the scaffold awaiting the fatal, final word, his physician in attendance felt his pulse and was astonished to find its beat was normal. There was a man proving the truth of the promise, 'As thy days, so shall thy strength be.'
(Deut. 33. 25)

### 658  Martyrs for Christ.

*One day in loved Jerusalem*
*There rushed a shrieking, maddened crowd*
*Upon a lowly kneeling form*
*Before his God and Saviour bowed:*
*And when with cruel stones they crushed*
*His beautiful and gentle life,*
*He prayed the Father to forgive*
*Their ignorance and raging strife.*
*This man was Stephen—born a Jew*
*Who died for Christ. Would I? Would you?*

*See! far upon a lonely isle*
*An aged man with snowy locks*
*Exiled to labour in the mines,*
*His only temple wind swept rocks.*
*'Twas he once leaned on Jesus' breast*
*And gazed with fond adoring eyes*
*Into that face where love divine*
*Still beams upon us from the skies.*
*This man was John beloved, a Jew,*
*Witness for Christ? Am I? Are you?*

*A Galilean fisher stood*
*Amid a fierce and angry throng.*
*No tremor spoke of hidden fear:*
*His face was peaceful, calm and strong.*
*And when they nailed him to a cross*
*As they had nailed his blessed Lord.*
*He gloried thus to die for Christ*
*And counted it a rich reward.*
*This man was Peter, born a Jew*
*Who died for Christ. Would I? Would you?*

*A captive, bound, was brought one day*
*To Nero's judgement seat in Rome;*
*For Christ he wore a heavy chain,*
*For Christ he had nor wealth nor home.*
*The noblest martyr Rome could boast*
*Of all the thousands that Rome slew,*
*The great apostle sent by God*
*To Gentiles with the message true.*
*This man was Paul, by birth a Jew,*
*Who died for Christ. Would I? Would you?*

(John 21. 18,19; 2 Tim. 4. 6; Rev. 1. 9)

### 659  Martyr's Hope—A.

Impressed by his lovely character, George Wishart's jailers asked if they could do anything for him. In response to his request, he was allowed to have the Lord's Supper the night before he was burned at the stake. The Christians who were allowed to attend that service with the man who in the sixteenth century gave up wealth and position for Christ's sake, said that he was overflowing with joy all evening. As they sat in the gloomy prison cell, the martyr spoke with great feeling about the love of the Lord Jesus in suffering

and dying for us, and he exclaimed with joy, 'To think I shall see Him in the morning.'
*Sunday School Times*
(Acts 7. 55-59)

### 660  Martyr's Reward.

Ignatius lived in Antioch and was martyred for his faith in Christ in A.D. 107.

On his arrival at Rome he was brought into the arena, and in the presence of the crowd calmly awaited his death. When the keeper of the lions came to loose them from their cages, the people grew wild with brutal joy and clapped and shouted, but the martyr stood firm. 'I am Christ's threshed wheat,' he said 'which the teeth of wild beasts must grind before it becomes bread.'

The awful spectacle was soon over, and before the people reached their homes Ignatius had won the crown he coveted and was at Home with the Lord.
(Rev. 2. 10)

### 661  Meekness.

Some words come by the accidents God provides. For a long time we had searched for a word adequate to express 'meekness.' Then we gave up (temporarily) and took a walk outside for a break. The grain-stalks left after harvesting were beginning to sprout again, so I said, 'Look, Kopta, they're sprouting.' 'No!' he said, 'they're iolo.' 'Iolo? What does that mean?' 'That is the word for new leaves when they are big enough and strong enough to bend and not break. We use it for people too, who are so strong inside that they don't need or want to fight you. But if a person is hard and brittle like a dead leaf, it means that he is not really strong.'

That is surely a better word for Bible meekness than anything we can say in English.
David B. Woodford

### 662  Meekness.

In the Spanish Bible the word for 'meek' in Matthew 5. 5 is 'Mauso', a word used to describe something that has been tamed or brought into submission. In South America, if you want to ride a horse and are not sure it has been broken in, the people assure you that they are giving you a horse that is 'mauso'. So the thought of submission is definitely implied in the verse, 'Blessed are the meek for they shall inherit the earth.' We find the same word in Matthew 11, where our Lord tells us He is 'meek and lowly in heart'. He was indeed the submissive One. He came to do the will of God. The chief business of the Christian is to do the will of God.

J. Manley

As meekness deepens, joy rises. It is the meek who increase their joy in the Lord, and in this way take root downward and bear fruit upward. Proud men despise meekness: it is shot at and hated like Joseph, but it is a fruitful bough by a well. Increase in joy comes from an increase in meekness.
(Isa. 29. 19; 2 Cor. 10. 1)

**663 Melody of Life.** Adelina Patti, the great singer, after her marriage to a certain Baron, left an order at home that her mail should be forwarded to the Cannes Post Office. On her arrival there she went to the post office, and asked if there were any letters for the Baroness Adeline Cederstorm-Patti. 'Lots of them,' was the reply. 'Then give them to me.' 'Have you any way of identifying yourself, Madam?' 'I have one of my visiting cards with me: will that do?' she asked. 'No, that is insufficient,' was the reply. 'You must have better evidence of your identity than that. Anyone could take one of these cards.'

She was at a loss for a moment, then she had a brilliant idea. She began to sing one of her well-known songs, 'A voice loving and tender'. She put her whole heart into the song and soon the whole post office was filled with silent people as they listened to those touching and beautiful words. As she finished, the old Postmaster came forward and said, 'It is indeed Madame Patti, no one else can sing that song like that.' Then she received her letters.

If we are to convince the world of the reality of Jesus Christ, and that we are indeed His disciples, it can only be by showing His power in our lives. Our claim must be substantiated by the melody of our life.
(Ps. 40. 1-3)

**664 Message of a Stray Bible.** Just before the final capture of the city of Lucknow by the British Forces, great fears were entertained as to the fate of two ladies who were known to be shut up in the immediate neighbourhood by the mutineers. A touching incident occurred during their captivity, and this was told at an annual meeting of the British and Foreign Bible Society.

'I was introduced to Mrs. Orr and Miss Jackson of whose preservation I wrote you an account in a former letter. They are comfortably lodged in a house near Bank's bungalow: but they evince in countenance and a painful air of suffering the effects of their long captivity. Their lives were spared indeed, but they were watched night and day by armed guards who did not hesitate to use gross and insulting language towards them, and whose constant delight was to tell them of the outrages and massacres which were taking place all over India during the time of our troubles. Their lives were preserved by the fidelity of Darogah, or by his desire to secure his personal safety in case the British became masters of the city. Day by day, before they were concealed in his house, they lived in expectation of death. In the midst of their captivity there was one source of consolation shut to them. They had no Bible and they felt the want exceedingly; but they could not remedy it, for any attempt to procure a religious book would only have increased the severities of their gaolers. Meantime, a little child, a Miss Christian, fell sick, and for several days they in vain sought assistance for her. At length, in a mood of contemptuous pity, the natives obtained the advice of a native doctor for the dying child, and this man sent some vile potion to her in a piece of paper torn from the first book he could lay his hands on. For a moment or two the printing on this fragment escaped attention; but as Mrs. Orr now drawing it from her bosom, placed it before us with an air of gratitude and reverence, I could well understand how it was that the words thus conveyed to them on the piece of paper seemed as promises from heaven, and bade them hope, and fear no more. Of the fragment thus conveyed to our countrywomen, I have procured an exact translation which I send herewith. It may be imagined how these words of comfort and assurance lighted up the prison—a handwriting on the wall in characters of fire, to illuminate the gloom of their dungeon:

' "I, even I, am He that comforteth you. Who art thou that thou shouldst be afraid of a man that shall die, and of the son of man that shall be made as grass; and forgettest the Lord thy Maker, that hath stretched forth the heavens and laid the foundations of the earth; and hast feared continually every day of the fury of the oppressor? The captive exile hasteneth that he may be loosed and that he should not die in the pit" (Isa. 51. 12-14). These words were accepted by our fellow-countrywomen as from heaven, and from that time they hoped on until they were rescued from the midst of the enemy.'
Narrated by the Earl of Shaftesbury

**665 Message of the Gospel.** We are not sent to preach sociology but salvation; not economics but evangelism; not reform but redemption; not culture but conversion; not progress but pardon; not the new social order but the new birth; not revolution but regeneration; not renovation but revival; not resuscitation but resurrection; not a new organization but a new creation; not democracy but the Gospel; not civilization but Christ. We are ambassadors, not diplomats.
(1 Cor. 15. 3,4)

**666 Messengers of God.** The wife of Robert Moffat, the missionary, stood outside the door of their hut with her baby in her arms, while her husband was busy outside the hut repairing a waggon. An African chief, with twelve attendants armed with spears, approached, and the attendants poised their spears opposite the missionary's breast. Dropping his tools and baring his breast, Moffat said, 'Strike if you will; but before you strike let me tell you that we have come here in the name of God as His servants and messengers to uplift and deliver you, and you cannot make us afraid or drive us out. All you can do is to kill us. Now drive your spear to my heart if you will. But when I am dead, others with the same spirit will come and take my place and carry on my work.'

Down went the spears in the dust, and the chief, turning to his attendants said, 'These men must have a thousand lives; they are indifferent to one, and there must be something in the doctrine of immortality that they are preaching to

us.' That was the turning point in Robert Moffat's mission to Bechuanaland, and from that time forth the Gospel began to prevail among that hardened tribe.
(Matt. 10. 28)

**667 Messiah's Song.** Around 1710 George Frederick Handel came to London. Everywhere people applauded him. For the next thirty years he wrote superb music for the nobility and royalty of England and the Continent. He almost completely dominated the world of music.

And yet all was not well. He was accomplished but he was arrogant; he was brilliant, but knew it himself. He was dominating and domineering, full of immense energy and immense temper, generous yet irascible. A host of enemies conspired to bring him down. The crash came in 1737. He was reduced to bankruptcy and on April 13 suffered a severe stroke. He was given little hope of recovery. But he did recover, and once more he turned with great gusto to composing operas. His star seemed to be rising again. Then Queen Caroline, his staunch patroness, died.

Handel, nearing sixty, far from well, weary, full of debt and disappointment felt deserted by man and God. 'Why did God permit my resurrection,' he cried, 'only to allow my fellow men to bury me again?'

One evening, returning to his shabby lodging in Brook Street, he found a large parcel on his desk. Hastily breaking the seal, he undid the wrappings and found a libretto, a *Sacred oratorio*, from Charles Jennens. Handel grunted. He didn't particularly want a religious composition. He snuffed out his candle and went to bed—but he could not sleep. He got up, lighted his candle again, and opened the manuscript. Words upon words reached his eye and moved his heart. 'He was despised and rejected of men . . . I know that my Redeemer liveth . . . Rejoice.'

With a trembling hand and a mind bursting with music he sat down at his desk, took pen, and began to write. With superhuman activity, page after page was filled with notes of music. Day after day the composer worked with feverish energy, scarcely taking time to eat or sleep. On the twenty-fourth day Handel gave up, fell exhausted on his bed and slept for eleven hours. But on his desk lay the score for *The Messiah*.

He played it in Dublin on April 13, 1742, the fifth anniversary of his stroke, and he continued to present it yearly. He conducted *The Messiah* for the last time in 1759, though blind and in great difficulty. At the words 'the trumpet shall sound' he hesitated and collapsed.

On April 13, the anniversary of his stroke twenty-two years previously, the anniversary of the first performance of the oratorio, he died. But *The Messiah* in all its glory, eloquent in faith and glorious hope, lives and will live.
*Gospel Witness*

(Job 19. 25)

**668 Mind Guarded.**

*I dallied with a doubtful thought; 'what harm
    can be,' said I,
'In merely thinking of a thing and letting it
    pass by?'
But ere I was aware, that thought had entered
    in my heart,
And firmly there ensconced itself, refusing to
    depart.
Anon it to a monster grew, it bound me foot
    and hand,
And in the kingdom of my mind established its
    command.
My will a helpless captive lay, I—powerless to
    be freed—
But for my God's delivering grace, had hopeless
    been indeed!
My Lord and Master, guard, I pray, the
    portals of my mind;
Grant that no soul-defiling shaft may easy
    entrance find!
But let the lovely things and true, the things of
    good report,
Where virtue is, or any praise, mould my
    most inward thought.*

(Prov. 23. 7)

**669 Mind Set on Things Above.** Dr Fullerton used to tell of a young army officer much addicted to gambling. He was very wealthy, owned a famous stud of horses, regularly attended the races and gambled on the winners. After his conversion he gave up all that and was never seen on a racecourse again. A young lady of his acquaintance met him one day and said, 'Captain, what's this I hear about you?' 'Oh, what are you hearing about me?' he asked. 'Well!' she said, 'I hear you have been converted: is that true, Captain?' 'It is perfectly true, Lady Betty.' 'O now,' she added, 'I am sure if there were a horse race anywhere near you would go just as you always did and put your money on your favourite horse, wouldn't you?' He said, 'Lady Betty, when I was a little boy, I was very fond of marbles, but when I got to be fond of horses, I forgot all about my marbles. Would you mind turning that over in your mind?'

She evidently did so, for soon after that Lady Betty, who was in the social whirl where she lived, was also converted. She was a delightful dancer and a skilful whist player. The captain met her some little time afterwards and said, 'Lady Betty, what's this I hear about you?' 'Oh, what are you hearing about me?' she asked the captain. 'I hear you have been converted; is that true, Lady Betty?' he asked. 'It is perfectly true Captain,' she said. 'Oh now, Lady Betty, I'm sure if there were a dance or a whist drive or a bridge party here tomorrow night you would be there, the charm and centre of attraction, as you used to be; now wouldn't you?' She replied, 'Captain, when I was a little girl I was very fond of dolls, but when I became fond of dancing, I forgot all about dolls. Would you mind turning that over in your mind?'

(Col. 3. 1,2)

**670  Mind Your Mind.** If scientists were able to build an electronic computer that matched the nerve connection of the human brain, they would need a skyscraper to house it, the power of Niagara Falls to run it, and the water of Niagara to cool it. Yet the Creator has compressed it all into the small space of a cranium.

It is often overlooked by Christians, however, that it is their responsibility to look after the brain that God has given them. Fatigue, due to lack of proper sleep, too much study, living on nerves during pressure periods, etc., may well have a serious effect upon the brain. Dr M. H. Nelson says, 'There is a limit of activity. If a person does not relax, the body and mind develop fatigue. The Christian who lets himself get fatigued is asking for trouble. Such a time is ideal for Satan to launch his attack.'

It is impossible to do one's best work for God when the mind is weary and there are ragged nerves. Rest is essential for the mind as well as the body.

(Mark 6. 31)

**671  Minister of Christ.** Dr F. W. Boreham started life at 14 as clerk in a brick company where he lost his right foot in a shunting accident. At 16 he entered the South London Tramways Company, and at 21 he was accepted into Spurgeon's College. Studying hard, he quickly showed his latent abilities when he took over the responsibilities of the student-pastorate at Theydon Bois. During his seventeen months' service, each week-end conversions and baptisms resulted in the doubling of church membership and a big forward move in the life of the church.

When the Principal of the College was appealed to on behalf of a small church in Mosgiel, N.Z., to find them a pastor, it was F. W. Boreham who seemed the obvious choice. Although he had not completed his three year course, the staff unanimously approved his selection, and at 24 years of age he took up his pastorate there.

In New Zealand, Tasmania and Australia he wrote his 46 books and produced articles for religious and national papers. What emerges from the years that follow is his prodigious industry, his painstaking verification of facts, his determination to eradicate natural disadvantages, his engaging modesty and humility, his breadth of reading and his wide catholicity of taste.

To conquer a monotonous delivery in a narrow voice-register, like Demosthenes centuries before, he declaimed on the seashore against the oncoming tide, with his young wife as critic and adviser.

When a noted barrister was defending a criminal case in the courts, he was present to learn all he could of the technique of voice production, gestures, and persuasive eloquence.

On his 70th birthday, at a luncheon organised in his honour and attended by 85 ministers and friends, in returning thanks for their appreciative remarks, he said, 'Christ is everything to me, and the desire of my heart has been to lead my hearers to Christ.' On a later occasion he said, 'If only the people could catch a vision of the Saviour, they would have no alternative but to lay their devotion at His feet. My soul has caught fire whenever I have exalted the Cross.'

At 88 came sunset and Home. They found in his desk several weeks' supply of articles and the complete arrangement for his funeral service.

Ransome W. Cooper

(1 Tim 4. 6.)

**672  Ministry of Angels.** In trouble from a very early age R——, from the worst city slum I have ever seen, arrived eventually in our Prison Bible Class at the age of seventeen, and made confession of faith in Christ. He had a long criminal record behind him.

On the morning of his release he arrived at the city railway station to find the gang of which he had been a deputy leader waiting to greet him. It took some courage to tell them that his connection with the gang was finished, and that from then on he would be living as a Christian. From that day his erstwhile friends became his worst enemies, and his life was constantly in danger.

Because of this we got him a job as a driver's mate on long-distance lorries, and I arranged that he would telephone from every night stop to let me know where he was, ask questions about the portion of Scripture he had been reading, and have a general chat. After about eighteen months of this, his mother became ill, and he felt it his duty to be at home with her. His next job was one that in the evenings and early mornings, he loaded milk delivery lorries in readiness for the early morning run. When the lorries had been loaded he was free to return home. At 2.30 a.m. one morning my telephone rang, and it was immediately apparent that R—— was in trouble. He explained that he had just left work to go home and had been chased along the street by his old gang who were brandishing razors and knives. He had just managed to find sanctuary in the telephone kiosk. Even as he was speaking, he said, they were trying to force an entry. His agonized call was, 'Sir, what can you do for me?'

The situation was too urgent to call the police, so I asked him to listen quietly while we prayed together. In a very few words we reminded the Lord of His promise, 'He will give His angels charge concerning thee.' I had scarcely finished when his voice came over the telephone again, full of tearful relief, 'O, sir, two of these angels you spoke about have just gone down the street and they're driving a police car, sir, and the gang has gone, and I'll get the police to take me home, sir. Thank you very much, sir!'

A few days later I met R—— dashing across the road to me through the traffic. His heart was full as he said, 'By here, sir, God fairly jumps to it when you tell Him what to do!'

Alex Allan

(Heb. 1. 14)

**673   Ministry of Angels.** I have never had any doubt about the ministry of angels in the present day, particularly towards those who are 'heirs of salvation'. Towards the start of my ministry of visitation in some of the less respectable parts of our large cities, the following incident happened in Glasgow.

A young man converted in prison returned home to tell his old gang associates that he would no longer be helping to terrorise the area, Later he was brutally beaten up because of his continued witness to the Lord Jesus, and eventually had to travel south to live in order to escape the fury of his ex-associates.

I went to visit him one dark evening, rather apprehensively, because it was not an area to visit during the hours of darkness. On this occasion, however, it was imperative that I should see him, and I ventured in, although I knew that the gang knew me and had vowed revenge on me for the change in their ex-leader.

On coming down from his house on the fourth floor I sensed a movement outside, and heard a whisper, 'Here he comes; close in and get him.' In the shaded light I caught a fleeting glimpse of a figure stealing towards the doorway, carrying a bicycle chain. To have retreated would have meant them following me and attacking me inside: so, with a brief prayer for help, I began to walk the twenty yards to my car with quaking dignity, and nothing happened until I had the key in the lock of the car door. Then pandemonium broke loose, and they swarmed round the car in which I was safely seated, with the engine running. Three of them jumped on the rear of the car as I drove away, but a quick swerve toppled them off and I was free. What kept them immobile during that twenty yard walk? The angel of the Lord encampeth round about them that fear Him and delivereth them.

Alex. Allan

(Ps. 34. 7)

**674   Ministry of Money.** The ministry of money is not understood or appreciated; men are purse-proud because they have no sense of stewardship. They think of their gains as their own, and of giving as an act of merit; and so become arrogant and sometimes defiant in their avarice. How quickly when God's Spirit possesses us do we see that nothing is our own, and so we, and all we have, belong to our Redeemer.

A. T. Pierson

(1 Tim. 6. 19)

**675   Minorities With God.** During the time Noah was building the ark he was very much in the minority, but he won. When Joseph was sold into Egypt by his brothers, he was a decided minority, but he won. When Gideon and his three hundred followers, with their pitchers and lamps, put the Midianites to flight, they were in an insignificant minority, but they won.

When David, ridiculed by his brothers, went out to meet Goliath, in size he was a decided minority, but he won.

When Martin Luther nailed his thesis on the door of the church he was a lonesome minority, but he won. When Jesus Christ our Lord was crucified by the Roman soldiers, he was a conspicuous minority, but He won. We Christians are in the minority today, but we shall win; 'if God be for us, who can be against us?'

*Christian Witness*

(Rom. 8. 31)

**676   Minute!—Just a.**

> *I have only just a minute.*
> *Only sixty seconds in it,*
> *Forced upon me—can't refuse it,*
> *Didn't seek it, didn't choose it;*
> *But it's up to me to use it,*
> *Give account if I abuse it.*
> *Only just a little minute*
> *But eternity is in it.*

(Ps. 90. 12)

**677   Miracle.** 'It took a miracle' is the chorus of a hymn. In his autobiography, George Beverley Shea tells an amusing incident in a story against himself. When in Great Britain with Dr Billy Graham on a Crusade in London, he sang on the first night a Gospel solo whose chorus is:

> *It took a miracle to put the stars in place:*
> *It took a miracle to hang the worlds in space;*
> *But when He saved my soul, cleansed and made*
>    *me whole,*
> *It took a miracle of love and grace.*

One lady who was present at the large meeting seemed greatly annoyed as she listened to the solo and wrote a letter of protest to Billy Graham, saying it was extremely unbecoming for a soloist from America to come to England and sing, 'It took America to put the stars in place: it took America to hang the worlds in space.'

George Beverley Shea remarked that it impressed on him the need for being absolutely clear in his articulation.

**678   Miracles—Great.** Moses spoke to the people of Israel in the plains of Moab, reminding them of God's dealings with them on the journey through the wilderness, and of the great miracles He had performed for them (Deut. 29).

On the march those who left Egypt for the promised land must have numbered over two million besides their flocks and herds. The number of fighting men was 600,000. As they marched five abreast, it has been computed that such a host must have covered about forty miles. A message from God communicated to Moses would take three hours to reach the perimeter of the camp, which would cover 500 square miles.

Major-General Wilson-Haffenden, reckoning on the basis of the requirements for an army in Burmah during the 1939-45 war, has calculated that a daily ration of 1000 tons of food would be required and 1800 tons of firewood to cook the flesh of the sacrifices offered and of the quails God supplied daily. Two million gallons of water would be needed for drinking and cooking alone, and that would not include the watering of the flocks and herds.

There is no record of shops, bakeries or stores being available to that vast company on their journey, and it is definitely stated that they had not eaten bread or drunk wine or liquor (Deut. 29. 6)

Apart from divine miraculous supplies of manna, quails and water, one wonders how the Israelites would have fared for a week, let alone forty years under wilderness conditions. (Deut. 29. 3)

**679  Miracles of Jesus.** On March 14, 1963, the following appeared in the *Daily Telegraph*.

'It seems to me that two considerations must ever lift the whole question of the credibility of miracles out of the realm of discussion on any one or two of them in particular.

'i. Christians accept the reality of the Incarnation. If God who is without body, parts or passions, has willed thus to appear in terms of humanity, taking upon Himself a human body, and has appeared in the human arena, you have a basic miracle with which anything else is incomparable.

'Seeing the Incarnation presupposes a purpose which must be endorsed in the judgement of those to whom He has come, that presupposition carries with it the strong likelihood that the whole of the mission will be endorsed by that which is obviously supernatural. . . .

'ii. You can never separate miracles from the ministry of Christ. A study of the Gospels puts it beyond any reasonable question that miracles were a normality of His life. It was not that He healed a few here and there, but wherever He went, as many as had need of healing. . . .

'Our Lord Himself is the greatest of miracles. Should we not expect that His footsteps should leave behind them at every point evidence not merely of His perfect humanity but of his undoubted Deity. Is not this what we find in the records of the Gospels?'

Preb. Colin Kerr

Christ's first recorded miracle was the changing of water into wine. In picturesque language Dryden described what took place in one of his essays: 'The conscious water saw its God and blushed.'

Nearly fifty years before that, Richard Crawshaw had written the same thing in a poem. An old Latin poem written in the Middle Ages contains the line:

'Lympha pudica Deum vidit et erubuit.' (John 2. 6-11; 3. 2)

**680  Mirror on the Compass.** A hunter related this amusing incident: Purchasing equipment for my first moose hunting trip in Alaska, I was baffled by a compass that had a mirror on the back. 'What's the mirror for?' I asked. 'Well,'

said the salesman, 'you look in there and it will tell you who's lost.' When I read this, I thought of the Bible. We all know that it is life's compass to show us the right way to think and talk and walk. But we often forget that it is a mirror as well. Is it not all too easy to study the Bible to be quick to point out to others where they are wrong, forgetting our own conduct?

'Never use the Bible as a compass without using it as a mirror before you give the reading of the compass to others.'

*New Life*

(James 1. 25)

**681  Misinterpreted Text.** Ebenezer Brown, son of John Brown of Haddington, who became a very great preacher, was in his boyhood very lively and given to pranks and practical jokes. There was a gathering of ministers for a special dinner at the Manse, and the services were long for a hungry boy. Ebenezer obtained his chance and carefully removed the meat from the meat pie that had been prepared for dinner, and carefully filled the dish with grass, replacing the crust. When the party gathered round the festive board and the crust was broken, the green grass appeared, with a card on which was inscribed, 'All flesh is grass.' (Isa. 40. 6)

**682  Missionaries Need Prayer.** Dr G. Campbell Morgan relates an experience he once had while in the house of a wealthy Christian. One morning at family prayers the brother prayed earnestly for the salvation of the heathen and for the missionaries. When prayers were over, one of the sons, a lad of ten, said to his father, 'Dad, I like to hear you pray for the missionaries.' The father, delighted, said, 'I am glad you do, my boy.' Then the boy replied, 'Do you know what I was thinking when you were praying? If I had your bank book, I would answer half your prayers'. (Phil. 4. 10)

**683  Missionary Accomplishments.** Dr David Livingstone's wife, Mary, the blue-eyed daughter of Robert Moffat, after her wedding in 1845 had many housekeeping chores, including bread-making, butter-churning, candle-moulding and soap-making, yet found time for teaching African children to read and write. Her husband added to his task of preaching the work of a farmer, a grower, a carpenter, a blacksmith and a doctor. 'We came nearly,' he said, 'to what may be considered as indispensable in the accomplishments of a missionary family in Africa; the husband to be a jack of all trades without doors, and the wife a maid of all work within.' (Eccl. 9. 10)

**684  Missionary Builder.** A retired Canadian lumber and building contractor received a letter from his missionary daughter regarding a building project in the Orient. Casually she added that she wished he were there to oversee the work. He wrote by reply that he was coming and would direct the building project. Six days a week he worked on the building. On Sunday he said, 'Now, dear, give me a boy who can speak a bit of English and load us up with Scripture portions and tracts.' One afternoon, coming back from a Sunday trek, the old gentleman fainted. When he revived, his daughter said, 'You must not do this any more, father'; he replied, 'I wouldn't do it for anyone else but Jesus.'

*The Herald*

(Col. 3. 23,24)

685  **Missionary Leper's Farewell Letter.** The following is the last letter written by John E. Davies, missionary to the Telugus in India, who died a leper:

'It is about fifteen years since I last saw you, so I appreciated your letter all the more. I have had a heavy cross to carry, but I am glad to tell you that His grace has been sufficient for me at every step of the way. At first I was somewhat rebellious, for I had great plans for the future. Many souls were turning to the Lord in all parts of the field, and I looked forward to the time when I should have the privilege of baptizing thousands.'

'I had said, "Lord, let Thy servant, filled with Thy Spirit, give all my thought, all my energy and my life for Thee." And He answered me. But instead of letting me serve Him as I had planned to do, He suddenly took me away from the work for ever. As I lay in the hospital in England, when the first horror of the final outcome was upon me, I thought sometimes that the Lord had forgotten and forsaken me, that He had hidden His face from me. But it was not so. The more sorrow I have had to bear, the easier it has become, and now I am rejoicing in my Saviour every hour. I know the time cannot now be long before I shall be with Him, but while I am in the body I cannot keep still. I must testify; I must tell of His great love for me and I have written a paper to be read at the Missionary Conference in India on "Filling full our place in life".

'You ask me how I am. I have lost my eyesight now and my voice; I have no feet or ankles; no arms; but my heart is far from dead. I still feel and long and sympathize. I still yearn for the extension of God's kingdom on earth as much as ever I did. I cannot read or write, but the kind sisters in charge of the hospital come and read to me, and write for me as I can find means to dictate to them. I have everything I need, and could not be more comfortable were I in my own home. While I live I expect to prepare others for India. And though I am slowly dying, I must keep on doing something to help on the Redeemer's kingdom when I have passed beyond.

'I know you will remember me in your prayers that I may be humble and patient and faithful to the end. I have no doubts in these days, and if I had my voice I should be singing all the day long. Sometimes I feel so happy that I long to go to my heavenly Home and be with my "Beloved" for ever.

'May the God of all comfort comfort you and grant you His grace, filling you with the sunshine of His presence, so that day by day you will be transformed into His likeness from glory to glory, is the prayer of

'Your brother in Christ's kingdom,
John E. Davies'

686  **Missionary On Furlough.**

*We call them home for such a needed rest,*
*Our missionaries, faithful and true;*
*Then we chase them about from east to west*
*To tell what the Lord can do.*

*At night they are speaking and visiting late,*
*By day many miles they must go;*
*Their schedule is full: they must keep every*
*date,*
*Never mind if they're weary or no.*

*We expect them to picture the heathen's dire*
*need*
*And thrill us with incidents true;*
*We drink in their message and bid them*
*Godspeed,*
*Never sensing how little we do.*

*Their love for lost souls is earnest and deep;*
*They pour out their hearts all aflame;*
*To them we must seem heavy with sleep*
*With no zeal the good news to proclaim.*

*The days of their 'rest' soon come to an end,*
*Their faces turn homeward again;*
*So with tiring farewells and 'God bless you's'*
*We send them to labour once more for lost*
*men.*

*They're speeding away to the harvest so white,*
*Soon to be in the place they love best;*
*But how can they go with new strength for the*
*fight*
*When their furlough's provided no rest.*

*If we 'homeland' Christians would faithfully do*
*God's will—if we served with true zest,*
*Then Christ's 'Come apart' would prove*
*blessedly true,*
*For His servants would have time to rest.*

L. W. Beckley

(Mark 6. 31)

687  **Missionary or no Missionary?** One day Dr Wilfred Grenfell, medical missionary to Labrador, was guest at a dinner in London, together with a number of socially prominent British men and women.

During the course of the dinner, the lady seated next to him turned and said, 'Is it true, Dr Grenfell, that you are a missionary?'

Dr Grenfell looked at her for a moment before replying, 'Is it true, Madam, that you are not?'

*Sunday School Promoter*

(John 17. 18)

688  **Missionary Pioneers.** Dugald Campbell, who crossed the Sahara Desert with the Gospel for the 'veiled Tuaregs' and other hostile tribes,

quoted the following lines as descriptive of this sort of work;

> There's a legion that never was listed,
> That carries no banner or crest;
> But split in a thousand detachments
> Is breaking the road for the rest.

We have known many of these pioneers in the past and it is a joy to recall their testimony.

Dear Frederick Stanley Arnot quoted his lines to a group of his early co-workers in Scotland as he returned on furlough from Africa:

> We have gleaned the sheaves together here
> And the joy has been passing sweet;
> But a deeper joy awaits us there
> When we meet at the Saviour's feet.

SO! 'Put a stout heart to a stey brae.' That was Livingstone's advice to Stanley.
(Rom. 15. 20)

### 689   Missionary Sisters

*Have you ever read the sorrow in a heathen*
*  woman's face*
*As you met her, eye to eye, amidst the throng?*
*She who is by sex your sister, though of a*
*  different race,*
*Have you ever wondered why she has no song?*
*It will take no occult power to fathom all her*
*  secrets deep,*
*And it needs no cruel probing just to know;*
*If you're filled with Christ's compassion and*
*  can weep with those that weep,*
*All her inmost soul will then to you outflow.*
*If you let Christ's love flow through you with*
*  a power she can feel,*
*She will follow close behind you as you go;*
*And if you but turn a moment you will meet*
*  her mute appeal*
*For a blessing that your shadow might bestow.*
*Yes, she feels you bear the comfort she has*
*  sought for years to find*
*In the temple where her gods sit row on row,*
*And somehow your very presence breathes a*
*  balm for troubled mind,*
*For she feels that you must understand and*
*  know.*

*She's a prisoner that beats against the very*
*  bars of life*
*And she longs for death, yet dare not, must*
*  not die;*
*She is cursed with cruel curses should she be*
*  a sonless wife,*
*And a baby daughter answer cry with cry.*
*She's the common drudge of yesterday and*
*  dreads the cruel morrow,*
*While today the weary hours drag like a chain;*
*And she prays to gods all deafened to her tale*
*  of sin and sorrow*
*Or if they hear, are heedless of her pain.*
*She's the daughter of her mother who before*
*  her trod the road:*
*She's the mother of a daughter who will know*
*All the depth of her own anguish, all the heavy,*
*  weary load,*
*All the bitterness—a heathen woman's woe.*

*No! 'tis not a heathen woman—'tis a piteous*
*  captive throng*
*In the deserts, jungles, paddy fields and marts,*
*In the lands that know not Jesus, lands of*
*  cruelty and wrong,*
*Where there is no balm for wounded, aching*
*  hearts.*
*Shall we let this stream flow downward in its*
*  widening, deathward way?*
*Shall we let this flood of misery hold this*
*  throng?*
*We can stem the deadly current if we go and*
*  give and pray:*
*They must join us in the glad redemption song.*

Mrs W. M. Turnbull in *Alliance Weekly*

690   **Missionary Zeal.** In November, 1882, D. L. Moody left Cambridge for Oxford and after the campaign several Cambridge students who were converted showed immediate awareness of a call to overseas service. Moody had said little at Cambridge about the foreign field.

At Brighton, Dixon Edward Hoste responded to Moody's appeal and went later as a missionary to China with the C.I.M. His brother, William Hoste, was then a student at Cambridge. In Moody's meetings at Stratford, C. T. Studd a backslider, was restored and offered for China. On February 4, 1885, the Cambridge seven went out.

Then the urge for foreign missionary service spread to America. Dr A. T. Pierson who had written a book—*Crisis of Missions*—addressed 1000 people at a Missionary Conference at Northfield on the subject—'The Hour of Advance'.
(Matt. 28. 18-20)

691   **Misunderstood.** Mrs C. H. Spurgeon had an experience that made her understand misunderstood people.

One who was at that time a welcome visitor at the home in Norwood narrated something that happened when he was there. Young Charles Spurgeon asked his mother for some eggs from the dairy that Mrs Spurgeon had. 'Yes, Charles,' she said, 'you may have them if you pay for them.' The visitor thought this strange. Later, rumours were circulated that Spurgeon and his wife were mean and grasping, because they sold butter, eggs and milk; but they gave no explanation and the critics continued to spread their aspersions. The explanation came at Mrs Spurgeon's death, when books were found containing all sales at the dairy and profits therefrom, all of which were devoted to the maintenance of two elderly widows of Welsh ministers. The cruel critics did not understand.

> *Not understood! The secret springs of action*
> *Which lie beneath the surface and the show*
> *Are disregarded; with self-satisfaction*
> *We judge our neighbours, and they often go*
> NOT UNDERSTOOD.

## 692　Misunderstood.

*Not understood we move along asunder:*
*Our paths grow wider as the seasons creep*
*Along the years! we marvel and we wonder*
*Why life is life, and then we fall asleep*
*Not understood.*

*Not understood, we gather false impressions*
*And hug them closer as the years go by,*
*Till virtues almost seem to us transgressions*
*And thus men rise and fall, and live and die*
*Not understood.*

*Not understood! Poor souls with stunted vision*
*Oft measure giants by the narrow gauge.*
*The poisoned shafts of falsehood and derision*
*Are oft impelled 'gainst those who mould the*
　　*age*
*Not understood.*

*Not understood! How trifles often change us!*
*The thoughtless sentence or the fancied slight*
*Destroy long years of friendship and estrange*
　　*us,*
*And on our souls there falls a freezing blight*
*Not understood.*

*Not understood! How many breasts are*
　　*aching*
*For lack of sympathy! Ah, day by day*
*How many sad and cheerless hearts are*
　　*breaking!*
*How many noble spirits pass away*
*Not understood!*

*O God! that men would see a little clearer*
*Or judge less harshly where they cannot see.*
*O God! that men would draw a little nearer*
*To one another! they'd be nearer Thee*
*And understood.*

(1 Cor. 4. 5)

## 693　Moment—In a.

*Quite suddenly—it may be at the turning of a*
　　*lane,*
*Where I stand to watch the skylark from out*
　　*the swelling grain*
*That the trump of God shall thrill me, with its*
　　*call so loud and clear,*
*And I'm called away to meet Him whom of all*
　　*I hold most dear.*

*Quite suddenly—it may be in His house I bend*
　　*my knee*
*When the Kingly voice, long-hoped-for, comes*
　　*at last to summon me;*
*And the fellowship of earth-life that has*
　　*seemed so passing sweet,*
*Proves nothing but the shadow of meeting*
　　*round His feet.*

*Quite suddenly—it may be as I tread the busy*
　　*street,*
*Strong to endure life's stress and strain, its*
　　*every call to meet,*
*That through the roar of traffic a trumpet,*
　　*silvery clear*
*Shall stir my startled senses and proclaim His*
　　*coming near.*

*Quite suddenly—it may be as I lie in dreamless*
　　*sleep,*
*God's gift to many a sorrowing heart, with no*
　　*more tears to weep,*
*That a call shall break my slumber and a voice*
　　*sound in my ear:*
*'Rise up, my love, and come away! Behold, the*
　　*Bridegroom's here!'*

(1 Cor. 15. 52)

**694　Moment—In a.** It is an interesting thought that the word 'moment' used by the Apostle Paul in 1 Corinthians 15. 51,52 is the translation of the Greek word 'atomos' the very word which has given us 'atom'. 'Behold I shew you a mystery; we shall not all sleep, but we shall all be changed in a moment . . .' To the prognostications of science what shall we say? None of us can deny that God in His omnipotence can use these very inventions of science to further His own purposes. He uses the wrath of man to praise Him. But, whilst recognizing that truth, we also have to add a further truth. As long as we believe in a God who is free and who is all powerful, then it is wrong to speak of a man-made Utopia or a man-made doom as being inevitable. That would be an admission that God has relinquished His control over the world. But such is not the case. God is still the Ruler of the universe, and when the time comes to fold up the pages of history and to bring to an end the things that are, that order will be issued not from Moscow nor from London nor from Washington, but from the throne of heaven. God has not delegated His authority to any other. He still remains in control of history and in the last analysis history is His story. That is why Christian people refuse to believe that this world can come to a premature end. That is why they are not driven to despair by the fantastic inventions of present-day science. They believe that God is still in control.
　　　　　　　　　　　　　　　Dr I. D. E. Thomas

(Rev. 19. 6)

**695　Money-Making.** A gentleman of Boston, U.S.A., an intimate friend of Professor Agassiz, once expressed his wonder that a man of such abilities as he (Agassiz) possessed should remain contented with such a moderate income. 'I have enough,' was Agassiz's reply, 'I have not time to make money. Life is not sufficiently long to enable a man to get rich, and do his duty to his fellow-men at the same time.' Christian, have you time to serve your God and yet to give your whole soul to gaining wealth?
　　　　　　　　　　　　　　　C. H. Spurgeon

(1 Tim. 6. 8-10)

**696　Money—Means of Grace.** To the unconverted money is a means of gratification—to the converted, a means of grace; to the one an opportunity of comfort, to the other an opportunity of consecration. So wrote Fred Mitchell.
　　What proportion of income, after deduction of income tax, should be set aside for church and philanthropic work? Some would say at

least a tenth based on the tithe of the old Testament, and there can be little doubt that if all Christians gave this proportion the Lord's work and His Church would suffer no lack. But if this means that, when we have given one tenth, or any other part, we can do what we like with the remainder, we certainly cannot invoke the teaching of the New Testament in support. The New Testament insists that ALL we are and have is a sacred trust from God. We must account to Him for all.

Said David Livingstone, 'I will put no value on anything I possess save in reference to the Kingdom of God.'

(Matt. 6. 19,20)

**697  Moon and Beyond.**  Interplanetary travel marks the advance of science in our day. Aeronauts who piloted planes through the air have, in this space age, been superseded by astronauts and cosmonauts who explore the moon and aim at exploring the planets and stars. Men have stood on the face of the moon, walked on its surface and come back with samples of moon rock to the earth to give their report. There is no record of communication ever having been established between the earth and the moon or any of the planets. We have never received a message from inhabitants of the moon or of any of the planets, if there are any. We do not even know if any are inhabited.

Yet we have a record in a book whose veracity has been firmly established, because it has stood the test of time, of One who came from a realm beyond our solar system which is not on the astronomers' maps and a message from heaven to the planet in which we live. His name, Jesus, was given to Him at His birth because He came from heaven to save His people on earth from their sins. The New Testament contains many of the messages He brought from heaven and declared on earth. So communication has been established between that realm far beyond the moon and this planet on which we live, not by scientific research but by divine revelation.

(John 3. 12,13)

**698  Moon-Explorers With Bibles.**  Not for the inhabitants of the moon, if there should be any, but for the astronauts themselves.

A new group of 'Gideons' met each Monday for prayer at Pasadena, Texas. One of them mentioned that he was praying about God's Word being aboard Apollo 8 on its flight to the moon. Another Gideon present, chief of the flight technical branch of the spacecraft Centre, said, 'Let me see what I can do. I know Commander Borman: he is a fine Christian. You claim Jeremiah 33. 3!' Look it up! It reads—'Call upon me and I will answer thee and show thee great and mighty things which thou knowest not.'

In early December he managed to contact Borman and asked, 'Do you have a copy of God's Word aboard?' Borman's reported reply was, 'No! I'm glad you reminded me of it.'

The result was that the Gideons presented all three astronauts with New Testaments which they took on the flight, and Commander Borman took also his own personal Bible. Non-combustible book coverings were provided. The passage read to the folks on earth was from Borman's Bible, the three reading one after the other, each a few verses from Genesis 1. 1-10. Then—'and from the crew of Apollo 8 we close with a Good-night. Good luck and a merry Christmas and God bless you—all of you on the good earth.'

**699  Morality—The New.**  God's standards of morals are set aside in favour of man's standards in a permissive society. Professor James Stewart warned that the great ideal of beauty, goodness and truth cannot be tampered with by society, even if that society is the most democratic in the world.

Today the dangerous idea is abroad that moral standards are relative and not absolute, set by society and not given by God. Many eminent teachers are propagating this infernal notion, and in this way playing into the hands of those who are out to disrupt the moral standards of our nation.

(Matt. 5. 17)

**700  More Than Conquerors.**  Demetrius laid siege to the ancient city of Rhodes. The citizens, hard pressed, made a sudden sortie, drove the beleaguering hosts from their walls and captured all their engines of war. From the material thus obtained, they made their famous Colossus, one of the seven wonders of the world, a huge bronze figure, 100 feet in height, bestriding the entrance to the harbour of Rhodes. The victors were thus 'more than conquerors' in that they turned the very weapons the enemy brought against them into good account for the glory of their city.

*Choice Gleanings*

(Rom. 8. 37)

**701  More to Follow.**  A benevolent person gave Rowland Hill a hundred pounds sterling to dispense to a poor minister, and thinking it was too much to send him all at once, Mr Hill forwarded five pounds in a letter with these words within the envelope—'More to follow'. In a few days' time the good man received another letter by post (and letters by post were rarities in those days) containing another £5 with the same motto, 'and more to follow'. A day or two after came a third and later a fourth, and still the same promise—'and more to follow'. By the time the whole sum had been disbursed to him the astonished minister had become very familiar with the cheering words—'And more to follow'.

Every blessing we receive from God comes with the self-same message from our Father—'More to follow'. 'Your sins are forgiven', but there's more to follow. 'Justified freely by His grace', but there's more to follow. 'Children of God by faith in Christ Jesus,' and still more to follow. 'Grace upon grace' and always more to follow.

*More and more, more and more, always more*
*to follow!*
*Oh what matchless boundless love! Still there's*
*more to follow.'*

(John 1. 16)

**702 Morning Star.** Dan Crawford used to tell about his Africans: when they were on the march and night was coming on, they would lie down to sleep, but before dropping off to sleep there would pass from group to group around the fires the word *Lutanda* (morning star). It was a laconic agreement to be up and ready to move when the morning star appeared.
*Choice Gleanings*

*He is coming, coming for us; soon we'll see His*
*light afar,*
*On the dark horizon gleaming, as the Bright and*
*Morning Star,*
*Cheering every waking watcher, as the star*
*whose kindly ray*
*Heralds the approaching morning, just before*
*the break of day.*

Many of the old expositors, like Benjamin Keach, were fond of dwelling on those metaphors that illustrate the bountiful provision in Christ. Of these the Morning Star is outstanding.
i. It is of the first magnitude. Christ exceeds all angels and men in surpassing splendour (Heb. 1. 1)
ii. It is of rare beauty and is said to have power to beautify plants (Zech. 9. 17)
iii. It has excellent properties and sends out beneficent influences toward the earth. So Christ is the source of all divine beneficent gifts (James 1. 17)
iv. It is both the Morning and the Evening Star, herald of dawn and guide at night. Jesus Christ is the Alpha and Omega, the File-Leader and Finisher of Faith.
v. Christ appears as the Morning Star before He rises as the Sun of Righteousness—as Morning Star to the Church (Rev. 22. 16), as Sun of Righteousness to the world (Mal. 4. 2)

**703 Morning Star Appearing.**

*When the evils of the earth were greatest*
*The Christ-child came from afar;*
*When the night of the world was darkest,*
*Shone forth the Bethlehem star:*
*Glory and peace was its message,*
*Love and goodwill to men—*
*A peace beyond our making,*
*A love beyond our ken.*

*Long has the vexed world waited*
*The peace that He came to bring;*
*Long have the turbulent peoples*
*Looked for a righteous king;*
*Long has His sad creation*
*Waited redemption's word;*
*Long have His faithful servants*
*Watched for their absent Lord.*

*Long—but the time draws nearer,*
*The Bridegroom comes from afar;*
*When the night of the age is darkest*
*We shall see the Morning Star;*
*Evil is growing stronger*
*And hearts are sick with fear;*
*But our hope is growing brighter*
*For we know that the hour is near.*
                                   Annie Johnson Flint
(Rev. 22. 16)

**704 Morning Watch.**

*Help me to be, to do, to say*
*All Thou hast planned for me today.*

*Give me the mind that learns Thy will,*
*Awaits Thy time, rests and is still.*

*Grant me Thy peace, whate'er befall,*
*Knowing that Thou art Lord of all.*

*Govern my temper, keep my tongue*
*For sake of those I dwell among.*

*Direct my eyes so prone to sin:*
*May my desires be pure and clean!*

*My wand'ring thoughts, oft my despair,*
*Keep specially within Thy care.*

*May I be gracious, thoughtful, kind,*
*To faults in others ever blind.*

*May Thy calm presence so control*
*And satisfy my longing soul,*
*That when I enter a crowded room,*
*They say, 'The man of God has come.'*

*When day is done, and I review*
*The tasks which I have had to do*
*May I be sure that it has passed*
*As if today had been my last.*
                                   Ransome W. Cooper
(Ps. 139. 23,24; 141. 3)

**705 Morning Without Clouds.**

*No clouds are there! No mystery and no*
*shadow;*
*No dark enigmas—hard to understand!*
*No tears are there, no weeping and no sadness,*
*For there—it is a cloudless, tearless land.*

*No clouds! No darksome clouds of lonely*
*sorrow;*
*No tragic hours of eating, mental pain;*
*No consciousness of human desolation,*
*Nor agony of heart can come again.*

*No clouds of anxious thought about some*
*morrow—*
*One's own, or others', e'er again can be;*
*No slow, incessant, taxing, wearing burden,*
*Since from the mortal frame all there are free.*

*No clouds! No clouds at all! The Saviour's*
*presence.*
*Seraphic music and angelic song,*
*And bliss beyond all human comprehending*
*Are 'mongst the joys which to those there*
*belong.*

(2 Sam. 23. 4)

## 706 Morning Without Shadows.

*No shadows there! They joyfully behold Him!*
*No cloud to dim their vision of His face!*
*No jarring note to mar the holy rapture,*
*The perfect bliss of that most blessed place.*

*No burdens there! These all are gone forever!*
*No weary nights, no long or dragging days;*
*No sighings there, or secret, silent longings,*
*For all is now unutterable praise.*

*No conflicts there! No evil hosts assailing!*
*Such warfare past—forever made to cease;*
*No tempter's voice is heard within those portals;*
*No foe lurks there to break the perfect peace.*

*No sorrows there! No sadness and no weeping!*
*Tears wiped away, all radiant now each face;*
*Music and song in happy, holy blending,*
*Fill all the courts of that sweet resting-place.*

                                    J. Danson Smith

(Rev. 21. 2, 3, 4)

## 707 Moses' Rods.

Moses has many titles. He is called the man of God, the servant of Jehovah, King in Jeshurun, a prophet with whom God spoke face to face, God's priest, God's chosen, author of the Pentateuch (2 Chron. 25. 4), a chronicler, the lawgiver, leader of Israel, a faithful steward: and he was 'learned in all the lore of the Egyptians'.

Moses made use of two rods, the first called 'the Rod from before the Lord': this was the priestly rod, the rod that budded, the rod of life and of grace. The other is called 'Moses' rod' the prophet's rod, and the symbol of law and government. This was the rod which was in Moses' hand when he was called to divine service. It was used to turn the river into blood, to bring upon Egypt the plagues of lice, lightning and locusts, to deliver Israel at the Red Sea and for Israel's supply at Marah.

(Exod. 4. 2)

## 708 Moslems' Statement of Faith.

'There is no god but Allah, and Muhammad is the apostle (prophet) of God.' This is the most often repeated sentence in the Arabic language. It is made up of seven Arabic words. Four state the unity of God and three declare the apostleship of Muhammad. Anyone who wishes to become a Moslem may do so by simply confessing this statement of faith. To the primitive mind this simplicity has a strong appeal. The word for witness is also poetic: 'there is no god if it be not The God' might be a literal rendering.

                                    J. Maynard Yoder

In the Arabic seven words are used to describe the faith of Islam.

Three words in Greek and in English—the exact rendering of the three Greek words—suffice for the Christian disciple. These are

Kurios = Lord:  the Christian's Confession:
Iesous = Jesus:  the Christian's Salvation:
Christos = Christ:  the Christian's Devotion.
'Sanctify Christ as Lord in your heart.'

(Rom. 10. 9; 1 Pet. 3. 15)

## 709 Mother of President Garfield.

In *From Log Cabin to White House* there is a fascinating story about President Garfield's inauguration. After the customary ceremonial the newly-acclaimed President stepped from the platform, put his arms round an elderly lady in the audience and placed a kiss on her cheek. That was his affectionate method of acknowledging his debt to his mother.

(Exod. 20. 12)

## 710 Mothers' Responsibilities.

A little girl was being importuned by a parish priest to attend his classes for religious instruction. She refused, saying it was against her father's wishes. The priest told her she should obey him rather than her father. 'Oh, sir,' replied the girl, 'we are taught in the Bible to honour our father and mother.' 'You have no business reading the Bible,' declared the priest. 'But, sir,' the child replied, 'our Lord said to search the Scriptures.' 'That was said only to the Jews, not to children who cannot understand it,' he said. 'But, sir,' the girl said eagerly, 'Paul said to Timothy—"From a child thou hast known the Scriptures." ' The priest had an answer for that too. 'Timothy was taught by the authorities of the church,' he explained, 'and trained to be a bishop.' The little girl knew her Bible so was able to have the last word. 'Oh no, sir,' she answered, 'he was taught by his mother and grandmother.'

(2 Tim. 1. 5; 3. 15)

## 711 Mothers Who Pray.

Dr Joseph Parker has written: 'Blessed are the men who have had praying mothers. The influence of that fact they cannot shake off. They may curse and swear, and go to the very boundary of the pit, and go into the pit, but I question whether through all their sufferings they can ever shake off the influence of having had a praying mother. The mother's devotion comes up in the boy's veneration, love of right, conscientiousness, magnanimous hope, gentle courage.'

J. Hudson Taylor owed much to his mother and her prayers. Once, when she was absent from home for several weeks, Hudson Taylor, being free and at leisure, picked up a tract one afternoon and determined to read only the story part and to stop before he came to the spiritual application. He felt, however, compelled to read on to the end, with the result that he decided to accept Christ as his Saviour that afternoon. He arranged with his sister Amelia that he would be the first to announce the news to their mother on her return. This he did and was surprised to learn that she already knew of his decision for Christ. Greater still was his surprise when he learned that no one had informed her. That afternoon when Hudson Taylor was converted, she had been praying for him and received the assurance from the Lord that he had become a Christian. What the world owes to Hudson Taylor's mother's prayers!

(1 Sam. 1. 27)

159

## 712 Motorist's Prayer.

*Grant me a ready hand, a watchful eye,*
*That none may suffer hurt when I pass by!*
*Thou givest life: I pray no act of mine*
*May take away or mar that gift of Thine.*

*Teach me to use my car for others' need,*
*Nor miss, through lack of wit or love of speed,*
*The beauties of the world, that thus I may*
*With joy and courtesy go on my way.*

G. Binnall

(Ps. 37. 5)

## 713 Mountain Removed.

One evening Frances Johnson, a missionary, was having evening devotions with her group of twenty girls in an orphanage in Poona, India. The Scripture she read was Matthew 21. 2,22: 'Jesus answered and said unto them, Verily I say unto you, If ye have faith and doubt not, ye shall not only do this which is done to the fig tree, but also if ye say unto this mountain, Be thou removed and cast into the sea; it shall be done. And all things, whatsoever ye shall ask in prayer, believing, ye shall receive.'

The town of Poona is built in the hills, and the orphanage had been built against the side of the mountain. The mountains in India have cold weather, and the sun set so early behind this one that the orphanage had very little sunshine. When Miss Frances had finished reading, Mona, one of the little girls, said, 'What about our mountain? If we pray, won't God remove it as He says?'

Frances hesitated, wondering if her own faith was strong enough to believe that the mountain really could be removed; but she must encourage the faith of her girls, so she answered, 'We shall pray about it.' Each little girl and their missionary then prayed that their mountain would be removed.

Next day the girls decided to help to answer their own prayers, so they took their sand buckets and shovels up the mountain side and filled the buckets and carried them down. After an hour or so they gave up.

Then came the excitement of Miss Frances leaving for two weeks. She was going to Bombay for a missionary conference; and as they waved goodbye they reminded her not to forget to pray about the mountain.

A few days after she was gone there was a knock at the door of the orphanage. An official-looking man had been sent by the British Government to see if they could have permission to level off the mountain behind the orphanage. They needed the earth to fill in on the other side as the sea had washed out the land. Of course, necessary steps were taken and permission was granted. In a few days bulldozers were at work and the girls were delighted as they saw the mountain being removed. What a surprise for Miss Frances when she returned! The mountain gone and now plenty of sunshine!

*The Prairie Overcomer*

## 714 Move—The Last.

There was once exhibited a remarkable picture entitled 'The Last Move'. It represents a young man playing chess with the devil. The chessmen were so arranged that seemingly the only move the young man could make at that time would cause him to be checkmated by the devil. A famous chess player went to see the picture and after studying the problem for some time had a chessboard brought to him, declaring, 'I can save that fellow.' Placing the men as in the picture, he so played the game as to bring out the young man victorious and Satan defeated.

What is Satan's last move with men? It is the terror of death. Having enticed man into sin, he was certain of closing up God's favoured creature to death irrevocably. But he was defeated when through death the Lord Jesus Christ brought his power to naught.

Selected

(1 Cor. 15. 55-57; Heb. 2. 14,15)

## 715 Music from our Lives.

A wealthy Englishman had added to his valuable collection a very rare violin which was coveted by Fritz Kreisler, the celebrated violinist. When the owner refused to part with it, Kreisler begged permission to play it just once. Permission was accorded him. He played it as only a genius can play, pouring his soul into the music.

The owner stood transfixed till the playing ceased. He was silent until Kreisler had tenderly returned the instrument to the antique box.

'Take the violin,' the Englishman burst out, 'it is yours: I have no right to keep it. It ought to belong to the man who can play it as you did.'

Ought not an instrument belong to a master who can draw the finest music from it? Ought not our lives belong to the Master who can draw the noblest harmonies from them?

(Rom. 6. 13)

## 716 Myself.

*God harden me against myself,*
*The coward with pathetic voice*
*Who craves for ease, and rest, and joys:*
*Myself, arch-traitor to myself,*
*My hollowest friend, my deadliest foe,*
*My clog whatever road I go.*
*Yet one there is can curb myself,*
*Can roll the strangling load from me,*
*Break off the yoke and set me free.*

Christina Rossetti

(Rom. 7. 24,25)

## 717 Name—Christ's Wonderful.

*And can the myriad tongues of earth*
*Frame words to speak the matchless worth*
*Of God's unique, begotten Son?*
*Can human language tell the sum*
*Or human thought begin to plumb*
*The Greatness of that worthy One?*

*Wonderful Counsellor, the Word*
*Revealing truths before unheard,*
*We worship, magnify, adore,*
*Spanning the gulf' twixt God and man,*
*Thus perfecting salvation's plan,*
*Thou wonderful, wise Counsellor.*
*The Mighty God, to Thee we bow,*
*Creator and Upholder Thou,*
*Whose Word is Thine almighty rod;*
*Yet dwelling in a tent with men,*
*Showing Thy glory, dying, then*
*Enthroned on high, O mighty God.*
*The Everlasting Father, Lord,*
*By the angelic hosts adored;*
*How much more Thy children, rather,*
*Laud Thy name who—wondrous story—*
*Bringest many sons to glory,*
*Thou Everlasting Father!*
*The Prince of peace, without one speck,*
*Our great King-Priest, Melchisedec,*
*Whose government must e'er increase;*
*In righteousness and peace He reigns,*
*Grace, love and truth divine maintains,*
*We worship Him, the Prince of peace.*

**Ray Guyatt**

(Isa. 9. 6,7)

**718  Name that is Matchless.** The Bible is a book of the Name and the names, the names of God and the names of men. As far as God and His Word are concerned, all is set forth in a Name. There are almost 3000 proper names in the Bible, and each has its own significance. Yet above them all there towers one matchless Name, a name divinely given, a name for ever unexcelled, the name of Jesus.

**Geoffrey Bull**

(Matt. 1. 21,23)

**719  Names of Jesus.** From the beginning to the end of the Bible it is the work of the Holy Spirit to reveal Christ, the Son of God. Our Lord is so lovely, so superlatively beautiful, so infinitely perfect, in all His virtues, attributes and graces, that they cannot be expressed in human language. The Holy Spirit, in framing in human language the excellency of Christ Jesus, ransacks every realm of creation for figures and types and illustrations of His loveliness. For this reason hundreds upon hundreds of names are applied to the Saviour, each one a descriptive title, each one serving as a window through which to behold new and different views of His infinitely many-sided loveliness and beauty. And so He is called by the Spirit in the Bible the Second Man, the last Adam, the Son of God, the Son of Man, the only Begotten of the Father, the First born from the dead. He is called the King of kings, the Captain of our Salvation, and the Head of the Church, the Messiah of Israel, the King of the Jews. His Name is called Wonderful, Counsellor, Mighty God, Everlasting Father and Prince of Peace. He is the Lamb of God, the Lion of the Tribe of Judah. He is the Chief Cornerstone, the Rock of Ages, the Head of the Corner and the Foundation Stone; He is the Sun of Righteousness,

the Bright and the Morning Star, the Beginning of the Creation of God, the Tree of Life. He is called the Prophet, Priest and King, the Angel of the Lord and the Angel of the Covenant, the Bread of Life, the Good, the Great and the Chief Shepherd, the Door, the Water of Life, the Word of God, and where shall we stop? For we might go on and on, for He is the Alpha and the Omega, the First, the Last, the Beginning and the End, yea, He is Altogether Lovely.

**M. R. de Haan**

(Matt. 1. 21,23; Luke 1. 32)

**720  Nazareth—Streets of.**
*When I am tempted to repine*
*That such a lowly lot is mine,*
*There comes to me a voice which saith,*
*'Mine were the streets of Nazareth.'*
*So mean, so common and confined,*
*And He the monarch of mankind,*
*Yet patiently He travelleth*
*Those narrow streets of Nazareth.*
*It may be I shall never rise*
*To place or fame beneath the skies,*
*But walk in straitened ways till death*
*Narrow as streets in Nazareth.*
*But if through heaven's arch I tread*
*And there forget to bend my head,*
*Then may I hear the Spirit's breath—*
*'Christ's were the streets of Nazareth.'*

(Luke 2. 51)

**721  Necessity of the New Birth.** Bishop Taylor Smith, when Chaplain General of H.M. Forces, was once preaching in a large cathedral, with the archdeacon seated on the preacher's left. His subject was the necessity of regeneration. To emphasize this he said:

'My dear people, do not substitute anything for the new birth. You may be a member of a church, but church membership is not new birth, and except a man be born again he cannot see the Kingdom of God.' Pointing to the archdeacon on his left, he continued, 'You may even be an archdeacon like my friend here and not be born again, and except a man be born again, he cannot see the kingdom of God. You might even be a bishop like myself and not be born again, and except a man be born again, he cannot see the kingdom of God.'

A day or so later he received a letter from the archdeacon in which he wrote, 'My dear Bishop, you have found me out. I have been a clergyman for over thirty years, but I have never known anything of the joy that Christians speak of; I never could understand it. Mine has been hard legal service. I did not know what was the matter with me, but when you pointed directly at me and said, "You might even be an archdeacon and not be born again," I realized in a moment what the trouble was—I had never known anything of the new birth.'

The next day both men got together over the Word of God, and after some hours the archdeacon told the Lord Jesus he would trust Him as his Saviour.

(John 3. 3)

## 722  Needs All Supplied.

*Lest I should lean on human strength to sow*
*Be Thou my strength;*
*Lest I should fall defeated by the foe*
*All the day's length,*
*Be Thou the arm that seals the victory,*
*For all I need, O Lord, is found in Thee.*

*And should I walk through cloud and darkness*
*    here*
*Be Thou my light;*
*Be Thou the calm that casts out every fear,*
*Be wisdom's sight.*
*Solve Thou the maze of life's perplexity,*
*For all I need, O Lord, is found in Thee.*

*Why should I set as goal some higher thing?*
*Be Thou my aim;*
*Be Thou the praise that makes my heart to*
*    sing*
*Of Thy dear name.*
*Thou art my righteousness eternally:*
*All that I need, O Lord, I find in Thee.*

Ruth G. Zivall

(Phil. 4. 19)

## 723  Net Menders.

*James and John were brethren by the sea.*
*They sat and searched their fishing nets to find*
*If there some broken strand or mesh might be,*
*Which they with patient, skilful hand might*
*    bind.*
*They were experienced fishers and they knew*
*That gaping nets let goodly fishes through.*

*So, while their partners fished, they in the boat*
*Together sat, a-mending nets; and He*
*Who could the toil of busy Peter note,*
*And called the bold apostle, 'Follow Me!'*
*Had also (Perfect Master!) work in view,*
*Suited for men like James and John to do.*

*Years have gone past: still John, with watchful*
*    eye,*
*Observes lest things should fray with wear and*
*    strain,*
*Still seeks the mender's gentle art to ply,*
*Still seeks to 'strengthen things that yet*
*    remain'.*
*With cords of love he threads his needle,*
*    'Truth';*
*He heals the schisms who mended nets in youth.*

*O Lord, I pray that in these latter days,*
*When many strive, and rashly tear and rend,*
*Thou wouldst raise up such men of tact and*
*    grace*
*The things that crumble and would part, to*
*    mend.*
*Teach us, O Lord, and let us not forget*
*Both how to fish for men and mend the net.*

James S. Tait

(Matt. 4. 21)

The same word translated 'mend' in Matt. 4. 21
is rendered 'restore' in Galatians. 6. 1.

## 724  Never Lonely.

*You'll never be lonely while Jesus is near;*
*His comforting presence casts out every fear;*
*And all through life's journey, whate'er may*
*    betide,*
*You'll never be lonely with Him by your side.*

*You'll never be lonely when you realise*
*That the great King of glory who built earth*
*    and skies*
*Is your constant companion, your Saviour and*
*    Friend;*
*You'll never be lonely right on to the end.*

*You'll never be lonely though sorrows oppress;*
*You'll never be lonely in pain or distress;*
*Your constant Companion, so loving and true,*
*Will loneliness banish while He walks with you.*

*You'll never be lonely because Jesus cares:*
*In mansions of glory a Home He prepares,*
*And there, reunited with loved ones above,*
*You'll never be lonely—redeemed by His love.*

(Heb. 13. 5,6)

## 725  New Birth Preached.

George Whitefield was always expatiating on one tremendous theme, John 3. 3—with an Indian in a canoe on one of the great American rivers, to black men in the Bermudas, to the aristocratic audience in the drawing-room of the Countess of Huntingdon. 'Why, Mr Whitefield,' inquired a friend, 'why do you preach so often on "Ye must be born again"?' 'Because,' was his answer 'ye must be born again.'

Bishop Taylor Smith was preaching one Sunday to a fashionable congregation in London, England. At the morning service he took for his text the words spoken by our Lord to Nicodemus, 'Ye must be born again.' After the service someone told him that they were not used to that kind of preaching in their church. It might be all right for the Salvation Army but not for a congregation such as theirs. That evening he preached again, this time from the words, 'Marvel not that I said unto thee, 'Ye must be born again." '

(John 3. 7)

## 726  New Captain—A.

Old 'Bust-me-up' was a queer shaped ugly old tugboat running between London and Portsmouth. She never came into port without colliding with some vessel and did some damage. Hence the name! But one day — to everybody's amazement — she came in straight as a die and glided gracefully to her berth. A sailor standing on the quay couldn't help shouting, 'Whatever's come to you, old Bust-me-up?' An old sailor shouted back, 'Got a new captain!' That was the secret of the change. And when Christ becomes our Captain, He controls us and changes our lives.

*Great Captain of salvation, now crowned with*
*    highest glory,*
*Joyful we raise our songs of praise, and lowly*
*    bow before Thee.*

*Choice Gleanings*

(Heb. 2. 10)

It is interesting to note that the word translated 'Captain' in Hebrews 2. 10 occurs four times in the New Testament, and every time is applied to the Lord Jesus Christ. It is translated 'Prince' in Acts 3. 15 and Acts 5. 31, 'Captain' in Hebrews 2. 10, and 'Author' in Hebrews 12. 2.

**727   New Testament Survey.**   The primitive Church depended on:
i. the Old Testament Scriptures; ii. apostolic doctrine (oral) of the life, teaching and redemptive work of Jesus Christ, and iii. direct revelation from God through His inspired prophets.

God providentially guided the early Church in its evaluation of books written so that books truly inspired were accepted and the rest rejected.
The Criteria of Canonicity were:
Agreement with the apostolic doctrine of the first century;
Authorship by an apostle or an apostolic delegate;
Date of writing within the apostolic period.

Mark was associated with Peter, Luke with Paul; and James and Jude, brothers of the Lord Jesus, were associates of the apostles in the church at Jerusalem.
The New Testament is the authoritative record and interpretation of God's revelation of Himself through Jesus our Lord. Most of it was written on papyrus in scroll form: some may have been put out in codex form, the pages being bound together. None of the original documents (autographs) is extant.
At first copies were made one by one; but later, a reader dictated to a room full of copyists. Human errors took place such as omissions, repetitions and even alterations, so each copy was checked against other manuscripts, sometimes several times. Later vellum (calfskin) and parchment (sheepskin) were used. Early MSS. were written in capital letters (uncials) and later in small letters (called cursives, which means running hand). The earliest MSS. in possession of modern scholars date from the second century. Primary sources are Greek MSS. early versions of translations into Syrian and Latin, writings of the early church fathers quoting New Testament writings, and readings from liturgies then in use. The earliest translations into English were Wycliffe's translation from the Latin in 1352, Tyndale's translation from Greek in 1525, the Roman Catholic Douay version in 1582, and the King James Version in 1611. Modern translations are numerous, some of them merely paraphrases.
Robert H. Gundry

**728   New Year Meditations.**

*O Lord, we know not how to face the year*
*That opens dark amidst the thunder's roar;*
*A silent dread, a pang of grief and fear,*
*A sigh of anguish, tears for joys now o'er—*
*How can we meet the future days alone?*
*How find the path, untrodden and unknown?*

*'Thou comest to us'—all things else are dim,*
*All things are shaking, night doth darkly brood;*
*The cup of sorrow filled up to the brim,*
*The powers of evil triumphing o'er the good;*
*Midst earthquake, fire and storm—a world*
*   distrest—*
*One voice speaks peace: Jesus Himself gives*
*   rest.*
                                                              J.H.S.
(Exod. 33. 16)

**729   News of a Great Discovery.**   Hulm, the great naturalist, tells us that if a wasp discovers a deposit of honey or other food, he will return to his nest and impart the good news to his companions, who will sally forth in great numbers to partake of the fare which he has discovered. Shall we, who have made a much greater discovery, be less considerate of our fellow-men than wasps are of their fellow-insects? The woman of Samaria went into the city and said 'Come, see a man which told me all things that ever I did: is not this the Christ?' Then they went out of the city and came to Jesus.
                                                   *Choice Gleanings*
(2 Kings 7. 9)

**730   Noah's Ark—Reported Discovery.**   From Istanbul, Turkey, came the word late last summer that Noah's Ark had been discovered resting on the side of Mount Ararat. There were two expeditions in search of the ark last summer season. One party was led by Eryl Cummings known as the world's greatest authority on Noah's Ark. He states that 185 individuals claim to have seen the Ark during the past 120 years. He returned from his latest expedition to Mount Ararat last August. Members of another expedition bored through the ice and brought up timber which may be from the Ark.
Mount Ararat has long been called 'Kui-inuh' by the Persians. The name means 'Noah's Mountain'. Another mountain in the Ararat region is called 'Sit-napistim,' meaning, 'the ship stopped'. There is a town in the region, named 'Kibotos,' meaning 'the Ark'. Another town carries a name which means 'the place of descent'.
The historian, Josephus, makes a statement that the remains of the Ark were still to be seen in his day, A.D. 90, in a place called 'the place of descent'. He also names various historians of an earlier date who testified to the fact. Thus Berorus, the Chaldean: 'It is said that there is still some part of this ship in Armenia at the mountain of the Corydaeans, and that some people carry off pieces of bitumen to use as amulets for averting mischief.' Nicolaus of Damascus, only thirty years before Christ, wrote: 'There is a great mountain in Armenia called Baris. One carried in an ark came on shore here after the Flood. Remains of the timber were a great while preserved here.'
Bitumen is subject neither to decay, oxidation nor attacks of insects. Huge timbers covered with it would be almost indestructible at the Ararat altitude. Ararat is four hundred miles north of Jerusalem.

It is of interest that Marco Polo wrote of the Ark. Speaking of the 'description of greater Armenia,' he says, 'And you must know that it is in this country of Armenia that the Ark of Noah exists (A.D. 1269) on the top of a certain great mountain on the summit of which, snow is so constant that no one can ascend; for the snow never melts, and it is constantly added to by new snow.'

There was a reported discovery of Noah's Ark ninety-five years ago. The government of Turkey sent commissioners to inquire into the reported destruction of some towns in the Ararat region, and to render relief to distressed villagers in the glens of the Ararat ranges. Due to the unusual inclemency of the season there had been some avalanches. Members of the expedition came upon a gigantic structure of very dark wood, embedded at the foot of one of the glaciers, with one end protruding, which they believed to be none other than the Ark. The place was given as in the department of Van, in Armenia, about forty leagues from the Persian frontier. The discovery was reported in the newspaper, the *Levant Herald*, and in *The British Prophetic Messenger*.

*Indian Christian*

(Gen. 8. 4)

**731 None but Christ.** The Christian martyr, John Lambert, was born during the reign of Henry VIII in the county of Norfolk, England, in a time of bitter persecution when many true Christians were being burnt at the stake. Educated at the University of Cambridge and converted through the preaching of Thomas Bilney, he joined William Tyndale who was then engaged in the translation of the New Testament. About the year 1532, while employed as a chaplain to the English at Antwerp, he was accused of teaching heresy and brought to England to be tried in the presence of the King, the Bishops and peers of the realm. He was charged with denying that the bread of the Sacrament was the real body of Christ. To this he replied that it was not possible for Christ's body to be in two places at one time, in heaven at the right hand of God and on earth in the Sacrament. He contended that the words, 'This is my body', are a figurative mode of speech where the thing signified is attributed to the sign, of which many examples could be deduced from the Scriptures. Enraged at the clear refutation of their doctrine, the court condemned him to death. He was hurried to Smithfield and there bound to the stake. In the midst of the fire his soul was joyful in the Lord and his lips filled with praise. To add to his torture two soldiers hoisted his body on their halberts, but the joyful martyr raised his arms and cried aloud, 'None but Christ, none but Christ!' In amazement the soldiers let his body drop into the flames which reduced it to ashes. The echo of his dying cry will live for ever: 'None but Christ, none but Christ.'

(Matt. 17. 8)

**732 None Like Christ.** Of John Brown of Haddington it could be said,

*So when a good man dies, for years beyond
   his ken
The light he leaves behind him lies upon the
   path of men.*

Toward the end of his life he said, 'Commend Jesus. I have been looking at Him for these many years and never yet could find a fault in Him. There is none like Christ, none like Christ, none like Christ; nothing like redemption through His blood, the forgiveness of sins according to the riches of His grace. There is no learning or knowledge like the knowledge of Christ; no life like Christ living in the heart by faith; no work like the service, the spiritual service of Christ; no reward like the free-grace wages of Christ; no riches or wealth like the unsearchable riches of Christ, no comfort like the consolations of Christ, no pleasure like the pleasure of fellowship with Christ.'

(Song of Solomon 5. 9,16)

**733 Nothing is Lost.**

*To talk with God no breath is lost; talk on,
   talk on.
To walk with God no strength is lost; walk on,
   walk on.
To wait on God no time is lost; wait on, wait
   on:
The work is quicker, better done, not needing
   half the strength laid on;
Work on, work on.*

*Martha stood, but Mary sat;
Martha murmured much at that;
Martha cared but Mary heard;
Listening to the Masters' word;
And the Lord her choice preferred;
Sit on, hear on.*

*Work without God is labour lost;
Full soon you'll learn it to your cost;
Toil on, toil on!*

*Little is much when God is in it;
Man's busiest day's not worth God's minute.
Much is little everywhere
If God the labour do not share;
In work with God there's nothing lost;
Who works with Him does best and most:
Work on, work on.*

(1 Cor. 15. 58)

**734 Nuclear Atheists.** Colonel John D. Craig, formerly of the U.S. Army, and photographer of the atomic explosions at Bikini and Eniwetok, made the following statement: 'There are no atheists among the nuclear scientists, not a single one!

'When they succeeded in splitting the atom, they realized that for the first time man had stepped into the realm of creation, that it was divine Sovereignty speaking to him, and that man had better listen to what the Creator was saying to him. For now two destinies were offered to man. The very power that was active in creation had been placed at his disposal, and he could use it for untold blessings or for his own undoing. Once more he had been confronted with the age-long alternative of choosing between life and death.'

These startling words coming from such a man should shake us out of our materialistic attitude of mind and make us realise that we have in the vast universe nothing less than the handiwork of God, the perfect Architect and Creator.

(Isa. 42. 5)

**735  Nuclear Dangers.** In the first speech President Kennedy of the U.S.A. made to the Ninety-nine Nations Assembly he said, 'The next ten months could decide the fate of man for the next 10,000 years,' and hoped we should not be remembered as the generation which turned this planet into a flaming pyre. During his short Presidency and almost within the ten months indicated in his speech, the Cuban crisis developed and might have led to a destructive nuclear war, which by divine Providence was averted. The time is not yet ripe in the divine purpose for the fulfilment of 2 Peter 3. 12.

**736  Nuclear Warfare.**
Mrs Nina Khrushchev, the quietly spoken wife of the former Russian Prime Minister, in a news dispatch from Moscow, acknowledging that there would be no defence in a nuclear war said, 'Therefore we are not building air raid shelters; we are not getting ready.' This homely friendly woman tersely stated again, 'There would be no defence in a nuclear war; there would be no place to hide.'

The build-up of British and U.S.A. nuclear weapons provides a total fire power of very many thousands of Hiroshimas. On August 6th, 1945, a city of 300,000—Hiroshima—was virtually levelled by the explosion of the second atom bomb. 70,000 people were killed instantaneously and 70,000 more were injured. Bodies were literally cooked, the brain cells seared and eyeballs melted and running down their cheeks.

Mr J. M. Davies, missionary in Kerala, India, stated that when, on one occasion, he read the words in Zechariah's prophecy—'This is the plague wherewith the Lord shall smite all the people that have fought against Jerusalem; their flesh shall consume away while they stand upon their feet, and their eyes shall consume away in their holes, and their tongue shall consume away in their mouth'—to an Indian army officer, he said it was an exact description of Hiroshima.

(Zech. 14. 12)

**737  Number of the Beast.** Some time ago a large Canadian newspaper ran an interesting news report under this headline: 'Will everyone have a number on his forehead?' It was a report on a meeting of the Computer Society of Canada held at Banff, Alberta. At this meeting Professor B. A. Hodson, director of the computer centre at the University of Manitoba, reportedly said: 'We find ourselves in a dilemma. We advocate an era in which everybody will have a number on his forehead and won't be able to do anything without. The centralization of government, business and credit records will help to bring this about. We are automating hospitals and changing our very society.'

It is easy to see that the Bible is 'ahead of the times'. It is indeed the inspired Word of God. We must prepare for the things yet to come.

H. H. Pohl

(Rev. 13. 16-18)

**738  Nuptial Day of Christ.**

*At last it dawns! that nuptial morning fair,*
*The day for which all other days were made;*
*In tender radiance stealing down the sky,*
*What hosts of glorious beings in light arrayed*
*Are gathering in their myriads, to await*
*The Bridegroom's coming in His royal state!*

*The mandate has gone forth! From gates of pearl*
*In shining legions through the air they press,*
*What joy triumphant lights each radiant brow,*
*In strength excelling and in holiness!*
*While, hark! the archangel's voice through*
*     heaven's vast space*
*Sounds its high summons to the angelic race.*

*In breathless expectation now they wait,*
*Deep silence broods o'er all the earth and sky,*
*When lo! a shout of rapture rends the air,*
*Of joy surpassing all yet known on high,*
*The Bridegroom's shout of victory as He leaves*
*     the throne*
*To welcome to the air His loved, His own.*

*What heart could e'er conceive, or tongue*
*     express*
*The heaven born ecstasy each saint shall feel,*
*When on his ear those thrilling accents fall,*
*Accompanied by the trumpet's last long peal;*
*Earth's million sleepers spurn the grave's*
*     disguise,*
*And, clad in Christ's own beauty, mount the skies,*

*Thrice blest are they who know the joyful*
*     sound,*
*The music of that tender Bridegroom call,*
*Whose hearts respond in deep adoring love,*
*'To Thee we come, our Lord, our Life, our All.'*
*Swift soar they upward through the ambient*
*     air,*
*Their cross for ever dropped, their crown how*
*     fair!*

*For ever with the Lord! Oh, bliss unknown,*
*And unimagined while in this time sphere!*
*To gaze for ever on His glorious face,*
*The music of His voice for ever hear;*
*Each soul so rapt in consciousness of Him,*
*That heaven's own glories by compare grow dim.*

*'Twere sight too fair for mortal eyes to view!*
*Where stands the Lamb amid that concourse*
*vast,*
*With all His matchless beauty now revealed,*
*God's masterpiece of Love unveiled at last;*
*In speechless adoration at His feet they fall,*
*And saints and angels crown Him Lord of all!*

*Immortal soul, whose eye now scans these lines,*
*What is the hope that's nearest to thy heart?*
*Should now the shout, the trumpet-call be*
*heard,*
*Wouldst thou take wing, all ready to depart,*
*To be with One unseen yet how adored,*
*And win Love's prize*—FOREVER WITH THE
LORD?

E.J.A.P.

(Song of Solomon 3. 11)

### 739 Obedience.

*I am not strong, I am not wise,*
*And many a path before me lies*
*Where I might stray*
*So, when I have to make a choice,*
*Help me to listen to Thy voice*
*And then obey.*

THIS IS MY PRAYER

(1 Sam. 15. 22)

### 740 Obedience Rewarded.

Many years ago a farmer noticed a party of horsemen riding in his direction. He had one field he was anxious that they should not ride over, so he sent a lad to the field, telling him to shut the gate, to watch it, and on no account to let it be opened.

Soon the huntsmen came up and ordered the gate to be opened. This the boy refused to do, stating the orders he had received which he could not disobey. After some argument one of the huntsmen said in commanding tones, 'My boy, you do not know me. I am the Duke of Wellington, and I command you to open the gate that I and my friends may pass through.'

The boy doffed his cap in deference to the famous hero of Waterloo, but answered respectfully, though firmly, 'I am sure the Duke of Wellington would not wish me to disobey orders. I must keep this gate shut and not allow anyone to pass except with my master's permission.'

Greatly pleased with the lad's loyalty to his master, the renowned General lifted his own hat to the lad and said: 'I honour the boy or man who cannot be frightened into doing wrong.' Handing the boy a sovereign, the Duke put spurs to his horse and with his friends galloped away.

It is essential for an overruling authority to maintain control of the gate of life and to that authority we must submit. Man normally comes under five authorities which claim obedience, each in its own sphere—his parents, employers, teachers, rulers and God; and obedience is the supreme test of faith in God. (Col. 3. 20,22; Heb. 13. 17; Acts 5. 29)

### 741 Obedience to Parents.

When General Havelock was a boy he was out on London Bridge one day with his father who, having some business to do, left him there and bade him wait there till he returned. The father was detained and forgot all about his son on the bridge. After he arrived home in the evening and had rested a bit, his wife asked, 'Where's Harry?' The father thought for a moment. 'Dear me!' said he, 'I quite forgot Harry. I left him on London Bridge and he must have been there these eight hours waiting for me.' Hurrying out, he found the lad just where he had left him in the morning, pacing to and fro like a sentinel on his beat.
(John 15. 10; Col. 3. 20)

### 742 Old Age.

Sir Walter Scott said in his last hours: 'I used to think a slight illness was a luxurious thing. It is different in the last stages. The old postchaise gets more shattered at every turn. Windows will not pull up; doors refuse to open or, being opened, will not shut again. There is one new subject of complaint every moment.

'The recollections of youth and health and uninterrupted activity, neither improved nor enjoyed, is a poor stream of comfort. Death has closed the long dark avenue upon loves and friendships, and I look at them as through the grated door.'
(Eccl. 12. 2-5)

### 743 Old Age.

*The sunny side of seventy! I've reached it long*
*ago,*
*And now I'm nearing eighty, with hair as white*
*as snow,*
*Eyes dim, joints still, back feeble—I seem in*
*evil case;*
*To sing of sunny seventy seems somewhat out*
*of place,*
*But is it? Pause and ponder what the good*
*Book has said*
*Of righteousness and glory crowning the hoary*
*head.*
*Think of the rocks and quicksands which I have*
*safely passed*
*By the Good Shepherd's guidance through many*
*a roaring blast*
*Now I am near the borders of the bright*
*shining land*
*Where blessed saints are waiting for me to*
*join their band—*
*For me—all believers cleansed in that marv'lous*
*flood*
*Which frees from all defilement,—e'en Christ's*
*atoning blood.*
*Does not that counterbalance the weakness of*
*my frame?*
*Oh, how the thought of glory has set my heart*
*on flame!*
*What though this mortal body, poor tenement*
*of clay,*
*'Neath death's dominion falling, should perish*
*and decay?*

*What matters? All is brightness, for thus*
  *proclaims the Word—*
*Absent from this poor body, then present with*
  *the Lord.*
*How glorious are my prospects—Lo! to faith's*
  *piercing view*
*Lie realms of brightest glory, scenes ever fair*
  *and new,*
*Where Christ in heavenly glory, the Lamb of*
  *God divine,*
*God's Son, His well-beloved, doth reign: and*
  *Christ is mine.*

Hector Maiben

(Prov. 16. 31; 2 Cor. 4. 16-18)

**744  Old Folks of Scripture.** Anna has an honoured place among the old folks of Scripture. The Bible list of senior saints is a long one, and the Old Testament in particular carries a long list of such names, which is not surprising when we remember the Old Testament story covers 4,000 years. The New Testament list is much shorter, but the names are very significant. Simeon was among the ancients. He, like Anna, filled an honourable role that self-same day in the Temple; he held the Child in his arms. Nicodemus was old—he said so to the Lord. Paul the apostle became Paul the aged. Peter too became old: his Master said he would. And John lived to a ripe old age. So Anna was in good company. But note one slight difference. Whilst the others were said to be old, we do not know precisely how old they were. We do, however, know Anna's age—84.

There are, of course, two Annas in the Bible, the Anna (Hanna) of the Old Testament, and the Anna of the New. The one was young and the other old; the one prayed and was given Samuel; the other fasted and prayed and was given to see God's unspeakable gift, her Saviour and ours. They both found their way to the Temple, the one for an annual visit, the other for her permanent abode. And then, when the Lord was brought there, she spake of Him. Let us do the same—let us speak of Him.

A. Soutter

(Luke 2. 25,26,36-38)

**745  Omnipresence of God.**

*If there be a God, the learned ones say,*
*He is 'billions and billions of light-years away'.*
*I'm not a scientist, but one thing I know,*
*The moment I send up a prayer from below,*
*That moment it reaches my Father who may*
*Be billions and billions of light-years away:*
*His Spirit pervades the fullness of space,*
*And instant connection He puts up apace.*
*Yea, this thing I know, I can converse with*
  *Him,*
*And closer is He than my life and my limb.*
*He guides me, instructs me, He answers my*
  *call;*
*He shows me what scientists can't see at all,*
*With their latest, most perfect, most power-*
  *fully made*

*Cameras, telescopes, and others to aid.*
*But, lacking the Light by Jesus Christ given,*
*And the current, His life, that links us to*
  *heaven.*
*Hath He not spoken His omniscient Word,*
*'Ere they call, I'll answer'? The eyes of the*
  *Lord*
*Scan every event, and each prayer that is*
  *said*
*Billions upon billions of light-years ahead.*
*Ye who would climb mountains and fly to the*
  *moon*
*And circle round planets, or even the sun,*
*Why are your minds so hermetically sealed*
*'Gainst knowledge that God has so freely*
  *revealed?*

H. Kaveri Bai

(Ps. 139. 7-10)

**746  One Fellowship.**

*In Christ there is no East and West,*
*In Him no South or North;*
*But one great fellowship of love*
*Throughout the whole wide earth.*

*In Him shall true hearts everywhere*
*Their high communion find;*
*His service is the golden chord*
*Close binding all mankind.*

*Join hands, then, brothers of the faith,*
*Whate'er your race may be.*
*Who serves my Father as a son*
*Is surely kin to me.*

(Gal. 3. 28,29)

**747  One in Christ.** It was Sunday morning in Kiangsu, China, during World War II. The service was in a little Chinese church. Suddenly there was excitement and suppressed cries of fear. Women clutched their babies. Men half rose from their seats. A Japanese soldier was walking down the aisle! Japanese troops had recently taken over Kiangsu. When the soldier reached the front of the church, he laid an offering on the table. All fear subsided when he said, 'I am a Christian. I desire to worship with you!' He opened a hymnbook at the hymn, 'Blest be the tie that binds'; and then the Japanese soldier and the Chinese Christians all sang together:

*Blest be the tie that binds*
*Our hearts in Christian love.*

Indian Christian

(Gal. 3. 28)

**748  One Tooth.** One Tooth, an old man living in a Papuan village in New Guinea, became a Christian. Subsequently he learned to read and then spent part of his time reading God's Word to fellow Papuans who came as out-patients to the hospital where he earned his living by cutting firewood. One day One Tooth was told that he had an incurable eye condition and he would soon be blind. The next morning the old woodcutter did not report for work but sent a young replacement instead. One Tooth had left for an unknown destination. After enquiries the doctor discovered that One Tooth was living in a desolate spot—the tribe's burial ground, which was under a taboo. A youth was supplying him with food, and one day a young man led the doctor to the hiding-place where he met the now blind One Tooth. 'What are you doing here? Why did you not stay at the hospital?' asked the doctor. One Tooth replied, 'Since you told me that I would be blind I have been here alone, reading God's Word and memorising it as much as I could: the passages about the Saviour's birth, His miracles, the Sermon on the Mount, the Cross and the Resurrection. I have learned some of the Psalms and the Old Testament stories. I have been repeating them from memory to the boy coming back to the hospital, doctor,' explained the old woodcutter. 'I won't be able to chop the wood, but I will be able to tell the out-patients about Jesus. When you told me that I would go blind I thought my work of sharing the message of the Bible was finished. But God has shown me that my work is just beginning. This I must do for God.'

Chairette

(Acts. 1.8)

**749   Opportunity.** The crosses of the two malefactors were equidistant from that of Christ. But one thief was saved; the other was damned. Each had the same opportunity. In the same land of Egypt Abram fell but Joseph rose to glory. The same sun melts the snow but hardens the clay. The same Red Sea became a wall of protection to the Israelites but a sepulchre to the Egyptians. The same cloud was light on the side of the Israelites but darkness on the side of the Egyptians who pursued the people of God. The same Word of God, when preached by Peter on the day of Pentecost, brought salvation to three thousand souls, but, when preached by Stephen before his martyrdom, hardened the heads and hearts of a great multitude, and increased their responsibility against the day of judgement.

V. P. Jacob

(Luke 23. 39-43)

**750   Original Sin.** Seth Joshua was once talking to a man who said to him: 'you know, I can't swallow what you preachers say about original sin.' Joshua replied, 'My friend, you don't need to swallow it: it is inside you already.'

(Ps. 51. 5; Rom. 5. 12)

**751   Others.** When William Booth, the founder of the Salvation Army, walked down the streets of Whitechapel in 1865, he looked out upon the godless multitudes through the eyes of a true evangelist. He hurried back to his West End home and said to his noble wife: 'Oh, Kate, I have found my destiny. These are

the people for whose salvation I have been longing all these years. I have offered up myself, and you, and the children to this great work.'

In a New Year message years later to all his people he sent only one word—'OTHERS': and later a Christian worker wrote a poem about this word, and concluded with the lines:

*'Others, Lord, yes, others! Let this my motto be! Help me to live for others that I may live like Thee.*

(Acts 10. 38; Rom. 15. 20)

**752   Others to think of.** Dr F. W. Boreham used to tell how in his New Zealand days, the opportunity came to him to revisit England. When the party reached Plymouth Sound they sent telegrams to their home folk telling them the exact time they might expect them the next day. The liner continued its voyage up the Channel but alas! down came the fog and down, too, went the anchor. The ship waited and waited.

'This is very exasperating,' observed Dr Boreham to the Captain. 'We sent telegrams from Plymouth telling the people at home when to meet us, and they'll be waiting on the docks now. Is there no possibility of getting on?' 'All very fine for you,' the skipper replied, 'You are in a 10,000 ton liner; and you would like me to go up the river crumpling everything we happen to strike, as though it was made of brown paper. No, no! we've got other ships to think of.'

'Many a time since then,' said Dr Boreham, 'when the thick fogs have enveloped me and I have been uncertain of my course, I have nevertheless been tempted to go full steam ahead. But I have recalled the old captain's words, "There are others to think of."'

(Phil. 2. 4)

**753   Outward Appearance.** Some time ago a great religious leader came to our State capital to speak at the Y.M.C.A. He had a terrific reputation as an evangelist, and to entertain him his sponsors called on me and said, 'Governor, would you have this man up for dinner before the evening meeting?' Of course I was delighted. The time came, and I rushed home from my office in high expectations to meet this dynamic speaker who had made such a wonderful record for his God. Right before me was a gnome-like creature not over five feet tall, who looked like something his mother would like to forget. My face registered my disappointment. My guest looked at me and said, 'Governor, isn't it wonderful what God can use?' And so it was.

Governor Arthur B. Langlie

(2 Cor. 10. 7-10)

**754   Outward Joy, Inward Sorrow.** In 1915, George Powell, a British actor, wrote a pop song that made him famous, and his father, Felix, composed the music to which it was sung all over Great Britain and by soldiers in the trenches in France. The song was—'Pack up your troubles in your old kit bag and smile, smile, smile.'

In February, 1942, twenty-seven years later, Felix Powell went to a recreation centre, sat down at the piano and sang, to the tune he had composed,

'*What's the use of worrying: it never was worthwhile;*
*So pack up your troubles in your old kit bag and smile, smile, smile.'*

Shortly after strumming out the words, he went into another room and shot himself. How sad! Overcome with worry and sorrow even while singing—'Smile, smile, smile'—he did not seem to know the only One who can banish grief and give lasting peace and satisfaction, the Lord Jesus Christ.
(John 16. 20,33)

**755 Overruling Hand of God.** Bernard Gilpin, sentenced in the reign of Queen Mary Tudor to die for his faith, repeated during his imprisonment each morning and each night, 'We know that all things work together for good to them that love God.' On his way to execution he fell and broke his leg, and was ordered back to prison where he moaned in pain. The jailer twitted him with his text. 'Ah!' he said, 'but it's true all the same.' And sure enough, it was, for while he lay in hospital, Queen Mary died, Elizabeth ascended the throne, and Bernard Gilpin was set at liberty.
(Rom. 8. 28)

**756 Oyster Supper.** Sir George Williams founder of the Y.M.C.A., when a young man, was greatly used in the warehouse where he was employed to the conversion of several young men. A scoffer by the name of Rogers vowed that he would 'take that nonsense out of them'. The young converts spent an evening in prayer and discussion as to how they might win the scoffer for Christ. Learning that the scoffer was very fond of oysters, George Williams said, 'Let's give him an invitation to an oyster supper.'

Rogers was casually informed that they were having an oyster supper and asked if he would like to join them. In a spirit of bravado he accepted the invitation and there discovered that Christians were not so stiff and starchy and long-faced as they were painted. Then he was invited to attend a prayer meeting and was there soundly converted. The young men's method of approach had disarmed his prejudice and led to his conversion.
(2 Cor. 12. 16)

**757 Pace-Setter—My.** In September, 1965, the *Christian Graduate* published the following paraphrase of Psalm 23 by Toki Miyashina of Japan:

*The Lord is my Pace-setter; I shall not rush.*
*He makes me stop and rest for quiet intervals:*

*He provides me with images of stillness which restore my serenity.*
*He leads me in ways of efficiency through calmness of mind, and His guidance is peace.*
*Even though I have a great many things to accomplish each day, I will not fret, for His presence is here.*
*His timelessness, His all-importance will keep me in balance.*
*He prepares refreshment and renewal in the midst of my activity by anointing my mind with His oil of tranquillity. My cup of joyous energy overflows.*
*Surely harmony and effectiveness shall be the fruits of my hours. For I shall walk in the pace of the Lord, and dwell in his House for ever.*

**758 Pardon Refused.** In 1830, a man named George Wilson was sentenced to be hanged for robbery and murder. Andrew Jackson, at that time President of the U.S.A. granted him a pardon. Wilson refused to accept it, and insisted that unless he did so it was not a pardon.

The Attorney General said the law was silent on the matter, and referred it to the Supreme Court. Chief Justice Marshall gave the following decision: 'A pardon is a paper the value of which depends on its acceptance by the person implicated. It is hardly to be supposed that one under sentence of death would refuse to accept a pardon, but if it is refused it is no pardon. George Wilson must be hanged.'
(Acts 10. 43)

**759 Pardon Undelivered.** 'We've a story to tell to the nations' is very often sung at missionary meetings. We would like to add this verse to the words already comprising the hymn:

*We've a pardon to give to the nations*
*Which was purchased at infinite cost,*
*A pardon as yet undelivered,*
*Which leaves them eternally lost.*

Jesus purchased that pardon by shedding His precious blood on the Cross. He committed this pardon to His Church as its only custodian, to deliver to a lost world, and bade them go and preach the gospel to every creature.
(Matt. 26. 28; Luke 24. 47)

**760 Parental Influence.** Dr S. D. Gordon in his *Quiet Talks on Home Ideals* says, 'A father and mother living together with their children, tender in their love, pure in their lives, strong in their convictions, simple and orderly in their habits, do infinitely more than presidents and governors, legislators and clergymen can do in making a strong nation.'
(Prov. 22. 6)

**761 Parenthood.** In a mothers' meeting there was a vigorous discussion on the theme— How early in a child's life ought one to begin to influence him toward God? After much spirited debate, a visiting grandmother was asked to make her comment. She said—in essence—'I began with my first child twenty years before she was born by giving myself to the Lord Jesus Christ.'

*Sunday School Times*

(2 Tim. 1. 5; 3. 15)

## 762 Parents of Retarded Children.   A parent writes:

I never knew the disappointment, heartbreak, rebellion, sacrifice and sometimes triumphant spirit that characterise the parents of a retarded child until after May 5, 1952, the day I learned I was the father of a mongoloid baby. There are many people and institutions to which to turn for guidance—specialists' clinics, children's homes, and a vast amount of literature. But the supreme problem is—How do I look upon this child, my child? Is God involved, or did the mathematics of the birth rate of retarded children just catch up with me? At this point the Bible is particularly relevant. When Moses protested to God that he was not eloquent, his protest brought forth the reply. 'Who hath made man's mouth? Or who maketh the dumb, or deaf, or the seeing, or the blind? Have not I, the Lord?' (Exod. 4. 11). The parent will either hate this kind of a God or come, perhaps slowly, to trust completely His wisdom and love. Job, having lost all but a critical wife, could finally say, 'What? shall we receive good at the hand of God and shall we not receive evil?' (Job. 2. 10). The biggest lesson learned is that, by following the pathway of acceptance and balanced understanding. Christian parents arrive at the place of being able to believe that 'all things work together for good to them that love God'.

Robert J. Lamont in *Christianity Today*
(Rom. 8. 28)

## 763 Parents' Primer.   The Police Department of Houston, Texas, prepared and published *The Making of A Delinquent* as a warning to parents indifferent to their children's welfare.

1 Begin at infancy to give the child everything he wants. In this way he will grow up to believe the world owes him a living.
2 When he picks up bad words, laugh at him. That will make him think he's amusing.
3 Never give him any spiritual training. Wait until he's twenty-one and then let him decide for himself.
4 Pick up everything he leaves lying about—books, shoes, clothes; do everything for him so that he will be experienced in throwing all responsibility on to others.
5 Quarrel frequently in his presence. In this way he will not be too shocked when the home is broken later.
6 Give the child all the pocket-money he wants. Never let him earn his own. Why

should he have things as tough as you had them?
7 Satisfy his every craving for food, drink and comfort. Denial may lead to harmful frustration.
8 Take his side against neighbours, teachers, policemen. They are all prejudiced against your child.
9 When he gets into serious trouble, apologise for yourself by saying, 'I could never do anything with him.'
10 Prepare for a life of grief. You are bound to have it.

*Reader's Digest*

(Prov. 23. 13)

## 764 Parents Who Pray.

*I wash the dirt from little feet and, as I wash,
  I pray,
'Lord keep them ever pure and true to walk
  the narrow way.'
I wash the dirt from little hands and earnestly
  I ask,
'Lord, may they ever yielded be to do the
  humblest task!'
I wash the dirt from little knees and pray,
  'Lord, may they be
In place where victories are won and orders
  sought from Thee.'
I scrub the clothes that soil so soon and pray,
  'Lord may her dress
Throughout eternal ages be Thy robe of
  righteousness.'*

*Ere many hours shall pass I know I'll wash
  those hands again,
And there'll be dirt upon the dress before the
  day shall end;
But as she journeys on through life and learns
  of want and pain,
'Lord keep her precious little heart cleansed
  from all sin and stain.
For soap and water cannot reach where Thou
  alone canst see:
Her hands and feet—these I can wash; I trust
  her heart to Thee.'*

B. Ryberd in *The King's Business*
(Prov. 31. 28)

## 765 Parousia of Christ.   Across the River Tyne from Newcastle is Sheriff's Hill, so called because in olden days when the judges came to hold the Assizes in the city, the Sheriffs of Newcastle rode out to meet them on that hill and to accompany them back to Newcastle.

The late H. P. Barker remarked that this is an illuminating picture of what is to happen when Christ comes again. The redeemed will meet Him in the air—His Sheriff's Hill—then He will return with His glorified saints to take possession of the earth, overcome His adversaries and establish His throne of judgement and of dominion. Of this the Apostle Paul reminds us in Colossians 3. 4; 1 Thessalonians 4. 15; 2 Thessalonians 1. 10.

**766 Parting Words.** A German princess, Marie Dorothea, taking leave of a Christian missionary, said, 'Christians never see each other for the last time: Adieu.' ('ADIEU' means literally—'To God'—I commend you.)
(2 Sam. 12. 23; Acts 20. 38)

**767 Partition Wall.** Christ has by His death broken down 'the middle wall of partition'. What was it?

It was the marble barrier which shut off the court of the Gentiles from the Jewish precincts of the temple in Jerusalem. Inscribed plaques warned the Gentiles against intrusion on pain of death. This prohibition and penalty was recognized as valid by the Roman authorities. In 1887 one of the plaques was found. It read: 'Let no one of any other nation come within the fence and barrier round the Holy Place. Whoever will be taken so doing will himself be responsible for the fact that his death will ensue.'
(Eph. 2. 14)

**768 Partners, First in Crime, Then in Christ.** C— and R— were the same age, had been brought up in the same street in Edinburgh, and were inseparable friends. They went to school together, played together, eventually got into trouble with the police together, were tried at the same court hearing and were sentenced to the same prison. Taking the morning service within the prison in August, 1969, and speaking on the theme, 'Does God care?'—from the incident of the storm on the lake and the disciples' question, 'Carest Thou not that we perish?' As we sang the closing hymn:

*God who made the earth, the air, the sky, the sea,*
*Who gave the light its birth,*
*Careth for me—*

C—was in tears, and I was not surprised when he told me at the afternoon Bible Class that he had surrendered to the Lord Jesus that morning. It was, however, surprising to hear just a few moments later that R—, who had been sitting on the opposite side of the Chapel in the morning service and had had no contact with C— since, had also accepted the Lord Jesus during that morning service. Without knowing what was in the mind of each other, they had both accepted Christ at approximately the same time. Released on the Wednesday of the same week, they returned home to Edinburgh. Just three weeks later, I received from R— a letter which I shall always treasure. It was a request that I should visit C—'s parents, and gave a heartbroken account of a midnight trip to the coast with a teenage church group, and of C— plunging to his death over a cliff edge which had crumbled under his weight.

The letter ended, 'I am heartbroken about this, but comforted to remember that the Lord Jesus said: I give unto My sheep eternal life, and they shall never perish, neither shall any man pluck them out of My hand.'

Alex. Allan

(John 10. 28)

**769 Passover.**

*Beneath the blood-stained lintel I with my*
*children stand:*
*A messenger of evil is passing through the land.*
*There is no other refuge from the destroyer's*
*face:*
*Beneath the blood-stained lintel shall be my*
*hiding-place.*

*The Lamb of God has suffered: our sins and*
*guilt He bore:*
*By faith the blood is sprinkled above our*
*dwelling door.*
*The foe who seeks to enter fears most that*
*secret sign:*
*Tonight the blood-stained lintel shall shelter*
*me and mine.*

(Exod. 12. 7)

**770 Password—The.** During the American Civil War a horseman found himself confronted by a sentry who pointed his gun and said, 'Halt! Who goes there?' 'A friend,' he replied. 'Approach and give the password.' 'Lincoln,' confidently said the horseman. The sentry said slowly, 'It is the wrong password, and if I did not know you, your life would pay the penalty. At the risk of my own life I spare yours. Go back and get the right word.' The horseman thanked the sentry and rode off, returning later with the right word—'MASSA-CHUSSETS'. 'Pass on! All's well!' was the reply, 'I cannot pass on,' said the rider, 'until I have given you a message. At the risk of your life you spared mine. Have you the right password for Heaven?' 'Yes, sir, I have.' 'What is it?' 'Jesus Christ, sir!' 'Where did you learn that?' 'In your Sunday School in Pennsylvania, sir!'
(1 Cor. 1. 18; 2. 2)

**771 Pastoral Work.** I have thought much of the glory of the pastor's gift. 'He gave some apostles, prophets, evangelists, pastors and teachers.' The Giver of these gifts exercised each one Himself. He was an Apostle (Heb. 3. 1), a Prophet (Acts 3. 22), an Evangelist (Luke 4. 18), a Teacher (John 3. 2), but He never says, 'I am the good Apostle, Prophet, etc.' He only says, 'I am the good Pastor; the good Pastor giveth His life for the sheep.'

This would appear to be in contrast with old-time pastors; with them the sheep died for the shepherd. Abel took a first born of his sheep. With Christ the Shepherd dies for the flock.

For many it is of vastly more value to care for souls, to visit and spend one's strength for the flock and its needs than to preach to audiences gathered to a regular meeting.

Harold St. John

(1 Pet. 5. 2-4)

**772 Pathway of Peace.** To be satisfied with your possessions but not contented with yourself until you have made the best of them; to despise nothing in the world except falsehood

and meanness; to fear nothing except cowardice; to be governed by your admirations rather
than by your disgusts; to covet nothing that is
your neighbour's except his kindness of heart
and gentleness of manners; to think seldom of
your enemies, often of your friends, and every
day of Christ, and to spend as much time as
you can, with body, soul and spirit, in God's
out-of-doors—these are the guide-posts on the
footpath to peace.

                                        Henry van Dyke
(Prov. 3. 17)

**773  Patience.**  There was once a household
so happy that for nine generations none of its
members had left it except the daughters that
marriage perforce took away. The fame of such
domestic bliss reached the ears of the Celestial
Emperor, so he sent to enquire the secret. The
old father of the house, taking a paper and
brush, printed many characters, then handed
his answer to the imperial envoy. When it was
unrolled, there was nothing there but the
character for 'PATIENCE' repeated 100 times.
(James 1. 4)

**774  Paul The Evangelist.**

*Oft when the Word is on me to deliver*
*Lifts the illusion and the truth lies bare;*
*Desert or throng, the city or the river*
*Melts in a lucid Paradise of air.*

*Only like souls I see the folks thereunder,*
*Bound who should conquer, slaves who should*
    *be kings—*
*Hearing their one hope with an empty wonder,*
*Sadly contented with a show of things—*

*Then with a rush the intolerable craving*
*Shivers throughout me like a trumpet call:*
*Oh, to save these! to perish for their saving,*
*Die for their life, be offered for them all!*

*Oh, could I tell, ye surely would believe it!*
*Oh, could I only say what I have seen.*
*How can I tell or how can ye receive it,*
*How—till He bringeth you where I have been?*

*Therefore, O Lord, I will not fail nor falter:*
*Nay, but I ask it, nay, but I desire—*
*Lay on my lips the emblems of the altar;*
*Seal with the sting and furbish with the fire.*

*Give me a voice, a cry and a complaining—*
*Oh, let my sound be stormy in their ears!*
*Throat that would shout but cannot stay for*
    *straining,*
*Eyes that would weep but cannot wait for*
    *tears.*

                                        F. W. Myers
(1 Cor. 9. 16)

**775  Peace.**

*Peace be to thy habitation, peace to all that*
    *dwell therein,*
*Peace the earnest of salvation, peace the fruit*
    *of pardoned sin,*

*Peace that speaks the heavenly Giver, peace*
    *to worldly minds unknown,*
*Peace divine that lasts for ever, peace that*
    *comes from God alone.*

(John 14. 27)

**776  Peace—Flower Of.**

*My soul, there is a country*
*Far beyond the stars,*
*Where stands a winged sentry*
*All skilful in the wars.*
*There above the noise and danger,*
*Sweet Peace sits crowned with smiles,*
*And One born in a manger*
*Commands the beauteous files.*
*He is thy gracious Friend,*
*And—O my soul, awake—*
*Did in pure love descend*
*To die here for thy sake.*
*If thou canst get but thither,*
*There grows the Flower of Peace,*
*The Rose that cannot wither,*
*Thy fortress and thy ease.*
*Leave then thy foolish ranges,*
*For none can thee secure*
*But One, who never changes,*
*Thy God, thy life, thy cure.*

                                        Henry Vaughan

**777  Peace, Perfect Peace.**  We made a discovery the other day; possibly some of our
readers also may not have noticed that the fine
hymn commencing: 'Peace, perfect peace' is a
dialogue, the first line of each verse closing with
a question mark—save the last verse. The
talented poet-bishop, Bickersteth, evidently
experienced a controversy in his own heart
between unbelief and faith, and gracefully
arranged it in poetic language. May not the
author have been contemplating some such
words as: 'Thou wilt keep him in perfect peace
whose mind is stayed on Thee: because he
trusteth in Thee,' when Unbelief butts in with
the words 'Peace, perfect peace, in this dark
world of sin?' insinuating the impossibility of
such blessedness. But Faith unerringly reveals
the fountain of all true peace and its locality:
'The blood of Jesus whispers peace within.'
    Unabashed, Unbelief raises a well-known
difficulty:
'Peace, perfect peace, by thronging duties
pressed?'
Faith does not deny facts, but gently replies:
'To do the will of Jesus, this is REST.'
    William C. Irvine in *The Indian Christian*
(Isa. 26. 3)

**778  Pen that Leaked.**  The late Dr F. B.
Meyer was frequently embarrassed and frustrated because, at an awkward, unexpected
time, his fountain-pen would suddenly spout
ink all over his fingers or soil a new shirt.
Finally, thoroughly disgusted with the pen's
behaviour, he put it in the back part of his desk.
Whenever he was preparing for a trip, he would

pass that particular pen by and take another in which he had complete confidence.

Using the leaky pen as an illustration, he would say, 'If that pen could have spoken, it might have asked me why I didn't use it more. And I would have replied, "Little pen, I would like to, but I cannot because you are not trustworthy."'

(Heb. 2. 1 (Margin))

**779 Perfection of Christ.** Jesus Christ is the only perfect Man. His perfection is seen in the combination in His life on earth of qualities regarded as incompatibles. These are:

*Solemnity and Joyfulness.* On his last journey to Jerusalem He was so solemn that His disciples were afraid; yet, in His last discourses, He repeatedly spoke of His joy.

*Aloofness and Sociability.* Rising a great while before day, He departed into a solitary place; yet, when invited, he was present at a marriage feast.

*Dignity and Humility.* His dignity is seen in His composed silence before Pilate; yet He said of Himself, 'I am meek and lowly in heart': and His humility is evident in all He did.

*Profundity and Simplicity*—The parables of Jesus are so simple that any child can understand them; yet so profound that they baffle every attempt to discover their inner meaning. These incomparable parables will hold and thrill the serious mind as long as language lasts.

*Severity and Tenderness*—He who lashed the hypocritical Pharisees with His words said to the poor adulteress, 'Neither do I condemn thee.' He who said to Peter, 'Get thee behind me, Satan,' said from the cross to John, 'Behold thy mother!'

*Energy and Restfulness*—The unceasing activity of Jesus was astonishing. From morn to night He travelled and taught, performing deeds of mercy. Yet there is no evidence that He was ever flustered or irritated. His experience was one of unbroken peace within.

*Haste and Leisureliness*—There was always a sense of urgency in His activities, and yet throughout there was an atmosphere of leisureliness. He was never too busy to attend to those who needed Him.

The character of Jesus was held in perfect equilibrium. He had no strong points because He had no weak ones. How different from ourselves. We are all conscious of weakness and defects.

(Mark 10. 32; John 2. 10; Mark 1. 35; John 15. 11; John 18. 9,10; Matt. 11. 29)

**780 Perplexity Overcome.** When Sir Hugh Foot was Governor of Cyprus, during a time of crisis, he received from Cornwall the following cable just when he was very hard pressed: 'FOOT, GOVERNMENT HOUSE, CYPRUS. SEE SECOND CORINTHIANS FOUR, VERSES EIGHT AND NINE.'

Opening his Bible at the passage his father, Isaac Foot, had indicated, he read: 'We are troubled on every side, yet not distressed; we are perplexed, but not in despair; persecuted, but not forsaken, cast down but not destroyed.'

From Cyprus to his father, who was a 78-year-old Methodist lay preacher, Sir Hugh replied: 'SEE ROMANS FIVE, VERSES THREE AND FOUR.'

The passage read, 'And not only so but we glory in tribulation also, knowing that tribulation worketh patience, and patience experience, and experience hope.'

*Time Magazine*

(2 Cor. 4. 8,9; Rom. 5. 3,4)

**781 Peter Sleeps.**

*The glory of the kingdom spread*
*Over the mountain's lofty head,*
*Lighting the rocky steeps;*
*And Jesus' robes were glistering white,*
*His face, the sun in all its might,*
*AND PETER SLEEPS.*

*'Tis night, and in Gethsemane*
*A prostrate form, in agony,*
*With bitter crying weeps;*
*The darkness deepens at His groan,*
*The darkest night this world has known,*
*AND PETER SLEEPS.*

*He lies upon the dungeon floor;*
*The guard quadrupled round the door*
*Its midnight vigil keeps:*
*Two chains of iron bind him fast;*
*Tomorrow morn may be his last,*
*AND PETER SLEEPS.*

*Nailed to a cross, by man contemned,*
*Head downwards, hangs a man condemned;*
*Darkness around him creeps.*
*Until the Lord from heaven descends*
*And till His shout the heavens rends,*
*'In Jesus' PETER SLEEPS.*

(Luke 9. 32; 22. 45; Acts 12. 6)

**782 Peter's Denial.**

*'Lord, let me only go with Thee,*
*Thy life if need be I'll defend,*
*And mine I'd give for Thy dear sake*
*Should any danger Thee attend.'*
*'Peter—impetuous thou art,*
*Thou dost not know thine inward heart!*

*'Thy lips shall have denied me thrice*
*Before we see the morning light.'*
*Then Peter followed from afar*
*To keep a watch throughout the night.*
*O Peter—ere this night is spent*
*What deep remorse thou could'st prevent!*

*He mingled with the crowd as one,*
*Then, face averted, loudly swore*
*He did not know his blessed Lord:*
*He had not seen this Man before!*
*—Grey streaks of light have touched the sky,*
*Then hark! there is a cock's shrill cry.*

*And when the raucous cock's crow rang*
*And stirred the morning echoes round,*
*Another heard, and only turned*
*To look at Peter without sound.*
*Oh, what a look! No words can say*
*The message it contained that day.*

*But Peter thus is not alone;*
*The heart of any man is weak.*
*If we would not betray His name*
*'Tis help from God that we must seek.*
*O man—Impetuous thou art,*
*Thou dost not know thine inward heart!*

                                        E. G. Richards
(Luke 22. 34,54-62)

**783  Phenomena Beyond Our Understanding.**
A Christian preacher was invited by the
Principal of an American High School to
address the 800 pupils under his care on the
topic—'A comparison between the miracles
seen in nature and those recorded in the Bible'.
Before he went on to the platform, a senior
pupil informed him that he did not accept the
bunk he expected would be handed out, and
only believed what he could understand. To get
his audience into a good mood and ready to
listen, he told them of the senior pupil who only
believed what he could understand. 'Perhaps,'
said the lecturer, 'our young friend would tell
us why it was that a black cow ate green grass
which makes white milk and yellow butter, and
then produces red hair on one of the folks who
ate the butter.' The amusing, though un-
scientific question brought great merriment to
the large audience. 'Then,' added the preacher,
'perhaps he would also explain why he blows
on his hands to warm them and on his coffee to
cool it. Most things can ultimately be explained,'
the speaker added, 'but we have to take many
things as we find them on trust and accept them
by faith.'

Directly on the theme of the lectures, he
pointed out the remarkable transformation
that takes place when a caterpillar (an uphol-
stered worm in a home-made casket) is changed
into a beautiful butterfly. Then, how do the
hairs on the caterpillar become scales, a million
to the square inch, on the butterfly, and how
are the caterpillars' many legs reduced to six on
the butterfly? How does the yellow colour
become a vivid red, and how does the crawling
instinct change to the flying instinct?

These miracles in nature we take for granted.
Can we not accept the recorded miracles
described in the Bible by faith?

**784  Philemon.**  Dr W. R. Matthews, Dean
of St Paul's, in the *Daily Telegraph*, November
6, 1965, said concerning the letter of Paul to
Philemon, which was the second lesson on
Sunday, November 7:

'Here is a precious first-hand record of
friendship in the Christian community of the
first century. We do not know whether Philemon
did what Paul asked, but it is reasonable to
suppose that he did, because he evidently kept

the letter. Perhaps the great fact that Philemon
must have carefully preserved the letter
suggests that it was the last that came from his
revered friend before his martyrdom.'

Professor F. F. Bruce asks the question:
'What did Philemon do when he read the letter?'
and remarks, 'We have no explicit information
that would enable us to answer the question
satisfactorily—apart from the fact that the
letter has been preserved. Philemon no doubt
treasured it. He would not have treasured it if
it had given him a guilty conscience every time
he came across it, because he had not treated
Onesimus as Paul asked him to.' He adds, 'But
Onesimus would treasure it even more; it was
his charter of emancipation.'

The names of *Philemon* and *Onesimus* are
interesting and significant.

*Philemon* means 'loving' and in the epistle Paul
again and again refers to his love. Several
common words contain the same derivative of
the same word for 'love'.—philanthropy,
philosophy, philately, for example.

*Onesimus* was a common slave name in the
days of the Roman Empire. A slave was
expected to be useful to his master, and
Onesimus means 'useful'.

**785  Physical Skill Rightly Used.**  D— was a
quiet lad, but his personality became completely
changed under the influence of alcohol and
drugs. When the police tried to arrest him for
breach of the peace (the offence for which he
was sent to prison), he threw five of them
through a plate glass window before reinforce-
ments managed to subdue him.

In prison he studied the Bible lessons and
listened attentively to the messages. He
eventually gave his heart to the Saviour and his
conversion was very real. There was still the
problem of excess energy, and as a pastime he
took up boxing. He succeeded so well in this
that, after only a year, he became a reserve for
the Scottish Amateur International team, and
all the time he was witnessing for Christ.

Eventually, as he continued to read his
Bible, he became convicted that the time he
was spending on this could be profitably spent
for the Lord Jesus, and he became associated
with a Church Youth Club where the children
almost idolised him for his efficiency in sport
and equally so for his fine Christian witness.

Now he is still a bright witness for the Lord
Jesus Christ in Australia, where he moved with
his wife shortly after their marriage which I had
the privilege of attending. To me he is an outstanding example of physical abilities chan-
nelled in the right direction, under the Lordship
of Christ.

                                        Alex. Allan
(1 Tim. 4. 8)

**786  Picture—A Hidden.**  Sir George Hayter,
a famous painter, when a guest in one of the
stately old homes of England, hesitated before
a study of still life—a basket of fruit—in the art
gallery of the house. As he looked more closely

174

at the picture, his host said, 'I do not think you will find that worth your time: it is a study quite without merit.' Hayter thought he saw a human eye looking at him through a plum, and asked his host, 'May I examine it a little more closely?' Permission was immediately granted, and, taking the picture out of the frame, he lifted a corner of the canvas with a sharp pen-knife. Then he asked, 'Do you know there is a picture under this?' There was hidden underneath the study of still life a Vandyke portrait of King Charles I. The early possessors, the Leigh family, were divided in their loyalty. The picture had been painted over to preserve it from possible harm, and forgotten.
(Matt. 13. 13,16)

### 787   Pierced Hands, Feet and Heart.

*His hands were pierced, the hands that made*
*The mountain range and verdant glade,*
*That washed the stains of sin away*
*And changed earth's darkness into day.*

*His feet were pierced, the feet that trod*
*The furthest shining star of God;*
*And left their imprint deep and clear*
*On every winding pathway here.*

*His heart was pierced, the heart that burned*
*To comfort every heart that yearned;*
*And from it came a cleansing flood,*
*The river of redeeming blood.*

*His hands and feet and heart, all three,*
*Were pierced for me on Calvary;*
*And here and now to Him I bring,*
*My hands, my feet, an offering.*
(Ps. 22. 16; John 19. 34)

### 788   Pilgrim Ways.

*Lord, since we sing as pilgrims,*
*O give us pilgrim ways,*
*Low thoughts of self, befitting*
*Proclaimers of Thy praise.*
*O make us each more holy,*
*In spirit pure and meek,*
*Much more like heavenly citizens*
*As more of heaven we speak.*
(1 Pet. 2. 11)

### 789   Pilgrimage. Dr W. Graham Scroggie has said: 'Christ has not promised His people a smooth passage, but only a safe landing. In embarking on the Christian life we are not guaranteed a sunlit sea, but rather are advised of a storm-tossed ocean; and it is far better to be in a storm with Him than in a calm without Him.'
(Matt. 8. 23-27)

### 790   Pilgrimage to Heaven.

*There is no solace on the earth for us, for*
*such as we*
*Who search for the hidden city that eyes may*
*never see:*
*Only the road and the dawn, the sun, the*
*wind and the rain,*

*And the watch-fire under stars, and sleep and*
*the road again.*
*We travel the dusty road till the light of the*
*day is dim,*
*And sunset shows us spires away on the*
*world's rim.*
*We travel from dawn to dusk till the day is*
*past and by,*
*Seeking the holy city beyond the rim of the*
*sky.*
Dr J. Masefield, O.M.

(Heb. 11. 13-16; 13. 14)

### 791   Pilot Missing. A missionary nurse in the hospital at Ajloun wrote: 'One evening late in February a pilot of a helicopter set off in heavy mist and rain from a point on the mountain not far away from us. On board with him was a doctor who had made a visit to see several patients at the post there. Not long after leaving, the pilot signalled that he was in difficulty and then no more was heard from him. Search-parties set out to try to find the missing ones, but without success. At 5.30 a.m. the next morning a second pilot took his own helicopter and continued the search, even though there was still heavy mist. His effort was successful and he located the plane. A party reached the spot on foot and found the body of the doctor and discovered that the pilot was living, though with serious head wounds. He was brought to us here and his injuries attended to. The second pilot made two visits to the hospital that day to find out the welfare of the injured man. The second pilot was King Hussein.'

There was another King, the King of kings, who came to seek and to save that which was lost.
*Practical Christianity*

(Luke 19. 10)

### 792   Plan and Pattern—Divine. The late R. J. Bryant, missionary in the Godavari Delta area of India, carried on for some years a small carpet industry. The pattern on each carpet was first planned out on paper—its shape, form and colour determined beforehand. All the working of each carpet was done from the back. Threads worked in and out sometimes seemed to the eye of the onlooker, unacquainted with carpet-making, just a tangle of threads with no pattern and no beauty. When the finished article was taken down from the frame the side of the carpet that had been hidden from view while it was being made revealed a perfect symmetrical pattern with no tangled threads, all according to the plan, and the whole finished carpet was a magnificent piece of work.
**A.N.**

*The work that Jesus Christ began,*
*The tangled thread which here we see,*
*Are but the weaving of a plan;*
*And perfect, too, the work will be,*
*Each thread in place, each colour true*
*To ring His praise the ages through.*
(Ps. 138. 8; Phil. 1. 6)

**793  Pleasing the Lord.** An Italian duke came upon a workman one day who seemed to be taking infinite care and pains in his work. He asked the labourer, 'For what will the box that you are making be used?' 'Flowers will be planted in it, sir.' Amused, the Duke continued, 'It will be filled with dirt. Why take such pains to make each joint and surface perfect?' 'I love perfect things,' the man replied. 'Ah, wasted effort! No one will observe its perfection. A mere flower box does not require such perfection.' 'But my spirit does;' insisted the man, 'do you suppose that the Carpenter of Nazareth ever made anything less perfect than He could?' Angrily, the Duke replied, 'Sacrilege! Your impudence deserves a flogging. What is your name?' The reply came—'Michelangelo'.
(Col. 3. 23)

**794  Pleasure in Life.** One of the poems of Philip Doddridge, who wrote the hymns 'O God of Bethel!' and 'O Happy Day!', which Dr Samuel Johnson liked very much was:

*Live while you live, the Epicure would say,*
*And seize the pleasures of the perfect day.*
*Live while you may, the sacred preacher cries,*
*And give to God each moment as it flies.*
*Lord, in my view let faith united be—*
*I live to pleasure as I live to Thee.*

(Rom. 6. 11; 8. 8)

**795  Poison in Books.** Mr Tom Olsen tells of a man who went into his library and took down a book from the shelf. As he did so he felt a slight pain, like a pinprick, in his finger, but paid no attention to it, thinking that perhaps some careless person had stuck a pin in one of the pages. Soon his finger, then his arm, then his whole body, began to swell, and in a few days he died. It was not a pin that was among the books but a tiny deadly serpent.

There are books that contain moral and spiritual poison more deadly than that snake's venom. Be careful what you read, and turn from all such poisonous literature.
(Acts 19. 19)

**796  Polished Shaft—A.** On the Sobat River and on the White Nile, stunted acacia and a few palms are the only wood available for use. None of these is any good for the natives' spear shafts, and a spear is useless without a good shaft. The Ethiopian native brings a bundle of small tree trunks from afar—1½ inches thick and about eight or ten feet long. They are crooked, a bend in them at every 6 inches, and covered with a rough bark.

He then drives a large number of pegs into smooth level ground in two parallel rows 1½ inches apart and three or four inches above ground. He passes each long rod through a fire until thoroughly heated, scrapes off the scorched bark and cuts off the worst bends. Then he heats each rod again, one by one, forces it between two parallel rows of pegs, straightening it and hardening the wood. He does this

several times until it is perfectly straight. Then he scrapes and shapes each with a sharp knife, tapering one end, and rubs on some abrasive until the rod is perfectly smooth. Oil is carefully rubbed in with much effort until the darkened wood shines. There must be no splinter to wound the user's hand. Now the spear point is fixed. The shaft is straight and true and the spear can go in a perfect arc and hit the mark.
(Isa. 49. 2)

**797  Politeness Wins.** An old man, telling what led him to the Saviour, said, 'Walking out one morning I met a bright-eyed boy. The little fellow stepped up to me and in the most polite manner imaginable said, "Please, sir, will you take a tract, and please, sir, will you read it?" I had always loathed tracts, and when offered one I sometimes swore dreadfully, but I could not swear at that gentlemanly little fellow with his kind "Please sir!" I took the tract and it was the means of leading me to Christ. The "Please, sir!" was the key that unlocked my hard old heart.'

*For—Hearts, like doors, open with ease*
*To very very little keys,*
*And these are 'Thank you!' and 'If you*
*  please!'*

(1 Pet. 3. 8)

**798  Pollution.** Excerpt from the *Manchester Guardian*, mid-September, 1968:

Paris, September 15
'Within the next two decades life on our planet will be showing the first signs of succumbing to industrial pollution. The atmosphere will become unbreathable for men and animals; all life will cease in rivers and lakes; plants will wither from poisoning.

'This frightening opinion has emerged from the Inter-Governmental Conference of Experts on the Scientific Bases for Rational Utilisation and Conservation of Biospheric Resources which has the most prolix title ever given to a Unesco symposium, but something extremely terse and telling to say.

'Natural sources, like minerals, are being swiftly depleted. Other natural products that renew themselves, such as forests, have not been given time to regrow. As cities spread in a monstrous fashion, the problem of refuse inherent in urban life attains the size of an insoluble problem. Carbon dioxide and all the hosts of airborne industrial wastes are fouling the atmosphere and poisoning fresh water. In the last twenty years the whole process has been accelerating at a crazy speed.'

But the growth of pollution has not been confined to the natural and material realms: it is much more serious in the moral and spiritual realms. Violence, murder, crime, immorality and dishonesty—indeed, every form of sin—have polluted the atmosphere of souls since the Fall of man.
(Rom. 1. 24-32)

**799 Porters—Bible.** The word in the King James Version of our Bibles that is translated 'PORTER' really means a doorkeeper. By derivation it is related to the word 'portal'. In the temple of Solomon the humble doorkeeper had an honourable place and a responsible work in the house of the Lord. In Nehemiah 12. 45 they receive honourable mention as doorkeepers of the ward of their God, along with the singers, some of whom are mentioned earlier as being over the business of the house of God. The porter's job was not carrying baggage, but keeping watch at the doors and gates of important places.

In meetings of the local church today, the saints owe much to the brothers who are 'on the door', welcoming friends as they arrive, distributing hymn books and making kindly enquiries concerning those who come and their relatives or friends who are on the sick list.

Palm 84 is a psalm of the sons of Korah who were content to be doorkeepers in the House of the Lord rather than be associated with those who, like their progenitor, Korah, opposed the divinely appointed order and were ambitious to rank along with God's chosen priests.

(1 Chron. 9. 19; Ps. 84. 10)

**800 Postponement Dangerous.** On October 8, 1871, D. L. Moody addressed the largest congregation he ever addressed in Chicago. His text was—'What shall I do then with Jesus who is called Christ?' Concluding, he gave the congregation this advice: 'I wish you would take this text home with you and turn it over in your minds, and next Sunday we shall come to Calvary and the Cross, and decide what to do with Jesus of Nazareth.' Ira D. Sankey sang the closing hymn.

Then the clang of fire-bells was heard. The great fire of Chicago laid Moody's hall in ashes, and over 1000 people perished, some of them among his audience. Moody said it was the greatest mistake he ever made—telling his hearers to postpone their decision till the following Sunday.

(Prov. 27. 1)

**801 Potter and Clay.**

*Thou, Lord, art the Potter and we are the clay,*
*And morning and evening, and day after day,*
*Thou turnest the wheel and our substance is*
*   wrought*
*Into form of Thy will, into shape of Thy*
*   thought.*
*Shall the clay to the potter make answer and*
*   say,*
*'Now, what dost Thou fashion?' Thy hand*
*   would not stay*
*Untiring, resistless, without any sound,*
*And true to its Master the wheel would go*
*   round.*
*How plastic are we as we lie in His hands?*
*And who, as the potter, the clay understands?*
*Thy ways are a wonder but oft, as a spark,*

*Some hint of Thy meaning shines out in the*
*   dark.*
*What portion is this for the sensitive clay*
*To be beaten and moulded from day unto day?*
*To answer not, question not—just to be still,*
*And know Thou art shaping us unto Thy will.*
*Thus, thus may we plead with Thee, workman*
*   divine,*
*'Press deep in our substance some symbol of*
*   Thine:*
*Thy name or Thine image, and let it be*
*   shown*
*Till Thou wilt acknowledge the work as*
*   Thine own.'*

(Rom. 9. 21)

**802 Potter's Hand—The.**

*I am a worthless piece of clay*
*Beneath the Potter's hand;*
*He works His sovereign will on me,*
*As He has wisely planned.*

*He knows what vessel He would make*
*According to His will,*
*And every turn of circumstance*
*Reveals His perfect skill.*

*Sometimes in pain He makes me lie,*
*And I, in arrant pride,*
*Resent the pressure of His hand*
*And fain would turn aside.*

*But gently He rebukes my fears,*
*And speaks with tender voice,*
*'My child, resent not what I do,*
*But make My will your choice.*

*'And when you see the vessel formed*
*My wisdom had in view,*
*You'll gladly bless the hours of pain*
*My love has sent to you.'*

*So let me then accept His will,*
*And offer no excuse,*
*For I shall be a vessel rare,*
*Fit for the Master's use.*

*I should not murmur or repine*
*Whate'er my earthly lot,*
*But wait till grace in heaven displays*
*What loving skill has wrought.*

A. Borland

(Jer. 18. 3,4)

**803 Poverty of Christ.**

*He who is the Bread of life often was hungry.*
*He who is the Water of life and dispensed it*
*   to others thirsted as He died.*
*Christ hungered as the Son of man and fed the*
*   the hungry as the Son of God.*
*He was often wearied, yet it is He who gives*
*   us rest.*
*He paid tribute to the Roman king, though He*
*   was King of kings.*
*Christ often prayed a night long but today He*
*   hears an instant of prayer.*
*Jesus wept, but He it is who will eventually*
*   dry all tears.*

*Thirty pieces of silver was the price of Him,*
*but now He can redeem all men, having paid*
*the price in full, His own precious blood.*
*Although He was the Good Shepherd, He was*
*slain as a Lamb.*
*As the Good Shepherd, He gave His life*
*for the sheep: as the Lamb of God, He*
*offered Himself as a sacrifice for sin.*
*He died, and because of His death we need*
*never die.*

(2 Cor. 8. 9)

**804  Power Over Sin.**  Within a week of my conversion I passed a picture store in St Louis and saw, hanging in a window, a picture of Daniel looking up in the den of lions and answering the king's question. I was a drunken lawyer before I was converted. No one had told me about the keeping power of Jesus Christ. I stood before that picture, and a great hope and faith came into my heart. I said, 'Why! these lions are all about me—my old habits and my old sins—but the God that shut the lions' mouths for Daniel can shut them for me!'

C. I. Scofield

(Dan. 6. 21,22)

God did not deliver Daniel from the lions' den but He did deliver him from the lions' mouths.

**805  Power Through Prayer.**  David Brainerd did his greatest work by prayer. He was in the depths of the forest alone, unable to speak the language of the Indians, but he spent whole days in prayer.

What was he praying for? He knew that he could not reach those savages. He did not understand their language. If he wanted to speak at all he must find somebody that would vaguely interpret his thought. Therefore he knew that anything he might do must be absolutely dependent upon the power of God. So he spent whole days praying simply that the power of the Holy Ghost might come upon him so unmistakably that these people should not be able to stand before him.

What was the answer? Once he preached through a drunken interpreter, a man so intoxicated that he could hardly stand up. That was the best he could do. Yet scores were converted through that sermon.

We cannot account for it, only that it was the tremendous power of God behind him. After he was dead, William Carey read his life and went to India. Robert McCheyne read his diary and went to the Jews. Henry Martyn read his journal and went to India. The hidden life in communion with God in trying to reach the source of power, is the life that moves the world.

S. D. Gordon

(Gen. 32. 28)

**806  Practical Christianity.**  The pastor of a coloured congregation was listening to the experiences of his people at a class meeting.

One woman spoke of the preciousness of the Bible and the Christian faith, and of all the comfort and joy she found from it. 'Delightful!' exclaimed the pastor. 'Now tell me about the practical side of it all. Does it make you kind in the home, cheerful at your duties, sweet and loving toward your husband?' Just then the pastor felt a tug at his coat tail and heard a male voice whisper, 'Press dem questions, pastor! Press dem questions! Dat's my wife.'

(Prov. 31. 27,28)

**807  Praise and Prayer.**

*My Lord who in the desert fed*
*On soul-sustaining heavenly Bread!*
*Words that were meat and drink to Thee—*
*Oh, let them daily nourish me!*

*And since the sword that served Thee well*
*In battling with the powers of hell*
*Is even now at hand for me,*
*Help me to wield it manfully.*

*But first, O holy, gracious Lord,*
*I pray Thee, let Thy Spirit's sword*
*Pierce heart and conscience till I see*
*Both what I am and ought to be!*

*Thy Word my rule and my delight,*
*My strength for service and for fight—*
*For this exhaustless treasure store,*
*My Lord, I praise Thee and adore.*

Frank Houghton

(Matt. 4. 4,7,10)

**808  Praise for God's Faithfulness.**  A poem written specially for the Centenary of Edgmond Hall, Eastbourne, in 1972.

*We gratefully acclaim Thy faithfulness,*
*Which down the years has lightened all our*
*way;*
*Thou art the God of wonder, love and grace,*
*Right joyfully we praise Thy name to-day.*

*What hath God wrought? we say with glowing*
*hearts;*
*What can He yet do? Faith at once replies.*
*We thank Thee for the past, but it departs;*
*'Tis to the future that we lift our eyes.*

*We would not limit Thee by feeble faith;*
*We say with Job, 'Thou canst do everything!'*
*We put our finger on Thy Word—'He saith'—*
*And lo! 'tis done! Lord, we our praises bring.*

*The enemy may come in like a flood;*
*Thou wilt unfurl Thy standard and take charge,*
*Turning what seems our peril to our good,*
*Cramped acres to a land exceeding large.*

*Thy faithfulness extends beyond the skies;*
*Though Satan rage, though kingdoms rise or*
*fall,*
*Come life, come death, with Him we too*
*shall rise*
*To find Thee then, as now, our all in all.*

Ransome W. Cooper

(Ps. 89. 1,2)

## 809   Praise Song—A.

*Father of all, whose mercy, ever tender,*
*Hath crowned with blessing all our fleeting*
*    days,*
*Accept the humble tribute that we render;*
*Receive our song of praise!*

*Safe through another year Thy power hath*
*    brought us;*
*Thy guiding hand has led us all the way;*
*And Thy kind care hath loving lessons taught us*
*With every passing day.*

*For every joy that tuned our hearts to singing,*
*For health, and friends, and days from trial*
*    free,*
*For wishes granted, our glad hearts are*
*    bringing*
*A song of praise to Thee.*

*And if for some of us the cup of sorrow*
*To our reluctant lips Thy hand hath pressed,*
*We bless Thy name, if on the dawning morrow,*
*We saw Thy will was best.*

*We thank Thee for the strength so timely given,*
*For promises of Thine that were our stay,*
*And for the precious hope of home and heaven*
*That cheers our pilgrim way.*

*For all Thy mercies, Father, we adore Thee!*
*With loving hearts our grateful song we raise,*
*And wait the day when, crowned with joy*
*    before Thee,*
*We'll give Thee nobler praise!*

(1 Sam. 7. 12)

## 810   Pray! Give! Go!

*Three things they had to do:*
*And we who serve Him here below*
*And long to see His kingdom come*
*May pray or give or go.*

*He needs them all—the open hand,*
*The willing foot, the praying heart,*
*To work together and to weave*
*A threefold cord that shall not part.*

*Nor will the giver count his gift*
*As greater than the worker's deed,*
*Nor he in turn his service boast*
*Above the prayers that voice the need.*

*Not all can go, not all can give*
*To speed the message on its way,*
*But, young or old or rich or poor,*
*Or strong or weak—we all can pray;*

*Pray that the gold-filled hands may give*
*To arm the others for the fray,*
*That those who hear the call may go,*
*And pray—that other hearts may pray.*

(Luke 10. 2)

## 811   Prayer Answered.
A young man in the State of Indiana left home for a business opening in Ohio. There a gentleman from his own native place found him, and was shocked to discover that he had become a profane swearer. Returning home, he felt constrained to tell the young man's pious parents of his awful degeneracy. They said little, so, in doubt whether they had understood him, the friend called the next day and repeated what he had told them. The father calmly replied, 'We understood you: my wife and I spent a sleepless night on our knees pleading on behalf of our son. About daybreak we received the assurance from God that James will never swear again.' Two weeks after, the son came home a changed man. 'How long since this change took place?' asked his rejoicing parents. He replied that just a fortnight before he was struck with a sense of guilt so great that he could not sleep, and spent the night in tears of repentance and prayer for pardon. There had been no time for any parental appeal, or even for a letter of remonstrance. While they were praying for him, God moved him to pray for himself.

Dr A. T. Pierson

(2 Tim. 1. 5)

## 812   Prayer Answered After Many Days.
When Judson was dying he heard from the lips of his wife, as she read from the newspaper, that some Jews in Turkey had been converted through the published account of his sufferings for the Gospel in Burmah. 'This awes me! This alarms me!' he said. 'Why,' said his wife, 'this is good news.' He replied, 'When I was a young man I prayed for the Jews and tried to go to Jerusalem as a missionary. But God sent me here to preach in Burmah and suffer torture in Burmese prisons. Now, by this means, God has brought Jews to repentance in Turkey. What awes me is this, that I never prayed earnestly for anything but it came, sooner or later, perhaps in the last way I could have imagined; but it came.'

(1 Cor. 15. 58; Col. 4. 12)

## 813   Prayer Answered in God's Own Way.

*He answered prayer!*
*Not in the way I sought:*
*Not in the way I had thought He ought!*
*But in His own good way; and I could see*
*He answered in the fashion best for me:*
*And I was glad that I had such a share*
*In His parental love and gracious care,*
*That thus He answered prayer.*

*He answered prayer!*
*But not in my brief hour:*
*I looked to see the fruit ere yet the flower*
*Had shed its gales of sweetness o'er my path!*
*But I have learned that slowest blossoms yield*
*The choicest fruit; and so I leave them there*
*Upon the boughs, assured that they will bear*
*In time my answered prayer.*

*He answered prayer*
*So sweetly that I stand*
*Amid the blessing of His wondrous Hand,*
*And marvel at the miracle I see,*
*The fashion that His love has wrought for me.*
*Pray on for the impossible and dare,*
*Upon thy banner this brave motto bear,*
*'My Father answers Prayer.'*

(Ps. 66. 19)

**814  Prayer Answered in God's Time.**  George Muller, founder of the Ashley Down Orphanages in Bristol, began to pray for five personal friends. After five years one of those whose salvation he desired came to Christ. After ten years two more were saved. For twenty-five years he continued praying for the other two, and then the fourth was saved. Until his death he did not cease to intercede for the conversion of the fifth. A few months after he died the fifth man was saved. Mighty in its working is the righteous man's prayer.
(James 5. 16,20)

**815  Prayer—Answers to.**

*The weary ones had rest, the sad had joy*
*That day, and wondered 'how?'*
*A ploughman, singing at his work, had prayed,*
*'Lord, help them now.'*

*Away in foreign lands they wondered how*
*Their simple word had power:*
*At home the Christians two or three had met*
*To pray an hour!*

*Yes, we are always wondering, wondering how,*
*Because we do not see*
*Someone, unknown perhaps, and far away*
*On bended knee.*

**816  Prayer Brings Revival.**  In striking contrast to the stories of student demonstrations of which so much has been heard of late, comes a thrilling account of an awakening among students at Asbury, an interdenominational college in Wilmore, Kentucky. What was evidently a movement of the Spirit of God resulted in classes being suspended for a week, and reached out to other colleges and communities from coast to coast.

It began at a morning chapel session. The programme was one of singing and personal testimony. Shortly before the end of the session, which usually lasted fifty minutes, a professor stepped forward and said: 'I wonder if there are any hungry hearts who would like to come and accept Christ as their personal Saviour.' The students began to pour forward and two lines were formed at either side of the auditorium. The power of the Spirit of God was evident and classes were suspended there and then for an indefinite period.

The meetings continued that night till the early hours of morning: townspeople joined the audiences, and the revival continued. The news spread and was publicised over the radio and television. Before the week of suspended classes was over, other states and colleges were affected. Prior to these events a group of students had been rising early for special prayer and Bible study.
(Ps. 85. 6)

**817  Prayer Changes Things.**

*Do you know what happened on that day*
*When, burdened for souls, you tried to pray?*
*Did you think you failed to touch the Throne*
*When your lips were dumb, your prayer a*
*    groan?*

*Over the sea in a hot, dry land*
*A sower sowed with faltering hand,*
*And lo! in that hour refreshing came:*
*God's servant spoke with a tongue of flame.*

*Souls long steeped in a land of night*
*Passed from gloom into marvellous light;*
*Away from idols they turned, to God,*
*Finding salvation in Jesus' blood.*

*'Twas your prayer that moved God's mighty*
*    hand,*
*And blessing poured down in a desert land.*

**818  Prayer—Ejaculatory.**  We use a picturesque and beautiful word when we speak of ejaculatory prayer. It comes from 'jaculum', a dart or arrow, and fittingly describes prayer which 'darts' up to God at all times. This is the true expression of the spirit of prayer, a spirit which in any moment of opportunity lifts itself up in a few words of prayer and intercession. We may turn every circumstance, experience and incident of the day into prayer, and find in 'the daily round, the common task', constant opportunities of ascending to God in prayer and praise.
W. Griffith Thomas
(Neh. 2. 4)

**819  Prayer—Ejaculatory.**

*I need not leave the jostling world*
*Or wait till daily tasks are o'er,*
*To fold my palms in secret prayer*
*Within the close-shut cloistered door.*

*There is a viewless, cloistered room*
*As high as heaven, as fair as day,*
*Where, though my feet may join the throng,*
*My soul can enter in and pray.*

(1 Thess. 5. 17)

**820  Prayer—Escape by.**  Three Scottish privates and a corporal had been cut off during a fierce engagement in a Belgian town one day, just before Dunkirk. Taking refuge in the loft of an empty house, they awaited what seemed to be certain death. Outside they heard the Germans setting fire to buildings, looting, killing. Suddenly the corporal said, 'Lads, it is time for Church parade; let us have a wee bit of service here; it may be our last.' The soldiers looked a bit astonished, but, placing their rifles in a corner, they stood to attention. The corporal took a small Testament from his breast pocket and turned the pages. As he read, loud shouts came from below. Doors banged, and glass was shattered. He finished and his grave face took on a wry smile. 'I am no good at this job, but we must finish it off. Let us pray.' The corporal stood with Bible in hand. The others knelt and bowed their heads. A little haltingly and very simply, he committed their way to God and asked for strength to meet their coming fate like men. Suddenly a heavy hand crashed open the door. An exultant exclamation in German was heard and then a gasp of surprise. Not a man moved and the corporal went calmly on. After a pause, he began, with great reverence, to repeat the Lord's prayer. A second later, hearing a click of heels, they knew the enemy was standing to attention. A moment of suspense, and then came the soft closing of the door and the sound of footsteps dying away. Gradually the sound of battle moved on. At dusk the four men ventured out, and, by making a wide detour worked around the flank of the enemy. They reached the British outposts in safety that night.

*Christian Readers' Digest*

(Ps. 66. 20)

## 821 Prayer—God Answers.

*I know not by what methods rare,*
*But this I know—God answers prayer.*
*I know not when He sends the word*
*That tells us fervent prayer is heard.*
*I know it cometh soon or late,*
*Therefore we need to pray and wait.*
*I know not if the blessing sought*
*Will come in just the guise I thought.*
*I leave my prayer with Him alone*
*Whose will is wiser than my own.*

(Ps. 34. 6)

## 822 Prayer—Ideal.

Maurice A. P. Wood, as he undertook the responsibility of ministering the good Word of God, prayed:

'Lord Jesus, make me humble: Lord Jesus, keep me human: Lord Jesus, make me holy. Then, Lord Jesus, help me to forget myself, in the joy of being a slave of Christ and a servant of God's people and a minister of Thy Gospel all my future days.'

(Phil. 2. 5; 1 Tim. 1. 12)

## 823 Prayer in a Prairie.

The miracle happened in the middle of 1964. On a tour of western countries I decided to cross Canada by rail, leaving Toronto by the Canadian Pacific Railway. I had heard a lot about this railway, together with the famous red-coated 'Mounties', in earlier years. It proved comfortable travel, and from the scenic dome of the train I gazed for hours at the surpassing beauty of Lake Superior and other Canadian lakes.

I broke my journey at Winnipeg where I had a busy interesting time. The next night I entrained again, undressed quickly and, I believe, put my purse under my pillow. It contained a number of dollars, incidentally the only foreign money I had in Canada and which would also have to do for ten days in the U.S.A.

The next day I was due at my destination, Calgary. I awoke early and after prayers and a quick wash I began to dress. My hand then customarily went under my pillow, but the purse was not there. I tried again—still no sign of the notes. I searched other parts of my bedding— with no result. Things were becoming serious. What I should have done, that I did not do: that is, report the loss to the railway authorities.

Imagine arriving at Calgary and telling my hosts that I had lost all my money on the train. Nothing for the rest of the Canadian trip; nothing for America! These were some of the thoughts that flooded my mind. They were terrible.

I turned my entire bedding upside down, but still could not find my purse. Then I prayed earnestly. I said something like this:

O Lord, Thou knowest that I have lost all my money. How can I face my friends in Calgary? Thou must act. Please restore to me all my money. Thou knowest where it is. In the Name of the Lord Jesus Christ, Amen!

That was my prairie prayer. A quiet peace entered my soul. I had a feeling that the purse would be found, and that, too, before I alighted from the train.

I went to breakfast, talked to an American farmer and his wife—they both were real Christians; but not a word did I tell them about my loss. We were now in the actual prairie country. We passed Medicine Hat, a place name that had much intrigued me during my days on a newspaper of Calcutta, and then Regina. We were approaching Calgary, but I was still penniless, or rather centless.

As breakfast and the talk about food for India were about to finish, a dark-skinned man, a west Indian, appeared in the doorway of the dining saloon. His name was Jack Holmes, and he was the railway porter in my part of the train.

'Have you lost anything, sir?' he enquired. Without saying 'Yes!' I was so overjoyed that I took it from him—the familiar black purse which my wife had bought me in Connaught Place, New Delhi, and I said, 'Thank you! I'll see you later.'

Then I told the American farmer and his wife. A little time afterwards I hurried back to my bunk, called for Holmes and asked him where he had found the purse. 'In your bedclothes,' he replied. Strange, I thought; I had searched everywhere. Knowing that I had lost the purse, he could have kept it. But the man was obviously honest. I had counted the money and found it correct to the last cent.

Jack Holmes then asked me a question: 'Why did you not report your loss to the railway?' I told him that instead of appealing to man I had appealed to God. Perhaps it did not make sense to him. I told him of how the Lord Jesus had died for everybody's sins, including Jack Holmes's. Christ was now risen and He wanted men and women to accept Him as their Saviour. I gave Holmes a New Testament, a gift of five dollars and a letter to the Canadian Pacific Railway telling them of their employee's honesty.

When the train arrived at Calgary, passengers began to remove their own luggage. But I stepped out like a lord! Another man had done it for me: that man was the smiling Jack Holmes.

James Pritchard

(Ps. 50. 15)

**824 Prayer in the Christian's Life.** There are many organizers but few agonizers; many who pay but few who pray.

Many are enterprising but few are interceding; many are entertaining but few intervening.

Don't mistake action for unction, commotion for emotion, reprisals for revivals. The secret of praying is praying in secret.

When payment has been made, the place is taken: when prayer has been made, the place is shaken. In the realm of effective praying, never have so many left so much to so few. Tithes may build a church but tears will give it life.
(Acts 4. 31)

**825 Prayer—Kepler's.** One of the astronomical works of the great Astronomer, Johann Kepler, ends with the following prayer:

It remains only that I should now lift up to heaven my eyes and hands from the table of my pursuits and humbly and devoutly supplicate the Father of lights. 'Oh Thou, who by the light of nature dost kindle within us a desire after the light of grace, that by this Thou mayest translate us into the light of glory! I give Thee thanks, O Lord and Creator, that Thou hast gladdened me by Thy creation, when I was enraptured by the works of Thy hands. Behold, I have here completed a work of my calling, with as much of intellectual strength as Thou hast granted me. I have declared the praise of Thy works to the men who will read the evidence of it, so far as my finite spirit could comprehend them in their infinity. My mind endeavoured to its utmost to reach the truth by philosophy, but if anything unworthy of Thee has been taught by me—worm born and nourished in sin—do Thou teach me that I may correct it. Have I been seduced into presumption by the admirable beauty of Thy works, or have I sought my own glory among men, in the construction of a work designed for Thy honour? O then graciously and mercifully forgive me, and finally grant me this favour, that this work may never be injurious, but may conduce to Thy glory and the good of souls.'
(James 1. 17)

**826 Prayer Meeting.** Two missionaries in Malaya (now Malaysia) had to go to the nearest town a considerable distance away across rough country to collect money which had come through for them to a bank there. They set off on foot early one morning, hoping to return the same day. Having arrived at the town and collected the money, they set off again on their trek across the wild and lonely country, only to find that they were too tired and too far away to reach their station that night. Committing themselves to God, they bivouacked on the hillside and soon fell asleep.

Morning came and they, surprised that they had not been disturbed by bandits or beasts, went their way and arrived safely at their mission station. Some weeks later a man came into the hospital for treatment. He stared at the missionary who attended him and said, 'I have seen you before.'

'No,' replied the missionary, 'I don't think we have met.' 'Oh, yes, we have,' said the man. 'You were camping on the hillside at such and such a place a few weeks back.' 'Yes, we were,' said the missionary. 'How did you know? We didn't see anyone.'

'I followed you with some of my companions from the town. We had seen you in the bank and knew that you had money on you. We waited till dark to creep upon you and rob you, but when we found you we daren't attack because of the soldiers.'

'Soldiers?' The missionary laughed. 'There were no soldiers with us, my friend.'

The bandit was adamant. 'There were—we counted them. There were sixteen, and they had swords.' The missionary humoured the man and dismissed it as a hallucination.

When he came on furlough to England some time later, he was telling the incident at a gathering in his home town. After the meeting, a man came up to him.

'What date was it that you camped out on the hillside?'

'I can soon tell you that,' said the missionary as he turned to his diary. 'It was on such and such a night.'

The questioner also turned up his diary. 'That night,' he said, 'we had our weekly meeting for prayer: your name was brought forward by someone and,' he added, 'there were sixteen of us at the meeting that night.'
*World Christian Digest*
(Acts 12. 5)

**827 Prayer—Men Of.** During the dark days of the American Civil War, Abraham Lincoln would say, 'I have been driven again and again to my knees because I did not know where else to go. Fondly do we hope, fervently do we pray, that the mighty scourge of war may speedily pass away.' When Gladstone was Prime Minister of Great Britain, his habits of prayer were well known to his biographer, John Morley. Now and then, for a day he would disappear from all who knew him. He was out seeking help from his Bible and prayer. During World War I, Marshal Foch was often missed from his general headquarters. Those who sought him found him on his knees in prayer, asking for God's blessing and guidance. In the face of what has been achieved when a few men prayed, think what it would mean if all men prayed.
*Sunday School Times*
(Ps. 50. 15)

**828 Prayer—Morse's.** A friend asked Samuel F. B. Morse, inventor of the telegraph, 'Professor Morse, when you were making your experiments did you ever come to a halt, not knowing what to do next?'

'O yes,' he replied, 'more than once.'

'And what did you do next at such times?'

'I may answer you in confidence, sir, but it is a matter of which the public knows nothing. Whenever I could not see my way clearly I prayed for more light. I made a valuable application of electricity. Flattering honours came to me from America and Europe on account of the invention that bears my name, not because I was superior to other men, but solely because God was pleased to reveal it to me.' The first message sent by the inventor on the Morse code was—'What hath God wrought?'

(Prov. 3. 5,6)

**829 Prayer Nourishes the Soul.** 'In God's name I beseech you, let prayer nourish your soul as meals nourish your body!' said the faithful Fenelon. Henry Martyn said, 'My present deadness I attribute to want of sufficient time for private devotion. O that I might be a man of prayer!'

Of this we are sure—the greatest undiscovered area in the resources of God is the place of prayer.

Leonard Ravenhill

(Ps. 42. 8)

**830 Prayer of Francis of Assisi.** Lord, make me an instrument of Thy peace. Where there is hatred, let me sow love. Where there is injury, pardon. Where there is doubt, faith. Where there is despair, hope. Where there is darkness, light. Where there is sadness, joy.

O divine Master, grant that I may not so much seek to be consoled as to console; to be understood, as to understand; to be loved, as to love; for it is in giving that we receive; it is in pardoning that we are pardoned; and it is in dying that we are born to eternal life.

**831 Prayer—Power of.** A marble cutter, with chisel and hammer, was changing a piece of stone into a statue. Looking on, a preacher said, 'I wish I could deal such clanging blows on stony hearts.' 'Maybe you could,' was the reply, 'if you worked, as I do, on your knees.'

(Mark 9. 27-29; James 5. 16)

**832 Prayer—Practice of.** A British soldier one night was caught creeping stealthily back to his quarters from the nearby woods. He was taken before his commanding officer and charged with holding communications with the enemy. The man pleaded that he had gone into the woods to pray by himself. That was his only defence. 'Have you been in the habit of spending hours in private prayer?' the officer growled. 'Yes sir!' 'Then down on your knees and pray now!' he roared. 'You never needed it so much!' Expecting immediate death, the soldier knelt and poured out his soul in prayer that could only have been inspired by the power of the Holy Spirit. 'You may go,' said the officer simply, when he had finished. 'I believe your story. If you hadn't drilled often, you could not do so well at review.'

*Sunday School Times*

(Dan. 6. 10)

**833 Prayers Unanswered.** The apostle Paul was importunate in his petition for deliverance from the sore trial of the thorn in the flesh. The Lord did not grant his request even after he had besought the Lord thrice to remove that painful bodily affliction. It seemed as if his prayer was unanswered, but the answer, continuous in its consoling efficacy, came to Paul in another way, for the Lord said, 'My grace is sufficient for thee: my strength is made perfect in weakness.' Charles Hodge's comment on this is, 'These words should be engraven on the palm of every believer's hand.'

So, sometimes in His great wisdom God refuses to give us the things we ask for that will be an injury to us; on the other hand, He may, at times, let us have the very thing we ask for so insistently, that we may feel the sting and misery of it and learn through pain and humiliation that God's will and way are always best.

'He gave them their request; but sent leanness into their soul.'

A.N.

(Ps. 106. 15; 2 Cor. 12. 8,9)

**834 Prayers Unanswered.**

*I thank Thee, God, for my unanswered prayers,*
*The foolish things I sought Thou hast denied;*
*The palace where I prayed I might abide—*
*For selfish ease, release from earthly care—*
*Relief from warning pain which I could bear,*
*For honours, riches, preferment and pride,*
*The world's applaudits like the rolling tide—*
*The purple robe of fame for me to wear.*
*How fatherly Thou art! How childish I!*
*Complaining for the sweets that do me harm;*
*No good thing dost Thou ever me deny,*
*All dangers fend and soothest each alarm.*
*O God, my earth desires are full of snares;*
*Forgive and do not answer all my prayers!*

(James 4.3)

**835 Praying Mother—A.** For me it had been a busy week-end. It was 1942 and the war was at its height. Now, late on Sunday evening, I caught the last train from London to the West. With difficulty I scrambled into a compartment already overfull with R.A.F. men returning from week-end leave. I was the only civilian. The only other passenger was a U.S. sailor, recalled from leave and now bound for Plymouth to rejoin his ship.

At Chippenham all the airmen alighted, leaving only the sailor and myself. Shortly afterwards he took from his pocket a wallet and from that a tract. Stretching himself comfortably on the seat he proceeded to read with evident interest. To my surprise it was a tract I knew—indeed I knew the author. It was entitled, 'What the Colonel said.' It told of how a Padre, addressing soldiers about to go into the battle line, assured them that if they fell in action, the sacrifice of their lives in a righteous cause would assure their entrance into heaven. However, before the parade was dismissed, the Colonel addressed his men. He said he did not wish to weaken the authority of the Padre but he felt he must tell them that the sacrifice of their lives would avail them nothing at all—that the Word of God declared that only through the sacrifice of Jesus, God's own Son, could remission of sins and eternal life be secured; that there is no other name given under heaven whereby we must be saved and that faith in Him alone would ensure peace with God now and certainty of heaven hereafter.

The sailor read the tract carefully, then, after a pause, began to read it through again. I watched him thoughtfully pondering those words, then he carefully replaced it in his wallet and put his wallet in his pocket again.

I leaned across and tapped him on the knee. He looked surprised as I said to him, 'Who do you think was telling the truth, the Padre or the Colonel?' After a moment he said, 'I think the Colonel was right and the Padre was wrong.' Nevertheless, he confessed that since he had been in the navy he had given little thought to these things. A most interesting conversation followed: I told him I knew the tract, and I knew the author, but more important still I knew the Saviour. He told me that a stranger on Paddington station pressed the tract into his hand as he boarded the train. I told him that I knew the publisher also and would be willing to give him a note of introduction to him since he lived in Plymouth, the very place to which he was journeying. Then I said, 'I wonder why God is so clearly showing His interest in you? A man in London, a man in the train, a man at your journey's end, all linked so clearly by one small tract—surely this is no mere coincidence. Why is God so concerned about you?'

I was due to alight at the next stop, Bath. Then, as the train slowed down, he looked at his wristwatch and slowly said, 'It is 1 a.m. here now: at this time every day since I joined the navy, my mother way over in the States has prayed for me—and she will be praying right now.'

That week-end his ship left Plymouth—the invasion of North Africa had begun, but a mother's prayers were surely being heard in heaven and answered on earth.        A. E. Barnes

**836  Preaching.** Samuel Chadwick, the noted Methodist Preacher, said: 'I would rather preach than do anything else in the world. I would rather preach than eat my dinner or have a holiday. I would rather pay to preach than be paid not to preach. It has its price in agony and sweat and tears, and no calling has such joys and heartbreaks, but it is a calling an archangel might covet. Is there any joy like that of saving a soul? Any thrill like that of opening blind eyes? Any reward like the love of children to the second and third generation? Any treasure like the grateful love of hearts healed and comforted?'
(Mark 16. 16; 2 Tim. 4. 2)

**837  Preaching for a Verdict.** In the early years of this twentieth century Donald McIntosh, a blind evangelist, made his mark in Scotland as a gifted preacher. Whatever his text, whatever his theme might be, he never failed in his preaching to impress upon his hearers the claims of Christ. Mr Asquith, at that time Chancellor of the Exchequer, heard Mr McIntosh preach repeatedly and remarked with true discernment, 'That man is always preaching for a verdict.'
(2 Cor. 5. 20)

**838  Preaching Salvation.**

*Oh let the Spirit all my powers inspire*
*To preach salvation, present, full and free;*
*Open my lips, bestow a tongue of fire,*
*A heart of love, in fellowship with Thee!*
*Give me to see, with faith's keen eagle eye,*
*The unseen worlds with all their weal and woe,*
*With Thee eternity of bliss on high,*
*Without Thee night, eternal night below.*

*I want to learn the value of one soul,*
*One soul that's saved, one soul for ever lost,*
*By pondering well its everlasting goal*
*And—more than all—what Thee its ransom cost.*
*O let Thy cross be e'er before my sight:*
*Teach me its endless wonders more to know,*
*Sin's righteous wage, love's all-surpassing might,*
*That I may far and wide Thy praises show.*

(Heb. 2. 3)

**839  Preaching The Word.** The photo of Glasgow's City motto brought to mind the last visit of the Pilgrim Preachers to the city. As the driver of their Gospel van, I had to apply for petrol coupons. The officer issuing the coupons said, 'There's no need of you in the city.'

'Oh yes, there is,' I replied, 'Your city's motto says: "Let Glasgow flourish by the preaching of the Word", but the latter part of the motto has been left out.'

Coupons were granted without a murmur.
          Dan Kerr in *The Christian Herald*
(2 Tim. 4. 2)

**840  Preaching to Sinners.** Daniel Webster, the famous American lawyer, during a summer holiday, went each Sunday to a little country church. His niece asked him why he went there when he paid little attention to far abler sermons in Washington.

'In Washington,' he replied, 'they preach to Daniel Webster the Statesman. This man has been talking to Daniel Webster the sinner and telling him of Jesus the Saviour.'
(Ps. 25. 8,9; 51. 13)

**841  Precepts of the Law.** The Jews in the Talmud have the saying, 'The whole law was given to Moses at Sinai, in six hundred and thirteen precepts.' David, in the fifteenth Psalm, brings them all within the compass of eleven. Isaiah brings them to six (Isa. 33. 15); Micah to three (Micah 6. 8); Isaiah again to two (Isa. 56); Habakkuk to this one, 'The just shall live by faith'. (Hab. 2. 4)
          Lightfoot

**842  Precious Things.** The most precious things in the world are often the product of the most adverse circumstances. Take pearls and diamonds, for instance. I have found pearls in the shell of an oyster. Scientists tell us that the pearl is the result of a speck of sand getting into the shell and irritating the fish so that it has to build a sort of protective covering around it. That in the end becomes the pearl.

In the case of diamonds it is intense heat and terrific pressure that make diamonds out of ordinary carbon. There are myriads of grains of sand and lots of pieces of carbon lying around that are never transmuted into precious stones. There is a parallel here of life. It is the finest character that is produced in the white heat of suffering and the intense pressure of circumstances. Remember that, if you are being called to endure burdens that seem at times greater than you can bear, it may be that God is preparing you by pressure and suffering to shine forth like a precious stone, a sparkling jewel for the King of kings.

Carl Osterlag

(Mal. 3. 16,17)

**843  Pre-existence of Christ.** Two men were debating the pre-existence of Christ on a railway station, one a Unitarian, the other a Christian. The former insisted that the Bible itself nowhere taught that Jesus had any existence before He was born into the world, and the latter affirmed that it did. When the Christian quoted texts such as—'In the beginning was the Word, and the Word was with God, and the Word was God', the other replied, 'In the mind of God, of course, but not actually.' So one text after another was swept out of the way. Another Christian man who had been listening to the argument stepped over and listened carefully. Both the debaters turned to him and said, 'What do you think?' 'Oh!' he said, 'one verse of Scripture settles that for me.' 'What verse is that?' they asked. 'Ye know the grace of our Lord Jesus Christ that, though He was rich, yet for your sakes He became poor that ye through His poverty might be rich.'

'Well!' said the Unitarian, 'I don't see what that has to do with it. That is not discussing the same question.' Even the Christian could not see that the verse quoted threw any light on the subject.

But the Christian who quoted it said, 'Gentlemen, think! It says He was rich, yet for our sakes became poor. Was He ever rich on earth? Was He rich when born in a cattle-shed and cradled in a manger? Was He rich when working in that humble village of Nazareth as a carpenter? Was He rich as He travelled on foot over the hills and through the valleys of Palestine? Was He rich when He said, "The foxes have holes and the birds of the air have nests, but the Son of man hath not where to lay His head?" The text says—"He was rich". When was He rich?' The Unitarian replied, 'I am not going to discuss that,' and walked off. The stranger boarded the train and, as it pulled out, the Christian was seen running after the Unitarian, saying, 'Tell me this—when was He rich?' But the Unitarian went on his way.

(2 Cor. 8. 9)

**844  Presence of God—The.**

*Fear thou not for I am with thee,*
*I thy God—be not dismayed:*
*Face the days that lie before thee,*
*Trust Me and be unafraid.*

*When the nights are darkest trust Me;*
*Trust Me when the days are bright.*
*'Tis My mighty hand upholds thee,*
*Though 'tis hidden from thy sight.*

*All the journey I am with thee,*
*All thy weakness I'll sustain;*
*Never shall My presence leave thee:*
*Trust Me still in joy and pain.*

*Trust Me when the shadows lengthen,*
*And the shades of night draw near;*
*I am with thee still to strengthen.*
*Trust in me and have no fear.*

*When for thee life's journey's ended*
*And thy days of service o'er—*
*With Me Who for thee has tended*
*Thou shalt be for evermore.*

J. C. Whitelaw

(Isa. 41. 10)

**845  Preserved by God.** Once when Charles Garrett was preaching to a large congregation about the mysterious troubles that often come to the Christian, he was saying that we were not exempt from trouble; 'whom the Lord loveth He chasteneth', and some converted men had more trouble after their conversion than before. He had known Christian men who were steeped in trouble—surrounded by it; trouble to the right, trouble to the left, trouble in front, trouble behind. Then an old man in the gallery who had served God for seventy years, shouted, 'Glory be to God, it's always open on top.' The old man was right, for there is one eye that never slumbers, one ear that ever hears, and one heart that ever feels—'He ever lives for us.'

Hy. Pickering

(Ps. 121. 3; Heb. 7. 25)

**846  Pride is Idolatry.** In his natural state every man born into the world is a rank idolator. Perhaps, indeed, we may not be such in the vulgar sense of the word. We do not, like the idolatrous heathen, worship molten or graven images. We do not bow down to the stock of a tree, to the stones set up on the roadside to measure the miles or kilometres, or to the work of our own hands. But what then? We have set up our idols in our hearts; and to these we bow down. We worship ourselves when we pay ourselves the honour that is due to God alone. Therefore, all pride is idolatry: it is ascribing to ourselves what is due to God alone.

(1 John 5. 21; 1 Pet. 5. 5)

185

**847   Pride the Oldest Sin.**   Pride is the oldest sin in the world. Indeed it was before the world. Satan and his angels fell by pride. They were not satisfied with their first estate. Thus pride stocked hell with its first inhabitants. Pride cast Adam out of paradise. He was not content with the place God assigned him. He tried to raise himself, and fell. Thus sin, sorrow and death entered in by pride.

Pride sits in all our hearts by nature. We are born proud. Pride makes us rest satisfied with ourselves—think we are good enough as we are—stop our ears against advice—refuse the gospel of Christ—turn every one to his own way. But pride never reigns so powerfully as in the heart of a young man.

J. C. Ryle

(Prov. 16. 18)

**848   Priesthood of Believers.**   All Christians are altogether priests, and let it be an anathema to assert there is any other priest than one who is a Christian, for it will be asserted without the Word of God.

Martin Luther

(1 Pet. 2. 5,9)

**849   Priests of Different Orders.**   Dr H. A. Ironside, with his wife and elder son, was at one time ministering the Word of God in the N.W. Provinces of Canada. Early one morning they were going by rail from a town in the south of the province to a larger city where he was to preach that night. When the train stopped at a wayside station, a missionary priest of the Franciscan Order boarded it. As he could not find a seat and as Dr Ironside and his wife and son were occupying two seats, Dr Ironside offered him the vacant seat, which he cordially accepted. His accent indicated that he was accustomed to speak in French, though his English was very good.

After the priest settled in, they chatted about things in general and finally the priest gave Dr Ironside the opportunity he wanted by enquiring whether they were residents in the province or tourists passing through. Dr Ironside replied that, though they were not tourists, their home being in California, they were in that province on special service. The priest then asked him if he was a commercial man representing some business firm and was told, 'Not exactly, though I represent a wonderful House and have splendid goods to display to those interested.'

Smilingly, the priest asked, 'What is your calling, if you don't mind telling me?' 'Well!' replied the doctor, 'I am a catholic priest engaged in missionary work.'

Looking up in surprise, the fellow-traveller glanced first at his collar, then at his wife and little boy, and said, 'I think you are joking. You surely are not a Catholic priest.'

'Yes,' replied Dr Ironside, 'I am indeed a priest, but a priest in the holy catholic Church. I am thoroughly serious in what I say.'

'But,' said the Franciscan, 'you are not wearing a Roman collar.'

'No! I did not say I am a Roman priest, but a priest of the catholic Church! Pardon me if I say that 'Roman' and 'catholic' do not fit very well together. One speaks of restricted communion, the other of a universal church.'

'Oh, I think I understand you. You are a clergyman in one of the sects of Protestantism.'

'No! I am not a clergyman but a priest. Perhaps I could make my position clearer if I tell you how I became a Christian and how I was made a priest.'

'I would be most interested if you care to tell me,' replied the Franciscan.

Dr Ironside then told him how, as a lad of fourteen, he read Romans 3 and learnt that he was a sinner, and then John 3. He read down to verse 18—'He that believeth in Him is not condemned', and then the light broke upon his soul, and he cried, 'Lord, I do believe and I trust Thy Word. I am not condemned.'

The Franciscan had listened very carefully and broke in with, 'I have never heard anything like this in all my life. You remind me of Saint Augustine. It was through the Book that light came to him without any individual speaking to him. And so with you—the light came through the Book. But what did you do next?'

'Well,' Dr Ironside replied, 'I sought out a little group of Christians with whom I soon had happy fellowship, and I continued studying my Bible. It was as I studied the First Epistle of the Apostle Peter that I made a very great discovery. I found out that I was not only a child of God, the possessor of eternal life, but that the moment I was saved I became a priest in the holy catholic Church. The apostle tells us in the second chapter, verse five, "Ye also, as living stones, are built up a spiritual house an holy priesthood, to offer up spiritual sacrifices acceptable to God by Jesus Christ", and in verse 9 he says, "But ye are a chosen generation, a royal priesthood, an holy nation, a peculiar people, that ye should shew forth the praises of Him who hath called you out of darkness into His marvellous light." From these Scriptures I learned that I am a priest, set apart in Christ Jesus as a worshipper, and that it is my blessed privilege to be Christ's representative in this world, seeking to make known the riches of His grace to others.'

Smiling, the Franciscan said, 'I understand now what you mean by saying that you are a catholic priest. But you are not a member of the true Church which Jesus Christ founded on Saint Peter.'

This led to a long, though friendly discussion as to the nature of the true Church, and also as to Peter's relation to it, and from that on to the new birth and the sacraments—particularly the real nature of the Lord's Supper and the purpose for which it was given. The Franciscan confessed frankly that he was at a loss in keeping up his side in such a discussion because he was not familiar with the Bible. He said that his studies had largely occupied him with the writings of the Fathers and the decrees of the church, and that he realized that he had not read the holy Scriptures as carefully as he should have done.

As they were about to separate, the Franciscan said, 'I wish you could come up to the monastery and spend the evening with me. I cannot ask the lady to come as it is contrary to the rules, but if you could possibly spare the evening I would be so glad to talk with you further.'

Dr Ironside assured him that he would enjoy spending such an evening, but a dinner appointment at his cousin's home and a preaching engagement made that impossible, He invited his fellow-traveller to come home with them, as he knew his relatives would gladly welcome him to dinner. That, too, the Franciscan priest was unable to do.

After another short talk they parted on very friendly terms and went their several ways.
(1 Pet. 2. 5,9)

**850  Priorities in Life.** The Christian life is not a hobby or a part-time occupation. Each should render full-time service for the Master whether occupied entirely in Christian work or in a secular vocation. It is vitally important, therefore, that we should know the mind of the Lord regarding every step of our lives. This will include the choice of a career, the place in which we live, the company of the Lord's people with whom we meet, our friendships, and especially the choice of a life partner.

What should be the guiding principle in our choice of a career? Many non-Christians put as their first consideration the salary, leisure time, prospects of advancement, etc., whilst others just drop into the first job that comes their way. The great question facing each young Christain should be—'To what is the Lord calling me?' His choice should be our first consideration. Outside of this we become only misfits and unhappy. The weight of responsibility for our vocation rests with the Lord who calls. Our responsibility is to follow His leading.

Dr A. H. Linton

(Matt. 6. 33)

**851  Priorities of Life.** It was opening night at Whitehall Theatre in the West End and a young woman of nineteen, who had the bright lights of the theatrical world as her cherished ambition, made her way with the throngs to the Corner House. As she sat awaiting her evening meal, she knew that the theatre was about the happiest place in the world. A new stage comedy was being presented and she felt inwardly glad, for it would help to lighten the hearts of war-weary Londoners. Victory had been won, but austerity still cast a grey pall over life. She realised, as an assistant stage manager, that she was contributing her part, for was she not responsible with others for the smooth handling of scenery, sound effects and lighting? Surely it was but a step towards a brilliant acting career. The gaiety and brightness and wonder of the play-world fascinated

and captivated her youthful life. Yet, on that particular afternoon in March, 1946, a wistful longing came over her and there was an intense desire for reality. She began to question what life was all about and why there was no lasting peace or satisfaction in her heart. Then what happened? Let her tell it in her own words:

'As I sat at the table I could see out of the corner of my eye a man with a large white Stetson hat waiting to be seated with his three companions, and to my surprise the hostess guided them to my table.

'The most prominent thing about my table companions was their friendliness and zest for life. We were soon talking and laughing as if we had known one another for years. And then I made a baffling discovery: they were headed toward a Youth for Christ Rally! Religion . . . and overflowing happiness? How did they fit in the same person? I'd never imagined such a combination.

'Leslie Rainey, the Stetson owner, talked enthusiastically about living for the Lord, and being saved. I'd never heard those expressions, but they evidently had something to do with knowing God in a personal way.

'I had to return to the theatre for the evening performance, while the fellows looked forward to attending the youth rally. But before we parted Les asked for my address, and we made an appointment for the following week.

'He carried a large umbrella and wore rubber overshoes. We strolled through St James's Park, passing the theatre where I had spent so many happy hours. Before long, the conversation turned from things of time to those of eternity, and Les began to show me how I could experience the joy and peace which he, himself, had received through knowing Christ Jesus as Saviour and Lord.

'Alone in my room that evening I made the decision that was to transform my whole life. As I knelt at my bedside, I knew that the Lord Jesus was in the room with me and He wanted me to turn my life over to Him. I came to Him as a little child and as He whispered to my heart, I simply said, "Yes, Lord!" When Christ came into my life, the sunlight of God streamed into my soul, and as the days went by and He became more precious to me, I began to understand God's plan of salvation.

'Meeting God like that changed a lot of things. I had been engrossed in theatre life, but its appeal began to wane. I felt that God wanted me to leave the theatre job and go to Bible School. I enrolled at Ridgelands Bible College to learn more of God's Word, and studied there until 1949. Then an unusual opportunity came to witness to my former stage associates.

'My life-verse is: "Seek ye first the kingdom of God and His righteousness and all these things shall be added unto you".'
(Matt. 6. 33)

**852  Prisoner's Conversion.** John, a child of incestuous relationship, abandoned by his mother at the age of two weeks, and from then until he was 3½ years of age reared in a children's Home in Ayrshire, had lived with six different sets of foster-parents. At 17 years of age I first met him in the Prison Bible Class. He was a difficult lad, unsettled and insecure, and prone to exaggerate wildly in order to draw attention to himself; but while in prison he made profession of faith in Christ and lived to prove the reality of his confession of faith. His faith was weak but sincere.

In spite of his difficult nature John was a lovable boy, and he spent many week-ends at our home since we were the only really settled friends he had in the world. He had a great love for animals and after a short time we were able to find him a job on a farm where he had his own room. The farmer and his wife, though they were not Christians, were sympathetic and kind. During his 2½ happy years on the farm he kept in close touch with us.

In August, 1972, we went on holiday for a few days, and on the Friday evening on our return, we were contacted by the police who said they had been trying to trace us during the few days of our absence. John had been calling incessantly for us from a hospital bed and had died just thirty minutes before we arrived back home. What had happened?

Earlier that week, while at work on the farm, he had drunk what he had thought to be lemonade but what proved to be the dreaded paraquat. The doctors had known from the start that there was no hope for him, and he died within four hours of admission. It was comforting to learn that during his last illness John had repeated over and over again the verse he most loved in the way we had taught him to say it: 'For God so loved John . . . that He gave His only begotten Son; that as John . . . trusts in Him, John . . . will never perish but John . . . will have everlasting life.'

At his funeral on a summer morning there were only five mourners, including a young ex-prisoner who had travelled fifty miles to be present: so the undertakers had to assist with the lowering of the coffin into the grave. John, rejected at birth and so friendless at death, was 'safe in the arms of Jesus'.

Alex. Allan

**853 Problem of Sin.** To deal with sin the Jews had a sacrificial system that had to be incessant in its performance, yet had proved ineffectual: for

*Not all the blood of beasts on Jewish altars slain*
*Could give the guilty conscience peace or wash away its stain.*

The cultured Greeks brought to bear on the problems of sin and of life and death a concentration of human effort along aesthetic and rational lines, but the dissoluteness of men in their most cultured cities was ample evidence of the failure of their system.

The Romans acknowledged the existence and misery of sin, but endeavoured to restrain it and wipe out its consequences by their emphasis on moral law and orderly government.

But the Gospel of Jesus Christ, not cluttered up with philosophical arguments or with the 'Do's' and 'Don'ts' of ethical homilies, states historical facts—'that Christ died for our sins according to the Scriptures, that He was buried, and that He rose again the third day according to the Scriptures'—is universal in its application and is made known to the nations of the world for the obedience of faith.
(1 Cor. 15. 3,4; Rom. 16. 26)

**854 Procrastination.** A letter was handed to Julius Caesar as he entered his chariot on the Ides of March to go to the Capitol in Rome. On his ears fell the words: 'Great Caesar! I beseech thee, read this missive without delay. Weighty matters depend on it.'

Caesar answered, 'I cannot tarry now. I shall read your missive later.'

When, shortly after, at the entrance to the Capitol, he fell down under the assassin's blows, the unopened note was found in his belt. It contained a warning which, if heeded, might have been the means of saving his life.
(2 Cor. 6. 2)

**855 Prodigal Son—A.** 'I will arise and go to my father.'

A young lad in his teens, with only one fellow-passenger, an older man who was an evangelist, occupied a compartment on a railway train. They had not spoken, but, as the young man was looking worried, the preacher asked sympathetically if there was anything wrong, and thus won the lad's confidence.

The youth opened his heart to the older man and told him he had run away from home and disgraced the family. Now he was repentant and wanted to return. His mother was willing to receive him back but the father would not hear of it. The boy's mother wrote to him and gave him some hope that she might be able to talk his father over, so the lad was going back in the hope that he would be forgiven and received. In her letter to her son his mother had said that if her husband relented she would hang a white rag on the solitary tree in the garden, which was visible from the passing trains. The preacher offered to look out and tell the young man what he saw in order to save him further emotional strain. As the train whizzed past the garden, the evangelist turned to the lad: 'Thumbs up! Cheer up!' he exclaimed, 'the tree is covered with white rags.' A welcome awaited the returning prodigal.
(Luke 15. 18)

**856 Prodigal Son—Story of the.** Here is an old negro preacher's outline of the narrative of the Prodigal son recorded in Luke 15. It is rather amusing.

1. HIS MADNESS:     *he cavilled:*
                    *he travelled:*
                    *he revelled.*

2. HIS SADNESS:                *he went to the*
                               *dogs:*
                               *he lost his togs:*
                               *he fed the hogs.*

3. HIS GLADNESS:               *he received the*
                               *seal:*
                               *he ate the veal:*
                               *he danced the reel.*

(Luke 15. 11-24)

**857 Profundity.** A diplomat once upbraided Abraham Lincoln for intimating that a certain Greek history was boring. 'The author of that history, Mr President,' said the diplomat, 'is one of the profoundest scholars of the age. Indeed, it may be doubted whether any man of our generation has plunged more deeply into the fount of learning.'

'Or come up drier,' quipped Lincoln.

It is a God-given art to present profound truths with clarity and in an interesting way.
(Isa. 28. 10)

**858 Promise of Christ's Presence.** The promise of our Lord Jesus to His disciples in Matthew 28. 20 was very precious to two Scottish missionaries, both doctors. Inscribed on the tombstone of Dr John Paton in Australia are those cheering words of promise that the veteran missionary to the New Hebrides had proved true again and again. He had quoted the words constantly in private conversation and in public address. 'Pleading the promise,' he said, 'I followed the Guide.'

They are found in Livingstone's journal in the British Museum. Of that unfailing promise he said, 'It is the word of a gentleman of the strictest and most sacred honour, and there's an end of it.'
(Matt. 28. 20; Heb. 13. 5)

**859 Proof by Performance.** Doré, the artist, faced by an immigration official, searched in vain for his passport. It was lost. Putting on an assuring smile, he turned to the officer and said, 'It's all right—I'm Doré the artist. Surely you will let me pass.' The official refused, then added, 'If you're Doré, prove it. Here's a pencil and paper. Draw me a picture!' A few strokes and the proof was there. The officer then exclaimed, 'Pass on, Doré. No other man could do that.'

John the Baptist sent messengers from his prison to ask Jesus, 'Art thou He that should come or look we for another?' To the imprisoned herald of the kingdom the messengers returned with the message, 'Show John again the things you hear and see. The blind receive their sight and the lame walk; the lepers are cleansed and the deaf hear; the dead are raised up, the poor have the gospel preached to them.'

The crowning evidence came when the crucified King burst the bands of death and rose from the tomb, Victor over death, hell and the grave.

*Message Of Victory*
(Matt. 11. 4,5)

**860 Proof by Skill.** The U.S.A. Immigration officer asked the tall young Pole, 'How much money have you?' 'None,' was the reply. Then the Pole argued that he had a friend in the States who would stand security for him: but the door of entry into the U.S.A. was closed fast against him. Finally, tapping the case under his arm, the young man pleaded, 'With this I can get anywhere.' Seeing the officer's curiosity, the young Pole produced a cornet and began to play the beautiful intermezzo from Cavalleria Rusticana. As he played, the room filled with people transfixed by the music. When he had finished, his audience broke into cheers. 'Go along,' said the official, 'you will never starve with a gift like that.'
(2 Tim. 2. 15)

**861 Prophecy and its Interpretation.** Mr E. W. Rogers has made twelve helpful suggestions as guides to the interpretation of prophecy. They are:

1 Every prophecy and prophetic technical word must be interpreted strictly in accordance with its context. If the context in the Old Testament differs from the citation of it in the new Testament, we may safely conclude that the original prophecy embodies a dual fulfilment, e.g. Joel 2. 28-32; Acts 2. 16-21. Thus some prophecies are capable of a partial as well as an ultimately complex fulfilment, e.g. Zechariah 9. 9-11; Matthew 21. 4,5. Such words as 'parousia', 'apocalypse', and 'epiphany' should be compared with reference to their context.

2 The pronouns used, and whether spoken in the third or first person, must also be considered. Indeed, all the usual points of grammar must be weighed, e.g. The Son of Man coming in Matthew 24 and 'I will come again' in John 14. 2,3.

3 Prophecy should be interpreted literally unless such literal interpretation is manifestly impossible because of absurdity. Metaphors and other figures of speech should be carefully distinguished from that which is literal. The Book of Revelation is full of symbols intermingled with that which is literal.

4 Prophecy is progressive—simple and concise in early parts of the Bible, gradually becoming more detailed. The Prophetic Word is a homogeneous whole.

5 Some prophecies—e.g. Genesis 3. 15—speak of apparently one event, the accomplishment of which is in two or more stages, e.g. Isaiah 61. 1,2.

6 The titles of divine Persons are significant—Son of Man, Saviour, Lord Jesus.

7 The persons of whom or to whom prophecies were spoken often represent a class.

8 The simpler the interpretation, the more likely it is to be the true one.

9 In interpreting prophecy it is absolutely essential to have regard to the various dispensations in which God acted in special ways with men.

10 The utmost care must be taken to keep strictly within the limits of the words of the prophecy under consideration.

11 Unless an Old Testament prophecy cited in the New Testament is specifically stated to have been fulfilled by such New Testament reference to it, the cited prophecy should not be regarded as exhausted by the New Testament application of it, but merely regarded as exemplifying the principle involved, e.g. 1 Corinthians 15. 54.

12 Those prophetic revelations called 'mysteries' should be interpreted as such for they relate to matters kept secret until the time of their disclosure.

In addition to the above, no system of prophetic interpretation can be right that ignores the God-given division of mankind—Jew, Gentile, Church of God.

Condensed from *The Harvester*

(1 Cor. 10. 32)

**862 Provision of God.** William Burton and his wife were missionaries in Africa. Mrs Burton was very ill, and often expressed her longing for an orange. Citrus fruit of any kind was good for her condition. The nearest orange trees were in Dan Crawford's orchard, which was a twenty-one days' jungle trek distant from their station. As Burton left to preach, depressed that he could not satisfy his wife's longing, she began to pray for some fruit. On his return he found that the Lord had supplied the need, for beside his wife's bed stood a full basket of beautiful oranges. Dan Crawford and his wife had been picking them half-ripe, and Mrs Crawford had said, 'Wouldn't it be nice to send some of these over to the Burtons?' They sent an African helper on the long journey with the oranges, and he arrived and delivered them while Mrs Burton was praying for them, and Mr Burton was preaching the Word. That night the two missionaries rejoiced as they recalled the Lord's promise, 'Before they call I will answer, and while they are yet speaking I will hear.'

(Isa. 65. 24)

**863 Pruning.** The chief tool of the vine-dresser is his knife. Pruning looks merciless and wasteful, but there is no random cutting; nothing is cut away but what it is gain to lose. Mr Cecil on one occasion, in deep dejection of spirit because of painful heart wounds, was pacing to and fro in a botanic garden in Oxford when he observed a fine specimen of the pomegranate almost cut through the stem. On asking the gardener for the reason, he received the following answer: 'Sir, this tree used to shoot so strong that it bore nothing but leaves. I was therefore obliged to cut it in this manner; and when it was almost cut through, then it began to bear plenty of fruit.'

Henry Durbanville

(John 15. 2)

**864 Psalm 23 in Lowland Scots.**

*I'm in the Maister's flock, He is my Herd,*
*And sin' He lo'es His ain, I've a' that's best;*
*By waters calm He airts my thowless feet,*
*And in the meadows fair He bids me rest.*

*He kens my failings, merks my ilka turn,*
*And whiles, when frae the track I gang astray,*
*Wi' tender care He tak's me in His airms,*
*And sets me doon in His ain righteous way.*

*Though death should cuist her shadow in my*
*    gait,*
*And eerie seem the valley, mirk and lang;*
*I'm suir nae han' daur fash or daunton me,*
*For Ye are there, my comfort and my sang.*

*Ye've gi'en me meat amang my verra foes,*
*Ye've shoo'ered your blessings on my*
*    worthless heid;*
*My cup o' joy is fu' and runnin' ower,*
*I've mair in Thee than meets my ilka need.*

*My Maister's guidness and His mercy strang*
*Has gane wi' me, and will through a' the days,*
*Till in His hame I dwell for evermair.*
*Mine be the bliss, but His be a' the praise!*

William Landles

**865 Punishment Borne for Others.** Many years ago the Emperor of China sent Wu Feng, his trusted representative, to rule over the tribesmen in the mountains of Formosa. Wu Feng proved to be a strict ruler who punished the tribesmen whenever they did wrong. But he was also fair and just, so that the people learned to love and respect him highly because of his kindness to them. He soon restored order among them.

They retained, however, one very wicked custom. Once every year they would swoop down from the mountains to cut off the head of the first man they encountered. Then they offered the head of the dead man as a sacrifice to their gods.

Wu Feng remonstrated with them. 'You should not kill people like that,' he exclaimed. 'It is sinful and senseless.' But they would not listen to him. Vainly he pleaded and threatened that these head-hunting expeditions should stop.

One day Wu Feng received a letter from the Emperor of China which said in part, 'Unless the head-hunting stops you will be brought back to China in disgrace.'

Following the receipt of the Emperor's letter the seventy-one year old Wu Feng sadly and disconsolately called his chiefs together. He had a plan to discuss with them.

'Honourable Chiefs,' he began, 'I have tried to be a kind and just ruler, but you still do not obey me. This practice must be stopped. Here, then, is my plan. Tomorrow night, when the moon is high, your tribesmen will take their last head. They will surround the crossroads near the village, where they will see a man dressed in white walking towards the crossroads. He will be your last victim. You may behead him, but after that your custom is to cease.'

The chiefs agreed and went home to prepare for the feast. At the appointed hour a lone figure, clad in white, walked slowly toward the crossroads. Hidden in the surrounding bush were numerous tribesmen prepared for the kill.

Amidst screaming and shouting, they charged as if in battle. There was a flash of moonlight on steel as one of the chiefs raised his axe and cut off the head of the lone stranger. Then quickly leaving the place of their murder, they carried their gory prize to a place in the bush where the feast had been prepared.

'Here's the head,' shouted one of the tribesmen, handing it to the big chief, so that he could carry it to be inspected by the light of the fire. But all at once the singing and shouting stopped and there was a great hush. As all eyes turned to the dead face, every man was shocked at what he saw. Their victim was their good and kind friend, Wu Feng. There was a smile on his still lips and he wore the calm and peaceful mien of one who had not been afraid to die.

The tribesmen looked at each other in dumb amazement. What had they done? Unwittingly they had killed their best friend. All the thrill and excitement of head-hunting was gone and they could not make merry that night. Thus it was that the last head was taken and the evil custom abolished. Wu Feng might have punished his tribesmen for their acts, but he chose rather to show them by offering himself, what a terrible crime they were committing.

Our blessed Lord Jesus Christ laid down His life so that we might forsake our sins and accept Him as our Saviour.
(Rom. 5. 8)

**866  Purity.** Story of the ermine and his little white coat.

Does the judge know the story of the spotless white fur that lines his robes of state? Does the society leader realize the sacrifice which makes possible the lovely ermine wrap which lies so gracefully about her shoulders? Do they know that the little animal whose coat they now wear, as he roamed the forest of Asia, was as proud as they—aye, very proud of his beautiful snowy coat? And do we wonder at it, for it is the most beautiful fur to be found in all the markets of the world?

Such pride does the little animal take in his spotless coat that nothing is permitted to soil it in the slightest degree. Hunters are well acquainted with this fact and take very unsportsmanlike advantage of this knowledge. No traps are set for him. Instead, they seek out his home—a tree stump, or rocky cleft, and then—be it said to their everlasting shame—they daub filth within and around the entrance. As the dogs are loosed and the chase begins, the little animal naturally turns to his one place of refuge. Reaching it, sooner than enter such a place of uncleanness, he turns to face the yelping dogs. He thinks that it is better to be stained with blood than to sully his white coat.

Only a little white coat, little ermine, but how your act condemns us! How often, in order to obtain something we desire, our character is sacrificed on the altars of worldly pleasure, greed, selfishness! Everything is lost when purity is gone—purity, which has been called the soul of character.
(1 Tim. 5. 22)

**867  Purpose for our Lives.** R. L. Stevenson once said, 'To be what we are and to become what we are capable of becoming is the only end of life.' The Apostle Paul, addressing the saints at Ephesus, said, 'Ye are His workmanship, created in Christ Jesus unto good works which God hath prepared beforehand that we should walk in them.' That is, there is a purpose for your life. Each Christian has something special to live for.

Charles Allen wrote in *The Reader's Digest*, 'When I realise that God made me as I am for a special purpose, there is no reason for me to resent the fact that He made other people for different purposes.'

Each of us should work towards forming in his own mind a clear picture of the person God created him to be. God had that picture in His mind before we were born. Let us pray that His mind will be in us. Ask yourself again and again, Why was I born? What can I best do and be? Get the picture focused sharply and fix it firmly.

'As a man thinketh in his heart, so is he.'
(Eph. 2. 10)

**868  Purpose of God and Plans of Men.** Before 1914, when the First World War commenced, Professor Stroeter, a prophetic teacher in Germany, was giving lectures, using a chart. Kaiser Wilhelm was a Bible student and used sometimes in those days to preach in the Palace Chapel. He invited Professor Stroeter to tell him what he was going to lecture about. The Professor was taken into the library and he spread out his chart.

'Do I understand you aright? Do you mean that Jesus Christ is coming back literally and all the kingdoms of the world will be destroyed, and He will set up His kingdom on the ruins of them all?' 'Exactly, your Majesty, exactly!' was the reply.

'Oh no!' said the Kaiser, 'I can't have that. Why, that would interfere with my plans.'
(Prov. 15. 22)

**869  Qualities to be Desired.** The godly Thomas Ken, writer of many fine hymns, wrote the following lines:

*Give me the priest whose graces shall possess*
*Of an ambassador the just address,*
*A father's tenderness, a shepherd's care,*
*A leader's courage which the cross can bear,*
*A ruler's awe, a watchman's wakeful eye,*
*A fisher's patience and a labourer's toil,*
*A guide's dexterity to disembroil,*
*A prophet's inspiration from above,*
*A teacher's knowledge and the Saviour's love.*

(2 Tim. 2. 24,25)

**870 Quarrel Among the Tools.** The carpenter's tools had a conference. Brother Hammer was in the chair. The meeting had informed him that he must leave because he was too noisy; but he said, 'If I am to leave, Brother Gimlet must leave too; he is so insignificant that he makes very little impression.'

Little Brother Gimlet arose and said, 'All right but Brother Screw must go also; for you have to turn him round and round again to get him anywhere.' Brother Screw then said, 'If you wish I shall go; but Brother Plane must leave also. All his work is on the surface: there's no depth in it.'

To this Brother Plane replied, 'Well, Brother Rule will have to withdraw if I do, for he is always measuring other folks as if he were the only one who is right.' Brother Rule then complained against Brother Sandpaper in these words, 'I don't care. He is rougher than he ought to be and rubs people the wrong way.'

In the midst of the discussion the Carpenter of Nazareth walked in. He had come to perform His day's work, so put on His apron and went to the bench to make a pulpit. He employed the screw, the gimlet, the sandpaper, the saw, the hammer, the plane, and all the other tools. The day's work over and the pulpit finished, Brother Saw arose and said, 'Brethren, I perceive that all of us are labourers together with God.'

How careful we should be not to find fault with any of God's tools, for they are of as much use to Him as we are, and His work cannot go on without them!

(2 Cor. 6. 1)

**871 Questing Spirit in Man.** When the first attempt was made to reach the moon, the *Belfast Telegraph* contained a paragraph with the heading and opening sentence—'Flight round the Moon' and 'there is a questing spirit in man which it is necessary to satisfy.'

Near the opening of one of his evangelistic crusades in England, Billy Graham said, 'Look at most of your songs: listen to them! They are asking, asking, asking.'

'What seek ye?' was the first question addressed by the Lord Jesus Christ to His disciples, the first Christians. They wanted to be with Him. (John 1. 38)

**872 Questions of Importance.** G. V. Wigram once asked an ex-Judge, Richard Hill, the following questions:

1 'Is Christ between you and the coming judgement of God?' The judge was able to reply: 'Christ has borne on the Cross all the judgement for me. I shall never come into judgement, for I have passed from death unto life.' (John 5. 24)
2 'Is Christ between you and your sins?' 'Yes,' was the answer. 'Christ died for my sins.' (1 Cor. 15. 3). 'Jehovah hath laid on Him the iniquity of us all.' (Isa. 53. 6)
3 'Is Christ between you and the law of God?'

This question was not answered so readily. 'Well,' said Judge Hill, 'it seems to be so according to the Scriptures, though I pray every week, "Lord, incline our hearts to keep this law." Still, Paul said, "Ye are become dead to the law" (Rom. 7. 4); and again "the law of the Spirit of life in Christ Jesus hath made me free from the law of sin and death." I think I heard someone say at your meetings the law is neither the ground of life nor the rule of life: Christ is both.'

4 'Very good!' said Mr Wigram. 'Now my fourth question—"Is Christ between you and the world?"' Yet with more hesitation came the reply, 'I hope so—it ought to be so. Is it not written, "Who gave Himself for our sins, that He might deliver us from this present evil world" (Gal. 1. 4) "The world is crucified unto me and I unto the world." (Gal. 6. 14).'
5 Then the final question: 'Is Christ between you and Richard Hill?' Judge Hill paused, then said, 'I fear I cannot go that far. I shall think about it and answer it to God.'

**873 Questions that Embarrass.** Uncle Willie had been visiting the best farm in the State, his own brother's. After he had gone, his nephew asked, 'Dad, is it true that you have the best farm in our State?' 'Yes, Willie!' 'Dad, is it true that you own a lot of houses and farms besides?' 'Yes!' 'Dad, is it true that you have insured everything and Mum and me too?' 'Willie, who's been talking to you?' asked his father. 'Well, Dad, I heard Uncle Willie say that you were so far-seeing and prudent that not a thing was uninsured, but you were very foolish indeed because you had no insurance on your soul. Dad, is that true?'

(Mark 8. 36,37)

**874 Quests for Other Worlds.**

*Man's discontent would search the stellar*
*spaces;*
*Urgent He wants 'midst other worlds to roam,*
*Perchance forgetting nothing good replaces*
*The world which God to man gave as his home.*
*Yet e'en while man explores the outer spaces,*
*Seeking his burning thirst to gratify,*
*We, who are Christ's, with eager upturned*
*faces*
*Wait the glad sight our hearts will satisfy.*

J. Danson Smith

(John 1. 38,39; 1 Thess. 1. 9,10)

**875 Quests of Life.** Jeremiah the prophet received a message from the Lord for his secretary, Baruch, who had become depressed because of his troubles and the condition of the nation of Israel, and possibly envious of others who were more comfortably placed than he. The message was—'Seekest thou great things for thyself: seek them not.'

This was the motto Thomas Ken chose for himself. He was appointed Bishop of Bath and Wells in 1685, and wrote some beautiful hymns, the best known of which is 'Glory to Thee, my

God, this night'. A model of Christian virtue and courage, he bore witness to his faith in every letter he wrote, heading each with the same words—'*Glory be to God*'. With such a desire that all his life might bring glory to God, self-seeking and self-glory were ruled out of his life and aspirations. On the fly leaf of his Greek New Testament was the Latin text in his own handwriting: ET TU QUAERIS TIBI GRANDIA? NOLI QUAERERE: which means— 'Seekest thou great things for thyself? seek them not.' His was not the selfish quest but the supreme quest: 'Seek ye first the kingdom of God and His righteousness.'
(Jer. 45. 5)

**876   Quietness.** A young doctor, while recovering from a serious operation at a hospital in Rochester, Massachussets, wrote in a letter to his parents:

'As a result of my being taken out of my busy practice I am learning the lesson of dependence upon the Lord, and realize it was all for a purpose. I am enclosing a poem someone sent me which expresses my experience:

*I needed the quiet, so He drew me aside*
*Into the shadows where we could confide;*
*Away from the bustle where all day long*
*I hurried and worried when active and strong.*
*I needed the quiet though at first I rebelled,*
*But gently, so gently, my cross He upheld*
*And whispered so sweetly of spiritual things.*
*Though weakened in body, my spirit took wings*
*To heights never dreamed of when active and*
        *gay;*
*He loved me so greatly He drew me away.*
*I needed the quiet—no prison my bed*
*But a beautiful valley of blessing instead,*
*A place to grow richer in Jesus to hide;*
*I needed the quiet so He drew me aside.*'

(Mark 6. 31)

**877   Race—The Chariot.** Professor E. M. Blaiklock points out that in expounding Philippians 3. 12-14, commentators generally have not marked the fact that Paul appears to have in mind, not the athletic contests of the Greeks from which he commonly drew illustrations, but the chariot racing of Rome. He was writing to a Roman colony: he was writing also from Rome itself: and never was there such rivalry of racing colours and circus fever as in the capital. The common talk of the soldiers of the guard would be of chariot racing, and Paul would gain an impression of this most perilous of sports.

Such a race as that which forms the substance of Paul's figure is described in *Ben Hur*. The charioteer stood on a tiny platform over sturdy wheels and axle. His knees were pressed against a curved rail and his thighs flexed. He bent forward at the waist, 'stretching out to the things before'. The reins were wound round the body and, as he stretched out hands and head over the horses' backs, the body, braced on the reins, formed a taut spring. It can easily be seen how completely the charioteer was at the mercy

of his team's sure feet and his own fine driving skill. Euripides in his *Hippolytus* describes how the hero fell and was killed. Ovid describes the same disaster. The driver, in his intense preoccupation, dare not cast a glance at the things behind. The roaring crowd, crying praise or blame, the racing of his rivals—all else had perforce to be forgotten. One object only held the driver's eye, the point to which he drove at the end of each lap.
(Phil. 3. 12-14)

**878   Radiance of Heaven.** When Adoniram Judson, the great missionary, was home on furlough on one occasion, he passed through the city of Stonington, Connecticut. A young boy playing about the wharves at the time of Judson's arrival was struck by the man's appearance. Never before had he seen such a light on any human face. He ran up the street to a minister to ask if he knew who the stranger was. The minister hurried back with him, but became so absorbed in conversation with Judson that he forgot all about the impatient youngster standing near him.

Many years afterwards that boy—who could never get away from the influence of that wonderful face—became the famous preacher, Henry Clay Turnbull. In a book of memoirs he penned a chapter entitled: 'What a boy saw in the face of Adoniram Judson.' That lighted countenance had changed his life. Did the radiance of Stephen's face change the outlook of Saul of Tarsus?
(Acts 6. 15)

**879   Radiant Joy of a Christian.** Dr G. Campbell Morgan told the story of a factory girl who, after she was saved, simply radiated Christian joy. One day, while waiting for a train at York station, she walked slowly up and down the platform to pass the time. A cultured lady, sitting on one of the platform seats observed her closely. Impressed by her happy face, she called to her, 'Excuse me, but what makes you so happy?' The girl asked, 'Was I looking happy? I didn't know it showed, but I certainly am. Would you like me to tell you why?' That gave her the opportunity of witnessing to the lady concerning the blessings of salvation and the joy it brings into life, with the result that her admirer was led to a personal acceptance of the Lord Jesus Christ.
(Prov. 16. 20; 2 Cor. 3. 18)

**880   Raised With Christ.**

*When Jesus died on Calvary,*
*I, too, was there;*
*'Twas in my place He stood for me,*
*And now accepted—even as He—*
*His right I share.*

*When Jesus rose with Life divine,*
*I, too, was there;*
*His resurrection power is mine,*
*And as the branches in the Vine,*
*His life I share.*

*When Jesus comes some day for me,*
*I shall be there;*
*With Him and like Him I shall be*
*And all His glorious majesty*
*I, too, shall share.*

*O blessed Life, so deep, so high!*
*Lord, keep me there;*
*Help me with Christ to live, to die,*
*And let me with Him by and by*
*His glory share!*

A. B. Simpson

(Rom. 6. 4; Col. 3. 1)

**881 Raising of Lazarus.** A modernistic lecturer was trying to prove that the eleventh chapter of John was written by someone who followed a tradition he had heard. He said that if Christ really had been there and knew that Lazarus had just died, he would not have needed to call his name. Would it not have been enough just to say 'Come forth?' With clever sophistry the lecturer sought to prove that for this reason the record did not ring true. Just then an elderly man stood up and said, 'I can give you the reason why the Lord called Lazarus by name. If He had merely said, "Come forth", then all the dead would have come out of their graves.' This simple statement rather punctured the lecturer, and made a big hole in his argument.

Yet the day is fast approaching when the same Person who raised Lazarus will speak another word of command, and all the dead in Christ will come forth: this will be the first resurrection. A thousand years later He will speak again and at His bidding all who have died in their sins will rise in the second resurrection and stand before the Great White Throne of judgement.

(John 11. 43)

**882 Rapture of the Saints.** A Christian physician died some time ago and his widow was sadly bereaved, but she was victorious in her sorrow. She kept up over his surgery door the little card he used when he was called out on business—'*Gone for a little while: will be back again soon.*'

Yes, believers who have died are gone for a little while. They are to be back soon with Him, for He says, 'We shall be caught up together in the clouds to meet the Lord in the air.'

(1 Thess. 4. 13-18)

**883 Rapture of the Saints.** On a visit to the great automobile factory in Detroit, Dr Donald Grey Barnhouse was fascinated by seeing train loads of scrap iron shunted on to the tracks over which an electro-magnetic crane was operating on elevated rails. With a flick of the switch, the operator in a cab on the crane brought the magnet over the cartload of scrap and turned on the power. Instantly the contents of the cart, with the exception of one or two small pieces, flew into the air to the magnet which then transported them to the maw of the furnace where the operator turned off the power, and the material dropped into the melting pot. One of the pieces not attracted by the magnet was a broomstick, the other a piece of copper tubing, neither of them iron or steel.

(1 Thess. 4. 17—'Caught up')

**884 Ready Answer—A.** A famous Jewish lecturer of Dubno had a driver who stopped en route to a lecture date and said, 'Rabbi, do me a favour. For once I'd like to be the one receiving all the honours and attention, to see what it feels like. For this one engagement, please change clothes with me. You be the driver and let me be the rabbi.'

The lecturer, a merry and generous soul, laughed and said, 'All right; but remember, clothes don't make a rabbi. If you're asked to explain some difficult passage of law, don't make a fool of yourself.'

The exchange was effected. The bogus rabbi was received with tumultuous enthusiasm, and obviously loved every minute of it. Finally, however, there came the dreaded moment when an extremely tricky question was put to him. He met the test nobly. 'A fine lot of scholars you are. Why, this is so simple that even my driver could explain it to you. Driver! come here and clarify the law for these dull-witted fellows.'

(Prov. 15. 23)

**885 Ready for His Return.** When Rupert Gibson's daughter was quite small, her father had to go away for quite a long time preaching in various places, and finally finished up in North Africa. When the great day came for him to return home he gave the date of his expected arrival, and Mrs Gibson dressed the little girl in a clean dress for Daddy's return. Unfortunately, things got a little mixed up and Mr Gibson had to cable home, 'Sorry, I shall not be home till Tuesday'—one day later. On Tuesday morning the best dress was put on again, but then again something happened and the plane could not take off. Once again he cabled, 'Sorry, delayed another day.' Eventually he arrived, and his little daughter, all spick and span, was waiting for him. Picking her up, he said, 'My word, don't you look lovely and clean and smart? What a lovely clean dress!' His wife remarked, 'That would never have happened if it had not been for you. She has never worn a dress and kept it clean for three days.' It was because she must be ready to meet Daddy when he came home, and look her very best.

(1 John 3. 2,3)

**886 Ready to Go or Stay.** The missionary motto of the Moravian Brethren was a picture representing an ox in the foreground standing between a plough on one side and an altar on the other. Underneath the picture, which spoke for itself, were the three words: '*Ready for either!*' It meant a lifetime of service and a life of sacrifice.

*Ready to go, ready to wait,*
*Ready a gap to fill;*
*Ready for service small or great,*
*Ready to do His will.*

*Ready to suffer grief and pain,*
*Ready to stand the test:*
*Ready to stay at home, and send*
*Others if He sees best.*

*Ready to speak, ready to think,*
*Ready with heart and brain;*
*Ready to start when He thinks fit,*
*Ready to stand the strain.*

　　　　　　　　　　　　　　A. C. Palmer

(Rom. 1. 15; 2 Tim. 4. 6)

**887　Ready to Meet God.** A miner in the
South of England was passing a meeting-house
one night and went in. The preacher was speaking of the holiness of God and the awful plight
of those still unprepared who might be called at
any moment to meet Him. He begged his hearers to ask themselves the question: 'Am I ready
to meet God?' He urged them to answer it now,
for now was the accepted time. God was willing
now: they were living men tonight: tomorrow
it might be too late.

The message touched the miner's conscience.
He knew he was not ready to meet God, for he
had lived a careless, godless life and dare not
meet God's holy gaze. His concern was how to
be at peace with God. He was so troubled that,
waiting till the rest of the people went out, he
approached the minister and confided to him
his fears. The faithful man of God tried to lead
him to the Saviour: 'He is your peace,' he said;
but the miner could not find peace. An hour
passed. 'Now,' said the preacher, 'it is late; go
home and seek the Saviour there.' 'No!' said
the miner, 'I beg you to stay a little longer; it
must be settled tonight.'

The minister explained the way of salvation
and prayed, but without result. Another hour
passed.

'You must go home,' he said, 'it is late, and I
can do no more for you: I cannot make the
way any clearer to you.'

'It must be settled tonight,' answered the
miner with increased earnestness.

Late as it was, the preacher felt that he could
not send him away. Once more he told him of
Jesus the Saviour and quoted promise after
promise. Once more he prayed, but in vain.
The minister grew more and more troubled.

'I must go,' said he with reluctance, 'it will
soon be morning. Go home: tomorrow night
there is a meeting here; maybe you will find
peace then.'

'Sir!' said the poor man, 'I cannot leave this
room until I find peace. Tomorrow it may be
too late, and I may be in hell. It must be settled
tonight.'

'By the help of God,' answered the preacher,
'it shall be settled tonight, and I will not leave
you until you find peace.'

After another presentation of the way, and
after further prayer, as the miner hung on to
the preacher's words with sobs and tears, at last
the light broke in on his darkness. 'I see it,' he
cried, 'my peace has been made with God. It is
settled. I have to thank God for it. I do! Praise
His Name! It is settled.'

Then they knelt again to thank God that He
had heard their prayer and saved the miner's
soul. Then they went on their way rejoicing.

The next day the miner went to his work, as
usual. During the day, as he went alone to fetch
some tools, a mass of rock fell on him and he
was buried in the debris.

(Amos. 4. 12)

**888　Reality of Conversion.** He was preaching
in the open air—a saved drunkard who had
formerly been a terror to himself, his family,
and his neighbours. He was telling in all
humility of spirit what great things the Lord
had done for him.

A sceptic in the crowd began muttering and
interjecting his infidel scoffs and jeers. 'It's all
fancy—just a dream,' he sneered.

A girl of ten years of age timidly touched him
and whispered: 'Please, sir, if it is a dream,
please don't wake him—that's my Daddy!'

That touched the scoffer's heart and conscience. He was later converted and found it
was not a dream, but a reality.

　　　　　　　　　　　　　　S. J. B. Carter

(2 Cor. 5. 17)

**889　Rechab's Successors.** At a public dinner
for General Harrison who later became President of the U.S.A., one of the guests rose and
drank to his health. Harrison replied by raising
a glass of water. Another man offered a toast,
saying, 'Will our honoured guest favour us by
drinking in response a glass of wine?' After
much urging he rose and said solemnly, 'Gentlemen, not a drop of liquor has ever passed my
lips. I made a resolve when I started in life that
I would avoid strong drink. I am one of a class
of seventeen who graduated from College
together. The other sixteen members now fill
drunkards' graves. I owe my health, my happiness and prosperity to my early resolution.
Would you urge me to break it now?' Hushed
silence came over the audience.

　　　　　　　　　　　　　　H.G.B.

(Jer. 35. 5,6)

**890　Recompensing Evil for Good.** One of
Abraham Lincoln's stories was about a poor
Springfield woman who complained to her
pastor about her worthless husband. He beat
her, she said, scolded the children, and refused
to work or take proper care of his family.

'Be patient with your husband,' the pastor
said, 'and set him a good example. In that way
you will heap coals of fire on his head.'

'That wouldn't do no good,' the woman
replied. 'I've already poured bilin' water on
him, and it don't scarcely take the dander out
of his hair.'

(Rom. 12. 20)

891 **Reconciliation.** The eldest son of a wealthy Christian grew up to be utterly selfish and a waster. He greatly resented the Christian atmosphere of his home, and at last he quarrelled violently with his father because he refused him all the money he demanded. The young fellow got together all the funds he could legitimately lay his hand on, left home in anger, and gave himself up to a reckless life. For a long time he continued his foolish course, and, in due time, all his money was finished and he was brought to the point of desperation. In his folly, he determined to return to his home and break into the house during the absence of the family on their summer holiday. He knew where he could obtain money, as he knew the combination of the letter-lock of his father's safe.

'My father has plenty of money,' he said to himself in his bitterness, 'and he brought me into the world; so he owes me a living, and I am going to have it.'

He succeeded in getting into the house and, opening the safe, began to search. He did not find the money he wanted but came upon some valuable papers, among which was his father's will. He began reading it with a curious eye. To his astonishment he found his name mentioned first among his father's heirs, with a large bequest set against it. The father with whom he had quarrelled, against whom he had shown such bitterness—could it be possible that he still cared about him, and was still intending to give him his inheritance in due time?

'Can it be,' he thought to himself, 'that my father still cares about me in spite of the shocking way I have treated him? Can it be that, in spite of all the dishonour I have brought upon the family name, he is still ready to treat me as his eldest son. As these thoughts rushed upon him, he was broken down and, in true repentance, went to the seaside resort where he knew his father was staying and was reconciled to his father.

(Rom. 2. 4)

892 **Recreation and Relaxation.** The late Professor A. Rendle Short once wrote:

'Too earnest people who never allow their minds any relaxation and have no sense of humour often come to a bad end.'

You cannot keep a bow taut all the time, and one who tries to go through life without taking time for relaxation is encouraging a mental breakdown.

The choice of recreation, however, is a problem to the Christian, and one that demands spiritual discernment. In this, as in other things, his first responsibility is to God and not to his brethren. Paul makes this very clear in the fourteenth chapter of Romans. 'Who are you to pass judgement on the servant of another?' This first responsibility to God carries with it an individual conscience.

(Rom. 14. 4)

893 **Redeemer—A Living.** After listening to a recital of Handel's *Messiah,* a musical friend asked if I had ever noticed where the highest note in the whole of the *Messiah* occurred. I suggested it might be in one of the great choruses, but I was wrong. The highest note is in the lovely and lofty air, 'I know that my Redeemer liveth', and is reached on the word 'risen'.

The composer realised that this one word is the key to the Gospel and to God's kingdom, and is proclaimed to all the world in the Gospel and in the message of Easter.

(Job. 19. 25)

894 **Redeemer—My.** Many poets have extolled Christ, the Kinsman-Redeemer. On December 20th, 1876, a poem was found in a piece of baggage rescued from the flaming wreckage of a train when a bridge collapsed in Ohio, and the train crossing the bridge plunged into the icy bed of the river. The poem was—'I will sing of my Redeemer and His wondrous love to me', and the poet was Philip P. Bliss, travelling with his wife to Chicago to fulfil an engagement at Moody's Tabernacle there. Bliss survived and climbed through the coach window looking for his wife whom he found in the wreckage. Reunited, they died together.

Charles Wesley's hymn—'O for a thousand tongues to sing my great Redeemer's praise!' also magnifies the Redeemer. The hymn was written on the first anniversary of Charles Wesley's conversion. John Wesley, the poet's brother, shortened it, making the hymn commence with the seventh stanza of the original poem.

Both these great poets had a personal and eternal interest in Christ as their Kinsman-Redeemer, and each could use the personal possessive 'MY'.

(Job 19. 25)

895 **Redeeming the Time.** A Christian writer tells of seeing recently an artist's drawing of an hour glass in which the sand was represented by dollar signs, and remarks that the artist had a point. Time is precious: indeed it is priceless. Every day, hour—and every minute that comes our way represents abundant wealth: and we must not forget that for each of us 'the sands of time are sinking'.

The late John F. Dulles once said, 'Time is the most valuable thing in life, and I don't want to waste it.' He proved that he meant what he said by travelling 559,988 miles on government business in six years. The attitude of Mr Dulles is actually the only sensible one. After all, each of us will have to give an account of our use of time, whether we look upon our minutes as treasures or as trifles.

After spending an evening too lightly, Robert Murray McCheyne wrote in his diary: 'My heart must break off from all these things. What right have I to steal and abuse my Master's time? "Redeem the time," He is crying to me.'

'Redeem' is the keyword to the Christian's attitude to time. The word gives direction and

demands diligence. We are in the market square of life: time is being put up for auction, and there are many bidders. We must redeem it, buy it up for ourselves in order that we may put it into the service of our Lord, but we must be alert, or others will put in their bid before us. Charles Cowman, missionary to the Orient, wrote to a friend, 'Be spiritually alert. God keep us from duties evaded, capacities wasted, opportunities neglected, the God-given life slipping away from our grasp.' It was the wail of an elderly woman, 'I have lost a day.' Let us see to it that we have not to say regretfully, 'I have lost a life.'
(Eph. 5. 16)

## 896 Reed—The Bruised.

'The bruised reed shall He not break!'
Another tramples it to take
The choicer stems to suit
His human talent, then intent
On making that fine instrument,
The ancient pipe or flute.

'The bruised reed shall He not break,'
But, undismayed by flaws, shall make
The weak excel the strong.
The injured reed shall be restored
And from its emptiness be poured
The ecstasy of song.

'The smoking flax shall He not quench,'
Though its black smudging breed a stench
That fouls and darkens night.
His care that noisome lamp shall claim;
His pruning hand shall tend the flame
To glow a shining light.

Sarah Elizabeth Sprouse
(Isa. 42. 3)

## 897 Reeds Bruised, Not Broken.

Reeds are of many varieties. Papyrus in Egypt was often made from them. Reeds growing on the banks of the Nile had a hard, outer covering and a pithy centre, and were both light and strong.

For paper-making the reeds must be crushed and bruised. Large canoes are built of papyrus in the River Nile. Long reeds are selected, feathery heads cut off, and then they are bound together with ropes. Reeds are slippery, so must be bruised by striking at the places where the strongest ties must come so that the rope can compass the pithy centre and take a firm grasp. This is necessary only for the outer layer that holds the whole together. The bruised reeds carry the constricting rope so that it does not slip.

O Jesus, keep me ever weak if human strength would doubt Thee,
Or subtle self-reliance seek to live for Thee, without Thee.
Thou wilt not break the bruised reed, so let me trust with meekness
Till men shall read Thy strength indeed made perfect in my weakness.

William Leslie
(2 Cor. 12. 9)

## 898 Reflecting Christ.

Being determined to perfect His saints God puts His precious metal into His crucible. But He sits by it, and watches it. Love is His thermometer, and marks the exact degree of heat; not one instant's necessary pang will He permit; and as soon as the dross is released so that He sees Himself reflected, the trial ceases. God's object is not only to remove alloy, but to develop all the possibilities of the precious metal of character.

A. T. Pierson

We take His name, but do we take His nature?
Can others see in us the Christ we own?
And from the way we talked with them and walked with them,
Would they have known.

Elizabeth Townsend
(Mal. 3. 3)

## 899 Rejection of Christ.

If you go, if you go,
You will pass by the cross on your way to the night:
You will pass with your eyes turned away from the light,
From the great revelation of measureless love,
From the hands that were wounded to lift you above,
From the heart that was broken that rivers of healing might flow.

If you go, if you go,
You have turned a deaf ear to His wonderful Word;
You have heard
How the Father has called through the voice of the Son,
How the sins of the world have been laid upon One,
How the gate of the Kingdom stands open to you,
And you know that the record is true,
That the life is for all who believe;
Yet you turn and reject Him, and will not receive.

If you go, if you go,
You have sealed your own doom,
You have taken your life in your hands,
You have spurned
All the pleading of wound-prints and thorns:
You have turned
To the midnight of gloom,
But oh! never because God appointed it so.
(Heb. 2. 3)

## 900 Religions of the World.

Of anybody who tells me of the world's religions I would ask a question or two. Where will be found, in all the religions of the world, any religion that teaches us these three great truths: First, that a deathless Man dies in order that other men may not die; Second, that a holy Man is made sin in order that sinners may be made righteous; and Third, that, instead of humanity seeking to placate God, God is reconciling man to Himself and is seeking to woo and win humanity?

There is nothing like it in all the religions of the world: it is absolutely unique. That is what Jesus Christ came to show us—that God is yearning over sinners, that, instead of any necessity for our doing something to reconcile God, He is beseeching us to be reconciled to Him; He has turned toward us, and all we need is to turn to Him, and the reconciliation is complete.

A. T. Pierson

(2 Cor. 5. 19,20)

**901 Remarkable Converts.** Who was 'holy John Gifford'? He was a rascal and a rogue turned saint, one whose conversion proves that God has no favourites. He was a remarkable convert. During the Royalist uprising in 1648, John Gifford was a major in the Royalist forces and took a prominent part in the engagement in Maidstone, where General Fairfax with his well trained Parliamentary troops won a decisive victory. Gifford was taken prisoner, and would have suffered the death sentence had not his sister engineered her brother's escape. He sought asylum in Bedford and lived the life of a profligate, one of whose chief delights was to persecute the Puritans of the city. In the mercy of God he was converted, and such was the change in his behaviour that he was respected for his purity. It was under his evangelical preaching that John Bunyan was converted, about whom Rudyard Kipling wrote:

> *A tinker out of Bedford,*
> *A vagrant oft in quod,*
> *A private under Fairfax,*
> *A minister of God.*

John Gifford is considered to have been the original of 'Evangelist' in *The Pilgrim's Progress.*

A. Borland

**902 Remembrance of Christ's Sufferings.**

> *Amidst the joy and gladness*
> *Each pang thou dost recall,*
> *Remembering the sorrow,*
> *The wormwood and the gall.*
>
> *Gethsemane and Calv'ry,*
> *The garden and the tree,*
> *The palace and the city,*
> *Are not forgot by Thee.*
>
> *The kiss and shameful spitting,*
> *The thorns and bloody sweat,*
> *The scourge and cruel mockings,*
> *Thou dost remember yet.*
>
> *By God and man forsaken,*
> *Midst crowds and yet alone;*
> *Without one eye to pity—*
> *'Tis thought of on the throne.*
>
> *And shall we not remember*
> *What Thou for us didst bear,*
> *And view with silent wonder*
> *Thine awful sufferings there?*

Ada R. Habershon

(Lam. 3. 19,20)

**903 Render Unto Caesar.** The daily press recently reported a find in Bangalore of nearly 250 silver coins in an earthen urn. Round in shape, and about the size of the present 25 Paise coins, they are around 2,000 years old and bear the image of Caesar together with the inscription 'Augustus Caesar Divine'. They belonged to the Roman Empire and the question of how they came to Bangalore and under what circumstances they were buried is arousing speculation. What interests us is the reminder they bring to us of our duty as Christians. Matthew 22. 16-21 tells us how the Herodians sought to catch the Lord in His teaching. They asked whether it was lawful to give tribute unto Caesar. Was it a similar coin to these that they handed Him on His request, 'Shew me the tribute money'? Looking at the image and superscription of Caesar, the Lord said, 'Render therefore unto Caesar the things which are Caesar's and unto God the things that are God's.' The Christian has a responsibility to his country and its rulers. He should seek to fulfil his obligations to them, at the same time remembering that man was made in the image of God, and the injunction of Romans 12. 1—'I beseech you, therefore, brethren, by the mercies of God, that ye present your bodies a living sacrifice, holy, acceptable unto God, which is your reasonable service.'

*Indian Christian*

(Matt. 22. 21)

**904 Repent or Perish.** Dr Evans, when a student at Moody Bible Institute, began talking to a man at the Pacific Garden Mission about his soul. The man argued, 'I don't believe the Bible: I'm an atheist.' Evans repeated the verse, 'Except ye repent, ye shall all likewise perish.' The man scoffed, 'I told you I didn't believe it.' Again Evans quoted, 'Except ye repent, ye shall all likewise perish.' The man was exasperated. 'You disgusting fellow, what's the use of telling me that?' Again Dr Evans repeated the Lord's words. Furious with rage, the man struck him between the eyes with his fist. Dr Evans got up and said graciously, 'Except ye repent, ye shall all likewise perish.'

The next night that man was in the Mission before the meeting began. He had not been able to sleep, he confessed, for everywhere he looked he saw the text—on his pillow, on the wall above his head, all over the room. After he got up and sat down to eat, he saw it inscribed on the breakfast table. He had come back that night to settle the whole matter, and knelt before God in sincere repentance.

(Luke 13. 3,5)

**905 Repetition of Words.** It has often been pointed out that on several occasions God repeats the name of a person He is addressing: for example—'Abraham, Abraham'; 'Martha, Martha'; 'Saul, Saul'. Sometimes He repeats a word more than twice. When God in His Word repeats a word, phrase or sentence, it is intended to give special emphasis. Instances of this are found in:

Isaiah 6. 3—Holy, holy, holy is Jehovah of hosts.

Jeremiah 22. 29—O earth, earth, earth, hear the Word of the Lord.

Ezekiel 21. 27—I will overturn, overturn, overturn.

Revelation 4. 8—Holy, holy, holy—a repetition of glory to be followed by divine judgement.

Revelation 8. 13—Woe, woe, woe—at the outpouring of God's wrath.

Revelation 18. 10,16,19—Alas, alas!—Alas, alas!—Alas, alas!—at Babylon's overthrow.

Revelation 19. 1,3,4,6—Alleluia! which means 'Praise the Lord!' repeated.

A.N.

**906  Reproach for Christ.** 'Without the camp' meant for the Lord 'outside the religious camp of Israel' in which He had been born, and which, despite its corruption, was dear to Him. And many Christians who have sought to live only for Jesus have found that the enmity of Christendom can be more acute even than that of the world, because there can be religious sin as well as other forms, and there has often been religious persecution.

Fred Mitchell

(Heb. 11. 26; 13. 13)

**907  Reproach of Christ.**

*Outside the camp unto Thy dear name,*
*This in Thy Word I see;*
*Unto that name—and to share in His shame,*
*Privileged place to be.*
*Feasting on Christ, His reproach to share,*
*Tempt not my soul away:*
*Nought can compare with the blessedness there—*
*Outside the camp to stay.*

*Outside the camp unto Thy dear name,*
*Blest gathering place for me:*
*Banner of love from His presence above,*
*Draw forth my soul to Thee.*
*Shame on my soul that I ever sought*
*Inside the walls to dwell;*
*Riches of grace, gazing there on His face:*
*Outside the camp all's well.*

*Outside the camp unto Thy dear name,*
*Lord, may I here be found,*
*Weaned from the world with its pomp and its fame,*
*Resting on holy ground.*
*Outside the camp, in Thy company till*
*Earth's little day is o'er,*
*Then, face to face, all Thy mercies to trace—*
*Inside the veil evermore.*

(Heb. 13. 13)

**908  Reproach of Christ.**

*He called me out, the Man with garments dyed,*
*I knew His voice—my Lord, the crucified;*
*He showed Himself, and oh, I could not stay,*
*I had to follow Him—had to obey.*

*It cast me out, the world, when once it found*
*That I within this rebel heart had crowned*
*The man it had rejected, spurned and slain,*
*Whom God in wondrous power had raised to reign.*

(John 17. 14)

**909  Rescue of a Jewel.** Dr Courtland Myers used to tell of a lady dressed in silks and satins standing on the kerb of a Paris street when to her horror a ring dropped from her finger into the filth of the gutter. It had a very valuable jewel in it. She stooped instantly. With the bent handle of her elegant sunshade she searched the gutter for it but could not find it. Then, as the astonished crowd looked on, she slipped the glove from her dainty white hand and with her delicate fingers searched through the water and mud until she found the lost jewel.

Dr Myers said, 'This is what we must do for the jewels of eternity—strip off formalism and search the very gutters of society for the lost gems of humanity as God did for us.'
(Luke 14. 23)

**910  Rescue The Perishing.**

*Oh! might I win from the burning flame*
*Some soul in sorrow and sin and shame,*
*Teach them to trust in the Saviour's Name,*
*Rescue some perishing soul!*

*Oh! might I melt some poor frozen heart*
*With love divine till the tear-drops start,*
*While they behold Thee as Thou art,*
*Tenderly seeking lost souls.*

*Oh! might I walk in the world's harsh light,*
*Washed in the blood, with my garments white,*
*Jesus my all and my heart's delight,*
*A witness to perishing souls.*

*Master, I yield Thee my life today;*
*Help me to labour and watch and pray:*
*Make me a blessing upon life's way,*
*Use me to perishing souls.*

(Luke 19. 10; 1 Cor. 9. 22)

**911  Rescued by a Raven.** In a little village near Warsaw lived a German peasant whose name was Dobry. Because of adverse circumstances he had got behind in paying his rent and the landlord was threatening to evict him. All his pleadings for an extension of time had been in vain, and the next day he and his family were to be turned out into the snow. Hearing the church bells chime for evening prayer, Dobry and his loved ones knelt to ask the Lord to supply their needs, for they were at the end of all human resources. After prayer they rose to their feet and sang the old hymn, 'Commit thou all thy griefs and ways into His hands.' As they finished singing, they heard a strange tapping at the window. Opening it, they found a raven that Dobry's grandfather had tamed many years before. It held in its beak a ring of great value set with many precious stones. An investigation disclosed that it had been lost that day by the king who was travelling through the town. When Dobry returned it, the king rewarded him with a large sum of money, sufficient to build a house of his own. To commemorate the wonderful events of that wintry night, a plaque was prepared on which was carved a raven with a ring in its beak, and underneath a stanza of the hymn they had been singing when the bird pecked at their window. Dobry recognized that even as the prophet Elijah had been divinely fed by the fowls of the air, he too had been rescued by a raven.

(1 Kings 17. 4)

**912 Response of Conscience.** A French chronicle of the thirteenth century related that Richard I of England was entrapped by his enemies while on his way home from the Crusades in December, 1192, and imprisoned in an Austrian castle. Richard had been very fond of music and, with his favourite minstrel Blondel, had composed and played many melodies. His subjects were in ignorance as to his whereabouts, and it seemed impossible for them to discover their lost monarch. Blondel set out to find him and played the tunes he had loved beneath the walls of the chief fortresses in Europe. At last he was rewarded by hearing an echoing strain come from the barred window of a dungeon cell in Durenstein Castle on the Danube. The same tune came floating through the grim bars in the prison wall, answering, note for note, to the music of the minstrel. Blondel recognized his master's voice and touch.

So it is with the Holy Scriptures. As they speak of our character and conduct, of our state and condition before God, our conscience, our moral monitor, answers back, note for note, word for word, the testimony which it bears.

R. McKee

(Rom. 2. 14,15)

**913 Rest in God.** George Herbert is a sure guide in the business of weariness. Have you ever read 'The Pulley'? He describes what God did when He at first made man. Into a glass of blessings He poured the world's riches, strength, beauty, wisdom, honour, pleasure. One thing was withheld—the treasure of Rest.

*For if I should, said He,*
*Bestow this jewel also on My creature,*
*He would adore my gifts instead of Me*
*And rest in Nature, not the God of Nature:*
*So both would losers be.*

*Yet let him keep the rest,*
*But keep them with repining restlessness.*
*Let him be rich and weary, that at least,*
*If goodness lead him not, yet weariness*
*Will toss him to My breast.*

So you see that weariness is a means to an end. It is not a wasteful substance. It is to lead us, in childlike simplicity, to the heart of One who said, 'Come unto Me, ye weary, and I will give you rest.'

T. Wilkinson Riddle in *The Witness*
(Matt. 11. 28; Heb. 4. 9)

**914 Restfulness.** Our lives these days are characterized by hurry and rush, by frenzied and feverish activity. With more and more machines, we have less and less rest. We have lost the art of being still. Some of us are like the indefatigable parish worker who was so busy that she did not have time to say her prayers. That is why God speaks to His children, saying, 'Be still and know that I am God.'

We live in an age which is dominated by the tyranny of the clock. Lewis Mumford regards the clock and not the machine as the characteristic symbol of the twentieth century. Our activities are dictated by the clock; we are continually reminded of the necessity for being 'on time', and of not 'wasting time': and yet, our chief complaint is that we never have time.

(Ps. 46. 10)

**915 Resting on Three Pillows.** 'How are you today, sir?' The speaker, a fine, stalwart young man, bent pitifully and reverently over the bed beside him as he spoke. The elderly invalid smiled faintly, but oh! so gently. 'My head is resting very sweetly on three pillows,' he replied, while a gleam of light illuminated the sunken eyes—'Infinite power, infinite love and infinite wisdom.'

L. O. Cooper

(Isa. 30. 15)

**916 Restoration to Health.** In the 1952 Keswick Convention the Bible Readings were taken by Dr W. Graham Scroggie who very ably dealt with the Epistle of Paul to the Romans. Some time later he was laid low with a serious illness, and many Christians prayed for his recovery. A few years later, restored to health, Dr Scroggie was again one of the Convention speakers at Keswick. Referring to his illness, he said that, under God, he owed his restoration to health to three things, namely, the saints' prayers, the doctor's pills and his wife's pillows.

**917 Resurrection—The.**

*Everything is new today,*
*Calvary's shadows flee away,*
*Flee before the rising Sun,*
*Love's redeeming work is done.*
*Past the shedding of His blood,*
*Risen is the Son of God.*

*Empty is the tomb where lay,*
*Waiting for the coming day,*
*His own body; while He went*
*Preaching to the spirits pent*
*In prison;*
*Now He's risen.*

Rolled away the mighty stone,
Snapt the Roman seal thereon;
Awful is the earthquake's roar
Heralding the promised hour.
Terror-stricken by the sound,
Roman soldiers, on the ground,
　　Lie around
　　Now are found
Holy angels set on guard,
　　Vigil keeping
O'er the tomb, wherein their Lord
　　Once lay sleeping.

　　In the dawning
　　Of the morning
Women to the grave repairing,
Precious spices now are bearing
To anoint the body of their Friend.
Is this the end?

'Whom seek ye?
Jesus seek ye!
The Living One among the dead?
Come ye near, behold His bed,
　　He's not here!'

They see the grave clothes lying orderly,
The napkin, likewise, folded separately;
But in that silent place
See not His lovely face,
　　For He's not there.

　　Listen!
　　He's risen!
　　Run and tell,
　　All is well,
　　He's conquered hell!

　　Yet one remains,
　　And she retains
　　A memory and a love,
　　All other loves above;
　　For from her heart
　　He bade depart
　　Seven devils,
　　Hellish perils!
　　Now He's gone,
　　She's left alone!
　　Will they return?
　　What then?
　　What then?

'Mary!' Oh that reassuring word!
'Rabboni!' She's worshipping her Lord!
　　That then!

And now good men, with hearts despairing,
Can scarce believe what they are hearing;
The grave is empty, gone is He?
Immediately they run to see;
Chastened, humbled, eager Peter;
John his fellow, younger, fleeter,
Gets there first, and stooping down,
Sees the shroud, 'yet went not in'.
Peter, breathless, follows after,
Enters in, sees not his Master,
Only grave clothes; relics they,
In the place wherein He lay,
Where loving hands had borne Him in,
Who His own self had borne their sin.
John the younger, loving, longing,
Enters now within the gloaming,

Grasps by faith the wondrous meaning,
　　Of the empty grave!
Came to him a revelation
Of the basis of Salvation;
Crucifixion! Resurrection!
　　Jesus lives to save!

So the wondrous confirmation
Of the glorious Resurrection;
First to Mary Magdalen,
Later He appears to men;
Two disciples, sadly walking
Toward their village home, are talking;
Someone comes and asks a question,
Joins them in their conversation,
Teaches them God's holy Word,
Solves the problem of their Lord;
It behoved the Christ to die,
Rise again, ascend on high.

Now the little journey done,
Entering the cottage home,
Two disciples and their Lord
Gather round the humble board.
He it is who takes the head
Of the table lately spread,
Gives God thanks and breaks the bread!
Suddenly their eyes are open!
Suddenly He vanished from them;
But they'd seen Him,
And they knew Him!

Banished all their groundless fears,
Christ has wiped away their tears,
Lasting joy dispels their sorrow,
They can't wait until tomorrow,
They, tonight, must run and tell
Christ has conquered death and hell.

All their thoughts on Jesus centre,
As the city gate they enter,
Onward, upward to the room
Where the chosen few had come.
Doors are barred for fear of Jews,
Tongues unloosed, Good news! Great news!
Actually they'd seen their Lord,
Listened to His holy Word,
Knew Him as He broke the bread,
Recogised their risen Head!

Even as they spake of Him,
He Himself had entered in,
Standing in majestic mien,
　　Among His own.
'Peace be unto you', He said,
'It is I, be not afraid;
Look upon my hands and feet,
Handle Me, for it is meet
That you be shewn
I'm flesh and bone,
　　And not a spirit!'

Then He asked them, Had they meat?
They watched wondering, while He ate,
Heard Him say He had fulfilled
What the prophets had foretold.
As He spake their minds were opened,
Knowledge of the Bible quickened:
By many proofs infallible
The story was reliable.

*After He'd endured His passion,*
*Without doubt the Lord had risen,*
*Granted His disciples vision,*
*Gave to them His great commission;*
*But first they must await the hour*
*When they would be endued with power,*
*So He spake to the Eleven,*
*Blessed them and went back to heaven.*

*Returning to Jerusalem,*
*They prayed and waited, all of them,*
*Until the power should fall on them.*
*Then suddenly like hurricane,*
*And tongues of fire the Spirit came;*
*He filled the house where they were staying,*
*He filled them each as they were praying,*
*And so united and empowered,*
*They straightway witnessed to their Lord!*

Douglas Brealey

(Acts 2. 32)

**918  Resurrection and Life—The.** A British soldier, struck down in the Battle of Inkerman, was just able to crawl to his tent, where he died. When found, he was lying on his face, his open Bible before him, his hand glued to the page by his life-blood which covered it. When his hand was lifted, the letters of the printed page were clearly traced on it, and with the ever-living promise on his hand, they laid him in a soldier's grave. The Bible words on his hands were—'I am the resurrection and the life; he that believeth on me, though he were dead, yet shall he live.'
(John 11. 25)

**919  Resurrection—The Greatest Miracle.** At a dinner party given by Lord Justice Darling, the talk turned on the Christian faith, especially the Resurrection. Placing his finger-tips together, assuming a judicial attitude, and speaking with a quiet emphasis that was extraordinarily impressive, Lord Darling said: 'We, as Christians, are asked to take a very great deal on trust; the teachings, for example, of Jesus and His miracles. If we had to take all on trust, I for one should be sceptical. The crux of the problem whether Jesus was, or was not, what He proclaimed Himself to be must surely depend upon the truth or otherwise of the last, final and greatest miracle, the resurrection.' He paused for a moment and went on: 'On that greatest point we are not merely asked to have faith. In its favour as a living truth there exists such overwhelming evidence, positive and negative, factual and circumstantial, that no intelligent jury in the world, examining the evidence, could fail to pronounce a verdict that the resurrection story is absolutely true.'
(1 Cor. 15. 20)

**920  Resurrection Message.** Eighteen hundred years ago a bereaved mother wrote to her friends who were in like case; her letter has been preserved in the dry sands of Egypt that we might know that our sorrows are as old as the race; the griefs that wring our hearts today are griefs that have wrung the hearts of mankind through the ages. This is what she wrote: 'Irene to Taonnaphris and Philon, Greeting! I was as much grieved and shed as many tears over Eumoiros as I shed for Didymus. I did everything that was fitting (referring apparently to the customary funeral rites) and so did my whole family. . . . But still there is nothing one can do in the face of such trouble. So I leave you to comfort yourselves.'

Some years earlier Paul had written to some folk whom he loved and who were mourning the loss of those dear to them and to him: 'the dead in Christ shall rise first. . . . Wherefore comfort one another with these words.'

C. F. Hogg

(1 Thess. 4. 16-18)

**921  Resurrection Morning.**

*On the resurrection morning*
*Jesus came forth from the tomb,*
*Met His doubting, sad disciples,*
*Banished all their fear and gloom.*

*'He is not here,' said the angel:*
*'See the place where He was laid.*
*Death by Him has now been vanquished:*
*There's no need to be afraid.'*

*On the resurrection morning*
*When our Lord shall come again,*
*All the dead in Christ shall meet Him*
*And the living with Him reign.*

*Christ the first fruits, we the harvest,*
*Fruit of all His toil and pain:*
*What a gathering of the ransomed!*
*What a triumph He will gain!*

*While we wait for His returning*
*'Mid the conflict and the strife,*
*Let our lamps be brightly burning*
*In this resurrection life.*

*In Him we shall be victorious*
*As we pass along life's way.*
*What a prospect! None so glorious*
*As the resurrection day.*

C. Cannons

(1 Cor. 15. 23)

**922  Resurrection of Christ.**

*To Joseph's tomb where none had lain*
*They carried Him whom foes had slain.*
*Men set a guard; men sealed the stone;*
*Men left Him there to sleep alone.*
*The sabbath passed: the first day came,*
*And Mary turned to hear her name.*
*While Salem slept, the Mighty dead*
*Had risen from His rocky bed.*
*In Him our hope, our longing are,*
*Who is our bright, our Morning Star.*

Dr Johnstone G. Patrick

(Matt. 28. 6)

**923  Resurrection of Jesus.**  A missionary and his colleagues were once witnessing a great religious parade in India. A bone of Buddha had been found and was being presented to the city with fanatical fervour. Thousands prostrated themselves before the sacred relic, bowing themselves in the dust. The missionary, turning to his friend, remarked, 'What a striking evidence is this of the difference between the two faiths. If any part of the body of Jesus was to be found it would cause not rejoicing, but dismay, for it would show that He had not risen from the dead.'

C. E. Tatham

(Luke 24. 3; 1 Cor. 15. 20)

**924  Resurrection of the Redeemer.**

*Oh, the anguish of Mary, the depth of despair*
*When she came to the tomb and the Lord was*
*    not there!*
*As she desolate stood with her balm and her*
*    myrrh*
*And the winding sheet only was waiting for her.*

*Oh, the blackness of death, oh, life's utter*
*    despair*
*Had she come to the tomb and the Lord had*
*    been there,*
*Lying wrapped in the sheet with the balm and*
*    the myrrh*
*And no risen Redeemer was waiting for her.*

Nicoll Robertson

(Mark 16. 1-6; John 20. 11-16)

**925  Reunion—Joy of.**  Dr David Livingstone decided to continue his service in Africa while Mary, his wife, took the children to Britain for three or four years. In April, 1852, they travelled together to Cape Town. Their hearts were sorely torn with anguish when Mary and their four children sailed for home.

Four and a half years later she went to Southampton to meet her returning husband. It was not in the least surprising that Mary had turned to the muse for help. After much hugging and kissing she gave David some verses she had written for him:

*A hundred thousand welcomes!*
*How my heart is gushing o'er*
*With the love and joy and wonder*
*Thus to see your face once more!*
*How did I live without you*
*These long, long years of woe?*
*It seems as if 'twould kill me*
*To be parted from you now.*

*Do you think I would reproach you*
*With the sorrow that I bore,*
*Since the sorrow is all over*
*Now I have you here once more?*
*And there's nothing but the gladness*
*And the love within my heart,*
*And the hope so sweet and certain*
*That again we'll never part.*

**926  Revelation in Creation and Incarnation.**

*God speaks each day a million words,*
*And those who listen hear His voice—*
*HIS sun, HIS breeze, HIS singing birds,*
*HIS gentle showers,*
*HIS dainty flowers,*
*HIS orchard sweet,*
*HIS fields of wheat.*
*(Thank Him, my soul; in Him rejoice!)*

*God speaks in majesty each night,*
*HIS voice is heard through all the earth;*
*HIS handiwork proclaims His might,*
*HIS evening star,*
*HIS Pluto, far,*
*HIS milky Way,*
*HIS Nebulae.*
*(Rejoice, my soul; proclaim His worth!)*

*From Nature men should all deduce*
*God's Wisdom and His mighty power:*
*Their unbelief is no excuse—*
*Their flagrant sin,*
*Black thoughts within;*
*Their conduct, rude,*
*Ingratitude.*
*(My soul, extol Him every hour)*

*At Bethlehem God bared His heart*
*In Christ, His Son, the Living Word;*
*Of human likeness He took part;*
*He taught and healed,*
*God's love revealed:*
*He died, now lives,*
*Salvation gives.*
*(My soul, O worship Him, thy Lord!)*

Marion Donaldson

(Rom. 1. 20; John 1. 18)

**927  Reverence.**

*'Tis not enough to bend the knee,*
*To bow the head and formal be;*
*God looks upon the heart.*
*He knows the wandering wish and thought,*
*The little sins men view as nought*
*When they from Him depart.*

*True reverence means a sense of sin*
*When we half-consciously begin*
*To leave His holy will.*
*True reverence grieves to grieve the Lord:*
*It seeks the fullest hearts accord*
*His precepts to fulfil.*

*Without true reverence who can learn*
*Or rightly good and bad discern?*
*We need the fear of God!*
*A holy awe is absent now,*
*But shall we cease our hearts to bow*
*When saved by precious blood.*

*Our Father, we to Thee draw nigh;*
*(And yet we know Thou art on high)*
*And humbly, boldly plead:*
*Be pleased to cause us more to feel*
*Thy greatness and in heart to kneel,*
*More conscious of our need.*

(Ps. 89. 7)

**928 Revival.** Revival does not just spring up, but:
If all the slumbering saints would wake up,
and all the lukewarm saints would fire up,
and all the dishonest saints would own up,
and all the disgruntled saints would sweeten up,
and all the discouraged saints would cheer up,
and all the depressed saints would look up,
and all the gossiping saints would shut up,
and all the dry bones would rise up,
and all the saints in debt would pay up,
and all true believers would stand up for Christ
    and the Faith,
then we might expect a revival.
(Ps. 85. 6; Hab. 3. 2)

**929 Revival—Basis of.** There never has been a spiritual revival which did not begin with an acute sense of sin. We are never prepared for a spiritual advance until we see the necessity of getting rid of that which has been hindering it, and that, in the sight of God, is sin. And with this consciousness the soul will cry out for Christ in all His fullness as Pardoner, Cleanser, Enricher, as Lord and Lover. And He is made all this to us, and much more by the Holy Spirit. Out of such an experience of Christ will grow every other experience, and no Christian who is living in the will of God will ever fail to fulfil all the obligations in the outlying fields of life.
                                Dr W. Graham Scroggie
(Ezra. 9. 8)

**930 Revival—Hindrances to.** An American minister said to Dr F. B. Meyer that he had pleaded with God for revival for many years but no revival came. Finally, in despair, he gathered his congregation around him and rolled the burden of the anxiety on his people, saying, 'I have done all I could; it is now for you to consider your attitude toward God.' Then there rose in that church meeting a grey-haired elder, highly respected by all, and said, 'Sir, I do not wonder that there is no revival here. There never will be so long as Brother Jones and I don't speak to one another;' and before all the assembled people the old man went to Mr Jones and said, 'Brother, forgive me. For ten years we have not spoken; let's bury the hatchet.' Thus they made peace. Then followed a great silence, and another, a deacon, arose and said, 'Pastor, there can be no revival in this place as long as I say fair things to your face and mean things about you behind your back. Forgive me!' He was readily forgiven, and for the next twenty minutes men rose to square accounts with their fellow Christian men, and women with women, and throughout an awful stillness filled the place. Then the Spirit of God came in mighty power, bringing revival.
                                F. B. Meyer
(Matt. 5. 23)

**931 Revival—Hindrances to.** Henry Moore-house, while still a young man, was conducting evangelistic meetings, but there was no revival.

God had given him precious reviving times in America and Great Britain, but now it seemed as if he were up against a stone wall. Day and night on his knees he searched his heart, crying, 'O God, why is there no revival?'

One day, walking along the street, he saw a large placard with the words: 'Henry Moore-house, the most Famous of all British Preachers.' At once he said to himself, 'That's why there is no revival!' He went at once to the campaign committee and said, 'Brethren, now I know why there is no revival. See how you have advertised me as the greatest of this and the greatest of that! No wonder the Holy Spirit cannot work. He is grieved because you haven't magnified the Lord Jesus Christ. I'm just a poor, simple, humble servant, preaching the glorious Gospel and saying, 'Behold the Lamb of God which taketh away the sin of the world!'
(John 16. 14)

**932 Revival—The Welsh.** In front of Moriah Chapel in Lughour, South Wales, which was built in 1892, is the statue of Evan Roberts, the young man so mightily used in the Welsh Revival, 1904-1905. At that time he was under deep conviction of sin and a tremendous struggle went on within him until he yielded to the claims of Christ and consecrated his life to the Lord's service. Yielded to God and filled with the Spirit, he preached with much power the Gospel of Christ, and many souls were saved through his preaching. The revival had to begin first in Evan Roberts.
(Hab. 3. 2)

**933 Rewards Unexpected.** A schoolboy came home for the holidays after three months and showed his report to his father. His father read it and said, 'Splendid, my boy.'

'Yes!' said the boy with pride, 'top of the class, Father, think of it.' 'That is splendid,' the father replied, 'I expect they will give you a reward for that.' 'No, Father, they are not giving prizes this term.' 'Oh, certainly you will be given a reward for it!' said his father.

Two or three days after the boy returned to school for the next term, the father received a letter full of anguish. 'They have moved me up into a new form, Father, where the work is too hard, and I am at the bottom of the form,' his son wrote. 'Please tell them to put me back in the form where I was top boy.'

The father wrote back, saying, 'My boy, I told you they would reward you.'

After two or three terms the boy came home and announced, 'Top of the form again, Father.' 'Well!' said the father, 'I expect they will reward you again.'

Sure enough, he got his reward by removal to a higher and harder form.

Is the work too hard for you? If so, the Lord is advancing and rewarding you, trusting you with harder work because He wants you to trust him more and to become 'more than conqueror'.
(2 Chron. 15. 7; Jer. 31. 16)

**934 Rich in Good Works.** Many years ago at a Bible reading in Dr Cronin's house, William Kelly suggested that the chapter, 1 Timothy 6, about riches was addressed—

i. At the beginning, to those who haven't them:

ii. at the end, to those who have them:

iii. in between, to the man of God in relation to both.

The former are warned against those who suppose that gain is godliness, but—in contrast —are told that godliness with contentment is great gain. Those who have riches are exhorted to 'do good, be rich in good works, ready to distribute, willing to communicate; laying up in store for themselves a good foundation against the time to come'. Timothy is warned about men who 'will be rich', who make it their object in life to acquire wealth, and also against the love of money. He is told to flee these things, and to follow after righteousness, godliness, faith, love, patience, meekness.

(1 Tim. 6)

**935 Rich in Heaven's Wealth.** Once a poor, rich man, walking over his estates, thinking to inspect the progress of his hired man digging a ditch through his land, found him singing at his work. As he approached he caught the words of the song:

*My Father is rich in houses and lands;*
*He holdeth the wealth of the world in His*
*hands.*
*Of rubies and diamonds, of silver and gold*
*His coffers are full—He has riches untold.*

*I'm the child of a King, the child of a King!*
*With Jesus my Saviour I'm the child of a King.*

'John,' said the rich man, 'why are you singing such nonsense; you are a poor ditchdigger.'

'Oh, but it's true!' was the reply. 'God is my Father, and He has given me so much for which to sing and praise Him. Yonder is my little cottage, and when my day's work is done, there stands Mary at the door to greet me with a kiss, and I sit down to a bountiful meal. Why shouldn't I sing for joy?'

Then the poor, rich man unburdened his heart, 'Yonder on the hill is my mansion; but they do not love me up there. They are only waiting for me to die to get my money. John, I wish I had what you have.'

(James 2. 5)

**936 Riches in Heaven.** A wealthy Norwegian farmer stood on the porch of his home, proudly surveying the broad, rich acres that he possessed. 'All this is mine,' he exclaimed. But alas like the rich man in the parable, he was absorbed with his wealth, while all the time forgetting God.

A short distance up the lane Old Hans, the farm-hand, had ceased from work, unpacked his lunch, and with his hands folded was now thanking God for all His goodness. Leaving the porch, the farmer stopped for a chat and, bursting in on the old man's meditation, asked Hans how he was keeping.

'Oh, is it you, sir?' Hans replied, looking up, 'I did not hear you coming. I have grown quite deaf lately and my eyesight is failing too.'

'But you look happy, Hans.'

'Yes, indeed, I am, sir. My heavenly Father has provided me with food and raiment, a good bed and a roof over my head; and that is more than my Saviour had when He was here on earth.'

The landlord glanced in disgust at the meagre lunch—a few slices of bread and a piece of fried pork. 'But how can you be thankful for such a poor lunch?' asked the farmer.

'Oh,' said Hans, 'it's the presence of my Saviour that adds sweetness to all He gives.'

Changing the subject completely, Hans then began to tell his employer of a dream he had on the previous night. 'I dreamt that I stood at the portals of heaven, so that I could see into the blessed city. Oh, sir, the glory and beauty no tongue can describe. Then I heard a voice saying, "The richest man in all the valley will die tonight." After that, the most wonderful music—a real Hallelujah chorus—burst upon my ears. Then I awoke. Sir, those words were so plainly spoken that I thought I should tell you. Perhaps it's a warning.'

The landlord's face turned pale and he tried to hide his fears as he hastily left the presence of the old man. During the rest of the day those words seemed to haunt the wealthy landowner —'the richest man in the valley will die tonight'. But this was only the dream of an old man, and certainly one that he did not believe.

Late that afternoon his brow was feverish and, believing the dream or not, he called for the doctor. Following a thorough examination and after hearing the dream, the doctor assured the farmer that the richest man in the valley would not die that night.

During the dinner hour and on into the evening the farmer and his doctor guest laughed and joked until almost ten, when they were startled by the ringing of the door-bell. The shrill sound dismayed the farmer and nervously he answered the door.

'Sorry to disturb you,' said the gentleman in the doorway, 'I just came to tell you that Old Hans died suddenly this evening, and to ask you to make funeral arrangements.'

So the old man's dream was true. The richest man in the valley had died. Though one of the poor of this earth, he was rich toward God, rich in faith. He was the happy possessor of something money could never buy—everlasting life.

(Luke 12. 21; James 2. 5)

**937 Riches of Heaven.**

*The riches of God's goodness*
*Are round us everywhere—*
*The earth, the sky, the water,*
*The sunshine and the air.*
*The needs of all His creatures*
*God always doth provide,*
*And the riches of His goodness*
*O'er all the earth abide.*

But He gives other riches—
The riches of His grace.
'Twas this that sent the Saviour
To die in sinners' place.
Forgiveness, peace, assurance,
Eternal life in heaven;
To all who will accept Him
Are riches freely given.

The riches of His glory
We here can't comprehend.
Christ in us is assurance
Of glory without end.
But there—in His own presence—
Our hearts shall understand
His love in fullest measure
And all the way He planned.

With sinless heart we'll serve Him,
With perfect knowledge blest,
With the ability to know
The fullness of His rest,
With no more sin, no sorrow,
But joy for evermore—
The riches of His glory
For us lie on before.

Mrs A. C. Murray

(Rom. 2. 4; Eph. 2. 7; Col. 1. 27)

## 938   Riches to Poverty.

'Though He was rich'—the Heir of all,
Lord of Creation—He
Who in the Father's bosom dwells
From all eternity,
Who flung the myriad stars in space
And called them all by name,
Who weighed the mountains in His scale
And gave the earth its frame;

The islands as a little thing
Were formed at His command;
He put His compass on the sea
And meted out the land;
The cattle on a thousand hills,
The silver and the gold,
Earth's rarest treasures all were His
Whose wealth was manifold:

Who ruled the mighty universe
And held it all complete,
While seraphim and angels bowed
In homage at His feet:
Who in that Paradise of bliss
Long before time began,
One in the mighty Trinity,
Devised redemption's plan.

Yet 'for your sakes' He left His throne,
Came down as Man to earth,
A child in Bethlehem's cattle shed,
Of holy virgin birth.
The foxes had their holes at night,
The little birds their nests;
But on the rugged mountain slopes
The Lord of glory rests:

Upon Golgotha's lonely hill
He bowed His head and died:
Redemption's work was now complete—
"Tis finished,' loud He cried.
We through His poverty made rich—

Richer we could not be—
Now heirs of God, joint-heirs with Christ
Through all eternity.

(2 Cor. 8. 9)

939   **Riches Untaxable.**   A tax collector once came to a minister in order to value his property.

'I am a rich man,' said the minister. The official quickly sharpened his pencil and asked, 'Well, what do you own?'

The preacher replied, 'I am the possessor of a Saviour who earned for me everlasting life and who is preparing for me a place in the eternal city.'

'What else?'

'I have a brave and pious wife, and, as Solomon says, "Who can find a virtuous woman, for her price is far above rubies." '

'What else?'

'Healthy, obedient children!'

'What else?'

'A merry heart which enables me to pass through life joyfully.'

'What else?'

'That is all,' replied the preacher.

The official closed his book, rose, took his hat, and said, 'You are indeed a rich man, sir, but your property is not subject to taxation.'

(Prov. 31. 10; Ps. 127. 3; Prov. 17. 22)

940   **Righteousness Practised.**   The late Dr F. B. Meyer narrated how one night, as he was preaching, a terrific conflict was going on within the heart of a leading lawyer in his congregation. A dying man had left valuable property and appointed him to manage it for his daughter until she came of age. Year after year he had profited by his trusteeship, greatly impoverishing the girl who knew nothing of what he was doing. As a result of the sermon in which the Word and will of God were emphasized, the lawyer first counted up all that he had wrongfully appropriated and, though it left him very much poorer, wrote out a cheque for its repayment. Then he went to the girl, confessed the wrong he had done her and refunded the money. Next day, with a truly repentant heart, a sense of divine forgiveness, and an indescribable glow of relief and tenderness, he came to the meeting and yielded himself wholly to the Lord.

(Matt. 5. 20)

941   **Risen With Christ.**

Risen with Christ, beyond all condemnation,
We stand in Him, completely justified;
Our sins, though many, are no more
    remembered,
For He has risen, who for them has died.
Risen with Christ, death has no power upon us;
Its claim in Him was fully met and paid.
Its sting is gone—it stands now but a portal
Through which we enter to the rest He made.
Risen with Christ, His perfect life supplying
The power to keep our faltering footsteps
    strong,
His wisdom knowing all the way before us
Which may be rugged but cannot be long.

*Risen with Christ, Earth's charms should not
  allure us;
Earth's sorrows should not plunge us in despair.
Our lives, hidden with Christ, are in His
  keeping;
The things of earth cannot molest us there.*

*Then may we truly set our heart's affection
On things above—where He for us now lives,
Our great High Priest, our Guide, our Guard,
  our Shepherd,
Thus will we know the peace and joy He gives.*

Mrs Alex C. Murray

(Col. 3. 1-5)

**942 Risk Worthwhile.** One night when storms
were beating in full fury, a wreck was firing the
minute gun and the lifeboat was manned and
sent out. Relay after relay rescued the whole
crew but one, and the lifeboat was being manned for the last trip, One young fellow, John
Holden, stepped in.

'John, don't go,' pleaded his mother. 'Your
father is dead, your brother William is lost at
sea, and I have no one left but you. Surely you
won't risk your life for only one.'

But John went. Slowly the lifeboat disappeared amidst mountains of foam. After
anxious suspense the boat returned. 'Is the man
saved?' was shouted from the shore. 'Yes,'
rang back the voice of John, 'and go and tell
mother it's William.'

(Rom. 11. 14)

**943 Rock—Crevice of the.** Many years ago
a poor widow was crossing a mountain pass in
the Highlands of Scotland. From the mountain
pass the widow's dwelling was ten miles off, and
no human habitation was nearer than her own.
She had undertaken a long journey, carrying
with her her only child, a boy of two years old.
The morning when the widow left her home
gave promise of a lovely day. Before noon, however, a sudden change took place in the weather.

Sudden gusts of wind began to whistle among
the rocks and to ruffle, with black squalls, the
surface of the lake. The wind was followed by
rain and the rain by sleet, and the sleet by a
heavy fall of snow.

Weary and wet and cold, the widow reached
the pass with her child. She knew that a mile
beyond it there was a mountain hut which
could give shelter; but the moment she attempted
to face the storm of snow which was rushing
through the gorge all hope of proceeding in that
direction failed. To turn home was equally
impossible. She must find shelter.

After wandering for some time among the
huge fragments of granite which skirted the base
of the overhanging precipices, she at last found
a sheltered nook. She crouched beneath a
projecting rock and pressed her child to her
trembling bosom. The storm continued to rage.
The snow was accumulating overhead. Hour
after hour passed. It became bitterly cold. The
evening approached. The widow's heart was
sick with fear and anxiety.

The child—her only child—was all she
thought of. She wrapped him in her shawl; but
the poor thing had been scantily clad, and the
shawl was thin and worn. The widow was poor,
and her clothing could hardly defend her from
the piercing cold of such a night as that. But
whatever might become of herself, her child
must be preserved. The snow, in whirling
eddies, entered the recess which afforded them
at best but miserable shelter.

The night came on. The wretched mother
then stripped off almost all her own clothing
and wrapped it round her child, whom, at last
in despair she put into a deep crevice of the
rock among some heather and fern. And now
she resolved at all hazards to brave the storm
and return home in order to get assistance for
her babe, or perish in the attempt. Clasping
her infant to her heart, and covering his face
with tears and kisses, she laid him softly down
in sleep and rushed into the snowy drift.

That night of storm was succeeded by a peaceful morning. The sun shone from a clear blue
sky, and wreaths of mist hung along the tops of
the mountains, while a hundred waterfalls
poured down their sides. Dark figures, made
visible at a distance by the white ground,
might now be seen with long poles examining
every hollow near the mountain pass. They are
people from the village who are searching for
the widow and her son. The night before, they
had gone forth with lanterns and searched in
vain.

Daylight brought hope. They have reached
the pass. A cry is uttered by one of the searchers
as he sees a bit of tartan cloak among the snow.
They have found the widow—dead! Her arms
were stretched forth as if imploring assistance!

Before noon they discovered her child by his
cries. He was safe in the crevice of the rock.

Dr A. I. Schofield

(Song of Solomon 2. 14)

**944 Room—Still Room.** 'Yet there is room!'
said the rich provider of the great supper in our
Lord's parable.

During Moody's gospel campaign in Britain
in 1843-73 Ira D. Sankey frequently sang as a
solo Tennyson's poem,

*'Late, late, so late, and dark the night and
  chill;
Late, late, so late, but we can enter still,'*

with a chorus—'Too late! too late! ye cannot
enter now.' The poem is based on the parable
of the Ten Virgins.

When the compilers of *Sacred Songs and
Solos* applied for permission to include the
poem in the collection, the copyright owners
refused to grant it. Then Dr Horatius Bonar was
asked to write a hymn on the same theme, and
it was included in the hymnal.

*'Yet there is room! the Lamb's bright hall of
  song
With its fair glory beckons thee along.
Room, room! still room! Oh enter, enter, now!'*

(Luke 14. 22)

**945 Royal Authority Essential.** The Duke of Somerset, in the reign of Edward VI, was one of the last men beheaded on Tower Hill. Just as the fatal moment was approaching, a mounted messenger in the service of the crown was seen riding toward the scaffold, following a number of officers who had ridden through the crowd to the same place. Thinking the messenger had been sent to stay the execution, the assembled crowd raised the cry, 'A pardon! A pardon!' The words reached the ears of the condemned duke. But popular opinion was mistaken: the king had not sent a message of pardon, so the cry of pardon was cruel mockery. The announcement by the crowd was false, lacking royal authority.

Pardon with the authority of the King of kings is found in Matthew 9. 6; Acts 13. 38,39.

**946 Royal Bible Readers.** The following narrative appeared in *The Christian Herald* of March 8, 1952:

A lorry driver stopped by the roadside to have lunch. A lady and gentlemen with two dogs approached, and the gentleman said, 'You have pulled up at a lovely spot.' The driver replied that it was, adding, 'I happen to know the Creator.'

'So do I,' came the reply from the gentleman who, turning to his wife, suggested they should sit down and rest as well. The driver left his lorry and said simply, 'Your Majesty!'

When the king learned that the driver had two girls (daughters), he said, 'I hope you are bringing them up to read the Bible.'

'Yes!' the driver said, 'we are in the Scripture Union.'

'So are we!' said the king: 'you are a wise father.'

Soon after, a present arrived for each of the two little girls.

Dan Kerr

(Acts 17. 11)

**947 Royalty Waits Outside.** King George V and Queen Mary were vacationing by the seaside in England. One night, when they were taking a walk along the sea front, the Queen sprained her ankle. It was important that they find a place for her to rest. The king finally spotted a little cottage. He helped his wife to the door and knocked. 'Who's there?' a voice called out. 'King George and Queen Mary,' was the reply. The voice from inside called again, 'You don't expect me to believe that, do you?' 'Come to the door,' the king commanded, 'and see for yourself.' The man of the house came and saw that his visitors were indeed the sovereigns of the realm. They were invited in and given the best hospitality that the poor couple could muster. For years the man and woman in the cottage by the sea retold the story of the night when they were visited by the king and queen. They always concluded, 'You know, we almost did not let them in.'

*Sunday School Times*

(Rev. 3. 20)

**948 Russia's Aims.** Peter the Great of Russia who died in A.D. 1725 had inserted in his will the following:

We must keep steadily extending our frontiers, northward along the Baltic and southward along the shores of the Black Sea. We must progress as much as possible in the direction of Constantinople and India. He who can get possession of these places is the real ruler of the world.

Russia must watch for and seize the favourable moment, and pour her already assembled hosts into Germany, while two immense fleets, laden with Asiatic hordes and convoyed by armed squadrons sweeping along the Mediterranean and the Atlantic, will overrun France on the one side, while Germany is overpowered on the other. When these countries are fully conquered, the rest of Europe must fall easily and without a struggle under our yoke. Thus Europe can and must be conquered.

(Dan. 11. 38)

**949 Sacrifice—A Worthwhile.** During the First World War, after a German attack, a soldier came back into the ranks and discovered that his pal with whom he had gone out had not returned. Immediately he asked permission to go back over the battlefield to find him, if that were possible. The officer advised against it, saying, 'Even if you find him it will not be worth it; and you will go at the risk of your life. But if you are determined, you may go.' The lad went off immediately, found his friend badly wounded, and was bringing him back to the lines. But before he reached them his friend died and he only just made it back to his own territory. The officer came over to see if he could help him, but seeing his life was ebbing out, said, 'I told you you had better not go. I warned you that you might lose your life. Was it worth while?'

'Yes, sir,' the soldier replied, 'it was worth while, for when I reached him, he said, "I knew you would come," and to hear those words from his lips was worth while.'

(John 15. 13)

**950 Sacrifice Offered.** Mrs Booth, wife of General William Booth, the founder of the Salvation Army, used to live in North London with their five children. She tells this story:

One wet day the children could not go out into the garden to play, so played indoors. They had a big Noah's Ark with animals, and were playing 'The Flood'. They lined up the animals two by two and got them into the ark, shut the door, and said, 'Now the next thing is the flood.'

In the bathroom there was a big concrete tank into which five or six children could enter at the same time. They put in the plug, got the taps going, and soon the ark was floating on the flood. A splashing good time!

Then they stopped the flood, pulled out the plug and slowly the ark subsided on Mount Ararat, the bath mat. Then they opened the door and let the animals out. Next thing—a sacrifice. Jumbo the elephant was too good and they could not spare Jacko the monkey. Suddenly Bramwell went dashing upstairs and fetched a white woolly sheep that had lost its head and tail and three legs. 'Will this do?' They all agreed and put it on the altar, lit the fire and offered the sacrifice.

Don't dare call that a sacrifice! David said, 'Neither shall I offer burnt offerings unto the Lord my God of that which doth cost me nothing.'

(2 Sam. 24. 24)

**951  Sacrificing of Animals.** The writer was able to visit the Kali temple in Calcutta recently. During this visit he was able to watch a devotee bring a young goat along as a sacrifice. The man reverently placed his hands on the head of the animal and made his confession over it. The priest then took the goat to the altar and with one sweep of the knife chopped its head off. As the blood poured from the body of the animal many women came forward and caught some of the blood in their hands and sprinkled themselves with it. It was an impressive scene, and it reminded one of the sacrifices of old that could never put away sin.

Sigma in *The Indian Christian*

We call to mind the two familiar verses of Isaac Watts:

*Not all the blood of beasts on Jewish altars slain*
*Could give the guilty conscience peace or wash*
*away its stain:*

*But Christ the heavenly Lamb, takes all our*
*guilt away,*
*A sacrifice of nobler name and richer blood*
*than they.*

(Heb. 10. 10-12)

**952  Safety, Certainty and Enjoyment.** It is well known that the late Queen Mary was in the habit of carrying a number of copies of the gospel booklet that bears this title in her handbag and judiciously giving them to people she met, with whom she was on speaking terms.

It may not be so well known that the late King George V, as well as Queen Mary, was saved through reading this booklet. A lady-in-waiting gave it to the queen who read it and asked the king to read it. Then they decided to ask the writer, George Cutting, to visit them. This he did and did not leave till both the king and queen were sure of their salvation.

The writer knows this to be true, as Mr Cutting was staying at her home at the time.

L. Freeman

**953  Saints in Circulation.** It is related that during the reign of Oliver Cromwell the government ran out of silver coinage. Cromwell sent his men to a cathedral to see if they could find any silver. They reported, 'The only silver we can find is in the statues of the saints standing in the corners.'

'Good,' he replied, 'we'll melt down the saints and put them into circulation!'

We might apply the words in a spiritual sense to ourselves, for surely one of the needs of the hour is that God's saints might be melted in revival fires and put into circulation to win lost souls.

(Acts 8. 4)

**954  Salvation—Not by Works.** George Goodman was in his office one day when a young man called to see him, ostensibly on legal business, but before long Mr Goodman perceived that the real reason for the visit was deep concern about his soul's salvation. 'What must I do?' queried the young man.

'What have you done?' asked George Goodman in reply.

The young man detailed a list of deeds he could reckon to his credit: he had prayed, read the Bible, paid his way, lived honestly with his neighbours and so on. 'What more can I do?' he exclaimed.

'I don't think you can do any more. You seem to have done more than I have,' replied Mr Goodman who asked him to repeat all he had done. As he finished, Mr Goodman said in a tone of sadness, 'No, I can't suggest any more you can do.' 'Then there is no hope!' said the young man in despair; and so saying he rose to go. 'Stop!' said George Goodman, 'I didn't say that. There is nothing you can do, but if I were to tell you of a work done for you, that would alter matters, don't you think?' The Lord's servant then told the enquirer the story of salvation; and the young man believed and was saved.

(Acts 16. 30,31)

**955  Salvation so Costly.** A preacher of the gospel went down a coal mine to preach to the men during their lunch hour. Afterwards he spoke to the foreman about his soul. The foreman said, 'This salvation is too cheap.' Without arguing the preacher said, 'How do we get out of this deep mine?' 'Why, that's simple,' said the foreman, 'we only have to step into this cage lift, press the button, and in a few seconds we are lifted to the top.'

To this the preacher replied, 'But that's too easy. Shouldn't I give a hand to help myself up?' 'No!' said the foreman, 'the engineers have done all the work necessary, and the cage has been tested and proved reliable. We only have to get in and go.' 'Then,' said the preacher, 'when God says, "Whosoever believes on the Son of God has everlasting life", how can you say it's too cheap? The cost of our salvation—the death of God's Son, Jesus Christ—is far above the cost to the engineers of providing this cage lift to take us to the surface: and you and I only have to trust ourselves to it.'

(John 3. 16; Eph. 2. 8)

**956 Salvation to the Uttermost.** Dr F. W. Boreham defines this as 'to the very last—unto the very last yard of the very last mile; to the very last minute of the very last hour of the very last day.'

On the threshold of his new life in Christ, J. B. Gough had a vision of three giants, tyrannical figures that arose and endeavoured to drive him back into slavery. Their names were Yesterday, Today and Tomorrow.

Giant Yesterday pointed out with terrific emphasis that the past is absolute, that what's done can never be undone, that:

*Wounds of the soul, though healed, will ache;*
*The reddening scars remain and make*
*    confession:*
*Lost innocence returns no more;*
*We are not what we were before*
*    transgression.*

To the end of his days Gough was haunted by the grim ghosts of seven terrible and remorseless years. He likened his life to a snowdrift that had been sadly stained, and could not be restored to its former purity and whiteness. 'The scars remain,' he used to say with bitter self-reproach. Giant Yesterday pointed to the black past derisively, held it up as a threat over the poor penitent's head, and told him in tones that sounded like thunder that there was no escape.

Giant Today pointed to things as they are. 'Look at yourself!' the tyrant exclaims. 'Facts are facts. Your present condition is a fact: how can you evade it?'

A series of visions came before Gough. Before him stood a bright, fair-haired blue-eyed, beautiful boy with rosy cheeks and pearly teeth, the perfect picture of innocence, peace, health, purity and joy. 'Who are you?' asked Gough. 'I am your past, I am what you were.'

Then another figure appeared. The youth had become a man who looked as if born to command. Intelligence flashed from his eyes; genius, trained and consecrated, marked his noble brow. 'Who are you?' asked Gough. 'I am your Ideal, what you might have been.'

Then there crept slowly into the bare room a wretched thing, unkempt, loathsome, manacled, with face furrowed and filthy, lips swollen and repulsive, brow branded with the stamp of sensuality, eyes glaring wildly and bleared and dim.' 'Who are you?' he asked. 'I am your Present: I am what you are!' By this impressive shadow-show Giant Today sought to frighten a trembling spirit from its rich inheritance.

Giant Tomorrow then addressed him. 'It is easy enough to be religious today, but what of tomorrow and the next day and all the days to come? If one temptation fails to overthrow you, another will surely bring you down.'

The Giants withdrew and in despair, thinking of the indelible past, humiliating present and unpromising future, distracted, Gough exclaimed, 'Oh wretched man that I am! I am

not able.' Then Faith stepped in with the assuring word from heaven itself, 'He is able to save to the uttermost all that come unto God by Him.'

(Heb. 7. 25)

**957 Samson Blind and Bound.** Three great truths concerning sin and departure from God evolve from the story of Samson's fall:

i.   Sin binds, steadily diminishing man's liberty and movement for God:
ii.  Sin blinds the eyes to a sense of purity and piety:
iii. Sin grinds its victims, compelling sinners to accept sin's debased currency as wages: for 'the wages of sin is death'.

John Milton in his Epic, *Samson Agonistes,* puts the following words into Samson's mouth:

*'Myself my sepulchre, a moving grave,*
*Prison within prison, inescapably dark!*
*Nothing of all these evils have befallen*
*Me but justly. I myself have brought them on—*
*Sole author I, sole cause! If aught seem vile,*
*As vile hath been my folly.'*

(Judge. 16. 21)

**958 Satisfaction More Than Contentment.**

*Earth might give contentment—satisfaction? No!*
*'Food and raiment' give me much of God to*
*    know:*
*But in Christ believing, standing by His side,*
*I, when changed and like Him, shall be*
*    satisfied.*

*Here, to be contented, God of me requires—*
*'Tis His will toward me, and all doubt retires,*
*But in resurrection, changed and glorified,*
*I at rest for ever shall be satisfied.*

*Till that hour contentment shall, through grace,*
*    be mine—*
*All my future welfare I to Him resign.*
*But when with my Saviour who for me has died,*
*I shall be made like Him, wholly satisfied.*

                                        Albert Midlane

(Ps. 17. 15)

**959 Satisfied.**

*I shall be satisfied—not with the blaze of glory*
*When that blest land first meets my wondering*
*    gaze,*
*Not with the soaring notes of angel chorus*
*Which fills the courts of heaven with Thy praise*

*I shall be satisfied—not with the joy of*
*    meeting*
*The ones I loved and lost while here below;*
*Not e'en with knowing all Thy thoughts towards*
*    me,*
*Not with the crown of life Thou wilt bestow.*

*I shall be satisfied—not with the things*
*    undreamed of*
*Thou hast prepared, though wonderful they be,*
*But in one great transforming revelation—*
*I shall be satisfied, oh Lord my God, with Thee.*

                                        Joan Suisted

(Ps. 17. 15)

**960   Saul's Conversion.**   Thrice narrated in the Acts of the Apostles is the remarkable conversion of Saul of Tarsus. Here is a poetic account of it.

*We sing the glorious conquest before Damascus'*
*    gate,*
*When Saul, the Church's spoiler, came breathing*
*    threats and hate;*
*The ravening wolf rushed forward full early to*
*    the prey;*
*But lo! the Shepherd met him and bound him*
*    fast that day.*
*O glory most excelling that smote across his*
*    path!*
*O light that pierced and blinded the zealot in*
*    his wrath!*
*O voice that spake unto him the calm reproving*
*    word!*
*O love that sought and held him the bondman*
*    of his Lord!*
*O wisdom ordering all things in order strong*
*    and sweet,*
*What nobler spoil was ever cast at the Victor's*
*    feet?*
*Lord, teach Thy Church the lesson, still in her*
*    darkest hour*
*Of weakness and of danger, to trust Thy*
*    hidden power;*
*Thy grace by ways mysterious the wrath of man*
*    can bind*
*And in Thy boldest foeman Thy chosen saint*
*    can find.*

                              J.E. *Choice Gleanings*

(Acts 9. 11,20)

**961   Scandal Avoided.**   Misjudged by a fellow missionary, Livingstone gave up his house and garden at Mabotsa, with all the money and toil they had cost him, rather than have any scandal before the heathen, and began in a new place the labour of house and school building, and gathering the people around him. Parting with his garden cost him a great pang. 'I like a garden,' he said, 'but Paradise will make amends for all our privations here.' His service thereafter and missionary achievements in Africa attest the wisdom of the step he took.
(Gen. 13. 8)

**962   Scenes to be Remembered.**

*Oh scene of love!*
*The broken bread and wine!*
*The memory of that love*
*Be ever mine!*

*That scene of hate—*
*The kiss, the sacred sign:*
*The memory of that hour*
*Be ever mine!*

*That scene—the cross!*
*What unknown woes were Thine!*
*The memory of such grief*
*Be ever mine!*

*Oh festal scene!*
*The branches and the vine!*
*The memory of the cup*
*Be ever mine!*

*Thy coming, Lord,*
*We hail with joy divine:*
*That blessed hope, O Lord,*
*Be ever mine!*

                              George Chesterman
(Matt. 26. 26-29)

**963   School of God.**

*Not for the wise the teaching,*
*But for the little child;*
*Not for the strong the guidance*
*But for the meek and mild.*
*The feast is for the hungry,*
*The treasure for the poor;*
*The naked and the outcast*
*Enter the open door.*
*The pure in heart behold Him,*
*From vultures' eyes concealed;*
*And to the bruised and bankrupt*
*The kingdom is revealed.*
*Philosophers may stumble*
*In daylight, like the blind,*
*While teachable disciples*
*The heavenly pathway find.*
*Where human wit is baffled*
*Love finds the golden key;*
*And with anointed vision*
*Reads heaven's mystery.*

*Say, wilt thou come and enter*
*This strange yet blessed school*
*Where only fools learn wisdom,*
*The wise becomes a fool:*
*Where littleness is greatness*
*And bigness becomes small;*
*Where pride strips off her glory*
*While nothingness gains all.*

(Matt. 11. 29)

**964   Scriptures—Christ in all.**
We see:
in the Pentateuch the Figures of the sufferings of Christ,
in the Psalms the Feelings of the suffering Christ,
in the Prophets the Forecasts of the sufferings of Christ,
in the Gospels the Facts of the sufferings of Christ,
in the Epistles the Fruits of the sufferings of Christ,
In the Book of Revelation the Fulfilment of the sufferings of Christ: and the Glory that should follow.
(John 5. 39; 1 Pet. 1. 11,12)

**965   Scriptures for Health.**   Some years ago a lady who told this story herself went to consult a famous physician about her health. She was a woman of nervous temperament whose many troubles had worried her to such an extent that her physical and mental health were threatened by the strain. She gave the doctor particulars of her symptoms and was astonished at his brief oral prescription: 'Madam, what you need is to read your Bible more.'

'But, doctor,' began the bewildered patient.

'Go home, and read your Bible an hour a day,' the physician reiterated with kindly authority: 'then come back to me a month from today.' So saying, he bowed her out of his surgery.

At first his patient was inclined to be angry. Then, as the prescription was so inexpensive, and as she had for a long time neglected Bible reading, which had been crowded out of her life by worldly cares, she went home and commenced conscientiously to try the doctor's remedy.

In a month she returned. 'Well,' said the physician, smiling as he looked at her face, 'I see you are an obedient patient and have taken my prescription faithfully. Do you feel as if you needed any other medicine now?'

'No, doctor, I don't,' she confessed honestly. 'I feel like a different person. But how did you know that is just what I needed?'

In reply, the physician turned to his desk. There, worn and marked, was an open Bible. 'Madam,' he said with deep earnestness, 'if I were to omit my daily reading of this book, I should lose my greatest source of strength and skill. I never go to an operation without reading my Bible. I never attend a distressing case without finding help in its pages. Your case called not for medicine but for sources of peace and strength outside your own mind. I showed you my own prescription and I knew it would cure.'

'Yet I confess, doctor,' said the lady, 'I came very near not taking it.'

'Very few are willing to try it, I find,' said the physician, 'but I know of many cases where it would work wonders if they would only take it.'

(Ps. 107. 20)

966  **Scriptures—How Produced.** The two great civilizations of the ancient world, both bounded by deserts, are those of the Nile and the Tigris-Euphrates. They dominate the early Scripture scene. Abraham lived in one, and his descendants were enslaved in the other. Further back in the shadows were the Hittites, whose very existence was once denied by some critics. Archaeological evidence has now confirmed the Scriptures in their reference to this race, and shown that they once had a capital surpassing even Babylon. The Hittites fell before the rising power of the Assyrians, a race of plunderers rather than Empire builders, who were the terror of the ancient world for centuries, though in constant conflict with the other great powers of Babylon and Egypt. In such a scene of fiercely contending giants the tiny race of Israel grew up and in the face of such powers God brought His people into the promised land.

It was during the earlier stages of this conflict of nations that a development took place which profoundly affected the production of the older Scriptures and indeed the material progress of the human race. It was the development of the alphabet. The international traders of the ancient world, the Phoenicians, found the hieroglyphs of Egypt and the cuneiform writing of Mesopotamia clumsy and difficult for their commercial purposes: there were invoices and accounts even in those early days. So they gradually developed the system of a symbol for a sound (an alphabet) instead of a picture for a word or syllable (an ideograph or ideogram). We so take the alphabet for granted that we find it difficult to imagine a world without it, though even today there is just one great language, Chinese, which is non-alphabetic.

Herbert Dennett

(2 Pet. 1. 20, 21)

967  **Secret Place—This.** During the World War, 1939-1945, under a pile of Government buildings in Storey's Gate off Whitehall, London, vast subterranean quarters with over one hundred and fifty rooms were in daily use. Winston Churchill called it 'This Secret Place': some called it 'the Hole'. In it were: a Map Room, with a great map of the world and its sea routes: a Cabinet Room where the enemy's strategy was debated by leading strategists, a Telephone Room, a Key Room for the purpose of holding regular communications with other rulers and all in secret.

Daniel, the prophet and Prime Minister, had his secret place, his telephone room in which he kept in touch three times daily with the God of heaven, and his map room, and he wrote also about God's Cabinet room.

(Dan. 4. 9; 6. 3,4)

968  **Seed of the Word of God.** Dr Alexander Maclaren used to tell of a man of great intellectual power whom he longed to win. To do so the famous preacher preached a whole series of sermons dealing with intellectual difficulties. To the doctor's delight the man came shortly afterwards and said he had become a convinced Christian and wanted to join the church. Overjoyed, the doctor said, 'And which of my sermons was it that removed your doubts?' 'Your sermons!' said the other, 'It wasn't any of your sermons. The thing that set me thinking was when I put out my hands to help a poor woman coming out of the church beside me, and stumbling on the steps, she said "Thank you!", and added, "Do you love Jesus Christ, my blessed Saviour? He means everything to me." I did not then, but I thought about it. I found I was on the wrong road. Though I still have many intellectual difficulties, He now means everything to me, too.' What a tiny seed! It can be carried in one sentence, yet it can change innumerable lives.

*Sunday School Times*

(1 Pet. 1. 23)

969 **Seek First.** A few years ago a young College graduate held a good job in a large city. He advanced rapidly in a well-known firm and because of his technical knowledge was able to close many large deals for his company. His superiors insisted that after closing a contract, or while working on one, this young employee should take his customers to the night clubs of the city at the company's expense. Needless to say, the firm was greatly surprised when the young man resigned his fine job. He explained that his home and his own self-respect meant more to him than a lot of money. He took a job in a smaller city at a greatly reduced salary but God blessed him with a happy Christian family. He laid hold on the principle, 'Seek ye first the kingdom of God and His righteousness, and all these things shall be added unto you.'

*The Challenge*

(1 Sam. 2. 30; Matt. 6. 33)

970 **Seeking Saviour—The.** Francis Thompson, who wrote *The Hound of Heaven*, was the son of a hard-working doctor in Lancashire, and his parents sacrificed much to educate him for a medical degree. He spent eight years at College, and failed each year. Opium was the cause of the slackening and deterioration of his mental powers, for after reading De Quincey's book, *Confessions of an Opium Eater*, he became, in modern parlance, a drug addict. The book had been presented to him by his mother before she died.

He was reduced to penury, sleeping at night on the London Embankment. One night a shoemaker laid his hand on Thompson's shoulder and asked him, 'Is your soul saved?' This was met by an angry reply, 'What right have you to ask that question?' 'Ah well!' replied the shoemaker, 'if you won't let me save your soul, let me save your body.'

So saying, he took him to his home, provided food and clothing and the chance of earning money. Thompson took to writing and sent his manuscript to Wilfred Meynell, editor of a London journal, in February, 1887. Later Thompson—ragged, unkempt, shirtless and barefoot, a wreck physically and socially, called to see Mr Meynell, who took him into his beautiful home, where he lived and wrote *The Hound of Heaven*, which Garvin called 'the most wonderful lyric in the language'.

Dr F. W. Boreham spoke of him as 'a moth of a man with the spirit of a seraph'. Professor Philps and Dr J. A. Hutton both compare *The Hound of Heaven* with Psalm 139. To write such a poem Francis Thompson must have experienced the miracle of conversion.

*I fled Him down the nights and down the days:*
*I fled Him down the arches of the years.*
*I fled Him down the labyrinthine ways*
*Of my own mind; and in the midst of tears*
*I hid from Him, and under running laughter*
*Up vistaed hopes I sped*
*And shot, precipitated*

*Adown Titanic forms of charmed fears,*
*From those strong feet that followed, followed*
*after.*

*That voice is round me like a bursting sea;*
*'Lo, all things fly thee, for thou fliest Me.'*
(Luke 19. 10)

971 **Seeking, Suffering, Saving.**
*Seeking? Yes, seeking! In infinite love*
*He came from the glories of heaven above,*
*Down to the stable—no room in the inn—*
*Seeking for me, a poor creature of sin.*

*Suff'ring? Yes, suff'ring! No pitying eye*
*To comfort His soul as He hung there to die*
*Alone on the cross of anguish and shame.*
*He was dying for me! Sound praise to His*
*Name!*

*Saving? Yes, saving! Now exalted on high*
*At the Father's right hand, He shall never-more*
*die.*
*He is able to save to the uttermost now*
*All who, believing, will at His throne bow.*

*Coming? Yes, coming! I know not how soon;*
*It may be at midnight, it may be at noon,*
*Perhaps in the twilight; but He's promised to*
*come*
*To call me away to His fathers' great home.*

E. B. Sprunt

972 **Self-Control.** 'I once remember,' said Henry Ward Beecher, 'that a man came to our house red with wrath, boiling over with fury. He had come to complain of a supposed grievance. My father listened to him with attention and perfect quietness until he got it all off his chest, and then said to him quietly in a low tone, 'Well, I suppose you only want what is just and right?' 'Yes!' said the man, but went on to state his case over again.

Very gently my father said to him, 'If you have been misinformed, I am sure you would be perfectly willing to know what the truth is.' He said he would. Then my father very calmly and gently presented the other side, and when he was through the man said, 'Forgive me, Doctor, forgive me!' Father had beaten him in his quiet, gentle way. That gave me an insight into the power of self-control. The Greek word translated 'temperance' means 'self-control'. (Prov. 16. 32; Gal. 5. 23; 2 Pet. 1. 6)

973 **Self-Effacement.** When a person is lecturing with a map or chart to illustrate his subject, he uses a pointer. His audience does not look at the pointer but at the places or words on the map or chart, even if the pointer be of solid gold.

Spurgeon said, 'When a dog is not noticed it doesn't like it, but when it is after a fox it doesn't care. When a minister is seeking for souls he does not think of himself. Self is forgotten in his single aim to save others.'

Not I but Christ: not I but the grace of God in me!
(1 Cor. 15. 10; Gal. 2. 20)

**974  Self-Effacement.** Some years ago Keith Beckwith, on his way to spend a few days of fellowship and encouragement with Christians in Poland, was killed in a head-on collision with a lorry near Poznan three days before Christmas, along with another O.M. leader, John Watts. Keith, converted at the age of eleven, studied at London University, and in 1963 joined the Operation Mobilisation movement in order to give his time and talents to the service of his Lord and Master, Jesus Christ. In addition to the general administration of the O.M. in Britain, he was studying three languages and writing to over twenty pen-friends in different lands. Besides this, he found time for a fervent life of prayer and public witness for Christ in universities and colleges.

Derek Virgin who knew Keith well and had been working with him for some months, wrote of him: 'I shall always remember Keith for his rejoicing heart, as only the Lord knew the responsibility and the burdens which were upon his shoulders. His smile was always a great encouragement, and was the means of sending many saints rejoicing in their walk with Jesus. Keith was one of those who took the Lord Jesus at His Word and followed Him, leaving behind his degree course to bury himself for the Master.

'George Verwer and I were cleaning out his office in Bolton. It really touched my heart to see the few items of clothing left in his office and the small space of floor where he slept. He really had forsaken all to follow Jesus. I have his personal timetable in front of me, and his day lasted from 6.30 a.m. well on into the night hours, often into the early hours of morning.'

Keith was always singing in Polish and had a deep love for the Polish people. May God raise up others with this same burden to encourage the believers in Poland and to carry the Gospel to the people of Poland!

**975  Sent.** 'So send I you.'

*So send I you to labour unrewarded,*
*To serve unpaid, unsought, unloved, unknown,*
*To bear reproach, to suffer scorn and scoffing,*
*So send I you to toil for Me alone.*

*So send I you, to bind the bruised and broken,*
*O'er wand'ring souls to work, to weep, to wake,*
*To bear the burdens of a world aweary:*
*So send I you to suffer for my sake.*

*So send I you to loneliness and longing,*
*With heart a-hung'ring for the loved and known*
*Forsaking home and kindred, friend and dear*
  *one,*
*So send I you to know my love alone.*

*So send I you to leave your life's ambition,*
*To die to dear desire, self-will resign,*
*To labour long, and love where men revile you,*
*So send I you to lose your life in mine.*

The response of the one sent is:

*'Christ the son of God hath sent me*
*Through the midnight lands:*
*Mine the mighty ordination*
*Of the pierced hands.*
*Mine the message, grand and glorious,*
*Strange, unsealed surprise,*
*That the goal is God's Beloved,*
*Christ in Paradise.'*

(John 17. 18)

**976  Septuagint—The.** This is the 'pre-Christian Greek version of the Old Testament Scriptures'.

The translators were approximately seventy in number, hence the name from Latin. It seems clear that Deissmann's original thesis must be modified in the direction of influence from the Septuagint and other Semitic influences, but there is no reason to rank New Testament Greek as something unique and unrelated to the total history of the language.

The Septuagint and the Hebrew Old Testament behind it, was the Scripture of the early Church. The writers did write the New Testament from the point of view of the Septuagint. Vocabulary and even syntax of the Greek New Testament draw upon the Septuagint; but even more important, the content of the New Testament is understood only in terms of the content of the Septuagint. It speaks to every person interested in understanding the message of the New Testament.
*The Bible Translator*

**977  Servant or Preacher.** Dr G. Campbell Morgan was called by the Lord from school teaching to the ministry. When he first heard this call and made his decision, he fell on his knees to pray. Just as if a voice were in the room with him, he heard the Lord say unto him: 'Which do you want to be—a servant of Mine or a great preacher?' Morgan wanted to be a great preacher, of course! But why could he not be both? A spiritual struggle ensued until it was impressed on him that God might want him to minister unknown and in an obscure place. Then he cried to God that his greatest wish was to be a servant of His. The Lord made Him a great preacher as well as His humble servant. If we are to be acceptable to Him, it is necessary that our highest wish shall be in conformity to God's will, whether our course leads to obscurity and trial or to prestige and blessing. (John 12. 26)

**978  Service for All.**

*We cannot all be heroes and thrill a hemisphere*
*With some great daring venture, some deeds*
  *that mock at fear;*
*But we can fill a lifetime with kindly acts and*
  *true;*
*There's always noble service for noble hearts*
  *to do.*

*We cannot all be preachers and sway with
    voice and pen,
As strong winds sway the forest, the minds and
    hearts of men;
But we can be evangels to souls within our
    reach,
There's always Love's own Gospel for loving
    hearts to preach.*

*We cannot all be martyrs and win a deathless
    name
By some divine enabling, some ministry of
    flame;
But we can live for truth's sake, can do for
    Christ and dare;
There's always faithful witness for faithful
    hearts to bear.*

(Heb. 6. 10)

**979  Service Humble.**  Professor F. F. Bruce
in his exposition of John 13. 13-15—our Lord's
words to His disciples in the upper room after
He had washed their feet—quotes a paragraph
from the biography of Robert Cleaver Chapman as follows!
    No task was too lowly for Chapman.
Visitors were particularly impressed by his
habit of cleaning the boots and shoes of his
guests. Indeed, it was on this point he met
with most resistance, for those who stayed
with him were conscious that despite the simplicity of his house he was a man of good
breeding, and when they heard him minister
the Word with gracious authority, they were
extremely sensitive about allowing him to
perform so menial a task for them. But he was
not to be resisted. On one occasion a gentleman,
having regard no doubt to his host's gentle
birth and high spiritual standing, refused to let
him take away his boots. 'I insist' was the firm
reply. 'In former days it was the practice to
wash the saints' feet. Now that this is no
longer the custom, I do the nearest thing,
and clean their shoes.'
    Then F. F. Bruce goes on to give the instance
of one of his friends who as a matter of course
cleaned the shoes of an elderly missionary who
was a guest in his home and who, as a young,
man, had stayed in Chapman's home and had
his shoes cleaned by the patriarch of Barnstaple.

**980  Sheep with the Broken Leg.**  A lady
climbing a mountain in Switzerland, came to
a shepherd's fold, walked to the door and
looked in. There sat the shepherd with his
flock lying around him. Near him, on a pile of
straw, lay a single sheep which seemed to be
in pain. Examining it more carefully, she saw
it had a broken leg, and, looking enquiringly
at the shepherd, asked, 'How did it happen?'
'Madam,' replied the shepherd, 'I broke its
leg.' Seeing the look of pain that overspread
the lady's face, he went on, 'Of all the sheep
in my flock, this one was the most wayward,
often wandering to the verge of perilous
cliffs or dizzy precipices. Not only was it disobedient itself, but it was continually leading

the rest of my sheep astray. I had had previous
experience with sheep of this kind, so I broke
its leg. The first day I went to it with food it
tried to bite me, so I left it alone for a couple
of days, then went back to it. Now it not only
takes the food I bring it, but licks my hands
and shows every sign of submission and even
affection. And now, let me tell you something.
When this sheep is well, as it soon will be, it
will be the model sheep of my flock, quickest
to hear my voice and closest in following me.
To the wayward ones it will be an example
and a guide, leading them in the path of obedience to my call, because it has been completely
transformed by its suffering.'
(Heb. 12. 11)

**981  Shepherd of Israel.**

*Thou Shepherd of Israel and mine!
The joy and desire of my heart!
For closer communion I pine,
I long to reside where Thou art;
The pastures I languish to find,
Where all who their Shepherd obey
Are fed, on Thy bosom reclined,
And screened from the heat of the day.*

*'Tis there, with the lambs of Thy flock,
There only I covet to rest,
To lie at the foot of the rock
Or rise to be hid in Thy breast;
'Tis there I would always abide
And never a moment depart,
Concealed in the cleft of Thy side,
Eternally hid in Thy heart.*

Charles Wesley

(Ps. 80. 1; Song of Solomon 1. 7)

**982  Shepherd Psalm.**  Psalm 23 may be
read as a meditation of the Lord Jesus as He
walked by faith in this world. He perfected
the life of faith, standing as Chief among
those who received a good report by it. He
addressed Himself to His journey in fullest
of confidence, though it may prove a long
and trying one. Every character of trial is
successively anticipated—want of provision,
need of restoration, the shadowy vale of death,
the presence of enemies. But the resources
of the hand that leads Him are felt to be
equal to all till the journey blessedly ends in the
house of the Lord. The Lord knew restoration
from soul-trouble in John 12. 27; and then
was He ready for the valley through which
He went, till in resurrection His cup ran over,
His table was spread in the presence of His
enemies and His head anointed, His consecration to office perfected, and the kingdom
by and by will display the cup, the table and
the anointing here anticipated in faith by Jesus.
    It may, however, be rather used as the lan-
guage of experience to any believer. We, who
are as weak as infants, may long to realize such
precious joy and liberty more and more richly.

J. G. Bellett

(Ps. 23)

**983   Shepherd Psalm—Red Indian Version.**
This version is now in the Indian section of
the museum at Banff, Canada. There is no
information as to how old it is, but it is
evidently a paraphrase written by a red-
skinned disciple of the Lord Jesus in speech
familiar to his fellows:

The Great Father is the Shepherd Chief. I am
His and with Him I want not.

He throws down to me a rope, the rope of
His love, and He draws me to where the grass
is green and the water is good and I go and lie
down satisfied.

Sometimes my heart is weak and falls down
but He lifts it up again and draws me into
a place between the mountains.

It is dark, there, but I will not draw back.
I will not be afraid, for it is there, between
those mountains, that the Shepherd Chief will
meet me and the hunger I have felt in my heart
all through life will be satisfied.

Sometimes He makes the love rope into a
whip but afterwards He gives me a staff to lean
on. He spreads a table before me with all kinds
of food. He puts His hand upon my head and
all tired is gone. My cup fills until it runs over.

What I tell you is true, I lie not. These roads
that are away ahead will stay with me through
this life and afterwards I will go to live in the
Big Tepee and sit down with the Shepherd
Chief for ever.

**984   Shepherd—The Lord is My.**   A Christian man, worn to a point near exhaustion,
came one summer to the range country of
southern Alberta, Canada, where he stayed
for several weeks, recovering his strength so
that he might go back to his work of rescuing
lost souls in the city. Each day he would take
long walks over the hills and across the empty
prairies, enjoying the solitude and the restfulness of that country. Then one day he met
a boy about fourteen years old, sitting on a
hillside watching a flock of sheep.

Sitting down beside the lad, he introduced
himself and spent an hour or more in his
company; and that was the beginning of a fine
friendship between the two, for each day the
man made it a point to seek out his shepherd-
boy friend and spend some time with him. He
learned that the boy had never been to Sunday
School, and that he knew nothing about the
Bible: so he began teaching him Psalm 23,
knowing that the boy would appreciate the
Shepherd's Psalm. Then he led him to a personal acceptance of Christ as his Saviour, and
there on the hillside, with the sun shining
warmly upon them and everything so comfortable and safe, he taught him to appropriate
the first statement in the psalm and to make
the great Shepherd his very own. Repeating
the opening words the boy touched his little
finger—'The': then at the second word 'Lord'
he clasped his second finger. When he came
to the fourth word 'my' he grasped his forefinger firmly in his right hand.

The man went back to his work in the city

but did not forget his shepherd boy. Returning
to the prairies another summer, he walked
over the familiar hills and down through
numerous small valleys in search of the boy.
He found the flock of sheep but no boy.
Approaching a shack on a hill, he knocked at
the door and asked the woman who opened it,
'Could you tell me where I might find the boy
who used to herd sheep near here?'

Bursting into tears, the woman silently
motioned him to enter and offered him a chair.
When she regained her composure, she said,
'That was my boy.' 'He was your boy?' the
man asked.

Then she told him of the late spring blizzard
that had struck the range land that year. The
boy had taken the sheep out to pasture, but
never came home. They went to look for him
and found he had gathered the sheep into a
safe place. They were all safe, but the boy was
dead under the snow. 'Then,' she said, 'it was
such an odd thing. I had knitted him a pair of
warm mittens and he had them with him, but
had removed them before he died and taken
hold of the forefinger of his left hand with his
right one, and there he lay like that. We couldn't
understand why he did that.' The man then
told her the story of how the boy had made
the Good Shepherd his.
(Ps. 23)

**985   Shepherd's Provision—The.**   Since the
Lord is my Shepherd, I shall not want:

Rest—'He maketh me to lie down'
Refreshment—'He leadeth me beside the still
  waters'
Restoration—'He restoreth my soul'
Guidance—'He leadeth me in the paths of
  righteousness'
Confidence—'I will fear no evil'
Companionship—'Thou art with me'
Comfort—'Thy rod and thy staff they comfort
  me'
Provision—'Thou preparest a table'
Unction—'Thou anointest my head'
Satisfaction—'My cup runneth over'
Protection—'Goodness and mercy shall follow
  me'
A home at last—'I will dwell in the house of
  the Lord for ever.'

H. A. Ironside

(Ps. 23)

**986   Shining Life—A.**   A Scottish missionary,
recently home on furlough from India, related
the following story:

While teaching a group of children one
day about Jesus, telling how good and kind
He is, how forgiving and merciful, she noted a
sudden and intense interest on their part:
but she was not prepared for what happened.
One small girl became extremely excited and
declared, 'I know Him. He lives right near us.'
Did ever human receive such praise as that?

S. D. Gordon

(Matt. 10. 25)

**987 Shining Light—A.** During a voyage to India I sat one dark night in my cabin, feeling thoroughly unwell. Suddenly the cry of 'Man overboard!' made me spring to my feet. 'What can I do?' I asked myself, and, instantly unhooking my lamp, I held it near the top of my cabin and close to my bull's eye window, that its light might shine on the sea and as near the ship as possible. In a half minute's time I heard a joyful cry, 'Its all right: he's safe.' I put my lamp back in its place. The next day however, I was told that my little lamp was the sole means of saving the man's life: it was only by the timely light which shone upon him that the knotted rope was thrown so as to reach him.

Spencer Compton

(Matt. 5. 16; Phil. 2. 15,16)

**988 Sign or Substance.**

*It is not for a sign we are watching,*
*For wonders above and below,*
*For pouring of vials of judgement,*
*For sounding of trumpets of woe.*
*It is not for a day we are looking*
*Nor even the time yet to be,*
*When the earth shall be filled with God's glory*
*As the waters cover the sea.*
*We wait for our Lord, the Beloved,*
*Our Comforter, Master and Friend,*
*The substance of all that we hope for,*
*Beginning of faith and its end.*
*We watch for our Saviour and Bridegroom*
*Who loved us and made us His own;*
*For Him we are looking and longing,*
*For Jesus and Jesus alone.*

(Phil. 1. 20,21)

**989 Silence Before God.** Luther's translation of Psalm. 46. 10 is—'Be silent to God and let Him mould thee.'

*The vessel must be shapen*
*For the joys of Paradise;*
*The soul must have her training*
*For the service of the skies;*
*And if the great Refiner*
*In furnaces of pain*
*Would do His work more truly,*
*Count all His dealings gain;*
*For He Himself hath told thee*
*Of tribulation here.*
*Be still and let Him mould thee*
*For the changeless glory there.*

*From vintages of sorrow*
*Are deepest joys distilled,*
*And the cup outstretched for healing*
*Is oft at Marah filled:*
*God leads to joy through weeping,*
*To quietness through strife,*
*Through yielding unto conquest,*
*Through death to endless life.*
*Be still! He hath enrolled thee*
*For the kingdom and the crown.*
*Be silent! let Him mould thee*
*Who calleth thee His own.*

*Such silence is communion,*
*Such stillness is a shrine,*
*The fellowship of suffering*
*An ordinance divine.*
*And the secrets of abiding*
*Most fully are declared*
*To those who with the Master*
*Gethsemane have shared.*
*Then trust Him to uphold thee*
*Mid the shadows and the gloom.*
*Be still! and He shall mould thee*
*For His presence and for Home.*

*For resurrection stillness*
*There is resurrection power,*
*And the prayer and praise of trusting*
*May glorify each hour.*
*For those who, with the risen One,*
*In risen life abide*
*There is a place of stillness*
*Close to His riven side.*
*Then let His love enfold thee;*
*Keep silence at His word.*
*Be still and He shall mould thee.*
*Oh! rest thee in the Lord.*

(Ps. 37. 7)

**990 Simplicity and Sincerity.**

*Simplicity sincerity—*
*Oh Lord! I ask of Thee*
*That Thou wilt grant these virtues*
*To me, even to me.*

*Simplicity—'sine plica'—*
*Two Latin words, they say,*
*That mean 'without a fold'—unclosed,*
*Open and clear as day.*

*Simplicity! Oh, let me be*
*Filled with this virtue sweet,*
*That it may be displayed in me*
*To everyone I meet.*

*Oh! let my personality*
*Be void of hidden things:*
*Let me be honest, open, Lord,*
*Clear as Thy crystal springs.*

*Sincerity! Lord, I ask of Thee*
*This virtue to bestow:*
*Give me an honesty of mind—*
*Straight, true, where'er I go,*

*That others may depend on me*
*Because they find sincerity,*
*And know that they can surely trust*
*Implicitly.*

*I would these virtues claim from Thee*
*As on through life I go.*
*To Thee be all the glory given*
*If Thou wilt grant it so.*

May Gorrie

(2 Cor. 1. 12)

**991 Simplicity in Preaching.** John Wesley was preaching once on a text, 'One thing is needful.' After the sermon a lady exclaimed with a tone of surprise, 'Is this the great John Wesley of whom we hear so much? Why, even the poorest and least educated might have understood him.' Replying to her, a Christian brother who had been in the audience said, 'Madam, in this Wesley displays his greatness, for while the poorest understand him, the most learned are edified.'

To this we may add a word from Martin Luther who said, 'When I preach I regard neither the Doctors nor the Magistrates of whom I have forty in my congregation. I have my eyes upon the children and the servant-maids. If the learned men are not well-pleased, the door is always open.'
(Neh. 8. 8)

**992   Sin.   What is sin? Sin is:**

**Earth's Deathblow,** marring its beauty, causing crops to fail, leaves to wither, thorns and thistles to thrive, clouds to darken the sky and floods to deluge the earth.

**A Nation's Shame.** It degrades the one who practises it, distresses the God-fearing, de-thrones the ruler who persists in it, deadens the national conscience and delights the scandal-monger.

**Man's Ruin.** It puts a gulf between the soul and God, transforms the innocent child into the hardened rebel, makes human reason a bewildered maze, the human heart a whirl-pool of tumultuous passions and the source of impure springs; and it is the spring of every tear, the germ of every disease, the core of every grief, and the worm that gnaws at the root of peace: it is the mother of the monster Death and the age-long grave-digger.

**God's Defiant Enemy,** violating His holy law, raising a rebel hand against His revealed will trampling on heaven's statute book and bring-ing down God's wrath and curse.

**Satan's Deadly Weapon,** his poisoned arrow that kills when it strikes, the burning flame that is never quenched, the builder of hell's prison-house, the forger of the chains of the eternally damned, the usher into that outer darkness where weeping for ever weeps, wailing for ever wails, teeth are for ever gnashed and memory for ever accuses.

**993   Sin Disease.**

*The worst of all diseases is light compared*
   *with sin:*
*On every part it seizes, yet rages most within.*
*'Tis dropsy, palsy, fever and ague all combined*
*And none but a believer the least relief can find.*

Sin is folly and those who indulge in it are fools. Sin promises pleasure and brings pain; it promises rejoicing and produces regrets; it offers delights and yields disappoint-ments. 'Sin, when it is finished, bringeth forth death,' eternal banishment from God who is Life.
(James 1. 15)

**994   Sin Found Out.** 'Be sure your sin will find you out.' The gloom of midnight may cover it; the silence of the grave may prevail over it; every eye that witnessed it may be glazed in death; the lip that could reveal it could be silent for ever; yet the sin of every transgressor will find him out. His own recollec-tion may fail him; his iniquities may fade from his memory; yet they shall turn up again. They all stand recorded in the book of God, and if not put away by the blood of Christ, they must be reckoned for in that day when the earth and the heaven shall flee away.

W.S.

*Be careful what you sow;*
*The weeds you plant will grow;*
*The scattered seed from thoughtless hand*
*Must gathered be by God's command.*

(Num. 32. 23)

**995   Sin Found Out.** In 1799 the *Nancy*, an American vessel, was carrying a contraband cargo to the West Indies. Hard pressed, the Captain threw overboard any papers that might possibly incriminate him.

He made the harbour all right but was under suspicion and committed for trial in the courthouse at Kingston. Producing a set of false papers prepared in the event of the ship being stopped at sea, he had almost succeeded in clearing himself when Lieutenant Hutton of H.M.S. *Ferret* appeared in court. While cruising off Port Royal, his crew had caught a shark and found in it a bundle of papers belonging to some ship. The ship's papers, produced at the crucial moment, brought consternation to the defence and satisfaction to the prosecution. The vessel was condemned and the skipper fined and imprisoned.

For some time the head of the shark was on show at Port Royal and is now in London in the United Service Museum.
(Num. 32. 23)

**996   Sin Plainly Defined.   Dr J. Wilbur** Chapman used to tell of a preacher who often spoke on the subject of sin, mincing no words but calling it 'that abominable thing that God hates'. One of his congregation came to him and urged him to stop using the ugly word. 'We wish,' he said, 'you would not speak so plainly about sin. Our young people, hearing you, will be more likely to indulge in it. Call it something else such as "inhibition", "error", a "fault" or a "mistake".'

Going to his medicine cupboard, the preacher produced a small bottle. 'This bottle,' he said, 'contains strychnine and has on it a red label marked "Poison". Would you suggest that I change the label and put on it one that reads "Wintergreen"?' The more harmless the name, the more dangerous the dose.
(Jer. 16. 10)

**997   Sincerely Mistaken.   Carbon dioxide** instead of oxygen was administered to a patient in a hospital in the State of New York, and death resulted almost instantly. The tragedy occurred while the patient was being prepared for a minor operation. A trained anaesthetist was administering a controlled mixture of oxygen and anaesthetic gas when the tank of oxygen became exhausted, and a new tank labelled 'Oxygen' was substituted.

Almost immediately, according to the police report, the patient died. The attending surgeon and hospital officials suspected some kind of accident and called the coroner. An autopsy revealed carbon dioxide poisoning. Upon examination the 'Oxygen' tank was found to contain carbon dioxide. The tank had been mislabelled before it reached the hospital. All was being done to discover how such a serious accident happened.

The manufacturer was sincere, the hospital authorities were sincere, the anaesthetist was sincere, and certainly the patient was sincere. All were sincerely mistaken.

In the matter of the soul's salvation, too, it is possible to be sincerely mistaken. There is but one way, and Jesus Himself said, 'I am the Way.'

**998  Singers on a Tenement Roof.**  One day, while on business in Glasgow, I was parking my car in the St George's Cross area, when I heard singing from somewhere in the distance. It was also attracting the attention of the passers-by. I was delighted to hear the words of our Prison Bible Class chorus, 'There is victory for me; there is victory for me; through the blood of Christ my Saviour there is victory for me.' It was being sung heartily by a number of voices. Eventually a passer-by spotted them and drew my attention to a group of men on the roof of a tenement, repairing storm damage after the severe winter gale of a few years ago.

Immediately they saw that my attention had been drawn to them, three of the young men waved their caps and called, 'It's grand to see you again, sir; don't worry about your car; nobody will touch it as long as we are here.' They were too far distant for me to recognize them, and I was in too great a hurry to climb any closer to them; but as I went down the street, it was to the accompaniment of 'I am so glad that our Father in heaven tells of His love in the Book He has given,' with its chorus ending 'Jesus loves even me'.

These three lads were evidently ex-prisoners, but it was equally evident that they had taught their workmates the words and tunes of the choruses and hymns they had learned in Bible Class at the prison. Who knows but that they may also have led some of them to the Saviour?

Alex. Allan

(Ps. 40. 2,3)

**999  Singing in Prison.**  A group of Christians who were in prison for their faith so sang and praised the Lord that they were brought before the Bishop and reprimanded. One of them wrote to a friend: 'The world wonders that we can be so merry under such extreme miseries, but our God is Omnipotent who turns our miseries into joy. I have so much joy that although I am in a place of darkness yet I cannot lament, but both day and night I am full of joy—never was so merry before. The Lord's Name be praised for ever.'

(Isa. 24. 15; Acts 16. 25)

**1000  Sinners Named.**  The following is an old story, amusing in its simplicity yet vouched for by the person who first narrated it.

In a poor district in London a group of children, after playing for some time in the street, began to feel chilly as the evening fell. Seeing a church building, they quietly slipped inside to get warm. The place was heated by a large, round stove near the back of the building, and the children sat on the seats nearest to the stove.

Scarcely had they seated themselves when the organ began to sound and the minister started to read Evening Prayer. After the hymn and prayer were over, the minister read from Luke 15; and as he read the words spoken concerning Jesus by the religious Pharisees— 'This man receiveth sinners and eateth with them'—one of the children, a little girl, pricked up her ears and listened very attentively to the Scripture lesson.

After the service was over, she went up to the minister and said, 'Sir, I didn't know that my name was in the Bible.'

'What is your name, dear?' he asked.

'Edith is my name, sir,' was her reply.

'No,' said the preacher, 'Edith doesn't come in the Bible.' 'Oh yes, it does, sir,' she replied 'you read it just now: "This man"—and you said it was Jesus Christ—"receiveth sinners and Edith with them".'

The similarity of sound had led to the little girl's mistake, but she was certainly not mistaken in her application of the words to herself; for the Lord Jesus still receives every sinner, be her name Edith or Mary, or be his name Tom or Henry, or what you will: He is ready to receive all who will come to Him as sinners to receive the salvation He offers.

(Luke 15. 2)

**1001  Slumber nor Sleep.**  A ship named the *Zamzam* was torpedoed. Passengers forced to leap into the sea were picked up by an armed freighter and placed in the hold of the ship. The next morning they asked each other, 'Were you nervous?' 'Were you cold?' 'Were you afraid?' 'Could you sleep?' An elderly missionary in reply said that the floor was terribly hard, but the Lord had reminded him of His words in Psalm 121: 'He that keepeth Israel shall neither slumber nor sleep.' Then, looking to the Lord, he had said, 'Lord, there really isn't any reason for both Thee and me to stay awake tonight. If Thou art keeping watch, I shall thank Thee for some sleep.' 'And,' said he, 'I got it.'

Paul S. Rees (adapted)

(Ps. 121. 4)

**1002 Small, Yet Made Great.** Paul, the great apostle, became so small that he could truthfully call himself 'less than the least of all saints', and, depend upon it, it was because of his smallness that God used him so much and lifted him so high.

The story of Naaman's cleansing in 2 Kings 5 shows the value placed by God on the small rather than on the great.

i. There was the little captive maid. She worked in Naaman's house faithfully and conscientiously to her mistress's satisfaction. This little maid set the wheels in motion that resulted in the Syrian General's complete recovery.

ii. Then there was the obscure prophet Elisha. The king of Israel thought so little of him that it never dawned on him to apply to that quarter for help.

iii. The next insignificant figure is the prophet's messenger, just called a 'messenger', sent to the door with the message to dip seven times in Jordan. Do you wonder that General Naaman squirmed?

iv. Naaman's servants said to their master, 'The prophet said to do only a small thing, not a big thing, so why not do it?' And the big man was wise enough to take the small men's advice.

A. Soutter (abridged)

(Jer. 30. 19)

What great things God did through Gladys Aylward, 'the small woman'!


**1003 Snakes and Sins.** Some years ago there lived in France a celebrated snake-charmer named Pamela. She was in the habit of taking her venomous pets to bed with her and letting them sleep by her side.

One morning she never awoke. Her lifeless body, swollen into a shapeless blue mass, was found by her friends. The snakes, so long tolerated and toyed with, had bitten her to death. Constant usage had caused her to regard them as harmless, but she had trifled with them once too often.

Not unlike Pamela's snakes are your sins. While your eyes are closed in sleep they surround you. One of these days, unless you get rid of them, they will be your ruin.

H. P. Barker

(James 1. 15)


**1004 Soldier—A Christian.** With acknowledgments to Andy Stewart who sings 'A Scottish Soldier'.

*There was a soldier, a Christian soldier,*
*Who travelled land and sea God's messenger*
*  to be.*
*There was none bolder his task to shoulder:*
*He'd preached the glad news free far, far from*
*  home.*
*He's seen Christ's glory, he's told the story*
*Of Jesus glorious, his Lord victorious:*
*And now he's lying Hell's hosts defying*
*Within a prison cell in Rome.*

*And now this soldier, this Christian soldier,*
*Who'd preached o'er land and sea salvation*
*  full and free,*
*Wears fetters galling, and death is calling*
*His martyr soul to free from that dark land.*
*His course completed, his foes defeated,*
*He now is full of zest to enter into rest*
*With Christ in glory, to tell his story,*
*Before his Captain's face to stand.*

*And now this soldier, this Christian soldier,*
*Will travel far no more: his battles all are o'er.*
*A sharp sword flashes: his spirit passes,*
*And then on heaven's shore his welcome home.*
*And there in glory he sings the story of Jesus*
*  glorious, his Lord victorious.*
*His labours cease now, he is at peace now*
*Far from those seven hills of Rome.*

*Because he knows Him whom he has believed*
*His commands received and His aims achieved*
*And fierce though many a conflict may have been,*
*He now rests in peace at home.*

A.N.

(2 Tim. 4. 7)


**1005 Soldier's Epitaph—Christian.**

*Here lies a good soldier whom all will applaud:*
*He fought many battles at home and abroad:*
*But the hottest engagement he ever was in*
*Was the conquest of self in the battle of sin.*


**1006 Somebody Touched Me.** Pierre Monteus, the London Symphony Orchestra's famous conductor, his wife and their French poodle were looking for a motel for the night. Driving up to a group of cabins, they saw a woman standing at the office door. As they approached, she said slowly, 'Sorry I have nothing.'

A young girl standing near by whispered to the woman, whose whole demeanour underwent an instant change. Making a sort of curtsey, she said, 'Excuse me, sir, I did not know that you were Someone. I think that I can accommodate you.'

Monteus's face became cold and withdrawn. Bowing in a most formal manner, he said, 'Madame, everyone is Someone. Au revoir.'

To the Lord Jesus Christ everyone is Someone, for He died for all. To him the poor woman with the issue of blood who touched the hem of His garment was Someone, for He said, 'Somebody touched me.' She was very sick and weak, and she was very poor, for she had spent all that she had. In the crowd she was Nobody: to the Lord she was Somebody.

(Luke 8. 46)


**1007 Song of Love.** The fisher folk who live along the shores of the Adriatic Sea have a custom, that when the shadows of twilight are gathering the families of the fishermen who are out at sea gather on the beach, build huge fires of driftwood, and sing their old folk songs round the fire. Thus the fishermen returning through the dusk, weary with their long day's toil, are guided by the fires and inspired by the songs of those they love, and they toil a little harder at the oars until they are safely home.

The story is told that many years ago a young man and his sweetheart came down to such a beach in the evening to say their farewells. Riding at anchor out in the bay was a ship on which he would be sailing at break of day, hoping to find his fortune in a far-off land. Then he would return and take her for his bride.

Gathering beachwood they built a fire, stood beside it and talked of their plans, and then he asked her to sing a love song that was dear to them both. As they plighted their vows anew, promising that each would be faithful and wait for the day when he would return, he asked her to sing the song once more.

He said, 'I will come back for you, and then I will take you to a beautiful home in that wonderland to which I am going. But when I am far away from you, I will be lonely, perhaps discouraged at times, and every day at this time I will be thinking of you as I have seen you here tonight. Then I will return at this same hour. Promise me that every evening you will come to this beach, build a fire and sing the song you have sung for me tonight. When I see your fire and hear your song, I shall know that you have been true and are waiting.'

Sadly the girl promised, and then with a last goodbye, he stepped into his boat and rowed away into the night. The next evening, true to her promise, the girl was at the beach, standing by her fire singing her song, thinking fondly of the one who was now far out to sea. Night after night found her keeping her tryst. Months slipped by, and then years, but still she watched beside her fire in the twilight and sang her song of love. Friends advised her to turn aside and find another, insisting that her lover had forgotten his promise and would never return. But her faith in him would not waver. He had promised; therefore he would come back for her.

One evening, more discouraged than usual, she came to her appointed place in the twilight. Hope seemed almost gone, but still she knew she must be true. The fire flickered in the wind, and she gathered wood for it a second time. She sang again the song she had sung so many times. As she was about to return to her home she heard the sound of oars out in the bay. Perhaps it was some late fisherman. But loving is not given up easily, and she kindled her fire anew and sang her song once more. Then he was there, taking her in his arms and telling her about the wonderful home he had built for her beyond the sea. 'I waited to see your fire and hear your song,' he said 'then I knew you had been faithful and were waiting.'

What was it Jesus said to His disciples? 'And if I go . . . I will come again and receive you unto myself, that where I am there ye may be also.'

(John 14. 3)

**1008 Songs in Prison.** A prisoner of war tells of his Christmas Eve in a wartime prison, to which he had been taken when he was recaptured after escaping from a P.O.W. camp. The prison was ruled by a discipline of fear, and his morale was at rock-bottom. Suddenly the atmosphere changed as a woman's voice singing 'Silent Night' floated across the courtyard from the women's cells. It seemed the most beautiful voice the recaptured prisoner had ever heard.

As gradually the singer's voice became stronger and clearer, other women's voices joined in, and one by one the male prisoners took their parts until there were hundreds of voices, all harmonising in that lovely carol. The prison guards called out 'Stop', but it seemed only half-heartedly, for they allowed the carol singing to continue. That night there was a peaceful quiet in the prison, and the prisoners enjoyed an unbroken night's rest.
(Acts 16. 25)

**1009 Sorrow's Lessons.**

*The night has passed, e'er filled with thoughts of day,*
*Earths' labours o'er, its sorrows passed away,*
*Earth's problems solved in heaven's eternal light,*
*Heaven's rest—reward of earth's sad, bitter fight.*

*Dark clouds have cast their shadows o'er the way,*
*Yet shadows prove a sun's benignant ray;*
*From 'neath the shadows, oft our eyes have seen*
*Showers of refreshment where but drought had been.*

*We cannot solve the mysteries of God,*
*But this we know—the hand that holds the rod*
*Is e'er controlled by heart of perfect love*
*And proves our sonship with our God above.*

*Oh, why such sorrow, why such bitter pain?*
*Why should we, loving, not be loved again?*
*Why should we lose thus those to us most dear?*
*Why dark to others that to us is clear?*

*Be still, my heart! for God is ever right;*
*'Tis thus He traineth through the darksome night.*
*He is the Master, we His scholars say,*
*'Lord, teach and train us for the coming day.'*

F. Howard Oakley
(Ps. 30. 5)

**1010 Souls for Shoes.** 'Stop him! Stop him!' the man shouted. While people jumped up to see what was happening, a long figure was, stretched out on a bench in the waiting-room sound asleep.

Outside, a burly policeman grabbed the fleeing man and he fell to his knees. 'What's this all about?' asked the policeman of the man who had started the chase. 'See! His shoes! He stole the man's shoes.'

The man on his knees held a paper bag in

one hand. The bag had held a pair of old shoes which lay on the platform. The policeman pulled him to his feet.

'Hold these shoes up.' They were dusty, grey and worn into holes. 'Very large! Very old!' mused the policeman. The accuser said, 'Perhaps his only pair. I saw this thief steal them Anyone can see they are old; and it's ready to snow.'

Another man agreed. 'I'd hate to walk out without shoes in this weather. The fellow ought to be whipped. The policeman led the thief back into the stuffy waiting room. The accuser pointed out the tall man sleeping on the bench. He had come in about eleven o' clock. The train was four hours late. He had taken off his shoes, put them under the bench, read a few minutes from his Bible, then used it for a pillow as he stretched out to sleep.

The policeman dragged the thief to the sleeping man, the crowd following silently.

An immaculately dressed man approached the policeman and asked where the porters were to carry his heavy bags. Told that as it was Christmas Eve, the porters had left for their homes at eleven o' clock, he muttered angrily, 'What nonsense!'

The stranger then awoke. Seeing the policeman and the thief before him, he got to his feet and asked in a deep, low, resounding voice, 'What's the matter?'

'This man stole your shoes.'

'Let him go! Let him go! They aren't worth 25 cents,' said the stranger.

'But you don't have any others,' suggested the accuser.

'That's true! The shoes are worn out. Let him go!'

The policeman turned to the thief. 'Take off your hat to a good man,' he commanded.

The thief took his hat off, looking more confused than frightened.

The policeman took out a pair of handcuffs and the bystanders drew back a few paces. The stranger took the policeman by the arm. 'Dont' do that,' he said.

'Don't punish him! I forgive him. Let him go!'

Then the accuser asked, 'You think it's no crime for a fellow to take your only pair of shoes when it's snowing.'

'Oh, no, no, no! I forgive him!'

'But he should be punished,' the policeman protested. 'I'll punish him,' said the stranger. 'O.K.! I'll give him over to you.'

As the group of people gathered round, the stranger got the thief to kneel down at the bench and to ask God to forgive him. The stranger knelt down, threw his arm across the thief's shoulders, and prayed to the God of all mercies, asking Him to make the thief's heart whiter than snow.

The thief began repeating the prayer in a low voice after him, and it deepened into a sinner's unashamed cry for forgiveness from the God of heavenly forgiveness.

The two men rose to their feet, their eyes wet and their faces radiant.

'What a miracle!' cried the stranger. 'Now I know why God brought me here, why He withheld the money for a bed. Sleeping on this bench has brought me happiness. It's Christmas and I can bring a treasure to the King and lay it on the Christ child's cradle—a soul forgiven.'

'Not just one soul but two souls,' rang out the voice of the wealthy business man. 'As you were praying, I knew I'd seen forgiveness and loving-kindness and faith for the first time, and I cried for forgiveness too.'

'I'm so happy,' said the stranger: 'two souls for a pair of shoes.'

'Whats' your name?' asked the business man. 'Yosef Benjamin.'

'He's going home with me,' announced the thief, 'I have a wife who prays.'

C. McManus

(Eph. 4. 32)

**1011   Sowing and Reaping.** When Horatio Bottomley, at one time editor of *John Bull*, was serving a prison sentence for embezzlement, one of his old acquaintances visited him in prison, and saw him busily sewing mail bags.

'What, Bottomley,' he said, 'sewing?'

'No!' was the reply, 'Reaping.'

There are some things we cannot possibly do. We cannot sow bad habits and reap a good character: sow jealousies and hatred and reap love and friendship: sow dissipation and reap a healthy body: sow deception and reap confidence: sow cowardice and reap courage: sow neglect of the Bible and reap a well-ordered life.

(Gal. 6. 7,8)

**1012   Sowing the Seed.**   It is said of Columbus that he carried the seed of flowers and scattered them around wherever his vessel anchored. This simple act of the explorer may have seemed insignificant to his associates but it left for Columbus a perpetual monument of beautiful flowers of Spain, blooming hundreds of years after his death in distant lands. Seed has the capacity to reproduce itself and multiply from year to year and so the reward of the sower abides perpetually. The labour of the builder may crumble and perish but the sower of good seed has an everlasting compensation.

Some years ago it was necessary to find traces of an old family who once were influential in a certain community. An investigator went to the district to try to find some information about the family. He searched the records but could find no trace of them whatever. He visited the supposed site of their ancient mansion. Not a stone remained to tell its place. Disappointed in these attempts he accosted an aged man: 'Do you know anything of the Findernes?'

'Findernes!' was the reply, 'We have no Findernes here but we have Findernes flowers.'

There was a clue. The old man led the way to a field where there were traces of an ancient terrace.

'There,' said he, pointing to a bank of garden flowers growing wild, 'there are Findernes flowers, brought by Sir Geoffrey Findernes from the Holy Land, and do what we will they will never die.'

Sir Geoffrey Findernes left a more lasting memorial than that written in the church records of the village, and more lasting than the walls of the stately mansion which bore his name. He sowed seed from Palestine around his dwelling and when everything else of him was forgotten the flowers of the Holy Land continued to grow and bloom, an undying monument to his memory.

No work is more noble or fraught with more blessed possibilities than the work of sowing the seed of the gospel. If you prayerfully scatter gospel tracts and preach Christ to others by lip and deed you will leave behind you, or carry with you, a more glorious reward than those who make millions or shape the destinies of nations. It is what you sow, not what you save that will leave the flowers of Palestine behind you and bless your memory.

The Lord Jesus called Himself a sower. He left no buildings or institutions behind Him to perpetuate His name. He did not organize His disciples into a fraternity. He merely sowed. He sowed the Word of God in the hearts of men and sowed Himself in the earth (John 12. 24). He went forth in sorrow, 'bearing precious seed'. He wept, He sighed, He was weary with His journey. It was His sowing time. But what a harvest from that sowing!

Leonard Sheldrake

(John 12. 24)

**1013 Sowing the Word.** At the time of the Nazi invasion of Poland, while people were fleeing, guns firing and shells bursting, a farmer was seen in his fields, busy sowing seed.

'How can you keep on working with war raging all around you?' he was asked. He replied, 'I plough and I sow. If I don't reap the harvest another will. My granary may burn, but grain in the soil will be safe and grow.'

If we sow the incorruptible seed of God's Word, we may be sure that His promise will be fulfilled: 'My Word shall not return unto me void but shall accomplish that which I please and prosper in that where to I sent it.' (Isa. 55. 11)

**1014 Space Travel.** In Antedeluvian times Enoch took right off and walked with God into the world of space. Abraham saw through the mysteries of time and grasped the pattern of the world to come, staking a claim therein. Elijah did not even have a count down when he took off into space. He just kept an appointment with God and mounted up in his chariot of fire. He was out of sight before anyone but Elisha knew what was happening.

Before the eyes of His disciples, from Mount Olivet our Lord Jesus was taken up into glory. Whether we die or remain until He returns, we who know Him will leave this little earth and be space-borne.

Earth satellites and moon rockets! These are child's play in comparison with God's place for his own in the world of space. God has always wanted us for Himself in the fullness of His universe. Faith opens to view the dimensions of a world to which no rocket will ever penetrate.
(Acts 1. 9)

**1015 Spending and Being Spent.** The prayer of the dedicated saint is:

*O Lord, please put me in Thy purse*
*And spend me somewhere in Thy universe.*

(2 Cor. 12. 15.)

**1016 Spirit—An Excellent.** Here are the outward expressions of an excellent spirit:

### i. Say Little!

*Winds the peaceful sea disturb and forests rend:*
*Give answer soft, venomed invective curb, and discord end*
*With grace, like sweet upon the bitter spirit.*

### ii. Serve All!

*The Master's plaudits to obtain: the Son divine*
*A slave became and shall remain: this mind be thine!*
*From this example let not earthly pride*
*Thy pure appreciative soul divide!*

### iii. Pass On!

*A pilgrim on thy heavenward way, seek not a name*
*Where others headlong rush into the fray for worldly fame!*
*Await thy Lord's 'Well done!' in quietness,*
*And not by words but actions love express.*

**1017 Spirit of God.** A new minister had come to minister in a certain church. His predecessor had introduced secular entertainments for his congregation, encouraged dancing among the young people to attract them, and organized fairs, festivals and bazaars to raise money. But the spirit of prayer and the operation of the Spirit of God were entirely absent.

The congregation was large and the members affluent. The new minister felt that it was all a deceptive external shell with true life absent. They had 'a name to live but were dead'. Accordingly, after much prayer, he began to preach against compromise with the world and the use of worldly methods, and to insist on a scriptural, spiritual life of prayer with the Holy Spirit in charge. As a result, his congregation dwindled and he emptied the building. A deputation of church wardens and others went to the bishop and protested. The wife of the bishop came to visit him and she enquired why he was following methods detrimental to the increase of the congregation.

He explained that the former ways were contrary to scripture, then, kneeling in prayer, earnestly asked light from the Lord. In the middle of the prayer, the lady said, 'Pray no longer: you are right and I am wrong.'

The number was reduced to two. They were in full sympathy and the three spent one and a half hours in prayer together, pleading with God to take charge by His Spirit of the church's witness. Soon a work of the Spirit began, and the place was filled with a new congregation. Some of the old members also returned. The Holy Spirit was recognized as the President in all the activities of the church. Boxes for offerings were placed at the door. The gospel was preached in its simplicity and souls were saved. God's blessing rested on the work. The men who had complained to the bishop were all converted, cleansed and filled with the Spirit of God. No appeals were made for money. They began the support of missionaries to other lands, and endeavoured to continue the Lord's work on apostolic lines.
(Eph. 5. 18; Acts 4. 31)

**1018 Spirit—The Holy.** The Holy Ghost from the day of Pentecost has occupied an entirely new position. The whole administration of the affairs of the Church since that day has devolved upon Him. . . . That day was the installation of the Holy Spirit as the Administrator of the Church in all things, which office He is to exercise according to circumstances at His discretion. Till the second coming of the Lord we live in the Pentecostal age and under the rule of the Holy Spirit.
(Acts 2. 32,33)

**1019 Spoiled Child.** Dr A. C. Dixon used to tell of a lady who had a very spoiled and wilful youngster. One day when a wasp flew in at the window, the boy, seeing its brilliant colours, began crying for it. At last the mother called to the servant who was tending the child 'What is that boy crying for? Will you please let him have it?' A few minutes later she was startled by a loud scream. 'What's the matter?' the mother exclaimed in alarm. 'He got what he wanted,' was the servant's calm reply.

**1020 Springs of Water.** While travelling in Norway one summer, we spent a day and a night on a little island off the eastern coast, to which we crossed from the mainland in a sailing-boat.

Soon after we arrived, our friends purposed to go for a walk, adding, 'Before we go anywhere else, we will show you the spring.' As we walked through the pine forest, we wondered what there was so special about this spring which we were going to see.

By-and-by we came out into an open part by the sea, and followed the shore for a distance; then we came to the spring. It was so small that we should certainly have passed it by had we been alone.

Just under the bank and only a few yards from the sea, was a little rocky basin, and into it the water came trickling in a tiny stream which seemed to come out of a hole in the rock. Our friends had brought a glass with them, and as we sat to rest we all drank of the cold sparkling water. They said, 'There is no water on the island so refreshing as this, and there is always water here in the hottest weather when all other springs are dried up, and in the coldest weather when all the water is frozen. It is always as you see it now; the rain does not increase it and the drought does not make it less.'

J. H. Lewis

(John 4. 14; 7. 37)

**1021 Stand Still.**

*O Lord, how can I stand,*
*When faithful servants weary in the fight,*
*When help is near and even day seems night,*
*With sorrows, yearnings, tears, o'er those who*
*    might*
*Yet stand for Thee?*

*Yea, Lord, I will obey,*
*For Thou hast promised those who wait on*
*    Thee*
*Shall strength renew; I'll look to Thee*
*For that which, unrevealed, shall yet be seen*
*Of that which Thou shalt do.*

*Yea, Lord, I can but rest,*
*Content to know Thy peace deep in my heart,*
*Thou who my wondrous heavenly lover art,*
*And then Thy rod the tossing seas shall part,*
*And I shall forward go.*

Shirley I. Woodfield

(Exod. 14. 13,15)

**1022 Stand Up for Jesus.** In Philadelphia, when Dudley Tyng preached to 5000 men, over 1000 confessed Christ. In the course of his sermon he said, 'I must tell my Master's errand and I would rather that this right arm were amputated at the trunk than that I should come short of my duty.'

During the following week he was involved in an accident when stroking a horse. His clothes became entangled in the cogs of the horse-powered corn sheller, his arm was mangled and he had to have it amputated. Shortly after, on his deathbed he said, 'Tell my brethren in the ministry to stand up for Jesus.' The following Sunday Dr Duffield took as his text the word 'Stand' in Ephesians 6. 14, and read the stanzas of a hymn he had written after the funeral.
(Eph. 6. 14)

**1023 Standards of Morality.** In 1963 Professor James Stewart, then Moderator of the Church of Scotland, wrote:

'The great moral ideal of beauty, goodness and truth cannot be tampered with by society, even if it is the most democratic in the world. Today the dangerous idea is abroad that moral standards are relative and not absolute, set by society and not given by God. Many eminent teachers are propagating this notion of moral standards set by society. In this way they may be playing into the hands of those who want to disrupt the moral standards of the country.'

Mr Phillips of Holyrood Church, Edinburgh, also spoke out:

'Society is corrupt and in desperate need of cleansing and healing. We call it a permissive society. It is well-named, for nothing is barred in belief or behaviour. History has shown that this is a frequent prelude to the decline and fall of empires and nations.'

Mr C. D. Alexander of Liverpool is even more forthright and searching:

'We are living in days of infamy and shame, and there are alarming tendencies in society. We are getting social rot in the community as the full effect of two generations without faith is being felt in Parliament and by the people, with bad and shameful laws being passed and the way of the transgressor, the Sodomite, the murderer, the bandit, the violent and the vicious made increasingly easy.'
(2 Tim. 3. 1,13)

**1024 Stars—Creator of the.** 'He made the stars also.'

Sir William Herschel, a Christian astronomer said, 'All human discoveries seem to be made only for the purpose of confirming more strongly the truths we get from on high, contained in the Sacred Writings.'

When a French infidel said to a Vendean peasant, 'We will pull down your churches, destroy your pictures, and demolish everything that reminds you of God,' the peasant replied, 'But you will leave us the stars.' Napoleon, when sailing on the Mediterranean toward Egypt, one night heard some of his officers deny the existence of God. Turning to them, and pointing to the cloudless heavens, he said, 'All very well, gentlemen! But who made the stars?'
(Gen. 1. 16; Ps. 19. 1)

**1025 Stars—Vastness of the.** Sir James Jeans commences one of his books with a staggering paragraph. He says, 'A few stars are known, which are hardly bigger than the earth, but the majority are so large that hundreds of thousands of earths could be packed inside each and have room to spare; here and there we come upon a giant star large enough to contain millions and milllions of earths. The total number of stars in the universe is probably something like the total number of grains of sand on all the sea shores of the world. Such is the littleness of our home in space, when measured up against the total substance of the universe.'
(Gen. 1. 16; Ps. 8. 3,4)

**1026 Step by Step.**

*He does not lead me year by year*
*Nor even day by day,*
*But step by step my path unfolds;*
*My Lord directs my way.*

*Tomorrow's plans I do not know,*
*I only know this minute;*
*But He will say, 'This is the way;*
*By faith now walk ye in it.'*

*And I am glad that it is so.*
*Today's enough to bear;*
*And when tomorrow comes, His grace*
*Shall far exceed its care.*

*What need to worry then, or fret?*
*The God who gave His Son*
*Holds all my moments in His hand*
*And gives them, one by one.*

Barbara C. Ryberg
(Ps. 37. 23; Prov. 20. 24)

**1027 Stoop of Love.** A Chinese Christian once was asked to tell the difference between Buddha, Confucius and Christ. He replied with an illustration. A man had wandered from the road and fallen into a hole so deep and slippery as to make escape impossible. He cried for help. Soon Buddha appeared and gazed down upon the helpless man in minutes of mute and comfortless contemplation. Finally he spoke and said, 'My poor man, such is the trickery of fate. Resign yourself to your doom.' With a shake of his head, he departed. Confucius came next and, seeing the man's plight, broke into a tirade. 'Fool! Why are you in the pit? Why did you stray from the road? Take my advice; if you get out of this pit, walk only in the centre of the road where there are no pits.'

The woeful cries of the man had but begun again when another came to the edge of the pit. Looking down, He saw the pitiful out-streched arms. Stripping the rich cloak from His back He leaped into the pit. Then the Son of God lifted the helpless man to His shoulders and bid him step up to the ground. When the man had scrambled to safety the Saviour said, 'Now, my son, take my cloak and go home.' So the love of God stooped to our misery. The Son of God not only gave His life to save us from the pit of sin, but He gave us the garment of His righteousness as well, and sends us on our journey to our home above.
(Luke 10. 33,34)

**1028 Stooping to Conquer.** When William the Conqueror landed in England, just prior to the great Battle of Hastings, he inadvertently slipped and fell upon his hands on the shore. His soldiers raised a loud cry of dismay, thinking that it was a sign of bad luck; but William replied, 'See, my lords, by the splendour of God, I have taken possession of

England with both my hands! It is now mine, and what is mine is yours.'

A greater than William the Conqueror came from heaven, humbling Himself even unto death, the death of the cross, where He wrought a mighty victory over Satan's forces as He stretched out His two hands. Those who trust in Him share His victory, for He says to them 'All mine is thine!'

(Phil. 2. 6-9)

## 1029   Story of the Saviour.

*'Twas Jesus my Saviour, the Lord from above,*
*Who came to display God's ineffable love:*
*My sins, red as crimson, He bore on the tree*
*And now, praise His name! there is pardon for*
   *me:*
*There's redemption and cleansing from sin*
   *through His blood.*
*And in Him, the Beloved, there's acceptance*
   *with God.*

*'Tis Jesus my Lord who arose from the grave,*
*Who lives, now exalted, the Mighty to save.*
*He succours us here with compassionate care*
*Till safely in glory, His Home we shall share.*
*Oh, what rapturous praise to our Lord shall*
   *resound*
*When with love in its fullness each heart shall*
   *abound.*

*Our praises shall rise to the Lamb that was slain;*
*Creator, Redeemer, the Prince that shall reign.*
*The earth will have peace in that glorious day*
*With evil restrained under Christ's righteous*
   *sway;*
*His authority owned as all men bow the knee*
*And confess with their tongue Jesus Christ*
   *Lord to be.*

                            James B. Naismith

(Phil. 2. 6-11)

## 1030   Strength of Love.
Rock is strong but iron cleaves it. Iron is strong but fire melts it. Fire is strong, but water quenches it. Water is strong, but clouds carry it away. Clouds are strong, but wind drives them. Winds are strong, but man can resist them. Man is strong, but fear casts him down. Fear is strong, but love casts out fear. Love is stronger: love is eternal.

*Love—strong as death, nay, stronger; love,*
   *mightier than the grave;*
*Broad as the earth and longer than ocean's*
   *wildest wave.*
*This is the love that sought us: this is the love*
   *that bought us:*
*This is the love that brought us*
*To gladdest day from saddest night,*
*From deepest shame to glory bright,*
*From depths of death to life's fair height,*
*From darkness to the joys of light.*

                            *Choice Gleanings*

(Song of Solomon 8. 6,7)

## 1031   Study of the Bible.
Luther said he studied the Bible in the same way as he gathered apples. First, he shook the whole tree that the ripest fruit might fall; then he climbed the tree and shook each limb; and when he had shaken each limb, he shook each branch, and after each branch every twig, and and then looked under every leaf. Let us search the Bible as a whole. Read it as you would read any other book, then study book after book, then chapters, paragraphs and texts.

(John 5. 39)

## 1032   Submission.
J. Hudson Taylor, founder of the China Inland Mission, is reputed to have said, 'The greatest mission in the world is Submission!' The most effective illustration of this is the reply of George Washington's mother to a distinguished French officer who at a banquet, asked her how she managed to rear such a splendid son. 'Sir,' she said, 'I taught him to obey.'

Submission to the claims of Christ brings remission of sins and admission into the family of God as His child.

(Ps. 86. 11)

## 1033   Substitution.
Returning home late one evening, the late Mr Harold St John found himself in a long queue waiting for a bus. When the bus arrived there was room for all in the queue except a well-dressed gentleman whom the conductor tried to prevent from boarding the bus, saying there was no seat available and standing was forbidden. The gentleman refused to alight, saying that his wife and children were on top and he had the money for their fares. The driver was called; a heated argument ensued; and driver and conductor announced that the bus would not proceed till the passenger had alighted.

Seeing that there might be considerable delay, Harold St John rose and addressed the people on the bus. 'Ladies and gentlemen,' he said, 'it looks as if we shall not get home very soon. The conductor is perfectly in order, for he is supporting the bye laws which forbid passengers standing on the bus. The passenger is equally right, for he is defending an older law, the law of humanity which forbids separating a man from his wife and children. I can see no way out except that I should give this gentleman my seat, then alight and wait for another bus. If I do this, the driver and conductor will be satisfied, the passenger will be content, and you will all get home in due time. Let me add one thing more. This is exactly what the Lord Jesus, my blessed Saviour has done for me, giving me His place in light and salvation, and taking the place due to me in death and darkness on the Cross.' As he alighted, the conductor was heard to say, 'Ain't he a kind bloke?'

(1 Pet. 3. 18)

**1034 Substitution Exemplified.** The tumbrils clattered over Paris streets, bringing victims of the Reign of Terror by the droves to the crowded dungeons. One night in July, 1794, an old man roamed the dark prison among his prisoner comrades. He came upon a sleeping figure at which he looked searchingly. Could it be? Yes, it was—his own son. Unknown to his father, the son had been seized and brought to this horrible place.

Overcome, the father sank down beside him, his heart mourning over the sad fate that had befallen his son. 'What can I do to save him?' he thought.

'We bear the same name,' he mused. 'Tomorrow I shall answer for him and go to the guillotine in his place.' Praying his son would not awaken, the father watched over him through the night. In the early hours of the morning three soldiers stamped into the dungeon. One called: 'Jean Simon de Loiserolle!'

The father sprang to his feet and answered clearly, 'Here!' On the way to the guillotine they passed through the bureau where the names were struck off. 'Jean Simon de Loiserolle, age thirty-seven?' the soldier intoned.

'That is my name,' answered the old man quickly, 'but my age is seventy-three.'

'Stupid mistake!' muttered the soldier, 'Seventy-three, not thirty-seven!' Seizing the pen, he made the correction and the father went to the guillotine where all was soon over.

The son awoke in the dungeon, expecting any moment to be called to his death. Finally, a fellow-prisoner told him: 'An old man watched beside you all night, and when the guard called your name this morning he answered for you and went to his death.'

'But I am Jean Simon de Loiserolle,' the son cried, but no one would listen. With bitter anguish he realised that his father had died for him. He waited, but three days passed; and with the execution of Robespierre, the Reign of Terror ended and the prisoners went free.

Jean Simon de Loiserolle, the son, solemnly vowed that every moment of his life should be worthy of his father's supreme sacrifice.

'Jesus Christ who loved me and gave Himself for me.'

(Gal. 2. 20)

**1035 Success out of Seeming Failure.** A Moravian missionary, George Smith, went to Africa. He had been there only a short time and had only one convert, a poor woman, when he was driven from the country. One day he was found dead. He had died praying for the dark continent. It seemed as if he had been a failure.

Yet, at the centenary of the founding of that mission, it was found that a company had found a copy of the Scriptures he had left in the place where he used to pray. They also found one aged woman who was his only convert. In summing up his brief life, they reckoned there were more than 13,000 living

converts from that life that had seemed a failure.

(Isa. 55. 11)

**1036 Succour When Needed.** At the battle of Crecy where Edward the Black Prince, then a youth of eighteen years of age, led the van, the king, his father, drew up a strong force on a rising ground and there watched the conflict, ready to send relief where it should be needed. The young prince, subjected to a heavy charge from the enemy and being in some danger, sent to his father for succour. As the king delayed sending it, the prince sent another messenger to request immediate assistance. To him the king replied:

'Go and tell my son that I am not so inexperienced a commander as not to know when succour is needed, nor so careless a father as not to send it.'

(1 Cor. 10. 13; Heb. 2. 17,18)

**1037 Sufferings of Christ—The.** T. T. Shields wrote, 'The sorrows of the Saviour challenge comparison; and the sacrifice of Calvary merits universal attention.'

Robert Browning called the sacrifice of Christ on the cross 'the transcendent act beside which the creation fades into a puny exercise of power'.

*There was never a Prince so royal,*
*So worthy of deathless fame:*
*There was never a friend so loyal—*
*Such an ocean of love in a name.*
*There were never such springs of sweetness,*
*Such streams of ineffable bliss,*
*Such powers of holy meekness*
*As welled in that heart of His,*
*Which moved His hands in weakness,*
*Overflowing His lips with grace,*
*Impelling His feet to mercy*
*And suffusing with love His face.*
*Yet never a friend did fathom*
*Such measureless depths of shame,*
*And never the vilest traitor*
*Did bear such a burden of blame.*
*There were never such rivers of sorrow,*
*There were never such floods of grief*
*As flowed from the hearts of sinners*
*Into His for their relief.*
*And where is the heart so hardened,*
*And who is so vile as he*
*Who beholdeth the Saviour suffer*
*And saith, 'It is nothing to me'?*

(Lam. 1. 12)

**1038 Summer Unending.** As Dr Rees was about to enter the pulpit to preach for the last time, a friend said to him 'You are whitening fast, Dr Rees!' The old Welsh pastor did not reply, but at the close of his sermon he said, 'There is a wee white flower that comes up through the earth at this season of the year, sometimes through the snow and frost. We are glad to see the snowdrop because it proclaims that summer is near at hand.

'A friend has reminded me that I am whitening fast. But do not heed that, brethren. To me it is proof that I shall have done soon with the cold east winds of earth, and that my eternal summer is at hand!'
(Song of Solomon 2. 11,12)

## 1039   Superlatives of Life.

*The greatest wisdom is to know*
*The love of God revealed below,*
*To know His Son who came in grace*
*And died to save a guilty race*
*From sin and endless woe.*

*The greatest blessing is to have*
*A living hope beyond the grave,*
*To have, when this short life is done,*
*A place with Christ beyond the sun*
*Who came in love to save.*

*The greatest joy that fills the breast*
*Is peace with God, through Christ possessed.*
*It makes the heart with rapture swell,*
*For oh! 'tis joy unspeakable*
*To be thus fully blessed.*

(Eph. 3. 19)

## 1040   Supersensitive.

*I've asked the Lord to take from me*
*The supersensitivity*
*That robs the soul of joy and peace*
*And causes fellowship to cease;*
*The things that people do and say*
*To foster hurt along the way.*
*I trust that by His Spirit sweet*
*I may those very people meet,*
*And show them that His love in me*
*Has won another victory.*

*The dart which carelessly they threw*
*Much closer to the Saviour drew*
*This heart, inclined to feel the pain*
*Of idle words they spoke in vain.*
*I asked him why it hurt so much*
*When they upon my life should touch:*
*Then quickly He revealed to me*
*My supersensitivity.*
*'Just leave it here,' He seemed to say,*
*'The victory can be yours today.'*

*'Remember that each idle word*
*My listening ear has also heard.*
*Before you brought that hurt to me*
*My eyes the one who spoke did see.*
*The victory is yours today*
*If you will put that hurt away,*
*Remembering that love will grow*
*If you will only show it.' So,*
*I've asked the Lord to take from me*
*All supersensitivity.*

*Ministry in Focus*

(1 Cor. 13. 5)

**1041   Supper of Remembrance.** These are minutes when the soul realises the presence of the Lord in a measure beyond all other hours. Then it is that the love of Christ melts our hearts and causes our eyes to overflow. Then it is that we look at the Man of Calvary. Then it is that we stoop to kiss the Conqueror's feet. Then it is that we see afresh the wounded hands, feet and side, and say with Thomas, 'My Lord and my God!'

J. B. Watson

(Luke 22. 19,20)

**1042   Supper—The Last.** A few days in Milan gave us time to see the famous painting of the Last Supper by Leonardo da Vinci. Actually it is done on a wall and is 24 feet long by 12 feet high. It is remarkable that when in the war bombs hit the building attached to the church, the walls at the ends of the building were the only parts not badly damaged. The other walls and roof were destroyed. The painting shows the twelve disciples seated on either side of the Lord and they are asking Him, 'Is it I?' while Peter is shown whispering to John to tell him to ask the Lord who will be the traitor. It is of course a work of man, but very cleverly done, and it certainly reminds us as we look on it of that sad hour when one of the twelve betrayed the Lord.

Hundreds of thousands of tourists visit this church to see the famous painting. When we visit places like these and those in Palestine which are called 'Holy Places', it brings real sadness to the heart to see how carelessly people look at places that remind them that Christ was once here, and yet so few seem to face the challenge of His life and death and bow their hearts to Him in surrender.

A. L. Goold

(John 13. 23-25)

**1043   Supper—The Lord's.** This is a simple ordinance, an act of remembrance and of holy communion. Paul calls it 'The Lord's Supper': Other names given to it are the Eucharist (thanksgiving), the Sacrament (sacred observance), Holy Communion.

The Council of Trent, composed of the Roman Church hierarchy, stated:
'By consecration of the bread and wine there takes place a conversion of the entire substance of the bread into the body of Christ, and the entire substance of the wine into the substance of His blood. This conversion is conveniently and appropriately known as Transubstantiation.'

Our objection to this statement is that the Lord Jesus said, 'This is My body'—not 'this becomes My body'.

The Lutheran church holds and teaches that in the Lord's Supper the body and blood of Christ are truly offered with those things that appear, namely the bread and wine. This is called Consubstantiation, but this too has no foundation in Scripture.

John Calvin considered the ordinance to be a special channel of blessing, but denied both transubstantiation and consubstantiation. Zwingli said, 'I believe that all the sacraments, so far from conferring grace, do not in themselves even distribute it. The Lord's Supper is a mode of recalling the death of Christ and confessing afresh our faith in Him.'

'In remembrance of me:' 'Ye do show forth the Lord's death till He come.'
(1 Cor. 11. 26)

### 1044 Supplies Continual.

*I praise Thee, Lord, and I am ever thankful*
*To know my flour barrel ne'er shall empty be;*
*And I am grateful that my cruse of oil*
*Shall ne'er run dry, for 'tis supplied by Thee.*
*Grant me assurance, Lord, that when supplies*
*   are lowest,*
*When in my heart I need so much to know*
*That every time I go unto my barrel*
*There'll be enough, even though it may be low.*

*And when I lift my little cruse of oil*
*But fear to tip it o'er lest it be dry,*
*Teach me to trust and simply turn it over*
*To see once more Thy bountiful supply.*
*Help me, O Lord, to never, never doubt Thee,*
*For Thou dost graciously supply my need,*
*And every day my barrel is replenished*
*And I have flour and oil enough indeed.*

                *Choice Gleanings*
(1 Kings 17. 16)

### 1045 Supplies Daily.

I have one preacher that I love better than any other on earth; it is a little tame robin that preaches to me daily. I put its crumbs upon my window sill, especially at night. It hops onto the window sill when it wants its supply and takes as much as it desires to satisfy its need. From thence it always hops to a little tree close by and lifts up its voice to God and sings its carol of praise and gratitude, tucks its little head under its wing and goes fast to sleep, and leaves tomorrow to look after itself.

                Martin Luther

*The birds without barn or storehouse are fed;*
*From them I have learned to trust for my bread.*

(Job. 12. 7)

### 1046 Surrender—Full.

J. W. Van De Venter was for some years a supervisor of art in the Public Schools of Sharon, Pennsylvania. As he had an outstanding evangelistic gift and was a keen personal worker, friends kept urging him to give up art teaching and become an evangelist. For five years he wavered, then, as he narrated in his own words, 'at last the pivotal hour of my life came, and I surrendered all. A new day was ushered into my life; I became an evangelist, and God caused me to sing songs I had never sung before.' One of these was the hymn, 'I surrender all'.
(Rom. 6. 13)

### 1047 Sweet Perfume.

*The perfume of a flower*
*Distils upon the air,*
*Its sweetness calls attention*
*To beauty hidden there.*

*So small and very fragile*
*Amid the tangled grass,*
*The bloom might go unnoticed*
*By those who quickly pass.*

*It gently gives a fragrance,*
*No effort on its part,*
*It's just the natural outcome*
*Of purity of heart.*

*The scent of flowers and spices*
*Float up to heaven above*
*When rising from the essence*
*Of God's own nature—love.*

*Frankincense the magi brought*
*Unto that manger bare,*
*Perfumed that humble stable*
*—And God Himself was there.*

*And Mary's costly ointment*
*Its odour spread abroad,*
*Refreshed the weary Saviour,*
*It showed she loved her Lord.*

*Then aromatic spices*
*Sweet sadness gently made,*
*Wrapped round the Saviour's body*
*As in the tomb He's laid.*

*So thus a Christian growing*
*In grace, from day to day,*
*Can emanate a sweetness*
*In a delightful way.*

              R. A. Claydon
(John 12. 3; 20. 39)

### 1048 Sword of the Spirit.

Dr Caesar Malan of Switzerland travelled in the same compartment of a Paris bound train as an infidel. The latter began to argue with Dr Malan about the Bible and Christianity. To each and all of the infidel's arguments Dr Malan replied with an exact quotation from the Scriptures, not once expressing his own opinion or trying to explain the Scriptures he quoted. In exasperation the infidel exclaimed, 'But I don't believe the Bible. What's the sense in your quoting it to me?' To this the Swiss doctor replied, 'If ye believe not that I am He, ye shall die in your sins'—the words of the Lord Jesus.

Ten years later Dr Malan received a letter from Paris. The writer—the former infidel—reminding him of their conversation in the train so long ago, said, 'You simply used the sword of the Spirit and stabbed me through and through. Every time I tried to parry the blade, you gave me another stab with the sword until I realized I was not fighting you but God.'

We cannot wield the sword of the Spirit unless we know how to use it: and we cannot use it unless we are familiar with it; therefore know your Bible.
(John 8. 24; Matt. 4. 4,7,10; Heb. 4. 12)

**1049 Sympathy—Royal.** Not far from Balmoral Castle there lived an aged widow whose only son was in feeble health. Queen Victoria used to visit that humble cottage and through her influence the sickly youth was sent to a warmer clime in the hope that his health might be restored. One morning, however, a letter in a stranger's handwriting conveyed to the widowed mother the sad news of her son's death in that distant land.

When the Queen heard of it, she hastened to the widow's side. The royal carriage drove up to the lowly dwelling and the neighbours saw the queen enter, and after a time leave the cottage. Curious to know what her Majesty had said or done, they asked the widow what the queen had said to her. She replied, 'She didna say a word. She jist sat doon by ma side, took ma haun in hers and squeezed it lovingly. Then the queen grat an' I grat, but naither o' us could say a word.'

That grip of the royal hand and the queen's silent tears spoke louder than words. They expressed the deep sympathy of one who herself was a widow and a bereaved mother, and could therefore sympathize with the sorrowing widow.
(Rom. 12. 15)

**1050 Synchronism.** A gentleman tells of an interesting visit to the observatory of Harvard University, just after a new astronomical instrument had been purchased. According to astronomical calculations contained in a little book ten years old, which calculations were based upon observations thousands of years old, a star was due in a certain position in the heavens at 5.20 p.m. When the hour drew near, the instrument was at once set in the determined position, and prone on his back under the eyepiece lay the enthusiastic professor. It was agreed that when the star crossed the spiderweb line streched across the lens of the instrument, the professor who was watching should pronounce the word 'Here!' It was also agreed that the assistant who watched the second-hand of the clock should let a hammer fall upon a marble table the instant the clock indicated 5.20. There was an impressive silence in the laboratory. But God's earth was moving through space and revolving upon its axis as He bade it do ages ago. Suddenly two sounds broke the stillness. One was the voice of the professor, saying 'Here', the other the sound of the hammer on the table, the two sounds simultaneous—at 5.20 p.m. If God guides the stars and calls them all by their names, does He not guide and care for each individual who obeys Him?
(Ps. 8. 3,4)

**1051 Tale-Bearers at Work.**

*A wood fire burns up quick and bright,*
*Sends forth a warm bright glow:*
*But soon more wood must be thrown in*
*Or out the fire will go.*

*So with the strife that spreads like fire:*
*It very soon will cease*
*If no tale-bearers are at work;*
*Then will come perfect peace.*

May Gorrie

(Prov. 11. 13; 20. 19)

**1052 Tale-Bearers—Dealing With.** A certain preacher had on his desk a special notebook labelled—COMPLAINTS OF MEMBERS AGAINST OTHER MEMBERS. When one of his people called to dilate on the faults of another, he would say, 'Well, here's my complaint book. I'll write down what you say and you can sign it. Then, when the time comes for me to take the matter up, I shall know what I expect you to testify to.'

The sight of the open book and the ready pen had its effect. 'Oh no, I couldn't sign anything like that,' and no entry was made. That preacher had his book for forty years, opened it probably about one hundred times, and never wrote a line in it.
(Prov. 26. 20; Matt. 18. 15)

**1053 Tale-Bearing.** The lines about the 'three narrow gates' have been often quoted:

*If you are tempted to reveal a tale someone*
*to you has told*
*About another, make it pass, before you speak,*
*three gates of gold,*
*Three narrow gates: First, 'Is it true?' Then,*
*'Is it needful?'*
*In your mind*
*Give truthful answers: and the next is last*
*and narrowest:*
*'Is it kind?'*

To these a few other lines may be added:

*And if to reach your lips at last it passes*
*through these gateways three,*
*Then you may tell, nor ever fear what the*
*result of speech may be.*

*A brother's future is at stake.*
*Before from him his name you take,*
*Ask yourself ere it is too late,*
*'Is it kind?'*
*For—better far be true and kind*
*And always act with Christlike mind.*

(Titus 3. 2; Prov. 26. 22)

**1054 Tarsus City.** Tarsus was the birthplace of the Apostle Paul who called it 'no mean city', one of no little importance. There in his youth Saul, whose name later was changed to Paul, imbibed Greek culture and logic. Paul was a Jewish Rabbi educated in the College of Gamaliel, a Greek scholar who could quote Greek poetry, and a Roman citizen.

The city of Tarsus was situated on the river

Cydnus, in the island of Cilicia and ten miles inland. Ramsay describes it as 'a city with its feet resting on a great inland harbour and its head reaching up to the hills'. In the middle of the ninth century B.C. it was raided by the Assyrian conqueror, Shalmaneser III. Later it became a border-line city between the Syrian and the Roman Empires. In 171 B.C. Antiochus Epiphanes conceded a large measure of autonomy to the city, and its constitution was reorganized to include the establishment of a ward of Jewish citizens, to whom Paul refers as his kinsmen.

The Romans first entered the region in 100 B.C. Tarsus was incorporated in the Roman Empire. The orator, Cicero, became Governor of Cilicia in 51 B.C. It was probably under Pompey that Roman citizenship was conferred on Tarsian Jews. In this University town, the resort of learned men, learning and debates flourished, and a school of Stoic philosophy was set up. In his youthful days in Tarsus Saul doubtless learnt the trade of leather working and weaving tent cloth from goat's hair which was called 'cilicium' from the name of the island.

(Acts 18. 3; 21. 39)

**1055 Teacher—The Best.** The world's teachers have hedged themselves about with a narrow circle of disciples, leaving the masses to take their chance. The Pharisee says that the people that do not know the law are cursed (John 7. 49). Plato says that it is not easy to find the Father of all existence; and when He is found, it is impossible to make Him known to all. Celsus charges this against Christianity, that woollen manufacturers, shoemakers, and curriers had become its zealous supporters. But it is the glory of Jesus that He pillaged truth's deepest mines of their golden ore, and minted it into common coin, which He threw in lavish handfuls among men. Only when they refused to hear did He hide His meaning in dark sentences; but wherever there was willingness to receive, He was prodigal to bestow. He set Himself to enwrap His teachings in the fascinating story, the pithy proverb, the sharp antithesis, the methods of speech dear to the crowds of every age, never lowering the truth by its dress, but hallowing the dress, just as common articles are counted heirlooms because once used by the hands of a prince.

F. B. Meyer

(Matt. 7. 28, 29)

**1056 Tears of the Preacher.** It is written about George Whitefield that when preaching to some coal miners who had just come from the mine, there were white streaks down their cheeks where tears had washed the coal dust. The word had penetrated their hearts and broken them down: but it first penetrated the heart of Whitefield, and broke him down.

Dr Timothy Stone visited the old church of Robert Murray McCheyne and was shown round by the aged sexton. Leading Dr Stone into the study and pointing to the chair, the sexton said, 'Sit there: that is where Mr McCheyne used to sit.' Then he continued, 'Now put your elbows on the table and bow your head upon your hands!' The visitor did so. 'Now let the tears flow; that is the way the minister used to do.'

Dr Stone was next taken into the pulpit, and the old sexton said, 'Stand there and lean your elbows on the pulpit. Put your face in your hands.' This done, the sexton continued, 'Now let the tears flow, as Mr McCheyne used to do.' Then the old man added a testimony which gripped the heart of his hearer, as he listened to the trembling voice saying, 'He called down the power of God upon Scotland, and it is with us still.'

(Luke 19. 41,42; Acts 20. 19)

**1057 Temptations Overcome.** Dr F. W. Boreham tells of a certain small town whose governing body decided to have a canal running down its central street. The bed was dug, and the city fathers thought they now had their canal. But soon a fungoid weed began to grow profusely in the canal bed, preventing the passage of boats. All sorts of remedies were suggested; acid was poured in but the weed, after disappearing for a time, began to grow more thickly than ever. The attempt was made to hack at the weed and uproot it, but soon it grew back as strong as before. Then some bright person suggested that willow trees be planted on the banks of the canal, and the weed disappeared. The nourishment that otherwise would have fed the weed now went to sustain the willow tree.

The incident has its parallel in real life. Some of the companions of the venerable Bede in north-east England came to him one day and said, 'We are harassed by many temptations which appeal to us so often and so strongly that they give us no rest. You do not seem to be troubled in this way, and we should like to know your secret. Don't these temptations that harass our souls ever come to you?' The old saint listened, smiled and said, 'I too know something of the temptations you speak of. But when temptations come knocking at the door of my heart, I always answer, "This place is occupied" and that is an end of it.'

(Rev. 3. 20)

**1058 Tenacity.**

*Somebody said it couldn't be done,*
*But they with a chuckle replied:*
*That maybe it couldn't, but at any rate*
*They wouldn't say 'NO' till they'd tried.*
*So they buckled right in with a bit of a grin—*
*If they worried, they hid it!*
*And they started to sing as they started the*
*   thing*
*That couldn't be done; and they did it.*

(Eccl. 9. 10)

**1059 Tent Folded Up.** Alexander Henderson, who died on August 16th, 1946, said, as he looked forward to being absent from the body, 'Never schoolboy more longed for the breaking-up than I do to have leave of this world.'

Both Paul and Peter use the figure of folding up a tent or tabernacle at death.

*Fold up the tent! The sun is in the west;*
*The house was only lent for my apprenticement,*
*And God knows best.*
*Fold up the tent!*
*Its pole all broken and its cover rent;*
*Its work is done.*

(2 Cor. 5. 1; 2 Pet. 1. 14)

**1060 Testimony of a Famous Comedian.** Dr G. W. Truett, in *The Prophet's Mantle*, published in the U.S.A., narrates this incident in the life of Sir Harry Lauder, the Scottish comedian.

'Harry Lauder and I were one day asked to be guests of three hundred officers during the First World War. Harry had just lost his son in the war in France. The men were very fond of the comedian, for he always entertained them; so they said to him, "Harry, we want you to sing for us: sing 'Comin' through the rye'." He said, "I canna sing for you, boys, I cannot sing. John, my boy, is dead out yonder in the field. I cannot sing today, but if you'll let me, I'll preach a little to you."

'Then we heard a sermon the like of which one rarely ever hears. He said, "Men, when I found John dead, the idol of my heart, John on whom I had built all my hopes, I had the choice of three roads: I could take the road of grief, or I could take the road of despair and commit suicide, or I could take the road of Jesus and give up to Him, and that is what I have done." With these few words he marvellously swayed that crowd of three hundred Army officers, and held them.'

(John 14. 6)

**1061 Testimony of a Polish Soldier.** I had the following experience in my early years during the first years of the last World War. Polish soldiers were billeted in the surrounding area, and a friend and I, both sixteen years of age, obtained literature in the Polish language from Mr Alex. McGregor and distributed it among the exiled soldiers. They were delighted to receive literature in their mother tongue.

No apparent results were seen from this distribution, and it was not until 1958— almost thirty years later—that we heard that the Lord had blessed this service. A friend, returning from a visit to Poland, told of a very active evangelical pastor he had met. Apparently he is being used greatly by the Lord in reaching his fellow-countrymen with the gospel. He gave his testimony of conversion to my friend, telling of being billeted in East Fife, homesick and almost in despair, when two 'children' came to visit the camp with evangelistic literature and New Testaments.

A few days later he was drafted to the battle-front, but in the meantime he had found the Saviour. He still possessed and treasured the tracts and New Testaments which had been handed to him so long before.

Alex. Allan

(Isa. 55. 11)

**1062 Testimony of an Old Soldier.** An old Confederate soldier from North Carolina, being in Philadelphia, visited John Wanamaker's Bible Class. At the close of the lesson an opportunity was given for testimonies, and a number of 'Grand Army' men took part. The old Southerner also gave his testimony. He said:

'Here is an old rebel who fought you North-erners hard in the war, and you beat him; but he doesn't have any hatred for you on that account. He loves you as fervently as he fought you in days gone by.'

The effect was electric. The old man's words of love captured every Yankee in the crowd.

(1 Pet. 1. 22)

**1063 Thankfulness.** Matthew Henry, the famous scholar and Bible commentator, was once accosted by thieves and robbed of his purse. He wrote these words in his diary:

'Let me be thankful first, because I was never robbed before; second, because, although they took my purse, they did not take my life; third, although they took my all, it was not much; and fourthly, because it was I who was robbed, not I who robbed.'

(1 Thess. 5. 18)

**1064 Thanksgiving.** During the memorable days of Dunkirk, a vicar walked into his church one summer evening and was surprised to find a small boy on his knees. After a while the boy stood up and hurried toward the door. At the door the vicar smiled and asked the boy what he had been doing. 'Sir,' was the reply, 'I've been coming every evening this week. You see, I was afraid my Daddy might be left on Dunkirk beaches, so I came to ask God to bring him safely home. He has: and so I came along this time just to say "Thank you, God!".'

(Phil 4. 6)

**1065 Thanksgiving.**

*As you seek for many blessings when you kneel*
*    in prayer,*
*Don't forget to add your thanks for gifts*
*    already there.*
*Great the blessings we receive as each new day*
*    unfolds,*
*Things we often take for granted, precious far*
*    than finest gold.*

*For the dawn and light of day and for the sun's*
*    warm glow,*
*For the silent dew that drops upon the earth*
*    below,*

*For the fresh sweet air we're breathing, for the
   birds that sing*
*For the growing trees and flowers and for the
   crystal spring;*

*For the golden sands that fringe around the
   sea so blue,*
*For the mountains and the hills, the stars and
   moonbeams too;*
*For the greatest gift of all, God's well-beloved
   Son*
*Who died on Calvary's cruel cross to save a
   world undone.*

*Never forget to offer thanks. Nothing could
   ever buy*
*All these many priceless blessings sent from
   God on high.*
                            May Gorrie
(Ps. 92. 1; 107. 1)

**1066 Thieves—Two Crucified.** As our Lord
Jesus hung on the cross between two thieves,
one on one side derided him: the other on the
other side decided to trust Him; and Jesus in
the centre divided them. So men are divided
for time and eternity by their attitude to the
crucified Christ.

Dr Alexander Smellie said of the thief who
repented and trusted Jesus, 'In the morning
the penitent thief was out of Christ: at noonday
he was in Christ: in the evening he was with
Christ.'

Dr Alexander Whyte said of him, 'This man
took heaven at a leap—from earth through
space to paradise.'

Is someone saying, 'I'm all right? You need
not trouble your head about me. I shall go
in for enjoying life while it lasts, and then at
the end, I quite mean to be saved—like the
dying thief, you know.'

'Yes, I see; but when the end comes what
dying thief will you be like? There were two of
them, you remember.'
(Luke 23. 42,43)

**1067 Thirst—Dying Of.** Seven young men
set out in a truck to hunt gazelle. They did not
return. At dawn next day planes and lorries
began the search. By noon hope that they could
be found alive in the stifling heart of that waste
of sand, scrub and stone, known as the Sahara,
was dwindling, but the search went on. At
three o'clock there was great excitement; an
abandoned lorry had been sighted. Later, three
miles from the lorry, three survivors out of an
original party of seven were found. They were
half dead and nearly mad.

Immediately the struggle to save their lives
began. While fluid dropped directly into their
veins, their bodies were washed repeatedly
with iced water. Then, in answer to the rescuers'
appeal, a helicopter arrived. Carefully and
gently the three men were placed aboard and
whisked away for further treatment.

The agonies of thirst suffered by these men
defies description. Few people have ever
experienced anything comparable and survived.
Yet, this is not the worst type of thirst. Physical
thirst, however tense, ends with this life.
Spiritual thirst can go on into eternity.

When on earth, the Lord Jesus Christ gave
a most graphic description of a man who left
this life with his thirst unquenched. On earth
that man had lived a life of luxury, surrounded
by every material comfort. His pre-occupation
with material things had crowded out any
thought of the life to come and preparation
for it. But the day came when he had to leave
this world and all the advantages he had
known here. He then discovered his great
mistake, for although he had been rich on
earth he now found himself a pauper. He
who had the choicest vintage on earth found that
he could not secure a drop of cold water to
cool his tongue.
(Luke 16. 24)

**1068 Thirst Quenched.** Entering a hotel in
America, a thirsty commercial traveller noticed
a drinking fountain with the invitation inscribed
above, 'Stoop and drink.' When he reached it,
he put out his hand to turn the water on but
found no handle. Then he looked for a button
to press or a plug to switch on, but found none.
The invitation seemed to mock him. Seeing no
other way, he then stooped and, as he did so,
the cold, clear water flowed and he was able
to drink. The fountain was controlled by an
electric eye so arranged that when a certain
beam of light was interrupted, a switch was
operated which opened the faucet.
(John 7. 37; Rev. 21. 6)

**1069 Thirst Quenched.** David Brainerd, who
became an orphan at 14, later a powerful
missionary, and who died at the age of 29, was
irritated by the text—'If any man thirst, let
him come unto me and drink'. At the age of
21 he felt like a man reeling on the edge of a
precipice. 'It seemed to me I was totally lost!'
he said. Reading a book entitled *A Guide to
Christ*, he came on the text again, and in a
greatly distressed and bewildered state of mind
and soul, he asked, 'What is it to believe?'
Again, on July 12, 1738, he was challenged
by the same text; and he saw there was only
one condition—'Thirst': only one command—
'Come': and only one way to satisfaction—
'Drink': and he came to Jesus and drank of
the life-giving stream. The text that had
challenged him now captivated him. In 1745,
when a young consumptive, he preached on
it again and again to North American Indians.
(John 7. 37)

**1070 Thoughts and Words.** There is an
eastern proverb—'Of thine unspoken word
thou art master; thy spoken word is master of
thee.' That just means that so long as we keep
a thought in our minds, it is our own, but if we
express that thought in audible words, it is
ours no longer. We can never retrieve it, and

it becomes a power for good or evil, as the case may be.

*Boys, flying kites, haul in their white-winged birds*
*But you can't do that when you're flying words.*
*Thoughts unexpressed may sometimes drop back dead,*
*But naught can kill them when they've once been said.*

(Ps. 34. 13; 1 Pet. 3. 10)

### 1071   Time Lost.

*Lost! Lost! Lost! A gem of countless price,*
*Cut from the living rock and graved in paradise,*
*Set round with three times eight large diamonds, clear and bright;*
*And each with sixty smaller ones, all changeful as the light.*

                                    Mrs L. H. Sigourne

(Ps. 90. 12)

*Grim Time moves on, and as we pass*
*Another milestone on life's way*
*And face the dim, outstretching years,*
*We hear our pitying Father say:*

*'Dwell not upon the futile past;*
*You may retrieve lost yesterdays:*
*I will restore the locusts' prey*
*And fill your lips with joyous praise.'*

*O trust your Saviour's boundless grace*
*Who pardons the remorseful years,*
*And let His sun shine on your face*
*And make a rainbow of your tears.*

                                    Agnes Gilmour Guthrie

(Joel 2. 25)

There is another side to the picture—for the unrepentant and unbelieving:

*If you in the morning throw minutes away,*
*You can't pick them up in the course of the day*
*You may hurry and scurry, and flurry and worry,*
*You've lost them for ever, for ever and aye.*

### 1072   Time—Redeeming the.
If you would redeem the time, begin the moment your eyes are open in the morning. Let no idle, foolish, hurtful thoughts be harboured for an instant, but begin at once to pray and to praise God, and to meditate on His glories, His goodness, His faithfulness and truth, and your heart will soon burn within you and bubble up with joy.
                                    S. L. Brengle

Chilo, one of the seven sages, when asked what was the hardest thing for a man to do, replied, 'To use and employ a man's time well!'
(Eph. 5. 16)

### 1073   Time—Stewardship of.

*Time is indeed a precious boon,*
*But with the boon a task is given:*
*The heart must learn its duty well*
*To man on earth and God in heaven.*

John Wesley was asked, 'Supposing you knew you were to die at 12 o'clock tomorrow night, how would you spend the intervening time?'

'Why, just as I intend to spend it now. I should preach this evening at Gloucester and again at 5 tomorrow morning. After that I should ride to Shaftesbury, preach in the afternoon and meet the societies in the evening. I should then repair to Martin's house, converse and pray with the family, as usual retire to my room at 10 o'clock, commend myself to my heavenly Father, lie down to rest and wake up in glory.'
(2 Cor. 5. 5,9)

### 1074   Time To Trust.

*When nothing whereon to lean remains,*
*When strongholds crumble to dust,*
*When nothing is sure but that God still reigns—*
*That is the time to trust.*
*'Tis better to walk by faith than sight*
*In this plan of yours and mine,*
*And the pitch black night when there's no other light,*
*Is the hour for faith to shine.*

\*   \*   \*

*I cannot understand the why and wherefore of a thousand things,*
*The crosses, the annoyances, the daily stings;*
*I cannot understand—but I can trust;*
*For perfect trusting perfect comfort brings.*

*I cannot see the end, the hidden meaning of each trial sent,*
*The pattern into which each tangled thread is bent;*
*I cannot see the end—but I can trust;*
*And in God's changeless love I am content.*

(Ps. 56. 3,11)

### 1075   Times—In God's Hand.

*Those twining threads that seem to tangle so,*
*Those winding paths that into shadows go,*
*Those broken chords and scattered notes that stray,*
*The seeming chance and mischance of life's day,*
*MY TIMES!*

*The weary hours that were so full of pain,*
*The days of joy that cannot come again,*
*Dark moments of suspense that slowly pass,*
*Sweet moments that, like daisies, star life's grass—*
*MY TIMES ARE IN HIS HAND!*

*Can the threads tangle which His fingers hold?*
*Can paths lead nowhere which His love controlled?*
*These drifting melodies His theme fulfil,*
*And chance and change are bounded by His will—*
*HIS HAND!*

*The hand that touched the leper in his need,*
*The tender hand that shields the bruised reed,*
*The mighty hand that brought the sea to calm,*
*The hand that bears the nail-print in its palm—*
*HIS HAND!*

*MY times upon that nail-print safely rest,*
*Close-folded in that hand that gives the best:*
*My 'how' and 'when' and 'wherefore' come to*
   *me,*
*Stamped with the love that went to Calvary.*
*MY TIMES ARE IN HIS HAND!*

                         Eva E. Ferguson
(Ps. 31. 15)

An African translation of 'My times are in Thy hand'—'My hows and whens and wherefores are in Thy hand.'

**1076 Tithing.** Years ago a young man knelt with his pastor and prayed, and he vowed to God to tithe his income. His first week's pay was £2, and he freely gave his tithe of twenty pence. Later on, as he grew older, his income increased and his tithe became £1.50 a week, and then £2 a week. He moved to another city where the Lord greatly prospered him, and his tithe pushed up to—first £10 a week, then £20, then £40, and finally £100 a week.

He became troubled over how much he was giving, so he sent word to his old pastor to come and see him. The pastor came, and at first they had a good time talking over old days. Finally, the prosperous business man came to his point. 'Do you remember the promise I made to the Lord years ago to tithe? Well, how can I be released from that?'

'Why do you want to be released?' asked the pastor.

'It's like this,' explained the man, 'when I first made the promise, I only had to give twenty pence a week; but now it is £100, and I can't afford to give away money like that.'

The pastor said that he doubted if it was right to ask God to release the man from his vow, but he said, 'I'll tell you what we can do. We can get down on our knees and ask the Lord to shrink your income down to the point where you again will only have to give Him twenty pence a week.'
(Gen. 28. 20)

**1077 Tithing.** John D. Rockefeller, Snr., was once asked if he tithed. He replied, 'Yes, I tithe. My first wages amounted to $1.50 per week. The first week I took the $1.50 home to my mother and she held the money in her lap and explained to me that she would be happy if I gave a tenth of it to the Lord. I did, and from that week to this day I have tithed every dollar that God has entrusted to me. If I had not tithed the first dollar I made, I would not have tithed the first million dollars I made. Train the children to tithe and they will grow up to be faithful stewards of the Lord.'
(Gen. 14. 20)

**1078 Together With God.** God never gives a command without giving with it the power to obey. A Scottish laird gave his old servant, Donald, a little farm. He said, 'Donald, I am going to give you that farm that you may work it for yourself and spend the rest of your days on your own property.' Donald replied, 'It's nae guid to gie me the fairm; I hae nae capital to stock it.' The laird looked at him and said, 'I think I can manage stock also.' 'Oh weel!' said Donald, 'if it's you an' me for it, I think we'll manage!'

                       G. Campbell Morgan
(Mark 16. 20)

**1079 Tokens and Wonders.** Most banks in India adopt the 'token' system for the payment of cheques. The Accounts section scrutinise the document and pass it for payment, but the Cash section are interested in the token number marked on the cheque and pay cash to the person who presents the small brass disc bearing the same number.

In Psalm 135. 9 we read, 'Who sent tokens and wonders into the midst of thee, O Egypt, upon Pharaoh and upon all his servants.' History, in Judaism, reveals that God first gave tokens and then did wonders on behalf of His people. The token was just a small assurance, like the brass disc in the bank, of the later and greater wonder that God was going to reveal—like the money given in exchange for the token from behind the counter. We must cash in on our tokens and draw upon God's wonders which He waits to work on our behalf.

                       S. J. W. Chase
(Exod. 4. 30)

**1080 Tomb—Most Magnificent.** No one who has visited the Taj Mahal in Agra, North India, can fail to be impressed by its magnificence and beauty. It is considered to be one of the world's most beautiful buildings, and after three hundred years retains its majestic splendour and whiteness.

Its name means 'Crown of the Palace'. The Mogul Emperor, Shah Jehan, had it built as a mausoleum for his favourite wife, Muntaz Mahal who died in 1611 at the age of 39. Its construction occupied nearly two decades and it cost what today would be the equivalent of twelve million pounds sterling. The domed tomb, with its four minarets, has an exterior of white marble and in its carved marble gates precious stones from every part of the Indian Empire are inset.

Over the tomb of Muntaz Mahal, in the Arabic language and script, are inscribed the lines:

             *     *     *

*I thought not that the sun could die*
*Nor stars from their bright spheres could fall;*
*Nor thought I that from earth could fly*
*The spirit of Muntaz Mahal.*

The Taj Mahal is an eloquent memorial to the love of a ruler for his wife. Human love is frequently displayed in sacrificial acts, in gifts of affection lavished upon its object and in costly memorials after the death of the loved one; yet it cannot prevent the icy hand of death from removing the object of its affection. But the love of God is bestowed on the lovely and unlovely, the lovable and unlovable in equal measure; 'for God so loved the world that He gave His only-begotten Son that whosoever believeth in Him should not perish but have everlasting life'.

The Emperor Shah Jehan could not restore life to his favourite wife. Jesus Christ, the King of kings who died and rose from the dead, gives eternal life to all who believe in Him. Only He can claim to be 'the resurrection and the life'.

(John 3. 16; 11. 25)

**1081  Tombstone Wisdom.** The following quaint lines are inscribed on a stone in Newlands Churchyard, Gloucester:

*Bold Infidelity, turn pale and die!*
*Under this turf an infant's ashes lie.*
*Say, is it lost or saved?*
*If death's by sin, it sinned because 'tis here;*
*If heaven's by works, it can't in heaven appear.*
*Ah—reason how depraved!*
*Revere the Bible's sacred page: the knot's*
*    untied—*
*It died through Adam's sin; it lives, for Jesus*
*    died.*

(Matt. 18. 10,11)

**1082  Tomorrow I'll Pray.**

*'Tomorrow,' he promised, 'Tomorrow, for God-*
*    sent revival I'll pray,*
*Tomorrow I'll plead as I ought to: I'm busy*
*    too busy, today!*
*Tomorrow I'll spend in my closet, tomorrow I*
*    humbly will bow':*
*Yet ever a voice kept on whispering, 'The*
*    Church is languishing now!'*
*Tomorrow, tomorrow, tomorrow—the delay oft*
*    repeated went on:*
*Tomorrow, tomorrow, tomorrow—till the years*
*    and the 'voices' were gone,*
*Till the Church its Lord had forgotten and the*
*    nation wallowed in sin,*
*Till millions had hopelessly perished whom the*
*    saved ones had not tried to win.*
*O members of Christ's mystic Body, O Church*
*    of the living God,*
*O evangelists, pastors and leaders, called to*
*    serve where apostles had trod!*
*The Spirit insistently whispers: answer not,*
*    'Tomorrow I'll pray.'*
*The voice of the Spirit reminds us the Church*
*    needs reviving today.*

(Prov. 27. 1; Ps. 85. 6)

**1083  Tomorrows of Life.** The oriental shepherd was always ahead of his sheep. He was down in front. Any attack upon them had to take him into account. Now God is down in front. He is in the tomorrows. It is tomorrow that fills men with dread. God is there already. All the tomorrows of our life have to pass Him before they can get to us.

F. B. Meyer

(Matt. 6. 34)

**1084  Tongue—Power of the,** It was a wise man who said, 'If I stop to think before I speak instead of afterward, I won't have to worry about what I said.'

In Germany, in the 1920s, there emerged a man to be universally known as Adolf Hitler and in Germany as the Führer. He was a fanatic, a Nazi, possessed of great powers of oratory. For two decades he whipped the German people into a frenzy until a normal nation became capable of inhuman conduct. As a result, millions of people perished and went to premature graves. History testifies to the depths of cruelty of which human nature is capable. Where does it originate? In the mind, and by the tongue of one man. 'The tongue . . . setteth on fire the course of nature.'

Robert Scott

(James 3. 6)

**1085  Touch of God.**

*God, touch my ears that I might hear*
*Above earth's din Thy voice ring clear:*
*God, touch my eyes that I might see*
*The tasks Thou'd have me do for Thee;*
*God, touch my lips that I might say*
*Words that reveal the narrow way;*
*God, touch my hands that I might do*
*Deeds that inspire men to be true:*
*God, touch my feet that I might go*
*To do Thine errands here below:*
*God, touch my life that I might be*
*A flame that ever glows for Thee!*

(Ps. 92. 3)

**1086  Town Clerk of Ephesus.** Cotton Mather used to say there was a man mentioned in Acts 19 to whom he was indebted for most of the success of his life, namely the town clerk of Ephesus whose wise counsel he took as his life rule. When business men consulted him, when philanthropists proposed schemes to him, when great commercial enterprises hung in the balance, he used to say to those around him, 'Gentlemen, if you have no objection, we will consult a little with the town clerk of Ephesus.' So he was never in a hurry, and mostly always right. The lesson, of course, is—Be quiet and calm in every circumstance, and do nothing rashly.

(Acts 19. 36)

**1087  Tract on Missions.** Early in 1819, while waiting to see a patient, a young physician in New York took up and read a tract on missions which lay in his room. On reaching home, he spoke to his wife of the question that had arisen in his mind. As a result, they set sail for Ceylon and later crossed to India as foreign missionaries. For thirty years the wife and husband laboured among the idolatrous Indians and then went to their reward.

Apart from what they did directly as missionaries, they left behind them several sons and two daughters. Each of their sons married and, with their wives and children, gave themselves to mission work. Several grandchildren of the first missionaries became missionaries in India, and carried on the great medical missionary work in Vellore, South India. To date over forty of the Scudder family have given over 1,000 years, all told, to the missionary cause. And it all began through a tract on missionary service.

**1088   Tract—Saved Through a.**   I met an old lady, now with the Lord, who told me she was saved at sixteen. She longed to do something for the Lord, but was very poor. One day she suddenly thought of some old magazines she had saved, went and sold them to a dealer who bought old paper, and with the few cents received, purchased a supply of tracts from the Bible and Book Store.

Later she was standing on a street corner with the tracts in her hand, when suddenly a man ran past her. She hesitated a moment, then ran after him and outran him, then asked if he would please take a tract. He thought perhaps he might, and ran on till he came to a light when he stopped and read it.

The following night she was in a mission and saw a man stand up. Imagine her wondering delight when she heard him say that on the previous night he was in great trouble and had decided to end his life. He had run down a street which ended in a cliff over which he was going to throw himself. He was running to keep his courage up when suddenly a girl outran him and asked if he would please take a tract. He did, and ran on, and when he came to a light thought he might as well see what the tract was about. The title was, 'I am not going to a Christless grave, are you?' He dared not go on to read the contents. Then he said, 'I invited the Lord into my heart by faith, and now all my troubles are over.' In her gentle way the old lady said to me, 'It was a great cheer to me.'

*Light and Liberty*

(Isa. 55. 11)

**1089   Transformed Dust.**

*If sunrise golden glorie's*
*And sunset's crimson gleams*
*Are re-flect light on air-borne dust,*
*Suspensed in sunlight beams,*
*Each sunrise holds a promise,*
*Each sunset proves a plan;*
*The light of heaven that transforms dust*
*Can also transform man.*

*Dust of the earth by nature,*
*If from the world set free,*
*I can reflect the character*
*Of Him who shines on me.*
*A son of dust and nothing*
*In darkness of the night,*
*But looking up on Jesus' face*
*I can reflect its light.*

*The transformation's simple:*
*Reflecting what I see,*
*I'm changed unto the character*
*Of Him who shines on me.*

F. Howard Oakley

(2 Cor. 3. 18)

**1090   Transformed Lives.**   A beautiful statue stood in the market place of an Italian city, the statue of a Greek slave girl, tidy and well-dressed. A ragged little child with hair all dishevelled, passing the statue one day, stopped and gazed at it in admiration. Captivated by its beauty, she stood transfixed, gazing at it long and lovingly. Moved by a sudden impulse she went home, washed her face and combed her hair. Another day she stopped again and viewed the statue admiringly. Then a new idea came into her little mind. Next day she washed and mended her dirty, tattered clothes. Each time she looked at that slave girl's statue she found something more beautiful to admire and copy until a complete metamorphosis had taken place in her.

(2 Cor. 3. 18)

**1091   Translating The Bible.**   No good work is easy work. Martin Luther translated the Bible into the German language, and that translation is one of the greatest books in the world. He said, 'I sweat blood and water in my efforts to render the Prophets into the vulgar tongue. How difficult it is to make these Jewish writers speak German!' Sometimes he occupied several weeks in hunting out and meditating upon the signification of a single word.

(Eccl. 9. 10)

**1092   Treasures.**   When a Roman lady of wealth and position was one day proudly displaying the contents of her jewel box to Cornelia, the latter drew her two small sons to her side, and said, 'Here are my jewels.' Cornelia was the mother of the Gracche, two men who were to sacrifice their lives in the service of the Empire.

When the King of Babylon sent ambassadors to Hezekiah, King of Judah, Hezekiah foolishly showed them all the treasures in his house. Manasseh, Hezekiah's son, was not a man in whom his pious father could boast. By human relationship he was dear as a child but he proved when he succeeded to the throne of Judah to be anything but a treasure.

The Christian has treasures to exhibit, not in pride or self-conceit in order to impress our neighbours, but in true humility befitting those who belong to Christ. In the monthly Christian magazine *The Harvester*, the writer of the article on 'Treasures' goes on to enumerate some of the treasures of those who are redeemed by the blood of Christ—the treasure of a wonderful body, the acme of creation, of a plastic, retentive mind, of a tender heart that is always impressionable, and of an immortal spirit that must live for ever.

(Isa. 39. 4)

**1093 Treasures of Darkness.** John Bunyan lay in Bedford jail for more than a dozen years. His earnest voice was stilled; and he, who, of all men in England of that day, was one of the best fitted to exhibit clearly the rich grace of God to sinful men was not allowed to speak at all. 'What a pity!' said some. 'What a mystery!' said others. It was neither a pity nor yet a mystery. In his prison he wrote his 'Immortal Dream', *The Pilgrim's Progress*, a book which has been many times more useful to the Church than all his preaching would have been. That book coming out of the darkness of his prison is one of the treasures of darkness. So also is some of the magnificent poetry of John Milton that emerged from the darkness of his blind eyes.

(Isa. 45. 3)

**1094 Trends of Events.** In writing on the signs of the times, Dr Donald Grey Barnhouse says that all we can look for in current events are tendencies which point in the direction of the prophetic Scriptures, noting where we might expect these trends to bring us. 'It is foolish,' he avers, 'to try to identify current events with the positive fulfilment of prophecy. All we may do is to see the direction of the flow and trend of movements in the light of the revelation given in the Scriptures.' By way of illustration he describes an incident which took place when he was travelling across South India. He says:

'It was night. There was a storm outside in the tropical darkness. Not a light was visible, not a star. Suddenly there was a flash of lightning. The whole black square of the scene outside the window became a picture. My eyes, like a photographic plate that is exposed for the fraction of a second, retained the etched image of the scene after the darkness had closed in again. There were clouds; there were high hills in the distance; there was a river; there were trees. I knew what kind of country we were approaching. We were entering the Nilgiri Hills. I had seen it on the map, even when I was in America, but now the lightning flash revealed the contours of the hills in the distance. What I had once known on the map by faith I could now glimpse in the far distance. I was sure that I was journeying toward a reality which had long been charted and which would surely be experienced.'

He then compared the map to God's prophetic plan in His Word, the approach to the Nilgiris to the movement of events toward the advent of Christ, the flashes of lightning to incidents taking place from time to time confirming faith in the promises and prophecies of Scripture, and the glimpses of light on the terrain through which he was travelling to the trends of current events today.

(Matt. 16. 3)

**1095 Trials of Life.**

*There must be thorns amid life's flowers, you*
   *know;*
*And you and I, wherever we may go,*

*Can find no bliss that is not mixed with pain,*
*No path without a cloud. It would be vain*
*For me to wish that not a single tear*
*Might dim the gladness that you hold so dear.*
*I am not wise enough to understand*
*All that is best for you. The Master's hand*
*Must sometimes touch life's saddest chords to*
   *reach*
*Its sweetest music, and His child to teach*
*To trust His love, till the long, weeping night*
*Is all forgotten in the morning light.*
*Trust, trust Him, then, and thus shall good or*
   *ill*
*Your trustful soul with present blessing fill.*
*Each loss is truest gain if, day by day,*
*He fills the place of all He takes away.*

(Heb. 12. 11)

**1096 Triumph Over Great Infirmity.** A minister in Melbourne relates the following:

'When I was in Melbourne, Australia, I kept hearing stories about a woman, a cripple, and I never believed them. I did not think the stories could be true. I went one day to offer comfort to her, but before I had been in the room ten minutes, I found it was I who was receiving instruction and help. When she was eighteen she was seized with a dread malady, and the doctor said that to save her life he must take off her foot. Both feet went. They followed the disease up the body, took off her legs to the knees, still followed it up, and as far as the trunk. Then it broke out in her hands. The first arm went to the shoulder, and the second to the shoulder, and when I saw her all that remained of her was a trunk. For fifteen years she had been there. I went to offer comfort, but I did not know how to speak to her or what to say. I found a room the walls of which were covered with texts, all of them radiating, and speaking of joy and peace and power. She lay in bed one day and asked what she could do, a dismembered woman without a joint in her body. Then inspiration came to her, and she got a friend who was a carpenter to come, and he fitted a pad to her shoulder, and then to that another, and a fountain pen, and she began to write letters with it. And remember, when you write, you write with your arm. She had to write; there was no joint, so she wrote with her whole body. I will undertake to say there is no woman who could write a letter one-half so beautiful from the point of view of caligraphy as that woman wrote in my presence, and she had got 1,500 or 1,600 letters from people who had been brought to Christ through the letters she had written in that way from that room. I said to her, 'How do you do it?' She smiled and replied, 'Well, you know Jesus said that they who believed in Him, out of them shall flow rivers of living water, and I believed in Him, and that is all.'

*The Reaper*

(John. 7. 38)

**1097 Troubled Heart Comforted—A.** Dr R. W. Dale lay dying, his faith failing. He woke after midnight in great pain and lay silently struggling with an unknown dread. At the height of the conflict it seemed as if Christ came to him and said, 'Let not your heart be troubled: believe in God; believe also in me.' That steadied him and he felt strong and safe in the love of Christ.

When Dr H. Grattan Guiness, in July, 1906, had news of the death of his daughter Lucy, he went off sorrowing to a quiet bay on a shore in New South Wales. There an old coloured lady with radiant, though wrinkled face, laid her hand on his shoulder and quoted the same words, 'Let not your heart be troubled: believe in God; believe also in me.' It was the message of God for him. He went and preached on the text—'Believe also in Me.'

(John 14. 1-3)

**1098 Trust with Joyfulness.** The author of the following lovely poetic paraphrase in the Doric of Scotland calls it very fittingly— 'LIPPENIN':

> *Though nae flouer come on the fig tree,*
> *Though nae grapes growe on the vine;*
> *Toom be a' the olive presses*
> *And the wheat-ears wilt and dwine.*
> *Suld nae flock at e'en be fauldit,*
> *And the byre nae lowin' hear;*
> *Still I'll trust in God my Saviour,*
> *Want, nor hunger, sall I fear.*
>
> *He's the spring o' a' my gledness,*
> *Gars my step wi' smeddum stert,*
> *Throwe the mirk His praise I'm singin',*
> *Softly singin' in my hert.*

(Hab. 3. 17-19)

**1099 Trust Versus Belief.** A party of visitors at the national mint were told by a workman in the smelting department that if the hand is dipped in water, the molten metal might be poured from the ladle over the palm without burning it. 'Perhaps you would like to try it'? he asked a gentleman in the party. 'No, thank you,' was the reply, 'I prefer to accept your word for it.' Then addressing the man's wife, 'Perhaps, madam, you will make the experiment.' 'Certainly,' she replied, bared her arm and thrust it into a bucket of water, then held it out calmly while the metal was poured on it.

'You see,' said the workman to the gentleman, 'you believed, but your wife trusted.'
(Ps. 40. 4; 125. 1)

**1100 Trust Withstanding Anger.** I once lived where my neighbour's garden was divided from me only by a very imperfect hedge. He kept a dog and his dog was a shockingly bad gardener, and did not improve my beds, So, one evening, while I walked alone, I saw this dog doing mischief and, being a long way off, I threw a stick at him, with some earnest advice as to his going home. The dog, instead of going home, picked up my stick and came to me with it in his mouth, wagging his tail. He dropped the stick at my feet and looked up to me most kindly. What could I do but pat him and call him a good dog, and regret I had ever spoken roughly to him? The dog mastered me by his trust in me. The illustration is to the point. If thou wilt trust God as that dog trusted me, thou wilt overcome. God will be held by thy trust in such a way that He could not smite thee, but must accept thee for Jesus' sake. If thou dost trust him, thou hast the key of His heart, the key of His house, the key of His heaven.

C. H. Spurgeon

(Isa. 26. 4)

**1101 Trustworthy Workman—A.** George, a lad of eighteen, was one of the first converts to Christ in our Prison Bible Class. While in prison, his father collapsed and died, and I was called in to help to comfort George who attributed his father's death to the worry caused by his own criminal record and the most recent episode which had brought him to prison. I accompanied him to his father's funeral which he attended under escort. The following Sunday he made a clear confession of faith in the Lord Jesus.

A profession made under psychological pressures of prison life has to be proved to be real by a continued witness over years within prison, or by a changed life after release. George was released, and over five years of liberty has proved the reality of his profession.

I got him a job with a joinery company, and when he was accepted for the job the director of the company made it very clear that he would never be allowed to work in an area from which valuables could be stolen, so he had to do the rough work outside, and gladly accepted this situation.

After two years I called on this same director to enquire about work for another lad, and was greeted with enthusiasm. The director was so impressed with the young ex-prisoner that he was now putting him out to all kinds of work. His expression was, 'If I had a job where the crown jewels were lying around unattended, it would be George I would send to it.' On one occasion George had found a large sum of money on a job he was doing, and had brought it back immediately. At meal hours George would always be found by himself enjoying his Gideon Bible.

Alex. Allan

**1102 Truth or Tradition.** Two men en route to Blairsville Intersection, an hour's run, by mutual consent were discussing a passage of Scriptures as translated in the Douay Version of the Bible. One was a Christian layman, the other a Roman Catholic clergyman. The former began: 'The question in mind is concerning a passage in the Gospel according to St John as translated in the accredited Douay Version of the Holy Scriptures, the fifth chapter and verse twenty-four. Perhaps you have a copy and we can read it together.'

'I do not have it with me,' the priest replied. The layman offered to quote it verbatim, asking the clergyman to check him if he discovered a misquote.

'Amen, amen, I say unto you, he that heareth My word and believeth Him that sent Me hath life everlasting and cometh not into judgment, but is passed from death to life.' The clergyman agreed that it had been correctly quoted.

'Well,' continued the other, 'I rather like this translation because it used the word "Judgment" for "Condemnation" which I am told is a more literal rendering of the text. But my difficulty is just here: according to this passage, the promise of eternal life is given by Christ to the one who hears His Word and believes in Him. The word "hath" is present tense, indicative mood, and means the present possession of eternal life. Is that how you understand it?'

'Well,' he replied slowly, 'I would not say that that is what it exactly means. I do not think that we should read quite so much into the verse.'

'But does it not say clearly "hath life eternal", and that through hearing the Word of God and believing the One who wrote it, this becomes a present possession?'

'Yes,' the clergyman agreed, 'according to the text, that seems to be the meaning, but the Church has never taught that. She believes that there are certain obligations to be fulfilled before eternal life is received.'

'You say "The Church" believes this', said the other, 'and I judge teaches it, which would be what is commonly known as tradition?'

'Yes, if you want to call it that,' the clergyman replied.

'Then the question seems to rest between believing the Word of God and the word of tradition, does it not?'

He agreed to this and then, arranging some papers on his lap, said he was en route to Pittsburgh where he was to lecture that night, and he did not have much time for review. (John 5. 24)

### 1103   Tryst To Keep.

*Dear loved ones, I am keeping a tryst 'twixt*
*thee and me*
*In company with angels who guard us o'er*
*life's sea;*
*And though you miss the footfall, and feel I've*
*gone away,*
*The thought that I'm in glory will help you*
*through the day.*

*Let not the clouds of sorrow bedim your*
*thoughts of home,*
*I would you'd catch the splendour that heaven*
*has alone:*

*The God of grace will hold you secure within*
*His care,*
*His Word will ever hasten the steps that lead*
*you there.*

*My work on earth is finished: I heard the*
*call—'Come Home',*
*You would not grudge promotion to your*
*beloved, your own;*
*Then hearken to the message, borne on the*
*wings of dawn—*
*God in His own good season will reunite His*
*own.*

*Life's span is just a moment, despite our count*
*of years;*
*He's promised 'joys eternal'—He'll wipe away*
*all tears;*
*In the gardens of tomorrow we'll walk and*
*happy be.*
*Dear loved ones, I am waiting to keep the tryst*
*with thee.*

M.R.

The above was found in the pocket of the late John Sylvester, much esteemed servant of Christ.
(Ps. 16. 11)

### 1104   Unchanged Sky—The.

It was Humboldt's first experience of an earthquake in South America. The air was filled with clouds of dust and the mountains were hurling their crags in the abysses; the birds were flying and screaming in the air with terror. The wild beasts fled from their caves and ran abroad in fear, and the very earth that seemed so solid was shaking like the ocean waves beneath his feet. Looking up to the sky, he saw that it alone was unchanged, calm, still, quiet and undisturbed by all the convulsions of the planet. There is always an uplook that is unchanged. There is a firmament as well as a throne that remains the same.

A. B. Simpson

*There is one amid all changes who standeth*
*ever fast,*
*One who covers all the future, the present*
*and the past;*
*It is Christ, the Rock of Ages, and He is the*
*first and last.*

(Heb. 12. 27,28)

### 1105   Unconscious Influence.

One of the solemnities of our life is that we are responsible, not only for what we purposely do, but also for what we unconsciously do. The shadow you cast when unwatched, when intent on no great errand but just living your ordinary life, speaking and acting without any thought of what comes of them, is helping or harming others.

M. M. G. Dana

*Only a look of anger, but it wounded a sensitive*
*heart;*
*Only a word of sharp reproach, but it made the*
*teardrop start.*

*Only a hasty, thoughtless word, sarcastic and*
*unkind,*
*But it darkened the day before so bright and*
*left a sting behind.*
*Only an act of kindness, but it lightened a heart*
*of grief;*
*Only a word of sympathy, but it brought one*
*soul relief;*
*Only a word of gentle cheer, but it flooded with*
*radiant light*
*The pathway that seemed so dark before, and*
*it made the day more bright.*

*Choice Gleanings*

**1106 Unequal Yoke.** A Christian girl told
C. H. Spurgeon that she was about to marry
a man who neither loved the Lord Jesus nor
attended church. He placed before her the
apostle's warning, 'Be not unequally yoked
together with unbelievers.' Then she tried to
assure Mr Spurgeon that her influence, when
they were married, would lift him up. The
preacher asked her to stand on a chair. 'Now,'
he said, 'you try to pull me up to your level.' She
tugged hard but her efforts were in vain.'
'Right,' he went on, 'now I'm going to pull
you down, but do all you can to remain on
the chair.' She tried hard, but all the trying
in the world didn't keep her there after the
first tug. 'That,' commented the wise pastor,
'is what will happen if you marry that man:
you won't lift him up but he will pull you down.'
(2 Chron. 18. 1,2; 2 Cor. 6. 14)

**1107 Unexpected—Expect the.** Travelling
through Kerala one often sees the road sign,
'Expect the unexpected', and one is reminded
by the tragedies that take place on the road,
that we must be prepared for the unexpected.
We must be prepared to be ushered, perhaps
rather abruptly, into the presence of our
Maker and God. The prophet Amos was
sent on a mission to Israel to reprove them
for their back-sliding and departure, and he
introduced his message with the words,
'Prepare to meet thy God, O Israel.' This was
not a gospel message proclaimed to the lost
and urging them to close in with God's wondrous offer of salvation. It was an urgent message
for the people of God.
(Amos 4. 12)

A. Soutter

**1108 Unfinished Task.**

*Facing a task unfinished*
*That drives us to our knees,*
*A need that, undiminished,*
*Rebukes our slothful ease,*
*We who rejoice to know Thee*
*Renew before Thy throne*
*The solemn pledge we owe Thee*
*To go and make Thee known.*

*We bear the torch that flaming*
*Fell from the hands of those*
*Who gave their lives proclaiming*
*That Jesus died and rose.*

*Ours is the same commission,*
*The same glad message ours;*
*Fired by the same ambition,*
*To Thee we yield our powers.*

*O Father who sustained them,*
*O Spirit who inspired,*
*Saviour whose love constrained them*
*To toil with zeal untired,*
*From cowardice defend us,*
*From lethargy awake!*
*Forth on Thine errands send us*
*To labour for Thy sake.*

Frank Houghton

(Acts 20. 24)

**1109 Uniformity is Not Unity.** The Ecum-
enical Movement is a human organization,
not a divine organism. True unity, the unity
of the Spirit, is organic, not organized; it is
not a union, and does not demand or entail
uniformity. Someone, referring to ecumenism,
made a blunder in naming it: he called it
'this mechanical movement'. It was an error
that partly expressed a truth, for organization
is a mechanical thing. Another, writing on
the subject, said, 'The idea of the reunion of
Christendom may seem magnificent, but it is
really mischievous. If it is carried out, it will
be a universal calamity, a compromise involving sacrifices which will be a betrayal of Christ.'
Nothing could be more destructive to the
unity of the Spirit than efforts to force all into
uniformity, for it is the Spirit who distributes
the various and manifold gifts to the members
of Christ's Mystic Body.
David, the author of the Psalm of fraternal
unity (Ps. 133) had known opposition from
his own family and division in the nation. He
calmed discord and anger and strife with chords
of music. The Psalm seems undoubtedly to
refer to the king's experience after the rebellion
of his son, Absalom, had been quelled: 'David
bowed the heart of all the men of Judah as
the heart of one man.' There must be unity of
heart and spirit, and ecumenism cannot produce that.
(2 Sam. 19. 14; Ps. 133. 1)

**1110 Unique Christ—The.** How difficult it
would be to name a noble figure, a sweet
simile, a tender and attractive relationship,
in which Jesus is not set forth to woo a reluctant
sinner and cheer a desponding saint! Am I
wounded? He is balm. Am I sick? He is medicine. Am I naked? He is clothing. Am I hungry?
He is bread. Am I thirsty? He is water. Am I
in debt? He is surety. Am I in darkness? He is
a sun. Have I a house to build? He is a Rock.
Must I face that black and gathering storm?
He is an anchor sure and steadfast. Am I to
be tried? He is an Advocate. Is sentence passed
and am I condemned? He is pardon.
To deck Him out and set Him forth, Nature
culls her finest flowers, brings her choicest
ornaments and lays these treasures at His
feet. The skies contribute the stars. The sea

gives up its pearls. From fields and mines and mountains, earth brings the tribute of her gold and gems and myrrh and frankincense: the clustered vine and the fragrant rose. He is 'the chiefest among ten thousand and the altogether lovely'.

Thomas Guthrie

(Song of Solomon 5. 16)

**1111 Unique Christ—The.** In the first half of this twentieth century, in the days when Mr Gandhi was fighting for the Independence of India and was almost an object of worship in his own country, an Indian Christian wrote a book entitled *The Unique Christ and the Mystic Gandhi*. In it Mr P. V. George, the author, showed from the Gospel records the uniqueness of the Lord Jesus Christ.

In the French New Testament, the equivalent of the word 'only-begotten' in the third chapter of St. John's Gospel, verse 16, is 'unique'.

Car Dieu a tellement aimé le monde qu'il a donné son fils *unique*, afin que quiconque croit en lui ne périsse point, mais qu'il ait la vie eternelle.

History has recorded the lives of many who for a time captured the world stage, but after their transient episodes were over Christ was still there. His personality proved an undeniable and formidable fact because He has outlasted the rise and fall of many empires and still maintains His impact on men. His story is History, and History is His story. Thinking men of all castes and creeds, friends and foes alike, unite in assigning to Jesus Christ a place unique in history. Horace Bushnell affirmed, 'His character forbids possible classification with other men.' Ernest Renan, the distinguished French infidel, philosopher and historian, testified to the uniqueness of the Lord Jesus in his unequivocal statement, 'He is the incomparable man to whom the universal conscience has decreed the title of the Son of God, and with justice.'

A.N.

(Luke 1. 31-35; Eph. 1. 21-23)

**1112 United Witness for Christ.** M—— was converted in prison, where he had been sent after conviction for offences committed under alcohol and drugs. His wife had threatened to leave him unless he changed his ways, but when he returned home confessing faith in Christ she decided that life with a Christian would be more restricting than life with a drunkard and drug-addict, and she left him for two and a half years. At this time they were both only seventeen years of age. M—— was shattered by this, but clung to his faith in the Lord Jesus, and began to mature considerably. Eventually he was baptized and received into the fellowship of a local church.

One night he telephoned to say that his wife had come back to him, and three weeks later he telephoned again—this time at 3 a.m.— to say that his wife had trusted the Lord

Jesus just ten minutes before. Since then, this couple have taken the area in which they live by storm, witnessing for the Lord Jesus and introducing Bible Lessons to their old school, to their neighbours, to old gang associates and to the youth of the area in general. They have seen a great many won for the Lord Jesus, and seem set on a lifetime of service for Him.

This is just another illustration of how the Lord overrules the most unlikely situations for His own glory.

Alex. Allan

**1113 Unity of Purpose.**

*'With one accord' within an upper room
The faithful followers of Jesus met.
One was the hope of every waiting soul
And on one object great each heart was set.*

*'With one accord'—until the mighty gift
Of Pentecostal power was outpoured;
Then forth as witnesses possessed of God
To preach the resurrection of the Lord.*

*'With one accord' within the House of God
A Hallelujah song was daily raised,
As with the voice of one, from vocal hearts,
Jehovah's name is glorified and praised.*

(Acts 1. 14; 2. 1)

**1114 Universe—The Wonderful.** Matter cannot be created or destroyed, but it can undergo a change in form. The same is true of Energy. Energy is necessary before matter can be produced, and matter is necessary for the production of energy. A small amount of matter, a kilogram—about 2.2 lbs—when the chain of fission is complete, will produce 25,000,000,000 kilowatt hours of energy. This is the equivalent of all the power stations in a country like the U.S.A., working at peak efficiency twenty-four hours daily without a stop for sixty days. In reverse, it would need 25,000,000,000 kilowatt hours of energy to bring into being 2.2 lbs of matter.

Now, ignoring all the stars and the planets in this galaxy, and considering only the planet earth on which we live, how much energy is needed to bring it into being? Its weight can be set down as 6,500,000,000,000,000,000,000,000 tons. Multiply this by 2240 to bring it to lbs. All the power stations in the world working non-stop for millions of years would not produce the energy needed to bring this little earth into existence. Where, then, did the power come from to bring the universe into being? The answer is—God spoke, giving expression to His power, and the worlds were born. Jesus Christ, the Word of God, by whom all things were made, is the very expression of the mighty power of God, and He deigns by His Spirit to live in the hearts of those who will yield themselves to Him.

(Gen. 1. 1-10; John 1. 1,2; Heb. 1. 1,2)

**1115 Unknown Warriors.** After the fall of France in the 1939-45 War, Winston Churchill said:

'This is no war of chieftains or of princes, of dynasties or national ambition; it is a war of peoples and of causes. There are vast numbers in every land who will render faithful service in this war, but whose names will never be known, whose deeds will never be recorded.

'This is a war of the unknown warriors; but let all strive without failing in faith or in duty.'

(2 Cor. 10. 3-6)

**1116 Unprofitable Lives.** A great philosopher said, 'I have spent my life laboriously doing nothing.' A great emperor said, 'I have tried everything and nothing is of any profit.' Goethe, the great German poet, said, 'My life has been a continual rolling of a stone uphill, which has continually rolled back.'

But Paul, the great Christian missionary, said, 'I have fought a good fight; I have finished my course; I have kept the faith. Henceforth there is laid up for me a crown of righteousness.'

Samuel Harris

(2 Tim. 4. 7,8)

**1117 Unquenchable Love.** Kipling in his volume *The Bridges of India*, tells of an incident that occurred when one of the great bridges was being built across the Ganges. The rain had produced a flooded condition; and when the roar of rushing waters was heard in the distance, all hands were called from the structure. The moments that followed were breathless in suspense. The reputation of the contractor was in the balance. Soon the great body of water struck the finished bridge and submerged it. Then it reappeared from amidst the foam, intact. The workers shouted with ecstatic joy, 'She stands! She stands!' In like manner the many waters could not quench the love of Christ, neither could the floods drown it.

*Sunday School Times*

(Song of Solomon 8. 7)

**1118 Ups and Downs.** Some years ago, George Cutting, in company with a few Christians, drove from Penzance in Cornwall to Land's End. Sitting with the driver, who drew attention to a church in the distance, saying, 'That church we shall presently pass, but between this point in the road and our arrival at the church we lose sight of it nine times.' Mr Cutting became curious to put the statement to the test.

They soon descended a small hill and lost sight of the church entirely. Once more, as they rose to the crest of the next hill, the building loomed in sight; again they dipped into the valley and again the church was hidden from their view till they reached the summit of the next slope and again could see the church. In this way they travelled on, sometimes losing sight of the building and then catching a fresh view, until they came to within a few yards of the ancient pile with its peculiar crosses and other things full in view. As the driver had said, they had lost sight of the old building nine times within three or four miles.

But how often did the church go up and down in that drive of three or four miles? Not once. The ups and downs were with us, not with the church.

Exactly! In the variable states of soul of which Christians speak, the ups and downs are with the believer, not with Christ. There are no ups and downs in God's thought of Christ's personal worth or in the value of His sacrifice. As we are accepted by Him on these grounds because we are 'in Christ', there can be no ups and downs in our acceptance.

(Eph. 1. 6)

**1119 Use and Usefulness.** It is a recognised fact that if a member of the body, an arm for example, is not used, or put to use, it eventually loses its ability to be used and to be useful, to function as it should as a member of that body. This is equally true in the spiritual realm. Every believer is a member of the Body of Christ, and unless he functions as such in the capacity and sphere assigned by God, he becomes an impotent drone, unable to be used and a drag on the rest of the body. I am sure that there is nothing that grieves the heart of God more than to see His children indolent, particularly in the service of God. Jeremiah (48. 10) says, 'Cursed be he that doeth the work of the Lord negligently' (marginal rendering).

Bishop J. C. Ryle once said: 'Never allow yourself to think that you can do too much— that you can spend and be spent too much for Christ's cause. For one man that does too much, I will show you a thousand that do not do enough. Fear not the reproach of men. Faint not because you are sometimes abased. Heed it not if you are sometimes called a bigot, enthusiast, fanatic, madman and fool. There is nothing disgraceful in these titles. They have often been given to the best and wisest of men.'

Never were there such doors of usefulness opened—never were there so many opportunities for doing good.

(2 Cor. 12. 15; Gal. 6. 9)

**1120 Valiant for Truth.** In *The Pilgrim's Progress* there is a beautiful description and account of a faithful and courageous pilgrim to whom John Bunyan gives the name—Valiant-for-truth. This was the passage read at the burial service of a very dear missionary colleague Crawford J. Tilsley in the Godavari Delta of Andhra Pradesh, South India. A nephew of Dan Crawford, the missionary in Africa who wrote the book *Thinking Black*, he was the great grandson of Mr and Mrs

William Bowden, one of the original pioneering couples who commenced the fruitful work in that area in 1836, and thus represented the fourth generation of missionaries in that part of India skirting the Bay of Bengal. Not only was Crawford Tilsley a man of great physical stamina but also a spiritual giant, answering to Bunyan's description of Valiant-for-truth. Although a diabetic for over forty years, he never allowed this to prevent his excelling in the service of his Lord and Master whom he loved and devotedly served. The valley of the shadow had no terrors for him: 'so he passed over, and all the trumpets sounded for him on the other side'. Another of our colleagues in the Godavari area, Roy German, still actively engaged for the Lord there, has written the following short account of what we all found Crawford to be:

'We shall always remember him as a devoted husband and loving father. But he was not only a dear father to his three children but also to at least twenty of us of a younger missionary generation in the Godavari Field. His own affairs were willingly put aside to listen patiently to the problems of a colleague and give godly counsel. He was a giant in his knowledge and use of the Telugu language and many of us were inspired to plod on with language study by his hearty, "You can do it!" He loved India and its people, for Christ's sake.'

**1121 Values—True Sense of.** Many, like the little girl in the following incident, have a false sense of values. We tend to cling with tightening grip to trivial things and lose what is infinitely more precious and lasting. Love of self, love of money, love of pleasure, hinder many from laying hold of eternal life and enjoying the life that is life indeed.

A little girl had accidentally dropped a small silver coin into her mother's prized vase. Naturally she put her little hand in to recover it, but found, as she gripped the coin and held it tight, that she was unable to withdraw her hand; so she screamed and struggled to get her hand out. Her cries attracted the other members of the family who all advised and pleaded with her to open her hand and then withdraw it with ease. But no! she would hold on to her precious little coin and continued to struggle, squirm and scream. Finally, the costly vase had to be broken and, with her fist tightly clenched, she exclamed 'I've still got it.' The far more costly vase was sacrificed for the sake of a paltry coin.

(1 Tim. 6. 10-12, 19)

**1122 Vanity of the World's Honours.** Do you remember that old Scythian custom, when the head of a house died? How he was dressed in his finest dress, and set in his chariot, and carried about to his friends' houses; and each of them placed him at his table's head and all feasted in his presence! Suppose it were offered to you, in plain words, as it is offered to you in dire facts, that you should gain this Scythian honour, gradually, while you yet thought yourself alive. Suppose the offer were this: you shall die slowly; your blood shall daily grow cold, your flesh petrify, your heart beat at last only as a rusty group of iron valves. Your life shall fade from you, and sink through the earth into the ice of Caina; but day by day your body shall be dressed more gaily, and set in higher chariots, and have more orders on its breast, crowns on its head, if you will. Men shall bow before it, stare and shout round it, crowd after it up and down the streets; build palaces for it, feast with it at their tables' heads all the night long; your soul shall stay enough within it to know what they do, and feel the weight of the golden dress on its shoulders, and furrow of the crown edge on the skull; no more. Would you take the offer verbally made by the death angel? Would the meanest among us take it, think you? Yet practically and verily we grasp at it, every one of us, in a measure; many of us grasp at it in its fullness of horror.

Every man accepts it who desires to advance in life without knowing what life is; who means only that he is to get more horses, and more footmen, and more fortune, and more public honour, and—NOT more personal soul. He only is advancing in life whose heart is getting softer, whose blood warmer, whose brains quicker, whose spirit is entering into living peace.

John Ruskin

(Eccl. 2. 1-11)

**1123 Vases Beyond Price.** An evangelist visited a man in a pottery district who, in his younger days, had been an infidel. The visitor gazed upon two magnificent vases contained in a glass case and remarked, 'What lovely vases! I suppose they are very valuable.' 'Yes!' was the reply. 'How much would you sell them for?' With a shake of the head, the man turned to the questioner, 'All the money in the world wouldn't tempt me to part with either of them,' he answered. 'Years ago I was a drunkard, a gambler, one who sold his soul to the devil. One day I was persuaded to attend a revival meeting. I did so, and on going home I passed a rubbish heap. I saw there a piece of clay. Evidently someone had thrown it away as useless. I picked it up, took it home, kneaded it and moulded it. Then I went to the wheel and out of that worthless piece of clay I made these two vases. I thought to myself that if I could do such a thing as that, God could do so with me. And therefore I placed myself in His hands, and He has made me a new man.'

*Prairie Overcomer*

(Jer. 18. 4,6; Eph. 2. 10)

**1124 Verse—The Added.** The American evangelist, and singer, Peter Bilhorn, who wrote the words and music of 'Sweet Peace', found a clipping from *Youth's Companion* with a poem by Hezekiah Butterworth, which he set to music.

Some weeks later Bilhorn was invited to conduct a gospel meeting in the Iowa State Prison at Fort Madison. Just before the close of the meeting the Chaplain said: 'Sing us one more song, Peter,' and without thinking where he was or how it would sound, the missioner picked up the sheet of the new song, seated himself at the organ and sang it to the prisoners.

When he had finished, a strange thing happened. A convict, a young man down in the centre, sprang to his feet and, holding on to the seat in front of him, said: 'Chaplain, Chaplain, is that true? If what he has been singing is true, there is no hope for me or a lot of us here.' And he dropped back into his seat with a sob.

Mr Bilhorn at once realised the dreadful blunder which he had made, but it was too late to explain or apologise. He went back to Chicago saying: 'It's not true; it's not true. There must be another verse added to that song.' A few days later he wrote:

> But the soul that comes to Jesus
> Is saved from every sin;
> And the heart that fully trusts Him
> Shall a crown of glory win.
> Then come to the dear Redeemer;
> He will cleanse from every stain;
> By the grace that He freely gives you
> You shall higher soar again.

Then he sat down and wrote to the Chaplain asking for the privilege of a return visit to the prison for another service. Three weeks later he was there. During the service he made his apology and sang the song with the new verse added.

But that is not the end of the story. In May, 1918, nearly twenty years afterward, Mr Bilhorn was at a camp in Illinois, singing for the Y.M.C.A. On a Sunday morning at the close of a meeting in the Tabernacle, a tall, splendid-looking officer in a colonel's uniform came down the aisle to the platform, put out his hand and said: 'Hello, Bilhorn. You don't remember me, but I do you. You visited Fort Madison prison eighteen years ago and sang about 'The Bird with the broken wing'. 'Yes,' said Peter, 'and every time I think of it I am filled with shame.' 'Well,' said the colonel, 'I am the man who asked if the song was true; and when you came back and then sang the new verse, I gave my heart to Jesus Christ. I am now the colonel of a regiment preparing to go overseas. By God's grace one can "higher soar again".'

Henry Durbanville

(Eph. 2. 10)

1125    **Vesture of Jesus Untorn.**  Our Lord's tunic, or inner vesture, was different from the other garments in that it was unseamed from the top, like the veil of the temple and the high priest's robe of the ephod (Exod. 39.

23). This intimate dress was the last thing to be taken from Him. His life He gave: no one could take that.

Some things we may reverently learn from such an object lesson:
1. Personally, the Lord Jesus had no need of it in the work He was finishing. As the last Adam He could be before His God unashamed in stainless holiness, as innately pure on Calvary's cross as in Bethlehem's manger. His purity was flawless. His Person undefiled. The Father's voice had pronounced His glad approval of His Son.
2. Substitutionally, He must have it. His native right to be clothed with light as with a garment He gave up when He chose the accursed death on the tree.
3. Typically, it is for us in its unrent perfection.
4. Actually, it fell by the chance of the dice to a soldier for whom the victim prayed and died.

A. C. Rose

(Matt. 27. 35)

1126    **Victory Complete.**

> O glorious blessed Saviour!
> I long to be with Thee:
> I long to sing Thy praises
> From every hindrance free;
> I long to praise more fully,
> To join that glorious song
> Of all the ransomed myriads
> Of that redeemed throng.
>
> I long to shout with triumph,
> 'Thy Victory is complete.'
> I long for crown of glory
> To cast it at Thy feet.
> Thou wondrous, peerless Saviour!
> Thou matchless Lover, Friend!
> Oh, let me join those praises
> That never, never end.
>
> Yes, let me swell the anthem
> Of praise, my Lord! to Thee.
> I know Thy worth exceedeth
> My thoughts whate'er they be;
> But too I know Thou'rt willing
> That I should join the song
> Of all Thy blood-bought people
> In that bright heavenly throng.
>
> With what transcendent rapture
> Thyself, Oh Lord! I'll see,
> When at that scene of glory
> A trophy I shall be!
> When on Thy hands once pierced
> I gaze with great delight,
> And see Thy face so lovely,
> Now crowned with glorious light!

F. Howard Oakley

(Rev. 5. 9,10)

1127    **Voice Clear and Clarion.**  In one of his discourses Dr Bartoli spoke of the wonderful tone of Dr Channing's voice. He said, 'Channing was an insignificant figure, short and slender, about a hundred pounds of flesh being the garment and instrument of his mighty soul. In the pulpit, however, he was of commanding height. He spoke with habitual rising inflection rather than cadence, which seemed to raise every listener to the skies; soft, yet audible; melting yet resonant; clear when it whispered and clarion when it rang. One day at his home an unbeliever complained of Christ's denunciation of the Pharisees as severe. Channing got the book, turned to the passage, and read the 'Woe unto you!' so solemnly, graciously and calmly. 'Oh!' said the infidel before the recitation stopped, 'if He spoke thus, my objection is withdrawn!' (Acts 2. 14)

### 1128 Vows of God—The.

O Christian! the vows of God are upon you. You are God's priest; act as such. You are God's king; reign over your lusts.

Banish for ever all thought of indulging the flesh if you would live in the power of your risen Lord. It were ill that a man who is alive in Christ should live in the corruption of sin. Surely, believer, from open lusts and sins you are delivered. Have you come forth from the lust of pride? Have you escaped from slothfulness? Have you been saved from carnal security?

Are you seeking day by day to live above worldliness, the pride of life and the ensnaring vice of avarice? These are the VOWS OF GOD that you took when you received Christ as Lord into your heart, His holy Spirit into your life, and the will of the Father to be your guide.

(Isa. 26. 13; Rom. 6. 12; 1 John 2. 15,16)

### 1129 Waggon-Plunderer's Conversion.

J—— was a vagrant lad of seventeen who had never known his parents and had lived rough for most of his life, apart from his terms in Approved Schools and other Institutions. Joining a local gang in Glasgow in a raid on railway waggons in a local siding, he was caught and sent to prison. There a latent tuberculosis came to light and he was sent to hospital. When I visited him there I found him semi-conscious, but in a lucid spell he recognized me and said, 'It's good of you to visit me, sir. I couldn't sleep last night, but I lay singing over in my mind the little songs you teach us in the Bible Class.' Then he repeated, word perfect, 'There's a way back to God from the dark paths of sin: there's a door that is open that all may go in. At Calvary's cross is where you begin, when you come as a sinner to Jesus': and then the chorus, 'I know a fount where sins are washed away'. He rallied after that and for several weeks I visited him, during which time it became clear that he had really trusted the Lord Jesus. This was surprising as he had only attended the Bible Class on three occasions before his illness; but he had grasped the gospel truth and found the Saviour. Shortly after this J—— died, and

that vagrant lad is now 'at home with the Lord'.

He had a fine sense of humour, as I recognized when he told me of his arrest. The gang had used him as a stooge, and he had the task of opening the first waggon. He described to me graphically the rest of the gang lurking back in the shadows while he went forward under the arc lights to open the door of the waggon. The police had been forewarned, and in J——'s words—'Withoot a word o' a lee, sir, it wis fou o' twinty p'licemen.' When asked what he did then, he said, 'I just stepped back and said, "I'm sorry, sirs: excuse me, sirs: I've opened the wrang waggon."'

Alex. Allan

### 1130 Waiting and Watching.

*It is not for a sign we are watching,*
*For wonders above and below,*
*For pouring of vials of judgement,*
*For sounding of trumpets of woe.*
*It's not for a day we are looking*
*Nor even the time yet to be,*
*When the earth shall be filled with God's Glory*
*As the waters cover the sea.*

*We wait for our Lord, our Beloved,*
*Our Comforter, Master and Friend,*
*The substance of all that we hope for,*
*Beginning of faith and the end.*
*We watch for our Saviour and Bridegroom*
*Who loved us and made us His own;*
*For Him we are looking and longing,*
*For Jesus, and Jesus alone.*

(John 14. 3)

### 1131 Waiting Upon The Lord.

*They that wait on the Lord*
*Shall all their strenth renew,*
*Succoured to win the fight*
*As life they battle through.*

*They that wait on the Lord*
*Shall mount on eagles' wings,*
*Soaring above the clouds,*
*Rising o'er earthly things.*

*They that wait on the Lord*
*Shall run nor weary be,*
*Drawing a power divine,—*
*Measureless, deep and free.*

*They that wait on the Lord*
*Shall walk and never faint,*
*Upheld by one unseen,*
*Leaning without restraint.*

*They that wait on the Lord—*
*Teach us to wait, we pray,*
*And prove the blessings from Thy}Word*
*By waiting day by day.*

May Gorrie

(Isa. 40. 31)

### 1132 Walking on Water.

One Sunday, in June, 1966, there was a gathering of distinguished people at an ashram near Bombay.

They had gathered to see a yogi defy gravity by walking twenty feet on water in a specially constructed steel tank, and each one of them had paid from 100 to 500 Rupees to witness this amazing feat. Before preparing for this most notable feat, the yogi amazed them by eating iron nails, crunching glass in his mouth, drinking poison, and walking on fire, without suffering any ill effects. Then they gathered before the steel tank to watch him walk on water. The swami made a speech to point out that he was a man who did what he said, and said what he did; and then climbed up to the top of the tank. He stood there for a quarter of an hour silently meditating, stepped boldly forward, and sank at once to the bottom of the tank which was filled with four feet of water.

Did you know that nearly two thousand years ago a Man really did walk on water? He did not walk on the surface of water that was only feet deep, but over the stormy waters of an inland sea, the sea of Galilee in Palestine. He walked on water to avoid popularity, for people, seeing some of the wonderful things He did, wanted to make Him king. He walked on water to meet and help His disciples whom He had sent off in a fishing boat to the other side of the lake.

His story is told in four little books called 'The Gospels' which have been more circulated throughout the world than any other books.

J. W. McMillan

**1133 Walking With The Great.** A young man with few friends, just beginning his business career on the London Stock Exchange, found his task very uphill. One day he obtained an introduction to Lord Rothschild and said, 'If in any way you can use your influence on my behalf, I shall esteem it a great favour.' Charmed with the young man's manner, Lord Rothschild said, 'Let us go for a little walk.' As they walked the full length of the Stock Exchange, the great financier encouraged the young man to open his heart to him. The return journey was made in the same fashion. When they were parting the young man said, 'I know you will help me all you can.' Lord Rothschild replied, 'I have done so already. Unless I am much mistaken, our walk together will bring you as much business as you can manage.' And so it proved. The old members of the Exchange seeing the two members engaged in close conversation as they walked together said, 'That young fellow is a coming man. See how Lord Rothschild has taken to him.' His success was assured from that hour.

The Christian's success is assured too, for he can truly say, 'I walk and I talk with a King.' That King is the Lord Jesus, greater and wealthier than all the Rothschilds in this world.
(Gen. 5. 24; 6. 9)

**1134 Wakefulness.** There are many ways of promoting Christian wakefulness. Among the rest, let me strongly advise Christians to converse together concerning the ways of the Lord. Christian and Hopeful, as they journeyed towards the Celestial City, said to themselves, 'To prevent drowsiness in this place, let us fall into good discourse.' Christian enquired, 'Brother, where shall we begin?' Hopeful answered, 'Where God began with us.' Then Christian sang:

*When saints do sleepy grow, let them come*
*   hither,*
*And hear how these two pilgrims talk together.*
*Yes, let them learn of them, in any wise;*
*Thus, to keep ope their drowsy slumbering eyes;*
*Saints' fellowship, if it be managed well,*
*Keeps them awake, and that in spite of hell.*

C. H. Spurgeon

(Mark 13. 32-37)

**1135 Warnings Rejected.** In a doctor's office these words were seen:

*God and the doctor we adore*
*On the brink of danger, not before.*
*The danger passed and things are righted—*
*God is forgotten, the doctor slighted.*

Johnstown, Pennsylvania, had an air of fear and dread some years ago, when the engineers notified its people that the great dam which had stood for many years was going to break in a few hours. Heavy rain had been falling for many days and the waters had backed up. When the engineers discovered a little crack in the dam, they cried, 'Flee for your lives, run to the hills! Rush to the mountains! The flood is coming.' But there were hundreds of people who said, 'Those young College students do not know what they are talking about! That dam has held all these years.' They stayed in their places of business and then—suddenly—there was a crash and a roar, and down the valley rushed millions and millions of gallons of water, sweeping some three hundred people to their deaths because they had not heeded the warning and had refused to leave.
(Gen. 19. 16,17,24,25)

**1136 Washing of Water.** Just a little while before the Chicago fire I said to my family one morning that I would come home early after dinner and take them out for a drive. My little boy jumped up and said, 'Papa, will you take us up to Lincoln Park to see the bears?' 'Yes, I'll take you up to Lincoln Park to see the bears.'

I hadn't more than left the house before he began to tease his mother to get him ready. She washed him, put a white suit on him and got him all ready. Then he wanted to go outdoors. When he was a little fellow he had a strange passion for eating dirt, and when I drove up to the house his face was covered with mud and his clothes were very dirty. He came running up to me and wanted me to take him in the carriage and go to Lincoln Park.

'Willie,' I said, 'I can't take you in that condition. You must be washed first.'

'No, I'se clean.'

'No, you are not; you are very dirty. You'll have to be washed before I take you out.'

'O, I'se clean; mamma washed me.'

'No,' I said, 'you are not.'

The little fellow began to cry and I thought the quickest way to stop him was to let him look at himself. So I got out the carriage, took him to the house, and showed him his dirty face in the looking-glass. That stopped his mouth. He never said his face was clean after he saw himself. But I didn't take the looking-glass to wash him with. I took him away to the water.

D. L. Moody

(James 1. 23,24; Eph. 5. 26)

## 1137 Watchman, What of the Night?

*The world's sad day wears to its eventide:*
*time steals away:*
*The shadows of the eve are stretched out wide:*
*wide, deep and grey.*
*In boding storms sinks down the cheerless light:*
*'The morning cometh!' also comes the night.*

*And still, 'mid portents of impending doom, men*
*make wild mirth:*
*Joy lights the festive chamber, and they grow*
*wanton on earth.*
*They plant, they build, choose Sodom's smiling*
*lot*
*And mock at sin, and say, 'Why comes He not?'*

*But lo! a gleaming from the Watchtower seen,*
*a star of dawn:*
*Long wild and weary has the darkness been—*
*'twill soon be gone.*
*The cherished ray that cheered through all the*
*night*
*E'en now seems blending with the eastern light.*

(Isa. 21. 11,12; 2 Sam. 23. 3,4)

## 1138 Water of Life.

In one of the sanguinary bayonet encounters so frequent in the terrible war of 1914-18 a certain young Englishman found himself face to face with a German officer armed with a sword. As they met with a terrific impact, the German's sword inflicted a nasty wound in the Englishman's thigh, whilst, the Englishman drove his bayonet through the German's chest, doing mortal injury. Becoming disentangled, they both fell to the ground. The tide of battle rolled over them, then receded, and there, amongst many others, they lay weak and helpless. The German officer said, 'How do you feel?' 'Pretty bad,' said the young Englishman. 'Anything you want?' asked the other, thoroughly at home in the English language. 'Just water,' was the reply; 'I am terribly thirsty.'

Though in evident pain the officer produced a water-botle, held it within reach of the Englishman's hand, saying, 'Drink this and live!'

With death written on his face, the officer drew out an English New Testament, turned over the leaves to a certain page, placed his thumb on a text on the open page, and said, 'Drink this and live for ever.'

(John 7. 37; 4. 13,14)

## 1139 Way of Salvation.

To the best of my knowledge James is not saved, but he certainly knows the message and the way of salvation.

He went through our prison Bible Class, and was then transferred to another, more leniently disciplined, establishment. I was asked to speak to the Bible Class there during the Chaplain's summer holiday, but when I arrived it was to discover that this worthy gentleman had returned home early, and was himself attending class that evening. He elected to speak to the boys himself.

He very pointedly addressed them as 'Christian gentlemen': 'Christians and gentlemen, don't forget, boys, that we are all the children of God from the moment of our birth; and if it sometimes seems otherwise, the Spirit of God lives in every person born into this world.' And so it went on, undermining the teachings of the Christian gospel. While this was going on I could see James sitting wriggling impatiently on his seat. Eventually the speaker noticed it too, and asked if he wanted to ask a question. The question was direct and deadly! 'Sir,' he said, 'why are you talking nonsense? We were taught in Mr Allan's Bible Class that we are all sinners, and that if we don't accept Jesus who died for us we will go to hell because of our sins.' 'And', turning to the boys, 'we all believe that don't we?' There was a chorus of assent. The speaker suddenly remembered a prior engagement and left.

Alex. Allan

## 1140 Way to Heaven—The.

The well-known preacher, John Wesley, once went to see a poor man who was reported to be rather weak in his intellect. Sitting down by his side he said, 'Well, my friend, what do you know of the way to heaven?' 'It seems to me,' replied the man after a moment's thought, 'there are three steps on that road: the first, out of self; the second, into Christ; the third, into heaven.' John Wesley said, 'I learnt more from that man than I have from many a volume of theology.' 'Out of my sin and into Thyself, Jesus, I come to Thee.'

(John 14. 5,6)

## 1141 Way to Heaven—Unknown.

A stranger, making his way one morning across Birkenhead Park, encountered four young men walking in the opposite direction, and solicited their help for guidance to his destination. Impressed by their unhesitating reply to his question, he thanked them for their help and the clarity of their directions, said a few words on general topics, then ventured to ask them, 'Had my destination been heaven, could you have directed me so promptly?'

'I'd have suggested going to church,' said the first.

'I think you ought to pray to God,' said the second youth.

Turning to the third young man, the stranger asked if he had any help to offer.

'Why, you must live a good life,' was his quite definite reply.

'Well, how would you direct me?' he asked the fourth, who replied in a very different tone and gave a very different answer: 'I don't know. Better ask a policeman.'

None of them had learnt Jesus said, 'I am the way, the truth and the life: no man cometh unto the Father but by Me.'

(John 14. 6)

**1142 Ways of Treating God's Word.** There are two ways of treating the seed. The botanist splits it up and discourses on its curious characteristics: the simple farmer eats and sows; sows and eats. Similarly there are two ways of treating the gospel. A critic dissects it, raises a mountain of debate about the structure of the whole and relationship of its parts; and when he is done with his argument he is done. He neither lives on it himself nor spreads it for the good of others. He neither sows nor reaps. The disciple of Jesus, hungering for righteousness, takes the seed whole; it is bread for today's hunger, and seed for tomorrow's supply.

W. Arnot

(1 Pet. 1. 23)

**1143 'We'—The Personal Pronoun.** To many a Bible translator, working at the task of making the Scriptures speak a language of Asia, or the Islands of the Pacific, or Africa, or Latin America, arise questions which have to be answered at every turn. For he finds himself faced with two different kinds of first person plural pronouns—one which includes the person spoken to (labelled by linguists 'inclusive') and one which excludes the person spoken to (labelled by linguists 'exclusive'). In Mark 9. 38 it might well be either inclusive or exclusive, but probably the better choice would be inclusive; i.e. 'we forbade him because he was not following you and us'.

At first glance the decision may not seem to be very difficult to make. Actually, however, the problems become very complex, involving interpretation of events in terms of the cultural context, details of the situation being described, the speaker's attitude toward his audience, and exactly what group he has in mind.

Velma B. Riskett

The learner of a language that has these two kinds of first person plural pronouns has to think when addressing God and when addressing his audience.

**1144 Wealth of God.** No rich man on earth could possibly be 'rich unto all that call upon him' very long. Too many would call upon him and they would call too often. He would do it to his ruin. But our God does not impoverish Himself by being rich unto all that call upon HIM. We are told that the original Greek of Romans 10. 12 is still more striking: 'Continually wealthy to all those who are continually invoking His aid.'

**1145 Wealth Unrealised.** A poor man and his wife lived on a small holding in Oklahoma, U.S.A. They had bought it during the depression years and subsisted somehow, but without any luxuries. One morning an engineer came up the path and asked if he might drill a test hole for oil under the kitchen floor. The couple found it difficult to decide, for the shack was all they owned, but finally gave him permission to drill the hole. He hit a gusher and the oil began to pour forth by the hundreds of barrels. Soon the couple were richer than ever they had been. They bought a modern home, a fine new car, and began enjoying a standard of living far higher than they had ever dreamed of.

One day the old man smiled reflectively and said to his wife, 'Just think—the oil was under our feet all the time, and all we had to do was to tap it.'

(Deut. 33. 24; Eph. 3. 8)

**1146 Wedding Anniversaries.** Married couples celebrate the anniversaries of their marriage as most people celebrate their birthdays: but how many know that names have been assigned to the number of years married, and what these names are? Here is a list of them:

> 1st year—PAPER
> 2nd year—COTTON
> 3rd year—LINEN
> 4th year—SILK
> 5th year—WOOD
> 6th year—IRON
> 7th year—COPPER
> 8th year—BRONZE
> 9th year—POTTERY
> 10th year—TIN
> 15th year—CRYSTAL
> 20th year—CHINA
> 25th year—SILVER
> 30th year—PEARL
> 35th year—CORAL
> 40th year—RUBY
> 45th year—SAPPHIRE
> 50th year—GOLD
> 55th year—EMERALD
> 60th year—DIAMOND

The list of names does not seem to go beyond that.

## 1147 Wedding—Golden.

*Golden thoughts come stealing down memory's*
*lane today*
*As on this fiftieth milestone you linger on your*
*way;*
*And as a curtain lifted the past is brought to*
*view—*
*The happy days and hours which long ago you*
*knew,*
*The dear forgotten faces again you seem to*
*see—*
*Old songs, old friends, old places pass by in*
*memory.*
*Life's sun will soon be setting: the thought*
*brings naught of pain,*
*For in yon land of gladness there waits eternal*
*gain.*
*Dear ones await up yonder whom you have*
*missed so long,*
*And oft you long to mingle with that triumphant*
*throng;*
*And deeper far the yearning to see His lovely*
*face*
*Who through the years has loved you and*
*saved you by His grace.*

Avis B. Christiansen

## 1148 Wedding—Silver.

*A quarter of a century you've walked life's way*
*together,*
*Through joy and sorrow, loss and gain, and*
*through all kinds of weather;*
*And, as you've shared its pain and grief, as well*
*as many a blessing,*
*You've found your gladness more complete,*
*your sadness less distressing.*
*For love can tinge the darkest cloud with glints*
*of heavenly sweetness*
*And add to e'en our deepest joys a sense of*
*rich completeness.*
*So on this silver wedding day life holds a fuller*
*meaning*
*Than e'er it did in bygone hours of wishful,*
*empty dreaming.*
*Our Father's hand has never failed in any kind*
*of trial,*
*And never, when His help you've sought, have*
*you met stern denial.*
*Today, with hearts still undismayed, you face*
*the unknown morrow,*
*Strong in His might and unafraid of turmoil,*
*pain and sorrow.*

**1149 Weeds and Fences.** There was a certain preacher who was reputed to be very wise in the settlement of church difficulties, so much so that all churches within reach, when in trouble, sought his counsel. This preacher, while living in the town, was the fortunate owner of a farm in the country, which was operated by a manager who lived on the premises. One day the preacher wrote two letters, one a letter to a church which had sought his advice in time of trouble, and the other a letter to his farm manager. Having the two letters completed, he put each into the wrong envelope, with the result that the farmer received the advice meant for the church, and the church that intended as direction for operating the farm.

When the letter came to the church, it was opened by the senior elder, and the church assembled to hear the preacher-counsellor's wisdom. The elder addressed the meeting to this effect:

Our brother whose counsel we sought has replied to our letter evidently in parabolic form, for this is his letter: 'KEEP DOWN THE WEEDS: KEEP UP THE FENCES: AND KEEP A SHARP LOOK-OUT FOR THE OLD BLACK BULL.' Having read the letter, the elder continued, 'My brethren, it is not difficult to interpret this parable. The weeds are causes of dissension, and we are advised therefore to see to it that no root of bitterness is allowed to grow up among us. The fences are undoubtedly intended to represent church discipline. The garden of the Lord must be separate from the world, and all that would injure the Lord's plants must be excluded. Therefore we must keep up the fences. Then, of course, my brethren, you will readily recognize who is meant by the big, black bull. That can be no other than the devil himself. What we are admonished to do, therefore, is to keep down all causes of possible dissension, maintain strict discipline, and always be on the alert to resist the approach of the devil. If we follow this advice, no doubt the garden of the Lord will prosper.'

After all, is it not possible that the preacher's letter to the manager of his farm was exactly the advice that the church, and every other church, too, required.

Dr Herbert Lockyer

(Heb. 12. 15; James 4. 7)

**1150 Welcome.** In an Aberdeenshire glen there is a wayside fountain with a drinking cup attached to it which bears the following inscription in the Gaelic language: 'Cead mille failte'—'a hundred thousand welcomes'. That motto is a fair interpretation of the invitations of the gospel; and responding to them, you will find yourself confronted with divine assurances.

Henry Durbanville

The measure of the welcome the Lord Jesus will give to His own may be seen in this: that He is coming out. He is coming right down, to receive and welcome them. How great is His expectancy! And how grand will be that meeting! As for His waiting people, they have the assurance that when they see Him they will be like Him.

A. Soutter

(John 14. 3)

**1151 Well-Doing.** 'Why, Auntie, you are putting some of your choicest rose bushes away in the backyard.' 'Yes, dear, and I am going to put some geraniums and some pinks and other lovely flowers which will bloom all summer out there, too. I know they seem to be out of sight,' Auntie said, 'but there's a woman who sits and sews day after day, week in and week out, at the upper window in the dingy house opposite, and I'm fixing that corner for her. She's always so busy and tired looking, and it may be that the flowers will put a bit of brightness into her life.'

> Then let no chance by me be lost
> Kindness to show at any cost;
> Remove some barrier from the road,
> Or brighten someone's heavy load.

(Gal. 6. 10)

1152  **Well Done!**  We see many a despised and once degraded heathen drawing near to 'the place that is called Calvary'; there to fall under the sweet compulsion of the cross, then to be linked by its blessed bond to the Redeemer and so to spend this little span of life in His service. 'That great day' will see many a strange reversal in positions: yet it is not too late to qualify for promotion. The lists are still open. Commissions are still being given to the rank and file. Napoleon said once, with a flash of genius, that every common soldier carried a Field-Marshal's baton in his knapsack. More truly, more certainly, each and every recruit carries undreamed-of possibilities in his heart. Commissions, and converts, and crowns of glory all may be his. Yet, surpassing all other honours is the King's 'Well done!'

Dr Northcote Deck
(Matt. 25. 21,23. Luke 19. 17)

1153  **Whales Have Swallowed Men.**  More than twenty-five centuries ago a Jewish prophet named Jonah was swallowed by a whale and vomited up on dry land.

Since 1880 three cases of men swallowed by sperm whales, all of whom survived, have been recorded. Marshall Jenkins, an American, while harpooning from a whaling boat, was swallowed by a whale, and after many hours, when the whale surfaced, was vomited up in the fish's death struggles.

James Bartley, a Britisher, on the whaling ship *Star of the East* was swallowed when harpooning. The whale was captured and cut up, and Bartley was found alive but unconscious within its stomach. For two weeks he was insane but recovered his reason and recounted his experiences. His face and hands were wrinkled and white through exposure to the whale's gastric juices.

An Arab swallowed by a whale in the Gulf of Akaba escaped by cutting his way out with a jack-knife.
(Jonah 1. 17; 2. 10)

1154  **What of the Night, Watchman?**

*What of the night, watchman, what of the night?*
*The wintry gale sweeps by,*
*The thick shadows fall and the night birds' call*
*Sounds mournfully through the sky.*

*The night is dark; it is long and drear,*
*But who, while others sleep,*
*Are that little band who together stand*
*And their patient vigils keep?*

*The heart's awake, and the strained eye,*
*And awake the list'ning ear;*
*For their Lord they wait, and watch at the gate*
*His chariot wheels to hear.*

*Long have they waited, that little band,*
*And ever and anon*
*To fancy's eye the dawn seemed nigh,*
*The night seemed almost gone.*

*And often through the midnight gale*
*They thought they heard at last*
*The sound of His train; and they listened again,*
*But the sound died away on the blast.*

*Ages have rolled, and one by one*
*These watchers have passed away;*
*They heard the call on their 'tent ears fall,*
*And they hastened to obey.*

*What of the night, watchman, what of the*
*    night?*
*The wild wintry gales sweep by;*
*When the darkest hour begins to lower*
*We know that the dawn is nigh.*

*Courage, ye servants of the Lord,*
*The night is almost o'er;*
*Your Master will come and call you home*
*To weep and to watch no more.*
(Luke 12. 37,38)

1155  **What Think Ye of Christ?**  T. De Witt Talmage, in reply to this question, calls up the following witnesses to give their testimony.

Isaac Watts—How do you feel concerning Him? And he writes,
'I'm not ashamed to own my Lord or to defend His cause.'

John Newton—What do you think of Him and His Gospel? And he writes,
'Amazing grace, how sweet the sound that saved a wretch like me!'

Charles Wesley—What do you think of Him? And he answers:
'Jesus, Lover of my soul, let me to Thy bosom fly.'

Ray Palmer—What do you think of Him? And he writes:
'My faith looks up to Thee, Thou Lamb of Calvary.'

Fanny Crosby—What do you think of Him? She replies:
'Blessed assurance, Jesus is mine: O what a foretaste of glory divine!'

But let us take higher testimony. David— What do you think of Him? The answer is:
'The Lord is my Shepherd, I shall not want.'

John—What do you think of Him? He answers:
'The root and the offspring of David, the bright and morning star.'

Paul—What do you think of Him? Even from the Roman prison he says:
'Christ is all in all.'
(Matt. 22. 42)

**1156 Where is He?** This poem, written by an anonymous sister in Devon, England, is based on the first New Testament question: 'Where is He that is born King of the Jews?'

*Where is He, born to be king?*
*In city great born in state*
*Amongst the mighty? Where is He?*
*Nay, not there: then where?*
*In village small, among the hay*
*In a cattle stall humbly He lay,*
*The Lord of all.*
*Where is He, now grown to manhood?*
*Moving in state in the city great?*
*In the city He is, His own by right,*
*But hounded by men misunderstood!*
*Can you see the sight?*
*He is crowned all right,*
*Clothed in robes of scarlet and purple hues:*
*And in Pilate's hall they mockingly call,*
*'Hail, King of the Jews.'*
*Then, stripped of the robe, bound, bleeding and*
*   bent,*
*Bearing a cross, thorn-crowned He went,*
*While they mocked Him still,*
*To the cross on a hill—*
*Him who had healed with compassion and skill*
*Those whom He met, the degraded and ill.*
*Why did they kill*
*Him on Calvary's hill?*
*Yes! but He went of His own free will,*
*For love led Him there*
*Our transgressions to bear;*
*For our sins to atone*
*He died there alone.*
*Then He rose in great power*
*That most wonderful hour.*
*But where is He now?*
*Where now is His place?*
*His thorn-scarred brow*
*Crowned with glory and grace,*
*At God's right hand*
*He sits to command.*
*In hearts He would live, in yours and in mine.*
*By His spirit divine.*
*He does live in mine,*
*Dispels fear and gloom:*
*He reigns there, the Lord who arose from the*
*   tomb.*
*Does He live in yours? Or have you no room?*

                              A Devon Christian Lady
(Matt. 2. 2)

**1157 Whither Bound.** While on the Nilgiri Hills, India, in the month of May, in one of the 1950s, we had the pleasure and privilege of meeting Rev. Francis W. Dixon, a well-known Keswick speaker. He narrated to us the story of the testimonies of several members of the Landsdowne Baptist Church, Bournemouth, where he is pastor, given at different times after the 1939-45 War. Those who testified had all been leading godless lives, with no concern as to their eternal destiny. They were all connected in some way with the war, and had served in various branches of H.M. forces, and when their conversion

took place, were passing through Sydney, Australia, where they stayed for varying periods of time. I cannot remember the details, and to recount each case of conversion would occupy too much space here: but the general pattern of conviction, conversion and committal to the Lord Jesus Christ was the same in each case.

Each had been accosted in the city of Sydney by an elderly Christian man who asked each the same question—on different occasions with days, weeks or months between—'If you were to die tonight where would your soul be, in heaven or in hell?' That was all, and there the contact ended. The question caused each to think seriously, and led to each of those service personnel accepting the Lord Jesus Christ as Saviour and in their subsequent testimonies owning Him publicly as Lord.

Mr Dixon went on to tell us that, when he later was in Sydney, he made it his business to find the aged Christian who had so faithfully spoken to each of those members of his congregation, and to visit him. When Mr Dixon recounted what those witnesses for Christ had said, the old man broke down in tears, and said, 'I have never before heard of conversions through my simple words of warning and witness, and it is a great cheer to me to know that the Lord has by His Spirit used my feeble testimony for His glory.'
                                                      A.N.

**1158 Widow's Meal—The.** I remember being much struck years ago by an incident related to me by a Highland shepherd on my uncle's estate of Arridilly, the facts of which he, a good Christian man, was quite prepared to vouch for.

Up on a lone hillside, and far removed from any other dwelling, there lived a poor lone widow, who for many a long year had learned to rest, in every difficulty and in all her need, upon Him who has somewhere said, 'Let thy widows trust in me.' It was in the depth of winter when the incident I am going to relate occurred, and the poor woman's stock, never very abundant, was reduced to its lowest by the difficulty of finding any employment at that season of the year. Unlike the widow in the Hebrew story, she actually found her barrel of meal fail, and when she had finished the last handful she went to bed, possibly with hope that she might be successful in earning a few pence on the morrow.

But when the morrow came, a terrific snow-storm swept over the land, and the lane leading to her little cottage was almost blocked with snow. It was quite beyond her slender powers to battle with the raging storm and make her way to some neighbour's house where at least she would be made welcome to a dish of porridge. There was only one Friend to whom she could apply, and in Him she had the most perfect confidence.

Accordingly she filled her pan with water, and put it upon the fire, and actually put the salt in the water. 'Noo,' she said to herself, 'I'll jist gang ben and ask the Lord for the meal.' So she retired into her inner chamber, and there with thanksgiving and praise she made her wants known to the Lord. She had not long been on her knees when there was a loud knock at the door. 'No an, Lord,' she said, 'Thou canst no hae sent the answer sae soon.'

But the knocking continued, and on her opening the door a buxom farmer's lass, who lived some distance off, flung down a sack of meal on the floor, exclaiming, 'Father sent ye that; and I think ye may be very grateful to me for bringing it here through all this terrible storm. Whatever possessed my father I don't know; but all morning he has been dinning into me about that sack of meal, and snow or no snow, I must be sure and fetch it to you; but it was a pretty hard job getting through the storm, I can tell you.'

With uplifted hands and eyes bedimmed with tears, the old body exclaimed, 'He's aye the same, Jeanie! Mony a long year hae I trusted Him and I ne'er found Him fail; and He's nae failed me noo. I put on the water and I put in the salt, and ne'er a grain o' meal had I in the hoose. Sae I was jist asking the Lord to send the meal when I heard ye knock at the door.'

Anon.

(1 Kings 17. 14)

**1159  Will of God.** The following lines, we are told, are written in the front of the Bible of Harold Wildish, missionary in Jamaica:

*I want my heart so rid of self that my dear*
*  Lord may come*
*And set up his own furnishings and make my*
*  heart His home.*
*And since I know what this requires, each*
*  morning while it's still,*
*I slip into that secret room and leave with Him*
*  my will.*
*He always takes it graciously, presenting me*
*  with His.*
*I'm ready then to meet the day and any task*
*  there is:*
*And this is how my Lord controls my interests*
*  and my ills*
*Because we meet at break of day for an*
*  exchange of wills.*

Cecil Rhodes once wrote, 'If there is a God and He cares for men, then the most important thing in the world is to find out what He wants me to do and to do it.'
(Acts 9. 6; Rom. 12. 2)

**1160  Will of God Accepted.** Back in the eighteenth century a young woman by the name of Anne Steele encountered one trial and disappointment after another. Being a devout Christian, she ever sought to raise a song of praise in her night of distress. Finally she was subjected to the 'acid test'.

Engaged to be married, she looked forward to the prospect with eagerness, making all the preparations with joy and happy anticipation. The day arrived and so did the guests, but the wedding had to be delayed because the groom was missing. After about an hour of waiting, a messenger brought the tragic news that the one to whom she was betrothed had drowned. Her reason almost fled at the sudden shock, but after a while, regaining her spiritual composure, she penned the hymn which is still found in many hymnbooks:

*'Father, whate'er of earthly bliss Thy sovereign*
*  will denies,*
*Accepted at Thy throne of grace let this petition*
*  rise:*
*Give me a calm, a thankful heart, from ev'ry*
*  murmur free;*
*The blessings of Thy grace impart and make me*
*  live to Thee.'*

(Col. 1. 9,10)

**1161  Will of God Greater Than His Work.** Miriam Booth, daughter of the founder of the Salvation Army, was a beautiful and cultured lady who began her Christian work with great promise and achieved unusual success. Then suddenly disease laid hold on her and brought her to the point of death. A friend visiting her one day said it seemed a great pity that a person with her capabilities should thus be hindered from doing the Lord's work. She replied with gentle graciousness, 'It is great to do the Lord's work but greater to do the Lord's will.'
(1 John 2. 17)

**1162  Will of God Known and Obeyed.** David Brainerd was waiting upon the Lord in order to ascertain His will concerning him. In 1742 he received a communication from Mr. Pemberton of New York to the effect that David Brainerd's presence was required for some important deliberation in connection with the sending of a Gospel Mission to work among the Red Indians of America. David Brainerd called together some Christian friends, read the letter in their hearing and solicited their counsel, prayer and co-operation. Then he bade them farewell. The die was cast and the Rubicon crossed: he became the apostle to the Redskins.

The late Tom Baird wrote:

*Dispose my will to will Thy will,*
*And then to will is well:*
*The willing will that wills God's will*
*Within God's will will dwell.*

**1163  Wind Cannot Be Explained.** Dr J. H. Jowett was engaged one Saturday morning in his study in meditation on the third chapter of John, the eighth verse, 'The wind bloweth where it listeth.' Although he considered long and carefully, somehow he could get no further, so he decided that he would go for a walk along the seashore. It was a bright spring morning, cool and clear. He saw the ships across the bay and the North Sea rollers breaking on the shore. He saw, too, seated by a breakwater, an old sailor, knife in hand, splicing rope. 'Ah,' said Dr Jowett, 'if any man can explain the wind, this is the man!' He went over to the sailor, sat down on the shingle by his side and said, 'Old man, can you explain the wind?' The old man looked out across the bay and saw the white sails of the ships billowing in the breeze. 'No,' he said, 'I cannot explain the wind but I can hoist a sail.' The doctor sprang to his feet. 'Thank you, my friend,' he said, 'I have my sermon.'

In every walk of life we are constantly using and profiting by powers that we cannot explain. Surely, then, we are foolish indeed if we pretend that we cannot lay hold upon the blessing that God has provided in Christ because we cannot explain just exactly how such a blessing can be brought about.

*Prairie Overcomer*

(John 3. 8)

**1164 Wings—Under God's.** An old puritan writer says: 'Under His wings we have curing and securing. Under the wings of the Almighty our wounds are healed and our alarms stilled, and a joyful confidence pervades the soul. We may be in the night but no terror will disturb us in the foreboding darkness. We may be in the broadening light but no arrow will wound us. We may be in the noontide, but no glare will blind us, no heat consume us.'

J. H. Jowett

(Ps. 91. 4-6)

**1165 Winning Souls for Christ.** C. H. Spurgeon uses an illustration borrowed from Dr Marigold's cart. When a cheapjack has a little knot of people round his van, he eyes them all and feels that the man who is standing over there is a butcher, and that young lad has more money than brains, and that the girl near him is out with her sweetheart and is soon to be married. Now, mark, he will hold up the exact articles which are likely to attract these customers, and in his harangues he will have jokes and telling sentences which will turn the butcher, and lad, and lass into purchasers. He cares not a jot for elegance, but very much for force. He knows that his trade will be better pushed by homely remarks and cutting sentences than by the prosiest prettinesses which were ever delivered; and he gains his end, which is more than those of you will do who talk to people about their souls with as much richness of diction as—

'*the girl who ate each pretty phrase let drop*
*A ruby comma, or a pearl full stop,*
*Or an emerald semi colon.*'

Dr Marigold is sharp and shrewd, because self-interest makes him so, and his extempory observations are so patly uttered and adroitly arranged, that he wins the attention of all, and the custom of many. Would to God that preachers and other workers for God had a tithe as much common sense as cheapjack and were half as earnest to bring men to Jesus Christ as cheapjack is to bring them to buy that tea tray and set of real china! O that we were as wise to win the ear and heart of the person with which we have to deal!

(Prov. 11. 30)

**1166 Winning Souls for Christ.** On his deathbed Dr Lyman Beecher told a fellow-minister, 'The greatest thing of all is not theology: it is not controversy; it is to save souls.' David Brainerd said, 'I cared not where I lived or what hardships I went through, so that I could but gain souls for Christ.' Gregory said, 'Of all sacrifices there is none in the sight of the almighty God equal to zeal for souls.'

Professor Smeaton of Edinburgh used to say, 'Gentlemen, reckon your ministry a failure unless souls are converted to Christ.'

'*Lead me to some soul today: O teach me,*
*Lord, just what to say:*
*Friends of mine are sunk in sin and cannot find*
*their way.*
*Few there are who seem to care, and few there*
*are who pray:*
*Melt my heart and fill my life: give me some*
*soul today.*'

(Prov. 11. 30; 1 Cor. 9. 19)

**1167 With it or With Him.** The great aim of many today is to be 'with it', that is, up-to-date, following the latest fashions, doing what others are doing. The two first Christians surged down with the crowds to the River Jordan to John the Baptist. But they had a different objective when John the Baptist focused their gaze on the Lamb of God: they wanted to be 'with Him'.

The president of one of the largest banks in New York said that after he had served for several years as an office-boy in the bank over which he became president, the then president called him into his office one day and said, 'I want you to come into my office and be with me.' The young man replied, 'But what do you want me to do?' 'Never mind that,' said the president, 'you will learn about that soon. I just want you to be in here with me.'

'That was the most memorable moment in my life,' said the great banker. 'Being with that man made me all that I am today.'

(John 1. 39; Mark 3. 14)

A.N.

**1168 Without Christ.** Without Christ religion is a sunless firmament; life is a dreary passage to a dreadful end; the home is no abode of peace; and prosperity is an adverse flood. Without Christ birth is no boon, life is no gain, and death is a downfall into an unfathomable abyss. Can I know this and not beseech men to make Christ their all?

Henry Law

(Eph. 2. 12)

**1169 Witnesses For Christ.** Jesus said to His disciples before He ascended to heaven from the Mount of Olives, 'Ye shall be witnesses unto me': and so they were.

Gibbon, the historian, wrote, 'In the early Church, it became the most sacred duty of the new convert to diffuse among his friends the inestimable blessing which he himself had received.'

Harnack avers, 'The great mission of Christianity was in reality accomplished by means of informal missionaries. Justin says so explicitly.'

It is said that by A.D. 49 the Gospel had reached the shores of India, and by A.D. 61 China had received the messengers of the Gospel.

Peter, John and the apostles were public witnesses, Stephen a persecuted witness who suffered martyrdom, Philip a personal witness and Luke, the beloved physician, a pen witness. (Acts 2. 32; 3. 15; 4. 33; 5. 32)

**1170 Woman.**

*Not from his head was woman took,*
*As made her husband to o'erlook;*
*Not from his feet, as one designed*
*The footstool of the stronger kind;*
*But—fashioned for himself—a bride,*
*An equal taken from his side.*

*The mate, the glory of the man—*
*Her place intended to maintain,*
*To rest, as still beneath his arm,*
*Protected by her lord from harm,*
*And never from his heart remov'd*
*As only less than God belov'd.*

Does this throw any light on the question of Woman's Lib?

But: 'When the woman saw that the tree was good for food, she took of the fruit thereof and did eat.' (Gen. 3. 6)

*She saw; she took; she ate;*
*Death enter'd by the eye;*
*And parleying in a tempted state,*
*We lust, consent and die!*
*But all mankind, restored,*
*Their Eden may retrieve;*
*And lo, by faith, we see our Lord,*
*We touch, and taste, and live.*

Gen. 2. 21; 1 Tim. 2. 14,15)

**1171 Wonderfully Made.** The New York Academy of Sciences propounded to scientists the following question: 'What single alteration would you make in the human body, if you had the power, that would be particularly useful to man at this critical time in his history?'

The scientists rose to the occasion with many fanciful suggestions, but not all were anxious to interfere with the original. Dr Albert Szent-Gyorgyi, a Nobel winner in medicine, replied: 'The main result of my research, stretching over more than five decades, is a deep admiration of the harmony and perfection of nature. My inability to improve on nature only made my silent admiration deeper.'

*Choice Gleanings*

(Ps. 139. 14)

**1172 Wonders in the Heavens.** In *The Evening Star*, published in Spencer, Indiana, U.S.A. in the year 1970, Dr Harold Hill of the Curtis Engine Company in Baltimore, Maryland—a consultant in the Space programme—related the following:

'Astronauts and scientists assembled at Green Belt, Maryland, were checking the position of the sun, moon and planets in space, and where they would be one hundred years from now. They explained, "We have to know this so that we don't send a satellite up and have it lump into something later on its orbits. We have to lay out the orbits in terms of the life of the satellite, and where the planets will be, so that the whole thing will not bog down."

'Computer measurement ran back and forth over the centuries and came to a halt, putting up a red signal to indicate that there was something wrong with the information fed into it. They then checked out on the computer itself and found it perfect. "What's wrong?" was the question asked. The answer was, "We have found there is a day missing in space in elapsed time." They scratched their heads but could find no answer.

'One man on the team said, "When I was in Sunday School they talked about the sun standing still." "Show us where that is in the Bible," the others asked. They got a Bible and found it in Joshua 10. 8 and 12. 13—the words of Jehovah—"ABOUT A WHOLE DAY"! They checked the computers, going back into the time it was written and found it close enough. Elapsed time in Joshua's day they found to be twenty-three hours and twenty minutes, but not a whole day. They noted the word "about" in the Biblical account. But they were still in trouble, for if you cannot account for forty minutes you will be in trouble one thousand years hence.

'The same man then remembered that it said somewhere that the sun went backwards ten degrees in the reign of Hezekiah, King of Judah. Ten degrees is equal to 40 minutes. Thus they found the missing twenty-four hours. Space travellers logged it in the Log book.'

(Isa. 38. 8; Dan. 6. 27)

Those who by faith believe the Bible to be the Word of God do not require any confirmation of such events and miracles recorded, but there are others who insist on scientific evidence of such happenings.

**1173 Word of a King.** A poor criminal stood before an eastern king trembling for his life. A moment later his head was to be severed from his body. He asked for a drink of water. They brought it, but his hand trembled so that he could not drink it. The king cried to him, 'Don't be alarmed; your life is safe till you drink the water.' In a moment the glass was shivered on the pavement and the water untasted; and, looking at the king, he claimed his royal word. The king bitterly smiled, but realized that he could not break his word, even to the criminal. If the word of a capricious king could shield a wicked man who trusted it, who would not fly for refuge to Him concerning whom the Scripture says, 'He that believeth in Him is not condemned.'

A. B. Simpson

(Eccl. 8. 4)

**1174 Word of God—Living and Powerful.** An educated Chinese gentleman, handed a copy of the Scriptures, was urged to read it carefully and thoughtfully. Some time later he came to his friend, asking, 'What is there about this Book that is different? In all my reading of Chinese literature I have read many good precepts but never, until I read this Book, have I been troubled in my mind when I have done wrong. Now whenever I do wrong I am troubled. Why is this book different from all other books that I have read?'

*Sunday School Times*

(Heb. 4. 12)

**1175 Word of God Printed.** A Moslem member of the House of Representatives in Lagos, Nigeria, has a nine-year-old daughter. In order to help her with her school studies he found himself reading the New Testament with her. The Spirit of God took a verse of Scripture and applied it directly to him. Night after night for some six months he sought and struggled until eventually, on his knees, he turned to Christ. Then he wrote what happened 'I have just received Jesus Christ into my heart and life, and I want to tell you something. If you had come to preach the gospel to me face to face, you would never have converted me; I would have out-argued you every time. But through the innocent hands of my little daughter there came into my home the printed Word.'

(John 5. 39)

**1176 Word of God Valued.** How highly do we value the Word of God? There is a man living in a suburb of Kansas City who lost both hands in an explosion while blasting stone. His face was much torn. Although surgeons did all they could for him his eyesight was utterly destroyed. He was young in the faith; the Bible was his delight, and his distress at being no longer able to read it was great. Hearing of a lady in England who read the Braille type with her lips, some friends ordered for him parts of the Bible in the Moon-raised type, and he could hardly wait till they arrived. What a disappointment then it was to find that the explosion had destroyed the nerves of his lips, and there was no sense of touch there! He wept over the Book, stooped to kiss

it farewell and happened to touch it with his tongue. His teacher was recalled, and he quickly learned to read the characters by running his tongue along them. Recently he said, 'I have read the whole Bible through four times, and many of the books of the Bible over and over again.' That man values and loves God's Word.

Chairette

The Bible, like some foods and drinks, creates an appetite for itself. The more we know of its marvellous message, the more we want to know, for the sweeter does it become.

G. M. Landis

(Jer. 15. 16; Ps. 119. 97)

**1177 Word Written and Incarnate—The.**

*O living Word, whose written Word is for our comfort given,*
*May we give heed as if we heard Thy voice that spoke from heaven!*

*Let us, as in a mirror, see the glory of our Lord;*
*And, as we gaze, transfigured be to His similitude!*

*From glory unto glory shine, as by the Spirit led,*
*Into the likeness, all Divine, of Christ, our risen Head.*

George Goodman

(2 Cor. 3. 18)

**1178 Work For All.** Sir Michael Costa, the celebrated conductor, was holding a rehearsal. As the mighty chorus rang out, accompanied by scores of instruments, the piccolo player ceased playing, thinking perhaps that his contribution would not be missed amid so much music. Suddenly the great leader stopped and cried out, 'Where is the piccolo?' The sound of that one small instrument was necessary to the harmony, and Sir Michael missed it.

In His great missionary programme for the world, God needs every Christian to do his part. So often we are tempted to think that because our part is so small we can drop out and never be missed. There is no need for unemployment in the Church of God or the service of Christ.

(Mark 13. 34)

**1179 Works and our Salvation.** William Wickham being appointed by King Edward to build a stately church, wrote on the windows, 'This work made William Wickham.' When charged by the king for assuming the honour of that work to himself as the author, whereas he was only the overseer, he answered that he meant not that he made the work, but that the work made him, having been very poor, and then in great credit. Lord, when we read in Thy Word that we must work out our own salvation, Thy meaning is not that our salvation should be the effect of our work, but our work the evidence of our salvation.

C. H. Spurgeon

(Phil. 2. 12,13)

**1180  World Population.** If all the people of the world were to stand in a continuous line spaced one yard apart, they would stretch more than 1½ million miles—more than the distance of three round trips to the moon, or a solid army in close formation marching four abreast, encircling the earth at the equator sixteen times. The rapid growth of world population some years ago was spoken of as 'mushrooming', but now it is 'exploding'.

The eminent British historian, Arnold Toynbee believes that if we have a nuclear war, too few people will be left to maintain civilization; but if we do not have such a war, too many people will make life on this planet impossible.

The population of the world at the beginning of recorded history is estimated to have been 125,000. At the time of Christ there were only two-thirds as many people on the whole earth as live in the U.S.A. today. It is reckoned that by A.D. 2000 the world's population will have exceeded 6½ thousand million.

The marshalling of figures relating to world population, world religions and world missions brings into sharp focus the responsibility facing God's people who desire to be obedient to the Great Commission.

**1181  World Problems.** Someone who visited Mr Dag Hammarskjöld, former Secretary-General of the United Nations, in his office at the U.N. before he was killed in a plane crash, found him greatly depressed. Looking from his window across New York, he said quietly, 'I see no hope of permanent World Peace. We have tried so hard and have failed so miserably. Then, pausing for a moment, he continued, 'Unless the world has a spiritual rebirth within the next few years, civilization is doomed.'

'Our interests are in ourselves: we are pre-occupied with material things. Our supreme god is technology: our goddess sex. Most of us are more interested in getting to the moon than in getting to heaven. We are more dedicated to material security than to inward purity. We give much more thought to what we wear, what we eat, what we drink and what we can do than to what we are. While we know more economics than ever before, the world has more poverty and hunger than ever before. With our space programme readying flights to the moon, we have not yet solved the basic problems of earth.' So wrote B.G. in *World Aflame*. Jean Paul Sartre, the French existentialist, said, 'There is no exit from the human dilemma.' Sir Winston Churchill said, 'Our problems are beyond us.'
(Isa. 32. 1,17)

**1182  World Trends Today.** H. G. Wells in *Mind at the End of its Tether*, his last legacy to the world, wrote:

'Our world is like a convoy lost in darkness on an unknown rocky coast, with quarrelling pirates in the chart room and savages climbing up the sides of the ship to plunder and do evil as the whim may take them. Where is the Captain? The ship is driving for the rocks, and man cannot stop it.'

Was he predicting the trend of the 1970s?

But there is an answer. There is at God's right hand in heaven a Man who, according to the purpose of God, is coming back to this earth to stop it and to bring peace and righteousness to this sin-weary earth—The Man Christ Jesus.
(Isa. 32. 1)

**1183  Worship—Centre of.** Service is centrifugal, that is, proceeding from the centre; but worship is centripetal, that is, proceeding towards the centre. The centre of Israel's worship was the ark of God, that pre-eminent type of our Lord Jesus Christ in the perfection of His deity, manhood, sacrifice, glory, mediatorship, the bridge across the gulf between God and man.

God's great House is silently building; we are like David's trusted men who ministered before the dwelling place of the tent with singing until Solomon had built the house; and then they waited on their office according to their order (1 Chron. 6. 32). We are often tempted to despise the humble tent which is our assembly, especially when human discord mars the harmony of the heavenly song, until we remember who it is who has made it His abiding place. For some, the tent is pitched in a heathen village, where the song is ceaselessly rivalled by the horrid noise of idolatry and devilry. For others it is pitched in the disquietude of a modern city, so different from Zion 'beautiful in situation'. But we know with increasing certainty that 'where two or three are gathered together in my name, there am I in the midst'. And He in whom dwells all the fullness of the Godhead bodily is enough.

A. C. Rose

(Ps. 122. 1; Matt. 18. 20)

**1184  Worship—Order Of.** Dr Stuart Holden, for many years a speaker at the annual Keswick Convention, wrote as follows on the order of worship:

'It is obvious that the ideal form of service is one in which all the members take individual part, each contributing something of ministry to the whole. Perhaps it is because this plan is no longer pursued in the church that many of the gifts of the Spirit seem now to have been lost. Where every member of an assembly is filled and controlled by the Spirit of God so that He speaks through one and another to the conviction, illumination and edification of all, there is a fullness of blessing that is not possible as a general rule where the majority of worshippers are silent and where the whole of the ministry is committed to one man.'
(1 Cor. 14. 26)

**1185 Worthwhile Duty—A.** The doctor was comfortably seated at the fireplace, thankful that for once he could spend the evening with his family and did not have to leave the comforts of home to go out in the pouring rain. Then there came a knock at the door. A poor widow who had walked five miles in the rain to the doctor's house stood shivering on the doorstep. 'My boy,' she cried, 'my Davie: he's dreadfully ill.'

To brave a night like this that a child might grow up to a life of poverty and misery! And he knew that a visit to a home like that would bring him in no fee. But he loved children and had a strong sense of duty: so he went. Davie's life was saved, and the child grew up to be the statesman, David Lloyd George.

The doctor, looking back to that night when he took that long walk in the drenching rain, would say, 'I never dreamed that in saving that child's life, I was saving the life of the future Prime Minister of Great Britain.' (Exod. 2. 3-6)

**1186 Wounds of Christ.**

*'Thy wounds, Thy wounds, Lord Jesus,*
*These deep, deep wounds will tell*
*The sacrifice that frees us*
*From self, and death, and hell.'*

H. A. Cameron writes, 'Wounds—according to the definition of the surgeon—are divisions of the soft part of the body by force applied externally, and they are classified by their different characters:
1. The Contused Wound—produced by a blunt instrument, the result of a blow by a rod.—(Matt. 27. 30)
2. The Lacerated Wound—produced by a tearing instrument, the result of scourging. —(Matt. 27. 26; John 19. 1)
3. The Penetrating Wound—caused by a sharp pointed instrument—the crown of thorns.—(Matt. 27. 29,30)
4. The Perforating Wound—piercing through the flesh: 'they pierced my hands and my feet'.— (Ps. 22. 16)
5. The Incised Wound—produced by a sharp-edged instrument—the spear thrust into His side.—(John 19. 34)
(Isa. 53. 5)

**1187 Writing of Christ.** 'Jesus stooped down and ... wrote on the ground' (John 8. 6). We are not told what words He wrote, but we know that when He stooped from heaven's glory to earth in His Incarnation He left His writing on the earth:
He wrote on Bethlehem the story of His birth; on Nazareth the story of His manhood; on Capernaum the story of His mighty works; on the lonely mountain side the story of His prayers; on Olivet the story of His tears; in Gethsemane the story of a broken heart; on Calvary the story of a finished work; on the throne of God the story of a World's redemption. He wrote on human hearts the story of the peace and love of God. He wrote on the ground of human need the omnipotence of God. He wrote it on the brow of the dead whom He raised to life, on the eyes of the blind to whom He gave sight, on the ears of the deaf and on the body of the leper. He wrote it on the heart of the woman of Samaria at Sychar's well, and on Zacchaeus's life, and on the heart of the weeping widow at Nain.

Heyman Wreford

**1188 Wrong Information.** A woman with her small babe was travelling by train through a northeastern state of the U.S.A. on a very wintry day. A terrific storm was blowing, snow was falling and sleet covered everything. The train made its way slowly because of the ice on the rails, and a snow-plough went ahead to clear the way. The woman seemed very nervous. She was to get off at a wayside halt, where she would be met by some friends, and she said to the guard, 'You will be sure and let me know the right place, won't you?'

'Certainly,' he said, 'just stay here until I tell you the right place.'

She sat rather nervously, and again said to the guard, 'You won't forget me.'

'No! Just leave it to me. I will tell you when to get off.'

A commercial traveller sat on the opposite seat. He leaned over and said, 'Pardon me, but I see you are rather nervous about getting off at your station. I know this line well. Your station is the first stop after the next city. Those guards are very forgetful; they have a great many things to attend to, and he may overlook your request, but I will see that you get off all right. I will help you with your baggage.'

'Oh, thank you,' she said. And she leaned back, greatly relieved.

By and by the name of the city the salesman had mentioned was called, and the latter said to the woman, 'Yours is the next station. Better get ready and I will help you to get off.' The train moved on and shortly afterwards came to a full stop.

The woman hurried to the end of the coach, the traveller carrying her bag. When they reached the door, there was no one there.

'You see,' said the traveller, 'these men are very careless. The guard has quite forgotten you.' But he opened the door, helped the woman with her baby down the steps and jumped on again as the train moved off.

A few minutes later the guard came through the train, and looking all about said, 'Why, that is strange! There was a woman here who wanted to get off at the next station. I wonder where she is?'

The traveller spoke up and said, 'Yes, you forgot her, but I saw that she got off all right.'

'Got off where?' the guard asked.

'When the train stopped.'

'But that was not a station! That was an emergency stop! The lights were only a track warning. Why, man, you have put her off in a wild district in the midst of all this storm, where there will be nobody to meet her.'

There was only one thing to do, and although it was a rather dangerous thing, they had to reverse the engine and go back some distance, and then they went to look for the woman. They searched, and finally somebody stumbled upon her body. She was frozen on the ground her babe dead in her arms. She was the victim of wrong information.

If it is such a serious thing to have wrong information in regard to temporal things, what about the great question of the salvation of our immortal souls? If men believe a false gospel, no matter who tells it to them, if they put their trust in something that is contrary to the Word of God, their loss will be not for time only, but for eternity.
(Luke 8. 18)

**1189  Wrong Inside.**  Old Thomas K. Beecher who could not bear deceit in any form, finding that a clock in his church was habitually too fast or too slow, hung a placard on the wall above it, bearing in large letters the words, 'Don't blame my hands—the trouble lies deeper.'

That is where the trouble lies with us when our hands or our feet or our lips, or even our thoughts do wrong. The trouble lies so deep that only God's miraculous power can deal with it. Sin indeed goes deep, but the power of Christ goes deeper.
(Jer. 17. 9; Rom. 7. 18,24)

**1190  Year—Threshold of the.**

*With bated breath we're standing*
*On the threshold of the year;*
*And glancing through the portals,*
*The road looks rough and drear.*
*For dark war clouds have gathered,*
*The sea and oceans roar,*
*And tempests wild are raging*
*Around Time's storm-swept shore.*

*The world is plunged in chaos,*
*In 'blood and sweat and tears',*
*While groans of dying millions*
*Are falling on our ears.*
*Unleashed, the powers of evil*
*Are stalking through the land,*
*While sin and death and sorrow*
*Are seen on every hand.*

*Men's hearts are growing harder*
*As swift the moments fly:*
*They list not to the warning—*
*'The soul that sins must die.'*
*A lost world rushes onward*
*Through ever-deepening gloom,*
*And soon will reach the vortex*
*That spells her awful doom.*

*But from the scene of turmoil*
*Our eyes would turn away*
*With longing expectation*
*To watch for break of day.*
*Lord Jesus, we are listening for*
*The sounding of Thy feet*
*Come skipping o'er the mountains*
*Thy bloodbought Bride to meet.*

(Rev. 22. 20)

**1191  Year—What is a?**

*What is a year?*
*It is a door*
*By which we reach new fields*
*Of service for our God and fellow-men,*
*A door by which we can explore*
*Wide spheres of usefulness*
*Our world to bless,*
*And reap the sheaves God's Word of witness*
*    yields.*

*It is a task*
*Set by the master of our souls,*
*A little part of our life's work below;*
*And so we ask*
*The holy wisdom which alone controls*
*Our labour, teaching what and where to sow*
*That the year, at its end,*
*May show God's glory and man's profit blend.*

                                    William Olney

(Ps. 90. 9,10,12)

**1192  Years Lost and Reclaimed.**  Young Augustine was a depraved youth living in open and abominable sin, but his godly mother, Monica, never ceased to pray for him.

One day in Rome he rose from his chair, went into the garden and threw himself on the ground. A voice seemed to say to him, 'Take up and read! Take up and read!' He took his scroll which opened at Romans 13. 14 and read the words the Holy Spirit used to his conversion. A life wasted by sin was thus transformed and the years that the locusts had eaten were restored.

Augustine from then onward lived for Christ and wrote 118 books, sermons, letters and notes that fill twenty immense volumes. After his conversion he lived many years as a committed Christian.

**1193  Young in Spirit.**  How can one stay young?
Stay Young—By continuing to grow. You do not grow old; you become old by not growing. By maintaining a cheerful attitude; keep in mind Proverbs 17. 22 'A merry heart doeth good like a medicine, but a broken spirit drieth the bones.'
By forcing your mind out of old ruts. Remember that beaten paths are for beaten men.
By keeping your heart young. Carl Sandberg wrote, 'It is not a bad practice for a man of many years to die with a boy heart.'
By knowing that 'they that wait upon the Lord

shall renew their strength: they shall mount up with wings as eagles: they shall run and not be weary; they shall walk and not faint' (Isa. 40. 31).

Remember that Goethe completed *Faust* at 82; Titian painted masterpieces at 98; Toscanini conducted at 87; Konrad Adenauer led West Germany at 86.

*Reader's Digest*

**1194 Young—Winning the.** F. H. Oakley who passed into the presence of the Lord in 1961, went to India as an accountant about the year 1900 and carried on business in the name of Oakley and Bowden for some years. Those who knew him were impressed by his versatility and his outstanding talents in many spheres. He was a grand preacher of the Gospel, a skilful painter and artist, an accomplished pianist, a gifted poet and a capable pharmacist and apothecary. A true Christian with the same motto as the Apostle Paul—'to me to live is Christ'—he not only lived in the sunshine of God's love himself but inspired others to do the same. He was honoured by King George V by being awarded the Kaiser-i-Hind Medal. Keenly interested in the large Anglo-Indian community in Madras, he proved to be to them a guiding influence and a friend in need, a father to the fatherless, though he himself never married, and a generous donor to help to alleviate the lot of the indigent.

Up to old age he devoted his entire life to win the young for Christ, and the motto of the 'Eversleigh Boys' Club' which he formed was 'Every boy for Christ.' All the young people loved him. One of his major aims was the building of Christian character among the youth of the city of Madras. He might with truth have sung every day of his life the chorus, not only 'Telling others', but 'Winning others'! 'My chief joy is winning others.'

(Prov. 11. 30; Prov. 22. 6)

**1195 Youth Outreach.** R—— was an only son, and through associating with bad company in a new area of Glasgow to which his parents had moved got himself into trouble with the police, and arrived in prison.

He studied the Bible Lessons carefully, and after some weeks said that he had accepted the Lord Jesus as Saviour. The reality of this has been amply demonstrated in his life since release from prison some five years ago.

He is an active member of a Glasgow centre Church, playing a prominent part in its youth outreach. He is a keen 'fisherman' on the streets of Glasgow before evening service every Sunday, and tells with great joy of an occasion when he managed to persuade five students of Glasgow University to attend the service with him, and all five visited the vestry at the end and accepted the Lord Jesus as Saviour.

He is a member of the Royal Navy Cadets, and made a firm friendship with a Roman Catholic lad who is also a Cadet. This lad, too, he brought to church and led to the Saviour.

At our last meeting in Glasgow he told of writing to a pen-friend in Germany, and of the German friend and his sister both being saved through this correspondence.

R—— is not only saved from a life of crime, but an active soulwinner in his own right.

Alex. Allan

(Prov. 11. 30)

**1196 Youth—Thoughtful or Thoughtless?** Want of thought is one simple reason why thousands of souls are cast away for ever. None are more in danger of this than the young. They know little of the perils around them; they hate the trouble of sober, quiet thinking, and so form wrong decisions and run their heads into sorrow.

The world is not one in which we can do well without thinking, and least of all do well in the matter of souls. 'Don't think,' whispers Satan. He knows well that an unconverted heart is like a dishonest tradesman's books; it will not bear close inspection. 'Consider your ways,' says the Word of God: 'stop and think; consider and be wise.' Well says the Spanish proverb, 'Hurry comes from the devil.' Just as a bad servant does wrong and then says, 'I never gave it a thought,' so young men run into sin and then say, 'I did not think about it: it did not look like sin.' Not look like sin! What would you have? Sin will not come to you, saying, 'I am sin!' It would do little harm if it did. Sin always seems good and pleasant and desirable at the time of commission. Remember the words of Solomon: 'Ponder the path of thy feet and let thy ways be established.'

Some, I dare say, will object that I am asking what is unreasonable; that youth is not the time of life when people ought to be grave and thoughtful. I answer that there is little danger of that being so in the present day. Doubtless there is a time for all things; but to be light and trifling is anything but wise.

Learn to be thoughtful and learn to consider what you are doing, and where you are going. Make time for calm reflection. Commune with your own heart and be still.

Bishop J. C. Ryle

(Hag. 1. 5,7)

**1197 Zacchaeus.**

*A little man, I could not see*
*The Christ who gave His life for me;*
*But though so little I could climb,*
*And up I scrambled just in time.*
*And then I saw the crowd who came*
*And One who set my heart aflame.*
*He would not know that I was there—*
*In fact, did anybody care?*
*Despised by men, yet full of pride—*
*Would the Lord Jesus too deride?*
*If only I had never been*
*So sinful and so very mean!*

*But lo! He stops and looks at me—*
*'Zacchaeus! come down from the tree;*
*I want to dine with you today*
*And in your heart to reign and stay.'*
*His voice was tender and so sweet.*
*I hastened down my Lord to meet.*
*He looked at me and then I knew*
*I had a friend my whole life through.*
*The gold I used to count as gain—*
*That thing to me—the very same*
*Became as dross when Christ came in*
*And cleansed my heart from every sin.*

G. V. B. Jennings

(Luke 19. 1-10)

**1198 Zeal for Souls.** A traveller was journeying in the darkness of night along a road that led to a deep and rapid river, which, swollen by sudden rains, was chafing and roaring within its precipitous banks. The bridge that crossed the stream had been swept away by the torrent, but he knew it not. A man met him, and after enquiring whither he was bound, said to him in an indifferent way: 'Are you aware that the bridge is gone?' 'No,' was the answer. 'Why do you think so?' 'Oh, I heard such a report this afternoon, and though I am not certain about it, you had perhaps better not proceed.'

Deceived by the hesitating and undecided manner in which the information was given, the traveller passed onward in the way of death. Soon another meeting him cried out in consternation, 'Sir, the bridge is gone!' 'Oh yes,' replied the wayfarer, 'someone told me that story a little distance back; but from the careless tone with which he told it, I am sure it is an idle tale.' 'Oh, it is true, it is true!' exclaimed the other. 'I know the bridge is gone, for I barely escaped being carried away myself. Danger is before you and you must not go on.' In the excitement of his feelings, he grasped the traveller by the arms, by the clothes, and besought him not to rush upon manifest destruction. Convinced by the earnest voice, the earnest eyes, the earnest gestures, the traveller turned back and was saved.

The intelligence in both cases was the same but the manner of its conveyance in the one gave it an air of a fable, in the other an air of truth.

It is only through a burning zeal for the salvation of the lost—a zeal glowing in the heart and flashing out in the look and action and utterance—that the confidence of unbelief can be overcome, and the heedless travellers of the broad way won to the path of life and happiness.

C. H. Spurgeon

(1 Cor. 9. 22)

**1199 Zeal in Action.** When the Spartans marched into battle they advanced with cheerful songs, willing to fight; but when the Persians entered the conflict, you could hear, as the regiments came on, the crack of whips by which the officers drove the cowards to the fray. You need not wonder that a few Spartans were more than a match for thousands of Persians, that in fact they were like lions in the midst of sheep. So let it be with the Church; never should she need to be forced to reluctant action, but full of irrepressible life, she should long for conflict against everything which is contrary to God. Were we enthusiastic soldiers of the cross we should be like lions in the midst of herds of enemies, and through God's help nothing would be able to stand against us.

C. H. Spurgeon

(Ps. 69. 9; John 2. 17; Tit. 2. 14)

**1200 Zigzag Path.** A zigzag path forward and backward is not always proof that the Lord is not leading. Man's wisdom is to decide where he is going and take the shortest, most direct route to his objective. That is not God's wisdom. It must have been tremendously trying to Moses, knowing the way out of Egypt and knowing the importance of getting out quickly, to follow the Lord's guidance when it seemed contrary to reason. But God was leading, and leading that Israel's triumph might be complete.

*We climbed the height by the zigzag path and*
*    wondered why—until*
*We understood it was made zigzag to break the*
*    force of the hill.*
*A road straight up would prove too steep for*
*    the traveller's feet to tread;*
*The thought was kind in its wise design of a*
*    zigzag path instead.*

(Exod. 13. 18; Ps. 78. 52,53)

# GENERAL INDEX

## General Index

## General Index

# INDEX OF PERSONS, PEOPLES AND PLACES

278

# INDEX OF TEXTS

**Index of Texts**

288

# Index of Texts